THE TIMETABLES OF™
JEWISH HISTORY

*A Chronology of the Most Important People
and Events in Jewish History*

JUDAH GRIBETZ

and Edward L. Greenstein and Regina Stein

SIMON & SCHUSTER
New York London Toronto Sydney Tokyo Singapore

for JESSICA

SIMON & SCHUSTER
Simon & Schuster Building
Rockefeller Center
1230 Avenue of the Americas
New York, New York 10020

SIMON & SCHUSTER and colophon are registered trademarks
of Simon & Schuster Inc.

Designed by Irving Perkins Associates
Manufactured in the United States of America

1   3   5   7   9   10   8   6   4   2

Library of Congress Cataloging-in-Publication Data
is available

ISBN 0-671-64007-0

INTRODUCTION

Owing to their long history and their wide dispersal, the Jews have been involved with many of the important movements and events in world history. From the emergence of the great monotheistic religions, based upon the Bible, to modern times, Jews have participated in almost every phase of human thought and activity. Although widely dispersed, Jewish communities influenced one another, and, in historical retrospect, Jews can trace continuities in their history and culture.

The Timetables of Jewish History™ offers a concise record of key figures and important events in the history of the Jewish people from earliest times to the present. Its format displays entries chronologically, when read vertically, and geographically, when read horizontally, thus allowing the reader to see important people, significant events, and works of cultural interest in their three-dimensional historical context.

The Jews have never been a people that "dwelt apart." For better *and* worse, they have been involved in the history of other nations more than any other people on earth. We therefore felt it important to outline world events ("General History") against which Jewish history has evolved. Our inclusion of general history is not intended to be universal or comprehensive; many significant events and achievements are omitted, and no slight to any culture is intended. Our general history entries are designed to give a useful background to Jewish history and culture and to identify parallels elsewhere in the world. The chronological organization of our book, which gives recognition to geographic distinctions, cultural significance, and general history, seems to us the most useful way to assist the reader in gaining a broad understanding of the Jewish experience.

The catastrophe of the Holocaust and the emergence of the State of Israel loom large in modern Jewish consciousness, and for that reason the modern period dominates this book. And, of course, in the present age, we have easier access to information.

We acknowledge that medieval Jewish history appears to be a litany of antisemitism and Jewish suffering despite our best efforts to portray the positive aspects and achievements of Jewish life. Yosef Yerushalmi, professor of Jewish History at Columbia University, has written that "the destruction of European Jewry was prepared, in many ways, by teachings of hostility in the Middle Ages whose own roots go back even earlier. If the Holocaust is not merely a Jewish issue, as it is surely not, but also a harrowing symptom of other malignancies deep in the heart of Western civilization, then all the prior evidence must be assembled." We have endeavored to present an array of evidence, mindful of his warning that we avoid reducing the Jews "to passive objects of history rather than active subjects."*

Further, we acknowledge that our historical data about the past grow more and more meager the further back we go. Especially in the ancient periods, we are often uncertain of the precise dates of various events and cultural achievements, and so they are often assigned to a round number such as the turn of a century. The dating and interpretation of many events are still the subject of lively controversy, and we have chosen what seems to us to be the most reliable dates.

The land of Israel is variously referred to as Israel, Canaan, the land of Israel, or Palestine, all of which are geographical designations. In today's world, using "Israel" or "Palestine" as the name of the area carries political connotations. Whatever term we use in any particular entry, we are proud to acknowledge that we regard the land of Israel as the site of the Jewish homeland and that it is therefore appropriate that the State of Israel be located in the land of Israel.

Non-Jews are identified by an asterisk, with the exception of officials of Christian churches and major figures of other faiths, whose religious affiliation is obvious.

Starting with 1933, where columns A through D align on months, column E (Jewish Culture) runs continuously without regard to month.

We have explored the questions "Who is a Jew?" and "What is Jewish culture?" in the course of determining whether it is appropriate to include a particular reference in this book. Jewish culture is an elusive concept. It has not developed in isolation but has occurred side by side with the development of other cultures. We have chosen to include contributions in the fields of religious and secular literature, art, and music, as well as social and natural sciences and medicine. We have selected persons identified as Jews who have made such contributions, as well as cultural events whose significance is distinctively Jewish.

In determining who is a Jew, another elusive concept, we have included persons identified as Jews either because of their commitment to Judaism and the Jewish community, or because others feel strongly that these people belong to Jewry. We have been guided in this decision by the comprehensive discussion of Jewish identity found in the *Encyclopaedia Judaica*.

One ponders the uses of Jewish history. Historian Lucy S. Dawidowicz suggests that "the historian's pursuit of knowledge is also a pursuit of truth, and that truth is often put in the service of what the historian holds dear. Since

The Study of Judaism, Bibliographical Essays in Jewish Studies, Vol. II (Anti-Defamation League of B'nai B'rith, 1976), pp. 12–13.

time immemorial, history has been used to celebrate, legitimate, and validate." She traced the evolution of Jewish historiography to the 19th century, when modern Jewish historical scholarship flowed from the pen of Heinrich Graetz. Graetz sought to communicate to his Jewish readers "a sense of the dignity and creativity of the Jews as a people and to demonstrate through his history that Judaism and its culture were still viable." Graetz wanted his non-Jewish readers "to see Judaism, not as a vestige of the denial of Christ, but as the animating and continuously creative force in the life and culture of the Jewish people."* So, too, are these the aims of the authors of *The Timetables of Jewish History*.

We believe the spread of Jewish knowledge to be an urgent priority in the Jewish and non-Jewish world today. We hope that the overview provided by the distinctive format of our book will satisfy readers' curiosity and enlarge their appreciation of the subject matter. Perhaps it will whet their appetites for more intensive inquiry. If so, this will provide the authors with great satisfaction.

In the preparation of this book we enjoyed the assistance and advice of Carla Glasser, Robert V. Rubin, David Robbins, Jessica Gribetz, our copy editor, Susan Winick, and our editor, Bob Bender. We are grateful that Gypsy da Silva has been our production editor. She has helped shape the final version of the book in ways we cannot begin to catalog. Stephen Kraft was our able cartographer. In gathering illustrations, we have been especially helped by Reuven Koffler of the Central Zionist Archives and by Barbara Kraft. We are most grateful for their sincere interest in our project.

*Lucy S. Dawidowicz, *What Is the Use of Jewish History?* (1992), pp. 4, 17–18.

List of Maps

List of Tables

A. General History	B. Jewish History	C. Jewish Culture	
Glaciers of the Ice Age have melted and receded. Dwellers of what is now northern Iraq begin to domesticate sheep.	Herding will be the occupation ascribed by the Bible to the earliest Hebrews and to Abel, son of Adam and Eve (Genesis 4:2).		-9000
		Farming culture establishes a permanent settlement, fortified in stone, at a site that will be called Jericho. Elsewhere in the land of Israel, people live in caves and forage, while at other sites herding of animals has begun.	-8000
Large Neolithic settlements appear in Anatolia, Asia Minor, some characterized by a technological innovation, pottery. In what is now southwestern Iran, farmers begin to cultivate wheat and barley. Agriculture will not spread to Europe or China for another 3,000 years.	Farming is said to be the occupation of Cain, son of Adam and Eve (Genesis 4:2).	Neolithic Jericho shows highly developed civilization, marked by animal domestication, cereal cultivation, toolmaking, and foreign trade.	-7000
Village culture, marked by painted pottery and craftsmaking, characterizes Upper Mesopotamia. Villages familiar with pottery emerge in Syria and along the Mediterranean coast.			-6000
In Egypt the earliest-known village culture appears in the Fayyum area of the Nile Delta.			-4300
The custom of burying the dead together with their possessions, enabling them to live in the next world, is already in evidence in Egypt.			-4000
Northern Mesopotamia is settled by the Subarians, an apparently central Asian people who may have given the idea of writing to the Sumerians who will supersede them.		Throughout the land of Israel, village culture is evident, with notable concentrations in the Negev and the Jordan Valley. Copper implements begin to be manufactured in the next few centuries.	-3500
The Sumerians (possibly Shinar in Genesis 11:2), a people of uncertain origins who settled southern Mesopotamia sometime before 4000 BCE, have by now built cities and irrigation canals. They invent or develop a system of writing, which will be further developed and stylized as cuneiform. They work in bronze and build cities. Their tradition ascribes the first fruits of civilization to the divine sage Uanna-Adapa, whose name may be reflected in the Greek Oannes and the Bible's Adam.		The early Bronze Age that runs the course of several centuries in Palestine is characterized by diverse painted pottery. Fortified cities begin to emerge, often built on a rocky hill. So do the cultic "high places" that will later incense Israel's prophets. Vines, for which Israel will later be renowned, are imported. Inhabitants speak an early form of western Semitic, from which Hebrew (Canaanite) will stem.	-3100
Upper and Lower Egypt are consolidated by Narmer* (Menes, traditional founder of the 1st Dynasty?) and trade begins with	In Hebrew, Egypt will still be known as the "Two Lands" (Mitsrayim).		-3000

	A. General History	B. Jewish History	C. Jewish Culture
-3000	Phoenicia and beyond. Although not as advanced in art and technology as Mesopotamia, Egypt devises hieroglyphic writing. The Indus River Valley begins to evolve a highly centralized civilization.		
-2900	Signs of a local flood are evident in the southern Mesopotamian city of Shuruppak, home of the Sumerian and Babylonian flood hero, parallel to the biblical Noah. The Sumerians associate the flood with a contemporary "deluge" of western Semites in the region.		
-2700	The Sumerian city of Uruk builds a six-mile-long protective wall around itself. The famed 18-foot-thick wall will be celebrated in the *Epic of Gilgamesh,** the legendary king of Uruk. Egyptians begin painting narrative scenes in their tombs.		
-2600	Egypt conquers its southern neighbor, Nubia. At the same time it is building settlements in the Nile Delta. Food staples are barley and beer. Pottery develops, giving rise to the myth that the god Khnum created humans on a potter's wheel. The 4th Dynasty of Egypt constructs pyramids for entombing its royalty, who are regarded as gods. Believing that a person exists so long as one's body is preserved, Egyptians bury their dead in dry sand and mummify them.	The balm that is brought down to Egypt in the biblical story of Joseph is surely meant for mummification.	Genesis 2 will describe Creation as "molding," a potter's activity.
-2500	Sumerian city-states develop a high level of culture, including literature. Kings organize irrigation and land tenure; priests run temples featuring *ziggurats* (temple towers). Hegemony passes from city to city. The several gods represent powers in nature; although the domain of many is cosmic, most are associated with a particular city. History is fated by the gods, and human law is meant to embody divine will. In Mesopotamia a Semitic people begins to emerge as dominant, having assimilated much of Sumerian culture, including cuneiform writing. Named for the city of Agade (Akkad in Genesis 10:10), these Akkadians forge a synthesis of Sumerian and Semitic religion.	THE ANCIENT NEAR EAST	
-2400	Egypt maintains extensive ties with Canaan, establishing an outpost in the Phoenician city of Byblos.	Many Canaanite city-states have emerged, most of them clearly Semitic.	

A. General History	B. Jewish History	C. Jewish Culture	
Copper is mined in the Sinai peninsula. The pharaoh is regarded in Egypt as a great god, owner of the entire land. The king of the Mesopotamian city of Lagash, Eannatum,* defeats the Elamites to the east and destroys their capital, Susa (biblical Shushan).	Genesis 47 will attribute the consolidation of Egypt's real and other property in the hands of the pharaoh to the program of Joseph.		**-2400**
Sargon* of Kish, reigning for half a century, builds an empire based in Akkad, reaching beyond Mesopotamia. An inscription boasts that he reached the cedar forests of Lebanon. Key to his administration is the establishment of a dynasty and appointment of cronies. A great Semitic city-state emerges in north central Syria: Ebla. Known through a recent discovery of over 16,000 cuneiform tablets, Ebla enjoys political and economic relations with Mesopotamia, Asia Minor, and Canaan.			**-2350**
Sargon,* now of Akkad, names his daughter Enheduanna* to the high priesthood of the Ur and Uruk cult centers. Composer of several Sumerian hymns, Enheduanna* is the earliest known author.			**-2320**
Akkadian king Naram-Sin,* long-lived grandson of Sargon,* sponsors a golden age of culture as a self-proclaimed divinity.			**-2280**
The Egyptian 6th Dynasty extends its control to the Sinai and Palestine.	Several cities in Palestine suffer destruction, possibly the result of invasion. Some, like Ha-Ai, will not be rebuilt until the Israelite period. Others, like Jericho and Hatzor, are resettled. Copper tools are now common, but solid houses are scarce, suggesting a population of herders.		**-2200**
Sweeping down from the Zagros Mountains, the Gutians help dissolve the Akkadian Empire. Indo-European Hurrians (biblical Horites), who may have also weakened Akkad, establish a strong presence across northern Mesopotamia.			**-2150**
The Old Kingdom of Egypt, collapsing from the weight of its overdemanding, overbuilding central authority, cannot restrain conflicts between Memphis and Thebes. A stable dynasty, inaugurating the so-called Middle Kingdom, is established at Thebes.			**-2130**

A. **General History**	B. **Jewish History**	C. **Jewish Culture**

-2100

The city-state of Ur overtakes Uruk (Erech in Genesis 10:10), which vanquished the Gutians, and builds a flourishing culture, superseding that of Sumer. Warfare is conducted by ass-drawn chariots, and an infantry, hurling javelins and thrusting short spears.

Struggle among rival kings throws Egypt into disarray. Land is held in a kind of feudal system.

The Egyptian wisdom text, the *Instructions of Merikare,** advises kings to suppress rebellion fiercely and reward allies; also, like the Bible, it claims a god prefers honorable conduct to the sacrifices of wrongdoers.

B. With Egypt and Mesopotamia in internal conflict, the western Semitic Amorites would seem to dominate Palestine.

-2050

Ur-Nammu,* king of Mesopotamian Ur, promulgates the first known law code and builds the great *ziggurat* that serves perhaps indirectly as a model for the biblical Tower of Babel.

The 11th Dynasty reunifies Egypt and renews its power.

The main stairway of the ziggurat *of Ur. (Permission of Jack Finegan)*

-2020

Ur-Nammu's* son Shulgi* develops Ur's trade and promotes literary productivity.

-2000

Assyria, composed of elements as diverse as Amorite and Hurrian in northeastern Mesopotamia, consolidates power and extends its trade, establishing a merchant colony as far west as Asia Minor, in Cappadocia.

In Egypt the god Amon is revered as preeminent in the world, as other nations in the Near East declare the greatest deity in their own pantheon to exert international power.

C. Seminomadic Amorites based in the Upper Euphrates region fan out and settle in southern Mesopotamia and in Syro-Palestine in the west, transforming its culture. This two-century movement may be reflected in the patriarchal migration from Mesopotamia to Canaan that is described in Genesis.

-1990

The political stability brought to Egypt by the 12th Dynasty facilitates a cultural renaissance, producing wisdom and other literary works, such as the tale of Sinuhe,* a palace official who had to flee Egypt and live in Phoenician exile until he was again welcome home.

-1975

The Egyptian Prophecy of Neferti* foresees a takeover of Egypt by Asians as well as a variety of natural catastrophes.

-1950

Elamites (from where Iran is today) raid Ur and destroy its power, opening the door for the spread of the Amorites. The graphic "Lamentation over the Destruction of Ur" is composed when Ur's

| | | | -1950 |

temples are rebuilt half a century later.

Babylonian mathematics has developed to high sophistication, at least in practice. It handles equations with two unknowns and solves the theorem later to be identified with Pythagoras.*

The Beni Hassan tomb painting depicts a group of Canaanites entering Egypt, their wares laden on asses. The early Hebrews resemble these Asiatics.

-1900

-1870

Lipit-Ishtar,* king of the city of Isin, promulgates a law code in Sumerian. About a century later, the first known Akkadian law code will be formulated in the city of Eshnunna. Both will have parallels in the earliest biblical code in Exodus 21–23.

Western Semites, perhaps Canaanites, bring their trades and wares to Egypt, as depicted in a tomb at Beni Hasan, Egypt.

The leading cities of Larsa and Isin break the peace of Mesopotamia by opening hostilities.

-1850

The land of Canaan from Sinai to southern Syria is subject to Egyptian control. The Egyptian Execration Texts show largely Semitic local rulers who were expected to be loyal to the pharaohs. They also attest heavy Canaanite settlement in the valleys and coastal plains, not the hill country that, according to Genesis, served as the favored territory of the Hebrew patriarchs. Among numerous Canaanite sites mentioned is one resembling Zebulon, one of the later Israelite tribes.

-1800

Under the unstable 13th Dynasty, Egypt's power wanes, paving the way for foreign rule.

-1780

Shamshi-Adad I* becomes king of Assyria; gaining control over all Upper Mesopotamia, he campaigns as far west as the Mediterranean.

-1750

The Hatti culture of Asia Minor, which carried on peaceful trade with Assyria, begins to be displaced by the Indo-European Hittites.

Zimrilim* wrests control of his native city, Mari, from Assyria. Mari, situated on the Upper Euphrates River, south of Harran, has an "Amorite" population, whose language and institutions, especially those of the local seminomadic tribes, resemble those described in the biblical narratives about early Israel. The chief local god is Dagan, otherwise known from later Canaan and Philistia (Dagon). In Mari's vicinity is the town of Nakhur, a name like that of Abraham's brother Nahor.

-1730

A. General History	B. Jewish History	C. Jewish Culture
-1730 Zimrilim* constructs a 300-room palace, some of whose walls are painted with frescoes. One depicts a Garden of Eden scene in which two cherubim (winged sphinxes) guard a tall tree. The archival remains include over 25,000 cuneiform tablets.		
-1728 Hammurapi,* king of Babylon, begins a campaign of conquest that will bring most of Mesopotamia under his rule.		
-1700 At Mari, seminomadic tribes remain outside but in commerce with the city. The Hebrew patriarchs, too, are said in Genesis to camp between cities. The Hittites in Asia Minor develop the military use of the chariot, a strategic advantage soon borrowed by Egypt and other Near Eastern powers. The various legendary tales of the partly divine Sumerian hero-king Gilgamesh* are composed into a long Babylonian epic about the human quest for immortality and its frustration.		
-1690 Hammurapi* promotes great achievements in building and literature. His code of 282 laws, meant to impress the gods as embodiments of justice, safeguard persons and property according to a specific social hierarchy, from palace and temple to private estate and from king and citizen to the middle-rank *mushkenum* and slave. Women may engage in business and own property.		The laws of Hammurapi may belong to the same tradition as the more egalitarian biblical codes such as Exodus 21-23.
-1675 A circle of huge monoliths is erected on Salisbury Plain, in England. The purpose of Stonehenge remains a mystery.		
-1670 The Hyksos, an Asiatic, possibly Canaanite, people, begin to govern Egypt.	Among the Hyksos who begin to govern Egypt is one Ya'qub-'al,* a name similar to Jacob. Early Hebrews may have entered Egypt during the Hyksos' rule.	
-1650 An ancient Sumerian story of a worldwide flood is written in Babylonia in the first Semitic version. Named for the human survivor-hero of the flood, Atrahasis* (the very wise), this epic explains the flood as a divine measure for controlling human overpopulation.		The biblical flood will be said to wipe out nearly all life on account of human corruption.
-1542 Native Egyptian control is restored when the Hyksos are driven out by Amosis.* In this so-called New Kingdom, Nubia is restored to		

A. General History	B. Jewish History	C. Jewish Culture	
Egypt and the capital is returned to Thebes.			**-1542**
Mursilis I,* king of the Hittites from Asia Minor, sacks Babylon, ending its first period of greatness.			**-1530**
Thutmose I* of Egypt, using the horse to military advantage, subjugates the land of Canaan to the Euphrates River in Syria.		The biblical "Song at the Sea" (Exodus 15) will praise God for throwing the pharaoh's "horse and rider" into the sea.	**-1525**
The earliest documented dynasty, the Shang, begins, marking the onset of the Bronze Age in China. It is uncertain if the Chinese learned of bronze production from the Middle East. Farmers raise wheat and barley more than rice. The religious cult involves human as well as animal sacrifices. The writing system is advanced.			**-1523**
After the Hittite plunderer of Babylon, Mursilis,* returns to Asia Minor, Gulkishar,* king of the Persian Gulf "Sealand" people, gains control of Babylonia.			**-1520**
An Indo-Aryan empire, the Mitanni, extends across Upper Mesopotamia, largely populated by Hurrians. The Kassites move down from northwestern Mesopotamia and seize Babylonia, where they will rule for centuries. The Indo-European Aryans invade India, using the same chariotry and technology by which they overtake Greece in the West. The Aryan tribal structure anticipates the Indian caste system. Their culture is reflected in the earliest passages of the Rig-Veda hymns.	Numerous Canaanite city-states are organized on a feudal model.	Canaan experiences an influx of Indo-Aryans and Hurrians (biblical Horites), leaving a tradition in Genesis that the land was populated by several different peoples. Hurrian laws, known from Nuzi, resemble certain biblical practices, such as the adoption of a servant as heir (Genesis 15). Nuzi also attests the custom of a man producing an heir through a concubine, which could provide a background for the Hagar stories in Genesis 16 and 21. Legal documents from the north central Syrian city of Alalakh allow a father to designate a younger son as legal heir, a practice attested in Genesis, as when Jacob favors his younger grandson Ephraim over Manasseh.	**-1500**
Queen Hatshepsut* of Egypt, who demands to be called "His Majesty" and has her likeness sculpted with a beard, undertakes an expedition to an East African land known as Punt, possibly the "Put" associated with Egypt in Genesis 10:6. This and other exploits she has depicted on the walls of the temples she builds.			**-1475**
Egyptian Pharaoh Thutmose III* begins a series of campaigns against Syrian and Phoenician cities, probably to offset growing Mitanni power.	Thutmose III* thrusts northward and lays siege to Megiddo, the fortified Canaanite town in the Jezreel plain.		**-1468**

	A. General History	B. Jewish History	C. Jewish Culture
-1450	The story of King Idrimi* of Alalakh tells how he, as a fugitive from Aleppo living seven years in Canaan, plans and executes his return to power in Syria. His story resembles those of Jacob and Moses in the Bible as well as the Egyptian story of Sinuhe.*	Canaan falls to Pharaoh Thutmose III,* who pushes his army up to the Euphrates River.	
-1410	The kings of the Mitanni Empire and Egypt end their long conflict and inaugurate a period of coexistence, sealed with royal marriages between the two nations.		
-1400	Crete, as well as Mycenean Greece and other Aegean lands, specialize in various crafts and market them all across the Mediterranean. Mycenean civilization is preserved as a memory in the Homeric epics.	Part of the cuneiform *Epic of Gilgamesh** is attested in the land of Israel at Megiddo, indicating cultural contact with Mesopotamia.	Alphabetic writing is being developed in northern Canaan. A cuneiform alphabet is used at Ugarit and a linear script in Phoenicia. This ancestor of Hebrew writing will be borrowed by the Greeks, through whom it will evolve into the Greek and Roman alphabets. Canaanite religion is concerned with producing fertility through the powerful rain god, Baal Hadad. In Ugaritic myth, Baal asserts his authority and recoups it through the help of the goddesses Asherah, Astarte, and Anath. Baal must subdue the flooding force of the sea god, Yam, and at the same time overcome the sapping power of the god of death, Mot. The father of the gods, El, functions in a more advisory and ceremonial way.
-1375		Though nominally under Egyptian control, Canaanite city-states fight for local hegemony, variously seeking support from the Hittites to the north or Egypt to the south and sometimes enlisting the aid of mercenaries called 'Apiru. The 'Apiru, a social class on the outskirts of civilization, are related to the Hebrews, according to some scholars. This century of turmoil is not reflected in the Bible's patriarchal stories, where Hebrews enjoy calm relations with local leaders and peoples.	
-1360	Pharaoh Akhenaten,* ruling from Amarna, where he has constructed a new city on the Middle Nile, elevates the sun disk, Aten, to preeminent divine status and worships it alone. The name of the traditional chief god of Egypt, Amun-Re, he erases from temples all over his land. Some find in this an incipient monotheism.		In saying that the Aten is the sole god giving life to peoples, animals, and plants everywhere, Egyptian hymns presage the solar imagery of the biblical Psalm 104.
-1355	Akhenaten* builds a temple to Aten at Karnak, where he sets the precedent of erecting royal statues of colossal size.		

A. General History	B. Jewish History	C. Jewish Culture	
The kingdom of Ugarit, located on the north Syrian coast, flourishes as a maritime center. Three large epics and other texts are written down in a language and style that in many respects anticipate biblical literature.	The Hittite king Shuppiluliuma,* taking advantage of Egyptian weakness under Akhenaten,* takes control of Syria and Phoenicia and stirs up tensions in Canaan.	David's lament over Saul and Jonathan (2 Samuel 1) seems directly dependent on the curse King Daniel imposes on the rain in the Ugaritic *Epic of Aqhat*.	-1350
Tutankhamen,* a son-in-law of Akhenaten* and Nefertiti* whose opulent tomb will remain unraided until 1922 CE, moves the royal residence back to the Nile Delta following what Egyptians see as Akhenaten's* heresy.			-1345
Resurgent Hittite power brings down the Mitanni Empire, while Assyria regains strength.			-1340
During a break in Egypt's dynastic succession, an army officer, Horemheb,* takes the throne. He dismantles the Karnak solar temple and otherwise seeks to obliterate the memory of Akhenaten* and his successors.			-1333
	Canaan again falls under Egyptian control, as Pharaoh Sethos I* retakes Beth Shean in the northern Jordan Valley. His conquest is commemorated there on a stela.		-1305
With the establishment of the Ramesside dynasty, Egypt plays host to groups of Asiatic Semites as well as African peoples. Inscriptions appear in Old South Arabian at Saba, which would seem to be the Bible's Sheba, in the southern Arabian peninsula. Some date this writing to the 8th century BCE.	The Canaanites specialize in international trade, marketing in particular the purple dye to which they owe their name.		-1300
Ramesses II* becomes pharaoh of Egypt and inaugurates a period of great building, including the colossal temple cut into a cliff above the Nile at Abu Simbel and the capital Avaris, called now the House of Ramesses.*	Among Ramesses' laborers are Asiatic 'Apiru. This may lie behind the biblical tradition (Exodus 1:11) that Hebrew slaves built the city of Ramesses.*		-1290
Ramesses II* of Egypt attempts to push his control north into Syria but is repelled by the Hittites.			-1285
Fearing a threat from Assyria to the east, the Hittites concede to a peace treaty with Egypt.			-1260
The Ramesside kings sponsor something of a cultural renaissance in Egypt.			-1250
Seaborne Greek troops sack the city of Troy on the western coast of Asia Minor. The events will be embellished in legends and achieve	If the general authenticity of the biblical tradition of the Exodus can be assumed to be correct, ancestors of the Israelites leave Egypt,	According to biblical tradition, the Hebrews leaving Egypt enter into a law-based covenant with their ancestral God at Mt. Sinai. They are	-1230

A. General History	B. Jewish History	C. Jewish Culture
-1230 their classic epic form in the 8th century BCE.	heading for Canaan. According to the Bible, these ancestors narrowly escape the pursuit of Egypt's chariots by crossing the Sea of Reeds.	led by a prophet, Moses. This God accompanies the Hebrews in their trek to Canaan.
-1220 Merneptah,* the Egyptian pharaoh succeeding Ramesses II,* repels an attack by seafaring people from the Aegean, possibly seeking a new home in the aftermath of the Trojan war. Assyria, under Tukulti-Ninurta I,* raids Babylon to the south and Hittite territories to the west. Moab and Edom, Israel's southeastern neighbors, emerge as new political centers. Ammon will emerge in the Transjordan, across from Jericho, within a century.	People from the Aegean will soon settle on the western coast of Canaan, where they will be known as the Philistines. Pharaoh Merneptah* claims victory over several sites and peoples in Canaan, including the territory of Israel. This is the earliest contemporary notice of Israel. According to tradition, the Hebrews, based at Kadesh on the Sinai–Negev border, meet resistance in trying to enter Canaan, so they circle the Dead Sea and encamp in Moab. The city of Jericho, which according to the book of Joshua was destroyed by the Israelites, shows no archaeological signs of ruin. Nearby Ha-Ai, whose destruction is likewise attributed to the Israelites, was ruined no later than 2500 BCE. Other sites, such as Hazor, Devir, and Lachish evidence destruction, but it is not clear at whose hands—Egypt's, the Philistines', other Canaanite states', or Israel's. Other sites said to fall to Israel, such as Gibeon and Hebron, do not yet exist. In the course of the next two centuries, Israel comprises a somewhat loose confederation of 12 tribes, though the identity of these tribes shifts. One gathers from the Book of Judges that in wartime Israel is united and led by a man or woman endowed with a divine charisma. In fact, the unity imputed to Israel in this period may be exaggerated; virtually every leader, or "judge," operates in the confines of one's own tribe.	The destruction of the Tower of Babel (Genesis 11) may recall the triumph of Tukulti-Ninurta I,* who may himself be recalled (in Genesis 10:8–10) as the legendary Nimrod.  *The Stela of Merneptah, in which the Egyptian king claims to have destroyed many peoples and places in the land of Canaan, including "Israel." The claims are surely exaggerated, but the mention of Israel indicates that a people of that name is located in Canaan at about 1230 BCE.* *Merneptah, very possibly the pharaoh who released the Hebrews from Egypt, in an Egyptian sculpture.* 
-1175 Under Ramesses III* Egypt is beset by attacks on all sides, including Libya to the west and the seafaring Philistines to the north. Plagued by domestic problems, too, Egypt is weakened.		
-1150 The Philistines set up a network of five cities—Ashdod, Ashkelon, Ekron, Gath, and Gaza—from which they expand to control a great deal of maritime and overland trade. They enjoy a monopoly on the manufacture of iron.	Israel begins to emerge as a network of settlements in the Galilean and central hill country. Details of Israel's origins and early development are obscure. Tribes form east of the Jordan River and join with Israel; the Bible reports Israelite victories against Transjordanian kings.	The tribes of Israel would seem to have mixed ethnic and geographical origins. They comprise substantial native Canaanite elements.

| | Deborah and Barak rally a number of Israelite tribes to defeat Canaanite forces at Mt. Tabor. Other stories about judges celebrate Israelite conquests of territory from Philistines (Shamgar, Samson), Ammonites (Jephthah), Moabites (Ehud), Midianites (Gideon), and others. | | **-1125** |

| The Arameans have emerged in Upper Mesopotamia and Syria, imposing pressure on the resurgent dynasty of Babylon. Although the Bible traces Israel's origins to Aram, mention of Arameans in Genesis is apparently anachronistic.

Taking advantage of the relative weakness of Assyria and Babylonia, the emergent Arameans establish small states in northwestern Mesopotamia, especially Syria. | YHWH is worshiped as Israel's national God, but Canaanite fertility rites are practiced, too. Figurines of goddesses are widespread, and Israel's prophets will repeatedly inveigh against the cult of the local rain god, Baal.

The tribes worship at a variety of shrines, each headed by a priestly family. It is possible that on the pilgrimage festivals, Pesah or Matsot (Passover); Shavuot (Weeks); and Harvest, or Sukkot (Booths), members of all tribes join to celebrate at a central shrine, such as Shechem, Gilgal, Bethel, or Shiloh. The ark of the covenant would be located at that shrine, removed only to accompany the Israelites in battle. Some attribute the Bible's earliest law code (Exodus 21–23) to the period of the tribal covenant. | The formation of the Israelite nation is recounted as the outcome of a holy war waged against Canaan by Israel's God, YHWH.

It may be the idea of being covenanted to God that confirms Israel's identity as a people. Law codes in the Pentateuch display a structure similar to Hittite and Assyrian treaties between overlord kings and their vassals. It would seem that Israel sees itself as the grateful vassal of YHWH, the God who liberated them from bondage. YHWH would then be perceived as Israel's king, enthroned between the cherubim on the ark containing the tablets of the covenant.

The earliest surviving Hebrew literature is, according to some, composed; it includes the "Song at the Sea" (Exodus 15), the "Song of Deborah" (Judges 5), and the testament of Jacob (Genesis 49). The archaic Psalm 29 depicts Israel's God as the power of a storm. The "Song at the Sea" seems to transform the pagan myth in which the storm god splits and subdues the sea god(dess); here, YHWH defeats the evil pharaoh of Egypt by splitting the sea and passing the Israelites through, moving from a struggle in nature to a conflict in history. | **-1100** |

Mt. Tabor, site of the battle between Deborah and Barak and the Canaanite army led by Sisera. (Israel Government Press Office)

| Control of Egypt is divided among Pharaoh Ramesses XI,* the high priest of the god Amun, and the viceroy of Nubia. | | | **-1090** |

| A papyrus relates that Wenamun,* an official of Egypt, is repeatedly rebuffed as he attempts to transact trade with Phoenicia. | The Philistines, the Bible recounts, inflict a severe military blow against Israelite forces at Aphek, capturing the ark of YHWH and destroying the shrine at Shiloh. The Philistines seem to have been seeking to control overland trade. | | **-1050** |

| | Saul leads Israelite forces in wresting Jabesh-Gilead from Ammonite hands; he is acclaimed king and anointed by the prophet Samuel. He builds a fortified palace on top of a formerly Philistine structure. | | **-1020** |

A. General History	B. Jewish History	C. Jewish Culture
-1010	A freebooter called David affiliates with Saul and attacks Philistine settlements. The Bible recounts that he later allies with the Philistine king of Gath, who grants him the town of Ziklag.	
-1005	Saul and his son Jonathan fall in battle against the Philistines at Mt. Gilboa.	The Bible ascribes to David a lament in which he lyrically curses Mt. Gilboa on which "the mighty have fallen."
-1004	David gains control of the territory of Judah, ruling as king from his capital, Hebron. According to biblical tradition, he had been anointed by the prophet Samuel. Northern Israel is ruled by Saul's son Ishbaal (Ishbosheth).	
-1003	Ishbaal is assassinated.	
-998	The northern Israelite tribes join Judah in recognizing David as king.	
-995	David outmaneuvers the Philistines, pushing deeply into their territory and keeping them at bay.	
-990	Using his private army, David conquers Jerusalem from the Jebusites. Centrally located between north and south, Jerusalem is made David's new capital. To reinforce his political control, David establishes the traditional covenant center at Jerusalem, installing the ark and priesthood there.	
-985	David overruns the remaining Canaanite enclaves, consolidating Canaan under his rule. He begins a campaign of imperial conquest, gaining control of the Transjordanian states of Ammon, Moab, and Edom and then turning north to conquer the Aramean states in Syria. These territories David makes tributary, while he makes a treaty with the Phoenician king, Hiram* of Tyre. David's empire reaches from Sinai to the Upper Euphrates River, the borders promised to the patriarch Abraham in Genesis. Judah and Israel are only a part of it.	
-980		David's state bureaucracy is modeled after Egypt's.
-970	Bolstered by sectional and economic grievances, David's son Absalom attempts to overthrow his father. After David puts down that rebellion, he must suppress another led by Sheba, who would have led northern Israel in seceding from the empire.	

A. General History	B. Jewish History	C. Jewish Culture	
	David's sons Adonijah and Solomon vie for succession to the throne, each supported by various palace officials.		**-968**
	An ailing David would seem to appoint Solomon as coregent, seeking to ensure the stability of the ruling house. After David's death, Solomon purges his rival Adonijah and his supporters.	It may be already in the Davidic or early Solomonic regime that a theology is promulgated in which YHWH promises to secure and perpetuate the Davidic dynasty (2 Samuel 7). The idea that YHWH chooses Mt. Zion as his abode serves the political interest of the Davidic kings.	**-967**
	Solomon seals alliances with other nations, often by marrying royalty, including a princess of Egyptian Pharaoh Siamun.* Despite efforts to strengthen fortifications, during his reign Edom and some Aramean states, such as Damascus, break away, eroding the empire.		**-960**
The Gezer Calendar, a stone tablet bearing the earliest extant Hebrew text, circa 950 BCE.	Solomon builds a port and merchant fleet at Ezion Geber on the Gulf of Aqaba. From there he conducts trade in precious stones and spices, deploying a Mediterranean fleet to trade in copper. His overland trade with Arabia is legendary, embodied in the Queen of Sheba* story. He brings wealth to his kingdom, though much of it is raised in taxation and state labor.		**-955**
	Solomon dedicates the most magnificent of his many buildings, the Temple of YHWH. Constructed on a Phoenician design and using Lebanon cedar, it reportedly houses the ark of the covenant constructed by the Israelites leaving Egypt with Moses three centuries earlier.	The oldest extant Israelite document that displays a meaningful message is written about this time. Inscribed in Hebrew on a piece of stone, the Gezer Calendar lists a series of agricultural activities that are performed every month or two during the course of a year. Although the Torah reckons the months from the spring, at Passover, here the counting begins in the fall.	**-950**
As Libyan presence grows strong in northern Egypt, a noble, Shoshenq,* takes the throne and inaugurates two centuries of Libyan dynastic rule there.			**-940**
		During the "golden age" of Solomon, the great biblical classics, the earliest patriarchal narratives (the work of the so-called Yahwist, or J) and the David narratives, are set in writing, according to many scholars. Psalmody and proverbial literature are also thought to flourish.	**-930**
	At Solomon's death, the northern Israelite tribes, long resentful of the Davidic–Solomonic regime for superseding tribal autonomy and imposing heavy taxation, refuse to acknowledge Solomon's son		**-928**

	A. General History	B. Jewish History	C. Jewish Culture
-928		Rehoboam as king. They anoint Jeroboam, son of Nebat, inaugurating the kingdom of Israel and sundering the empire.	
-926		Rehoboam of Judah takes control of the small territory of Benjamin north of Jerusalem as a buffer.	
-923		Pharaoh Shoshenq* of Egypt (known in the Bible as Shishaq) campaigns as far north as Megiddo, leaving a wide path of destruction in his wake. He would seem to target the kingdom of Jeroboam more than that of Rehoboam, who paid the pharaoh heavy tribute. Perhaps on account of Egypt's internal weakness, Shoshenq* does not establish control over Israel and Judah. He leaves a victory stela in Megiddo and lists Israelite towns on the record of his conquests in Karnak, Egypt.	 *Prisoners taken captive by Pharaoh Shoshenq on his campaign into Judah, as depicted on a relief in the Temple at Karnak, about 923 BCE. (Staatliche Museen zu Berlin-Preussischer Kulturbesitz)*
-922		Jeroboam I moves his capital from Shechem, the well-known cultic center, which would appear to have been damaged by Shoshenq,* to Tirzah. He establishes two new shrines at both ends of his kingdom, Bethel and Dan. To rival the Jerusalem Temple, where YHWH rests between the cherubim, Jeroboam sets up a calf at each shrine to serve as a pedestal for YHWH's presence.	The Book of Kings, written from a Judean perspective, will portray Jeroboam's act as idolatry and condemn all northern Israelite kings for following this policy.
-906		Jeroboam's son Nadab is assassinated by one of his officers, Baasha, who rules as king in his stead.	
-905		King Asa of Judah (908–867 BCE) repels the attack of Zerah* the Ethiopian, which may have been instigated by Pharaoh Osorkon I* of Egypt.	
-886		King Asa of Judah prevents King Baasha of Israel (906–883 BCE) from forcibly reclaiming the territory just north of Jerusalem by enlisting the aid of King Benhaddad I* of Damascus.	
-884	Ashurnasirpal II* begins to extend Assyrian control across Upper Mesopotamia, campaigning as far west as Phoenicia. He turns terror and cruelty into standard military procedure.		
-882		Baasha's son Elah is assassinated by one of his officers, Zimri. Zimri, however, cannot withstand the attack on Tirzah by another officer, Omri, who becomes king of Israel.	

A. General History	B. Jewish History	C. Jewish Culture	
	King Omri (882–871 BCE) forges alliances with his neighbors, marrying his son Ahab to the princess of the Phoenician port of Sidon, Jezebel.* Ahab and Jezebel's daughter Athaliah will be married to the son of King Jehoshaphat of Judah, Jehoram.		**-876**
	Omri reconquers some Transjordanian territory from Moab for Israel. The Book of Kings passes over this event, but it is recorded in the monument of King Mesha* of Moab.	Omri begins building a new capital at Samaria. The fortified palace, which will be completed by Ahab, features furniture with ivory inlays. Omri and Ahab also build a summer palace at Jezreel and fortify other cities.	**-875**
	Ahab would seem to share the kingship of Israel with his father, Omri.		**-873**
Benhaddad II* of Damascus (d. 842 BCE) begins extending the dominion of his father, reaching northern Syria.			**-870**
	King Jehoshaphat (870–846 BCE), enjoying a period of relative strength and prosperity, reforms the judicial system of Judah, according to Chronicles. (Jehoshaphat's name means "YHWH judges.")	Ahab's reign (873–852 BCE) is remembered as one pervaded by the pagan Baal cult, promoted by Queen Jezebel.* The case for YHWH is fought by the legendlike wonder-working prophet Elijah of Gilead. According to the Bible, Elijah confronts the Israelites, asking how long they will flit back and forth like a fickle bird between worshipping their God or the Canaanite–Phoenician Baal.	**-860**
Rule of Assyria falls to Ashurnasirpal's* son, Shalmaneser III,* who embarks on a series of annual campaigns to conquer the Aramean states to his west.			**-859**
Shalmaneser III* of Assyria succeeds in overtaking Bit-Adini, an Aramean state he annexes to his empire. This act of aggression may be recalled in Amos 1:5, where God declares he has removed "him who holds the scepter from Bet Eden."			**-855**
	An attempt to overrun the western states of the Middle East by Shalmaneser III* of Assyria is thwarted at Qarqar by a coalition of kings including Ahab of Israel and his former enemy, Benhaddad II* of Damascus. Ahab brings 2,000 chariots and 10,000 soldiers with him to the battle. Ahab's prominence is attested by the Assyrian chronicle, though the entire event is ignored by the Book of Kings.		**-853**
	Ahab's son Jehoram (851–842 BCE) is blocked by King Mesha* from restoring Moab to Israelite control.		**-850**

	A. **General History**	B. **Jewish History**	C. **Jewish Culture**
-850		King Jehoram of Judah (851–843 BCE) loses control of Edom, sacrificing the southern port of Ezion Geber.	
-845	The king of Moab, Mesha,* has an inscription carved in a meter-tall monument in which he explains that Omri, king of Israel, had subjugated his land because the national god of Moab, Chemosh, was angry with it. Mesha* describes the buildings he has dedicated to Chemosh for having restored to Moab the territory the Israelites had occupied during the reign of Ahab. The text is the only extensive one in Moabite, a language very similar to biblical Hebrew.		
-842	Hazael,* an army officer, assassinates and seizes the throne of Damascus from Benhaddad II.*	Jehu, an army general, overturns the regime of the Omride dynasty of Israel, purging the royal family, including King Ahaziah of Judah, cousin of King Jehoram of Israel. The Book of Kings depicts Jehu as a devotee of YHWH, supported by the prophet Elisha. Queen Athaliah takes over the throne of Judah, becoming its only non-Davidic and female monarch. She reportedly introduces Phoenician cultic practices.	 *King Jehu of Israel is depicted in a relief on a stela of King Shalmaneser III, bowing down before his Assyrian overlord. (British Museum)*
-841	Shalmaneser III* of Assyria makes a successful campaign to the west, exacting tribute from various Phoenician cities as well as from King Jehu of Israel.		
-836		Athaliah's seven-year-old nephew, Joash, is crowned king of Judah, and Athaliah is executed.	
-835		The militant Hazael* of Damascus staves off further Assyrian aggression and seeks to dominate the kingdoms of Israel and Judah.	
-827	Rebellions at home preoccupy Shalmaneser III* of Assyria, leaving Hazael* of Damascus to pursue his military efforts against the states of Israel and Judah to his south.		
-814		By the end of Jehu's reign, Israel's Transjordanian holdings have been swept away by Hazael* of Damascus, leaving Israel weak and vulnerable. Judah under Joash has also paid tribute to Hazael.*	
-805	Adad-Nirari III,* whose mother, the legendary Semiramis,* ruled until he came of age, begins leading Assyria on a reconquest of Syria. Assyria continues to seek access to Mediterranean shipping and a		

A. General History	B. Jewish History	C. Jewish Culture	
strategic position between Egypt and Asia Minor.			**-805**
The state of Damascus falls to Adad-Nirari III* of Assyria.	Although Adad-Nirari III* of Assyria will exact tribute from Israel and Judah, too, the Israelite states enjoy a respite from Aramean pressure.	The Second Book of Kings (13:4–5) takes a theological view: YHWH had punished Israel for its cultic sins by placing it in the hands of Aram; but in response to the prayer of King Jehoahaz, YHWH sends a "savior" (the Assyrian king) to remove the Aramean overlord.	**-802**
	Jeroboam II ascends the throne of Israel beside Joash (or Jehoash). During his long individual reign (786–746 BCE) the former borders of Israel, from Syria through the Transjordan, are restored.		**-789**
	War between Joash of Israel (800–784 BCE) and Amaziah of Judah (798–785 BCE), possibly provoked by the latter in conjunction with the reconquest of Edom, leaves Judah defeated.		**-788**
	Upon the assassination of his father Amaziah, Uzziah (785–733 BCE) governs Judah alone. During his reign the territory of Edom and the southern port of Ezion-Geber are restored to Judean control.		**-785**
The festival of Zeus at Olympia is celebrated with military and athletic games. The custom of holding these games every four years sets the precedent for the Olympics of the 20th century CE.			**-776**
The Chou dynasty shifts eastward, having brought China a feudal form of organization.			**-771**
	When King Uzziah of Judah catches leprosy, his son Jotham governs for him.		**-758**
The various states of Syria maintain relative independence from a weakened Assyria.	The power vacuum benefits the kingdoms of Israel and Judah.		**-754**
The great Greek epic poems attributed to Homer,* the *Iliad* and the *Odyssey*, are composed. They render a legendary account of the events surrounding the sacking of Troy around 1230 BCE.		The kingdoms of Israel and Judah enjoy an epoch of military security and economic prosperity. The arrogance, corruption, and disparities between rich and poor that ensue prompt condemnation from the prophets Hosea, Amos, and, a generation later, Isaiah ben Amoz.	**-750**
	After Jeroboam II dies, the throne of Israel is overturned several times in rapid succession.		**-748**
Babylonian astronomers devise a lunar calendar with a system for adding (intercalating) months over a 19-year period to adapt to the solar			**-747**

	A. General History	B. Jewish History	C. Jewish Culture
-747	year. Jewish scholars will develop a similar system a millennium later, around 250 CE.		
-745			Amos, a prophet from the Judean village of Tekoa, attacks the northern Israelite shrines for maintaining a strong cult while failing to engender social and economic justice among the people. He threatens Israel with disaster on account of such moral corruption. The priest of the temple of Bethel, Amaziah, expels the prophet from the northern kingdom.
-744	Tiglath-Pileser III,* who usurped the Assyrian throne, begins an aggressive program for restoring territories north, west, and south to Assyrian control.		
-743		King Uzziah (or Azariah) of Judah leads a group of local armies against the advance of Tiglath-Pileser III* in northern Syria. Ahaz takes the throne of Judah to replace his father Jotham, who dies as regent of his father King Uzziah.	
-738		Tiglath-Pileser III* exacts tribute from Menahem ben Gadi of Israel (747–737 BCE) and other local rulers. Menahem has little choice but to submit to Assyrian domination.	
-735	Two Arabian queens, Zabibe* and Samsi,* are cited by Tiglath-Pileser III.*	Pekahiah, son of Menahem, king of Israel, is assassinated by an army officer, Pekah ben Remaliah, who overtakes the throne, hoping through alliance with Rezin,* the Aramean king of Damascus, to free Israel from Assyria. Pekah (735–732 BCE) of Israel and Rezin* of Damascus invite King Ahaz of Judah to join them against Assyria. When Ahaz, fearful of Assyrian reprisal, refuses, Pekah and Rezin* attack Judah. His kingdom at stake, Ahaz requests intervention from Tiglath-Pileser III* of Assyria.	The prophet Hosea blames political disorder within northern Israel on religiocultural decay. He foresees the destruction of Israel by Assyria as severe divine punishment. Hosea articulates the covenantal relation between YHWH and the people Israel as a marriage in which YHWH expects fidelity in the form of exclusive worship.
-734			The prophet Isaiah warns King Ahaz not to appeal to Tiglath-Pileser III* for aid against the Aramean–Israelite onslaught, urging him to trust instead in YHWH. He foresees an era of international peace in which Jerusalem with its Temple will serve as spiritual center. It is known from Assyrian sources that Ahaz pays tribute to the Assyrian king during his campaign against Philistia.
-733		Tiglath-Pileser III* invades Israel, gradually overrunning the country from the Mediterranean to the Transjordan. Israel's new king,	

A. General History	B. Jewish History	C. Jewish Culture	
	Hosea ben Elah (732–724 BCE), who murdered his predecessor Pekah, submits and renders tribute to the Assyrian overlord.		-733
Damascus falls to Tiglath-Pileser III,* and its king, Rezin,* is killed. Tiglath-Pileser III* deports many Arameans and reorganizes the Aramean states.			-732
The throne of Babylon is seized by a rebel hostile to Assyria, drawing Tiglath-Pileser III's* attention.			-731
Northern Egypt, ruled in a quasi-feudal manner by various Libyan kings, is subjugated by the Ethiopian king of Sudan and southern Egypt, Piankhy.*		Assimilating to Assyrian culture, King Ahaz introduces certain pagan ritual practices in Judah and the Jerusalem temple. He depletes the royal treasury making tribute payments to Assyria.	-730
Tiglath-Pileser III* takes over Babylonia, ruling it under the name Pulu.*			-729
	Hosea, king of Israel, banking on support from Egypt, rebels against Assyria by withholding tribute from its new king, Shalmaneser V.*		-726
	Shalmaneser V* invades Israel, taking control of the entire north except for the capital, Samaria.		-724
Sargon II* seizes the throne of Assyria upon the death of Shalmaneser V.* Sargon II* takes credit for the downfall of Samaria and deportation of 27,290 northern Israelites, which may have been accomplished by his predecessor.	Samaria falls to the Assyrian army. Large numbers of Israel's population are deported to northern regions of the Assyrian Empire, and other peoples are transplanted in northern Israelite territory. The deported Israelites—the so-called 10 lost tribes—assimilate into their new localities.		-722
Merodach-Baladan* succeeds in breaking Babylonia away from Assyrian control.			-721
A battle between Assyria and the joint forces of Elam and Babylonia at Der, near Iran, is indecisive.	In the course of putting down rebellions in the Aramean state of Hamath and in Gaza, Sargon II* reorganizes Israel as a new province of Assyria.	The prophet Micah castigates the Judean clergy for venality, while both he and Isaiah ben Amoz caution Judean society on the growing disparity between rich and poor. Micah, even more than Isaiah, forecasts severe devastation for Jerusalem, not unlike that suffered by Samaria.	-720
Rebellions by Assyrian vassals in Asia Minor and Syria prompt Sargon II* to campaign there. He then turns to the troublesome Urartu and destroys it.			-717
Egypt falls entirely into the hands of the Ethiopian dynast, Piankhy's* brother Shabaka.*			-716

	A. General History	B. Jewish History	C. Jewish Culture
-715		King Hezekiah of Judah (727–698 BCE), laden with Assyrian taxes and chastened by the recent downfall of northern Israel, promotes religious reform while seeking an opportunity to achieve national independence.	
-714	Ashdod and other non-Israelite dominions in the area of Judah rebel against Assyria with the promise of Egyptian support.		Isaiah tries to persuade Hezekiah to abstain from the rebellion against Assyria led by the city of Ashdod. YHWH, Isaiah affirms, will alert Hezekiah when the time to rebel is at hand. The prophet Isaiah walks naked and barefoot to symbolize to Judah the emptiness of Egypt's promise of support for a rebellion against Assyria.
-712		Sargon II* puts down the rebellion of Ashdod and allied parties, making some of them provinces of Assyria. Although Judah is involved, along with Edom, Moab, and Ammon, it is not made an Assyrian province.	
-710		Hezekiah seeks to incorporate remaining northern Israelites into his realm. For the most part, they refuse.	Hezekiah removes from Judah Assyrian images and other cult objects tinged with paganism; he attempts to eliminate worship at shrines outside Jerusalem.
-709	Sargon II* of Assyria seizes dominion of Babylonia from Merodach-Baladan.*		
-705	Sargon II,* killed in battle, is succeeded by his son Sennacherib.* Exploiting Assyrian vulnerability, Merodach-Baladan* of Babylonia enlists international support for rebellion against Assyrian rule.		
-704		King Hezekiah of Judah joins various Phoenician cities and other local regimes in rebelling against Assyrian domination. Doing his part, he imprisons the Philistine king of Ekron, who supports Assyria.	The Judean prophet Isaiah urges Hezekiah not to rely on Egypt and to avoid war with Assyria.
-702			Fearing Assyrian reprisal, Hezekiah constructs a tunnel leading water from the Siloam pool into Jerusalem. It would be vital in case of a siege. A contemporary Hebrew inscription marking the completion of the tunnel will come to light in 1880 CE.
-701	Sennacherib* crushes the Phoenician port of Tyre, leading other local states to surrender meekly to Assyrian authority. Sennacherib* deposes Merodach-Baladan* of Babylonia.	Sennacherib* penetrates Lachish with battering rams and devastates it, as he does other Judean cities and towns. He lays siege to Jerusalem, withdrawing only after Hezekiah has paid heavy tribute and restored the king of Ekron to his throne. The Bible tells of a divine plague that prompts the Assyrian army to leave.	The prophet Isaiah breaks with past custom and encourages Hezekiah to rebel against Assyria. Arrogant Assyria, Isaiah affirms, will be brought down while YHWH will protect his holy seat in Jerusalem. The doctrine of Zion's inviolability may be bound up with the idea that the Davidic dynasty will reign forever.

A. General History	B. Jewish History	C. Jewish Culture	
Sennacherib* places his son Ashur-nadin-shum* on the throne of Babylon. The military technique of lining spear-wielding soldiers across a battlefield protects Greece from invading armies and prepares Greece for overseas conquest. Leading families share government of cities in a form of oligarchy that anticipates democracy. Hesiod,* the Greek theologian, asserts that the gods reward and punish people according to a moral calculus and advises his contemporaries to learn the means for material, and hence moral, success.	Sennacherib* records in his annals that he trapped Hezekiah in Jerusalem "like a bird in a cage," exacting considerable booty, including some of Hezekiah's daughters.	*King Sennacherib of Assyria reviews captives from Judah on this wall relief. (British Museum)* 	-700
	Manasseh, who succeeds his father Hezekiah as king of Judah, accepts the fact of Assyrian lordship.	Manasseh will go beyond his grandfather Ahaz in introducing pagan rituals and symbols into Judah and the Jerusalem Temple. One striking innovation is the astral cult, possibly influenced by Assyria.	-698
Elam supports a Babylonian uprising against Assyria, removing Ashur-nadin-shum* and replacing him with a Babylonian.			-694
Sennacherib* crushes Babylon, destroying and plundering the capital. Pharaoh Taharqa* of Egypt challenges Assyrian hegemony, but Sennacherib* defeats him.			-689
Following the murder of the Assyrian monarch Sennacherib,* his son Esarhaddon* becomes king and asserts firm control.			-681
Esarhaddon* defeats the pharaoh Taharqa* and subjugates Egypt.	Manasseh assists the Assyrian army in its campaign against Egypt.		-671
An Egyptian rebellion against Assyria led by Taharqa* is put down by Esarhaddon's* son and successor, Ashurbanipal* (669–627 BCE).			-667
A further rebellion by Egypt prompts the Assyrian army to destroy Thebes and with it the 25th Dynasty.			-663
A growing Aramean population, known as the Chaldeans, are among those who disturb the peace of Assyrian rule in Mesopotamia.			-660
King Psammetichus I* (664–610 BCE) of Egypt consolidates sufficient power to achieve independence from Assyria.			-655

	A. General History	B. Jewish History	C. Jewish Culture
-652	Shamash-shum-ukin,* brother of King Ashurbanipal* and regent of Babylon, leads a rebellion against Assyria with the support of the Elamites and Chaldeans. Hearing of the Babylonian uprising, Psammetichus* of Egypt incites a wave of rebellion among small states in Syro-Palestine. Arabs from the Syrian desert begin to raid the Transjordan as far south as Edom.	King Manasseh of Judah may respond to Egyptian incitement to join the rebellion against Assyria.	
-650	In Greece, following a nearly successful revolt by serfs, or helots, Sparta concentrates on becoming a soldier-state. The central European Celts, making use of their metallurgical skill, extend their domain to the Atlantic.		
-648	After a protracted struggle, King Ashurbanipal* retakes Babylon.		
-646	Ashurbanipal* reasserts Assyrian control of the states in the Syro-Palestine region, including Judah.		
-640	Ashurbanipal* destroys Elam and its capital, Susa. Lydia extends its domain in Anatolia once the Cimmerians are routed by Assyria. Lydia will develop extensive trade during the next century and invent the use of coins.	Elamites and others suppressed by Ashurbanipal* are deported to and resettled in Israel. King Amon, son of Manasseh, is assassinated after a two-year reign. His younger brother Josiah, though only eight, is made king of Judah.	
-635	King Ashurbanipal* collects in Nineveh a vast library of Mesopotamian literature reaching back to antiquity. Most of the tablets are copied by his scribes.		
-628		Seeing the Assyrian Empire wane, King Josiah begins to assert Judean nationalism. He takes control of Samaria and other northern Israelite areas and removes ritual elements associated with Assyria.	In the spirit of a general ancient Near Eastern turn toward classical culture, Josiah would seem to be reviving an ideal past, such as that of Moses or David.
-626	Following the death of Ashurbanipal* in 627 BCE, Nabopolassar* wrests Babylon from Assyria, which had been racked by internecine struggle for a few years. He founds the Neo-Babylonian Empire.		
-625			The prophets Zephaniah and Jeremiah threaten national catastrophe if Judeans do not abandon all pagan practice and immoral conduct. Jeremiah, it would seem, lends strong support to Josiah's reform.

		In conjunction with King Josiah's reform, a *book of instruction* (torah) is publicly read. The book calls for elimination of all foreign cult forms, specifying astral worship among other items, and prohibits all but one central shrine. Josiah applies the book's program, destroying all shrines except the Jerusalem Temple, eradicating the rural priesthood, and assembling Israelites in Jerusalem to celebrate the spring festival of Pesah (Passover) (2 Kings 22–23). The book Josiah "found" is probably the core of Deuteronomy.	**-622**
The Mesopotamian creation myth, *Enuma elish*, is performed as part of the Babylonian New Year festival. Originating in the preceding millennium, the myth relates that Marduk, chief god of Babylon, is ensconced in his temple and adored by the other gods after he has created the world from the corpse of the goddess of the watery chaos, Tiawat.		The Book of Ruth may be composed at about this time. An idyllic story about the bond between a Judean woman, Naomi, and her Moabite daughter-in-law, Ruth, and the kindness in turn by the Bethlehem noble, Boaz, who redeems Naomi's land and marries Ruth to preserve the name of Ruth's late husband, the tale takes on political import when in the end it is recounted that King David is descended from Ruth and Boaz. Some scholars think the book was written to oppose the measures against intermarriage by Ezra and Nehemiah in the 5th century. In Jewish tradition Ruth is the model convert, committing herself to the God, people, and land of Israel. The Book of Proverbs is compiled from various older and younger collections of Hebrew proverbial wisdom, probably within a century of this date. The universal character of the pragmatic advice that is offered in the book accords with the appearance of Phoenician influence in Chapters 1–9 and of borrowing from the Egyptian *Wisdom of Amen-em-opet** in Chapters 22–24. In the form of counsel addressed to a young man, Proverbs holds that pious and correct behavior will bring one prosperity.	**-620**
Psammetichus I* of Egypt sends troops to aid Assyria in repelling a further Babylonian assault. Egypt apparently fears growing Babylonian power.			**-616**
The Medes overtake the Assyrian capital, Asshur.			**-614**
A coalition of Babylonia and Media destroy the Assyrian stronghold of Nineveh. King Ashur-uballit II* leads the Assyrian army in a retreat west to Harran.			**-612**

	A. General History	B. Jewish History	C. Jewish Culture
-609	The remaining Assyrian army is destroyed by the Babylonian alliance at Carchemish. Pharaoh Necho II* of Egypt (610–594 BCE) leads an army to Carchemish to assist the Assyrians and reestablish hegemony in Syro-Palestine. They fail against a powerful Babylonian force.	King Josiah of Judah, apparently supporting Babylon, attempts to thwart Pharaoh Necho II's* effort to aid the Assyrians. Meeting Necho at Megiddo, Josiah is slain. Returning from Syria to Egypt, Necho II* appoints Josiah's son Jehoiakim as a puppet king over Judah.	The prophet Nahum sees divine retribution in the utter fall of Assyria. His prophecy gloating over Nineveh's downfall may have anticipated the event in 612 BCE.
-608			Jeremiah decries rampant immorality. Many Judeans, it would seem, are not convinced by Josiah's reforms.
-607	King Nabopolassar* and his son Nebuchadrezzar* assert Babylonian strength to the north in Armenia.		
-605	The Babylonian army led by Nebuchadrezzar* routs Egyptian forces stationed at Carchemish, Syria.		
-604		Nebuchadrezzar II* (605–562 BCE), now king of Babylon following his father's death, campaigns from Syria through Israel, ravaging much of Philistia. King Jehoiakim of Judah submits to Babylonian control.	
-601		Near the Egyptian border the armies of King Nebuchadrezzar* and Pharaoh Necho II* fight to a draw. When the Babylonians return home, King Jehoiakim decides to withhold tribute and rebel.	
-600	In eastern Persia Zarathushtra, known to the Greeks as Zoroaster, teaches that two divine powers, one light and good, the other dark and evil, struggle within the world. The Judean prophet in Babylonian exile may be responding to this idea when he insists that Israel's one God "forms light and creates darkness, makes peace and creates evil" (Isaiah 45:7), but the dating of Zarathushtra is uncertain. As romantic songs flourish in Greece, the female poet Sappho* of Lesbos writes of love between women. Male homosexuality revolves around the all-male athletic arena and may be reflected in the contemporary development of nude sculpture.		A history of Israel is composed in the spirit of the Book of Deuteronomy, showing that since the time of settling their land the Israelites suffered calamities when they neglected or violated the covenant with YHWH. Written from a Judean perspective, in which the northern kingdom of Israel continually displeases God for worshipping elsewhere than Jerusalem, the history will be revised to include events surrounding the fall of Judah. The fall of Jerusalem is attributed not to the conduct of the recent King Josiah but to the sins of his father Manasseh. The Deuteronomistic history comprises what are now the Books of Joshua, Judges, Samuel, and Kings.
-598		When King Jehoiakim dies, perhaps the victim of assassination, he is succeeded by his son Jehoiachin. An army is sent by King Nebuchadrezzar* from Babylon to suppress the Judean rebellion.	

A. General History	B. Jewish History	C. Jewish Culture	
	Judah surrenders to Nebuchadrezzar's* army; King Jehoiachin and many other leading citizens, including a young priest named Ezekiel, are exiled to Babylon. Zedekiah, uncle of Jehoiachin, is appointed king of Judah.		-597
	An insurrection in Babylon is joined by some Judeans.		-595
Pharaoh Psammetichus II* is preoccupied with securing the southern territory of Egypt.	Judah and some local states, hearing of the insurrection against Babylon, plan their own revolt. The plot fails to materialize, and King Zedekiah reassures King Nebuchadrezzar* of his loyalty.	The prophet Jeremiah wears an ox yoke to symbolize his advice to submit to the yoke of Babylon.	-594
In Athens Solon* promulgates socioeconomic reforms such as the abolition of indentured slavery and the inclusion of poor citizens in the electorate.		Ezekiel begins to prophesy to his fellow Judean exiles in Babylon. The prophet envisions YHWH visiting him from Jerusalem in a heavenly chariot, which will later become the object of Jewish mystical speculation. He regurgitates a message of Jerusalem's doom, written on a scroll Ezekiel is said to eat. Although he affirms the possibility of last-minute repentance, he foresees catastrophe as he mimes to his audience the impending siege and exile of Jerusalem.	-593
	King Zedekiah consults with the imprisoned prophet Jeremiah about the wisdom of rebelling against Babylonian domination. The prophet, fearing catastrophe, cautions against such a move. Zedekiah, under pressure from the aristocracy to conserve Judean wealth and probably relying on Egyptian support, rebels.		-589
	The Babylonian army lays siege to Jerusalem in January and destroys other Judean towns. Letters written by Judean officers near Lachish report that the fire signal of nearby Azekah has gone out. In July the Babylonian army repels an Egyptian force and resumes the siege of Jerusalem.	Many leading Judeans affirm that YHWH would not allow the holy city of Jerusalem and its Temple to be violated. The prophets Jeremiah and Habakkuk insist that YHWH would destroy the city himself for violations of the covenant.	-588
	By July Jerusalem is worn down. The shortage of supplies grows so severe that children are reportedly cooked for food. The Babylonians break into the city and exile King Zedekiah. In August King Nebuchadrezzar's* commander, Nebuzaradan,* sets fire to Jerusalem and its Temple. Judean officials are executed or		-587

	A. General History	B. Jewish History	C. Jewish Culture
-587		exiled to Babylonia with thousands of other Judeans. Judah is made a province of Babylonia.	
-586		Judean nationalists assassinate the appointed governor of Judah, Gedaliah, as a Babylonian collaborator. Other Babylonian supporters flee to Egypt, taking the prophet Jeremiah with them.	When news of Jerusalem's destruction reaches the Babylonian exiles, Ezekiel comforts his compatriots, envisioning a return from exile and a rebuilt Israelite homeland. The prophet depicts the future redemption as a divine refurbishing of the exiles' "dry bones" with sinews, flesh, and the breath of new life.
-585	King Nebuchadrezzar* blocks the emerging Median empire based in Ecbatana from controlling the northern frontier as far as Lydia in western Asia Minor. The Phoenician city of Tyre withstands a Babylonian assault, despite the dire predictions of the prophet Ezekiel.		
-582		The Babylonian army deports more Judeans in reprisal for Gedaliah's death.	
-580		The exiled Judeans are settled together near Babylon; they build houses, raise families, and earn livelihoods farming and trading. Pharaoh Apries* establishes a colony of Judean mercenaries at Elephantine, an island in the Middle Nile.	Some Judeans and northern Israelites continue to make offerings at the ruins of the Jerusalem Temple. The Book of Lamentations may comprise liturgies recited to commemorate the Temple's destruction. "A sin has Jerusalem sinned; for that she has been cast aside" (Lamentations 1:8).
-575	The city-state of Athens begins minting coins.		
-568	King Nebuchadrezzar* of Babylon sends an army to check Egyptian expansion into Asia.		
-560	Athens' governance is taken over by Pisistratus,* a revolutionary "tyrant" who transfers wealth of the powerful to the lower classes.	King Jehoiachin of Judah is freed by Nebuchadrezzar's* short-lived successor, Evilmerodach.*	
-556	Nabonidus,* an Aramean from Harran, seizes the throne of Babylonia, which had been unstable since Nebuchadrezzar's* death. Nabonidus alienates many Babylonians by promoting the supremacy of the moon god, Sin, and by excavating various temples to identify their builders. He spends a decade at Teima in northern Arabia, establishing military outposts along caravan routes. Among these far-flung soldiers are, it would seem, Judeans.		

| | | With Nabonidus* in Teima, Belshazzar,* his son, governs Babylon. Nabonidus* will be identified in the Book of Daniel with his predecessor Nebuchadrezzar,* the king who went mad, living like a beast in Arabia, and Belshazzar* will be represented as the king whose writing on the wall Daniel interprets. | **-553** |

| A Persian named Cyrus,* or Kurash,* takes over the Median Empire in Ecbatana.

Greek colonies proliferate in southern Italy and elsewhere along the Mediterranean Sea from Spain to the Black Sea, easing the overpopulation of the Greek mainland and stimulating trade. | | Judeans in Israel and the Diaspora consolidate their traditions. In addition to revising the Deuteronomistic history, scribes compile and edit prophetic books while others put the priestly material of the Torah into unified literary form. A history of Israel and its covenant, from the creation of the world through the exile of Judah, is composed out of these and other narrative and legal materials. The first five books, known as the Torah of Moses, place a core of God's laws in the center, providing a revealed constitution to the restoration community and Jewish centers outside Judah, too.

Two thin silver strips are inscribed with versions of the priestly benediction attested in Numbers 6. The strips are rolled up and are probably worn around the neck as amulets by members of a wealthy Jerusalem family living at what is now called Ketef Hinnom. The inscriptions are the earliest extant documents containing part of the Torah. | **-550** |

| Cyrus* wrests Lydia in western Asia Minor from Babylonia. He proceeds to expand his dominion north- and eastward. | | | **-546** |

| The Greek philosopher Xenophanes,* settled in Italy, posits a single God as the eternal substance at the root of all things. | | Some Judean exiles have lost faith in the God of their ancestors, YHWH, who allowed their homeland to be ravaged. An anonymous prophet, known as the Second Isaiah, eloquently argues that YHWH had planned the exile as a punishment and has now planned a restoration. As the sole creator of the world, YHWH has the power to manipulate all history (Isaiah 40–48). | **-545** |

| Cyrus'* army defeats Babylon at Opis on the Tigris River. Cyrus* claims that Marduk and the other Babylonian gods gave him victory to undo the abominations perpetrated by Nabonidus*; he does in fact | | The Second Isaiah has told his fellow Judean exiles that YHWH has been granting victories to Cyrus* so that he will overthrow Babylon and restore them to their homeland. The exiled Judeans have more than paid | **-539** |

	A. General History	B. Jewish History	C. Jewish Culture
-539	seem to have been aided by the Marduk priests of Babylonia. Cyrus* appoints his son Cambyses* as regent of Babylon.		for their past sins, so "Mother Zion," now forgiven by her "husband" YHWH, will welcome home her once wayward "children." The people of Israel may then fulfill their mission to be a "light unto the nations" (Isaiah 49:6).
-538		Cyrus* releases the Judean exiles to return to Jerusalem and rebuild it as part of his policy toward ethnic and religious groups. A member of the Judean royal family, Sheshbazzar, is assigned to repatriate the temple vessels.	
-530	Cambyses* succeeeds to the throne of his father when Cyrus* dies in battle.	The administration of communal and judicial affairs among the Judean exiles is performed by a council or tribunal of "elders," in conformity with general Persian practice.	The returnees from Babylon try not to intermingle with Judeans who were not exiled, who were thought to have corrupted the covenant tradition.
-525	Egypt falls to Cambyses* and becomes a province of Persia.	The small community of returnees from Babylon faces hardships due to difficult economic conditions and hostility from the Samarians who were not exiled. Rebuilding the Temple is hindered.	
-522	When Cambyses* dies, an army officer from the royal family, Darius I,* seizes the throne. Throughout the Persian Empire, rebellions break out.		
-520	Darius I* establishes control of his empire.		The prophets Haggai and Zechariah* interpret the upheavals in Persia as a sign of YHWH's return to the historical stage. They press the Judeans to resume construction of the Temple under the leadership of a scion of the Davidic line, Zerubabbel.
-515	*King Darius of Persia reviews prisoners as depicted on a relief high on the Behistun cliff.*	The newly completed Temple is dedicated as Passover is observed. Davidic kingship under Zerubbabel is not restored.	Jews begin replacing the personal name of God, YHWH, with more general epithets such as "God of Israel." From around 200 BCE some Jews read Adonai (My Lord) for YHWH, a practice that continues to this day. According to the Mishnah (200 CE), YHWH is pronounced only by the high priest in the Temple's Holy of Holies on the Day of Atonement.
-511	The city-state of Sparta attacks its rival, Athens.		
-510	Democracy is extended in Athens to all native-born, free, adult males. Leadership revolves, assigned by lot.		
-500	Darius I's* empire extends from the Indus River Valley to Libya. He controls it through a system of 20 satrapies and a corps of spies.		The age-old problem of evil, of why the righteous suffer and the wicked thrive, is pointedly addressed in the Book of Job. A legendary tale

A. General History	B. Jewish History	C. Jewish Culture	
Edomites inhabit southern Israel having been pushed northward by the Arab occupation of their territory. In India followers of Gautama* develop Buddhism, and those of Mahavira,* Jainism. Buddha,* a non-Aryan, particularly opposes the caste notion. The Upanishad texts in Sanskrit idealize personal efforts to transcend material existence.		written in the Persian period describes a pious Gentile who refuses to curse God even after he has been bereaved of his estate and his children. This tale has been subverted by a dramatic poem in which Job insists that God is persecuting him unjustly and demands that God defend Job's suffering. The book refutes the notion held by Job's challengers that all suffering signifies divine punishment for sinning.	**-500**
Ionia begins its rebellion against Persian domination.			**-499**
Confucius* (d. 479 BCE) stresses interpersonal ethics and urges his fellow noblemen in China to serve as role models. His teaching that political rule rests on a moral foundation will be elaborated a century later by Mencius.*		The earliest of the 100 Aramaic papyruses and 350 Aramaic ostraca found at Elephantine is executed. Nearly all these documents reflect the legal and political activities of the 5th-century Jewish colony, which largely follows common Aramaic practice. In contrast to later rabbinic law, for example, women engage in business and initiate divorce actions. These Jews live among Gentiles and evidence no use of Hebrew. Among their literary texts is an Aramaic version of the proverbs of the Assyrian courtier, Ahiqar.*	**-495**
The army of Darius I* is repelled from Greece by Athenians at Marathon. Enriched by newly discovered silver, Athens builds an extensive navy.	Judah's numbers grow as more exiles return from Babylon. It would seem the high priest administers Persian rule, accusing local Jews of sedition to ensure Persian support.		**-490**
Xerxes I* succeeds to his late father Darius'* throne. He suppresses a revolt in Egypt.		Xerxes* is probably the King Ahasueras (Persian, Khshayarsha) remembered in the biblical story of Esther.	**-486**
The Persian emperor Xerxes* puts down a revolt in Babylonia and proceeds on a protracted campaign against Greece.			**-482**
Xerxes* destroys the Babylonian capital built by Nebuchadrezzar,* a famed "wonder of the world."			**-478**
Herodotus* writes a history of Greece's wars with Persia that encompasses two centuries of Middle Eastern life and lore. Opposing the school of Xenophanes,* the Greek philosopher Heraclitus* maintains that reality is grounded not in the permanent, but in change.			**-475**
Xerxes'* army is defeated at the Eurymedon River and must withdraw from Europe.			**-466**

	A. General History	B. Jewish History	C. Jewish Culture
-460	With the aid of the Libyan Inaros* and the Greek navy, Egypt drives Persia from the Nile Delta. The rebellion is short-lived as Persian forces kill Inaros* and allied Phoenicians cripple the Greek fleet.		
-455		An inscription attests to a Jewish community in Sardis, in western Asia Minor.	From the archive of the Murashu* family in Nippur, in which at least 100 Jews are named, it is clear that Jews lease and own Babylonian land, sometimes in conjunction with Gentiles, and engage in agriculture, tax collecting, and other occupations. Perhaps as a response to the prophet Jeremiah's call to the Babylonian exiles to pray for the welfare of their new country (Jeremiah 29:7), some Jews name their sons Shulum-Babli, "Welfare of Babylon." It is common for Jews with Babylonian names to give their children Hebrew ones, expressing perhaps their increased security in the Diaspora.
-450	While Greek city-states remain largely at peace, Athens enjoys its "golden age," as philosophy, mathematics, art, and drama by such playwrights as Aeschylus* (d. 456 BCE) and Euripides* (first staged 455 BCE) and poetry by Pindar* and others collectively represent the epitome of Western culture.	Judeans, feeling threatened by hostile elements, fortify Jerusalem. Persian subjects in Samaria accuse them of rebelling.	The prophet Malachi condemns what he sees as materialism and a breakdown of family morals in Judah.
-449	Athens and Persia declare a truce.		
-445		A Jewish official of the Persian court, Nehemiah, is sent to Jerusalem to rebuild its fortifications and supervise the community. Judah is separated from Samaria as a province of Persia. The territory from Hebron south to Egypt is governed by Geshem* the Arabian.	
-437		Despite repeated harassment by Sanballat, governor of the Samarian province, and Tobiah, governor of the Transjordanian province, Nehemiah completes the Jerusalem wall.	
-433		When Nehemiah returns to Babylon, Jerusalem's high priest Eliashib gives the Transjordanian governor, Tobiah, quarters in the temple.	
-432	A masterpiece of Greek architecture, the Parthenon is completed atop the acropolis in Athens.		
-431	Greek states begin a fierce and protracted conflict for hegemony known as the Peloponnesian War.	Nehemiah is reappointed to Jerusalem. Upon his arrival, Nehemiah expels Tobiah and enforces observance of the Sabbath and the ban on intermarriage.	

A. General History	B. Jewish History	C. Jewish Culture	
The Greek philosopher Democritus* proposes that matter is composed of atomic structures.			**-430**
	The priest-scribe Ezra arrives in Judah, authorized by the Persian government to instruct all those professing to be Jews in the Laws of Moses and to exact observance of his interpretation of these Jewish laws. Ezra compels Jews to divorce their gentile wives and otherwise to commit themselves to Mosaic law and support of the Temple.	Ezra and Nehemiah assemble the Jews on the Festival of Sukkot (Booths) for reading and explicating the Torah of Moses (see Nehemiah 8). Ezra's exegesis (*midrash*; see Ezra 7:10) of the Torah may be seen as the beginning of classical Judaism, a religion that determines the will of God through textual interpretation rather than prophecy. Ezra will be viewed in rabbinic tradition as the prototypical rabbi.	**-428**
A series of plays by Aristophanes,* beginning now and continuing for decades, ridicule the warring Greeks and even their gods.		The Jews at Elephantine, at Aswan, Egypt, practice a distinctly unorthodox religion. While they sacrifice to YHWH at their own temple according to the ordinances of the Torah, they make offerings to local pagan gods, too, and invoke their names in oaths.	**-425**
		Yedoniah, priest of the Jewish community at Elephantine, is ordered by the local Persian satrap Arsames* and Nehemiah's successor Hananiah in Jerusalem to observe the Passover according to Mosaic law.	**-419**
	An anti-Jewish attack in Egypt incited by the priests of the local god Khnum destroys the temple at Elephantine.		**-411**
	The Jerusalem high priest Yochanan has his ambitious brother Joshua killed, prompting the Persian governor Bagoas to repress Jewish activities.		**-410**
	Elephantine Jews seek assistance to rebuild their temple from the Persian governor of Judea, Bagoas,* and the sons of Sanballat, governor of Samaria, having failed to receive support from the Jerusalem high priest Yochanan. Their bid is approved, and the temple is reconstructed. To assuage the local pagan priests and the Jerusalem priests, however, the Jews are forbidden to make animal offerings.		**-408**
The Peloponnesian War ends, decimating Athens, favoring Sparta, but overall weakening Greece to the advantage of Persia. In his history of the war, Thucydides* exposes the internal politics of Athens as well as the broader political scene. Artaxerxes II* succeeds Darius II* as king of the Persian Empire.			**-404**

A. General History	B. Jewish History	C. Jewish Culture

-404 Egypt under Amyrtaeus* liberates itself from Persian control.

-401 Artaxerxes II's* brother Cyrus* leads an army of 13,000 Greek mercenaries in an unsuccessful revolution. The story of the Greeks' hard march home is recorded in the "Anabasis" by Xenophon.*

-400

Jews continue to live in the land of Israel far beyond the borders of Judea. They inhabit the coastal towns as well as the Transjordanian region of Tob, home of the aristocratic Tobiad family. Some, like the legendary Tobit from the Galilean hills, make pilgrimage to the Jerusalem Temple.

A history of the Jews from the beginning of humankind up to the leadership of Ezra is composed. This work, the biblical Book of Chronicles, emphasizes the continuity between the people and institutions of the restored Judean community and the Second Temple with those prior to the destruction of the First Temple. The founder of the legitimate royal house, King David, is accredited with establishing the entire Temple cult.

Aramaic, the lingua franca of the Persian Empire, increasingly serves as a spoken language of Judea. Hebrew is written in the square letters developed for Aramaic (recalled in Daniel 2:4).

Collections of religious songs, many used in temple worship, are assembled by cultic personnel into what will become the biblical Book of Psalms. Traditionally ascribed to King David, the psalms appear to stem from various stages in Israel's history. The Psalms include prayers and hallelujah hymns related to the temple service, but many take the form of personal supplications expressing a profound faith that God will deliver the pious from distress.

-399 Citizens of Athens condemn their leading philosopher, Socrates,* to death. Socrates* challenged the underlying premises of the Sophists, utilizing a searching method of questioning to be known as the *Socratic method*, and he shifted the emphasis in philosophy from metaphysics to ethics. Chief among his disciples is Plato.*

-380 Plato* develops his theory that the higher reality comprises ideal forms of those that we directly perceive. This view will influence Philo of Alexandria's interpretation of Judaism as well as some medieval Jewish thought.

-360 A revolt against Artaxerxes II* by western Asian satraps is put down when Egypt, facing unrest at home, pulls back its support.

A. General History	B. Jewish History	C. Jewish Culture	
Philip II* becomes king of Macedonia.			**-359**
Pharaoh Teos* taxes Egypt heavily to pay the Greek mercenaries he will need to bring Syro-Palestine back under Egyptian control. He is removed in favor of his son Nectanebo II.*			
Artaxerxes III* establishes his position as Persian king by purging the rest of his family. He puts down local rebellions with similar resolve.			**-358**
Aristotle,* a student of Plato,* takes a far more empirical approach to understanding reality and the sciences. He endeavors to treat each branch of knowledge systematically. For him, the highest good is to contemplate the principle of existence, the prime mover from which it derives. Aristotle's thought, translated by Arab philosophers, will make a profound impact on medieval Jewish thinking. The increasing Hellenization of Italy and other Mediterranean lands shifts the centers of trade from Greece to its colonies.	Artaxerxes III* settles some Judeans in northern Persia, extending the Diaspora.	The Book of Tobit, part of the Apocrypha, is composed in Aramaic (though it survives only in Greek and Hebrew fragments among the Dead Sea Scrolls). Weaving together a variety of folklore motifs and drawing on biblical history, the bittersweet story relates the misfortunes of the family of Tobit, a Jew in the long-gone Assyrian Empire and uncle of the legendary sage Ahiqar. The tale bespeaks the irony of a pious Jewish life, as Tobit, for example, is blinded by bird droppings after having made extraordinary efforts to bury the Jewish dead at Nineveh. Tobit reveres the Jerusalem Temple but does not journey there. Angels and demons appear routinely; an organized Jewish community is not in evidence. Hope is expressed that gentile nations will come to acknowledge the sovereignty of Israel's God, echoing perhaps the sentiment of Zechariah 14:9.	**-350**
Successful diplomacy between Athens and Philip* of Macedon occasions the great orator Demosthenes'* "On the Peace."			**-346**
Artaxerxes III* of Persia destroys the rebellious Phoenician port of Sidon and proceeds to reconquer Egypt.			**-343**
Persia under Artaxerxes III* retakes Lower Egypt.			**-341**
The Latins open rebellion against Rome.			**-340**
Philip II* of Macedon defeats the Athenian league at the battle of Chaironeia and gains control of all Hellas.			**-338**
Philip* of Macedon is murdered in advance of his campaign against Persia. His son Alexander* (333–323 BCE) inherits his kingship.			**-336**

	A. General History	B. Jewish History	C. Jewish Culture
-333	Alexander* of Macedon (to be known as Alexander the Great), having successfully invaded Asia Minor, leads his army down the coast of Syria and Phoenicia, conquering each city in his path. While Phoenician cities like Sidon welcome Alexander's army, others, like Tyre, offer unsuccessful resistance. In November, Alexander* the Great defeats the army of Darius III* of Persia in Syria, thus inaugurating his conquest of the Near East.		
-332		During his seven-month siege of Tyre, the army of Alexander* the Great takes over Samaria and Judea. Gaza submits to Alexander's* siege after two months, clearing his path to Egypt. Jewish tradition relates a meeting between Alexander* and the high priest of Jerusalem, Jaddua. The governor of Samaria, Sanballat III, reportedly sends troops to assist Alexander* in the conquest of Tyre.	
-331	Alexander* the Great conquers Egypt handily, founding the city of Alexandria. In October, with an army now including Jewish mercenaries, Alexander* the Great defeats Darius III* of Persia near Mosul and takes over Babylon.	Alexander* suppresses a rebellion in Samaria and settles some Macedonians in that part of Israel. A group of Samarians escapes to a cave near Jericho, but the Macedonians find and kill them.	Alexander's* Jewish soldiers refuse to cooperate in rebuilding the pagan Babylonian temple, Esagila.
-330	When Darius III* is assassinated, Alexander* the Great gains complete control of Persia. He aims to unite Macedonians and Persians as one people. Alexander* administers Persia through its system of satrapies. He appropriates Persian wealth by converting its precious metal into Greek coinage.	In early Hellenistic Alexandria Jews are naturalized, enjoying full political rights. By the second quarter of the next century new Jewish residents are regarded as noncitizens so that two Jewish classes evolve.	The Macedonians newly settled in Samaria introduce foreign worship that the native Samaritans find alien. The latter have been serving the God of Israel for generations. Accordingly, they withdraw and begin building their own temple in Shechem, a cultic site ordained by Deuteronomy. Though disdained by the Jews in Jerusalem, they regard themselves as truly Israelite. The Samaritan version of the Torah makes Shechem the site of YHWH's chosen shrine.
-325	Alexander* the Great halts his campaign into India and establishes a capital in Babylon, where he plans a movement into Arabia.	The small province of Judea (Ioudaia) thrives under Alexander,* who leaves taxes as they are. Unlike elsewhere, Judeans all enjoy citizen status, undivided into classes.	
-323	When Alexander* the Great dies of malaria in Babylon, his generals Ptolemy,* Seleucus,* Antigonus,* and others, known as the "successors" (diadochi), murder his heirs and vie for control of the Greek Empire.		

A. General History	B. Jewish History	C. Jewish Culture	
Ptolemy,* one of the leading successors to Alexander,* establishes control of Egypt, keeping his eye on Syro-Palestine.			**-320**
Antigonus,* a successor to Alexander,* drives his rival Seleucus,* satrap of Babylon, out of Asia Minor and embarks on a conquest of the Mediterranean Coast down to Gaza.	Antigonus* appoints his son Demetrius* governor of Palestine.		**-317**
		Aristotle* engages in dialogue with a Jew in Asia Minor, according to Clearchus* of Soli, a disciple of Aristotle. The Greek is characterized as a sage, the Jew, as a wonder worker. Jews, however, gain a reputation in Greece as Eastern philosophers.	**-315**
Ptolemy* and Seleucus* defeat Demetrius* at Gaza. Ptolemy* takes control of Palestine, and Seleucus* proceeds to conquer Babylon. Antigonus* leads an army into Syria and Palestine, forcing Ptolemy* back to Egypt.	Many Jews supportive of Ptolemy* return with him to Egypt, according to Josephus.		**-312**
Thwarted in an attempt to dominate the Nabateans, Antigonus* establishes outposts such as Pella to control caravan routes in the Transjordan.	Antigonus* would seem to govern Judea and Samaria through districts or hyparchies. Jerusalem may well have been administered by a council led by the high priest Onias I (323–301 BCE), son of Jaddua. This council would be the Great Assembly of rabbinic tradition and forerunner of the Sanhedrin.	Outside the borders of Judea proper, some Jews worship at altars other than the Jerusalem Temple, as excavations at Lachish and Arad show.	**-311**
The Greek philosopher Epicurus* establishes a school in Athens, teaching his followers to diminish their desires so as to increase their contentment and that a person disintegrates at death. His ideas may bear a kinship to those of the Bible's philosopher, Qohelet (Ecclesiastes).			**-306**
Ptolemy I,* surnamed Soter (Savior), makes himself king of Egypt, adopting the prerogatives of the pharaohs to own all lands and control trade.		The stories comprising Chapters 1–6 of the Book of Daniel are by now composed. They are written in Aramaic. The series of tales features the young Judean exile Daniel and his three companions, each of whom has a Babylonian name in addition to his Hebrew one. Despite the efforts of the Babylonian kings Nebuchadrezzar* and Belshazzar* and Darius* the Mede to try their faith, the Jewish youths remain steadfast in their religion and prove the universal power of their God. Daniel foretells the fall of the kingdoms of Babylon, Media, and Persia. These chapters will be joined to Daniel 7–12 in 165 BCE,	**-305**

A. General History	B. Jewish History	C. Jewish Culture
-305		when the fall of Antiochus IV* is similarly envisioned.
-301 Seleucus* claims rule over Syria and Palestine after a victory against Antigonus* at Ipsus, in Phrygia. While the rivals are engaged in battle, Ptolemy* seizes control of Palestine.	Ptolemy* captures Jerusalem and exiles possibly thousands of Judeans to Egypt.	
-300 The Chinese *Tao te ching*, ascribed traditionally to Lao-tzu* of the 5th century BCE, teaches that good and evil, life and death, and other concepts exist relative to each other in pairs and that behind the illusory appearances that people ordinarily perceive lies the absolute Tao, which can be contemplated only mystically.	Seleucus* induces Jews to settle new cities, such as Antioch, that he founds in Asia and Syria. The Jews of Antioch form a special political body.	Hecataeus* writes in his history of the world that Egypt had long ago expelled the Jews, whose leader, Moses, founded Jerusalem. His (mis)information apparently derives from Egyptian priestly lore. According to Hecataeus'* Greek outlook, Moses and the priests after him presented the Torah as divine revelation in order to lend the law authority among the people. An unknown author of uncertain date writes a critique of Babylonian idolatry, apparently addressed to fellow Jews. The Epistle of Jeremiah survives only in its translation in the Greek Bible.
-290 Manetho,* an Egyptian priest, writes a history of his nation in Greek, establishing the division of eras by royal dynasties. He would seem to identify the 2nd-millennium Hyksos with the Hebrews.		
-286 Ptolemy I Soter* has gained control of the ports of Sidon and Tyre, giving him hegemony over both land and sea trade routes and providing his regime with great wealth.		
-279 The Gauls invade Greece but are repelled at Delphi. Undaunted, they proceed to invade Asia Minor.		
-278 After defeating the Nabateans, Ptolemy II* Philadelphus closes off the Transjordanian trade route and redirects it through Gaza, an area under his immediate control.	To fortify Palestine, Ptolemy II* builds and rebuilds cities such as Acco (which he calls Ptolemais), Beth-shean, and Rabbah (modern Amman, which he calls Philadelphia).	
-275		A group of Aramaic texts revolving around the biblical character Enoch, who was "taken" to heaven by God, begins to be composed and collected. The full collection, called 1 Enoch, survives only in an Ethiopic version. In describing the astronomical structure of the sky, an early section anticipates the Book of Jubilees and Dead Sea Scrolls in assuming a solar calendar, not the lunar one of the Bible. The nature of the calendar will become a major bone of contention among Jewish sects.

A. General History	B. Jewish History	C. Jewish Culture	
Ptolemy II* defends his rule against the Seleucids in the First Syrian War (274–272 BCE).			**-272**
The Mauryan king Asoka* adopts Buddhism and attempts to govern India by superseding the caste hierarchy.	Economic development under the Ptolemies attracts many Greeks to cities lying on trade routes in the Transjordan and on the Mediterranean Coast. Jerusalem and Judean villages remain relatively un-Hellenized.		**-270**
Rome extends its control to all southern Italy.			**-268**
The Ptolemaic regime imposes taxes on slaves, materials, and livestock, requiring residents of Syria and Phoenicia to report on all taxable animals. Fraud is severely punished.	The Greek overlord is interested chiefly in revenue, otherwise allowing Jews autonomy to follow their religious law.		**-264**
		Ptolemy II* abolishes the practice of mortgaging persons, even oneself, to pay debts. Although the Torah is more flexible on this, the Hellenistic norm of pledging property for personal credit becomes entrenched in Jewish law.	**-261**
Ptolemy II* wages the Second Syrian War against the Seleucid Antiochus II,* recent successor to his father Antiochus I,* and Antigonus Gonatas* of Macedon.	The Ptolemaic regime raises funds through heavy taxation, using local collectors or "tax farmers"; the Jerusalem priesthood pays tribute by levying a land tax. Poorer farmers are driven into slavery.	The Book of Qohelet (Ecclesiastes) is, according to many, composed at about this time. The author appears familiar with Jerusalem and takes a cynical view toward people's ability to change fate. Observing the oppression of the poor and the inevitability of corruption, he advocates accepting and taking advantage of what one has. He challenges the traditional belief in a morally concerned God, noting that death awaits good and bad alike. Qohelet displays a later Hebrew style influenced by Aramaic.

Following an ancient tradition of translating laws, Jews of Alexandria, Egypt, render the Torah (five books of Moses) in Greek. According to the legend preserved in the pseudepigraphic Letter of Aristeas from the next century, King Ptolemy II* commissioned the translation from 72 Jewish scholars from Jerusalem who completed the task in 72 days. The translation, known therefore as the Septuagint (Seventy), reflects a text of the Torah slightly different from the traditional Jewish (Masoretic) text but occasionally anticipates interpretations codified in later rabbinic law. The translation is careful not to use terms associated with paganism in describing worship of God. Reflecting Hellenic aesthetics, the Septuagint translates not that God saw creation was "good" but that it was "beautiful." The Septuagint will serve | **-260** |

A. General History	B. Jewish History	C. Jewish Culture
-260		Greek-speaking Jews for centuries and will be adopted by the early Christian church.
-259	Zenon* is dispatched from Egypt to Judea on a treasury matter of Ptolemy II.* His records are an important source of information about political and economic life in Judea.	
-253	Following the Second Syrian War (260–253 BCE) Ptolemy II* marries his daughter Berenice* to the Seleucid king, Antiochus II.*		
-250	Among the technological innovations of the Ptolemies are the foot-driven potter's wheel and a semienclosed, longer-lasting oil lamp.	Egypt's Jews, living largely in the western delta and bearing Greek names, worship in prayer houses. The only part of their liturgy known is the Ten Commandments followed by the Shema (as attested in the 2nd-century BCE Nash Papyrus). Since it does not depend on a central temple, prayer increasingly becomes the major mode of worship among Jews, even in the land of Israel.	The tale of Susannah circulates with the Aramaic stories of Daniel 1–6. In a twist on the episode about Joseph and Potiphar's* wife in Genesis 39, the Jewess Susannah piously withstands the advances of lecherous town elders. Condemned to death, Susannah is saved by the wisdom of Daniel. The story, preserved only in Greek, illustrates a degree of Jewish self-government as justice is rendered by a court of elders who require the testimony of two witnesses in accordance with the Torah. In the Septuagint's version of the Ten Commandments in Deuteronomy, the Hebrew original is expanded to include a prohibition of Dionysian rites. Hellenistic Jews all over engage in pagan practices without abandoning their observance of Jewish worship.
-246	Ptolemy III* succeeds to his father's throne in Egypt. The murder of Antiochus II* and his wife Berenice,* Ptolemy III's sister, in Syria triggers the Third Syrian War, another struggle for control of Syro-Palestine, this against Seleucus II.*		
-241	Seleucus II,* facing a challenge to his throne by his brother Antiochus Hierax,* cedes control of much of Syria and Asia Minor to Ptolemy III.* Carthage sues Rome for peace, ending the First Punic War. Rome had waged war against Carthage in 264 BCE to increase her wealth and has now acquired Sicily as a province.	Onias II, high priest in Jerusalem, trusting that Ptolemy III* would lose the Third Syrian War, stops paying tribute to Egypt. A victorious Ptolemy III* transfers political power in Judea to Joseph, son of Tobias, a Jerusalem supporter of Hellenism with roots in Transjordan. The Tobiads will retain economic and political influence until their power is dissolved by the Maccabees a century later.	
-239		As tax farmer of Syro-Palestine for the Ptolemaic regime, Joseph, son of Tobias, governs with a strong hand. He builds Jerusalem into a	

A. General History	B. Jewish History	C. Jewish Culture	
	commercial center, enhancing its Hellenistic character.		**-239**
Rome seizes the islands of Sardinia and Corsica from her rival, Carthage.			**-238**
With Greece the scene of major intercity hostilities, Rome forges alliances with several Greek cities.			**-228**
Antigonus Doson* of Macedonia forms the Hellenic League and embarks on campaigns to control independent Greek city-states.			**-224**
Antiochus III* consolidates the Seleucid regime and plans an assault on Egypt.			**-223**
When Ptolemy III* dies and is succeeded by young Ptolemy IV Philopator,* Antiochus III* embarks on the Fourth Syrian War, wresting control of Antioch and Mediterranean port cities with little difficulty. He will rename his domain Coele-Syria and Phoenicia. Philip V* becomes king of Macedon. The contest for hegemony among him, the Seleucid Antiochus III,* and Ptolemy IV* upsets the traditional balance of power in the Hellenistic world. Following a long period of conflict, the Chin dynasty comes to dominate all of China. The northern border is protected by the Great Wall. The feudal system will be replaced by regional bureaucracies.			**-221**
	Simon II, son of Onias II, serves as high priest in Jerusalem (220–190 BCE), the last undisputed one. He gains a reputation as a defender of the Jewish faith; rabbinic literature recalls him as Simon the Just of the Great Assembly.	The peace and prosperity of the Ptolemaic regime may have as much as trebled the Judean population. Among the improvements in agriculture is a device for sowing seed together with plowing, a technique known in Mesopotamia for centuries.	**-220**
The Carthaginian general Hannibal* invades Italy when the First Punic War with Rome breaks out.	Antiochus III* leads an army through Ptolemaic strongholds in northern Israel and the Jordan Valley and then reconquers much of the Transjordan, restoring to Philadelphia its earlier name, Rabbat-Ammon.	According to a papyrus, a Judean man Jonathan is sued by his Greek wife Helladote* concerning her dowry, a Hellenistic innovation in Jewish law anticipating the rabbinic *ketubbah*.	**-218**
Having rebuilt his army, Ptolemy IV* defeats Antiochus III* at Raphia, near the Negev–Sinai border.		Ptolemy IV's* defeat of Antiochus III* would seem to be reflected in Daniel 11:10–13, with a note that the "king of the North" will have his comeuppance.	**-217**
Hannibal* of Carthage leads his army toward Rome.			**-211**

A. General History	B. Jewish History	C. Jewish Culture
-210		The Testaments of the Twelve Patriarchs, preserved in Greek by the Byzantine church, is composed in Hebrew. Representative of Jewish fictional elaboration of scripture, the Testaments present Jacob's 12 sons each telling a confessional narrative about his life and offering ethical advice to his heirs, anticipating the literary genres of the confession and the Jewish ethical will. Among the virtues advised are restraint in drinking and sex.

Demetrius* writes a chronological account of biblical history in what is the first known Jewish composition in Greek. He makes a point of calculating the time from the fall of the kingdoms of Israel and Judah to the reign of Ptolemy IV.* In his spare comments on the narrative, he seeks to resolve difficulties. |
-206 Rebellion touched off by the severe economic demands of Ptolemy IV's* wars results in an independent southern Egypt, with pharaohs ruling at Thebes for 20 years.		
-202 Following the defeat of Hannibal* and the Second Punic War, Rome turns against Philip V* of Macedon, who had been an ally of Hannibal.* He is also an ally of Antiochus III,* the Seleucid ruler of Syro-Palestine, against Ptolemy V.*		
-201 The Greek isle of Rhodes seeks the aid of Rome in its war against Philip V.*	Antiochus III,* having strengthened his regime and army, invades Israel, regaining its control from the Ptolemies. Only Gaza, a major Egyptian port, offers substantial resistance before being taken.	
-200 The Laws of Manu* formalize Hindu doctrine in India.	Jerusalem suffers considerable damage as a scene of conflict between Ptolemaic and Seleucid forces. To gain favor, Antiochus III* reduces taxes and plans for rebuilding the Temple. The restoration earns the high priest Simon the plaudits of Jesus ben Sira, the Apocrypha author.

Antiochus III* endows Judea with political privileges as an "ethnos" and at the same time demands Jews' obedience to their ancestral law, the Torah. The charter Antiochus III* issues provides that the Jewish council of elders, the *gerousia*, continue to govern. To ensure that the Temple functions properly, Antiochus III* grants a substantial subvention for animal, incense, and other offerings and safeguards ritual purity by excluding tainted animals from Jerusalem and prohibiting | The popular story of Bel and the Dragon, which is preserved only in Greek, reflects Jewish disdain of the surrounding paganism. Daniel, the Jewish hero of faith, refuses a royal order to bow to a statue of the Babylonian god, Bel. Using a stratagem anticipating a famous rabbinic legend about Abraham, Daniel sprinkles ashes in front of the statue and proves by telltale footprints that it is the priests and not the god who eat the food offerings laid before it. Although angry pagans throw Daniel in a lions' den, he is miraculously untouched and is served kosher (Judean) food by the prophet Habakkuk.

Jews incorporate motifs from many pagan myths in developing their own biblical interpretation (*midrash*). Borrowing from the Greeks, Jews |

A. General History	B. Jewish History	C. Jewish Culture	
	aliens and impure Jews from the Temple's inner court. Judean inflation is dissolved by the Seleucids. A class of Jewish entrepreneurs forms a nouveau riche class, provoking resentment (such as one finds in the Book of Ecclesiastes and the Wisdom of Ben Sira) by less successful Judeans. Foreign slaves abound; occasionally Judeans will emancipate them.	elaborate the Tower of Babel story (Genesis 11) to tell that the builders were giants who survived the Flood and who meant to ascend to heaven by the tower. A version of this Hellenistic *midrash* appears in later rabbinic literature: God blows the tower over by wind and the Babylonian plan to avenge the Flood is foiled. The first part of the present book of 1 Enoch is assembled. The author, who sees himself as a prophet touring the world from heaven to the underworld, attributes evil to human rebelliousness and to the primeval rebellion of some angels. Good angels bring the biblical Flood to rid the world of corruption.	**-200**
Ptolemy V's* efforts to hold on to parts of Palestine fail, and Antiochus III,* the clear victor of the Fifth Syrian War, extends his dominion up to the border with Egypt.			**-198**
The Romans assist Greek cities in the Aegean to thwart the aggression of Philip V* of Macedon, ally of Antiochus III.* Rome assumes control of Philip V's* holdings outside Macedon.	Antiochus III* settles groups of Jews in northern sites, such as Carduchi (Kurdistan), to help maintain peace. Jews, who are encouraged to practice their traditional law, show allegiance to the Seleucid regime and serve reliably as troops.		**-197**
With Carthage long subdued, Rome sends Cato* to Spain to suppress rebellion there.	Antiochus III* and Seleucus IV* promulgate decrees, preserved on the Hefzibah Inscription, protecting Jewish citizens from trespasses by the Seleucid army.		**-195**
The Roman army, having broken its alliance with Antiochus III* in 193 BCE, defeats him at Magnesia.		Jesus ben Sira(ch), a learned scribe, composes a proverbial wisdom book, stressing Jewish piety and praising the heroes of Israel's past. For him traditional religious wisdom (Torah) as much as secular knowledge is the mark of culture. He writes admiringly of Aaron and other priests, ending with an encomium for Simon II the Just. Like Simon, as cited in the rabbinic *Ethics of the Fathers*, Ben Sira calls for gracious acts (*hesed*) among people. This Hebrew work will be translated into Greek by Ben Sira's grandson in 135 BCE; no complete Hebrew version will survive, but the Christian church will preserve it in Greek.	**-190**
At Apamea Antiochus III* submits to Rome, surrendering his son, later to be known as Antiochus IV Epiphanes,* as a hostage and paying enormous tribute.			**-188**
In order to pay the tribute he owes Rome, Antiochus III* attempts to plunder a temple treasury in Elam (modern Iran), but he is killed			**-187**

	A. General History	B. Jewish History	C. Jewish Culture
-187	there. He is succeeded by his firstborn, Seleucus IV Philopator.*		
-180		Seleucus IV* sends an official, Heliodorus,* to reappropriate surplus funds (provided by the king) from the Jerusalem Temple treasury. The high priest Onias III (190–174 BCE), who favors the Ptolemies and fears antagonizing the local aristocracy, refuses.	Worship in the Jerusalem Temple comprises an animal offering and libations made by priests and psalm singing by the Levites. In response the people bow down, then recite benedictions and a communal prayer for the well-being of Israel and the city of Jerusalem. This brief prayer will be developed into the center of Jewish liturgy after the destruction of the Temple (70 CE), the *Tefillah* (prayer) or *Amidah* (said while standing). The priests conclude by giving the prostrate people the threefold divine blessing (Numbers 6:23–26).
-177	Antiochus IV Epiphanes* is released by Rome; he settles in Athens.		
-176	Seleucus IV* is assassinated by his officer, Heliodorus,* who is blocked from seizing power by Antiochus IV Epiphanes,* Seleucus IV's brother and ultimately his successor (176–164 BCE).	Jerusalem high priest Onias III travels to Antioch to account for his refusal of funds to Seleucus IV.*	
-175		Antiochus IV* extends citizenship to all inhabitants of the Seleucid Empire who take on a Greek life-style, an offer that appeals to increasing numbers of Jews. Some surgically undo their circumcision in order to play in the gymnasium games.	The Book of Jubilees is composed in Hebrew; it is ascribed to an angelic revelation to Moses. The book elaborates the narratives of Genesis and Exodus, injecting its own, more puritanical morals. On the one hand, it attests to later rabbinic practices such as the grace after meals. On the other, its prohibition of marital intercourse on the Sabbath, which is reflected later among the Samaritans and Karaites, will be opposed by the rabbis. Concerned with establishing chronology, Jubilees divides history into septennial periods and uses a solar calendar instead of the Bible's lunar one. The book and solar calendar will find a place within the Dead Sea sect. The complete text survives only in an Ethiopic version. The Book of Jubilees reflects the type of scriptural interpretation (*midrash*) that would come to characterize rabbinic exegesis. For example, the Bible (Genesis 4) does not describe the slaying of Abel by Cain in detail. Jubilees holds the murder weapon was a stone, since metal implements were first made by Cain's descendant Tubal-Cain (Genesis 4). As poetic justice, Cain, says Jubilees, was slain by stone, when his house collapsed on him. *Midrash* typically fleshes out scripture by filling in gaps, resolving inconsistencies, and tying up loose ends.

A. General History	B. Jewish History	C. Jewish Culture	
		A Jewish philosopher in Alexandria, Aristobulus, pioneers a tradition in Jewish thought in which Greek philosophy derives its truth from the Torah. According to Aristobulus, Plato* and Pythagoras* received their teaching from Moses. In *An Explanation of the Mosaic Scripture* he reiterates the biblical "wisdom" idea that fear of God leads to moral knowledge but adopts a nonanthropomorphic understanding of God and a symbolic interpretation of the Sabbath.	**-175**
	Jason, son of Onias III, is appointed high priest in Jerusalem. He offers to increase his tribute if Antiochus IV Epiphanes* will construct a gymnasium and otherwise Hellenize the Jewish capital.		**-174**
	Menelaus bribes Antiochus IV* to appoint him high priest, even though he lacks the proper pedigree. Jason flees to the Transjordan.		**-172**
Antiochus IV Epiphanes,* the Seleucid ruler of Syria, leads an army as far as Alexandria. In exchange for peace Egypt's King Ptolemy VI* becomes Antiochus IV's* vassal.	Menelaus, supported by the Tobiad family, has the rival Onias III executed in Antioch.	Yosi ben Yoezer (d. c.160 BCE), a protorabbinic sage, together with Jesus ben Sira and others represent a relatively new emphasis in Hellenistic Judaism on widespread Jewish engagement in the study and discussion of Torah as a mine of Judaic culture. Jewish law begins to become the province of all Jews, not only priests. Heliodorus'* retreat from the Temple treasury a decade earlier is elaborated in a popular Jewish story in Greek, preserved in 2 Maccabees. A phantom horse and rider accost Heliodorus,* who recognizes the specter as a warning from God.	**-170**
	Jason returns to Jerusalem seeking to overthrow Menelaus. It would seem that a Seleucid army repels Jason, who dies in Sparta. Perceiving Jason's revolt as a sign of Judea's disloyalty, Antiochus IV* plunders the Jerusalem Temple.		**-169**
Antiochus IV* advances toward Egypt to put down Ptolemy VI's* rebellion. Rome, fearing a takeover of Egypt would render Antiochus IV* too powerful, orders him back to Syria.	After Rome foils his campaign against Egypt, Antiochus IV* builds a Greek fortress in Jerusalem, the Acra. Samaritans ask Antiochus IV* to release them from the Judean tax and protect their worship from the pressure of Hellenizers.	Menelaus and his Hellenizing cohort seek to remove the distinctive character of Jewish worship by calling God "Zeus Olympius," establishing pagan altars, sacrificing pig, and persecuting hostile Jews. Later Jewish histories blame such abominations directly on Antiochus IV.*	**-168**

-167

-165

The head of Antiochus IV, the Seleucid ruler against whose policies the Maccabees first rebelled.

A passage from the pseudepigraphical Enoch material foresees not only Jewish deliverance from Antiochus IV* but an awakening of the dead. This, together with the latter half of Daniel, is the first clear Jewish reference to resurrection.

The Hasmonean family of priests in the Judean town of Modein leads a rebellion against the Hellenistic regime in Jerusalem. Joined by the traditional religious group of Hasideans (pietists), the Hasmoneans seek to thwart Hellenization of the national religion and remove oppressive taxation. According to 1 Maccabees, the revolt begins when the Hasmonean patriarch Mattathias slays a Jew making a sacrifice ordained by Antiochus IV.*

When Mattathias dies, leadership of the Hasmonean revolt falls to one of his five sons, Judas. He is nicknamed the Maccabee (the Hammer).

Judas the Maccabee wages successful guerilla war against Seleucid troops stationed in Judea while Antiochus IV* is fighting Parthians in the east.

Antiochus IV* sends Syrian troops led by Ptolemy,* Nicanor,* and Gorgias* to suppress the Maccabean revolt. Judas defeats them near Emmaus. The Syrian regent, Lysias,* himself leads a force to Judea, where a peace is made with Judas.

After Seleucid troops massacre a band of Hasideans on the Sabbath, Mattathias decides that his followers may defend their lives even on holy days.

A strong sense of imminent apocalypse is reflected in the Testament of Moses, a Hebrew or Aramaic work surviving only in Latin. Antiochus IV's* persecutions are explained as divine punishment for Jewish sins, but God will soon destroy the oppressors and their idols.

The chapters forming Daniel 7–12 are composed in Hebrew rather than Aramaic, a sign perhaps of Jewish nationalism. The texts depict the succession of empires up through the Macedonians as a series of beasts, with the impudent and blasphemous Antiochus IV* the last and least among them (in Daniel 7 he is no more than a puny horn with a big mouth). God with the help of angels will relieve the pious of persecution and bring an end to human rule. Daniel 7–12 is joined to Chapters 1–6, which exemplify the faith of the oppressed pious, producing the biblical Book of Daniel.

The Scroll of Esther is composed in Hebrew sometime in the preceding two centuries. It relates a fabulous tale of how the Jews of Persia are saved from antisemitic attacks instigated by the courtier Haman* by a Jew, Mordechai, and his ward Esther, who becomes queen of Persia by winning a beauty contest. In a happy reversal, the Jews best their enemies, and Mordechai replaces Haman.* Persian Jews celebrate their survival in the festival of Purim and urge Jews everywhere, for all time, to observe the holiday by drinking and sending gifts to the poor. The role of the deity in saving the Jews is only implied in the narrative; God's name is not mentioned.

A. General History	B. Jewish History	C. Jewish Culture	
	When Antiochus IV* dies, he is succeeded by his son Antiochus V.* The latter honors the peace with the Maccabees, which would seem to have Roman backing, and grants religious freedom to Judea.	The Maccabees purify and rededicate the Jerusalem Temple in December. A commemorative celebration, attended by many later legends and traditions, is ordained: Hanukkah (Dedication). An eight-branched menorah, symbolizing the Temple, is kindled for eight nights, acknowledging the miraculous role of God in the Maccabean triumph.	-164
	Judas the Maccabee attempts to seize the Seleucid fortress in Jerusalem, the Acra. He is repelled and pursued by a force commanded by Lysias,* who has appointed himself regent for Antiochus V.*		-163
A general of Antiochus IV,* Philip,* had been named regent for Antiochus V*; he takes control while Lysias* fights the Maccabees in Judea. Lysias* returns to regain his power but is in turn eliminated together with Antiochus V* by Antiochus IV's* brother Demetrius I Soter* (162–150 BCE).	Lysias,* having to return to Syria, offers peace to the Maccabees. Seeing religious freedom restored, the Hasideans abandon the revolution. Demetrius I* appoints Alcimus high priest. Judas the Maccabee takes Jerusalem to prevent Alcimus from functioning. Alcimus seeks aid from Demetrius.*		-162
	Judas the Maccabee defeats a Seleucid army led by Nicanor* near Beth-Horon. Judas strengthens his position by allying with Rome. Demetrius'* general Bacchides* defeats and kills Judas the Maccabee near Jerusalem. Alcimus is reinstated as high priest. Jews are first documented in Rome as members of a political delegation sent by Judas the Maccabee. The Jews there constitute the oldest continuous Diaspora Jewish community in the world.	The Maccabean defeat of the Seleucid army is commemorated in an annual festival, Nicanor Day.	-161
	With the Hellenists recouping power in Jerusalem, the leader of the Maccabees, Jonathan, holds out in the Transjordan.	Jews build a temple and make offerings to God at Leontopolis, Egypt; it survives over 200 years. The Book of Judith is composed in Hebrew though it is preserved only in Greek and through references in rabbinic literature. A mishmash of historical data and biblical motifs, the story tells of an observant and pious Jewish woman who uses her beauty to win her way into the Assyrian army camp and behead its general, Holofernes.* The tale is set in the Persian period, but it would seem to address the Maccabean war against the Seleucids. The woman, named Judith (Jewess), is, like her	-160

	A. General History	B. Jewish History	C. Jewish Culture
-160			people, an unlikely champion against a mighty power; her victory is therefore a triumph of God.
-156		Jonathan reestablishes himself just north of Jerusalem at Michmash with the consent of Bacchides.* He cannot resolve severe economic conditions in Judea.	
-153	Alexander Balas* wrests control of the Seleucid Kingdom from Demetrius I* with backing by a Roman Senate eager to weaken a rival state.	Jonathan the Hasmonean is permitted to muster an army in return for supporting Demetrius I.* Jonathan takes over Jerusalem.	
-152		In return for his support, Alexander Balas,* now in control of the Seleucid Kingdom, appoints Jonathan high priest in Jerusalem and later governor of Judea. Many Jews challenge Jonathan's legitimacy and further diverge into different parties and sects.	
-150			Important Jewish sects of the Roman period may originate in the era of Jonathan. The Sadducees, who would seem to trace a priestly pedigree to the Davidic high priest Zadok, comprise aristocrats who oppose messianism, apocalyptic, and other disturbances of the status quo. The Pharisees are diverse "middle-class" Jews who affirm an ancient oral tradition and adopt such notions as afterlife and resurrection. The Essenes aspire to a high level of ritual purity, espouse pacifism, and live communally. The community that settled at Qumran by the Dead Sea sees itself as the true Israel, living a strictly regulated life of high ritual purity and using a solar calendar. The sect's founder, the Teacher of Righteousness, or Right Teacher, may have been an enemy of Jonathan, whom he regarded as an illegitimate priest. Most Jews under Rome belong to none of these groups.
-146	Rome beats down rebellions in Greece and takes it over entirely. Carthage, an ally of some Greek cities, is destroyed.		
-145	Assisted by Ptolemy VI* of Egypt, Demetrius II* regains the Seleucid throne from Alexander Balas.*	Jonathan controls the Acra fortress. Demetrius II* confirms him in his priestly post and extends his political regime into Samaria.	
-142	Trypho* replaces Seleucid King Demetrius II* with Antiochus VI,* son of Alexander Balas,* only to murder him and seize the throne himself.	Implicated in the power struggle for control of the Seleucid Kingdom, Jonathan the Hasmonean is killed by Trypho.* Jonathan is succeeded by the surviving Hasmonean brother,	

A. General History	B. Jewish History	C. Jewish Culture	
	Simon. Through political maneuvering, Simon takes over all direct taxation, replacing the Seleucid land-lease tax with the traditional tithe. 1 Maccabees declares, "The yoke of the Gentiles was removed from Israel."		**-142**
The Parthians under Mithridates I* take over Babylonia.			**-141**
		Simon the Maccabee builds a mausoleum for his parents and brothers, following recent Hellenistic Jewish practice. In biblical times corpses were buried directly in the ground. From 200 BCE bones were gathered in ossuaries. The Hellenistic innovation preserves the individuality of the deceased.	**-140**
		Jews erect public altars to their God in Rome, hoping to spread their religion.	**-139**
Trypho* is overthrown in Syria by a brother of Demetrius II,* Antiochus VII.* Like his brother, Antiochus VII.* is beset by the Parthians. Wearing down the Seleucid regime is fostered by Rome.	In the midst of his struggle with Trypho,* Antiochus VII* grants Simon the privilege of minting coins. Once his power is assured, Antiochus VII* demands that Simon restore the cities of Gadara (Gezer) and Joppa (Jaffa) and the Acra to the Seleucids and pay heavy tribute. When Simon refuses, Antiochus VII* sends an army led by Cendebaeus.* Simon's sons Judas and John defeat the Seleucid army.		**-138**
	Simon is killed in a coup d'état engineered by his son-in-law Ptolemy, commander of Jericho. Simon's son John takes charge in Jerusalem, suppressing the attempted coup. The Great Assembly ratifies the regime of John, now also called Hyrcanus. Antiochus VII* lays siege to Jerusalem and imposes heavy tribute on John Hyrcanus. Rome orders the siege lifted. John allies with the Parthians against Antiochus VII.*		**-134**
The Parthians kill Antiochus VII* in combat, and Demetrius II* regains the Seleucid throne.	John Hyrcanus solidifes his domain by conquering the Transjordan, Beth-Shean, and Shechem, where in an act of religious rivalry he razes the Samaritan temple. He forcibly circumcises the Idumeans of the southern Transjordan, leading them to think of themselves as Jews.		**-128**
		A letter is sent to the Jews of Egypt, ordaining that they celebrate the eight-day Festival of Sukkot (Booths) in the month of Kislev (December). The observance would seem to be a precursor of Hanukkah.	**-124**

	A. General History	B. Jewish History	C. Jewish Culture
-120		Having been rejected by and rejecting of Judean Jews for over three centuries, the Samaritans will remain a separate group.	The Samaritans fix in writing their own version of the Torah, using the archaic angular Hebrew script that Judeans had replaced centuries earlier with the square Aramaic lettering that has persisted until today.
-115	Recouping losses, the Parthians control trade routes from the Middle East to China. King Mithradates II* suppresses the Arabs and maintains peace with Rome.		
-110		John Hyrcanus alienates many Jews by looting the tomb of David to pay his mercenaries. The Pharisees reject him, and he allies with the Sadducees.	
-104		Aristobulus I, king of Judea (104–103 BCE), succeeds his father John Hyrcanus, consolidating his power by imprisoning his mother and executing his brother Antigonus. He conquers the Galilee and forcibly circumcises the populace, many of whom are Jews.	
-103		When Aristobulus dies, his widow, Salome Alexandra, marries his brother Alexander Janneus, appointing him both king of Judea and high priest. This offends traditionalists, the Pharisees in particular, as the Torah forbids priests from marrying widows. Alexander Janneus conquers the coastal city of Ptolemias (Acre), with the support of Queen Cleopatra III* of Egypt. He proceeds to establish control over both sides of the Jordan and the Mediterranean Coast, seeking to develop maritime trade. For this purpose he also mints coins.	
-102	Rome captures Cilicia and virtually completes its conquest of the eastern Mediterranean coastlands.		
-100	Germanic tribes originally from Scandinavia settle around the Rhine River.		The Letter of Aristeas, purporting to date from about 250 BCE but written later by a Jew, legitimizes the Greek translation of the Torah, the Septuagint. It relates a legend according to which the translation was made for King Ptolemy II Philadelphus* by 72 Judean scholars, each of whom miraculously produced the same text. The Book of 1 Maccabees is composed in Hebrew, though it survives only in Greek. This history of the Hasmonean rebellion against Antiochus IV* begins with the religious zeal of Mattathias and ends with the high priesthood of John

A. General History	B. Jewish History	C. Jewish Culture	
		Hyrcanus. Emphasis is placed on the salvation of Judea by God through the military efforts of Judas the Maccabee and his brothers and on salvaging the proper high priesthood. The book may serve as an apology for Alexander Janneus, whose priesthood is widely challenged.	-100
		The Book of 2 Maccabees is composed in Greek; it summarizes a five-volume history by Jason of Cyrene of the Maccabean uprising and its background. This work elaborately tells of Jewish martyrdom in the face of Seleucid persecution, relating the famous story of the pious Hannah who encouraged each of her sons in turn to die for his religion. Such faith will be rewarded by bodily resurrection. Because this history focuses on the accomplishments of Judas the Maccabee and on none of the Hasmonean priests, it may serve to challenge the priesthood of Alexander Janneus.	-95
	In an open challenge to Alexander Janneus's legitimacy as high priest, Jews reportedly pelt him with citrons (etrogim) during the Festival of Sukkot. He responds with mass executions.		-90
Rome puts an Italian revolt, the so-called Social War, to rest by granting citizenship in exchange for peace.			-89
Civil war leaves Rome under the Senate and consul Sulla's* rule. When he travels to Greece the following year, his supporters in Rome are slain.	While Alexander Janneus is fighting Nabateans, a Judean rebellion breaks out. The rebels call upon the Seleucid king, Demetrius III,* for aid. Alexander regains Judean support, and Demetrius* retreats. Alexander crucifies 800 rebels, many of them probably Pharisees, in Jerusalem.		-88
		In retelling the story of Jacob's daughter Dinah (Genesis 34), the poet Theodotus has the patriarch insist on the conversion of Dinah's would-be husband.	-85
Mithradates VI* of Pontus and Ptolemy IX,* governor of Cyprus, wrest control of most of Greece and Asia Minor. Sulla,* the Roman consul, concedes their conquest.			-84
	The Nabatean king, Aretas III,* having conquered most of Syria, invades Judea and defeats Alexander Janneus near Lydda.		-83

	A. General History	B. Jewish History	C. Jewish Culture
-82	Following renewed civil hostilities, Sulla* regains control of Italy for the Roman Senate.	Alexander Janneus makes peace with Aretas III,* leaving himself in control of nearly all of Israel and the Transjordan. He embarks on a campaign to conquer and Judaize independent Greek cities in the Transjordan.	
-80			The Book of 3 Maccabees is composed in Greek. The book strings together a series of tales related to diverse periods in which persecution of Jews in Ptolemaic Egypt for their distinctive religious practices is thwarted by acts of God.
-77			A Greek translation of the Scroll of Esther includes six additions, highlighting the efficacy of prayer and the national level of gentile persecution of Jews. One addition deals with the problem of Esther's intermarriage.
-76		Alexander Janneus is killed in a campaign in the Transjordan. He is given a royal burial in Jerusalem. His widow, Salome Alexandra, succeeds his rule, appointing her son Hyrcanus II high priest. To maintain domestic order, it would seem, Salome shows favor to the Pharisees, giving them representation in the Sadducee-dominated assembly (*gerousia*) and releasing their allies in prison. Salome Alexandra (139–67 BCE) becomes queen of Judea. A strict observer of religious traditions, she supports the Pharisees' demand that they control Temple practices and the fixing of the calendar. The 1st-century CE historian Josephus will praise her for keeping the nation at peace.	
-75			The so-called Damascus Document is composed in Hebrew; a version will be found in the late 19th century CE in the Cairo Genizah and seven copies will be discovered among the Dead Sea Scrolls. The text interprets several biblical prophecies to describe the sojourn of a disaffected Jewish sect in "Damascus" and the antagonism between its leader, the Teacher of Right, and the Jerusalem priesthood. Giving a strict reading to the Torah, the Document delineates some of the laws the group is to observe as it awaits its messianic vindication by God. The Qumran Rule of the Community is assembled. This manual of conduct describes the

A. General History	B. Jewish History	C. Jewish Culture	
		Dead Sea sect's reclusive move to the wilderness and delineates its hierarchy and regimen. The rules aim to segregate this exclusive covenant of God from the corruption of outsiders and their ways.	-75
Successful Roman commanders Crassus* and Pompey* assume a reinvigorated consulship of Rome.			-70
	When Queen Salome dies, her younger son, Aristobulus II, wrests the kingship and high priesthood from Hyrcanus II by force of arms. This turn of events deals a blow to the Pharisees, as Aristobulus II is allied with the Sadducees.		-67
The Roman general Pompey* defeats Mithradates* of Pontus, in northern Asia Minor, clearing his path to the Near East.			-66
	Hyrcanus II attempts to regain power with the help of the Nabatean king, Aretas III,* who lays siege to Aristobulus II in Jerusalem. Both Hyrcanus and Aristobulus II seek support from Rome.		-65
	Pompey* subjugates Syria and eliminates the Seleucid regime, bringing with that control of Judea.		-64
	Pompey* declines to throw support to Aristobulus II until he subjugates the Nabateans. Aristobulus II, impatient, fortifies himself in Judea. Pompey invades, captures the Jerusalem Temple, and violates its Holy of Holies. Pompey* restores Hyrcanus II to the high priesthood, but he strips Judea of all political holdings except Judea, Galilee, and Idumea, which is controlled by the powerful Antipater. Imposing heavy tribute, Pompey* ends the Hasmonean regime and makes Judea a vassal state. Pompey* marches Aristobulus II and other Judean captives through Rome. These become the core of Rome's growing Jewish community.		-63
Caesar,* now Roman governor of Spain, Crassus,* and Pompey* agree to share power in Rome as a triumvirate.		The idea of an anointed savior (Messiah) from the house of David is first attested in the pseudepigraphic Psalms of Solomon.	-60
Crassus* is slain in battle with the Parthians; Caesar* attempts to impose order on Gaul.			-53
	Jews increase their numbers in Rome into the ten thousands,	The most extensive biblical commentary to be found among the	-50

A. General History	B. Jewish History	C. Jewish Culture
-50	building several synagogues. From here they spread to other towns in Italy, to Spain, and to North Africa.	Dead Sea Scrolls, the pesher of Habakkuk, is composed. Like other Dead Sea pesher texts, the commentary interprets a prophet, in this case the late 7th-century Habakkuk, to speak directly of the history and imminent future of the Qumran sect. This pesher finds in Habakkuk reference to the conflict between the sect's founder, the Teacher of Right, and a failed Jerusalem high priest (probably the Hasmonean Jonathan or Simon) as well as the quasi-apocalyptic onslaught of the Roman army (Habakkuk's Kitteans). The pesher of Nahum finds a reference to the "wrathful lion," Alexander Janneus, crucifying masses of Jews who oppose him, in all likelihood the Pharisees. In the pesher's view, this is divine retribution for their false teaching. Other Qumran Bible interpretation foretells the eschatological appearance of a Messiah of the house of David and a priestly Messiah. The sect can trust these interpretations because, according to the pesher of Habakkuk, God told the Teacher of Right the true meaning of the prophets' "mysteries." In the Hymn, or Thanksgiving, Scroll, the speaker calls himself an interpreter of mysteries who heals the pious and repels the wicked. The pious are members of the sect, the True Israel.
-49	Following his conquest of Gaul, Julius Caesar* defies the Roman Senate, crosses the Rubicon River into Italy, and, together with Mark Antony,* assumes dominion of Rome.		
-48	Julius Caesar* defeats his rival Pompey* at Pharsalus, Greece, and becomes uncontested head of the Roman Empire. Caesar* returns Cleopatra VII* to the throne of Egypt.		
-47		In exchange for Hyrcanus II's support of Julius Caesar* during his Egyptian campaign, Caesar* appoints Hyrcanus ethnarch of the Jews. One of the Idumean Antipater's sons, Herod, defeats and executes a Jewish army in the Galilee. The Jewish court in Jerusalem, the Sanhedrin, summons Herod to account. Herod appears with armed guards. Fearing civil war, Hyrcanus II stops the trial. Herod is appointed administrator of Coele-Syria and Samaria by Sextus Caesar.*	

A. General History	B. Jewish History	C. Jewish Culture	
			-44
Having successfully routed the armies of the Roman Senate and the late Pompey* in North Africa and Spain, on March 15 Julius Caesar,* made emperor for life, is murdered in Rome. East Asians called the Hsiung-nu are driven west by the Chinese to Turkestan. Around 200 CE, these "Huns" will push the Goths further westward, wreaking havoc in the Roman Empire.			
			-42
The new Roman triumvirate, Octavian,* Mark Antony,* and Lepidus,* defeat Brutus* and Cassius* at Philippi. Antony* is given control of the Near East.			
			-41
	Jews appeal to the Roman ruler, Mark Antony,* to suppress the troublemaking Herod. Herod, too, asks Antony* for recognition; he and his brother Phasael are appointed tetrarchs of Judea.		
			-40
Romans, using slave labor, construct straight, paved roads four feet thick for mobilizing their military machine and facilitating trade.	With the help of Antigonus, son of Aristobulus II, the Parthians conquer a large area of the Near East. Judea falls to them; Hyrcanus II and Phasael are captured; Herod flees. Antigonus is made king of Judea and high priest. The Roman Senate names Herod king of Judea; he must wrest control from Antigonus.	The pseudepigraphical Psalms of Solomon are composed in Hebrew by Pharisees or others with similar views. They seek deliverance from God while ascribing Jewish suffering under oppression to sin.	
			-38
The Roman army defeats the Parthians, on whose support Antigonus depends.	Herod conquers all of Palestine but Jerusalem.		
			-37
Mark Antony* weds the Egyptian queen Cleopatra VII,* galvanizing his control of the Near East. This move provokes his rival in Rome, Octavian,* whose sister is also married to Antony.*	Herod, with Roman help, overruns Jerusalem and has Antigonus beheaded.	The Pharisees Shemaiah and Pollio (Avtalyon), well known from the rabbinic *Ethics of the Fathers*, favor Herod's victory as divine punishment for Judaism under Antigonus.	
			-35
	To increase his popular support, Herod had married Miriamne, a granddaughter of the Hasmonean, John Hyrcanus II. Her brother, Aristobulus, became high priest through the influence of Cleopatra VII.* Now, as Aristobulus gains in popularity, Herod has him drowned in the bath.		
			-31
Octavian's* navy defeats Antony* at Actium. Antony* and Cleopatra VII* commit suicide, and Egypt falls to Roman control.	Following the defeat of Antony,* Herod, who had been away fighting the Nabateans during the battle of Actium, pledges allegiance to Octavian* and so maintains his position.		

	A. **General History**	B. **Jewish History**	C. **Jewish Culture**
-30	Priesthood of the various Roman gods is not, as in Israel, hereditary but falls to those powerful or wealthy enough to obtain it.	As part of his effort to establish a splendid Oriental court, Herod brings in the Greek historian Nicolaus* of Damascus, who records Herod's reign within his history of the world.	A Jewish prediction incorporated into book 3 of the Sibylline Oracles (compiled c.500 CE) foretells the establishment of God's kingdom following the imminent Roman takeover of Egypt. Elsewhere the book praises Jewish piety and exhorts Gentiles to abandon their idolatrous ways.
-27	Octavian* is made emperor under the name Augustus (the Exalted). Octavian,* who had the year before asserted his primacy in Rome by purging the Senate, now, as emperor, shares authority over the provinces with the Senate. When the Senate confers on him the name "Augustus," he is worshipped in the provinces, whose people view him as their benefactor. Within Rome Augustus* promotes traditional religion. Augustus* patronizes the classical poets Horace* and Virgil* and the historian Livy,* whose *History of Rome* reflects upper-class interests. Virgil* (70–19 BCE) glorifies this Augustan age by composing the epic *Aeneid*.		
-25		To relieve a national famine, Herod uses silver and gold from his palace to buy food in Egypt. Remnants of the Jewish military force sent by King Herod with Aelius Gallus* to conquer southern Arabia settle there after the expedition is defeated.	
-24	Himyarite Arabia defends against the bid of Aelius Gallus* to extend Augustus Caesar's* dominion there.		
-22		Herod begins constructing the Roman port of Caesarea on the Mediterranean. He also rebuilds the fortress of Samaria, renaming it Sebaste in honor of Augustus.* Herod builds fortresses and cities all over the land, calling two of them Herodium. On a hill overlooking the western side of Jerusalem, he constructs a lavish palace. His magnificent refurbishing of the Temple will be completed in 64 CE, long after his death. To finance these projects Herod raises taxes, holding back at times to stave off rebellion.	
-19	Augustus* reforms Roman family law, seeking to control promiscuity and promote childbearing. Abroad, his aide, Marcus Agrippa,* suppresses unrest in Spain.		
-18		The sons of Miriamne, Herod's wife, Alexander and Aristobulus,	

| | return from Rome, where Herod had sent them to be raised. Herod marries off the former to the princess of Cappadocia, the latter, to his own niece. When he later suspects them of disloyalty, he has them executed in Sebaste. | | **-18** |

| | Excavations in Jerusalem attest to many opulent homes with private reservoirs and mosaic floors. Though heavily taxed, farmers thrive on the relative peace during Herod's rule.

The Boethos family from Egypt gains prominence in the Jerusalem priesthood, later rivaling the priestly dynasty of Hanan. The Temple priesthood is rife with nepotism and other political abuse. | Herod formally opens his port of Caesarea, which includes a pagan temple.

Owing perhaps to their popularity and early support, the Pharisees gain influence under Herod. Herod respects Jewish law by prohibiting foreigners from the Temple but antagonizes many by installing a Roman eagle there and selecting his own high priests. | **-10** |

| | Herod executes a punitive raid against the Nabateans. | | **-9** |

| | Judas the Galilean leads a rebellion provoked by the effort of the Syrian legate, Quirinius,* to take a Jewish census. Successful Roman suppression of this revolt does not disquiet the spirit of Jewish rebellion. | | **-6** |

| | Alleging disloyalty of his son Antipater, Herod has him killed. He names another son, Archelaus, his successor.

When Herod dies and is interred at Herodium, outside Jerusalem, a rebellion erupts, put down temporarily by Archelaus. Archelaus travels to Rome for confirmation as ruler. Varus,* governor of Syria, attempts to keep the peace, which is broken by revolts in Judea and Galilee. With the aid of the Nabatean king, Aretas IV,* Varus* suppresses rebellion and crucifies 2,000.

At Herod's death a former slave of the king, Simon, pretends to kingship in the Transjordan, anticipating the revolt of Simon bar Giora, another leader of the lower classes.

Emperor Augustus* in Rome hears and settles the dispute over Herod's succession, dismissing a request from some Judeans to reject Herod's family. The region is divided among Herod's three sons: Judea, Samaria, and Idumea to Archelaus; Galilee to Herod Antipas; and the Lebanon districts to Philip. | 
Herodium. A modern view. (Israel Government Press Office) | **-4** |

	A. General History	B. Jewish History	C. Jewish Culture
1			The Greek story of Joseph and Asenath resolves the apparent problem that in Genesis the patriarch Joseph marries the daughter of an Egyptian priest. Here Asenath* embraces the reputedly compassionate, patient God of Joseph before her marriage. The story, in which Asenath's exemplary conversion brings her immortality, may serve as a tract for proselytes.
4	Roman Emperor Augustus* adopts his stepson Tiberius,* who has demonstrated military capabilities in central and eastern Europe.		
5			A retelling of Genesis is composed in Aramaic and is found among the Dead Sea Scrolls. Similar to works such as 1 Enoch and Jubilees, the Genesis Apocryphon has Noah born of angels and Abram a healer and dream interpreter.
6		Roman Emperor Augustus* reorganizes Judea as a Roman province after Samaritans and Judeans adamantly protest the administration of the ethnarch, Herod's son Archelaus. The capital is moved from Jerusalem to more Hellenized Caesarea. Herod's other sons, Herod Antipas and Philip, continue to govern Galilee and Transjordan, respectively. A Roman census drives home the provincial status of Israel and, according to the Jewish historian Josephus, sparks the seditious Zealot movement. Led by Judah of Gamala and Zadok the Pharisee from Jerusalem, the Zealots see Jewish freedom and hastening the reign of God as intertwined goals.	
10	One-third of Roman Italy, or 2 million people, are slaves, many knowing harsh conditions from birth. Law advantages the upper class of freemen.		In his Jerusalem academy the Babylonian scholar Hillel formulates seven principles for broadening the interpretation of the Torah. They are essentially rules of deduction and analogy similar to those used elsewhere in the classical world. A major legalist, Hillel is famous for his epigrams. Among them are "If I am not for myself, who will be?" and "What is hateful to you, do not do to your fellow. That is all the Torah; all the rest is commentary. Go and learn it!"
14	When Augustus* dies in Rome, he is succeeded by his adopted son Tiberius,* who tries to hold the empire together by curbing spending.		

A. General History	B. Jewish History	C. Jewish Culture	
		The Pharisaic leader Hillel issues decrees to ease economic distress. Lenders would refuse to make loans to the poor close to the sabbatical year, when, according to the Torah, unpaid debts are to be forgiven. Hillel institutes the *prozbul*, by which the loans are channeled through a court that is not subject to the sabbatical year restriction.	**15**
	Jews of Syria and Judea ask Rome for a substantial tax reduction. In addition to provincial tax levies, they have been paying heavy duty on commerce between provinces, often collected by Jewish officials, and serving in state labor. Roman governors like Pontius Pilate* (26–36) dip into the Jerusalem Temple's treasury for emergency funds.		**17**
Hero of Rome's wars in Germany, Tiberius'* adopted son Germanicus* leads Roman forces in quieting Asia Minor and Syria, where he will die the next year.			**18**
	Emperor Tiberius* removes Jewish missionaries from Rome. Proselytization of Romans by Jews had gone on for at least 150 years and will continue strongly enough to provoke comment from Roman authors such as Tacitus* and Juvenal.*		**19**
	The Jewish court of 71, the Sanhedrin, performs secular administration in Judea but issues religious policy for all imperial Jews. Headed by the high priest, but comprising Jews from all over the area with a significant and influential contingent of Pharisees, the Sanhedrin regulates Temple matters and fixes the calendar. Criminal cases are handled by the Roman courts, but capital cases involving the Temple remain under Jewish jurisdiction. Other Jewish cities, like Tiberias, have a local administration (*boule*) and popular assembly.		**20**
		Herod Antipas, tetrarch of Galilee, climaxes his building achievements by completing Tiberias, which rivals Sepphoris as the northern capital. Rabbi Yohanan ben Zakkai leaves the Jerusalem academy of Hillel to serve as judge in the Galilean town of Arav. He has difficulty teaching that Torah study and strict observance, rather than messianic hope, bring salvation. He cultivates an important disciple there, the faith healer Hanina ben Dosa.	**22**

	A. General History	B. Jewish History	C. Jewish Culture
25	The Han dynasty of China, which ruled from 206 BCE through 9 CE and made Confucianism public policy, is restored.	As many as 3 million Jews, many originating outside the Judeans themselves, populate the Roman Empire from Italy to Armenia.	The Testament of Moses, composed first as an apocalyptic vision of the downfall of Antiochus IV* ca. 165 BCE, is updated to assure Jews that an apocalypse will follow the death of Herod.
26		Pontius Pilate* is appointed governor of Judea by Emperor Tiberius.* Perhaps under the influence of Tiberius'* deputy Sejanus,* Pilate insults Jewish religious sensibilities by introducing Roman symbols in Jerusalem and striking coins bearing pagan images. A huge Jewish demonstration at Caesarea induces him to remove from Jerusalem banners depicting the emperor.	
29		Herod Antipas has John the Baptist executed for speaking publicly against Antipas' marriage to his sister-in-law, Herodias, in violation of Jewish law. The Jewish historian Josephus will suggest Antipas may have feared the size of John's following.	
30		Pontius Pilate* has a Jewish preacher from Galilee, Jesus of Nazareth, crucified in April. Only the late Christian Gospel of John will involve the Pharisees in his trial. Jesus had proclaimed the imminence of the kingdom of God as a relief to the poor in particular. Jesus' followers, calling themselves Nazarenes, regard him as the anointed descendant of King David, or Messiah, foreseen as a redeemer in biblical prophecy.	Philo of Alexandria, a well-born Jew with a classical Greek education, writes allegorical interpretations of the Torah, based on the Septuagint translation. He devotes books to the lives of the patriarchs as embodiments of ethical and philosophical values and to the life of Moses the lawgiver. His commentary on the Torah highlights what he interprets as its philosophical import, and his doctrine of the Logos has a significant influence on Christian theology. It is the Church that preserves his writings in Greek and Armenian. The Testament of Job expands the biblical story, making Job king of Egypt and his interlocutors, kings. Satan repeatedly attempts to discomfit Job, but Job insists that the way of piety will triumph. Remarkably, Job bequeaths his magical knowledge to his daughters, not his sons.
31	When the Roman imperial deputy Sejanus* assumes too much authority, Emperor Tiberius* has him killed.		
35			The king of Adiabene, Izates II,* converts to Judaism despite political hardships he incites. He has his sons educated in Jerusalem, and his dynasty will support the Jewish revolt against Rome.

A. General History	B. Jewish History	C. Jewish Culture	
	Pilate* is dismissed as governor following a protest of his cruelty by Samaritans.		36
The new Roman emperor Gaius Caligula* (37–41) declares himself a god and begins a reign of terror.	Agrippa, another son of Herod, is named king of Judea by Emperor Gaius Caligula.*		37
	In Alexandria, Egypt, Jews are attacked pogrom-style on the pretext that they refuse to worship Emperor Caligula.* Another attack follows a few years later.		38
	Jews of Yavneh destroy an altar set up by Emperor Caligula* to himself. In retribution, Caligula* orders the governor of Syria, Petronius,* to place a gold statue of himself in the Jerusalem Temple. Besieged by Jewish protesters at Acco, Petronius* has second thoughts. King Agrippa travels to Rome, persuading Caligula* to cancel the plan.		39
Most followers of Jesus are Jews, many of whom, like James, called the brother of Jesus, adhere to the traditional Commandments. Saul of Tarsus, who studied with Rabban Gamaliel in Jerusalem, begins preaching to Gentiles under the name of Paul that Jesus' death atoned for human sin and that faith in Jesus' divinity redeems without observance of the Torah. New Christians, accordingly, do not become Jews.	Yohanan ben Zakkai returns to Jerusalem and shares leadership of the Pharisees. He and Simon ben Gamaliel send letters to various communities advising them on proper observance.	Concerned with the suffering of pious Jews, possibly at the hands of Caligula,* a Jew assumes the identity of King Solomon and composes in Greek a book of wisdom promising that in contrast to appearances the good are rewarded and pass directly into an immortal state. The Wisdom of Solomon is influenced by the so-called suffering servant passages in Isaiah 52–53 and reflects views, such as the critique of paganism, similar to those of the Christian Paul.

Composed in Greek, 4 Maccabees is perhaps a reaction to the acts of Caligula.* Influenced by Greek philosophy, it attributes the choice of martyrdom to the control of the emotions by reason. | 40 |
	Agrippa happens to be in Rome when Claudius* is made emperor. In return for helping persuade the Roman Senate to abandon the idea of restoring the republic, Agrippa is granted the areas of Judea and Samaria by Claudius,* making him king of all Israel.	King Agrippa I respects Jewish religious sensibilities in Jerusalem by minting coins there with no image on them and by adhering while there to Jewish practice. At the Mediterranean port of Caesarea he promotes Hellenism.	41
	Agrippa I exhibits the ambition to become the most powerful ruler of the East. His plans to build a fortification wall around Jerusalem and host a summit meeting of local kings in Tiberias are quashed when the governor of Syria, Marsus,* complains to Emperor Claudius.*		42
	When Agrippa I dies, his son Agrippa II continues to wield power in the northern part of the country. Rome, however, returns Judea to its		44

	A. General History	B. Jewish History	C. Jewish Culture
44		own provincial administration under procurator Fadus* (44–46). Procurator Fadus* executes a would-be Messiah, Theudas, who proposed to turn the Jordan River dry.	
46		The procurator of Judea, Tiberius Alexander (46–48), who is of Jewish descent, crucifies two sons of the Zealot leader Judah of Gamala.	
50	The sacred Indian *Bhagavad-Gita* text reflects an ethic in which the caste system headed by the Brahman priests again prevails.	The large Jewish community of Egypt is estimated by Philo of Alexandria as 1 million. The Jews' numbers are increased through proselytization. Jews, who have lived in Greece since the 3rd century BCE, reside in all major cities and the islands. Among the Pharisees' supporters are members of restrictive ritual communities called *havurot*. Though not priests themselves, members of a *havura* observe temple laws, such as tithing scrupulously, and maintain a strict state of purity at meals.	The Testament of Abraham is composed at a date uncertain. The text is preoccupied with the inevitability of death, as an angel prepares Abraham to die. As consolation, the patriarch is given an advance tour of heaven. There angels are described writing down people's good and bad deeds and balancing them on scales. Literacy is emphasized in Judea through education of children in reading, Jewish law, and history; following the destruction of the Jerusalem Temple in 70, the high priest Joshua ben Gamla will order universal education from age six.
52		Clashes between Galilean pilgrims to Jerusalem and Samaritans confound procurator Cumanus* (48–52). Rome replaces him with Felix* (52–60).	
54	When Roman Emperor Claudius* is murdered by his wife, Agrippina,* his adopted son Nero* succeeds him. In 59 Nero* will have Agrippina* killed.		
58	Roman legions destroy the Armenian capital, Artaxata.	Felix* has difficulty suppressing increased Jewish unrest throughout the land of Israel despite his frequent recourse to bloody measures. He settles a conflict between the gentile majority and Jewish minority for control of Caesarea by sending in troops and massacring Jews.	
60	Paul (formerly Saul) of Tarsus, Asia Minor, is jailed for his own protection in Caesarea by Roman authorities. A missionary of the Jerusalem Christian church who had preached the abrogation of the laws and rituals of the Torah and faith in Jesus as the Messiah in Asia Minor and Syria, Paul was accosted by Jews on a visit to the Jerusalem Temple, leading to his arrest. Paul	The Jerusalem Temple is the site of tension between the high priest and common priests, who fail to receive their due of tithes, and between priests and Levites, who seek equal status. Jerusalem becomes increasingly anarchic.	Jewish mysticism focuses on the seven heavens of God on the one hand and the divine chariot described in Ezekiel 1 on the other. When the Temple is destroyed in 70, many will ask how the Romans could burn a temple with God resident in it. Some mystics will reply that God had already abandoned the Temple, ascending in his chariot.

A. General History	B. Jewish History	C. Jewish Culture	
authors a number of arguments for Christianity in letter form; they will become the earliest documents included in the New Testament.			**60**
The Christian missionary Paul is imprisoned in Rome, where he will die, perhaps during Nero's* persecutions of Christians there.	James, the "brother" of Jesus who with Peter leads the Christian community in Jerusalem, is executed by priestly authorities in Jerusalem.		**62**
For nine days in July Rome burns. While some hold Emperor Nero* responsible, Nero* blames Christians, who are then persecuted.		*A Christian depiction of Jews, portrayed here in "St. Paul Disputing with the Jews," 1150. (Victoria & Albert Museum, London)*	**64**
	Groups of Jews plan to overthrow Roman rule in Judea. Jewish rebels belong to two basic groups. The Galilean *Sicarii*, led first by Menahem, seek more to overturn society; the Jerusalem-based Zealots, led by Eleazar ben Hananiah, include disgruntled priests but are more religiously motivated. One of the two largest cities in Galilee, Sepphoris, remains loyal to Rome during the Jewish revolt while Tiberias mostly joins the rebellion. Estimates of the Jewish population by the contemporary historian Josephus reach into the millions. While these may be exaggerated, Jews densely populate Judea, the near Transjordan (Peraea), and Galilee. The Roman historian Tacitus* claims 600,000 Jews are in Jerusalem at the time of the revolt.	Pliny* describes Jerusalem as the best-known city of the Orient. The next largest Judean city is Jericho in the Jordan Valley. While most of the land engages in agriculture, Jericho is distinguished by lush orchards.	**65**
Emperor Nero* ends his conflict with the Parthians by recognizing the king of Armenia but sends legions across the Caucasus Mountains just in case.	Gentile residents of Caesarea win citizenship from Rome and force Jews out. This, compounded by Procurator Florus'* appropriation of funds from the Temple, triggers a clash between Jews and Roman troops in Jerusalem. As the fighting escalates, Florus* flees. Restive Jews ask Agrippa II to see the emperor; when he and other Jerusalem leaders fail to act, rebel leader Eleazar ben Hananiah stops Temple offerings on behalf of Rome and has the Roman troops in Jerusalem slain. News travels, and the revolt spreads throughout Israel. Cestius Gallus,* the Roman legate in Syria, musters Roman troops in Acco to suppress the Jewish revolt, but local Jewish fighters force their retreat. Inspired by the Jewish revolt in Israel, Jews in Alexandria, Egypt, seek to further their civic rights. The Roman governor, Julius Tiberius,* rebuffed in an effort at		**66**

A. **General History**	B. **Jewish History**	C. **Jewish Culture**

66

| | appeasement, sets his troops on them. Many thousands are slaughtered by soldiers and anti-Jewish citizens. | |

67

| | In February Rome responds to the Jewish revolt by sending the general Vespasian* and 60,000 soldiers. They overtake the Jewish stronghold Jotapata in western Galilee and capture their commander, Joseph ben Mattathias. Joseph, better known as the historian Flavius Josephus, persuades his captors to have him chronicle the war attached to the unit of Vespasian's* son, Titus.* Within the year Vespasian's* army dominates the rest of Galilee. Jewish diehards like John of Giscala hasten to Jerusalem to share in its defense.

Steeling themselves for a Roman attack, the Zealots struggle against other Jewish rebels for control of Jerusalem. When the other rebel groups mount an assault on their stronghold in the Temple, the Zealots, with the aid of reinforcements from Idumea and John of Giscala, rout them and execute their leaders, Hanan ben Hanan and Joshua ben Gamla. Zealot leader Eleazar ben Simon, populist leader Simon ben Giora, and John of Giscala continue their strife and fail to unite the Jews against Rome. | Simon bar Giora declares the freedom of all Jewish slaves. Many Jews had sold themselves and their families to pay off heavy debts. |

68

| In June, in the face of a coup, Nero* commits suicide. Vespasian* and Vitellius* vie to succeed him. | | |

69

| Vespasian,* whom the Roman army in the East had declared emperor, returns to Rome in December and seizes the emperor's throne. By spring Titus* assumes the task of suppressing the Jewish revolt. | | |

70

The Menorah of the Second Temple is conveyed to Rome, as depicted in a relief on the Arch of Titus, 70 CE.

| | Titus* lays siege to Jerusalem in the spring and struggles to breach its defenses. Initially frustrated, he surrounds the capital with a wall, hoping to starve the defenders.

In early Av (midsummer) Titus* takes the Temple Mount and burns down the Jerusalem Temple. A month later the Romans overcome the last Jewish defenders of the upper city.

The fall of Jerusalem leads to removal of the Jewish aristocracy and high priesthood from the Sanhedrin. Under rabbinic control, courts operating by *halakhah* are established, providing alternatives to | When the Temple is destroyed, synagogues already function in Caesarea, Dor, Tiberias, Capernaum, and elsewhere.

A Jewish rebel against Rome composes a scroll enumerating 36 days on which it is forbidden to fast. Megillat Ta'anit (Scroll of the Fast), written in Aramaic, includes a number of holidays commemorating victories of the Maccabees and their successors in the 2nd century BCE. Among the dates are the 25th of Kislev, Hanukkah; the 13th of Adar, Nicanor* Day, when the Syrian general was defeated by the Maccabees; and the 22nd of Shevat, when Roman Emperor Caligula* |

70

Roman jurisprudence. To impose greater uniformity, disputes between the houses of Hillel and Shammai are decided in favor of the former. The Romans would seem to endorse the Pharisaic party as the popular Jewish group most sympathetic to Roman rule.

Traditions differ on whether Rabban Yohanan ben Zakkai, vice president of the Sanhedrin and a long-standing proponent of pacifism toward Rome, left or was smuggled out of Jerusalem before its fall to the Romans, perhaps as early as 68, or whether he was taken captive to the coastal town of Yavneh during the fall. In any event, he reestablishes an academy at Yavneh from which the Sanhedrin continues to announce the calendar to all Jewry.

rescinded his order to install his statue in the Jerusalem Temple. An important historical source, the scroll may have been written to inspire Jewish fighters with victories of the past.

Rabban Yohanan ben Zakkai at Yavneh helps reconstruct Judaism to flourish after the destruction of the Jerusalem Temple by permitting such rituals as blowing the *shofar* (ram's horn) on the New Year and carrying the *lulav* (palm branch) on the Festival of Sukkot (Booths) outside the Temple precincts. He has the priests bless the community of Israel wherever they may be.

71

Returning to Rome to march in triumph, Titus* appoints Sextus Lucilius Bassus* to defeat the remaining Jewish rebel fortresses at Herodion and Masada west of the Dead Sea and Machaerus east of it.

After the Jewish revolt, Rome stations its 10th legion in Israel, placing the burden of providing for its needs, including forced labor, on the Jewish population. Believing that the gods of Rome had defeated the God of Israel, Rome imposes a tax on Jews throughout the empire to support the temple of Jupiter Capitolinus in Rome.

Rome confiscates many Judean farms, leasing them to Jews through gentile *conductores*, whom the Jews call *oppressors*. Many Jews retain title to their lands, but they must pay a land tax in addition to a poll tax, unlike other Roman subjects. Eventually, many Jewish captives are redeemed and return home, assisting in replanting and repopulating the country.

The Masada fortress. A modern view of its ruins. (Israel Government Press Office)

72

When Bassus* dies following the capture of Herodion and Machaerus, the task of overpowering Masada falls to Flavius Silva.*

73

The Romans sweep through Qumran and other last-ditch outposts near the Dead Sea. After a long siege, Roman troops mount a ramp and break into the Masada fortress. They find hundreds of defenders, led by Galilean rebel Eleazar ben Yair, dead, having chosen to take their own lives rather than fall into Roman captivity. Fearing contamination by Roman hands, the Qumran sect had secreted its sacred scrolls in caves, some in jars. These Dead Sea Scrolls will be rediscovered beginning in 1947.

	A. General History	B. Jewish History	C. Jewish Culture
73		Refugee Zealots from the Judean revolt come to Egypt and incite rebellion among poorer Jews. In response to Jewish unrest, Emperor Vespasian* closes the temple in Leontopolis, which was built for Egyptian Jewry by Jerusalem high priest Onias IV in 145 BCE.	
75			*The Book of Biblical Antiquities*, falsely ascribed to Philo of Alexandria, selectively retells the Bible's story, highlighting Abraham's resistance to paganism and the role of Moses as covenant mediator. Apparently composed in Hebrew, the book survives only in a Latin version. The term *rabbi* comes to identify sages carrying on the Pharisaic tradition.
79	The volcano Mt. Vesuvius erupts in Italy on August 24.		The Jewish collaborator with Rome, Flavius Josephus, completes a detailed history, *The Jewish War* and his *Antiquities of the Jews*, which provide invaluable information, especially from Hasmonean times on. Though tending to show Rome in a favorable light, Josephus writes with great sympathy for the Jews and their culture. *The Jewish War* explains Rome's destruction of Jerusalem as an unfortunate but necessary act of divine retribution and the Romans as normally hospitable to the Jews.
80	Following a fire in Rome, the Colosseum is opened.	Gamaliel II, son of Rabban Simon ben Gamaliel, takes over control of the Yavneh academy from Yohanan ben Zakkai at about this time and reasserts the authority inherited from the Jerusalem Sanhedrin.	
85	Rome completes its conquest of the British isles.		
90	The early Christian Gospel of Matthew blames the destruction of the Temple on the Jews' rejection of the Torah as embodied in Jesus and of the biblical prophets before him. The bishop of Rome, Clement, models the Christian church on the model of Greek city government.	Visits from Palestinian rabbis help maintain religious ties between Egyptian and Judean Jewry.	A number of authors attempt to make theological sense of Jerusalem's fall. Pretending to be Baruch, the scribe of Jeremiah the prophet who witnessed the destruction of Jerusalem by the Babylonians, an apocalyptic author uses that event to represent indirectly the Roman destruction of Jerusalem in 70. In 2 Baruch God assures the scribe that the punishment will be followed by forgiveness, that the suffering righteous will receive an eternal reward. God advises Baruch to fast in anticipation of the apocalypse. A similar work, 4 Ezra, is set in the Babylonian exile. Like 2 Baruch, 4 Ezra traces human sinfulness to the pattern set by Adam and insists that proper divine retribution and reward will obtain only in a predetermined

A. General History	B. Jewish History	C. Jewish Culture	
		end of time at which a Davidic Messiah will bring down the Roman Empire. The Apocalypse of Abraham has God show the patriarch how the Temple's destruction resulted from improper cultic practices.	**90**
Domitian,* Titus'* terror-wielding brother, is murdered in Rome, bringing the Flavian dynasty to an end.			**96**
The Roman taste for death, represented in mass gladiator fights, engenders more horrific entertainment, such as pitting slaves and Christians against wild animals.	With the Flavian dynasty gone, Rabban Gamaliel, son of Rabbi Simon ben Gamaliel, a supporter of the Jewish revolt and former head of the Sanhedrin, replaces Rabbi Yohanan ben Zakkai as president of the Sanhedrin. Rabban Gamaliel draws other sages to Yavneh and reasserts its authority. Members of this body are distinguished by learning rather than position and are ordained with the title *rabbi* (master, teacher). Gamaliel and other sages travel even to far-flung Jewish communities to preside over their affairs and collect funds. Power struggles between Hillelites and Shammaites continue; ultimately a cohead of the Sanhedrin, priestly Rabbi Eleazar ben Azariah, is elected alongside Rabban Gamaliel.		**98**
The Roman historian Tacitus,* with a perspective reflecting old Republican values, describes the surrounding world as decadent.	In order to segregate Jewish Christians, the Yavneh sages stiffen certain separatist regulations and introduce a prayer against heretics into the central *Amidah* liturgy. The oldest known synagogue in western Europe is constructed at Ostia, Italy, near the mouth of the Tiber River. The edifice will be expanded in stages over several centuries. Its ruins will be excavated in 1961.	The Yavneh sages transform the Temple-based Passover ritual to a family meal in which the erstwhile lamb offering is recognized only symbolically and the story of God's deliverance from Egypt, the Haggadah, is recited. The ritualized meal is fixed as the *seder*. Rufus of Samaria is the earliest known Jewish physician and medical writer. His commentaries in Greek on the works of Hippocrates* are quoted by the 2nd-century Greek physician Galen.* The literary art of the creation account in Genesis is praised in the Latin essay "On the Sublime," traditionally ascribed to the Roman author Longinus.*	**100**
	Trajan* conquers the Nabateans, taking over and further enhancing the Transjordanian trade routes. This has the effect of diverting revenues from Judea.		**106**
		Yavneh sages head local houses of study, *batei midrash*; among them are Rabbi Akiba in Benei Berak, Rabbi Eliezer ben Hyrcanus and Rabbi Tarfon in Lydda, and Rabbi	**110**

A. General History	B. Jewish History	C. Jewish Culture
110		Ishmael in southern Kefar Aziz. While Rabbi Akiva somewhat mystically draws significance out of every letter of the Torah, Rabbi Ishmael asserts that "the Torah speaks in ordinary language." These schools include both full-time younger students and others who attend after work. Schools take meals together, and disciples are encouraged to emulate their teachers' conduct even in mundane matters. Nahum of Gimzo, a town in central Israel, interprets the minutiae of Scripture without concern for context. His disciple, Rabbi Akiva, will follow his practice of atomizing the words of the Torah and explicating every particle.
111	Alexandrian Jews appeal to Emperor Trajan* for extension of their civic rights.	
115	Trajan* leads his fleet down the Tigris River, capturing Persia from the Parthians within the year.	Trajan's* general, Lucius Quietus* the Moor, puts down a Jewish revolt in Mesopotamia and turns then to Judea, where insurgents have been meeting on the Temple Mount and in Galilee. Quietus* (Kitos* in Jewish tradition) executes some of the leaders and erects an idol on the Temple Mount. Jews in Alexandria and Cyrenaica (west of Egypt on the north African coast) open a revolt against Roman authority, partly in resentment of Greek privileges, partly out of messianic hopes. The revolt spreads to Libya, Cyprus, and Mesopotamia; it finds support among gentile peasants.	
116	Amid widespread rebellion against Rome in the Near East, Jewish insurgence triggers revolts in Egypt and Cyprus.		
117	New Roman Emperor Hadrian* seeks to maintain order in his domain by helping to rehabilitate ravaged localities.	Emperor Hadrian's* benign policies toward the provinces are seen in Judea as a commitment to rebuild the Temple. In short time, Hadrian decrees that the Temple may not be rebuilt and that circumcision is forbidden throughout the empire. The Jewish revolt, which has brought devastation to many areas, is suppressed by Hadrian.* In the wake of the rebellion, Jews in Cyprus are wiped out and forbidden to return.	

A. General History	B. Jewish History	C. Jewish Culture	
	Jews angered by Hadrian's* restrictions secretly plan rebellion, occasionally carrying out guerilla attacks against occupying Roman troops.	A Roman proselyte to Judaism, Aquila of Pontus, translates the Torah into Greek in a manner that reflects the interpretations of the Yavneh sages. Under the influence of Rabbi Akiba, he renders the Hebrew virtually word for word. Whereas Christians adopted the Septuagint, Jews made use of Aquila's version.	120
	When Hadrian* is away from the East, Jews openly revolt. They are led by Simon bar Kosiba, dubbed Bar Kokhba (Son of a Star), who, together with the priestly sage Eleazar of Modein, commands the Jewish army and even strikes "freedom" coins from their headquarters near the Dead Sea at Ein Gedi. Many of the sages back the revolt; Rabbi Akiba calls Bar Kokhba "Messiah." Documents found at the Muraba'at caves and Wadi Hever, south of Qumran, show that Bar Kokhba seeks to redistribute land that, due to economic depression, had fallen to Roman hands.	 *Bar Kokhba letter fragment from Wadi Muraba'at; it begins: "From Simon son of Kosiba . . ." Circa 133 CE. (Israel Museum)*	132
	The governor of Syria, Publius Marcellus,* leads a contingent of legions from Syria, Egypt, and Arabia against the Jewish army. The Jews defeat them and proceed to engage the Romans in the Mediterranean Sea.		133
	The governor of Britain, Julius Severus,* is dispatched with a number of European legions to join the war against the Jewish rebels. Overtaking Galilee, the Roman army pursues the Jews to their fortress southwest of Jerusalem, Betar.		134
	Following a long siege, in the summer the Jewish rebels at Betar fall to the Romans. The Roman historian Dio Cassius* counts all Jewish casualties at over 600,000. Thousands are enslaved. Hadrian* punishes the revolt by transforming Jerusalem into a pagan city, Aelia Capitolina, and forbidding Jewish assembly, even in schools or at the Temple Mount. He has leading exponents of rebellion, including many sages such as Rabbi Akiba, executed.	Dismayed at the Hadrianic persecutions and martyrdom of sages, some, like the scholar Elisha ben Abuya, lose faith in God's saving power. Elisha is remembered in rabbinic tradition as a heretic who denies divine providence.	135
	Upon Hadrian's* death, his successor, Antoninus Pius,* loosens former restrictions on Palestinian Jews, allowing ritual circumcision again.	As Roman restrictions ease, remaining sages reconstitute the Sanhedrin at various towns in the Galilee. Among them is Rabbi Akiba's protégé, Rabbi Meir, whose	138

A. General History	B. Jewish History	C. Jewish Culture
138		wife, Beruriah, daughter of the martyred Rabbi Hananiah ben Teradyon, is also a Torah scholar.
150	Rabban Simon ben Gamaliel, a member of the revolutionary Sanhedrin who may have gone into hiding, takes charge of the new Galilean Sanhedrin at Usha. He reestablishes its power to fix the calendar despite initial resistance from the Babylonian exilarch. Rabban Simon includes Babylonian authorities in the Sanhedrin by introducing a tradition of bringing the presiding judge of the rabbinic court from Babylonia.	The first extant Jewish chronology of the world, *Seder Olam Rabbah*, is composed. Based on biblical ages and reckonings, it places the Exodus from Egypt at 2,448 years after creation, 500 years after the birth of Abraham.
161	Roman Emperor Marcus Aurelius,* a famed philosopher, is preoccupied until his death in 180 with provincial revolts. Building up roads and cities, Rome nevertheless spreads its trade throughout Europe and Britain.		
162	The Parthians invade Armenia, signaling a rebellion against Roman rule that will last two years.		
173	Revolt against Rome erupts in Egypt.		
175	Rome restores its control over Egypt.		The Greek physician Galen* distinguishes between Greek thought, in which the gods do not interfere with the mechanical order of the universe, and Jewish thought, in which the Creator may miraculously intervene.
180	The Sibylline Oracles foretell the fall of haughty Rome in tones reminiscent of the biblical prophet Isaiah.		
188	Rome puts down a revolt in Germany.		
193	Septimus Severus* becomes emperor of Rome after besting his rival Pescennius Niger,* who had been named emperor by the Roman legions in Syria.	Severus* shows constant favor toward the Jewish population of Israel for having supported him against the hostile Niger.*	
195		The patriarch (*nasi*, or prince) Rabbi Judah, son of Rabban Simon, extends the Sanhedrin's powers of taxation and the jurisdiction of Jewish courts, making good advantage of Emperor Severus'* favor. Rabbi Judah's imposition of death sentences is tolerated by Rome.	
200		Diverse and populous Babylonian Jewry, whose main occupations are agriculture and commerce, is headed by an exilarch (Aramaic, *resh galuta*), who holds court in Oriental fashion.	The Jewish mystical doctrine that elect individuals would behold God in an enormous human form is by now well developed. Based on imagery of the Song of Songs and

A. General History	B. Jewish History	C. Jewish Culture	
	The Jews at Beth-Shean, an ancient city south of the Sea of Galilee, erect a Roman theater with a seating capacity of almost 5,000.	other sources, the embodiment of the doctrine in *Shi'ur Qomah* (Measure of Stature) will become a central tract in later Kabbalah. The original Hebrew documents survive only fragmentarily. The text of the public Aramaic translation of the Torah is written down in Israel. The Aramaic rendering, or *targum*, has perhaps for centuries accompanied the reading of the Torah in the synagogue. Part of a *targum* of Job, for example, is found among the Dead Sea Scrolls. The practice of publicly reading the Torah along with a *targum* continues until the present among Yemenite Jews. The version of the written translation known as Targum Onkelos becomes the official one in the Babylonian rabbinic academies; its interpretation of the Torah's Hebrew often reflects rabbinic views.	**200**
The Antonine Constitution, promulgated by Emperor Caracalla,* extends Roman citizenship to all sectors of the empire except subject peoples. While the edict grants personal benefits to property holders, it makes them responsible for imperial taxes and services. Persians rebel against their Parthian overlords.	Jews in the Roman Empire share in the newly granted citizenship. Some Jewish landowners leave Israel to escape responsibility for local Roman levies.		**212**
		Rabbi Judah the Nasi publishes the Mishnah (Teaching), an arrangement of rabbinic law including written collections and oral traditions of the past several generations. Its six parts (*sedarim*, or orders) comprise: Seeds (agriculture), Festivals, Women (marriage, divorce), Torts, Holy Matters (Temple cult, food regulations), and Purity Matters. Written in a crisp contemporary Hebrew style, the Mishnah formulates legal opinions in textbook manner and often records dissenting views. It legislates for a Jewish community in Israel as if it were still revolving around the Jerusalem Temple.	**215**
		An academy is founded in Sura by Abba Arikha, who is known as Rav (Rabbi). Rav, who had returned from studying in Israel, sets the Mishnah of Rabbi Judah the Nasi at the center of the curriculum and assumes other Palestinian traditions. The rival academy in Nehardea is led by Samuel.	**219**

	A. General History	B. Jewish History	C. Jewish Culture
220	The Han dynasty falls, effected largely by regional power conflicts that will leave China a divided land until 569. The political tremors touch off philosophical challenges to Confucianism as forms of Buddhism and Taoism flourish. Eastern Emperor Licinius* issues anti-Christian measures.	After the death of Rabbi Judah the Nasi, rabbis of the Sanhedrin, led by Haninah bar Hama at Sepphoris, succeed in governing themselves, leaving political matters to the patriarch, now Rabban Gamaliel. Since local judges are also rabbis, the Sanhedrin insists on sharing powers of ordination with the *nasi*.	The leading Babylonian Jewish sage, or *amora*, Samuel declares that "the law of the state is the law," underlining the obligation of Babylonian Jews to pay land and poll taxes and to obey local economic regulations.
224	The Sassanids rise to power in Mesopotamia, overthrowing the Parthians and reestablishing Zoroastrianism.		
226		The Zoroastrian regime of the Sassanids restricts the jurisdiction of Jewish courts, especially over capital matters.	
230	The Persian Sassanid king Ardashir* besets Roman outposts in Mesopotamia, leading eventually to the capture of Antioch in Syria. In tribute to his continuing conquests and building activities, Ardashir* will be memorialized in legend.	In Israel Rabbi Judah succeeds Rabban Gamaliel as *nasi*.	A literary companion to Rabbi Judah the Nasi's Mishnah is compiled. This supplement, the Tosefta, which is three times the Mishnah's length, presents more material of the later Mishnaic sages, including Rabbi Judah the Nasi himself, and serves both to add to and elaborate on the material in the Mishnah. The Tosefta may be viewed as the first stage in the evolution of the Palestinian and Babylonian Talmudim as extended commentaries on the Mishnah.
232	The Roman army, led by Emperor Severus Alexander,* counterattacks the Sassanians in the Near East, but they are repelled.		
235	In the midst of conflict between the army and the Roman Senate, Emperor Severus Alexander* is murdered, introducing anarchy in place of the Severan dynasty. Aggression by Parthians in the East and Teutons in the West bedevil emperors, who replace each other in relatively rapid succession.		
240	The Persian prophet Mani* begins to spread an international religion embracing elements of Zoroastrianism, Buddhism, and Christianity. Mani* teaches that human souls need to escape the evil world of matter and disparages life as such. Manicheism will pose a threat to official religion in both Rome and Persia.	Rome's need to sustain its far-flung troops in times of rampant foreign aggression imposes heavy burdens on Palestinian Jews, especially farmers, to provide revenues and supplies. Many Jews, hard-pressed, leave the country.	The Christian church father, Origen,* who had studied Hebrew in the land of Israel, completes an edition of the Hebrew and Greek versions of the Hebrew Bible, the Hexapla, in Alexandria, Egypt. Origen* lays out the versions in six parallel columns, including a phonetic transcription of the Hebrew into Greek letters. He also indicates differences between the Hebrew source and Greek translations. The monumental work, the remains of which greatly assist Bible scholars today, is meant to inform Christians in their quarrels over Scripture with Jews.

A. General History	B. Jewish History	C. Jewish Culture	
Newly elected Roman Emperor Philip* the Arabian establishes peace between eastern Roman forces and the Sassanians before leaving for Rome.			**244**
		Jews at Dura-Europos, a Roman outpost on the Upper Euphrates River, complete construction of their synagogue, remarkable for its ubiquitous wall paintings and its preservation in sand in the face of Sassanian destruction in 256. The large synagogue hall is oriented toward Jerusalem in the west, where a niche for the Torah is set in the wall. The paintings depict numerous biblical scenes from the stories of Genesis through the tale of Esther and the Book of Maccabees, though some of the motifs are pagan in origin.	**245**
New Roman Emperor Decius,* concerned over the success of Christian missionaries in the empire and viewing Christianity as a state within the Roman State, systematically persecutes Christians.			**249**
Neoplatonism, an amalgam of Greek philosophy and pagan lore, is developed as a means for mystical union by Plotinus.* Its ideas of spheres emanating from the divine center and of elevating the soul toward the divine through purification will influence Spanish Jewish mysticism. More immediately, it will stimulate the development of the Christian Eucharistic rite whereby bread and wine are transubstantiated into the body and blood of Jesus, to be consumed by the worshipper who seeks divine grace.	Roman Emperor Decius* exempts Jews from a libation ordained to demonstrate allegiance to the empire.	Nonlegal teachings of prerabbinic and rabbinic sages, mostly worldly and spiritual wisdom in epigram form, are edited into Pirkei Avot (Chapters of the Fathers), and appended to the Mishnah. Characteristic is the observation that the world exists by virtue of three things: *torah* (study), worship, and kindness toward others. A rabbinic elaboration of the Chapters, called Avot de-Rabbi Nathan, composed somewhat later, would seem to be based on an earlier form of the Chapters than the Mishnah's. It quotes the sage Elisha ben Abuya, who is regarded as a heretic in rabbinic tradition for his denial of divine providence.	**250**
Roman persecution of Christians subsides as Emperor Decius* is slain by Goths, who beset Rome's European dominions.			**251**
	Jews in Cappadocia, Asia Minor, knowing of the Sassanid regime's religious intolerance, attempt to thwart the advance of King Shapur I* (241–272). The Persian slaughters 12,000 of them.		**252**
		Under the leadership of exilarch Rav Huna (257–297), the Sura academy exercises authority throughout Babylonian Jewry.	**257**
	When Palmyran troops sack the Nehardea academy in Babylonia, it		**259**

	A. General History	B. Jewish History	C. Jewish Culture
259		moves to Pumbaditha under Rav Judah bar Ezekiel.	
260	Sassanid King Shapur I* defeats an invading Roman force led by Emperor Valerian* himself. Valerian* dies in captivity and is buried beside the ancient Persian kings as a showpiece.	When Palmyra achieves temporary independence (until 272), Jews enjoy political influence in the Arab-dominated city, giving rise to a legend that Queen Zenobia* (267–272) converted to Judaism.	
269	The Roman army finally defeats the Goths in the Balkans.		
270		The Sanhedrin, now at Tiberias, is headed by Rabbi Yohanan ben Nappaha, who maintains routine communication with sages in Babylonia and issues numerous halakhic opinions.	Academies continue to flourish in various towns in the Galilee and Judea.
273	Palmyra, independent under King Odenathus* and then Queen Zenobia* since 260, is reconquered by Rome.		
278	Roman Emperor Probus,* having removed the threat of Germans and Goths from Gaul, turns his attention to Asia Minor.		
288	Roman Emperor Diocletian* pacifies the Near East by setting up a government in Armenia in coordination with Sassanian King Vahram II* and by suppressing a revolt in Egypt. Order will not last a decade.		
297	Diocletian's* lieutenant in the Near East, Galerius,* combats Persian forces while in Egypt revolt breaks out again, drawing a Roman army led by Diocletian* himself the next year.		
300		Diocletian* divides the land of Israel into three administrative areas: central Palaestina Prima, with Caesarea its capital; northern Palaestina Secunda, with Beth-Shean its capital; and southern Palaestina Tertia, with its capital in Petra. Bureaucracy is increased; craftsmen are organized into guilds to facilitate taxation. Jews begin using more Hebrew and the Hebrew, rather than Greek, forms of their names.	An Aramaic translation of the Prophets, used in the synagogues of Israel, is brought to Babylonia, where it is reworked over many generations and fixed as the standard Targum Jonathan to the Prophets, an official counterpart to Targum Onkelos to the Torah. A translation of the Bible into an eastern Aramaic dialect of Syria, Syriac, is completed. The relatively literal translation, called the Peshitta, shows the influence of the Greek Septuagint and some rabbinic interpretation. Nevertheless, a direct Jewish role in the translation is disputed and the effort is generally attributed to Christians in Edessa.
303	Diocletian* resumes the persecution of Christianity suspended by Emperor Gallienus.* The preceding		

A. General History	B. Jewish History	C. Jewish Culture	
emperors' military disasters had confirmed Christians' faith that God was requiting their oppressors.			**303**
Diocletian* abdicates the imperial throne, dividing his power among three subordinate "colleagues." The Empire will not be united under a single ruler again until 324.	The Council of Elvira, Spain, forbids Christians to live or eat with Jews. During the preceding century Jews had settled in Spain in larger numbers and many other inhabitants had become Christian.		**305**
Roman "Caesar" (a subimperial title) Galerius* decrees the end to persecution of Christians. The edict will take effect in the western empire, not the eastern.			**311**
Constantine,* vying with other generals to be Roman emperor since 306, conquers Italy and secures his regime. Son of a Christian mother, he begins promoting Christianity in his domains.			**312**
In the wake of conflicts to control the Roman Empire, Constantine,* emperor of the West, agrees that Licinius* will govern the East. Armed struggle between them will nevertheless erupt in the next year. A bishop of the Church, Donatus, contends that temporal authorities can have no control over ecclesiastical property. Despite censure, scores of bishops come to share the Donatist view.	The Roman church, enjoying new power from Christian Emperor Constantine,* more aggressively proselytizes and derogates Jews. While the Church is dedicated to stamping out paganism, it tolerates Jews so that they may witness the return of Messiah Jesus.		**313**
	Constantine* begins a series of edicts oppressive to Judaism, including a prohibition against male converts and the manumission of slaves circumcised by their Jewish owners.		**315**
Eusebius (260–339), church father and bishop of Caesarea, writes *Onomasticon*, a work of biblical place names that serves as an important source of information on Palestine in the 4th century. Constantine* removes his eastern coemperor, Licinius,* liquidates pagan temples, and uses their funds for building Christian churches in Asia Minor, Syria, and Judea.			**324**
Three hundred Christian bishops join Constantine* at Nicaea, northwestern Asia Minor, to adopt a creed affirming that Jesus Christ is of the "same substance" as God, his father. The third part of the Christian Trinity, the Holy Ghost, will also be declared to be of that substance at the Council of Constantinople in 381.			**325**

	A. General History	B. Jewish History	C. Jewish Culture
330	Constantine* founds the Byzantine imperial capital of Constantinople.		
337	Upon the death of Constantine,* governance of the Roman Empire is divided among his three sons.	Constantius,* who succeeds his father, Constantine,* in the East, extends his anti-Jewish legislation, forbidding female converts, intermarriage with Christians, and Jewish ownership of slaves. Jews are labeled a "pernicious sect."	
338	Bishop Eusebius of Caesarea uses his biography of Constantine* to draw the ideal image of a Christian monarch.		Under the leadership of Rava, the Babylonian Pumbaditha academy moves to Mahoza, on the Tigris River.
340	A monastic movement of Christian ascetics, strong in the Fayyum, northwestern Egypt, spreads north to Judea, Syria, and Asia Minor.		
350		Emperor Constantius* and his mother Helena,* a devout Christian who eventually moves to Israel, build churches in Bethlehem and Jerusalem. A Jewish apostate named Joseph constructs churches in the Galilee with imperial support.	
351		Jews in Sepphoris, northern Israel, encouraged by rebellions against Byzantine authority in the west and the Persian onslaught, overcome the local imperial troops. As rebellion spreads through Galilee, the eastern governor, Gallus,* sends an army that destroys many Jewish centers, such as Beth-shearim, burial site of many Jewish nobles.	
352	With both his brothers out of the way and insurgents defeated, Constantius* rules the entire Roman Empire alone from Constantinople.		
358		The *nasi* Hillel II fixes the Jewish calendar on the basis of astronomical calculations. Diaspora Jews no longer depend on the Sanhedrin for new moon announcements, which had been outlawed by Constantius II.*	
360	New emperor of the West, Julian,* known later as "the Apostate," follows the old Greek cult, disparaging Christianity and admiring Jewish ritual. Julian's preference for paganism has been typical of many upper-class Romans.		
362		Emperor Julian,* to suppress Christianity and win Jewish favor on the eve of his war against Persia, announces his intention to rebuild the Jerusalem Temple and places a deputy in charge. Jews begin expelling Christians from Jerusalem.	

A. General History	B. Jewish History	C. Jewish Culture	
	Persian Jews seeking to make pilgrimage to Jerusalem during Julian's* war with Shapur II* (309–379) are slain by Persians.		362
Julian* is killed in Mesopotamia by a Christian Arab under his command. Persia and Rome make peace.			363
The Roman army makes Valentinian* emperor of Rome; he appoints his brother Valens* (364–378) emperor in Constantinople. The division of the empire into West and East is complete.			364
	Valens* prohibits imperial troops from lodging in synagogues; he also exempts Jews under the aegis of the *nasi* from serving on municipal councils.		368
Germans begin crossing the Rhine and settling in the Roman Empire proper.			370
		Rav Ashi heads the Sura academy (until 427), compiling and editing Babylonian discussions relating to the Mishnah into a dialectical commentary. Following the order of the Mishnah and modeled on the Palestinian Talmud, the commentary becomes the basis of the extensive Babylonian Talmud. Rich in legend and lore, the essentially legal material reflects local Babylonian concerns and interpretations. The heavily intellectual character of the arguments, attempting to harmonize traditions and attribute them to leading sages or schools, reflects the belief that one serves God with the mind as well as the heart.	371
Upon the accession of the teenage emperor Gratian,* Roman leadership is contested among generals and the army is fragmented.			375
The Visigoths, who will later wreak havoc on Rome, are pressed westward across the Danube River by the Huns.			376
The new Roman emperor, Theodosius I,* restores the power of the Christian church. Under his tenure the Church will obtain tax-exempt status and the right to maintain its own courts.			379
	The *nasi* Gamaliel ben Hillel consults regularly with the Roman jurist in Antioch, Libanius.*	The Palestinian, or Jerusalem, Talmud, is edited, mainly in Tiberias. It arranges two centuries of rabbinic discussion in the form of a commentary on the Mishnah. Much of the Palestinian Talmud	380

	A. General History	B. Jewish History	C. Jewish Culture
380			serves as material for the Babylonian Talmud, but only the first four divisions of it survive, and not all of them intact. A product of the land of Israel, the Palestinian Talmud includes commentary on the first order of the Mishnah, "Seeds," dealing with agriculture, a section the Babylonian Talmud does not treat.
385		The empire imposes the "colonate" law in Palestine, restricting tenant farmers from leaving the land they work.	
387		In Antioch, Syria, church father John Chrysostom preaches a series of virulent sermons against Jews.	
388		The synagogue in Callinicum, Mesopotamia, is burned and pillaged by Christians at the instigation of their bishop. Emperor Theodosius I* of Rome orders the bishop to rebuild the synagogue and punish the perpetrators. St. Ambrose (339–397), who was then bishop of Milan, writes to the emperor objecting to the penalty, saying those who protect synagogues become allies of the Jews and therefore enemies of Christ.	
395	At the death of Emperor Theodosius I,* who had made a point of persecuting paganism, the empire is again divided between East and West. Under Alaric* the Bold, the Visigoths grow more assertive in their demands for Roman-held lands.		
400	The Roman Senate is bloated with hereditary officials, exploiting their position for personal gain. Local administrators enter the priesthood as a source of income. The peasantry seeks refuge from taxation in the Church, the army, and the cities. Piracy is on the rise.	The king of Himyar, on the southwest coast of Arabia, Ab Karib As'ad,* converts to Judaism and maintains strong contacts with Tiberias. Himyar's fortunes decline with those of Rome and the expansion of the Church.	A largely halakhic (legal) *midrash* of most of the Book of Exodus is compiled in Israel. This work, later called the Mekhilta of Rabbi Ishmael, a leading sage of the 2nd century, assembles a number of interpretations from the period of the Mishnah (*beraitot*) according to the synagogue Torah divisions of the Book of Exodus. A century later, another *midrash* of Exodus, the Mekhilta which will be attributed to the 2nd-century sage Rabbi Shimon bar Yohai, borrows from the aggadic (homiletical) portions of the Mekhilta of Rabbi Ishmael but extends the *aggadah* to the balance of the Book of Exodus. A very early work of Jewish mystical speculation on creation, *Sefer ha-Yetsirah* (*Book of Creation*), would seem to be taking shape in the land of Israel. Influenced apparently by Gnosticism, it holds that creation occurred by means of the 22 letters of the Hebrew alphabet and 10

A. General History	B. Jewish History	C. Jewish Culture	
		phases (*sefirot*) of metaphysical development, the first at least emanating from God. Brief and opaque, this tract becomes the object of medieval Kabbalistic interpretation and study.	400
The Visigoths, following the raids of Vandals and other northern "barbarians," sack Rome, opening the way for the dissolution of the western Roman Empire.			410
	The patriarch Cyril* expels Jews from Alexandria, Egypt, for a time. For the first time, Roman imperial laws expressly prohibit construction of new synagogues. Lawful protection is afforded only to old ones.		415
The Visigoths under Ataulf,* brother-in-law and successor of the slain conqueror, Alaric* the Bold, establish a kingdom in Spain.	Jews, many of them wealthy landowners, on the isle of Minorca off Spain are ordered to convert to Christianity by Severus, bishop of Majorca. Some escape, others fight to the death, and others comply.		418
	A Christian monk, Barsauma of Nisibis, leads a rampage against Jews throughout Palestine, demolishing synagogues.		419
As a result in part of Sassanian persecution of Christians, war erupts between Byzantium and Persia, leading to the latter's defeat in 422 and tolerance of Christianity.			421
A law code is issued under Byzantine Emperor Theodosius II.*		Sifra, an almost verse-by-verse legal *midrash* of the Book of Leviticus, compiled mostly from *beraitot* (rabbinic sources from the Mishnaic period), is composed, probably in Israel.	425
Augustine completes his 22-book systematization of the Church and its theology, *The City of God*. He began writing this work shortly after the collapse of the city of Rome.			426
The Vandals cross over to Africa from Spain, which they have occupied for 20 years. By 440 they will have dominion over all northern Africa.	Emperor Theodosius II* (408–450) decrees that the Sanhedrin surrender funds collected for the patriarch, abolishing in effect the Jewish patriarchate. Rabbi Gamaliel, the last *nasi*, had already been demoted in 415. The Church had been seeking to eliminate the Davidic position of patriarch because it seemed to challenge the Christian idea of the Messiah.		429
In North Africa, Martianus Capella* lays down the seven liberal arts, which will become the scholastic curriculum of the West through the 19th century. The disciplines are	The Christian population of Israel grows significantly; church prelates prevent Emperor Theodosius II* from protecting Jews from attack.		430

	A. General History	B. Jewish History	C. Jewish Culture
430	grammar, dialectics, rhetoric, arithmetic, geometry, astronomy, and music.		
431	A Christian missionary from Wales, later known as St. Patrick, begins organizing the Church in Ireland.		
438		Theodosius II* decrees that Jews may neither hold any public office—lest they insult Roman law or Christianity—nor build synagogues.	
439	Carthage, the North African Phoenician colony and now the last significant stronghold of the old Roman regime, falls to the northern barbarians.		
440	Sassanid ruler Yazdigar II* enhances the power of the Zoroastrian priests in Mesopotamia, leading to persecution of Christians and other religious minorities.		
450	The Hindu philosopher and scientist Panini* composes in India a system of epigrammatic rules (sutras) that form the grammar of the Sanskrit language. The grammar explains how the rules operate on abstract, underlying word forms in a certain sequence to produce the language. Panini's* system anticipates the "generative" grammar of Noam Chomsky (b. 1928) in the latter half of the 20th century.	Jews extend and improve agriculture and refurbish synagogues in the land of Israel, taking advantage of political and theological divisions in the Church.	Legal midrashim to the books of Numbers and Deuteronomy are composed, probably in the land of Israel. Comprising various Hebrew sources, the Sifrei to Numbers and Deuteronomy comment on the legal material but also treat narrative passages in their aggadah. The Sifrei to Numbers, sharing certain features with the Mekhilta of Rabbi Ishmael on Exodus, would appear to stem from a different tradition from the Sifrei to Deuteronomy, which may rather reflect the school of Rabbi Akiva, Ishmael's rival.
451	To increase the Church's control over its members, a council at Chalcedon, in northwestern Asia Minor, divides the empire into five sees, each governed by a patriarch. The council is marked by a lasting controversy between Afro-Asian Christianity and the Roman church over the nature of Jesus' divinity, or humanity. The influential Pope Leo I's (440–461) doctrine of the Trinity holds sway.		
453	The Huns, led by the fierce Attila,* overrun Gaul but are stopped by the Spanish-based Visigoths.		
455	Rome is raided by the Vandals. Byzantine Emperor Valentinian III* decrees that all bishops are subordinate to the Church of Rome.		
456		Yazdigar II* forbids Jews in Mesopotamia from observing the Sabbath.	

A. General History	B. Jewish History	C. Jewish Culture	
	Yazdigar II* is succeeded by his son Firuz,* whom Jewish sources refer to as "the Wicked" for banning Jewish worship and study, also perhaps because Firuz* murders his brother in 459 to secure his throne. Jews are placed under the jurisdiction of Persian courts, and Jewish children are often compelled to receive Zoroastrian education.		**458**
	Firuz's* persecution of Mesopotamian Jewry enters a vehement stage, called by the Babylonian Talmud "the year of the destruction of the world." Synagogues and schools are demolished. Many Jews flee to Arabia and India.		**468**
	Firuz* executes the sage Huna, son of the Jews' exilarch Mar Zutra.		**470**
		Genesis Rabbah, a collection of *midrash* interpreting the first book of the Bible almost verse by verse, is compiled in Israel. At the opening of sections a *midrash* is often presented like a sermon. Sometimes several *midrashim* of the same verse or phrase are given, reflecting the principle that Scripture can have many simultaneous meanings. The *midrash* Leviticus Rabbah is composed in the land of Israel. Comprising a series of 37 sermons taking the beginning of the weekly Torah reading, according to the triennial cycle, as the point of departure, the *midrash* repeatedly communicates the need for holiness to be expressed in the lives of ordinary Jews in the wake of the loss of the Temple in 70. A similar *midrash*, Pesikta de-Rav Kahana, consists of homilies on the festivals and special Sabbaths and may have the same provenience.	**475**
With the blessing of eastern emperor Zeno,* the German Odovacar* seizes control of Italy, deposing the emperor of the West.			**476**
Barbarians slay Sassanid King Firuz* and continue to plague Persia.			**484**
New Sassanid ruler Kovad I* adopts the teaching of the prophet Mazdak,* whose religion shows signs of Manicheism, and begins persecuting those who refuse his doctrines.			**488**
The Ostrogoths take over Italy.			**489**
	Exilarch Mar Zutra forms an autonomous Jewish kingdom based		**495**

495		in Mahoza. He levies taxes and raises a defense army.

496 The powerful Frankish king, Clovis,* galvanizes power in western Europe by converting to Christianity and winning some support from the Church. Within decades his Merovingian house will govern all of Gaul and Germany.

497 Sassanid ruler Kovad I* is deposed and imprisoned.

499 The last head of the Sura academy, Rabina, continues the compilation and editing of the Babylonian Talmud. The Talmud is still a fluid composition as opinions and contributions of later sages are introduced. In the succeeding generations, the Babylonian Talmud takes shape according to involved yet intricate literary structures known as *sugyot* (lessons). In Babylonia nonlegal, aggadic rabbinic material is not edited into separate *midrash* collections but is included within the Talmud itself.

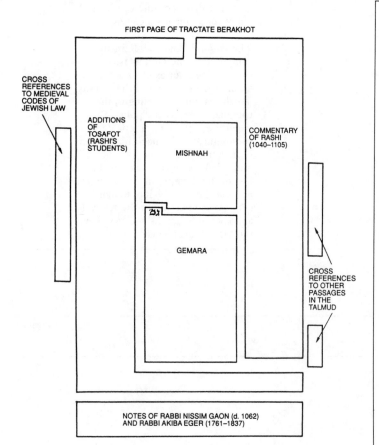

FIRST PAGE OF TRACTATE BERAKHOT

CROSS REFERENCES TO MEDIEVAL CODES OF JEWISH LAW

ADDITIONS OF TOSAFOT (RASHI'S STUDENTS)

MISHNAH

COMMENTARY OF RASHI (1040–1105)

GEMARA

CROSS REFERENCES TO OTHER PASSAGES IN THE TALMUD

NOTES OF RABBI NISSIM GAON (d. 1062) AND RABBI AKIBA EGER (1761–1837)

A. General History	B. Jews in Europe	C. Jews in the Middle East and North Africa	D. Jewish Culture	
Cassiodorus'* *History of the Goths* portrays King Theodoric,* who reigns over Italy from 493 to 526, as the champion of the historic Roman Empire.			Liturgical poetry, *piyyut* (a Greek-derived term), is finely developed, at first, it would seem, in Israel. Composed in learned Hebrew or Aramaic, *piyyut* draws on and plays with biblical expressions and incorporates rabbinic exegesis (*midrash*). *Piyyut* was first introduced to stand in for nonfixed parts of the synagogue service (in an era when worshipers did not have prayer books), but it came to embellish parts of the Sabbath and especially festival liturgy when prayers became more standard. Earlier *piyyutim* are anonymous, but there now begin to appear works by the great classic *payyetanim*, Yosi ben Yosi, Yannai, and Eleazar ben Kalir. *Piyyut* continues to flourish through the Middle Ages, especially in Mediterranean lands, from Israel to Spain.	500
		Restored to his throne, Sassanian ruler Kovad I* overruns the Jewish kingdom and executes Mar Zutra and his grandfather, Rav Haninah. Jewish schools and synagogues are shut down. Jewish leaders flee eastward and found a new academy near Apamea.		502
	The Visigoths' law code forbids Jews in Spain from building synagogues, owning Christian slaves, and holding public office. Jews in Visigoth Spain pay a special tax but generally fare better than the laws would allow.			506
		Yusuf As'ar Dhu Nuwas,* king of the independent kingdom of Himyar, in southern Arabia, converts to Judaism before he ascends the throne. He is one of several Himyarite kings to embrace Judaism.		517
	The synagogues of Ravenna are set afire by Christians. Theodoric,* who reigns over Italy, compels the Christians to pay for their rebuilding.			519
The Bulgars follow hordes of Goths and Huns in raiding the eastern Roman Empire.		The Sanhedrin in Palestine appoints as *nasi* Mar Zutra, posthumous son of the Babylonian exilarch.	An elaborate mosaic floor is laid in the synagogue at Beth Alfa, southwest of the Sea of Galilee. The three	520

	A. General History	B. Jews in Europe	C. Jews in the Middle East and North Africa	D. Jewish Culture
520	Imru al-Qays* (d. 540) composes some of the earliest classical Arabic poetry.		In Mesopotamia communal institutions like the exilarchy and the learning assembly (*kallah*), in which many Jews attend an academy preceding the holidays of Rosh Hashanah and Pesah, resume.	panels depict the holy ark of the synagogue, the signs of the zodiac, and Abraham's binding of Isaac.
527	Justinian* succeeds to the imperial throne of his adoptive father, Justin,* at Byzantium.		Justinian* proceeds to issue anti-Jewish legislation.	
529	Justinian* sets out to convert all pagans to Christianity by force.			
530	Partly in reaction to Himyarite persecution of Arabian Christians, Christian Abyssinia invades Arabia up to Mecca.			
533	Eastern Emperor Justinian* embarks on a reconquest of the western imperial lands. Fierce Ostrogothic resistance draws out the Gothic War over decades.			
534	Justinian* completes the codification of Roman law as an absolutist system. It will serve as the basis of later European codes. He also engages in extensive building projects in Constantinople, defining the Byzantine style.			
535	The Christian monk Benedict (d. 547) has established a discipline of behavior for his monastery near Naples. The Rule of St. Benedict will become common among monks by the late 9th century.			
537			Justinian* decrees that Byzantine Jews must maintain municipal government even though they may hold no positions in it.	
540	Preoccupied with his campaigns in the west, Justinian* loses the Balkans to Slavs and Syria to the Iranians. He will not realize his dream of uniting the western and eastern imperial domains.			
550				The biblical Song of Songs is interpreted verse by verse as an allegory of the

The sacrifice of Isaac (Genesis 22) is depicted in this mosaic from the Beit Alfa synagogue floor. (Institute of Archaeology, Hebrew University of Jerusalem)

A. General History	B. Jews in Europe	C. Jews in the Middle East and North Africa	D. Jewish Culture	
			covenantal love between God and the people of Israel in the Palestinian *midrash* composition, Song of Songs Rabbah. The "lily among the thorns" (2:2), for example, is decoded as the Hebrews in Egypt in need of redemption by God.	**550**
		Justinian* resolves a Jewish dispute about whether the Torah may be read in the synagogue in Greek translation by forbidding the Mishnah as man-made law and bidding Jews pay heed to prophecies concerning Jesus the Messiah. The Greek translation should attract Jews to Christianity.		**553**
For the next two centuries popes in Rome will seek confirmation from the emperor in Byzantium.				**555**
		Palestinian Jews join Samaritans in fighting imperial measures against their practices, including destruction of synagogues.		**560**
The Lombards take over northern Italy.				**568**
During the long reign of Chosroes I,* the Persians import such Indian tales as *Sindbad the Sailor* and disseminate the game of chess.				**570**
The Sassanian king Chosroes I* reclaims southern Arabia from Abyssinia.				**575**
	Christians destroy the synagogues in Clermont-Ferrand. Bishop Avitus forces over 500 Jews to accept baptism. Those who refuse flee to Marseilles.			**576**
New Sassanian ruler Hormuzd IV* restores influence to the Zoroastrian "magi" in Persia.		Jewish institutions in Babylonia are again beset. The Pumbaditha academy moves to Firuz-Shapur, which is under Arab control.		**580**
	A wealthy Jewish trader, Priscus, is made to debate the merits of Judaism with Frankish King Chilperic.* Though successful in the disputation, Priscus is later murdered by an apostate Jew.			**581**

	A. General History	B. Jews in Europe	C. Jews in the Middle East and North Africa	D. Jewish Culture
582		Frankish King Chilperic* attempts to convert all Jews in his realm. According to the *History of the Franks* composed by Gregory, bishop of Tours (573–594), Jews live in Marseilles, Orleans, Tours, and other localities.		
587	The Arian king of the ruling Visigoths, Reccared,* joins the Catholic church.			
589		The Catholic Council of Toledo, with the assent of King Reccared,* decrees that children of Jewish–Christian marriages must be baptized.		
590	Sassanian ruler Chosroes II* (590–628) shows tolerance to minorities.		Jewish institutions in Mesopotamia prosper again; both leading academies function.	
600	Under Pope Gregory I (590–604) the papacy becomes the supreme authority of the western Church.	Pope Gregory I establishes a policy of converting Jews to Christianity by restricting Jewish religious activity on the one hand and proffering political and economic inducements to converts on the other. Setting official papal policy toward Jews, he orders that Jews be protected from violence but enjoins, too, that they not attain status equal to that of Christians.		
602	A revolt in the east against Emperor Maurice* provides an occasion for Persia to reconquer Syria and Asia Minor. Persia will soon press on to overtake Egypt.			
612		Spain's new Visigoth king, Sisebut,* decrees that all debts to Jews are released; to keep title to their land, Jews must convert to Christianity.		
613		Visigoth King Sisebut* gives Jews the ultimatum of converting or leaving. Some Jews leave Spain; others are baptized and remain.		
614	The Persian army's advance against the Byzantine Empire reaches Israel.		Jews, some with messianic expectations, join Persian forces in overtaking the Galilee, then Judea and Jerusalem. When Jerusalem falls, the Persians place it in the Jews' charge. Under the leadership of Nehemiah ben	

A. General History	B. Jews in Europe	C. Jews in the Middle East and North Africa	D. Jewish Culture	
		Hushiel, the Jews oust Christians and their churches from Jerusalem.		**614**
		Through a rapprochement with Persia, Christians regain control of Jerusalem. Jews mount a counterstruggle, but they are defeated and their leader, Nehemiah, is killed.		**617**
In Arabia, Muhammad, the Prophet of Islam (Submission to Allah), fails to fire up a following in his native Mecca and leads a migration (Arabic, *hejira*) from Mecca to Medina, a formerly Jewish center ripe for religious leadership. Established in Medina, Muhammad organizes the Muslim community through law and government. His teachings, embodied in the Koran, involve divergent versions of biblical narrative and claim Islam as the authentic continuation of the faith of Abraham. Major Jewish rituals are supplanted by new Islamic rites, which include five prayers daily, charity, the month-long fast of Ramadan, and a pilgrimage (Arabic, *haj*; compare Hebrew *hag*) to Mecca once in a life, as well as abstinence from pork and wine and the institution of holy war (Arabic, *jihad*).		Jews on the Arabian Peninsula join their allied Arab tribes, Banu al-Aws and Banu Khazraj, in showing support to Muhammad. Byzantine Emperor Heraclius* marches as far as Ecbatana and imposes peace on Persia, restoring control of Israel to Christian hands.		**622**
		Shoring up power, Muhammad drives the Jewish tribes out of Arabia in the course of four years.		**624**
	Byzantine Emperor Heraclius* orders that Jews throughout his realm, which extends as far as Spain, convert to Christianity.			**628**
		Emperor Heraclius* arrives in Israel to restore Christian holy relics to Jerusalem. Welcomed by Jews and hosted by Benjamin of Tiberias, Heraclius* agrees to pardon Jewish opponents. After Heraclius* visits the Church of the Holy Sepulchre in Jerusalem, he is pressured by Christian clerics to break his oath. Jews are expelled from the Jerusalem area, and some must flee for their lives.		**629**

	A. **General History**	B. **Jews in Europe**	C. **Jews in the Middle East and North Africa**	D. **Jewish Culture**
630	After nearly a decade of combat, Muhammad overtakes Mecca and rids it of paganism, extending Islam to virtually all the Arabian Peninsula.			
632	Upon the death of Muhammad, nomadic and other groups seek independence from Islam. Muhammad's successor, Abu Bakr,* restores discipline by force, extending control from Byzantium to the Persian Gulf.			
633		The Council of Toledo, Spain, adopts the new Church policy of eschewing forced conversion of Jews. However, Jews who had already converted, even by force, may not return to Judaism; their children must be raised as Christians.		
634	The caliph (divine deputy) Omar,* succeeding the late Abu Bakr,* begins a pattern of dispatching small armies throughout the Middle East, bringing it all under his power in a few years.			
638		The Council of Toledo, under the sway of King Chintila,* forbids any but Catholics from living in Spain. Many Jews adopt Christianity rather than leave.	The Muslims conquer Jerusalem and, being more tolerant of Judaism than Christianity, allow Jews to resettle there.	
639			Babylonian Jews assist the Arabs in their conquest of Persia, expecting from them a policy of tolerance.	
640			Upon the Arab conquest, Bustanai ben Haninai is appointed exilarch in Babylonia and is given a Persian princess as a wife.	Descendants of Bustanai's gentile wife later succeed him as exilarch, posing a halakhic problem that will occupy the *geonim*, or deans, of the rabbinic academies.
642	After three years of Arab forays, all Egypt falls under Muslim control.			
644	The caliph Omar* is murdered at prayer in Medina and is succeeded by Uthman* of the Meccan Umayyad family.			

A. General History	B. Jews in Europe	C. Jews in the Middle East and North Africa	D. Jewish Culture	
The Muslims complete their conquest of Mesopotamia by defeating the last Sassanian king, Yazdagird III.* By this time Zoroastrian traditions have been set in writing in the *Avesta*, influenced perhaps by the model of Christian Scripture.				**651**
	The Council of Toledo reprimands the Visigoth royal authorities for permitting Jewish observance. King Recceswinth* insists that converted Jews remain loyal Catholics and prohibits circumcision and the keeping of Jewish holy days.			**653**
Uthman* is killed by a lot of disgruntled Muslim nobles. His successor, Ali,* Muhammad's son-in-law, attains power in spite of fierce opposition by the prophet's widow, Aisha,* in the Battle of the Camel.				**656**
		The caliph Ali ibn Talib* is hailed by 70,000 or more Jews at his conquest of Firuz Shapur. Jews generallly favor the new Arab rulers of what is now called Iraq.		**658**
The culturally enlightened Umayyad caliphate of Syria constructs the Al-Aqsa mosque on the Jerusalem Temple Mount, the far end of Muhammad's "night journey" in Islamic tradition.				**660**
The Umayyad governor at Damascus, Mu'awiya,* gains full power over Islamic lands after Ali's* assassination.				**661**
Papal diplomacy persuades English clerics to accept the Roman church.				**664**
			Huna and Rabba, the *geonim* (deans) of the Sura and Pumbaditha academies, issue a decree liberalizing the conditions in which a woman may sue for divorce in the Jewish courts.	**670**

	A. General History	B. Jews in Europe	C. Jews in the Middle East and North Africa	D. Jewish Culture
680		The Council of Toledo, under King Erwig's* influence, holds Catholic clergy responsible for converting the Jews.		
690			A sectarian Jew, Obadiah, leads a failed revolt against the Baghdad caliph Abd al-Malik.*	
691	The Umayyad caliph Abd al-Malik* builds the Dome of the Rock over the stone Muhammad was said to have touched in Jerusalem on his "night journey," on the site of the former Jewish temples. The magnificent Muslim edifice dwarfs local Christian churches.			
693		King Egica* bans forced conversion of Jews in Spain but imposes heavy taxes and severe economic restrictions on them, hoping they will freely convert to Christianity.		
694		Fearing Jews will aid the imminent Muslim invaders, King Egica* places Spanish Jews in slavery and has their children raised by Christians. Many Jews fail to escape.		
700	The so-called Covenant of Omar, attributed to the Muslim conqueror, segregates but tolerates non-Muslims under Arab sovereignty—so long as the "infidels" pay their heavy taxes. Such tribute purchases Muslim "protection" (dhimma). Western churches have ceased to use only wine imported from Israel in the Eucharist rite, perhaps because trade with the Middle East has been curtailed under Islamic conquest.	The Arab conquerors establish numerous military towns in their western domains. Owing to Arab policies on agriculture ("infidels" must pay heavy poll and land taxes) and widespread communication among Jews in diverse communities, Jews are attracted to the towns, where they engage in commerce and all manner of urban occupation.	Arab conquests along the Mediterranean induce Jews to populate more inland cities.	Local legal precedents are compiled in Palestine in *The Book of Acts for Citizens of Israel.* Surviving fragments show a reaction against women seeking greater social independence.
711	Muslim armies led by Tarik bin Ziyad* overrun Spain, leading many Visigoth nobles to flee. With this conquest, the Muslim Empire extends from Spain to India.	Jews, or crypto-Jews, assist the Muslim conquerors of Spain by serving in military outposts or supplying them. Some lay claim to abandoned Visigoth estates; a number of refugees return from North Africa.		

A. General History	B. Jews in Europe	C. Jews in the Middle East and North Africa	D. Jewish Culture	
Emperor Leo III* repels Arab forces from Constantinople.		The caliph Omar II* oppresses all minorities in Babylonia, including Jews, excluding them from government appointments and compelling them to wear distinctive dress.		**717**
An Anglo-Saxon monk to be known as Boniface embarks on a decades-long campaign to Christianize western Europe.				**718**
			The *midrash* Pirkei de-Rabbi Eliezer is composed in the land of Israel. Assuming the form of a discourse by the 2nd-century sage Rabbi Eliezer ben Hyrcanus, the *midrash* retells the narrative of the Torah in a manner reminiscent of such postbiblical works as Jubilees and Enoch. It apocalyptically envisions the fall of the Umayyad caliphate.	**725**
Byzantine Emperor Leo III* forbids making Christian images. The iconoclast movement associated with this and other policies claims that iconic representations of Jesus imply he is not divine.				**726**
Arab conquest of Frankish territory is repelled at Tours by Charles Martel.* Charles* repays his soldier-knights with fiefs expropriated from church holdings.				**732**
The British scholar-monk Bede completes his much admired *Ecclesiastical History of the English People* in Latin.				**735**
The Caspian kingdom of the Khazars loses a second long war against the Muslims.	The Khazars' defeat may influence their subsequent conversion to Judaism.			**737**
	Bulan,* one of the rulers of the Khazar Empire, which covers a large segment of southern Russia from the Lower Volga to the Crimea, formally adopts Judaism. His example is followed by many of his subjects, although he has made no effort to impose the Jewish religion upon			**740**

	A. General History	B. Jews in Europe	C. Jews in the Middle East and North Africa	D. Jewish Culture
740		the pagan masses or the Christian and Muslim minorities.		
750				A leading scholar from Babylonia, Ahai of Shabha, composes a series of ethical and halakhic discourses, *She'iltot* (*Questions*) in Aramaic. The homiletical text, only part of which survives, includes scores of talmudic laws, for which he provides scriptural derivations. Among the laws are decisions of the *geonim* and early talmudic material that sometimes differ from the version published in the Babylonian Talmud.
751	Muslim troops vanquish a Chinese army north of the Jaxartes River, in China.			
754	Seeking political power, the pope sends Pepin III,* whom the Church had made king in Paris in 751, a forged document, the Donation of Constantine, establishing papal supremacy over temporal rulers.			
755		The Umayyad regime in Cordoba, Spain, founded by Abd al-Rahman,* allows Jews to work in all occupations. The regime's tolerance attracts many Jews from elsewhere.		
759	The Frankish king Pepin III* beats back the Muslims from Provence and the Lombards from southern Italy in return for papal support.			
760				The *gaon* of the Sura academy, Yehudai bar Nahman, composes in Aramaic a digest of talmudic law, the *Halakhot Pesukot* (Law as Decided) to answer fundamental questions at a time when few copies of the Talmud are available.
765			A century later, the Jewish sect known as the Karaites, or Scripturalists, will identify with traditions ascribed to Anan. Early Karaites, who may be influenced by Islam's attachment to the text of	Anan ben David, a Babylonian Jew probably residing in Baghdad, founds a sect named for himself, holding that the more flexible rabbinic interpretation of the Bible perverts its meaning and

A. General History	B. Jews in Europe	C. Jews in the Middle East and North Africa	D. Jewish Culture	
		its scripture, the Koran, and by other Muslim beliefs, would seem to consist of Jews turning away from the populous rabbinic centers in Babylonia. Karaism will soon spread throughout the Middle East, manifested in a variety of sects. Anan's descendants settle in Egypt.	calling for observance of the Torah according to its plain sense. For example, whereas the Torah forbids making fire on the Sabbath, rabbinic law would permit the use of fire for light and heat provided it was set before the holy day began. Anan would prohibit fire altogether. His law code survives.	765
As part of the Carolingian Renaissance, Charles,* king of the Franks, has the scholar monk, Alcuin of York, establish a palace school for the liberal arts, a prototype of the university. Schools will spread the study of the Bible and writings of the church fathers.				782
		After a period of relative toleration, Babylonian Jews are subject to a heavy tax and other restrictions by the fanatical caliph Harun al-Rashid.* Political infighting cripples the Jews' ability to protest.		786
Byzantine Empress Irene* has the Council of Nicaea overthrow the iconoclasm that Emperor Leo III* had championed. This radical move renews power struggles in the eastern empire.				787
Scandinavian shipbuilders devise a shallower, faster craft; the Vikings use it to advantage in raiding Europe and establishing outposts along its coastal areas and rivers during the next two centuries. Vikings colonize England, Normandy, Paris, and even North Africa.				790
The gradual disintegration of the Roman–Byzantine Empire culminates in the crowning of Charlemagne,* king of the Franks, as emperor of the West. He forms the Holy Roman Empire, comprising northwestern Europe as far south as northern Spain and Italy. The Carolingians replace Germanic trial by ordeal with a predecessor of the jury system.	Jews move up the Rhine Valley to Flanders and eastward to what will become Germany, populating most large cities. Jews call the area of France and Germany Ashkenaz. Isaac, a Jewish emissary from Rome to the caliph Harun al-Rashid,* returns from Baghdad with an elephant for newly			800

	A. General History	B. Jews in Europe	C. Jews in the Middle East and North Africa	D. Jewish Culture
800	The Old English epic, *Beowulf*, written down about this time, describes the heroic exploits of a Scandinavian warrior king.	crowned Emperor Charlemagne.*		
808			Idris II* admits Jews to Fez, North Africa, a community that will produce many leading Jewish scholars.	
810		Although Charlemagne* engages Jews in trade and has them at his court, he prohibits Jews from employing Christians on their holy days and from buying church lands.		
820	Emperor Louis the Pious* (778–840), Charlemagne's* scholastic son, offers exemplary protection to Jews, allowing them to own property and shielding them from hostile church officials. He appoints a magister Judaeorum to oversee these protections.	The archbishop of Lyons, Agobard, attempts to restrict Jewish merchandising and convert Jewish children by force, but imperial authorities stymie him. Arguing that Jews exert a negative influence over Christians, he composes six anti-Jewish tracts.		
825	Under the caliph al-Ma'mun* (813–833) many works of Greek philosophy and science and Persian literature are translated into Arabic, as are the Hebrew Bible and Christian Scriptures.	The Jewish slave trade, licensed by the crown, comes under the fire of the archbishop of Lyons, Agobard. Jews would sell pagan Slavs sold to them by Christians to Muslims in Africa and Asia. Agobard protests the trade of Christians or Christian converts. Jewish commerce follows Muslim trade routes as far as China. The Holy Roman Emperor Louis* the Pious, beholden to Jewish merchants, encourages Jewish trade, even in slaves. His Charter of Protection also relaxes political restrictions on Jews, allowing them some juridical autonomy over the objections of Agobard, archbishop of Lyons.	The exilarch, leader of the Jewish community in Babylonia, loses official recognition by the Muslim rulers as the sole authority entitled to speak on behalf of the entire Jewish community. Disputes among Christian leaders lead to this change. Jews continue to respect the authority of the exilarch.	In Basra, a town on the Persian Gulf, Simon Kayyara compiles a code of Jewish law following the general sequence of the Babylonian Talmud. This work, *Halakhot Gedolot* (Important Laws), will be edited in Spanish and Ashkenazic versions and influence subsequent codifiers.
833	Louis the Pious* is deposed as Holy Roman Emperor by a group of nobles and churchmen.			
839	Vikings make raids from Scandinavia into the European continent, establishing a strong mercantile presence down the rivers of central and eastern Europe.	A former bishop in the Frankish court of Louis* the Pious comes to Saragossa, converts to Judaism, and changes his name from Bodo to Eleazar. He engages in an		

A Christian bishop redeeming Christian slaves from a Jewish merchant, as depicted on the door of a church in Gniezno, Poland, 12th century. (Bildarchiv Photo, Marburg, Germany)

A. General History	B. Jews in Europe	C. Jews in the Middle East and North Africa	D. Jewish Culture	
	extended polemic with a Cordoban Christian, Alvaro.*			**839**
A countrywide peasant revolt led by one Abu Harb* wreaks havoc on Jerusalem, raiding mosques and churches.				**841**
The Treaty of Verdun divides the empire of Louis* the Pious among his three sons: Charles* the Bald receives Gaul; Louis,* Germany; and Lothair,* the Rhine Valley into Italy (later named for him, "Lorraine"). As another sign of the empire's dissolution, spoken Latin is superseded by early French, German, and other dialects.				**843**
		Jews and other minorities in Babylonia are required to wear a yellow headcovering or patch by the caliph al-Mutawakkil.* Enforcement of the Jewish dress code may be lax, but such humiliating restrictions are repeatedly reissued. The caliph al-Muqtadir* (908–932) will impose the yellow stigma on Jewish physicians and tax collectors. Nonetheless, Jews hold official appointments under most caliphs. A Karaite sect is founded in Ramleh, Israel, by Malik al-Ramli.	Paltoi, the *gaon* of the Babylonian Pumbaditha academy, sends a Talmud with some explanatory notes in response to a request from rabbinic savants in Spain. Until the spread of paper in the following century, copies of the Talmud are hard to come by. Spanish students rely on digests of talmudic law composed by *geonim* and other sages. Various homiletical *midrashim* on the Torah are set down in the land of Israel, many ascribed to Rabbi Tanhuma. This family of *midrash* collections will be composed in different forms as Midrash Tanhuma, a source of *aggadah* widely used in subsequent centuries. Karaism, the Jewish movement that bases its observance on a strict reading of the written Torah rather than on rabbinic interpretation, is defined philosophically and institutionally by Benjamin ben Moses Nahawendi, a Persian Jew. Unlike other Karaites, who oppose all rabbinic teaching, Benjamin adopts rabbinic practice where the written Torah does not spell it out.	**850**

	A. General History	B. Jews in Europe	C. Jews in the Middle East and North Africa	D. Jewish Culture
853				Natronai, son of former *gaon* Hilai, becomes *gaon* of the Sura academy. Perhaps the first *gaon* to write responsa in Arabic, Natronai advises the Jews of Lucena, Spain, among others. His responsa help fix the standard order of prayers and insist that the prophetic reading (*haftarah*) be chanted after the Torah on the Sabbath and holy days. He declares that all Jews, not only rabbis, should study the Babylonian Talmud.
858	Pope Nicholas I campaigns to centralize temporal power in churchmen's hands. When incursions from north and east upset the political order, the Church seeks to rebuild local authority.			
860				Amram, *gaon* of the Sura academy, compiles the laws governing prayer and an "order" of the liturgy, or *seder*. Sent by request to Jews in Spain, Amram's *seder* has wide influence in Europe as well as the Middle East.
863	A Greek missionary, known later as St. Cyril, invents an alphabet in which the Slavs can read the Christian Bible; the Cyrillic alphabet becomes the standard Slavic script.			
873			Anti-Jewish policies intensify when Byzantine Emperor Basil I* compels many Jews to convert.	
878			Ahmad ibn Tulun* brings Jerusalem under the dominion of the Cairo caliphate. It will remain largely under Egyptian governance until the Ottoman conquest of 1516. The Umayyad capital in Israel had been established at Ramleh about 700, from which time Jerusalem's political importance had declined.	
887	Nordic incursions get the better of Charles* the Fat, king of the Franks, who turn to Odo,* count of Paris, to defend them.			

A. General History	B. Jews in Europe	C. Jews in the Middle East and North Africa	D. Jewish Culture	

In the next two years the Roman papacy changes six times, as the Carolingians and other power brokers vie for a century to control it.

896

The imam (supreme authority) of the Shi'ite Zaydi sect begins the conquest of Yemen. The Zaydi rule intermittently until the kingdom is overthrown in the revolution of 1962.

897

Having suffered the depredations of Nordic Vikings, eastern Magyars, and Arabs, the Carolingian Empire teeters on the brink of collapse.

The Christian monastery is transformed from Benedictine insularity into an institution serving the community outside.

Jewish slave merchants have been losing trade to enterprising Italian Christians.

Sometime during this century, Jews from northern France and northern Italy, speaking a language called Laaz, begin speaking earliest Yiddish as a result of contacts with persons speaking the German language.

Babylonian Jewish bankers take on wealthy Jewish merchants who invest heavily as silent partners. The Baghdad caliphate and other Muslim regimes often finance their projects through their Jewish "court bankers."

The essential shape of the Passover liturgy, the Haggadah (Narration), has by this time been formed; the earliest surviving example is found in the order of the prayers of Saadiah Gaon. The Haggadah accompanies the Passover meal, the *seder*, providing the blessings, prayers, and explication that make up the evening celebration of the festival. The structure of the seder is laid out in the Mishnah (c.215), and the Haggadah text incorporates versions of Mishnaic passages and classical rabbinic *midrash*. The core of the Haggadah is the narrative of the Israelite Exodus from Egyptian bondage, which is midrashically elaborated to magnify the power of God. The Haggadah expresses the perennial Jewish hope for redemption from persecution. Parts of the Haggadah will be added throughout the Middle Ages. Illustrating the text of the Haggadah will become an important Jewish art form.

A Persian Karaite scholar, Daniel ben Moses al-Qumisi, settles in Jerusalem and heads the *Avelei Zion* (Mourners of Zion) group. Devoting himself to biblical commentary, Daniel holds that when the Temple of Solomon was destroyed by the Babylonians, the Torah was removed from the control of Israel's priests and entrusted to the lights

900

THE JEWISH WORLD, 7TH TO EARLY 11TH CENTURY

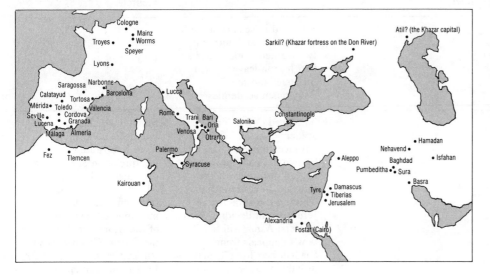

	A. General History	B. Jews in Europe	C. Jews in the Middle East and North Africa	D. Jewish Culture
900				of every Jew. A strong rationalist, Daniel interprets the Bible's "angels" as natural forces. The earliest surviving illuminated text of the Hebrew Bible is written and decorated by Karaites in Cairo, Egypt.
911	A Viking chieftain, Rollo,* seizes the area that will become Normandy, compels the king to grant it to him as a fief, and turns his dukedom into a battleground for decades.			
916	The great Arab historian and commentator on the Koran at-Tabari* completes his extensive annals of the Muslim political and religious leaders.			
920	Arabs seeking to control Mediterranean trade and travel obstruct Christian pilgrims in the Alps as well as shipping by sea.	It may be now that Rabbi Moses of Lucca, Italy, together with his son Kalonymus, moves to Mainz, where the family, including many scholars, will be pillars of German Jewish culture. Kalonymus' responsa, dating to around 940, are the oldest native products of Ashkenazi Jewry.		Saadiah ben Joseph (882–942), an emerging scholar in the Fayyum area of Egypt, writes the first of his philological works, a Hebrew dictionary, the *Agron*. He will later revise this aid to Hebraists and Hebrew poets in Arabic. He himself will compose many liturgical poems in Hebrew.
921			Schooled in science as well as rabbinics and author of two learned works, Saadiah ben Joseph leaves Egypt for Israel and the Babylonian academies.	
922			The head of the Jerusalem academy, Aaron ben Meir, advances the ritual calendar by two days and provokes a heated dispute with the Babylonian academies. Touting the authority of Jerusalem in deciding such matters, Aaron will not bow to appeals from Saadiah ben Joseph, now in Babylonia. As a result, Jews in Israel keep the New Year on Tuesday while those in Babylon keep it on Thursday.	Much of Saadiah's linguistic work intends to favor Rabbanite interpretation of Scripture over that of the Karaites, who do not accept rabbinic tradition. Saadiah's monumental translation of the Bible into Arabic, the Tafsir (Commentary), still serves traditional Jews from Arab lands. Little of his extensive Bible commentary survives, but his exegesis is addressed by many interpreters of the Spanish school, such as Abraham ibn Ezra.
923				Saadiah ben Joseph, newly appointed *gaon* of the Pumbaditha academy, writes *The Book of Sacred*

A. General History	B. Jews in Europe	C. Jews in the Middle East and North Africa	D. Jewish Culture	
			Times, settling the calendar controversy in favor of the Babylonian tradition.	**923**
		Saadiah, though lacking a geonic pedigree, is appointed head of the Sura academy by the exilarch David ben Zakkai. He raises funds and recruits students from as far as Spain.		**928**
The caliphate in Cordoba, Spain, is assumed by the tolerant Abd al-Rahman II,* who provides political stability and promotes culture.				**929**
The great Muslim philosopher al-Farabi* is much sought after in the Middle East. A master of Greek learning and Aristotle* in particular, he produces Arabic treatises on a variety of subjects, from music to logic, and toward the end of his life (d. 950) a number of original philosophical studies, where the influence of Plato,* too, is evident.		A personal dispute leads David ben Zakkai to remove Saadiah from the Sura academy. Saadiah names David's brother as rival exilarch.	Saadiah Gaon, in the tradition of Amram Gaon, arranges the laws of prayer and many individual prayers in his *siddur* (prayer book). The Palestinian tradition of reading the Hebrew Bible is consummated in the work of Aaron ben Moses of the Ben-Ashers, a family in Tiberias that for two centuries had been standardizing the biblical text and its chanting. Aaron ben Moses establishes an authoritative text by indicating with diacritical marks and marginal notations how precisely to vocalize, accentuate, and sing the Hebrew. The tradition of preserving the text of scripture and its vocalization is known as the Masorah and the traditional text is called Masoretic. The Ben-Asher standard will be compared and followed for centuries prior to the invention of printing.	**930**
		Byzantine Emperor Romanus I* (920–944) orders the conversion of Byzantine Jewry to Christianity. His decision may be prompted by a political need to legitimate his rule as well as considerations concerning ecclesiastical alliances.	Deposed as *gaon* by political enemies, Saadiah devotes himself to philosophy, composing *The Book of Beliefs and Opinions*. The Arabic original will influence Jewish Neoplatonists such as Bahya Ibn Paquda, but it will attain lasting significance only after its translation into Hebrew in 1186. Saadiah affirms reason as a source of knowledge alongside	**932**

	A. General History	B. Jews in Europe	C. Jews in the Middle East and North Africa	D. Jewish Culture
932				revealed tradition and distinguishes rational from nonrational divine commandments. He delves into the abstract nature of God and the dual nature of humanity, which has both body and soul.
935				A scathing Karaite polemic against Saadiah Gaon and the Rabbanite belief in the oral Torah is composed in rhymed Hebrew verse by Salmon ben Jeroham, probably in Babylonia. The poem is called "The Wars of the Lord."
940		A Cordoban Jew, Hasdai ibn Shaprut, becomes the caliph's physician and rises to leading positions in customs and diplomatic service. Appointed head of the Jewish community, Hasdai sponsors Jewish scholars and poets.		
945			A fanatical Shi'ite Persian house, the Buwayhids, governs Iraq, subjecting Jews as well as Sunni Muslims and Christians to extra taxes for a century. The Jewish exilarchate is abolished.	
950	The king of the Germans, Otto I* the Great (936–973), invests the clergy with their symbols of power, asserting the superiority of the crown.			The leading Karaite scholar of Babylonia, Jacob al-Qirqisani, from an area near Baghdad, completes at about this time two erudite works in Arabic: *The Book of Lights and Watchtowers*, a code of Karaite law with a history of the sect in its diverse forms, and *The Book of Gardens and Parks*, a commentary on the nonlegal sections of the Torah.
953				An unknown Jew in southern Italy composes a history of the Jews in Rome, culminating with the fall of Masada in the Jewish revolt against Rome in 73. Based on Josephus' contemporary account of that war, this pro-Jewish history written in classical Hebrew style will be attributed to Josephus by medieval Jews and called *Josippon*. Translated into several languages, *Josippon* provides medieval Jewry

A. General History	B. Jews in Europe	C. Jews in the Middle East and North Africa	D. Jewish Culture	
			with its primary history of Second Temple times.	953
Otto* the Great beats back the Magyars and rids central Europe of Arab marauders, winning him acclaim in western Europe, too.	A rabbi from Italy, Moses ben Hanokh, is appointed rabbi of Cordoba by Hasdai ibn Shaprut. Rabbi Moses opens an academy and serves as decisor of *halakha*, weaning Spanish Jewry from the authority of the Babylonian *geonim*.			955
		According to Jewish historical tradition, Joseph ibn Abitur explicates the Talmud for the caliph of Cordoba in Arabic.	A Spanish Jewish scholar, Menahem ibn Saruq, composes the first biblical dictionary written in Hebrew, the *Mahberet*, under the patronage of Hasdai ibn Shaprut. Limited by the theories of Saadiah Gaon, who failed to recognize the triconsonantal basis of Hebrew roots, Menahem preserves many traditional interpretations and, because he writes in Hebrew rather than Arabic, serves as a standard reference for Jewish exegetes in 11th- to 12th-century France. Dunash ben Labrat, who had studied with Saadiah Gaon in Baghdad, composes Hebrew poetry using Arabic forms under the patronage of Hasdai ibn Shaprut. A superior linguist, Dunash writes a tract criticizing 200 points in Menahem's *Mahberet*. Students of Menahem and Dunash continue the debate.	960
Otto* the Great of Germany has the pope in Rome anoint him emperor of the West.				962
The Byzantine navy under powerful Emperor Basil II* breaks Arab control of Cyprus and Crete, a critical step in reversing the Muslim conquest. Through dramatic developments in art and commerce, the long reign of Basil II* (963–1025) marks a Macedonian Renaissance.	Jews and other merchants of Flanders are placed under the authority of the bishop of Magdeburg by the Holy Roman Empire. This is part of the gradual Jewish expansion from the Rhine basin to regions both to the south and the east.		When Rabbi Moses ben Hanokh dies, he is succeeded by his son, Hanokh, further establishing a native Spanish Judaism.	965
			Sherira succeeds his father, Hanina, as *gaon* of the Pumbaditha academy. He issues a remarkable number of legal responsa,	968

	A. General History	B. Jews in Europe	C. Jews in the Middle East and North Africa	D. Jewish Culture
968				many composed together with his son and appointed successor, Hai. Stressing the traditional importance of learning, Sherira Gaon disqualifies a prayer leader who does not understand the content of the liturgy. He also writes a number of biblical and talmudic commentaries. He will die in 1006 at age 100.
969	Egypt, which experienced relative freedom for a century, is overtaken by the Arab Fatimids of Tunisia; they build a new Cairo.			
975	Under John I Tzimisces,* the eastern empire strikes back against the Muslim conquests by driving Byzantine armies through Syria and as far as Jerusalem to the south and Baghdad to the east.		Karaite propagandist Sahl ben Matsliah writes a letter in Hebrew attacking a partisan of Saadiah Gaon, Jacob ben Samuel of Cairo, who lambasted Sahl for missionizing among Rabbanite Jews.	Reflecting his Karaite interest in the language of the written and not the oral Torah as the immediate source of Jewish authority, David Alfasi, hailing from Fez, Morocco, and working in Israel, composes a dictionary and grammar of biblical Hebrew in Arabic. An expert linguist, Alfasi compares Aramaic, Arabic, and later Hebrew in order to elucidate Scripture's meaning. *The Book of Remedies* by Shabbetai Donnolo (913–c.982), Italian physician, is the oldest Hebrew medical work in Europe and the earliest medical work written in Italy (and probably in any Christian land of the West) in any language after the fall of the Roman Empire. Well versed in rabbinic literature, he also writes a commentary on the ancient mystical work *Sefer ha-Yetsirah*.
980				The Karaite scholar Japheth ben Ali, a native of Basra living in Jerusalem, translates the Bible into Arabic and composes biblical commentaries in Arabic that are distinguished by their plain-sense approach and contributions to Hebrew philology. Some will be rendered into Hebrew. A sharp critic of Saadiah Gaon, Japheth's work will be cited by such Rabbanite authors as Abraham ibn Ezra.

A. General History	B. Jews in Europe	C. Jews in the Middle East and North Africa	D. Jewish Culture	
			A blind but highly influential scholar from Mosul, Hefets ben Yatsliah, authors a lengthy compilation of talmudic law. Written in Arabic, *The Book of Precepts* explains the biblical basis of the laws using the tally of 613 commandments.	**985**
The Capetian dynasty succeeds the remarkable Carolingians in France, maintaining modest autonomy of the empire through control of churches and an army.			Sherira, *gaon* of the Pumbaditha academy, writes an important letter (*iggeret*) to a Jew in Kairouan, North Africa, tracing the evolution of the Talmud and discussing the editorial role of the *saboraim* in the later stages.	**987**
The conversion of Vladimir I* of Kiev to Greek Orthodoxy marks a significant step in the re-Christianization of the East.				**989**
Western Emperor Otto III* together with his former tutor, Pope Sylvester II, plan to herald the millennium by converting Slavs, Vikings, and other non-Christians in Europe. The plan dies with them just after the year 1000.		The expansion of the Byzantine Empire into Asia under Basil II* draws Jewish (and Christian) traders in its wake.		**995**
			Samuel ben Hophni becomes *gaon* of the Sura academy, following the philosophical and scholastic trends set by Saadiah. Among his numerous and diverse works is the first introductory text to the study of Talmud. His Bible commentary, distinguished by its systematic approach, survives only in fragments and references in later commentaries.	**997**
			Hai, son of Sherira and son-in-law of Samuel ben Hophni, becomes the last, highly influential *gaon* of the Pumbaditha academy. Serving for 40 years and authoring numerous responsa, Hai confirms the superiority of the Babylonian Talmud over its Palestinian counterpart in deciding Jewish law.	**998**
Government in Spain becomes increasingly decentralized as the locus	A synagogue is built in Cologne. It will be remodeled beginning in		Gershom ben Judah, rabbi and head of an academy in Mainz, Germany, takes	**1000**

	A. General History	B. Jews in Europe	C. Jews in the Middle East and North Africa	D. Jewish Culture
1000	of power shifts to diverse cities, some Muslim, some Christian, some Berber, some Slavic. Eastern Emperor Basil II* reextends Christian dominion to the Caucasus region. Leif Ericson's* Viking expedition reaches North America, calling it Vineland.	1096 after some damage by the crusaders. It will be remodeled again in 1280 and used until 1349, when the Jews will be expelled after a pogrom. From 1372, after readmission, it will be used until 1426, when the synagogue will be put to town use. It will be excavated in the 1950s.		pains to establish good manuscripts of the Bible, Mishnah, and Talmud. Relying little on the Babylonian *geonim*, his teaching becomes preeminent among Franco-German Jewish scholars, especially through the commentaries of a student of his disciples, Rashi. Two famous decrees are attributed to Rabbenu Gershom: a ban on bigamy and on reading someone else's letters. Some of his liturgical poems (*piyyutim*) are standard among German Jews.
1007			Karaite authorities in Jerusalem declare the Hebrew month of Adar to be Nisan, the succeeding month, according to their practice of proclaiming the spring when the barley begins to ripen. Passover, falling in mid-Nisan, replaces the holiday of Purim, which falls in mid-Adar and is therefore not observed this year. In 1061 and other years when the barley ripens late, an extra month is intercalated so that Karaites and Rabbanites celebrate Passover a month apart. Such discrepancies exacerbate sectarian friction.	
1008			The caliph of Egypt, Al-Hakim bi-Amar Allah,* a member of the more radical Shi'ite Muslim group rather than the more tolerant Sunni majority, marks Jews by enjoining them to dress publicly in black and hang on their necks the image of a calf, a reminder of Israel's sinful worship of the Golden Calf during the Exodus.	
1009				Following the Masoretic tradition of Aaron Ben-Asher, a manuscript of the entire Hebrew Bible is written. It is the oldest extant text of the full Bible, called the Leningrad Manuscript after the location of the library where it is housed. Another Ben-Asher manuscript of about the same age becomes the

A. General History	B. Jews in Europe	C. Jews in the Middle East and North Africa	D. Jewish Culture	
			possession of Syrian Jews. This text, the *Aleppo Codex*, is apparently the one used as a standard by Maimonides in the next century. It will be nearly half-burned when the Aleppo synagogue is attacked in 1948; it is preserved in Israel.	**1009**
	Provoked by the conversion of a priest in Mainz, Germany, to Judaism, Emperor Henry II* expels all Jews from Mainz. The expulsion will soon be rescinded.			**1012**
	The right of Jews to own land is legalized in Leon, Spain.			**1017**
Normandy is becoming a powerful feudal state by imposing heavy obligations on landless knights seeking their own fiefs. Its culture is enriched by monastic schools. Ibn Sina,* known later in Europe as Avicenna* (980–1037), works as a physician in the courts of petty eastern rulers and composes works of philosophy and science prolifically. His philosophical writing synthesizes Greek with Islamic thought, and his medical textbook will be used in translation in Europe into the 17th century.		Jewish travelers and merchants from Attalia are captured by Arab raiders and taken to North Africa. The Jews of Alexandria ransom them for a large amount of money, confirming that community's high financial standing.	A school of Karaite linguists thrives in Jerusalem. Led by Joseph ben Noah, a grammarian and commentator on the Torah, it produces Abu al-Faraj Harun and Joseph ben Abraham Hakohen, who also compose studies of biblical Hebrew and Bible interpretation. Their works, written largely in Arabic, are for the most part lost.	**1020**
		When the caliph Al-Hakim* disappears, the humiliating impositions on Egyptian Jewry are stopped.		**1021**
Under the new German emperor, Conrad II,* the Benedictine monastery at Cluny, Burgundy, builds itself into the preeminent cultural force in the West.		Jarah Bedouins ravage Jewish settlements in Israel, exacerbating already depressed conditions.		**1024**
		A Rabbanite Jew from Fez, Solomon ben Judah, assumes the gaonate in Jerusalem, exerting strong influence over Egyptian Jewry as well. He favors tolerance toward Karaism, but his views are not widely shared.		**1025**

	A. General History	B. Jews in Europe	C. Jews in the Middle East and North Africa	D. Jewish Culture
1027		A Jew from Cordoba, whose literary and political talents are recognized by the Berbers, works his way up to become vizier of Granada. Samuel ibn Nagrela, called ha-Nagid (the Commander) by fellow Jews, will lead Berber troops against the Arab army of Seville in 1038 and will follow this success with other campaigns.		
1030				Abulwalid Merwan ibn Janah, a Spanish Jewish physician and Hebraist who had studied with the poet Isaac ibn Mar Sha'ul, is engaged in writing in Arabic two major books on biblical Hebrew. His grammar, *The Book of Embroidery*, incorporates the insight of his predecessor Judah ibn Hayyuj, who recognized, through comparison with Arabic, that all Hebrew verbs are constructed on a pattern of three root consonants. His lexicon, *The Book of Roots*, utilizes the same insight and, like the grammar, includes a substantial amount of original analysis, much of it significant even today. The two books of Ibn Janah, known by Jews as Rabbi Jonah, will be translated over a century later by the Ibn Tibbon family.
1032	The important Syrian city of Edessa and its region are incorporated into the Byzantine Empire.			
1033		A Jew in Taranto, Italy, buys a plot of land with two vineyards. In contrast to western Christendom, there is nothing in Byzantine law to prevent Jews from holding land and engaging in agriculture.		
1035		Jews under the protection of King Sancho* of Castile are driven from the royal domain at his death; scores are slain.	The rulers of Fez are overthrown and 6,000 Jews are slaughtered.	
1038		Samuel ha-Nagid leads Granada to victory against Almeira near El Fuente. Seeing the triumph as vital to Jewish life in Spain,		

A. General History	B. Jews in Europe	C. Jews in the Middle East and North Africa	D. Jewish Culture	
	Samuel proclaims a Second Purim to celebrate the victory.			**1038**
			The rabbinic scholar and author in Kairouan Hananel ben Hushiel composes a commentary on the Babylonian Talmud with emphasis on its laws. Hewing closely to the perspectives of the Babylonian *geonim*, Hai in particular, and making reference to the Palestinian Talmud, Rabbenu Hananel's commentary becomes widely studied. The Jerusalem Karaite scholar, Joseph ben Abraham al-Basir (the Blind), composes several books of religious philosophy in the tradition of Muslim Mu'tazilite rationalism. Among his views is that God is motivated by wisdom to behave only according to what is just and to give humanity commandments so that they will do the same.	**1040**
		Fractious relations between the *gaon* Solomon ben Judah, who had been compelled to move to Ramleh, and Nathan ben Abraham, head of the rabbinic court in Jerusalem, are suppressed by the Fatimid regime. Nathan is made Solomon's successor.		**1043**
		Riots in Constantinople lead to the expulsion of aliens, including many Arabs, Armenians, and Jews, who are blamed for the disturbances.		**1044**
Emperor Henry III* settles a three-way struggle for the papacy among Roman nobles by placing a series of German bishops on the throne, culminating in 1049 in the appointment of his relative, Leo IX, who will reassert papal prerogatives. The enhanced power of king and Church is reflected in the fortresslike Romanesque architecture that spreads throughout western Europe.		A Karaite community is well established in Constantinople under the leadership of the renowned sage Tobias ben Moses Hama'atik (the Translator), who hailed from Egypt and studied with the Karaite master Joseph al-Basir in Jerusalem. He translates al-Basir's works into Hebrew and contributes significantly to the Karaite legal tradition, which is oral but supposedly based on Scripture.		**1045**

	A. General History	B. Jews in Europe	C. Jews in the Middle East and North Africa	D. Jewish Culture
1049			Rule over 15 Jewish families in Chios, an island in the Aegean Sea off the west coast of Turkey, is transferred to the monastery there, and by 1062 the Jews are obligated to reside in the premises belonging to the monastery. The secular authorities support this transfer because they prefer that Jewish taxes go to the monastery rather than to some potential enemy of the ruler.	Samuel ha-Nagid, the Cordoban Jewish statesman, completes his synthesis of talmudic law, *Hilkhata Gavrata*. Samuel's differences with geonic law draw some fire, leading him to apologize in poetry. A highly accomplished poet, his work displays literary inventiveness and worldly interests.
1050	As successful farmers market their produce for local consumers, towns crop up throughout western Europe. Many cities are dominated by the wealthy who control the merchant guilds. New trade routes facilitate cross-European commerce.		Local civil strife prompts the Jews of Basra on the Persian Gulf, many of them artisans and merchants, to find other homes in Israel and elsewhere.	Nissim ben Jacob succeeds Hananel in Kairouan as the leading rabbinic authority. Under the patronage of Samuel ha-Nagid, Nissim conveys the teaching of Hai Gaon to Spanish academies. Among Rabbenu Nissim's many works is a wide-ranging and influential miscellany called *Megillat Setarim* (The Scroll of Secrets) written part in Hebrew and part in Arabic.
1054	Pope Leo IX insists that the Roman See dominate the emperor and the Byzantine patriarch, causing a lasting schism in the Church.			Ahimaaz ben Paltiel, poet of southern Italy, compiles *Megillat Ahimaaz* (The Scroll of Ahimaaz). Written in rhymed Hebrew, it chronicles his family from the 9th century to his own time. Once dismissed as legend, it is believed to be a reliable source of the history of the Jews in southern Italy and North Africa.
1055	The Turkish tribe of Seljuks, en route toward conquering the Near East as far as China, makes a pact with the Abbasid caliph in Baghdad and promotes traditional Islamic norms, including repression of non-Muslims in their domain.	Samuel ha-Nagid leads Granada to victory in its conflict with the rival city-state, Seville. In a celebratory poem Samuel attributes his triumph to special divine providence.		At about this time, Solomon ibn Gabirol (c.1020–c.1057), the master Hebrew poet hailing from Malaga, Spain, composes in Arabic an extensive metaphysical work, translated into Hebrew as *The Source of Life* and into Latin as *The Fountain of Life*. Gabirol, who displays a mystical strain in both his secular and religious poetry, dwells in his philosophy on the relations of matter and form. In Latin this work will find many medieval Christian readers who will not discern that its author, Avicebron, is a Jew.

A. General History	B. Jews in Europe	C. Jews in the Middle East and North Africa	D. Jewish Culture	
	Peter Damiani,* a fervent church reformer from northern Italy, writes two tracts degrading Judaism. These documents and others by subsequent clerics will provide a rationale for Christians to attack Jews during the Crusades. The idea is taking hold in Christianity that the severe God of the Old Testament (Hebrew Bible) has been superseded by the loving God of the New Testament.	A dispute breaks out between rabbinic Jews and Karaites in Thessalonica, Greece, over the dates of the festival calendar. The Karaites complain to the authorities about the Rabbanites and the latter are fined. This fine becomes a yearly tax interpreted by the community as punishment for tolerating heresy.		**1060**
		The Seljuk–Abbasid alliance upholds orthodox Islam by closing all taverns in Baghdad, including those of Jews.		**1062**
	The Lombard duke of Benevento, seeking to please his Norman masters, subjects Jews to forced conversion.			**1065**
William* the Conqueror invades England from Normandy and establishes dominion there. This and other blows to Viking colonies drive the Norse folk back to Scandinavia. William* proceeds to impose Norman culture and feudal structure on the Anglo-Saxons.	Jews follow William* the Conqueror and establish a Franco-Jewish community in England. Muslims riot against Jews in Granada, resentful of their prosperity and position. Many Jews, including the much-abused Joseph ha-Nagid, Samuel's son and successor, are slain.			**1066**
As Byzantine conquests return to Muslim hands, the eastern emperor will seek help from the pope in Rome.	Granada falls to the Almoravides, and the Jewish community is destroyed. The prominent Ibn Ezra family is one of those forced to flee. Moses ibn Ezra, celebrated Hebrew poet, remains behind until 1095, when he begins to wander throughout Christian northern Spain bemoaning his loss of wealth and homeland. William* the Conqueror brings Jews to England from Rouen, France, and settles them in London and Oxford. They serve as financiers of the realm. An important Jewish academy is founded in Troyes, capital of Champagne, by a vintner educated in Mainz and		Rashi composes commentaries on most of the Bible. His Torah commentary, the most widely studied by Jews until today, mixes contextual, plain-sense interpretation with traditional rabbinic legal and homiletical (midrashic) exegesis. His commentary on the Babylonian Talmud, completed after his death by his grandson Rabbi Samuel ben Meir (Rashbam) and others, has been of fundamental importance. A major Ashkenazic authority on Jewish law, Rashi incorporates halakhic rulings in his Talmud commentary and issues many responsa. The Karaite sage, Jeshua ben Judah, a disciple of	**1070**

	A. General History	B. Jews in Europe	C. Jews in the Middle East and North Africa	D. Jewish Culture
1070		Worms, Solomon ben Isaac, later known as Rashi (1040–1105). His most prominent students are relatives, particularly his sons-in-law and then grandsons. Together they and their students build the French school of text interpretation, emphasizing the role of context (*peshat*) in their commentaries.		Joseph al-Basir in Jerusalem, composes an extensive treatise against the common Karaite expansion of the Torah's incest laws to prohibit marriage with female relatives beyond those specified in Leviticus. Jeshua's view against this expansion, called *rikkuv*, becomes Karaite law.
1071	The Turks strike a severe blow against the Byzantine imperial forces at the Battle of Manzikert.		The Jewish community of Jerusalem is disbanded when it is overrun by the Seljuk Turks.	
1074	The Seljuk official Nizamu-l-Mulk* appoints the mathematician, Omar Khayyam,* also known as the great poet of the *Rubaiyyat*, to reform the calendar. Nizamu also founds an important university in Baghdad and in general sponsors culture and learning.			
1075	Pope Gregory VII (1073–1085) promotes monastic ideals throughout Christian Europe while reforming the clergy itself.		The restrictions of al-Mutawakkil* against Babylonian Jews are revived by the caliph al-Muqtadi.*	
1076	German Emperor Henry IV* summons an ecclesiastical synod at Worms to depose Pope Gregory VII, who has been opposing lay investiture of clerics. Gregory VII is unmoved, and in the following year the emperor will seek his pardon.		Nicephorus III* captures Constantinople and as a by-product of prolonged fighting, the Jewish quarter is severely damaged. Christian property, too, suffers.	
1077			Homes of Karaites and Jews in Pera, the northern suburb of Constantinople, are burned during an uprising against Byzantine authorities.	
1084		The bishop of Speyer, Germany, grants the Jews a Charter of Protection in order to attract them to the city. Jews coming there from Mainz seek the assurance of a wall to surround their neighborhood, one of the specific rights granted by the charter. It is renewed in 1090 by Henry IV.*		
1085	King Alfonso VI* of Castile captures Toledo from the	Jews help finance the army of King Alfonso VI* of		

A. General History	B. Jews in Europe	C. Jews in the Middle East and North Africa	D. Jewish Culture	
Moors and restores Christian rule to Spain. The caliph of Baghdad, al-Muqtadi,* reenacts the Covenant of Omar, forcing non-Muslims to wear an insignia on their turbans and forbidding them to build their homes taller than those of neighboring Muslims.	Castile, as they are said to have aided the unsuccessful Spanish liberator El Cid* some years before.			**1085**
William* registers all English property in the *Domesday Book*.				**1086**
	William* the Conqueror's son and successor, William Rufus,* shows a sympathy for Jews and taxes the Church, raising the ire of Anselm, archbishop of Canterbury, who is ineffective in opposing him.			**1087**
	Rabbi Isaac Alfasi arrives in Spain from North Africa, from which he was expelled by the Muslim authorities. Born (1013) in Algeria and schooled in rabbinics in Kairouan, Alfasi establishes an academy in Lucena where he teaches such luminaries as Rabbi Judah Halevi, the great poet and philosopher.		Author of numerous responsa in Arabic and Hebrew in the style of the *geonim*, Rabbi Isaac Alfasi (later known as "the Rif") composes a Hebrew digest of the Babylonian Talmud's laws, *Sefer Hahalakhot* (The Book of the Laws), which is a major work of talmudic interpretation and legal source for Maimonides.	**1088**
A school of law has been established at Bologna. It will produce many of Europe's bureaucrats during the next century. The main textbook is the rediscovered code of Justinian, embellished by contemporary legal commentary, like the Bible.			Nathan ben Abraham, who will succeed in 1095 to be chief judge of the Palestinian rabbinic court, composes a concise commentary on the Mishnah in Arabic. Nathan relies on the Talmud and the *geonim* of Babylonia rather than on the native traditions of Israel.	**1090**
	The king of Castile and Leon, Alfonso VI,* bows to political pressure to withdraw Jewish civil rights. Alfonso VI* had appointed Jews to diplomatic posts as well as tax collection against the advice of Pope Gregory VII.			**1091**
Pope Urban II proclaims the First Crusade. In the spirit of Pope Gregory, Urban II seeks to assert papal supremacy in the East as well as the West.	Gilbert of Crispin (c.1046–1117), Abbot of Westminster, writes *Discussion Between a Jew and a Christian*, a record of a friendly disputation	Reports reach western Europe of depradations against Christians and their institutions in Israel, mainly by Muslims but also by Jews.		**1095**

	A. General History	B. Jews in Europe	C. Jews in the Middle East and North Africa	D. Jewish Culture
1095	Preaching Christian knightly ideals, the crusaders cross Europe, gathering the masses along the way, to reconquer the Holy Land from the Muslim "infidels."	between Crispin and a Jew from Mainz with whom he did business. The Jew has deep knowledge of Jewish and Christian religious literature.		
1096	In response to appeals from Christians in the Middle East, armies are formed in France and Germany to embark on the First Crusade.	In May, members of the First Crusade attack and kill Jews in Speyer and Worms, and in Mainz and Cologne, where the local bishops are powerless to protect them. Jews in Regensburg (Ratisbon) are forced to convert. Many Jews inflict their own deaths as martyrs (*al kiddush hashem*, "to sanctify God's name"). The massacres stop when the crusaders are met by Hungarians who will not tolerate the violence.		Jews in subsequent generations will refer to Jewish martyrdom during the First Crusade as another *Akedah*, the biblical binding of Isaac.
1097	Crusader forces capture Nicaea, where crusader Peter* the Hermit's army had been destroyed.	Rouen's Jewish community will continue to flourish judging by the evidence of a new synagogue or house of study constructed during the following decade. It will be excavated in 1976.		
1098	Crusaders overtake Antioch, Syria, in June.			
1099	After routing an army from Egypt at Ashkelon, the crusaders return to Europe.		Jerusalem falls to crusaders led by Godfrey* of Bouillon in July. Jews and Karaites are herded into a synagogue and burned. Jews will rebuild and continue to settle in Jerusalem; the Karaite community is wiped out.	
1100	Partly as a result of overpopulation, peasants in western Europe seek to make arable forests, swamps, and other uncultivated land as they found more and more settlements. In the course of this century, the feudal system of landed lords and dependent serfs will develop.	Jews from Normandy and elsewhere in western Europe settle most major towns in central England. Henry I* (1100–1135) grants significant rights to Jews.		Ashkenazic (Franco-German) rabbis begin exploring halakhic ways of legitimizing usury. The traditional liturgy and laws concerning holiday and daily ritual practice are set down in the *Mahzor Vitry* by Simha ben Samuel of Vitry, France, a colleague of Rashi's. Reflecting the views of the Rashi school and resembling in part Rashi's order of prayers, *Siddur Rashi*, this basic composition will be amended and supplemented for centuries.
1101	Fatimid Muslims counterattack crusader			Nathan ben Yehiel of Rome completes his

A. General History	B. Jews in Europe	C. Jews in the Middle East and North Africa	D. Jewish Culture	
positions in Israel, scoring some successes.			dictionary of the Talmudim and *midrashim*, the *Arukh*. Educated by his father, head of the Rome yeshiva, and by Moses the Darshan in Narbonne, Nathan incorporates broad knowledge of talmudic interpretation, Jewish law, and etymology in many languages to compose this fundamental research tool. It is still used in updated scholarly editions. Nathan has headed the Rome yeshiva with his brothers Daniel and Abraham from 1070 and will continue to do so until his death, about 1110.	**1101**
As the Muslim counter-Crusade surges, the crusader-appointed king of Jerusalem, Baldwin* of Boulogne, holds on but suffers severe losses.			An Italian priest converts to Judaism and moves to Constantinople to pursue his studies. Known as Obadiah the Proselyte, his Jewish endeavors in Baghdad and later Egypt are chronicled in a Hebrew autobiography, preserved in the Cairo Genizah.	**1102**
The crusader army of Raymond* of Saint-Gilles lays siege to Tripoli.	Henry IV* of Germany permits Jews forcibly baptized during the First Crusade to return to Judaism. His attempt to include Jews in the "Peace of the Land of Mainz," which protects unarmed Christians during a period of feudal wars, does not succeed.		Leadership of the talmudic academy in Lucena, Spain, passes to Rabbi Alfasi's student Rabbi Joseph ibn Migash, who will hold that position until his death in 1141. Little of his work survives, but he is renowned as Spain's greatest rabbinic scholar. Among his students is Maimonides' father.	**1103**
Baldwin* of Boulogne overtakes the stronghold at Acre.				**1104**
Norway's King Sigurd* embarks on a pilgrimage to Jerusalem.				**1107**
	The poet Judah Halevi leaves his medical practice in Toledo upon the murder of his patron, Solomon ibn Ferrizuel, a nobleman close to the court of King Alfonso VI.* He travels around the Mediterranean, engaging in trade. He is close to the biblical commentator Abraham ibn Ezra, another itinerant scholar.			**1108**
Frankish crusaders capture Tripoli in July.	At the death of King Alfonso VI,* Jews, once protected by the crown, are			**1109**

	A. General History	B. Jews in Europe	C. Jews in the Middle East and North Africa	D. Jewish Culture
1109		attacked in Toledo. Anti-Jewish legislation is soon revived.		
1110				Abraham bar Hiyya, a Jewish astronomer, mathematician, and philosopher in Barcelona, composes the first Hebrew encyclopedia, *Yesodei ha-Tevuna u-Migdal ha-Emunah* (The Foundations of Understanding and the Tower of Faith), including articles on the various sciences and arts; only fragments survive. Bestirred by conflicts between Turks and crusaders in the Middle East, in *Megillat ha-Megalleh* (The Scroll of the Revealer), Abraham calculates the imminent coming of the Messiah. He holds the public office of captain of the bodyguard, the Arabic title of which is "Savasorda."
1111	Pope Paschal II, a reformer in the tradition of Gregory VII, reaches an accord with German Emperor Henry V.* Paschal will soon repudiate it under pressure from his cardinals, who do not accept his doctrine that the Church and its clergy should not own land.			
1115	Crusaders under Baldwin* of Le Bourg, successor to Baldwin* of Boulogne, recapture eastern Asia Minor from Armenians.	Friction between Muslims and Jews in Aragon is addressed by its king, Alfonso I,* who grants limited but equal rights to both groups. In Tudela, Alfonso forbids Muslims to own houses or mosques within the city walls but restricts Jews from owning Muslim slaves and insulting Muslims. Christian rulers in Spain favor Jews in return for support of their conquests.		
1119	Syria is the arena of bitter fighting between crusaders including Baldwin* of Le Bourg and Muslim chiefs.			
1120			Many Jews from Muslim lands begin to settle in Byzantium in this decade because of the relatively good conditions that prevail there and the need to escape the religious	

A. General History	B. Jews in Europe	C. Jews in the Middle East and North Africa	D. Jewish Culture	
		persecutions of the Egyptian caliph al-Hakim.*		**1120**
The Concordat of Worms denies Emperor Henry V* the right to invest clergy but grants him virtual veto power over papal appointees within his domain.				**1122**
Egyptian forces in the eastern Mediterranean are defeated by crusaders from Venice and France.				**1123**
	Records of a Jewish gate in Kiev, Russia, attest to the presence of a Jewish community.			**1124**
After Henry V's* death, German feudal lords elect his successor and set limits on royal power.				**1125**
Muslims regain control of Aleppo for the second time in four years.				**1128**
	An allegation that a Jew killed a sick man brings a 2,000-pound fine on London's Jews.			**1130**
	The count of Barcelona, Ramon Berengeur IV,* appoints a politically experienced Jew, Eleazar of Saragossa, as steward. Jews commonly serve administrations in Spain through their knowledge of Arabic and the sciences.			**1131**
Henry I* of England conquers Normandy back from his brother Robert.* He dies and is replaced by a nephew, Stephen of Blois,* elected by the barons.			Samuel ben Meir, a northern French Jewish sheep farmer by trade, authors a commentary on the Torah that supplements that of his grandfather and teacher, Rashi. Dealing exclusively in the contextual (*peshat*) approach, Samuel, later known as Rashbam, opposes his interpretation to the classical rabbinic mode, *midrash*, often diverging from Rashi's explanations. Rashbam's comments occasionally react to Christian uses of the Bible.	**1135**
Geoffrey* of Monmouth develops the popular legends about the 5th-century King Arthur in his *History of the Kings of*				**1136**

	A. General History	B. Jews in Europe	C. Jews in the Middle East and North Africa	D. Jewish Culture
1136	*Britain.* The Arthurian romance will soon be expanded in French by Chrétien de Troyes* and inspire Wolfram von Eschenbach's* *Parzifal* in German.			
1137			Jews in Seleucia, on the southern coast of Asia Minor, encourage fellow Jews to move there and share their prosperous conditions, according to a letter preserved in the Cairo Genizah.	
1139	The kingdom of Portugal is established on the Iberian Peninsula under King Affonso.* A Jew, Yahya ibn Yaish, is appointed treasurer.			Judah Halevi completes his classic and influential philosophy of Judaism. Composed in Arabic as *The Book of Argument and Proof in Defense of the Despised Faith*, it will become known as *The Kuzari* after its translation into Hebrew in about 1160. The book takes the form of dialogues between the king of the Khazars and an Aristotelian philosopher, a Christian, a Muslim, and a Jew, each of whom presents the merits of his own beliefs. Dissatisfied with the former three speakers, the king extends his dialogue with the Jew, learning of the many facets of his faith. For Halevi, Jews have a unique, inherent prophetic sense enabling them to experience the divine presence, the *Shekhinah*, a source of authority greater than the reason of the philosophers.
1140	A code of canon (church) law authorized by the pope is produced by the Italian legal scholar Gratian,* who employs the dialectical method in use in the French academies, such as the newly founded University of Paris, a school of higher learning sponsored by the Church. The method resolves conflicts among older church documents and traditions. Such academic methods of study may influence the development of the talmudic Tosafot among French Jewish scholars.		The great poet and philosopher Judah Halevi reaches Egypt en route to the land of Israel, his Zionist destination. He will die in Israel within the year; it will be told that he was trampled to death by an Arab rider in Jerusalem.	A significant and influential method of Talmud study is developed by Rashi's grandsons, Jacob Tam and his brothers Samuel ben Meir and Isaac ben Meir. Taking off on a comment by Rashi, they seek to identify and then resolve apparent contradictions between Rashi's interpretation and a Talmud passage, between different Talmud passages, or between Rashi or the Talmud and scholars of the Babylonian tradition such as Hananel and Alfasi, whose works are becoming more available in France. These additional comments, known as

The scholar Peter Abelard* (d. 1142) composes the autobiographical *History of My Calamities*, demonstrating the individuality of the human personality and undermining Platonic idealism. Abelard* is tried for heresy by the anti-intellectual mystic, Bernard of Clairvaux, and forced to recant. Bernard himself propounds the revolutionary idea—for a Christian—that one can transcend the flesh in this life through mystical union with God. He also espouses the cult of the Virgin Mary and accuses fellow clerics of serving the Antichrist.

Tosafot, set the model for Talmud study in France and Germany for over two centuries, eventually becoming composed into a running commentary that is printed opposite Rashi's in standard Talmud editions.

1140

Abraham ibn Ezra (1089–1164), scientist, poet, and Hebrew grammarian, like his friend Judah Halevi a native of Tudela, leaves Spain for the life of a wandering Jewish scholar, writing Bible commentaries on request and translating important works in Arabic such as some of Judah ibn Hayyuj's treatises on biblical Hebrew. Spending time in Italy, Germany, and France, Ibn Ezra applies his linguistic expertise and rationalist bent toward interpreting the Torah and other biblical books in classic contextual (*peshat*) style. Ibn Ezra's observations will interest Benedict Spinoza and other modern readers for their hints that Moses did not write certain verses of the Torah. He also writes on Hebrew grammar, mathematics, and other subjects.

A Jerusalem Karaite, Elijah ben Abraham, writes a history of Jewish sectarianism, *Hilluk*, describing the four contemporary Jewish sects—Rabbanites, Karaites, Tiflisites, and Mashwites—and tracing the schism between Rabbanites and Karaites to the division of the Israelite monarchy after Solomon's death in 928 BCE.

Edessa, a Christian center in eastern Asia Minor that had been recaptured by the crusaders in 1098, is overtaken by Muslims.

In reponse to the appeal of the beset "Latin Kingdom of Jerusalem," as the Christian domain in Jerusalem is called, church leader Bernard of Clairvaux exhorts European Christians to embark on the Second Crusade.

Jews in Norwich, England, are accused of murdering a Christian child for alleged ritual use of his blood. This first in a series of blood libels is based on an ancient charge to defame Judaism and the Christian story of the torture and execution of Jesus. The Norwich blood libel, like those that follow in Gloucester (1168), Winchester (1192), and elsewhere, incites violence against Jews.

Over 800 of Judah Halevi's Hebrew poems survive. Reflecting current Arabic and Hebrew genres and forms, the poems range from secular compositions in praise of love and wine and tributes to friends and colleagues living and dead to liturgical *piyyutim* of a markedly sorrowful type. His fervent hope for messianic redemption is expressed, too, in his "Songs of Zion," envisioning Israel in the

1144

A. General History	B. Jews in Europe	C. Jews in the Middle East and North Africa	D. Jewish Culture

1144

East as a haven for Jews from the many vicissitudes of the West.

Antisemitic caricature of the family of Isaac son of Jurnet of Norwich, 1233. (Public Record Office, London)

1146

The bishop of Freisling, Otto, of the royal German house of Hohenstaufen, takes a dim view of earthly government in his historical survey, *The Two Cities*. At the accession in 1152 of his nephew Frederick,* Otto will bid his church support what he envisions as constructive imperial power.

Heeding the cry of Pope Eugene III to recapture Edessa and other Near Eastern Christian centers from the Muslims, Christian soldiers embark on the Second Crusade.

Local governments in Germany and Austria (Cologne, 1266; Austria, 1316; Winterthur, 1340) grant Jews a monopoly in usury as a result of the condemnation of Christian usury by Bernard of Clairvaux and others. Some cities actually force Jews to lend money to Christians (Cologne, 1250; Passau, 1260; Regensburg, 1328).

Despite some attacks against Jews in the Rhineland, these crusaders are less distracted than their predecessors by calls to avenge the wounds of Jesus by letting the blood of Jews.

1147

Crusaders from western Europe are thwarted by the Turks in Asia Minor.

1148

Crusade leaders including King Louis VII* of France hold an assembly in Jerusalem.

When Cordoba falls under Almohad control, the Jewish rabbinic judge Maimon takes leave with his family, which includes a brilliant son, born in 1135, who will become known as Moses Maimonides.

The preeminent Karaite book of theology, *Eshkol ha-Kofer*, is written in Hebrew by the sage Judah ben Elijah Hadassi in Constantinople. Explaining the interpretive methods of the Karaites, Hadassi delineates all their commandments and legal traditions and the reasons for them. Although he criticizes talmudic lore, he shares rabbinic beliefs in magic and astrology.

1150

The papacy will for the first and only time be held by an Englishman. Adrian IV will be assisted by university-trained John* of Salisbury, who will return to England in 1153 to serve as secretary to the archbishop of Canterbury and then his successor, Thomas à Becket. John* criticizes the university for debating what is true instead of teaching it.

A conference of rabbis (synod) is held at Troyes, France. Convened by Jacob ben Meir (Tam) and his brother Samuel ben Meir (Rashbam), they discuss questions of Jewish law relating to informers and litigation by Jews in non-Jewish courts. It is believed to be the first Ashkenazic rabbinical synod.

Restrictions on Babylonian Jews are largely lifted by the caliph al-Muqtafi.* According to the traveler Benjamin of Tudela, the succeeding caliph, al-Mustanjid,* is disposed toward Jews and studies their Torah in Hebrew.

An important Bible interpreter in the tradition of Rashi, Eliezer of Beaugency, France, composes commentaries on Isaiah, Ezekiel, and the 12 minor prophets. He explains the Bible independently of rabbinic *midrash* and pays unusual attention to the editing of the prophetic books and matters of history.

A. General History	B. Jews in Europe	C. Jews in the Middle East and North Africa	D. Jewish Culture	
In northern France, epics applauding local feudal lords, *chansons de geste*, are sung. In Spain the epic *El Cid* recalls the warrior of the preceding century.		Byzantine Jews, many of whom work in trade guilds making textiles and tanning leather, number about 85,000, about 0.5% of the empire's entire population; 10% of these Jews are Karaites. In Egypt, 40,000 Jews comprise 1% percent of the populace; Syria's 40,000 Jews make up 1.5% of the total. Byzantine Jewry uses Hebrew rather than Grecized names for centuries.		**1150**
The accession of the powerful Frederick I* of Barbarossa in Germany puts an end to decades of conflict between rival houses and strikes a balance between the imperial regime and the various feudal lords.				**1152**
		The Second Crusade is consummated with the recapture of Ashkelon, the Mediterranean port in Israel, from Muslim control. As the crusaders fortify it, Jews repopulate it and other cities, except Jerusalem, which is still restricted.		**1153**
Most of Syria apart from the Christian stronghold of Antioch has fallen under the control of Muslim leader Nur ed-Din.* The English barons restore a strong centralized government by electing Henry II,* grandson of Henry I,* king.				**1154**
	Count Ramon Berenguer IV* of Barcelona contracts with his Jewish physician Abraham Alfaquim for construction of a public bath. In exchange, Abraham and his family are guaranteed one-third the profits and a ban against the building of any competing baths in Barcelona.	The family of Maimon settles in Fez, Morocco, where many Jews had converted to Islam. Son Moses studies rabbinics under Rabbi Judah ibn Susan, as well as medicine and other sciences. He continues to compose his Arabic commentary on the Mishnah.	Rabbi Abraham ben David, trained in talmudic scholarship at Narbonne and later applauded as a critic of Maimonides' code of Jewish law, founds an academy at Posquieres that attracts students throughout Europe. Rabad, as he is called, composes commentaries on tractates of the Talmud and, most unusually, on the Mishnah alone and on *midrashim*. Preeminent legal authority in Provence, Rabad trains many rabbis and issues numerous halakhic opinions.	**1160**

	A. General History	B. Jews in Europe	C. Jews in the Middle East and North Africa	D. Jewish Culture
1161				Abraham ben David ibn Daud, physician and philosopher (1110–1180), composes *Sefer ha-Kabbalah* (The Book of Tradition) in Toledo. This important historiographic work traces an unbroken Jewish tradition from biblical to contemporary times, for which it is an invaluable resource. Its polemic maintains that Rabbanite Judaism and not Karaism is the faithful heir to this tradition and that the center of the tradition has now moved from Babylonia to Spain. Judah ibn Tibbon of Spain is commissioned to translate Bahya ibn Paquda's *Hovot ha-Levavot* (Duties of the Heart) from Arabic to Hebrew. He also translates Judah Halevi's *Kuzari* and Saadiah Gaon's *The Book of Doctrines and Beliefs*.
1162		In Spain the first Jewish bailiff, a high official responsible primarily for fiscal matters, is appointed by King Alfonso II* of Aragon. He is Yahia ben David of Monzon.		
1163			The Jews are given permission by Emperor Heaou-tsung* to erect a synagogue in Kaifeng, ancient capital of Honan Province, China. It is destroyed when the Yellow River floods in 1279; it will be rebuilt and destroyed repeatedly.	
1165			The Jews of Yemen are forced to convert to Islam as a result of the fanaticsm of the Shi'ite Muslims. Maimon and his sons Moses and David leave Fez, making their way to Acco, in Israel. Their exodus may have been triggered by the martyrdom of Rabbi Judah ibn Susan.	
1166			Moses Maimonides settles in Fostat (Old Cairo), breaking the dominant influence of the Karaites there. Supported by his brother David's trade in precious stones, Moses	Moses Maimonides' reputation as a preeminent scholar of *halakhah* will soon bring him queries from communities as remote as Provence and Yemen and from

A. General History	B. Jews in Europe	C. Jews in the Middle East and North Africa	D. Jewish Culture	
		completes his Mishnah commentary.	authorities as established as Samuel ben Ali, *gaon* of Baghdad. Over 460 of his responsa are published. He also writes, in Arabic, his own enumeration of the 613 injunctions of the Torah, *The Book of the Commandments*.	1166
Egypt, beset by a Frankish attack, seeks help from Nur ed-Din* in Syria.			Maimonides completes his Arabic commentary on the Mishnah, *The Book of Light*. He incorporates material he had been gathering from his education in Spain and his sojourn in Israel. The commentary is to serve as an explication of the Mishnah and an introduction to more advanced talmudic study. His prologue to Tractate Sanhedrin, chapter 10, forms the basis of Maimonides' influential 13-principle creed, "I believe . . ." (*Ani Ma'amin*). He writes, too, that revelation is not literal, that the Torah's statement "God said" is a metaphor for prophetic communication.	1168
Thomas à Becket, archbishop of Canterbury, chief prelate of England, is murdered for his refusal to grant traditional clerical powers to King Henry II.*	The Jews of Tudela move into the citadel. In exchange for defending the citadel, the Spanish king guarantees to repair and maintain the walls and grants Jews the right to defend themselves against any mob violence. The settlement of Jews inside fortresses is common in Spain.	Following a tense period, Jews repopulate Basra, south Babylonia. Benjamin of Tudela reports 10,000 Jews there at the time of his visit.	Isaac ben Abba Mari, originally from Marseilles, composes an encyclopedia of everyday *halakhah*, arranged by topic, *Sefer ha-Ittur*. Isaac draws on both Talmudim, geonic responsa, and the writing of contemporary Franco-German and Spanish authorities. Ashkenazic rabbis continue this tradition of collecting halakhic precedents.	1170
The vizier of Egypt, a Kurd called Salah al-Din* or Saladin, dethrones the Fatimid sultan and returns Egypt to the dominion of the Abbasid house in Baghdad, which will rule there until the Mamluk conquest in 1250.	The Jews of Rouen are burned to death. The murderous blood libel against Jews that first appears in Norwich, England, in 1144 spreads to the European continent beginning at Blois, France.			1171
		Moses Maimonides writes an important letter (*iggeret*) to the Jewish community of Yemen, encouraging them to remain faithful to tradition in the face of increased pressure by Shi'ite Muslims to convert and to resist the appeal of a false Messiah in their midst.	Returning to Tudela, Spain, from about a decade of travel through southern Europe and the Middle East, Benjamin ben Jonah writes up a summary of his journeys that will become a widely printed and translated book and a paramount source for	1172

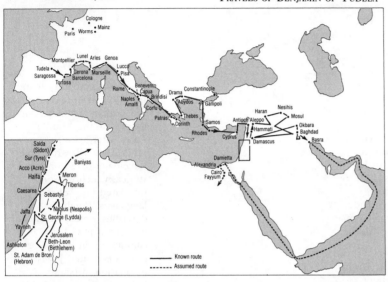

TRAVELS OF BENJAMIN OF TUDELA

Cologne
Mainz
Paris · Worms
Montpellier · Lunel · Arles · Genoa
Tudela · Gerona · Lucca
Saragossa · Barcelona · Marseille · Pisa
Tortosa · Rome · Benevento
Naples · Capua · Drama · Constantinople
Amalfi · Brindisi · Abydos · Gallipoli
Corfu · Thebes · Samos · Antioch · Aleppo · Haran · Nesihis
Patras · Corinth · Rhodes · Cyprus · Hammati · Mosul
Damascus · Okbara · Baghdad · Basra
Damietta
Alexandria · Cairo · Fayyum

Saida (Sidon)
Sur (Tyre)
Acco (Acre) · Baniyas
Haifa · Meron
Caesarea · Tiberias
Sebastye
Jaffa · Nablus (Neapolis)
Yavneh · St. George (Lydda)
Ashkelon · Jerusalem · Beth-Leon (Bethlehem)
St. Adam de Bron (Hebron)

— Known route
---- Assumed route

	A. General History	B. Jews in Europe	C. Jews in the Middle East and North Africa	D. Jewish Culture
1172				modern historians centuries later. Benjamin thoughtfully describes the people and politics of the numerous places he visits, giving special attention to the Jewish communities. He details many sites in the land of Israel though he dilates most on the court of Baghdad.
1174	Saladin,* sultan of Egypt, seizes power in Syria when its ruler, Nur ed-Din,* dies, thereby positioning himself to battle the crusaders in Israel.			
1175		A spiritual movement spreads throughout Germany placing special emphasis on ascetic practices and martyrdom (*Kiddush ha-Shem*). It makes use, too, of Jewish mystical sources. Led by Rabbi Samuel ben Kalonymus, the Hasidei Ashkenaz (Franco-German Pietists) will flourish for about a century. The synagogue at Worms is completely rebuilt. Believed to have been erected in 1034, it was badly damaged by rioters during the Crusades of 1096 and 1146. It will be damaged again during the riots of the Black Death (1348–1350), and rebuilt in 1355. In 1623–1624, a chapel will be added, named after Rashi, who had studied in Worms in the 11th century. The synagogue will be burned by the Nazis on *Kristallnacht* (Night of the Broken Glass) in 1938 and damaged further by Allied bombing in 1945. After World War II, it will be faithfully restored.		Petahiah, a wealthy Jew from Regensburg and scion of Tosafists, embarks on a journey to the Middle East. After his return, other Jews will write up a travelogue based on his stories, which will be translated into several languages. Petahiah describes a prosperous and influential Jewish community in Babylonia but a decimated Jewish population in Israel following the Crusade of 1099. Joseph ben Isaac of Orleans, known as Joseph Bekhor Shor, combines the interpretive method of *peshat* as developed in the school of Rashi with homiletics and anti-Christian polemic to write an original commentary on the Torah. His explanations display a rationalism associated with the Spanish tradition, although some of them apply the talmudic method of the Tosafot. Joseph was a student of Rabbi Jacob Tam, and his son Abraham is quoted in the Tosafot comments on the Talmud.
1176		The concept of Jews as serfs of the ruler is first formulated. The law of Teruel, Spain, states that "the Jews are the serfs of the king and the absolute property of the royal treasury." This notion provides a theoretical basis for humiliating Jews while protecting them and their possessions for the sovereign's benefit.		

A. General History	B. Jews in Europe	C. Jews in the Middle East and North Africa	D. Jewish Culture	
The Treaty of Venice leaves Italy in the hands of local rulers and the pope, frustrating Frederick* Barbarossa's plans of expanding imperial control.				**1177**
	The Third Lateran Council summoned by Pope Alexander III adopts a canon concerning relations with Jews. Jews are prohibited from having Christian servants; the testimony of Christians is to be accepted against Jews in all lawsuits; Jews who convert to Christianity are not to be deprived of their possessions.			**1179**
About this time, the great Persian poet Nazami* composes an epic poem about the popular 5th-century Sassanid king, Vahram.*			Babylonian Jews are reported to be universally well versed in Scripture, each Jew capable of chanting from the Torah correctly. Baghdad alone boasts of ten yeshivot.	**1180**
The great Muslim philosopher Ibn Rushd,* known later in Europe as the premier interpreter of Aristotle,* Averroës,* serves as medical adviser to Marrakesh,* the chief judge of Cordoba.	Jews are expelled from France by King Philip Augustus* and their lands are confiscated. Emperor Frederick I* issues the Confirmation of Rights of the Jews of Regensburg. It includes a guarantee that Jews may live according to their own laws and customs and that they and their property would be protected.	 *The expulsion of the Jews from France in 1182, depicted in the 1321* Grandes Chroniques de France. *(Bibliothèque Royale Albert I, Brussels)*		**1182**
	When Aaron of Lincoln, England, a Jewish moneylender whose records have survived, dies, 430 people owe him 15,000 pounds, the equivalent of three-quarters of the annual revenue of the English exchequer. The exchequer claims his property and debts.	Moses Maimonides is appointed physician to the Egyptian vizier Al-Fadil.* Moses had turned to medicine after his brother David, source of his livelihood, drowned. As a physician, Moses was able to achieve preeminence in the Fostat community and find time to continue his scholarship. He writes extensively on medical subjects as well as Judaic ones. His treatises, discussing topics from asthma to sexual intercourse, include a guide that lays importance on care of both body and soul for maintaining good health.	Moses Maimonides completes his comprehensive 14-volume code of Jewish law, the *Mishneh Torah* (Second Torah), which stands as one of Judaism's most magnificent achievements. Written in lucid Hebrew style "for young and old" alike and arranged by subject, this code incorporates talmudic and geonic *halakhah* and constitutes a major source. Because it obviates study of the Talmud itself and does not typically justify its statements, Maimonides' code immediately begins to provoke controversy. Zerahiah ben Isaac, a leading talmudic scholar and bilingual poet from Gerona, completes a	**1185**

	A. General History	B. Jews in Europe	C. Jews in the Middle East and North Africa	D. Jewish Culture
1185				two-part legal interpretation of the Talmud at odds with that of Alfasi, *Ha-Ma'or* (The Light).
1187	From his base in Syria, Saladin* raids Israel on horseback, removing Christian control from all but a few towns on the Mediterranean Coast.			
1189	In reaction to Saladin's* recapture of the Holy Land, the king of England, Richard I* the Lionhearted, leads a Third Crusade to wrest it from Muslim hands.			
1190		Anti-Jewish riots break out following the coronation of Richard* the Lionhearted. Fleeing to a castle in York but unable to gain help, Jews led by Rabbi Yom Tov of Joigney slay themseves.	Following his conquest of Jerusalem from the crusaders, Saladin* permits Jews to resettle there.	
1191	Saladin* succeeds in destroying the crusader fortifications in Ashkelon, but after a two-year bloody standoff against the Christians in Acre, he signs a truce with crusader Richard* the Lionhearted, leaving the coastal towns from Jaffa up to Tyre in Christian hands. Richard* will soon return to Europe.			
1195				Moses Maimonides completes *The Guide for the Perplexed*, the most important work of medieval Jewish thought. In it Maimonides addresses the philosophically initiated, explaining the Bible and Judaism within an Aristotelian framework common among contemporary Muslim thinkers. Those parts of Scripture that may seem to contradict reason and philosophical truth should be understood metaphorically or symbolically. God is an incorporeal prime mover who created the world from nothing. Humans enjoy divine providence in proportion to their intellectual faculties. *The Guide* will soon be translated twice into

A. General History	B. Jews in Europe	C. Jews in the Middle East and North Africa	D. Jewish Culture	
			Hebrew, reaching a wide audience of Jews.	**1195**
	Between 1198 and 1231 the king and princes of France conclude 18 different pacts in which they agree to return fleeing Jews to the sovereign who "owns" them.			**1198**
With Jerusalem under the control of Saladin's* brother and successor, Malik al-Adil,* and Richard* the Lionhearted dead, European leaders plan another crusade.			Samuel ibn Tibbon of Spain is given permission by Maimonides to translate the latter's *Guide for the Perplexed* from Arabic to Hebrew. Maimonides contributes many of his own suggestions to the translation.	**1199**
Mongol hordes invade Russia.	Following the destruction of the Karaite community of Jerusalem in the First Crusade, a disciple of Jeshua ben Judah, Sidi ibn al-Taras, returns to his native Castile, Spain, and teaches Karaism. Upon his death, his wife, known as "the Teacher," continues his effort and establishes herself as an authority in her own right. The popularity of Karaism in Spain will provoke Rabbanite Jews to seek the expulsion of Karaites by the Christian king.

Rabbi Judah ben Samuel, known as "he-Hasid" (the Pietist), leads from his center in Regensburg the Hasidei Ashkenaz movement. Teaching the religious value of self-restraint, Judah is the main author of the Pietists' manual, *Sefer Hasidim*. A more mystical work of his, *Sefer ha-Kavod* (The Book of the Divine Glory), survives only in references. His commentary on the Torah contains the daring thesis that certain passages postdate Moses. | | Rabbi David Kimhi (1160–1235) of Provence, the most accomplished of a family of Hebrew linguists and exegetes, composes biblical commentaries that stress scientific philological analysis to determine the *peshat* (contextual meaning) of the text. In addition to his grammar of Hebrew, *Mikhlol*, and his dictionary, *The Book of Roots*, his commentaries on Genesis, the Prophets, Psalms, and Chronicles are extensively studied by both Jews and Christians. Kimhi occasionally introduces rabbinic *midrash* and anti-Christian polemic.

Samson ben Abraham of Sens, France, a pupil of Rabbi Jacob Tam and Isaac ben Samuel of Dampierre, composes a Talmud commentary in the Tosafist tradition, known as Tosafot Sens. Famous as an admiring critic of Maimonides, Samson moves to Israel.

An influential book comprising various sorts of Jewish mystical speculation and interpretations of *Sefer ha-Yetsirah* is composed in a difficult mixture of Hebrew and Aramaic in southern France. This relatively short work, *Sefer ha-Bahir* (The Book of the Bright), features esoteric explanations of the biblical commandments and manipulations of the names of God for magical | **1200** |

	A. General History	B. Jews in Europe	C. Jews in the Middle East and North Africa	D. Jewish Culture
1200				purposes. *Sefer ha-Bahir* develops the *sefirot* (phases) of *Sefer ha-Yetsirah* into a set of 10 fundamental attributes and powers emanating from God through which the world takes its form.
1202				Meir Abulafia of Toledo (c.1180–1244) writes to the followers of Maimonides in Lunel, France, criticizing the latter's *Mishneh Torah* for omitting mention of the doctrine of the resurrection of the dead. Maimonides is also attacked for not citing the sources for his legal decisions.
1204	Crusader forces capture Constantinople, leaving Baldwin* of Flanders emperor there.	The existence of a synagogue in Vienna is recorded. The Jewish community of Vienna remains the primary area of Jewish settlement in Austria from the late Middle Ages onward.	Crusaders set Constantinople's elegant Jewish quarter ablaze. According to tradition, the remains of Moses Maimonides are interred in Tiberias.	
1205		The Toledo synagogue, now known as Santa Maria La Blanca, is erected. It will be confiscated from the Jews in 1405 or 1411, following anti-Jewish attacks. From 1554 to about 1600, it will be a convent for reformed prostitutes. In the mid-19th century, it will become a national monument and will be restored.		
1206		King Philip Augustus* of France assigns special officials the task of recording documents of indebtedness, with special fines to be imposed against those who falsify the amounts or conditions of loans. A rate of interest Jews may charge is fixed and the types of objects acceptable as pledges are restricted.		
1209	Pope Innocent III launches the Albigensian Crusade, which lasts until 1229, and either destroys or subdues various Pietist sects including the Albigensians, Cathars, and Waldensians, all of whom reject papal authority.	The papacy recognizes the Franciscan order established by Francis of Assisi. This Roman Catholic order of friars joins the persecution of Jews instigated by the Dominicans. Their spirituality, however, seems to influence 13th- and 14th-century Spanish Jewish mysticism.		

A. General History	B. Jews in Europe	C. Jews in the Middle East and North Africa	D. Jewish Culture	
Asserting the power of his papacy, Innocent III excommunicates Holy Roman Emperor Otto IV.*			Influenced by the great Rabbanite Hebrew poets of Spain, the Egyptian Karaite physician Moses ben Abraham Dar'i composes a collection (*diwan*) of 544 lyric poems in Hebrew. Among them is a diatribe against an age when women dominate men.	**1210**
		A group of 300 French and English rabbis settle in Palestine.		**1211**
	Jews are first documented in Switzerland. By 1241 the Jews of Basle are listed among the contributors to the imperial tax.			**1213**
King John* of England accedes rights to his nobles by signing the Magna Carta.	The Fourth Lateran Council summoned by Pope Innocent III (1198–1216) adopts four canons concerning Jews. (1) Jews must wear a mark on their clothing to separate them from Christians. (2) Jews may not exact immoderate usury from Christians, and Christians may not do business with Jews who do not obey church instructions. (3) Jews may not hold public office. (4) Converts to Christianity must desist from Jewish observances.			**1215**
Pope Honorius III recognizes the Dominican order. Charged with fighting heresy, it soon directs much of its energy against the Jews, censoring Hebrew books, preaching conversionist sermons, and writing anti-Jewish polemics.		The poet Rabbi Judah Alharizi (1170–1235) visits Israel and makes note of an invitation issued by Saladin* after he captured Jerusalem, for Jews to return to Jerusalem, especially those Jews who were refugees from the crusader period.		**1216**
Francis of Assisi (c.1181–1226) arrives in Acco on a pilgrimage.				**1219**
	The Assembly of the Jewish communities of Speyer, Worms, and Mainz adopts a tax ban against anyone who lies to the community about how much money one has. In many communities stringent measures are adopted to ensure a fair distribution of the tax burden among all its members.			**1220**

	A. General History	B. Jews in Europe	C. Jews in the Middle East and North Africa	D. Jewish Culture
1221	The Mongols capture Persia.			
1222	Chinggis Khan* attacks India.	The Council of Oxford, convened by Stephen Langton, archbishop of Canterbury, introduces into England the discriminatory legislation of the Fourth Lateran Council of 1215. The restrictions include the prohibition of building new synagogues and the requirement of Jews to wear the Jewish badge, which in England took the form of two tablets of stone. This same Langton is responsible for dividing the Bible into chapters to serve the needs of the concordance he commissioned for use in disputations.		
1223	Emperor Frederick II* invades Jerba and transfers its population—including Jews—to Palermo.	French royal ordinances begin to give evidence of the desire to abolish Jewish usury as much as possible.		
1224			An Arab historian claims that there is not a single synagogue in the entire Maghreb. This may reflect the Jewish fear of provoking their Muslim enemies by worshiping publicly.	
1228		The English chronicler Roger* of Wendover records the legend of the Wandering Jew in his *Flores Historiarum.* Based upon the New Testament (John 18:20–22 and Matthew 16:28), the legendary personage, named Ahasuerus, is condemned by Jesus to wander until his Second Coming for having rebuffed or struck him on his way to the Crucifixion. Wendover* reports the Wandering Jew to have been seen in Armenia. The story or folktale gave expression to medieval anti-Jewish feeling and flourished well into the 20th century.		
1230		The Treaty of Melun is signed. It is the culmination of a long-developing policy by which the king and most French lords pledge themselves not to steal		Jacob Anatoli, physician, translator, and scholar, arrives in Naples from France. Invited by Emperor Frederick II* to serve as a physician, he engages in scholarly work.

126

A. General History	B. Jews in Europe	C. Jews in the Middle East and North Africa	D. Jewish Culture	
	each other's Jews. The law is based on the doctrine that kings and barons are masters over their Jewish serfs and the owners of their property.		He translates Averroës'* works into Latin and writes a homiletical work, *Malmad ha-Talmidim* (*A Goad to Scholars*), which argues for a philosophical and ethical understanding of the Bible and prayers.	**1230**
	Pope Gregory IX commissions the distinguished jurist Raymond* of Penaforte to compile an authoritative collection of ecclesiastical law. Completed in 1234, the "Decretales" become the recognized statement of church law. Its section on the Jews collects and restates Jewish rights and restrictions from earlier ages.			
	The Altneuschul (Old New Synagogue) of Prague, a landmark of Jewish settlement in medieval Europe, is believed to be a remodeled synagogue erected in 1230, according to recent scholarship. It is the oldest functioning synagogue in Europe, as the Worms synagogue was destroyed and rebuilt.			
Venice becomes the first European power to open a consulate in Tunis. It is followed by Marseilles, Genoa, Pisa, Sicily, and Aragon.		The political situation of the Jews in Tunis begins to ease as Europeans establish political and economic ties to the area.		**1231**
Pope Gregory IX prohibits the study of Aristotle* and other philosophical works as heretical.	Rabbi Solomon bar Abraham of Montpellier issues a ban against the study of philosophy and the reading of Maimonides' *Guide for the Perplexed* and *Sefer ha-Madda*. The works of Maimonides are burned by the Dominicans in Provence. Whether this takes place at the initiative of Maimonides' Jewish opponents or the Dominicans remains unclear.	The Jewish community of Marrakesh, Morocco, is reestablished after having been banned by the Almohades. However, massacres ensue, caused by Muslim political revolt and popular hatred of Jews.		**1232**
	The Statute of the Jewry is issued in England. These laws deal with registration of Jewish loans, limits on interest rates, articles forbidden to pawn, and threats of expulsion for Jews who are disloyal or do not "serve" the king.			**1233**

	A. General History	B. Jews in Europe	C. Jews in the Middle East and North Africa	D. Jewish Culture
1233		Emperor Frederick II* grants the Jews of Jerba who had been relocated to Palermo permission to form a separate congregation.		
1234		Jews are forbidden to live in Newcastle. Similar prohibitions in the English cities of Derby (1261), Romsey (1266), and Cambridge (1275) do not, however, prohibit Jews from continuing to retain ownership of their property there.		
1236	Christians led by Ferdinand III* of Castile capture Cordoba.	Emperor Frederick II* extends the concept of Jews as "serfs of our chamber" from Sicily to the entire Holy Roman Empire north of the Alps. Control and ownership of Jews is part of the power struggle between the emperor and the pope. Emperor Frederick II* investigates the blood libel and declares the charge baseless. Though Pope Innocent IV also condemns the charge, the libels continue well into the modern era. Pope Gregory IX, in a letter to Louis IX* of France, condemns the "excesses" of the Fifth Crusade in its violence against Jews. Three years earlier he had complained about Jews holding public office, proselytizing among Christians, circumcising Christian slaves, and employing Christian servants and nurses. An anti-Jewish riot in Narbonne, in southern France, initiated after a Christian fisherman is killed by a Jew in a private dispute, is subdued by the governor of the city. The community proclaims and celebrates the Purim of Narbonne, i.e., a Second Purim to commemorate deliverance from this crisis.		
1238	The Mongols capture Moscow.	Frederick II* grants a charter to the Jews of Vienna.	A rabbinical conference (synod) is held at Crete. It adopts a series of ordinances designed to strengthen the piety of local Jews. The synod was	

A. General History	B. Jews in Europe	C. Jews in the Middle East and North Africa	D. Jewish Culture	
		convened at the suggestion of Rabbi Baruch ben Isaac, who visited the island on his way to Palestine from northern Europe and was dismayed at the lax religious and moral behavior of the Jewish community. It is believed to be the first rabbinical synod held in southern Europe.		**1238**
	Prince Archambaud de Bourbon,* expressing an increasingly popular attitude among European rulers, decrees that Jews dwelling in his lands must "make their livings from permissible activities and commercial transactions, refraining completely from the extortion of usury." Pope Gregory IX (1227–1241) orders the kings and bishops of France, England, Spain, and Portugal to confiscate Hebrew books. "The outstanding reason that Jews remain obstinate in their perfidy is the influence of their books; they should, therefore, be forced to give up their books." Following his authorization, the Talmud is condemned and burned in France and Rome. James I* of Aragon issues the edict of Valencia in which he grants Jews rights and protections. The king is anxious for Jews to resettle the lands reconquered from the Muslims. This charter later serves as a model for others granted to Jews in the towns of Aragon.			**1239**
The Mongols capture Kiev.	A public disputation takes place in Paris between Jews and Christians after a Jewish convert to Christianity, Nicholas Donin, condemns the Talmud as anti-Christian. It results in the confiscation and burning of all available copies of the Talmud by the Dominicans.		Around this time, Zedekiah ben Abraham Anav, an Italian talmudist, writes *Shibbolei ha-Leket* (*The Gleaned Ears*), a halakhic compendium on the liturgy and the holidays. Referring to the custom of Rome, where he lived, the work contains detailed explanations of individual prayers; a commentary on the Passover Haggadah; and the laws relating to the Sabbath, holidays, and fasts.	**1240**

	A. General History	B. Jews in Europe	C. Jews in the Middle East and North Africa	D. Jewish Culture
1241		The Tartar invasion of Poland brings suffering and devastation to many of the cities in its path affecting many Jews as well. Unlike Jews of Germany and possibly Hungary, Polish Jews are not accused of conspiring with the Tartar invaders. Jews support the Mongolian armies led by Ogdai Khan* as they attack and plunder Silesia and Breslau. Khazars and Jews from the Caucasus probably fight on the Mongolian side, expecting the war to herald the messianic age.		
1243		The first recorded charge of Jewish desecration of the Host takes place in Germany. Jews are accused of accepting the doctrine of transubstantiation and torturing the Host in the same way that they tortured Jesus. Many German Jewish communities are destroyed in the wake of this accusation.		
1244		Duke Frederick II* of Babenberg grants the *Fredericianum* charter to all the Jews of Austria. It becomes the model for other 13th-century European Jewish charters of privileges.		
1247		Pope Innocent IV orders the cessation of the burnings of the Talmud. He bases his decision on the Constitution of the Jews issued by Pope Innocent III, whereby Jews are to be protected not because of any intrinsic right to protection but "only on account of the humane feelings" of Christianity.		
1248	Seville falls to the Christians led by Ferdinand III* of Castile.		Shipping records attest to Jewish economic activity in the North African port cities of Bougie, Algiers, and Teues.	
1250	The Mamluk Empire comes to power and is ruled by a military elite of Turkish-speaking former slaves. They rule Egypt,	The first blood libel takes place in Spain in Saragossa. Such accusations, however, are rare in Spain.		In the beginning of what is described as the Old Yiddish period, Yiddish-speaking Jews from Ashkenaz make contact

A. General History	B. Jews in Europe	C. Jews in the Middle East and North Africa	D. Jewish Culture	
part of Libya, Syria, Israel, and western Arabia until the Ottoman conquest of 1517.			with Slavic-speaking Jews in southeastern Germany, Bohemia, and later in Poland. The Old Yiddish period lasts until about 1500, and a relatively uniform literary language emerges.	**1250**
	A synagogue is erected in Buda, in the southern part of the castle district, on the right bank of the Danube River. The Jews will be expelled in 1360, and when they return in 1364, they will build synagogues in the northern part of the castle district.			**1251**
	Louis IX* orders the expulsion of all Jews from France except those engaged in manual labor. Though unenforced, the order results in financial extortion, social oppression, and bodily injury. Henry III* issues a series of decrees in England prohibiting construction of new synagogues, forbidding employment of Jewish servants and nurses by Christians, and requiring the wearing of a distinctive marking by Jews on their clothing.			**1253**
	An interregnum in Germany begins that lasts until 1273 and brings with it lawlessness and anarchy. Burghers attack the nobility, and the mobs attack the Jews in Augsburg, Arnstadt, Weissenberg, and Coblenz. Jews are often dependent on a strong central authority for physical protection and suffer severely in its absence.			**1254**
	The Jews of Lincoln, England, are accused of crucifying a Christian child and then removing his intestines for use in witchcraft.			**1255**
The Mongols led by Hulagu Khan* capture Baghdad and put an end to the Abbasid caliphate.				**1258**
The Mamluks stop the Mongols.	Judah ben Lavi de la Cabaleria is appointed to		Isaiah ben Mali di Trani the Elder (c.1200–c.1260),	**1260**

	A. General History	B. Jews in Europe	C. Jews in the Middle East and North Africa	D. Jewish Culture
1260	The Tartars destroy Jerusalem.	an office equal to that of minister of finance in the Spanish kingdom of Aragon. From the end of the 13th century, however, Jewish influence begins to decline in Aragon.		Italian halakhist who wrote many *pesakim* (decisions) and commentaries on the Talmud, dies. He traveled to Greece and Palestine and was in contact with Jewish scholars in Germany. His grandson, Isaiah ben Elijah di Trani the Younger (d. c.1280), will also write important novellae on the Talmud.
1263	The Mamluks defeat the Mongols at Ayn Galud (now Ein Harod), Palestine, establishing their unchallenged control of the Levant. They bring political stability, economic decline, martial rule, and Muslim fanaticism to Israel.	A disputation takes place in Barcelona between Moses ben Nahman (Nahmanides) and the Jewish convert to Christianity, Pablo Christiani.* The Spanish law code *Las Sieta Partidas* is formulated. It grants Jews religious freedom provided they do not attack Christianity. It seeks to prevent blood libels and forced conversions while emphasizing Jewish subjugation to Christians.		Shemtov ben Joseph Falquera (c.1225–c.1290) of Spain completes his *Ha-Mevakkesh* (*The Inquirer*). The purpose of the author is to instruct people in the right way of conduct. It is divided into two epistles, in the form of a series of dialogues between a young inquirer in search of wisdom and knowledge and various representatives of pursuits and occupations in life and of the sciences.
1264		The Jews of London are massacred during Easter as a result of a dispute between a Jew and a Christian over interest on a debt. Many later flee from there to Normandy. Conflict breaks out in the Jewish community of Saragossa, Spain, over the method for apportioning taxes. When complaints reach James II* that the tax burden is being unfairly shifted from the rich to the middle and lower classes, he rules that all tax payments be based on individual declaration under oath of personal assets rather than by tax assessors appointed by the *kahal* (communal organization). Prince Bolislas* the Pious of Kalish grants the Jews of his principality (Great Poland) a charter patterned on that granted by Frederick* of Austria in 1244. It serves as the model for Jewish privileges in other parts of Poland and signifies the beginning of large settlements of Jews in Poland.		

A. General History	B. Jews in Europe	C. Jews in the Middle East and North Africa	D. Jewish Culture	
	A church synod in Breslau, Poland, resolves to separate Jews from Christians by restricting their area of residence and imposing special attire on Jews. The synod also forbids the farming out of customs, tolls, and revenues to Jews because it claims that these put Jews in administrative positions and make Christians subservient. These restrictions were often repeated but rarely enforced. Pope Clement IV (1265–1268) issues the bull Turbato Corder, which extends the authority of the Inquisition over Jews who proselytize, Jewish converts who revert to Judaism, and Christians who convert to Judaism.	Nahmanides (Rabbi Moses ben Nahman, 1194–1270), Spanish rabbi and scholar, arrives in Palestine, settling in Jerusalem and later Acco. He was exiled from Spain because of his disputations with the Church. He becomes the leader of Jewish life in Palestine.		**1267**
Southern Morocco is conquered from the Almohades by Abu Yusuf,* who establishes the Merinid line.	Rent charges are prohibited in England and those already in existence are annulled. This ended the Jewish financial practice in which money would be lent in exchange for the creation in perpetuity of an annual rent charge on the borrower's land.	The Merinids prove friendly to the Jews of Morocco. Jews become stewards, counselors, and courtiers. A Hebrew inscription found on the island of Chennamangalam proves the existence of Jews along the west coast of India. Jewish, Christian, and Muslim travelers and geographers also report the existence of Jewish communities from the 12th to the 14th centuries.		**1269**
			Nahmanides (1194–1270), having moved to Palestine, completes his monumental commentary on the Torah. It draws heavily on rabbinic sources, reflects his belief in mystical doctrines such as transmigration of souls, and rejects the rationalism of Maimonides. It responds explicitly to the commentaries of Rashi and Ibn Ezra, generally favoring the former. In the introduction, Nahmanides states his intention to comfort the Jews in exile.	**1270**
Thomas Aquinas* (1225–1274), Christian philosopher, completes his Summa Theologica in Paris. He presents an introduction to theology, doctrine, and morals that				**1272**

	A. General History	B. Jews in Europe	C. Jews in the Middle East and North Africa	D. Jewish Culture
1272	reveals close knowledge of Maimonides, Ibn Gabirol, and other Jewish philosophers.			
1274	Khubilai Khan* leads the Mongols in an unsuccessful attempt to invade Japan.	Thomas Aquinas* permits sovereigns to treat Jewish goods as their own property since "in consequence of their sin [of rejecting and crucifying Jesus] Jews were destined to perpetual servitude." Since those who benefit from Jewish property, however, are profiting from usury, Aquinas* encourages them "to compel Jews to work for their living . . . rather than to allow them to live in idleness and grow rich from usury."		Rabbi Joseph ben Abraham Gikatilla (1248–c.1325) of Spain completes his *Ginnat Egoz* (*The Garden of Nuts*), a mystical work dealing with the symbolism of the Hebrew alphabet and divine names. A student of Abraham ben Samuel Abulafia (1240–c.1290), he gains renown as a leading mystic and Kabbalist paving the way for the appearance of the Zohar. His most influential work is *Sha'arei Orah* (*Gates of Light*), which explains the mystical symbolism of the *sefirot* (divine emanations).
1275	Marco Polo* arrives in China.	King Edward I* of England issues the *Statutun de Judeismo* (Law regarding Jewry) prohibiting Jewish usury. No debts bearing interest are to be collected. Jews may reside only in those royal cities and boroughs in which there is an *archa*, i.e., a coffer for the deposit of Jewish bonds. Jews are permitted, however, to be merchants and craftsmen or cultivate lands that they may lease for ten years. The law permitting cultivation of lands is to expire in 1290.		
1276	Sultan Ya'qub,* founder of the Merinid dynasty, which rules the western Maghreb from 1269, transfers his capital to Fez, expanding the city beyond its walls.		A massacre of Jews takes place in Merinid Fez, Morocco, as the result of a rumor accusing a Jew of improper behavior toward a Muslim woman.	
1278			Pedro III* of Aragon (1276–1285) orders his army and navy to grant safe passage to Jews from Tripoli, thereby confirming continued Jewish settlement there.	
1279		Pedro III* compels Jews to attend sermons by friars in Spanish synagogues. This is in keeping with the bull issued by Pope Nicholas II (1277–1280) in 1278 instructing that preachers be sent all across Europe to convert the Jews. Pedro's* action leads to anti-Jewish riots.		The only known Hebrew translation of the popular legends of King Arthur is made by an anonymous translator from a now lost Italian source. The Hebrew manuscript later comes into the possession of the Vatican.

A. General History	B. Jews in Europe	C. Jews in the Middle East and North Africa	D. Jewish Culture	
The Catalonian nobility revolt against Pedro III.*	As a result of the rebellion by the Spanish nobility, Jewish officials are given responsibility for administration of taxes and finances, arms supply, and judiciary appointments. At the same time, however, every opportunity is taken to fine Jews for disobeying the laws governing interest. Abraham ben Samuel Abulafia (1240–c.1291), a Kabbalist who came to Italy from Spain via Palestine and Greece, goes to Rome upon being moved by a prophetic vision with the intention of urging Pope Nicholas III to account for and ameliorate the sufferings of the Jews. He is arrested and condemned to death. After a short stay in prison, he is released when the pope dies. Abraham was called a charlatan by Solomon ben Abraham Adret of Barcelona, the leading rabbinical authority of the times.			**1280**
	Rabbi Todros ben Joseph Abulafia of Toledo, Spain, calls for social and moral reforms. He proposes appointment of weight and measure inspectors and imposition of fines on anyone caught swearing or cursing. The community agrees to prohibit Jews from owning unmarried Muslim female slaves and employing unmarried Jewish women in order to avoid immoral behavior.			**1281**
	Pedro III* forbids the Dominicans from continuing their inquisition of a group of Barcelona Jews accused of hiding Jewish converts to Christianity. The king fears that success of the inquisition will result in fewer Jews who can be taxed by the royal treasury.	Riots break out against Jews in Baghdad. Sparked by *An Examination into the Inquiries of the Three Faiths* by Sa'd ben Kammuna (d. 1285), which contained passages critical of Islam, these riots spread and result in a purge of Jewish officials throughout Iraq and Iran.		**1284**
Philip IV* the Fair begins his rule of France. It will last until 1314.				**1285**
	The Jews of Munich are accused of murdering Christian children and drinking their blood.	The explorer Marco Polo* makes reference in his *Travels* to a Jewish community in China	Rabbi Moses de Leon (d. 1305), a mystic in Guadalajara, Spain, completes a commentary	**1286**

	A. General History	B. Jews in Europe	C. Jews in the Middle East and North Africa	D. Jewish Culture
1286			numerous enough to exert political influence.	on the Torah, the Zohar (The Book of Splendor). Presenting the Aramaic work as a copy of esoteric revelation from the 2nd-century rabbi Simeon bar Yohai, de Leon interprets the Torah in an allegorical, symbolic, mystical manner. Building on earlier Kabbalistic works, the Zohar deals with the nature of God; the secrets of the divine names; the nature and destiny of the human soul; the importance of the Torah; the mysteries of Creation, the Messiah, and redemption. The reputation of the Zohar will grow over the centuries and it remains the central text of Jewish mysticism.
1287		The king of Aragon issues a proclamation guaranteeing his protection to Jews coming to settle there.		
1288		The rulers of Naples issue their first expulsion edict against the Jews of southern Italy. They issue similar edicts against Jews under their rule in France.		
1289		King Edward I* of England orders the arrest of all the Jews of Gascony and the seizure of their property. They were then expelled. His motive seems to have been purely financial.	Both Jews and Christians serve in the Mongol administration in Iraq with Jewish influence reaching its peak under the rule of Arghun Khan* (1284–1291). He appoints Sa'd al-Dawla, a Jewish scholar and physician, vizier over all of the Ilkhanid state in 1289.	
1290		Edward I* issues an edict in July banishing all Jews from England. This is the first of the general expulsions of the Middle Ages, and more than 4,000 Jews will leave for France, Flanders, and Germany by November 1, All Saints' Day. Reasons for the expulsion include failure of previous efforts to restrict Jewish usury, insincerity of Jewish converts to Christianity, and growth of a new middle class, which makes Jews economically unnecessary.		
1291	Acre is destroyed, bringing an end to the crusader domination of Palestine.			Hillel ben Samuel (c.1220–c.1295), physician, talmudic scholar, and

A. General History	B. Jews in Europe	C. Jews in the Middle East and North Africa	D. Jewish Culture	

1291

D. Jewish Culture: philosopher who lived in Italy, completes *Tagmulei ha-Nefesh* (*The Rewards of the Soul*), in which he deals with the nature of the immortality of the soul. Influenced by the works of Averroës* and Thomas Aquinas,* he nevertheless remains faithful to the Jewish tradition.

1292

A. General History: Roger Bacon* (c.1214–1292), a Franciscan scientist and theologian who arduously pursued experimentation in science and is the first European to describe the process of making gunpowder, dies.

1293

B. Jews in Europe: The destruction of most of the Jewish communities in the kingdom of Naples, which had begun in 1290, is culminated. This destruction of the cradle of Ashkenazic culture in southern Italy is accompanied by the conversion of many Jews to Christianity.

1295

A. General History: The Ilkhanid dynasty in Iraq becomes permanently Muslim, returning Jews and Christians to their subservient *dhimmi* status.

B. Jews in Europe: The Jewish communities of Castile experience a wave of messianic fervor that culminates in the appearance of the "Prophet of Avila." Though illiterate, he is said to experience visions and revelations in which an angel dictates *The Book of Wondrous Wisdom* to him. The entire literary genre of popular eschatology is condemned by the leading Spanish rabbi, Solomon ibn Adret (c.1233–1310).

1296

The Jewish Population in Western and Central Europe 1300 CE		
Country	*Jews*	*General Population*
France (including Avignon)	100,000	14,000,000
Holy Roman Empire (including Switzerland and the Low Countries)	100,000	12,000,000
Italy	50,000	11,000,000
Spain (Castile, Aragon, and Navarre)	150,000	5,500,000
Portugal	40,000	600,000
Poland-Lithuania	5,000	500,000
Hungary	5,000	400,000
Total	450,000	44,000,000

D. Jewish Culture: The community of Nuremberg begins recording communal entries in a *Memorbuch* (*Memorial Book*). Running up to 1392, it contains lists of communal benefactors and a martyrology that summarizes persecutions in France and Germany from the First Crusade of 1096 to the Black Death of 1349. Memorial books abound especially in Ashkenazic communities, and their lists of local martyrs and records of persecutions are read in the synagogue during memorial services.

	A. General History	B. Jews in Europe	C. Jews in the Middle East and North Africa	D. Jewish Culture
1298		A German knight named Rindfleisch,* in response to a series of blood libels and accusations of Jewish desecration of the Host, begins to instigate the massacre of thousands of Jews in 146 communities in southern and central Germany by going from town to town inciting the burghers to attack the Jews. Among the communities affected are Rottingen, Wurzberg, Nuremberg, and Bavaria. Emperor Albert I* of Austria tries to contain the massacres, but his proclamation is largely ignored.		
1299	Mongols invade Syria with help of Armenians and Druze.			
1300		A synagogue is erected by the Jews of Sopron, Hungary. A second synagogue will be erected nearby in about 1350. The street will become known as Jews' Street. The Jews will be expelled in 1526. Both synagogues will be rediscovered in the 1950s and 1960s. Pope Boniface VIII (1294–1303) orders the expulsion of Jewish and Christian usurers from Avignon. Boniface VIII's most important decision affecting the Jews is that Jews who are baptized, even in infancy, must remain Christians.		An extensive rabbinic commentary on the Torah is compiled in Yemen by David ben Amram Adani. This Midrash Hagadol (Great Midrash) for the most part excerpts classical rabbinic texts but contributes original interpretations, too. In the 19th and 20th centuries, scholars will sometimes compare this work to correct faulty editions of the classical texts it quotes.
1301	The Mamluks institute a policy of strict enforcement of the Pact of 'Umar and add further restrictions against non-Muslims. Yellow turbans must be worn by Jews and no non-Muslim home may be higher than that of a Muslim.	A document from Cologne refers to "the leaders and the Warden [parnass] and all the community of the Jews" speaking together. Well-defined Jewish institutions of self-government emerge in central Europe in the 13th century, increasing the power of the community over the individual. The non-Jewish burghers of Breslau, in their attempt to monopolize retail trade, prohibit Jews from retail sale of textiles. A similar prohibition will be introduced in Warsaw in 1461. Attacks on Jewish		

A. General History	B. Jews in Europe	C. Jews in the Middle East and North Africa	D. Jewish Culture	
	retail trade will peak in the late 15th and early 16th centuries. Jews are also engaged in foreign trade, which is more profitable and less controlled.			**1301**
Dante Alighieri* (1265–1321), the great Italian poet, is exiled from Florence when the supporters of Pope Boniface VIII (1294–1303) gain power. His *Divine Comedy* describes the journey through hell, purgatory, and up to paradise. In his journey through hell, he encounters heretics, usurers, and counterfeiters, but mentions no Jews among them.	With the ascent of Ferdinand IV* (1302–1312) of Castile, Christian opposition to Jewish courtiers mounts. Ferdinand IV* refuses to submit to pressure to discontinue using Jews as tax farmers and courtiers because he fears the financial loss that will result.			**1302**
	Pope Clement V becomes the first pope to try to force the Jews to stop lending money for interest to Christians by threatening economic boycott.		Under the leadership of Rabbi Solomon ben Adret (c.1250–1327), a great German talmudist and communal leader, a proclamation of 36 rabbis is issued prohibiting the study of philosophy and natural sciences (except medicine) to anyone under 25 years old. The ban is also supported by Rabbi Asher ben Yehiel in Germany.	**1305**
	Philip IV* expels the Jews of France. They number approximately 100,000 at that time.			**1306**
	The body of Rabbi Meir ben Baruch of Rothenburg (1215–1293) is ransomed 14 years after his death and buried in Worms. A leading talmudist and legal authority of his generation, he was imprisoned by the emperor in the fortress of Enzisheim. The rabbi, who died in prison, would not permit the Jewish community to ransom him alive for fear that it would lead to repeated imprisonment of Jews.			**1307**
The seat of the papacy moves to Avignon due to political conditions in Rome. The tenor of the papacy is overwhelmingly French until it moves back to Rome in 1377.	The Order of Teutonic Knights, rulers of East Prussia since the 13th century, prohibits Jews from entering the territory.	The Tunisian treasury confiscates goods of Majorcan Jews because of hostilities between King Jaime II* (1291–1327) of Majorca and Tunis.		**1309**

	A. General History	B. Jews in Europe	C. Jews in the Middle East and North Africa	D. Jewish Culture
1310				The Golden Haggadah, the earliest extant illuminated Sephardic Haggadah, is believed to have been executed in Barcelona between 1310 and 1320. It contains 15 full-page miniatures illustrating the biblical story from Adam to the Exodus from Egypt, in addition to the text of the Passover Haggadah.
1312		A Spanish ecclesiastical council is held in Zamora. It demands enforcement of laws prohibiting Jews from holding public office, total segregation of Jews from Christians, distinct Jewish clothing, prohibitions against building new synagogues, and other laws. While the synod's impact is unclear, it does reflect growing animosity toward Jews.		
1314	Revolts against Philip IV* in France lead to the granting of a variety of charters of liberties to clergy, nobility, and bourgeoisie in each major province and region of the country.			
1315		Jews expelled from France in 1306 are invited to return. Unlike earlier expulsions, only a few return.		
1317				Joseph ben Abba Mari ibn Kaspi (c.1279–1340) of Spain writes *Sefer ha-Sod* (*The Book of the Secret*). A great admirer of Maimonides, he rejects the popular allegorical method in his Bible commentaries and believes that Aristotle's* philosophy was not only consonant with but was derived from Jewish sources.
1321		Around this date Abner of Burgos, a Spanish Jewish Kabbalist and scholar, converts to Christianity. He becomes known as Alfonso of Valladoid and his anti-Jewish polemics constitute the earliest outline for the plan against the Jews, which was carried out in 1391. Another Jewish apostate, Don Solomon Halevi,		Immanuel ben Solomon of Rome (1260–c.1328, Immanuel the Jew) leaves Rome for northern Italy, probably as a result of a papal edict of expulsion. His most important work is the *Mahberot* (*Compositions*), a collection of poems, which is a fusion of Italian, Latin, and Jewish cultures. His last *mahberet*, *Tofet and Eden* (*Hell and Paradise*),

A. General History	B. Jews in Europe	C. Jews in the Middle East and North Africa	D. Jewish Culture	
	becomes Bishop Pablo de Santa Maria of Burgos, another vocal opponent of Judaism.		an imaginary journey to heaven and hell, is modeled on Dante's* *Divine Comedy.* He never knew Dante,* and his heaven includes rabbis, patriarchs, and righteous Gentiles.	1321
	Charles IV* expels the French Jews for the second time.		Estori ha-Parhi (1280–1355), first topographer of Palestine, who was born in France and settled in Palestine in 1312, writes *Sefer Kaftor va-Ferah* (*A Knob and a Flower*), which presents the results of his travels throughout the country. It determines the names of towns and villages, describes Palestinian geography and natural history, and identifies some 180 ancient sites.	1322
The established guildsmen of Florence pass a law prohibiting all associations not already chartered. It is one indication of the growing power of the guilds in Europe.				1324
		Jews are called to Peking to assist the imperial army at a time when the power of the Mongolian dynasty is declining. Jews are called again in 1354. They are referred to in the documents as *Djuttudu* (*Yehudim*). Elsewhere in 1704 they are called *Tiao-kin-Kiao,* "the sect who extracts the sinew," referring to the biblically derived law making the hindquarter inedible until the sciatic nerve is removed.	Levi ben Gershom (1288–1344), philosopher, Bible commentator, mathematician, and astronomer, completes his major philosophical work, *Milhamot Adonai* (*The Book of the Wars of the Lord*). The last great Jewish Aristotelian, Gersonides breaks with his teachers by applying his belief in the dynamic advancement of science and knowledge to traditional problems of immortality of the soul and the nature of heavenly bodies. Little is known of his life in his native France. His views expose him to accusations of heresy.	1329
The Kamakura shogunate is overthrown in Japan.	Casimir* the Great (1333–1370) comes to power in Poland and brings with him a sympathetic attitude toward Jews, whom he sees as more loyal and dependable than the German burghers in his struggle for power against the Church. Polish Jews benefit from the trend toward Poland's unification achieved by Casimir.*			1333

	A. General History	B. Jews in Europe	C. Jews in the Middle East and North Africa	D. Jewish Culture
1335	The Franciscans establish their first monastery in Jerusalem.			Jacob ben Asher (c.1270–1340), halakhic authority, completes his *Arbaah Turim* (*Four Columns*). In 1303 he moved to Toledo from Germany. His legal code is divided into four sections dealing with daily practices and holidays, permitted and prohibited foods, family law, and civil law. It becomes the accepted code for German Jews and the foundation for later popular codes.
1336	Pedro IV* (1336–1387) reigns in Aragon. His policy toward the Jews of Spain is generally favorable and a reflection of his own financial interests.			
1346			Ibn Batuta,* an Arabian envoy, makes reference to Jews in China.	
1347		The first ritual murder accusation takes place against Jews in Poland.		
1348	The Black Death reaches Europe from central Asia. Provence sells the city of Avignon to the French States of the Holy See. It remains under their control until 1791, during the French Revolution.	Though the Black Death strikes Jews as well as non-Jews, the Jews are accused of causing it by poisoning the wells. Despite the attempts by Pope Clement VI in Avignon, Carl IV* of Germany, and King Pedro IV* of Aragon to defend the Jews against the mobs, many perish. The plague is a decisive turning point in the political, economic, and cultural status of the Jews in Castile and Aragon. King Alfonso XI* of Castile prohibits Spanish Jews and Muslims from lending money for interest or collecting their debts. They are permitted to purchase land. The law is opposed by both Jews and Christians, and in 1351 the Cortes (Parliament) of Castile will call for its abolition.		
1350				At about this time, Samson ben Isaac of Chinon (c.1300–c.1350), French Tosafist, writes *Sefer Keritut* (*The Book of a Love Covenant*). It is the first work on talmudic methodology written by a

A. General History	B. Jews in Europe	C. Jews in the Middle East and North Africa	D. Jewish Culture	
			Tosafist. It will first be published in Constantinople in 1515 and then be frequently republished.	**1350**
Boccaccio* (1313–1375), Italian scholar and poet, completes the *Decameron*. Acknowledging both man's power and limitations, it portrays alternately tragic and comic views of life and helps lay the foundations for the humanism of the Renaissance.				**1353**
	The Jewish Council of Aragon Communities appeals to the king and to Pope Clement VI to defend them against Christian mob violence and to issue a papal decree making it impossible to blame entire communities if one member harms a Christian. The most daring request is that the pope not allow the inquisition into heresy to be applied to the Jews, since "it is impossible to classify as heresy on the part of the Jew what he holds to be justified according to his own faith." Jews are readmitted to Zurich after being expelled in the wake of the Black Death. Though persecutions against Jews are widespread in Switzerland in this era, most localities readmit them within a few decades.	Under Sultan al-Malik al-Salih* new restrictions are imposed on non-Muslims in Egypt–Syria. Jewish women may appear in public only with yellow garb and are barred from bathing with Muslim women. Turbans worn by *dhimmi* (Christian and Jewish) men are limited in size, and these men are forced to wear special neck rings in public baths.		**1354**
Charles IV* issues the Golden Bull in Germany establishing the Holy Roman Emperor's election by the seven rulers of the electoral states. The bull transforms the empire from a monarchy into an aristocratic federation.				**1356**
	Don Samuel Halevi Abulafia (c.1320–c.1361) builds the El Transito synagogue in Toledo, Spain. As finance minister and advisor to King Pedro* the Cruel (1350–1368) of Castile, he is also responsible for negotiating a political treaty with Portugal in 1358. He dies in prison in 1360–1361 though the reason for his			**1357**

143

	A. General History	B. Jews in Europe	C. Jews in the Middle East and North Africa	D. Jewish Culture
1357		arrest and torture is not known. After the expulsion of 1492, the synagogue is transformed into a church. It has been restored and since the 1960s is a Jewish museum.		
1360	A peace treaty is signed between Abu Ishaq Ibrahim,* sultan of Tunis and Bougie, and Pedro IV* of Aragon.		Catalan and Tunisian Jews are mentioned repeatedly in the peace treaty between Tunis and Aragon. Promises of protection and safe passage attest to the growing involvement of Jews in trade between these regions.	
1362				Rabbi Moses ben Joshua Narboni (c.1290–after 1362) of Spain completes his commentary on Maimonides' *Guide for the Perplexed*. An ardent follower of Averroës'* rationalist system, Narboni believes that the Bible has one level of meaning for the masses and another esoteric one for the intellectual elite.
1364	The University of Cracow is founded.	The University of Cracow is located on the Jewish street of Cracow in houses that had been bought or requisitioned from Jews. The *kampsor* (banker of students) was a Jewish moneylender appointed by Casimir* the Great, who set the maximum rate of annual interest for student loans at 25%.		
1367		The Jews of Hungary are expelled. The Jews of Carpentras, in Provence, build a small two-story synagogue. The women are accommodated in the basement, with the men on the floor above where the ark is located. A matzah bakery and ritual bath are built within the immediate vicinity. The synagogue, as well as a neighboring one constructed in Cavaillon in 1499, will be periodically restored and remain in use today.		
1370		Kings and princes in Saragossa end a 30-year policy of granting communal tax exemptions		In Damascus, Joseph ben Eliezer Bonfils (Tov Elem) writes a supercommentary on the Torah commentary

144

A. General History	B. Jews in Europe	C. Jews in the Middle East and North Africa	D. Jewish Culture	
	and bestowing communal offices on favored Jewish craftsmen. The policy had long been condemned by the duly appointed and elected Jewish communal officials.		of Abraham ibn Ezra (1089–1164). *Zafenat Pa'ne'ah* (*Resolution of Enigmas*) challenges Mosaic authorship of portions of the Torah and defends Ibn Ezra against charges of heresy.	1370
	Rabbi Isaac ben Sheshet Perfet (1326–1408) becomes rabbi of Saragossa, Spain. His responsa deal with religious and social questions addressed to him by Jews throughout the world. They reflect a desire for stricter observance of religious law and concern for the behavior of communal administrators.			1372
	The *Catalan Atlas*, an important work of cartography, is prepared by Abraham and Judah Crescas in Spain using data provided by Marco Polo.* Judah is hired by Henry* the Navigator (1394–1460) to produce maps at the royal school for mariners at Cape Saint Vincent. Jewish artists in Spain also work on illuminated manuscripts and the mixing of colors.			1376
	The Cortes of Burgos revokes the law imposing collective fines for the murder of a Jew and thereby eliminates a major deterrent to anti-Jewish mob violence in Spain.			1377
Wenceslaus IV* becomes German emperor. Peace loving but an incompetent ruler, he is deposed in 1400.	The archdeacon of Ecija, Ferrant Martinez,* begins preaching vehemently anti-Jewish sermons in Seville, calling for the destruction of all synagogues and total isolation of the Jewish community.			1378
	King John I* of Castile prohibits Spanish Jews from reciting the passage condemning heretics in the *Amidah* prayer, from judging Jewish criminal offenses, and from circumcising Muslim slaves.			1380
	The Jews of Strasbourg are expelled.			1381

	A. General History	B. Jews in Europe	C. Jews in the Middle East and North Africa	D. Jewish Culture
1383		The government empowers leaders of the Jewish communities of Aragon to sentence *malshinim* (informers) to exile, mutilation, or death solely at their discretion, with the sentence to be carried out by royal officials.		
1384		Jews are expelled from Lucerne. The rise of the artisan classes, combined with a new tolerance for Christian moneylenders who charge interest, undermine the foundations of Jewish life. The Jews are also expelled from Berne (1408 and 1427), Fribourg (1428), Zurich (1436), and Geneva (1490).		
1385		King Wenceslaus IV,* concerned with restoring his income from German Jews, reaches an agreement with the League of Swabian Cities whereby the king would cancel a quarter of all the debts owed by the Christians to Jews and the cities would pay the king 40,000 guilders. In many cities Jews not only lose their money as a result but are imprisoned and have their property confiscated.		Rabbi Shem Tov ben Isaac ibn Shaprut writes *Even Bochan* (*The Touch Stone*), a work representative of Jewish apologetics in 14th-century Spain. In addition to answering the anti-Jewish arguments raised by Christians, it specifically responds to the doctrines of the apostate Abner of Burgos.
1386		An attack by the lower classes within the Jewish community of Barcelona against the long-standing oligarchy of a few aristocratic families proves successful. In smaller communities where the lower classes are usually without representation, social tensions continue to grow.		
1387	Geoffrey Chaucer* (c.1343–1400), English poet, begins writing his unfinished *The Canterbury Tales*. They are a collection of stories told by pilgrims of diverse class and background on their way to Canterbury. Poland and Lithuania unite and give boyars and clerics total exemption from state service, personal service, and certain taxes, thereby placing more burden on the peasants. Poland absorbs Galicia.	Geoffrey Chaucer's* *Canterbury Tales* includes "The Prioress's Tale," which centers around the murder of an innocent young Christian boy by wicked Jews. Though the Jews had been expelled from England in 1290, Chaucer's* tale refers to the story of Hugh of Lincoln, one of the earliest blood libels in Europe.		

<table>
<tr><td></td><td>A charter of rights and liberties is granted to the Jews of Grodno. Unlike Polish Jewry, the Jews of Lithuania are full burghers and enjoy all economic and settlement rights. They share equal status with the townsfolk in commerce, crafts, and agriculture. In Grodno, they are centrally situated next to the town citadel by the river in the municipal market.</td><td></td><td>**1389**</td></tr>
</table>

A. General History	B. Jews in Europe	C. Jews in the Middle East and North Africa	D. Jewish Culture	
	A charter of rights and liberties is granted to the Jews of Grodno. Unlike Polish Jewry, the Jews of Lithuania are full burghers and enjoy all economic and settlement rights. They share equal status with the townsfolk in commerce, crafts, and agriculture. In Grodno, they are centrally situated next to the town citadel by the river in the municipal market.			**1389**
	Anti-Jewish riots break out in Seville and spread throughout Spain leaving synagogues destroyed and Jews killed or forced to convert. In 1390 both the king, John I* of Castile, and the archbishop had died. The former was succeeded by a minor and the latter by Ferrant Martinez,* a Jew-hater. Economic hardship, famine, and high prices also contribute to the anti-Jewish atmosphere.	Refugees from anti-Jewish riots in Spain settle in Algeria. Rabbi Isaac ben Sheshet Perfet (1326–1408), Rabbi Simon ben Semah Duran (1361–1444), and other leading rabbinic authorities make Algeria the spiritual center of North Africa (the Maghreb).		**1391**
	King John I* of Aragon (1387–1396) directs the reestablishment of the Jewish community of Barcelona by allotting a new residential area and synagogue and restoring all the earlier privileges in an effort to bolster the revenues and honor of the city. Very few Jews return to Barcelona due to the strong opposition of the local Christian population. The city council of Cracow rules that a Jew who bought a house from a Christian must sign a promise to resell it only to a Christian. This policy is designed to limit the growth of the Jewish population by limiting the availability of housing.			**1392**
	Pesach-Peter, a German Jewish convert to Christianity, attacks the *Aleinu* prayer as derogatory of Christianity. As a result of the ensuing controversy, Rabbi Yom Tov Lipmann Muelhausen is imprisoned and composes a defense of Jewish ethics, the Bible, and Talmud called *Sefer ha-Nitsahon* (*The Book of Triumph*).			**1394**

	A. General History	B. Jews in Europe	C. Jews in the Middle East and North Africa	D. Jewish Culture
1397	The Medici bank of Florence is established with branches in Rome, Naples, Venice, and Genoa. It spreads throughout Europe (Bruges, London, Avignon, Milan, and Lyons) in the 15th century and soon controls production from raw materials as well as finance and exchange.			Profiat Duran, known also as Isaac ben Moses ha-Levi Efodi (d. c.1414), completes *Kelimmat ha-Goyyim* (*The Shame of the Gentiles*). As one of the many Spanish Jewish converts to Christianity after the persecutions of 1391, Duran later returns to Judaism, attacking Christianity and defending Judaism in this very popular work.
1399		Anti-Jewish measures lead to the establishment of Italian Jewish synods to ensure centralized leadership of the community. These synods are called throughout the 15th and early 16th centuries to solve special problems.		
1407		Although anti-Jewish riots break out in Poland, the economic and social success of Polish and Lithuanian Jewry continues to lead German Jews to believe Poland to be the safest place for them.		
1410				Rabbi Hasdai ben Abraham Crescas of Spain (c.1340–c.1410) completes *Or Adonai* (*The Light of the Lord*). In this critique of Aristotelianism, the rationalism of Maimonides and Gersonides, Crescas discusses the major philosophical questions and concludes that love of God rather than knowledge of God is the ultimate good and goal of the Commandments.
1412		Laws are introduced in Spain restricting the places where Jews may live in an attempt to isolate and confine them. This begins the Jewish emigration from Spain to North Africa, other Muslim countries, and Palestine.		
1413		Disputation at Tortosa begins. Called by Pope Benedict XIII as an attempt to convert the Jews, the disputation revolves around accusations that the Talmud blasphemes against Christianity. Drawing on		

A. General History	B. Jews in Europe	C. Jews in the Middle East and North Africa	D. Jewish Culture	
	arguments taken largely from Raymond Martini's* *Pugio Fidei* (*Dagger of Faith*), the Jewish convert to Christianity Joshua Lorki uses rabbinic literature in his attempt to prove that Jesus is the Messiah.			**1413**
John Huss* (c.1369–1415) is burned at the stake. Founder of an influential Christian reform movement that emphasizes the Hebrew Bible and rejects the adoration of saints and relics, he and his followers are accused of Judaizing.	Antipope Benedict XIII in Avignon issues a bull prohibiting the employment of Jews in the making of crucifixes and other Christian ceremonial objects. The bull is evidence that Jews had heretofore participated in such arts and crafts.			**1415**
	Delegates from Jewish communities in Italy meet in Bologna and Forli (1418) to respond to the anti-Jewish preaching of the Franciscans. These meetings result in pro-Jewish bulls by Pope Martin V (1417–1431), who tries to control their preaching.			**1416**
		Regulations against both Christian and Jewish *dhimmis* in Egypt are intensified in retaliation for the subjugation of Muslims in the Christian kingdom of Abyssinia.		**1419**
	From the beginning of the 1420s, the Hussite revolt in Bohemia and Moravia leads to increased suspicion and religious zealotry against the Jews of central Europe. A Polish church council in Kalish resolves to limit the interest rate on money lent by Jews and to forbid Jews from lending money on mortgages. These stipulations are later incorporated into Polish governmental legislation.			**1420**
Peking is established as the capital of China.	The Jews of Vienna are massacred and later banned from the city. Their property is confiscated by Duke Albert V,* who is badly in need of money. Jews are also expelled from Linz (1421), Cologne (1424), Augsburg (1439), Bavaria (1442 and 1450), and the crown cities of Moravia (1454).			**1421**

	A. General History	B. Jews in Europe	C. Jews in the Middle East and North Africa	D. Jewish Culture
1424		Alfonso V* grants a special "privilege" to the municipality of Barcelona, forever banning the establishment of a Jewish community there.		
1426	The Franciscan chapel on Mt. Zion in Palestine is seized by the Muslim authorities. Local Jews are blamed for instigating the action.			
1428			Transportation of Jews to Palestine comes to a virtual halt by order of the pope. Since sea traffic with Palestine flows through the port cities of Italy, the pope has a major impact on that traffic.	Rabbi Joseph Albo of Spain (c.1380–1444) completes *Sefer ha-Ikkarim* (*The Book of Dogmas*). Based in large part on the works of Hasdai Crescas and Simeon ben Tzemah Duran, Albo succeeds in systematizing and popularizing his philosophy of Judaism as revolving around three basic principles: God's existence, revelation, and reward and punishment.
1429		Pope Martin V issues a bull forbidding the Franciscans to preach against Jews, infringe on their religious rights, interrupt their relations with their neighbors, or exclude them from normal activities. Though it is a sweeping measure of protection, it remains largely unenforced.		
1430		The synagogue of Tomar, northeast of Lisbon, is believed to have been built between 1430 and 1460. It will be used until the expulsion of 1496. In 1922, a Jewish mining engineer from Poland, Samuel Schwarz (1880–1953), will purchase the building and open it as a museum.		
1438			The first *mellah* is established in Fez. This Jewish area is located next to the government administrative center to protect the Jews from mob violence. This *mellah* becomes the model for others in Morocco, though those established in the 16th and 17th centuries are designed to ostracize rather than protect the Jews.	
1439		A Jewish bank opens in Fano under a detailed agreement with the city		

A. General History	B. Jews in Europe	C. Jews in the Middle East and North Africa	D. Jewish Culture	
	fathers. This *condotta* requires an investment of 3,000 ducats capital by the Jewish owner. As a rule, the prescribed interest rate of Italian Jewish banks varies between 15% and 25% and is much lower than rates set by Christian moneylenders.			**1439**
	The Jewish community of Troki, Lithuania, is the only one to be put under the Magdeburg law. This law puts German burghers and their Polish followers in a privileged position that almost totally exempts them from the jurisdiction of the local authorities and empowers them to resist Jewish competition.			**1441**
	A synod of the Jewish leaders of communities in Castile is held in Valladoid. It deals with compulsory taxation to support Torah study, appointment of judges and other functionaries, and the measures to be taken against informers and those who appeal to non-Jewish courts. Pope Eugenius IV (1431–1447) issues an edict forbidding Italian Jews to build new synagogues, lend money for interest, hold public office, or testify against Christians. Though originally holding a favorable attitude toward Jews, Eugenius changed his view probably as a result of the severe attitude toward Christian heresies adopted by the Council of Basle (1431–1437). Jews respond to the anti-Jewish edicts of Pope Eugenius IV by meeting in Tivoli and later in Ravenna (1443). Their lack of success causes many Jews to move to other areas in Italy.			**1442**
			Isaac, or Mordecai, Nathan, a rabbi and physician in Arles, compiles the first concordance to the Hebrew Bible. Primarily for the use of Jews in disputations with Christian scholars,	**1445**

	A. General History	B. Jews in Europe	C. Jews in the Middle East and North Africa	D. Jewish Culture
1445				Nathan lists occurrences of Hebrew words according to the Christian order of biblical books and introduces the 13th-century Christian chapter divisions into a Jewish work on the Bible. Nathan's concordance, *Me'ir Nativ* (*Illuminator of the Path*), will serve as the basis for later Christian and Jewish Bible concordances.
1447	The Poles choose the Lithuanian Grand Duke Casimir* as their king thereby uniting Poland and Lithuania.			
1448			The Mamluk sultan Jaqmaq* issues a decree prohibiting Jewish and Christian physicians from treating Muslim patients.	
1449		Violent clashes break out in Toledo between "old" and New Christians, or Marranos. The latter include many Jews who convert under pressure and are never accepted by the larger Christian community. Though never officially recognized by the Church, the concept of *Limpiezza di sangre* (purity of blood) had begun to develop among the "old" Christians in their attempt to distinguish between themselves and the Marranos. The Jews of Bavaria are expelled.		
1450	Pope Nicholas V founds the Vatican Library.			
1453	The Ottomans under Muhammad II* capture Constantinople. They institute millets for non-Muslims thereby dividing the Orthodox, Armenian, and Jewish populations along religious lines and giving each community's religious leaders sole authority over the secular and religious affairs of the community.	The Jews are expelled from Breslau as a result of a ritual murder libel. The libel is encouraged by John* of Capistrano (1386–1456) who preached hatred against the Jews throughout Italy from 1417 onward and then extended his efforts from Austria and Germany to Poland in his attempt to defend the true Christian faith against the Hussite heresy.	The conquest of Constantinople by the Turks increases the role of Polish Jewish merchants who trade in textiles, grain, cattle, and produce across the vital overland route through Poland, linking the Ottoman Empire with central and western Europe. Ottoman attitudes toward the Jews, with the exception of the *jizya* (poll tax), are quite liberal but grow worse with the breakdown of central authority toward the end of the century. Rabbi Moshe Kapsali, chief rabbi of Constantinople, is	

A. General History	B. Jews in Europe	C. Jews in the Middle East and North Africa	D. Jewish Culture	
		confirmed in his office by the Ottomans. Jewish communities must pay a special tax, *ravakcesi* (rabbi's asper), for the privilege of having a rabbinic authority in the various communities of the Ottoman Empire.		1453
	A dispute arises concerning the German Jewish synod of Bingen. It is just one of many conflicts that arise with the trend toward centralized leadership after the Black Death of 1348 and the resulting massacres. Centralization is seen as a threat to the authority of individual local sages.			1455
Johann Gutenberg* prints the first surviving dated book in Mainz, a Latin translation of Psalms.				1457
			The Italian Jew Fra Mauro prepares a famous map that places Jerusalem at the center of the world, a practice discontinued by the late Renaissance.	1459
Ivan III* the Great (1462–1505) rules Russia.	Pope Pius II praises the burghers of Frankfurt for forcing the Jews to live in an area beyond the city walls and apart from the Christian community. *Monti di pieta* (piety funds) are established in northern and central Italy. Advocated by the Franciscan monks, these public institutions provide interest-free loans in places where Jews are practicing moneylending. Jewish loan-bankers become economically superfluous and are more easily subject to expulsion. Without interest, however, the funds soon dissipate and by the beginning of the 16th century the pope permits them to charge a low rate of interest.			1462
	A papal legate arouses the Polish population to set off on a new crusade against Turkey. When a mob unites with the crusaders to organize a pogrom against the Jews of Cracow, King Casimir IV* fines the city council heavily to guarantee that peace prevails.			1463

	A. General History	B. Jews in Europe	C. Jews in the Middle East and North Africa	D. Jewish Culture
1464				A Chair of Hebrew is established at the University of Bologna. The revival of Hebrew study is motivated not only by theological considerations, but also by the secular interest in antiquity that characterizes the Italian Renaissance.
1465	The Merinid dynasty, which has ruled Morocco since 1269, comes to an end.		The appointment of a Jew, Aaron ben Batash, to the vizierate under the Merinid sultan Abd-al Haqq* leads to the former's death and to anti-Jewish riots and massacres in Fez and throughout Morocco.	
1468				Joseph ben Meshullam writes a satire, *Alilot Devarim*, in Italy. The author explains the title to mean "words of battle and anger." A convinced rationalist, he condemns mysticism, superstitious customs, and pilpul, the method of talmudic study then gaining in popularity.
1470				Isaac ben Moses Arama (c.1420–1494), Spanish rabbi and philosopher, writes *Akedat Yitzhak* (*Binding of Isaac*), a philosophical and allegorical commentary on the Torah. It becomes popular and influential, dealing with such major philosophical questions as faith and reason, allegory, articles of faith, the relation of scripture to philosophy, providence, and the immortality of the soul.
1471	Muhammad al-Shaykh al-Wattasi* comes to power in Morocco and rules until 1554.	Secularization of the papacy reaches its climax with the rise of Pope Sixtus IV leaving the Jews of central and northern Italy free from persecution. Protection of Jewish life, property, and business affairs also guarantees a continual source of tax revenues for the papal treasury.	Jews who had earlier fled to Spain from Morocco are welcomed back under the Wattasids' rule. Spanish and Portuguese Jews will also be welcomed here when they are expelled from Spain and Portugal in 1492 and 1496, but there will be conflict between them and the established Jewish community.	
1473			Muslim fanatics destroy the Jerusalem synagogue and the authorities demand heavy payment from the Jewish community in exchange for permission to rebuild it.	The first two Hebrew presses, one in Reggio di Calabria and the other in Pieva da Saca, are established. Other Hebrew presses in Italy are founded in Naples and Mantua. Early in the 1480s the Soncino family will begin es-

A. General History	B. Jews in Europe	C. Jews in the Middle East and North Africa	D. Jewish Culture	
			tablishing Hebrew presses in Italy and later in Constantinople and Salonika.	1473
	The Jews of Trent are tortured and expelled as the result of a blood libel inspired by the preaching of the Franciscan, Bernardino da Feltre. The missing Christian child, Simon,* is canonized in 1582. In 1965 the Church withdraws this proclamation of sainthood and acknowledges that a judicial error had been committed against the Jews of Trent in this trial.		Judah Messer Leon, Italian rabbi, scholar, and man of letters, writes *Sefer Nofet Tzufim* (*The Book of the Honeycomb's Flow*), a treatise on Hebrew style, applying categories of rhetoric derived from Greek and Latin authors to classical Jewish—mainly biblical—literature. In addition to this volume, Judah writes works on philosophy, science, and general Judaica.	1475
	Pope Sixtus IV authorizes Ferdinand* and Isabella,* rulers of Spain, to organize an Inquisition to extirpate false Christians.		Abraham Zacuto (1452–c.1515), Spanish astronomer and historian, completes *Ha-Hibbur ha-Gadol* (*The Large Treatise*), his major astronomical work. It is translated into Spanish, Latin, and Arabic. The world explorers Christopher Columbus* and Vasco da Gama* are influenced by Zacuto and his work.	1478
	Queen Isabella* of Castile instructs her court painter to prohibit Jews from painting the figures of Jesus or Mary. Spanish Jews sculpt Christian figures and are engaged in the making of crucifixes.			1480
	The earliest auto-da-fé of the Spanish Inquisition takes place in Seville. After the judicial sentence is pronounced, the "heretics" are turned over to the secular authorities who burn the victims at the stake. The Church does not want to be formally associated with the shedding of blood.	The Jewish traveler Joseph di Montagna of Italy visits Safed. He writes that there are 300 Jewish households within the city and surrounding villages. Most of the Jews in the Galilee are vendors of cheese, oil, spices, and fruit.		1481
	The Jews are expelled from all of Andalusia. With the appointment of the Dominican Tomas de Torquemada as inquisitor-general of both Castile and Aragon, the measures taken against Jewish converts suspected of secretly adhering to Jewish practices become increasingly severe.			1483
The Angevin rule in England ends, and the Tudors rise to power.	The Jews of Cracow, under pressure from the non-Jewish merchants and			1485

	A. General History	B. Jews in Europe	C. Jews in the Middle East and North Africa	D. Jewish Culture
1485		artisans, sign an agreement with the townsfolk renouncing their participation in commerce and restricting themselves to moneylending and trade in abandoned pledges and the handicrafts made by poor Jewish women. It is the success of the Jews in every branch of commerce that leads to the increased tension between them and the townsfolk. In 1495 the Jews will be expelled from Cracow.		
1486	The Florentine philosopher, poet, and scholar Pico della Mirandola* (1463–1494) writes *Oration on the Dignity of Man*, which synthesizes the works of earlier philosophers.	Luis de Santangel (d. 1498), comptroller general to Ferdinand* and Isabella* of Spain, and a descendant of a *converso* family, meets Christopher Columbus* and influences the Spanish monarchs to support his explorations. He will lend considerable sums to finance Columbus'* historic voyage of 1492 resulting in the discovery of the American continent. Another *converso*, Gabriel Sanchez* (d. 1505), who will be treasurer of the kingdom of Aragon, will also assist Columbus.*		
1488		Obadiah of Bertinoro (c.1450–c.1516), Italian rabbi and Mishnah commentator, writes a letter describing the social and economic condition of Jews in Palermo, Sicily. They are "poor craftsmen . . . copper and iron smiths and porters and men engaged in all kinds of heavy work. They are despised by the gentiles, being all ragged and filthy. . . . They must wear a red cloth. . . . They are required to work for the king . . . dragging the fishing boats ashore, building up embankments, or things of that kind." Later in the year he emigrates to Palestine, where he becomes the leader of the Jewish community. There, too, he writes of widespread Jewish poverty.		The first complete edition of the Hebrew Bible is printed in Soncino, Italy. It is the work of Abraham ben Hayyim, Italian pioneer of Hebrew printing from Pesaro, whose services were secured by the Soncino family, noted printers of Hebrew works. The edition is vocalized with cantillation.
1489			Obadiah of Bertinoro writes of Jews of Aden who came to Jerusalem: " and they tell that there are many large Jewish communities . . . those people are inclined to be black . . . they possess no	

tractates of the Talmud
. . . all of them are versed
in Maimonides.''

1489

The Jews of Ravenna, in
northern Italy, are expelled
and their synagogue is
destroyed at the instigation
of Bernardino of Feltre
(1439–1494), Franciscan
friar. Bernardino, who
inspired the blood libel
accusation of 1475 at
Trent, preached
throughout northern Italy
with other Franciscan and
Dominican itinerant
preachers against the
Jewish moneylenders.
Their goal was the
expulsion of Jews from
Italy. The Jews were
expelled from Perugia in
1485, from Gubbio in
1486, from Campo San
Pietro in 1492, and from
Brescia in 1494. Bernardino
was beatified after death
and debeatified in 1965.

Rabbi Elijah Delmedigo
(1460–1497) completes his
Behinat ha-Dat (*The
Examination of Religion*) in
which he shows that the
Zohar could not possibly
have been written by
Simeon bar Yohai because
it quotes rabbis who lived
long after his time.
Delmedigo, who holds a
chair of philosophy at the
University of Padua, is a
major influence on Pico
della Mirandola.*

1491

THE JEWISH WORLD, CIRCA 1490

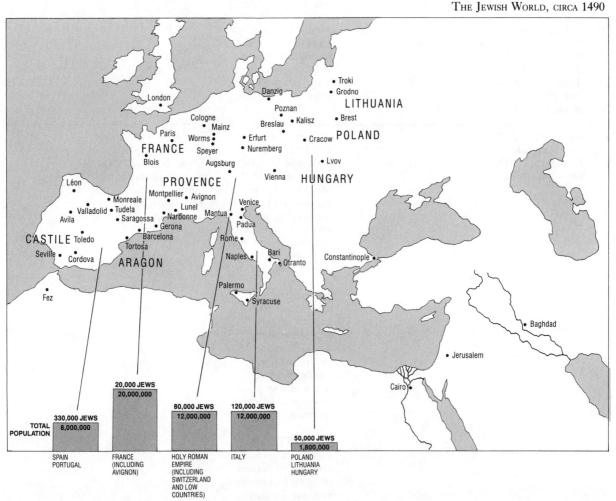

	A. General History	B. Jews in North and South America	C. Jews in Europe	D. Jews in the Middle East and Elsewhere	E. Jewish Culture
1492	The Christian reconquest of Spain culminates in the capture of Granada, the last Muslim territory in the Iberian peninsula. Christopher Columbus* (1451–1506), Italian explorer in the service of Spain, in search of a western route to Asia, discovers various islands in the Caribbean. This first of four voyages to the New World (between 1492 and 1504) leads to permanent European settlement in the Americas.	Christopher Columbus* utilizes the nautical tables developed by Abraham Zacuto, Spanish astronomer and historian, and the nautical instruments developed by his pupil, the scientist and physician Joseph Vicinho, on his voyages to the New World. During this year, when the Jews are expelled from Spain, Zacuto emigrates to Portugal where he becomes court astronomer.	The Jews of Spain are expelled. The exodus of about 100,000 Jews begins in May, and by July 31 the last Jew leaves Spain. The majority flee to Portugal, where they will be expelled in 1496–1497, and to North Africa and Turkey. Turkey is the only major country that openly welcomes Jews. The Jews of Sicily and Sardinia, territories ruled by Spain, are expelled by the general edict expelling all Spanish Jews.		Ladino (Judeo-Spanish) begins to emerge as a specifically Jewish language of Jews of Spanish origin. It preserves many of the forms of Spanish from the 14th and 15th centuries and diverges increasingly from Castilian Spanish as Jews settle further away from Spain.
1494	French armies invade Italy. The Prussian Code and later the Muscovite Law Code of Ivan III* (1497) document the decline of the peasants into serfdom.		The Jews of Florence and other Tuscan towns are expelled when the Medici fall from power. They will return to power in 1513 and bring with it the return of the Jews.		
1495	King Emanuel I* the Fortunate rules Portugal and will reign until 1521.		The Jews are expelled from Lithuania by Grand Duke Alexander.* Motivated by the opportunity to enrich the royal treasury, religious intolerance, and possibly the fear of Jewish proselytizers who had penetrated the highest circles of court, aristocracy, and church, the decree is soon revoked, and in 1503 traditional Jewish privileges will be renewed and confiscated property returned. Charles VIII* of France occupies the kingdom of Naples, bringing looting, new war taxes, and persecution against the Jews, many of whom had settled	The Jews who fled from Spain and Portugal in the 1490s are well received in Constantinople. They assist in the creation of a local arms industry.	

A. General History	B. Jews in North and South America	C. Jews in Europe	D. Jews in the Middle East and Elsewhere	E. Jewish Culture	
		there as refugees from Spain. The Jews will be expelled from Naples in 1510 and again in 1541.			**1495**
		In December, King Emanuel I* the Fortunate of Portugal orders the expulsion of all Jews from the country. The expulsion is to be completed by November 1497. The expulsion results from his desire to unite with Spain. The consent of Spain is dependent on the expulsion of Portugal's Jews. He later resolves to keep the Jews in his country for economic reasons and utilizes persuasion and torture, with little success, to turn them into legal Christians.

Emperor Maximilian I* (1493–1519) expels the Austrian Jews from Styria and Carinthia. His action is instigated by the estates who resent debts owed the Jews and promise to reimburse the emperor for any Jewish revenues lost as a result of the expulsion. | | Don Isaac Abrabanel (1437–1508) completes *Mayyenei ha-Yeshuah* (*Fountains of Salvation*). In the wake of the expulsion of the Jews from Spain in 1492, this Spanish rabbi, religious philosopher, biblical exegete, and communal leader seeks to comfort the survivors by predicting the imminent coming of the Messiah and redemption. His biblical commentaries are influenced by those of Isaac Arama (c.1420–1494) and Levi ben Gershom (1288–1344). Rejecting philosophical rationalism and allegory, Abrabanel draws on contemporary social and political realities to elucidate biblical passages.

The Kabbalah is discussed in the *Apologia* of Pico della Mirandola,* famous Florentine philosopher and poet of the Renaissance. His interaction with a number of contemporary Jews and study of Jewish texts leads to his development of the Christian Kabbalah. Pico* attempts to confirm the truth of the Christian religion from the foundations of Jewish Kabbalah. | **1496** |
| | | Before setting out on his sea voyage, Portuguese explorer Vasco da Gama* consults with Abraham Zacuto, the Spanish astronomer and historian, now the Portuguese court astronomer. Zacuto instructs da Gama's* sailors in the use of his tables, maritime | | | **1497** |

	A. General History	B. Jews in North and South America	C. Jews in Europe	D. Jews in the Middle East and Elsewhere	E. Jewish Culture
1497			charts, and his newly developed astrolabe. In 1497, when Portuguese King Manuel* forces all Jews to convert, Zacuto leaves for North Africa.		
1498	The Portuguese explorer Vasco da Gama* discovers a route to India around the Cape of Good Hope.		The German emperor approves expulsion of the Jews of Nuremberg. A combination of growing capitalism and popular religious hatred motivates the expulsion.	Vasco da Gama's* naval expedition captures a Jew in Goa and brings him to Portugal where he converts to Christianity. His parents had come to Goa from Poland.	
1499	The first known edition of *La Celestina* by the Spanish *converso* author Fernando de Rojas (c.1465–1541) is published. This early Spanish literary work earns Rojas the title "father of the Spanish novel."				
1500			A disputation takes place in Ferrara between Christians and Abraham Farissol (c.1451–c.1525) of Avignon. Farissol defends Jewish moneylending for interest, arguing that it does not differ from the universally accepted practices of renting a house or hiring a worker for a fair price or wage. Rabbi Asher Lemlein, a false Messiah, begins preaching in northern Italy of repentance and the coming of the Messiah. Of Ashkenazic origin, he extends his ideas into Germany. This year becomes known, even among Christians, as the "year of the repentance."		The Middle Yiddish period begins. It is noted for the increasing numbers of Yiddish speakers and the vigorous expansion of narrative and expository prose throughout German and eastern European territories. This period will last until about 1700, when the Modern period will begin. The Modern period will witness the slow decline of Yiddish in western Europe.
1503			The Polish monarchy appoints Rabbi Jacob Polak "Rabbi of Poland." The emergence of a chief rabbinate, supported by the crown, allows		

A. General History	B. Jews in North and South America	C. Jews in Europe	D. Jews in the Middle East and Elsewhere	E. Jewish Culture	
		the development of a form of Jewish self-government.			**1503**
				Abraham Zacuto, Spanish astronomer and historian, completes *Sefer Yuhasin* (*Book of Genealogies*) in Tunisia. This history of rabbinic scholars who transmitted the Oral Law includes information on events in Jewish history until his own time and a chronology of world events. The work will first be published in 1566 in Constantinople.	**1504**
				The Jewish poet Solomon ben Mazzal Tov, apparently one of the Spanish exiles, establishes in Constantinople one of the first printing presses in Turkey. Many of his religious and national poems adopt the rhythms and melodies of Turkish and Arabic folk songs.	**1505**
		Hebrew language and general Judaica interest Christian scholars. The German Christian humanist Johannes von Reuchlin* (1455–1522) writes a grammar of Hebrew, *Rudimenta Hebraica*, for use by other Christian scholars. He also writes *Arte Cabalistica*, which shows that Kabbalah is in total harmony with Christianity.			**1506**
				Elijah Levita (c.1468–1549), Italian grammarian and philologist, writes *Bove-Bukh*, a secular literary romance in Yiddish. It is believed to be an adaptation of an Italian version of an Anglo-French romance. The popularity of the tale	**1507**

	A. General History	B. Jews in North and South America	C. Jews in Europe	D. Jews in the Middle East and Elsewhere	E. Jewish Culture
1507					results in the name becoming a synonym for any fantastic tale.
1508		The bishop of Cuba writes to Spain that practically every ship arriving in Havana is filled with Hebrews and New Christians, Jews converted to Christianity by force, despite edicts that no Jews, Moors, or other heretics or their fourth-generation descendants could reside in any part of the Spanish Empire in the New World.		Ahmad al-Wansharisi,* editor of the collection of legal opinions, *The Marvelous Touchstone*, dies. This voluminous work promotes the strict application of Islamic laws to Moroccan Jews, a policy enforced throughout the late medieval and early modern periods.	
1509	Henry VIII* accedes to the throne of England (1509–1547).		Johannes Pfefferkorn, an apostate, obtains approval from the German emperor Maximilian* for the confiscation of Jewish writings. He is prevented, however, from burning the Talmud and Kabbalah through the arguments of Johannes Reuchlin,* who sees these works as favorable to Christianity and confirming its claims to truth.	Sultan Bayezid II* (1481–1512) welcomes Spanish and Portuguese Jewish refugees to Greece and Turkey, where they could openly profess Judaism.	
1510	Tripoli is captured by Spain. It remains under Christian rule until 1551.		With the defeat of the French in Naples, King Ferdinand* establishes it as the largest principality in Italy and expels the majority of Jews living south of Rome. They will be expelled from Naples again in 1541.	Goa is established as the seat of Portuguese rule in India, leading to the influx of many Spanish and Portuguese Jews until the establishment there of the Inquisition in 1560.	
1511				Tetuan, in Spanish Morocco, becomes an important Jewish maritime community. It becomes a center of Jewish culture and over time its Jews emigrate to South American and North African cities.	
1513	Italian writer and statesman Niccolo Machiavelli* (1469–1527) writes *The Prince,*				

A. General History	B. Jews in North and South America	C. Jews in Europe	D. Jews in the Middle East and Elsewhere	E. Jewish Culture	
expounding his political theory of the state.					1513
		The edict of expulsion of the Jews of Naples (1510) is extended to include New Christians.	A group of *conversos* (New Christians) settle in Marrakesh, where they share their expertise in the weapon and metal industries with the Muslims.		1515
		In Italy, the practice of confinement of Jews in a separate area of the community outside of which they are not permitted to live begins. The policy is designed to gain maximum economic advantage from a Jewish presence, including special taxes, while ensuring that Jews have little social contact with the population. In Venice, the area is called the *ghetto* (foundry). Over time, the word *ghetto* becomes a general European term for the enclosed quarters of the Jews.	Palestine becomes part of the Ottoman Empire. This further increases the movement of Jews from Spain and Portugal to the Holy Land and strengthens commercial ties between this Jewish community and those of Egypt and Syria, making the city of Safed an important commercial and cultural center.		1516
Martin Luther* (1483–1546), German religious reformer, posts his 95 theses against indulgences on the church door in Wittenberg. The Ottoman Turks destroy the Mamluks and conquer Syria and Egypt.		In Italy, Daniel Bomberg* (d. 1549), the first Christian merchant to found a Hebrew press, prints an edition of the Hebrew Bible with the commentaries of Rashi, Ibn Ezra, David Kimhi, and Gersonides. He also publishes the Babylonian and Palestinian Talmudim for the first time (1521–1522).			1517
The Polish serfs become permanently bound to the soil and lose the legal protection of the king. Their obligations to the landowners increase steadily from this point.		Johannes Reuchlin* writes *De accentibus et orthographia linguae hebraicae.* In addition to discussing the Hebrew language and Masorah, this is one of the best known of the early specimens of Masoretic cantillation.			1518

	A. General History	B. Jews in North and South America	C. Jews in Europe	D. Jews in the Middle East and Elsewhere	E. Jewish Culture
1519		New Christians are among the first Spaniards to come to Mexico. They accompany Hernando Cortes,* the conquistador, who conquers the country.	The Jews of Regensburg are expelled as a result of their alleged responsibility for 40 years of social and economic decline in the city.		
1520	Martin Luther* is excommunicated. The rule of Suleiman I* the Magnificent of the Ottoman Empire begins. He reigns until 1566 and is regarded as the greatest of the sultans.	Inquisition proceedings are commenced against the Marranos in Cuba.	Josel of Rosheim (c.1478–1554), the chief spokesman for German Jewry, succeeds in influencing Holy Roman Emperor Charles V* (1518–1556) to renew earlier privileges and letters of protection to German Jews. As the Reformation gains force, however, and becomes more vehemently anti-Jewish, Josel cannot prevent the expulsion of the Jews from Saxony in 1537. Scarcely 120 Jewish families remain in all of Alsace. Most will be expelled during the second half of the 15th century.		Solomon ibn Verga (c.1450–c.1525), a Spanish Jew who came to Italy, writes *Shevet Yehuda* (*The Rod of Judah*), an essay on the persecutions of the Jews, which some claim to be the first work on Jewish history since Josephus' *Antiquities* over 1400 years before. It asks why Jews are hated and suggests divine punishment as its cause as well as the relevance of secular factors. The book will be published in Turkey by his son in 1554. *Mahzor Romania*, the Byzantine prayer book, is first printed in Constantinople. Hebrew rather than Greek remains the language of prayer. The appearance of the word *heretics* in the condemnation against slanderers in the *Amidah* prayer may be a reference to the Karaites.
1521		To limit the presence in Mexico of a growing number of New Christians, Spain closes the newly conquered territory to all those who cannot show four generations of Catholic ancestors. Some Spanish and Portuguese New Christians continue to arrive in Mexico as they manage to procure appropriate certificates through corruption.		The Turks conquer Belgrade and transfer thousands of Jews and Christians to Ottoman cities such as Izmir, Salonika, and Istanbul. The Ottomans consider these Jews politically reliable and economically beneficial.	
1522			Jacob ben Joseph Pollak (c.1460–after	The Jewish population of Safed	Joseph Caro (1488–1575), codifier

A. General History	B. Jews in North and South America	C. Jews in Europe	D. Jews in the Middle East and Elsewhere	E. Jewish Culture	
		1522), Polish halakhic authority, is compelled to leave the yeshiva in Cracow he established as a result of a lawsuit. From this time, all traces of him disappear. His method of dialectical Talmud study (*pilpul*), as well as his own erudition, made this yeshiva a center of European learning.	is numbered at over 300 households, making it equal to that of Jerusalem. By the mid-16th century it numbers 8,000–10,000 Jews, mostly Sephardim. By the early 17th century the community will be numbered at 20,000–30,000.	of Jewish law and Kabbalist, begins writing *Beit Yosef* (*House of Joseph*) in Adrianople, which he completes in 1542 in Safed. It is a commentary on the *Arbaah Turim* (*The Four Columns*), Jacob ben Asher's (c.1280–1340) code of Jewish law. Caro investigates the source of every practical law from its talmudic origins, traces its development, mentions divergent views, and recommends the appropriate practice. His *Shulhan Arukh* (*The Set Table*), completed in 1555, is a digest of *Beit Yosef*.	**1522**
		Martin Luther,* German religious reformer, writes *Jesus Christ Was a Jew by Birth*. It argues for the conversion of Jews not through persecution and cruelty but through the belief that "if the Jews are treated in a friendly fashion and are instructed from Holy Writ, many of them will become worthy Christians."		Elijah Capsali (c.1483–1555), rabbi of Candia, Crete, writes *Seder Eliyahu Zuta* (*The Minor Order of Elijah*) in which he describes the history of the Ottoman Turks down to his own day with special reference to the Jews. It includes an account of Spanish Jewry, especially during the expulsion. This work is believed to be the first effort to write Jewish history within the context of general history. In 1508, Capsali went to study at the yeshiva in Padua and in 1517 wrote *Divrei ha-Yamin le-Malkhut Venezia*, a chronicle of Venice and the condition of the Jews in the Venetian dominions.	**1523**
		The old established Jewish families of Rome come to terms with the *transmontani* (those from over the mountains), the newcomers from France and Germany who have heretofore	Ahmed Shaitan,* the governor of Egypt, revolts against Suleiman* the Magnificent, the Turkish sultan, imprisons 12 Jews in an attempt to extort money, and	In Italy, Abraham ben Mordecai Farrisol (1451–c.1525) writes *Iggeret Orhot Olam* (*The Ways of the World*). This first Jewish cosmography charts not only the	**1524**

	A. General History	B. Jews in North and South America	C. Jews in Europe	D. Jews in the Middle East and Elsewhere	E. Jewish Culture
1524			not been accepted into the leadership of the community. Roman Jewish self-government is now apportioned among its Italian, Spanish, Sicilian, and German Jews. David Reuveni (d. c. 1538), claiming to be a messenger of the king of the lost tribes of Israel, appears before Pope Clement VII and proposes a military treaty between the Jews and the Christians against the Muslims. With the pope's support, Reuveni is received by King John III* of Portugal and arouses great messianic fervor among the Marranos there. He later dies a prisoner in Spain charged with encouraging New Christians to return to Judaism.	threatens to annihilate the Jewish community of Cairo. His revolt is crushed and he is beheaded. An Egyptian Purim, i.e., a Second Purim, is proclaimed by the Jews of Egypt to commemorate the event. A Megillat Mitsrayim (Scroll of Egypt) is written, which is publicly read when the holiday is celebrated each year on the 28th of Adar.	places mentioned in the Bible, but the new route to India discovered by the Portuguese and the islands of the New World as well. David Reuveni writes of his travels to Pisa, Italy, where he observes educational attainments of women. He met a young lady who read the Bible and prayed daily. He also met a woman who was a schoolteacher.
1525	William Tyndale* (c.1490–1536) completes his translation of the New Testament into English. It becomes the basis for most subsequent English translations, particularly the King James Version of 1611.		Solomon Molcho (c.1500–1532), pseudo-Messiah, converts to Judaism and settles in Salonika, where he preaches and writes of the coming redemption. Born in Lisbon of Marrano parents, as Diogo Piros, he was a Christian courtier. In 1529, he will return to Italy and approach Emperor Charles V* (1519–1566) at Regensburg to discuss a plan for Jews to join the war against the Turks. He will be arrested by the emperor.	A conflict erupts in Fez between the native Jewish population and the newer community of exiled Spanish Jews over ritual slaughter. The dispute continues to split the community for 10 years until it will be finally resolved in favor of the exiles.	
1526			Emperor Charles V* issues a general safe-conduct to the Portuguese New Christians in Antwerp, bringing many Marranos who settle and conduct business there. By 1550 these Jews will be accused of aiding	Rabbi Elijah Mizrahi, chief rabbi of Istanbul, dies. Due to disagreement within the community, no new chief rabbi is selected until 1834 when one is imposed by the sultan.	The Prague Haggadah, containing the oldest known printed Yiddish poem, is published.

A. General History	B. Jews in North and South America	C. Jews in Europe	D. Jews in the Middle East and Elsewhere	E. Jewish Culture	
		the Reformation and an edict of expulsion will force them from Antwerp until the Peace of Westphalia of 1648.			**1526**
	The first auto-da-fé in America is held in Mexico City when two Jews, including the conquistador Hernando Alonso, are burned at the stake by order of the Dominican Fray Vicente de Santa Maria, who exercises inquisitorial powers.				**1528**
The Ottomans lay siege to Vienna but are forced to retreat.		The Scuola Grande Tedesca, the oldest of the five main synagogues in the Venice ghetto, is opened. This main Ashkenazic congregation will be followed by the smaller Ashkenazic Scuola Canton in 1531; Scuola Spagnola, the largest, in 1555 or 1584; Scuola Levantina in 1538; and Scuola Italiana in 1575. All are virtually unrecognizable from the outside, being established above the top floors of existing buildings in observance of the rabbinic precept that they be higher than their surroundings. The interiors are beautifully appointed.			**1529**
				The first Hebrew press is opened in Poland in Cracow. Others follow in Brisk (1546) and Lublin (1550).	**1530**
Huldreich Zwingli* (b. 1484), Protestant reformer of Switzerland, dies.			A Franciscan friar is permitted to preach in the synagogue in Fez. He does not succeed in persuading Jews there to convert.	Records show earliest information about a Jewish play in Europe. Marino Sanuto,* an Italian historian, mentions a Purim play he witnessed in the ghetto of Venice. Plays with biblical themes are very popular in Europe.	**1531**

	A. General History	B. Jews in North and South America	C. Jews in Europe	D. Jews in the Middle East and Elsewhere	E. Jewish Culture
1532			Solomon Molcho (c.1500–1532), pseudo-Messiah, is burned at the stake by the Inquisition in Mantua. Arrested by Emperor Charles V* and sent to Mantua, he dies after refusing to revert to Christianity.		Jacob Azulai, the earliest known of an Italian family that makes majolica seder plates, makes his seder plate in Padua. It will be displayed in the Jewish Museum of Vienna.
1533	Ivan IV* the Terrible rules Russia until 1584. The Act of Appeals cuts all ties between the English church and Rome.				
1534	The first complete edition of Martin Luther's* German translation of the Bible is published.		A pogrom breaks out against the Jews of Plock. Dozens of pogroms, blood libels, and charges of desecration of the Host are recorded in Poland starting from the mid-16th century.	Moses Hamon (c.1490–c.1554), court physician to Suleiman* the Magnificent, accompanies Suleiman* on his attack of Persia. Descended from a Spanish and Portuguese family of court physicians to the sultans, Hamon assists fellow Jews in need and obtains a firman from the sultan protecting Jews from blood libels. He maintains a yeshiva in Salonika, assists in the publication of Jewish books, and owns a rare manuscript collection.	Rabbi Anshel of Cracow publishes *Mirkevet ha-Mishneh*, an alphabetical concordance of the Bible, with Yiddish translation. It is the first book printed in Yiddish.
1535	Spain, under King Charles I,* conquers Tunis.			Jews in Tunis flee the Spanish conquest. Some Jews are killed, others are sold into slavery. About 150 Jews are redeemed by Jewish communities in Naples and Genoa.	Judah Abrabanel (known in the Christian world as Leone Ebreo, c.1460–c.1523) writes *Dialoghi di Amore* (*Dialogues about Love*). Published in Rome, it is a Neoplatonic treatise on love by a leading philosopher of the Renaissance. This work becomes a classic of Renaissance literature. Judah is the son of Don Isaac Abrabanel. Solomon ben Moses ha-Levi Alkabez

A. General History	B. Jews in North and South America	C. Jews in Europe	D. Jews in the Middle East and Elsewhere	E. Jewish Culture	
				(c.1505–1576) arrives in Safed where he writes mystical poetry including "Lekhah Dodi" ("Come My Beloved"), which gains immediate popularity and is integrated into the Kabbalat Shabbat (Friday evening) service.	**1535**
			Suleiman* the Magnificent begins construction of the wall surrounding the Old City of Jerusalem. It is completed in 1542 and, along with Suleiman's* repair of the sewers and cisterns, makes Jerusalem more attractive to Jewish settlers.		**1536**
		The Polish Sejm (Diet) prohibits the leasing of royal revenues to Jews. Public revenues and monopolies on land, mills, inns, breweries, distilleries, salt, customs duties, and taxes are often leased to Jews in Poland–Lithuania as part of a system called *arenda*. The growing power of the nobility leads to their competing with the Jews for these leases.	Jacob Berab of Safed attempts to reinstitute rabbinic ordination. Basing himself on the authority of Maimonides, a need on the part of penitent Marranos for this authoritative institution, and a growing messianic fervor, Berab gets ordained and proceeds to ordain four of his own students. The plan fails, however, due to the opposition of the scholars of Jerusalem led by Levi ben Habib.	Elijah Levita (c.1468–1549), Italian grammarian and philologist, writes *Masoret ha-Masoret* (*The Traditions of the Biblical Text*) in which he is the first to point out that, contrary to traditional views, the vowel points and accent marks in the biblical text were introduced by the Masoretes of Tiberias. They did not originate in the Sinai period, but in posttalmudic times.	**1538**
		The Polish king transfers jurisdiction over the Jews to the nobles on whose private estates they live. This enables Jews to settle and live free of the pressures from the burghers in new settlements in the south and southeast. From the mid-18th century, half to three-quarters of all Polish Jews will live on privately owned estates.			**1539**

	A. General History	B. Jews in North and South America	C. Jews in Europe	D. Jews in the Middle East and Elsewhere	E. Jewish Culture
1540	The Society of Jesus is founded by Ignatius Loyola* (1491–1556). Fueled by militant loyalty to papal dogma and traditional devotion, the Jesuit movement grows rapidly and gains great influence.				
1541	Charles V* of Spain attempts to capture Algiers. The Jews ally with Algerian Muslims and the Spanish attack is successfully repelled.		The Venetian Senate grants Levantine Jews permission to reside temporarily in Venice. This privilege comes in response to the increasing participation of Sephardic Jews in Balkan commerce and is an attempt by Italian princes to improve their economies at the expense of local interests. Jews are expelled from Naples and areas under its jurisdiction. They will be readmitted in 1735.		Elijah Levita, Italian grammarian and philologist, writes *Tishbi*. It provides explanations of 712 words, partly biblical and mostly talmudic and posttalmudic, of special importance. It is published with a Latin translation and is an important work in the research of Hebrew grammar. The numerical sum of the word *tishbi* is 712. Rabbi Shalom Shakhna ben Joseph (d. 1558) is appointed chief rabbi of Lesser Poland. His yeshiva and rabbinical court in Lublin draw students from all across Europe and make Lublin a center of religious learning and Jewish communal activity.
1543			Martin Luther,* German religious reformer, expresses open enmity for the Jews. Though he at first hoped that the Reformation's return to a pure biblical Christianity would attract Jews, Luther responds to the failure of these missionary attempts with vehement antisemitism. He writes *About the Jews and Their Lies*, a pamphlet described as the first work of modern antisemitism.		
1544	Charles V,* Catholic emperor of the German empire, accords the Jews his				The first Yiddish translation of the Torah with prophetic readings and the

A. General History	B. Jews in North and South America	C. Jews in Europe	D. Jews in the Middle East and Elsewhere	E. Jewish Culture	
protection, prohibiting all banishments not approved by him. After his abdication in 1556, expulsions will be renewed.				Five Scrolls appears in Germany. Many of the Yiddish translations of biblical books are composed for women to displace the German stories, fables, and tales that they are reading.	**1544**
		According to the records of the Lisbon Inquisition, a small crypto-Jewish community resides in Bristol, England, until 1555. Martin Luther* writes to Joachim II* (1535–1571) of Brandenburg to express his anger at the latter's having readmitted the Jews to his territory. Unlike the expulsions from c.1470 to 1520, those that follow are often instigated by religious and temporal rulers as well as by popular antisemitism.			**1545**
The Council of Trent begins its work of Counter-Reformation. Ottomans conquer Yemen.				A Yiddish translation of *Josippon* is published in Zurich. Yiddish translations of *Sefer ha-Yashar* (1670), Solomon ibn Verga's *Shevet Yehudah* (1591), and David Gans' *Tzemah David* (1698) set the foundation for historical writing in Yiddish.	**1546**
After 30 years of fighting, the Ottomans control much of Hungary and successfully demand tribute.				The oldest medieval encyclopedia to be printed, written by Gershon ben Solomon of Arles between 1242 and 1300, appears in Venice. *Sha'ar Ha-Shamayim* (*The Gates of Heaven*), written in Hebrew, serves as a popular summary of the natural sciences, astronomy, and theology for centuries.	**1547**

	A. General History	B. Jews in North and South America	C. Jews in Europe	D. Jews in the Middle East and Elsewhere	E. Jewish Culture
1548			Josel of Rosheim (c.1478–1554), the great *shtadlan* and leader of German Jewry, defends the Jews of Colmar. As on many occasions, his argument against expulsion and attack is based on a combination of continuity of imperial privileges, the humanist concept of equality of the human race, and biblical proofs that appeal to Protestants.		
1549		Thomas de Souza serves as the first Spanish governor-general of Brazil.		Suleiman* the Magnificent builds a wall around Safed and stations troops there to protect the inhabitants from thieves. This makes Safed the best-protected town in Palestine.	The commentary of Obadiah of Bertinoro (c.1450–c.1516) on the Mishnah is published in Venice. Completed in Jerusalem, his work is the standard commentary on the Mishnah, as is Rashi's on the Talmud. The lucid commentary relies heavily on Rashi and the rulings of Maimonides.
1550	The Tartars raid China.	According to some sources, Mexico City has more Spanish New Christians than Spanish Catholics.	One hundred fifty-five Jewish families are expelled from the Palatinate, the principal Calvinist state in Germany. Though John Calvin* (1509–1564), French church reformer, is more moderate than Luther* in his animosity toward the Jews, this does not influence the city council, clergy, or populace of Geneva to readmit the Jews expelled in the 1490s.		Moses ben Jacob Cordovero (1522–1570) of Safed completes his first major work on the Kabbalah, *Pardes Rimmonim* (*Pomegranate Orchard*). A teacher of Isaac Luria (1534–1572), the major Kabbalistic scholar of Safed, Cordovero writes commentaries on the Zohar in which he tries to synthesize the various approaches to Kabbalah into a unified system.
1551			The grand duke of Tuscany issues a charter to attract Sephardic Jewish merchants from the Balkans to Pisa. They proceed to trade with Dalmatia using the overland routes to Ancona and Pesaro.		

A. General History	B. Jews in North and South America	C. Jews in Europe	D. Jews in the Middle East and Elsewhere	E. Jewish Culture	
		King Sigismund II* (1548–1572) of Poland–Lithuania permits the Jews to choose their own chief rabbi rather than imposing one on them. The crown has appointed the chief rabbi since 1503			**1551**
Pope Julius III, convinced that the Talmud attacks Christianity, authorizes the confiscation and burning of thousands of volumes of the Talmud in Rome. Similar public burnings take place in Bologna, Ferrara, Mantua, and Venice.		The Jewish community of Ottoman Salonika numbers over 20,000, making it one of the largest Jewish communities in the world. Moses Isserles (1525 or 1530–1572), Polish rabbi and codifier, builds a synagogue in Cracow in memory of his first wife. It will still be in use after World War II. It is the yearly custom of Polish Jews to visit his grave alongside the synagogue on the Lag ba-Omer holiday. Isserles is considered the "Maimonides of Polish Jewry" and is best known as the author of the *Mappah* (*Table Cloth*) to Joseph Caro's *Shulhan Arukh* (*Prepared Table*), a supplement to the code for use by Ashkenazic Jews.		Samuel Usque's *Consolacam as tribulacoens de Israel* (*A Consolation for the Tribulations of Israel*), written in Portuguese, is published in Ferrara. A Marrano who fled the Inquisition, Usque's work encompasses a review of the whole of Jewish history, in the form of a pastoral dialogue between three allegorical characters. He seeks to assure the Jews that they had not been abandoned by God. Burning the Talmud in Italy and forbidding its printing results in its elimination from educational curricula and replacement by various talmudic codes, particularly Isaac Alfasi's *Halakhot*, for nearly two centuries. The Marrano printer Abraham Usque publishes the Ferrara Bible, a literal Spanish translation from the Hebrew. It differs greatly from the Vulgate and challenges the latter's authority in its attempt to win the Marranos back to Judaism.	**1553**
		A delegation of Italian Jews meets in Ferrara to discuss the papal banning of the Talmud. They adopt a rabbinic ordinance, which is recognized by the government, establishing a system of internal control		Joseph ha-Kohen (1496–1578) of Italy completes *Divrei ha-Yamim Le-Malkhei Zarefat U-le-Malkhei Bet Ottoman ha-Togar* (*History of the Kings of France and the Ottoman Sultans*). Focusing primarily	**1554**

	A. General History	B. Jews in North and South America	C. Jews in Europe	D. Jews in the Middle East and Elsewhere	E. Jewish Culture
1554			over the printing of Hebrew books. Three rabbis and a lay leader must authorize the printing. Rabbis in charge of the inspection are empowered to punish offenders through excommunication. Similar rules will be adopted in Padua in 1585; by the Council of Four Lands in Poland in 1594; by the Jewish community of Frankfurt in 1603; and by the Sephardic community of Amsterdam in 1639.		on the Crusades, Ha-Kohen explains the suffering of the Jews in this period as a result of the historic struggle between Asia and Europe, Islam, and Christianity. In 1558 he will write *Emek ha-Bakha* (*The Vale of Tears*), a history of Jewish suffering since the fall of the Second Temple. *Shevet Yehudah* (*The Scepter of Judah*), written by Solomon ibn Verga, exiled Spanish historiographer, is published in Adrianople. It is an account of historical Jewish suffering generally and of the Spanish expulsion in particular. The account is interspersed with imaginary disputations and deliberations. It will be reprinted in many languages and achieve wide popularity.
1555	The Peace of Augsburg establishes the principle that the ruler of each territory determines the religion practiced in that territory.		Cardinal Caraffa becomes Pope Paul IV. His bull *Cum nimis absurdum* brings religious and economic restrictions against the Jews of papal lands. His papal bull reviews all earlier papal restrictions on Jews and, for the first time, requires all Jews within the papal states to live in enforced ghettos and limits their economic relations with Christians to the selling of used clothes.		Judah Leone Sommo (1527–1592), Italian Hebrew poet and dramatist, writes *An Eloquent Marriage Farce* in the style of a Renaissance comedy; it is believed to be the first Hebrew play. In 1565, he will write *Dialogues on the Art of the Stage*, which are important discussions on Renaissance theater.
1556				Responding to persecutions by Pope Paul IV against the Jews of Ancona, part of the papal states, Doña Gracia Mendes (1510–1569), a former Marrano and prominent leader of the Istanbul Jewish	

			community, tries to impose an economic boycott against the port of Ancona and economically reward the community of Pesaro for receiving Ancona's Jewish refugees. The plan fails because of internal Jewish division over its efficacy and fear of further persecution.	**1556**
		Pope Paul IV (1555–1559) places the Talmud on the *Index librorum prohibitorum*, which lists the Hebrew books banned to that time. Pope Pius IV (1559–1565) and Pope Gregory XIII (1572–1585) will permit the printing and use of the Talmud provided any expression or passage the censors deemed insulting toward Christianity be eliminated and the book not be titled Talmud, but rather Gemara, Shishah Sedarim, or Limmud. Even with these caveats, the Talmud will not be printed in Italy. The last edition of the *Index* in 1948 will still include books written by Jews.		Pope Paul IV permits the first printing of the Zohar (*The Book of Splendor*), the primary text of medieval Jewish mysticism, in Mantua and Cremona at the same time that he authorizes the burning of 12,000 Jewish books in Cremona, because he is persuaded the Zohar contains no defamation of Christianity.	**1559**
			Doña Gracia Mendes and her nephew Don Joseph Nasi (c.1524–1579), wealthy former Marranos, apply to the Turkish authorities for permission to resettle Jewish refugees from Spain and Portugal in Tiberias. Turkish authorities grant permission despite Muslim opposition. City walls for the Jewish settlement are completed in 1565. The economic foundation of the community is based on the presence of	In Cremona, Italy, Judah Loeb Bresch publishes a Yiddish translation of the Torah, the Five Scrolls, and the Haftarot. It is believed to be an improved version of a 1544 Yiddish translation by Michael Adam, a convert. Abramo Dall'Arpa (c.1542–c.1577), one of the outstanding harpists of his time, plays before the duke of Mantua. Other members of this Italian Jewish	**1560**

	A. General History	B. Jews in North and South America	C. Jews in Europe	D. Jews in the Middle East and Elsewhere	E. Jewish Culture
1560				Jewish craftsmen, plantations for growing silkworm, and merino wool from Spain.	family are also noted musicians.
1563	The Council of Trent concludes its third and final session and Pope Pius IV issues the bull *Benedictus Deus*, which, along with the revised *Index librorum prohibitorum*, confirms the reassertion of papal authority and conservatism.		Ivan IV* the Terrible conquers Polotsk and forces the Jews to adopt Greek Orthodoxy. Three hundred resist and are drowned in the Dvina River. Poland will recapture Polotsk in 1579, and the forced converts and others again will publicly profess Judaism.		
1564	John Calvin* dies in Geneva. The Jesuits come to Poland. They succeed through their schools and colleges in promoting religious intolerance. Protestants are restricted from being burghers and members of the guilds in many cities.				Hayyim ben Joseph Vital (1542–1620) begins to study Kabbalah in Safed. He becomes the primary pupil of Isaac Luria. After his master's death, Vital tries to become the sole interpreter of Luria's Kabbalistic system, since the latter left no writings of his own.
1565					Joseph Caro's (1488–1575) *Shulhan Arukh* is first printed in Venice.
1566					Maimonides' "Thirteen Principles" appears in the Venice Haggadah. This is probably the earliest statement of these principles in doctrinal form.
1567				Turkish tax records list the Jewish population of Safed as 143 Portuguese families, approximately 300 Spanish, 80 Italian, and less than 50 German and Hungarian. By the 1560s, Jews comprise about half the population of approximately 10,000 in Safed. Although ransacked by Bedouin and Druze, causing many Jews to flee, Safed becomes	

A. General History	B. Jews in North and South America	C. Jews in Europe	D. Jews in the Middle East and Elsewhere	E. Jewish Culture	
			a Jewish religious and intellectual center in the 16th century.		**1567**
		The Jewish district of Lublin assumes the character of a quasi-independent Jewish municipality. It is typical of the cities in which Jews and burghers reach a general agreement concerning the location of the Jewish quarter and the commercial activities of its inhabitants.	The Paradesi synagogue in Cochin, India, is built.		**1568**
The Union of Lublin creates a firmly established federation between Poland and Lithuania. It becomes a multinational state, the second largest in territory and sixth largest in population throughout Europe.	Philip II* of Spain orders the Inquisition to be established in the Americas.	Pope Pius V (1566–1572) issues the bull *Hebraeorum Gens*, expelling the Jews from all the localities in the papal states with the exception of the port city of Ancona and the city of Rome. The expulsion applies to the papal states of France–Avignon and the Comtat Venaissin as well. The Jews of Lvov are given complete control over the election of community officials, their communal archive, communal property, and provision of welfare services. This privilege is soon granted to other Polish Jewish communities.		At about this time, Isaac Luria, Kabbalist, settles in Safed. Luria was born in Jerusalem and raised in Egypt by his Sephardic mother after the death of his Ashkenazic father. Referred to as Ha-Ari (the Sacred Lion), Luria is the foremost Kabbalist of his day. It is Luria's doctrines of *zimzum* (divine contraction) and *tikkun* (restoration) that, though based on earlier ideas, give rise to a new and profoundly influential form of Jewish mysticism.	**1569**
		The Stara (Old) medieval synagogue of Kazimierz, a suburb of Cracow, is remodeled by the Italian architect Matteo Gucci. He places a parapet on the synagogue, which is useful for defense of the community. The synagogue, being the oldest in the community, is the center of Jewish life. It remains standing		Hayyim ben Bezalel (c.1520–1588), talmudic scholar and rabbi of Friedberg, Germany, writes *Vikkuah Mayim Hayyim* (*Dispute over Living Waters*), a criticism of the codification of Jewish law undertaken by Moses Isserles and by Joseph Caro. He believes that publication of definitive codes undermine the study	**1570**

	A. General History	B. Jews in North and South America	C. Jews in Europe	D. Jews in the Middle East and Elsewhere	E. Jewish Culture
1570			today as an official museum of Jewish history.		of the Talmud and ignore differences between the various local customs.
1571		An independent tribunal of the Holy Office of the Inquisition is established in Mexico City. The burning at the stake of several New Christians, however, had begun as early as 1528.	The Venetian government, at war with Turkey, resolves to expel all Jews from the city of Venice and the Adriatic Islands. Though the expulsion is not enforced, it reflects the impact of the Counter-Reformation and the papal willingness to sacrifice local commercial interests to doctrinal necessities.	The conquest of Cyprus by the Turks is followed by an imperial order to settle Jews in these newly acquired provinces for economic reasons. A similar order follows the Turkish capture of Rhodes in 1523.	
1572	The St. Bartholomew's Day massacre of Protestants in Paris signifies the beginning of a violent stage in the Counter-Reformation, bringing religious warfare to Europe for over 70 years. Poland becomes a republic with the extinction of the Jagiellonian dynasty (1386–1572). It is ruled by the landed gentry in a parliament (Sejm) with a king elected by the nobility.		Duke Emmanuel Philibert* of Savoy invites Levantine Jews and Marranos to settle in Nice to develop Levant trade and set up textile factories. Though he guarantees Jews protection against the Inquisition, he withdraws the guarantees in 1574 under pressure from the pope. The leaders of the Netherlands revolution against Spain turn to the Jews for material assistance.		
1573			Elector Joachim II* expels the Jews from Brandenburg, Germany. Between 1573 and 1581, the Cinque Scole synagogue is erected in the ghetto of Rome. When the ghetto was established in 1555, the Jews were permitted to have only one synagogue. Later, Pope Pius V agreed to have one building house five separate synagogues. The Cinque Scole satisfied the literal restriction but permitted Jews of ethnic, linguistic,		

A. General History	B. Jews in North and South America	C. Jews in Europe	D. Jews in the Middle East and Elsewhere	E. Jewish Culture	
		and social differences to establish Castilian, Catalan, Sicilian, Temple, and New congregations. The Cinque Scole will be demolished in 1910.			**1573**
Tunisia is the last country in North Africa to fall under Ottoman rule.			Murad III* (1574–1595) is the first Ottoman sultan to enforce the sumptuary laws requiring non-Muslims to wear distinguishing dress and prohibiting the building or repair of synagogues.		**1574**
		There are 150,000 Jews living in Poland out of a total population of 7 million.		Azariah dei Rossi (c.1511–c.1578), Italian scholar and physician, publishes *Me'or Einayim* (*Light for the Eyes*), a series of historical essays. Using classical Greek, Latin, Christian, as well as Jewish sources, dei Rossi's work is the first since antiquity to deal with the Hellenistic–Jewish scholar Philo and to subject the Jewish calendar to historical scrutiny. On account of his critical method and refusal to accept rabbinic legend as literal truth, the work is banned in many Jewish communities. Dei Rossi's insights on biblical poetics anticipate the work of Bishop Robert Lowth (1710–1787), who makes reference to him. Elijah ben Moses de Vidas, Kabbalist of Safed, writes *Reshit Hokhmah* (*The Principles of Wisdom*), a book on morals in Judaism that includes Kabbalistic theories. It will enjoy great popularity and will be printed 40 times.	**1575**
			A thousand Jewish families of Safed are ordered to relocate to Famagusta, Cyprus.		**1576**

	A. General History	B. Jews in North and South America	C. Jews in Europe	D. Jews in the Middle East and Elsewhere	E. Jewish Culture
1576				The order will later be rescinded by Sultan Murad III,* who is generally favorable toward the Jews.	
1577		Spanish laws forbidding Jews to emigrate to the colonies of the Western Hemisphere are repealed as they are ineffective.	The Jews are readmitted to the bishopric of Hildesheim. The position of Jews in other bishoprics, such as Mainz, Speyer, and Strasbourg, also improves as a result of the decline in the Protestant challenge to the prelate-princes of the German ecclesiastical states. The Jews are readmitted over the strong objections of the local citizenry. Rudolph II,* the Hapsburg emperor, grants the Jews of Bohemia a charter of privileges. He appoints Marcus Meisel (1528–1601) financier of the crown. Meisel is regarded as the first Court Jew, a merchant-financier with court connections, who will be a key figure in central European life from 1650 to 1750. Rabbinic and lay leaders of Prague sign an ordinance whereby holding communal office is dependent on election by the majority of the community and limited to one year. As in Poland–Lithuania, the Jews of Bohemia and Moravia must struggle with the state for the right to complete independence in electing communal leaders. Daniel Rodriguez, a Dalmatian Marrano, is authorized by the		The first Jewish printing press in Palestine is established in Safed.

A. General History	B. Jews in North and South America	C. Jews in Europe	D. Jews in the Middle East and Elsewhere	E. Jewish Culture	
		Republic of Venice to create the new port of Split. Jews are involved in rerouting trade down the Balkan rivers.			**1577**
The Battle of the Three Kings (Sebastian* of Portugal, his ally, Muhammad al-Shaykh,* and Abd al-Malik*) at Alcazarquivir leaves the latter's uncle Ahmad* in control of Morocco.		Two Marranos forewarn the Jews that Sebastian* intends to baptize them by force if he is victorious. After his defeat, the Jews of Morocco proclaim a Second Purim, called either *Purim Sebastiano* or *Purim de los Cristianos*, to commemorate deliverance from this event.			**1578**
The seven northern Netherlands provinces form the Union of Utrecht. They thereafter expel the Spanish from the Lowlands.		Marrano immigration into France increases dramatically as a result of intensified Inquisition pressure on the Marranos of Portugal.			**1579**
The ruler of Portugal cedes his throne to Philip II* of Spain. Spain absorbs Portugal into a union.	Portuguese Jews begin to enter colonial Argentina. They settle mostly in Buenos Aires, Cordoba, and Tucuman and are involved primarily in commerce and trade. They are not permitted to live openly as Jews.	The Council of the Four Lands emerges in Poland. Based on the periodic sessions of the rabbis and communal leaders at the fairs of Lublin and Jaroslaw, the council consists of two bodies: a parliament of heads of principalities, selectmen, and representatives, and a supreme court of elected judges. It deals with matters affecting Polish Jewry as a whole, disputes between lands or communities, and appeals by individuals against decisions of other courts or rabbis.		Eliezer ben Elijah Ashkenazi (1513–1586), Polish rabbi, writes a commentary on the Torah, *Ma'aseh Adonai* (*Deeds of God*). He follows a rationalist trend in rabbinical scholarship and calls for individual freedom in biblical research. "Let us not permit the opinion of someone else—even if of an earlier generation—to hinder us from research. . . . Research and choose: for that you have been created and reason has been given you from heaven."	**1580**
The Dutch proclaim their independence from Spain.		Pope Gregory XIII renews the prohibition against Jewish doctors treating Christian patients. The integrity of the Jewish doctors is defended by David de Pomis in *De Medico Hebraeo enarratio apologetica*,			**1581**

	A. General History	B. Jews in North and South America	C. Jews in Europe	D. Jews in the Middle East and Elsewhere	E. Jewish Culture
1581			which will be published in Venice in 1588.		
1582			A general synod of German Jewry meets to restore a comprehensive judicial and financial system for all of German Jewry. It establishes five principal rabbinic courts in Frankfurt, Worms, Fulda, Friedberg, and Guenzburg. This action reflects a general revival of Jewish life in Germany in the late 16th century.		Rabbi Solomon ben Joshua Adeni (1567–c.1625) enters the Safed yeshiva of Rabbi Hayyim Vital. Adeni later writes a commentary on the Mishnah. His use of primary sources and variant manuscripts of the text and earlier commentaries results in a commentary known for its fidelity to the plain meaning of the text.
1584	An expedition sent by Sir Walter Raleigh,* English explorer, to the New World lands in Virginia. In 1585, his colonists will settle on Roanoke Island.				
1585	The Spanish troops of Philip II* occupy Antwerp causing trade and financial activity to shift to Amsterdam.	Joachim Gaunse, a mining technologist from Prague, comes to America to serve as the metallurgist at Roanoke Island, Virginia, in the colony founded by Sir Walter Raleigh.* Gaunse is the first recorded Jew in English-speaking North America. Remaining for less than one year, he returns to England, where in 1589 he will be indicted as a Jew for blasphemy. Gaunse is credited with revolutionizing England's copper smelting industry.			
1586			The last meeting of Jewish delegates from throughout the Jewish communities of Italy takes place. Though there is an attempt to centralize Jewish self-government in Italy in the 15th and 16th centuries, the emphasis remains primarily on local institutions rather	The Jews of San'a, Yemen, are persecuted by the iman who accuses them of aiding the Turks. Regulations about special Jewish garments and headgear are imposed. The Nahmanides synagogue, established about	

A. General History	B. Jews in North and South America	C. Jews in Europe	D. Jews in the Middle East and Elsewhere	E. Jewish Culture	
		than on regional or supraregional organization.	1266, is confiscated by the Arabs under the rule of Jerusalem's governor, Abu Sufain,* and converted to a warehouse.		1586
The first important play of Christopher Marlowe* (1564–1593), *Tamburlaine the Great*, is performed. Marlowe* is the greatest figure in Elizabethan drama before Shakespeare* and establishes the use of blank verse in the English theater.			Bezalel Ashkenazi (c.1520–c.1591/94), leader of the rabbis of Jerusalem, appeals to Italian Jewry to finance the restoration of the Nahmanides synagogue in Jerusalem. Though the synagogue is not restored, Ashkenazi is responsible for several communal reforms including the stipulation that one-sixth of all funds for Jerusalem collected overseas by Ashkenazic emissaries be allocated to the Sephardic community.	Salomone De'Rossi (c.1570–c.1630) enters the service of Duke Vicenzo I* of Mantua as a singer and musician. He becomes the leading Jewish composer of the late Italian Renaissance.	1587
The English navy defeats the Spanish Armada, thereby preventing Spanish involvement in English affairs and heralding the decline of Spanish influence in central Europe.		Jan Zamojski* founds the town of Zamosc, Poland, and gives Sephardic Jews the same rights as other burghers. While some cities and towns forbid Jewish settlement, they are the exceptions rather than the rule from the 16th to 18th centuries.		*Mishlei Shu'alim* (*Fox Fables*) is translated into Yiddish and becomes part of European Jewish culture. It is believed to have been written by Rabbi Berechiah ben Natronai ha-Nakdan at the end of the 12th or beginning of the 13th century when fox fables were very popular. A Hebrew printing was done in Mantua in 1557.	1588
The Jew of Malta, a romantic tragedy by Christopher Marlowe,* is performed. It is a portrait of Barabas, a wicked Jewish merchant. Like Shakespeare's* Shylock, Barabas has a beautiful daughter, Abigail, who becomes a Christian.					1589
At about this time, the plays of William Shakespeare* (1564–1616), English		Marranos of Portuguese and Spanish origin begin to settle in		The first printed collection of *tehinot* is composed by Abraham Apteker	1590

	A. General History	B. Jews in North and South America	C. Jews in Europe	D. Jews in the Middle East and Elsewhere	E. Jewish Culture
1590	poet and dramatist, are performed. The most widely known author in all English literature, he establishes drama as a respected literary medium.		Amsterdam after the northern provinces of the Netherlands declare their independence of Catholic Spain. They do not openly reveal themselves as Jews. Under the leadership of Mordecai Jaffe (1530–1612), 30 leading Polish rabbis issue an ordinance "that no rabbi shall receive rabbinic office for money [given] before or after, or through other conditions that bring monetary profit." Jaffe's compendium of Jewish law, *Levushim* (*Garments*), becomes very popular and further enhances his rabbinic reputation.		and printed in Prague. This genre of personal supplications and petitions flourishes alongside the formal prayer book. They are usually written in Yiddish and often composed by women. Jacob Ashkenazi of Janow writes *Ze'enah u-Re'enah* (*Come and See*), a Yiddish work that receives widespread popularity among women and from which they learn biblical stories and observations on Jewish customs and morals. The oldest existing edition dates from 1622.
1592					David Gans (1541–1613) of Prague, scholar and chronicler of Ashkenazic Jewry, completes *Tsemah David* (*Offspring of David*). Written "for householders like myself," this history is divided into two separate parts, Jewish history from Creation to his own time and a general history of gentile nations and emperors.
1593	Joseph Justus Scaliger* (1540–1609) is appointed to a professorship at the University of Leiden in the Netherlands. Believing that all Latin Bible translations are corrupt, Scaliger advocates study of Hebrew by biblical scholars. He favors resettlement of Jews in western Europe not only for economic reasons, but also because non-Jews "need to learn from them."		Marcus Meisel, Prague financier and the first Court Jew, comes under the direct protection of the emperor, gaining the status of a noble. This unprecedented privilege comes in recognition of Meisel's financial services to the crown. He is also an unstinting supporter of the Jewish community and its institutions. Pope Clement VIII (1592–1605) expels the Jews living in all the papal states		

A. General History	B. Jews in North and South America	C. Jews in Europe	D. Jews in the Middle East and Elsewhere	E. Jewish Culture
		except Rome, Avignon, and Ancona.		**1593**
		Jews are invited to settle in Leghorn, the main port of Tuscany, in central Italy, where they are granted full religious liberty and civil rights. The Medici, rulers of Leghorn, sought to develop it into a center of commerce. In 1600, about 100 Jews will live there. Their number will grow to about 3,000 in 1689 and 5,000 at the end of the 18th century. It is the only large Italian city without a closed ghetto.		
		Dr. Roderigo Lopes (1525–1594), physician to Queen Elizabeth I* of England since 1586 and one of about 80 Marranos known to live in London during her reign, is executed on a false charge of attempting to poison the queen. His fate causes the Marrano community to dwindle away.		*Hizzuk Emunah* (*The Strengthening of Faith*), an apology of Judaism written by Isaac ben Abraham of Troki (c.1533–c.1594), a Karaite scholar from Lithuania, is completed by his pupil after his death. Conversant with Catholic and Protestant theologians, Troki attacks Christianity and the Gospels as illogical and inconsistent. His apology of Judaism will be adopted by rabbinic Jews in their disputes with Christians. **1594**
		King Henry IV* (1589–1610) issues privileges to the Jews of Metz, guaranteeing them the right to practice Judaism openly. This contributes to Metz becoming a major Jewish community in 17th-century Europe. A Portuguese Marrano Jewish community is established in Amsterdam. In the wake of the Dutch extension of their		**1595**

	A. General History	B. Jews in North and South America	C. Jews in Europe	D. Jews in the Middle East and Elsewhere	E. Jewish Culture
1595			blockade of Antwerp, which prevents ships from entering or leaving the Flemish seaports with Portuguese colonial goods. The Catholic church establishes the *Index Expurgatorius* (*Sefer ha-Zikkukh*) of Hebrew books, which lists books that may not be read without having individual passages deleted or revised before publication. Official revisers, sometimes apostate Jews, are appointed to censor the books according to regulations in *De correctione librorum* (Regarding the correction of books). The Casale Monferrato synagogue in Piedmont is built. Typical of Italian synagogues in northwestern Italy during the Renaissance period, it is located in a courtyard. The main entrance door does not open from the street as the Jews are concerned for their security and laws in many communities forbid Jewish prayer to be heard by Christians.		
1596	William Shakespeare* writes *The Merchant of Venice*. At its core is the best-known Jew of English literature, Shylock, the moneylender of medieval legend who seeks his pound of flesh. Shylock's beautiful daughter Jessica elopes with a Christian.	Luis de Carvajal the Younger, his mother and three sisters are burned at the stake in Mexico. His uncle, Luis de Carvajal, is governor of part of northeastern Mexico. The Governor discovered their inclination toward Judaism.			
1597			Nine hundred Jews are expelled from Milan, now under Spanish rule.		

A. General History	B. Jews in North and South America	C. Jews in Europe	D. Jews in the Middle East and Elsewhere	E. Jewish Culture	
The Edict of Nantes is issued by Henry IV* in France granting religious and political freedom. Boris Godunov* becomes czar (1598–1605) of Russia.				Rabbi Judah Loew ben Bezalel (Maharal of Prague, c.1525–1609) writes *Be'er ha-Golah* (*Well of Exile*) in which he condemns religious fanaticism and religious compulsion. He pleads that each nation be permitted to preserve its own faith. He writes extensively against the outdated educational methods and curriculum of his day and the emphasis on *pilpul*. He is also renowned as the creator of the legend of the Golem, an inert creature brought magically to life to protect the Jews of Prague from their enemies.	**1598**
				Rabbi Judah Loew ben Bezalel writes *Netsah Yisrael* (*Eternal One of Israel*), a Jewish theory of the history of civilizations, in which he maintains that God will not forsake his people, that the Messiah will come, and that the Temple in Jerusalem will be rebuilt. He believes that Palestine is the natural territorial center of the Jewish people.	**1599**
The English East India Trading Company is chartered.		The Jewish population of Czechoslovakia grows from a few dozen in 1564, to over 3,000 due largely to immigration by Polish Jews. This first important buildup of Jewish population west of Poland since the 13th century marks the beginning of the reversal of Jewish migration from west to east. Under the Polish Arenda system, Jews lease estates from the Polish			**1600**

	A. General History	B. Jews in North and South America	C. Jews in Europe	D. Jews in the Middle East and Elsewhere	E. Jewish Culture
1600			nobility at fixed rates for a specified number of years in order to manage them and receive income from them. Inns and flour mills often come to be leased to Jewish families. Jews sell liquor and commodities to peasants and buy their agricultural produce.		
1601			Marranos, given permission to leave Spain and Portugal after selling their property, begin to settle in the German cities of Hamburg, Altona, and Glueckstadt, as well as in Denmark. Though they arrive as Christians, they soon begin to live openly as Jews. Upon the death of Marcus Meisel, Court Jew to the Hapsburg Emperor Rudolph II,* his estate is seized by the state. Meisel spent large sums on the Prague Jewish community and financed Jewish communities in Poland and Palestine.		
1602	The Dutch East India Company is founded.		A community of Jews lives openly in Amsterdam, possibly as early as 1591. Their commercial activity flourishes with their ties to Jews in central and eastern Europe, Italy, North Africa, and even Portugal from where they had earlier been expelled.		Moses ben Hanokh Altschul (c.1546–1633) writes *Brant Shpigl* (*The Burning Mirror*), the first comprehensive book of ethics written in Yiddish. Typical of a series of Yiddish morality works of the late 16th and early 17th centuries, it is directed at women who cannot read Hebrew. These books become popular among German Jews. The oldest printed edition of the *Maaseh-Buch* is published in Basle. A collection of 257

A. General History	B. Jews in North and South America	C. Jews in Europe	D. Jews in the Middle East and Elsewhere	E. Jewish Culture	
				tales of anonymous authorship, dating from around 1580, it is a treasure of Yiddish folktales and novellas, weaving together foreign and Jewish motifs for popular entertainment.	**1602**
		The last meeting of the comprehensive German Jewish synod takes place. It had begun meeting in the 11th century, but with the gradual decline of central rule in Germany, the Jewish community switches to a form of regional organization that proves more viable.		In Italy, despite much opposition, Leone Modena (1571–1648) has a choir accompany the service in the synagogue in Ferrara. The harpsichord accompanies synagogue services on weekdays and Simhat Torah in Sephardic synagogues in Venice, Amsterdam, and Hamburg.	**1603**
			Safed is attacked by Druze. Weakened by plague in 1602, Safed is seized repeatedly by the Druze (1628, 1636), and the Jewish community is plundered, forcing many Jews to flee.		**1604**
Peace is established between China and Japan.		Polish and Lithuanian Jewry introduce the *heter iskah*. This regulation allows one Jew to participate in the transactions of another by advancing money in return for a specified percentage on the capital investment. It is necessary at this time of rapid development of Jewish business to deal with the biblical prohibition of lending money at interest to a fellow Jew.			**1607**
Ben Jonson* (1572–1637) writes *The Alchemist*. Along with *Volpone* (1606) and other plays, the popularity and esteem that his writings inspire give Jonson* a reputation in England second		Vladislav,* a Polish prince, is elected czar of Russia. He stipulates that no non-Orthodox denomination be allowed in Russia and that "Jews must not be admitted to the Muscovite		Seligmann Ulma writes *Der Tsukhtshpigl* (*The Mirror of Virtue*). Published in Germany, it is a Yiddish reworking of rhymed maxims and moral lessons collected from	**1610**

	A. General History	B. Jews in North and South America	C. Jews in Europe	D. Jews in the Middle East and Elsewhere	E. Jewish Culture
1610	only to Shakespeare.*		Empire whether on business or for any other purpose."		talmudic and posttalmudic literature and is typical of a very popular literary genre.
1611	The King James, or Authorized Version, of the Bible is published in England. The work of 47 scholars laboring in six groups at three locations for seven years, its powerful style makes it the generally accepted English translation for three centuries.				
1612			There are 10 Jewish brokers among the 300 members of the Amsterdam mercantile exchange.		Samuel Edels (Maharsha, 1555–1631), leading Polish Talmud commentator, begins publication of *Hiddushei Halakhot* (*Halakhic Insights*), an explanation of the talmudic text in accordance with the view of Rashi and the Tosafists. His work, completed in 1621, is included in almost every edition of the Talmud.
1613	After a period of instability, Michael Romanov* is crowned czar of Russia. He rules until 1645, and the Romanov dynasty will remain in power until 1917.			Julius Aleni, a Jesuit missionary and Hebraist, visits the synagogue of Kaifeng after his predecessor, Father Ricci (1581–1610), is visited in Peking by a Jew from Kaifeng.	
1614	*The plunder of the Jewish Quarter of Frankfurt by a mob led by Vincent Fettmilch. Engraving by G. Keller.*		A Frankfurt mob, led by Vincent Fettmilch,* plunders the Jewish quarter and expels the Jews. Hapsburg Emperor Matthias* returns the Jews to their homes and hangs the leaders of the mob. The event is thereafter celebrated as the Purim of Vincent.		Yom Tov Lipmann Heller (1579–1654), Moravian rabbi, writes *Tosefot Yom Tov* (*The Glosses of Yom Tov*). Published in Prague, this commentary on the Mishnah becomes very popular due to its clarity of language and style. In some cases Heller defends his views against the opinions of the sages.
1615			Hugo Grotius* (1583–1645), Holland's leading		

A. General History	B. Jews in North and South America	C. Jews in Europe	D. Jews in the Middle East and Elsewhere	E. Jewish Culture	
		jurist, reports on the findings of his commission appointed to consider a petition of Jews who fled from Spain and Portugal and who seek asylum in Holland. They decide in favor of admission, to permit freedom of worship subject to prohibition of mixed marriages, and to limit the number of families to 300 in Amsterdam and 200 in the provinces. The report is adopted as the Dutch recognize the value of the mercantile experience of the Jews. A bitter struggle breaks out in Frankfurt over the oligarchic rule that controls the Jewish community. The Council of Four Lands intervenes and eventually brings about an agreement to hold annual elections and ensure rotation of officers, common practices in the communities of Poland. The conflict continues until 1628.			**1615**
An Italian nobleman, Pietro della Valle,* locates the ruined remains of ancient Babylon. His later discovery of cuneiform inscriptions from various Mesopotamian sites spurs archeological interest in the Middle East among Europeans.		Rabbi Isaac Uziel (d. 1622), who left North Africa for Amsterdam in 1606, where he became a teacher and rabbi of the Neveh Shalom congregation, writes of the Jews in Amsterdam: "At present people live peaceably in Amsterdam. . . . Each may follow his own belief, but may not openly show that he is a different faith from the inhabitants of the city."	Sir Thomas Roe,* an English traveler, confirms the existence of Jews in northern India under Mogul rule. Mainly of Persian and Khurasan origin, Jews establish communities in Old Delhi, Lahore, Agra, Fatehpur, and Kashmir.	Leone Modena, Italian rabbi and scholar, writes *Historia de'riti Ebraici*. This systematic description of Jewish customs is one of the earliest modern attempts to describe Judaism to non-Jews. Its popularity will be bolstered by translation into English (1650), French (1671), Dutch (1683), and Latin (1693).	**1616**
The Thirty Years' War (1618–1648) begins with the Bohemian king, Ferdinand II,* trying to impose Catholic rule in his lands, and		The Thirty Years' War gives rise to a group of German Jewish financial dynasties such as those founded by Behrend Levi			**1618**

	A. General History	B. Jews in North and South America	C. Jews in Europe	D. Jews in the Middle East and Elsewhere	E. Jewish Culture
1618	the Protestants revolt in Bohemia and Austria. The conflict quickly widens, fueled by political, territorial, and economic ambitions.		(b. c.1600), Mordechai Gomperz (d. 1664), and Samuel Oppenheimer (1630–1703). They begin as military purveyors and become Court Jews responsible for supplying whole armies, a process that peaks in the 1670s and continues until the end of the War of the Spanish Succession (1713).		
1619					Rabbi Joel Sirkes (Bach, 1561–1640) is appointed head of the yeshiva in Cracow. Best known for his *Bayit Hadash* (*A New House*), a critical and comprehensive commentary on Jacob ben Asher's *Arba'ah Turim*, Sirkes renders many controversial legal decisions and trains some of the leading rabbis of Poland.
					Shalem ben Joseph Shabazi, the greatest of Yemenite Jewish poets, is born. In hundreds of Hebrew and Arabic poems, Shabazi uses mystical symbolism to express love of God and yearning for the Messiah. He also writes communal songs, wedding poems, love songs, and didactic poems.
1620	Pilgrims land at Plymouth Rock and establish the first permanent settlement by Europeans in New England.				
1621	The Dutch West India Company is established.\n\nWilliam Bradford,* governor of Plymouth, New England, invites neighboring Native Americans to join the		King Ferdinand II* gives the Jews of Vienna a new quarter for residence outside the city walls.		

A. General History	B. Jews in North and South America	C. Jews in Europe	D. Jews in the Middle East and Elsewhere	E. Jewish Culture	
Pilgrims in celebration of the first Thanksgiving. The three-day festival of feasting in gratitude for the bounty of the season is modeled on the biblical Festival of Sukkot.					**1621**
		The Hapsburg emperor licenses a consortium to manage the minting of silver coinage in Bohemia. Among its most prominent members is Jacob Bassevi (1570–1634), one of the first European Jews to be ennobled, who serves as financial advisor to the project. The coinage issued is extremely debased and results in legal action being taken against the members of the consortium.	The forced conversion of Persian Jews to Islam begins and does not abate until 1629. These Jews come to be known as *Jadid al-Islam* (New Muslims). Though they practice Islam in public, they retain their allegiance to Judaism, which they continue to practice in secret.		**1622**
		Bohemian Jews are now permitted to deal in grain, wine, and cloth. They had previously been barred from such trade, but Ferdinand II* (king of Bohemia, 1617–1637; Holy Roman Emperor, 1619–1637) eases these restrictions to reward the Jews for the cash and supplies that they had provided to his army.

An assembly of Lithuanian Jews separates from the Council of Four Lands and begins to function independently. It will meet until 1764 and have significant influence over Lithuanian Jewish life. | | Isaiah Horowitz (c.1565–1630), rabbi and head of a yeshiva in Poland, completes *Shenei Luhot ha-Brit* (*Two Tablets of the Covenant*, also known by the acronym Shelah) in which he popularizes many of the mystical ideas of Lurianic Kabbalah and makes them accessible to Polish Jewry.

The Council of Four Lands limits the number of musical compositions sung in the Sabbath service, evidence of an abundance of musical creativity on the part of synagogue cantors. | **1623** |
| The Dutch drive the English out of the East Indies spice trade.

The Dutch establish a colony called New | | The Jews of Vienna are given a separate district in which they are permitted to build a synagogue, something prohibited since 1421. The local | | Salomone De'Rossi (c.1570–c.1630), leading Jewish composer of the Italian Renaissance, writes *Canti ha-Shirim Asher* | **1624** |

	A. General History	B. Jews in North and South America	C. Jews in Europe	D. Jews in the Middle East and Elsewhere	E. Jewish Culture
1624	Netherlands, with the town New Amsterdam on the lower end of Manhattan Island in New York. Cardinal Richelieu enters and comes to dominate the royal council in France.		citizenry protest, but the Jewish quarter, under control of the imperial chancery rather than the city council, flourishes. In Amsterdam, Uriel da Costa (1585–1640) completes his *Examen dos Tradicioens Phariseas Conferidas con a Ley Escrita*. Da Costa is excommunicated, and the book is prohibited and burned by the leaders of the Jewish community because of its attacks on rabbinic authority and the doctrine of the immortality of the soul as biblically derived. Born in Portugal to a Marrano family, da Costa moved to Amsterdam to practice his own version of Judaism but came into repeated conflict with rabbis.		*li-Shelomo*, a collection of synagogal choral compositions. It is the first Hebrew book to be printed with musical notations. One of a number of Italian Jewish court musicians, most of De'Rossi's secular music is not composed specifically for Jews.
1625	John Donne* (1572–1631) writes *Four Sermons on Special Occasions*. Along with his secular and metaphysical poetry, Donne's* sermons bring him a reputation as a leading poet and prose writer of England.			Muhammad ibn Farouk* of Nablus purchases the office of pasha. He imprisons the Jewish leaders in Jerusalem, confiscates property, and imposes heavy taxes on the Jewish community. By 1663 most of Jerusalem's Jews have fled to Ramleh.	
1626					Manasseh ben Israel (1604–1657), Amsterdam scholar, founds the first Hebrew printing press in Amsterdam. Discarding the Venice type, he has his own type cast, which becomes dominant throughout Europe. He follows the Dutch style of book design and illustration, often including a portrait of the author in the frontispiece. He will publish Hebrew Bibles and prayer

A. General History	B. Jews in North and South America	C. Jews in Europe	D. Jews in the Middle East and Elsewhere	E. Jewish Culture	
				books in various languages, including a Yiddish book of religious customs, *Book of Minhagim*, in 1645.	**1626**
		The Jews of Holland respond to a call for aid by the Jews of Venice on behalf of Jews in Jerusalem who suffer at the hands of the despotic Turkish governor, Muhammad ibn Farouk.* Jewish communities makes a practice of collecting funds annually to support the Jews of Israel. The Jewish Council of Lithuania decides to send emissaries to the communities to ensure fair apportionment of communal taxes. After 1648, the worsening condition of the Jews of Poland and Lithuania makes equitable collection of these taxes even more difficult. Emperor Ferdinand II* grants Jews the right to trade at all the fairs in Bohemia and Silesia. This privilege, in gratitude for a loan to the emperor, greatly increases Jewish trade in central Europe.			**1627**
Ferdinand II* of Germany issues the Edict of Restitution, which returns to Rome church lands seized by Protestants.				Joseph Solomon Delmedigo (1591–1655), rabbi, mathematician, astronomer, and philosopher, writes *Elim* (an allusion to Exodus 15:27), an answer to questions put to him by a Karaite scholar from Lithuania. Delmedigo is one of the most interesting Jewish personalities of his time, possessing a wide range of knowledge. Born in Candia of a distinguished family,	**1629**

	A. General History	B. Jews in North and South America	C. Jews in Europe	D. Jews in the Middle East and Elsewhere	E. Jewish Culture
1629					he studied astronomy and medicine in Padua and lived in Egypt, Constantinople, Poland, Hamburg, and Amsterdam.
1630		The short-lived Dutch conquest of northeastern Brazil leads to the establishment of the first Jewish community in the New World. It ends in 1654 when Brazil comes under Portuguese rule and the Inquisition is reintroduced.	Austrian soldiers capture Mantua and sack the Jewish quarter. Though the surviving Jews are then expelled, they are soon allowed to return due to the intervention of the Jewish leaders of Vienna with the emperor. An outbreak of plague leads to a severe reduction in trade and industry throughout Italy. This reinforces the already existing interest of Italian princes in Jewish immigration and succeeds in attracting Jews from Spain, Brazil, Holland, and North Africa from approximately 1645 to the late 1660s.		Joseph Juspa ben Phineas Seligmann Hahn (Nordlingen, 1570–1637), German rabbi of Frankfurt, completes *Yosif Omets* (*May He Increase in Strength*), a popular work on the laws and customs of Jews throughout the year. It is a rich source of information on the practices of and events affecting this significant Jewish community.
1633			Antonio Fernandez Carvajal (c.1590–1659), Portuguese Marrano merchant, moves from Rouen to London where he engages in large-scale trade with the East and West Indies. Carvajal is head of the crypto-Jewish community in London at the time Manasseh ben Israel undertakes his mission, in 1655, to obtain the readmission of Jews to England. Under the influence of Cardinal Richelieu, Louis XIII* dismisses charges of Judaism against New Christians in France. In this half-century French crypto-Jews come to practice Judaism more openly.		

A. General History	B. Jews in North and South America	C. Jews in Europe	D. Jews in the Middle East and Elsewhere	E. Jewish Culture	

| | | | | In Lublin, Moses Moravchik publishes a pamphlet entitled "How to Organize Learning," which is critical of elementary Jewish schooling in Germany and eastern Europe. The private heder (one-room schoolhouse) is deficient because of improper programs and methods of instruction and the teacher's desire to promote pupils for fear of losing them and their instruction fees. | **1635** |

| Roger Williams* (c.1603–1683), who came to America in 1630 with the Puritan founders of the Massachusetts Bay colony, is banished from the colony for heresy and founds the tolerant town of Providence in the Rhode Island colony. Rhode Island will be the first settlement in New England to allow a Jewish community, in Newport.

Peasant revolts break out in southern and western France. | | 

Manasseh Ben Israel (1604–1657). An etching by Rembrandt van Rijn. | | Manasseh ben Israel, Amsterdam scholar, writes *The Creation Problem* in Latin, which is directed to non-Jews. It contains a preface written by influential humanist writer Caspar Barleus,* who implies that Christians do not have a monopoly on piety and that Jews and Christians might live "as friends before God." Barleus* is rebuked by many.

Rembrandt van Rijn* etches a portrait of Manasseh ben Israel, Amsterdam scholar, who is his friend and neighbor. | **1636** |

| | | Simone Luzzatto (1583–1663), rabbi in Venice for 57 years after his ordination in 1606, writes *Essay on the Jews in Venice*, the first apologetic work urging toleration of the Jews through use of economic arguments. He argues for better treatment of Italian Jewry based on their economic usefulness, diligence, faithfulness, and antiquity. Unlike foreign merchants, the Jews have no homeland of their own to which they might wish to | | | **1638** |

	A. General History	B. Jews in North and South America	C. Jews in Europe	D. Jews in the Middle East and Elsewhere	E. Jewish Culture
1638			transfer the wealth they have gained in Venice.		
1639	The Ottoman Turks capture Iraq from Persia.	Jews settle in Surinam. They come from Brazil and Holland and set up sugar cane plantations. An auto-da-fé is held in Lima, Peru, after the discovery of Jews among the Portuguese merchants of Lima. Seven Jews are burned at the stake including Manuel Bautista Perez, the city's wealthiest merchant, and the physician Francisco Maldonado de Silva.	A Sephardic synagogue in Amsterdam is opened, replacing three synagogues that amalgamated into one congregation. It will be sold in 1675 and be replaced by a new Sephardic synagogue capable of serving a larger community.		
1640	Portugal revolts against Spain and reestablishes its throne.		Uriel da Costa, excommunicated in 1624, rejoins the Amsterdam Jewish community but must submit to flogging in the synagogue. The humiliation leads to his suicide. Da Costa becomes an example of a freethinker opposing religious orthodoxy.		
1644			Antonio De Montezinos (d. c.1650), a Marrano traveler, reports to Amsterdam Jews, including Manasseh ben Israel, of his trip to South America in 1641–1642 in which he discovered the "ten lost tribes of Israel" in what is now Ecuador. He swore that he saw a group of natives who could recite the Shema and were aware of other Jewish rituals.		Leone Modena, Italian rabbi, writes *Magen VaHerev* (*Shield and Sword*), a polemical work in which he claims that Jesus never considered himself the Son of God. He also states that the main tenets of Christianity stem from a much later date and were heavily influenced by pagan beliefs and customs.
1648	The Peace of Westphalia ends the Thirty Years' War.		Led by Bogdan Chmielnicki,* Ukrainian peasants, helped by Dnieper cossacks and Tartars from the Crimea, revolt against Polish landlords and their Jewish agents for the treatment received under the Arenda system of land use.		Rembrandt van Rijn* etches *The Jews in the Synagogue*, a scene believed to be of everyday Jewish life in Amsterdam. The figures have been identified as Ashkenazic Jews who, in 1648, were granted permission to construct a

A. General History	B. Jews in North and South America	C. Jews in Europe	D. Jews in the Middle East and Elsewhere	E. Jewish Culture	
		The main victims are Jews, with whom they have the most contact, and it is believed that 100,000 Jews are killed and 300 communities destroyed. Combined with the later Muscovite invasions of Poland, the mass destruction leads to large-scale migration of Jews from the east to Germany and western Europe. The Council of Mechanics in England adopts a resolution in favor of religious tolerance "not excepting Turkes, nor Papists nor Jewes." As a result of the Thirty Years' War (1618–1638), Livorno becomes the major Mediterranean shipping port, and the Jewish merchant population flourishes there.		synagogue of their own. Some critics believe that the men in fur caps may represent Polish Jews who, in 1648, fled their homeland, which was being overrun by cossacks. Naphtali ben Jacob Bacharach writes *Emek ha-Melekh* (*Valley of the King*), which is published in Germany. This work popularizes and spreads the mysticism of Lurianic Kabbalah to the lands north of the Alps.	**1648**
	Solomon Franco, a Jew, arrives in Boston from Holland with a consignment of goods. He proposes to settle in the colony. His request is denied by the Puritan authorities, and he is given several weeks' subsistence until he secures passage for return to Holland. There is a huge auto-da-fé in Mexico City. Only 13 of the 109 victims are "reconciled" and escape execution.	Joanna and Ebenezer Cartwright,* two English Baptists living in Amsterdam, submit a petition requesting the readmission of Jews to England. Jewish life flourishes in Poland–Lithuania despite the heavy losses during the Chmielnicki massacres. This is due to the support of the nobles who are committed to furthering settlement in the east and to the Polish kings who adopt favorable policies toward the Jews in order to advance their own mercantile interests.			**1649**
	Jews of Dutch Brazil (Recife and Mauricia) number about 650. Many had died during war with the Portuguese or had returned to Holland.	From 1650 to 1700, Jewish merchants in Amsterdam are among the first groups to engage in modern capitalistic activities. Their special industries are		The Council of Four Lands, the governing body of Polish Jewry, proclaims a fast to be celebrated each year on the 20th of Sivan to commemorate the Chmielnicki pogroms	**1650**

The Jews in the Synagogue. An etching by Rembrandt van Rijn.

	A. General History	B. Jews in North and South America	C. Jews in Europe	D. Jews in the Middle East and Elsewhere	E. Jewish Culture
1650			tobacco, printing, and diamonds. They trade with the Iberian Peninsula, England, Italy, Africa, India, and the East and West Indies. They are active in the stock market, owning a quarter of the shares of the East India Company. Manasseh ben Israel, Amsterdam scholar who advocates the readmission of the Jews to England, writes *The Hope of Israel*. Dedicated to Parliament, the book reports the "discovery" in South America by Antonio De Montezinos of the lost ten tribes. He uses this "evidence" of the worldwide dispersal of the Jews as an argument to convince Oliver Cromwell* to permit their return to England, then the only country without Jews. The Messiah would come when the Jews were dispersed throughout the world. The book influences English theologians, and he is invited to visit England. Frederick William,* the great elector of East Prussia from 1640 to 1688 who inherited principalities in western Germany, permits Polish Jews to trade but not reside in Brandenburg for seven years. He renews the privilege in 1660.		of 1648. Although contemporary *selihot* are composed, the communities of Poland follow the custom of Rabbi Yom Tov Lipmann Heller to recite the *selihot* composed in the 12th century after the burning at the stake of the French Jews of Blois. The fast day will be observed in eastern Europe until the outbreak of World War II.
1651	The Navigation Act is passed in England. It stipulates that all goods imported into England must be carried on English ships or ships from the country of origin. It is intended to limit Dutch involvement in shipping. Thomas Hobbes* (1588–1679), English	Jews come to Curaçao by agreement with the Dutch West India Company after the Dutch acquire it from Spain in 1643. The Sephardic Jewish community there becomes the largest in the West Indies. Other Jewish communities are established in Barbados, Jamaica,	Sephardic Jewish shippers in Amsterdam seek to have Jews readmitted to England. They hope to circumvent the Navigation Act and regain their foothold in international shipping by establishing themselves or their relatives in London.		

A. General History	B. Jews in North and South America	C. Jews in Europe	D. Jews in the Middle East and Elsewhere	E. Jewish Culture	
political philosopher, writes *Leviathan*. It uses secular and utilitarian arguments to defend the absolute power of the state. The book is peppered with biblical prooftexts that are excised in most modern editions.	Martinique, and Tobago.				**1651**
The Anglo-Dutch wars begin. They last until 1674 and result in the division of America and the East Indies into colonial spheres of influence by the two powers.		The Jewish community council of Lithuania undertakes supervision of a program sponsored by various communities to aid 2,000 needy refugees from the Chmielnicki pogroms and to raise money needed to ransom Jewish prisoners. Jews of Italy, Constantinople, Amsterdam, and Hamburg send aid as well.			**1652**
Oliver Cromwell* rules as lord protector of England until his death in 1658.				Nathan Hannover (d. 1683), of Polish origin but forced to wander through Europe because of the Chmielnicki pogroms, writes *Yeven Metsula* (*Deep Mire*). The book is a chronicle of the events that led up to the depredations. He attempts to prove from Scripture that the pogroms were foreseen by King David. This popular book will be translated into several languages and go through many editions well into the 20th century.	**1653**
After many years of guerilla warfare, the Dutch in Brazil are defeated by the Portuguese and capitulate in January.	Following the Portuguese victory in Brazil, the Dutch, including all Jews, are required to leave Brazil within three months. The majority leave for Amsterdam, some sail to the Caribbean islands, and some leave for the Dutch colonial town of New				**1654**

	A. General History	B. Jews in North and South America	C. Jews in Europe	D. Jews in the Middle East and Elsewhere	E. Jewish Culture
1654		Amsterdam (New York). On July 8, Jacob Barsimon arrives in New Amsterdam aboard the ship *Peartree* from Holland, about two months before 23 Jews arrive from Brazil. Regarded as the earliest Jewish settler of New Amsterdam, he was a champion of equal rights for Jews, insisting with Asser Levy on the right to stand guard duty in place of paying a special tax. In September, the French privateer *St. Catherine* brings 23 Jewish refugees to New Amsterdam from Recife in Brazil. Peter Stuyvesant* (1592–1672), the governor of New Amsterdam, greets the Jewish refugees from Brazil with unexpected hostility. Although they are Dutch subjects, he protests to the Dutch West India Company against their settlement. He calls them "a deceitful race" who should not be allowed "to infect and trouble this new colony."			
1655	Sweden invades Poland as part of the Russian–Swedish War.	In April, the Dutch West India Company advises Peter Stuyvesant* that Jews may remain in New Amsterdam, "provided the poor among them shall not become a burden to the company or the community, but be supported by their own nation." The Amsterdam Jewish community, some of whom had investments in the company, had intervened on their behalf. The letter	Jews carry arms and assist in the defense of Poland, and city officials frequently train Jews in the use of firearms. Many Jewish communities are struck hard by the war. Manasseh ben Israel arrives in England from Amsterdam to petition Oliver Cromwell* to formally readmit the Jews to England. Cromwell* favors their readmission and convenes a Whitehall		Manasseh ben Israel, Amsterdam scholar, writes and publishes *Piedra Gloriosa*, an apocalyptic treatise based on Daniel's interpretation of Nebuchadnezzar's* dream, for which Rembrandt van Rijn* etched four illustrations. Three of the images relate to biblical references to a stone with spiritual qualities, which Manasseh believes to be messianic symbols. It is only one of three

A. General History	B. Jews in North and South America	C. Jews in Europe	D. Jews in the Middle East and Elsewhere	E. Jewish Culture	
	mentions the loyalty of the Jews to the Dutch in Brazil and their capital investments in the company. England captures Jamaica, in the West Indies, from Spain.	conference to consider the petition. Sensing negative reaction, including opposition of London merchants who fear Jewish economic competition, he dissolves the conference and arranges an informal Jewish presence in England.		times Rembrandt* illustrates a book. It represents, also, the collaboration of a Protestant and Jew on a religious theme.	**1655**
	In June, Peter Stuyvesant* is ordered to allow the Jews of New Amsterdam to engage in trade and to own real estate. However, other restrictions prevail, and Jews are barred from holding civic office and from conducting religious services.	In March, a group of Marranos already settled in London, joined by Mannaseh ben Israel, petition Oliver Cromwell* for the right of religious practice. Later that year, the petition is assented to by the Council of State. Although not a formal action, the settlement of Jews in England is, thereafter, never questioned. Mannaseh's theological arguments, potential economic benefits, and a general trend toward religious tolerance are factors in this decision. Baruch de Spinoza (1632–1677) is excommunicated from the Amsterdam Jewish community on the accusation that he denies the divine inspiration of the Torah, the existence of angels, and the immortality of the soul. He is the first Jew known to have rejected his faith and withdrawn from Jewish society without adopting another religion. He becomes an outstanding figure in world philosophy.	The Jews of Isfahan are expelled or forced to convert to Islam. Under Shah 'Abbas I* (1588–1629), Jews, Armenians, and other Christians had been allowed to settle in the Iranian capital. In 1661 the remaining Jews will be allowed to practice Judaism openly if they agree to pay the poll tax arrears and wear a distinguishing patch on their outer garments.	Manasseh ben Israel publishes *Vindiciae Judaeorum*, an important apologetic work he wrote during his mission to England. It refutes all anti-Jewish libels, especially the blood libel, and emphasizes the material benefits that acceptance of the Jews may bring to a state. A book of Spanish poetry by Jacob de Pina, a Marrano merchant, is confiscated and burned by the leaders of the Amsterdam Jewish community, who describe it as "lascivious." Though more open than the Jewish communities of Poland or the Balkans, internal Jewish censorship is also practiced in central and western Europe.	**1656**
	Asser Levy (d. 1681), a member of the first group of Jews to arrive in New Amsterdam in 1654, wins the right to serve in the militia, after contesting, in 1655, a	The United Netherlands affords Dutch–Jewish subjects the same rights of protection and respect as any other citizen when residing abroad or undertaking			**1657**

	A. General History	B. Jews in North and South America	C. Jews in Europe	D. Jews in the Middle East and Elsewhere	E. Jewish Culture
1657		tax assessed against Jews who were refused that right. In 1661, he will become the first Jew to own a house in New Amsterdam or anywhere in North America.	commercial or other ventures by sea or land. This is in recognition of the value of their connections with the Islamic world of the East and the Iberian world of the West. The king of Spain refuses to permit Jewish residents of the Netherlands to reside and engage in commerce in Spain and Portugal. The Peace of Muenster (1648) required this of him for all subjects of the Netherlands. In response, the States General of the Netherlands issues a Declaration Protecting the Interests of Jews Residing in Holland. Antonio Fernandez Carvajal (c.1590–1659), Marrano merchant, is one of the lessees to a plot of land outside of London for use as a Jewish cemetery. Late in 1656, he leased a house on Creechurch Lane, London, which the Jews of London converted into a synagogue. The synagogue will be enlarged in 1674.		
1658			Jews are permitted to graduate in medicine from the university at Koenigsberg, the capital of East Prussia.		Joseph Athias establishes a printing press in Amsterdam. Unlike Manasseh ben Israel, who was not admitted to the Bookseller's Guild, Athias is admitted to the guild in 1661 and is the first Jewish printer to engage in letter casting, publishing, and book selling. His first book, in 1658, is a prayer book according to the Sephardic rite. In 1659, he will publish a commentary on the Torah. He prints many Christian Bibles for export and

A. General History	B. Jews in North and South America	C. Jews in Europe	D. Jews in the Middle East and Elsewhere	E. Jewish Culture	
				will announce, in 1687, that he has exported more than a million Bibles to England and Scotland.	**1658**
	An entry in the General Court of Hartford, noting the arrest of "David the Jew" for peddling, is the first record of a Jew living in Connecticut.	The Jews in the small villages of Bohemia begin meeting as a separate regional council apart from Prague to avoid being totally dominated by this largest Jewish community in Europe. Together with the Council of Moravia, these groups supervise Jewish affairs in the *landjudenschaften* of central Europe.			**1659**
Charles II* (1660–1685) is recalled from exile and restored to the throne of England.		Restoration of the Stuart monarchy brings a challenge to the newly reestablished Jewish community in London when King Charles II* is petitioned to expel them. The fact that Jewish cloth merchants are underselling established London merchants is brought as proof that Jews endanger the economy. Charles II,* more interested in vital cloth exports, rejects the petition. Irish records relate the existence of a Jewish house of worship on Crane Lane, Dublin. It serves a community of Spanish and Portuguese Jews, some of whom were refugees from the 16th-century Inquisition in the Canary Islands. The community virtually disappears by 1790, due to the disastrous social and political conditions prevalent at that time.	Tiberias is completely destroyed in the wake of Bedouin tribal wars and remains in ruins for the next 80 years.		**1660**
Passage of the Toleration Act in England gives	The Jews of Jamaica benefit from England's efforts to	Hector d'Azevedo is sent by the States General of the		Joseph Athias, publisher and printer in Amsterdam,	**1661**

	A. General History	B. Jews in North and South America	C. Jews in Europe	D. Jews in the Middle East and Elsewhere	E. Jewish Culture
1661	Protestant dissenters the freedom to worship openly as long as they profess belief in the Trinity. The Corporation Act of England bars from membership in municipal and commercial corporations anyone who refuses to take Communion as prescribed by the Church of England.	increase the size of the island's population. England bestows upon all settlers and their children the rights and privileges of "natural born subjects of England." However, higher taxes on Jews are imposed. They will be maintained until 1740.	Netherlands to negotiate a peace treaty with Algiers. Other Jewish negotiators include Isaac Saportas and David Torres. They also negotiate the release of Christian prisoners		publishes a Bible, prepared under the editorship of Professor Johannes Leusden* of Utrecht, in an edition of 3,000 copies. It is the first Hebrew Bible to have the verses numbered.
1662	William Hemings* writes an English drama, *The Jewes Tragedy*, which is based on the Jewish revolt against Rome as described by Josephus and *Josippon*.		John Greenhalgh* writes of his visit to London's Creechurch Lane synagogue: "I counted about or above a hundred right Jews, one proselyte among them, they were all gentlemen [merchants], I saw not one mechanic [laborer] among them."		
1663			French King Louis XIV* (1643–1715) rejects a proposal that Jews from Amsterdam be permitted to settle in Dunkirk. Though the Jews would have brought trade with them, Louis XIV* cannot tolerate their demand to practice Judaism publicly. Israel Aron, military contractor and purveyor to the mint, is permitted by Frederick William,* great elector of East Prussia from 1640 to 1688, to settle in Berlin. He becomes Court Jew to Frederick William.*	Many Jews fall victim to the intermittent war between the Turks and Christians in the Mediterranean, with Malta being a major base of slave trade. A description of a Malta slave prison notes, "Jews, Moors and Turks are made slaves here and are publicly sold in the market." The Malabar Coast in India comes under Dutch rule. Jews prosper, especially in Cochin, attracting Jewish immigrants from all over the world. They establish close ties to the Jewish community of Amsterdam.	
1664	The Conventicle Act is passed in England prohibiting all religious services other than those of the Church of England. Dutch New Amsterdam falls to		The earl of Berkshire* attempts to extort a large sum of money from the Jewish community of England by threatening to apply the Conventicle Act to Jewish worship. The Jews appeal to	The French consul in Algiers estimates the Jewish population at 10,000 to 12,000. Although they are despised by the Muslim Turks, some Jews hold key positions at court.	

A. General History	B. Jews in North and South America	C. Jews in Europe	D. Jews in the Middle East and Elsewhere	E. Jewish Culture

1664

the English and renamed New York.		the king and are reassured by the privy council that the law will not be used against them. Moses Jacobson de Jong, a Jewish merchant from Amsterdam, is permitted by the elector of Brandenburg to settle in the Baltic port of Memel, where he becomes the most important merchant.		

1665

	The Jews of New York obtain the right of freedom of worship and other advantages of English citizenship from Richard Nicholls,* the first English governor. The British colony in Surinam grants free exercise of religious rites to Jewish settlers.	In October, reports of the coming of the Messiah, in the person of Shabbetai Zevi (1626–1676), and his prophecies, visions, and miracles, sweep across Europe from one end to the other. Messianic fervor engulfs all classes of Jews in both the Ashkenazic and Sephardic communities. Lvov, Livorno, and other communities send envoys to Smyrna to pay homage to "our king."	Shabbetai Zevi, who was born in Smyrna and trained as a rabbi, travels to Gaza to visit Nathan of Gaza (1643–1680), a Kabbalist renowned for his visions. Shabbetai hopes Nathan will cure him of his mental sickness. Nathan encourages Shabbetai's delusions and leads him to proclaim himself, in May, Messiah of the Jews. Despite opposition of Jerusalem's rabbis, Nathan promotes Shabbetai's "visions" and arouses the emotions of the common people in Gaza and Hebron.	

Engraving of Shabbetai Zevi (1626–1676), sketched by an eyewitness in Smyrna, 1666.

	A. General History	B. Jews in North and South America	C. Jews in Europe	D. Jews in the Middle East and Elsewhere	E. Jewish Culture
1665			There is widespread popular indignation of Christians at the insolence of Jews in their belief that the Messiah had come in the person of Shabbetai Zevi. Riots occur in Pinsk, Vilna, and Lublin and across southern Germany. Alarmed Jewish communal officials seek government protection.	Shabbetai Zevi, after the announcing of his messiahment, moves back to Smyrna where he becomes head of that community.	In about 1665, Rembrandt van Rijn* paints *The Jewish Bride*. Some believe it to be a portrait of Daniel Levi de Barrios (1635–1701) and his second wife. Barrios was born in Spain and lived in Italy and Tobago before settling in the Netherlands, where he achieves fame as a poet and playwright.
1666			In April, Sir John Finch,* an Englishman, reports to London from Florence that many families of Jews have come to Leghorn from Rome, Verona, and Germany to "embarque to find their Messia."	In September, Shabbetai Zevi is summoned to Constantinople by the sultan. Given the choice of death or conversion to Islam, he converts on September 15 after denying he ever made messianic claims. His conversion disillusions the entire Jewish Diaspora. The Sabbatean movement survives the debacle of his apostasy and his death in 1676 and continues for a century.	
1667	John Milton* (1608–1674), English poet, writes *Paradise Lost*, which is steeped in biblical and Judaic lore. His drama *Samson Agonistes* is a powerful description of the biblical hero who, like Milton, must deal with his blindness.				
1669			Louis XIV,* under the influence of his minister of trade and finance, Jean-Baptiste Colbert* (1619–1683), agrees to allow a group of Jews from Leghorn to settle in Marseilles on a trial basis in the hope that they will stimulate trade with North Africa and the Levant. His expectation is	The Jews are expelled from Oran in Algiers for social, political, and economic reasons. They are also accused of passing information to Muslim enemies.	

A. General History	B. Jews in North and South America	C. Jews in Europe	D. Jews in the Middle East and Elsewhere	E. Jewish Culture	
		fulfilled, but the Jews will be expelled in 1682 due to Louis'* increasingly militant Catholicism. Bishop Count Kollonch urges the expulsion of all Austrian Jews before a special commission for Jewish affairs appointed by Leopold I.*			**1669**
				Baruch de Spinoza writes *Tractatus Theologico-Politicus*, whose purpose is "to explain that in a free state every man should be entitled to think what he wishes, and also to declare what he thinks." He is the first Jewish scholar to propose a scientific critical approach to the Bible. He strives to identify the authors of the biblical books and their dates of composition.	**1670**
	The governor of the British West Indian colony of Jamaica rejects a petition urging the expulsion of the Jews, writing that "his majesty could not have more profitable subjects than the Jews and the Hollanders."	The Grote Sjoel (Great Synagogue), an Ashkenazic synagogue in Amsterdam, is opened. The Great Elector Frederick William,* ruler of East Prussia from 1640 to 1688, issues an edict permitting 50 wealthy Jewish families from Austria to settle in Brandenburg. They may engage in trade, buy houses and shops, but may not open a synagogue. In September, Abraham Riess and Benedict Veit are issued a writ of privileges to remain in Berlin, marking the foundation of the Berlin community.			**1671**
		Of Amsterdam's 200,000 people, about 7,500 are Jews.			**1672**

	A. General History	B. Jews in North and South America	C. Jews in Europe	D. Jews in the Middle East and Elsewhere	E. Jewish Culture
1672			William of Orange,* later William III* of England, who leads the coalition against Louis XIV's* armies, is financed and provisioned by Dutch Sephardic Jews. Chief among them are Antonio Alvarez Machado and Jacob Pereira.		
1673	The Test Act in England disqualifies from political and civil service duties anyone who refuses to take Communion as prescribed by the Church of England. It will be repealed in 1828. The Declaration of Indulgence of Charles II,* which had guaranteed the right of public worship to Catholics and dissenters in England, is revoked.		Leaders of the Jewish community in England are prosecuted on the charge of gathering to worship illegally. Upon petition, the king drops the proceedings. Jews are permitted to settle in Denmark. This decision is intended to revive trade with Spain and Portugal by attracting Sephardic Jews from Hamburg, but more Ashkenazic than Sephardic Jews respond. Samuel Oppenheimer (1630–1703) is imperial war purveyor to the Austrian monarchy's struggle against the attempt of Louis XIV* of France to dominate the continent.		
1674	The duke of York* grants full religious liberty in the colony of New York.	A tax list discloses the presence of two Jews in Boston.	Of the 69 major investors in the Dutch West India Company, 11 are Jews. Their investment is relatively modest.		The Spanish-born writer Daniel Levi de Barrios records that a number of newcomers to the Portuguese community of Amsterdam are talented singers and musicians. Spanish and Portuguese refugees arriving in central Europe are often cultural trendsetters.
1675	The idea of a comprehensive Jewish literature is introduced to the Christian world by Guilio Bartolocci* (1613–1687), Italian		The Portuguese synagogue (Esnoga) of the Jews of Amsterdam is opened across the canal from the smaller Ashkenazic	Lancelot Addison,* English Christian minister, writes *The Present State of the Jews*, in which he describes the North African Jewry. After	The Amsterdam printing press of David de Castro Tartas (c.1625–c.1700) prints *Gazeta de Amsterdam*, the

A. General History	B. Jews in North and South America	C. Jews in Europe	D. Jews in the Middle East and Elsewhere	E. Jewish Culture	
Christian Hebraist and bibliographer and scriptor at the Vatican library. His *Bibliotheca Magna Rabbinica* will be completed by his students in 1693.		Grote Sjoel erected in 1671. Designed by Elias Bouman, it replaces the old Sephardic synagogue in use since 1639. Both synagogues are taller than the buildings in the surrounding Jewish neighborhood. The synagogue seats over 1,200 men and 400 women. It is the largest synagogue in the world.	witnessing the education of the Jewish children in the Maghreb, he writes, "There is no boy in the world who can at the age of 13 give such an accurate account of the laws of his faith as can the Jewish boy."	earliest Spanish Jewish weekly newspaper. Addressed to the Marrano Diaspora and specializing in mercantile news, it continues publication in Amsterdam until 1690. Tartas also prints seven sermons delivered at the new Portuguese synagogue, illustrated with eight engravings by Romeyn de Hooghe.*	**1675**
			A new wave of persecutions against the Jews of Yemen begins as the imam attempts to exile all non-Muslims. He destroys all synagogues and expels all Jews. In about 1680, the Jews will be permitted to return to their abandoned homes.		**1676**
	A Jewish cemetery is opened in Newport, Rhode Island. It later is the subject of a poem by Henry Wadsworth Longfellow.*				**1677**
	About 300 Jews live in Barbados, an island of the British West Indies. The first settlers, who had arrived in 1655, were ex-Marranos who escaped from Brazil after its reconquest by the Portuguese from the Dutch.			Joseph ben Solomon Calahora (Joseph Darshan, 1601–1696) publishes *Yesod Yosef* (*Foundation of Joseph*) in Frankfurt. His book becomes one of the most popular ethical writings in eastern Europe.	**1679**
		An epidemic strikes Prague, killing thousands of Jews. Funds are collected from Jewish communities across Europe in response to the crisis.		In Amsterdam, Shabbetai ben Joseph Bass (1641–1718) publishes *Siftei Yeshenim* (*The Lips of the Sleeping*), a bibliographic handbook of some 2,000 titles. This is the first Jewish bibliography written in Hebrew and serves as the basis for all later works in the field.	**1680**

	A. General History	B. Jews in North and South America	C. Jews in Europe	D. Jews in the Middle East and Elsewhere	E. Jewish Culture
1681			Johann Christoph Wagenseil* (1633–1705), German Christian Hebraist, writes *Flaming Arrows of Satan*, a collection of works written by Jews for use in Christian–Jewish disputations. His objective is to make Christians aware of Jewish objections to Christianity. He appends a refutation for use by Christians.		
1682	The oldest known etchings of Dutch Jewish life are published by Johannes Leusden* in his *Philogus Hebraeo Mixtus*. A Christian from Utrecht, he went to Amsterdam in 1649 for the special purpose of learning more about Jews.		Pope Innocent XI (1676–1689) abolishes Jewish loan-banks in Rome. In 1683 he extends the ban to Ferrara and other Jewish ghettos under his authority. Prohibited from shopkeeping and most trades and crafts, the Roman Jewish community shrinks, while the Jews of northern Italy begin entering commerce and industry.		
1683			About 300 families in Salonika convert to Islam and join with Shabbetai Zevi's original fellow converts to form the crypto-Jewish sect, known as the *Doenmeh*, which survives to the 20th century.		
1685	James II* succeeds to the throne and attempts to restore Catholicism to England by suspending laws against Catholics and appointing them to positions of power in the Church, the universities, and the army. The Edict of Nantes, issued in 1598 to grant religious freedom in France, is revoked.		Thirty-seven Jewish merchants are arrested and charged with failure to attend the Church of England, an omission punishable by fine since the days of Elizabeth I.* James II,* interested in protecting non-Anglicans, orders the charges dropped. Revocation of the Edict of Nantes leads to a massive exodus of Huguenots from France and extensive damage to trade and industry.		

212

A. General History	B. Jews in North and South America	C. Jews in Europe	D. Jews in the Middle East and Elsewhere	E. Jewish Culture	
		In panic, the government cancels an expulsion of Jewish families.			**1685**
		A Christian–Jewish disputation takes place in the Netherlands between Isaac Orobio de Castro (1620–1687) and the liberal Protestant preacher Philipp van Limborch* in the presence of English philosopher John Locke* (1632–1704) and is published as an exchange of letters. Orobio is one of a group of Jewish polemicists.	The first Jewish settlers in Surat, India, arrive from Amsterdam. Jewish merchants are attracted by the lucrative trade in diamonds and pearls.	The first newspaper in Yiddish, the *Dienstagische und Freitagishe Kurant*, begins twice-weekly publication in Amsterdam. Publication ceases in 1687.	**1686**
				Uriel da Costa's (1585–1640) autobiography, *The Ideal of Human Life*, is published. Of Portuguese Marrano background, he lived in Amsterdam and had been idealized as a victim of religious bigotry and obscurantism.	**1687**
The Glorious Revolution in England brings to the throne the Protestant William* of Orange who expands political and religious freedom.		William* of Orange's invasion of England is largely financed by the Lopez Suasso family. Joseph Penso de la Vega (1650–1692), writer and merchant born in Amsterdam of Marrano parents, writes *Confusion de confusiones*, the first book on the stock exchange, which describes the operations of the Dutch trading companies.			**1688**
Letter Concerning Toleration, written by the English philosopher John Locke,* proclaims that no one, not even a Jew, "ought to be excluded from the civil rights of the Commonwealth because of his religion." Along with his *Essay Concerning*			Abraham Navarro, a Portuguese Jew from London, is appointed ambassador to the Mogul emperor Aurangzeb* by the East India Company.		**1689**

	A. General History	B. Jews in North and South America	C. Jews in Europe	D. Jews in the Middle East and Elsewhere	E. Jewish Culture
1689	*Human Understanding* and *Two Treatises of Government* (both published in 1690), the letter makes Locke a major influence in the 18th-century Enlightenment.				
1693			Jacob Sasportas (c.1610–1698) becomes rabbi of Amsterdam. A strong opponent of the Sabbatean movement, his *Zizat Novel Zevi* (*Wilted Flowers*), a collection of Sabbatean pamphlets along with his answers to them, is a major source for the study of early Sabbateanism.		
1695		There are 103 Portuguese Jewish and German Jewish families comprising 570 persons in the Dutch colony of Surinam. They own more than 40 sugar cane plantations and have 9,000 slaves. By 1730, they will own 115 of the colony's 400 plantations.			The Amsterdam Haggadah is the first ever to be illustrated with copper engravings. They are the work of a convert to Judaism, Abraham ben Jacob, who came to Amsterdam from Germany and who copied scenes from biblical engravings of a Christian artist, Matthew Merians.* These illustrations will appear in many Haggadot even into the 20th century.
1697			In an effort to displace Holland as the leading money market in the world, the London Stock Exchange reserves about 10% of its seats for Jewish brokers, even though the entire Jewish status in England is under debate. This limited percentage will remain in effect until 1830. Augustus II* is crowned king of Poland and reigns until 1733. He agrees to the demand by the nobility that Jewish economic rights be curtailed		

A. General History	B. Jews in North and South America	C. Jews in Europe	D. Jews in the Middle East and Elsewhere	E. Jewish Culture	
		and forbids Jews to farm royal revenues and royal estates. The 17th and 18th centuries bring many inconsistencies. Pro- and anti-Jewish laws are sometimes issued simultaneously by the same body or individual.			**1697**
		On a visit to Amsterdam, Czar Peter* the Great is presented with a petition by the mayor of Amsterdam, Nicolaes Witsen,* on behalf of leading Amsterdam Jews seeking admission of Jews to Russia. Peter* rejects the petition claiming "the time has not yet come to bring these two nationalities together."			**1698**
The Treaty of Karlowitz restores most of Hungary, Transylvania, Croatia, the Morea, and Dalmatia from Ottoman to western rule. It comes in the wake of the failure of a second Ottoman siege of Vienna (1683) and signals the decline of the Ottoman Empire.		Johann Andreas Eisenmenger* (1654–1704), professor of Hebrew at Heidelberg University, writes *Judaism Unmasked*. It misquotes and mistranslates talmudic statements to support his claim that the Black Death was caused by Jewish poisoning of wells and that medieval blood libels were true. Upon Jewish representations to the emperor that it would inflame antisemitism, its publication is delayed until 1711 when Eisenmenger's* heirs secure publication.			**1699**
Approximately 275,000 people live in the American colonies. Russia, Poland, and Denmark fight Sweden as the Great Northern War begins. They seek to break Swedish supremacy in the Baltic area.		Solomon de Medina (c.1650–1730) becomes the first openly identified Jew to be knighted in England. A Dutch Jew, he had moved to London to serve as the representative of the Machado and Pereira families, the primary purveyors to William III.*	Judah Hasid (c.1660–1700), believed to be a Sabbatean preacher in Poland, leads the first organized Ashkenazic emigration to Palestine. Of the 1,300 emigrants from Poland and Germany, several hundred die en route	David Estevens (c.1670–c.1715), artist of Marrano origin, paints the portrait of Rabbi David Nieto in London. He studied with the French artist Jacques d'Agar* in Copenhagen.	**1700**

	A. General History	B. Jews in North and South America	C. Jews in Europe	D. Jews in the Middle East and Elsewhere	E. Jewish Culture
1700			The first population census of Berlin records about 1,000 Jews.	and Judah himself dies shortly after arrival in Jerusalem. After his death, disputes will erupt and some will return to Poland, others will remain in Jerusalem, and some will convert to Christianity.	
1701			The Sephardic community of London erects the Bevis Marks synagogue and moves from the synagogue on Creechurch Lane. The synagogue is erected beyond the city limits, where Jews could not yet acquire property, and in a lane because Jews were not allowed to build a synagogue on the nearest public street.		
1703	Local tax collectors in Jerusalem begin a four-year revolt against the emissaries of the sultan who come to collect the land tax.		Upon the death of Court Jew Samuel Oppenheimer, the Habsburg Austrian monarchy repudiates its debts to him despite his great service rendered as military contractor to the state. His death brings deep financial crisis to the state.	Anti-Jewish violence and Jewish communal debt increase in Jerusalem as a result of the tax revolt. Many Jews abandon the city, leaving only the poor behind. Only with the intervention of a committee of rabbinic leaders of Constantinople is a fiscal policy for payment of the community's large debt to Arab moneylenders implemented and an economic basis reestablished.	
1705	Pirates from Tripoli capture a ship bearing gifts from the governor of Egypt to the ruler of Tunisia, Ibrahim al-Sharif* (1702–1705). Ibrahim* responds by laying siege to Tripoli until forced to retreat.			Jews in Tripoli aid in defense of the city and celebrate Ibrahim al-Sharif's* retreat annually in a festival called Purim al-Sharif.	Zevi Hirsch Koidonover (d. 1712) writes *Kav ha-Yashar* (*The Measure of Righteousness*). Written in his native Vilna, it is published in Frankfurt. It reflects the gloomy, rigorous, and mystic spirit of European Jewry resulting from its suffering and persecution. This very popular ethical work demands penitence and strict

216

A. General History	B. Jews in North and South America	C. Jews in Europe	D. Jews in the Middle East and Elsewhere	E. Jewish Culture	
				attention to fulfillment of the Commandments. It is replete with stories about demons, transmigrations of the soul, and similar superstitious beliefs current in this age.	**1705**
		Jacques Christian Basnage* (1653–1725), Protestant theologian living in Holland, begins publication of his popular seven-volume *History and Religion of the Jews from the Time of Jesus Christ to the Present*. Completed in 1711, it is the first attempt to give a full history of the Jews.			**1706**
		The free port of Hamburg issues an ordinance by which the Jews are forbidden to build a synagogue, attend private services in greater numbers than 10 families, marry Christian women, live elsewhere than in Neustadt (the slum area), exhibit any ostentation in dress, and other similar restrictions.			**1710**
	The New York Jewish community contributes 5 pounds 12 shillings for building the steeple of Trinity Church.	*Judaism Unmasked*, written in 1699, is published in Berlin.			**1711**
England and France sign the Peace of Utrecht, ending the War of the Spanish Succession and the attempts at continental expansion by the great powers. It marks the rise of English trading rights in Spanish America and the decline of the Dutch.					**1713**
	Susanna Haswell Rowson* writes *Slaves in Algiers*, the first American play to contain Jewish characters. The villain is a Jew,	John Toland* (1670–1722), English political philosopher and follower of the Enlightenment, publishes anonymously *Reasons*		David Nieto, *hakham* of London's Spanish and Portuguese synagogue from 1701 until his death, writes *Matteh Dan* (*Dan's Staff*), in	**1714**

	A. General History	B. Jews in North and South America	C. Jews in Europe	D. Jews in the Middle East and Elsewhere	E. Jewish Culture
1714		described as a forger and crook who cheats Gentiles but who, like Shakespeare's* Shylock, has a beautiful daughter who wishes to convert to Christianity.	*for Naturalizing the Jews in Great Britain and Ireland.* He argues that an increase in Jewish immigration will bring economic prosperity to England. It receives little positive comment. Frederick William I,* ruler of Prussia from 1713 to 1740, issues an edict designed to restrict or even reduce the number of Jews in Prussia. Only one son may inherit the father's right of residence. The second son has to possess 1,000 taler and pay 50 to be granted the right of residence, and the third son twice these amounts. The Heidereutergasse synagogue, the first community synagogue in Berlin, is opened. Authorized by King Frederick William I* of Prussia, who attends its dedication, it will be the only synagogue in which religious services are permitted by the Nazis after the beginning of World War II.		which he defends rabbinic Judaism against criticism of ex-Marranos, who find the rabbinic tradition novel and unacceptable. Catherine da Costa (1678–1756) paints a portrait miniature of her son Abraham. Daughter of Fernando Mendez, court physician to English king Charles II,* she is the first Jewish woman artist whose work has survived.
1715			Nehemiah Hayon publishes *Oz le-Elohim* (*Might Belongs to God*) in Germany, the only overtly Sabbatean work to be published after 1666. Hayon brings the copies of the book to Amsterdam and initially is supported by the Sephardic community, as its then leading rabbi was a Sabbatean. Hayon ultimately is forced to leave Amsterdam. The Sabbatean controversy continues		

A. General History	B. Jews in North and South America	C. Jews in Europe	D. Jews in the Middle East and Elsewhere	E. Jewish Culture	
		in Holland and elsewhere in Europe and the Middle East.			**1715**
The Peace of Passarowitz ends war between the Holy Roman and Ottoman empires.		The Peace of Passarowitz between Austria and Turkey permits Turkish Jews to live and trade in Austria. In 1736, a Turkish community is founded in Vienna by Diego d'Aguilar (1699–1759).			**1718**
		The journey of Abraham Levi of Horn (1702–1785) begins. His travels through Germany, Bohemia, Hungary, Austria, Syria, and Italy become the basis for an important Yiddish travelogue, *Rayze-Bashraybung.* He records the use of musical instruments: "organs, cymbals, harpsichords and strings every Friday for greeting the Sabbath."		Glueckel of Hameln (1645–1724), businesswoman and Yiddish memoirist, completes writing her memoirs. Begun in 1691 out of despair at the death of her husband, her description of 17th- and 18th-century Jewish life in Hamburg (her birthplace), Altona, Hameln, Hanover, Berlin, Amsterdam, and Metz (where she lived from 1690 until her death) is an important source of central European Jewish history and culture.	**1719**
		A new influx into England of New Christians fleeing renewed oppression by the Inquisition in Spain and Portugal begins. It more than doubles the English Sephardic population of about 1,000 people before it ends in about 1735. Ashkenazic immigration from Germany, Holland, and Poland is much greater and continues until approximately 1830.			**1720**
Johann Sebastian Bach* (1685–1750) completes his *Brandenburg Concertos.* Along with his Mass in B Minor and other works, they earn him the reputation of the foremost composer of the Baroque era.		The Lithuanian Jewish communities appeal to the treasury tribunal against the five main communities that dominate the Lithuanian council, claiming that taxes have been illegally collected and the tax			**1721**

	A. General History	B. Jews in North and South America	C. Jews in Europe	D. Jews in the Middle East and Elsewhere	E. Jewish Culture
1721			burden unequally apportioned. Social and economic tensions and charges of corruption are common in many communities.		
1722		Judah Monis (1683–1764) is converted to Christianity in Boston and thereafter appointed instructor in Hebrew at Harvard College. In 1723, he receives a Master of Arts degree from Harvard.			
1723			Sephardic Jews in Bordeaux are granted legal residence. Diego d'Aguilar, Marrano financier, reorganizes the Austrian state tobacco monopoly, which he holds from 1723 to 1739. He also raises large loans for the Austrian imperial treasury.		The life and customs of Dutch Jewry in the early 18th-century are depicted by Bernard Picart* (1673–1733), a French artist who settled in Amsterdam in 1710. He publishes *Ceremonies and Religious Customs of the World's Peoples*, which includes sketches of Jews in their homes and the synagogues.
1724			Daniel Defoe's* (c.1660–1731) novel *Roxana* includes a vicious and criminal Jew.		
1725	Italian philosopher Giambattista Vico* (1668–1744) writes the *New Science*. This pioneering work in the philosophy of history later influences the French philosopher Auguste Comte* (1798–1857), the German philosopher Karl Marx (1818–1883), and probably the Galician Jewish philosopher Nachman Krochmal (1785–1840).		The rabbis of Hamburg, Altona, and Landsbek relax the communal rules governing Jewish dress and annul the ban on attending the opera and theater. At the same time, there is general condemnation of those actions viewed as antitraditional and imitative of a non-Jewish life-style.		
1727			The Familiants Law is passed in Austria, permitting only the oldest son of each Jewish family to marry. The law remains in effect until 1848.		

A. General History	B. Jews in North and South America	C. Jews in Europe	D. Jews in the Middle East and Elsewhere	E. Jewish Culture	
		All Jews are formally banished from Russia.			**1727**
				Jacob Basevi Cervetto (1682–1783), Italian-born violoncellist and composer, arrives in London. He introduces the violoncello in England and plays in the orchestra of the Theatre Royal, Drury Lane, which he will later manage.	**1728**
Benjamin Franklin* (1706–1790) begins publishing *Poor Richard's Almanack*, a collection of proverbs that gains wide popularity.			The Jews of Constantinople send money to the Jews of Hebron caught in the middle of a war between local Arab tribes that are extorting large sums.		**1729**
	The Sephardic (Shearith Israel) congregation in New York opens the Mill Street synagogue, which is the first synagogue in North America. The synagogue compound includes a schoolhouse and a ritual bath.	Frederick William I,* ruler of Prussia, promulgates a new, contradictory Jewry law that prohibits Jews from engaging in all crafts (except seal engraving) competing with Christan guilds and from peddling and dealing in a large number of goods. Jewish merchants are encouraged to invest in manufacturing, as well as moneylending.		Jacob Culi (c.1685–1732), rabbi and editor, publishes a commentary on Genesis and a portion of Exodus as the first volumes in a series of Ladino (Judeo-Spanish) Bible commentaries known as *Me'am Lo'ez*. He hopes this work will assist the Jewish masses to become familiar with traditional Judaism. It will become very popular among the Jews of Turkey and the Balkans.	**1730**
England grants a royal charter to James Oglethorpe* for an English colony in Georgia. It is the last of the original 13 American colonies to be settled.	The Sephardic community of Curaçao erects a synagogue, Mikve Israel, in the town of Willemstad.	Leaders of the Jewish community of London give financial support to poor Sephardic refugees to settle in Georgia and other New World Sephardic communities. They seek to alleviate some of the financial drain of their own community, but the flow of Jews fleeing the poverty of Italy, Turkey, North Africa, and Gibraltar will continue into the 19th century.			**1732**

A. General History	B. Jews in North and South America	C. Jews in Europe	D. Jews in the Middle East and Elsewhere	E. Jewish Culture
1733	Georgia, last of the thirteen English colonies on the North American continent, is founded by James Oglethorpe.* It is considered a strategic emplacement against the Spanish in Florida and a refuge for the improverished of England. London's Sephardic community sends 42 Jews to Savannah, Georgia.	Joseph Suess Oppenheimer (Jude Suss, c.1698–1738), is put in charge of the finances of the duke of Württemberg. Oppenheimer has little connection to traditional Jewish observance and cultivates his social position among the non-Jewish aristocracy.		
1734		Moses Hayyim Luzzatto (1707–1746), Italian poet, dramatist, and mystic, is put under the ban (*herem*) by Italian rabbis fearing a new messianic pretender for practicing sorcery and pronouncing incantations.		
1735	Judah Monis, instructor in Hebrew at Harvard, publishes *A Grammar of the Hebrew Tongue*. It is the first book that uses Hebrew type to be published in America.			*Title page of a Hebrew Grammar published in Colonial America by Judah Monis (1683–1764).*
1736		Israel ben Eliezer (c.1700–1760), later known as Ba'al Shem Tov, "the Besht," begins founding the Hasidic movement in eastern Europe. He developed the concept of the *zaddik*, the saintly person who mediates between the Upper and Lower worlds, and a revolutionary form of popular prayer based upon religious feeling and devotion in addition to the words of prayer. Hasidism emphasizes joyful worship of God in prayer and in all of one's actions.		
1738		Joseph Suess Oppenheimer, Court Jew to the duke of Württemberg* since		

A. General History	B. Jews in North and South America	C. Jews in Europe	D. Jews in the Middle East and Elsewhere	E. Jewish Culture	
		1732 and financier to other leaders in southern Germany, is arrested after the duke's sudden death in 1737. He is tried and hanged for embezzling state revenues and other crimes. He has been hated by many for his role in planning and implementing radical economic reforms.			**1738**
		Jews are expelled from the Ukrainian and White Russian territories annexed by Russia. The decree will be executed in 1740, resulting in the expulsion of 292 men and 281 women scattered throughout 130 manorial estates.			**1739**
The War of Austrian Succession begins after Maria Theresa* becomes the Habsburg ruler (1740–1780). Frederick II* the Great (1712–1786), king of Prussia from 1740–1786, invades Silesia.	The English Parliament passes the Plantation Act, permitting the naturalization of immigrants to the American colonies, including Jews, after seven years of residence.	Israel Ba'al Shem Tov, the founder of Hasidism, establishes himself at Medzibezh, Podolia, where he remains until his death. His study and prayer room (*bet midrash*) is a simple unadorned building. Followers of Hasidism gather in nondescript and austere houses (*shtiebls*) for prayer, study, and assembly. Inner fervor and joy are what matter. The nondistinctive *shtiebl* makes no contribution to synagogue architecture.	As a result of an initiative by Bedouin Sheikh Daher-al-Omar* to develop the Galilee region, Rabbi Haim Abulafia settles in Tiberias. With the sheikh's help, Abulafia builds a synagogue, houses, and shops and rebuilds the wall around the Jewish quarter. He creates an economic base for the community by developing farming, trade, and crafts.	Moses Hayyim Luzzatto (1707–1746), Italian poet and Kabbalist, writes *Mesillat Yesharim* (*The Path of the Upright*) while living in Amsterdam. This ethical work, written in Hebrew, will become one of the most influential books read by eastern European Jewry in the late 18th and 19th centuries.

The earliest known cantorial manual is written by Judah Elias of Hanover, Germany. | **1740** |
| | | Diego d'Aguilar, Marrano financier, and Issachar Berush Eskeles use their influence to prevent expulsion of the Jews from Moravia.

Reiterating the policy of 1727, Czarina Elizabeth Petrovna* orders all Jews immediately deported, together with all their property, from the entire Russian Empire, which now | | | **1742** |

	A. General History	B. Jews in North and South America	C. Jews in Europe	D. Jews in the Middle East and Elsewhere	E. Jewish Culture
1742			includes the Ukrainian and White Russian territories. Elizabeth* strictly adheres to this policy and thousands of Jews are deported.		
1743					She'erit Yisrael (The Remnant of Israel) by Menahem Mann ben Solomon Halevi Amelander (d. 1767) is published in Holland. Conceived as a Yiddish continuation of Josippon to modern times, it contains much valuable material on the Jewish communities of Germany, Poland, and Holland.
1744			England's Parliament rejects a bill that would admit Jews to the Levant Company. The English merchants fear that since the Turkish merchants are primarily Jewish, they will trade with their fellow Jews in England at the expense of the non-Jewish merchants. The Jews are expelled from Prague by Queen (later, Empress) Maria Theresa.* Though based on rumors of Jewish disloyalty during the French and Prussian conquest, the expulsion makes Jews the scapegoat for Austria's military debacle. It will be reversed in 1748.		
1745	Frederick II* conquers Silesia, making Prussia a great European military power.		When the city of London is panicked by the Jacobite uprising, the financier Samson Gideon (1699–1762) raises 1,700,000 pounds to assist the government in restoring stability.		
1746					A manuscript of David Conforte's (1618–c.1690) major

A. General History	B. Jews in North and South America	C. Jews in Europe	D. Jews in the Middle East and Elsewhere	E. Jewish Culture	
				work *Kore ha-Dorot* (*Summoning the Generations*) is published in Venice. This book by the Sephardic rabbi and literary historian surveys Hebrew literature from the talmudic period to the present and is especially important for its information about Mediterranean Sephardic scholars in the 16th and 17th centuries.	**1746**
Pope Benedict XIV decides that once a child is baptized, even against the prescriptions of canon law, he is to be educated under the Church.					**1747**
David Hume* (1711–1776), Scottish historian and philosopher, writes *An Enquiry Concerning Human Understanding*. He is best known for his empiricism and philosophical skepticism.	Peter Kalm,* Swedish university professor who mingled among the Jews of New York during his visit to North America, observes: "They [the Jews] enjoy all the privileges common to other inhabitants of this town and province."	Abraham Gradis, a Jewish merchant of Bordeaux who owned and operated most of the merchant ships sailing between France and New France, founds the Society of Canada to encourage trade with Canada.		Contemporary Jewish customs are portrayed without negative prejudice by Johann Bodenschatz* (1717–1797), a German Protestant theologian. His four-volume work on the subject contains many informative engravings.	**1748**
	Jews in Charleston, South Carolina, found Congregation Kahal Kadosh Beth Elohim.	Under Austrian Empress Maria Theresa,* a special edict is issued encouraging Jews to engage in manufacturing.			**1749**
Denis Diderot* (1713–1784) and D'Alembert* begin publication of their *Encyclopedie* in France. One of the first attempts to summarize knowledge in the arts, history, philosophy, and sciences, it will be completed in 1780.		Frederick II,* king of Prussia, issues a charter dividing Jews according to their economic value to the state. The "specially" privileged are allowed temporary residential rights. The "generally" privileged, a few valuable industrialists, are allowed full rights of residence and occupation. Even this group is restricted to the number of children permitted to live		The first talmudic encyclopedia in alphabetical arrangement, *Pahad Yitshak* (*Awe of Isaac*), written by Isaac Lampronti (1679–1756), rabbi and physician of Ferrara, begins publication. *Pahad Yitshak* is a comprehensive encyclopedia of *halakhah*, including material from the Mishnah, Talmud, and responsa literature. Lampronti devotes special attention to the	**1750**

	A. General History	B. Jews in North and South America	C. Jews in Europe	D. Jews in the Middle East and Elsewhere	E. Jewish Culture
1750			with them, and they have no hereditary right of residence.		responsa literature of the Italian rabbis.
1751		Jews settle in Halifax, Nova Scotia, which was founded by the British in 1749. Halifax attracts Jewish merchants from Newport, Rhode Island, whose families were from England.	Jacob Emden (1697–1776), rabbinical scholar and anti-Sabbatean polemicist, accuses Rabbi Jonathan Eybeschuetz (c.1690–1764) of the Three Communities, Altona, Hamburg, and Wandsbeck, of Sabbatean sympathies on the evidence that he distributed amulets to ward off sickness. Jewish communities throughout Poland and Germany are drawn into the controversy with attacks, proclamations, and excommunications abounding on both sides.	Shalom Sharabi (1720–1777) becomes head of Yeshiva Bet El in Jerusalem. Born in Yemen, Sharabi acquires a reputation as a pious Kabbalist, and his life comes to be embellished by legends and miraculous tales.	
1753			The English Parliament enacts a Jewish naturalization bill (the "Jew Bill"), which provides foreign-born Jews the privileges enjoyed by their native-born children. Intense anti-Jewish economic and religious prejudice results in its immediate repeal. The prohibition against Jews participating in the British Levant Company is lifted. Out of fear of extensive Jewish involvement in trade along the eastern Mediterranean, Jews who now join the company are prohibited from employing Jewish agents in the East. Tobias Smollet's* (1721–1771) novel *The Adventures of Ferdinand Count Fathom* includes the benevolent Joshuah Manasseh, who insists on lending the hero money without interest.		Hayyim Joseph David Azulai (1724–1806), born in Jerusalem but widely traveled, begins his literary diary, *Ma'agal Tov* (*Good Path*), in which he records information on Jewish scholarship, history, and folklore. Covering a period of 25 years (through 1778), it is an invaluable source on Hebrew manuscripts located in Italy, Holland, and France.

A. General History	B. Jews in North and South America	C. Jews in Europe	D. Jews in the Middle East and Elsewhere	E. Jewish Culture	
		Jean Astruc* (1684–1766), French biblical scholar, publishes an anonymous biblical treatise expressing the view that while Moses composed the Law, he utilized older sources in the Torah's narrative, each using a different name for God. Astruc* is regarded as a main founder of biblical higher criticism.			**1753**
		Gotthold Ephraim Lessing* (1729–1781), German Protestant dramatist and philosopher, publishes *The Jew*, the first play in modern times that includes an unambiguous portrayal of a Jew as a man of virtue.			**1754**
	Congregation Shearith Israel of New York opens a synagogue community all-day school. In addition to Hebrew, such general subjects as Spanish, English, writing, and arithmetic are taught. The school will last until the American Revolution, when most of the city's Jews leave New York.	Jacob Frank (1726–1791) returns to Podolia, where he was born, after many years of traveling in the Balkans and Turkey and initiates a new movement of Sabbatean fervor. The Frankist movement quickly spreads to other parts of the Ukraine and Poland. Frank will be excommunicated by a rabbinical court in Brody in 1756, convert to Christianity, and join with Christians in attacking rabbinic Judaism.			**1755**
The Seven Years' War begins in Europe, North America, and India. France, Austria, Russia, Sweden, Saxony, and, later, Spain oppose England, Prussia, and Hanover. The war includes colonial rivalry between England and France and struggle for power in Germany		In his *Complete Works*, Voltaire* (1694–1778), French philosopher and leading critic of European society before the French Revolution, says of the Jews: "We find in them only an ignorant and barbarous people, who have long united the most sordid avarice with			**1756**

	A. General History	B. Jews in North and South America	C. Jews in Europe	D. Jews in the Middle East and Elsewhere	E. Jewish Culture
1756	between Austria and Prussia.		the most detestable superstition and the most invincible hatred for every people by whom they are tolerated and enriched."		
1757			Bishop Dembkowski of Kamenets Podolski forces Jewish communal leaders into a disputation with Frankists that results in the confiscation and burning of the Talmud in Kamienec and Podolia. The bishop unexpectedly dies in November at the very time of the burnings, and the Frankists lose their protector. The rabbinical community resumes its condemnation of the sect.	Samuel Abraham (d. 1792), probably of Polish birth, arrives in Cochin, India. A leading merchant, trading chiefly in timber for shipbuilding, he serves both the Dutch and English East India companies. His Hebrew letter (c.1790) to a New York synagogue will be the first known contact of Jews of Cochin with those of the Western Hemisphere.	
1759	The British defeat the French near Quebec.	Moses Malkhi of Safed is the first Palestinian emissary to the New World. He visits New York's Shearith Israel congregation for four months, where he helps them arrange their religious affairs. He also visits Newport, Rhode Island. Permanent Jewish settlement of Canada follows the British conquest of New France. The most well-known settler was Aaron Hart, a commissary officer in the army of General Amherst.	The Catholic clergy of Lvov arrange for a second disputation between Frankists and anti-Frankists. According to one account, the disputation ends when the traditional Jews persuade the Catholic clergy that the Frankists have no sincere intention of converting to Catholicism. Cardinal Lorenzo Ganganelli (later Pope Clement XIV) issues a report condemning blood libel accusations.	An earthquake devastates Safed, Palestine, killing 2,000, among them 190 Jews.	Solomon da Costa Athias (1690–1769) presents the newly opened British Museum with his collection of Hebrew manuscripts and bound volumes.
1760	The British capture Montreal. The French surrender Detroit to the British. The entire province of Canada is surrendered by the French to the British. George III* becomes king of Great Britain and Ireland.		Upon the death of the Ba'al Shem Tov, the Hasidic preacher Dov Baer of Mezhirech (c.1710–1772) succeeds to leadership of the Hasidim. The *Maggid* (Preacher) of Mezhirech, as he is called, disseminates the teaching of his master throughout eastern Europe.	*Hakham* Isaac, son of David Nieto, writes to the Jews of China on behalf of the London Jewish community, asking for information on their origin. A similar letter is sent by way of Canton in 1815, but no reply is received.	

A. General History	B. Jews in North and South America	C. Jews in Europe	D. Jews in the Middle East and Elsewhere	E. Jewish Culture	
	An anonymous English translation of *Evening Services for Rosh-Hashanah and Yom Kippur* is printed in New York. The translation is attributed to Isaac Pinto (1720–1791), a merchant. In 1766, a second volume, *Prayers for Sabbath, Rosh-Hashanah and Yom Kippur*, translated by Isaac Pinto, will be published. They are the first translation of a prayer book into English but do not appear in England, which has a larger Jewish community.				1761
Jean Jacques Rousseau* (1712–1778), French philosopher, publishes the *Social Contract*, a treatise on the origins and organization of government and the rights of citizens. Catherine* the Great becomes czarina of Russia.	Rabbi Raphael Hayyim Isaac Carigal (1729–1777), Palestinian rabbi from Hebron, visits Curaçao in the West Indies, the largest Jewish community in the Western Hemisphere, to raise funds for his community.			Isaac de Pinto, philosopher and economist of Portuguese background who lived mostly in Holland, writes *Apologie pour la nation juive* (*Apology for the Jewish Nation*), a defense against Voltaire's* defamation that is more a defense of Sephardim, whom he describes as cultured and enlightened, than of Judaism. He suggests that antisemitic diatribes are justified against Ashkenazim.	1762
The Treaty of Paris ends the Seven Years' War. France cedes its territories east of the Mississippi River, except New Orleans, to Britain. Spain gives Florida to Britain in return for Cuba and the Philippines. Prussia retains Silesia.	The Jews of Newport, Rhode Island, dedicate a synagogue designed by America's leading architect, Peter Harrison* (1716–1775). It becomes known as the Touro synagogue in recognition of its first minister, Isaac Touro, and his sons Abraham and Judah (1775–1854), who provide funds for the ministry and building maintenance. The congregation is Sephardic.			Abraham Ezekiel (d. 1799), an English silversmith, and his brother Benjamin build the synagogue in Exeter. His son Abraham (1757–1806), a silversmith, watchmaker, scientific optician, and painter of miniature portraits, engraves bookplates and portraits by Sir Joshua Reynolds* (1723–1792).	1763

	A. **General History**	B. **Jews in North and South America**	C. **Jews in Europe**	D. **Jews in the Middle East and Elsewhere**	E. **Jewish Culture**
1764	Britain enacts the Sugar Act and Currency Act to raise money in the American colonies to pay the war debt. The Colonies protest against the acts.		The Polish Sejm abolishes the Council of Four Lands and all Jewish provincial councils because they are no longer reliable sources of government income or instruments for conducting Jewish affairs. Instead, a poll tax is to be collected by the authorities themselves from each individual community. This puts an end to government recognition of Jewish centralized institutions that has existed for almost 200 years.	Nahman of Horodenka (d. 1780) and Menahem Mendel of Peremyshlany (b. 1728), notable Hasidic rabbis, lead a group of Hasidim to Palestine and settle in Tiberias.	
1765	Britain enacts the Stamp Act. The Virginia Assembly opposes the act. The Congress in New York City adopts the Declaration of Rights and Grievances. The Colonial policy of nonimportation of British goods is implemented.	There are 10 Jews among the 375 signers of the Non-Importation Agreement of Philadelphia following the Stamp Act. This agreement is in protest of the "restrictions, prohibitions and ill-advised regulations" British policy had imposed on the colonies.	Denis Diderot,* French philosopher and rationalist, includes an article on the Jews in volume 9 of his encyclopedia. He admires Jews as the oldest nation still in existence, the life of Moses, and the "natural" religion of the patriarchs. However, he asserts that Judaism contains defects peculiar to an ignorant and superstitious nation.		Aaron Beer (1739–1821) is appointed chief cantor of the Heidereutergasse synagogue in Berlin. Beer, who composes some of his own melodies, has a very extensive liturgical repertoire that he varies constantly to prevent the congregation from singing with him.
1766	Britain repeals the Stamp Act. Britain enacts the Declaratory Act, stating its right to enact laws for the colonies.				
1767	Britain enacts the Townshend Act, requiring the colonies to pay import duties on tea and other goods. The colonies revive their nonimportation policy.				Moses Mendelssohn (1729–1786), spiritual leader of German Jewry, writes *Phaedon*, a defense of the immortality of the soul and the existence of God. Written in German, it is well received in the gentile world.
1768	The Civil War begins in Poland. An anti-Russian group supports Poland's independence. Catherine* the Great sends Russian troops	The Jews of Montreal establish the Spanish and Portuguese Shearith Israel congregation, the first Jewish congregation in	Rival gangs of the Haidamaks, consisting of cossacks and peasants, invade eastern Poland, leaving up to 20,000 Poles and Jews dead.	The Jews of London send money to help ransom Jewish slaves in Malta.	Jacob Emden (1697–1776), rabbinical scholar and anti-Sabbatean polemicist, writes *Mitpahat Sefarim* (*The Cover of Books*),

A. General History	B. Jews in North and South America	C. Jews in Europe	D. Jews in the Middle East and Elsewhere	E. Jewish Culture	
to suppress the uprising.	Canada. They adopt the form of service of New York's Shearith Israel congregation.			which is critical of the Zohar. He questions its antiquity and its sanctity.	**1768**
		John Caspar Lavater* (1741–1801), Swiss clergyman, publicly challenges Moses Mendelssohn to defend the superiority of Judaism to Christianity. In 1770, Mendelssohn publishes his reply to Lavater,* politely declining to accept the challenge because polemics on religious questions are contrary to the spirit of tolerance and also imprudent for a Jew.	*Moses Mendelssohn (left) sitting opposite John Caspar Lavater, Lutheran theologian. Gotthold Lessing, Protestant dramatist and philosopher, is standing. Etching is after a painting by Moritz Oppenheim.*		**1769**
	Probably the earliest American version of the Jewish international conspiracy theory is recorded by Congregationalist Minister Ezra Stiles.*	Baron D'Holbach* (1723–1789), French philosopher, writes an essay, *The Spirit of Judaism*. He attacks Judaism as being filled with self-interest and avarice.			**1770**
		Voltaire* writes his *Letter of Memmius to Cicero*, in which he adopts the pose of an ancient Roman reporting on the Jews. "They are, all of them, born with raging fanaticism in their hearts, just as Bretons and Germans are born with blond hair. I would not be in the least bit surprised if these people would not some day become deadly to the human race."			**1771**
The first partition of Poland occurs. Part of Belorussia and Lithuania is ceded to Russia; Galicia, to Austria; and other territories, to Prussia. Poland loses about one-third of its territory.		The duke of Mecklenburg-Schwerin issues a decree prohibiting Jews from burying their dead before the third day after death, lest live people be accidentally declared dead and buried. Though Moses Mendelssohn is asked by the Jewish	Hayyim Joseph David Azulai, rabbi and sometime Palestinian emissary, reports on one of his travels that the Jewish community of Tunis is thriving religiously and has over 300 rabbis and sages. Tunis carries on the traditions and institutions of Jewish		**1772**

	A. General History	B. Jews in North and South America	C. Jews in Europe	D. Jews in the Middle East and Elsewhere	E. Jewish Culture
1772			community to intercede on its behalf, he thinks the decree is sound rather than oppressive and refuses. The rabbinic leaders of Vilna, including Elijah ben Solomon Zalman (1720–1797), the Vilna Gaon, put the Hasidim under rabbinic ban. This is soon repeated in other communities. The Hasidim are accused, among other things, of contempt for the Oral Law and its scholars, of organizing separatist congregations, changing the traditional form of the prayers, and disregard of religious transgressions. The decree does little to stop the movement's spread, though it is reissued in 1781.	learning from Kairouan after the latter's decline in the 11th century.	
1773	Britain enacts the Tea Act. Colonial anger results in the Boston Tea Party, as the British tea shipment is dumped into Boston Harbor.	On May 28, Rabbi Raphael Hayyim Isaac Carigal, Palestinian rabbi from Hebron, preaches a Shavuot sermon in the Newport, Rhode Island, synagogue in the presence of the governor. While in Newport, Carigal becomes friendly with Ezra Stiles,* later to become president of Yale University.			
1774	Britain enacts the Intolerable Acts to punish the colonies. The first Continental Congress meets in Philadelphia. A petition of grievances is sent to the king of England. Louis XVI* becomes king of France.	Columbia (Kings) College of New York graduates its first Jewish student, Isaac Abrahams (1756–c.1832).	The Marseilles Chamber of Commerce tries to reduce Jewish participation in trade with North Africa by limiting Jewish residence in Marseilles to three days.		
1775	The American Revolution begins, as minutemen fight the British at Lexington	Frances Salvador (1747–1776) is elected as a delegate to the South Carolina	Pope Pius VI, who reigns until 1799, issues his Edict on the Jews, which	Algerian Jews led by Rabbis Nehoray Azubib and Jacdo ben Naim proclaim	

A. General History	B. Jews in North and South America	C. Jews in Europe	D. Jews in the Middle East and Elsewhere	E. Jewish Culture	
and Concord. The second Continental Congress meets and appoints George Washington* as head of the Continental Army. Spain fails in its attempt to capture Algiers.	Provincial Congresses of 1775 and again in 1776. He is the first Jew to hold elective office in America. In 1776, he will be the first Jew to die in the American Revolutionary War, being killed and scalped by the Tory-led Cherokees.	revives and consolidates medieval restrictions and degradations of the Jews, including the prohibition on the erection of tombstones over Jewish graves.	two days of celebration in gratitude for their miraculous escape from Spanish conquest.		**1775**
The Continental Congress adopts the Declaration of Independence. The British capture New York City and are victorious in the Battle of Long Island. Revolutionary forces are victorious in the Battle of Trenton.	When the British occupy New York, Rev. Gershom Mendes Seixas (1746–1816), spiritual leader of Congregation Shearith Israel, flees to Connecticut, carrying with him Torah scrolls and other sacred objects of the synagogue.	Pope Pius VI orders the issuance of an edict in Avignon, prohibiting the forced baptism of Jewish children.			**1776**
The Continental Congress adopts the Articles of Confederation. The American Revolutionary War continues.	The Jews of New York are granted equality under the law as the New York State Constitution abolishes religious discrimination. Two brothers, Solomon and William Pinto, graduate from Yale University.		Menachem Mendel of Vitebsk (1730–1788), Hasidic leader, accompanied by Abraham of Kalisk and Israel of Polotsk, leads a group of 300 Jews to settle in Palestine. He will become the leader of the Hasidic community there while remaining the spiritual leader of the Hasidim in Belorussia.		**1777**
The Continental Congress enters into alliance with France. The American Revolutionary War continues. The War of Bavarian Succession begins between the Holy Roman Empire and Prussia over Bavaria. Catherine II* divides Russia into provinces and classifies their inhabitants into various categories.	American Revolutionary War soldiers Colonel Mordecai Sheftall and his son, Sheftall Sheftall, are taken prisoner during the capture of Savannah, Georgia, by the British.	David Friedlaender (1750–1834), communal leader and disciple of Moses Mendelssohn, establishes a modern Jewish school in Berlin, which will exist until the Nazi period. Other modern schools emerge, supported and sometimes demanded by the German and Austrian governments. Catherine II* of Russia classifies rich Jews as merchants to be included within the guilds, while other Jews are classified as		Jewish pictorial art in medieval Hebrew Bibles is recognized in a monograph by the German Christian Hebraist Olaus Gerhard Tychsen.* His monograph is believed to be the first investigation of early medieval Jewish art.	**1778**

	A. General History	B. Jews in North and South America	C. Jews in Europe	D. Jews in the Middle East and Elsewhere	E. Jewish Culture
1778			burghers. Thus, Russia becomes the first European country in which Jews are permitted to elect or to be elected to guild councils and municipalities.		
1779	The American Revolutionary War continues. Spain declares war on England. The War of Bavarian Succession ends with Prussia retaining Bavaria.	Philip Minis (1734–1789), reputed to have been the first white child born in Savannah, Georgia, assists the French in a failed effort to recapture Savannah from the British. Solomon Bush (1753–1795) is made a lieutenant colonel in the Continental Army. He holds the highest rank by a Jewish officer in the American Revolutionary Army.	Gotthold Ephraim Lessing,* German Protestant dramatist and philosopher, writes *Nathan the Wise*. Nathan, modeled after Moses Mendelssohn, whom Lessing* greatly admires, is the spokesman for tolerance, brotherhood, and the love of humanity. The success of the play is a landmark in modern German history.	 *Moses Mendelssohn (1729–1786). Contemporary engraving.*	
1780	The American Revolutionary War continues. The British capture Charleston. Benedict Arnold* commits treason. Johann Gottfried Eichhorn* (1752–1827), German biblical scholar, begins publication of his *Introduction to the Study of the Old Testament*. Completed in 1783, it is a pioneering study of the Bible, free of church dogma, and influences a wide public, including Moses Mendelssohn and his fellow biblical commentators.	Captain Lushington's* Company, made up of American Revolutionary War volunteers from Charleston, South Carolina, includes some 20 Jews and is known as the "Jew Company." On September 25, Benedict Arnold* writes George Washington,* advising that his Jewish aide, Major David Salisbury Franks (c.1743–1793), has been unaware of his (Arnold's) treasonous behavior. Gershom Mendes Seixas becomes minister of Congregation Mikveh Israel in Philadelphia.			Jacob Joseph of Polonnoye (d. c.1782), who in 1741 came under the influence of the Ba'al Shem Tov, publishes *Toldot Yaakov Yosef* (*History of Jacob Joseph*), the first work to outline the basic teachings of Hasidism. Elijah ben Solomon Zalman, the Vilna Gaon, expresses interest in secular sciences as an aid to the understanding of the Torah. He believes "all knowledge is necessary for our Holy Torah and is included in it."
1781	The German philosopher Immanuel Kant* (1724–1804) writes the *Critique of Pure Reason* in which he claims the existence of God cannot be demonstrated	Haym Salomon (1740–1785), who arrived in New York from Poland in 1772, assists Robert Morris,* superintendent of finance, in raising funds to finance the	At the request of Moses Mendelssohn, Christian Wilhem von Dohm* (1751–1820), the German diplomat in the court of Frederick* the Great, writes *On the*		

A. General History	B. Jews in North and South America	C. Jews in Europe	D. Jews in the Middle East and Elsewhere	E. Jewish Culture

1781

empirically. For Kant,* ethics born of human autonomy is valued above law, and Christianity, which is based on ethics motivated by love, is a truer form of religion than Judaism, which is based on law.

Hostilities of the American Revolutionary War end with the surrender of the British at Yorktown to combined American and French forces. The Articles of Confederation are ratified.

patriot cause in the Revolutionary War. He advances over $200,000 to help provision the armies. On two occasions, in September 1776 and August 1778, he is arrested by the British on suspicion of espionage. In 1778, he was sentenced to death but escaped. He will die bankrupt.

Improvement of the Jews as Citizens, a plea for Jewish civil liberties. He writes condescendingly that the Jews are no worse than Christians and that their condition results from their own superstitious religion. Holding up the example of American Jewry, Dohm* argues that equal treatment for Jews is achievable.

Joseph II* (1741–1790), king of Germany (1764–1790) and Holy Roman Emperor (1765–1790), begins a series of reforms designed to make Jews more useful to the state. He abolishes the yellow badge and body tax and introduces measures of general educational reform. He also forbids the use of Yiddish and Hebrew in the public and commercial records of the Jews. His Edict of Tolerance applies the principles of the Enlightenment to the Jews of his empire.

The roof of the early 18th-century wooden synagogue at Wolpa is redesigned, making it the most beautiful of all wooden synagogues in eastern Europe. In these forest-covered countries, timber is the primary building material for synagogue construction from the mid-17th to late 18th centuries. Emigration, impoverishment of those Jews who will remain, and the plunder of wars will result in the destruction of all wooden synagogues by the end of World War II.

A. General History	B. Jews in North and South America	C. Jews in Europe	D. Jews in the Middle East and Elsewhere	E. Jewish Culture
1782		Naphtali Herz Wessely (1772–1805), Haskalah poet and educator, writes *Divrei Shalom ve-Emet* (*Words of Peace and Truth*), in which he endorses educational reforms for Jewish children that had been introduced in Austria under the Edict of Tolerance by Emperor Joseph II.* This first work in Hebrew on Jewish education proposes a course of Jewish study that would combine the religious with the secular and also advocates the study of the Bible in German. He is opposed by Orthodox rabbis who fear his ideas would foster assimilation. Russian Jewish merchants and burghers must live in towns and not in villages. This law is later expanded to banish Jews from the villages and causes further economic decline.		Abraham Abramson (1754–1811), German medalist, is appointed royal medalist. He is one of a group of German Jewish itinerant craftsmen who execute commemorative medals and wax portraits.
1783	The American Revolution ends as Britain recognizes U.S. independence at the signing of the Treaty of Paris. Frederick II* of Prussia tries to form a union of Prussian princes to thwart advances of the Holy Roman Emperor. Russia annexes the Crimea.	Johann Gottfried Herder* (1744–1803), German Protestant theologian and philosopher, writes *The Spirit of Hebrew Poetry*, in which he lauds the genius of Hebrew poetry from biblical to rabbinic times. Herder* calls for complete emancipation of German Jews.		The Society for the Proponents of the Hebrew Language (Hevrat Doreshei Leshon Ever) is founded in Koenigsberg by Isaac Abraham Euchel (1756–1804). Later that year, it begins publication of *Ha-Me'assef* (*The Collector*), the first secular Hebrew monthly magazine, which appears intermittently until 1811. It becomes the symbol of the Haskalah movement. Lorenzo Da Ponte (1749–1838) is appointed librettist to the Imperial Opera of Vienna. Born in Italy to a family that later converts to

A. General History	B. Jews in North and South America	C. Jews in Europe	D. Jews in the Middle East and Elsewhere	E. Jewish Culture	
				Christianity, Da Ponte writes the libretti for some of Wolfgang Amadeus Mozart's* (1756–1791) most famous works including *Marriage of Figaro* (1784) and *Giovanni* (1787). Da Ponte is instrumental in bringing the first performance of *Don Giovanni* to America.	**1783**
	David Salisbury Franks, a Revolutionary War officer, is appointed vice-consul in Marseilles. He is the first Jew to be appointed to a U.S. diplomatic post.				**1784**
The Virginia Statute of Religious Liberty is adopted by the General Assembly. It guarantees freedom of worship; prohibits public support of religious institutions; and provides that religious opinions and beliefs shall not diminish, enlarge, or affect civil capacities. It serves as a precedent for the federal Constitution of 1791 and inspires European liberal thought.		The London Court of Aldermen prohibits baptized Jews from taking the Christian oath required of those seeking the privileges of a freeman of the city. The London merchants hope thereby to limit Jewish influence in international trade by eliminating those Jewish tradesmen for whom baptism is an economic rather than religious act.		Joseph ben Moses Hayyim Baruch's *Praises of Jerusalem* is published in Leghorn. Its description of the holy places in Jerusalem results in the work achieving great popularity and being published in 10 editions.	**1785**
Delegates to the Constitutional Convention draft and sign the U.S. Constitution, which is sent to the states for ratification. It contains the clause, "no religious test shall ever be required as a qualification for any office or public trust under the United States." This law does not supersede rights of the individual states, although most of them emulate the federal model.

Joseph II* appoints Wolfgang Amadeus Mozart* as chamber | Although Article VI of the U.S. Constitution abolishes any religious test "as a qualification to any office," Maryland and North Carolina continue to restrict the right of Jews and other religious dissidents to hold public office, maintaining that the Constitution applies only to federal offices. Maryland will abolish the restriction in 1826 and North Carolina in 1868. | On the eve of the French Revolution, there are about 40,000 Jews in France. About 30,000 are German-speaking Jews who live in the border provinces of Alsace and Lorraine. Several thousand Sephardim live in Bordeaux and Bayonne. The majority are treated as second-class citizens. The 800 Parisian Jews have no legal status.

Count de Mirabeau* (1749–1791), statesman of the French Revolution, writes *On Moses* | | | **1787** |

237

	A. General History	B. Jews in North and South America	C. Jews in Europe	D. Jews in the Middle East and Elsewhere	E. Jewish Culture
1787	composer to the Austrian Empire. He creates such works as *The Marriage of Figaro* (1786) and the *The Magic Flute* (1791) but dies in abject poverty.		*Mendelssohn and Political Reform of the Jews*, in which he argues that to make Jews better citizens, all debasing distinctions against them should be banished and all avenues of subsistence and livelihood be opened to them. Joseph II* requires Jews to be liable for military service and to adopt German-sounding family and personal names to be selected from a government-prepared list. Frederick William II,* ruler of Prussia from 1786 to 1797, introduces a period of reform. He repeals the *leibzoll* (body tax) for foreign Jews. In May 1791 he will grant full citizenship to Daniel Itzig and his family. In 1792 he will abolish collective responsibility and liability of the Jewish community for nonpayment of taxes and crimes of theft.		
1788				At least six Jewish convicts arrive at Botany Bay, New South Wales, Australia.	
1789	George Washington* and John Adams* are chosen president and vice president of the U.S. The first 10 amendments (Bill of Rights) to the Constitution are adopted by Congress. The Estates General meet in Versailles. The French Revolution begins. The National Assembly adopts the Declaration of the Rights of Man.	In Philadelphia, a public feast and parade is held to celebrate the new Constitution, and although the Jews are few in number, there is a special table where the food conforms to the Jewish dietary laws.	In August, the Declaration of the Rights of Man, which prefaces the French Constitution, is adopted by the revolutionary National Assembly, and states that no man ought to be "disturbed" because of his religious beliefs. During the debate on the "Jewish question" before the French General Assembly, Count Stanislas de Clermont-Tonnerre*		

A. General History	B. Jews in North and South America	C. Jews in Europe	D. Jews in the Middle East and Elsewhere	E. Jewish Culture	
		(1757–1792), French revolutionary, pleads for equal rights for Jews: "The Jews should be denied everything as a nation but granted everything as individuals." The French General Assembly grants civil and political rights to Protestants; the deputies from Alsace and Lorraine refuse to agree to the emancipation of Jews. Mateusz Butrymowicz* (1745–1814), Polish reform leader, publishes "A Way of Transforming the Jews into Useful Citizens of the Country." He advocates assimilation.	 *The New Great Synagogue at Duke's Place is opened. Engraving by Pugin and Rowlandson.*		**1789**
Edmund Burke,* English statesman, writes *Reflections on the Revolution in France*, a critique of its excesses. The French National Assembly adopts a constitution establishing a limited monarchy.	The first U.S. federal census estimates a Jewish population between 1,300 and 1,500. Jews comprise about 1/30th of 1% of the total population of 3,929,214. George Washington,* in replying to congratulatory letters sent to him by Jewish congregations on his election to the presidency, stresses his belief in religious freedom. His letter to the Jewish congregation of Newport, Rhode Island, includes the now well-known phrase "To bigotry no sanction," which he quotes from the letter from the congregation.	The French National Assembly grants "active" citizenship to Sephardic Jews from Bordeaux, Bayonne, and Avignon. These Jews dissociate themselves from the emancipation efforts of their Ashkenazic brethren in Alsace and Lorraine. The new Duke's Place synagogue, the Great Synagogue of London's Ashkenazic community, is opened. It seats 500 men and 250 women in the gallery. In 1809, Thomas Rowlandson* and A. C. Pugin* will depict the interior. Pugin will accurately draw the architecture, but Rowlandson will draw the worshippers in disagreeable caricature.		Solomon Maimon (c.1753–1800), philosopher born in Poland who later studies in Berlin, writes *An Essay on the Transcendental Philosophy*, which is praised by Immanuel Kant.* In his later writings, he will achieve a synthesis of rationalism and Judaism. A Hebrew reader for children, *Avtalyon*, written by Aaron Wolfsohn-Halle (1754–1835), is published in Berlin. Containing tales from the Bible, proverbs, animal fables, and a section on history, it is utilized by modern schools founded by disciples of Moses Mendelssohn.	**1790**
The states of the U.S. ratify the Bill of Rights, which becomes part of the U.S. Constitution adopted in 1787.	The Jews of Surinam own 46 of 600 sugar cane plantations. Slave trade will be abolished in 1819 and slaves will be	In January, the Jews of Paris appear before the Paris Commune to urge the emancipation of all Jews of France.			**1791**

	A. General History	B. Jews in North and South America	C. Jews in Europe	D. Jews in the Middle East and Elsewhere	E. Jewish Culture
1791	The First Amendment guarantees the equality of all U.S. citizens, regardless of religion. Vermont becomes the 14th state of the U.S. King Louis XVI* attempts to flee France. He is restrained and forced to accept the Constitution.	emancipated in 1863. As sugar cane exports diminish, the Jewish community will decline.	In September, the French General Assembly admits all Jews (Ashkenazim and Sephardim) to full emancipation. Czarina Catherine* the Great, in reponse to complaints from Moscow merchants, decrees that the economic rights granted to Jews as members of guilds of merchants relates only to the territories newly taken over.		
1792	Kentucky becomes the 15th state of the U.S. France declares war on Austria and Prussia. Austria and Prussia wish to restore Louis XVI* to his throne, and the duke of Brunswick, commander of Prussian and Austrian armies, issues a manifesto threatening destruction of Paris if Louis XVI* is harmed.			Samuel Aaron Romanelli (1757–1817), Italian Hebrew poet and traveler, writes *Massa ba-Arav* (*The Travels of the Jews in the Arabic Countries*), a description of internal Jewish life in Morocco and their relations with the wider society.	Daniel Mendoza (1764–1836) becomes English boxing champion. Known as the father of scientific boxing, he becomes the first boxer to receive royal patronage. Proud of his heritage and calling himself Mendoza the Jew, he assists in easing the position of Jews in England.
1793	The U.S. Congress passes the Fugitive Slave Act, making it unlawful to prevent the arrest of or assist runaway slaves. The monarchy is abolished in France. King Louis XVI* and Marie Antoinette* are executed. The Republic is established, and the Committee of Public Safety begins the Reign of Terror. The Second Partition of Poland takes place. Russia obtains most of Lithuania and western Ukraine. Prussia gets Danzig and Great Poland.	A Jewish witness, Jonas Phillips, is fined 10 pounds by a Pennsylvania court for refusing to testify on Saturday. Thomas Paine,* among the intellectual leaders of the American Revolution, writes *The Age of Reason*. He is contemptuous of Christianity, Judaism, and the Bible. Paine believes that practicing Jews are a danger to enlightened society.	Johann Gottlieb Fichte* (1762–1814), German philosopher who reveres the Bible but rejects the Jewish religion, writes the essay *On the French Revolution*, in which he argues against granting civil rights to the Jews as long as one Jewish idea remains with them but distinguishes this view from human rights, which must be given to them, "for they are human beings and their malevolence does not justify our becoming like them."		Solomon Maimon (c.1753–1800), Polish-born philosopher known for his knowledge of German culture and philosophy, writes his autobiography. It describes his estrangement from traditional Judaism and is an important source of knowledge of Judaism and Hasidism in eastern Europe. Lazarus Bendavid (1762–1832), German mathematician, educator, and philosopher, writes *Notes Regarding the Characteristics of Jews*, in which he calls for the abolition of ritual laws of Judaism. He believes religious reform is the only

A. General History	B. Jews in North and South America	C. Jews in Europe	D. Jews in the Middle East and Elsewhere	E. Jewish Culture	
				feasible way of slowing the growing tide of conversion to Christianity.	**1792**
The Qajar dynasty rises in Iran. Rivalry among French political groups results in the execution of leaders and followers. The French army defeats the Austrians and advances along the Rhine. Thaddeus Kosciusko,* Polish military leader, wages an unsuccessful national uprising against the Russians and Prussians. Kosciusko* had fought in the American Revolution. In London, William Blake* (1757–1827) completes his *Songs of Innocence and Experience.* They are followed by *Milton* and *Jerusalem.* Though his poetry and engravings are steeped in biblical imagery, his views on biblical laws and commandments are very negative.	Congregation Beth Elohim of Charleston, South Carolina, dedicates its synagogue building, the second oldest in the United States. It will be destroyed by fire in 1838 and replaced in 1841 by a Greek revival synagogue building, which still stands today. A drawing by Solomon Nunes Carvalho (1815–1894) of the exterior of the synagogue survives the fire.	Richard Brothers* (1757–1824), a retired navy captain, begins prophesying that he has been sent by God to redeem England and return the Jews to the Holy Land, where he will rule over them until the Second Coming. His pamphlet, *Revealed Knowledge of the Prophecies and Times*, is one of many popular millenarian works dealing with Jewish restoration. Richard Cumberland's* (1732–1811) English play *The Jew* includes a sympathetic portrayal of the Jew Sheva. "Everybody rails at us, everybody points us out for their may-game and their mockery. If your playwrights want a butt, or a buffoon or a knave to make sport of, out comes a Jew to be baited and buffetted through five long acts, for the amusement of all good Christians." Berek Joselewicz (c.1770–1809), military leader, organizes a Jewish legion to participate in the unsuccessful national uprising against Russia and Prussia led by Thaddeus Kosciusko.* In May 1809, Joselewicz will be killed in battle. Czarina Catherine II* issues a decree establishing the Russian Pale of Settlement in the area outlined by the boundaries of the former Polish kingdom. It will be consolidated by	After a short period of relative tolerance under the rule of Sunni Muslim Nadir Shah* (1736–1747), the status of Iranian Jews deteriorates sharply until the Qajar dynasty ends in 1925.		**1794**

	A. General History	B. Jews in North and South America	C. Jews in Europe	D. Jews in the Middle East and Elsewhere	E. Jewish Culture
1794			stages in the course of the 19th century until its dissolution in 1917. In Vilna, Elijah Ben Solomon Zalman, the Vilna Gaon, calls for the public burning of the *Testament of Rabbi Israel Ba'al Shem Tov*, the Hasidic leader.		
1795	The Third Partition of Poland takes place. All of Poland is divided among Russia, Prussia, and Austria. The third French Constitution creates the Directory government. The war continues against Austria, England, and Sardinia. Prussia and Spain make peace. The Netherlands, occupied by France, is reconstituted as the Batavian Republic. Napoleon Bonaparte* subdues a royalist uprising.	A group of Ashkenazim from the Mikveh Israel synagogue in Philadelphia break away and form their own synagogue, Rodeph Shalom (Pursuer of Peace), which will be the first in America to follow the Ashkenazic form of service. This begins a trend that becomes the norm, namely, the founding of synagogues according to the traditions of the members, even where there are other synagogues in the community.	The Third Partition of Poland culminates a process bringing hundreds of thousands of additional Jews under Russian rule. Though by law Jews have been prohibited from living in Russia for hundreds of years, Russia now has the largest Jewish population in the world.		Marcus Eliezer Bloch (1723–1799), Berlin physician, completes his 12-volume history of fishes, begun in 1781, which is superbly illustrated and classifies over 1,500 species of fish. After his death, his marine collection will become a part of the Berlin Zoological Museum.
1796	John Adams* (Federalist) and Thomas Jefferson* (Democratic–Republican) are elected president and vice president of the U.S. George Washington's* Farewell Address as U.S. president warns against U.S. involvement in foreign affairs. Tennessee becomes the 16th state of the U.S. Edward Jenner,* English physician, performs the first innoculation against smallpox. French forces under the command of Napoleon Bonaparte* defeat the Austrians in Italy. Sardinia makes peace.		Between 1796 and 1798 French troops led by Napoleon Bonaparte* liberate many Italian ghettos. With the founding of the Batavian Republic, the Jews are granted full civil rights. When Hasidim spread a rumor that the Vilna Gaon regrets his stand against Hasidism, he replies, "it is the duty of every believing Jew to repudiate and pursue them . . . because they have sin in their hearts and are like a sore on the body of Israel."	Samuel Ezekiel Divekar (d. 1798) builds a Bene Israel synagogue in Bombay, India. The Bene Israel moved to Bombay gradually from the Konkan coastal villages. They also had contacts with the Cochin Jews. By 1947, they will number 24,000.	Peter Beer (c.1758–1838), Austrian educator, publishes a history of the Jews, *Toledot Yisrael*, which becomes the prototype of biblical history textbooks used in Europe until the 20th century. Shneur Zalman of Lyady (1745–1813), founder of Habad Hasidism, publishes *Tanya*, a systematic exposition of Habad Hasidism, which emphasizes learning and the intellectual aspects of Judaism as much as its spiritual side. It is studied daily by his adherents. Judah Leib ben Ze'ev's (1764–1811) Hebrew grammar, *Talmud Leshon Ivri* (*Learning the Hebrew*

A. General History	B. Jews in North and South America	C. Jews in Europe	D. Jews in the Middle East and Elsewhere	E. Jewish Culture	
Napoleon* obtains armistices from the king of Naples and the pope. Austrian forces defeat the French in southern Germany. Spain joins France in a war against England.				*Language*), is published in Breslau. It serves as the main source for the study of Hebrew in eastern Europe for a century.	**1796**
The Treaty of Campo Formio brings peace to Austria and France. The third edition of the *Encyclopedia Britannica* ends its detailed history of the Jews with the destruction of the Second Temple in 70. The following 17 centuries are summarized in one paragraph.	Solomon Etting (1764–1847) appeals to the Maryland state legislature on behalf of a "sect of people called Jews, deprived of invaluable rights of citizenship and praying to be placed on the same footing as other good citizens." A three-decade struggle begins with this petition, which will end successfully in 1826. *The Algerine Captive*, a novel written by Royall Tyler* (1757–1826), who later becomes chief judge of the Vermont Supreme Court, tells the story of a ship's doctor whose ship is captured by Algerian pirates. The doctor meets a Jewish merchant, Adonah, who promises to help him escape but instead robs him. Adonah is the first modern Jew mentioned in American fiction.	From 1797 to 1799, the French Revolutionary Army brings temporary emancipation to the Jews of Italy. The first Reform congregation in Europe, Adas Jeshurun, is established in Amsterdam. Reform adapts Jewish tradition to contemporary life and sensibilities.		Phinehas Elijah Hurwitz (1765–1821), European Hebrew writer and Haskalah advocate, writes *Sefer ha-Berit (The Book of the Covenant)*. Aimed at a popular audience, it is an anthology of the sciences and deals also with metaphysical issues. He urges Jews to engage in manual labor and not only in study and commerce, which encourages antisemitism.	**1797**
The U.S. Congress enacts the Alien and Sedition Acts, restricting political opposition and permitting arrest and deportation of dangerous aliens. Virginia and Kentucky adopt resolutions declaring these acts unconstitutional. Eli Whitney* builds a factory for the mass production of firearms near New Haven, Connecticut. He is acknowledged as the "father of mass production."		With the French expulsion of the pope from Rome, Jews are granted equal rights, and all earlier special laws relating to their status are revoked. Nahman of Bratslav (1772–1811), Hasidic zaddik, visits Palestine. His attachment to Palestine is both spiritual and physical. "If one wishes to be a true Jew, that is to go from level to level, it is impossible without	Shalom ha-Cohen (d. 1836), an Arabic-speaking Jew from Aleppo, Syria, becomes the first Jewish merchant to settle in Calcutta, India.	In an essay on Moses Mendelssohn, Isaac D'Israeli (1766–1848), English writer and father of Benjamin Disraeli, attacks rabbinic Judaism and praises Mendelssohn for promoting acceptance of European culture by Jews. While many English Jews cease traditional observances, most do so with no attempt to find intellectual justification for their actions.	**1798**

	A. General History	B. Jews in North and South America	C. Jews in Europe	D. Jews in the Middle East and Elsewhere	E. Jewish Culture
1798	The French capture Rome and invade Switzerland. Napoleon* attacks the British Empire through the invasion of Egypt. Horatio Nelson,* British admiral, defeats the French fleet in the Battle of the Nile. England, Austria, Russia, Naples, Portugal, and the Ottoman Empire estabish the Second Coalition against France.

Napoleon* ends the slave trade in the Mediterranean. Many Jews had been victims. | | Eretz Israel. This Eretz Israel, plainly and simply, with these houses and yards."

The Hasidim complain to the Russian–Lithuanian governor that they are being persecuted by the Vilna kehilla board. Both Hasidim and Mitnaggedim involve the government in disputes within the Jewish community. | | *Sefer Vikkuah* (*The Book of Disputation*), written by Israel Loebel, rabbi, preacher, and dayyan in Novogrudok since 1787, is published in Warsaw. Loebel is an opponent of Hasidism, and his work compares Hasidism with occasional heretical sects that had arisen throughout Jewish history. He attacks their principle that prayer is more important than Torah study and their leaders as ignoramuses who exploit the masses. His book is banned by Hasidim, who buy up and destroy almost all the copies printed.

Sefer Me'or Einayim (*The Book of the Light of Eyes*), written by the Hasidic leader Rabbi Menahem Nahum of Chernobyl (1730–1787), is published. His commentary interprets the Torah according to basic Kabbalistic and Hasidic teachings. He stresses people's moral attributes. |
| 1799 | Napoleon* returns to France, overthrows the Directory, and establishes the Napoleonic Consulate, with himself as First Consul.

The French armies are defeated in Italy and the old regimes returned to authority.

Napoleon's armies enter Israel, taking Jaffa on March 6. In April, Kleber* leads a French military force to victory near Mt. Tabor. With the help of British armies and supplies, the Turks hold Napoleon* off at Acre. On April 26 | In Charles Brockden Brown's* (1771–1810) novel *Arthur Mervyn*, written in two parts and completed in 1800, the hero marries Achsa Fielding, a rich Jewish widow. The poet Shelley* is reported to have been displeased by the transfer of the hero's affections from a simple peasant girl to a rich Jewess. | As a result of the restoration of the old rulers in Italy, the Jews are again ghettoized and the restrictions against them reimposed.

The first blood libel case in Russia occurs south of Vitebsk, near Senno, on the eve of Passover. The accused are released. | The Jews of Israel support Napoleon* and send a delegation to explain the messianic hopes embodied in his conquest. | |

					1799
Napoleon* abandons Acre and withdraws with his troops to Egypt.					

					1800

In the U.S. presidential election, Thomas Jefferson* and Aaron Burr* each receive 73 votes in the electoral college.

The U.S. moves the seat of government from Philadelphia to Washington, D.C.

France defeats the Austrians at the Battle of Marengo. They conquer Italy, seize Munich, and defeat the Austrians at the Battle of Hohenlinden.

During the first decade of the 19th century, Charleston, South Carolina, contains about 500 Jews and is the largest, wealthiest, and most cultured Jewish community in the United States.

Benjamin Nones (1757–1826), who fought for the patriot cause with distinction during the Revolutionary War, is attacked in a Federalist publication for being a Jew, a Republican, and poor. In his reply, he defends his faith and expresses his belief in a democratic republic where men have rights and his disdain for monarchies where men "live but to experience wrongs."

About 600 Jewish households in Amsterdam—predominantly Ashkenazi—are earning their livelihood from diamond polishing. The craft was brought to Holland in the 1590s by Flemish Christians from Antwerp. For many years, they succeeded in denying Jews admission to the guild.

Gabriel Romanovich Derzhavin* (1743–1816) issues a report of his investigation of the Jewish problem in Russia made on behalf of the czar, which blames the Jews for the sufferings of the peasantry. He suggests that Jews be divided into four estates according to income and place of residence and "New Russia" be made available for Jewish agricultural colonization.

World Jewish Population, 1800

Total World Population	720,000,000
Total World Jewish Population	2,500,000

Place	Number	% of World Jewry
Near East (including Turkey)	1,000,000	40.0
Russian Poland & Western Russia	800,000	32.0
Austria (including Galicia)	300,000	12.0
Bohemia & Moravia	70,000	2.8
Hungary	100,000	4.0
Prussia	100,000	4.0
France (including Alsace)	80,000	3.2
Holland	50,000	2.0

Note: At the beginning of the 19th century, only two cities of the world contained more than 10,000 Jews: Amsterdam, with a Jewish population in 1797 of 23,104, and Constantinople. The Jewish population in the United States is estimated at 2,000.

	A. General History	B. Jews in North and South America	C. Jews in Europe	D. Jews in the Middle East and Elsewhere	E. Jewish Culture
1801	The U.S. House of Representatives elects Thomas Jefferson* as president and Aaron Burr* as vice president. The U.S. sends naval ships to the Mediterranean in response to the pasha* of Tripoli's demand that U.S. ships pay more tribute to the pirates of the Barbary States (Morocco, Algiers, Tunis, and Tripoli). France surrenders to the British in Egypt. Czar Paul I* of Russia is assassinated. He is succeeded by his son, Alexander I.*	The Hebrew Orphan Society of Charleston, South Carolina, is organized. It is an early example of American Jewish philanthropic activity. Reuben Etting (1762–1848) is appointed U.S. marshall for Maryland by President Thomas Jefferson.* Long involved in politics, he becomes the first Jew to hold public office.	Israel Jacobson (1768–1828), German financier and pioneer of Reform Judaism, establishes a school for Jewish children in the small town of Seesen in Lower Saxony. The curriculum is mostly secular and vocational in the anticipation it would enhance the prospects of emancipation.		John Braham (c.1774–1856), English tenor and son of the chorister of London's Great Synagogue, returns to England after a European tour and is hailed as the most remarkable singer of his time.
1802	Thomas Jefferson,* in his letter of reply to an address of the Danbury, Connecticut, Baptist Association, interprets the religious freedom provision of the First Amendment to the federal Constitution as setting up "a wall of separation of church and state." The Treaty of Amiens among France, England, and Spain restores the conquests to France. Napoleon* becomes First Consul of France for life. He becomes president of the Italian Republic. France signs a treaty returning Egypt to the Ottoman Empire. France subdues a black rebellion in Haiti.	Simon M. Levy is a member of the first graduating class of West Point.	Solomon Hirschel (1762–1842) is appointed rabbi of the principal London synagogue, the Great Synagogue, and becomes the first formally recognized chief rabbi of Great Britain. Johann Gottfried Herder* (1744–1803), German philosopher and theologian, publishes an essay in which he calls for total emancipation of the Jews. Hayyim ben Isaac Volozhiner (1749–1821), Russian rabbi and educator, founds a yeshiva at Volozhin. It becomes the prototype of the great yeshivot of eastern Europe in the 19th and 20th centuries.		THE JEWISH WORLD OF EUROPE, NORTH AFRICA, AND THE MIDDLE EAST AT THE BEGINNING OF THE 19TH CENTURY 
1803	The U.S. negotiates the Louisiana Purchase and obtains the Louisiana Territory from France for $15 million.		A special committee appointed by Czar Alexander I* (1801–1825) in 1802 studies the question of the status of the Jews. Some argue for reformation of the		Aaron Chorin (1766–1844), a Hungarian rabbi who advocates reforms in Judaism, publishes *Emek ha-Shaveh* (*Valley of Equals*) in Prague, which

A. General History	B. Jews in North and South America	C. Jews in Europe	D. Jews in the Middle East and Elsewhere	E. Jewish Culture	
Ohio becomes the 17th state of the U.S. War between France and England is resumed.		Jewish way of life before assimilation, while others argue that assimilation would naturally follow the granting of rights. Those advocating the first view prevail.		attacks customs he believes have no basis in Judaism. He abrogates the Kapparot ceremony, abolishes the *Kol Nidrei* prayer, and permits prayer in the vernacular and the use of the organ on the Sabbath. He is attacked by Orthodox Jewish circles.	**1803**
Thomas Jefferson* is reelected U.S. president, and George Clinton* is elected vice president. Napoleon Bonaparte* is proclaimed emperor of France. The Napoleonic Code is promulgated. Spain, allied with France, declares war on England. 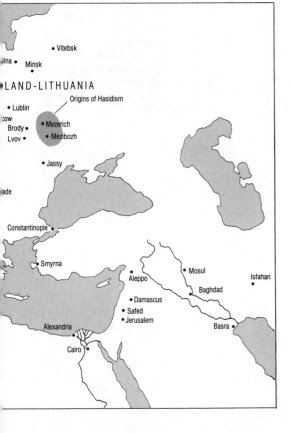		Czar Alexander I* promulgates the first Constitution of the Jews. Jews are denied the right to hold leases on land or to operate taverns; they are to be expelled from villages and sent to larger towns and cities, i.e., confined to the Pale of Settlement. Jews are granted access to public schools in an effort to foster conversion. Tax exemption is offered to those who will move to southeastern Russia to farm the land. These measures will fail as few attend public school or emigrate south. Judah Leib Nevakhovich (1776–1831), an early Russian Jewish *maskil*, publishes a pamphlet in Russian and Hebrew, *The Outcry of the Daughter of Judah*, calling on Russians to treat Jews with sympathy and tolerance and rejecting demands of Christians that Jews be converted. In about 1809, he will convert to Lutheranism, resulting in the rejection by many Jews of the Haskalah movement.		The "Maggid of Dubno," Jacob ben Wolf Kranz (1741–1804), dies in Poland. Famous as a preacher in Dubno, where he served 18 years, he composed homilies that the laymen could understand and encouraged the masses through use of a wide knowledge of fables, stories, and parables. However, his homilies are not simplistic and include ethical and halakhic principles. His works will be printed posthumously by his son.	**1804**
Tripoli grants free passage to U.S. ships in the Mediterranean, as a			Naphtali Busnach, the chief aide of the Bey of Algiers, is assassinated, and		**1805**

	A. General History	B. Jews in North and South America	C. Jews in Europe	D. Jews in the Middle East and Elsewhere	E. Jewish Culture
1805	peace treaty ends the Tripolitan War. However, the piracy of the Barbary States lasts until 1815. The Ottoman sultan appoints Muhammad Ali* pasha of Egypt.			hundreds of Jews are massacred by janissaries (i.e., soldiers of the Ottoman Empire), who resent the favors the Jews receive from the Dey.	
1806	Prussia declares war on France. The French defeat the Prussians at the Battle of Jena. Napoleon* occupies Berlin. The British blockade the French ports. Napoleon* promulgates the Berlin Decree, which initiates the Continental System, i.e., the closure of Continental ports to British ships.		In May, Napoleon,* on his return from victory at Austerlitz, receives complaints from Strasbourg citizens about the "usurious" activities of Jewish moneylenders in Alsace and Lorraine. He issues a decree convening an Assembly of Jewish Notables from all over the French Empire and the kingdom of Italy to clarify relations between the state and the Jews. In July, the Assembly of Jewish Notables, consisting of 112 Jewish community leaders, meets in Paris, elects Abraham Furtado (1756–1817) its president. In September, Napoleon* issues a call for a Sanhedrin to be held in 1807. In October, Count Clemens Metternich,* then Austria's ambassador in Paris, writes of Napoleon's* plans for an invasion of central Europe. "There is no doubt that he will not fail to present himself as a liberator to . . . its immense Jewish population." Moses Sofer (Hatam Sofer, 1762–1839), leader of Orthodox Jewry's effort to frustrate the emerging Reform movement, is appointed rabbi in Pressburg, the most important community		Moses Lopez, of Newport, Rhode Island, compiles the first American printed calendar (*Luah*) of Hebrew dates. Charles Towne (1781–1854), a London-born painter, begins to exhibit his paintings of animals and landscapes at the Royal Academy. *Sulamith*, the first German-language Jewish periodical, begins publication in Dessau. Edited by David Fraenkel (1779–1856), one of its founders, it supports the modernization of Jewish education and religious reforms. It will cease publication in 1833.

A. General History	B. Jews in North and South America	C. Jews in Europe	D. Jews in the Middle East and Elsewhere	E. Jewish Culture	
		in Hungary. He establishes a yeshiva, which becomes the center of his activities against the Reform movement. Sofer opposes halakhic innovation and does not involve himself in the struggle for emancipation.			1806

A. General History	B. Jews in North and South America	C. Jews in Europe	D. Jews in the Middle East and Elsewhere	E. Jewish Culture	
The U.S. Congress passes the Embargo Act, prohibiting trade with any foreign country. This act is aimed at preventing England and France from interfering with U.S. trade. The French defeat the Russians at the Battle of Friedland. Napoleon* signs the Treaty of Tilsit with Russia and Prussia. France occupies Portugal.	Ezekiel Hart, of Three Rivers, and the son of Aaron Hart, the first Jew to have settled permanently in Canada, is elected to the Parliament of Lower Canada. However, he does not take his seat as he would not be sworn in "on the true faith of a Christian."	In February, the Sanhedrin convened by Napoleon* meets in Paris. Chaired by David Sinzheim (1745–1812), rabbi of Strasbourg, it consists of 80 delegates, including 46 rabbis. They affirm Jewish political loyalty, assert that they "no longer form a nation within a nation," and publicly condemn moneylending at high rates of interest. At this time, Napoleon's* armies are in Warsaw and the grateful Jewish community undertakes to provision his army. Augustin Barruel* (1741–1820), French Jesuit antirevolutionary, advises the French government of an alleged world Jewish conspiracy. His accusation receives the endorsement of Pope Pius VII and is believed to be the cause of Napoleon's* decision to dissolve the French Sanhedrin. Barruel's* fantasies are an early example of the world "Jewish plot" theme.		Judah Leib ben Ze'ev begins publication in Vienna of *Ozar ha-Shorashim* (*Treasury of Roots*), a Hebrew–German and German–Hebrew dictionary that forms the basis for modern Hebrew terminology in linguistics. It will be completed in 1808.  *Opening session of the Sanhedrin convened by Napoleon. A contemporary engraving.* Tadeusz Czacki* (1765–1813), Polish Christian historian, writes a book on Jews and Karaites. It is the first comprehensive account of Polish Jewry. Manasseh ben Porat (1767–1831), an early Russian *maskil*, writes *Pesher Davar* (*Solution to a Problem*), calling for some change in the *halakhah* toward increasing rationalism. This work is suppressed by Orthodox rabbinical circles.	1807

A. General History	B. Jews in North and South America	C. Jews in Europe	D. Jews in the Middle East and Elsewhere	E. Jewish Culture
1808 James Madison* is elected U.S. president, and George Clinton* is reelected vice president.

The U.S. prohibits the importation of African slaves.

France invades Spain, and Napoleon* installs his brother as king of Spain. The English land in Portugal and defeat the French.

The Portuguese court, including about 15,000 courtiers, flees from Napoleon's* armies to Brazil. | Polonies Talmud Torah is established in New York. It is named after Myer Polony, who had died in 1801 and left a bequest of $900 to Congregation Shearith Israel, the Spanish and Portuguese synagogue of New York, for the establishment of a Jewish communal day school. It is the first Jewish school on record in the U.S.

In attacking Voltaire's* derogatory attitude toward the Bible and the Jewish people, John Adams* (1735–1826) writes to a friend: "How is it possible this old fellow should represent the Hebrews in such a contemptible light? They are the most glorious nation that ever inhabited this earth. The Romans and their Empire were but a bauble in comparison of the Jews." | Napoleon* issues two edicts regulating the position of the Jews. The first edict declares Judaism to be an "official" religion and creates a consistory of French Jews headed by a central consistory in Paris and 13 regional consistories to supervise Jewish religious life. The second, the "Infamous Decree," imposes control over Jewish loans, requires special permits to engage in trade, and forbids settlement in northeastern France. It will be abolished in 1818.

Francois Fourier* (1772–1837), French social reformer, writes a book that identifies commerce as the source of all evil and the Jews as "the incarnation of commerce."

Israel Jacobson, German court banker and pioneer of Reform Judaism, convenes a group of Jewish notables in Kassel to introduce religious, civic, and moral reform among the Jews. His gathering is viewed with suspicion by Orthodox Jews.

A survey of 16 Jewish communities in the Russian provinces of Vitebsk and Moghilev records their decision not to create any secular schools and to limit their children only to religious education.

Baruch of Medzibezh (1757–1810), Hasidic zaddik and grandson of the Ba'al Shem Tov, founder of modern Hasidism, regards himself as the leader of Hasidism by hereditary right, | For three years, beginning in 1808, some disciples of the Vilna Gaon, the *perushim*, emigrate to Palestine and settle in Safed. Israel of Shklov (d. 1839), talmudic scholar from Lithuania, arrives in 1809 and becomes the leader of the *Kolel ha-Perushim*. Within seven years their numbers increase from 200 to 700. This emigration is believed to be the beginning of the modern settlement of Israel.

The Sultan of Morocco, Mulay Suleiman,* orders the enclosure of Jews into mellahs in the cities of Tetuan, Rabat, Sale and Mogador. He seeks to seal Morocco off from foreign influence and to reduce trade with Europe. | In Galicia, Mendel ben Jehudah Loeb Levin (1749–1826) publishes *Heshbon ha-Nefesh* (*Soul Searching*), a guide to Jewish ethics and self-improvement based on the works of Benjamin Franklin.* |

A. General History	B. Jews in North and South America	C. Jews in Europe	D. Jews in the Middle East and Elsewhere	E. Jewish Culture	
		acquires wealth by accepting gifts from Hasidic pilgrims seeking his blessing, and holds court in his mansion. His behavior is deplored by other Hasidic leaders.			**1808**
The duke of Wellington leads British and Portuguese forces in driving the French out of Portugal, invades Spain, and defeats the French at the Battle of Talavera. Napoleon* captures Vienna, defeats the Austrians at the Battle of Wagram, and forces them to cede territory at the Treaty of Schonbrunn. He annexes the papal states.	An enemy of Jacob Henry, a Jewish member of the North Carolina legislature's lower house, demands that Henry vacate his seat, because the state Constitution forbids civil office to non-Protestants. Henry objects and is permitted to retain his seat. However, the objectionable state constitutional clause will remain in effect until 1868, when the right to hold office will be granted to Jews.			*Shirei Tif'eret* (*Poems of Glory*) by Naphtali Herz Wessely (1725–1805) is published in Prague. A major literary work of the German Haskalah, it is a long epic on the life of Moses and the Exodus from Egypt. Wessely is a pioneer in Jewish education and wrote biblical commentaries, including a commentary on Leviticus, for Mendelssohn's commentary and translation of the Bible, the Bi'ur.	**1809**
Argentina, Chile, Colombia, and Venezuela estabish autonomous governments.	Argentina gains independence. Despite the fact that immigration is open as of 1812 to anyone from a country at peace with Argentina and the Inquisition there is abolished in 1813, it is only in 1853 that the Constitution guarantees complete religious freedom to all residents.	Israel Jacobson, German financier, opens a synagogue on the grounds of the school he founded in 1801 in Seesen, Lower Saxony. A pioneer in Reform Judaism, he established his school for children, and his synagogue and its services, conducted in German, are strongly influenced by Protestant practices. In 1813, Jacobson's privileged status will come to an end, and he will move to Berlin.		In Germany, Adolf Martin Schlesinger (1768–1848) establishes the music publishing firm Schlesinger'sche Buch und Musikalienhandlung. It publishes music by Beethoven* and Bach.*	**1810**
James Madison* is reelected U.S. president and Elbridge Gerry* is elected vice president. The War of 1812 between the U.S. and England begins. Louisiana becomes the 18th state of the U.S.	Hannah Adams* (1755–1831), considered to be the first American woman professional writer, writes *History of the Jews from the Destruction of Jerusalem to the Nineteenth Century*, which includes a chapter on the Jews in the New World. She is associated with efforts to pro-	During Napoleon's* fateful invasion of Russia, most Russian Jews remain steadfastly loyal to the czar. Czar Nicholas I* will note in his diary during an 1816 visit to Jewish areas, "Surprisingly . . . in 1812 they were very loyal to us and assisted us in every possible way even at the risk of their lives."			**1812**

	A. General History	B. Jews in North and South America	C. Jews in Europe	D. Jews in the Middle East and Elsewhere	E. Jewish Culture
1812	Napoleon* invades Russia. The duke of Wellington* leads British and Portuguese forces in defeat of France in Spain. They enter Madrid.	mote Christianity among American Jews. However, she expresses concern that some American Jews are becoming nonbelievers, and she fears that Jewish faithlessness might spread to Christian circles.	The Jews of Prussia receive a grant of civil rights from Frederick William III.* They are granted freedom of trade, movement and residence. However, they are still denied the right to hold state positions. Württemberg, Baden, and Bavaria do not grant their Jews these freedoms. The Russian Pale of Settlement takes its final form. Jews are confined to 25 western Russian provinces and cannot travel, let alone live, outside the Pale without official permission. The authorities impose limits on the occupations Jews can engage in within the Pale.		
1813	The U.S. fleet under Commodore Perry* defeats the British in the Battle of Lake Erie. The War of 1812 continues. Austrian, Prussian, and Russian armies decisively defeat the French at the Battle of Leipzig. Wellington* leads the invasion of France from Spain.	Mordecai Manuel Noah (1785–1851), U.S. politician, editor, and playwright, is appointed as U.S. consul at Tunis, the first major diplomatic post awarded a Jew.	Isaac D'Israeli explains his indifference to formal Judaism to the board of the Bevis Marks synagogue in London as the reason for his refusal to act as warden. He remains a Jew, yet, in 1817, he will baptize his famous son, Benjamin (1804–1891). *Unser Verkehr* (*Our Visitors*), a play written by Karl Sessa* (1786–1813), is widely performed in rural southern Germany. Sessa,* an antisemitic German physician, ridicules the greed, vulgarity, and immorality of postemancipation Jewry. The play is the inspiration for many of the antisemitic caricatures found in German literature.		Joseph Perl (1773–1839), leader of the Galician Haskalah movement, establishes in Tarnopol the first modern Jewish school in Galicia. The curriculum includes both general and Jewish studies.
1814	The British capture Washington, D.C., and burn the White		Rabbi Akiva Eger (1761–1837), German rabbi, is		Liepmann Fraenckel (1774–1857), a Jewish miniature

A. General History	B. Jews in North and South America	C. Jews in Europe	D. Jews in the Middle East and Elsewhere	E. Jewish Culture	
House. The U.S. fleet defeats the British on Lake Champlain. The Treaty of Ghent ends the War of 1812. Napoleon* abdicates and is exiled to Elba as the Allies capture Paris. Louis XVIII* is restored to the French throne. The First Peace of Paris deals generously with France—it is not occupied or forced to pay indemnity. The victors convene the Congress of Vienna to discuss the remaking of Europe. Pope Pius VII revives the Inquisition and restores the Jesuits and the Index.		appointed rabbi of the Posen district over the objections of Reform movement leaders. He establishes a yeshiva and is a leading opponent of the Reform movement. Nevertheless, he responds to demands for a modern curriculum in Jewish schools. Rahel Varnhagen (1771–1833), German socialite, converts to Christianity. Her home is the informal gathering place for literary, social, and political sages of the day, both Jewish and non-Jewish.		painter, is commissioned by the Danish court to paint King Frederick VI* and members of his family.	**1814**
Two weeks after the Treaty of Ghent is signed, U.S. forces under General Andrew Jackson* defeat the British at the Battle of New Orleans. The Algerine War ends as the U.S. naval forces under Stephen Decatur* force the dey of Algiers and leaders of Tripoli and Tunis to sign treaties ending U.S. tribute. Brazil is granted equality with Portugal. The British and Prussian armies defeat the French at the Battle of Waterloo. Napoleon* is exiled to St. Helena. The Second Peace of Paris is signed. The Congress of Vienna redraws the map of Europe. The German states group themselves into a loose association of	Mordecai Manuel Noah is recalled as the U.S. consul to Tunis by Secretary of State James Monroe,* giving Noah's religion as the ostensible reason for termination of his appointment. Noah is also charged with fiscal malfeasance and is cleared after investigation.	The Congress of Vienna gives witness to the formation of the German Confederation. The Confederation rejects Prussia's proposal that the Prussian decree of 1812 be applied to Jews throughout the Confederation. Participants at the Congress of Vienna, including Metternich* and Talleyrand,* attend the receptions of Fanny Arnstein (1757–1818) at her famous salon. Although she adopts the ways of contemporary non-Jewish society, she retains elements of loyalty to Judaism. She renders financial support to Wolfgang Amadeus Mozart* (1756–1791). Israel Jacobson, German financier and pioneer of Reform Judaism, opens a "private" Reform synagogue in his Berlin home. Several			**1815**

	A. General History	B. Jews in North and South America	C. Jews in Europe	D. Jews in the Middle East and Elsewhere	E. Jewish Culture
1815	39 kingdoms, duchies, principalities, and free cities, known as the German Confederation. It is dominated by Prussia and Austria. The Netherlands and Poland are created as kingdoms. Sweden retains Norway.		months later, the government prohibits the holding of services in private homes. Shalom Rokeah (1779–1855), rabbi in Belz, is recognized as a zaddik. Thousands of Hasidim become his followers, and Belz becomes the center of Galician Hasidism. English poet Lord Byron* writes his *Hebrew Melodies*, some of which express sympathy for the plight of the Jews.		
1816	James Monroe* and Daniel D. Tompkins* are elected president and vice president of the U.S. Indiana becomes the 19th state of the U.S.		The Jewish population of Berlin is 3,373 or 1.20% of the total population. Jakob Friedrich Fries* (1773–1843), German antisemitic philosopher popular with nationalistic students, writes *On the Danger to the Well-Being and Character of the Germans Presented by the Jews*, in which he protests the emancipation of the Jews. "Judaism . . . should be completely extirpated. In fact, improving the condition of the Jews in society means rooting out Judaism, destroying the whole lot of deceitful, second-hand pedlars and hawkers."		The Palatine Library of Parma acquires Giovanni Bernardo de'Rossi's* (1742–1831) library of several thousand Jewish manuscripts and books. De'Rossi,* an Italian Christian Hebraist, sold his collection to the duchess of Parma, who donated it to the library.
1817	Mississippi becomes the 20th state of the U.S. Jose de San Martin* leads a revolutionary army over the Andes and defeats the Spanish in Chile at the Battle of Chacabuco. David Ricardo (1772–1823), British economist, writes *Principles of Political*	The Pennsylvania State Supreme Court affirms the conviction of Abraham Wolf, a professing Jew, for "having done and performed worldly employment on the Lord's Day, commonly called Sunday."	Benjamin Disraeli is baptized into the Church of England. In Ferrara, Italy, the five-year-old daughter of Angelo Ancona is forcibly taken from her parents, with church approval, on the grounds that when she was two months old she was privately baptized by her nurse.		

A. General History	B. Jews in North and South America	C. Jews in Europe	D. Jews in the Middle East and Elsewhere	E. Jewish Culture	
Economy and Taxation. Ricardo's theories transform economic speculation into a scientific discipline. He left the faith in 1793, yet he consistently fought for the removal of Jewish disabilities. He will enter Parliament in 1819.		The Society of Israelitic Christians is founded by Czar Alexander I* of Russia for the purpose of promoting conversion of Jews to Christianity. There are few Jewish converts, and the society will be disbanded in 1833. Czar Alexander I* issues an edict directing that Jews not be accused of murdering Christian children "merely upon the basis of the ancient tradition that they required Christian blood" and orders a fair investigation in each case.			**1817**
Illinois becomes the 21st state of the U.S. Independence of Chile is assured as the Spanish are defeated at Maipu.	John Adams* (1735–1826), a champion of religious freedom, writes to Mordecai Manuel Noah: "I wish your nation may be admitted to all the privileges of citizens in every country of the world. This country has done much. I wish it may do more, and annul every narrow idea in religion, government and commerce." Only three Jewish families remain in Newport, Rhode Island. The first Jewish choir in the U.S. is organized at Congregation Shearith Israel in New York.	King Frederick William III,* ruler of Prussia, excludes Jews from academic positions and dismisses Jewish officials from state positions. He actively encourages conversion to Christianity and prohibits conversion to Judaism. Services begin at the New Israelite Temple Association of Hamburg. Founded by 66 laymen, it institutes the first systematic Reform synagogue service. It attempts to enhance the service by emphasizing decorum, abbreviating the service, and introducing a choir and organ and a sermon and prayer in the vernacular. Ludwig Boerne (1786–1837), German political essayist, converts to Christianity and founds *Die Waage*, a periodical that publishes his cultural and political writings.		Leopold Zunz (1794–1886), one of the founders of the Science of Judaism in Germany, writes his first work, *Studies in Rabbinical Literature*, a review of postbiblical Jewish literature. In this pioneering work, Zunz argues that Jewish literature should include the humanities and natural sciences and not be confined merely to the religious and halakhic tradition. Eliezer Liebermann, talmudic scholar, is enlisted by the founders of the Hamburg Reform synagogue to prepare a halakhic defense of Reform. He writes *Nogah ha-Tsedek* (*The Light of Righteousness*) and *Or Nogah* (*The Light of Splendor*).	**1818**

A. General History	B. Jews in North and South America	C. Jews in Europe	D. Jews in the Middle East and Elsewhere	E. Jewish Culture
1818		A leader of German liberals, he converts not out of religious conviction but to gain wider acceptance of his views. During the 19th century, at least 250,000 Jews convert to Christianity.		

A. General History	B. Jews in North and South America	C. Jews in Europe	D. Jews in the Middle East and Elsewhere	E. Jewish Culture
1819	Alabama becomes the 22nd state of the U.S. Simon Bolivar* defeats Spanish forces and becomes president of Greater Colombia (Venezuela, Colombia, Ecuador, and Panama).	William Davis Robinson,* a Christian merchant, writes "A Plan for Establishing a Jewish Settlement in the United States," urging Jewish sponsors to transport Jews from Europe and settle them in an agricultural colony in the upper Mississippi territory. Alfred Mordecai, of Richmond, Virginia, graduates from West Point, the highest-ranking student in his class.  *Anti-Jewish riots in Germany. A contemporary print.*	Anti-Jewish riots— so-called Hep! Hep! riots—break out in Germany and spread to Denmark. They are the result of accusations of economic exploitation of Christians by Jews resulting from the granting of commercial and civil rights to Jews. Authorities exploit the riots to argue that emancipation of the Jews increases social tensions. Hep! Hep!, a slogan used by the rioters, is of crusader origin, developed from the initials of the words *Hierosolyma est perdita* (Jerusalem is lost). The Society for Culture and the Scientific Study of the Jews is founded in Berlin by Leopold Zunz and others. Its purpose is to demonstrate the universal value of Jewish knowledge. The society will be dissolved in 1824. The Hamburg Reform synagogue introduces a new prayer book. Mention of the Messiah and return to the Holy Land are omitted. The rabbinic court of Hamburg publishes *Eleh Divrei ha-Beit* (*These Are the Words of the Covenant*), which contains the responsa of 22 of Europe's leading rabbis opposing the Hamburg reforms as		Mordecai Manuel Noah produces his play *She Would Be a Soldier*, one of the first American plays to draw exclusively upon American materials. It is set at the time of the Battle of Chippewa (July 5, 1814) when, led by General Winfield Scott,* Americans redeemed earlier defeats of the Canadian campaign. Rebecca Gratz (1781–1869) serves as the model for the character Rebecca in Sir Walter Scott's* (1771–1832) novel *Ivanhoe*. Scott's Jews are different from earlier stereotypes, and they preach peace and respect for human life to the murderous Christian knights. Washington Irving,* who knew Gratz from Philadelphia, informed Scott* of her noble character. Joseph Perl, leader of the Galician Haskalah movement writes *Megalleh Temirin* (*The Revealer of Secrets*), a satirical polemic against Hasidism.

A. General History	B. Jews in North and South America	C. Jews in Europe	D. Jews in the Middle East and Elsewhere	E. Jewish Culture	
		based on a misinformed reading of *halakhah* and as creating a schismatic threat to the unity of the Jewish people.			1819
James Monroe* and Daniel D. Tompkins* are reelected president and vice president of the U.S.

The U.S. Congress passes the Missouri Compromise. The Mississippi Valley north of latitude 36 degrees 30 minutes will be closed to slavery.

Maine becomes the 23rd state, a free state, of the U.S.

The liberal rebellion in Naples forces the Spanish Bourbon king to grant a constitution. Revolutionary movements occur in Piedmont, Spain, and Portugal. | The American Society for Meliorating the Conditions of the Jews is founded by Frederick Frey (1771–1850), who before his conversion to Christianity was Joseph Samuel Levy. This missionary society will function for half a century without much success. *Israel Vindicated*, published in New York to counteract the society's missionary activities, argues that religious freedom in America implies the absolute equality of all religions before the law.

At the dedication of a synagogue in Savannah, Georgia, Jacob de la Motta preaches: "On what spot of this habitable globe does an Israelite enjoy more blessings, more privileges, or is more elevated in the sphere of preferment." | At the suggestion of Czar Alexander I,* the Vilna Kahal places smuggling from the neighboring provinces in Prussia under a religious ban. The Minsk community fails to follow Vilna's example. | | Isaac Marcus Jost, first major historian of the Jews in the modern period, begins publication of his *History of the Israelites*. The work of this German scholar appears in nine volumes and covers the period from the Maccabees to 1815. In 1846–1847, he will add three more volumes dealing with his own time. Jost condemns the Pharisees and rabbis for promoting Jewish separatism and considers Jewish nationhood to have ended with the destruction of the Second Temple. His works remain untranslated from the German. | 1820 |
| Missouri becomes the 24th state, a slave state, of the U.S.

The Greek War of Independence begins. | | Isaac Bernays (1792–1849) is appointed rabbi of Hamburg. He opposes the Reform movement in his community and formulates a "modern Orthodoxy," which influences his disciple, Samson Raphael Hirsch (1808–1888).

During the Greek revolt, Greek Jews are loyal to the Ottomans and support their rule. Five hundred Jews are massacred in Peloponnesus by Greek rebels. | | Isaac Samuel Reggio (1784–1855) begins to publish the first modern Italian translation and Hebrew commentary on the Torah. He will also publish for the first time *Kol Sachal* and *Ari Nohem* by Leone Modena (1571–1648) and found the rabbinical seminary in Padua. | 1821 |

	A. General History	B. Jews in North and South America	C. Jews in Europe	D. Jews in the Middle East and Elsewhere	E. Jewish Culture
1822	Brazil becomes independent of Portugal. The Rothschild family launches a huge Russian loan of 10 million pounds. It helps Russian reconstruction and currency stabilization after the Napoleonic Wars.	Three years after Leopold Zunz and other German Jews found the Society for Culture and the Scientific Study of the Jews, they write to Mordecai Manuel Noah in the U.S. They ask for "every particular information . . . of the Jews" and how "emigration may be connected with the welfare of those who may be disposed to leave a country where they have nothing to look for but endless slavery and oppression."	The synagogue on Rue Notre Dame de Nazareth in Paris is opened. Situated in a courtyard behind a street-type façade and seating 1,000, it is the first synagogue of historical and architectural significance built by the consistory. It will be closed in 1850, having fallen into a state of decay. Abraham Mendelssohn (1776–1835), German banker and son of Moses Mendelssohn, and his wife convert to Christianity "because it is the religious form acceptable to the majority of civilized human beings." They rear their children, Fanny (1805–1847) and the well-known composer Felix (1809–1847), as Protestants in order to improve their social opportunities.		The first issue of *Zeitschrift fuer die Wissenschaft des Judentums*, the journal of the Society for Culture and the Scientific Study of the Jews, is published. Edited by Leopold Zunz, the first issue of the short-lived journal includes a programmatic manifesto by Immanuel Wolf, "On the Concept of a Science of Judaism." "Scientific" study is aimed at securing equal rights for Jews. *Alfei Menasheh* by Manasseh of Ilya (1767–1831) is published in Lithuania. A student of the Vilna Gaon, Manasseh wants to reconcile Hasidim and Mitnaggedim, *maskilim* and traditionalists, for the good of the community. He calls for Jews to engage in productive labor and obtain basic secular knowledge to improve their social condition.
1823	U.S. President James Monroe* announces the Monroe Doctrine, which unilaterally warns European nations not to interfere in the Western Hemisphere. The U.S. renounces any intention of interference in internal European concerns.	Solomon H. Jackson (d. 1847), the first Jewish printer in New York, edits and publishes *The Jew*, the first Jewish periodical in the U.S. The prime purpose of this periodical, which survives for two years, is to refute missionary attacks on Jews.	In Velizh, in Vitebsk Province, Jews are accused of killing a Christian child around Passover time. The investigation and trial of this blood accusation will last over 10 years. Jews are imprisoned and the town's synagogues closed before an investigation by a czarist official, N. Mordinov,* establishes the falsity of the accusation. However, Czar Nicholas I* will refuse to renew the edict of 1817, and blood libels remain an instrument of anti-Jewish agitation until the end of the czarist regime.	A group of Habad Hasidim emigrate from Europe to Palestine and settle in Hebron. The community remains in Hebron until the Arab riots of 1929. "The Affair of the Hats" almost results in the severing of diplomatic relations between Tunisia and European nations. The Bey had compelled his Jewish subjects to wear distinctive hats. A Jewish-British subject is arrested for wearing a European hat. He will be released after Britain protests. Thereafter all foreign nationals will be exempt from the law.	Isaac Baer Levinsohn (1788–1860), a founder of the Russian Haskalah, writes Te'udah be-Yisrael (*Testimony in Israel*), in which he severely criticizes the traditional school system, advocates study of the Hebrew language as the "bond of religion and national survival" and of the sciences, and urges manual labor and farming, and deplores petty trading. The Orthodox prevent its publication until 1828. The book has a great impact on Russian Jewish life. Judah Leib Miesis (1798–1831), leader of Galician Haskalah

A. General History	B. Jews in North and South America	C. Jews in Europe	D. Jews in the Middle East and Elsewhere	E. Jewish Culture	
				movement, writes *Kinat ha-Emet* (*The Zeal for Truth*), in which he condemns Hasidism and Kabbalah as superstitious nonsense and many aspects of rabbinic Judaism as legalistic and contrary to common sense. His views are considered so extreme that many fellow *maskilim* dissociate from him.	**1823**
None of the four U.S. presidential candidates obtains an electoral majority.	When Congregation Beth Elohim of Charleston, South Carolina, rejects demands for reform, 47 members, led by Isaac Harby (1778–1828), secede and organize the Reformed Society of Israelites. This is the first American attempt at Reform Judaism. Reformers demand change in religious practice, not theological dogma, i.e., a shorter service, improved decorum, English translation to accompany Hebrew prayers, and an English sermon.	Karl Marx (1818–1883) is baptized. His father, Heinrich, although trained as a lawyer, could not practice law as a Jew in Trier, Prussia. He therefore baptizes his family into Christianity.			**1824**
The U.S. House of Representatives selects John Quincy Adams* as president of the U.S. John C. Calhoun* was elected vice president in the 1824 election. The Erie Canal opens and accelerates the growth of New York as the port through which the produce of the American West is exported. Czar Nicholas I* (1825–1855) ascends the Russian imperial throne.	Mordecai Manuel Noah proposes "a city of refuge for Jews," called Ararat, on Grand Island in the Niagara River near Buffalo. Contemplated as a temporary refuge for the Jews until they could return to Palestine, the plan is ridiculed by the European Jewish press and is never implemented. Congregation B'nai Jeshurun is founded in New York by a group of German Jewish (Ashkenazi) members of the Spanish–Portuguese	Heinrich Heine (1797–1856), German poet and essayist, is baptized into Christianity. He refers to the act as "an entrance ticket to European society." His conversion fails to advance his academic career, and in 1831 he leaves for Paris, never returning to Germany. A leader of the Young Germany movement, the author of "Lorelei" is later recognized as one of Germany's greatest men of letters. Paul Pestel,* one of the revolutionary		Michael Beer (1800–1833), German playwright and poet, achieves great praise from Johann Wolfgang von Goethe* upon the production of his drama *Der Paria*, a protest against Jewish suffering and a plea for Jewish emancipation.	**1825**

A. General History	B. Jews in North and South America	C. Jews in Europe	D. Jews in the Middle East and Elsewhere	E. Jewish Culture
1825	Congregation Shearith Israel, who seceded from that synagogue to form their own congregation. In 1826, they will acquire a former church on Elm Street and remodel it as a synagogue. The Sephardic congregation Mikve Israel of Philadelphia dedicates a new synagogue on Cherry Street. It is the first building in Philadelphia exhibiting Egyptian Revival features. It seats over 190 men and 160 women.	leaders of the unsuccessful Decembrist uprising against Czar Nicholas I,* advocates in his treatise *Russian Truth* the abolition of Jewish autonomy and their complete integration or, as a more desirable alternative, transplanting the Jews to Asia Minor and establishing an independent Jewish state there.		
1826	The Maryland "Jew Bill," proposed by Thomas Kennedy,* is enacted into law. It removes political disabilities of Jews from the Maryland Constitution. The test oath is eliminated, and Jews are permitted to hold public office. Thomas Jefferson* responds to the receipt of Isaac Harby's discourse delivered on the first anniversary of the founding of the Reformed Society of Israelites in Charleston. He writes, "I am little acquainted with the liturgy of the Jews or their mode of worship but the reformation proposed and explained . . . appears entirely reasonable. Nothing is wiser than that all our institutions should keep pace with the advance of time and be improved with the improvement of the human mind."	English Jews are no longer required to take a Christian oath as part of the naturalization process. The last recorded auto-da-fé of the Spanish Inquisition takes place in Valencia, Spain. Between 1481 and 1826, there were 2,000 autos-da-fé with about 30,000 persons being put to death. In Vienna the Seitenstettengasse synagogue is opened. Led by Isaac Mannheimer (1793–1865), its moderate Reform services, held in Hebrew without organ music and marked by decorum, become the model for all synagogues in the Austrian Empire. The synagogue is concealed from the street because Austrian authorities refuse to permit non-Catholic religious buildings to be visible to the public. A modern Jewish school is founded in		Solomon H. Jackson, the first Jewish printer in New York, publishes *The Form of Daily Prayers According to the Custom of the Spanish and Portuguese Jews.* It contains the traditional prayers in Hebrew, revised and edited by E. S. Lazarus (the grandfather of poet Emma Lazarus), and an English translation by the publisher-printer himself. Yiddish textbooks that emphasize the subject of writing are introduced into Jewish secular education. The first to appear, known as *Brifnshteler*, is written by Abraham Leon Dor.

A. General History	B. Jews in North and South America	C. Jews in Europe	D. Jews in the Middle East and Elsewhere	E. Jewish Culture	
		Odessa by Simhah Pinsker (1801–1864) and other leaders of the Haskalah. It expands instruction in the sciences and languages at the expense of Jewish studies.			**1826**
		Czar Nicholas I* of Russia issues the Cantonist Decrees: At age 18 Jews are conscripted for 25 years of service; they can be taken at age 12 for preparatory service; like others, they can send substitutes, but they have to be Jews. It results in a class struggle among Jews. Jewish authorities favor wealthy and educated Jews with exemption. Between 1827 and 1856, when the conscription ends, about 60,000 Jews will be conscripted, with perhaps half converting to Christianity.	Between 1827 and 1839, largely through the diplomatic efforts of Britain's Lord Palmerston, the Jewish population of Jerusalem increases from 550 to 5,500.	Dr. Isaac Hays, ophthalmologist, becomes editor of the *Philadelphia Journal of the Medical and Physical Sciences*. He changes its name to *The American Journal of Medical Sciences*. He will remain its sole editor until 1869. The journal is the acknowledged forerunner of the *Journal of the American Medical Association* and is commonly known in the history of medicine as Hays' Journal.	**1827**
Andrew Jackson* is elected president and John C. Calhoun* is reelected vice president of the U.S.		A chair of Hebrew is established at the University College in London, which attracts Jewish teachers and students.			**1828**
The Catholic Emancipation Act in England permits Catholics to sit in Parliament and hold public office.	Reverend Isaac Leeser (1806–1868), who was born in Germany and brought to the U.S. in 1824 by an uncle living in Richmond, Virginia, is appointed *hazzan* of Philadelphia's Mikve Israel synagogue at the age of 23.	Upon the success of the movement to emancipate Catholics in England, Robert Grant* and Thomas Babbington Macaulay* introduce similar legislation in the House of Commons on behalf of Jews, as did the duke of Sussex* in the House of Lords. This legislation will pass in the Commons in 1833 but be continually rejected in the House of Lords until 1858. The yeshiva at Metz achieves the status of Rabbinical Seminary (Ecole Rabbinique)		Mendes I. Cohen (1796–1879), of a U.S. banking family from Baltimore, travels abroad until 1835. He is the first American to explore the Nile River. He will present his collection of Egyptian artifacts to Johns Hopkins University. The library of David Oppenheim (1664–1736), rabbi of Prague, is sold to Oxford University. Numbering over 7,000 volumes and 1,000 manuscripts, it comprises a substantial part of the Hebrew	**1829**

Isaac Leeser. (Library of Congress)

	A. General History	B. Jews in North and South America	C. Jews in Europe	D. Jews in the Middle East and Elsewhere	E. Jewish Culture
1829			of France. It will transfer to Paris in 1859. The Storch synagogue in Breslau opens, named after a Jewish merchant who built it at his own expense and rented it to the community. The government permits the construction of this large building in the belief that Jewish activities could be more closely watched when diverse small synagogues will be closed.		collection of the Bodleian Library. The first modern rabbinical seminary is founded in Padua as the Instituto Convitto Rabbinico, through the efforts of Isaac Samuel Reggio and under the direction of Lelio Della Torre (1805–1871) and Samuel David Luzzatto (Shadal, 1800–1865). It will close in 1871 and be revived in 1887 in Rome as the Collegio Rabbinico Italiano.
1830	Revolution in France brings Louis Philippe,* "the Citizen King" to the throne. The French invade Algeria and occupy Algiers. The Belgians revolt against the Kingdom of the Netherlands and declare independence. The Poles rebel in Warsaw against Russian rule.	Cincinnati's Holy Congregation of Children of Israel is incorporated by an act of the Ohio legislature. The congregation had been formed in 1824 and will build its first synagogue in 1836. Congressman Richard Johnson* reports in Congress against petitions to halt the transportation of mail on Sundays. "The Constitution regards the conscience of the Jew as sacred as that of the Christian, and gives no more authority to adopt a measure affecting the conscience of a solitary individual than that of a whole community."			Abraham Firkovich (1786–1874), Karaite leader born in Poland, visits Palestine and collects numerous manuscripts. He wishes to prove that the Karaites had entered the Crimea from Byzantium and that they converted the Khazars to Judaism. He quarrels with Rabbanites and stimulates scholarly interest in the Karaites, although the authenticity of some of his discoveries is disputed.
1831	The Belgian constitution proclaims equality for all its citizens. Uprisings in the central Italian communities of Modena, Parma, and the papal states are suppressed by Austrian forces. Italy's nationalist movement continues.	The Supreme Court of Pennsylvania decides that the conscientious scruples of a Jew against appearing in court to attend the trial of his case on the Jewish Sabbath is no ground for postponing the judicial process.	It is decided that anyone who wishes to be admitted to the freedom of the city of London can take the oath in a way that will not offend his religious faith. This enables Jews and others to engage in retail trade in London.	The Egyptian leader Muhammad Ali* ejects the Ottomans from Palestine. Until the return of the Ottomans in 1841, the social and legal status of Christians and Jews is improved under Egyptian rule. Neveh Shalom is erected in Calcutta, India. It is the	Solomon Judah Leib Rapoport (Shir, 1790–1867), who will become chief rabbi of Prague in 1840, sets a new standard of critical rabbinic scholarship by the publication of bibliographical studies of rabbinic leaders of the geonic period, then a relatively obscure

A. General History	B. Jews in North and South America	C. Jews in Europe	D. Jews in the Middle East and Elsewhere	E. Jewish Culture	
Giuseppe Mazzini,* Italian revolutionary, founds Young Italy, aimed at achieving Italian unification under a republican form of government. The Russians suppress Polish rebellion.	Isaac Leeser, *hazzan* of Congregation Mikveh Israel of Philadelphia, becomes the first American Jewish minister to institute regular preaching in English as a feature of Sabbath services. Canada's legislature enacts a law "declaring persons professing the Jewish religion capable of holding any office or place of trust." Jews of Canada thus achieve political emancipation 27 years before the Jews of Great Britain.	Judaism is granted equal legal status with other religions in France. King Louis-Philippe* agrees to include the expenses of the Jewish Consistory, particularly the salaries of rabbis and religious officials, in the national budget. The expenses had been borne by members of the Jewish faith. Gabriel Riesser (1806–1863), leader of the German Jewish emancipation, demands Jewish emancipation in his *Verteidigung der Buergerlichen Gleichstellung der Juden* (*The Defense of the Civil Equality of Jews*). He argues for Jewish citizenship in Germany as a matter of right and not in exchange for conversion to Christianity.	community's first synagogue and is named in honor of its founder, Shalom ha-Cohen.	period of Jewish history. He outlines the migration of rabbinic scholarship from Palestine through Italy to central and western Europe and from Babylonia through North Africa to Spain. Giacomo Meyerbeer (Jacob Liebmann-Beer, 1791–1864), German composer, composes *Robert le Diable*, the first in a series of successful French grand operas. Meyerbeer assists other composers, including Richard Wagner.* He remains faithful to Judaism and so, is attacked by Wagner.*	**1831**
Andrew Jackson* is reelected president and Martin Van Buren* is elected vice president of the U.S.		Abraham Geiger (1810–1874), German rabbi and leader of the Reform movement, becomes rabbi in Wiesbaden, where he institutes his first efforts to introduce reform of the synagogue services. Leopold Zunz, among the founders of the Science of Judaism in Germany, writes his *History of the Jewish Sermon*. Written in response to the attempt of the Prussian government to suppress the "innovation" of the vernacular sermon in the synagogue, Zunz shows that preaching in the language of the country is as old as the synagogue itself.	David Sassoon (1792–1864), a Baghdad Jewish merchant, settles in Bombay, India. An influx of Baghdadi Jews to Bombay follows, and the Sassoons become the leaders of the Jewish community. They found a successful merchant house and soon become known as the Rothschilds of the East. Israel Bak (1797–1874), who immigrated to Palestine from Berdichev, establishes a Hebrew printing press in Safed. In 1841, he will establish the first—and for 22 years, the only—Hebrew printing press in Jerusalem.		**1832**

	A. General History	B. Jews in North and South America	C. Jews in Europe	D. Jews in the Middle East and Elsewhere	E. Jewish Culture
1833		The Supreme Court of South Carolina rejects the plea that Sunday laws contravene the federal Constitution and upholds the conviction of Alexander Marks for keeping his store open on Sunday under an ordinance of the town council of Columbia, South Carolina. The Reformed Society of Israelites of Charleston, South Carolina, dissolves as the city declines because of economic conditions. Penina Moise (1797–1880), U.S. poet and teacher, publishes a volume of her poems, *Fancy's Sketch Book*. Five are of Jewish interest. Her book is believed to be the first book by a Jewish woman to be published in the U.S.	Thomas B. Macaulay,* in a speech in the English Parliament, refutes the arguments against granting full rights to the Jews: "In the infancy of civilizations, when our island was as savage as New Guinea, when letters and arts were still unknown to Athens, when scarcely a thatched hut stood on what was afterwards the site of Rome, this condemned people had their fenced cities, their splendid Temple."		Benjamin Disraeli, British statesman, after touring the Holy Land, writes *Alroy*, a novel of 12th-century Jewish messianism. The novel describes its hero's attempt to restore Jerusalem to the Jews. Moritz Daniel Oppenheim (1799–1882), German painter, paints *Return of a Jewish Volunteer from the Wars of Liberation to His Family Still Living According to the Old Tradition*. Oppenheim is the first professing Jew to achieve fame as an artist and is well known for his genre paintings of Jewish domestic life.
1834	The states of the German Confederation form a German Customs Union with free trade. The ensuing years see strong economic growth. Prussia emerges as the dominant German power. Austria remains aloof of the union.	The House of Rothschild, European Jewish international bankers, is appointed fiscal agents of the U.S.			
1835	Felix Mendelssohn, German composer and grandson of Moses Mendelssohn (1729–1786), who was baptized in 1816, revolutionizes orchestral playing by becoming one of the first independent baton-wielding conductors.		A new group of Ashkenazic Jews immigrates to Ireland from England and founds a synagogue that later becomes known as the Dublin Hebrew Congregation. Czar Nicholas I* of Russia issues a new Jewish statute, which redefines boundaries of the Pale of		Jacques Halevy's (1799–1862) opera *La Juive* creates a new French opera form. Abraham Geiger begins publishing the *Wissenschaftliche Zeitschrift für Jüdische Theologie* (*The Scientific Journal for Jewish Theology*), a major

A. General History	B. Jews in North and South America	C. Jews in Europe	D. Jews in the Middle East and Elsewhere	E. Jewish Culture	

THE PALE OF SETTLEMENT

Settlement and suspends expulsions of Jews from villages to cities; prohibits Jewish males from marrying under age 18 and females under 16; restricts Jewish employment of Christian domestics and the erection of synagogues near churches. The Kahal is responsible for tax collection and enforcement of law. These regulations break down in execution.

platform for the Reform movement. Geiger condemns the obligatory observance of Jewish laws and encourages the adaptation of Judaism to modernity through the removal of all national symbols from the liturgy.

Israel Aksenfeld (1787–1866), Russian author, writes *Der Ershter Yidisher Rekrut* (*The First Jewish Recruit*). This is the first attempt to use Yiddish to ridicule Hasidism and convince the masses of the virtues of Haskalah.

1835

Martin Van Buren* is elected president of the U.S. Richard M. Johnson* is chosen by the Senate to be vice president as no vice-presidential candidate receives an electoral majority.

Turkish authorities create the office of chief rabbi. The first chief rabbi is appointed for Istanbul and later for provincial capitals and other major towns.

Arkansas becomes the 25th state of the U.S.

The University of London is founded. It is the first institution of higher learning not affiliated with any particular religious group.

About 10,000 Boer (Dutch) farmers and cattlemen begin the Great Trek north and east of South Africa's Cape Colony to escape British rule. They found Transvaal, Natal, and the Orange Free State.

The Board of Deputies of British Jews is recognized by an act of Parliament. Tracing its origins back to 1760, the board is a representative body of both Ashkenazic and Sephardic congregations whose sole concern is relations with the non-Jewish world.

Czar Nicholas I* introduces a special censorship of Jewish books. Many are publicly burned on the advice of corrupt Christian censors or ignorant converts. All Jewish printing presses, with the exception of the Vilna press, are closed. In 1847, an additional press will be allowed in Zhitomir. These restrictions severely limit the publication of Haskalah literature.

Zevi Hirsch Kalischer (1795–1874), Orthodox rabbi and early Zionist thinker, asks the Rothschild family in Frankfurt for funds to purchase land in Palestine for colonization by the Jews. He believes in redemption through natural causes. It can only be achieved through Jewish settlement in Palestine.

Samson Raphael Hirsch, leading German Orthodox rabbi, writes *Nineteen Letters of Ben Uziel*, a presentation of Orthodox Jewish faith. Benjamin, "the perplexed," expresses the doubts of a young Jewish intellectual. He is answered by Naphtali, the traditional spokesman, who discusses the relationship of Judaism to world culture.

1836

Michigan becomes the 26th state of the U.S.

August Belmont (1816–1890) arrives in New York City

Jews are enabled to receive academic degrees from the

An earthquake devastates Safed, in Palestine, killing

Samson Raphael Hirsch, leading German orthodox

1837

	A. General History	B. Jews in North and South America	C. Jews in Europe	D. Jews in the Middle East and Elsewhere	E. Jewish Culture
1837	The rebellion against Britain's colonial government in Upper and Lower Canada is unsuccessful. Victoria* (1819–1901) becomes queen of Great Britain and Ireland. Benjamin Disraeli is elected to the British Parliament as a Tory.	from the Rhenish Palatinate to set up shop as a private banker and American agent for the Rothschilds.	University of London, but are still prohibited from studies at Oxford and Cambridge. Moses Montefiore (1784–1885), a wealthy English businessman and philanthropist, is elected sheriff and knighted by Queen Victoria. Charles Dickens* (1812–1870) begins serialization of his novel *Oliver Twist*, which includes Fagin, the Jewish villain who is a corrupter of youth and a receiver of stolen goods. To Dickens,* that class of criminal almost invariably is Jewish.	5,000, among them 4,000 Jews. Joseph Sundel Salant (1786–1866) arrives in Jerusalem from Lithuania. Salant's humility and great learning make him the ideal ethical man in the eyes of his student Israel Lipkin Salanter (1810–1883), founder of the Musar movement.	rabbi, writes *Horeb: A Philosophy of Jewish Laws and Observances*, a halakhic interpretation of Judaism. Publication of the German Jewish periodical *Allgemeine Zeitung des Judentums* (*German Journal of Judaism*) begins in Leipzig under the editorship of its founder, Ludwig Philippson (1811–1889). It is the first modern Jewish periodical to discuss current affairs, including news of American Jewry. It will cease publication in 1922. Wilhelm Beer (1797–1850), German astronomer, and Johann H. Madler* publish their studies of the moon. Their map of the visible lunar surface is the standard work for many years. A mountain on the moon will be named for Beer.
1838	The first British consulate is established in Jerusalem.	A group of 13 Jews from New York establish an agricultural colony in Wawarsing, Ulster County, New York, which they name Scholem (Peace). Although it will fail after five years, it has the distinction of being the first of many 19th-century settlements of its kind. The first Jewish Sunday School in the U.S. is founded in Philadelphia by Rebecca Gratz for instruction in Jewish history and related subjects.	Abraham Benisch (1814–1878) and others form Die Einheit (The Unity) in Vienna, a secret society whose purpose is to encourage organized Jewish immigration to Palestine. Solomon Judah Rapoport, a noted proponent of Haskalah, becomes rabbi of Tarnopol. His appointment is met with hostility by the Hasidic and traditional circles whom he had so often opposed in the pages of *Kerem Hemed* (*Delightful Vinyard*), which he edits.	The consul in the newly established British consulate in Jerusalem is instructed by Foreign Secretary Lord Palmerston* to devote part of his duties "to afford protection to the Jews generally."	Isaac Leeser, U.S. rabbi and educator, publishes a six-volume Sephardic prayer book in Hebrew, accompanied by English translation. Isaac Nordheimer (d. 1842), professor of Oriental languages at what is now called New York University, writes *A Critical Grammar of the Hebrew Language*, the first major work of Jewish scholarship published in America. He is acknowledged as the only Jewish Hebraist of quality in America. In Italy, Samuel David Luzzatto ("Shadal," 1800–1865) publishes

A. General History	B. Jews in North and South America	C. Jews in Europe	D. Jews in the Middle East and Elsewhere	E. Jewish Culture	
				Atticisme et Judaisme, in which he rejects Haskalah rationalism. The immutable nature of Judaism, unlike the philosophy of Greece, guarantees morality and justice. Isaac Baer Levinsohn, a leader of the Russian Haskalah, writes *Beit Yehudah* (*House of Judah*), in which he argues that Judaism should not be limited to "divine religion," but includes "civic religion," which involves the practices of society and the sciences required for its maintenance and development.	**1838**
Abd al-Majid* (1823–1861), sultan of Turkey from 1839 to 1861, proclaims the Hatti-i-Sherif, a declaration of rights for all citizens without distinction of religion or race. The British occupy Aden for use as a coaling station and to guard the entrance to the Red Sea.			The entire Jewish community of Meshed, Persia, is forced to convert to Islam. They continue to observe Judaism in secret, although they are publicly devout Muslims. Jews comprise the majority of Aden's 500 inhabitants.	Judah Alkalai (1798–1878), Sephardic rabbi of Semlin (in the Balkans) and early Zionist thinker, writes his first book, *Darkhei No'am* (*Paths of Pleasantness*), a Ladino–Hebrew textbook, in which he espouses a revolutionary concept of redemption. He interprets repentance, the precondition for redemption, in the literal sense, i.e., return. The return he espouses is the general return of all Jews to the land of Israel.	**1839**
William Henry Harrison* and John Tyler* are elected president and vice president of the U.S. The British Parliament adopts the recommendations of the Durham Report of 1839 and unites Upper and Lower Canada with the Act of Union.	In the U.S. one-third of the grandchildren of the Jews during the time of the American Revolution have left the Jewish community by 1840. During the 1840s, the word *Jew* comes into use as a verb in popular parlance. *To Jew* means to strike a sharp bargain or to employ questionable ethics in business dealings.	Jews throughout the world anticipate that the Jewish year 5600 (1840 CE) would mark the arrival of the Messiah. The belief is based on statements in the Talmud (Tractate Sanhedrin 99a) and the Zohar (I:117a). The Reform religious movement is introduced in England with the founding of the West London synagogue.	Upon the murder of a Capuchin friar and his servant in February, the Jews of Damascus are accused of blood libel—using their blood for Passover preparation. Several Jews are arrested and tortured. Some confess and others die or convert. Sixty-three Jewish children are held as hostages.	Solomon Alexander Hart (1806–1881), English painter, becomes the first Jewish member of the Royal Academy. Hart will visit Italy in the 1840s and later paint *The Feast of the Rejoicing of the Law at the Synagogue in Leghorn* (1850). He serves as a professor of painting and as librarian at the Royal Academy.	**1840**

	A. General History	B. Jews in North and South America	C. Jews in Europe	D. Jews in the Middle East and Elsewhere	E. Jewish Culture
1840		During August and September, mass meetings of American Jews are held in New York, Philadelphia, Charleston, Cincinnati, Savannah, and Richmond to protest the Damascus blood libel. President Martin Van Buren* had already ordered the American consul in Egypt to protest. This is the first organized protest of American Jewry, then numbering about 15,000, on behalf of their overseas brethren.	The synagogue in Dresden, designed by the Protestant architect Gottfried Semper,* is opened. His treatment of the synagogue interior is believed to be the introduction of Oriental Revival architecture. Rabbi Zacharias Frankel (1801–1875) is the congregation's leader.	In August, a Jewish delegation led by Britain's Sir Moses Montefiore and the French lawyer Adolphe Cremieux (1796–1880) secures the release of the captives of the Damascus blood libel and persuades the sultan of Turkey to issue an edict forbidding the circulation of blood libels.	The publication of *Archives Israelites de France*, a French-language Jewish monthly, begins in Paris. Founded by Samuel Cahen (1796–1862), it advocates religious reform. It will cease publication in 1935.
			Baron Jozsef Eotvos* (1813–1871), Hungarian statesman, writes *Emancipation of the Jews*, in which he argues for emancipation without conditions as the way to their betterment and assimilation.	Britain's Lord Palmerston* instructs his ambassador in Constantinople to pressure the Turks to allow European Jews to settle in Palestine.	Jacob Henle (Friedrich Gustav, 1809–1885), German anatomist and pathologist, writes *Pathological Investigations*, in which he argues that infectious diseases are transmitted by living organisms. The grandson of a rabbi, he was baptized at the age of 11. His contention will be proved 40 years later by his pupil Robert Koch.*
		Abraham Joseph Rice (1802–1862) arrives in the U.S. to serve as rabbi of the Baltimore Hebrew Congregation. Born and educated in Bavaria, he is the first traditionally ordained rabbi to serve in the U.S. and is recognized as the rabbinic authority in the U.S. by Orthodox Jews.	The czarist government of Nicholas I,* under the guidance of Sergei S. Uvarov,* minister of education from 1833 to 1849, undertakes a large-scale effort to induce Jews to establish schools devoted to secular subjects taught in Russian. The schools are shunned by Jews.	The first Hebrew printing press in India is established in Calcutta by a Jew from Cochin.	Judah Alkalai, Sephardic rabbi of Semlin and early Zionist thinker, writes *Shelom Yerushalayim* (*Peace of Jerusalem*). He advocates repentance, which can be implemented by the establishment of a tithe that will be directed toward the rebuilding of Jerusalem.
			Louise Lady Rothschild founds the Jewish Ladies' Benevolent Loan Society and the Ladies' Visiting Society. They are the first independent Jewish women's philanthropic associations in England. Modeled on Christian charitable organizations, they encourage thrift and self-sufficiency among their clients with a patronizing tone that often causes resentment.		Heinrich Heine, German poet and essayist, writes *The Rabbi of Bacherach*, a historical novel in which he defends the cause of Jewish emancipation.
1841	U.S. President William Henry Harrison* dies one	Isaac Leeser, U.S. rabbi, formulates a program for a	Max Lilienthal (1815–1882), German rabbi and	Turkish authorities appoint the first chief rabbi in Jerusalem.	Publication of the *Jewish Chronicle* weekly newspaper

A. General History	B. Jews in North and South America	C. Jews in Europe	D. Jews in the Middle East and Elsewhere	E. Jewish Culture	
month after inauguration. Vice President John Tyler* succeeds to the presidency. President John Tyler,* in a message to Congress, invites immigration to the U.S.	federation of American synagogues to deal with transcongregational problems while guaranteeing congregational autonomy. The effort fails, as American Jews believe the establishment of any ecclesiastical authority whatsoever to be alien to the American spirit of liberty. Alfred Mordecai drafts the first *U.S. Army Ordnance Manual*. A foremost weapons expert, he is offered the position of chief of ordnance for the Confederacy at the beginning of the Civil War by Jefferson Davis.* In 1861 he will resign from the army, being one of 30 southern officers who are unable to fight for the North against their families or for the South against the flag. James Joseph Sylvester (1814–1897), British mathematician and Fellow of the Royal Society, is appointed professor of mathematics at the University of Virginia. Within the year, he leaves the university, either because his outspoken abhorrence of slavery or because his violent response to antisemitic threats made by students threatens his safety. In 1877, he will return to the U.S. to join the faculty of Johns Hopkins University.	educator, is commissioned by Russia's minister of education Sergei S. Uvarov,* to propagate secular schools for Jews. After a few years, Lilienthal acknowledges that the government's main objective is conversionist rather than enlightenment. In 1844, he will flee Russia and emigrate to the U.S.	The Jews of Capetown, the oldest Jewish community in South Africa, organize the Capetown Hebrew Congregation.	begins in London. This first permanent Anglo-Jewish periodical is the oldest continuing Jewish publication in the world. Samuel Joseph Fuenn (1818–1890), Russian Haskalah scholar, begins publication in Vilna of *Pirhei Zafon* (*Flowers of the North*), the first Hebrew literary magazine in Russia, together with L. Hurwitz. Publication will cease in 1844.	**1841**
	The first Jewish day school is established in New York by	Led by Theodor Creizenach (1818–1877), the		Abraham Dov (Adam) Lebensohn (1794–1878),	**1842**

	A. General History	B. Jews in North and South America	C. Jews in Europe	D. Jews in the Middle East and Elsewhere	E. Jewish Culture
1842		Congregation B'nai Jeshurun, the city's first German Jewish congregation. Studies include formal instruction in Hebrew and religion in addition to elementary English education. Baltimore's Har Sinai Verein becomes the first congregation to be founded as a Reform congregation in the U.S. In 1855, it will bring to America and to its pulpit one of the intellectual giants of Reform Judaism, David Einhorn (1809–1879). Boston's first synagogue, Ohabei Shalom, is established, adopting the ritual of Jews of southern Germany.	Reform Jews of Frankfurt found a society to promote a program rejecting talmudic Judaism, traditional observance, and belief in the Messiah. Israel Lipkin Salanter, Lithuanian rabbi, founds the first Musar society in Vilna. The movement is a reaction to Hasidism, the contemporary yeshiva curriculum, and the growing threat of secularism. It advocates moral earnestness as a required addition to ritual observance and talmudic learning. His teachings become an integral part of many yeshiva curricula.		Hebrew poet of the Russian Haskalah, publishes his first collection of poems. Lebensohn is the first Russian Hebrew poet of any significance.
1843		The first of the Jewish fraternal orders in the U.S., the Independent Order of B'nai B'rith, is founded in New York by 12 German Jews. Its first president is Isaac Dittenhoefer, succeeded by Henry Jones, who is credited as chief founder. The statutes of Connecticut are amended to permit the lawful incorporation of Jewish congregations.	Bruno Bauer* (1809–1882), German Protestant theologian and antisemitic leader of the Young Hegelians, writes *On the Jewish Question*, in which he demands that Jews abandon Judaism and transform their plea for emancipation to a campaign for liberation from religion. Karl Marx responds with an essay describing the evil of Judaism as social and economic, not religious. He calls for the elimination of Judaism as a prerequisite for the liberation of all mankind. "Money is the jealous God of Israel. . . . In emancipating itself from hucksterism and money, and thus from real and practical Judaism, our age would emancipate itself." Czar Nicholas I,* in the effort to prevent		Isaac Leeser, U.S. rabbi, founds the first Jewish journal in the U.S., *The Occident and American Jewish Advocate*, a traditional monthly edited by him until his death, when it ceases publication.

A. General History	B. Jews in North and South America	C. Jews in Europe	D. Jews in the Middle East and Elsewhere	E. Jewish Culture	
		smuggling, orders the total elimination of Jews from the western frontier districts, resulting in the uprooting of thousands of Jews. The Rothschild family makes an unpublicized intercession.			**1843**
James K. Polk* and George M. Dallas* are elected president and vice president of the U.S. Samuel F. B. Morse* uses his telegraph system to send the first famous message, "What hath God wrought?" from Washington, D.C., to Baltimore.	Mordecai Manuel Noah, U.S. editor and politician, speaks before large and distinguished audiences in New York, including the Roman Catholic bishop and influential Protestant ministers, urging the idea of Palestine as a national home for the Jews. Jews of Charleston, South Carolina, protest Governor James Hammond's* Thanksgiving message calling for special prayers "to God their creator, and his son, Jesus Christ, the redeemer of the world." Hammond* ignores their protests, and Thanksgiving comes and goes unobserved in the Jewish community.	Nathan Marcus Adler is elected chief rabbi of the British Empire. Educated in Germany and of enlightened Orthodoxy, he is mainly responsible for the establishment of Jews' College in London in 1855. A rabbinical conference initiated by Ludwig Philippson (1811–1889) is held at Brunswick to discuss a proposal for reform. One hundred sixteen Orthodox rabbis attack the conference for its rejection of Jewish tradition and declare that nobody may "abrogate the least of the religious laws." The Russian government abolishes the Kahal and transfers the role of Jewish communal supervision and tax collection to the municipalities and the police. The Russian government imposes a special tax on the wearing of distinctive Jewish clothing. Jewish leaders of Frankfurt, Konigsberg, London, and Paris submit a petition to Czar Nicholas I* asking that Jews be allowed to leave Russia without hindrance.		Benjamin Disraeli writes *Coningsby*, a novel whose hero, Sidonia, is modeled on Lionel de Rothschild (1808–1879). *L'Univers Israelite*, a French-language Jewish monthly, begins publication in Paris. Founded as a rival to the Reform-minded *Archives Israelites* (1840), it is a conservative religious publication and is the vehicle for expressing the views of the chief rabbis of France. It will cease publication in 1940. Publication of *Ben Chananja*, the first Hungarian Jewish learned periodical, commences. Its contributors are Hungarian scholars, and the journal has correspondents in Jerusalem, Berlin, New York, and other cities with large Jewish communities. It will cease publication in 1867.	**1844**
Florida becomes the 27th state of the	The Baltimore Hebrew	Alphonse Toussenel* (1803–1885), writer	France reorganizes the communal	Isaac Leeser, U.S. rabbi and educator,	**1845**

	A. General History	B. Jews in North and South America	C. Jews in Europe	D. Jews in the Middle East and Elsewhere	E. Jewish Culture
1845	U.S. Texas accepts annexation and becomes the 28th state of the U.S. The U.S. Supreme Court, in *Permoli* v. *Municipality*, 3 Howard 609, rules that the Constitution leaves the protection of religious liberties exclusively to the states and imposes no "inhibition" on state conduct respecting religion. Justice Joseph Story* even doubts whether the spirit of religious equality underlay the Constitution. Failure of the potato crop leads to the Great Famine in Ireland. During 1845–1846, it kills nearly 1 million Irish and drives another million abroad.	Congregation opens a synagogue on Lloyd and Water streets. Seating over 280 persons, it is of Greek Revival design. The round windows of the façade and the window over the ark are laid out in the shape of the shield of David, the first public display of the design in the U.S. David Levy Yulee (1810–1866), a prominent lawyer, is elected to the U.S. Senate as the first senator from the state of Florida after its admission to the Union. In 1846, he will renounce Judaism and marry the daughter of the former governor of Kentucky and assume the name of Yulee. His children are raised as Christians. From 1841 to 1845 he was the Florida territory's delegate to Congress, where he urged Florida's admission to the Union.	and disciple of French Utopian socialist Francois Fourier,* writes *The Jews, Kings of the Epoch*, an attempt to intertwine anticapitalism with antisemitism. It becomes a leading textbook for antisemites. A conference of 31 rabbis interested in Reform, the Reform Rabbinical Conference, is held in Frankfurt. They agree to eliminate references to messianism and restoration of sacrifices from theprayers, to utilize the triennial cycle of Torah readings, to gradually abolish Hebrew as the language of prayer, and permit the use of the organ in the synagogue. The objective is to strengthen Judaism by adapting it to the modern needs of the new generation. Zacharias Frankel, chief rabbi of Dresden, withdraws from the Reform Rabbinical Conference in Frankfurt in protest against its rejection of messianic belief and the commitment to the use of Hebrew in the liturgy. He describes his middle ground as "positive-historical Judaism," which must be preserved while Judaism adjusts to the spirit of the times.	structure of Algerian Jewry by creating consistories in Algiers, Oran, and Constantine on the French model, headed by a chief rabbi and lay leaders.	establishes the first Jewish Publication Society to promote Jewish literature by reprinting books issued by a similar project in London called the Cheap Jewish Library. After 14 small volumes of popular literature known as the Jewish Miscellany Series are published, the project ends when its stock is destroyed by fire in 1851. Isaac Leeser, U.S. rabbi and educator, publishes an English translation of the first five books, or *Humash* (the Pentateuch), of the Bible. The entire Bible in English translation takes Leeser 17 years to complete and becomes the standard American Jewish translation until the Jewish Publication Society translation of 1917. Leopold Zunz, one of the founders of the Science of Judaism in Germany, writes *Contributions to History and Literature*, in which he shows the breadth of Jewish literature and its place in the general culture. Meir Aron Goldschmidt (1819–1887), Danish journalist and novelist, writes *A Jew*, a novel of Jewish family life in Denmark. His novels are the first Danish works to achieve international critical acclaim.
1846	Iowa becomes the 29th state of the U.S. The U.S. war with Mexico begins. Congress fails to enact the Wilmot Proviso, which would	Reverend Isaac Mayer Wise (1819–1900), who will become the leader of Reform Jewry in the U.S., arrives in the U.S. from Bohemia and heads a congregation	The special Jewish oath in law courts is abolished in France. A result of extended efforts by the lawyer Adolphe Cremieux, it brings complete equality to French Jews, who are no	The Jewish community of San'a, Yemen, is required to clean all the city's sewers. The order will remain in effect until 1950.	Judith Cohen Montefiore (1784–1862) anonymously writes *A Jewish Manual*, the first book of guidelines for the social conduct of women published in

A. General History	B. Jews in North and South America	C. Jews in Europe	D. Jews in the Middle East and Elsewhere	E. Jewish Culture	
outlaw slavery in any territory acquired from Mexico.

The appearance of the sewing machine gives impetus to the ready-to-wear clothing industry. | in Albany, N.Y. Among reforms introduced by Wise are a mixed choir, mixed seating, and confirmation.

Fifteen Jews found Kehillath Anshe Ma'arav (The Congregation of the People of the West), the first congregation in Chicago. Jewish settlers were recorded in Chicago as early as 1832, a year before Chicago was incorporated as a town and five years before Chicago had 5,000 inhabitants and became incorporated as a city.

The first Ashkenazic synagogue of English, German, and Polish Jews is established in Montreal, Canada. Later known as Sha'ar ha-Shamayim congregation, it occupies rented quarters until its first building is erected in 1860. | longer singled out as a separate group in any legislation.

A third conference of German rabbis interested in Reform is held at Breslau. Attended by 25 rabbis, they reject the suggestion that the Sabbath be transferred to Sunday, the civil day of rest. They agree to abolish the second day of the holidays and many mourning customs.

Jacob Isaac Altaras (1786–1873), French philanthropist, proposes to officials of Czar Nicholas I's* government the resettlement of Russian Jews in Algeria. At first, the Russians demand a per capita ransom for exit permits but later agree to some emigration on condition that the émigrés lose their Russian citizenship. Francois Guizot,* French foreign minister, vetoes the scheme, asking Altaras "Do you mean to Judaize Algeria?"

Zacharias Frankel, leading German rabbi, declares: "for the Russian Jews there is only one way out; to leave Russia and settle under a sky where the law recognizes human rights." | | England. Lady Montefiore sets an example for Jewish women by attending synagogue services despite her family's protest that, by tradition, women do not belong in the synagogue. | **1846** |
| | A rabbinic court (Bet Din) is established in New York under the leadership of Rabbi Max Lilienthal and includes Rabbi Isaac Mayer Wise among its members. It meets only on one occasion.

The Shaaray Tefila congregation of New | Baron Lionel de Rothschild is elected to the British Parliament but is not allowed to take his seat because he will not take the Christian oath. This prompts a parliamentary dispute, which is resolved in 1858 when the oath is | | Benjamin Disraeli writes *Tancred*, a novel in which he favors restoring national independence to the Jews and criticizes assimilationist Jews ashamed of their heritage. He includes his impressions of Jerusalem, which he visited 15 years before. | **1847** |

	A. General History	B. Jews in North and South America	C. Jews in Europe	D. Jews in the Middle East and Elsewhere	E. Jewish Culture
1847		York dedicates its Wooster Street synagogue. The congregation employs Leopold Eidlitz (1823–1908) as one of its architects. Eidlitz, born in Prague, is probably the first Jewish architect to practice in the U.S. The Harmonie Club, the most prestigious of the Jewish clubs, is organized in New York.	amended and Rothschild is permitted to take his seat in Parliament. Samuel Holdheim (1806–1860) is appointed rabbi of the newly founded Reform congregation in Berlin, which under his leadership becomes the center of radical Reform. The Prague Jewish community establishes a hostel for needy Jewish patients at the Carlsbad Spa. It is the first Jewish institution of its kind.		Meir Halevi Letteris (c.1800–1871), Hebrew poet and editor, is awarded a gold medal by the Austrian emperor Franz Joseph* for his collection of German poems *Sagen aus dem Orient* (*Legends of the Orient*). An exponent of the Haskalah, Letteris writes most of his poetry in Hebrew. He will edit the Hebrew text of the Christian Bible in 1852 for the British and Foreign Bible Society in London. This edition will be known as the Letteris Bible.
1848	Zachary Taylor* and Millard Fillmore* are elected president and vice president of the U.S. Wisconsin becomes the 30th state of the U.S. The first women's rights convention takes place in Seneca Falls, New York. It drafts the *Declaration of Sentiments and Principles*, which marks the founding of the women's rights movement in the U.S. The February revolution of workers in France causes the abdication of King Louis Philippe.* The counterrevolution in June subdues the workers. In December, Prince Louis Napoleon Bonaparte* (1808–1873), nephew of Napoleon I,* becomes president of the Second French Republic. In March, revolutions occur in the German states. They are inspired by liberal democratic principles. In May,	Warder Cresson (1798–1860), of a Quaker family from Philadelphia, who went to Jerusalem in 1844 to convert Jews to Christianity, is converted to Judaism. Returning to the U.S. in 1849 to settle his affairs, he will successfully fight his family's efforts to declare him insane. He will move to Palestine in 1852 and promote Jewish agricultural colonization of the land. South Carolina Appellate Judge John O'Neale* reverses the decision of a magistrate who held that Solomon Benjamin, a Jew in Charleston, did not violate a local ordinance by selling a pair of gloves on Sunday. He declares that only police power, and not a constitutional question, is involved. Jews argue that Sunday laws are not a proper use of police power—the laws are actually intended to be religious regulations. Not only are Jews	A small congregation of Jews secretly worships in an underground synagogue in an unnamed Spanish city, according to reports in the London *Jewish Chronicle*. With the promulgation of the Piedmontese constitution, the Jews of the Piedmont region in northern Italy are granted full emancipation. Gabriel Riesser (1806–1863), a veteran in the battle for Jewish rights, is elected deputy-speaker of the all-German parliament convened in Frankfurt. Despite protracted debate, he succeeds in guaranteeing that the future constitution will contain a clause granting equal rights to all men, regardless of their religion. Leopold Kompert (1822–1886), German Jewish writer, deeply disappointed by the anti-Jewish riots that		Isaac Leeser, U.S. rabbi, publishes a one-volume edition of the Ashkenazic daily prayer book in Hebrew and English. Paul Julius Reuter (1816–1899) establishes Reuter's News Agency in Germany. Born Israel Beer Josaphat, he was baptized in 1844, when he assumed the name Reuter. Isaac Meir Dick (1814–1893), Russian Hebrew and Yiddish writer, reputed to be the first popular writer of Yiddish fiction, writes *Tractate on Poverty* in Hebrew, a satire on Russian Jewish society in the guise of a talmudic parody. Dick introduces the sentimental story, as well as historical and humorous tales, into Yiddish literature.

A. General History	B. Jews in North and South America	C. Jews in Europe	D. Jews in the Middle East and Elsewhere	E. Jewish Culture

1848

A. General History	B. Jews in North and South America	C. Jews in Europe
the Frankfurt Parliament drafts a constitution for a united Germany, but the attempt to unite Germany under a liberal parliamentary system soon fails. In March, the liberal revolution in Austria causes the emperor to abdicate and Metternich* to resign. The counterrevolution later in the year succeeds and Franz Josef* becomes emperor. Throughout the year, political and social rebellions sweep Italy, Bohemia, Hungary, Denmark, and Schleswig-Holstein. They fail. In September, Switzerland becomes one federal union under a new constitution. Karl Marx and Friedrich Engels* publish *The Communist Manifesto*, the best-known work on modern socialism.	subject to pecuniary loss and inconvenience if they keep their own Sabbath, but as non-Christians their claim to equality is weakened. Ernestine Potovsky Rose (1810–1892), Polish-born daughter of an Orthodox rabbi and the first nationally prominent Jewish feminist in America, argues for women's rights at the Seneca Falls convention. She states in 1851 that to deny women suffrage guarantees "freedom and power to one half of society, and submission and slavery to the other."	accompanied the revolutions, calls for an organized "On to America" movement of German Jews. Abraham Kohn (1807–1848), district rabbi of Lvov (Lemberg), dies of food poisoning two years after founding a Reform synagogue. He attempted to have the civil authorities prohibit Jews from wearing traditional dress and from observing traditional customs. Upon his death, his leading Orthodox opponent, Jacob Naphtali Herz Bernstein (1813–1873), is arrested upon suspicion of foul play. He will later be released. The first of Russian state-sponsored Jewish schools is established in Russia. Conceived by Count Sergei S. Uvarov,* minister of education, the schools are meant to wean the Jewish population away from Judaism and ultimately draw them toward Christianity.

1849

A. General History	B. Jews in North and South America	C. Jews in Europe	E. Jewish Culture
The Frankfurt Parliament adopts a constitution, which includes religious equality, for a united Germany. Frederick William IV,* king of Prussia, refuses to accept the designation as emperor of the Germans. The German unification founders. Hungary declares its independence. Louis Kossuth* is elected president. The Austrians, assisted by the Russians, defeat the Hungarian army. Hungary returns to the Habsburg rule.	There are Jewish storekeepers in almost every one of the towns and trading posts that spring up during the Gold Rush in the West. There are, however, very few Jewish prospectors for gold. Abraham Joseph Rice resigns his position at the Baltimore Hebrew Congregation and opens a dry goods store. He writes to a friend in Germany: "The religious life in this land is on the lowest level, most people eat foul food	Achille Fould (1800–1867), manager of the Fould–Oppenheim French banking house, is appointed minister of finance by President Louis Napoleon* of France. Fould serves in this capacity on three separate occasions until his retirement in 1867. The Danish constitution, adopted June 4, 1849, includes a refusal to recognize the inequality of any person on the basis of religious grounds. This clause is	The publication of *The Asmonean*, a journal of Orthodox Judaism, begins in New York. It will last until 1858 when its English Jewish editor, Robert Lyon, dies. Isidor Bush (1822–1898), upon his arrival in New York from Austria, founds the liberal German weekly *Israel's Herold*, which is the first American Jewish weekly. It fails after three months of publication.

	A. General History	B. Jews in North and South America	C. Jews in Europe	D. Jews in the Middle East and Elsewhere	E. Jewish Culture
1849	Emperor Franz Joseph* of Austria grants his people a constitution that includes a statement that "civil and political rights are not dependent on religion."	and desecrate the Sabbath in public. . . . Thousands marry non-Jewish women. Under these circumstances my mind is perplexed and I wonder whether it is even permissible for a Jew to live in this land." August Belmont, banker and political leader, marries Caroline Slidell Perry,* Episcopalian daughter of Commodore Matthew Perry.* He establishes himself in Christian society, although he never denies his Judaism. His children, however, are baptized.	considered an act of Jewish emancipation. The Hungarian Diet passes a resolution granting the Jews equal rights. Only 3% of Russian Jewry possesses any capital at all, while the rest live a miserable existence according to findings of the Russian scholar B. Miliutin.* Leon Mandelstamm (1819–1889), Russian scholar who was appointed to be in charge of Jewish affairs in the ministry of education as the successor to Max Lilienthal, publishes a Hebrew reader *Alef-Bet* for use by children in government schools in Russia.		From 1849 to 1853, Abraham Dov Lebensohn, Russian Hebrew poet of the Haskalah period, publishes, together with others, an edition of the Bi'ur, the commentary and translation of the Bible by Moses Mendelssohn, with additional commentaries. The work finds a wide audience in Russian Jewry and assists in the development of the Haskalah.
1850	U.S. President Zachary Taylor* dies and is succeeded by Vice President Millard Fillmore.* Ernestine Potovsky Rose, leading feminist, assists in organizing the National Woman's Rights convention held in Massachusetts. She campaigns for women's property rights, suffrage, and reform of the divorce laws. The Compromise of 1850 passes Congress after a debate on slavery. California becomes the 31st state as a free state. New Mexico and Utah territories are organized, and they are permitted to make their own decision on slavery. A more effective Fugitive Slave Act requires citizens of the free states to turn in runaway slaves, and slave	The California Gold Rush of 1849 causes an influx of Jews in the 1850s into California, especially San Francisco, where they establish themselves mostly as merchants and shopkeepers. By the end of the 1850s, the percentage of Jews in San Francisco— between 6 and 10% —is higher than in New York. The *New York Herald*, which in 1840 had sympathized with the Jews of Damascus, reopens the blood libel charges with a lurid front page story of how the atrocious murder of a Catholic priest and his servant had been perpetrated by Jews. New York's Congregation Anshe Chesed opens its new synagogue on Norfolk Street near Houston Street. German Gothic in	As the Swiss constitution grants religious freedom only to Christians, a treaty of commerce between the U.S. and Switzerland guarantees treaty rights to Christians alone. Since Switzerland is a federal republic, its cantons have the right, which some exercise, to refuse entry and commercial privileges to foreign Jews. Despite repeated protests, the U.S. does not renounce the treaty. Richard Wagner* (1813–1883), German composer, writes *Das Judentum in der Musik* (*Judaism in Music*). It blames Jews for the early negative reception of his music and claiming that Jewish composers Felix Mendelssohn and Giacomo Meyerbeer are not truly creative.	 *The Peddlar's Wagon, about 1850. (Library of Congress)*	*The Vale of Cedars*, a novel written by Grace Aguilar (1816–1847), an English author of Portuguese Marrano heritage, is published posthumously. It is a romantic picture of Marranos in Spain that remains popular for many years and is translated into Hebrew and German.

A. General History	B. Jews in North and South America	C. Jews in Europe	D. Jews in the Middle East and Elsewhere	E. Jewish Culture	
trade is terminated in the District of Columbia.

Frederick William IV,* king of Prussia, presents his own plan for German unification. He abandons his proposal in the face of opposition from Austria. | design, with twin towers, it seats 700 men and 500 women.

Bitter opposition to Rabbi Isaac Mayer Wise's advocacy of Reform at Albany's Congregation Beth El leads to physical violence at the Rosh Hashanah service, causing the police to close the synagogue. Rabbi Wise and 77 congregants withdraw from Beth El and found Anshe Emeth.

B'nai B'rith starts the Maimonides Library Association in New York. Members make use of the circulating library and enjoy social evenings of entertainment, as well as lectures. | Raphael Jonathan Bischoffsheim (1808–1883), who moved to Brussels from Germany in 1830 after Belgium became independent, helps to found the National Bank of Belgium. | | Moritz Steinschneider (1816–1907), father of modern Jewish bibliography, writes an article on Jewish literature that is published in the great General Encyclopedia of Sciences and Arts, edited by Johann Gottfried Gruber* and Johann Samuel Ersch.* In 1857, it will be translated into English from the German and titled Jewish Literature from the 8th to the 18th Century. | **1850** |
| The new Prussian constitution, enacted after the reconsolidation of monarchal rule following the revolutionary upheavals, contains a clause recognizing Christianity as the official state religion. It contradicts an earlier clause from the 1848 constitution, which recognizes the equal status of all religions, but this earlier clause is not removed. | Sabato Morais (1823–1897) is appointed rabbi of Congregation Mikveh Israel in Philadelphia, succeeding Isaac Leeser. Born and educated in Leghorn, Italy, he served as assistant rabbi in London's Bevis Marks synagogue until his arrival in the U.S. | Sir David Salomons (1797–1873), prominent in English finance and commerce, is elected to Parliament. He is forced to withdraw from his seat in the House of Commons because he refuses to recite the conclusion of the oath "on the true faith of a Christian." After the 1858 amendments regarding the oath, he will sit in Parliament from 1859 until his death.

Samson Raphael Hirsch is appointed rabbi of the Adass Yeshurun conregation in Frankfurt, a post he holds for 37 years until his death. Here he develops his views on neo-Orthodoxy, an educational system embodying the principles of halakhic Judaism in harmony with the modern world.

The first Jewish secular school opens | | Paul Julius Reuter moves his news-gathering agency to London. He is soon serving newspapers on the European continent and later expands to America and the Far East.

Zacharias Frankel, German rabbi and scholar, founds the Monatsschrift für Geschichte und Wissenschaft des Judentems (Monthly for the History and Scientific Study of Judaism), which becomes the world's major Jewish scholarly periodical. It will cease publication in 1939.

Guide to the Perplexed of the Time by Nachman Krochmal (1785–1840), Galician philosopher and historian, is edited and published 11 years after his death by Leopold Zunz. His is the first systematic philosophy of Jewish | **1851** |

	A. General History	B. Jews in North and South America	C. Jews in Europe	D. Jews in the Middle East and Elsewhere	E. Jewish Culture
1851			in Bucharest, Romania. It is established by Julius Barasch (1815–1863), physician and communal leader. In Russia a plan for Jewish classification designed to separate the "useful" Jews from the "exploiters and parasites" goes into effect despite opposition from local officials and the Council of State. Due to the Crimean War and the death of Nicholas I,* this plan is never implemented.		history. The history of every nation undergoes three periods: growth, blossoming, and decay. However, Israel, unlike other nations, always rises again to begin the cycle anew. In Galicia, the journal *He-Halutz* (*The Pioneer*), dedicated to social and religious reforms, is founded by Isaac Erter (1791–1851) and Joshua Heschel Schorr (1818–1895). The *maskilim* again plead for study of languages, artisanry, and crafts among Jews so that they can become productive laborers in society.
1852	Franklin Pierce* and William R. King* are elected president and vice president of the U.S. Benjamin Disraeli becomes chancellor of the exchequer and leader of the British House of Commons when his Tory party assumes power. The French approve a new constitution and the establishment of the Second Empire. President Louis Napoleon* proclaims himself Emperor Napoleon III.* Count Camillo Benso di Cavour* becomes prime minister of the kingdom of Sardinia. He supports the Risorgimento, the movement that leads to the unification of Italy in 1870, and modernizes the government and economy.	The first eastern European Orthodox synagogue in the U.S., the Beth Hamedrash Hagadol (Great House of Study), is established in New York. Abraham Joseph Ash (1813–1888), one of its founders, serves as rabbi. The first Jewish hospital in America (Jews' Hospital) is established in New York. In 1866, it will be renamed Mt. Sinai Hospital. Judah Philip Benjamin (1811–1884), a noted lawyer from Louisiana who had been elected to the Louisiana state legislature in 1842, is elected to the U.S. Senate. After his election, outgoing U.S. President Millard Fillmore* offers him a seat on the U.S. Supreme Court, confident that the Senate would confirm the newly elected southern senator. Benjamin	An important catacomb with Jewish inscriptions is found in Venosa, in southern Italy, attesting to the wide Jewish culture in Italy.	Judah Alkalai, Sephardic rabbi who was raised in Jerusalem and influenced by events surrounding the Damascus blood libel of 1840, visits England to win support for the settlement of Jews in Palestine as the primary solution to the Jewish problem. His efforts in England and elsewhere in Europe bring few results. Isaac Leeser, U.S. rabbi and educator, suggests that western Jews attempt to establish contact with the recently discovered Jewish colony in K'ai-Feng, China. Leeser is motivated by the effort to forestall Christian missionary activity.	A prayer book prepared especially for women, *Roochamah: Devotional Exercises for the Use of the Daughters of Israel, Intended for Public and Private Worship on the Various Occasions of Women's Life*, is edited by Reverend Morris J. Raphall (1798–1868) of New York.

A. General History	B. Jews in North and South America	C. Jews in Europe	D. Jews in the Middle East and Elsewhere	E. Jewish Culture	
	declines the offer. He will be reelected in 1858.				**1852**
The U.S. purchases territory in what is now southern New Mexico and Arizona from Mexico. Known as the Gadsden Purchase, it is the last contiguous addition to the U.S. continental boundaries.

The Argentine constitution of 1853 affords complete religious freedom for all residents. However, it declares that the government must support Roman Catholic worship and that the president-must be Roman Catholic.

The Crimean War begins as Turkey declares war on Russia.

Comte Joseph de Gobineau* (1816–1882), French diplomat, writes *Essai sur l'Inegalite des Races Humaines* (*Essay on the Inequality of the Human Races*), which is the first systematic presentation of general racist theory. It has a great influence on German antisemites. | Oheb Shalom is organized in Baltimore and becomes the first positive-historical (Conservative) congregation. Its pulpit is headed by Benjamin Szold (1829–1902). Szold will edit a prayer book, *Abodath Israel*, which in English translation comes to be known as the Jastrow prayer book, and will be used by many moderate Reform and Conservative congregations.

Solomon Nunes Carvalho (1815–1897) accompanies General John C. Fremont* on his fifth exploratory expedition designed to map out the U.S. transcontinental railway route, serving as the first official photographer of a U.S. exploratory expedition. | Jewish elementary secular schools in England begin to receive parliamentary grants. The "voluntary" schools sponsored by the various religious denominations will continue to receive government financial support even after 1870 when a general system of public education is introduced in England.

Three Jews of the town of Saratov, Russia, are accused and convicted of the ritual murder of two Christian children. It is the only instance of a blood libel conviction in Russia and causes a revival of the blood libel charge throughout Russia. A government commission investigates and in 1860 will conclude that guilt had been established. | I. Camondo & Cie., an Ottoman banking house, established by Abraham de Camondo (1785–1873) and his brother, finance the Ottoman Empire during the Crimean War, which will end in 1856. De Camondo, a philanthropic leader of the Turkish Jewish community, is known as the Rothschild of the East. | Abraham Benisch founds the *Hebrew Observer* as a rival journal to the *Jewish Chronicle* in London. In 1854, the two journals will merge as the *Jewish Chronicle and Hebrew Observer* under the editorship of Benisch.

Heinrich Graetz (1817–1891) begins publication, completed in 1876, of his 11-volume *History of the Jews*. Graetz, the major Jewish historian of the 19th century, attempts to write the history of the Jews as a living people, guided by divine providence. The work will be translated from German into many languages.

Abraham Mapu (1808–1867), Russian Haskalah educator, writes *Ahavat Zion* (*The Love of Zion*), the first Hebrew novel. Set in biblical times, it will be translated into many languages, including English, and published in 16 editions. | **1853** |
| The U.S. Congress enacts the Kansas–Nebraska Act, which establishes territories of Kansas and Nebraska and allows them to decide whether to permit or prohibit slavery. The act repeals the Missouri Compromise of 1820 and is condemned by abolitionists. The Republican party, which advocates abolition of slavery, and the Native American, or Know-Nothing, party are formed. | There are seven Jewish schools in New York, where religious and secular studies are taught, with 35 teachers for 857 pupils. By 1860, with the creation of public schools, all will be closed.

In his will, Judah Touro (1775–1854), New Orleans merchant, donates several hundred thousand dollars to Jewish and non-Jewish charitable institutions. It is the largest sum that | The Jewish Theological Seminary is established in Breslau, Germany, under the leadership of Zacharias Frankel. A traditional institution, it is nevertheless organized along modern lines and includes critical scholarship to reflect positive-historical Judaism.

Rabbi Naphtali Zevi Judah Berlin (1817–1893) becomes head of the yeshiva | Charles Dyte takes a leading part in the Eureka Stockade, the gold diggers' revolt against unjust government licensing in the gold fields of Ballarat, Central Victoria, Australia. Dyte later becomes the town's mayor. In 1859, Ballarat will count 347 male Jews in its population. | Edward Bloch (1816–1881) establishes a printing company in Cincinnati that publishes books and newspapers of Jewish content in English and German, including *The American Israelite* and *Die Deborah*. | **1854** |

	A. General History	B. Jews in North and South America	C. Jews in Europe	D. Jews in the Middle East and Elsewhere	E. Jewish Culture
1854	Britain and France ally with Turkey and declare war on Russia. Allied troops land in the Crimea and lay siege to Sevastopol. Russia evacuates the Danubian principalities, which neutral Austrian forces then occupy. The great library of the Assyrian king Ashurbanipal* is discovered at the ruins of Nineveh.	anyone in the U.S. has yet donated to charity. Included in his will is the sum of $60,000 for the relief of the poor in Palestine to be used at the discretion of Sir Moses Montefiore. Isaac Mayer Wise becomes rabbi of Congregation B'nai Yeshurun in Cincinnati, where he remains until his death in 1900. While there, he begins to publish the *Israelite* as a weekly platform for his ideas.	at Volozhin and transforms it into a spiritual center for all Russian Jewry. He requires his students to devote attention to the interpretation of the Scriptures, an innovation for yeshiva study, in addition to intensive talmudic studies.		
1855	Castle Garden, located at the tip of Manhattan Island, becomes the nation's first formal immigrant receiving station. Before it will close in 1889, a total of 8,280,000 immigrants will enter America through its doors. It has the virtue of being within walking distance of the Lower East Side. Sardinia enters the Crimean War allied with Britain, France, and Turkey. Czar Nicholas I* dies. Alexander II* becomes czar of Russia. The Russians abandon Sevastopol. Alexander II* begins peace negotiations to end the war. Ferdinand de Lesseps,* French engineer and diplomat, is granted the concession to build the Suez Canal.	A rabbinical conference is held in Cleveland, Ohio, at the urging of Rabbi Isaac Mayer Wise, to organize a central religious body and to define American Judaism. Wise has the conference recognize the authority of the Talmud as well as the divine character of the Bible in an effort to allay fears of the Orthodox. The conference fails as Isaac Leeser does not trust a group led by Wise to be even mildly Orthodox. Acceptance of the authority of the Talmud is denounced by radical Reformers led by Rabbi David Einhorn. Speaker William Stow,* of the California state legislature, during a debate of a bill to forbid trading on Sundays, accuses Jews of economic parasitism and disloyalty.	Jews' College, for the training of rabbis, is founded in London. A demographic survey in Frankfurt reveals that the average life span of Jews is 48 years 9 months and of non-Jews, 36 years 11 months. Jewish fertility in Europe is no higher than that of non-Jews, but among Jews, there is a drop in infant and adult mortality resulting from care of the young and sick, family stability, fewer illegitimate children, infrequency of venereal disease, and alcohol abstinence. A special Russian committee of theologians and Orientalists issues a report that there is no evidence to indicate that Jews use Christian blood or are involved in ritual murder.		Samson Raphael Hirsch, leader of German Orthodoxy, establishes a coeducational school in Frankfurt that includes a program of Jewish and secular subjects. Daniel Chwolson (1819–1911), Russian Semitic scholar, upon conversion to the Russian Orthodox church, is appointed professor of Hebrew, Syriac, and Chaldaic philology at the University of St. Petersburg.
1856	James Buchanan* and John C. Breckinridge* are elected president and vice president of the U.S.	August Bondi (1833–1907) and his business partners, Theodore Weiner and Jacob Benjamin, who are opposed to	Czar Alexander II* (1855–1881) of Russia abolishes the cantonist system of recruiting Jews for military service and		Rabbi David Einhorn, of Baltimore, publishes a Reform prayer book, *Olat Tamid* (*Daily Offering*),

A. General History	B. Jews in North and South America	C. Jews in Europe	D. Jews in the Middle East and Elsewhere	E. Jewish Culture	
Border warfare breaks out in the Kansas territory between pro- and antislavery factions, including John Brown's* abolitionist forces. The Congress of Paris brings an end to the Crimean War. The independence and integrity of the Ottoman Empire are recognized by the European powers. The Ottoman sultan guarantees the rights of all subjects. The Danubian principalities (later Romania) are placed under the guarantee of the European powers with their status to be determined later. The Italian National Society is founded. Aimed at the unification of Italy, it is supported by Cavour* and Garibaldi.*	slavery, join John Brown's* abolitionist forces in Kansas. They take part in the battles of Black Jack and Osawatomie, against proslavery forces. The Orthodox Ashkenazic Sons of Israel congregation is founded in Toronto, Canada. In 1875, it will become known as the Holy Blossom Temple and evolve into a Reform congregation during the first quarter of the 20th century. Kate E. R. Pickard* writes *The Kidnapped and the Ransomed*, a narrative of the personal recollections of Peter and Vina Still* who escaped to the North after 40 years in slavery. Their escape in 1850 was made possible by two Jewish shopkeepers, Joseph and Isaac Friedman, of Tuscumbia, Alabama. Of the approximately 90 slave narratives published, the Still narrative is the only one involving Jewish slaveholders. The Friedmans, however, bought Peter Still in order to free him afterward. Sabato Morais, rabbi of Congregation Mikveh Israel in Philadelphia, denounces the evils of American slavery from his pulpit.	makes them equal with the rest of the nation regarding military conscription. Nathaniel Hawthorne* (1804–1864) is a guest at a formal dinner given by David Salomons, first Jewish lord mayor of London. Hawthorne's* dislike of Jews is revealed in his *Passages from the English Notebooks* (1870), which describes his views of the lord mayor's brother and sister-in-law. "The sight of him justified me in the repugnance I have always felt towards his race."		predominantly in German, which is more radical in theology than his rival Wise's *Minhag Amerikah*. In addition, he begins publication of a monthly German-language journal, *Sinai*. His prayer book is used only by his own congregation and he will suspend publication of the journal in 1862. *Ha-Maggid* (*The Declarer*), the first weekly Hebrew newspaper, begins publication in Lyck, East Prussia. In 1858, David Gordon (1831–1886) will become editor, and the paper will grow in importance as a source of news of Jews throughout the world, and specialize in Judaic studies. After the 1881 pogroms in Russia, the paper will advocate Jewish nationalism and settlement in Palestine. It will cease publication in 1903.	**1856**
The U.S. Supreme Court renders the *Dred Scott* decision and holds that Congress had no right to prohibit slavery in the territories. Antislavery forces are outraged. Henry Rawlinson,* first decipherer of	Uriah Phillips Levy (1792–1862), who was one of 200 U.S. officers dismissed to improve the efficiency of the Navy, is restored to active duty by a naval court of inquiry. At the court's hearing, George Bancroft,* who was Navy		Despite vigorous French protests, Batto Sfez, a Tunisian Jew, is executed for having blasphemed Islam. Napoleon III* sends a French naval squadron to Tunisia. The Bey is coerced to adopt to Pacte Fondamental, which grants equal rights to	Rabbi Isaac Mayer Wise publishes *Minhag Amerikah* (*The American Rite*) in Hebrew and German, a radical revision of the traditional prayer book. He abolishes those prayers that refer to the sacrificial system, prayers for the coming of the	**1857**

	A. General History	B. Jews in North and South America	C. Jews in Europe	D. Jews in the Middle East and Elsewhere	E. Jewish Culture
1857	the Old Persian inscription of Darius I* and of Babylonian cuneiform, and three other scholars convince the Royal Asiatic Society in London that cuneiform has been interpreted.	secretary in 1845–1846, testifies to a strong prejudice against him, due in major part to "his being of the Jewish persuasion." A naval officer since 1817, he was a leader in the fight to abolish flogging. Adah Isaacs Menken (1835–1868), U.S. actress, is converted to Judaism in Cincinnati, Ohio. Proud of her religion, she leads a protest against the exclusion of Jews from England's House of Commons.		all, including the Jews. Muslims object and insurrection follows.	Messiah, and prayers for a restoration to Palestine. In San Francisco, Rabbi Julius Eckman (1805–1877) begins publication of *The Weekly Gleaner*, the first Jewish newspaper on the West Coast of the U.S. He served as rabbi in congregations in San Francisco, California, and Portland, Oregon. Judah Leib Gordon (1831–1892), Hebrew poet and Haskalah leader, writes *Judah's Parables*, a compilation of known fables such as Aesop's, as well as those written by him, which are derived from the Bible and the Midrash.
1858	Abraham Lincoln* (1809–1865) achieves national fame from the Lincoln–Douglas debates held during the Illinois senatorial contest. However, Douglas* wins reelection. Minnesota becomes the 32d state of the U.S.	President James Buchanan* refuses a request of American Jewish community leaders to intercede with the Vatican on behalf of the abducted Italian child, Edgardo Mortara. Intervention might alienate Irish Catholics who are loyal Democratic supporters. Paulson Dietrich dies in a Catholic hospital in St. Louis after having been involuntarily baptized and is buried in a Catholic cemetery. After determined efforts by Jews, his body is exhumed and reburied in a Jewish cemetery. This event is considered the American counterpart of the Mortara case. Reform and Traditional religious elements, including Rabbis Isaac Leeser	In Bologna, under papal rule, police seize six-year-old Edgardo Mortara from his family and take him to the House of Catechumens in Rome, relying on the testimony of a Christian servant that she had baptized him as an infant. Despite worldwide protests, he is handed over to a monastery and raised as a Christian. Isidore Cahen (1826–1902), French journalist and editor of the monthly *Archives Israelites*, publishes an appeal for the creation of an international committee for Jewish defense and suggests it be named Alliance Israelite Universelle. Pierre Joseph Proudhon* (1809–1865), leader of 19th-century French socialism,	The first synagogue is established in Aden. The British occupied the harbor of Aden in 1839. As a result of British rule, Jews from Yemen and Egypt emigrated to Aden.	The publication of *Hebraeische Bibliographie*, the first journal to be devoted in its entirety to Jewish bibliography, begins in Berlin. Edited by Moritz Steinschneider, it will be issued six times a year from 1858 to 1882. *The Watchman of the House of Israel* by Isaac Erter (1791–1851), Haskalah satirist who writes in Hebrew, is published. The book contains five previously written satires. Living in Brody, Erter directs his sharp humor against Hasidic superstition, hypocrisy, and ignorance. L.F.J.C. de Saulcy,* the French consul in Jerusalem, publishes *Histoire de l'art judaique*. On the basis of

| | and Isaac Mayer Wise, convene the Cleveland Conference. Recognizing that unity requires compromise, Leeser attends a conference planned and dominated by Reform Jews and Wise accepts the Talmud as the authoritative interpretation of the Bible. The conference does not lead to unity.

Judah Philip Benjamin, U.S. senator from Louisiana, is publicly offered the post of ambassador to Spain by President James Buchanan.* Benjamin decides to remain in the Senate and declines the offer.

Rabbi Joseph Saul Nathanson (1808–1875) of Lemberg responds to an inquiry by Rabbi Judah Mittelman of New York, who asks whether Protestant church buildings offered for sale may be converted to synagogue use. "Since the building does not contain any likeness or image, it is permitted to turn it into a house of study (and prayer) and it is, in fact, a virtue thus to sanctify God's name." Jewish congregations frequently use former church buildings. | accuses the Jews of "having rendered the bourgeoisie, high and low, similar to them, all over Europe." In his posthumously published diary, he wrote that the Jews were an "unsociable race, obstinate, infernal. . . . We should send this race back to Asia, or exterminate it."

The Tempelgasse synagogue in Vienna is opened. | | archaeological discoveries, he concludes that the Jews carried the arts to a high degree of perfection, and he rejects the notion that there was no art among the ancient Hebrews. | **1858** |

Judah Philip Benjamin, undated. (Library of Congress)

| John Brown,* hoping to start a slave insurrection, seizes the U.S. arsenal at Harpers Ferry. He is captured and later hanged for murder, treason, and conspiracy. | Representatives of 25 congregations from 14 U.S. cities resolve to create the Board of Delegates of American Israelites. The Mortara Affair highlighted the absence of any representative body to communicate the | The Jewish Board of Guardians is established by the synagogues of London to facilitate a more efficient administrative system of charitable aid to the poor. | | Moritz Steinschneider is appointed lecturer at the Veitel-Heine-Ephraimsche Lehrenstalt in Berlin. He will teach there for 48 years, and his students will include Solomon Schechter, Ignaz | **1859** |

	A. General History	B. Jews in North and South America	C. Jews in Europe	D. Jews in the Middle East and Elsewhere	E. Jewish Culture
1859	Oregon becomes the 33rd state of the U.S. Austrian forces invade Piedmont. France assists the Sardinians and declares war on the Austrians, whom they defeat. An armistice is signed. Venice remains with Austria, which cedes Lombardy to Sardinia. Charles Darwin* writes his *On the Origin of Species*, in which he develops his theories of evolution and natural selection.	views of the American Jewish community to the government, and the board is created for that purpose, as well as to gather statistical information and to arbitrate disputes between congregations. A Jewish child is secretly baptized by his nurse in New York and is forcibly taken from his parents by Catholic authorities. The child is returned to his family by a court order. Israel Joseph Benjamin (1818–1864), Romanian explorer and writer, begins a three-year journey throughout the U.S. In 1862 he will publish a description of his travels, which is the first comprehensive report on American Jewish communities.	The Dohany Street synagogue in Pest, Hungary, a double-turreted Moorish-style structure seating over 2,500 persons, is opened. The synagogue project was led by Rabbi Low Schwab (1794–1857), who became chief rabbi of Pest in 1836. He fashioned a compromise between Orthodox- and Reform-minded Jews, resulting in a community synagogue with an unabridged Hebrew service but a male choir, low gallery parapets, an organ, and sermons in the vernacular. Czar Alexander II* allows "useful" Jews to live outside the Pale of Settlement. Judah Leib of Lublin Eger (1816–1888) assumes the role of Hasidic zaddik upon the death of Menahem Mendel of Kotsk and propounds his own Hasidic teachings. His moral integrity is noted even by those opposed to Hasidism.		Goldziher, Judah L. Magnes, Alexander Marx, Henry Malter, and others who become leading scholars. Robert Remak (1815–1865), German neurologist, is appointed associate professor of medicine at the University of Berlin. One of the first Jews permitted to lecture at the university, he makes important discoveries in nerve and muscle diseases.
1860	Abraham Lincoln* and Hannibal Hamlin* are elected president and vice president of the U.S. Condemning Lincoln's* attack on slavery, South Carolina secedes from the Union. Garibaldi,* Italian revolutionary, leads the Thousand Red Shirts in conquest of Sicily and Naples. King Victor Emmanuel II* of Sardinia joins forces with Garibaldi* to defeat the papal forces.	Lewis Naphtali Dembitz (1833–1907) makes one of the three speeches nominating Abraham Lincoln* for president at the Republican National Convention. Active in Jewish communal affairs, he will be a founder of the Jewish Theological Seminary of America. On the eve of the Civil War, most of the more than 16,000 peddlers in the U.S. are Jews. On February 1, Rabbi Morris J.	The Alliance Israelite Universelle, the first modern international Jewish organization, established as a direct result of the Mortara Affair of 1858, is founded, with Paris as its headquarters, to defend the civil rights and religious freedom of the Jews all over the world. The alliance works through diplomatic channels, helping Jews to emigrate, and promotes the education of young Jews.		The first prayer book for Jewish children, *Order of Prayers for Hefzi-Bah Hebrew School, Temporarily Compiled for the Devotion of the Solemn Holidays of the Year 5621*, is published in San Francisco. The first Hebrew book written and printed in America is published. It is Joshua Falk's *Avney Yehoshua*, a homiletical commentary on the *Ethics of the Fathers*. The publication of *Der Israelit*, a

A. General History	B. Jews in North and South America	C. Jews in Europe	D. Jews in the Middle East and Elsewhere	E. Jewish Culture	
	Raphall, of Congregation B'nai Jeshurun in New York, delivers an invocation at the opening session of the 36th U.S. Congress. He is the first rabbi to have this honor. Congregation Shearith Israel, the Sephardic congregation of New York, opens a new synagogue on West 19th Street near 5th Avenue. It introduces the neobaroque design to the U.S. Israel Joseph Benjamin, a Romanian Jew traveling throughout America, causes a controversy in New Orleans when he objects to the contemplated erection of a statue in tribute to the philanthropist Judah Touro (1775–1844). When asked, leading rabbis throughout the world confirm his opinion that Jewish law prohibits a sculptural monument in honor of a Jew. August Belmont, American banker, becomes chairman of the Democratic National Committee. During his 12 years as chairman, his party never wins the presidency. In his romantic novel *The Marble Faun*, Nathaniel Hawthorne* introduces his only depiction of a Jewish woman in the character of Miriam.	Dr. Hayyim Lorje, of Frankfurt, forms the Society for the Colonization of Palestine. Lorje publishes articles in the Jewish and non-Jewish press and recruits men of reputation throughout Europe to his organization. However, not a single settlement is established in Palestine, and his society will die in 1865. Ignaz Kuranda (1812–1884), Viennese Jewish communal leader, forces a libel suit from Sebastian Brunner* (1814–1893), leading antisemitic journalist. The trial is of great interest to eastern European Jewry, and Kuranda is acquitted.		German-language Jewish weekly, begins in Mainz. Founded by Marcus Lehmann (1831–1890), an Orthodox rabbi, it becomes the leading Orthodox newspaper in Germany under the leadership of Jacob Rosenheim (1870–1965). It will cease publication in November 1938. Moritz Steinschneider completes a catalog of Hebrew books in the Bodleian Library, which documents the English library's great Judaica collection up to 1732. With this catalog, written in Latin, Steinschneider puts Hebrew bibliography on a scholarly basis. In the 1860s, Berl (Margolis) Broder (c.1815–1868), Yiddish composer and folk singer, organizes the Broder Singers, who tours Galicia, Hungary, and Romania, entertaining the public with Yiddish folk songs, many written by Broder himself. Alexander Zederbaum (1816–1893) begins publication of *Ha-Meliz* (*The Advocate*), a Hebrew weekly newspaper, in Odessa. Two years later, *Kol Mevasser*, a Yiddish supplement, will be added. The paper supports the Haskalah movement, becomes the organ of the Hibbat Zion (Love of Zion) movement in Russia and publishes the early writings of Ahad ha-Am and Bialik. It will cease publication in 1904.	**1860**

	A. General History	B. Jews in North and South America	C. Jews in Europe	D. Jews in the Middle East and Elsewhere	E. Jewish Culture
1860					The publication of *Razsvet* (*Dawn*), the first Jewish weekly written in the Russian language, begins. The decision to spread Russian among the Jewish masses, few of whom speak the language, is aimed at the elimination of antisemitism. Within the year its defense of Jewish civil rights will bring conflict with the government censor, and it will cease publication.
1861	Alabama, Arkansas, Florida, Georgia, Louisiana, Mississippi, North Carolina, Tennessee, Texas, and Virginia secede from the Union. They form the Confederate States of America with Jefferson Davis* and Alexander H. Stephens* elected as president and vice president. The U.S. Civil War begins. Kansas becomes the 34th state of the U.S. The kingdom of Italy is proclaimed. Czar Alexander II,* in response to growing industrialization and the need of factory owners for free labor, emancipates the peasants of Russia. He is called the Czar Liberator.	On January 4, Rabbi Morris J. Raphall, of New York, America's best-known Orthodox rabbi, delivers a sermon arguing that Judaism does not forbid slavery, adding that he is speaking only of biblical times. During the Civil War, Raphall will support the Union. His son, Alfred, will become a Union officer and lose an arm at Gettysburg. On January 15, the *New York Daily Tribune* publishes a reply to Morris J. Raphall's proslavery sermon, written by Michael Heilprin (1823–1888), editor and lay scholar. He calls it a "divine sanction of falsehood and barbarism." David Einhorn of Baltimore becomes the first rabbi to take issue with Raphall. As a result, Einhorn has to flee to Philadelphia. In January, the *Boston Transcript* editorially characterizes the support of Senator Judah Philip Benjamin of Louisiana and the southern Jews for secession from the Union as indicative	The Jews of the South German state of Baden are granted full civil rights. Solomon Judah Rapoport, chief rabbi of Prague and pioneer of critical Jewish scholarship, defends Zacharias Frankel's work on the Mishnah against attacks on dogmatic grounds by Samson Raphael Hirsch. Like Hirsch, he is an Orthodox rabbi, but Rapoport believes in free inquiry into traditional sources. Czar Alexander II* forbids the conversion of Jewish children under 14 without the consent of their parents. During the Civil War, approximately $200 million in U.S. bonds are sold in Frankfurt for the Union cause through the efforts of Joseph Seligman (1819–1880) of J & W Seligman & Co. Banking House. These sales are characterized as scarcely less important than the Battle of Gettysburg.	The newly adopted Tunisian constitution makes no distinction between Tunisian Muslims and Jews. Article 86 states: "All subjects of the Tunisian Regency, no matter of what religion, have the right to complete security of person, property, and of honor." The Magen David synagogue is established in Bombay by Jewish immigrants from Baghdad.	The publication of *Die Neuzeit* (*Modern Times*), a German-language Jewish weekly directed at the Jews of Austria–Hungary, begins in Vienna. Founded and edited by Leopold Kompert and Simon Szanto (1819–1882), it is politically liberal in viewpoint and advocates religious reform. In 1882, Adolf Jellinek (c.1820–1893) will succeed as editor. It opposes secular Jewish nationalism and Zionism. It will cease publication in 1903. Joseph Natonek (1813–1892), Hungarian rabbi and early Zionist, writes *The Messiah—or On the Emancipation of the Jews*, an essay in which he advocates national emancipation rather than cultural emancipation as the means of solving the Jewish question. *Serkele*, a Yiddish comedy by Solomon Ettinger (1803–1856), Polish Yiddish poet and dramatist, is published five years after his death. Serkele is an ambitious woman who pursues wealth and power. Ettinger

1861

A. General History

(no entry)

B. Jews in North and South America

of the disloyalty of all American Jews. Isaac Mayer Wise expresses outrage and points to the widespread support of the Republican party by thousands of northern Jews. Senator Andrew Johnson,* who in 1864 will be elected vice president, attacks Benjamin: "He sold out the old [government]; and he would sell out the new if he could in so doing make two or three millions."

In March, Judah Philip Benjamin is appointed attorney general in the newly created Confederate government by President Jefferson Davis.* In 1862, he will be appointed secretary of state, a post he will hold until the collapse of the Confederacy in 1865. He will flee to England, where he will develop a distinguished career in law.

In April, *Slavery Among the Ancient Hebrews from Biblical and Talmudic Sources*, written by Moses Mielziner (1828–1903), rabbi of Copenhagen, appears in *The American Theological Review*, a Christian journal, in English translation. It influences the Christian abolitionist movement.

C. Jews in Europe

(no entry)

D. Jews in the Middle East and Elsewhere

(no entry)

> HEAD QUARTERS, 13TH ARMY CORPS,
> DEPARTMENT OF THE TENNESSEE.
> Oxford, Miss., Dec. 17th, 1862.
>
> GENERAL ORDERS,
> No. 12.
>
> 1. The Jews, as a class, violating every regulation of trade established by the Treasury Department, and also Department orders, are hereby expelled from the Department.
> 2. Within twenty-four hours from the receipt of this order by Post Commanders, they will see that all of this class of people are furnished with passes and required to leave, and any one returning after such notification, will be arrested and held in confinement until an opportunity occurs of sending them out as prisoners unless furnished with permits from these Head Quarters.
> 3. No permits will be given these people to visit Head Quarters for the purpose of making personal application for trade permits.
> BY ORDER OF MAJ. GEN. U. S. GRANT.
>
> JNO. A. RAWLINS,
> Assistant Adjutant General.
>
> (OFFICIAL:)
> *Paul S. Tipton*
> Assistant Adjutant General.
>
> HEAD QUARTERS, 13TH ARMY CORPS,
> DEPARTMENT OF THE TENNESSEE,
> Holly Springs, Miss., Jan. 6, 1863.
>
> GENERAL ORDERS,
> No. 2.
>
> In pursuance of directions from the General-in-Chief of the Army, General Orders No. 12, from these Headquarters, dated Oxford, Miss., December 17th, 1862, is hereby revoked.
>
> BY ORDER OF MAJ. GEN. U. S. GRANT.
>
> JNO. A. RAWLINS,
> Assistant Adjutant General.
>
> [OFFICIAL:]
> *Loyd Wheaton*
> Capt & A. Assistant Adjutant General.

E. Jewish Culture

influenced Mendele Mokher Seforim (Shalom Abramowitsch, 1835–1917).

Daniel Chwolson, leading Russian Semitics scholar and apostate, publishes *On Several Medieval Accusations Against the Jews*, denouncing blood libel accusations against the Jews. It is written after the 1853 blood libel in Saratov.

The text of General Order No. 12 issued by General Ulysses S. Grant—a repetition of his Order No. 11—issued on Dec. 17, 1862, and its revocation on Jan. 6, 1863, persuant to the order of President Abraham Lincoln.

1862

A. General History

The Civil War rages throughout the U.S. Confederate forces led by General Robert E. Lee* begin the invasion of the North. General Ulysses S. Grant* (1822–1885) leads the Union forces in the Department of Tennessee. The Union fleet under Admiral David G.

B. Jews in North and South America

Lobbying by Jews and presidential intervention cause Congress to amend a law specifying that army chaplains had to be ministers of "some Christian denomination." It is changed to read "some religious denomination," thus permitting the appointment of

C. Jews in Europe

Moses Hess (1812–1875), German Socialist, whose views influenced two major political movements, Zionism and Communism, writes *Rome and Jerusalem*, an analysis of the contemporary Jewish condition and an argument for the establishment of a

D. Jews in the Middle East and Elsewhere

France places the Algerian consistories under the authority of the central consistory in Paris. Algerian Jewry becomes an official branch of French Jewry.

The first Alliance Israélite Universelle school is founded in Tetouan, Morocco.

E. Jewish Culture

Sarah Bernhardt (1844–1923), French actress, the daughter of a Jewish mother, and one who identifies with her Jewish heritage, makes her debut in the Comédie Française.

The Mekize Nirdamim Society (Rousers of Those

	A. General History	B. Jews in North and South America	C. Jews in Europe	D. Jews in the Middle East and Elsewhere	E. Jewish Culture
1862	Farragut* captures New Orleans. Otto von Bismarck* (1815–1898) is appointed prime minister of Prussia. The Danubian principalities of Moldavia and Wallachia unite and are recognized by the Ottoman sultan as Romania.	Jewish military chaplains. As food shortages and inflation hamper the Confederate cause, southerners seek scapegoats. The *Richmond Examiner* focuses on Jews as the worst "speculators" and "extortioners." In December, General Ulysses S. Grant* issues Order No. 11 expelling the Jews "as a class" from the area under the jurisdiction of the Union Army's Department of Tennessee. Jews, including former Union soldiers, are physically uprooted from Paducah, Kentucky, and Holly Springs and Oxford, Mississippi. Grant* is seeking to curb trade with the Confederate enemy and apparently succumbs to the anti-Jewish prejudice of military officers and civilian officials. Emil S. Heineman and Martin and Magnus Butzel form the clothing manufacturing firm of Heineman, Butzel & Co. in Detroit, Michigan, which supplies uniforms for the Union Army. The first minyan of Jews in Argentina is organized in Buenos Aires.	Jewish state in Palestine. "Neither religious reform nor baptism, neither Enlightenment nor Emancipation will open the gates of social life before the Jews."	The number of French-oriented schools will grow rapidly, and by World War I there will be a network of over 100 schools in North Africa, Persia, the Balkans, and throughout the Turkish Empire. Zvi Hirsch Kalischer (1795–1874), Orthodox rabbi and early Zionist thinker, writes *Derishat Ziyyon* (*Inquiry for Zion*), in which he argues for the redemption of the Jews through the return to Palestine. The Jews should create an economically viable homeland through agricultural settlement. He will assist in the creation of an agricultural school that will open at Mikveh Israel in 1870, sponsored by the Alliance Israelite Universelle.	Who Slumber) is founded in Germany. Its purpose is to publish Hebrew works of classical Jewish literature, especially unpublished manuscripts. In 1934, the society will move to Palestine. Anton Rubinstein (1829–1894), Russian pianist and composer who, with all his family, had been baptized into the Russian Orthodox church in 1831, establishes the St. Petersburg Conservatory and becomes its first director. Peter Tchaikowsky* is one of his pupils. Samuel David Luzzatto, Italian religious thinker who teaches at the Italian Rabbinical College in Padua, publishes *Lectures on Israelite Moral Theology*. He strongly believes in tradition, revelation and the election of Israel. The Torah must not be rationalized and subjected to historical evolutionary relativism, nor can morality be separated from religion.
1863	The Civil War continues to rage throughout the U.S. The Union defeats Confederate forces at the Battle of Gettysburg, Pennsylvania. The Confederates retreat into Virginia. Union forces led by General Ulysses S. Grant* capture Vicksburg, Mississippi. President Lincoln*	On January 3, Cesar Kaskel, Paducah merchant, who informed the American Jewish community of General Grant's* Order No. 11, heads a delegation of Jews who meet with President Lincoln* to advise him of the purposeful discrimination of the order. Lincoln*	Ferdinand Lassalle (1825–1864), German Socialist leader, founds the General German Workers Association, from which emerges the German Social Democratic party. In the 1840s he developed his theory of democratic and industrial socialism founded on the rule of law. Although	Sir Moses Montefiore, supported by the British government, petitions Sultan Muhammad IV* of Morocco to guarantee the safety and tranquility of Morocco's Jews. In February 1864, the sultan will issue a royal decree announcing the protection of Jews from injustice	Judah Leib Gordon, Hebrew poet and Russian Haskalah leader, writes "Awake My People," a poem that becomes the motto for a generation of "enlightened" Jews. He exhorts his Jewish reader: "Be a man in the street and a Jew at home, a brother to thy [non-Jewish]

A. General History	B. Jews in North and South America	C. Jews in Europe	D. Jews in the Middle East and Elsewhere	E. Jewish Culture	
issues the Emancipation Proclamation, freeing slaves in the southern states. West Virginia becomes the 35th state of the U.S. It broke away from Virginia in 1861. Poles in Russian Poland revolt. The revolution spreads to Lithuania and White Russia.	directs that the order be rescinded. Jews own 18 of the 20 old-clothes stores advertising in the *New York Herald* in May. With Chatham Street as the center, old-clothes stores are a major Jewish business in New York. The Emanu-El synagogue is erected in Victoria, British Columbia, Canada. Jews from England, Poland, Germany, and the U.S. emigrated to British Columbia following the discovery of gold in the Fraser River country, and they play a prominent part in the early social, economic, and political life of the colony. Lumley Franklin will be elected mayor of Victoria in 1866.	trained for a rabbinical career, he became estranged from Judaism and in 1860 wrote: "I can well affirm that I am no longer a Jew. . . . I see in them nothing but the very much degenerated sons of a great but vanished past." The Jews of Turin begin construction of a synagogue designed by Alessandro Antonelli to include seats for 1,000 men, a gallery for women, a school, a bakery, a ritual bath, a rabbi's residence, and other meeting rooms. By 1869, after many grandiose design changes, they will exhaust funds for the project, and in 1877 it will be taken over by the municipality and completed in 1889. A more modest Moorish Revival synagogue will be opened in 1878. Ernst Renan* (1823–1892), French philosopher, writes *Life of Jesus*, in which he asserts his theory of Semitic racial inferiority. The book is widely read in 19th-century France.	and oppression in accordance with Islamic law. Shortly thereafter, he will nullify the decree. The degraded status of Jews will continue until the French takeover of Morocco in 1912.	countrymen and a [faithful] servant to thy king." The Society for the Promotion of Culture among the Jews of Russia is founded in St. Petersburg. J.Y. Guenzburg (1812–1878), banker and philanthropist, is its first chairman. Its aim is the Russification of Jews, yet it subsidizes scholarly publications of the Haskalah movement. The publication of *Havazzelet*, a Hebrew monthly newspaper, begins in Jerusalem. Founded by Israel Bak, it becomes embroiled in controversy with *Ha-Levanon*, a rival newspaper founded a few months earlier by Jehiel Brill (1836–1886). The Ottoman authorities will force both to cease publication in 1864. The publication of *Havazzelet* will resume in 1870 and exist primarily as a weekly until 1910. It attacks financial corruption in Jerusalem and the secular character of Zionism.	**1863**
The Civil War continues. General Ulysses S. Grant* becomes commander-in-chief of the Union Armies. The Union Army captures Atlanta and marches through Georgia to the sea. Abraham Lincoln* is reelected president and Andrew Johnson* is elected vice president of the U.S. Nevada becomes the 36th state of the U.S.	The Knesseth Israel synagogue in Philadelphia is opened. With twin towers and bulbous tops, it inaugurates the Moorish Revival style in the U.S. It bears a striking resemblance to the synagogue constructed in 1839 in Kassel, Germany. The Hebrew Free School is established in New York's poor neighborhoods to counteract schools founded by Christian missionaries.	The Jews of the South German state of Württemberg are granted full civil rights. The writings of Rabbi Abraham ibn Ezra influence the English poet, Robert Browning* (1812–1889). Browning, who writes his most famous poem on a Jewish theme, "Rabbi Ben Ezra," is strongly sympathetic to the Jews. Meir Loeb ben Jehiel Michael		Isaac Meir Dick, popular Yiddish story writer of the Russian Haskalah, enters into a contract with the Romm publishing house to write a 48-page novelette each week. His stories are read by thousands of men and women. Mark Antokolski (1843–1902), Russian sculptor, is awarded the Great Silver Medal of the Academy of Art in St. Petersburg for his wood bas-relief *The Jewish Tailor*. Born in	**1864**

	A. General History	B. Jews in North and South America	C. Jews in Europe	D. Jews in the Middle East and Elsewhere	E. Jewish Culture
1864	The Russians crush the Polish revolt and begin Russification programs in Poland.		Malbim (1809–1879), who became chief rabbi of Bucharest in 1858, is freed from imprisonment on the intervention of Sir Moses Montefiore. Head of the Orthodox wing of the community, he opposed Reform innovations, including the proposed construction of the Choral Temple. Reform leaders had falsely denounced him to the government as disloyal. Malbim was a noted Bible commentator. Isaac Elhanan Spektor (1817–1896), recognized as Russian Jewry's greatest authority on rabbinic law for almost half a century, becomes rabbi of Kovno, where he serves until his death. He publicly proclaims the religious duty of settlement in Palestine. Charles Dickens'* novel *Our Mutual Friend* includes Mr. Riah, the Jewish benefactor of society and ally of the innocent. Dickens* has Mr. Riah say: "Men find the bad among us easily enough. They take the worst of us as samples of the best; they take the lowest of us as presentations of the highest; and they say 'All Jews are alike.'"		the Vilna ghetto, he chose his career against the wishes of his Orthodox parents and becomes one of the most famous artistic personalities of the 19th century. His sculptures embody social and human ideals.  The Jewish Tailor, *a wood bas-relief by Mark Antokolski (1843–1902).*
1865	In February, Judah Philip Benjamin, realizing the weakness of the Confederacy, calls for the emancipation of the slaves on condition that they join the fight against the Union. He is censured by the Confederate Senate	Senator Grimes* of Iowa introduces a proposed constitutional amendment to adopt Christianity as the state religion of the U.S. Jewish leaders protest and the Senate Judiciary Committee tables the proposal.			Abraham Abraham (1843–1911) and Joseph Wechsler establish a dry goods store in Brooklyn, New York, which develops under the name Abraham & Straus into Brooklyn's largest department store.

A. General History	B. Jews in North and South America	C. Jews in Europe	D. Jews in the Middle East and Elsewhere	E. Jewish Culture

for his proposal. Several weeks later the Confederate legislature passes a limited Negro enlistment bill in the effort to bolster General Robert E. Lee's* military forces.

In April, the U.S. Civil War ends with the surrender of the Confederate armies. President Lincoln* is assassinated. He is succeeded by Vice President Andrew Johnson.* In December, the 13th Amendment to the Constitution, prohibiting slavery, is ratified.

The passage of a special law permits non-Catholics in Chile to practice their religion in private homes and to establish private schools.

Prussia defeats Austria in the Seven Weeks' War and drives it out of the German Confederation. Prussia creates a North German Confederation of states north of the Main River, which flows through Frankfurt.

Although American Jews had participated in 1854 in the founding of the Arion Choral Society (German Gesang Verein), by 1866 the society resolves to refuse further admissions to Jews. Many newspapers editorialize against this infringement of the American spirit.

B'nai Yeshurun, the first Moorish Revival synagogue in the U.S., known as Rabbi Isaac Mayer Wise's Plum Street Temple, is dedicated in Cincinnati, Ohio.

The Temple Emanu-El on Sutter Street in San Francisco is opened. Jewish symbols—the shield of David and tablets of the Law—are publicly displayed on this twin-tower building with "golden globes." Services are in the Reform tradition. The synagogue will burn down in the earthquake of April 1906.

Gerson Bleichroeder (1822–1893), merchant banker, serves as Otto von Bismarck's* financial adviser and helps him raise funds for the Prussian war against Austria.

The Oranienburgerstrasse synagogue in Berlin, a Moorish Revival synagogue crowned with a bulbous dome, is opened. It is the largest synagogue in the world, seating over 3,200, and is equipped with the most modern lighting and ventilating systems. It will be set afire on *Kristallnacht* in 1938, damaged again by Allied bombing in World War II, and remain as a skeleton in East Berlin.

Switzerland eliminates restrictions on Jewish residence in response to pressure from foreign governments. Full emancipation will be achieved in 1874.

The Choral Temple, constructed by the

Congregation B'nai Yeshurun, the Plum Street Temple, Cincinnati. (Library of Congress)

Congregation Temple Emanu-El, Sutter Street, San Francisco, 1866. (Library of Congress)

Wilhelm Steinitz (1836–1900), chess master, born in Prague, resettles in London, where he wins the world chess championship and retains the title until he is defeated in 1894 by Emanuel Lasker (1868–1941).

Moritz Daniel Oppenheim's (1799–1882) canvases of Jewish genre scenes, painted in Germany, are repeated in gray gouache to permit photographic reproduction. They are distributed in the U.S. in an album as *Family Scenes from Jewish Life of Former Days.*

Solomon Sulzer (1804–1890), Austrian cantor and composer of Reform liturgical music, publishes his second volume of *Shir Ziyyon* (*Song of Zion*), the earliest complete and organized repertory in Hebrew to be arranged for cantor and male choir. He officiates at the New Synagogue in Vienna from 1826 to 1881.

	A. General History	B. Jews in North and South America	C. Jews in Europe	D. Jews in the Middle East and Elsewhere	E. Jewish Culture
1866			Reform-minded German–Austrian community of Bucharest, Romania, is opened.		
1867	The U.S. buys Alaska from Russia for $7.2 million. The U.S. Congress passes three Reconstruction Acts over President Andrew Johnson's* vetoes. The Ku Klux Klan is formally organized at Nashville, Tenn. Nebraska becomes the 37th state of the U.S. Charles Warren,* an Englishman, undertakes the first archaeological explorations in Jerusalem. The British North America Act creates the dominion of Canada, consisting of the provinces of Quebec, Ontario, Nova Scotia, and New Brunswick. As a result of the Compromise of 1867, Austria–Hungary liberalizes itself into a multinational empire. Karl Marx, German philosopher and leading theorist of modern socialism, writes the first volume of *Das Kapital*, his major work.	It is reported that Cornelius Cole,* U.S. senator from California and lobbyist for the purchase of Alaska from Russia, credits Louis Goldstone, an agent for California fur houses who visited Alaska several times, as the most original and active mover in the plan to buy Alaska after the Civil War. Isaac Leeser creates a rabbinical school, Maimonides College, in Philadelphia, where he serves as provost. The school lasts for only six years, closing in 1873 without having graduated or ordained a student. Morris Rich (1847–1928), who emigrated to the U.S. in 1860 from Hungary, opens Rich's Retail Store in Atlanta, Georgia. It becomes the first in a chain of department stores in the South that becomes known for good labor relations and liberal credit terms. Rich and his brothers started as peddlers in Cleveland, Ohio.	The Jews of Austria receive full rights as the new constitution of Austria–Hungary abolishes religious discrimination. Louisa Lady Goldsmid, active in the founding of the first women's college at Cambridge University in England, joins in supporting the Reform Bill and women's suffrage. Hebrew culture is recognized when Matthew Arnold* (1822–1888), English Victorian poet, writes his elegiac poem "On Heine's Grave."	Jean Henri Dunant* (1828–1910), Swiss Protestant philanthropist and founder of the International Red Cross, describes his plans for the resettlement of Jews in Palestine. His association would acquire land, build a Jerusalem–Jaffa railroad, and develop agriculture in Palestine. His efforts are unsuccessful, and he blames his failure on Jewish indifference to the colonization plan.	Nathan Mayer (1838–1912) writes *Differences*, a novel about Jews, North and South, during the Civil War period. It is described as the first novel by an American Jew about American Jews considered to have literary merit. It is serialized by Isaac Mayer Wise in *The Israelite* before being published in book form. Julius Sachs (1832–1897), German botanist, is appointed professor of botany at Würzburg. He is credited with being the creator of experimental botany, and under his leadership Würzburg becomes an international center for plant physiology.
1868	General Ulysses S. Grant* and Schuyler Colfax* are elected president and vice president of the U.S. Benjamin Disraeli, British statesman and novelist, serves a brief term as prime minister of Great Britain.	North Carolina adopts a new state constitution that finally eliminates the religious test disqualifying Jews from holding state public office. The first congregation, Congregacion Israelita de la Republica Argentina,	The liberal trend in Austria continues with the annulment of the agreement with the Vatican, resulting in the removal of education and matrimonial law from church control. The principle of legal equality without regard to religion is strengthened.	Bukharan Jews begin emigration to Palestine from Russia. In 1892, they will found the Bukharan Quarter of Jerusalem, which they name Rehovot.	Adolf Neubauer (1831–1907), European scholar who settled in England in 1865, becomes Semitics librarian at the Bodleian Library at Oxford. In 1884, he will be appointed reader in rabbinic literature at the university. He enriches the library's

A. General History	B. Jews in North and South America	C. Jews in Europe	D. Jews in the Middle East and Elsewhere	E. Jewish Culture	
	is founded in Buenos Aires. It deals with such matters as marriage and burial of dissidents in the cemetery. Temple Emanu-El on 5th Avenue and 43rd Street in New York is opened. This Moorish Revival synagogue, with services in the Reform tradition, seats 1,800 on the floor and 500 in the gallery. It is designed by Leopold Eidlitz. S. A. Bierfield, a young Russian Jewish owner of a dry-goods store in Franklin, Tenn., known as a Radical Republican, employs a Negro as a clerk. On August 16 he and his clerk together are murdered by the Ku Klux Klan.	Under the pseudonym Sir John Retcliffe, Hermann Goedsche,* German novelist, writes *Biarritz*, a novel that contains the chapter "In the Jewish Cemetery in Prague." Thirteen Jews representing the 12 tribes and those in exile swear all the world will be their slaves within the next century. By 1872, this fictional episode is believed to be true and will later be used to demonstrate the authenticity of *The Protocols of the Elders of Zion*. After the emancipation of the Jews, the Hungarian government convenes a General Jewish Congress to regulate internal Jewish affairs. Attended by 220 delegates (126 Reformers [Neologists] and 94 Orthodox), it erupts into conflict. The government allows two organizations to exist, the Reformers and the Orthodox, and status quo and Hasidic congregations are recognized.		 *Temple Emanu-El, Fifth Avenue and 43rd Street, New York, 1868. (Library of Congress)*	collection of Judaica, particularly from the Cairo Genizah. Seligman Isaac Baer (1825–1897), German liturgical scholar, publishes an edition of the prayer book with commentary, which is accepted as the standard prayer book, or *siddur*, text for the Ashkenazic community. Leopold Auer (1845–1930), Hungarian violinist and teacher, is appointed soloist of the Russian Imperial Orchestra and professor at the St. Petersburg Conservatory shortly after his baptism into the Russian Orthodox church. His pupils include Mischa Elman, Jascha Heifetz, and Nathan Milstein. The publication of *Ha-Shahar* (*The Dawn*), a Hebrew-language monthly, begins in Vienna. Founded and edited by Perez Smolenskin (c.1840–1885), it becomes the leading Hebrew literary exponent of the later Haskalah movement and of early Jewish nationalism. It will cease publication in 1885.	**1868**
The Suez Canal is opened. Susan B. Anthony* and other activists including Ernestine Potovsky Rose found the Women's Suffrage Society in the U.S.	President Ulysses S. Grant,* after being advised by American Jews of a contemplated expulsion of 20,000 Jews from an area in southwestern Russia, intervenes with the czarist government. The expulsion is halted as a consequence of American concern. The Ohio Supreme Court overturns a	The North German Confederation, under the leadership of Chancellor Otto von Bismarck,* abolishes all remaining civil and political disabilities due to differences in religious affiliation. Shomer Yisrael (Guardian of Israel), an assimilationist movement, is organized in Galicia, as Jewish political		Moritz Steinschneider, father of modern Jewish bibliography, is appointed assistant in the Royal Library of Berlin, a position he holds until his death. Mendele Mokher Seforim, Russian Yiddish and Hebrew writer, writes *Fishke the Lame*, a tender idyllic tale of two beggars, one lame	**1869**

	A. General History	B. Jews in North and South America	C. Jews in Europe	D. Jews in the Middle East and Elsewhere	E. Jewish Culture
1869		lower court's decision and sustains the Cincinnati Board of Education decision to dispense with all Bible readings in the public schools. Rabbi Isaac Mayer Wise is a leader in the fight to prohibit Bible reading in the public schools. He advocates an American public life that is religiously neutral. The first statement of the position of Reform Judaism in America is published at a conference of Reform rabbis in Philadelphia under the guidance of Rabbis David Einhorn and Emil G. Hirsch. Rabbi Isaac Mayer Wise, who wished a conference that would result in a broad union of American Jews, does not attend.	activity intensifies after the adoption of the Austrian constitution of 1867. It favors German cultural orientation and publishes a weekly, *Der Israelit*. Jacob Brafman (c.1825–1879), Russian apostate and antisemite, publishes with government support *The Book of the Kahal*, in which he reproduces many excerpts from the minute book of the Minsk community; he claims the minutes, which he has doctored, reveal the Jews' wish to exploit the general population. The book receives widespread approval. Mikhail Bakunin* (1814–1876), Russian revolutionary and founder of anarchism, responding to a letter from Moses Hess, states that the Jews are a nation of exploiters and are opposed to the interests of the proletariat.		and the other hunchbacked, as seen against the background of beggars and paupers Mendele associated with in his younger years. He also writes a Yiddish play, *The Tax*, in which he denounces the infamous meat tax that fell heaviest on the poor.
1870	The New York Elevated Railroad Co. opens a new era of intraurban mass transportation. The Franco-Prussian war breaks out. The German victory leads to the consolidation of the German Empire. A bloodless revolution in France deposes Napoleon III,* and the Third French Republic is established. The First Vatican Council proclaims the dogma of papal infallibility, i.e., the pope cannot make a mistake when authoritatively defining matters of faith and morals.	Joseph Seligman declines the post of secretary of the treasury, offered by his friend, President Ulysses S. Grant.* President Ulysses S. Grant* appoints Benjamin F. Peixotto (1834–1890), grand master of the Order of B'nai B'rith, American consul in Bucharest, Romania. Since the U.S. budget makes no provision for such a consular office, B'nai B'rith defrays expenses of the office for five years. During 1870 and 1871, Simon Sterne (1839–1901) serves as secretary to the	The United Synagogue, a union of England's Ashkenazic synagogues, is established pursuant to an act of Parliament. Adolphe Cremieux, French lawyer, statesman, and Jewish leader, signs as minister of justice in the French Republic a governmental decree that confers French citizenship on the Jews of Algeria. The Jews of Italy are finally emancipated with the abolition of the ghetto in Rome. The rights gained in the 1790s	Alliance Israelite Universelle establishes an agricultural school, Mikveh Israel, near Jaffa. Rabbi Akiva Schlesinger (1832–1922), Orthodox rabbi of Pressburg, emigrates to Palestine. He seeks refuge from the modernism and secularism spreading throughout Europe.	August Brentano (1831–1886), who emigrated to the U.S. from Austria in 1853, establishes Brentano's Literary Emporium, which later becomes New York's leading bookstore. Julius Bien (1826–1909), lithographer, cartographer, and president of B'nai B'rith from 1854 to 1857 and 1868 to 1900, produces the maps and atlases accompanying the U.S. federal census reports. He continues to do so for each decade up to 1900.

A. General History	B. Jews in North and South America	C. Jews in Europe	D. Jews in the Middle East and Elsewhere	E. Jewish Culture	
	Committee of Seventy, which will help overthrow New York's notorious Tweed Ring.	and lost upon the fall of Napoleon I* were regained in 1848 in Tuscany and Sardinia; in 1859 in Modena, Lombardy, and Romagna; in 1860 in Umbria; in 1861 in Sicily and Naples; and in 1866 in Venice.		Israel Hildesheimer (1820–1899), rabbi and leader of German Orthodox Jewry, founds the *Juedische Presse*, a weekly published in Berlin. From its outset the paper supports settlement in Palestine.	**1870**
		The Hanover synagogue, designed by the architect Edwin Oppler (1831–1888), who rejected the prevalent Moorish style of synagogue architecture as having "not the slightest relationship to Jewry," is opened. The synagogue is of Romanesque design.		Elie de Cyon (1842–1912) becomes the first Jewish professor in Russia when he is appointed to the chair of physiology at St. Petersburg University.	
		The Great Synagogue in Stockholm is opened. It is a freestanding structure seating more than 830, located on a side street in the center of the city.		Moses Leib Lilienblum (1843–1910), Hebrew writer, political journalist, and leader of the Hibbat Zion movement, writes *Kehal Refa'im* (*The Community of the Dead*), a political satire in which he calls for the normalization of Jewish life through participation in agricultural labor, commerce, and industry.	
There is a panic on Wall Street. A five-year economic depression begins. The notorious Tweed Ring in New York is overthrown. Tammany boss William Marcy Tweed* is indicted for fraud. The ring defrauded the city of at least $30 million. The new Third French Republic suppresses the Paris Commune. Prussia defeats France in the Franco-Prussian War. France cedes Alsace–Lorraine to Germany. Otto von Bismarck,* chancellor of the	The Rodeph Shalom congregation in Philadelphia opens a new synagogue building on Broad and Mt. Vernon streets, built in the Moorish Revival style. The congregation, largely of German immigrants and led by Rabbi Marcus Jastrow from 1866 until 1892, strives to remain in the Orthodox tradition.	The English Parliament passes the Universities Tests Act of 1871, which opens all lay posts at Oxford and Cambridge to men of all creeds on equal terms. Sir George Jessel (1824–1883), is appointed solicitor general, the first Jew to hold a ministerial office in England. In 1873, he will be appointed master of the rolls, which ranks next in order of precedence to the chief justiceship. The Anglo-Jewish Association is established in Great Britain to represent English-speaking		Zvi Hirsch Bernstein (1846–1907), who arrived in New York from Russia in 1870, founds *Ha-Zofe ba-Arez ha-Hadashah* (*The Observer in the New Land*), the first Hebrew newspaper in the U.S. Publication will cease in 1876. Emil Bessels (1847–1888), German physician, explorer, and naturalist, sails on the U.S. vessel *Polaris* with Captain Francis Hall's* expedition to the North Pole. After traveling farther north than any other explorer by ship, Hall* dies, the *Polaris* is wrecked in	**1871**

	A. General History	B. Jews in North and South America	C. Jews in Europe	D. Jews in the Middle East and Elsewhere	E. Jewish Culture
1871	North German Federation, persuades the southern states to join his federation. The Second German Empire, with King William I* of Prussia as emperor and Bismarck* as its "Iron Chancellor," is proclaimed. Charles Darwin* writes *The Descent of Man*, in which he applies his theories of evolution to humans.		Jews and to protect underprivileged Jews in eastern Europe, North Africa, and the Middle East by means of education and diplomacy. The Jews of Bavaria are accorded full rights. Jews become emancipated in all territories of the new German Empire. In reality, Jews are excluded from the officer corps, major administrative posts, foreign service, and teaching positions below the university level with few exceptions. The first modern Russian pogrom takes place in Odessa, instigated mainly by Greek merchants out of commercial rivalry.		polar ice, and Bessels is rescued with other crew members. In 1873, Bessels will be accused of murdering Hall* but will be adjudged innocent by an inquiry of military surgeon generals. Judah Leib Gordon, Hebrew poet, despairing of the Jewish community ever integrating into Russian society because of the growth of antisemitism and the ineptness of Russian liberalism, and despairing also of the indiscriminate assimilationist trends of the *maskilim*, composes *For Whom Do I Labor?*
1872	Ulysses S. Grant* is reelected president and Henry Wilson* is elected vice president of the U.S. British archaeologist George Smith* finds the Mesopotamian flood story among the cuneiform tablets unearthed at Nineveh. Similarities to the biblical account are quickly seen.	A provision in the Tennessee state constitution that the legislature should be opened in prayer by a "Christian" minister is eliminated. Immediately thereafter, a rabbi is invited to offer the invocation at the legislature's next session. Central Synagogue–Congregation Ahavath Chesed at Lexington Avenue and 55th Street in New York is opened. Constructed in the Moorish Revival style, this Reform synagogue seats 1,500 persons. It remains the oldest synagogue building in continuous use in New York. Albert Jacob Cardozo (1828–1885), a judge of the New York Supreme Court, resigns during the exposure of the Tweed Ring	A higher school for the scientific study of Judaism (Hochschule für die Wissenschaft des Judentums) is established in Berlin. It is the first rabbinical seminary to train Reform rabbis. One of its first teachers is Abraham Geiger. Israel Hildesheimer, rabbi and leader of German Orthodox Jewry, establishes Palaestina Verein, whose object is to raise the educational and vocational standards of the Jews of Jerusalem. Gerson Von Bleichroeder (1822–1893) is raised to German nobility. A leading German merchant banker, he became a private banker and financial adviser to Otto von Bismarck.* A Reform synagogue opens in Breslau. Designed by the		Jehiel Brill, Hebrew journalist, begins publication of his periodical *Ha-Levanon* (*The Lebanon*) in Mainz, Germany. It strongly supports Jerusalem Orthodoxy, including *halukkah*. Max Buedinger (1828–1902), German historian, is appointed professor of history at Vienna University, after converting to Protestantism. Ferdinand Julius Cohn (1828–1898), German botanist and bacteriologist, initiates a systematic classification of bacteria. His research establishes bacteriology as a science. In 1851, he was appointed lecturer in botany at the University of Breslau and in 1872 is the first Jew in Prussia granted the rank of professor.

A. General History	B. Jews in North and South America	C. Jews in Europe	D. Jews in the Middle East and Elsewhere	E. Jewish Culture	
	scandals. He is the father of Benjamin Nathan Cardozo (1870–1938), leading U.S. jurist and legal philosopher, who will serve on the U.S. Supreme Court from 1932 until his death.	architect Edwin Oppler, it resembles a Rhenish Romanesque cathedral. The Rumbach Street synagogue in Budapest, an Orthodox synagogue seating 1,160, is opened. Judah Leib Gordon, Hebrew poet and Haskalah leader, is appointed secretary of the Jewish community in St. Petersburg and director of the Society for the Promotion of Culture among the Jews. He influences the poetry and nationalist outlook of Hayyim Nahman Bialik (1873–1934).		Yehiel Michael Pines (1843–1913), Russian Hebrew writer, publishes *Yaldei Ruhi* (*The Children of My Spirit*), in which he criticizes the assimilationist and religious reformist tendencies of the Haskalah. He believes changes in *halakhah* could occur without affecting the sanctity of Jewish religion. His ideas are expanded by Ahad ha-Am. Abraham Firkovich (1786–1874), Karaite scholar, writes *Avnei Zikkaron* (*Stones of Remembrance*), which describes his travels and archaeological studies. After his death, scholars prove that his material contains many forgeries.	**1872**
	The Union of American Hebrew Congregations is founded in Cincinnati by 34 congregations from the West. Its aims are to establish a Jewish theological seminary, "to preserve Judaism intact," and to publish books for Sabbath schools "without, however, interfering in any manner whatsoever with the affairs and management of any congregation." The leading proponents and organizers of the union are Rabbi Isaac Mayer Wise and Moritz Loth, the president of his Cincinnati congregation, B'nai Jeshurun.	Rabbi Israel Hildesheimer founds a seminary for the training of Orthodox rabbis in Berlin. The seminary's curriculum is organized on the premise that Orthodoxy is compatible with the scientific study of Jewish sources.	Julius Vogel (1835–1899), journalist and statesman, becomes prime minister of New Zealand and serves until 1875 and briefly in 1876. He laid the foundations for centralized governmental administration and a national education system. Born in London, he emigrated first to Australia in 1852 and then to New Zealand in 1861.	Hermann Cohen (1842–1918), German philosopher, is appointed instructor in philosophy at the University of Marburg. He establishes the Marburg school of neo-Kantian philosophy. He will retire in 1912 and establish a second career as a Jewish philosopher, teaching at the Berlin Hochschule. Mendele Mokher Seforim, Russian Yiddish and Hebrew writer, writes *The Nag, Or Against Cruelty to Animals*, a popular allegory on the persecution of Jews in czarist Russia and an indictment of the Haskalah attitude that if the Jew Europeanizes himself, he will gain acceptance in society. Israel Meir ha-Kohen, leading	**1873**

	A. General History	B. Jews in North and South America	C. Jews in Europe	D. Jews in the Middle East and Elsewhere	E. Jewish Culture
1873					Orthodox rabbi and moralist, anonymously publishes his first book in Vilna, *Hafez Hayyim*, which discusses the need for careful observance of the laws of slander, gossip, and talebearing. He becomes known by the name of this book.
1874	Benjamin Disraeli becomes prime minister of England and holds the office for six years.	The United Hebrew Charities of New York is established. The first Young Men's Hebrew Association (YMHA) is founded in New York. By 1890 the YMHAs will number more than 120 branches, and cultural activities will include lectures, discussions, classes, and free Jewish libraries. The Merriam Co. is prevailed upon to eliminate from the *Webster Dictionary* the term *to Jew*, which had been defined as "to bargain."	The synagogue on Rue de la Victoire in Paris is opened. Designed by the architect Alfred Aldrophe (1834–1895), it is located on a relatively narrow street, as the government does not want the building to be visible on a well-traveled thoroughfare. It can accommodate upward of 5,000. The new Swiss constitution finally establishes religious liberty, thereby extending equal treatment to Jews. This is the culmination of American and western European nations' repeated requests to treat Jewish citizens on a par with non-Jewish citizens. Switzerland is the last country in central Europe to legally emancipate its Jews. A new Russian law provides exemptions from military service for educational purposes, resulting in a flow of Jews into Russian schools.		Camille Pissarro (1830–1903), French painter born in the Virgin Islands into a Sephardic family from Bordeaux, becomes a founder and leader of the Impressionist movement. He was a teacher of Paul Cézanne* and Paul Gauguin.* He is considered the first major Jewish painter, yet he painted not a single Jewish subject. Emile-Auguste Begin (1802–1888) becomes librarian at the Paris Bibliothèque Nationale. Jacob Hamburger (1826–1911), German rabbi, begins publication of the first encyclopedia in German on Jewish subjects. Leopold Auerbach (1828–1897), German physician and biologist, publishes a treatise that is the basis for the new science of cellular biology.
1875	U.S. President Ulysses S. Grant* expresses his opposition to any religious instruction in the public schools. Under the leadership of Prime Minister	Hebrew Union College, the first successful rabbinical school in the U.S., is founded by the Union of American Hebrew Congregations, with Isaac Mayer Wise,	Joseph Deckert,* Viennese Catholic clergyman, publishes an account of an alleged ritual murder. Rabbi Joseph Samuel Bloch (1850–1923) takes legal action against	Sir Charles Warren,* English archaeologist, writes *The Land of Promise: or, Turkey's Guarantee*, in which he proposes that a British company be created to colonize	Adolphe Opper Blowitz (1825–1903), chief Paris correspondent of the London *Times*, originates the technique of interviewing prominent

A. General History	B. Jews in North and South America	C. Jews in Europe	D. Jews in the Middle East and Elsewhere	E. Jewish Culture	
Benjamin Disraeli, England acquires dominant control of the Suez Canal with the financial help of the Rothschilds, so as to protect the vital route to India, the heart of the British Empire.	the leader of American Reform Judaism, as its president.

The Reverend Dwight L. Moody,* popular evangelical Protestant minister, continually preaches the accusation of deicide, the Jewish killing of Christ, to tens of thousands during meetings held in major U.S. cities. Moody* advocates a religious Protestant base for American society and appeals to middle-class native-born Americans. | him, and Deckert* is found guilty of slander.

Anthony Trollope's* novel of London life, *The Way We Live Now*, includes the Jewish financial villain, Augustus Melmotte. Melmotte was based on Albert Grant, born Abraham Gotheimer (1831–1899), who became a member of Parliament and the general manager of Credit Mobilier in London, which floated fraudulent companies. He died a pauper. | Palestine "with the avowed intention of gradually introducing the Jew, pure and simple, who is eventually to occupy and govern this country." | personalities, such as Bismarck,* the sultan of Turkey,* and Pope Leo XIII.

Karl Goldmark (1830–1915), Hungarian composer and son of a cantor, who settled in Vienna, composes the opera *The Queen of Spades*.

Lev Levanda (1835–1888), Russian author and publicist, writes *Turbulent Times*, a novel describing the Polish uprising of 1863. An advocate of Russification and assimilation, he will join the Hovevei Zion movement after the pogroms of 1881. | **1875** |
| Samuel J. Tilden,* Democratic candidate for U.S. president, receives a majority of the popular votes over Rutherford B. Hayes,* Republican candidate. Disputes over fraudulent election practices and electoral votes cause a final decision to be made by Congress. In March 1877, Hayes* is declared president and William A. Wheeler,* vice president.

Colorado becomes the 38th state of the U.S.

Abdul Hamid II* becomes the Ottoman sultan. The Ottoman constitution is proclaimed. | The Ethical Culture movement, an American nontheistic humanist movement, is founded by Felix Adler (1851–1933). Adler is the son and chosen successor of Samuel Adler, the rabbi of Temple Emanu-El in New York. Among Adler's followers, Jews of German background are prominent in New York and Protestants of German background are prominent outside New York.

Herman Melville* (1819–1891), U.S. novelist and poet, known for his masterpiece *Moby-Dick*, writes a book-length poem, *Clarel*, based on a trip to Palestine and the Levant in 1856 and 1857. His portrayal of Jewish characters displayed sensitivity to their persecution and hardship in Palestine. | George Eliot's* (1819–1880) novel *Daniel Deronda* is published. The hero prepares to go to Palestine to restore a political existence to his people and make them a nation again. Eliot's* work has the practical effect of stimulating the Zionist renaissance.

The Belgian government officially recognizes the Consistoire, which means that Jewish religious officials, like those of other sects, are to be paid by the state.

Prussia adopts the Law of Secession, which abolishes compulsory membership in the community, required since 1847. Jews are permitted to disassociate for religious reasons and yet be recognized as Jews. The law was requested by some Orthodox leaders, including Samson Raphael Hirsch, and forms the legal basis for a separate | Jews in the Ottoman Empire are granted equal rights. There are four Jewish representatives in the parliament. | Moses Jacob Ezekiel (1844–1917), the first American sculptor of international reputation, executes a monument, *Religious Liberty*, which the B'nai B'rith commissioned for the Philadelphia Centennial Exposition of 1876.

Emile Berliner (1851–1929), U.S. inventor, begins refining Alexander Graham Bell's* newly invented telephone, and his innovations make the telephone practical for long-distance use.

Eugen Goldstein (1850–1931), German physicist, proves that the radiation in a vacuum tube produced when an electric current is forced through the tube starts at the cathode. He introduces the term *cathode ray* to describe the light emitted. His studies become highly significant for the study of radiation in general. | **1876** |

	A. General History	B. Jews in North and South America	C. Jews in Europe	D. Jews in the Middle East and Elsewhere	E. Jewish Culture
1876			Orthodox movement. The vast majority of Jews remain within the general congregational community, which is permitted by law to tax for its support.		Abraham Goldfaden (1840–1908) initiates the professional Yiddish theater after observing the Broder Singers. He conceives the idea of combining the songs with prose dialogues woven into a plot.
1877	The first great railway strike and other strikes throughout the U.S. result in great violence, loss of life, and property destruction. The Russo-Turkish War begins. The Russians invade Romania.	New Hampshire modifies its constitution to eliminate a religious test that had disqualified Jews from holding state public office. Joseph Seligman, eminent banker, is refused admission to the Grand Union Hotel, the leading hotel resort in Saratoga Springs, New York, by Henry Hilton,* business manager of the A.T. Stewart retail merchant interests. The event sparks a boycott by Jews of the A.T. Stewart Co. Bret Harte (1836–1902), who is one-fourth Jewish, writes the satirical poem *That Ebrew Jew!* to protest the anti-Jewish discrimination displayed against Joseph Seligman. Harte ridicules Henry Hilton's* vague distinction between acceptable "Hebrews" and unacceptable "Jews." Jews, Seventh-Day Adventists, and other Saturday Sabbath observers prevail upon Senator Horace Gates Jones* to introduce a bill in the U.S. Congress for the protection of seventh-day observers, but the bill dies.	A rabbinical seminary is founded in Budapest. Wilhelm Bacher (1850–1913), Hungarian Semitics scholar, is appointed to the faculty, where he teaches *midrash*, biblical exegesis, Hebrew poetry, and grammar. He will serve as head of the seminary from 1907 to his death.	The poverty of Jews in Palestine is confirmed by a survey that reports that almost one-half of the Jewish population in Jerusalem is supported by public funds, i.e., *halukkah*. Julius Blum (1843–1919), known as Blum Pasha, Austro-Hungarian banker who worked in Egypt, becomes Egyptian under secretary of finance and until 1890 will be instrumental in rehabilitating the country's economy. Samuel Isaac Joseph Schereschewsky (1831–1906) is appointed Episcopal bishop of China. Born in Lithuania, he emigrated to the U.S. in 1854, converted to Christianity in 1855, and went to China as a missionary in 1859. He translated the Bible into Mandarin Chinese.	James Joseph Sylvester (1814–1897), British mathematician, is appointed the first professor of mathematics at Johns Hopkins University. In 1878, he will found, edit, and contribute to the *American Journal of Mathematics*, the first U.S. research journal in mathematics. Karl Emil Franzos (1848–1904), Austrian novelist and journalist, writes *The Jews of Barnow*, a fictional account of Hasidic life in Czortkow, his hometown, on the Russo-Galician border. He is critical of traditional life in the shtetl. His popular stories aid in the dissemination of the negative image of unassimilated Jews of eastern Europe. Jacob Dineson (1856–1919) writes *The Beloved and the Pleasant or the Black Youth*, a sentimental Yiddish novel that sells over 200,000 copies. Abraham Goldfaden, Yiddish playwright, writes *Shmendrik*, a satirical comedy whose title hero becomes a synonym for a gullible, good-natured person. Leopold Ullstein (1826–1899), scion of a family of German newspaper publishers, buys his first newspaper, the *Neues Berliner*

Cartoon from Puck, *1877, lampooning the Grand Union Hotel affair in Saratoga Springs, New York. (Library of Congress)*

A. General History	B. Jews in North and South America	C. Jews in Europe	D. Jews in the Middle East and Elsewhere	E. Jewish Culture	
				Tageblatt. He and his five sons will develop their publishing business so that by 1927 they will employ 8,000 people, including 200 editors and a news agency with 250 correspondents throughout the world.	**1877**
The European powers convene the Congress of Berlin, with German Chancellor Bismarck* as the "honest broker." Serbia, Montenegro, and Romania become independent states. Austria occupies Bosnia and Herzegovina. Bulgaria becomes three territories. Britain occupies Cyprus. The Ottoman Empire is left with a few fragments of territory in Europe. The Russo-Turkish War ends with the Treaty of San Stefano. British Prime Minister Disraeli insists that the treaty be submitted to the great powers. At the Congress of Berlin, Russia is forced to renounce her domination of the Balkans obtained as a result of the treaty.	A survey by the Union of American Hebrew Congregations reports 270 congregations and 230,000 Jews in the U.S. during 1875–1878. This is the first effort to ascertain the size of the U.S. Jewish population. The Board of Delegates of American Israelites goes out of existence as it merges with the Union of American Hebrew Congregations when a number of eastern congregations join the union. Gustav Gottheil (1827–1903), U.S. Reform rabbi, writes *The Position of the Jews in America* in the *North American Review*. He notes that "when the Jew attempts to . . . mix freely with his neighbors, he is repelled and unceremoniously shown back to his own tribe; and if he keeps there, he is accused of hereditary and ancestral pride." *Gwendolyn: A Sequel to George Eliot's Daniel Deronda*, written anonymously and published in the U.S., is a virulently antisemitic novel responding to George Eliot's* sympathetic treatment of Jews.	Jewish communal leaders advise leaders of European powers at the Congress of Berlin of the plight of Jews in the Balkan countries and seek a guarantee of equal rights for all races and creeds in the peace treaty. The congress recognizes the independence of Romania, Serbia, and the territories of Bulgaria on the condition of granting civil rights to Jews. Romania refuses to meet its obligations for several more decades. A group of Jewish communal leaders submits a memorandum to the Congress of Berlin requesting that the Jews of Palestine be permitted to establish a constitutional Jewish monarchy. The memorandum is not discussed on the floor. Adolf Stoecker* (1835–1909), court chaplain to the German emperor, founds the Christian Social Workers' party, composed of artisans, small shopkeepers, and professionals who resent the economic mobility of Jews. He becomes the first to use antisemitism as a means of gaining a political following. The Great Synagogue on	Petah Tikvah, a Jewish farming community, is established in Palestine. Yehiel Michael Pines, Russian writer, settles in Palestine as director of the Sir Moses Montefiore Testimonial Fund. The fund grants aid for the construction of houses in Jerusalem and purchases land for Bilu settlements. Emin Pasha (1840–1892), Austrian traveler and explorer, born Eduard Schnitzer of Jewish parents but later baptized, is appointed governor of the Equatorial Province of Egypt by General Gordon.* A noted explorer of Central Africa, he will be murdered in 1892 by slave traders whose activities he opposed.	Sir Ernst Joseph Cassel (1852–1921), British banker, marries Annette Maxwell.* His granddaughter, Edwina (1901–1960), will marry Lord Louis Mountbatten,* the uncle of Queen Elizabeth II.* Cassel will leave Judaism and die a Roman Catholic. The collection of Jewish art assembled by Joseph Strauss (1827–1870), a noted French conductor of the mid-19th century, is exhibited as part of the Universal Exhibition of 1878 in Paris. This is the first public exhibition of Jewish art. The collection is purchased by the Rothschilds and donated to the Musée de Cluny, Paris. Maurycy Gottlieb (1856–1879), Polish painter, paints *Jews Praying on the Day of Atonement*, which includes a self-portrait. Although his career lasts only four or five years, as he dies at the age of 23, he is unusually prolific. He is known for his psychologically realistic portraits. Mendele Mokher Seforim, Russian Yiddish and Hebrew writer, writes *Travels of Benjamin the Third*. Mendele continues	**1878**

	A. General History	B. Jews in North and South America	C. Jews in Europe	D. Jews in the Middle East and Elsewhere	E. Jewish Culture
1878		Osman Bey, a pseudonym for Frank Millinger, a swindler of Jewish origin, writes an antisemitic tract, *The Conquest of the World by the Jews*, which is published in St. Louis.	Tlomacka Street in Warsaw is opened. Sponsored by culturally assimilated and wealthy Jews, the interior has 1,100 men's seats and includes a choir loft for an all-male choir and an organ, which is not played on the Sabbath.		the Haskalah tradition of satirizing folk beliefs in the person of a timid and vacillating Yiddish adventurer who wanders through the Pale of Settlement everywhere encountering superstition, backwardness, and uncleanliness.
1879	Germany and Austria–Hungary establish an alliance. It is created as a result of tension with Russia and remains in force until 1918. In New York, the dumbbell design wins a competition for a tenement design on a 25-by-100-foot lot. It becomes the model for future building, especially on the Lower East Side, until prohibited in 1901. Thomas A. Edison* invents the first practical electric incandescent lamp.	The Union of American Hebrew Congregations meets in an atmosphere of harmony between East and West in New York. It has 118 member congregations located in all parts of the U.S., a little more than half the total number of U.S. congregations, and they are fairly representative of organized Jewish life in the U.S. Henry Adams* (1838–1918), who became a historian of reputation and a well-known antisemite, writes of Jews while visiting Spain: "I have now seen enough of Jews and Moors to entertain more liberal views in regard to the Inquisition, and to feel that, though the ignorant may murmur, the Spaniards saw and pursued a noble aim." Austin Corbin,* president of the Long Island Rail Road and the Manhattan Beach Co., publicly proclaims his intent to bar Jews from a proposed fashionable hotel and beach in Brooklyn. In an interview in the *New York Herald*, Corbin states: "We must have a good place for society to patronize. I say we cannot do so and have Jews.	Heinrich von Treitschke* (1834–1896), German historian, justifies German antisemitism and attacks the refusal of Jews to assimilate into German society and culture and their desire to establish a "mongrel" German–Jewish culture. He coins the slogan "The Jews are our misfortune." Because of his scholarly reputation, antisemitism acquires the cloak of respectability. He also attacks Heinrich Graetz (1817–1891), the historian of the Jews, accusing him of hatred of Christianity and Jewish nationalism. William Marr* (1818–1904), German antisemitic agitator, coins the term *antisemite*, through the founding of the League of Anti-Semites, the first attempt to organize a popular political movement founded on antisemitism. Mahzike Hadas, an Orthodox political movement, is organized in Galicia. Led by Simon Schreiber (the son of Hatam Sofer) and Joshua Rokeah (1825–1894), the rabbi of Belz, its objective is to protect the religious character of the	A group of American Jews who emigrated to Jerusalem attempt to form an American *kollel* (i.e., an ethnic community living primarily from charitable contributions from their country of origin). The attempt fails, due to the opposition of the general organization, Vaad ha-Kelai, which was founded in 1866, and is in direct competition for American funds.	Philip Cowen (1853–1943), in cooperation with a group of prominent New York Jews, founds *The American Hebrew*, a weekly newspaper that covers Jewish events from throughout the world and maintains good literary standards. Cowen will edit and publish the weekly for 27 years. Max Liebermann's (1847–1935) painting *Jesus in the Temple* is shown in Munich. His portrayal of Jesus as a Jewish boy surrounded by Jewish-looking rabbis results in an antisemitic campaign against him. He will achieve great fame, becoming the president of the Berlin Academy of Art in 1920. The Nazis will oust him from the presidency in 1933 and will remove his paintings from all German museums. Eliezer Ben-Yehuda (1858–1922), Hebrew writer and lexicographer, writes *A Burning Question*. It propounds for the first time the idea of a national spiritual center in Palestine. A community must be established in Palestine, so that even those who remain in the Diaspora would know that they

A. General History	B. Jews in North and South America	C. Jews in Europe	D. Jews in the Middle East and Elsewhere	E. Jewish Culture	
	They are a detestable and vulgar people."	community from the assimilationist orientation of the rival Shomer Israel and Aguddat Ahim movements.		belong to a people living in its own land with its own language and culture.	1879
James A. Garfield* and Chester A. Arthur* are elected president and vice president of the U.S.

Benjamin Disraeli resigns as prime minister of Great Britain after his Tory party loses a general election. He is succeeded by William Gladstone.* | A tabulation of American Jewish business firms reports that 50% are engaged in clothing and allied occupations. Eighty percent of all retail and 90% of all wholesale clothing firms in New York are owned by Jews. Non-Jewish observers believe the clothing industry to be a Jewish monopoly.

The Hebrew Orphan Society, located on Amsterdam Avenue and 138th Street in New York, opens to house homeless Jewish children. It will remain in use until 1941.

Lew Wallace* (1827–1905) writes Ben-Hur, an extraordinarily popular religious novel that sells over 2 million copies. It is essentially a story of conversion by Jews, such as Ben-Hur, to Christianity. To Wallace,* Judaism is a preparation for Christianity. | Theodor Mommsen* (1817–1903), German historian and classical scholar, writes Another Word About Our Jewry, an essay in which he publicly attacks Heinrich von Treitschke's* antisemitic writings. Although he is supportive of Russian Jewry, Mommsen* urges Jews to assimilate.

Hermann Cohen, German philosopher, defends Judaism from the antisemitic attacks of the historian Heinrich von Treitschke.* Cohen professes German Jewry to be totally integrated into German society without any double loyalty but a community that takes its religion seriously.

The Société des Etudes Juives is founded in Paris by Isidore Loeb (1839–1892), Zadoc Kahn (1839–1905), and Israel Levi (1856–1939) to promote the study of Judaism and revive interest in French Jewry. The publication of its journal, Revue des Etudes Juives, begins. The journal appears until World War II. Resuming after the war, it will merge in 1961 with Historia Judaica.

Aguddat Ahim (The Brotherhood), an assimilationist movement, is organized in Galicia. It favors Polish cultural orientation. | | Joseph Breuer (1842–1925), Austrian physician, treats a patient suffering from hysteria by having her relate her fantasies, at times using hypnosis. He communicates his treatment to his friend Sigmund Freud (1856–1939), and Freud begins similar treatments for his patients.

Jacob Barth (1851–1914), one of the most important Semitic linguists of his time, is appointed associate professor of Semitic philology at the University of Berlin. He also teaches Hebrew, biblical exegesis, and Jewish philosophy at the Orthodox Rabbinical Seminary founded in Berlin by his father-in-law, Azriel Hildesheimer.

Moritz Benedict Cantor (1829–1920), professor of mathematics at Heidelberg, Germany, begins publication of his four-volume History of Mathematics. Cantor developed set theory in mathematics.

Eduard Strasburger, German botanist, is appointed professor at the University in Bonn. Under his leadership, Bonn becomes a world center in the emerging science of cell biology. In 1882, he will coin the terms cytoplasm, for the part of the cell within the membrane but outside the | 1880 |

	A. General History	B. Jews in North and South America	C. Jews in Europe	D. Jews in the Middle East and Elsewhere	E. Jewish Culture
1880			By 1884, as a result of increased antisemitism in Poland, many of its adherents become Zionist in outlook, and the organization dissolves. Prior to the pogroms of the 1880s, the famous Russian sculptor Mark Antokolski is attacked by the nationalist press. He is described as a Jew who has no right to portray non-Jewish religious figures, such as Jesus and John the Baptist. He leaves Russia for Paris. George Meredith's* (1828–1909) English novel *The Tragic Comedians* includes Alvan, a romantically attractive Jew.		nucleus, and *nucleoplasm*, for the material within the nucleus. Jacob Meijer de Haan (1852–1895), Dutch painter and businessman, begins living with Paul Gauguin* in Brittany and provides financial assistance to enable Gauguin* to pursue his career in painting. Abraham Goldfaden, Yiddish playwright, writes *The Fanatic, or The Two Kuni-Lemls*, a satiric comedy modeled after Moliere.* Eliezer Ben-Yehuda writes two articles in *Havazzelet*, advocating the use of Hebrew as the language of instruction in the Jewish schools of Palestine. Michael Heilprin, scholar and encyclopedist who emigrated to the U.S. from Hungary in 1856, publishes *Historical Poetry of the Ancient Hebrews Translated and Critically Examined*, an early example of serious Jewish scholarship in the U.S.
1881	U.S. President James A. Garfield* is assassinated and is succeeded by vice president Chester A. Arthur.* Czar Alexander II* is assassinated by revolutionaries of the Narodnaya Volya (People's Will) organization, which includes a young Jewish woman, Gesia Helfman. Tunisia becomes a French protectorate under the terms of the Treaty of Bardo.	The Russian Relief Fund in New York writes to the French Alliance Israelite Universelle asserting that it lacks sufficient resources to help the Russian immigrants. "It was understood that you were to send us only the strong and able-bodied. . . . The great bulk settle in this city and crowd the filthy tenements in a certain section on the East Side. . . . Many are sent over	On the eve of mass immigration of Jews to England from eastern Europe, English Jewry numbers 65,000; three-quarters are English born; two-thirds live in London. After the assassination of Czar Alexander II,* a wave of pogroms occurs throughout more than 100 Russian communities. They are inspired or	Eliezer Ben-Yehudah settles in Jerusalem and begins writing in favor of new agricultural settlements and revival of spoken Hebrew and against the *halukkah* system. Yemenite Jews begin to emigrate to Palestine. By 1914, about 3,000, or between 5 and 10% of Yemen's Jews, will have emigrated. They are spurred by a wave a messianic fervor as well as by	*The Tales of Hoffmann*, an opera by Jacques Offenbach (1819–1880), French composer, is completed after his death and achieves great popularity. Born in Cologne, he is the son of a poor synagogue cantor and music teacher. *Egyenloseg*, a weekly Jewish newspaper written in Hungarian, begins publication in Budapest. Representing the

Cartoon from Puck, *1881, by Frederick Burr Opper and Joseph Keppler, depicting Uncle Sam as a modern Moses, permitting the children of Israel to reach the promised land.* (Library of Congress)

A. General History	B. Jews in North and South America	C. Jews in Europe	D. Jews in the Middle East and Elsewhere	E. Jewish Culture	
	here purposely, merely to relieve the European communities."	condoned by the minister of the interior, Ignatiev.*	harsh and unstable conditions of Jewish life in Yemen.	non-Orthodox sector of Hungarian Jewry, it is assimilationist, championing religious equality for Jews and complete integration into Hungarian life. It is anti-Zionist. It will cease publication in 1938.	**1881**

A. General History

B. Jews in North and South America

here purposely, merely to relieve the European communities."

The Hebrew Emigrant Aid Society is established in New York to help the newly arriving Russian Jews. Although ambivalent about the wisdom of encouraging refugees, the society renders financial aid to Jews who arrive in 1881–1882 until they can find jobs. The society will disband in early 1883.

Herman Rosenthal (1843–1917), who arrived in the U.S. from Russia earlier in the year, establishes the first Am Olam colony in the U.S. at Sicily Island, Louisiana. It consists of 32 families from Russia. In the spring of 1882, they will leave the site as a result of a disastrous Mississippi River flood.

Nina Morais, of an established Philadelphia Sephardic family, writes an article, *On Jewish Ostracism in America*, in the *North American Review*. Her view is that antisemitic Christian teachings repeated in nursery rhymes, the public schools, combined with missionary exhortation, Jewish manners, and ignorance about Jews, result in overt social discrimination.

The government of Argentina appoints a special agent in Europe to attract Russian Jewish immigrants.

C. Jews in Europe

condoned by the minister of the interior, Ignatiev.*

Am Olam (the Eternal People), a Russian Jewish society, is formed in Odessa to encourage the settling of Jews on the land in the U.S. in the form of Socialist communes. Between 1881 and 1882 groups are also founded in Yelizavetgrad, Kiev, and Kremenchug. Several communes are established in the U.S. The movement will dissolve in 1890.

With the beginning of mass emigration of Russian Jews, organized Jewish communities in Germany, France, and England, anxious to help the victims of pogroms but afraid they might engulf their countries, create a network of organizations to facilitate their emigration to America.

Otto von Bismarck,* chancellor of the German Empire, ignores a petition of 250,000 signatures demanding the dismissal of Jews from all government positions and the halting of Jewish immigration.

Richard Wagner* German composer, in an essay, *Know Thyself*, applauds political antisemitism, deplores the granting of civil rights in 1871, and attacks Jews as the "demon causing mankind's downfall." Wagner's* political writings will greatly influence Adolf Hitler (1889–1945).*

D. Jews in the Middle East and Elsewhere

harsh and unstable conditions of Jewish life in Yemen.

E. Jewish Culture

non-Orthodox sector of Hungarian Jewry, it is assimilationist, championing religious equality for Jews and complete integration into Hungarian life. It is anti-Zionist. It will cease publication in 1938.

The publication of *Voskhod* (*Sunrise*), a Jewish periodical written in Russian, begins in St. Petersburg. Established by Adolph Landau (1842–1902), with government authorization, it appeals to the Jewish intelligentsia. It opposes Zionism, as well as total assimilation, hoping for emancipation. Publication will cease in 1906.

Isaac Jacob Reines (1839–1915), then a rabbi in the Vilna district, completes *Hotam Tokhnit* (*Seal of Perfection*), a major halakhic work that introduces new methodology in contrast to the *pilpul* system, and is based on a pure logical approach, which he utilizes in all his writings, and which impresses western European Jewish circles.

The Barnato brothers (Barney [1852–1897] and Henry), South African diamond mining magnates, form the Barnato Diamond Mining Co., which rivals the DeBeers Mining Co. of Cecil B. Rhodes.* The two companies will amalgamate in 1888.

Joseph Unger (1828–1913), Austrian jurist and statesman, is appointed president

	A. General History	B. Jews in North and South America	C. Jews in Europe	D. Jews in the Middle East and Elsewhere	E. Jewish Culture
1881			Karl Eugen Duehring* (1833–1921), German economist and philosopher, writes the first of a series of tracts on racial antisemitism. The "Jewish type" presents not only a cultural threat but, mainly, a biological danger to the German people, especially so when they convert to Christianity and gain entry to previously closed circles. Duehring* will have a leading influence on the development of German antisemitism.		of the Imperial Court. He holds this post until his death. He converted to Roman Catholicism.
1882	The U.S. Congress enacts the Chinese Exclusion Act, which halts for 10 years the immigration of Chinese laborers. It is the first of a series of acts based on racist concepts that will be added to U.S. immigration policies in the following decades. The first general federal immigration law is enacted. It does not change the basic policy of unlimited immigration and is designed to exclude only individual undesirables: lunatics, convicts, idiots, and persons likely to become public charges. Italy, Austria–Hungary, and Germany form the Triple Alliance. British forces suppress an Egyptian nationalist revolt and occupy Cairo.	The *Jewish Messenger* and *American Hebrew* news magazines editorialize against the Chinese Exclusion Act. Leopold Morse (1831–1892), of Massachusetts, one of the two Jews in Congress, adds his opposition to Chinese exclusion, calling it "dishonorable" and "un-American." Emma Lazarus (1849–1887), U.S. poet, writes an article in *Century Magazine* defending Judaism and the Russian Jew from an earlier article that placed the onus for Russian pogroms on the Jews themselves. Later in the year, she commences writing, in the *American Hebrew*, a series of 16 articles envisioning Palestine as a secure haven for the oppressed Russian Jews. She opposes emigration to the U.S., where society is "utterly at variance with their time-honored customs and most sacred beliefs."	In January, a group of young Russian Jews meets in the Kharkov home of Israel Belkind (1861–1929) and found the Bilu movement. Bilu, the Hebrew initials of "House of Jacob, come ye and let us go," is a return-to-Palestine movement. Later in the year, the first group of 14 arrives in Palestine and begins work at the Mikve Israel Agricultural school. The first non-U.S. B'nai B'rith lodge is founded in Germany. Nathan Birnbaum (1864–1937), Ruben Bierer (1835–1931), and Moritz Schnirer (1861–1941) found Kadimah (Eastward, or Forward), the first Jewish nationalist students' association, at Vienna University, to encourage settlement in Palestine. As Passover draws near, a blood libel accusation is made against 15 Jews in Tiszaeszlar, a small Hungarian village,	Rishon Le-Zion, the first settlement in Palestine established by pioneers from outside the country, is founded by 10 Russian Jews. In the first year of its creation, the population grows to 100 when Bilu settlers join the village after receiving agricultural training at Mikve Israel. Nissim Behar (1848–1931) becomes headmaster at the newly founded Alliance Israelite Universelle School in Jerusalem. Its modern methods will be applied in schools throughout Palestine.	The first professional performance of a Yiddish play in New York, *The Witch*, written by Abraham Goldfaden, includes Boris Thomashefsky (1868–1939) in the cast. Thomashefsky arrived in New York from the Ukraine in 1881. The Slobodka Yeshiva, an advanced school for young adults, is founded in Lithuania by Rabbi Nathan Zevi Finkel (1849–1927), a leader of the Musar movement. In 1897, the yeshiva will split over a controversy. Those loyal to Rabbi Finkel will join the renamed Yeshiva Keneset Israel, while others will organize Keneset Bet Yizhak. By 1924, Rabbi Finkel's school will open a branch in Hebron, Palestine. Rabbi Finkel will join the Hebron school in 1925. Leon Pinsker (1821–1891), a Russian physician who observed the participation of Russian liberal intellectuals in the

1882

B. Jews in North and South America

Moritz Loth, president of the Union of American Hebrew Congregations, proposes that Jewish refugees from Russia be led into agricultural pursuits. The executive board rejects the proposal.

Russian Jewish Am Olam agricultural colonies at New Odessa, Oregon; Cremieux, South Dakota; and Cotopaxi, Colorado, receive financial assistance from the French Alliance Israelite Universelle but will all fail within a few years.

The first Hovevei Zion (Lovers of Zion) group is organized in New York.

Abraham Cahan (1860–1951) leaves Russia and arrives in New York. He will become a leading journalist, Socialist leader, and novelist.

C. Jews in Europe

when a 14-year-old Christian girl disappears. They will be acquitted, but the incident causes a widespread outburst of antisemitism in Hungary.

The Moorish Revival synagogue of Florence is opened. David Levy willed his entire estate for the building of a temple worthy of the city.

An assembly of 40 Russian Jewish leaders in St. Petersburg adopts a resolution rejecting "completely the thought of organizing emigration" as it was incompatible with "the historic rights of the Jews in their present fatherland."

Czar Alexander III* (1881–1894) promulgates the May Laws, prohibiting Jews from settling outside towns and hamlets, from conducting business on Sundays and Christian holidays, and introducing a *numerus clausus* in Russian schools. The Jewish flight from Russia is intensified.

Algernon Charles Swinburne* (1837–1909), English poet, expresses sympathy for victims of the Russian czar in his poem "On the Russian Persecution of the Jews."

E. Jewish Culture

pogroms of Odessa, writes *Auto-Emancipation*, in which he analyzes the psychological and social roots of antisemitism and concludes that assimilation is impossible. The Jews would have to emancipate themselves in their own land. He writes in German in the hope of securing the support of Western Jews.

> *First "Aliyah" to Palestine, 1882–1904*
> Number: 25,000
> Origin: Individuals and small groups of Eastern Europeans, inspired by the Hibbat Zion and Bilu movements, who established the early moshavot.

1883

A. General History

The Brooklyn Bridge opens, linking the island of Manhattan with Brooklyn and the rest of Long Island. Designed by John Roebling,* it is the longest suspension bridge in the world.

B. Jews in North and South America

The U.S. House of Representatives adopts a resolution urging the Garfield administration to use its influence with Russia to stop anti-Jewish discrimination and persecution.

Century Magazine publishes Emma

C. Jews in Europe

Ernest Renan* (1823–1892), French Orientalist and philosopher, writes an essay, *Judaism: Race or Religion?* in which he popularizes the myth that Aryans and Semites form distinct, antithetical races. He is the first to question the ethnic purity of

D. Jews in the Middle East and Elsewhere

The Keneset Eliyahu synagogue is erected in Bombay, India.

A 4th-century synagogue with a beautiful mosaic floor is discovered at Hamman-Lif, near Carthage, North Africa.

E. Jewish Culture

Emma Lazarus writes "The New Colossus," a sonnet to be auctioned as one of many literary contributions by prominent American authors in the effort to raise funds for the pedestal of New York's Statue of Liberty. Forgotten for 20 years, the

A. General History	B. Jews in North and South America	C. Jews in Europe	D. Jews in the Middle East and Elsewhere	E. Jewish Culture
1883	Lazarus' article *The Jewish Problem*, in which she calls for the establishment of an independent Jewish nationality in Palestine. The first graduation class dinner of the Hebrew Union College causes a religious uproar because nonkosher food is served. Rabbi Isaac Mayer Wise, the college's president, who had arranged the banquet, had previously clashed with traditionalists with his disparagement of what he called "kitchen Judaism." The incident encourages the withdrawal from the Union of American Hebrew Congregations of some of the traditionalists and increases the reluctance of others to cooperate with Wise. Isaac Mayer Wise delivers a series of Friday evening lectures in Cincinnati entitled "Judaism and Christianity, Their Agreements and Disagreements." He hails the freedom that permits a Jewish lecturer to compare the two faiths publicly and dispassionately.	eastern European Jews because of their alleged Khazar antecedents. August Rohling,* professor of Catholic theology at Prague University, offers to testify on oath at the Tiszaeszlar blood libel trial that Jews practice ritual murder. He is challenged in the press by Rabbi Joseph Samuel Bloch, who accuses him of perjury. Rohling* sues Bloch for libel but will withdraw his charges during the trial's last stages, where Protestant theologians Franz Delitzsch* and Hermann L. Strack* discredit Rohling.* Esra, an association for the support of Jewish farmers in Palestine and Syria, is founded in Berlin. Its aim is the support of small-scale settlement, i.e., infiltration, without prior international agreement. One of its founders is Willi Bambus (1863–1904), who will later oppose Theodor Herzl's (1860–1904) political Zionism. Moses Leib Lilienblum, Hebrew writer, political journalist, and leader of the Hibbat Zion movement, and Leon Pinsker found the Zerubbabel Zionist Society in Odessa, which becomes the center for contacts with other Zionist groups. The pogroms of 1881 convinced Lilienblum that there was no remedy for antisemitism in the Diaspora and that settlement in Palestine was the only solution.		poem will be rediscovered and inscribed at the statue's base. Joseph Pulitzer* (1847–1911), son of a Jewish father and Roman Catholic mother and U.S. newspaper editor and publisher, buys the *New York World* newspaper. His mass-appeal journalism, including crime stories, comic strips, and strong editorials, results in greatly increased circulation. Pulitzer* bought his first newspaper, the *St. Louis Dispatch*, in 1878 and merged it with the *Post*. By 1881, the *Post–Dispatch* was very profitable. Max Nordau (1849–1923), philosopher and physician, writes *The Conventional Lies of Our Civilization*, an attack on the hypocrisy and intellectual dishonesty of society's institutions. At the time, Nordau is an assimilated intellectual. The Dreyfus Affair will result in his return to Judaism and Zionism. Sholom Aleichem (Shalom Rabinovitz, 1859–1916), Yiddish writer, publishes his first Yiddish story, *Two Stones*, a sentimental romance, in the St. Petersburg Yiddish weekly *Dos Yidishe Folksblat*. Isaac Ruelf (1831–1902), German-born rabbi of Memel, writes *Aruhat Bat Ami*, an essay advocating the establishment of a Jewish state in Palestine with Hebrew as its

A. General History	B. Jews in North and South America	C. Jews in Europe	D. Jews in the Middle East and Elsewhere	E. Jewish Culture	
				language as the way of solving the Jewish problem in Europe. He brought the plight of Russian Jewry to the attention of the West and organized many relief projects on their behalf. He will become one of the few Western rabbis to strongly oppose anti-Zionist rabbis.	**1883**
Grover Cleveland* and Thomas A. Hendricks* are elected president and vice president of the U.S.	Anna Dawes,* daughter of a U.S. senator from Massachusetts, writes an essay, *The Modern Jew*, in which she asserts that Jews are unassimilable in Western society. The remedy lies in the colonization of Jews outside the modern national states.	Joseph Samuel Bloch is elected to the Austrian Parliament from a predominantly Galician Jewish constituency and gains a reputation as a defender of Jewish rights. A pogrom occurs in the Kanavino quarter of Nizhni Novgorod (now Gorki). This pogrom marks the end of the first wave of pogroms in Russia. The first conference of Hovevei Zion (Lovers of Zion) groups is held in Kattowitz, a German Silesian city. Led by Leon Pinsker, 32 delegates (22 from Russia and the rest from Germany, England, France and Romania) attend and agree to finance Jewish settlement in Palestine. Pinsker calls for Jews to return to agriculture in Palestine but does not stress the goal of a national renaissance and political independence, as he hopes to gain support of western European Jews.	Gederah, a moshav on the coastal plain of Palestine, is founded by members of the Bilu movement from Russia. Yehiel Michael Pines, director of the Sir Moses Montefiore Testimonial Fund, purchased the land for them. The Magen David synagogue is erected in Calcutta, India. The Beth Israel synagogue is founded in Nagasaki, Japan, under the initiative of Elias Sassoon.	Leopold Damrosch (1832–1885), who left Germany to settle in New York in 1871, directs the first German opera season at the Metropolitan Opera House. Naphtali Herz Imber (1856–1909), Hebrew poet, writes "Ha-Tikvah" ("The Hope"), which appears in his first volume of poems, and is dated "Jerusalem 1884." It becomes the national anthem of the Jews and of the state of Israel after its founding. Solomon Reineman of Galicia, who had arrived in Rangoon, Burma, in 1851 as a British army supplier, writes *Solomon's Travels*, which is the first Hebrew account of Burma and its towns.	**1884**

The first conference of the Hovevei Zion at Kattowitz, November 1884. Leon Pinsker (front row, fifth from left), Rabbi Samuel Mohilever (front row, fourth from left).

A. General History	B. Jews in North and South America	C. Jews in Europe	D. Jews in the Middle East and Elsewhere	E. Jewish Culture	
Trade and navigation on the Congo and Niger river basins and the intention of the great powers to suppress slavery are discussed at the Berlin Conference on Africa, attended by	Beth Hamedrash Hagodol (Great House of Study), founded in New York in 1852 as the first Russian Orthodox synagogue in the U.S., acquires and remodels the	Otto von Bismarck,* chancellor of the German Empire, supports the expulsion from Germany of 30,000 Russian and Austrian citizens, one-third of whom are Jews.		Kasriel Zvi Sarasohn (1835–1905), who arrived in New York from Russia in 1871, founds the *Yiddisches Tageblatt*, the first Yiddish daily newspaper in the world, in New York.	**1885**

	A. General History	B. Jews in North and South America	C. Jews in Europe	D. Jews in the Middle East and Elsewhere	E. Jewish Culture
1885	world powers. The conference, in effect, stimulates the partition of Africa by the great powers by stating that recognition of territorial claims would not be recognized unless the claimed-for region is effectively occupied by the great power.	Norfolk Street Baptist church. Rabbi Kaufmann Kohler (1843–1926) assembles 19 rabbis of the Union of American Hebrew Congregations in Pittsburgh. Chaired by Rabbi Isaac Mayer Wise, but dominated by Kohler, they adopt a radical statement of principles of Judaism, called the Pittsburgh Platform. It asserts that the Jews are not a nation, but a religious community; dismisses a return to Zion; and rejects regulations of diet, purity, and dress. Rabbi Alexander Kohut (1842–1894), of New York's Ahavath Chesed congregation, criticizes the Reform Judaism he observes in the U.S. "A reform which seeks to progress without the Mosaic rabbinical tradition . . . is a skeleton of Judaism without . . . spirit and heart." President Grover Cleveland* appoints Anthony M. Keiley* ambassador to the Austro-Hungarian Empire. Keiley's marriage to a Jewish woman causes Vienna to reject the nomination. Henry Harland* (1861–1905), writing under the Jewish-sounding pseudonym Sidney Luska, writes *As It Was Written: A Jewish Musician's Story*, the first novel to depict the life of New York's German Jews for the general public. It sells 50,000 copies.	Louise Lady Rothschild establishes the West Central Friday Night Club in London to meet the social, educational, and recreational needs of eastern European Jewish immigrant girls. Constance Rothschild Battersea founds in London the Jewish Ladies Society for Preventive and Rescue Work, later renamed the Jewish Association for the Protection of Girls and Women. It is the first Jewish organization to publicly acknowledge the existence of Jewish prostitutes and the trafficking in unsuspecting eastern European Jewish girls. Battersea opens rescue homes and an industrial training school to care for and educate these girls. Jews are drafted into the Bulgarian army for the first time during the war between Serbia and Bulgaria.		It attains wide readership and will be published until 1928 when it will merge with the *Morning Journal*. Oscar S. Straus (1850–1926), a lawyer, writes *The Origin of the Republican Form of Government in the United States of America*, in which he develops the thesis that the Hebrew commonwealth depicted in the Bible was the model for the political institutions of the early American colonies and for the first state and national constitutions. Nathan Birnbaum founds and edits the first Jewish nationalist journal in German, *Self-Emancipation*, where he will introduce the word *Zionism* in its columns (1890). It attempts to bridge the ideological gap between eastern and western European Jewries on Zionist issues. It will be published intermittently until 1895. Edmund Menahem Eisler (1850–1942), Slovakian author who writes in German, anonymously publishes *Ein Zukunftsbild* (*A Sign of the Future*), a novel that envisions the exodus of Jews from Europe to a Zionist Utopia, where Hebrew is the national language. The novel falls into obscurity until rediscovered in 1954.

A. General History	B. Jews in North and South America	C. Jews in Europe	D. Jews in the Middle East and Elsewhere	E. Jewish Culture	
	The Rise of Silas Lapham, written by William Dean Howells* (1837–1920), is first serialized in *Century Magazine*. The Laphams discuss selling their Boston home and moving to a better neighborhood because the Jews "have gotten in." After criticism from Jews, Howells* drops the passage from the book version.				**1885**
The American Federation of Labor is organized by Samuel Gompers (1850–1924) and Adolph Strasser (1844–1939). Strasser is a leader of the International Cigar Makers Union, which is largely Jewish. The first settlement house in the U.S., the Neighborhood Guild, is founded on New York's Lower East Side by Dr. Stanton Coit.* The Statue of Liberty is dedicated in New York Harbor. General Georges Boulanger* is appointed French minister of war. He becomes the symbol of the desire for revenge against Germany.	The Jewish Theological Seminary of America is founded in New York, with Rev. Sabato Morais as its head. Founded by moderate traditionalists of the historical school, including Alexander Kohut and H. Pereira Mendes (1852–1937), its aim is to train rabbis "in sympathy with the spirit of conservative Judaism." The Pittsburgh Platform and the retreat from tradition of the Union of American Hebrew Congregations and the Hebrew Union College impel the establishment of the seminary. Etz Chaim, the first yeshiva for talmudic studies in the U.S., is founded in New York. The first synagogue to be erected on New York's Lower East Side by eastern European Jews, the Eldridge Street synagogue, Khal Adath Jeshurun with Anshe Lubz, opens. The congregation was founded in 1856. Designed by the architectural firm of Christian Brothers, it is a late version of the Moorish Revival style.	Edouard Drumont* (1844–1917), French antisemite, writes *La France Juive*, a two-volume study describing France as being controlled by Jews in the political, cultural, social, and economic spheres. It is said to be the most widely read book in France. *La Croix*, a French Catholic daily newspaper founded by the Assumptionists in 1883, bestows praise on Edouard Drumont's* antisemitic study, *La France Juive*. By 1890 it will have a daily circulation of 140,000 and frequently attack Jews and Judaism.		*The Menorah*, a monthly magazine, is founded by the B'nai B'rith. It is edited by Benjamin F. Peixotto. It will later be called the *National Jewish Monthly*. Lyman Bloomingdale (1841–1905) and his brother, Joseph (1842–1904), open Bloomingdale Brothers Department Store on its present site in midtown Manhattan. *Ha-Yom* (*The Day*), the first Hebrew daily newspaper, begins publication in St. Petersburg. It will last for only 25 months but have great influence on the Hebrew press. It is edited in the style of a European daily newspaper in clear and simple Hebrew. Benjamin Szold (1829–1902), U.S. rabbi and scholar, publishes a commentary on the biblical Book of Job.	**1886**

A. General History	B. Jews in North and South America	C. Jews in Europe	D. Jews in the Middle East and Elsewhere	E. Jewish Culture
1887 Germany enters into the bilateral Reinsurance Treaty with Russia. Under the pseudonym Doktoro Esperanto, Ludwik Lazar Zamenhof (1859–1917), Polish physician and philologist, publishes *International Language*, an outline of a new language based on the principal European languages but with a simple and regular grammar and with basic word formation rules from which an extended vocabulary can be derived from a small number of basic words. The founder of the Esperanto language remains close to Judaism and is an early member of the Hovevei Zion.	Moses Weinberger (1854–1940), who arrived in New York in 1880 from Hungary as a newly ordained Orthodox rabbi, writes *Jews and Judaism in New York*. Unable to obtain a pulpit, he was involved in various businesses, and this account, written in Hebrew, describes a city where religious observance is minimal and that lacks Jewish education. To Weinberger, New York is a world turned upside down, "where people walk on their heads," and he advises potential observant immigrants to stay home. Six model tenement buildings on Cherry Street, on New York's Lower East Side, are erected to house eastern European Jews by the Tenement House Building Co., formed at the urging of Dr. Felix Adler. Adler founded the Society for Ethical Culture in 1876. The Hebrew Actors Union is established to redress the problem that most of the actors on the Yiddish stage are paid subsistence wages. The union is the first actors' union in the U.S.	The second Hovevei Zion conference is held at Druskieniki. Rabbi Samuel Mohilewer (1824–1898) wants to transform it into a religious movement led by rabbis but is opposed by secular delegates. A compromise results in Leon Pinsker remaining the head of the organization, with a board including three rabbis chosen to ensure that settlement in Palestine is carried out in a traditional Jewish spirit. Russia adopts restrictive quotas on Jewish enrollment in general schools and universities.	Eliezer Ben-Yehuda and David Yellin (1864–1941) publish the first children's book in Palestine, *Mikra Le-Yaldei Benei Yisrael*. A Jewish necropolis is discovered at Tell Al-Yahudiyya, Egypt. It includes 80 Jewish tombstones.	*Der Judischer Courier*, a Yiddish daily newspaper, is established in Chicago. Albert Abraham Michelson (1852–1931), U.S. physicist, and Edward Morley* determine that light travels with the same velocity in any direction under any condition. The experiment proves a starting point for the theoretical developments of 20th-century physics. Cyrus Adler (1863–1940), U.S. scholar and communal leader, is awarded the first Ph.D. degree in Semitics from Johns Hopkins University. He will become librarian of the Smithsonian Institution in 1892. Emile Berliner, U.S. inventor, improves Thomas A. Edison's* phonograph by introducing a flat disk instead of a wax cylinder. His patent will be acquired by the Victor Talking Machine Co. Dankmar Adler (1844–1900) and his architect partner, Louis Sullivan* (1856–1924), introduce a new concept in office architecture, the steel-framed skyscraper. Isidor (1845–1912) and Nathan (1848–1931) Straus, who became partners with R. H. Macy* in 1874, become sole owners of the department store. They develop it into the world's largest.

A. General History	B. Jews in North and South America	C. Jews in Europe	D. Jews in the Middle East and Elsewhere	E. Jewish Culture	
				An Anglo-Jewish Historical Exhibition is held in London, featuring Anglo-Jewish history and Jewish ritual art. The exhibition includes the Joseph Strauss (1827–1870) collection of ritual art shown in Paris in 1878.	**1887**
Benjamin Harrison* is elected president of the U.S., defeating President Grover Cleveland* by 233–168 electoral votes. However, Cleveland* receives a popular vote of 5,540,050 to Harrison's 5,444,337. German Emperor William I* dies. He is succeeded by his son Frederick III,* who dies. In June, his son William II,* "the Kaiser," succeeds. All major European powers attend a convention at Constantinople and declare the Suez Canal neutral and open to all merchant and naval vessels during peace and war.	Secretary of State Bayard* instructs the U.S. minister to Turkey, Oscar S. Straus, to protest limitations on U.S. Jewish citizens' rights to take up residence or engage in commerce in Jerusalem. The United Hebrew Trades is organized in the U.S. under the leadership of Bernard Weinstein, Jacob Magidoff, Morris Hillquit, and Henry Miller, with the direct assistance of Samuel Gompers. It is one of a number of "national" foreign-language labor federations formed in the United States during the second half of the 19th century. Rabbi Jacob Joseph (1848–1902), communal preacher and religious judge in Vilna, accepts the call of an association of 16 Orthodox congregations in New York to become their chief rabbi. Initially well received in the community, he becomes embroiled in the effort to supervise the *kashrut* of meat and the ensuing widespread opposition to the imposition of a meat tax. In 1895, kosher butchers will defy his authority, and he will be left in financial distress and hampered by serious illness.	Baron Maurice de Hirsch (1831–1896), German financier, establishes the Baron de Hirsch Foundation to foster educational work among the Jews in Galicia and Bukovina.	The first Palestinian B'nai B'rith lodge is founded in Jerusalem.	The Jewish Publication Society of America is founded for the purpose of publication in English of books of Jewish content. The society's first book, Lady Katie Magnus' *Outline of Jewish History*, will be published in 1890. Isaac Markens, a New York newspaperman, writes *The Hebrews in America*, the first history by a Jew of the Jews in America.  *Title page of the first volume of Sholom Aleichem's Yiddish annual,* Di Yidishe Folksbibliotek. Sholom Aleichem founds *Di Yidishe Folksbibliotek* (*The Popular Jewish Library*). It is a turning point in modern Yiddish literature. The first volume includes works by Mendele Mokher Seforim and Isaac Leib Peretz. A second volume will appear in 1890. As his financial fortunes take a turn for the worse, no further volumes will be published. Amy Levy (1861–1889), British novelist and poet, writes *Reuben Sachs: a Sketch*, a novel of the materialistic values of two wealthy London Jewish families. It is believed that the novel influenced the writings of Israel Zangwill (1864–1926). Levy was the first Jewish woman to go up to Newnham College, Cambridge.	**1888**

	A. General History	B. Jews in North and South America	C. Jews in Europe	D. Jews in the Middle East and Elsewhere	E. Jewish Culture
1888		Henrietta Szold (1860–1945) and a group of friends from the Baltimore Hebrew Literary Society organize a night school for Russian immigrants. It will develop into a model program of Americanization of immigrants. Annie Nathan Meyer (1867–1951), graduate of Columbia University's Collegiate Course for Women, founds Barnard College in New York. Meyer's efforts open the door to a college education for many Jewish women. An antisemitic novel, *The Original Mr. Jacobs*, written by Telemachus Thomas Timayenis,* is published in New York.			
1889	North Dakota, South Dakota, Montana, and Washington become the 39th, 40th, 41st, and 42nd states of the U.S.	The Central Conference of American Rabbis is organized. Isaac Mayer Wise becomes president of this organization of Reform rabbis and holds office until his death in 1900. A Hebrew Institute is founded on New York's Lower East Side by a group of German Jews that includes Jacob Schiff (1847–1920) and Isidor Straus to implement an Americanization program for the eastern European immigrants. In 1891 it will be housed in an impressive building and will be renamed the Educational Alliance in 1893. Moisesville, the first Jewish agricultural settlement in Argentina, is established in the	Russian and Galician Jewish students studying in Berlin found the Russian–Jewish Scientific Society. They support Zionism and engage in debate with the majority of Russian Jewish students who support socialism and cosmopolitanism. Mordecai Eliasberg (1817–1889), Latvian rabbi and an early Hovevei Zion member, opposes ultra-Orthodox rabbis who demand cessation of agricultural work in Palestine during the sabbatical year and urges farmers not to abide by their injunctions. Benei Moshe, a small, exclusive club, is founded in Odessa by Ahad ha-Am as a result of dissatisfaction with the Zionist	Ahad ha-Am (Asher Ginsberg, 1856–1927), Hebrew essayist and leader of the Hibbat Zion movement, publishes his first important essay, *The Wrong Way*, in which he attributes the difficulties of Jewish settlement in Palestine to the weakness of the national consciousness among Jews. Alfred Beit (1853–1906), South African financier, is cofounder with Cecil Rhodes* of the British South Africa Co., which administers the territory that will become known as Rhodesia and later Zimbabwe.	The *Jewish Quarterly Review* is founded, financed and coedited by Claude Montefiore (1858–1938), English theologian and leader of radical liberal Judaism in England. Coedited with Israel Abrahams (1858–1924), it is the principal scholarly Jewish journal in English during its publication in England until 1908. In 1910, a new series of the *Quarterly* will begin publication in the U.S. at Dropsie College, under the editorship of Cyrus Adler and Solomon Schechter. Jozef Israels (1824–1911), founder and leading member of the Hague school of 19th-century Dutch painting, paints *A Son of the Ancient Race*, a compassionate depiction of a forlorn

A. General History	B. Jews in North and South America	C. Jews in Europe	D. Jews in the Middle East and Elsewhere	E. Jewish Culture	
	Santa Fe Province by 136 Russian Jewish families, numbering 800 persons.	leadership for their neglect of education as a precursor to a Palestinian settlement. The group will last for eight years, found Hebrew schools in Jaffa and in the Diaspora, and establish the Ahiasaph Publishing House in Warsaw.		second-hand clothes dealer in Amsterdam's Jewish quarter. He is best known for his paintings of Dutch peasants and fishermen in the Netherlands coast. Only four of his paintings relate to Judaism.	**1889**

A. General History	B. Jews in North and South America	C. Jews in Europe	D. Jews in the Middle East and Elsewhere	E. Jewish Culture	
Idaho and Wyoming become the 43d and 44th states of the U.S.

Ellis Island in New York Harbor becomes the port of entry for immigrants, replacing Castle Garden at the tip of Manhattan, which had been the major entry station for immigrants since 1855.

Bismarck* is dismissed as chancellor of Germany by Emperor William II,* who is determined to rule the empire. | Jacob A. Riis* (1849–1914) writes *How the Other Half Lives*, an exposé of ghetto conditions in New York, which includes a description of the overcrowding in the Jewish quarter of the Lower East Side where "nowhere in the world are so many people crowded together in a square mile as here."

Beth Israel Hospital, the first Jewish hospital on New York's Lower East Side, is organized. It provides services for Orthodox Jews, such as kosher food and places for eastern European physicians, which are not available at Mt. Sinai Hospital.

"Mother" Frederika Mandelbaum of New York's Lower East Side becomes one of the nation's leading dealers in stolen goods. When indicted, she flees to Canada, where she spends the rest of her life.

The cloakmakers in New York stage their first great strike. Joseph Barondess (1867–1928) is one of the leaders.

Twenty-one clothing manufacturers in Rochester, New York, organize a Clothing Exchange, | Charles Smith,* U.S. minister to Russia, denies reports of oppression of Jews.

Ready for the Sabbath Eve in a coal cellar. Photograph by Jacob A. Riis.

The Odessa Committee, the organizational headquarters of the Hibbat Zion movement, is founded with the permission of the Russian authorities. The full name is the Society for the Support of Jewish Farmers and Artisans in Syria and Palestine. Leon Pinsker is the first chairman. Its aim is to assist Jews who settle in Palestine to work productively, especially in agriculture. It will exist until 1919.

During the 1890s, sugar refining plants in the Ukraine owned by Israel Brodski (1823–1888) and his sons produce approximately one-quarter of the sugar refined in Russia. | Haderah, a village on the coastal plain in Palestine, is founded by members of Hovevei Zion from Vilna, Kovno, and Riga.

The Hebrew Language Committee is founded in Palestine by Eliezer Ben-Yehuda, pioneer of modern Hebrew, David Yellin, and others. Ben-Yehuda will preside until his death. At its beginning, the committee establishes Hebrew terms needed for daily use and creates a uniform pronunciation for Hebrew speech. | Cyrus Adler, curator of the department of antiquities at the Smithsonian Institution, is appointed special commissioner of the proposed Columbian Exposition by President Benjamin Harrison.* He travels for 15 months throughout the Near East, visiting Turkey, Egypt, Algeria, Tunisia, Morocco, and Syria (including Palestine), to secure exhibits and their participation in the exhibition.

Simeon Singer (1848–1906), English rabbi, edits and translates the daily *siddur* into English. Known as Singer's Prayer Book, it will go through 27 editions and over 500,000 copies and enjoy great success both in England and the U.S.

Jozsef Kiss (1843–1921), Hungarian poet, founds *A Het* (*The Week*), a leading literary journal, which reflects new trends in the literature of western Europe. The first professing Jew to receive fame as a Hungarian writer, his poems reflect a love of Jewry and are about the deterioration of traditional Jewish family life, | **1890** |

	A. General History	B. Jews in North and South America	C. Jews in Europe	D. Jews in the Middle East and Elsewhere	E. Jewish Culture
1890		with Henry Michaels as president. In 1891, they will stage a lockout that undermines the strength of organized labor in the city. The Grandview House opens. It is the earliest boarding house in the Catskill Mountains of New York State to cater to a Jewish clientele. In Spokane, Washington, Ray Frank becomes the first American woman to deliver a *Kol Nidrei* sermon. Though Frank takes courses at the Hebrew Union College, she never graduates. She rejects several invitations to serve as rabbi.	The Brodskis employ thousands of Jewish workers. Their property will be confiscated after the Russian Revolution in 1917.		antisemitism, social change, and the difficulties of economic life in the city. José Maria Miro,* Argentinian novelist, writes *La Bolsa*, a novel that contains several antisemitic passages adapted from Edouard Drumont's* *La France Juive*. The novel is published by the influential newspaper *La Nación* and will be reprinted many times.
1891	A New Orleans mob lynches 11 Italian immigrants after they are acquitted on the charge of murdering the chief of police. A year later the U.S. will pay an indemnity to their families. S. R. Driver* (1846–1914), professor of Hebrew at Oxford, writes *An Introduction to the Literature of the Old Testament*. His *Introduction* adopts the source critical approach of Wellhausen* but emphasizes exegesis more than history.	Congress enacts an immigration law, including provisions for rejection of immigrants who are paupers or likely to become public charges. Charles Foster,* secretary of the treasury, states that immigrants aided by private organizations are to be considered "assisted immigrants" and, as such, refused admission. B'nai B'rith and other Jewish organizations assert that Jewish immigrants will not become members of a dependent class. They "are instantly taken charge of by their brethren. . . . This is done without asking for any subvention from National or State revenues." Joseph Barondess, labor organizer, is convicted of extortion as a result of charges brought by the cloak	Hermann Adler (1839–1911) is elected chief rabbi of the British Empire, succeeding his father, Nathan Marcus Adler. He is generally credited with securing recognition of the chief rabbi being the main representative of English Jewry. He does not gain the confidence of the Russian Jews who arrive in great numbers during his tenure, and he opposes political Zionism, calling it an "egregious blunder." Baron Maurice de Hirsch, German financier, establishes the Jewish Colonization Association (ICA) to foster Jewish emigration from Russia to Argentina for agricultural resettlement. The ICA is formed after the Russian government refused his offer of $10 million to establish a	Ahad ha-Am, Russian Hebrew essayist and Zionist who develops the Hebrew essay into a fine literary form, on return from his first visit to Palestine writes *The Truth from Palestine*. He criticizes the cultural and economic deficiencies of the first Jewish settlements in Palestine and draws attention to the need to recognize and respect the large Arab population.	The Jewish Publication Society of America begins publication of an abridged version of Heinrich Graetz's *History of the Jews*. It will be completed in 1898 with the publication of the sixth volume. Jacob Gordin (1853–1909), who arrives in the U.S. from Russia this year, writes a Yiddish play, *Siberia*. The play tells of the ordeal of a Russian Jew who in his youth had been sentenced to Siberia, later escapes and assumes a new identity, becomes wealthy, and is later betrayed to the police by a business rival. It is commissioned by Jacob P. Adler (1855–1926), who performs the leading role. Alexander Harkavy (1863–1939), Yiddish lexicographer who left Russia for the

1891

B. Jews in North and South America

manufacturers. Sentenced to a 21-month term, he is pardoned by New York's Governor Sulzer,* who acted upon a petition signed by 15,000 persons.

The Baron de Hirsch Fund is incorporated in New York State to administer the proceeds of a $2.4 million endowment established by Baron Maurice de Hirsch, the German financier. The fund establishes farm colonies and vocational schools to assist eastern European Jewish immigrants.

The Educational Alliance Art School is established on New York's Lower East Side under the leadership of Henry McBride,* art critic of the *New York Sun*. Among the first teachers and pupils are Jacob Epstein and Jo Davidson. The school will be suspended in 1905 because of financial difficulties.

The Jewish Prisoners Association is founded in New York by the Jewish Ministers Association to minister to the needs of Jewish prison inmates and to combat missionary efforts.

Beth El synagogue, on 5th Avenue and 76th Street in New York, is opened. Designed by Arnold Brunner (1857–1925), probably the first American-born Jewish architect, this Reform congregation will merge with Congregation Emanu-El in 1927. The building will be razed in 1947.

C. Jews in Europe

modern education system for the Jewish masses in Russia.

One hundred ten thousand Jews emigrate from Russia.

On the first day of Passover, the Russian government orders the expulsion of Jews from Moscow. Over 10,000 Jews, about one-half of the Jewish population, are expelled.

The Jewish Historical Ethnographic Commission is founded in St. Petersburg. This first eastern European Jewish scholarly group is similar to Jewish historical societies then being organized in Europe and the U.S. Their apologetic purpose is to demonstrate in their countries the antiquity of Jewish settlement and to highlight Jewish loyalty and patriotism.

The Great Synagogue on Arkhipova Street in Moscow is opened. A dome crowned outside by a six-pointed star is built above the four-columned neoclassical facade. The authorities, displeased by this display of Jewish identity, require the dome to be demolished. During the period of expulsion of Jews from Moscow, the synagogue will be closed. It will reopen in 1906.

A blood libel charge against Jews on the Greek island of Corfu results in the large-scale emigration of the island's 5,000 Jews.

E. Jewish Culture

U.S. in 1881, writes his English–Yiddish dictionary, the first of its kind. In 1898 he will write a Yiddish–English dictionary, and in 1925, a trilingual Yiddish–English–Hebrew dictionary.

Isaac Leib Peretz (1852–1915), leading Yiddish writer, writes *Pictures of a Provincial Journey*. Working with a group doing a statistical survey, Peretz undertook a journey through the small Jewish towns of Poland. In addition to collecting data for the projected census, he notes his impressions of Jewish shtetl life.

Population of Palestine, 1856–1947			
Year	Jews	Non-Jews	Total
1856	10,500		
1882	24,000		
1895	47,000		
1914	85,000		
1922	83,790	668,258	752,048
1931	174,606	858,708	1,033,314
1936	384,708	981,984	1,366,692
1942	484,708	1,135,297	1,620,005
1947	614,239	1,319,434	1,933,673

	A. General History	B. Jews in North and South America	C. Jews in Europe	D. Jews in the Middle East and Elsewhere	E. Jewish Culture
1891		Congregation Anshe Maariv (KAM), in Chicago, opens a synagogue designed in the functional style by Dankmar Adler and Louis Sullivan.* Adler's father is the rabbi of the congregation.			

B. Jews in North and South America

B'nai Israel synagogue in Salt Lake City, Utah, is opened.

William E. Blackstone,* Chicago Christian evangelist and businessman, initiates a petition to President Benjamin Harrison,* signed by 413 leading American Christian and Jewish leaders, urging the restoration of the Jews to Palestine as a primary solution to the problem of Jewish persecution in czarist Russia.

Ignatius Donnelly* (1831–1901), U.S. populist political leader, writes a Utopian novel, *Caesar's Column*. To Donnelly,* Jews are in control of the economy yet are the brains of the revolution against capitalism. Some historians assert that the novel's antisemitism served as the basis of the populist antisemitism of the 1890s.

Goldwin Smith,* noted British historian from Oxford who taught at Cornell University, writes *New Light on the Jewish Question*, published in the *North American Review*, in which he challenges the patriotism of Jews and argues that Russian persecution had been greatly exaggerated and that if persecution did, indeed, exist, one should look to the Jew for the cause.

President Benjamin Harrison,* in his annual message to Congress, notes that the U.S. expresses its concern to Russia of its harsh treatment of the Jews. "No race, sect or class has more fully cared for its own than the Hebrew race. . . . It is estimated that over 1,000,000 will be forced from Russia within a few years. . . . the sudden transfer of such a multitude under conditions that tend to strip them of their small accumulations and to depress their energies and courage is neither good for them nor us."

	A. General History	B. Jews in North and South America	C. Jews in Europe	D. Jews in the Middle East and Elsewhere	E. Jewish Culture
1892	Violence erupts at a strike of steelworkers at the Carnegie plant in Homestead, Pennsylvania, protesting wage cuts. Several Pinkerton detectives hired by Carnegie are killed. The state militia restores order. The strike is broken. Alexander Berkman (1870–1936), anarchist, attempts to kill Henry Clay Frick,* general manager of the Carnegie Steel Corp., during a steelworkers' strike at Homestead, Pennsylvania. He will serve 14 years in prison and upon his release resume a close relationship with Emma Goldman (1869–1940), fellow	The Workmen's Circle is founded in the U.S. to promote Yiddishist and Socialist ideas among the masses of Jewish laborers. The American Jewish Historical Society is founded under the initiative of Oscar S. Straus and Cyrus Adler. The society aims to counter the alien image of the Jew in the U.S. The Hebrew Free Loan Society of New York is founded by immigrant Jews. Starting with a capital investment of $95, by 1990, the society was lending over $3 million annually without interest	Edouard Drumont,* French journalist, founds *La Libre Parole*, a daily newspaper that expresses his antisemitism. On the eve of the 1893 elections, the German Conservative party holds a conference at Berlin's Tivoli Hall at which it adopts an antisemitic program. "We combat the obtrusive and debilitating Jewish influence on our popular life." Adolf Wolff Buschoff, a butcher and former *shohet* of the town of Xanten, Germany, is the victim of a blood libel. Accused of murdering a		The publication of *Tsukunft* (*Future*), a Yiddish monthly literary magazine of Socialist leanings, begins in New York. In 1913, Abraham Liessen (1872–1938) will become its editor, a post he will hold until his death. Jacob Gordin, Yiddish playwright who arrived in New York from Russia in 1891, writes *The Jewish King Lear*. Starring Jacob P. Adler, Gordin bends Shakespeare's plot to a Russian Jewish setting, where an old, wealthy Jew is tormented by the ingratitude of his daughters. Gordin and Adler are credited with inaugurating the

A. General History

anarchist. They will be deported to Russia following the Palmer raids of 1919.

Grover Cleveland* is elected president of the U.S., defeating Benjamin Harrison* by 277–145 electoral votes. The popular vote is Cleveland,* 5,554,414 to Harrison,* 5,190,801.

The House of Representatives refuses to allocate funds for food transports to Russia because of the czarist regime's treatment of Jews.

B. Jews in North and South America

or service charge.

Congregation Knesseth Israel opens a synagogue in Philadelphia on North Broad Street.

Paul Haupt* (1858–1926), head of the Oriental department at Johns Hopkins University, writes *The Mesopotamian Plan*, a pamphlet advocating the resettlement and colonization of Russian Jews in Syria and Mesopotamia. Haupt* writes at the suggestion of Cyrus Adler, his student and friend, and obtains the support of Oscar S. Straus and Mayer Sulzberger (1843–1923), American Jewish leaders. Haupt* had earlier studied Mesopotamia as a region for possible German colonization at the request of Bismarck.*

Theresa Serber Malkiel (1874–1949) founds the Woman's Infant Cloak Maker's Union. Malkiel also founds the Socialist Women's Society of New York.

C. Jews in Europe

Christian boy, he is arrested and released for lack of evidence. Later in the year, he is again arrested, tried, and found innocent by a jury.

Andrew D. White,* former president of Cornell University and ex-minister to Berlin, is appointed minister to Russia at the urging of leading American Jews. He reports on the persecution of Jews in Russia and ably defends the victims.

Harold Frederic* (1856–1898), *New York Times* foreign correspondent, writes *The New Exodus: Israel in Russia*. It describes his travels in Russia in the 1880s and includes reports of persecution of Russian Jews. American Jewish leaders underwrote his trip to Russia.

The Strashun library of Vilna is opened to the public and is named after Mathias Strashun (1819–1885), talmudic scholar and bibliophile who donated his library of over 5,700 volumes to the Vilna community.

E. Jewish Culture

golden age of Yiddish theater in New York. He will write more than 100 plays for the Yiddish stage.

Israel Zangwill, English author, writes *The Children of the Ghetto: A Study of a Peculiar People*. This first British novel to depict the life of eastern European Jewish immigrants in the ghetto of London's East End becomes a best-seller.

Max Nordau, Zionist, philosopher, and physician, writes *Degeneration*, in which he denounces major figures and trends in European art and literature and predicts the coming of an unprecedented human catastrophe.

David Schwarz (1845–1897), Austrian inventor and timber merchant, designs a cigar-shaped airship with an aluminum framework. His designs are sold to Count Zeppelin.*

Sholom Aleichem begins his series of Menakhem Mendl letters exchanged between him and his wife Sheineh Sheindel. Mendl is the typical *luftmensch* of the Pale of Settlement struggling to make his fortune. The series will continue until 1913.

Waldemar Mordecai Haffkine (1860–1930), Russian-born bacteriologist, develops the first effective vaccine against cholera at the Pasteur Institute in France. The vaccine begins to be used throughout India.

A. General History	B. Jews in North and South America	C. Jews in Europe	D. Jews in the Middle East and Elsewhere	E. Jewish Culture
1893 Financial panic on Wall Street ushers in an economic depression. The World Parliament of Religions at Chicago's World's Columbian Exposition brings together representatives of dozens of faiths including a large percentage of women of many faiths. France and Russia enter into a dual alliance.	Adolf Stoecker,* German politician and world "leader of the Jew baiters," visits the U.S. In two New York speeches he explains his hatred of Germany's Jews, charging them with absorbing Germany's wealth while at the same time promoting a Marxist revolution. The National Council of Jewish Women is founded by Hannah G. Solomon and Sadie American (1862–1944) after they participated in the Parliament of Religions at Chicago's World's Columbian Exposition. Its program calls for Jewish women's study, schools, philanthropy, and exchange of ideas. The Jewish Chautauqua Society is organized by Henry Berkowitz (1857–1924), U.S. Reform rabbi. Its aim is to popularize knowledge of Judaism through home reading courses and summer assemblies. The Jewish Prisoners Association of New York is reconstituted as the Society to Aid the Jewish Prisoner. The society is the cornerstone of New York Jewry's efforts to eliminate Jewish criminality. Edward King* (1848–1896), labor reformer familiar with New York's Lower East Side, writes *Joseph Zalmonah*, a novel of Russian Jewish immigrant labor strife, patterned on the life of the Jewish trade unionist Joseph Barondess.	The Jewish Historical Society of England is founded. Lucien Wolf (1857–1930) serves as its first president. In London, Lily Montagu (1873–1963) creates the first English multipurpose Jewish girls' educational society, social club, and settlement house by transforming the small West Central Jewish Girls Club. It becomes a model for Jewish Girls Clubs in England. The Central Union of German Citizens of Jewish Faith (Centralverein) is founded in Berlin to fight antisemitism and to protect and strengthen Jewish social and civic status. It will be dissolved by the Nazis in 1938. Candidates of the German antisemitic political parties receive 262,000 votes and win 16 seats in the German parliament. Max Isidor Bodenheimer (1865–1940) and David Wolffsohn (1856–1914) found a Hibbat Zion society in Cologne, Germany, which becomes the nucleus of the German Zionist Federation. Switzerland is the first modern country to outlaw *shehitah* (ritual slaughter). An anti-*shehitah* movement began in Germany in the mid-19th century. Other countries which will later ban *shehitah* include Norway (1930), Nazi Germany (1933), Sweden (1937), and Fascist Italy (1938).	Louis-Gustave Binger (1856–1936), French explorer, is appointed first governor of the Ivory Coast. Binger's expeditions in West Africa from 1887 to 1889 enabled France to annex the Ivory Coast in 1891. Its capital, Bingerville, is named in his honor.	Ephraim Benguiat's collection of Jewish ritual art is exhibited at the World's Columbian Exposition in Chicago. The collection will be acquired by the Jewish Theological Seminary of America in 1925. Moritz Steinschneider, father of modern Jewish bibliography, publishes *The Hebrew Translations of the Middle Ages and the Jews as Interpreters: A Contribution of the Literary History of the Middle Ages, Mostly from Manuscript Sources*. This work contains a wealth of information about the transmission of philosophy and sciences throughout the Middle Ages, discussing the works of Greeks, Arabs, Jews, and Christians. Alexander Bihari (1856–1906), Hungarian genre painter, paints his masterpiece, *Sunday Afternoon*, which is housed in Budapest's National Gallery. Abraham Leib Shalkovich (Ben-Avigdor, 1867–1921) establishes the Ahi'asaf Publishing House in Warsaw. Regarded as the founder of modern Hebrew publishing, he produces attractive and reasonably priced Hebrew books.

A. General History	B. Jews in North and South America	C. Jews in Europe	D. Jews in the Middle East and Elsewhere	E. Jewish Culture	
	Charles P. Daly* writes *The Settlement of the Jews in North America*, a history of the Jews in the U.S. It contains a forward by Max J. Kohler (1871–1934), attorney and communal leader, underscoring the importance of presenting facts to disprove antisemitic charges.	Israel Meir ha-Kohen, leading Orthodox rabbi and moralist, pleads that those who must leave for America for economic reasons should leave their children behind and return to eastern Europe after achieving success. The Great Synagogue in St. Petersburg is opened. Popularly known as the Baron Ginsburg synagogue, it has 1,200 seats.			**1893**
In July, Major Esterhazy* (1847–1923), French army officer, offers his services to the German military attaché Lieutenant Colonel von Schwartzkoppen* (1850–1917) with the intention of passing on military secrets. The Immigration Restriction League is formed by nativists in Boston as a lobby for a national policy of restrictive immigration. Distinguishing between "old" and "new" immigrants, Prescott F. Hall* defines their agenda as whether the country "be peopled by British, German and Scandinavian stock, historically free, energetic, progressive, or by Slav, Latin and Asiatic races, historically downtrodden, atavistic, and stagnant." Nicholas II* (1894–1917) succeeds his father, Alexander III.* He is the last czar of Russia.	A report by a New York State legislative committee investigating municipal corruption in New York (the Lexow Committee) discloses a sizable Jewish criminal element on Manhattan's Lower East Side. The report startles the New York Jewish community. The Baron de Hirsch Agricultural School is opened in Woodbine, New Jersey. It is the first American secondary school teaching agricultural subjects. Temple Tifereth Israel opens in Cleveland, Ohio, and is designed in the Romanesque style of synagogue architecture.	On October 15, Captain Alfred Dreyfus (1859–1935), probationary officer on the French general staff, is accused of passing military secrets to the Germans and is arrested. On November 9, weeks before the trial of Alfred Dreyfus, the French antisemitic newspaper *La Libre Parole* proclaims that all of Jewry is behind "the traitor." On December 19, the first court-martial of French Army Captain Alfred Dreyfus is begun in closed session and completed on December 22. General Auguste Mercier* (1833–1921), minister of war, orders incriminating documents to secretly be made available to the judges, who convict Dreyfus and sentence him to perpetual deportation and military degradation. George Du Maurier's* (1834–1896) novel *Trilby* includes	Jews are among the earliest settlers in Bulawayo, Rhodesia. A congregation is formed. The first white child born there is Jewish. The first newspaper published is Jewish owned and edited.	The Central Conference of American Rabbis (Reform) publishes the *Union Prayer Book* as the liturgy of the Reform movement. A radical departure from the conventional *siddur*, it shortens the *musaf*, abbreviates the *amidah*, and reduces the Hebrew prayers. It is more akin to David Einhorn's radical *Olat Tamid* than the traditional *Minhag Amerikah* of Isaac Mayer Wise. Moses Mielziner (1828–1903), U.S. rabbi and professor of Talmud and rabbinical literature at the Hebrew Union College since 1879, writes *Introduction to the Talmud*, which becomes a popular reference book. The University of California establishes a Semitics department through the efforts of Jacob Voorsanger (1852–1908), rabbi of Temple Emanu-El of San Francisco. He serves as professor. Meyer Kayserling (1829–1905), German historian who specializes in the history of	**1894**

A. General History	B. Jews in North and South America	C. Jews in Europe	D. Jews in the Middle East and Elsewhere	E. Jewish Culture
1894		Svengali, the eternal Jewish alien who belongs to an inferior race and whose occult exploits are designed to corrupt the pure white race, personifed in the novel's heroine, Trilby.		Spanish Jewry and the Marranos, writes *Christopher Columbus and the Participation of Jews in the Spanish and Portuguese Discoveries*. Kayserling was commissioned by Oscar S. Straus to write a book about the Jewish involvement in the discovery of America.

Bernard Berenson (1865–1959), U.S. art historian, writes *The Venetian Painters of the Renaissance*, the first of a series of books that establish him as an authority on Italian Renaissance art.

Otto Brahm (1856–1912), German stage director, takes over Berlin's Deutsches Theater for the production of modernist playwrights Henrik Ibsen* (1828–1906), Gerhart Hauptman* (1862–1946), and Arthur Schnitzler (1862–1931). Brahm's productions make Berlin one of Europe's theatrical centers.

The Sarajevo Haggadah, a Spanish illuminated 14th-century manuscript, reaches the Sarajevo Museum when a child of the city's Sephardic community brings it to school to be sold after the death of his father leaves his family destitute. This Haggadah is the best-known Hebrew illuminated manuscript.

Sholom Aleichem begins writing the first episode of the life of Tevye the Dairyman. Tevye, the father of seven |

A. General History	B. Jews in North and South America	C. Jews in Europe	D. Jews in the Middle East and Elsewhere	E. Jewish Culture	
				marriageable daughters and husband of an ailing wife, is the symbol of the Jewish pauper with a philosophical bent whose faith sustains him and who refuses to accept defeat. The series will continue until 1914 and appear in Yiddish newspapers and Aleichem's books. Isaac Leib Peretz (1852–1915), leading Yiddish writer, publishes *Yom Tov Bletlakh* (*Little Pages for Festivals*), a series of essays calling for a cultural revival in eastern European Jewish life.	**1894**
The first volume of *The Woman's Bible* by Elizabeth Cady Stanton* is published in the U.S. Many references blame the subservient status of contemporary women on Judaism and the role of women in the Hebrew Bible. Auguste and Louis Lumière,* French movie film pioneers, invent the cinematograph.	The leaders of the Boston Jewish community federate their charities to improve inadequate philanthropic administration and organize an annual campaign for funds. The Cincinnati community will follow in 1896.	On January 5, the degradation ceremony of court-martialed Captain Alfred Dreyfus is held at France's Ecole Militaire. On April 13, court-martialed French army captain Alfred Dreyfus is placed in solitary confinement on Devil's Island, off the coast of French Guiana.		Sears, Roebuck Co. opens a mail-order business that revolutionizes retail merchandising in the U.S. Julius Rosenwald (1862–1932), U.S. clothing merchant, purchases a one-quarter interest in the company. He will become company president in 1909. Rosa Sonneschein (1847–1932) founds the *American Jewess*, the first English-language Jewish feminist journal in the U.S. It appears monthly through 1899 and advocates social, political, and religious emancipation for Jewish women.	**1895**

The degradation ceremony of Captain Alfred Dreyfus, from The Graphic.

	Lillian Wald (1867–1940), U.S. social worker, founds the Henry Street Settlement on New York's Lower East Side. Born into a wealthy German Jewish family in Rochester, Wald chooses to become a nurse and resolves to bring nursing care	Theodor Herzl, then Paris correspondent of the Viennese newspaper *Neue Freie Presse* and affected by the antisemitic outbursts at the Dreyfus trial, considers the "Jewish problem." In May he meets with philanthropist Baron Maurice de		The Central Association of German Citizens of the Jewish Faith begins publication of a German-language Jewish monthly, *Im Deutschen Reich*. In 1922, it will be renamed *Central-Vereins-Zeitung* (*C.V. Zeitung*). It is assimilationist in

	A. General History	B. Jews in North and South America	C. Jews in Europe	D. Jews in the Middle East and Elsewhere	E. Jewish Culture
1895		and hygienic instruction to the new immigrants living in the tenements. She campaigns for improved sanitation, pure milk, and the control of tuberculosis. Herman Ahlwardt* (1846–1914), German antisemitic politician who had been imprisoned for libeling Jews, visits the U.S. to organize an antisemitic movement. He is denounced by prominent American Christian clergymen, and his public appearances are marked by near riots. The popular humor magazine *Life* publishes a cartoon showing an obviously Jewish man reading an oculist's chart. The oculist asks him to read the lines on the chart, and the man replies, "I can see noddings but the one at the bottom," which is a dollar sign. The cartoon is typical of the stereotype that appears frequently. Simon Wolf (1836–1923), U.S. communal leader, writes a study of Jews in the American armed forces from 1774 to 1865, *The American Jew as Patriot, Soldier and Citizen*, to counter arguments that Jews lacked patriotism. The Women's Christian Temperance Union, founded in Ohio in 1874, votes to admit Catholic and Jewish women.	Hirsch but fails to arouse his interest in a plan to resettle the Jews of Europe in a country of their own. Karl Lueger* (1844–1910), head of the antisemitic Christian Social party in Austria, is elected mayor of Vienna. Emperor Franz Joseph* refuses to confirm the appointment. The Hungarian parliament grants Jews full equality with the Christian religion through the efforts of Hungarian Magyar nationalists who seek support from the Jews, who comprise 5% of the population. Together, they make up a majority of the country. Jews are an active element of the Hungarian economy and their assistance is sought in the effort to break away from dependence on Austrian economic hegemony. In November, Theodor Herzl discusses the idea of a Jewish state with Max Nordau at the suggestion of a friend who is concerned about Herzl's mental health. Nordau, philosopher and physician, concludes the meeting by exclaiming, "If you are insane, we are insane together. Count on me."		viewpoint and an anti-Zionist rival of the *Juedische Rundschau* (1896). It has the largest circulation of any Jewish newspaper in Germany. It will cease publication in 1938. Otto Lilienthal (1848–1896), German aeronautical engineer, and his brother Gustav design and fly the first glider that can soar above the height of takeoff. He will die in a crash of a glider flight. The Jewish origin of the Lilienthal brothers has been disputed.
1896	William McKinley* is elected president of the U.S.,	Congress enacts an immigration bill containing a literacy	In March, Lieutenant Colonel Marie-Georges	A group of American immigrants, numbering	Abraham Cahan writes *Yekl, A Tale of the New York Ghetto*, a

A. General History	B. Jews in North and South America	C. Jews in Europe	D. Jews in the Middle East and Elsewhere	E. Jewish Culture

A. General History

defeating William Jennings Bryan.*

Utah becomes the 45th state of the U.S.

Nobel Prizes are established under the bequest of Swedish scientist Alfred Nobel* (1833–1896) for achievement in physics, physiology or medicine, chemistry, literature, and peace.

The revived Olympic games are conducted in Athens, Greece.

The moving picture inventors, the Lumière* brothers, film the *Jerusalem Railroad Station*, the first movie filmed in Palestine.

B. Jews in North and South America

test suggested by the Immigration Restriction League as a device to exclude "undesirable" southern and eastern Europeans. The draft bill permits entry only of those who are literate "in the English language or the language of their native or resident country or in some other language." Senator Henry Cabot Lodge* has the phrase "or in some other language" deleted, which aimed at Jews fleeing Russia who are literate in Yiddish but not in Russian. The clause is restored after a public outcry.

A second New York State legislative inquiry into municipal corruption in New York (the Mazet Committee) reports evidence of active Jewish participation in prostitution, extortion, and petty crime.

Cyrus Adler, U.S. scholar and communal leader, writes to Theodor Herzl outlining his program for the resettlement of eastern European Jewry in Syria and Mesopotamia rather than Palestine. He encloses Paul Haupt's *Mesopotamia Plan* of 1892 and suggests that the plan be discussed at the forthcoming first Zionist Congress. Herzl will not reply to Adler until the end of 1899.

C. Jews in Europe

Picquart* (1854–1914), the new chief of the French military information service, identifies Major Esterhazy* as a German spy on the basis of a *petit bleu* (express letter). Picquart* slowly realizes that all the evidence brought against court-martialed Captain Alfred Dreyfus, especially the *bordereau* (memorandum), was the work of Esterhazy.*

On October 27, Lieutenant Colonel Picquart* is relieved of his post at the French military information service. Generals Gonse* and Boisdeffre* are responsible for his transfer.

On November 6, Bernard Lazare (1865–1903) publishes his brochure, *A Judicial Error: The Truth on the Dreyfus Affair*, in Brussels, which raises the antisemitic issue from the Jewish point of view: "Because he was a Jew he was arrested, because he was a Jew he was convicted, because he was a Jew the voices of justice and of truth could not be heard in his favor." It becomes a rallying point for the revision of Dreyfus' trial.

Theodor Herzl writes *The Jewish State: An Attempt at a Modern Solution of the Jewish Question*, in which he states that antisemitism will never disappear, that the Jews were "one nation," and there could be no solution to the Jewish question except by the creation of a

D. Jews in the Middle East and Elsewhere

approximately 1,000, found an American *kollel* in Jerusalem. Known as Kollel America Tifereth Jerusalem, it overcomes opposition from the general organization, Vaad ha-Kelai.

The Cairo Genizah, a storehouse of literary and historical documents, is rediscovered by Solomon Schechter (1847–1915), then reader in rabbinic and talmudic literature at Cambridge University, who arranges for the transfer of about 100,000 pages to Cambridge.

Solomon Schecter examining Cairo Genizah documents at Cambridge, England about 1898.

E. Jewish Culture

grim story of Jake and his wife who are alienated by the process of Americanization. William Dean Howells,* preeminent American man of letters, reviews Cahan's book and Stephen Crane's* *George's Mother*. He asserts that their fiction has "drawn the truest pictures of East Side life." Howells* directs public attention toward Cahan.

Israel Abrahams, English scholar, writes *Jewish Life in the Middle Ages*. In 1902, he will succeed Solomon Schechter at Cambridge University, where he will serve until his death.

Jacob Sandler (d.1931), composer and music director, composes the song "Eili Eili," with words by Boris Tomashefsky, for the M. Horowitz operetta *The Hero and Bracha or the Jewish King of Poland for a Night*. It becomes a world-famous Jewish song.

Juedische Rundschau (*Jewish Observer*), journal of the German Zionist Federation, begins publication. It has a circulation of over 30,000 and appears twice weekly when it ceases publication in 1938. Its last editor is Robert Weltsch.

A. General History	B. Jews in North and South America	C. Jews in Europe	D. Jews in the Middle East and Elsewhere	E. Jewish Culture
1896		Jewish state. The book arouses enthusiasm among Zionists throughout Europe. It will appear in 80 editions in 18 languages.		Solomon Mandelkern, an author and scholar from Russia working in Leipzig, completes *Heikhal Hakodesh* (*Temple of the Holy*). This concordance includes all Hebrew and Aramaic words in the Hebrew Bible, arranged by grammatical form. It will be revised six times from 1925 to 1967 and serve as a fundamental tool for studying the Bible and its language.

Title page of Theodor Herzl's The Jewish State: *first edition, Vienna, 1896. (Central Zionist Archives)*

Isaac Levitan (1861–1906) is appointed professor of landscape painting at the Moscow Art Academy. His works portray the sad and heavy monotony of the vast Russian steppes.

Ha-Shiloah (*The Wellspring*), a Hebrew literary and cultural monthly, begins publication. It is first edited by Ahad ha-Am in Odessa and Warsaw and is considered the principal vehicle of cultural Zionism. In 1903, he will be succeeded as editor by Joseph Klausner (1874–1958). From 1920 until it ceases publication in 1926, it is edited and printed in Jerusalem.

A. General History	B. Jews in North and South America	C. Jews in Europe	D. Jews in the Middle East and Elsewhere	E. Jewish Culture
1897	In March, Grover Cleveland,* in one of his last acts as president, vetoes the immigration bill that would make mandatory a literacy test for immigrants. He describes the measure as an unworthy repudiation of the country's historic role as an asylum for the oppressed.

French archaeologists discover the stela containing the Code | At almost the same time as the First Zionist Congress is taking place at Basel, the Central Conference of American Rabbis, the rabbinic organization of American Reform Judaism, adopts a resolution totally disapproving of any attempts for the establishment of a Jewish state.

Frank Moss,* former chief counsel to the | In June, upon hearing that Theodor Herzl is scheduling a Zionist congress to be held in August in Munich, German Reform and Orthodox rabbis join in protest. Herzl transfers the congress to Basel.

On July 13, Auguste Scheurer-Kestner* (1833–1899), vice president of the French senate, becomes convinced of the innocence of | | Abraham Cahan is hired as a police reporter for the *New York Commercial Advertiser*, an avant-garde daily newspaper, by its managing editor, Lincoln Steffens* (1866–1936).

The *Forward*, a Yiddish daily newspaper, begins publication in New York. Abraham Cahan is one of its founders and will edit the paper from 1903 to 1951. |

A. General History	B. Jews in North and South America	C. Jews in Europe	D. Jews in the Middle East and Elsewhere	E. Jewish Culture

1897

A. General History

of Hammurapi* in the ancient Elamite and Persian capital of Susa.

B. Jews in North and South America

New York State Mazet Committee inquiry into New York municipal corruption, writes *The American Metropolis*, a 3-volume work describing various aspects of New York. Moss calls the Lower East Side a center of crime and describes Russian and Polish Jews as "the worst element in the entire make-up of New York life."

Theodor Herzl addressing the First Zionist Congress in Basel, Switzerland, in August 1897. (*Central Zionist Archives*)

The Rabbi Isaac Elhanan Theological Seminary for the advanced study of Talmud is founded in New York. In 1915, it will merge with Yeshiva Etz Chaim, which was founded in 1886 as an elementary school. The merger forms the nucleus of Yeshiva University.

Congregation Shearith Israel of New York moves to a new synagogue building on Central Park West and 70th Street, designed in classical Roman Revival style by Arnold Brunner. This change in Brunner's later synagogue design is influenced by the findings of exploration of ancient synagogues in the Galilee built in the Greco-Roman tradition.

B'nai B'rith, the oldest and largest Jewish fraternal organization in the

C. Jews in Europe

Captain Alfred Dreyfus.

In August, the First Zionist Congress convenes in Basel, Switzerland, under the leadership of Theodor Herzl. Delegates from 16 countries adopt the Basel Program advocating large-scale migration and settlement of Palestine, which could only be achieved through the political assistance and consent of the community of nations. Herzl wrote in his *Diaries*: "In Basel I founded the Jewish State. If I were to say this aloud I would meet with general laughter; but in another five years, and certainly in another fifty years, everyone will be convinced of this."

Hermann (Zevi Hirsch) Schapira (1840–1898) presents his idea for a general Jewish fund to the First Zionist Congress in Basel. The fund, to which Jews throughout the world would contribute, would expend two-thirds of its resources in purchasing land in Palestine and the other third for maintenance and cultivation of this land. The Fifth Zionist Congress (1901) will adopt the proposal and thus establish the Jewish National Fund.

Moritz Guedemann (1835–1918), chief rabbi of Vienna, writes *Nationaljudentum* (*National Judaism*) in which he attacks Theodor Herzl's recently published *The Jewish State*. Herzl sought his

E. Jewish Culture

The Jewish Times, the first Jewish newspaper in Canada, begins weekly publication. In 1915, it will merge with the *Canadian Jewish Chronicle*, which will begin publication in 1914. It will become a monthly in 1970.

Marcus Samuel (1853–1927), British industrialist, founds the Shell Oil Co. He will become lord mayor of London in 1902 and Viscount Bearsted in 1925.

The publication of *Die Welt* (*The World*), a Zionist weekly newspaper, founded by Theodor Herzl, begins in Vienna. It will move to Cologne in 1905 and to Berlin in 1911. Publication will cease in 1914. Among its editors are Martin Buber, Jacob Klatzkin, and Nahum Sokolow.

Sigmund Freud, Austrian psychiatrist, develops the essential elements of psychoanalysis. He undertakes his own self-analysis.

Max Grunwald (1871–1953), German rabbi, historian, and folklorist, establishes a Jewish folklore society and edits its scholarly journal. He is credited with stimulating the first serious attempts at the collection and description of Jewish folklore.

Gustav Mahler (1860–1911), composer and conductor who was born in Bohemia, is appointed director of the Vienna Court Opera. To secure this position, Mahler converts to Catholicsm.

A. General History	B. Jews in North and South America	C. Jews in Europe	D. Jews in the Middle East and Elsewhere	E. Jewish Culture
1897	U.S., permits ladies' auxiliaries to its lodges for the first time. The first chapter of B'nai B'rith Women will be formed in 1909.	support along with that of Baron de Hirsch and Baron Rothschild. Guedemann concludes there is no such thing as a Jewish people and Jews should devote their energies to the abolition of nationalism.		Jakob Wasserman (1873–1933), German novelist, writes *The Jews of Zirndorf*, his first novel, about the changing Jewish life in his native province of Franconia. His later novels, including *The World's Illusion* (1920), become best-sellers. He espouses assimilation and decries Jewish nationalism and Zionism. The Nazis will burn his books.

Karl Lueger,* head of the antisemitic Christian Social party in Austria, is elected mayor of Vienna. Emperor Franz Joseph* confirms the appointment after having refused to do so since he was first elected in 1895. Lueger* will hold office until his death.

On November 15, Mathieu Dreyfus, brother of court-martialed Captain Alfred Dreyfus, publicly denounces Major Esterhazy* as the author of the *bordereau*.

The first comprehensive Russian census counts 5.2 million Jews in the Russian Empire. All but 300,000 live within the Pale of Settlement. Those outside the Pale include 60,000 Georgian and "mountain" Jews of the Caucusus, and 50,000 in Central Asia and Siberia.

The Bund, the general league of Jewish workingmen in Russia and Poland, is founded. It is a social democratic (Marxist) labor organization. Founded a year before the Russian Social Democratic party, it evolves a multilayered program that combines agitation on behalf of

The German government finances test flights of a dirigible designed by David Schwarz. The test flight is made after his death and is observed by Count Zeppelin,* who bought his plans and designs. He will modify and rebuild Schwarz's dirigible, naming it "the Zeppelin."

A Jewish museum is opened in Vienna. It is the first actual Jewish museum, with its own occasional publications.

Illustration by E. M. Lilien for Morris Rosenfeld's Songs of the Ghetto. *Two immigrants to the New World, having been classified as "paupers," are being returned to Russia. Their despair is reflected in the skeletal face of Death* (upper right). *(Library of Congress)*

A. General History	B. Jews in North and South America	C. Jews in Europe	D. Jews in the Middle East and Elsewhere	E. Jewish Culture	
		the Russian proletariat, defense of the specific interests and rights of Jewish workers, and the fight against anti-Jewish laws.			**1897**
The U.S. battleship *Maine* is blown up in Havana Harbor, Cuba. The Spanish–American War begins. U.S. fleets destroy Spanish fleets in the Philippines and Cuba. The war ends, and Spain gives up claim to Cuba and cedes the Philippines, Puerto Rico, and Guam to the U.S. The U.S. annexes Hawaii. The first German Navy Law begins expansion of the German navy and the start of the naval race with Great Britain. The Russian Social Democratic Workers party is formed. Anglo-Egyptian forces led by British General Kitchener* invade and occupy the Sudan. French forces occupying Fashoda, on the Nile in the south of Sudan, evacuate, and avert war between Great Britain and France.	Fifteen Jewish sailors lose their lives aboard the U.S. battleship *Maine*, which is sunk in Havana Harbor. It is reported that there are over 500 Spanish Jews engaged in commerce in Cuba and that five or six Jewish families are among the island's wealthiest. Jews are among the founders of the commercial cane sugar fields and the first sugar refineries. Eastern European immigrants to the U.S. organize a Union of Orthodox Congregations, whose viewpoint clashes with that of the Union of American Hebrew Congregations (Reform). The *Atlantic Monthly Magazine*, in its July issue, publishes *The Russian Jew in America* by Abraham Cahan. He writes of "a tenement house kitchen turned, after a scanty supper, into a classroom, with the head of family and his boarder bent over an English school reader," as typical rather than exceptional activity. David Blaustein (1866–1912) is appointed superintendent of New York's Educational Alliance. Located on the Lower East Side, it serves eastern European immigrants as they acculturate to the U.S.	On January 13, the French journal *L'Aurore* publishes "J'Accuse" by Emile Zola* (1840–1902). The letter proclaims the innocence of court-martialed Captain Alfred Dreyfus and accuses his denouncers of malicious libel. On January 11, Major Esterhazy* is tried and summarily acquitted at a court-martial. In February, Emile Zola* is tried in Paris for libel. He is found guilty, fined, and sentenced to one year in prison. In July, French Minister of War Godefroy Cavaignac* (1853–1905) presents forged evidence against Captain Alfred Dreyfus in the French Chamber of Deputies. Jean Jaures* (1859–1914), the Socialist leader, publicly demonstrates the falseness of the evidence. In August, Lieutenant Colonel Henry* (1847–1898) confesses to French Minister of War Cavaignac* his perjuries against Captain Alfred Dreyfus. He is interned at a military prison, where he commits suicide. The Second Zionist Congress convenes in Basel under Theodor Herzl's leadership. The congress decides to encourage settlement in Palestine, even in	In January, the Dreyfus Affair causes antisemitic riots in Algeria. On October 3, Turkey refuses permission to American Jews to land in Palestine. Apparently alarmed at the influx of Jews into Palestine, even French, English, and Italian Jews are compelled to seek assistance from their consuls before being allowed to land at Jaffa. In November, Theodor Herzl confers with German Kaiser Wilhem II* during his visit to Palestine. He fails to win the kaiser over to the Zionist cause.	Leo Wiener (1862–1939), later to be professor of Slavic studies at Harvard, translates into English the Yiddish verses of Morris Rosenfeld (1862–1923). Rosenfeld worked in New York's sweatshops since his arrival from Russia in 1886. *Songs of the Ghetto* sings the woes of workers and satirizes social injustice. An edition will be illustrated by Ephraim Moses Lilien (1874–1925), German artist. Lewis Naphtali Dembitz, U.S. Jewish communal leader, writes *Jewish Services in Synagogue and Home*, a popular volume. He is greatly admired by his nephew, Louis D. Brandeis (1856–1941), who changes his middle name from David to Dembitz. Jacob Schiff, U.S. investment banker and philanthropist, purchases the library of Moritz Steinschneider. Steinschneider, the father of modern Jewish bibliography, lives in Berlin in very modest circumstances. Schiff wills the library to the Jewish Theological Seminary of America. Solomon Schechter is discouraged by the irreligion of Zionist leaders. Believing that without religion the Jewish nationality could not	**1898**

A. General History	B. Jews in North and South America	C. Jews in Europe	D. Jews in the Middle East and Elsewhere	E. Jewish Culture
1898	The first organized Jewish college campus group, the Zeta Beta Tau fratenity, is founded under a Hebrew name, Zion be-Mishpat Tipadeh (Zion shall be redeemed by justice, Isaiah 1:27), in New York. Its purpose is to encourage the study of Jewish history and culture among Jewish students but is soon converted into a Greek letter fraternity.	the absence of political guarantees, and to engage in cultural activities. On the basis of a report by David Wolffsohn, the congress decides to establish the Jewish Colonial Trust, to assist financially in the development of Palestine.		survive, he writes, "I have spent nearly 50 years on the study of Jewish literature and Jewish history; I am deeply convinced that we cannot sever Jewish nationality from Jewish religion."

The first organized Jewish college campus group, the Zeta Beta Tau fratenity, is founded under a Hebrew name, Zion be-Mishpat Tipadeh (Zion shall be redeemed by justice, Isaiah 1:27), in New York. Its purpose is to encourage the study of Jewish history and culture among Jewish students but is soon converted into a Greek letter fraternity.

The Federation of American Zionists is organized under the presidency of Professor Richard J. H. Gottheil (1862–1936) of Columbia University. By 1900 it will have a membership of 8,000.

Responding to the program of the Second Zionist Congress, the Union of American Hebrew Congregations, the synagogue organization of American Reform Judaism, adopts a resolution: "We are unalterably opposed to political Zionism. The Jews are not a nation, but a religious community."

Joseph Simon (1851–1935), a native of Germany who arrived in Portland at age six, serves as U.S. senator from Oregon until 1903. A major figure in Republican politics in Oregon for 30 years, he will serve as mayor of Portland from 1909 to 1911.

C. Jews in Europe

the absence of political guarantees, and to engage in cultural activities. On the basis of a report by David Wolffsohn, the congress decides to establish the Jewish Colonial Trust, to assist financially in the development of Palestine.

The first conference of Russian Zionists is held secretly in Warsaw. Ahad ha-Am discusses his differences with Theodor Herzl. The demand of Orthodox rabbis to supervise cultural activities causes friction.

On September 3, French Minister of War Cavaignac* resigns and his statement is posted throughout France.

On September 26, the French cabinet submits the file of court-martialed Captain Alfred Dreyfus to the criminal chamber of the Court of Appeal for revision.

As a result of the czarist policy of pauperization of the Jews, the number of Jewish paupers increases by 27% in the years between 1894 and 1898, according to the Russian economist A. Subbotin.*

The Bund is admitted to the newly formed Russian Social Democratic Workers party as the sole representative of the Jewish proletariat.

Nachman Syrkin (1868–1924), founder of Socialist Zionism, writes *The Jewish Question and the Socialist Jewish State.*

E. Jewish Culture

survive, he writes, "I have spent nearly 50 years on the study of Jewish literature and Jewish history; I am deeply convinced that we cannot sever Jewish nationality from Jewish religion."

Lilian Mary Baylis (1874–1937) assists in managing the Victoria Theatre in London. Under her guidance the "Old Vic" becomes well known as the home of Shakespeare. She will become sole manager in 1912.

Izhac Epstein (1862–1943), pioneer in modern Hebrew education who emigrated to Palestine in 1886 from Russia, writes *Ivrit be-Ivrit* (*Hebrew in Hebrew*), in which he advocates explanations to be made only in the language that is being taught. His work has a fundamental influence on Hebrew teaching.

Abraham Cahan, editor and author, writes *The Imported Bridegroom, and Other Stories of the New York Ghetto.*

Abraham Hayyim Rosenberg (1838–1928), Hebrew writer and printer, begins publication of a biblical encyclopedia, *Ozar ha-Shemot* (*Treasury of Names*), which will be completed in 10 volumes in 1922. He emigrated to the U.S. from Russia in 1891, and his Hebrew printing press in New York probably prints more Hebrew works than any similar establishment.

1898

Theodor Herzl meets Kaiser Wilhelm II at Mikveh Israel, Palestine. This photomontage was made after the photographer failed to capture the actual event. (Central Zionist Archives)

C. Jews in Europe

A Russian ideologist, he believes a classless Jewish society and national sovereignty are the only means of completely solving the Jewish problem.

E. Jewish Culture

Moritz Lazarus (1824–1903), German philosopher and psychologist, writes *The Ethics of Judaism*, which will be translated into English by Henrietta Szold. He emphasizes the religious character of obligation in Jewish ethics and prefers moderate rabbinical thinking to prophetic fervor.

1899

A. General History

Emile Loubet* (1835–1929) succeeds Felix Faure,* who died on February 16, as president of the French Republic.

Houston Stewart Chamberlain* (1855–1927) writes *Foundations of the 19th Century*. This work, which combines German nationalism, racist theories of Nordic superiority, and antisemitism, becomes the source of Nazi ideology. It will be admired by Kaiser William II* and Adolf Hitler* (1889–1945). Chamberlain,* British by birth and German by choice, is Richard Wagner's* (1813–1883) son-in-law.

The First Hague Peace Conference establishes a Permanent Court of International Justice and Arbitration.

Anglo-Egyptian joint rule over the Sudan is established.

The Boer War in South Africa begins.

B. Jews in North and South America

Abram S. Isaacs, in the first volume of *The American Jewish Year Book* (5660), writes of the Jews in the U.S. that the "flag of Zionism continues to be unfurled by earnest advocates. The body of adherents is made up from among our Russian brethren. . . .With the exception of a few leaders, like Prof. Gottheil and Rev. Stephen S. Wise, . . . the movement has failed to influence American Jewish sentiment; and it will have to detach itself from the fantasy of a Judenstat, and devote itself wholly to practical and practicable colonization, if it hopes to secure a larger following in this country."

William Z. Ripley* writes *The Races of Europe: A Sociological Study*, in which he concludes that the Jews are not biologically a distinct race. His progressive view, however, is marred by his description of the

C. Jews in Europe

On June 3, the French Court of Appeal revokes the verdict of 1894 against Captain Alfred Dreyfus and orders him to face another court-martial at Rennes.

In August, the second court-martial trial of Captain Alfred Dreyfus begins at Rennes. Dreyfus is again found guilty, this time with extenuating circumstances, and sentenced to 10 years in prison.

The Third Zionist Congress meets in Basel under Theodor Herzl's leadership. The congress decides that Herzl is to attempt to obtain a charter from the Turkish government. It is decided to use Colonial Trust funds only for settlement activities in Palestine and Syria.

On September 9, the trial of Leopold Hilsner begins in Kuttenberg, Bohemia, on the accusation of ritual murder of a young

E. Jewish Culture

The first volume of *The American Jewish Year Book*, published by the Jewish Publication Society of America, appears under the editorship of Cyrus Adler.

A dramatization by Israel Zangwill of his novel *Children of the Ghetto* is performed at the National Theatre in Washington, D.C.

Leo Wiener, later to become professor of Slavic studies at Harvard, writes *The History of Yiddish Literature in the Nineteenth Century*. He visited Europe in 1898 to gather material for his study and received 1,000 Yiddish books from the Asiatic Museum at St. Petersburg, which formed the basis of the Yiddish collection at Harvard University.

Arnold Bogumil Ehrlich (1848–1918), Russian-born Bible scholar who emigrated to the U.S. in 1878, begins publication in Berlin of a Hebrew commentary, *Mikra ki-Feshuto* (*The Bible*

A. General History	B. Jews in North and South America	C. Jews in Europe	D. Jews in the Middle East and Elsewhere	E. Jewish Culture

1899

A. General History

Adversaries are the Boer republics in the Orange Free State and Transvaal and the British colonies in South Africa.

Filipinos, disappointed with the terms of the peace treaty between Spain and the U.S., begin a three-year rebellion against U.S. rule.

B. Jews in North and South America

Jews' "physical degeneracy"—their short stature and deficient lung capacity—and his fear that the "great Polish swamp of miserable human beings" will drain itself off into the U.S.

Samuel Clemens (Mark Twain, 1835–1910) writes the essay "Concerning the Jews" in *Harper's Magazine.* He asserts that their contributions to commerce, the arts, science, and learning are way out of proportion to their numbers. The essay also contains an unfortunate stereotype that the Jews have an unpatriotic disinclination to stand by the flag as a soldier, a charge he will retract in 1904.

The National Jewish Hospital for Consumptives is opened in Denver, Colorado.

The National Conference of Jewish Charities (later known as the National Conference of Jewish Social Service) is organized in the U.S.

Frank Norris* (1870–1902) writes *McTeague,* his most widely read novel, which contains a viciously antisemitic stereotype, the red-haired junk dealer Zerkow, who is insanely money mad.

C. Jews in Europe

woman in Polna. Hilsner is convicted and sentenced to death.

On September 19, French President Loubet* pardons Captain Alfred Dreyfus.

On September 29, Chief Rabbi Moritz Guedemann takes an oath declaring the ritual murder charge against Leopold Hilsner a fabrication at a public mass meeting in Vienna. The crown prosecutor later determines that there are insufficient grounds for a criminal libel action against Guedemann on the charge of having vilified the Catholic church by his denial of the "blood accusation."

On October 10, the Semitic Section of the International Congress of Orientalists at Rome unanimously adopts a resolution declaring the ritual murder charge against the Jews as baseless.

More than a week of anti-Jewish riots begin on October 18 in about 40 towns in Bohemia and Moravia.

Samuel Hirsch Margulies (1858–1922), Galician rabbi and scholar, becomes head of the Collegio Rabbinico Italiano in Florence. He trains many rabbis and is instrumental in reviving Italian Jewish cultural life.

Sir Otto Jaffe (1846–1929), Irish industrialist, becomes lord mayor of Belfast. In 1904, when Belfast's

E. Jewish Culture

in Its Plain Meaning), on the Bible. It is regarded as an important contribution to modern biblical exegesis. He applies textual criticism and comparative philology to the Bible, then unusual for a Jew. He converted to Christianity and worked with Franz Delitzsch,* German scholar and missionary, and renounced his apostasy only when arriving in New York.

Charles Proteus Steinmetz (1865–1923), electrical engineer, arrives in the U.S. from Germany. He becomes chief consulting engineer to the General Electric Co., and his studies on the theory of alternating current are said to have led to the development of the modern electrical industry.

Solomon Schechter publishes his edition of the Hebrew original of the Wisdom of Ben Sira from manuscripts he discovered in the Cairo Genizah.

Mordecai Zeeb Feierberg (1874–1899), Hebrew writer, writes an autobiographical novel, *Whither?,* which is widely read in eastern Europe. It is the story of the alienation of Nahman, the hero, from the Jewish community and his efforts to rejoin it. At the end, he exhorts the Jews to return to Palestine, not only to escape persecution, but to build a new

A. General History	B. Jews in North and South America	C. Jews in Europe	D. Jews in the Middle East and Elsewhere	E. Jewish Culture	

| | | Jewish population will number over 1,000 as a result of Russian Jewish immigration, he will finance the construction of the community's second synagogue and lead the effort of uniting the new immigrants with the community's German Jewish founders. | | society. The novel is published shortly after Feierberg's death.

Moses Jacob Ezekiel, American sculptor, models a bust of Isaac Mayer Wise, which is probably the first three-dimensional bust of a living rabbi created by a Jew.

Isaiah Bershadsky (1871–1908) writes his Hebrew novel *Be-Ein Mattarah (To No Purpose)*. Published in Russia and set in the Pale of Settlement, it deals with the social and ideological problems of Hebrew teachers facing the question of Zionism. The novel creates the prototype of the Jewish social misfit. | **1899** |

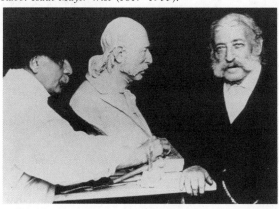

Moses Jacob Ezekiel (1844–1917) models bust of Rabbi Isaac Mayer Wise (1819–1900).

| The world Jewish population is about 10,600,000. From 1800 to 1900 it increased more than four times (from about 2,500,000), or somewhat more rapidly than the general population.

A nationalist uprising in China (the Boxer Rebellion) is crushed by an international expeditionary force.

The International Ladies' Garment Workers' Union (ILGWU) is founded. By 1903, it will have nearly 10,000 members, about a third of whom were women.

William McKinley* is reelected president of the U.S., defeating William Jennings Bryan.*

American archaeologists complete their excavation of ancient | The Jewish Agricultural Society is organized by the Baron de Hirsch Fund to promote farming among Jews in the U.S.

Henry M. Goldfogle (1856–1929), born in New York, who was a practicing lawyer and a municipal court judge, is elected to the U.S. House of Representatives from the Lower East Side. He will serve until 1915 and again from 1919 to 1921.

Bernard Felsenthal (1822–1908), Reform rabbi of Chicago, is excoriated by many Reform colleagues for his support of Zionism, as he asserts that the best answer for persecution lay in Zionism.

Jacob David Willowski (Ridbaz, 1845–1913), the well-known Russian | In March, several Jews of Konitz, West Prussia, are charged with the ritual murder of a 19-year-old youth. Anti-Jewish riots ensue. They are acquitted of the blood libel charge, although one is sentenced to prison for denying he knew the victim. He will later be pardoned. On May 1, a Court of Cassation reverses the Kuttenberg ritual murder conviction of Leopold Hilsner and orders a new trial, excluding the ritual murder charge. In November he will be sentenced to death as an accomplice to murder. The sentence will later be commuted to life imprisonment after Austrian Emperor Franz Joseph* refuses to confirm the death sentence.

David Blondes of Vilna is accused of wounding his | Baron Edmund de Rothschild announces that he will donate his Palestine colonies to the Jewish Colonization Association.

Pardes, a cooperative society for the marketing of citrus, is founded in Petah Tikvah, Palestine, by a small group of orange growers. | *The Boston Jewish Advocate*, a weekly Jewish newspaper printed in the English language, is established.

Ost und West, an illustrated modern German Jewish monthly with contributions by artists, writers, and scholars, begins publication in Berlin, Germany.

David Belasco's (1853–1931) play *Madame Butterfly* is performed in New York. The play will later become famous as Giacomo Puccini's* (1858–1924) opera.

Isidor Kaufmann (1853–1921), painter of Jewish genre subjects who was born in Hungary and settled in Vienna in 1876, paints *Yeshivah Boy at Study*. He traveled to the shtetls of Galicia, Poland, and Hungary | **1900** |

A. General History	B. Jews in North and South America	C. Jews in Europe	D. Jews in the Middle East and Elsewhere	E. Jewish Culture
1900 Nippur, revealing a bounty of Sumerian texts.	rabbi of Slutsk, while on a visit to the U.S., addresses a convention of Orthodox rabbis and declares that anyone who emigrated to America is a sinner. It is not only home that the Jews left behind in Europe, it is their Torah, their Talmud, their yeshivot—their entire Jewish way of life. In 1903, he will emigrate to the U.S. to become chief Orthodox rabbi in Chicago. He will leave the U.S. in 1905 for Palestine. Jacob Hollander (1871–1940), political economist, is appointed treasurer of Puerto Rico by President William McKinley.* He will devise Puerto Rico's revenue system.	maidservant to extract blood for Passover matzot. He is acquitted of the blood libel but convicted of wounding his servant. In 1902, after an appeal and retrial, he will be vindicated after it is established that the victim's wounds were self-inflicted. The Jews' Free School in London's East End with 3,000 pupils is the largest school in England and, reportedly, the largest Jewish teaching center in Europe. The Fourth Zionist Congress convenes. It is held in London to acquaint the British public with the aims of Zionism. The Orthodox delegation, led by Rabbi Isaac Jacob Reines of Russia, demands that the Zionist organization cease its cultural program for fear that such activity would have an antireligious character. The congress expands its program to include economic activities for the improvement of conditions in the Diaspora. On December 27, a Law of Amnesty is passed in France for all infractions of law committed in connection with the Dreyfus Affair. Captain Alfred Dreyfus requests and is granted an exception in order to pursue his case for exoneration.		to observe the customs and lives of Orthodox Jews. His paintings are popular with assimilated Jewish middle-class urban dwellers who are nostalgic for their past. Sigmund Freud, Austrian psychiatrist and originator of psychoanalysis, writes *The Interpretation of Dreams*, a report of his studies of dreams in terms of hidden symbols that reveal the unconscious mind. Isaac Blaser (1837–1907), Russian rabbi, writes *Or Yisrael* (*Light of Israel*), an exposition of the Musar movement, founded by his mentor Rabbi Israel Lipkin Salanter (1810–1883).

MAJOR JEWISH CITIES, 1900

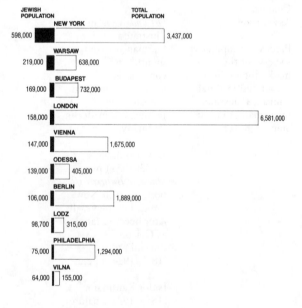

JEWISH POPULATION | TOTAL POPULATION
NEW YORK 598,000 / 3,437,000
WARSAW 219,000 / 638,000
BUDAPEST 169,000 / 732,000
LONDON 158,000 / 6,581,000
VIENNA 147,000 / 1,675,000
ODESSA 139,000 / 405,000
BERLIN 106,000 / 1,889,000
LODZ 98,700 / 315,000
PHILADELPHIA 75,000 / 1,294,000
VILNA 64,000 / 155,000

WORLD JEWISH POPULATION, 1900

TOTAL WORLD POPULATION 1,800,000,000

TOTAL WORLD JEWISH POPULATION 10,602,500

AMERICAS
1,175,000 JEWS

A. General History	B. Jews in North and South America	C. Jews in Europe	D. Jews in the Middle East and Elsewhere	E. Jewish Culture
1901 The Filipino insurrection against the U.S. ends. Military rule is replaced by civil government.	The Industrial Removal Office is organized by the American Jewish community to assist in settling immigrants	In August, Jewish students at Russian universities are restricted to 3% of the student body, and Jews are excluded entirely	In May, Theodor Herzl meets the Sultan Abdul Hamid* of Turkey in Constantinople and fails to gain approval for the creation of a	The 12-volume *Jewish Encyclopedia*, under the editorship of Isidore Singer (1859–1939), begins publication in the U.S. Completed in

A. General History	B. Jews in North and South America	C. Jews in Europe	D. Jews in the Middle East and Elsewhere	E. Jewish Culture	1901

The commonwealth of Australia is created. It is the second dominion within the British Empire.

U.S. President William McKinley* is shot by anarchist Leon Czolgosz* on September 6. He dies on September 14 and is succeeded by Vice President Theodore Roosevelt.*

Seth Low* is elected mayor of New York on a reform ticket opposed to the Tammany bosses. Jacob A. Cantor (1854–1921), a New York State senator, joins Low's reform ticket and is elected borough president of Manhattan.

The New York State legislature enacts the Tenement House Law of 1901, which prohibits further construction of dumbbell tenements, requires a separate water closet in each apartment, and improves other housing standards.

throughout the U.S. It "removed" from congested East Coast cities some 100,000 persons, or nearly 7% of all Jewish immigrants, between 1901 and 1914.

In Nome, Alaska, a Hebrew Benevolent Society is formed. The society purchases a Sefer Torah, and holds services during the High Holy Days.

Frank Norris* writes *The Octopus*, a novel dealing with the raising of wheat in California and the ranchers' struggle against the monopolistic practices of the railroad owners. The novel contains a money-obsessed character, S. Behrman, who is not mentioned as a Jew, but who exhibited the traits of the antisemitic stereotype.

from the University of Moscow.

Ivan Bliokh (1859–1942), Russian banker and pacifist, underwrites publication of five-volume work that analyzes the economic conditions of Russia's Jews and outlines their great contributions to the Russian economy. Written after the pogroms of the 1890s, its purpose was to end government discrimination of Jews. The work was confiscated by the government, but many copies survived.

Simon Dubnow (1860–1941), Russian historian, conceives of the political theory called *Autonomism*, a program for the future of the Jews. They were to exist as a national cultural entity but were to remain politically and territorially members of the states in which they lived.

Hilfsverein Der Deutschen Juden (The German–Jewish Defense Organization) is founded and concentrates its activities on education in the Balkans and the Middle East. By World War I it will have established about 50 schools, including 29 in Palestine.

Martin Buber (1878–1965), German philosopher, is appointed editor of *Die Welt*, the central weekly organ of the Zionist movement. He emphasizes the need for cultural and educational creativity.

Jewish state in Turkish-held Palestine.

In December, Jewish services for the first time are openly held in Manila, the Philippines.

Sir Aurel Stein, during explorations in Khotan, in China's Sinkiang Province, finds a Persian document in Hebrew script, part of a business letter written in 718. This find indicates that Jews visited China as early as the 8th century.

1906 with the aid of hundreds of scholars in the U.S. and abroad, this English-language encyclopedia attempts to include all Jewish knowledge.

The Jewish Morning Journal, a Yiddish daily newspaper, begins publication in New York. From 1916 to 1938, it will be edited by Jacob Fishman (1878–1946). It will merge with the *Jewish Day* in 1953 and cease publication in 1971.

The Maccabaean, a Zionist monthly, is founded in the U.S. under the editorship of Jacob De Haas (1872–1937) and Louis Lipsky (1876–1963).

Harry Clay Adler (1865–1940) becomes chairman of the board and general manager of the *Chatanooga Times* of Tennessee, a daily newspaper owned by his brother-in-law, Adolph S. Ochs.

The first Yiddish production of William Shakespeare's *Merchant of Venice* is given at the People's Theatre on New York's Lower East Side. Jacob P. Adler plays Shylock, a role that brings him world fame.

Meyer Guggenheim (1828–1905), who immigrated to the U.S. from Switzerland in 1848, takes control of the American Smelting and Refining Co. together with his sons, Daniel, Murray, and Solomon, by owning $45 million in stock.

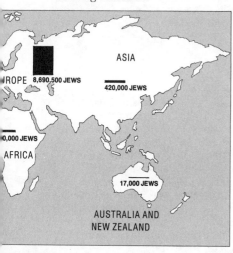

EUROPE 8,690,500 JEWS

ASIA 420,000 JEWS

0,000 JEWS

AFRICA

17,000 JEWS

AUSTRALIA AND NEW ZEALAND

A. General History	B. Jews in North and South America	C. Jews in Europe	D. Jews in the Middle East and Elsewhere	E. Jewish Culture
1901		The Fifth Zionist Congress convenes in Basel, Switzerland. The Democratic Faction, consisting of Chaim Weizmann (1874–1952), Martin Buber, Leo Motzkin (1867–1933), and others demand that the Zionist organization conduct cultural activities, separate Zionism from religion, and undertake research into suitable ways of settling in Palestine. Orthodox opposition to the faction arises, fearing the secularization of the movement. The Jewish Museum and the Society for Exploration of Jewish Antiquities are established in Frankfurt, Germany. Heinrich Von Coudenhove-Kalergi* (1859–1906), Austrian diplomat, publishes *Anti-Semitism Throughout the Ages*, in which he regards the antisemitic movements to be the result of envy, intolerance, and lack of education. He traces its roots to fanaticism instilled in children when taught that Jews crucified Christ.		They become the "copper kings" of the era. Israel Elyashev (Baal-Makhshoves, 1873–1924), Yiddish literary critic, publishes his first Yiddish critical reviews. Trained as a physician, he becomes the first critical master of modern Yiddish literature.
1902	The U.S. Congress establishes the Philippine Islands as an unincorporated territory. U.S. Secretary of State John Hay,* at the direction of President Theodore Roosevelt,* dispatches a note to American envoys in European capitals. Aimed at Romania,	Hutchins Hapgood* (1869–1944), a reporter for the *New York Commercial Advertiser*, publishes a collection of sympathetic sketches of life on the Lower East Side. Hapgood* was introduced into the area by Abraham Cahan. His book, *The Spirit of the Ghetto*, is illustrated with drawings by	Sir Marcus Samuel is elected lord mayor of London. The First Conference of Jewish Women in England establishes the Union of Jewish Women in Great Britain. It remains a social service organization of and for upper-class Jewish women until World War I.	Moshe Wallach (1866–1957), a German physician who settled in Jerusalem in 1891, establishes a modern hospital, Shaare Zedek (Gates of Righteousness) outside the old city in Jerusalem. He received financial support from the Jewish communities	Abraham Cahan returns to the *Forward* as its editor. He had participated in the founding of this New York Yiddish daily and was editor for several months in 1897. He will remain its editor until his death in 1951. Lillian Wald, U.S. social worker,

Title page of The Spirit of the Ghetto *by Hutchins Hapgood. The sweatshop worker is drawn by Jacob Epstein.*

A. General History	B. Jews in North and South America	C. Jews in Europe	D. Jews in the Middle East and Elsewhere	E. Jewish Culture

A. General History

which refused to enter into a naturalization treaty with the U.S., it declares that the U.S. will not countenance any distinction between citizens on the basis of religion.

The South African (Boer) War ends with the Treaty of Vereeniging. The Boers accept English sovereignty.

An Anglo-Japanese alliance is formed.

B. Jews in North and South America

Jacob Epstein, who uses his earnings to study sculpture in Europe.

The first U.S. collegiate Zionist society, the Students' Zionist Society, is founded at the City College of New York.

The Jewish Theological Seminary of America in New York is reorganized with Solomon Schechter as president of its faculty, Cyrus Adler as chief executive, and Louis Marshall (1856–1929) as chairman of the executive committee. In 1901, Adler encouraged business leaders, including Jacob Schiff, the Lewisohns, and the Guggenheims, to endow the seminary and to enable an invitation to Dr. Schechter to revive the institution.

New York Congressman Henry Goldfogle introduces a resolution in the House of Representatives requesting information from the Department of State as to whether American citizens of the Jewish faith holding passports issued by the U.S. government are excluded from Russia and what action the U.S. government has taken concerning such discrimination.

At the annual convention of the Central Conference of Reform Rabbis, question of whether to transfer the Sabbath from Saturday to Sunday is widely discussed, and the issue is deferred for later

C. Jews in Europe

Claude Montefiore and Lily Montagu found a radical Reform movement in England, the Jewish Religious Union. At first, it runs services supplementary to those of existing synagogues. In 1911, the union will establish the Liberal Jewish Synagogue. It advocates the equality of women in the synagogue and community.

Juedischer Verlag, the first Zionist publishing house in western Europe, is established by members of the Democratic Faction at the Fifth Zionist Congress. The Verlag will publish literary, cultural, and artistic accomplishments of the Jewish people. Ephraim Moses Lilien, illustrator and printmaker and the first artist to become involved in the Zionist movement, serves as manager, editor, and publicity agent, as well as illustrator.

The Second Conference of Russian Zionists is held publicly in Minsk. Control of cultural activity dominates the debate. Ahad ha-Am and Nahum Sokolow (1859–1936) demand national cultural activity. Sokolow is a pioneer in Hebrew journalism. They are opposed by the Orthodox. In a compromise, two committees for cultural activity— traditional and secular—are created.

All Jews residing in the surroundings of Kiev, Russia, are ordered to leave immediately.

D. Jews in the Middle East and Elsewhere

of Amsterdam and Frankfurt.

The first synagogue in Hong Kong is dedicated.

Joseph Chamberlain* (1836–1914), Britain's colonial secretary, meets Theodor Herzl to discuss Herzl's plan to establish a self-governing Jewish colony at El-Arish in the Sinai Peninsula. The site is rejected by authorities in Egypt, because the colony would have to draw off large amounts of Nile water for irrigation.

E. Jewish Culture

introduces the idea of the school nurse in the U.S.

Old New Land, Theodor Herzl's Zionist novel, is published. His novel prophesies social and technological achievements of Palestinian settlement on a cooperative basis, calls for Arab and Jewish tolerance, but reveals a lack of awareness of Jewish tradition and culture and ignores the significance of the Hebrew language to the Zionist movement.

The first source book for the study of the history of medieval German Jewry is published. The collection of sources was gathered by Julius Aronius (1861–1893) and serves as a model for similar works produced in other countries.

Emile Durkheim (1858–1917), French sociologist, becomes professor of sociology and education at the Sorbonne, in Paris. A leader in the field, he emphasizes the role of philosophical criticism and anthropology in sociology.

Solomon Reinach (1858–1932), French archaeologist, delivers a series of lectures culminating in 1903 at the Ecole du Louvre on the history of art. Subsequently published under the title *Apollo*, it achieves widespread popularity as a manual of the history of art throughout the ages.

	A. General History	B. Jews in North and South America	C. Jews in Europe	D. Jews in the Middle East and Elsewhere	E. Jewish Culture
1902		resolution. The conference will go on record in favor of strengthening the "historical Sabbath." Factory workers of R. Hoe & Co. cause a riot at the funeral procession of Chief Rabbi Jacob Joseph on New York City's Lower East Side. The quelling of the riot results in charges of police brutality against Jews. Jewish women on New York's Lower East Side initiate a successful boycott of kosher butchers to protest the rising cost of kosher meat. Eastern European Orthodox rabbis found the Union of Orthodox Rabbis (Agudat ha-Rabbanim) in the U.S. It will be led for many years by Rabbi Israel Rosenberg (1875–1956). Oscar S. Straus is appointed by President Theodore Roosevelt* to the Permanent Court of International Arbitration of the Hague. Jewish settlements in Moiseville and Mauricio, Argentina, founded under the auspices of Baron Maurice de Hirsch, and housing over 340 European immigrant families, report successful agricultural achievements.	The Artisans Bill is enacted into law in Romania, which contains requirements making it impossible for Jewish tradesmen to obtain the right to work and hastens Jewish emigration. Isaac Jacob Reines, a rabbi in Lida, convenes a conference of Orthodox rabbis and lay leaders in Vilna, from which the religious Zionist movement, Mizrahi, is formed. Their motto is "The land of Israel for the people of Israel according to the Torah of Israel." These Orthodox opponents to the Democratic Faction of the Fifth Zionist Congress defend political Zionism but oppose the cultural activity of the Zionist Organization. During the year, Reines writes *A New Light on Zion*, in which he counters Orthodox rabbinic opposition to Zionism. Max Regis,* a notorious antisemite and former mayor of Algiers, is tried and sentenced to three years' imprisonment in France for libels against Jews.		Giuseppe Ottolenghi (1838–1904) is named minister of war of Italy. An army officer, he is the first Jew to serve on the general staff. He achieved the rank of lieutenant general.
1903	The U.S. supports the revolution in Panama and recognizes the new republic of Panama. An agreement with Panama gives the U.S. a 10-mile-wide strip for construction of a canal connecting	The American section of Mizrahi, the religious Zionist organization, is established. The first national Jewish sorority to be formed in the U.S., the Iota Alpha Pi, is	In Kishinev, Bessarabia, a pogrom results in 45 Jewish dead, 86 seriously wounded, 500 other casualties, and 1,500 shops and homes plundered or destroyed. Agents of the Russian Interior	One hundred Jews flee Taza, Morocco, and report that the occupying troops of the sultan had massacred a number of Jews, violated women and girls, and pillaged the shops.	"The New Colossus," a poem written by Emma Lazarus (1849–1887) in 1883, is engraved on a bronze plaque and placed on the base of the Statue of Liberty in New York Harbor.

A. General History	B. Jews in North and South America	C. Jews in Europe	D. Jews in the Middle East and Elsewhere	E. Jewish Culture

A. General History

the Atlantic and Pacific oceans.

Germany, Austria–Hungary, and Italy renew their Triple Alliance. This renewal is repeated in 1912.

A German firm begins construction of the Berlin–Baghdad railway.

The U.S. Department of Commerce and Labor is created.

The Ford Motor Co. is created.

The Wright* brothers achieve their first successful heavier-than-air flight.

The Lumière* brothers produce photographic plates in color.

The first moving picture to tell a story, *The Great Train Robbery*, is produced.

B. Jews in North and South America

organized at Hunter College in New York.

Kaufmann Kohler becomes president of the Hebrew Union College in Cincinnati, Ohio. A distinguished scholar, he is determined to raise the institution's academic standards and ensures that the college will be a Reform institution.

Alexander Marx (1871–1953), historian and librarian, is appointed librarian and teacher of history at the Jewish Theological Seminary of America. When he arrives from Germany, the seminary library contains three manuscripts and 5,000 volumes. At the time of his death, the library will possess 8,500 manuscripts and 153,000 volumes.

The southern New Jersey farming village of Woodbine, supported by the Baron de Hirsch Fund, becomes the first all-Jewish municipality in the U.S.

On June 3, Lyman Abbott,* respected voice of American Protestantism, writes that the Jews were responsible for the death of Jesus.

Twenty-five Jewish bakers in Newark, New Jersey, strike in response to the refusal of their employers to grant them Saturday as a holiday.

Jews comprise 50% of the 5,000 to 6,000 physicians in New York, according to the estimate of Dr.

C. Jews in Europe

Ministry and local officials were apparently involved in the pogrom's preparation. It was preceded by antisemitic attacks in a government-supported newspaper edited by P. A. Krushevan.*

After the Kishinev pogrom, Hayyim Nahman Bialik, Russian Hebrew poet, begins writing "poems of wrath." At first, he writes "Al ha-Shehitah" ("On the Slaughter"), in which he accuses the perpetrators. Later, in the summer, he writes "Be-ir ha-Haregah" ("In the City of Slaughter"), a denunciation of the submission to the massacre, which spurs Jewish youth to organize a self-defense group. Translated into Russian by Vladimir (Ze'ev) Jabotinsky (1880–1940) and into Yiddish, this poem establishes Bialik's reputation as the national poet of the Jewish people.

Leo Tolstoy,* Russian literary master, notes that the "outrages at Kishinev are but the direct result of the propaganda of falsehood and violence which our Government conducts with such energy" and Maxim Gorki,* Russian author, states that "cultivated society is no less guilty of the disgraceful and horrible deeds committed at Kishinev than the actual murderers and ravishers."

The Bund is expelled from the

D. Jews in the Middle East and Elsewhere

Jews hover over victims killed in the Kishinev pogrom, 1903.

E. Jewish Culture

The Semitic Museum building at Harvard University, funded almost entirely by the generosity of Jacob Schiff, is dedicated.

Jacob P. Adler stars as Shylock in *The Merchant of Venice* in a New York Broadway production. Adler speaks his lines in Yiddish with an English-speaking cast. He also opens his Grand Theatre on New York's Lower East Side. It is the first playhouse built specifically for the Yiddish stage.

Barney Dreyfuss (1865–1932), owner of the National League Pittsburgh Pirates baseball team, proposes that his National League champion meet the American League champion, the Boston Red Sox, in a series of games, the first World Series.

Mayer Sulzberger, U.S. communal leader, donates his collection of 3,000 rare books to the Jewish Theological Seminary of America.

Morris Joseph (1848–1930), English Reform rabbi, writes *Judaism as Creed and*

A. General History	B. Jews in North and South America	C. Jews in Europe	D. Jews in the Middle East and Elsewhere	E. Jewish Culture
1903	Isaac M. Rubinow (1875–1936), U.S. economist and social worker. Roger Mitchell* writes *Recent Jewish Immigration to the United States* in *Popular Science Monthly*, in which he describes the Jews of New York's Lower East Side as vulnerable to chronic disease and physical breakdown. "Their mental processes were not of the Western order, but, after all, the Hebrew is only more or less modified Oriental still." Owen Wister* (1860–1938), U.S. author, writes *Philosophy Four*, a novella of undergraduate life at Harvard, which portrays patrician antisemitism of two Harvard upper-class students toward Maironi, a poor, aspiring Jewish classmate. Henrietta Szold is granted permission to attend classes at the Jewish Theological Seminary of America "only after she had assured its administration that she would not use the knowledge thus gained to seek ordination."	Russian Social Democratic Labor party at its Second Congress for its exposition of nationalist positions. Theodor Herzl visits Russia to seek Russian intervention with Turkey on behalf of his Zionist proposals to secure Jewish settlement in Palestine, and to permit open Zionist activity in Russia. He meets with Russian Interior Minister, Plehve,* who is believed to be responsible for the Kishinev pogrom. Joseph Chamberlain* Britain's colonial secretary, suggests to Theodor Herzl the consideration of a self-governing Jewish settlement in an uninhabited region of Uganda (now Kenya). The Chamberlain–Herzl negotiations of the "Uganda scheme" are the first recognition of the president of the Zionist organization as representing the Jewish people. The Sixth Zionist Congress convenes in Basel. Theodor Herzl brings the Uganda scheme before the congress as a temporary measure, emphasizing that Palestine remains Zionism's final objective. Herzl is supported by Max Nordau, who terms the Uganda scheme a *Nachtasyl* (refuge for the night), and is opposed by Russian Zionists. A pogrom in Gomel leaves eight Jews dead and 100 injured. For the first time a Jewish self-defense group fights the attackers.		*Life*, a popular formulation of Judaism as practiced in England. Marcus Jastrow, rabbi and scholar, completes *A Dictionary of the Targumim, the Talmud Babli and Yerushalmi, and the Midrashic Literature.* *Jewish History: An Essay in the Philosophy of History*, by the Russian historian Simon Dubnow, is published in English translation. A Jewish museum is founded in Danzig. In 1939, at the outbreak of World War II, the collection will be shipped to the Jewish Museum in New York.

A. General History	B. Jews in North and South America	C. Jews in Europe	D. Jews in the Middle East and Elsewhere	E. Jewish Culture	
		Vladimir Lenin* (1870–1924), Russian revolutionary, writes *The Position of the Bund in the Party* in the magazine *ISKRA*. He opposes antisemitism but insists that the Jews must undergo a more radical and cultural transformation than other Russians. A synagogue in Szeged, Hungary, is opened under the leadership of Rabbi Immanuel Loew (1854–1944). Seating over 1,100, it includes stained glass windows that depict a thematic cycle inspired by Jewish literary sources.			**1903**
Great Britain and France enter into their Entente Cordiale. In February, the Russo-Japanese War begins. The Japanese attack Port Arthur. In May, the Japanese defeat the Russians at the Yalu River and occupy Dairen. They begin the siege of Port Arthur. In July, the Trans-Siberian Railroad, linking the Ural Mountains to Russia's Pacific coast, is completed after 13 years of construction. The first subway in New York, from City Hall to 145th Street, opens. Theodore Roosevelt* is elected president of the U.S., defeating Alton B. Parker.* Lincoln Steffens* (1866–1936) writes *The Shame of the Cities*, a journalistic exposé of municipal and business	Jacob Schiff, of the then Jewish banking firm of Kuhn, Loeb & Co., takes a leading role in underwriting a bond issue of $200 million for Japan during the 1904–1905 Russo-Japanese War. He was deeply angered by the antisemitic policies of the Russian regime. Alarmed by the prostitution problem in New York, the Baron de Hirsch Fund founds the Clara de Hirsch home for immigrant girls. Martin Behrman (1864–1926) is elected mayor of New Orleans, Louisiana, and serves four terms until his defeat in 1920. Myra Kelly,* an Irish public school teacher, publishes *Little Citizens*, a collection of her short stories of the lives of Jewish school-children on New York's Lower East Side.	A synagogue is dedicated in Lisbon, the first opened in Portugal since the expulsion in 1498. Theodor Herzl dies on July 3. A conference of Mizrahi Zionists convenes at Pressburg, Hungary. Rabbi Isaac Jacob Reines presides. He is a staunch Zionist and has been a supporter of Theodor Herzl. The aim of Mizrahi is to counteract the irreligious declarations of many Zionist spokesmen and to make it possible for the Orthodox to remain in the movement. Two thousand observant Jews in London's East End attack the members of the Social Democratic Club in their clubhouse for disregarding the Day of Atonement. Karl Lueger,* antisemitic mayor of Vienna since 1897, urges Christians to	Aharon David Gordon (1856–1922), Hebrew writer and Zionist thinker, leaves Russia to settle in Palestine. Although 48 years old, he works on the land. His writings advocate that Jewish workers in Palestine must find their way to a just society through a life of labor. The Gordonia Zionist youth movement will be founded in Galicia in 1925. Jacques Faitlovitch (1881–1955), who studied Oriental languages in Paris, embarks on his first trip to Ethiopia, where he spends 18 months studying the beliefs and customs of the Falashas. He believes the Falashas are Jews and that it is not enough to study them. World Jewry has an obligation to save them from extinction. Faitlovich will organize pro-Falasha committees in Europe, the U.S., and Palestine.	Mayer Sulzberger, U.S. jurist and communal leader, donates 26 ceremonial objects and his Hebrew book collection to the library of the Jewish Theological Seminary of America. He recommends that the seminary begin to organize a Jewish museum. Ralph David Blumenfeld (1864–1934) becomes editor of the *London Daily Express*. Until his retirement in 1932, he edits the paper for mass appeal and raises its circulation to 2 million daily. Arthur Ruppin (1876–1943), German sociologist and Zionist leader, writes *The Jews in the Modern World*, the first work of Jewish sociology to be based on demographic and statistical study. Nahum Slouschz (1871–1966), Semitic scholar, is appointed to a newly founded chair of Hebrew	**1904**

A. General History	B. Jews in North and South America	C. Jews in Europe	D. Jews in the Middle East and Elsewhere	E. Jewish Culture

1904

A. General History

corruption in the U.S.

The Iman Yahya* of Yemen leads a revolt against Ottoman rule. The Turks will finally evacuate the country in 1911.

B. Jews in North and South America

"The Scattered Nation," a classic philo-Semitic lecture delivered many times by North Carolina Senator Zebulon B. Vance* (1830–1894), is published. He praised the Jewish love of learning and their ability to flourish despite persecutions throughout the centuries.

Thirty-seven families, numbering 267 persons, from Bessarabia found an agricultural colony in the state of Rio Grande do Sul, Brazil. It is named Philippson, after its initiator.

C. Jews in Europe

avoid Christmas shopping at Jewish shops. Lueger* has a profound influence on young Adolf Hitler.*

Prime Minister Arthur James Balfour* (1848–1930) submits a restrictive Aliens Bill to Parliament designed to regulate immigration to Great Britain. The bill is withdrawn after it is attacked by Winston Churchill* (1875–1965) and other opposition leaders as inhuman and antisemitic.

Michael Davitt* writes *Within the Pale*, a U.S. correspondent's account of the Kishinev massacres of 1903, in which he concludes that the pogrom had been planned "with the passive connivance of the Chief of Police and the active encouragement of some of his officers."

Forty-three pogroms throughout Russia during the year are recorded in *The American Jewish Year Book (1906–1907)*. They included Ostrovitz on August 13, when 20 Jews are killed; Ovidiopol on November 4, when 11 are killed and over 200 wounded; and Slonim on November 16, when many are killed. Mobilization of reservists for the unpopular war in the Far East often leads to the pogroms by the reservists. The antisemitic press accuses the Jews of deliberately bringing about the war with Japan.

The Temple Israelitico in Rome is

E. Jewish Culture

language and literature at the Sorbonne. In 1902, he wrote *The Renascence of Modern Hebrew Literature*, which will be translated into English by Henrietta Szold in 1909. In 1919, he will settle in Israel, where he will revive the Palestine Exploration Society.

Second "Aliyah" to Palestine, 1904–1914
Number: 40,000
  Origin: Russians, labor and social Zionists, disillusioned by wave of pogroms that followed 1905 Revolution

---

A. General History	B. Jews in North and South America	C. Jews in Europe	D. Jews in the Middle East and Elsewhere	E. Jewish Culture	
		opened. Situated on the bank of the Tiber, it is of classical design. Bertha Pappenheim (1859–1936), leader of the German Jewish feminist movement and social worker, founds the Jewish Women's Organization. Her social work energies are directed against prostitution, white slavery, and illegitimacy. In 1914, near Frankfurt, she will establish a home for unwed mothers, delinquent women, prostitutes, and their children.			**1904**
In January, Russia surrenders Port Arthur to the Japanese. In January, unrest and strikes by workers results in bloodshed in Russia. Unrest and disorder continue throughout the year. In March, the Japanese defeat the Russian armies at Mukden, China. In May, the Japanese navy destroys the Russian fleet in the naval battle in the Tsushima Straits. In September, the Treaty of Portsmouth ends the Russo-Japanese War. U.S. President Theodore Roosevelt* mediates the settlement and will be awarded the Nobel Peace Prize in 1906. In October, under the pressure of a great general strike and public demonstrations, Czar Nicholas II* issues the October Manifesto, promising basic freedoms to the	Isidor Rayner (1850–1912) is elected U.S. senator from Maryland and serves until 1912. On Thanksgiving Day, at a New York celebration of the 250th anniversary of the settlement of the Jews in the U.S., President Theodore Roosevelt* sends a letter in support of Russian Jewish immigration. He writes that from Colonial days the Jews "have become indissolubly incorporated in the great army of American citizenship. . . . This is true not only of the descendants of the early settlers and those of American birth, but of a great and constantly increasing proportion of those who have come to our shores within the last twenty-five years as refugees reduced to the direst straits of penury and misery." Louis Marshall, on the occasion of the 250th anniversary of American Jewish settlement, is invited	A pogrom occurs in Zhitomir at the Russian government's instigation. Jewish self-defense efforts limit the number of Jews killed to about 15. In May, 52 Russian Jewish communities present a Declaration of Jewish Citizens to representatives of the czar, signed by 60,000, urging that civil rights be extended to Jews so they can have a normal existence in Russia. The Seventh Zionist Congress convenes in Basel under the leadership of Max Nordau. It rules out any alternative to Palestine as the Zionist objective, rejecting the Uganda scheme. A minority, headed by Israel Zangwill, secede and found the Jewish Territorial Organization. Zangwill argues that the essence of Zionism is not organically connected to Palestine and that the Zionist effort can be directed to any	Ha-Poel ha-Za'ir (The Young Worker) labor organization is founded in Palestine by the pioneers of the Second Aliyah. It seeks to initiate the principle of labor into the work program of Zionism, transforming it from a means of livelihood into a supreme value. Its members are among the founders of Kibbutz Deganyah and of the first moshav. In 1930, it will merge with Ahdut ha-Avodah, and the Israel Labour party, Mapai, will be created. The Temple of Onias is excavated by Flinders Petrie* (1853–1942), British Egyptologist, near Heliopolis, Egypt. Several inscriptions testify to the existence of ancient synagogues.	The Union of American Hebrew Congregations (Reform) creates a Board of Editors of Religious School Literature, which pioneers the writing and publication in English of textbooks, curricula, and teacher's guides. Abraham Cahan writes *The White Terror and the Red*, a fictionalized account of the revolutionary movement in Russia and the attitude and participation of Jews in the movement. Charles S. Bernheimer (1868–1960), U.S. social worker, edits *The Russian Jew in the United States*, containing studies of social conditions in New York, Philadelphia, and Chicago, with a description of rural settlements. Contributors include Henrietta Szold, Abraham Cahan, Isaac M. Rubinow, and Louis Lipsky. New York's Little Gallery of the Photo-Secession is	**1905**

A. General History	B. Jews in North and South America	C. Jews in Europe	D. Jews in the Middle East and Elsewhere	E. Jewish Culture
1905 whole population and creating a parliament, the Duma. In December, the Russian government suppresses an insurrection of workers in Moscow. The army restores order in the provinces. The first Moroccan crisis occurs. Germany opposes French ambitions in Morocco. Sun Yat-sen* founds a revolutionary league aimed at expelling the Manchus from China. The Norwegian union with Sweden is dissolved. Norway becomes a monarchy. Lewis W. Hine,* pioneer in photojournalism, starts photographing working conditions in American factories and mines, as well as conditions at Ellis Island and in the tenements. The first use of the term *picture story* occurs in connection with his work.	by *Harper's Weekly* to write on the Jews' financial position in the U.S. Marshall's article dispels the myth that all Jews are wealthy and that they control the economic wealth of the country. He maintains that the Jews are hardworking, self-reliant and patriotic. Solomon Schechter, chancellor of the Jewish Theological Seminary of America, joins the American Zionist Federation. The next year he will write *Zionism: A Statement*. His endorsement of the doctrine of Jewish national restoration in Palestine adds the support of the Conservative movement to the growth of Zionism in America. In December, more than 100,000 New Yorkers stage a demonstration to express their anger and their sorrow due to the pogroms in Russia. Rabbi Jacob David Willowski (Ridbaz, 1845–1913), who came to the U.S. from Russia in 1903 to accept an appointment as the chief rabbi of a group of Orthodox congregations in Chicago, leaves for Palestine where he founds a yeshiva in Safed. He leaves in despair of the future of Judaism in the U.S. In 1904, he wrote: "There are many God-fearing Jews in this land. When they see what is happening to their children, they curse the day they came to this land."	country suitable for mass settlement and national autonomy. David Wolffsohn is elected president of the Zionist organization and moves its center from Vienna to his native Cologne. Ber Borochov (1881–1917), Russian Socialist Zionist leader, writes *On the Question of Zion and Territory*, an essay that outlines his opposition to the Uganda scheme. In August, the Aliens Bill, passed by Britain's Parliament, becomes law to be effective on January 1, 1906. Its primary aim is to prevent mass immigration, largely Jewish, from Russia. Britain's Prime Minister Arthur James Balfour declares in the House of Commons, "the treatment of the [Jewish] race has been a disgrace to Christendom." He is invited by the *London Jewish Chronicle* to explain how his sympathy for persecuted Jews could be reconciled with a policy designed to refuse asylum to them. Government-inspired pogroms take place in 660 Russian Jewish communities during the course of one week, resulting in about 1,000 dead, 7,000–8,000 wounded, and widespread property damage. Among the communities affected is Odessa, where at least 300 are killed and thousands wounded. The Russian Jewish Bund, which was formed in 1897 as		founded by Edward Steichen* and Alfred Stieglitz (1864–1946) at 291 5th Avenue, where photography as well as the works of American and European artists, such as Pablo Picasso* and Henri Matissse,* are exhibited. Stieglitz fights for the recognition of photography as an art, and he is the first photographer whose photographs are accepted by American museums. Elkan Adler (1861–1946), English lawyer, bibliophile, and world traveler, writes *Jews in Many Lands*, which includes descriptions of Jewish life in Palestine. The Warburg Bibliothek is founded by Aby Warburg (1866–1929), German historian of art and civilization, in Hamburg, Germany. Its purpose is to trace the influence of classical antiquity on subsequent civilizations. The Bibliothek will be transferred to London and renamed the Warburg Institute upon the advent of Adolf Hitler.* Rabbi Leo Baeck (1874–1956), German theologian, writes *The Essence of Judaism* as a reply to Protestant theologian Adolf von Harnack's* *The Essence of Christianity*. Baeck argues that Judaism is the religion of reason, while Christianity is the religion of romantic irrationalism.

1905

A. General History

B. Jews in North and South America

The New York Board of Regents censures State Librarian Melvil Dewey* in response to a petition from a group of leading Jews, because he operates a summer hotel that baldly advertises its anti-Jewish exclusionary policies.

The Workmen's Circle (Arbeiter Ring) is incorporated in the U.S. as a fraternal society created for mutual aid and the promotion of cultural activities in Yiddish.

The Union of American Hebrew Congregations purchases an 18-acre tract of land opposite a park in Cincinnati near the University of Cincinnati for a new campus of the Hebrew Union College.

Edith Wharton* (1862–1937), U.S. novelist, writes *The House of Mirth*, a novel of an unmarried, socially prominent New York woman who seeks marriage with a man of wealth. One of her suitors is Simon Rosedale, a vulgar, rich Jew, a repugnant character whose life is dominated by moneymaking and a determination for social success.

C. Jews in Europe

the first Jewish Socialist party, has 30,000 members. Its influence on Russian socialism is evident as the general Russian Socialist party has 50,000 members.

Count Vladimir Lamsdorf,* Russia's minister of foreign affairs, tries to persuade the czar that the revolution of 1905 had been directed by the forces of world Jewry, led by the Alliance Israelite Universelle, "which possesses giant pecuniary means, disposes of an enormous membership, and is supported by Masonic lodges of every description."

The first Russian public edition of *The Protocols of the Elders of Zion* appears. This antisemitic forgery purports to show the existence of an international Jewish conspiracy aimed at worldwide domination. It is believed that an unknown author developed *The Protocols* in Paris at the end of the 19th century at the behest of the Russian secret police, who sought to influence Czar Nicholas II.

Isaac Jacob Reines, Orthodox rabbi and leader of the religious Zionist movement, founds a modern yeshiva in Lida, a town in the province of Grodno, which meticulously adheres to tradition and in which secular and vocational studies are taught together with religious studies.

In the wake of the Dreyfus Affair,

E. Jewish Culture

Albert Einstein (1879–1955), while working at the Patent Office in Berne, Switzerland, publishes *The Special Theory of Relativity*, which includes his famous $E = mc^2$ equation showing that mass and energy are relative with respect to time.

Sigmund Freud, Austrian psychiatrist, writes *Three Essays on the Theory of Sexuality*, in which he elaborates on the importance of infantile sexuality and the Oedipus complex.

Adolf von Baeyer (1835–1917), German organic chemist, is awarded the Nobel Prize in chemistry for the advancement of organic chemistry and the chemical industry through his work on organic dyes and hydroaromatic compounds.

Samuel Hirszenberg, Polish painter who was among the first to depict the sad plight of the Jews in Russian-dominated Poland, paints *The Black Banner*, showing the anguished expression of black-clad Hasidic men carrying a coffin.

	A. General History	B. Jews in North and South America	C. Jews in Europe	D. Jews in the Middle East and Elsewhere	E. Jewish Culture
1905			France passes a law separating church and state, and the Consistoire of French Jews becomes a voluntary organization.		
1906	In April, San Francisco is devastated by the most severe earthquake in U.S. history. The ensuing fire destroys most of the city's central area. In May, the first elected Duma, the imperial Russian legislature, convenes. In July, the czar dissolves the first Russian Duma. The Algeciras Conference reaffirms French and Spanish control in Morocco. In October, Georges Clemenceau* (1841–1929) becomes prime minister of France and appoints Colonel Marie-Georges Picquart* minister of war.	In April, the San Francisco earthquake and fire result in the destruction of three synagogues, the B'nai B'rith library, school buildings and the clinic of the Emanu-El Sisterhood. On June 22, Congress passes a joint resolution declaring "that the people of the United States are horrified by the reports of the massacre of Hebrews in Russia, on account of their race and religion" and expresses sympathy with the sufferers. On November 11, the American Jewish Committee is founded in New York in the aftermath of the Kishinev pogrom. The founders include Jacob Schiff, Louis Marshall, Oscar S. Straus, Cyrus Adler, and Mayer Sulzberger. Oscar S. Straus is named secretary of commerce and labor by President Theodore Roosevelt.* The first Jew named to a cabinet post, he will serve until March 1909 and is noted for his opposition to exclusionist immigration policies, including those affecting the Japanese. Sholom Aleichem moves to New York, where he hopes to achieve financial success by writing for the Yiddish theater.	In May, there are 12 Jews elected to the first Russian Duma, including Maxim Vinawer (1862–1926), Shmarya Levin (1867–1935), and Leon Bramson (1869–1941). In June, a pogrom takes place in Bialystok, resulting in over 200 dead and hundreds injured, despite spirited Jewish self-defense efforts. The newly formed Duma orders an investigation. In July, the Duma Commission investigating the Bialystok pogrom lays blame on the Russian government. On July 12, after a new inquiry, the French Court of Appeal proclaims the innocence of Captain Alfred Dreyfus. He is reinstated in the French army and is made Chevalier of the Legion of Honor at the Ecole Militaire. In August, a pogrom occurs in Siedlce in which about 30 Jews are killed and 180 are wounded. At about this time, the second wave of pogroms in Russia ends. Pogroms begin again after the downfall of the czar in 1917. The founding conference of the Po'alei Zion (Zionist Socialist Workers) of Russia is held at Poltava. Ber Borochov, founder of	In April, the U.S. delegate to the Conference on Morocco held at Algeciras, Spain, on instruction from the State Department, has a clause inserted in the treaty guaranteeing the security and equal privileges of the Jews in Morocco. In September, David Ben-Gurion (1886–1973) leaves Russia and settles in Palestine and works in the orange groves of Petah Tikvah and in the wine cellars of Rishon le-Zion. Aaron Aaronsohn (1876–1919), Palestinian agronomist and, later, founder of the espionage group NILI, discovers wild emmer wheat in the Galilee. This discovery earns him a reputation in scientific circles. Boris Schatz (1866–1932) emigrates to Palestine from Bulgaria, where he was head of the Royal Academy of Art in Sofia, and founds the Bezalel School of Arts and Crafts in Jerusalem. The school develops a national artistic style combining Near Eastern forms with European techniques.	The *Forward* begins publishing the "Bintel Brief" ("Bundle of Letters") when editor Abraham Cahan senses a need for his immigrant readers to have a place to air their problems. Bertha Kalich (1875–1939), the first Yiddish actress in the U.S. to gain recognition on the English stage, is the heroine in an English production of Yiddish playwright Jacob Gordin's *Kreutzer Sonata*. The play preaches women's rights to human fulfillment. Benjamin Altman (1840–1913) moves his large department store, known as B. Altman & Co., to 5th Avenue in New York. It becomes the first department store to be established in a residential area. The London Whitechapel Art Gallery holds an exhibition of Jewish art and antiquities, which includes the works of contemporary Jewish artists. Martin Buber, German philosopher who became a student of Hasidism, writes *The Tales of Rabbi Nachman of Bratslav*, a retelling of the Hasidic leader's tales. This book will be followed in 1908 by his *The Legend of the Baal-Shem*.

346

1906

B. Jews in North and South America

In the summer of 1907 he will return to Europe bitterly disappointed. He will return to New York in December 1914.

In an exchange of letters with New York's Temple Emanu-El, Rabbi Stephen S. Wise (1874–1949) insists on the right to advocate his personal views as a condition of his accepting an offer of the pulpit. As a result, he is not offered the pulpit and in 1907 will found his own Free Synagogue.

The Central Conference of American Rabbis (Reform) issues a statement that the Bible should not be read in U.S. public schools where different views have to be treated impartially.

The first Jewish collegiate association in the U.S., the Menorah Society, is founded at Harvard by Henry Hurwitz (1886–1961). He hopes to nourish an interest in Jewish studies, and ultimately win a "rightful place for the field of Jewish history and culture in the university." The Menorah movement will spread to about 30 universities in the next two decades.

The "white slave" traders in Argentina organize themselves into the Zwi Migdal Society. It protects them through bribery of the authorities. As they are ostracized by the Jewish community, the Society supplies religious services such as a separate

C. Jews in Europe

the party and Yiddish scholar, outlines the program of the party, which is a synthesis of Marxist and Zionist ideologies.

In December, the third conference of Russian Zionists is held in Helsinki, Finland. Meeting after the revolution of 1905, pogroms, the death of Theodor Herzl, and the growing influence of competing ideologies among the Jewish masses, it resolves to "work in the present" without rejecting the fundamental Zionist aim of "negating the Diaspora." Zionists are to organize Diaspora Jewry as a national minority who will be provided with the cultural, material, and political means to assist in the creation of a proper national life in Palestine.

Simon Dubnow, Russian Jewish historian and political ideologist, founds the Folkist (Jewish People's) party. Its goal is the attainment of Jewish autonomy in Russia. Nationalities would be granted full autonomy in the realms of education and culture by a constitutional government that would deal with matters of general concern. The party will achieve little political influence.

Winston Churchill,* as undersecretary for the colonies, publicly supports Israel Zangwill's Jewish Territorial Organization, whose objective is autonomous Jewish settlement within the British Empire.

E. Jewish Culture

August von Wassermann (1866–1925), German bacteriologist and immunologist, develops his famous test for syphilis.

Henri Moissan (1852–1907), French inorganic chemist, is awarded the Nobel Prize for chemistry for his investigation and isolation of the element fluorine.

Salomon Hugo Lieben (1881–1942), historian of Bohemian Jewry, founds and directs the Prague Jewish Museum.

A 16-volume Russian Jewish encyclopedia begins publication under the editorship of Judah Leib Katznelson (1846–1917), Simon Dubnow, David Guenzburg (1857–1910), and Abraham Harkavy (1835–1919).

The Gesamtarchiv der Deutschen Juden (The Complete Archive of German Jewry) is established in Berlin. Until taken over in 1938 by the Nazis, this archive contains the records of hundreds of German Jewish communities. Its first director is Eugen Taeubler (1879–1953). The Nazis will make extensive genealogical use of these records. The remains of the archive, including records of 800 former Jewish communities in Germany, will be transferred to Jerusalem in 1954 and become the Central Archives for the History of the Jewish People.

	A. General History	B. Jews in North and South America	C. Jews in Europe	D. Jews in the Middle East and Elsewhere	E. Jewish Culture
1906		synagogue and cemetery. The Society will be dissolved by the government in 1930.			
1907	The U.S. Congress establishes the Dillingham Commission, headed by Senator William P. Dillingham* of Vermont, to investigate the impact of immigration upon the well-being of the nation as an outgrowth of the failed renewed attempt to establish a literacy test. It is composed of six experts appointed by Congress and three by President Theodore Roosevelt* and will present its conclusions in 1910. Oklahoma becomes the 46th state of the U.S. Japanese immigration to the U.S. is restricted by a "gentlemen's agreement." Walter Rauschenbusch* (1861–1918) writes the manifesto of the Protestant Social Gospel movement, *Christianity and the Social Crisis.* In February, the Second Duma, the imperial Russian legislature, is elected. It is dissolved in June. The Third Duma is then elected under a new electoral law and serves until 1912. In August, the Anglo-Russian agreement completes the Triple Entente, whose members are France, Great Britain, and Russia.	The New York City Board of Education, in response to protests from Jewish religious organizations, adopts a resolution prohibiting the singing of sectarian hymns or songs, the reading of religious books other than the Bible, and the holding of sectarian or religious exercises at the beginning of the winter vacation in the public schools. Three members of the faculty of the Hebrew Union College—Henry Malter (1864–1925), Max L. Margolis (1886–1932), and Max Schloessinger (1877–1944)—resign because of their Zionist sentiments, which run counter to President Kaufmann Kohler's and the board's anti-Zionist views. In May, the State Department issues a directive informing passport applicants that passports will not be issued to former Russian subjects or to Jews intending to visit Russia, unless the Russian government consents. The directive is changed after a protest by the American Jewish Committee that the directive imposes an unconstitutional religious test. Harvard University President Charles E. Eliot,* in an address to the university's Menorah Society, notes that there are 60 Jews among a student body of	The Eighth Zionist Congress convenes at The Hague, in the Netherlands, under the leadership of David Wolffsohn. Chaim Weizmann speaks of "synthetic Zionism" merging political and practical Zionism into an organic whole. A Palestine office is opened in Jaffa, headed by Arthur Ruppin, to direct agricultural settlements. Leopold Jacob Greenberg (1861–1931), English journalist and early supporter of Theodor Herzl (1860–1904), and friends buy the *London Jewish Chronicle* to ensure that the Zionist cause would have an adequate public forum in Great Britain. He serves as editor of the weekly until his death. Max Isidor Bodenheimer, German Zionist leader, becomes director of the Jewish National Fund. During his administration, which lasts until 1914, the fund acquires lands upon which Deganyah, Kinneret, and Merhavyah are built, and it loans money to help found Tel Aviv. In October, Ernesto Nathan (1845–1921) is elected mayor of Rome, holding office until 1913. The Italian government abandons the plan to send former Treasury Minister Luigi	Yitzhak Ben-Zvi (1884–1963) leaves Russia and settles in Palestine. In 1952, he will be elected the second president of Israel. The first Jews settle in the Belgian colony of the Congo in Africa.	The first Hebrew encyclopedia, *Ozar Yisrael* (*Treasury of Israel*), edited in 10 volumes by Judah David Eisenstein (1854–1956), begins publication in New York and is completed in 1913. Alfred Stieglitz, U.S. photographer who fought for the recognition of photography as an art, produces his most famous photograph, "The Steerage," as a passenger aboard the SS *Kaiser Wilhelm II.* Albert Abraham Michelson, U.S. physicist, is awarded the Nobel Prize for physics for his studies in measuring the velocity of light, which furnished much of the experimental base for the special theory of relativity. An 1873 graduate of the U.S. Naval Academy, he also taught there. From 1892 until 1929, he is a professor at the University of Chicago. His is the first Nobel Prize given to an American other than the Nobel Peace Prize bestowed upon President Theodore Roosevelt* in 1906. Bernard Berenson, U.S. art historian, begins his long association with Joseph Duveen (1869–1939), the English art dealer. Berenson's certification of the genuineness of Italian Renaissance paintings enables

A. General History	B. Jews in North and South America	C. Jews in Europe	D. Jews in the Middle East and Elsewhere	E. Jewish Culture	
Universal suffrage is instituted in Austria.

The Second Hague Peace Conference fails to secure limitations on armaments. The conference codifies the rules of war.

New Zealand becomes a dominion within the British Empire. | 2,200, whereas there was not a single Jew in attendance when he was a student at the University.

The Galveston Project, proposed and financed by Jacob Schiff, is an effort to divert European Jewish immigration to the U.S. from the large cities of the East Coast to the sparsely populated Jewish communities in the southwestern states. Galveston, Texas, is selected as the port of entry. The Jewish Territorial Organization, headed by Israel Zangwill, undertakes to sponsor and oversee the project. Five thousand immigrants will pass through Galveston until the outbreak of World War I ends the movement.

Dropsie College for Hebrew and Cognate Learning opens in Philadelphia with Cyrus Adler as its president. A postgraduate institution in all branches of Jewish learning and Semitic studies, it is established with funds provided under the will of Moses Aaron Dropsie (1821–1905), a Philadelphia lawyer.

The Hawthorne School, America's first all-Jewish reformatory, is established in New York by German Jews in the effort to prevent juvenile delinquency.

Henry James* (1843–1916), U.S. novelist and critic, writes *The American Scene* upon his return to America after two decades abroad. He | Luzzatti (1841–1927) to Russia to negotiate a commercial treaty between the countries, as Russia intimates that a Jew would be an unacceptable emissary.

Adolph Buechler (1867–1939), Hungarian-trained rabbi and historian, becomes the principal of Jews' College in London. | | both of them to amass fortunes.

Irving Berlin (Israel Baline, 1888–1989), famous American popular songwriter and son of a cantor, publishes his first song, "Marie from Sunny Italy."

Isaac Leib Peretz, leading Yiddish writer, writes *At Night in the Old Market*, a Yiddish drama that portrays a deeply pessimistic panorama of Jewish life in Poland. Scenes from all segments of Jewish life, past and present, the living and dead, the real and unreal, are blurred.

Israel Meir Ha-Kohen, leading Orthodox rabbi and moralist, completes publication of his *Mishnah Berurah*, a six-volume commentary on the *Shulhan Arukh*. Begun in 1894, the *Mishnah Berurah* is an authoritative reference on halakhic matters.

Carl Watzinger* (1877–1948), German archaeologist, and Heinrich Kohl* publish the findings of their excavation of ancient Galilean synagogues, which reveal sculpted friezes. | **1907** |

	A. General History	B. Jews in North and South America	C. Jews in Europe	D. Jews in the Middle East and Elsewhere	E. Jewish Culture
1907		is astonished by the alien quality of American cities, especially "the extent of the Hebrew conquest of New York."			
1908	In October, Austria annexes Bosnia and Herzegovina. Tension with Russia ensues. William Howard Taft* is elected president of the U.S., defeating William Jennings Bryan.* The Model T automobile is introduced by the Ford Motor Co.	In January, there is a rent strike on New York's Lower East Side. In June, the platform adopted at the Republican National Convention includes a plank addressed to restriction of travel by American Jews in Russia. "We . . . pledge ourselves to insist upon the just and equal protection of all our citizens abroad. It is the unquestioned duty of the Government to procure for all our citizens, without distinction, the rights of travel and sojourn in friendly countries." In July, the platform adopted at the Democratic National Convention includes a plank addressed to the restriction of travel by American Jews in Russia. "We . . . insist upon the just and lawful protection of our citizens at home and abroad, and to use all proper methods to secure for them, whether native-born or naturalized, and without distinction of race or creed, the equal protection of the law and the enjoyment of all rights and privileges open to them under our treaty." New York's Police Commissioner Theodore A. Bingham* claims in an article, "Foreign Criminals in New York," published in the *North American Review*, that Jews,	Morris Benedikt (1849–1920) becomes the sole owner of the *Neue Freie Presse*, the most influential newspaper in the Austro-Hungarian Empire. Affiliated with the newspaper since 1872, he opposed Zionism and would not permit its literary editor, Theodor Herzl (1860–1904), to publish anything in support of Zionism. The first international conference to discuss the role of Yiddish in Jewish life convenes in Czernowitz, Bukovina. Nathan Birnbaum, leading central European Jewish intellectual, suggested the conference while on a visit to the U.S. Attended by 70 delegates, the conference adopts a resolution calling Yiddish "a national language" rather than "the national language" out of deference to Hebraists. The daily newspaper *L'Action Française* is founded by the French antisemitic movement Action Française following the Dreyfus Affair. Its principal theorist is Charles Maurras.*	Arthur Ruppin, German sociologist and Zionist leader, establishes the Palestine Land Development Co. and negotiates the acquisition of large tracts of land in the Jezreel Valley. Ruppin is acknowledged as the "father of Zionist settlement" and is instrumental in purchasing land in Haifa and in the Rehavia quarter of Jerusalem as well as in the area of Mount Scopus, where the Hebrew University will be built.	Louis D. Brandeis, a lawyer who will be the first Jew appointed to the U.S. Supreme Court, submits what becomes known as the "Brandeis brief" to the U.S. Supreme Court in *Muller* v. *Oregon*. He uses statistical analysis to buttress moral and social arguments in defending a state law limiting the working hours of women. Leo Buerger (1879–1943), U.S. physician, accurately describes a rare noninflammatory vascular condition of the extremities that becomes known as Buerger's disease. Paul Cassirer (1871–1926) establishes a publishing house in Germany that publishes works of modern artists. His Berlin art gallery is the first to exhibit in Germany the paintings of Paul Cézanne,* Vincent van Gogh,* Claude Monet,* and Edouard Manet.* The Jewish Historical-Ethnographical Society is founded in St. Petersburg, Russia. Salwian Goldstein (1855–1926), historian, is one of the founders and is director of its archives. Joel Engel (1868–1927), composer, founds the Society for Jewish Folk Music in Moscow. In 1912, he

A. General History	B. Jews in North and South America	C. Jews in Europe	D. Jews in the Middle East and Elsewhere	E. Jewish Culture
	although comprising only 25% of the city's population, furnished 50% of all criminals. Denounced by Jewish groups, Bingham* retracts his charges. Prescott F. Hall,* a foe of unrestricted immigration, writes *Immigration and Its Effects Upon the United States*, in which he claims that New York's Jews are degenerative physically, as well as politically and morally. He further claims the Jews' desire for "racial and religious purity" impedes their assimilation into American society. *The Melting Pot*, a play about Jewish life in New York by Israel Zangwill, English author active in Jewish public life, opens in Washington, D.C., with President Theodore Roosevelt* in attendance. Its assimilatory theme receives Jewish criticism. In 1909, Judah L. Magnes (1877–1948), will say the play asks the Jew to give up his identity.			will accompany Solomon Zainwil Rapaport (S. Anski, 1863–1920) in his ethnographical expedition to South Russia, where he will collect many Jewish folk songs. Paul Ehrlich (1854–1915), German chemist, is awarded the Nobel Prize for physiology or medicine for his research in the mechanics of immunology. He was a pioneering researcher in the fields of hematology, immunology, and chemotherapy. Actively involved in Jewish affairs, he was associated with the early efforts to create a Hebrew University in Jerusalem. Gabriel Lippmann (1845–1921), French physicist, is awarded the Nobel Prize for physics, for his research in the field of color photography. In 1886 he was appointed professor of experimental science and director of the research laboratories at the Sorbonne. He held these positions until his death. Enrico Castelnuovo (1839–1915), Italian author, publishes his most famous novel, *The Moncalvos*, which includes a discussion of early 20th-century Zionism. The publication of *Haynt* (*Today*), the leading Yiddish daily newspaper in Warsaw, begins. By 1914, its circulation will be over 100,000. It supports Zionist ideology and fights Jewish assimilationists. Its main competitor, *Der Moment* (*The*

A. General History	B. Jews in North and South America	C. Jews in Europe	D. Jews in the Middle East and Elsewhere	E. Jewish Culture

1908

Founders of Tel Aviv casting lots for building sites. Photo by Abraham Soskin (d. 1963).

Founding of Deganyah, the first kibbutz in Palestine. (Central Zionist Archives)

Moment), will be founded in 1910. Publication of both newspapers will cease in 1939 upon the Nazi invasion of Poland.

Peretz Hirschbein (1880–1948), Yiddish playwright, organizes a professional Yiddish drama group in Odessa. For the next two years he will travel with them throughout Russia producing Yiddish plays of quality.

Elie Metchnikoff (1845–1916), Russian biologist, is awarded the Nobel Prize for physiology or medicine for his research in the mechanics of immunology.

1909

A. The National Association for the Advancement of Colored People (NAACP) is founded in the U.S.

Admiral Peary* arrives at the North Pole.

Prince Bulow,* German chancellor since 1900, resigns.

B. The Kehillah, a representative body of New York Jews, is founded as result of the Bingham Affair. The founding conference is attended by 300 delegates representing 222 Jewish organizations, excluding Socialists, who do not join. Judah L. Magnes, U.S. rabbi and communal leader, is elected chairman and will remain its head until the end of the Kehillah in 1922.

In November, 20,000 shirtwaist makers of the International Ladies' Garment Workers' Union (ILGWU), mostly Jewish girls, go on strike in New York. The strike is called "the Uprising of the Twenty Thousand." The strike will be settled in February 1910, with 339 of the 353 members of the manufacturers association signing up with the ILGWU.

C. The Ninth Zionist Congress convenes in Hamburg, Germany, under the leadership of David Wolffsohn. The congress decides to begin a cooperative settlement in accord with a plan of Franz Oppenheimer (1864–1943), German sociologist and economist.

Herbert Samuel (1870–1963), British statesman, is appointed Britain's first Jewish cabinet minister.

Jehiel Heilprin establishes a Hebrew kindergarten in Warsaw, Poland, which serves as a model for other institutions in eastern Europe.

D. The City of Tel Aviv is founded.

The first kibbutz, Deganyah, is founded in Palestine.

The society Ha-Shomer (The Watchmen) is founded in Palestine to guard Jewish settlements. They replace non-Jewish guards, speak Arabic, and dress to blend into the environment. It is the Jewish community's first fighting force and will be disbanded in 1920.

Hermann Burchardt (1857–1909), German explorer, is murdered by marauders in the Arabian Desert betweeen Mecca and San'a. He brought the all-but-forgotten Jewish community of Yemen to the attention of world Jewry.

E. Professor Louis Ginzberg (1873–1953), preeminent scholar of rabbinic literature who teaches at the Jewish Theological Seminary of America, begins publication of his *Legends of the Jews*. It combines legends, folklore, and fairy tales contained in texts ranging from rabbinic to Christian into a continuous narrative of biblical personages and events.

Al Jolson (Asa Yoelson, 1886–1950), the son of a cantor, puts on blackface in a San Francisco vaudeville show and ignites a national song craze.

James Oppenheim (1882–1932), a social worker who headed the Hudson Guild's east side settlement house, writes *Dr. Rast*, a collection of short stories portraying incidents in the life of a

1909

B.

The workers will win a 52-hour week, four paid legal holidays, improvements in working conditions, and methods of settling wage disputes.

Ray Stannard Baker* (1870–1946), U.S. journalist, writes "The Disintegration of the Jews" in *The American Magazine*. He describes the Orthodox Jew arriving in New York "five hundred years from the Middle Ages" bringing "his tribal instincts and his tribal conception of God with him, and the first thing he does is to attempt to set up and continue his tribal institutions."

Two groups fostering aid to Jewish immigrants are merged to form the Hebrew Sheltering and Immigrant Aid Society (HIAS).

Mordecai M. Kaplan (1881–1983), U.S. rabbi and educator, becomes head of the newly formed Teachers Institute of the Jewish Theological Seminary of America at the invitation of Solomon Schechter.

Jack London* (1876–1916) writes *Martin Eden*, a semiautobiographical novel about a writer's struggles in which he associates "ghetto" Jews with the "weak races." He describes a Jew seen at a Socialist meeting as "a symbol. . . of the whole miserable mass of weaklings and inefficients who perished according to biological law in the ragged confines of life. They were the unfit."

E.

German Jewish doctor practicing on New York's Lower East Side.

Jacob Marinoff (1869–1964), Yiddish poet and editor who emigrated from Russia to the U.S., founds the Yiddish weekly *Der Kundes* (*The Stick*). It is a journal of Yiddish wit, humor, and satire. The name is later changed to *Der Groyser Kundes* (*The Big Stick*). Publication will cease in 1927.

Julius Rosenwald, U.S. merchant and philanthropist, on assuming the presidency of Sears, Roebuck and Co., converts it into the largest mail-order house in the world.

Abraham Arden Brill (1874–1948), Austrian-born psychoanalyst, introduces Sigmund Freud's writings to the English-speaking world by translating into English Freud's *Studies in Hysteria*. Freud and C. G. Jung* (1865–1961) visit the U.S. and lecture at Clark University. In 1910, Freud's *Five Lectures on Psychoanalysis* will be published.

Paul Ehrlich, German chemist and Nobel Prize winner, discovers salvarsan, also known as 606, a "magic bullet," or cure, for syphilis. It is the beginning of modern chemotherapy.

Leon Bakst (1867–1924), Russian artist, begins executing theater decorations in Paris for Sergey Diaghilev's* Russian ballet.

	A. General History	B. Jews in North and South America	C. Jews in Europe	D. Jews in the Middle East and Elsewhere	E. Jewish Culture
1909		The Jewish population of Buenos Aires, Argentina, is estimated at 40,000. The first Jewish community organization in Chile, the Sociedad Unión Israelita de Chile, is founded. The Jewish Colonization Association (ICA) acquires 231,810 acres in the Quatro Irmaos area of Rio Grande do Sul, Brazil, for farming. By 1915, 1,678 persons will settle there. By 1930, there will be very few Jewish settlers and, in 1965, the land will be sold and ICA activities will cease.			Isaac Leib Peretz, leading Yiddish writer, publishes two volumes of stories, *Hasidic* and *Folktales*. They are considered the major work of his career. He uses Hasidic folk tales and material as an instrument to express his own views that Europe's Jews are natural, healthy human beings who create a rich and varied culture even in the midst of oppression. He also writes *The Golden Chain*, a Yiddish play focusing on a Hasidic rabbi's determination to prolong the Sabbath into seven days of the week so as to make all of life a sacred celebration.
1910	The Dillingham Commission, appointed by the U.S. Congress in 1907 to investigate the impact of immigration on the well-being of the nation, publishes its conclusions that the new immigration was essentially different from the old and less capable of being Americanized. Critics argued that despite its scientific pretensions—it employed a staff of about 300 and published its results in 42 volumes—the report made certain that the conclusions would confirm its prejudgment. The Union of South Africa is formed on the basis of racial segregation. Eugene Ely* flies his airplane off the temporary flight deck of the U.S. cruiser *Birmingham* anchored at Hampton Roads, Virginia, anticipating the birth of the aircraft carrier. Japan annexes Korea.	Judah L. Magnes resigns as rabbi of New York's leading Reform congregation, Temple Emanu-El. He assumed the pulpit in 1906 and preached that the tide of assimilation engulfing the native-born generation could be stemmed only by the return to a more traditional form of Judaism. Samson Benderly (1876–1944) is appointed director of the newly founded Bureau of Jewish Education in New York. Organized by the Kehillah it is the first such bureau in the U.S. and the prototype of similar agencies throughout the country. Mordecai M. Kaplan, U.S. rabbi and later founder of the Reconstructionist movement, and Bernard Crouson conduct the first community survey of Jewish education in New York. They find 200,000 Jewish children of school age,	The 11th edition of the *Encyclopaedia Britannica* contains the entry "Anti-Semitism" written by Lucien Wolf, British journalist and Anglo-Jewish historian. Jews are expelled from Kiev, Russia. Montague Burton (1885–1952) establishes a clothing factory in Leeds, England. He founds a chain of stores that employs over 20,000 people and is known for its well-made, inexpensive men's clothes. Luigi Luzzatti becomes prime minister of Italy. An economist and lawyer, he was elected to Parliament in 1871, where he will sit until 1921, when he will be elevated to the Senate. He is minister of the treasury on three occasions and also minister of agriculture. He supports Zionist enterprises in Palestine.	Aaron Aaronsohn, agronomist, establishes an agricultural experimental station at Athlit, Palestine, with financial assistance from American Jewish leaders. He had been the guest of the U.S. Department of Agriculture in 1909.	*La America*, the first Judeo-Spanish–language weekly newspaper, begins publication in New York. Published and edited by Moise Gadol (1884–1941), it appears intermittently until 1925. Cyrus Adler transfers *The Jewish Quarterly Review*, a scholarly journal, from England to Dropsie College, Philadelphia. Fanny Brice (1891–1951), U.S. singer and comedienne, tours in a burlesque show, *The College Girl*. She sings one of Irving Berlin's songs, "Sadie Salome, Go Home," with a Yiddish accent, which inaugurates her career as a singer of Yiddish-type comic songs. Montague Glass (1877–1934), U.S. writer, publishes *Potash and Perlmutter*, a collection of his short stories. Abe Potash and Mawruss Perlmutter, two partners in the cloak

A. General History	B. Jews in North and South America	C. Jews in Europe	D. Jews in the Middle East and Elsewhere	E. Jewish Culture	
The International Psychoanalytical Association is founded. C. G. Jung* is the president.	with only 21 to 24% receiving some Jewish education. Sixty thousand cloak makers of the ILGWU, mostly Jewish, strike for two months against mostly Jewish manufacturers. Communal leaders Louis Marshall and Louis Kirstein (1867–1942) suggest Louis D. Brandeis as mediator, who brings about an end to the strike by concluding a Protocol of Peace. The protocol was a pioneering achievement in the history of American union and management relations, providing for a method of settling disputes by mediation and arbitration. Louis D. Brandeis meets Jacob De Haas, publisher of the *Boston Jewish Advocate*, who awakens Brandeis' interest in Zionism. The first American Yiddish secular school system is established by the Labor Zionist movement. In New York, a city with over a million Jews, there are only 200 Jews on the 10,000-man police force. The largely Irish police force is one cause of the interethnic tensions experienced by the Jews.			and suit trade, are comic types, but as presentations of the American Jew they are nonetheless caricatures. A Jewish museum is founded in Warsaw and named after Matthias Bersohn (1823–1908), an art collector who donated his collection to the Jewish community. Otto Wallach (1847–1931), German organic chemist, is awarded the Nobel Prize for chemistry for his pioneer work in the field of alicyclic compounds. His work forms the basis for the development of the perfume industry. Paul Johann Ludwig Heyse (1830–1914), German author, is awarded the Nobel Prize for literature. Eliezer Ben-Yehuda, Hebrew lexicographer who is considered the father of modern Hebrew, begins publication of his *Complete Dictionary of Ancient and Modern Hebrew*. Comprising 17 volumes, it is completed in 1959 by his widow and son. Albert Gerchunoff (1889–1950), Argentine writer, publishes Los Gauchos Judios, a series of sketches of Jewish life in the Argentine farming communities.	**1910**
The Mexican Revolution takes place between 1911 and 1920. Italy and Turkey war over Libya. Italy defeats the Turks and occupies Libya. The Russians invade and occupy northern Persia.	Jewish charities in major U.S. cities establish the National Desertion Bureau to consolidate their efforts on a national scale, locating runaway immigrant husbands and forcing them at least to contribute to the support of their families.	The 10th Zionist Congress, named the Peace Congress for its absence of friction, convenes in Basel under the leadership of David Wolffsohn. Discussions of practical activities, Hebrew culture, and relations with the Arabs take place. The Zionist headquarters is moved		Maurice Fishberg (1872–1934), U.S. physician and physical anthropologist, writes *The Jews: A Study of Race and Environment*, in which he describes Jews as a genetically heterogenous people, similar to the varied physical types among whom they have lived throughout the Diaspora, and not a	**1911**

A. General History	B. Jews in North and South America	C. Jews in Europe	D. Jews in the Middle East and Elsewhere	E. Jewish Culture
1911 Norwegian explorer Roald Amundsen* reaches the South Pole. The Second Moroccan Crisis takes place. Germany accepts the French principle of a protectorate over Morocco. France cedes to Germany territory in French equatorial Africa. Al-Fatah (the Young Arabs), a secret Arab nationalist movement, strongly anti-Zionist, is started in Paris.	A fire at New York's Triangle Shirtwaist Factory, a typical sweatshop, results in the deaths of 146 mostly Jewish and Italian young immigrant women. The tragedy leads to the appointment of a state Factory Investigation Committee headed by Senator Robert F. Wagner* and Assemblyman Alfred E. Smith.* Some reforms follow. The U.S. abrogates the Russo-American commercial treaty of 1832. Technically, the treaty is abrogated on the narrow issue of passport discrimination against American Jews. Behind the move is a determination to relieve the plight of Russian Jews. The State Department opposed abrogation, arguing that quiet diplomacy would be more effective, U.S. commercial interests would be harmed, the U.S. had no right to interfere in internal affairs of a foreign country, and antisemitism would increase both in the U.S. and Russia. Victor Berger (1860–1929), Socialist leader and journalist, is elected to the U.S. House of Representatives from Wisconsin, becoming the first Socialist to serve in Congress. The New York State Section of the National Council of Jewish Women creates a Department of Immigrant Aid to deal with the problem of prostitution among immigrant Jewish girls. The department maintains contact with 300 U.S. cities in an effort to find clients	to Berlin, and Otto Warburg (1859–1938) is elected president. Mendel Beilis (1874–1934) is accused in Kiev, Russia, of the ritual murder of a 12-year-old boy. Tried in 1913, after two years of investigation, violent antisemitic propaganda within Russia, and worldwide protests, he will be acquitted. Solomon Zainwil Rapaport, Russian writer and folklorist, heads an ethnographic expedition financed by Baron Horace Guenzburg and travels throughout the Russian villages in Volhynia and Podolia from 1911 to 1914 collecting folklore material. Werner Sombart* (1863–1941), a German economic historian, writes *The Jews and Modern Capitalism*, in which he argues that because Jews were excluded from the system of medieval commerce, they broke it up and substituted modern capitalism, with unlimited competition as the only law. It will be translated into English in 1913 and later discredited because of its use by the Nazis.		pure-blooded race nor a separate subrace. Irving Berlin composes the music and writes the words to "Alexander's Ragtime Band," which becomes America's most popular Tin Pan Alley song. Alfred Fried (1864–1921), Austrian pacifist, and Tobias Michael Carel Asser (1838–1913) are two of three awardees of the Nobel Peace Prize. Fried is the founder of German and Austrian peace societies. Asser, of Dutch origin and a member of The Hague Permanent Court of Arbitration, arbitrated the dispute between Russia and the U.S. over fishing rights in the Bering Straits. Sigmund Freud and his colleagues C. G. Jung* and Alfred Adler (1870–1937) have a falling out, mainly on the issue of Freud's theories on infantile sexuality. Hayyim Nahman Bialik, Hebrew poet, coedits *Sefer ha-Aggadah* (*Book of Legends*), organizes the legends and folklore of the Talmud and *midrash* by topic, and translates Aramaic texts into Hebrew.

A. General History	B. Jews in North and South America	C. Jews in Europe	D. Jews in the Middle East and Elsewhere	E. Jewish Culture	
	homes, jobs, training, and medical care.				1911
Woodrow Wilson* is elected president of the U.S., defeating William Howard Taft* and Theodore Roosevelt.*

New Mexico becomes the 47th and Arizona the 48th state of the U.S.

The U.S. occupies Nicaragua.

The Balkan Wars, involving Turkey, Bulgaria, Greece, Serbia, Montenegro, Albania, and Romania take place between 1912 and 1913. The Balkan states are victorious; Turkey withdraws from the Balkans.

The fourth Duma, the imperial Russian legislature, is elected and sits until 1916.

The Treaty of Fez resolves the Moroccan crisis. The French protectorate is established over Morocco. Germany receives territorial concessions in the Congo.

The African National Congress, a nonviolent movement opposed to white racist policies in South Africa, is founded. | Solomon Schechter, president of the Jewish Theological Seminary of America, resigns from the Board of the Educational Alliance, founded by assimilated German Jews to assist in the Americanization of eastern European Jewish immigrants living on New York's Lower East Side. Schechter believes the religious activity of the alliance is perfunctory. He writes: "The great question before the Jewish community . . . is not so much the Americanising of the Russian Jew as his Judaising. . . . the problem is whether we are able to keep the immigrant within Judaism after he has become Americanised."

The Young Israel, a modern Orthodox movement, is founded on New York's Lower East Side. The founders are Orthodox Americanized youth who feel themselves to be part of American society and who wish to remain Orthodox but reject many of the folkways and practices of their parents.

Horse poisoning reaches its peak in New York's Jewish neighborhoods when an average of 12 horses per week are poisoned. The poisonings are called Yiddish Black Hand.

Herman Rosenthal, well-known Jewish gambler, is murdered hours before he is to testify before a grand jury on police–underworld ties in New York. He had charged Police Lieutenant Charles | England's Liberal Jewish Synagogue, established in 1911, installs Israel I. Mattuck (1883–1954), ordained at the Hebrew Union College of Cincinnati, Ohio, as its rabbi.

The Jewish League for Woman Suffrage is founded in England. It combines the demand for parliamentary suffrage with the goal of furthering the improvement of Jewish women in the community.

Agudat Israel (Association of Israel) is founded in Kattowitz, Upper Silesia, at a convention attended by 227 Orthodox Jewish leaders from Russia, Austria, Hungary, Germany, and Palestine. Its purpose is to reaffirm the unimpeachable authority of the Torah and *halakhah* and to counter advances made by assimilation, Reform trends, the Bund, and especially Zionism. It opposes Zionism for its efforts to establish a secular society in Palestine.

Blau-Weiss, a Jewish youth movement, is founded in Germany and Czechoslovakia. It assists assimilated youth to find their way back to the Jewish people and Zionism.

At the age of 70, German philosopher Hermann Cohen leaves the university at Marburg to teach at the Berlin Hochschule. In 1914, he will visit Polish Jews in Vilna and Warsaw, which will affect and change his | | Mary Antin (1881–1949), who emigrated to the U.S. from Poland in her early years, writes her best-selling autobiography, *The Promised Land*. In it she praises the free opportunity and enlightenment of the U.S. as contrasted with the repression of the Old World. She advocates assimilation and discarding Jewish customs and beliefs of the past. Almost 85,000 copies will be sold, and the book will be used as a civics class text in public schools.

David Ignatoff (1885–1954) begins publication in New York of the Yiddish journal *Schriften* (*Writings*). Appearing irregularly, it publishes original works by young writers, translations of world literature, and reproductions of works by Jewish painters.

Fanny Brice, U.S. singer and comedienne, invents Baby Snooks as part of her vaudeville act. In 1936, she will introduce this precocious little-girl character to radio listeners.

Carl Laemmle (1867–1939) founds Universal, the first large Hollywood movie studio.

Josef (Yossele) Rosenblatt (1882–1933) emigrates to New York from Russia to serve as cantor for Congregation Ohab Tzedek, located in Harlem. He is paid the handsome sum of $2,400 a year. He becomes widely | 1912 |

A. General History	B. Jews in North and South America	C. Jews in Europe	D. Jews in the Middle East and Elsewhere	E. Jewish Culture
1912	Becker,* head of an antivice squad, with being his silent partner in illegal gambling activities. After several trials, Becker* will be convicted of conspiring to murder Rosenthal and executed in July 1915. A Bureau of Social Morals is sponsored by the New York Kehillah. This "Jewish police station" exists for five years and surveys activities of local Jewish criminals and then reports to the police. The bureau is formed as a consequence of the Rosenthal–Becker affair and concern over widespread Jewish criminality. Abe Shoenfeld is a salaried investigator, and Harry Newberger is counsel. Big Jack Zelig, Jewish pickpocket and gangster, is assassinated on New York's Lower East Side. Thousands attended the funeral to pay tribute to Zelig, who had rid the neighborhood of Italian hoodlums. The Central Conference of American Rabbis, leaders of American Reform Judaism, issue a warning to Jews not to affiliate with the Christian Science Church. Some Jews divided their allegiance between Judaism and Christian Science, which appealed to Jews seeking health and peace of mind. Morris Raphael Cohen (1880–1947), philosopher who emigrated to New York with his parents from Russia in 1892, is appointed to the	attitude toward Judaism. A synagogue in Trieste is opened. Constructed of Istrian limestone, the exterior style is late Roman of a type found in 4th-century Syria. Angelo-Raphael Chaim Sacerdoti (1886–1935) is appointed chief rabbi of Rome. Under Benito Mussolini* (1883–1945), he is instrumental in passing a law requiring all Italian Jews to belong to one of the 26 united communities unless they renounce Judaism, thereby encouraging expanded participation in Jewish communal life.		known in the U.S. and Europe through many concert tours. Casimir Funk (1884–1967), U.S. biochemist, while doing research at the Lister Institute in London on the disease beriberi, discovers a substance that prevents the disease. He calls it "vitamin." His further research on the importance of vitamins will help develop the field of nutrition and modern dietetics. The Hebrew art magazine *Mahmadim* (*Delights*) is published in Paris. Arthur Schnitzler (1862–1931), Austrian physician and playwright, writes *Professor Bernhardi*, a play dealing with the problems of medical ethics and antisemitism. The hero is a physician who prevents a Catholic priest from administering the last rites to a dying patient, as he believes it may subject him to unnecessary suffering. As the physician is Jewish, he is subjected to antisemitic attacks. Jascha Heifetz (1901–1987), violinist and child prodigy who was born in Vilna, Russia, performs at Berlin's Academy of Music while only 11 years of age. He will become a U.S. citizen in 1925.

A. General History	B. Jews in North and South America	C. Jews in Europe	D. Jews in the Middle East and Elsewhere	E. Jewish Culture	
					1912
	department of philosophy of the City College of New York. He influences thousands of City College students. Henrietta Szold organizes Hadassah, the Women's Zionist Organization of America, to provide modern medical and health care to the people of Palestine. It will become the largest Zionist organization in the world.				
					1913
The 60-story Woolworth Building in New York, designed by Cass Gilbert,* is completed. It remains the world's tallest building until 1929. American and European contemporary art is displayed at the Armory Show in New York.	Solomon Schechter founds the United Synagogue of America, the lay organization of the Conservative movement. Schechter hopes the organization will be acceptable to Orthodox as well as Conservative congregations. On April 27, Mary Phagan,* a 14-year-old employee, is found murdered in the basement of the National Pencil Factory in Atlanta, Georgia. Leo M. Frank (1884–1915), Brooklyn-reared and northern-educated superintendent and part owner of the factory, is arrested for the crime. In August, Leo M. Frank is convicted of the murder of Mary Phagan* after a jury trial in Atlanta, prosecuted by the state solicitor general, Hugh M. Dorsey.* The state relied mainly on the testimony of an ex-convict employee, James Conley,* who was suspected to be the true culprit. The U.S. Congress passes a joint resolution requesting European powers to compel Romania to	The 11th Zionist Congress convenes in Vienna under the leadership of Otto Warburg. It decides to establish a Hebrew university in Jerusalem and devote further attention to settlement. Joseph H. Hertz (1872–1946), the first graduate of the Jewish Theological Seminary of America in 1894 and rabbi of New York's Orach Hayim synagogue, is elected chief rabbi of the United Hebrew Congregations of the British Commonwealth. Rufus Daniel Isaacs (1860–1935), the first marquess of Reading, is appointed lord chief justice of Great Britain, the only Jew ever to hold that post. He will also serve as special envoy to the U.S. during World War I, viceroy to India (1920–1926), and, in 1931, foreign secretary. He is active in Zionist affairs. Vladimir Lenin,* Russian revolutionary leader of the Bolshevik faction of the Social Democratic Workers' party, writes *Critical Remarks on the National Question*, in which he advocates	Eliezer Ben-Yehuda, Hebrew writer, leads the "war of the languages" in defeating the plan of the Hilfsverein der deutschen Juden (Relief Organization of German Jews) to introduce German as the language of instruction in their planned Haifa Technion in Palestine. Henry Polak, close associate of Mohandas K. Gandhi* (1869–1948) during the period 1906 to 1914 when he struggled for the rights of Indians in South Africa and developed his doctrine of satyagraha, writes that "those non-Indians who have taken a leading part in the effort to expose and do away with this persecution are most of them members of our faith."	*Yankel Boyle* (*Village Youth*), by Leon Kobrin (1872–1946), Yiddish playwright and novelist, has a successful run in New York and Europe. It is a dramatization of his 1899 novel of a handsome Jewish fisherman and his tragic love affair with a Christian girl. Kobrin, who came to the U.S. in 1892, writes more than 20 plays about American Jewish life. Samuel Goldwyn (1882–1974), a glove salesman; his brother-in-law, Jesse Lasky (1880–1958), a vaudeville promoter; and Cecil B. de Mille* produce the first feature-length movie, *The Squaw Man*. Bela Schick (1877–1967), pediatrician, while teaching in Vienna, develops a skin test for the detection of diphtheria. In 1923 he will become chief pediatrician at New York's Mt. Sinai Hospital. Ismar Elbogen (1874–1943), German Jewish scholar, publishes *Der Juedische Gottesdienst*, a comprehensive history of Jewish liturgy.	

A. General History	B. Jews in North and South America	C. Jews in Europe	D. Jews in the Middle East and Elsewhere	E. Jewish Culture
1913	end Jewish discrimination. New York State enacts a civil rights law at the urging of the American Jewish Committee that prohibits owners of hotels or places of public accommodation from excluding persons because of race, color, or creed and from advertising any discriminatory or exclusionary practices. B'nai B'rith establishes the Anti-Defamation League, which is designed to combat antisemitism in the U.S. Henry Hurwitz organizes the Intercollegiate Menorah Association in the United States. The Semitics Division of the Library of Congress is founded. It includes both Arabic and Hebrew materials and is given its impetus by the donation of a collection of 10,000 Hebrew books by Jacob Schiff. Israel Schapiro (1882–1957) heads it until 1944. Isidore "Izzy the Painter" Stein, leader of an arson trust, is arrested and convicted, together with several other arsonists, of setting many fires in the Jewish neighborhoods of Harlem in New York. The National Federation of Temple Sisterhoods is founded. Carrie Obendorfer Simon, the first president, calls on the Reform synagogue to "provide a place of equal privilege, prayer, activity and responsibility for the Jewess."	assimilation as the solution to the Jewish question and considers the Bundist nationality policy as a political and ideological threat to the revolutionary cause. Lenin opposes antisemitism not only because it is morally wrong, but because it heightens Jewish national consciousness and impedes assimilation. Joseph Stalin* (1879–1953), Russian revolutionary, writes *Marxism and the National Question* with Vladimir Lenin's* approval, in which he criticizes the Bund's nationalist policy. He maintains that to be a nation there must be a community of language and a common territory. Carl E. Brandes (1847–1931) begins a second period of service as finance minister of Denmark. He will administer neutral Denmark's finances during World War I.		The publication of the complete Yiddish works of Shalom Abramowitsch (Mendele Mokher Seforim) in 16 volumes is completed. A three-volume edition of his complete Hebrew works was published in 1911. Beginning in 1890, Mendele recast his Yiddish works into Hebrew and reedited his Yiddish fiction while he continued his original writings. David Bergelson (1884–1952), Russian Yiddish writer, writes *Nokh Alemen* (*After All*), his first novel. The novel describes the slow decay of the Jewish bourgeoisie in a Ukrainian provincial town through the eyes of its heroine, Mirl Hurvits, the secularly educated daughter of a prominent family. During World War II, Bergelson will be active in the Jewish Anti-Fascist Committee. He will be imprisoned by Stalin* and killed with other leading Jewish writers in 1952. Mark Gertler (1891–1939), English artist, paints *The Rabbi and His Grandchild*. His early works are influenced by his life in poverty in the Whitechapel ghetto. As he achieves great early success and is welcomed into the intellectual, social, and artistic elite of London society, he abandons overtly Jewish subjects. Plagued by deteriorating health and decreasing success, he will commit suicide in 1939. Samuel Niger (Samuel Charney, 1883–1955), Yiddish literary critic, edits *Der Pinkes*, the first modern anthology

1913

E. Jewish Culture: of the history of Yiddish literature, language, folklore, and criticism, which includes studies and a bibliography by Ber Borochov. In 1920, Niger will leave Europe for the U.S. and join the staff of the New York Yiddish daily *Der Tog* (*The Day*), where he will become a respected Yiddish literary critic.

1914

A. General History

Archduke Franz Ferdinand,* heir to the Austro-Hungarian throne, is assassinated at Sarajevo by a Serbian nationalist.

In August, World War I breaks out between the Allies (Great Britain, France, Russia, Belgium, and Serbia) and the Central Powers (Austria–Hungary and Germany). In November, Turkey enters the war as a Central Power ally.

The U.S. proclaims itself neutral in World War I.

The Allies blockade Germany.

The Russians mount an offensive against Germany to relieve the French front. The German counteroffensive defeats the Russians at Tannenberg.

In September, the first German advance into France is halted at the Battle of the Marne, and prolonged trench warfare is begun on the western front.

In December, Great Britain establishes a protectorate over Egypt.

The Amalgamated Clothing Workers of America is established.

B. Jews in North and South America

One hundred fifty American Zionists meet in New York and found the Provisional Executive Committee for General Zionist Affairs. Louis D. Brandeis is elected president. The headquarters of the World Zionist Organization is in Berlin; the members of its executive are on both sides of the belligerents; the U.S. is the greatest of the neutral countries and can oversee the Zionist settlements in Palestine.

The Joint Distribution Committee is organized for the relief of Jewish war sufferers, with Felix M. Warburg (1871–1937) as chairman. It represents the American Jewish Committee, Orthodox groups, and labor elements. As the U.S. is neutral, it is able to work on both sides of the front, distributing funds to Russia, on the one hand, and to Poland (via Germany) and to Turkish-controlled Palestine, on the other. The "Joint" disbursed some $15 million in cash or kind during 1914–1918, as well as transmitting private funds from U.S. families to European relatives.

C. Jews in Europe

The German General Staff addresses a proclamation to Russian Jews calling for an uprising against the Czarist regime and promising equal rights to all Jews in territories captured from the Russians.

Russians attack Lemberg (Lvov) and drive Austrian troops out of eastern Galicia. Hundreds of thousands of Jews are subjected to Russian rule.

Chaim Weizmann, who was living in England since 1906 and was a member of the science faculty of Manchester University, interests C. P. Scott,* editor of the English newspaper *The Manchester Guardian*, in the Zionist cause. Scott* puts Weizmann in contact with Herbert Samuel, a member of Britain's war cabinet. They discover they have similar Zionist views.

Marcus Ehrenpreis (1869–1951), Swedish rabbi, is appointed chief rabbi of Stockholm and serves until 1941.

D. Jews in the Middle East and Elsewhere

After Turkey enters World War I on the side of the Central Powers, David Ben-Gurion and Yitzhak Ben-Zvi, Zionist leaders in Palestine, submit a proposal to Turkish authorities for the creation of a Jewish Legion attached to the Turkish army. The proposal will be canceled after initial approval when the Turkish authorities begin their repressive measures against the Jews of Palestine.

After Turkey enters the war on the side of the Central Powers, 6,000 Russian Jews are ordered expelled from Jaffa, and 700 are immediately deported by ship to Alexandria, Egypt. Within one month, 7,000 Jews flee Palestine to escape Ottoman rule. Thousands of Jews who remain in Palestine apply for Ottoman citizenship to avoid disaster.

E. Jewish Culture

The publication of *Der Tog* (*The Day*), a Yiddish daily newspaper of high literary and journalistic standards, begins in New York. It will merge with the *Jewish Morning Journal* in 1953 and cease publication in 1971.

Elmer Rice (Elmer Reizenstein, 1892–1967), U.S. playwright, writes his first play, *On Trial*, a murder mystery. It is the first play on the U.S. stage to use the flashback technique to present scenes described by trial witnesses.

Harry Hershfield creates a new comic strip character, Abie Kabibble, for his comic strip, "Abie the Agent." Described as the first adult comic strip in America, Abie Kabibble is depicted as "the wandering Jew taking a short rest in the suburbs of the world."

Israel Abrahams, reader in rabbinic and talmudic literature at Cambridge University, writes *Notes to the Authorized Daily Prayer Book* (Singer's Prayer Book). The *Notes* becomes a popular addition to the widely used prayer book, which was first translated into English and edited by Rabbi Simeon Singer

	A. General History	B. Jews in North and South America	C. Jews in Europe	D. Jews in the Middle East and Elsewhere	E. Jewish Culture
1914		Socialist Meyer London (1871–1926) is elected to the U.S. House of Representatives from New York's Lower East Side. He is the first Jew of Russian birth to serve in Congress. He will be reelected in 1916 and 1920. Paul Moritz Warburg (1868–1932), U.S. banker, is appointed by President Woodrow Wilson* as one of the five members of the first Federal Reserve Board. Grossinger's, located on 1,200 acres in the Catskill Mountains, opens as a boarding-house for Jewish vacationers. It will develop into a large-scale resort of national reputation.			(1848–1906) in 1890. Singer was Abrahams' father-in-law. David Bomberg (1890–1957), described as the first native-born English painter of outstanding ability, organizes an international Jewish section in an exhibition, 20th-Century Art, held at London's Whitechapel Art Gallery. This is the first collection of modern Jewish art exhibited in England. Marc Chagall (1887–1985), Russian-born painter, has his first one-man show in Berlin's gallery Der Sturm.

1914   C. Jews in Europe

Robert Barany (1876–1936), Austrian otologist, is awarded the Nobel Prize for physiology or medicine for his research in ear diseases. Barany serves as a surgeon in the Austrian army during World War I and is captured by the Russians, who will release him in 1915 upon learning of his winning of the Nobel Prize.

Jacob Landau (1892–1952), Austrian journalist and publisher, founds the first Jewish international news service, the Jewish Correspondence Bureau, at The Hague. In 1919, it will be reestablished in London as the Jewish Telegraphic Agency. It will move to New York in 1922. In addition to its wire services, it will publish the *Jewish Daily Bulletin*, beginning in 1924.

Simon Dubnow's *History of the Jews in Russia and Poland* is published in Russian and later translated into several languages.

The Jewish Palestine Exploration Society (after 1948, called the Israel Exploration Society) is founded in Jerusalem. In 1919, Nahum Slouschz will revive the society's activities, which were curtailed during World War I.

	A. General History	B. Jews in North and South America	C. Jews in Europe	D. Jews in the Middle East and Elsewhere	E. Jewish Culture
1915	In February, the first submarine campaign against merchantmen is begun by Germany. In April, Germans introduce the use of poison gas warfare on the western front. Allied troops land at Gallipoli, on the Asian side of the Dardanelles Strait, beginning a campaign against the Turks.	Tom Watson,* populist and anti-Catholic Georgia politician, conducts an antisemitic campaign against Leo M. Frank in his weekly *Jeffersonian Magazine* urging the execution of "the filthy perverted Jew of New York." The circulation of the magazine rose from 25,000 to 87,000 during the period of Watson's* crusade against Frank.	Herbert Samuel presents a memo to fellow British cabinet ministers concerning a Jewish national home in Palestine under British trusteeship after World War I, which prepares the way for the Balfour Declaration. In August, the Russian government in effect abolishes the Pale of Settlement as thousands of expelled or refugee Jews from	In February, Djemal Pasha,* Ottoman military governor of Palestine, begins a campaign to terrorize Palestine's non-Turkish population. Zionist activities are curtailed. Newspapers, schools, banks, and political offices are closed. Jewish leaders, including David Ben-Gurion and Yitzhak Ben-Zvi, are exiled. The hardships of war cause food shortages and starvation.	Folksbiene, a Yiddish theater company operating under the aegis of the Workmen's Circle, is organized in New York. It is probably the oldest surviving English or Yiddish theater company in New York. Henry Hurwitz founds *The Menorah Journal*, a magazine of Jewish opinion that becomes one of the outstanding Jewish publications of

A. General History	B. Jews in North and South America	C. Jews in Europe	D. Jews in the Middle East and Elsewhere	E. Jewish Culture	
					1915

A. General History

In May, Italy leaves the Triple Alliance and declares war on Austria–Hungary.

President Woodrow Wilson's* strong reaction to the sinking of the *Lusitania* and the *Arabic*, with loss of American lives, results in Germany modifying its unrestricted submarine warfare.

During the summer, the Turks deport and massacre Armenians, whom they accuse of aiding the Russians.

Haiti is occupied by the U.S. as marines are sent to protect U.S. interests.

The Ku Klux Klan is refounded by William J. Simmons.* It directs its activities at foreigners, Catholics, blacks, and Jews, who they claim challenge American social and moral norms.

The Birth of a Nation, a movie by D. W. Griffith,* is first shown. This three-hour account of the Civil War and Reconstruction, starring Lillian Gish,* condones racism.

B. Jews in North and South America

In May, the U.S. Supreme Court denies Leo M. Frank's appeal of his conviction for the murder of Mary Phagan.* Frank alleged he was not given a fair trial. Justices Charles Evans Hughes* and Oliver Wendell Holmes* dissent from the Court's opinion.

In the May issue of *Harper's Monthly Magazine*'s "Editor's Easy Chair," William Dean Howells* dicusses the New York literary scene and writes: "Very possibly there may be at this moment a Russian or Polish Jew, born or bred on our East Side, who shall burst from his parental Yiddish, and . . . slake our drought of imaginative literature." Bernard Malamud was born in Brooklyn in 1914; Saul Bellow is born near Montreal in 1915; Arthur Miller, in Harlem in 1915; Herman Wouk, in the Bronx in 1915; and Alfred Kazin, in Brooklyn's Brownsville section in 1915.

On June 21, Governor John Slaton* of Georgia commutes Leo M. Frank's death sentence to life imprisonment.

In June, Solomon Schechter, head of the Jewish Theological Seminary of America, at his last public address, warns against "the Institutional Synagogue [a synagogue center] in which the worship of God must become in the end subordinated to the material service of man and his amusements."

C. Jews in Europe

the battle zones flee into the interior of Russia. It is argued that Jewish residence outside the Pale was authorized in response to pleas from English and French Jewish financiers of the Russian war effort, as well as for technical military reasons.

In September, when the great German offensive against Russia ends, the Germans occupy the important Jewish centers of Warsaw, Vilna, Kovno, and Grodno.

D. Jews in the Middle East and Elsewhere

In the spring, Joseph Trumpeldor (1880–1920), one of the more than 10,000 Palestinian Jewish deportees lodged in Egyptian refugee camps, meets Vladimir (Ze'ev) Jabotinsky, then a Russian newspaper correspondent, and they collaborate in the effort to create a Jewish Legion to fight with the Allies to liberate Palestine from the Turks. The British respond by forming the Zion Mule Corps, a special transportation unit, led by Colonel John Henry Patterson,* with Trumpeldor second in command. The Mule Corps, 500 strong, serves with distinction in the Gallipoli campaign and will be disbanded early in 1916.

As a result of the intercession of Henry Morgenthau, Sr. (1856–1946), U.S. ambassador to the Ottoman Empire in Constantinople, Turkey eases repressive measures against Jews in Palestine and halts expulsions and arrests. Morgenthau arranges for U.S. naval vessels to bring food supplies to Palestine.

Sir Henry McMahon,* British high commissioner for Egypt, writes to the sharif of Mecca that Britain would support Arab independence in the Turkish Asiatic provinces where Britain is free to act without detriment to the interests of her French ally. The British later will reject the Arab claim that their pledges to the Zionists are not binding as they were subsequent to this assurance. The

E. Jewish Culture

the world. He remains editor until his death.

Joseph Goldberger (1874–1929), a physician who immigrated to the U.S. from Hungary, discovers that pellagra is caused by a vitamin deficiency.

The Ben Uri Society is formed in London to further the advancement of art among the eastern European immigrants.

Richard Willstaetter (1872–1942), German organic chemist, is awarded the Nobel Prize for chemistry for his research on plant pigments, especially chlorophyll. Although he is awarded the civilian Iron Cross during World War I for his work on gas masks, the Nazis will force him to leave Germany in 1939.

Matthias Mieses (1885–1945), Yiddish philologist, writes a pioneering work on the origin of Yiddish, *Entstehungursache der judischen Dialekte* (*Developmental Origins of Jewish Dialectics*), which is credited with establishing the academic field of comparative Jewish linguistics. In 1908, he delivered the first ever scientific analysis of Yiddish at the Czernowitz Conference. He will die on the way to Auschwitz in the last days of World War II.

Horace M. Kallen (1882–1974), U.S. philosopher and educator, writes an essay, *Democracy versus the Melting Pot*, in *The Nation* magazine, in which he formulates his theory of "cultural pluralism." He refuses to accede to the doctrine of

A. General History	B. Jews in North and South America	C. Jews in Europe	D. Jews in the Middle East and Elsewhere	E. Jewish Culture

1915

B. Jews in North and South America

Louis D. Brandeis, leader of American Zionism and prominent lawyer, addresses a conference of Reform rabbis on the subject of divided loyalties. "There is no inconsistency between loyalty to America and loyalty to Jewry. The Jewish spirit, the product of our religion and experiences, is essentially modern and essentially American. . . . Indeed, loyalty to America demands . . . that each American Jew become a Zionist."

Leo M. Frank is kidnapped from the state prison farm in Milledgeville, Georgia, and lynched by a mob. He is the only Jew ever to be murdered by a lynch mob in the U.S. Governor Slaton's* commutation of Frank's sentence will end his political career, and in 1916, Frank's prosecutor, Hugh M. Dorsey,* will be elected governor of Georgia.

Bernard Revel (1885–1940) begins reorganizing the Rabbi Isaac Elchanan Theological Seminary and merges it with Yeshiva Etz Chaim (an Orthodox secondary school).

Moses Alexander (1853–1932), Democrat, is elected governor of Idaho. He is the first Jewish governor of an American state and serves for two terms (1915–1919). Previously he had been elected mayor of Boise, Idaho, in 1897 and helped organize the first synagogue in that state.

D. Jews in the Middle East and Elsewhere

correspondence will remain secret until 1938.

Aaron Aaronsohn, agronomist, together with family and friends, establishes the NILI (acronym for its Hebrew password) espionage group in Palestine, which supplies intelligence to the British campaign against the Turks in Palestine.

The lynching of Leo M. Frank on August 16, 1915.

David Ben-Gurion and Itzhak Ben-Zvi arrive in New York from Egypt after being deported from Palestine by the Turkish authorities for conspiring against the Ottoman rule in order to establish a Jewish state. They direct their efforts to the preparation of young Jews for settlement in Palestine. In 1917, Ben-Gurion will marry Paula Munweis in New York. Ben-Gurion and Ben-Zvi will leave for Egypt in 1918 to join the Jewish Legion and fight alongside the British army.

E. Jewish Culture

assimilation in any form, including the melting pot. To assure everyone his full rights in a democracy, each American should be encouraged to have a direct and respected relationship to his ethnic group. The democratic objective is "a cooperation of cultural diversities."

| A. General History | B. Jews in North and South America | C. Jews in Europe | D. Jews in the Middle East and Elsewhere | E. Jewish Culture |

1916

Yiddish Daily Newspapers Published in New York City—1916

Name	Date Established	Publisher and Editor	Political and Religious Orientation	Circulation, 1916
Jewish Daily Forward (*Forverts*)	1897	Established by: Forward Association Editor: Abraham Cahan	Socialist Anti-Zionist Nonreligious	198,982
Jewish Morning Journal (*Der Yiddisher Morgen Journal*)	1901	Established by: Jacob Saphirstein Editor: Peter Wiernik	Republican Zionist Orthodox	111,000
The Truth (*Der Warheit*)	1905	Established by: Louis E. Miller Editor: I. Gonikman	Nonpartisan Zionist Liberal	89,000
The Day (*Der Tog*)	1914	Established by: Judah Magnes, Herman Bernstein, Morris Weinberg Editor: William Edlin	Nonpartisan Zionist Liberal	81,000
Jewish Daily News (*Yiddishes Tageblatt*)	1885	Established by: K.H. Sarasohn Editor: Gedalia Bublick	Republican Zionist Orthodox	58,000

The total daily circulation 537,982. This is the year of peak circulation of Yiddish dailies published in New York City. The daily circulation of *The New York Times* is 340,000.

A. General History

In January, the Allies evacuate the Gallipoli Peninsula in the Dardanelles, as their campaign against the Turks ends in failure.

In February, the Battle of Verdun rages on the western front as Germany attacks French positions. The battle lasts until December, with over 700,000 casualties.

In May, the British and German battle fleets clash at the Battle of Jutland in the North Sea.

In May, Great Britain and France, having secretly agreed to partition the Middle East, secretly sign the Sykes–Picot Agreement, later to be approved by Russia and Italy. France is to control Syria and Lebanon; Britain would control Mesopotamia and the ports of Haifa and

B. Jews in North and South America

In January, Louis D. Brandeis is nominated to the U.S. Supreme Court by President Woodrow Wilson.* He is confirmed four months later by the Senate, which battles over the appointment of a lawyer of reform reputation, who is also a Jew. *New York Times* publisher Adolph S. Ochs opposes the nomination. The *Times* editorializes that "to place on the Supreme Bench judges who hold a different view of the function of the court, to supplant conservatism by radicalism, would . . . strip the Constitution of its defenses." Brandeis will serve until 1939.

In March, a preliminary conference of the American Jewish Congress is held in Philadelphia. Reflecting the desire

C. Jews in Europe

Eugen Rosenstock-Heussy, German philosopher who converted to Christianity, and Franz Rosenzweig (1886–1929), Jewish philosopher, exchange 21 letters while both are serving in the German army at the front in World War I. The exchange is considered a disputation attempting to prove the superiority of their respective religions.

Hermann Cohen, German philosopher, publishes an article rejecting Zionism. To Cohen, this national conception of Judaism is a betrayal of the messianic ideal.

Germany and Austria establish a semi-autonomous Polish state on territories formerly held by Russia.

E. Jewish Culture

Elias Tobenkin (1882–1963), U.S. novelist, writes *Witte Arrives*, a novel of the acculturation of Emil Witte, a Jewish immigrant who arrives in the U.S. at the age of seven and marries into an old New England family. Witte leaves Judaism but retains his Jewish awareness. In the end, a rift develops between Witte and his non-Jewish wife.

Martin Buber, philosopher and Zionist thinker, founds *Der Jude*, which becomes the most well-known central European Jewish monthly magazine.

The Amsterdam Stedelijk Museum's exhibit The Disappearing Ghetto draws attention to the disappearance of the Jewish community's historical resources.

1916

A. General History

Acre. An Arab state would be created in the interiors of Syria and Mesopotamia. The Russian zone would run along the Black Sea to the Caspian Sea and the Italian zone, along the northern Mediterranean shore.

In June, the Russian attack against Austria is repulsed with heavy losses. By August, the Russian army begins to break up.

In May, Italy enters the war against Austria–Hungary.

Woodrow Wilson* is reelected president of the U.S., defeating Charles E. Hughes.* The Democrats retain control of Congress.

Margaret Sanger (1883–1966) opens the first U.S. birth control clinic in Brooklyn.

B. Jews in North and South America

for a democratically elected group to express the will of the Jewish community, it adopts a program for convening a congress that would labor "for the attainment of full rights for Jews in all lands, for national rights wherever such are recognized, and for the furtherance of Jewish interests in Palestine." Louis D. Brandeis is selected as the chairman of the organizing committee.

Yiddish schools are organized in the U.S. by the Workmen's Circle as afternoon schools supplementary to public education.

In November, the Jewish vote in the U.S. presidential election is estimated at 55% for Woodrow Wilson* and 45% for Charles E. Hughes.*

Simon Bamberger (1846–1926) is the first Democrat and non-Mormon to be elected governor of Utah. He is also a founder of Utah's first Jewish congregation.

Madison Grant,* respected anthropologist, writes *The Passing of the Great Race*, an enormously popular anti-immigration book. "The new immigration contained . . . the weak, the broken, and the mentally crippled of all races drawn from the lowest stratum of the Mediterranean basin and the Balkans, together with hordes of the wretched, submerged populations of the Polish ghettos. Our jails, insane asylums, and almshouses are filled with this human flotsam and the whole tone of American life . . . has been lowered and vulgarized by them."

E. Jewish Culture

The exhibition leads to the founding of the Jewish Museum in Amsterdam.

Hermann Struck (1876–1944), German painter and etcher, produces *Sketches from Lithuania, White Russia and Kurland*. He will settle in Palestine in 1923.

The Jewish Ethnographic Museum is opened in Petrograd (St. Petersburg). The collections of the ethnographic expeditions of 1912 through 1914 led by Solomon Zainwil Rapaport (S. Anski) throughout the Ukraine, Podolia, and Volhynia form the core of the museum. During the 1930s, most of the collection will be transferred to the Leningrad State Museum.

El Lissitsky (1890–1941) and Issachar Ryback (1897–1935), Russian Jewish artists, study and explore the architecture and folk art of the wooden synagogues along the Dnieper River, including copying the wall paintings of the famous Mohilev synagogue.

Population of New York City *The World's Largest Jewish City in the 20th Century*			
Year	*Total Population*	*Jewish Population*	*% of Jewish as % of Total*
1900	3,437,000	598,000	17.4
1910	4,767,000	1,252,000	26.5
1920	5,620,000	1,643,000	29.2
1930	6,930,000	1,877,000	27.1
1940	7,455,000	2,085,000	28.0
1950	7,892,000	2,110,000	26.7
1960	7,782,000	1,836,000	23.6
1970	7,895,000	1,990,000	25.3
1981	7,071,000	1,114,600	16.0
1990	7,322,600	1,027,000	14.0

A. General History	B. Jews in North and South America	C. Jews in Europe	D. Jews in the Middle East and Elsewhere	E. Jewish Culture

A. General History

In January, British forces clear the Sinai Peninsula of all organized Turkish forces.

In February, Germany resumes unrestricted submarine warfare.

In March, the Revolution begins in Russia. Czar Nicholas II* abdicates. Alexander Kerensky* heads the provisional government.

In April, the U.S. declares war against Germany.

In April, Vladimir Lenin* is permitted by the Germans to return to Russia. The Germans hope he will facilitate negotiations between Russia and the Central Powers.

In April, British forces in Palestine are placed under the command of General Edmund Allenby* after two attacks against Gaza fail to dislodge the Turks.

In May, following a stalled French offensive on the western front, there are mutinies in the French army.

In May, the Selective Service (military draft) begins in the U.S.

In May, the U.S. sends Henry Morgenthau, Sr., former ambassador to Turkey, to Europe to explore the possibility of a separate peace with Turkey. Great Britain opposes the move, as Turkey would retain control over Palestine as well as Armenia and Syria. The British persuade Chaim Weizmann to meet with Morgenthau to dissuade him. They meet in Gibraltar in

B. Jews in North and South America

The Jewish population of 3,388,951 comprises 3.27% of the total U.S. population of 103,690,473.

In July, the Conservative movement's lay organization, the United Synagogue of America, adopts a resolution reaffirming "its faith in the fulfillment of our ancient Zionist hope in the early restoration of Palestine as the Jewish homeland as the means for the consummation of the religious ideas of Judaism." The resolution is adopted over the objection of a determined minority led by the seminary's president, Cyrus Adler.

In July, the United Synagogue of America establishes a standing committee on the interpretation of Jewish law. Consisting of five members "learned in the Law," it is chaired by Louis Ginzberg. It issues responsa covering issues of concern to America's growing movement of Conservative Jews.

The Jewish Center, on New York's Upper West Side, is opened with Mordecai M. Kaplan as its rabbi. It is the first synagogue center in the U.S., built at Kaplan's suggestion for the creation of a new kind of synagogue that would be a "veritable sanctuary of the Jewish spirit, where everything of Jewish value would be represented."

The National Jewish Welfare Board is established in order to care for the religious needs of Jews in the

C. Jews in Europe

In April, the provisional government of Russia issues a decree abolishing all restrictions on the rights of Russian subjects enacted by existing laws that had been based on national origin and religion.

Jews of the Ukraine are greatly affected by civil war in Russia. Various armies fight in the area: the Ukrainian army under the command of Simon Petlyura* (1879–1926); the Red Army; the counterrevolutionary White Army under the command of Anton Denikin*; and independent units commanded by local leaders, including Ataman Grigoryev.* All engage in pogroms against the Jews.

David Sterenberg, a painter, leaves Paris and returns to Russia, where he becomes the director of the Soviet Commission on Culture.

Sarah Schnirer (1883–1938), a seamstress, recognizing the neglect of religious education for girls, organizes a school in Cracow, Poland, for 30 girls. A network, known as Beth Jacob schools, develops. By 1938, in Poland alone there will be 230 schools with 27,000 students.

Samuel Schwarz (1880–1953), a Polish mining engineer living in Portugal, discovers a group of Marranos living in Belmonte, at the Spanish border. They marry only among themselves, observe certain Jewish rituals and festivals, and keep the Sabbath.

D. Jews in the Middle East and Elsewhere

In February, Mark Sykes* (1879–1919), adviser on Middle Eastern affairs to Britain's Prime Minister Lloyd George,* opens negotiations with Zionist leaders that were to lead to the Balfour Declaration. The British want to protect their interests in the Suez Canal area by placing the whole of Palestine under their control. To extricate themselves from the terms of the Sykes–Picot Agreement, they enlist Zionist support in favor of British trusteeship instead of French rule over Palestine.

In April, the Turkish military authorities order the remaining Jews of Jaffa out of the city as they prepare for the British military offensive. The 9,000 Jews flee north, where they suffer from disease and starvation.

In July, the original draft of the Balfour Declaration includes three elements: (1) the reconstitution of Palestine as a whole as the Jewish national home; (2) unrestricted Jewish immigration rights; (3) internal Jewish autonomy. This text is later modified as a result of the opposition to Zionism of some British Jews led by Edwin Montagu (1879–1924), who is a member of the cabinet.

In August, the British announce the formation of a regiment of Jewish volunteers to fight in the war. Composed primarily of Jews from Britain and former members of the Zion Mule Corps, it is

E. Jewish Culture

The Jewish Publication Society of America issues a new English translation of the Bible, which replaces Isaac Leeser's translation published 60 years earlier. The translators are a group of American Jewish scholars, with Max L. Margolis serving as editor-in-chief. This translation becomes the standard English version of the Masoretic text.

Abraham Cahan publishes *The Rise of David Levinsky*, a novel depicting a young Russian immigrant's evolution into a rich American clothing manufacturer. Written in English, it is an unromanticized story of an immigrant who found fortune but not happiness. It is a realistic description of New York's Lower East Side between the 1880s and World War I. Although later considered among the best novels of American business, when first published, it is criticized by many who believe it will spur antisemitism.

Edna Ferber (1887–1968), U.S. novelist, writes *Fanny Herself*, her only novel with a Jewish milieu and in which Jewish characters are central. Fanny Brandeis, of a Jewish family in Wisconsin, is a successful businesswoman who gives up her career for marriage.

Benny Leonard (Benjamin Leiner, 1896–1947), born on New York's Lower East Side, wins the World Lightweight Boxing Championship, a title he retains until his retirement in 1925.

A. General History	B. Jews in North and South America	C. Jews in Europe	D. Jews in the Middle East and Elsewhere	E. Jewish Culture

1917

A. General History

July, and Morgenthau agrees to drop his mission.

In June, combat training is begun in France for U.S. troops.

In July, a Russian offensive on the eastern front ends in total failure. A complete breakup of the army ensues.

In October, British forces led by General Edmund Allenby* capture Beersheba, force the Turks to evacuate Gaza, and make preparations for an attack on Jerusalem.

In November, the Bolsheviks, led by Vladimir Lenin* and Leon Trotsky (Lev Davidovic Bronstein) (1879–1940), seize power in Russia. The provisional government dissolves.

In December, peace negotiations between Russia and the Central Powers begin.

On December 9, British forces under General Edmund Allenby* attack and occupy Jerusalem as the Turks evacuate the city.

The enactment by the U.S. Congress of a literacy test for immigrants overrides President Woodrow Wilson's* veto. President Grover Cleveland* vetoed a similar bill in 1897, as did President William Howard Taft* in 1913 and President Wilson* in 1915 and 1917.

The Charlie Chaplin* film *The Immigrant* is released.

Pulitzer Prizes in journalism and letters are created from

B. Jews in North and South America

General Edmund Allenby, commander of allied forces that expelled Turks from Palestine, entering Old City of Jerusalem.

armed forces of the U.S.

The Federation of Jewish Philanthropies is established in New York to create order out of the chaos of Jewish philanthropic agencies competing for contributions and duplicating services.

The Central Conference of American Rabbis (Reform) adopts a prosuffrage resolution. Despite the individual involvement of noted Jewish men and women in the women's suffrage campaign, no American Jewish woman's organization officially supports it,

> Foreign Office,
> November 2nd, 1917.
>
> Dear Lord Rothschild,
>
> I have much pleasure in conveying to you, on behalf of His Majesty's Government, the following declaration of sympathy with Jewish Zionist aspirations which has been submitted to, and approved by, the Cabinet
>
> "His Majesty's Government view with favour the establishment in Palestine of a national home for the Jewish people, and will use their best endeavours to facilitate the achievement of this object, it being clearly understood that nothing shall be done which may prejudice the civil and religious rights of existing non-Jewish communities in Palestine, or the rights and political status enjoyed by Jews in any other country"
>
> I should be grateful if you would bring this declaration to the knowledge of the Zionist Federation.

The Balfour Declaration. November 2, 1917.

D. Jews in the Middle East and Elsewhere

designated the 38th Batallion of the Royal Fusiliers, in deference to anti-Zionist Jews who strove to limit the Jewish character of the unit. The battalion will be transferred to Palestine in June 1918, where it will be joined by the 39th Battalion of Royal Fusiliers.

In October, Turkish authorities uncover the NILI espionage group, led by Aaron Aaronsohn, a spy ring of Palestinian Jews who were furnishing British authorities with military information. Several members are caught and killed, including Sarah Aaronsohn, Aaronsohn's sister; Avshalom Feinberg; Na'aman Belkind; and Yosef Lishansky. Aaronsohn advised the British not to attack the Turks through Gaza but rather to outflank them with a surprise attack on Beersheba. He gave vital information on the sites of desert wells, enabling passage through the desert.

On November 2, the British government issues the Balfour Declaration, viewing "with favor the establishment in Palestine of a national home for the Jewish people, and will use their best endeavors to facilitate the achievement of this object, it being clearly understood that nothing shall be done which may prejudice the civil and religious rights of existing non-Jewish communities." It no longer considers Palestine as *the* national home and makes no reference to unrestricted Jewish

E. Jewish Culture

Herbert Bayard Swope (1882–1958), U.S. journalist, wins the first Pulitzer Prize for reporting for his war dispatches from Germany to the *New York World*.

The Jewish Museum in Berlin is founded. It will be confiscated by the Nazis in November 1938.

The Yiddish State Theater and Habimah Theater, a Hebrew theater, are established in Moscow.

Amedeo Modigliani (1884–1920), Italian painter and sculptor, holds his only major one-man show in Paris. It is a failure. It is only after his death that the greatness of his work will be recognized. Modigliani is a member of the Circle of Montparnasse with fellow Jews Chaim Soutine (1893–1943) and Jacques Lipchitz (1891–1973), but his Jewishness never appears directly in his work.

A. General History	B. Jews in North and South America	C. Jews in Europe	D. Jews in the Middle East and Elsewhere	E. Jewish Culture	
Joseph Pulitzer's* (1847–1911) $2 million bequest to the Columbia School of Journalism.	and prosuffrage resolutions introduced prior to 1917 were rejected by the Central Conference.		immigration and internal rule.		**1917**

In January, an elected Constituent Assembly meets in Russia. The Bolsheviks, who are in a minority, dissolve it.

In January, the Ukraine declares independence from Russia and concludes a separate peace with Germany and Austria. Three years of warfare ensue. The Bolsheviks seize Kiev in February but are ejected by the Germans. In November, Ukrainian Socialists, led by Simon Petlyura,* seize power. In December, the French occupy Odessa.

In January, a summary of American war aims, the Fourteen Points, is issued by U.S. President Woodrow Wilson.* The 14th point is the formation of an association of nations to guarantee the independence and territorial integrity of all nations.

In March, Russia signs a separate peace treaty at Brest-Litovsk, with the Central Powers. It accepts great territorial losses, ceding the Baltic provinces, its part of Poland, and its protectorate over Finland.

In March, a civil war breaks out in Russia. Allies give assistance to the counterrevolutionary (White) armies. British and American troops land in Murmansk; Japanese and American troops, in Vladivostock; French troops, in Odessa, where they

---

In March, Henry Morgenthau, Sr., resigns from the presidency of New York's Free Synagogue over differences with Rabbi Stephen Wise on the support for Zionism.

In September, President Woodrow Wilson* announces his approval of the Balfour Declaration in an open letter to Rabbi Stephen S. Wise.

On December 15, 400 delegates to the American Jewish Congress meet in Philadelphia. One hundred were chosen by the national organizations, and 300 were popularly elected by 335,000 voters. Julian Mack is elected president; Louis Marshall, vice president, and Jacob Schiff, treasurer. The Congress decides to send a delegation to the Paris Peace Conference to secure the rights of Jews in Europe and to cooperate with the World Zionist Organization for recognition of claims of Jewish people in Palestine under the Balfour Declaration.

The Federation of American Zionists is reorganized and renamed the Zionist Organization of America.

There are 24 Yiddish theaters in America. Eleven are in New York with the balance in Chicago, Philadelphia, Boston, and Detroit.

In January, a Jewish Commissariat and Yevsektsiya (Jewish sections of the Communist party) are established in Russia. They are to integrate the Yiddish-speaking masses into the revolution. They dismantle the traditional social organizations and close the yeshivot and other educational institutions. At the same time, they create a Jewish Communist culture, including publishing houses, a Yiddish press and theater, and educational institutions. In 1930, all national sections, including Yevsektsiya, will be abolished.

In April, on the recommendation of the regiment's adjutant, who is a Jew, Adolf Hitler* is awarded the Iron Cross, First Class, for bravery in the service of the German army.

In July, the Soviet government, under Vladimir Lenin's* leadership, issues resolution defining perpetrators and instigators of pogroms as enemies of the revolution who have to be outlawed. This policy results in sympathy of many Jews on behalf of the new regime but does not reduce antisemitism.

Simon Diamanstein (1886–1937), Russian Communist leader who was an assistant to Joseph Stalin,* becomes editor of the Yiddish newspaper *Der Emess* (*The Truth*). The paper directs

---

In March, a Zionist Commission appointed by the British government, headed by Chaim Weizmann, reaches Palestine. It is an advisory body to the British military government on all matters relating to Jews.

In May, the British permit the formation of a battalion of Jewish volunteers from Palestine to fight in the war. Formed into the 40th Battalion of Royal Fusiliers, it is trained and deliberately kept in reserve in Egypt. It will be sent to Palestine to join the 38th and 39th battalions in December 1918, after the armistice with Turkey is signed. In the beginning of 1919, the three battalions will number 5,000 men and their name will be changed to the Judean Regiment. Most will be demobilized by the end of 1919 as a result of an unsympathetic British policy.

Four thousand American Jewish volunteers arrive in Britain and are formed into the 39th Battalion of Royal Fusiliers, led by Lt. Col. Eliezer Margolin (1874–1944). They were recruited under the leadership of Pinhas Rutenberg, David Ben-Gurion, and Yitzhak Ben-Zvi. Some of them will take part in the British campaign in Palestine.

In June, Chaim Weizmann meets Emir Feisal,* son of

Maurice Schwartz (1890–1960), Yiddish actor, establishes the Yiddish Art Theater in New York, located at the Irving Place Theater. He will later build a theater on Second Avenue, and his company will last until 1950, performing in a manner described as "something worth respecting" by *New York Times* drama critic Brooks Atkinson* in 1947. His greatest success will be *Yoshe Kalb*, dramatized in 1932 from the novel by Israel Joshua Singer (1893–1944).

Isaac Rosenberg (1890–1918), English poet, painter, and soldier, is killed on the western front. He had served on the front since August 1916 and composed what are believed to be the best "trench" poems written in English, including "Dead Man's Dump," describing the predicament of all soldiers.

Mani Leib (1883–1953), Yiddish poet, coedits *Insel*, an anthology of Di Yunge, the American Russian literary movement. Leib emigrated to the U.S. in 1905 after participating in the Russian revolutionary movement and becomes a leading figure of the Yunge group of poets, who are influenced by European literary movements, with romanticism and art for art's sake as guiding principles.

1918

A. General History	B. Jews in North and South America	C. Jews in Europe	D. Jews in the Middle East and Elsewhere	E. Jewish Culture
1918				

A. General History

join German troops in the Ukraine, although they are still at war with them. By the end of 1920, the Bolsheviks are victorious, and the counterrevolution collapses.

In March, Leon Trotsky becomes the people's commissar for military affairs, organizes the Red Army, and directs military operations on the various civil war fronts in Russia.

In March, President Woodrow Wilson* appoints Bernard Baruch (1870–1965) head of the War Industries Board, with the power to mobilize the American wartime economy.

In May, Germany breaks through the Allied lines on the western front and reaches the Marne.

In May, the U.S. enacts the Sedition Act, which permits imprisonment of antiwar Socialist leaders.

In July, the Russian royal family is executed by the Bolsheviks.

In July and August, the turning point of the war takes place at the Second Battle of the Marne, as the Allies turn back the Germans.

In September, the German government is pressed for an armistice by General Ludendorff.*

On November 11, an armistice is signed between the Allies and Germany, and World War I is ended.

In November, a revolution breaks out

B. Jews in North and South America

Josef (Yossele) Rosenblatt, famed European cantor who had settled in the U.S. in 1912, rejects the Chicago Opera Association's offer of a large fee to perform as Eleazar in Fromental Halevy's opera *La Juive*. Rosenblatt advises that it would be inappropriate for a synagogue cantor to act in an opera.

Walter Rauschenbusch,* an important American Protestant theologian, writes that the Jews "were the active agents in the legal steps which led to the Christian Savior's death."

The Jewish Women's League of the United Synagogue of America is founded by Mathilde Schechter. It will later be known as the Women's League for Conservative Judaism.

C. Jews in Europe

Communist propaganda against religion, Zionism, and the Bund. Diamanstein will be executed during the Stalin purges, and the newspaper will cease publication in 1938.

Louis Bernheim (1861–1931), lieutenant general in the Belgian army, commands three Belgian divisions in Flanders in the final advance on German lines during World War I.

Otto Bauer (1881–1938), Austrian Socialist leader, succeeds Victor Adler as Socialist party leader and foreign minister of Austria. He will remain leader of Austria's Socialists until forced to flee the country in 1934 when the Austrian republic collapses. A leading Marxist Socialist theoretician, he cofounded the Socialist journal *The Struggle* in 1907. Like Adler, he believed assimilation to be a historical necessity for the Jews.

Hirsch (Zevi) Perez Chajes (1876–1927) is appointed chief rabbi of Vienna, a post he holds until his death. A leading Zionist, in 1921 he will be elected chairman of the Zionist Actions Committee, serving until 1925.

Over 1,172,000 Jewish soldiers served in the Allied and Central Powers forces in

D. Jews in the Middle East and Elsewhere

Sharif Hussein* of Mecca, the leader of Arab nationalism, at Aqaba. Feisal* pledges support of the Zionist aims in Palestine on condition that Arab nationalist aims are met in Syria and Iraq. Feisal* fails to achieve support from the Allies on his aims. He considers himself released from his pledges to Weizmann.

Chaim Weizmann meets Emir Faisal, son of Sharif Hussein of Mecca, the leader of Arab nationalism, at Aqaba.

On July 24, 12 foundation stones of Hebrew University are laid on Mt. Scopus in Jerusalem. Chaim Weizmann initiated the establishment of the university, which will open in April 1925.

E. Jewish Culture

Irving Berlin writes and stars in the all-soldier revue *Yip, Yip, Yaphank*, which features his famous army song "Oh, How I Hate to Get Up in the Morning."

Fritz Haber (1868–1934), German physical chemist, is awarded the Nobel Prize for chemistry for his synthesis of ammonia from its elements, which is of invaluable assistance to the German war effort in World War I. Although he left the Jewish faith, he will refuse to dismiss his Jewish colleagues from the Kaiser Wilhelm Research Institute in Berlin, which he will head, when the Nazis come to power. He will choose, instead, to go to Switzerland, where he will die.

Richard Beer-Hofmann (1886–1945), Austrian playwright, publishes his play *Jacob's Dream*, the first of a biblical trilogy. It is based on the conflict between the brothers Jacob and Edom, their reconciliation, and Jacob's covenant with God at Beth-El. Jacob is foretold the future of his descendants, a people wandering on earth who would be the guardians of a precious moral heritage, God's witnesses on earth. His second play, *The Young King David*, will be completed in 1933, shortly before his works are burned by the Nazis.

Marc Chagall is appointed director and commissar of fine arts in Vitebsk's Art Academy. His paintings are placed on exhibit at the

A. General History	B. Jews in North and South America	C. Jews in Europe	D. Jews in the Middle East and Elsewhere	E. Jewish Culture	
in Germany and Kaiser William II* flees the country. Albert Ballin (1857–1918), German shipping magnate and confidant of Kaiser William II,* entrusted with negotiations for an armistice and peace preparations, commits suicide. In November, Kurt Eisner (1867–1919), German Socialist leader and head of the revolutionary movement in Munich, becomes prime minister of the new Republic of Bavaria. In November, the Hapsburg monarchy ends and the new nations of Hungary, Czechoslovakia, Austria, and Yugoslavia are created. The Second Polish Republic is established. During World War I, the Allies mobilized 42,189,000 soldiers, and 4,489,000 were killed. The Central Powers mobilized 22,850,000 and 3,132,000 were killed. Over 6,642,000 civilians died in the war. A worldwide influenza epidemic results in the death of 20 million people by 1920, including 500,000 in the U.S.		World War I, including czarist Russia, 450,000; Austria–Hungary, 275,000; the U.S., 250,000; Germany, 90,000; Great Britain, 50,000; France, 35,000. Over 15,000 American Jewish soldiers and 10,623 German Jewish soldiers were killed. The ratio of the German Jewish dead to the ratio of the Jewish population far exceeds the total German ratio of the war dead. The legend of the stab in the back (Dolchstosslegende) is propagated by the defeated German army and elements of the German right. The Jews are identified as principally responsible for Germany's defeat and for preventing German recovery. Ernst Bloch (1885–1977), German Marxist philosopher, writes *The Spirit of Utopia*, a blend of Jewish mysticism, Christian heresy, Marxist utopia, expressionist literature and revolutionary politics. It includes a chapter in which he hopes for the renewal of Judaism.		Winter Palace in Leningrad. *Baginnen* and *Eigenes*, literary magazines, are published in Kiev. Jacob Klatzkin (1882–1948), Russian-born Zionist philosopher, writes an essay describing his Zionist position: Only land and language make a nation. Abstract religious or cultural ideas are abnormal. The Jews need to reacquire their land and again speak Hebrew, their language. The Judaism of the Diaspora is not worthy of survival. All Jews must emigrate to Palestine or they will disappear by intermarriage.	**1918**
In January, peace negotiations open in Paris. In February, at the urging of U.S. President Woodrow Wilson,* delegates to the Paris Peace Conference in Versailles agree to create a League of Nations as part of the general peace treaty. Kurt Eisner, prime minister of the	In January, George Louis Beer (1872–1920) serves as chief of the colonial division of the American delegation at the Paris Peace Conference. He is believed to have originated the use of the term *mandate* to promote the welfare of colonial natives. From January 7 to 13, Jews are beaten in the streets of Buenos	In January, a pogrom occurs in Zhitomir in which 80 Jews are killed. In March, when Simon Petlyura's* soldiers capture the city from the Red Army, a pogrom results in the murder of 317 Jews. Rosa Luxemburg (1871–1919) and Karl Liebknecht,* revolutionaries and leaders of the German Communist party, are killed in Berlin while	On January 4, Chaim Weizmann and Emir Feisal,* son of Sharif Hussein* of Mecca, sign an agreement, arranged by the British, in London, envisaging a common stance at the upcoming Paris Peace Conference. The Jews are guaranteed free immigration and settlement on the land of Palestine. Arab tenant farmers will be safeguarded on their	George Gershwin (1898–1937), U.S. composer, writes his first song, "Swanee," made famous by Al Jolson. Fannie Hurst (1889–1968), a third-generation Ohioan, publishes *Humoresque*, a volume of short stories. The collection includes eight stories of New York's Jews.	**1919**

A. General History	B. Jews in North and South America	C. Jews in Europe	D. Jews in the Middle East and Elsewhere	E. Jewish Culture
1919				

A. General History

Bavarian Socialist republic, is assassinated.

In March, the Communist International (Comintern) is founded in Russia.

Benito Mussolini* founds the Fascist party in Italy.

Bela Kun (1886–1939) becomes dictator of the Communist regime in Hungary, which holds power until August.

In April, the Bolsheviks expel the Allies from Russia and establish the Soviet republic.

In June, the Treaty of Versailles is signed. Germany cedes Alsace–Lorraine to France and western Prussia to Poland. It loses its colonies and limits its army to 100,000 men. The left bank of the Rhine is demilitarized. Germany undertakes to pay reparations.

In July, the new German republic adopts the Weimar Constitution. Hugo Preuss (1860–1925), minister of the interior, headed the committee that drafted the constitution. An authority on constitutional law, Preuss was denied a professorship at the Berlin University because of his religion and liberal views.

In August, the White Army led by Anton Denikin* conquers the Ukraine but is expelled by the Bolsheviks in December.

In September, President Woodrow Wilson* tours the

B. Jews in North and South America

Aires, Argentina, as a pogrom follows a general strike. Anti-Russian fervor after the Russian Revolution stimulated antisemitism and the charge that Bolshevik Jews, led by Pinie Wald, attempted to seize control of the country.

President Woodrow Wilson* meets with the American Jewish Congress delegation to the Paris Peace Conference and advises: "I am persuaded that the Allied nations with the fullest concurrence of our own Government and people are agreed that in Palestine there shall be laid the foundation of a Jewish commonwealth." He tells Rabbi Stephen S. Wise, "Don't worry, Dr. Wise, Palestine is yours."

Julius Kahn (1861–1924), Republican congressman from California, presents a petition to President Woodrow Wilson* signed by nearly 300 anti-Zionist American Jews opposed to a Jewish homeland in Palestine.

Under the leadership of Louis D. Brandeis, the American Zionist movement grows from 12,000 members and a budget of $15,000 in 1914 to 176,000 members and a budget of $3 million in 1919.

The Rabbinical Assembly of America is established. It is the central organization of Conservative rabbis.

Emma Goldman and Alexander Berkman, U.S. anarchists who had been imprisoned

C. Jews in Europe

in government custody. An internationalist, Luxemburg had no interest in a specifically Jewish labor movement and was devoid of Jewish national sentiments.

Ukrainian soldiers who are followers of nationalist leader Simon Petlyura* massacre 1,700 Jews in the Ukrainian town of Proskurov. The next day, they conduct a pogrom at the neighboring town of Felshtin and kill an additional 600 Jews.

A Ukrainian band of peasants conducts a pogrom in Trostyanets, killing over 400 Jews.

The Soviet authorities commence the destruction of Russian Zionism, the strongest political element of Russian Jewry.

The Comité des Délégations Juives is formed at the Paris Peace Conference, representing Jews from the U.S., Canada, Palestine, Poland, Russia, Romania, Austria–Hungary, Turkey, Italy, Greece, and the Ukraine. It submits two memoranda to the conference, one on the civil and cultural rights of Jews in various countries and the other on the historic claim of the Jewish people to Palestine. The international treaties guaranteeing rights of all minority groups is considered a major achievement of the Comité.

Gustav Landauer (1870–1919), who served as minister of

D. Jews in the Middle East and Elsewhere

land and assisted in their economic development. Britain will arbitrate disputes. Feisal,* on his own, attaches a codicil to the Arab version. The agreement is conditioned on the Arabs obtaining independence in Syria.

In February, Chaim Weizmann heads the Zionist delegation at the Paris Peace Conference in Versailles, where he urges an international ratification of the Balfour Declaration.

In March, Emir Feisal* writes to Felix Frankfurter (1882–1965), of the American Jewish delegation to the Paris Peace Conference, that the Zionist proposals submitted to the conference are moderate and proper. "We wish the Jews a hearty welcome home. . . . There is room in Syria for us both. Indeed, I think that neither can be a real success without the other."

In July, Arab nationalists, at a Syrian Congress, pass a resolution against the creation of a Jewish commonwealth in the southern part of Syria, known as Palestine.

By midyear, Emir Feisal,* having failed to obtain Arab independence and Zionist assistance in his dispute with the French in Syria, terminates public meetings with Zionists. He becomes disillusioned with his Zionist connection and warns the Zionists to moderate their claims in Palestine and agree to consider

E. Jewish Culture

Moshe Leib Halpern (1886–1932), Yiddish poet who emigrated to the U.S. in 1908 from Galicia, publishes his first collection of poems, *In New York*, which establishes his reputation as a major Yiddish poet.

Franz Rosenzweig (1886–1929), German philosopher and theologian, completes *Star of Redemption*, begun in the trenches of eastern Europe during World War I. Influenced by his cousin Eugen Rosenstock-Huessy, Hermann Cohen, and Martin Buber, he was on the verge of converting to Christianity when he began a "return" to Judaism. His *Star* comprises three elements—man, the universe, and God—related to each other through the three processes of creation, revelation, and redemption. His book influences Jewish intellectuals.

Jacob Kramer (1892–1962), British immigrant painter, paints *The Day of Atonement*, typical of the works for which he becomes best known, using simplified, angular forms to recall the deeply religious life of the past.

Max Beckmann (1884–1950) paints *Synagogue* in a somber and foreboding mood. He teaches at the Frankfurt Art School from 1915 to 1933 when he will be dismissed by the Nazis. The synagogue that was the subject of the painting will be destroyed with other Frankfurt synagogues by the Nazis on *Kristallnacht*, November 9, 1938.

1919

U.S., crusading for Senate approval of the League of Nations. He suffers a stroke and abandons the tour.

In September, Adolf Hitler,* employed by the German army as an education officer to report on subversive movements, attends a meeting in Munich of the German Workers' party, the precursor of the Nazi party, and joins it. At this time, he writes a response to an inquiry on the "Jewish question," his earliest extant political statement, in which he advocates rational antisemitism. At first, the emancipation of the Jews should be legally rescinded, "but the final objective must be the complete removal of the Jews."

The first successful U.S. tabloid newspaper, the *New York Daily News*, is established.

Walter Gropius* (1883–1969) establishes the Staatliche Bauhaus in Weimar. The Bauhaus revolutionizes the teaching of fine arts, architecture, and design.

Jewish delegation to the Paris Peace Conference, 1919. Chaim Weizmann is seventh from right. (Central Zionist Archives)

for antiwar activities, are deported to the Soviet Union.

Jewish educational summer camping is begun in the U.S. with the founding of CJI Camps (later Cejwin) by the Central Jewish Institute of New York.

Hanane Caiserman (1884–1950), who left Romania in 1911 for Montreal, helps organize the Canadian Jewish Congress. He becomes general seretary and serves as such until his death.

Victor Berger, U.S. congressman from Wisconsin, is convicted and sentenced to 20 years in prison for violation of the Espionage Act. A Socialist, he opposed U.S. involvement in World War I. His conviction will be overturned by the U.S. Supreme Court in 1921, and a year later he will be reelected to Congress, where he will serve until 1928.

culture and education in the Bavarian Socialist republic, is murdered by counterrevolutionary soldiers after the overthrow of Kurt Eisner's regime. A friend of Martin Buber, he opposed Buber's support of Germany's World War I policies and was a leading opponent of war and an advocate of a united Europe.

In June, the Paris Peace Conference promulgates the principle of minority rights as an instrument of internal peace in multinational states. Jews are specifically mentioned in treaties with Poland and Turkey, but the safeguards are intended to benefit Jews in all the new or newly enlarged European countries. Czechoslovakia and Estonia will live up to the guarantees, while Romania and Poland will sabotage minority rights and the equality of their Jewish citizens.

All Jewish religious communities in the Soviet Union are dissolved, their property is confiscated, and most synagogues are closed.

The counterrevolutionary Russian White Army conducts a pogrom in Fastov, killing over 1,500 Jews. The White Army conducts similar pogroms all over Russia.

During the summer, a Ukrainian band of peasants led by Grigoryev,* who seceded from the Red Army in May, conducts pogroms in 40 communities and kills about 6,000 Jews.

Palestine as part of Greater Syria.

Louis D. Brandeis and Chaim Weizmann meet for the first time, in London, during the summer. Brandeis is on his way to Paris, the site of the Peace Conference, and then to Palestine.

Ahdut ha-Avodah, the Zionist Socialist Labor party, is founded in Palestine. It includes 80% of all Jewish workers.

Akiva Jacob Ettinger (1872–1945) founds Kiryat Anavim on the rocky hills near Jerusalem, which becomes a model for hill settlements throughout Palestine. An agricultural expert, he plays a prominent role in land purchase and settlement on behalf of the Jewish National Fund.

Religion of Reason Out of the Sources of Judaism, written by German philosopher Hermann Cohen (1842–1918), is published posthumously. Cohen was the leader of the neo-Kantian school of philosophy, but he differed with Kant on the approach to Judaism. Kant considered Judaism an obsolete religion. Cohen attempted to present Judaism as a religion of reason.

A Jewish museum is founded in Vilna by the Society of Lovers of Jewish Antiquities. In 1920, it will be named for Solomon Zainwil Rapaport (S. Anski), Russian writer and folklorist, following his death. A second Jewish museum in Vilna will be founded about 1930 by the Institute for Jewish Research together with an institute for the study of Jewish art.

The Archives of the World Zionist Organization are established in Berlin. In 1933 they will be moved to Jerusalem and become the Central Zionist Archives.

Sholem Asch (1880–1957) writes *Kiddush ha-Shem*, a story of Jewish martyrdom in 17th-century Poland and the Ukraine, which is one of modern Yiddish literature's earliest examples of a historical novel. It will be translated into English in 1926.

The publication of *Haaretz* (*The Country*), a Hebrew daily newspaper, begins in Jerusalem. It will move to Tel Aviv in

	A. General History	B. Jews in North and South America	C. Jews in Europe	D. Jews in the Middle East and Elsewhere	E. Jewish Culture
1919	Adolf Hitler* is recruited by the German army's political branch in Munich as an education officer and disseminator of the legend of the stab in the back, which holds Jews responsible for Germany's defeat and economic ills.		During the year, 685 pogroms and 249 lesser riots occur against the Jews of the Ukraine. Nathan Birnbaum, an early leader of Zionist ideology who later withdrew from Zionism to become a leader of Orthodox Judaism, becomes the first general secretary of the Agudat Israel World Organization. Arturo Carlos de Barros Basto (1889–1961), Portugese soldier of Marrano descent, converts to Judaism. He works toward the revival of Judaism among Portuguese Marranos and founds a synagogue at Oporto.		1923. It is independent and liberal in orientation. Its literary supplement features the best Hebrew writers and scholars, both from Palestine and the Diaspora.

> *Third "Aliyah" to Palestine, 1919–1923*
> *Number:* 35,000
> *Origin:* Young pioneers (*halutzim*) mainly from Russia, Poland and Rumania

	A. General History	B. Jews in North and South America	C. Jews in Europe	D. Jews in the Middle East and Elsewhere	E. Jewish Culture
1920	U.S. Attorney General A. Mitchell Palmer* directs "Red-scare" arrests and deportations of Communists, anarchists, and labor leaders throughout the country. The 18th Amendment to the U.S. Constitution, the Prohibition amendment outlawing alcoholic beverages, goes into effect. However, article 7 of the National Prohibition Act of 1920 permits every family to use up to ten gallons of wine annually for religious purposes. The National Socialist German Workers' party (later to be known as the Nazi party) publishes, in Munich, a 25-point program. The main thrust is nationalist, the creation of a "Great Germany." No Jew can be a member of the party, and all Jews who had come to Germany since 1914 should be forced to	Henry Ford's* weekly newspaper, the *Dearborn Independent*, begins publishing a series of almost 100 articles entitled The International Jew, including reprinting *The Protocols of the Elders of Zion*. It enjoys a peak circulation of 500,000. Jews institute a communitywide boycott of Ford autos. The Jewish vote in the U.S. presidential election is estimated at 43% for Warren E. Harding,* 38% for Eugene V. Debs,* and 19% for James M. Cox.* The American Academy for Jewish Research is established, with Louis Ginzberg as president. Its purpose is to foster and promote the cause of Jewish learning and research. Director Frank Borzage's screen adaptation of Fannie Hurst's *Humoresque* wins praise from the	Winston Churchill* writes in Britain's *Illustrated Sunday Herald* that "no thoughtful man can doubt the fact that they [the Jews] are the most formidable and the most remarkable race which has ever appeared in the world." The *Times* of London publishes "The Jewish Peril," an editorial that assumes the authenticity of *The Protocols of the Elders of Zion*. It asks, had England "escaped a Pax Germanica only to fall into a Pax Judaica?" It is believed that the editorial resulted from the fear of the spread of communism throughout Europe and the prominence of some Jews, by origin if not by allegiance, in revolutionary leadership positions. Adolf Hitler* speaks in Munich on the subject, Why We Are Against the Jews. He states that his Nazi party "will free you	Arabs attack Jewish settlements in Galilee. Joseph Trumpeldor and five others are killed during the defense of Tel Hai. The attack is a minor incident in the Arab–French conflict over control of Syria. In April, Sir Herbert Samuel is appointed the first British high commissioner in Palestine by Prime Minister Lloyd George.* He arrives in Palestine in June and serves until 1925. Arabs riot in Jerusalem on the festival of Nebi Mussa. This first violent Arab attack on Zionism is in response to British policy and Jewish immigration. Seven Jews are killed and 200 wounded. As British police are unable to maintain order, Vladimir (Ze'ev) Jabotinsky organizes a Jewish self-defense group. He is arrested and sentenced to 15 years' imprisonment by British military forces.	Isaac Baer Berkson (1891–1975), U.S. educator, writes *Theories of Americanization*, in which he applies the American theory of cultural pluralism to the problems of Jewish education. Anzia Yezierska (1885–1970), U.S. writer, publishes *Hungry Hearts*, a collection of her short stories about Lower East Side ghetto life and sweatshops. Her book will be purchased by Hollywood filmmakers, and she will receive a contract to write for the movies. Franz Rosenzweig, German philosopher and theologian, organizes the Freies Juedisches Lehrhaus (Independent House of Jewish Learning) in Frankfurt, which becomes a center of adult Jewish education for assimilated Jews in search of their past. Nahum Glatzer, Gershom Scholem

1920

A. General History

leave. At this time, the party has 60 members.

After the Bolsheviks defeat the White Army in the civil war in White Russia and the Baltic states, the Soviet government recognizes the independence of Estonia (February), Lithuania (July), Latvia (August), and Finland (October).

The U.S. Senate fails to ratify the Treaty of Versailles and the covenant establishing the League of Nations.

Poland attacks Russia in an attempt to wrest the Ukraine from the Bolsheviks. They quickly overrun the country, but the Russians counterattack and by August are on the outskirts of Warsaw. The Poles, aided by the French, force the Russians back. The Treaty of Riga, which will be signed in March 1921, defines the boundary between the two countries.

At the San Remo Conference, the Allies divide the Middle East into mandates. The British obtain Palestine and Iraq. The French acquire Syria and Lebanon.

Under the Treaty of Trianon between the Allied powers of World War I and Hungary, Romania is awarded substantial territory from Hungary, including Transylvania.

Danzig is proclaimed a free city as provided by the Versailles treaty. It is placed under the protection of the League of Nations.

B. Jews in North and South America

New York Times for its vivid Lower East Side atmosphere and genuine acting. It is the tale of a young Jewish boy (Gaston Glass) pushed by his Yiddishe mama (Vera Gordon) to become a great violinist.

C. Jews in Europe

from the power of the Jews" and demands "the removal of the Jews from the midst of our people."

During the year, 142 pogroms and 36 lesser riots occur against the Jews of the Ukraine.

G. K. Chesterton* (1874–1936), English journalist and author noted for his antisemitic views, records his visit to Palestine in *The New Jerusalem*, in which he expresses his admiration for the Zionist ideal of emancipation through physical toil.

D. Jews in the Middle East and Elsewhere

He will be pardoned in 1921.

At the London Zionist Conference, Max Nordau urges the immediate immigration of 600,000 Jews to Palestine to create a Jewish majority before the development of Arab resistance. This would enable the establishment of Jewish political independence. He later will write: "We need the unoccupied land of Palestine to settle millions of our. brethren. The danger of slaughter and tragedy looms over them in the Ukraine. Poland is plotting to choke them slowly through economic boycott and Austria–Hungary and Germany seek to drown them in the darkness and shame of the ghetto."

At a meeting of the World Zionist Conference in London, Louis D. Brandeis seeks the concentration of Zionist activity on the economic development of Palestine, based mainly on private enterprise, led by experienced businessmen such as James de Rothschild (1878–1957) and Lord Mond. He argues that the political functions of the movement should be ended and transferred to the mandatory government. His suggestions are not accepted and lead to the cleavage between the Brandeis and Weizmann groups.

Histadrut, the General Federation of Jewish Labor, is founded in Palestine. It is a general labor organization in which

E. Jewish Culture

(1897–1982), and Eric Fromm are among the Jewish intellectuals attracted to the Lehrhaus.

The Dybbuk, a play written by Solomon Zainwil Rapaport (S. Anski) in Russian is performed in Yiddish by the Vilna troupe. Rapaport developed its theme from the folklore legends he amassed during his leadership of the Jewish ethnographic expedition from 1911 to 1914. Its first American production will be in 1922 at Maurice Schwartz's Yiddish Art Theater in New York.

Marc Chagall executes large paintings for the Jewish State Theatre in Moscow. Directed by Alexander Granowsky (1890–1937), the theater presents works mainly by Jewish authors.

Joseph Hayyim Brenner (1881–1921), a major figure in modern Hebrew literature, writes *Breakdown and Bereavement*, a novel describing the transition of a pioneer from an agricultural settlement to Jerusalem. Brenner is noted for portraying the bleak and difficult life in Palestine during the early 20th-century. Brenner fled Russia for England in 1905. He settled in Palestine in 1909.

Samuel Hugo Bergman (1883–1975), librarian at the Prague University library, emigrates to Palestine and becomes the first director of the National and University Library.

	A. General History	B. Jews in North and South America	C. Jews in Europe	D. Jews in the Middle East and Elsewhere	E. Jewish Culture
1920	The French occupy Damascus and depose Feisal* as king of Greater Syria. In March, Feisal* had been proclaimed king by the Arabs, but Britain and France refuse to recognize him.

American women gain the right to vote, as the 19th Amendment to the U.S. Constitution becomes effective.

Eight Chicago White Sox baseball players are indicted on charges they had conspired with gamblers to fix the 1919 World Series.

The Republican Warren G. Harding*–Calvin Coolidge* U.S. presidential ticket defeats the Democrat ticket of James M. Cox*–Franklin D. Roosevelt.* | | | all political parties can cooperate on labor, economic, and cultural questions.

The Haganah, a Jewish defense organization, is established under the initiative of the Palestinian labor movement.

A Palestine Arab Congress held at Haifa founds the local Arab nationalist movement.

The institution of two chief rabbis in Palestine, one Ashkenazic and one Sephardic, and rabbinical courts are given legal status by a mandatory ordinance, with jurisdiction over matrimonial law and religion. The first chief rabbis are Rabbi Abraham Isaac Kook (1865–1935), Ashkenazic, and Rabbi Jacob Meir (1856–1939), Sephardic.

During the year, Yehoshua Hankin (1864–1945), who arrived in Palestine in 1882 from the Ukraine and who was instrumental in purchasing land for Jewish settlement on behalf of the Jewish National Fund, purchases 51,000 dunams in the Jezreel Valley, on which En-Harod, Tel Yosef, Nahalal, and other agricultural settlements are later founded. During his lifetime, he will purchase over 600,000 dunams of land for settlement. | The Hebrew Union of Artists is founded in Jerusalem with the objective of disseminating "works of art and fine taste in the Hebrew spirit." |
| **1921** | In January, Adolf Hitler's* party, the National Socialist Workers' party (later known as the Nazi party), holds its first national congress in Munich. Although | In January, President Woodrow Wilson,* former President Taft,* Cardinal O'Connell of New York, and 116 other prominent Americans of the Christian faith | During the Russian civil war, ending in 1921, there are 2,000 pogroms in Poland and the Ukraine. Half a million Jews are left homeless; 30,000 Jews are killed directly and | In March, Winston Churchill,* British colonial secretary, visits Palestine and concludes an agreement with Abdullah ibn Hussein* (1881–1951) | Herman Bernstein (1876–1935), U.S. journalist, writes *The History of a Lie*, an account of how *The Protocols of the Elders of Zion* is a forgery. |

A. General History

attendance is meager, Hitler* and the party receive press attention.

U.S. General Billy Mitchell* demonstrates the destructive power of aircraft by sinking captured German warships by bombing.

After the U.S. Senate rejects the Versailles treaty, the U.S. signs a separate peace treaty with Germany. The treaty neither recognizes the League of Nations nor reparations.

The Quota Act of 1921 (the Johnson Act) is signed by President Warren G. Harding* following a veto in the last days of President Woodrow Wilson's* administration. This act provides that the number of immigrants admitted in any one year could not exceed 3% of their ethnic stock in the U.S. in 1910. Although a temporary measure, it is a turning point in the U.S. immigration policy, since the 1910 census indicated larger numbers of northern and western Europeans than those of eastern or southern European stock.

The Chinese Communist party is founded. Sun Yat-sen* proclaims the nationalist government in Canton.

Emir Feisal* is proclaimed king of Iraq by the British mandatory authorities. He emphasizes equality of all Iraqis and serves until his death in 1933.

B. Jews in North and South America

issue a protest against "what is apparently an organized campaign of anti-Semitism."

At the June convention of American Zionists, a majority of delegates do not support Louis D. Brandeis' proposal of financial autonomy of the American Zionist Organization, fearing it would weaken the World Zionist Organization. Brandeis resigns from the leadership role.

Benjamin Nathan Cardozo (1870–1938), judge of the New York Court of Appeals and later to become an associate justice of the U.S. Supreme Court, writes his classic philosophic essay, *The Nature of the Judicial Process*.

Albert Einstein, world-renowned physicist living in Germany, accepts an invitation of Chaim Weizmann and accompanies him on a visit to the U.S. to raise money for the Hebrew University and the Jewish National Fund.

In July, George F. Moore* (1851–1931), Harvard professor of Hebrew, Bible, and rabbinics, criticizes Catholic and Protestant scholarship of early Christianity and rabbinic Judaism as being "primarily apologetic or polemic rather than historical." According to Moore,* Judaism can be understood only on its own merits by a study of its own sources and not by an attempt to find its relationship to the Christian faith.

Julian Morgenstern becomes president of Hebrew Union

C. Jews in Europe

an additional 120,000 die from wounds or as a result of illnesses contracted during the pogroms.

Beginning in 1921 and continuing until 1924, the Joint Distribution Committee establishes medical stations, loan cooperatives, and vocational training schools in Russia and expends over $25 million to help Russian and Polish Jews.

Philip Graves,* Constantinople correspondent of the *London Times*, demonstrates that *The Protocols of the Elders of Zion* is a forgery, having been plagiarized from a French political pamphlet written in 1864 by Maurice Joly* (d. 1879), who attributed ambitions of world domination to Napoleon III.*

In September, the 12th Zionist Congress convenes in Carlsbad, under the leadership of Chaim Weizmann. The movement is consolidated under Weizmann's leadership and the hope of political cooperation with the British under the impending mandate.

Julius Brutzkus (1870–1951) is appointed minister for Jewish affairs in the Lithuanian government and in 1922 is elected to the Lithuanian Parliament.

A central Yiddish school organization is formed in Poland with a network of 69 Yiddish elementary schools and 35 kindergartens located in 44 cities.

D. Jews in the Middle East and Elsewhere

to place Transjordan under his rule under the terms of the British mandate over Palestine. Transjordan had been considered part of Palestine in all deliberations with the Zionists.

Sir Herbert Samuel, British high commissioner in Palestine, appoints Haj Amin al-Husseini* an Arab nationalist, Grand Mufti (expounder of Muslim law) of Jerusalem.

Arab riots result in 47 Jewish fatalities in Palestine. Forty-five Jews are killed at a hostel for new immigrants in Jaffa. On the sixth day of riots, Sir Herbert Samuel, the high commissioner, suspends Jewish immigration in an effort to appease Arab grievances. Joseph Hayyim Brenner, Hebrew writer, is among those murdered.

David Ben-Gurion is elected secretary-general of Histadrut, which he and Berl Katznelson (1887–1944) head for almost 14 years.

King Feisal* of Iraq appoints Sir Sassoon Heskel as his first finance minister. He is the only Jew ever to hold cabinet rank in Iraq.

Kibbutz En-Harod, the first large kibbutz (215 members), is founded in the Jezreel Valley. Within several years, 20 settlements are founded in the Jezreel Valley.

An edict is issued in Yemen requiring all Jewish orphans who are minors to convert to Islam.

E. Jewish Culture

Ben Hecht (1894–1964), U.S. journalist, novelist, and playwright, publishes his first novel, *Erik Dorn*, the story of a Jewish intellectual who gives up his wife and mistress for the excitement of the European revolution. Hecht made use of his experiences as a *Chicago Daily News* foreign correspondent in Berlin in 1918 and 1919.

Albert Einstein, German physicist, is awarded the Nobel Prize in physics for his explanation of the photoelectric effect, which contributes to the foundation of the quantum theory, and not for his discovery of the theory of relativity.

Alter Kacyzne (1885–1941), Yiddish writer and professional photographer, is commisssioned by the Hebrew Immigrant Aid Society (HIAS) to photograph the emigration process from Poland as it was facilitated by HIAS. His photographs of Jewish life in Poland are featured in the *Forverts* (*Froward*) in New York until his death at the hands of Ukrainian collaborators who will kill him as he flees the Germans in World War II.

Leivick Halpern (H. Leivick, 1886–1962), Yiddish poet and playwright, writes *The Golem*. The play is first performed in 1924 in Moscow in a Hebrew production by the Habimah repertory theater. Its theme, mankind's yearning for redemption, centers on the creation of a golem by Rabbi Judah

	A. General History	B. Jews in North and South America	C. Jews in Europe	D. Jews in the Middle East and Elsewhere	E. Jewish Culture
1921		College, succeeding Kaufmann Kohler.

Reform and Conservative rabbinical leaders oppose the sacramental wine exception to the Prohibition amendment in response to concern for abuse. Dr. Louis Ginzberg writes responsa officially sanctioning grape juice, as he concurs that unfermented wine possesses the same status as fermented wine in regard to its use for religious purposes. The Orthodox community publicly insists on using wine for religious purposes, taking advantage of the federal law's exception.

The Hebrew Theological College, a seminary for the training of Orthodox rabbis, is established in Chicago, Illinois.

The Boston Hebrew Teachers' College is founded, and in 1927 it will receive a state charter enabling it to confer degrees.

John Dos Passos* (1896–1970), U.S. novelist, writes *Three Soldiers*, which shows the effects of World War I on the character of three soldiers. It includes an antiwar, radical Jewish soldier, Eisenstadt, who is Jew-baited by his fellow soldiers. | | Bank Hapoalim (The Workers' Bank) is established by the Histadrut with the assistance of the World Zionist Organization as a central credit resource for its cooperative and settlement activities.

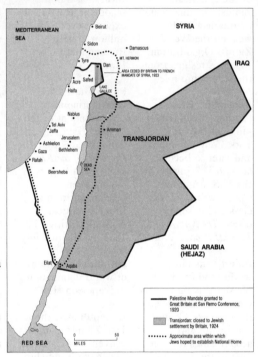

PALESTINE MANDATE GRANTED TO GREAT BRITAIN, 1920 | Loew (1512–1609) of Prague to defend the Jewish community. Born in Russia and active in the Bund, Leivick was arrested in 1906, imprisoned, and exiled to Siberia. He escaped to the U.S. in 1913.

The First Art Exhibition at the Tower of David in Jerusalem includes the debut exhibition of the Hebrew Union of Artists, a gallery of international artists, and an exhibit of Islamic art. The event stirs national sentiments. Jewish artists exhibited include Israel Paldi (1893–1979), Zeev Raban (1890–1970), Abel Pann (1883–1963), and Boris Schatz.

The publication of *Hadoar* (*The Post*), a Hebrew periodical, begins as a daily newspaper in the U.S.. In 1922, it will cease daily publication and resume as a weekly under the auspices of the Histadruth Ivrit of America. In 1971, on its 50th anniversary of publication, it will be the only Hebrew weekly in the U.S.

Abraham Shlonsky (1900–1973), Israeli poet and literary editor, returns to Palestine fom Russia and engages in road building in the Jezreel Valley. Calling himself "the road-paving poet of Israel," he will spearhead the revolt against the school of Bialik and will play a central role in the modernization of Hebrew poetry. |
| 1922 | In February, the Washington Conference concludes with a naval armaments treaty. | President Harding* signs the Lodge–Fish Resolution, a joint resolution of Congress that gives formal | On June 22, Walter Rathenau (1867–1922), an industrialist who in February became the | The League of Nations incorporates the Balfour Declaration into its final approval of the | El Lissitsky, Russian painter who brought Russian constructivist art to western Europe, illustrates a book of |

A. General History	B. Jews in North and South America	C. Jews in Europe	D. Jews in the Middle East and Elsewhere	E. Jewish Culture

1922 (right margin)

A. General History

Japan is to reduce the size of its fleet.

In February, Egypt is declared independent as Great Britain ends its protectorate.

In April, Germany and the Soviet Union sign the Treaty of Rapallo. They mutually cancel all prewar debts and renounce all war claims. It is the first major recognition of the Soviet Union.

In April, Joseph Stalin* becomes general secretary of the Communist party in the Soviet Union.

In October, Benito Mussolini's* Fascists march on Rome. The Italian king grants him dictatorial powers.

In December, the Union of Soviet Socialist Republics is formed. The union includes Russia, the Ukraine, White Russia, and Transcaucasia.

Kemal Ataturk* abolishes the sultanate and proclaims Turkey a republic. He is elected the first president.

Radios are found in approximately 3 million American homes.

B. Jews in North and South America

American approval to the establishment in Palestine of a national home for the Jewish people. However, the House Committee on Foreign Affairs made it clear that the resolution "expresses our moral interest . . . (and) commits us to no foreign obligations or entanglements."

The American Jewish Congress becomes a permanent organization, representing Zionist-minded immigrant Jews from eastern Europe.

Mordecai M. Kaplan founds the Society for the Advancement of Judaism, a synagogue located in New York, at which his philosophy of Judaism, known as Reconstructionism, is practiced. He believes the present generation, while revering the ideals and rituals of the past, is free to make its own changes in light of its own needs.

The Jewish Institute of Religion is founded in New York by Stephen S. Wise for training rabbis primarily for the Reform movement.

As the proportion of Jews at Harvard College exceeds 21%, a quota limiting the number of Jewish students is imposed. Harvard President A. Lawrence Lowell* defends the idea of a quota, writing to a Jewish graduate of "a rapidly growing anti-Semitic feeling in the country" and suggesting that if "every college in the country would take a limited proportion of Jews, . . . we should go a long way toward eliminating race

C. Jews in Europe

first Jew to be appointed foreign minister of Germany, is assassinated by antisemites.

Adolf Hitler,* in conversation with Major Josef Hell,* advises that if he wins power, "the annihilation of the Jews will be my first and foremost task. . . . They cannot protect themselves and no one will stand forth as their protectors."

Hilaire Belloc* (1870–1953), English Catholic author, writes *The Jews*, in which he expresses a belief in the Jewish world conspiracy canard.

James Joyce* (1882–1941), Irish novelist, publishes *Ulysses*, generally regarded as the greatest 20th-century novel written in English. Joyce describes the purpose of the book as "the epic of two races [Israel–Ireland] and at the same time the cycle of the human body as well as a little story of a day." The central character of the novel is Leopold Bloom, an Everyman figure, in an Irish nation and society where Jews are few in number.

John Galsworthy's* (1867–1933) English play *Loyalties* depicts Ferdinand DeLevis, the Jewish victim of a robbery at a country house party. The other guests band together to defend the thief because he is one of them, while the Jew is an alien. Galsworthy* will be awarded the Nobel Prize for literature in 1932.

D. Jews in the Middle East and Elsewhere

British mandate over Palestine.

Winston Churchill,* British colonial secretary, issues the Palestine White Paper. It reaffirms that the Jews are in Palestine as of right and not on sufferance, restricts the Jewish National Home to the area west of the Jordan, limits Jewish immigration to the economic capacity of the country to absorb new arrivals, and pledges nondomination by the Jews of the Arab population.

Haj Amin Al-Husseini,* Palestinian Arab nationalist leader, who in 1921 was appointed Grand Mufti of Jerusalem by High Commissioner Sir Herbert Samuel, is appointed president of the Supreme Muslim Council. The administrative and financial power of this post combined with his religious position leads to his leadership of Palestinian Arab nationalism.

Kibbutz Bet Alfa is founded in Palestine by pioneers from Poland. It is the first settlement of the Kibbutz Arzi ha-Shomer ha-Za'ir movement.

Ahad ha-Am, Hebrew essayist and leader of Hibbat Zion movement, settles in Palestine, where he remains until his death. Born in Russia, he moved to England in 1907.

E. Jewish Culture

stories written by Ilya Ehrenburg (1891–1967). In 1914, he explored Russian Jewish folk art and thereafter illustrated Jewish children's books employing folk motifs. In 1919, in like style, he illustrated the "Had Gadya" song, which is included in the Passover Haggadah.

The publication of *Morning Freiheit* (*Freedom*), a Yiddish daily newspaper, begins in New York. It is founded by the Jewish section of the American Communist party.

A Yiddish translation of the Bible by Solomon Bloomgarden (Yehoash, 1872–1927) begins appearing in the New York Yiddish daily, *Der Tog* (*The Day*). It is regarded as a masterpiece of translation and is printed, in parallel Hebrew and Yiddish texts, in tens of thousands of copies and distributed throughout the world. Serialization continues until 1927.

Ludwig Lewisohn (1882–1955), teacher and writer, who came to Charleston, South Carolina, in 1890 with his parents from Berlin, writes an autobiographical memoir, *Up Stream*, in which he describes his student years at Columbia University and the antisemitism that barred his way to university teaching in his chosen field of English literature. He is described as the first Jewish intellectual to achieve national literary and cultural influence.

Niels Bohr (1885–1962), Danish physicist, is awarded

A. General History	B. Jews in North and South America	C. Jews in Europe	D. Jews in the Middle East and Elsewhere	E. Jewish Culture
1922	feeling among the students." Numerous U.S. colleges and universities also adopt quota systems. New York State broadens its kosher food laws, originally enacted in 1882, by passage of a law requiring establishments selling kosher and nonkosher food to clearly identify the products, prohibiting the fraudulent sale of products as being kosher when they are not, and defining the term *kosher* as food prepared "in accordance with the Orthodox Hebrew religious requirements." The New York statute becomes the model for laws enacted by other states. The Central Conference of American Rabbis (Reform) votes to ordain women, but the Board of Governors of the Hebrew Union College rejects their recommendation. The question will not rise again until 1972. Rabbi Morris and Tehilla Lichtenstein found Jewish Science. Based on Mary Baker Eddy's* Christian Science, it teaches that God rather than modern medicine is the source of physical and mental health. Tehilla Lichtenstein becomes the leader of the movement when her husband dies in 1938.			the Nobel Prize in physics. The son of a Jewish mother, in 1943 he will escape from the Nazis in Denmark and thereafter become a consultant to the Allies' atomic bomb project. Chaim Soutine, French painter, is "discovered" by the American art collector Albert C. Barnes,* who purchases more than 50 of his paintings, thus affording him financial security. Soutine, born and raised in Russia, moved to Paris in 1913, where he became a member of the Circle of Montparnasse with his friend Amedeo Modigliani. An expressionist, he utilizes violent color to express the agony depicted in his paintings—all broken, twisted, and distorted. He never paints a specifically Jewish picture. Joseph Klausner (1874–1958), historian, literary critic, and Zionist, writes *Jesus of Nazareth: His Life, Times, and Teachings,* the first study of Jesus written in Hebrew by a modern Jewish scholar. He claims that Jesus was a proud Jew who never abandoned Judaism and never considered himself as the Jewish Messiah. He also claims that Jesus was executed by Pilate the Roman and not by Jews. Dvir, a Hebrew publishing house, is founded in Berlin by Hayyim Nahman Bialik and others. In 1924 it will begin publishing in Tel Aviv.

A. General History	B. Jews in North and South America	C. Jews in Europe	D. Jews in the Middle East and Elsewhere	E. Jewish Culture	
In January, France and Belgium occupy the Rhineland when Germany fails to make its reparation payments. In June, Germany's currency is rapidly becoming worthless. In just three weeks, it loses half its value. In August, U.S. President Warren G. Harding* dies. He is succeeded by Vice President Calvin Coolidge.* In November, Adolf Hitler* is arrested after leading an unsuccessful attempt by his Nazi party to seize power in Munich. At the time of this "Beer Hall Putsch," the Nazi party has 70,000 members in Bavaria. Hitler* is jailed in Landsberg and the Nazi party is banned. Ladislav Grabski* becomes prime minister of Poland. The economic crisis affecting the country since its founding in 1918 continues.	The Reform movement's Union of American Hebrew Congregations and Central Conference of American Rabbis establish the Commission on Jewish Education, headed by Emanuel Gamoran (1895–1962). Gamoran supervised the establishment of a complete curriculum for the Reform religious school and developed textbooks for classes from nursery through adult Jewish education. The B'nai B'rith Hillel Foundation is founded to serve the needs of 400 Jewish students at the University of Illinois at Urbana. Modeled after the Methodist Wesley Foundation, its objective is to counteract the indifference of young Jews to their own tradition and culture. The Hillel movement thereafter will spread to college and university campuses throughout the U.S. The first congress of the World Council of Jewish Women meets in Vienna. Organized by the National Council of Jewish Women in the U.S., it is chaired by Rebekah Kohut (1864–1951) and brings together 200 Jewish women from over 70 countries to deal with issues concerning social justice for Jewish women.	In August, the 13th Zionist Congress convenes in Carlsbad under the leadership of Chaim Weizmann. A proposal to include non-Zionists in the Jewish Agency, newly created from the Zionist Organization, pursuant to Article 4 of the mandate "to secure the cooperation of all Jews who are willing to assist in the establishment of the Jewish National Home," is debated and arouses opposition. Kurt Yehudah Blumenfeld (1884–1963), German Zionist leader, becomes president of the German Zionist Federation. He holds this post until 1933, when he leaves to settle in Palestine. He has an influence on Zionist activities of assimilated western European Jews, including Albert Einstein. The first issue of the antisemitic newspaper *Der Sturmer*, edited by Julius Streicher* (1885–1946), is published in Nuremberg Germany. The banner slogan of the newspaper is "The Jews Are Our Misfortune." Betar (an abbreviation of Berit Trumpeldor), a Zionist youth movement, is founded in Riga, Latvia. It is a fusion of Vladimir (Ze'ev) Jabotinsky's nationalist and self-defense ideas with those of Joseph Trumpeldor. At the Agudat Israel congress, Meir Shapira (1887–1934), Polish rabbi, proposes that every Jew undertake to study each day the	On September 29, the Palestine mandate is ratified by the council of the League of Nations. Vladimir (Ze'ev) Jabotinsky, Zionist leader, resigns from the Zionist Executive and leaves the Zionist Organization. He disagrees with what he terms Zionist acquiesence to Britain's disregard of its obligations under the mandate. In November, he publishes two articles in which he asserts that Arab nationalist emotions would foreclose a voluntary agreement between Jews and Arabs over Palestine. Only an "iron wall of Jewish bayonets" could force them to accept the Jewish presence. During the year, the Jewish community in Palestine undergoes a severe economic crisis. There is famine in the settlements, and thousands are unemployed in the cities. Israel Zangwill, English author, states that Palestine would never be "Jewish nor national nor a home; it is simply another outpost in the diaspora."	Elmer Rice, U.S. playwright, writes *The Adding Machine*, an expressionist play satirizing the machine age. Mr. Zero, an accountant for 25 years, is discharged when his employer installs adding machines and kills his employer in a fit of insanity. Mr. Zero is returned to earth as an industrial slave. Samuel Ornitz (1890–1957), U.S. writer, writes *Haunch, Paunch and Jowl*, a highly realistic novel of political corruption on New York's Lower East Side. Its first-person narrator, Meyer Hirsch, is born into the corruption of his neighborhood and spends his time alternately studying and stealing, doing so well that he is able to rise from street urchin to shady lawyer to Superior Court judge. The novel achieves critical as well as commercial success. Eddie Cantor (Isidor Iskowitch, 1892–1964), U.S. comedian and vaudeville performer, stars in *Kid Boots*, a musical that runs on Broadway for three years. The New York Giants baseball team uncovers a long-ball hitter named Moses Solomon. They call him "the Rabbi of Swat" and tout him as the Jewish Babe Ruth. Solomon does not pan out. Peretz Hirschbein, U.S. Yiddish playwright, writes *Green Fields*, a pastoral romance of Levi Yitskhok, an unwordly young scholar, and Tsine, the farmer's daughter. In 1937, it will be made into a Yiddish film.	1923

	A. General History	B. Jews in North and South America	C. Jews in Europe	D. Jews in the Middle East and Elsewhere	E. Jewish Culture
1923			same *daf yomi* (daily page), of the Talmud. Ladislav Grabski,* Poland's prime minister until 1925, introduces a system of taxation and other economic policies that impose severe financial burdens on Jewish merchants and shopkeepers, driving many of them to economic ruin. In 1924, when immigration to the U.S. will be severely limited, many Polish Jews begin emigration to Palestine. George Lukacs (1885–1971), Hungarian philosopher, writes *History and Class Consciousness*, an elitist interpretation of the role of the Communist Party in the labor movement. He will later repudiate this work.		Martin Buber, German philosopher, publishes *I and Thou*, which formulates his philosophy of dialogue. Otto Meyerhof (1884–1951), German biochemist, is awarded the Nobel Prize in physiology or medicine, in recognition of his research in the chemistry of muscles. He will leave Germany in 1938 for Paris, and when the Nazis conquer France, he will escape to the U.S. Jakob Steinhardt (1887–1968), German painter who is one of the finest woodcut artists of modern times, illustrates the Passover Haggadah. His World War I German military service on the eastern front brought him into contact with Jewish life in Lithuania. In 1933, upon the rise of Adolf Hitler,* he will emigrate to Palestine where he will teach at the Bezalel school. Otto Rank (Rosenfeld, 1884–1939), Austrian psychoanalyst and protégé of Sigmund Freud, writes *The Trauma of Birth*, an open challenge to psychoanalytic orthodoxy. It will lead to his break in 1926 from the circle around Freud.
1924	In January, Vladimir Lenin* dies and a power struggle in Soviet Union ensues, pitting Joseph Stalin,* Lev Kamenev (1883–1936), and Grigori Zinoviev (1883–1936) against Leon Trotsky. Kamenev and Zinoviev will be executed in the Stalin* purges of the 1930s and Trotsky's	The College of Jewish Studies is founded in Chicago, Illinois, by the Board of Jewish Education, to train teachers and to foster Jewish studies. Its first leader is Alexander Dushkin, who serves until 1935. The Jewish vote in the U.S. presidential election is estimated at 51% for Davis,*	Zevi Hirsch Belkowsky (1865–1948), chairman of the Zionist Central Committee of Russia, is arrested for his Zionist activities and sentenced to deportation to Siberia. His sentence is commuted, and he is banished from the Soviet Union and settles in Palestine.	Jacob Israel De Haan (1881–1924), Dutch journalist and lawyer who emigrated to Palestine in 1919, is assassinated by a Zionist group, the first political murder in the Yishuv. After his arrival, he affiliated with the Agudat Israel and criticized the way in which Zionism ignored the interests of Orthodoxy and the	Cyrus Adler, chancellor of the Jewish Theological Seminary of America, and Felix Warburg purchase Ephraim Benguiat's collection of Jewish ceremonial art, the first major acquisition of the Jewish Museum of New York. Benguiat's collection, brought to the U.S. from Smyrna in 1890, was exhibited

A. General History	B. Jews in North and South America	C. Jews in Europe	D. Jews in the Middle East and Elsewhere	E. Jewish Culture	

murder in 1940 will be ordered by Stalin.*

President Calvin Coolidge* signs the Immigration Act of 1924, which reduces the national origins figure of the 1921 act to 2% and moves the base date back to 1890. Using the 1890 base date, when the foreign-born from southern and eastern Europe were much fewer, it effectively ends the era of unrestricted immigration, including mass Jewish immigration, to the U.S.

Republican Calvin Coolidge* is reelected U.S. president, defeating the Democratic ticket of John W. Davis* and Charles W. Bryan.*

In December, Adolf Hitler* is released from the Landsberg prison. At this time, the Nazi party has drastically declined in membership.

Ibn Saud* drives Sharif Hussein* from Mecca.

Mustafa Kemal,* first president of the Turkish Republic, abolishes the Ottoman caliphate.

27% for Calvin Coolidge,* and 22% for LaFollette.*

The women's branch of the Union of Orthodox Jewish Congregations of America is founded.

Centos, a federation for the care of orphans in Poland, is established with nine regional committees. The American Joint Distribution Committee had assumed the care of children orphaned during World War I and in 1924 transferred that responsibility to Centos. The Centos orphanage in Warsaw is directed by Janusz Korczak (1879–1942).

Between 1924 and 1936, about 14,000 Soviet Jewish families are settled on collective farms in the Crimea and Ukraine through a cooperative effort of the Soviet Society for the Settlement of Jewish Toilers (KOMZET) and the American Joint Agricultural Society (Agro-Joint), a subsidiary of the Joint Distribution Committee, which funded the project. The project is headed by Joseph A. Rosen, a U.S. agronomist. The Agro-Joint work will cease in 1938, when large numbers will have left the colonies. Most of the others will be murdered by the Nazis.

Arab population. His criticism appeared in non-Jewish newspapers, and he was believed to have secret contacts with Arab nationalists to harm Zionist interests and with mandatory authorities.

The Slobodka Yeshiva opens a branch school in Hebron, Palestine, after the Lithuanian government discontinues its policy of exempting yeshiva students from military service.

The U.S., as a nonmember of the League of Nations, formally approves the Palestine mandate in a special convention with Great Britain.

Hayyim Nahman Bialik, Hebrew poet, settles in Tel Aviv, Palestine, and becomes the center of Hebrew cultural activity. He moved from Berlin, where he lived and established his publishing firm, Dvir, after he left Russia in 1921.

1924

at the Chicago World Columbia Exhibition in 1892–1893. It was later catalogued by Adler in 1901 when Adler was affiliated with the Smithsonian Institution of Washington, where the collection remained until purchased in 1924.

George Gershwin, U.S. composer, creates his best-known work, *Rhapsody in Blue*, for Paul Whiteman's* jazz band with piano.

Richard Simon and M. Lincoln Schuster establish Simon and Schuster publishing company. Their first title is *The Cross Word Puzzle Book*, which brings the popular new word game out in book form for the first time.

Serge Koussevitsky (1874–1951), son of a Russian violin teacher and klezmer musician, moves to the U.S. to become the conductor of the Boston Symphony Orchestra. He will be the foremost American conductor to introduce new U.S. music and will hold this post until his retirement in 1949.

Edna Ferber, U.S. novelist, writes *So Big*, a novel describing the life of widowed Selina DeJong, a former schoolteacher, who achieves success for herself and her son in a community of truck farmers who do not understand her fine qualities. Ferber will receive the 1925 Pulitzer Prize for the novel and is the first Jewish writer to receive the prize.

Samuel Goldwyn and Louis B. Mayer (1885–1957) found the Metro–Goldwyn–Mayer

A. General History	B. Jews in North and South America	C. Jews in Europe	D. Jews in the Middle East and Elsewhere	E. Jewish Culture

1924

Lord Arthur Balfour addressing the opening of the Hebrew University in Jerusalem. Seated around the table starting on the right with Chaim Weizmann with hand on chin, are Sir Herbert Samuel, Field Marshal Edmund Allenby, Chief Rabbi Abraham Isaac Kook, Chief Rabbi Jacob Meir, Ahad Ha-am, Chaim Nahman Bialik, and Judah Magnes.

film company and Harry Cohn (1891–1956) founds Columbia Pictures in Hollywood.

Harold Abrahams, British athlete, becomes the first European to win an Olympic sprint event when he wins the 100-meter dash.

The publication of *Kirjath Sepher*, a Hebrew bibliographical quarterly, begins in Jerusalem, under the auspices of the Jewish National and University Library.

1925

Paul von Hindenburg* (1847–1934) is elected president of Germany and serves until 1934.

Adolf Hitler* publishes the first part of *Mein Kampf* (*My Struggle*), written while he was imprisoned at Landsberg. The second volume will be published in December 1926.

The Treaty of Locarno is signed by the European nations, including Germany, guaranteeing the frontiers of western Europe. Germany and France mutually agree not to make war against each other.

There is an Arab revolt against the French in Damascus, anti-British riots in Baghdad, and civil war in the Arabian Peninsula. Ibn Saud* takes control of the entire Arabian Peninsula.

The New Yorker magazine is founded and edited by Harold Ross* (1892–1951). An urban weekly, it gives special attention to culture, fiction, verse, and special

The U.S. Supreme Court, in *Hygrade Provision Co.* v. *Sherman*, upholds the New York kosher food law statute, rejecting the arguments that the statute was unconstitutional because the terms *kosher* and *Orthodox Hebrew religious requirements* were too vague to be used as legal standards.

Willa Cather* (1873–1947), U.S. novelist, writes *The Professor's House*, which includes the Jewish character Louie Marsellus, an engineer who is portrayed as a money-maker rather than a creator. Cather's* writings contain many insensitive references to Jews. One of her biographers attributes Cather's* attitude to her resentment of the marriage of Isabelle McClung,* the woman she most loved, to Jan Hambourg, a Jewish professional violinist.

Edward Ellsberg, U.S. naval officer who will retire as a rear admiral in 1951, is the first person to be

In August, the 14th Zionist Congress convenes in Vienna, under the leadership of Chaim Weizmann. Weizmann's proposal that the Jewish Agency be composed of equal numbers of Zionists and non-Zionists meets strong opposition.

The Estonian Parliament confirms the law of national cultural autonomy and four minorities—Russian, German, Swedish, and Jewish—are recognized. Estonia is the only eastern European country to fulfill its obligations to its national minorities.

The Institute for Jewish Research (YIVO) is founded in Vilna, Poland, as an educational institute for the study of Jewish history, language, and culture.

Sergei Eisenstein (1898–1948), Russian film director, directs *Battleship Potemkin*, which greatly influences filmmaking, with his realistic portrayal of crowd scenes. Eisenstein is the son of a Jewish

In April, the Hebrew University is opened in Jerusalem.

Vladimir (Ze'ev) Jabotinsky founds the Federation of Revisionist Zionists in opposition to official Zionism at a Paris convention of his followers. He calls for the establishment of a Jewish state in Palestine on both sides of the Jordan within its historic borders.

Berit Shalom (Peace Association) is founded in Jerusalem by Arthur Ruppin. It favors a binational state in the whole of Palestine, with Jews and Arabs equally sharing power regardless of respective population size. It ceased to exist in the mid-1930s.

A record number of Jews, 35,000, come to Palestine, mainly from Poland. Poland suffers a continuous economic crisis, and economic sanctions affect Jewish enterprises. These emigrants to Palestine are mainly urban dwellers who settle in the cities in what

Israel Davidson (1870–1939), professor of medieval Hebrew literature at the Jewish Theological Seminary of America, begins publication of his four-volume *Thesaurus of Medieval Hebrew Poetry*. Completed in 1938, it lists 35,000 poems and prayers from the postbiblical era until the beginning of the Haskalah period.

Sophie Tucker (1884–1966), singer, introduces "My Yiddishe Mama," which together with "I'm the Last of the Red Hot Mamas" (1928) become two of the songs with which she is closely identified.

The first volumes of the Bible translated into German by Martin Buber and Franz Rosenzweig are published. After the death of Rosenzweig in 1929, Buber will continue the task alone and complete the translation in 1961 in Israel. The translation seeks to preserve the sounds and rhythms of the original Hebrew and reflects the translators

A. General History

articles on topical themes.

B. Jews in North and South America

awarded the Distinguished Service Medal in peacetime. He led the rescue efforts to raise the sunken submarine USS *S-51* off the coast of Block Island.

Sinclair Lewis,* U.S. novelist, writes *Arrowsmith*, a novel of the career of a man of science. Arrrowsmith studies with and is influenced by Max Gottlieb, a devoted Jewish émigré scientist from Germany.

F. Scott Fitzgerald,* U.S. novelist, writes *The Great Gatsby*, a novel portraying wealthy society on New York's Long Island during the jazz age. A leading character is the gambler Meyer Wolfsheim, who is described as a "flat-nosed Jew" with "tiny eyes" and "two fine growths of hair which luxuriated in either nostril."

Pioneer Women, the Women's Labor Zionist Organization, is founded in the U.S. Though it emphasizes Socialist and feminist causes at its birth, by the end of World War II it will expand its program of cultural and welfare projects in the U.S. and Israel.

C. Jews in Europe

father and non-Jewish mother.

The Jewish population of Berlin is 172,672, or 4.30% of the total population. They comprise 30.6% of German Jewry.

Germany's Jews in Modern Times	
Population	
1871	512,158
1880	562,612
1890	567,884
1900	586,833
1910	615,021
1925	564,379
1933	503,000
1939	234,000
1941	164,000
1969	30,000

D. Jews in the Middle East and Elsewhere

becomes known as the Grabski aliyah. In late 1923 Tel Aviv had 16,500 residents. At the end of 1925, its population is 40,000.

Reza Shah,* the founder of Iran's Pahlavi dynasty, grants the Jews political status equal to that of all other citizens of the country. They are allowed to buy and own property and engage freely in business and trade.

E. Jewish Culture

belief in the originally oral nature of the Bible.

Lion Feuchtwanger (1884–1958), German novelist, writes *Jude Suess* (titled *Power* in the 1927 U.S. edition), a novel about the 18th-century Court Jew, Joseph Suess Oppenheimer, who aroused the enmity of the populace and was eventually executed. In 1939, the Nazis will use this best-seller as the basis of an antisemitic film.

The Trial, a novel by Franz Kafka (1883–1924), is published posthumously by his friend Max Brod (1884–1968). Some critics have interpreted the novel as a parable about a Jew waiting in vain for Gentiles to tell him on what terms they might accept him.

The Jewish Theater founded by Alexander Granovsky (1890–1937) in 1918 becomes the Jewish State Theater for the Soviet Union in Moscow. Granovsky presented works by Jewish authors including Sholom Aleichem, I. L. Peretz and Scholem Asch. He will leave the Soviet Union in 1928 and continue his career in Berlin.

James Franck (1882–1964), German physicist, is awarded the Nobel Prize in physics, sharing the award with Gustav Hertz (1887–1950) for their discovery of the laws governing the impact of the electron on an atom. Franck will leave Germany in 1933 for the U.S. when the Nazis come to power, while

	A. General History	B. Jews in North and South America	C. Jews in Europe	D. Jews in the Middle East and Elsewhere	E. Jewish Culture
1925					Hertz, the son of a Jewish father, will adopt Christianity and remain in Germany throughout World War II.

Sigmund Freud, Austrian psychiatrist and originator of psychoanalysis, writes *An Autobiographical Study*. He writes: "My parents were Jews, and I remained a Jew myself." Though not a practicing Jew, estranged from Judaism and indifferent to Zionism, he rejects baptism and is a loyal member of the Jewish community.

Simon Dubnow, historian, begins publication of his massive 10-volume *World History of the Jewish People*, completing it in 1929. Written in German, it will be translated into Russian, Hebrew, Yiddish, and English. An 11th volume, updating it to World War II, will be published in 1940. The history emphasizes political and demographic changes rather than religious and literary developments. In 1940, he will be murdered by the Nazis.

Davar (*Report*), a Hebrew daily newspaper, begins publication in Tel Aviv. Edited by Berl Katznelson, it is the first daily of the entire labor movement.

The Palestine Historical and Ethnographical Society is founded. In 1936, it will begin publication of *Zion*, a scholarly quarterly. |
| **1926** | Marshall Jozef Pilsudski* (1867–1935) leads a military revolt against | Herman Bernstein, U.S. journalist, institutes a lawsuit against Henry Ford,* | Simon Petlyura,* Ukrainian nationalist leader at the time of a wave of pogroms in | Morris A. Cohen, "Two-gun Cohen" (1887–1970), becomes general in the Chinese | Radio station WEVD is founded in New York by the same Socialist organization |

A. General History	B. Jews in North and South America	C. Jews in Europe	D. Jews in the Middle East and Elsewhere	E. Jewish Culture
Poland's government. He becomes dictator of Poland.

Paul Josef Goebbels* (1897–1945) is appointed Nazi party leader in Berlin, Germany.

Hirohito* becomes emperor of Japan. | whose news magazine, *The Dearborn Independent*, helped to circulate the antisemitic forgery *The Protocols of the Elders of Zion* and other antisemitic articles based on it.

Benjamin Nathan Cardozo is elected chief judge of New York's highest court, the Court of Appeals. He has been serving as an associate justice of that court since 1913.

The Synagogue Council of America is established. Composed of Orthodox and non-Orthodox organizations, it is an attempt to assert the place of the synagogue among the agencies of the American Jewish community.

Rabbi Israel H. Levinthal, spiritual leader of the Brooklyn Jewish Center, defends synagogue centers from attack as detracting from the centrality of religion in American Jewish life. "If the Synagogue as a Beth Hatefilah [house of worship] has lost its hold upon the masses, some institution would have to be created that could and would attract the people so that the group consciousness of the Jew might be maintained. . . . It is true that many will come for other purposes than to meet God. But let them come."

A religious census report indicates 3,118 congregations and 1,782 synagogue buildings. The estimated Jewish population of the U.S. is 4.1 million. | 1919–1920 against the Jews of the Ukraine, is assassinated on a Paris street by Shalom Schwartzbard in revenge for the murder of his Ukrainian relatives. In 1927, Schwartzbard will be acquitted by a Paris court after a dramatic trial, which will receive documented evidence of the terrible slaughter of the Jews in the Ukraine.

The Amici Israel is founded in Rome by Catholic clergy to foster a better understanding of Judaism. It reaches a membership of 2,000 clergymen. On March 21, 1928, the Vatican will proscribe this group as "contrary to the spirit of the Church." In the same decree it proscribes antisemitism. | Nationalist party. Sun Yat-sen* became friendly with Cohen while in exile in Canada in 1908 and invited him to China in 1922. Cohen assists in organizing and training the Nationalist army and takes part in campaigns against the Japanese and Chinese Communist rebels. | that publishes the Yiddish daily newspaper, *Forward*. Its call letters honor the memory of Socialist leader, Eugene V. Debs.* WEVD specializes in Yiddish-language programming.

David Sarnoff (1891–1971) creates the first U.S. radio chain, the National Broadcasting System, as a component of the Radio Corp. of America. Sarnoff will become president of the corporation in 1930.

George Sidney, as Cohen, and Charles Murphy,* as Kelly, star in the silent film *The Cohens and the Kellys*. It proves to be a successful example of the many films highlighting the relationships between the members of two minority groups, the Jews and the Irish.

Edna Ferber, U.S. novelist, writes *Show Boat*, a novel describing three theatrical generations, including life on a Mississippi River showboat.

Elizabeth Stern (1889–1954), using the pseudonym Leah Morton, writes *I Am a Woman—and a Jew*, a semiautobiographical account of an eastern European Jewish woman's struggles in the U.S. The account makes her a role model for many other American Jewish women.

Raphael Soyer (1899–1988), U.S. painter, paints the *Dancing Lesson*, a direct, almost primitive depiction of his family's attempts at Americanization. Soyer and his |

	A. General History	B. Jews in North and South America	C. Jews in Europe	D. Jews in the Middle East and Elsewhere	E. Jewish Culture
1926		The National Council on Jewish Education is founded. Its goal is to improve the quality of Jewish education in the U.S. A study of the effects of the prohibition amendment reveals heavy traffic in bootlegging liquor on New York's Lower East Side. Abner Zwillman (Longy Zwillman), Irving Wexler (Waxey Gordon, 1888–1952), and Arthur Flegenheimer (Dutch Schultz) are among the most notorious bootleggers. Ernest Hemingway* (1899–1961) writes *The Sun Also Rises*, a novel of expatriate Americans in Europe leading a futile and empty life after World War I. The novel includes overtones of antisemitism in its treatment of Robert Cohn. Sephardic Jewish immigrants to Venezuela, who arrived in Caracas from North Africa at the turn of the century, found a mutual aid society. In 1929 they will acquire cemetery grounds and in 1935 build a synagogue.			artist-brothers, Moses and Isaac, came to the U.S. in 1913. Consistently a realist painter, in the 1930s he will depict life in New York, especially that of the unemployed and lower-paid workers. *The Castle*, a novel by Franz Kafka (1883–1924), is published posthumously by his friend Max Brod. Leo Blech (1871–1958) is appointed conductor of the Berlin State Opera. He will be forced to resign by the Nazis in 1937 and flee to Sweden in 1941, where he becomes conductor of the Stockholm Royal Opera. In 1949 he will return to Germany to once again conduct the Berlin State Opera. Isaac Babel (1894–1941), Russian Jewish author, writes *Red Cavalry*, a volume of stories of his experiences in the Russian Revolution and of Jewish life in his native city of Odessa. In 1939 he will be arrested and accused of Trotskyism and in 1941 murdered by the Stalin* regime. In 1954, he will be "rehabilitated."
1927	Charles A. Lindbergh* (1902–1974) flies the first solo airplane flight across the Atlantic from New York to Paris.	Henry Ford* publicly apologizes for having published antisemitic propaganda in his newspaper, *The Dearborn Independent*. The document of apology was drafted	The 15th Zionist Congress convenes in Basel under the leadership of Chaim Weizmann. It is preoccupied with the severe economic crisis and unemployment	The Jewish community in Palestine suffers a severe economic crisis. Large-scale unemployment leaves many homes abandoned and shops	Alexander Marx and Max L. Margolis, U.S. scholars, write the one-volume *History of the Jewish People*, a history with special emphasis on economic and social

A. General History

Joseph Stalin* gains control of power in the USSR as Leon Trotsky and his group are expelled from the Communist party.

Chiang Kai-shek* comes to power in China.

The Holland Tunnel under the Hudson River, the first underwater tunnel for vehicles, is opened in New York.

The first demonstration of television takes place in the U.S.

New York Yankee outfielder Babe Ruth* sets a record when he hits 60 home runs in one season.

B. Jews in North and South America

by Louis Marshall of the American Jewish Committee.

Charles A. Levine is the first to fly over the Atlantic as a passenger. He travels 3,903 miles (a world record at the time) from New York to Eisleben, Germany, with Clarence Chamberlain* as pilot. Levine financed this pioneer flight himself.

Three Jewish interns are assaulted at Kings County Hospital in Brooklyn, New York. The incident is an example of prejudice against Jewish doctors in a city hospital in a borough with a large Jewish population. The mayor orders an investigation and the superintendent is suspended but is later reinstated.

George F. Moore,* Harvard professor of Hebrew, Bible, and rabbinics, publishes his two-volume study, *Judaism in the First Centuries of the Christian Era*, a study of the creative accomplishments of the early talmudic age.

Fourth "Aliyah" to Palestine, 1924–1932

Number: 88,450
Origin: Mainly middle class immigrants from Poland in wake of economic measures adopted by the government against Jewish middle class; also about 9,000 Sephardic and Oriental Jews from Turkey, Bulgaria and Yemen.

C. Jews in Europe

in Palestine.

Hillel Zeitlin (1871–1942), Polish Yiddish journalist, writes in the daily newspaper *Der Moment* of early acts of Nazi vandalism in Jewish cemeteries in Germany. He warns that Jews will be the first victims of Nazi atrocities, castigates Western culture for remaining mute, and predicts that the whole world will be engulfed in the Nazi degeneracy. He will be killed by the Nazis on the way to Treblinka.

Joseph Isaac Schneersonn (1880–1950), the Lubavitch Rebbe, obtains permission to leave the Soviet Union with the assistance of Mordecai Dubin (1889–1956), Agudat Israel leader who serves in the Latvian House of Representatives from 1919 to 1934. Schneersonn goes to Riga, Latvia, where he organizes new Habad centers. In 1934, he will settle in Poland. During World War II, he will escape to the U.S.

D. Jews in the Middle East and Elsewhere

and factories closed. While 2,700 immigrants arrive, 7,000 leave the country. A small faction of left-wing pioneers, led by Mendel Elkind, become disillusioned with Zionism and leave for the Soviet Union, where they establish a Hebrew-speaking communal farm, Via Nova, in the Crimea. It will be disbanded in 1932, and its leaders purged by Joseph Stalin.*

Tnuva, a cooperative which markets the agricultural products of Jewish settlements in Palestine is founded.

E. Jewish Culture

life, which becomes the standard history for the general reader.

Al Jolson, the son of a cantor, stars in *The Jazz Singer*, the first significant feature-length sound motion picture. The main character is Jakie Rabinowitz, modeled after Jolson himself, a Lower East Side youngster who is torn between his drive for a successful musical career on Broadway and his devotion to his cantor father and his religious obligations. The film is based on a story by Samson Raphaelson.

Jerome Kern (1885–1945), U.S. composer, composes *Show Boat*, the first modern American serious musical play, together with librettist Oscar Hammerstein II (1895–1960). It is adapted from the novel by Edna Ferber. Songs include "Ol' Man River," "Why Do I Love You," and other classics that result in Kern being considered the father of modern American theater music.

Bennett Cerf, Elmer Adler, and Donald Klopfer found the Random House Publishing Company in New York City.

Henri Louis Bergson (1859–1941), French philosopher, is awarded the Nobel Prize in literature. The son of a Warsaw Jew, in his later years he is attracted to Catholic mysticism but refuses to convert. As he expresses in his will of 1937, "I wanted to remain among those who tomorrow will be the persecuted ones."

	A. General History	B. Jews in North and South America	C. Jews in Europe	D. Jews in the Middle East and Elsewhere	E. Jewish Culture
1927					The last volume of *Remembrance of Things Past*, a novel by Marcel Proust (1871–1922), French writer, appears five years after his death. Begun in 1913 by Proust, the son of a Catholic father and Jewish mother who was raised as a Catholic, the novel has three main Jewish characters, including the assimilated Charles Swann, a sympathetic character believed to be Proust's own alter ego.
1928	The Nazi party wins 12 seats, including a seat for Adolf Hitler,* in the Reichstag elections. Party membership exceeds 100,000.

The First Five-Year Economic Plan begins in the Soviet Union. Private trade is suppressed, and agriculture is collectivized.

During the presidential campaign, Governor Alfred E. Smith* of New York, the Democratic candidate, is charged with being disqualified for the presidency because, as a Roman Catholic, he owed a "higher loyalty" to the pope. Smith* asks an adviser, Joseph Proskauer (1877–1971), to draft the reply article in the *Atlantic Monthly* magazine. The article receives great praise and, years later, Smith will disclose the article's authorship.

Herbert Hoover* (secretary of commerce) and running mate, Senator Charles Curtis* of Kansas, defeat Democrat and Catholic New York | Arnold Rothstein (1882–1928), U.S. underworld figure credited with putting crime on a corporate basis, is murdered. The son of respected and well-to-do Orthodox Jews, Rothstein became known as the J. P. Morgan of the underworld.

The Jewish vote in the U.S. presidential election is estimated at 72% for Alfred E. Smith* and 28% for Herbert Hoover.*

Yeshiva College opens with Bernard Revel as its head. It is the outgrowth of the Rabbi Isaac Elchanan Theological Seminary and is the first liberal arts college under Jewish auspices, combining traditional religious education with secular studies on the college level.

The Rabbinical Assembly, the organization of Conservative rabbis, establishes the Committee on Jewish Law to replace the United Synagogue's committee. This committee of rabbis is designed to reflect the diversity within the Conservative | Adolf Hitler* associates the degeneration of Germany with German Jewry. "In Germany today, German interests are no longer decisive but rather Jewish interests."

Leon Blum (1872–1950) is among the founders of the Socialist Pro-Palestine Committee. In 1936, he will become the Socialist premier of France.

The rabbis of both the Orthodox and liberal wings of Hungarian Jewry sit in the upper chamber of the Hungarian Parliament as representatives of the Jewish community.

The Soviet Union begins the project of settling Jews in the Birobidzhan region of eastern Siberia. Of the 654 settlers who arrive in the spring, only about 325 are left by October. | The Habimah Theater, originally founded in 1917 in Moscow, moves to Tel Aviv.

French archaeologists begin excavating the north Syrian port of Ras Shamra and discover the ancient north Canaanite metropolis of Ugarit, where significant literary and administrative documents are found. | Ludwig Lewisohn, U.S. novelist and essayist, writes *The Island Within*, a novel whose theme decries the assimilation of Jews as "protective mimicry." Assimilated Jewish intellectuals are "drained of anything of their own." The Jew should return to the inner life of the Jewish community from the inhospitable Gentile world.

Louis Wirth (1897–1952), U.S. sociologist, writes *The Ghetto*, a study of the Jewish settlement in Chicago's West Side. He views Jews as steadily progressing from self-segregation to acculturation to assimilation, a process that might be interrupted temporarily by prejudice and discrimination.

Eddie Cantor, U.S. comedian and vaudeville performer, stars in the Broadway show *Whoopee*, which features the song "Makin' Whoopee."

A German *Encyclopedia Judaica* begins publication under the editorship of Jacob Klatzkin, |

A. General History	B. Jews in North and South America	C. Jews in Europe	D. Jews in the Middle East and Elsewhere	E. Jewish Culture	
Governor Alfred E. Smith* and vice presidential candidate Senator Joseph T. Robinson* of Arkansas.

Walt Disney* (1901–1966) releases the first Mickey Mouse animated movie cartoon. | movement. Only a unanimous opinion will be authoritative. Lacking unanimity, the questioner will receive majority and minority opinions.

The National Conference of Christians and Jews is established with the purpose of eradicating prejudice from the American scene. | | | Nahum Goldmann (1895–1982), and Ismar Elbogen (1874–1943). The rise of the Nazi regime prevents its completion. Only 10 volumes appear, through the letter *L*.

The Case of Sergeant Grischa, written by Arnold Zweig (1887–1968), German novelist and playwright, is published in an English translation. It is an antiwar novel and a searing indictment of Prussian justice. After the rise of Adolf Hitler,* Zweig will leave Germany for Palestine, where he will never feel at home. He will become sympathetic to communism, and return to live in East Germany.

Kurt Weill (1900–1950), composer, writes the music for Bertolt Brecht's* *Threepenny Opera*. A social satire, it is an outstanding success in Germany, where it has over 4,000 performances in one year. He will arrive in the U.S. in 1935 from Germany, after the Nazis seize power, with his wife, Lotte Lenya, where he will continue his career. He writes the music for successful musical comedies, including *Knickerbocker Holiday* (1938) and *One Touch of Venus* (1943).

Yehuda Burla (1886–1969), Palestinian writer who became the first modern Hebraist to deal with the life of Middle East Sephardim, writes his first novel, *His Hated Wife*. It deals with the life of a Sephardic Jewish family from Morocco living in Jerusalem. | **1928** |

	A. General History	B. Jews in North and South America	C. Jews in Europe	D. Jews in the Middle East and Elsewhere	E. Jewish Culture
1929	Heinrich Himmler* (1900–1945) becomes head of the SS, which numbers 280 men. The Great Depression begins with the Wall Street crash. A demand proposed by Adolf Hitler's* Nazi party that Germany repudiate its Versailles debts receives 6 million of the required 21 million votes at a national referendum. Although the vote fails, Hitler* attracts the attention of many Germans frustrated by the nation's economic ills. The Lateran Treaty restores the temporal power of the pope, who is to rule over Vatican City, a small part of Rome, and define the relationship of the Church in the Fascist state. Leon Trotsky is exiled from the Soviet Union. He settles in Turkey. Mohandas K. Gandhi,* Indian nationalist leader, conducts a civil disobedience campaign between 1929 and 1931. The Academy Awards, or "Oscars," are presented in Hollywood for the first time to recognize outstanding filmmaking.	The *Morning Freiheit*, the New York Communist Yiddish daily, initially supports the Jews during the Arab riots in Hebron and throughout Palestine. When the Soviet Union supports the Arabs, the paper reverses itself and supports the Arabs, resulting in a Jewish boycott of the newspaper. Abraham Reisen (1876–1953), Lowick Halpern (H. Leivick), and other writers on the staff of the New York Communist Yiddish daily, *Morning Freiheit*, resign in protest of the newspaper's support of the Arabs during the riots in Palestine. This adherence to the Communist party line alienates many readers and causes a sharp decline in circulation from its peak readership of 14,000. *Disraeli*, a critically acclaimed and financially successful sound film, portrays Benjamin Disraeli sympathetically and stresses his Jewish origins. George Arliss* wins an Oscar as Disraeli.	The 16th Zionist Congress convenes in Zurich, under the leadership of Chaim Weizmann. A debate over enlargement of the Jewish Agency with non-Zionist members ends with their addition to comprise one-half its membership. Kurt Tucholsky (1890–1935), German satirist and journalist, writes *Deutschland, Deutschland uber Alles*, which criticizes the German military, churches, police, Paul von Hindenburg,* trade union leaders, and the Social Democrats. Although he abandoned Judaism in 1911, his writings arouse antisemitism. In 1929 he settles in Sweden, and despairing of the rise of Nazism, in 1935, he will commit suicide.	Arab riots throughout Palestine result in over 130 Jewish deaths. A pretext for the riots is a dispute on the rights of Jews to pray at the Wailing Wall in Jerusalem. Jewish defense forces contain rioters, except in Hebron, where 60 Jews are killed, and in Safed, where 18 are killed. In Hebron, eight Americans who were students at the American-supported Slobodka Yeshiva are among those killed. After Arab riots, the Palestinian Communist party appoints an Arab majority to its Central Committee and continues to represent official Soviet policy in support of the Arab population. The B'nei Akiva (Sons of Akiva), the youth movement of Ha-Po'el ha-Mizrahi, under the spiritual leadership of Rabbi Abraham Isaac Kook, is founded in Jerusalem. The mosaic floor of the ancient synagogue at Bet Alpha in Palestine is discovered by Nahman Avigad and Eliezer L. Sukenik (1889–1953) of the Hebrew University. The mosaic panels include the offering of Isaac, the signs of the Zodiac, and the ark of the synagogue and represent a folk art that developed among the Jewish villages of Galilee in the Byzantine period.	Professor Louis Ginzberg, talmudic scholar and master of *halakhah*, who teaches at the Jewish Theological Seminary of America, lectures on the significance of the *halakhah* for Jewish history at the Hebrew University in Jerusalem. Ginzberg argues that *halakhah* is the living expression of the inner life of the people whose important enactments are rooted in the economic, social, and political realities of the day. It is not the creation of the House of Study without any connection to daily life. Ludwig Lewisohn, U.S. novelist and essayist, writes his second autobiographical memoir, *Mid-Channel*, in which he describes his discovery of his Jewish heritage after years of unconscious behavior as an assimilated Jew. Elmer Rice, U.S. playwright, writes *Street Scene*, a tragedy of New York slum life describing the love of Samuel Kaplan, a Jewish youth, for Rose Maurrant, an Irish girl. The play wins him the Pulitzer Prize. Harry A. Wolfson (1887–1974), Harvard professor of Hebrew literature and philosophy since 1925, publishes *Crescas' Critique of Aristotle*, a critical edition of a portion of Crescas' "Or Adonai" translated into English with extensive notes explaining his thoughts.

NBC radio starts broadcasting "The Goldbergs." The show, which Gertrude Berg (1900–1966) writes and in which she stars as Molly Goldberg, becomes an immediate national hit, running for 4,500 separate broadcasts over the next 17 years.

George Gershwin, U.S. composer, is commissioned by the New York Metropolitan Opera to compose a Jewish opera, *The Dybbuk*, a project that did not proceed.

Myron Brinig (1896–1991) writes *Singermann*, a novel depicting a Romanian Jewish family that settles in Silver Bow, a Montana mining town. Largely autobiographical, it paints a grim picture of the life of second-generation American Jews in Butte, Montana, with intermarriage and the collapse of parental authority among its themes. In 1932, he will write a sequel, *This Man Is My Brother*.

Louis Bamberger (1855–1944), founder of Bamberger's Department Store in Newark, New Jersey, and his sister, Mrs. Felix Fuld, give $5 million for the establishment of the Institute for Advanced Study at Princeton, New Jersey.

Edward L. Bernays (b. 1891), a leading public relations counselor of major American corporations and regarded as the originator of the field of public relations, writes *Crystallizing Public Opinion*, the first book on the subject.

The Marx brothers, the U.S. vaudeville and motion picture comedy team composed of Chico (1891–1961), Harpo (1893–1964), Groucho (1895–1977), and Zeppo (1901–1979), star in *The Cocoanuts* (1929). It will be followed by *Animal Crackers* (1930), the film version of their Broadway comedy hit show and other film comedies: *Monkey Business* (1931), *Horse Feathers* (1932), *Duck Soup* (1933), and *A Night at the Opera* (1935). A fifth brother, Gummo (1894–1977), left the act before it reached Broadway.

Manfred Joshua Sakel (1900–1957), Austrian psychiatrist, introduces insulin shock for the treatment of schizophrenia. In 1936, he will emigrate to the U.S.

Waldemar Mordecai Haffkine, Russian-born bacteriologist, establishes the Haffkine Foundation in Lausanne, Switzerland, stipulating that its funds be used for religious, scientific, and vocational education in eastern European yeshivot.

Itzik Manger (1901–1969), Yiddish poet, publishes his first volume of poems, *Shtern Ofyn Dakh* (*Stars on the Roof*). He achieves great popularity with his ability to combine eastern European folk sources with sophisticated motifs of contemporary European poetry.

A. General History	B. Jews in North and South America	C. Jews in Europe	D. Jews in the Middle East and Elsewhere	E. Jewish Culture	
In the October Reichstag elections, the number of Nazi party seats rises from 12 to 107. With more than 6 million votes, it becomes the second-largest party in Germany's Reichstag. General disorder follows, with a confrontation between the Nazis and the Communists. The Sturmabteilung (SA), or brownshirts, now numbers over 100,000 men and is larger than the regular army.

Alfred Rosenberg* (1893–1946), an early Nazi antisemitic propagandist, writes *Myth of the Twentieth* | At the annual meeting of the Rabbinical Assembly (Conservative rabbis), Rabbi Louis Epstein (1887–1949) suggests a way to solve the problem of the *agunah*—the woman who, according to Jewish law, is unable to remarry if her husband is presumed dead with no witnesses to his death.

Salo Wittmayer Baron (1895–1989) joins the faculty of Columbia University as the first incumbent of the Miller Chair of Jewish History, Literature, and Institutions. It is the first chair in | All Jewish sections of the Communist party in the Soviet Union, the Yevsektsiya, are abolished.

Yehezkel Abramsky, rabbi of Slutsk and Smolensk who publishes a periodical dedicated to strengthening Torah study in the Soviet Union, is arrested as a counterrevolutionary and sentenced to hard labor in Siberia. After two years he is released and assumes a rabbinic post in London.

German sociologist Ernest Kahn calculates that due to | The Shaw Commission, appointed by Great Britain to report on the causes of the August 1929 Arab riots in Palestine, finds that Arab anti-Jewish hostility results from the Arabs' political and economic frustration. It criticizes Zionist immigration and land purchase policies that give the Jews unfair advantages.

Great Britain's Labor government publishes the Passfield (Sidney Webb*) White Paper, the first direct sign of British anti-Zionism in a state paper. It | Charles Reznikoff (1894–1976), U.S. poet and novelist, writes *By the Waters of Manhattan*, a realistic, autobiographical novel of immigrant life. The novel is devoted to his mother's hard life in the shtetl and later, in poverty, in the U.S. and to her son's development and education.

Michael Gold (Irwin Granich, 1893–1967), writes *Jews Without Money*, a semiautobiographical novel. Gold's Lower East Side is a world of prostitution, crime, corruption, sweatshops, and | 1930 |

	A. General History	B. Jews in North and South America	C. Jews in Europe	D. Jews in the Middle East and Elsewhere	E. Jewish Culture
1930	*Century*, in which he argues that the "Aryan race" is the creator of all values and culture, whereas the "Jewish race" is the corrupter of these values. It is the duty of Germany to subdue Jewry's drive for world domination. The book is regarded as fundamental Nazi thinking. Great Britain agrees to support Iraq's admission to the League of Nations in 1932. Maxim Litvinov (1867–1951) is appointed foreign minister of the Soviet Union. In 1933, he will personally conduct the negotiations leading to the establishment of diplomatic relations between the U.S. and the Soviet Union. Pro-Western in orientation, he will be replaced by V. M. Molotov* in May 1939, when Stalin* collaborates with Hitler's* Germany. Haile Selassie* becomes emperor of Ethiopia.	Jewish history at a secular university in the Western world. A *New York Times* editorial approves of the Passfield White Paper. It states that a temporary ban on Jewish immigration would prove invigorating to Jews, Arabs, and the Palestinian economy. The Jewish Colonization Association (ICA) settlement in Argentina peaks with over 20,000 settlers farming about 1,235,000 acres of land.	German Jewry's low birth rate, each family would have to average seven children in order to preserve their numbers. German Jewry's low birth rate is typical of Western Jewry. Salman Schocken (1877–1959) founds the Institute for Research in Hebrew Poetry in Berlin. Heinrich Brody (1868–1942) is appointed its head. The institute will move to Jerusalem in 1933. Italy enacts a law standardizing the legal status of Italian Jewish communities. They must join the Union of Italian-Jewish Communities, the central representative body; election of local leaders is required; mandatory contributions are established; the role of rabbis is defined; and the law decrees that the community is subject to the protection and supervision of the state. Rabbi Meir Shapira founds a yeshiva in Lublin, Poland. It is equipped with an excellent library, spacious living and dining areas, and attractive lecture halls. He is opposed to the unattractive surroundings and poor amenities of most European yeshivas. Hannah F. Cohen becomes the first woman elected to the presidency of the Board of Guardians in England. She promotes progressive social service projects and preventive health care during her 10-year tenure.	threatens the Jews with an embargo on additional land purchases and recommends cessation of Jewish immigration, as there is Arab unemployment. It is criticized as a departure from British obligations under the mandate. Chaim Weizmann resigns the Jewish Agency posts in protest. South Africa adopts a Quota Act, under the leadership of Daniel F. Malan,* minister of the interior, that greatly restricts Jewish immigration.	crowded tenements. He is a leader of the Communist literary movement. The novel is translated into 15 languages, and the English edition goes through 11 printings in its first year and 17 printings in a decade. Meyer Waxman (1887–1969), U.S. rabbi and scholar, begins publishing his *History of Jewish Literature*. It is a detailed survey of Jewish literary creativity from the close of the biblical period to the present. A five-volume revised edition will be completed in 1960. Meyer Levin (1905–1981), U.S. novelist and journalist, writes *Yehuda*, the first novel published in English about a kibbutz in Palestine. Arthur Fiedler (1894–1979) is appointed conductor of the Boston Pops Orchestra. He will lead the orchestra for almost 50 years and achieve wide acclaim for his television and outdoor Boston Esplanade performances of classical, semiclassical, and popular music. Karl Landsteiner (1868–1943), U.S. medical scientist, is awarded the Nobel Prize in physiology or medicine for his discovery of four different groups of human blood. In 1940, with Alexander S. Wiener, he will discover the Rh human blood factor. He dies a Roman Catholic.

1930

Theodor Lessing (1872–1933), German philosopher, writes *Jewish Self-Hatred*, an analysis of Jewish intellectuals who are afflicted with self-hatred, a sickness he has experienced. He writes that the return to the land of Palestine will renew the Jewish people, forced to live an unnatural life in Europe. As a student, he converted to Christianity but later embraced Zionism and returned to Judaism. In 1933, he will be assassinated by Nazi agents.

Lion Feuchtwanger, German novelist, writes *Success*, which describes the moral corruption of Germany after the First World War that gave Adolf Hitler* a boost and an advantage. It is considered the first anti-Nazi novel ever written.

Ambroise Vollard,* French art dealer, commissions Marc Chagall to illustrate the Bible. The 105 etchings for the Bible will be finished in 1956 and published by Teriade in 1957.

The publication of *Tarbiz* (*The Disseminator*), a Hebrew quarterly for Judaic studies, begins in Jerusalem under the auspices of the Hebrew University. It is edited, until 1952, by Jacob Nahum Epstein (1878–1952), professor of talmudic philology and one of the quarterly's founders.

A. General History	B. Jews in North and South America	C. Jews in Europe	D. Jews in the Middle East and Elsewhere	E. Jewish Culture
King Alfonso XIII* is deposed and Spain becomes a republic. Adolf Hitler,* head of the National Socialist German Workers' (Nazi) party, meets German president Paul von Hindenburg.* The meeting results in according respectability to Hitler* and his party. Manchuria is invaded by Japan. The International Olympic Committee designates Berlin, Germany, as the site for the 1936 Olympic games. The Empire State Building in New York, the world's tallest structure, opens. It is 1,245 feet tall. The George Washington Bridge, connecting New York and New Jersey across the Hudson River, opens. Its main span is 3,500 feet long.	William Faulkner* (1897–1962), U.S. novelist, writes *Sanctuary*, a sadistic horror story that includes a Jewish lawyer from Memphis as an unsavory character who exacts sexual favors from a client as payment for his services. King Vidor's* *Street Scene*, a film adaptation of Elmer Rice's play, presents the issue of American antisemitism. The character Abraham Kaplan is the first Hollywood portrayal of the Jew as a Socialist. It also depicts a love affair between Kaplan's son, Sammy, and Rose Moran (Sylvia Sidney) and introduces words like *kike* and *yid* to the screen. Raoul Walsh's* *The Yellow Ticket* is a film denunciation of brutal Russian antisemitim. The film's Jewish heroine, Marya Kalish (Elissa Landi), kills her tormentor, Baron Andreff (Lionel Barrymore*), after joining with British journalist Julian Rolfe (Laurence Olivier*) to write a series of articles exposing conditions of life in Russia.	The 17th Zionist Congress convenes in Basel under the leadership of Chaim Weizmann. Criticism of Britain's Palestine policy and of Weizmann's trust in British promises results in his failure to be reelected president of the Zionist Organization. He is succeeded by Nahum Sokolow. The breach between the revisionists and Mapai continues. The Soviet Union makes clear its opposition to Zionism and support of a national liberation movement of the Arab masses. The attitude of the Communist International toward Zionism is published in Arabic in *Ila al-Aman* (*Forward*), the organ of the Communist party in Palestine. The first world conference of Betar, the Zionist revisionist youth movement, is held in Danzig, with 87 delegates from 21 countries. Vladimir (Ze'ev) Jabotinsky is elected head of Betar, whose world membership is 22,300.	British Prime Minister Ramsay MacDonald* clarifies the Passfield White Paper in the form of a letter to Chaim Weizmann by stating that immigration to and acquistion of land in Palestine by Jews would not be curbed and the positive obligations of the mandate can be fulfilled without jeopardizing the rights of the Arabs. Mohandas K. Gandhi,* Indian leader, issues an anti-Zionist declaration. Betar units join dissident Haganah members in Jerusalem and establish the separate underground organization, Irgun Zevai Leumi. Saul Tchernichowsky (1875–1943), Hebrew poet and physician, leaves Europe to settle in Palestine.	Elmer Rice, U.S. playwright, writes *Counsellor-at-Law*, which follows the career of George Simon, Simon's snobbish wife and her children who snub their stepfather because he is Jewish. In 1933, it will be adapted to the screen under the direction of William Wyler (b. 1902), starring John Barrymore* as Simon. George Gershwin composes the music and George S. Kaufman (1889–1961), Ira Gershwin (1896–1983), and Morris Ryskind the text of the musical comedy, *Of Thee I Sing*. It is the first musical to win a Pulitzer Prize. Eddie Cantor, U.S. comedian and singer, begins a very popular radio career as the host of "The Chase and Sanborn Hour." This weekly variety show will continue for almost two decades under various titles with Cantor as host. A retrospective exhibition at the Berlin National Gallery of the work of Lesser Ury (1861–1931) to

1931

	A. General History	B. Jews in North and South America	C. Jews in Europe	D. Jews in the Middle East and Elsewhere	E. Jewish Culture
1931		Irving Wexler (Waxey Gordon), underworld racketeer, becomes head of the bootleggers in the New York metropolitan area. He is also alleged to be the head of a nationwide narcotics ring. In 1932, he will be indicted and convicted of tax evasion and sentenced to 10 years in prison.	Fritz Lang, German film director, directs *M*, a film depicting a child murderer. It stars Hanna Meron as the child and Peter Lorre (1904–1964) as the child murderer. Lang, son of a Jewish mother, will flee Germany in 1933 and become a successful U.S. film director. Meron will leave Germany for Palestine in 1933, where she becomes the star of the Cameri Theater in Tel Aviv. Lorre will leave Germany in 1934 and become a notable Hollywood actor.		celebrate his 70th birthday becomes a memorial to Ury. Ury lived in poverty, and his paintings were unrecognized until late in his life, when he achieved fame for his cityscapes of street life in Berlin. Otto Heinrich Warburg (1883–1970), German biochemist, is awarded the Nobel Prize in physiology or medicine for his discovery of the nature and mode of action of the respiratory enzyme. He was baptized, did research at the Kaiser Wilhelm Institute in Berlin, and will be left undisturbed by the Nazis during the Hitler regime. The Institute for Jewish Research (YIVO) of Vilna begins the monthly publication of the *YIVO Bleter*, its scholarly journal in Yiddish. From 1940, it will be published as a biannual in New York. Max Weinreich (1894–1969) is editor from 1931 to 1950. Arthur Ruppin, sociologist and Zionist leader, publishes *The Sociology of the Jews* in two volumes, the first major work on the subject.
1932	Germany defaults on its World War I reparations payments. German Chancellor Heinrich Brüning* demands of Disarmament Conference negotiators that Germany be granted military equality and that the Versailles restraints on Germany be abrogated. Adolf Hitler* overcomes an obstacle to German leadership	A Council of Jewish Federations and Welfare Funds is organized to give organizational expression to the national scope of Jewish philanthropy in the U.S. David Dubinsky (1892–1982), U.S. labor leader, becomes president of the International Ladies' Garment Workers' Union. He will hold this position until 1966.	Youth Aliyah, a program to resettle and train Jewish youth in Palestine, is founded by Recha Freier in Germany. With Adolf Hitler's* rise to power in 1933, it becomes a large-scale project under the leadership of Henrietta Szold. By 1970 it will have resettled over 125,000 Jewish children in Israel.	Chaim Arlosoroff (1899–1933), political secretary of the Jewish Agency Executive, writes a confidential memorandum to Chaim Weizmann, in which he advocates a transition period of organized revolutionary rule of the Jewish minority to develop Palestine and save as many Jews as possible in the face of an approaching world war and emerging Arab nationalism.	Ben Shahn (1898–1969), U.S. artist, paints a series of gouaches on Nicola Sacco* and Bartolomeo Vanzetti* that are featured in a one-man show at New York's Downtown Gallery. Later in the year he will exhibit two mural panels on the Sacco* and Vanzetti* trial at the Museum of Modern Art. George S. Kaufman and Edna Ferber

A. General History	B. Jews in North and South America	C. Jews in Europe	D. Jews in the Middle East and Elsewhere	E. Jewish Culture	
					1932

A. General History

when he becomes a German citizen by being appointed a representative of the Brunswick state government to Berlin.

In March, Paul von Hindenburg* defeats Adolf Hitler* in Germany's presidential election, but without an absolute majority. He receives 49.6% of the vote to Hitler's* 30%. In a runoff election held in April, von Hindenburg* is reelected German president. He receives 53% of the vote, but Hitler* increases his vote to 37%. Franz von Papen* (1879–1969) becomes chancellor.

In July, the Nazis win 230 seats in Reichstag elections, becoming the largest party, but receive only 37% of the vote. Hermann Goering* (1893–1946) is elected president of the Reichstag.

In August, Germany's President Paul von Hindenburg* rejects Adolf Hitler's* demand that he be named chancellor of Germany.

James "Jimmy" Walker,* mayor of New York, resigns from office. He is facing a removal hearing before Governor Franklin D. Roosevelt* on charges of corruption in office.

Democratic presidential candidate Franklin D. Roosevelt* pledges the New Deal program, which calls for federal support of the economy and social programs.

Democrat Governor Franklin D. Roosevelt* and John

B. Jews in North and South America

Benjamin Nathan Cardozo, chief judge of New York's Court of Appeals, is appointed associate justice of the U.S. Supreme Court upon the nomination of President Herbert Hoover.*

Lower Canada enacts legislation giving full civil rights to Jews, including the right to sit in Parliament and hold public office.

The popular film *Symphony of Six Million* is based on a story by Fannie Hurst and is considered Hollywood's last serious portrait of Jewish family life for 20 years. Felix Klauber (Ricardo Cortez), caught up in the ambition to succeed in America, becomes a doctor who moves his practice from Hester Street to West End Avenue to Park Avenue, leaving behind his ghetto family.

The Jewish vote in the U.S. presidential election is estimated at 82% for Franklin D. Roosevelt* and 18% for Herbert Hoover.*

D. Jews in the Middle East and Elsewhere

The November issue of the *Annals of the Academy of Political and Social Science* is devoted to discussion of the Palestine question.

Victor Jacobson (1869–1935), representative of the Zionist Organization to the League of Nations in Geneva, writes a memorandum advocating a "territorial solution" to the Arab–Zionist impasse in Palestine. He calls for the establishment of two separate, "sovereign, autonomous" entities or cantons in Palestine. The proposal is rejected by the Zionist leadership.

An American–French expedition discovers the ruins of a synagogue built in 245 CE at Dura-Europos, an ancient city on the Euphrates River. In a remarkable state of preservation, its walls are covered with frescoes depicting scenes of the Bible, giving evidence of Jewish pictorial art in antiquity.

E. Jewish Culture

write a play, *Dinner at Eight*, which has a successful Broadway run.

"Brother, Can You Spare a Dime," a song by lyricist E. Y. "Yip" Harburg and composer Jay Gorney, epitomizes the Depression.

The Jewish Museum in London is founded by Cecil Roth (1899–1970) and Wilfred S. Samuel (1886–1958) when Woburn House, the communal center, is opened.

Louis Golding (1895–1958), English novelist, writes *Magnolia Street*, a novel of Anglo-Jewish life, based on his memories of Manchester and the relations between Jews and non-Jews on Magnolia Street between 1910 and 1930. It becomes an international best-seller.

Hermann Broch's (1886–1951) novel *The Sleepwalkers*, a trilogy whose theme is the decay of values in the 20th century, is published in English. Through the efforts of James Joyce* and other writers of note, this Austrian novelist will be released from prison in 1938 and emigrate to the U.S.

Hayyim Isaac Bunin (1875–1943), expert on Habad Hasidism, begins publication of *Mishneh Habad*, describing Habad doctrines, sources, and sayings. Bunin will be murdered by the Nazis at Treblinka.

The Tel Aviv Museum of Art is founded under the initiative of Meir Dizengoff

	A. General History	B. Jews in North and South America	C. Jews in Europe	D. Jews in the Middle East and Elsewhere	E. Jewish Culture
1932	N. Garner* of Texas, his running mate, defeat President Herbert Hoover* and Vice President Charles Curtis.* The Democrats win overwhelming control of both houses of Congress. France and the Soviet Union, concerned over Germany, sign nonaggression and conciliation pacts. Oliveira Salazar* becomes premier of Portugal and begins a 36-year reign as dictator. Ibn Saud* becomes king of Saudi Arabia.				(1861–1937), the city's mayor. It opens with a one-man show by Reuven Rubin. Rubin's work exemplifies an effort to create a national style of Israeli art. The publication of the *Palestine Post*, an English-language daily newspaper, founded and edited by Gershon Agron (1894–1959) and Ted R. Lurie, begins in Jerusalem. In 1950 it will become the *Jerusalem Post*.
1933	The Good Neighbor policy toward Latin America is announced by U.S. President Franklin D. Roosevelt.* The Soviet Union is recognized by the U.S., ending a long period of estrangement. Trade relations are opened. Prohibition comes to an end with the ratification of the 21st Amendment to the U.S. Constitution. U.S. unemployment is estimated to be 13 million. The U.S. gold standard is abandoned and currency is devalued. The Great Plains of the U.S. are turned into a dust bowl as a result of harsh droughts between 1933 and 1936. Benjamin V. Cohen (1894–1983) and Thomas G. Corcoran,* advisers to President Franklin D. Roosevelt,* draft the Securities Act of 1933. They are credited,	Morris Raphael Cohen (1880–1947) and Salo Wittmayer Baron found the Conference on Jewish Relations in New York. Its goal is to assemble reliable data on the position of the Jew in the modern world, enabling it to combat Nazi propoganda. In 1939, it will begin publication of a scholarly quarterly, *Jewish Social Studies*. DAIA, the representative body of Argentine Jewry officially recognized by the government, is established.	On the eve of Adolf Hitler's* rise to power, it is estimated that approximately 503,000 Jews live in Germany. They comprise less than 1% of the total German population of 65 million. About 99,000 (19.8 %) of Germany's Jewish population are eastern European nationals. The rate of intermarriage reached 60% by 1932. The Jewish population of Berlin is 160,564. The archbishop of Munich, Michael Cardinal von Faulhaber, delivers Advent sermons defending the Jews. The Nazis burn works by the noted artist Marc Chagall in Mannheim, Germany. After Adolf Hitler* rises to power, Max Liebermann is ousted from the presidency of the Berlin Academy of Art and his paintings are removed from German museums. The Warburg Bibliothek is transferred from	The construction of a modern harbor at Haifa in Palestine is completed. Egged, a public transport cooperative, is founded in Palestine and establishes branches throughout the country. French archaeologists begin excavating the ancient northwest Mesopotamian city of Mari. They will unearth over 20,000 tablets from the early 2nd millennium BCE, as well as the palace of Zimrilim. Reform Judaism is introduced into South Africa by Rabbi Moses C. Weiler, who is a moderate Reformer and Zionist in sentiment.	Solomon Grayzel, U.S. rabbi, historian, and editor, publishes his doctoral dissertation, *The Church and the Jews in the XIIIth Century*. His study of papal documents sheds new light on the relationship of the Roman Catholic church and the Jews during the years 1198–1254. Irving Fineman writes *Hear Ye Sons*, a novel of ghetto life in 19th-century Russian Poland, where Jews maintained a way of life in beauty and dignity despite oppression and persecution. Ernest Bloch (1880–1959), Swiss composer who emigrated to the U.S., composes "Sacred Service," a Sabbath morning composition for orchestra and mixed chorus. A number of his compositions are specifically Jewish. Jerome Kern, U.S. composer of popular music, composes the song "Smoke Gets in

1933

A. General History

also, with drafting other New Deal legislation, such as the Securities Exchange Act of 1934, the Public Utility Holding Company Act of 1935, and the Fair Labor Standards Act of 1938.

The first All-Star baseball game is played in Chicago, Illinois.

Romanian Prime Minister Ion Duca* is assassinated by the Iron Guard, an extreme nationalist group.

C. Jews in Europe

Germany to London and renamed the Warburg Institute.

Bruno Walter (1876–1962), music conductor in Berlin and Leipzig, is forced to leave Germany by the Nazis. He will settle in the U.S. in 1939.

Leo Baeck, Berlin Reform rabbi, announces the end of the 1,000-year history of Germany's Jews. As president of the representative body of German Jews, he refuses invitations to leave the country and declares that he will remain with the last group of German Jews. Baeck will be sent to the Theresienstadt concentration camp in 1943 and survive the war.

Martin Buber, having been forced by the Nazis to leave his position as professor of religion at Frankfurt University, is appointed head of the newly created central office for adult education in Germany. He travels throughout Germany, teaching, lecturing, and encouraging the Jewish community.

The Nazis force Theodor Lewald, president of the German Olympic Committee, to resign, as one of his grandparents was Jewish.

Edgar Ansel Mowrer,* U.S. foreign correspondent, argues in his book *Germany Puts the Clock Back* that the Nazis aim "was the extermination, permanent subjugation or the voluntary departure of the Jews from Germany."

E. Jewish Culture

Your Eyes" with Otto Harbach.

Sidney Kingsley, U.S. playwright, writes *Men in White*, about the crisis in the life of a surgeon. It wins the Pulitzer Prize.

Marvin Lowenthal (1890–1969), U.S. editor and communal worker, writes *A World Passed By*, a popular informal history of Jewish life in Europe and North Africa over the centuries.

Nathanael West (Nathan W. Weinstein, 1903–1940), U.S. novelist, writes *Miss Lonelyhearts*, a sad satire of a newspaperman involved in the lives of writers to his lovelorn column.

Sholem Asch's Yiddish novel *Three Cities* is published in English translation. It describes Jewish life in St. Petersburg, Moscow, and Warsaw during the first two decades of the 20th century.

Yoshe Kalb, a novel by Israel Joshua Singer, Polish Yiddish novelist who emigrates to the U.S. in 1933, appears in English translation. Set in the rabbinic courts of 19th-century Galician Hasidism, it depicts a mystic, an ascetic son of a rabbi, who commits adultery with his young mother-in-law and exiles himself, spending the rest of his life waiting for redemption that never comes.

Jacob Z. Lauterbach, U.S. talmudic scholar, publishes a critical edition, introduction, and translation of the *Mekhilta de-Rabbi Ishma'el*.

A. **General History**	B. **Jews in North and South America**	C. **Jews in Europe**	D. **Jews in the Middle East and Elsewhere**	E. **Jewish Culture**

Jan. 1933

A. General History

Adolf Hitler* becomes chancellor of Germany, the head of the German government.

E. Jewish Culture

The ancient Jewish law code, the Mishnah, becomes available to the general reader through a standard translation by the English Christian Hebraist Herbert Danby* (1889–1953).

Feb. 1933

A. General History

On February 4, Adolf Hitler* issues a decree giving the German government power to ban political meetings and to suppress publications deemed harmful to the public interest.

On February 27, a fire at the German Reichstag is denounced by Adolf Hitler* as a Communist plot to disrupt new elections. Hitler* demands new laws permitting arbitrary imprisonment without warrant or trial. Later evidence proves Nazi responsibility for the fire.

Germany's President, Paul von Hindenburg,* signs an emergency decree suspending constitutional guarantees of free speech, right of assembly, a free press, and right of privacy. Communist Reichstag members are arrested.

> *Jewish Emigration from Germany, 1933–1939*
>
> Between April 1933 and May 1939, 304,500 Jews emigrated from Germany (including areas occupied by Germany in May 1939). They emigrated to:
>
> | | |
> |---|---:|
> | U.S. | 63,000 |
> | Palestine | 55,000 |
> | Great Britain | 40,000 |
> | France | 30,000 |
> | Argentina | 25,000 |
> | Brazil | 13,000 |
> | South Africa | 5,500 |
> | Italy | 5,000 |
> | Other European countries | 25,000 |
> | Other South American countries | 15,000 |
> | Other | 8,000 |
> | Total | 304,500 |

E. Jewish Culture

Sir Francis Eugene Simon (1893–1956), German physicist, leaves Germany for the Clarendon Laboratory in Oxford, England. A leader in the science of thermodynamics, during World War II he will perform important research in the development of the atomic bomb.

Gertrude Stein (1874–1946), U.S. author and art critic who settled in Paris in 1902, writes an autobiographical study, *The Autobiography of Alice B. Toklas*, which describes her life in Paris. She is a prominent expatriate and is the center of a celebrated literary and artistic circle.

Gershom Scholem is appointed professor of Jewish mysticism and Kabbalah at the Hebrew University in Jerusalem. He left Germany for Palestine in 1923. He demonstrates that there is a constant mystical stream within Jewish tradition. In 1941, he will publish *Major Trends in Jewish Mysticism* and in 1973, his study, *Sabbatai Sevi: The Mystical Messiah (1626–1676)*, will be published in the U.S.

Mar. 1933

A. General History

The Nazi vote in the last Reichstag elections increases to only 44%. Together with other parties, Adolf Hitler* forms a majority and alters the German constitution, introducing the Third Reich.

On March 10, the first concentration camp is established in Germany by the SS at Dachau, near Munich. It exists until captured by the Americans on April 29, 1945. It is estimated that more than 40,000 will be killed at Dachau, of whom 80–90% are Jews.

C. Jews in Europe

Syndicated U.S. columnist Dorothy Thompson* visits Germany and reports on the situation of the Jews. "It's an outbreak of sadistic and pathological hatred."

Albert Einstein, who was teaching abroad when Hitler* assumed power, resigns his position at the Royal Prussian Academy of Sciences and accepts a position at the Institute for Advanced Studies in Princeton, New Jersey. He will never return to Germany.

E. Jewish Culture

Saul Aaron Adler (1895–1966), of the Hebrew University Medical School, is awarded the Chalmers Gold Medal of the Royal Society of

A. General History	B. Jews in North and South America	C. Jews in Europe	D. Jews in the Middle East and Elsewhere	E. Jewish Culture	

| | | | | | **Mar. 1933** |

U.S. Secretary of State Cordell Hull* pressures the press to adopt "a spirit of moderation" toward Germany. He suggests that conditions may not have been "accurately" and "authoritatively" reported and believes that the "gravity" of press reports have not been borne out by the facts.

U.S. Jewish leaders threaten a counterboycott of German goods at a mass rally in New York at the Madison Square Garden. The boycott is to last as long as a proposed Nazi boycott of German Jewish businesses. In response, the Nazis limit their boycott to one day.

Tropical Medicine and Hygiene for his studies on the transmission of the kala-azar disease by the sandfly.

| | | | | | **Apr. 1933** |

On April 26, the Nazis take over the German State Secret Police (Gestapo).

Three days after the German boycott of Jewish businesses and stores, the *Christian Science Monitor* accuses the Jews of the U.S. of exacerbating the situation by demanding official condemnation of Germany. Its editorial exonerates the non-Jewish world of responsibility for antisemitism by declaring that it is Jews' "commercial clannishness which . . . gets them in trouble."

H. R. Knickerbocker,* foreign correspondent, reports in the *New York Evening Post* "that all of Germany's 600,000 Jews are in terror."

The *Christian Century*, the most prominent American Protestant journal, reports that too many Jews in Germany are radical or Communist and accepts this claim as justification of Adolf Hitler's* attitude toward them.

The Nazis stage a one-day boycott of all Jewish stores, doctors, and lawyers. Nazi leaders begin urging expulsion of Jews from schools and universities. The *Volkischer Beobachter*, the Nazi newspaper, declares that the boycott "is to be regarded merely as a dress rehearsal for a series of measures that will be carried out unless world opinion, which at the moment is against us, definitely changes."

Robert Weltsch (1891–1982), German Zionist journalist, writes an article in *Judische Rundschau*, a German Zionist monthly magazine, "Wear It with Pride, the Yellow Badge," which becomes the slogan of Jewish resistance to Nazi oppression.

A new German civil service law, the first anti-Jewish ordinance, is passed barring from public employment anyone who is not of "Aryan descent." This act gives legal status to the concept of racial difference between German Jews and all other Germans.

On April 13, German Jewish leaders establish a Central Bureau for Relief and Reconstruction. Its

Nazi SA guards at the entrance of a Jewish store on April 1, Boycott Day. The sign reads: "Germans beware! Do not buy from Jews!"

A. General History	B. Jews in North and South America	C. Jews in Europe	D. Jews in the Middle East and Elsewhere	E. Jewish Culture
Apr. 1933		objective is to extend legal and economic assistance to Jews who lost their jobs or who were forced to leave their places of residence. The Nazi government passes a law against the excessive number of "students of foreign race" in German schools and universities. German Jews are considered "of foreign race," even though German Jews have lived in Germany for over 1,000 years.		
May 1933	Japan leaves the League of Nations.	On May 12, Walter Lippmann (1889–1974), one of America's most influential columnists, writes that he is convinced that Adolf Hitler* wants peace and accuses the Jews of causing their own suffering. Felix Frankfurter is so incensed by his friend's column that he does not speak to him for over three and a half years. The *New York Times* editorializes that dispatches of news reporters from Germany are truthful and not exaggerated. Jacob R. Marcus (b. 1896), Hebrew Union College history professor, writes an article in the *American Scholar* supporting a Jewish national home in Palestine and urges American Reform Jews to join the Zionist movement.	On May 10, the Nazis arrange the public burning of books by Jewish and non-Nazi authors in great bonfires throughout Germany. A committee of French Jews protests anti-Jewish discrimination in Germany to the League of Nations. They complain on behalf of Franz Bernheim of Upper Silesia, who is dismissed by the Nazis from his job because he is Jewish, and argue that it violates the German–Polish convention of 1922 guaranteeing equal rights to minorities. The League upholds Bernheim, and Jews in Upper Silesia will enjoy equal rights until the expiration of the convention on July 15, 1937. The Central British Fund for German Jewish refugees is created. It guarantees the British government that refugees from Nazism will not become a public burden. At the beginning of World War II, when their number reaches 60,000, the	 *Nazis burn banned books of Jewish and non-Jewish authors at Berlin's Opera Square, May 10, 1933.*	

A. General History	B. Jews in North and South America	C. Jews in Europe	D. Jews in the Middle East and Elsewhere	E. Jewish Culture
		government begins to subsidize the fund.		**May 1933**
	On June 12, reports in the *New York Times* describe the denial of Nazi terror against the Jews as more shocking than the terror itself.		Chaim Arlosoroff, Mapai Zionist and head of the Jewish Agency's political department, is murdered in Tel Aviv. Abraham Stavsky, Zevi Rosenblatt, and Abba Ahimeir, revisionists, are accused, but the crime has never been solved. Arlosoroff was a protégé of Chaim Weizmann.	**June 1933**
On July 8, Germany and the Vatican sign a concordat, in which Germany agrees to respect Catholic rights and institutions in Germany but will limit activity it considers political. The concordat's effect is to undercut efforts of anti-Nazi churchmen to retain basic freedoms in Germany. On July 14, the Nazi party becomes the only legal political party in Germany. The Staatliche Bauhaus faculty closes the school in Germany under Nazi pressure. Many artists begin emigration to the West.		*Newsweek* magazine reports the arrest of 200 Jewish merchants in Nuremberg for "profiteering," the beating of American Jews in Berlin, and the closing of the Jewish Telegraphic Agency offices in Germany. During this same period, the *Christian Science Monitor* publishes a series describing life in Germany as normal and serene, with most Jews "not in any way molested."		**July 1933**
		The 18th Zionist Congress convenes in Prague under the leadership of Nahum Sokolow. Conflict between the revisionists and labor heightens. Moshe Sharett Shertok, 1894–1965) is elected head of the Jewish Agency's political department, succeeding Chaim Arlosoroff. Several American Jewish organizations, including the Jewish War Veterans and the American Jewish Congress, led by	Zionist leaders enter into an agreement with Nazi authorities to facilitate German Jewish emigration to Palestine by allowing the transfer of their capital in the form of German goods. Many oppose the "transfer agreement" (Ha'avarah) as standing in contradiction to the boycott against Germany. Others believe the argument for rescue and for building a haven in Palestine for those threatened is more convincing. In 1935,	**Aug. 1933**

403

	A. **General History**	B. **Jews in North and South America**	C. **Jews in Europe**	D. **Jews in the Middle East and Elsewhere**	E. **Jewish Culture**
Aug. 1933			Samuel Untermyer and Abraham Coralnik, declare a boycott against Nazi Germany. In October, the American Federation of Labor announces its support of the boycott of Nazi goods. Reinhold Niebuhr* (1892–1971), professor at the Union Theological Seminary, writes in the *Christian Century* magazine of his visit to Germany. "With unexampled and primitive ferocity," Jews were "arrested, beaten and murdered, with no public protest." He writes of the capitulation of the German churches, Protestant and Catholic, to Nazism and Jew-hatred.	the agreement will be approved at the 19th Zionist Congress.	
Sept. 1933		Theodore Dreiser* (1871–1945), well-known U.S. novelist, writes in the *American Spectator* magazine. "My real quarrel with the Jew is not that he is inefficient or ignorant or even unaesthetic. It is really that he is too clever and too dynamic in his personal and racial attack on all other types of persons and races." He proposes that their situation in the world today could be overcome by their gathering in a state of their own.		*Fifth "Aliyah" to Palestine, 1933–1939* *Number:* 215,222 *Origin:* Mainly from all countries of Central Europe, including beginnings of Youth Aliyah, in wake of persecution by Nazi Germany and other anti-Semitic governments; from Germany (44,420) and Poland (over 90,000); also including over 15,000 Sephardic and Oriental Jews from Yemen (over 7,000), Turkey and Bulgaria.	
Oct. 1933	Germany withdraws from the Disarmament Conference and from the League of Nations.			In the last week of October, Arabs riot in Jerusalem, Nablus, and Jaffa in reaction to the increase in the number of Jewish immigrants to Palestine.	
Nov. 1933	In a national plebiscite, over 90% of the German electorate approves Adolf Hitler's* decision to withdraw from the League of Nations.				

A. General History	B. Jews in North and South America	C. Jews in Europe	D. Jews in the Middle East and Elsewhere	E. Jewish Culture	
Fiorello H. La Guardia* (1882–1947) is elected mayor of New York. Born to a mother of Jewish descent and an Italian father, he serves for three terms, until 1945.					**Nov. 1933**
Mustafa Kemal,* the first president of the Turkish republic, abolishes the Ottoman caliphate. The censorship of U.S. motion pictures is begun by the Catholic League of Decency. The *Partisan Review*, an American literary magazine, is founded. Identified with left-wing politics, it is edited for many years by Philip Rahv, one of its founders.	The Jewish Labor Committee is organized under the leadership of B. Charney Vladeck (1886–1938). It represents the Amalgamated Clothing Workers, the United Hat, Cap and Millinery Workers, the Workmen's Circle, and the International Ladies Garment Workers Union. The committee is aloof to Zionism. T. S. Eliot* (1888–1965), poet and critic, publishes *After Strange Gods*, a collection of lectures, in which he observes that "reasons of race and religion combine to make any large number of free-thinking Jews undesirable" in the U.S. Eliot* will win the Nobel Prize for literature in 1948. *The House of Rothschild* wins an Academy Award nomination for best film of the year. A theme in this film of the famous Jewish banking house is the gaining of rights for Jews. Max Gordon (1902–1989), cabaret owner, opens the Village Vanguard in New York's Greenwich Village. A Lithuanian immigrant who came to New York by way of Oregon, Gordon is responsible for launching the careers of many entertainers, including Betty Comden, Adolph Green, Judy Holliday,	The Jewish Central Information Office is founded in Amsterdam as an archive of materials on contemporary Jewish history, antisemitism, and the Nazi persecution. Founded by David Cohen (1883–1967) and Alfred Wiener (1885–1964), its director, it will be transferred to London in 1939 and later renamed the Wiener Library.	The Daniel Sieff Research Institute is established at Rehovot. It is founded with the financial support of the Sieff family of England. Chaim Weizmann heads the scientific staff. In 1949, it will become the Weizmann Institute of Science.	Max Baer (1909–1959) wins the world heavyweight boxing title on June 14 by knocking out Primo Carnera* of Italy in the 11th round at New York's Madison Square Garden. Baer, who wears a Star of David on his boxing trunks, loses the championship the following year to James J. Braddock.* Henry "Hank" Greenberg (1911–1986), first baseman of the Detroit Tigers baseball team who is hitting .338 with 25 home runs, does not play on Yom Kippur although the team is in the midst of the pennant race. His decision causes great interest and is probably the first time in American history that widespread attention is called to Jewish religious practice. The Tigers win the American League pennant. Mordecai M. Kaplan, U.S. rabbi, writes *Judaism as a Civilization*. He interprets Judaism as a religious civilization that reveres the past ideals and rituals of Judaism, but whose present generation is free to make its own changes in light of its own needs. To Kaplan, Judaism encompasses the whole of life, art, drama, music, and folk customs. Henry Roth (b. 1906), U.S. novelist, writes	**1934**

	A. General History	B. Jews in North and South America	C. Jews in Europe	D. Jews in the Middle East and Elsewhere	E. Jewish Culture
1934		Johnny Mathis,* and Harry Belafonte.* In the 1950s, the Village Vanguard will present modern jazz and gain a reputation as the premier jazz nightclub in the world.			*Call It Sleep*, a novel of two years of immigrant life on New York's Lower East Side in about 1912 as seen through the eyes of six-year-old David Schearl. Although it is well-reviewed, Roth's only work falls into obscurity until it is revived, to wide critical acclaim, in the 1960s.
Jan. 1934	Germany and Poland enter into a 10-year nonaggression pact. Poland becomes the first country to enter into a friendly agreement with the Hitler* regime.				Daniel Fuchs, U.S. novelist, writes *Summer in Williamsburg*, the first novel of the Williamsburg Trilogy, which describes life in the Jewish slums of the Williamsburg neighborhood in Brooklyn, New York. The other two novels of the trilogy are *Homage to Blenholt* (1936) and *Low Company* (1937).
May 1934			The Nazi newspaper, *Der Sturmer*, devotes a special edition, of which 130,000 copies are printed and sold, to blood libel accusations against the Jews, utilizing infamous medieval cartoons showing Jews using human blood in the observance of religious customs. The Birobidzhan area of the Soviet Union is granted the status of a Jewish autonomous region, despite the fact that the Jewish population is less than 20% of the total. The Jewish population is about 8,200, whereas the goal was to have about 50,000 by this date.		Nathanael West, U.S. novelist, writes *A Cool Million*, a savage satire of the Horatio Alger story and of American gullibility to demagogery, in which antisemitism plays a useful role. George Blumenthal (1858–1941), U.S. banker and senior partner of Lazard Frères, becomes president of New York's Metropolitan Museum of Art. He is also president of Mt. Sinai Hospital.
June 1934	Adolf Hitler* orders the killing of Storm Troop leader Ernst Roehm* (1887–1934), together with many of his followers ("The Night of the Long Knives"), whom he viewed as his enemies in the Nazi party.				Max Weber (1881–1961), U.S. painter and sculptor whose avant-garde work is at first harshly criticized but later receives widespread acclaim, paints *The Talmudists*. His Jewishness is a part of his artistic life. In 1955, he will be elected a member of the National Institute of Arts and Letters.
July 1934	Austrian Chancellor Engelbert Dollfuss* (1892–1934) is assassinated as an attempted coup by Austrian Nazis fails.				

A. General History	B. Jews in North and South America	C. Jews in Europe	D. Jews in the Middle East and Elsewhere	E. Jewish Culture	
Adolf Hitler* becomes president of Germany upon the death of Paul von Hindenburg.* Eighty-eight percent of the voters, in a plebiscite, affirm Adolf Hitler* in his new role as chancellor and president of Germany.			Three days of anti-Jewish riots in the Algerian city of Constantine result in 23 Jews killed and 38 wounded.	Lillian Hellman (1905–1984), U.S. playwright, writes *The Children's Hour*, a psychological drama based on an actual case in Edinburgh, Scotland, about a schoolgirl's charges of lesbianism against two of her teachers. This is her first performed work.	**Aug. 1934**
The Soviet Union enters the League of Nations.				Harry A. Wolfson, Harvard professor of Hebrew literature and philosophy, writes *The Philosophy of Spinoza*, a two-volume discussion of the content and structure of Spinoza's reasoning.	**Sept. 1934**
Adolf Hitler* secretly orders the rapid expansion of the German military and the creation of an air force.				Alfred Gerald Caplin (Al Capp, 1909–1979) creates Li'l Abner, a comic strip character who satirizes the American political and social scene. "Li'l Abner" is widely syndicated throughout the U.S. press.	**Oct. 1934**
Winston Churchill* warns in a parliamentary speech that Germany is building a modern air force that will endanger Great Britain.				Lion Feuchtwanger, German novelist, writes *The Oppermans*, which depicts the fate of a sophisticated German Jewish family at the time of Adolf Hitler's* rise to power. In 1983, it will be adapted to television by a West German production company.	**Nov. 1934**
Sergei Kirov,* the Leningrad party leader, is assassinated under Joseph Stalin's* orders. His death is considered the beginning of 25 years of terror in the Soviet Union, in which Stalin* wipes out real or imagined enemies, perhaps in the millions.		Revisionist Zionists begin to enroll at the Italian maritime school at Civitvecchia. This collaboration between Italian Fascists and revisionist Zionists is based on their ideological differences with Great Britain. In 1938 the Zionist relationship with the school will end. By the end of 1934, more than 50,000 of the 500,000 Jews of Germany have emigrated.		Andre Citroen (1878–1935), French industrialist, introduces front-wheel drive for his automobiles. Bruno Schulz (1892–1942), Polish writer and artist, publishes a collection of short stories, *Cinnamon Shops*. Although his literary output will be small, as he will be killed by the Nazis, his works are considered significant contributions to Polish	**Dec. 1934**

	A. General History	B. Jews in North and South America	C. Jews in Europe	D. Jews in the Middle East and Elsewhere	E. Jewish Culture
Dec. 1934					literature. *Cinnamon Shops* will be translated into English in 1980 as *Streets of Crocodiles*.
1935	Karl Barth* (1886–1968), Protestant theologian who opposes Adolf Hitler,* is expelled from Germany to his native Switzerland. He helps to found the Confessing Church, which deems Hitler* and his Nazi ideology incompatible with the Christian commitment to the teachings of Jesus. The Committee for Industrial Organizations (CIO) is established by U.S. industrial unionists within the American Federation of Labor (AFL). FM radio is perfected by Edwin Armstrong.*	The Reconstructionist movement, under the leadership of Mordecai M. Kaplan, issues a platform that calls for the establishment of a Palestinian commonwealth as indispensable to Jewish life in the Diaspora. Kaplan also begins publication of the *Reconstructionist* magazine. Alfred Eisenstaedt, described as the father of photojournalism, leaves Nazi Germany for the U.S., where he joins the staff of *Life* magazine. During his 40-year career with the magazine, his photographs are featured on 90 *Life* covers. His work as a press photographer in Germany was influenced by Erich Salomon (1886–1944). The Rabbinical Council of America, composed of English-speaking Orthodox rabbis, is organized. Wilbur J. Cohen (1913–1987) assists in drafting the Social Security Act of 1935. Sinclair Lewis,* U.S. novelist, writes *It Can't Happen Here*, a novel that deals with the rise and establishment of a Fascist dictatorship in the U.S. James T. Farrell,* U.S. novelist, completes his trilogy of novels, *Studs Lonigan*, which describes Chicago's Irish lower middle class and includes a portrayal of their attitude toward their Jewish neighbors.	Yellow benches for the segregation of Jews are set up in Berlin parks and labeled "Only for Jews." The second world conference of Betar is held in Cracow, Poland. Vladimir (Ze'ev) Jabotinsky propounds the text of the Betar ideology, whose first paragraph states: "I devote my life to the rebirth of the Jewish state, with a Jewish majority, on both sides of the Jordan." Revisionists convene a conference in Vienna and establish the New Zionist Organization.	Haifa becomes the terminus of a pipeline transporting crude oil from Iraq to the Mediterranean. Rabbi Amram Blau leaves the Agudat Israel movement and founds the extreme anti-Zionist Hevrat Hayyim (Association of Life), which later becomes Neturei Karta (Guardians of the City), in Jerusalem. During the year, 69,000 immigrants, the largest number ever to arrive until then, reach Palestine. Mostly from Poland and Germany, they raise the population of Tel Aviv to 150,000. Coffeehouses, as in Vienna and Berlin, spring up throughout the city, which in 1931 was a provincial township of 50,000.	*Porgy and Bess*, a folk opera about the life of southern blacks by George Gershwin and his brother Ira has its premiere. It is based on the 1925 novel *Porgy* by DuBose Heyward.* *Waiting for Lefty* and *Awake and Sing*, two well-known plays of Clifford Odets (1906–1963), proletarian dramatist, are performed by New York's Group Theater. *Waiting for Lefty*, about a strike in the taxi industry, stars Elia Kazan.* *Awake and Sing* concerns a Jewish working-class family in the Bronx and features Morris Carnovsky, Stella and Luther Adler, and John Garfield (Julius Garfinkle, 1913–1952). Rabbi Isidore Epstein (1894–1962) begins supervision of an English translation of the Babylonian Talmud, published by the Soncino Press in England. The project will be completed in 1952. The Jewish Museum of Amsterdam holds an exhibition in honor of the 250th anniversary of the Ashkenazic congregation. It is the museum's first major exhibition. Abraham Reisen, Yiddish poet and short story writer, completes the third volume of his memoirs, *Episodes of My Life*. Born in Russia, he emigrated to the U.S. in 1914, where he began writing for Yiddish

A. General History	B. Jews in North and South America	C. Jews in Europe	D. Jews in the Middle East and Elsewhere	E. Jewish Culture	
				dailies. His memoirs are an important source for the history of Yiddish literature and its important personalities.	**1935**
A plebiscite held in the Saar region, under League of Nations auspices, returns the province to the control of Nazi Germany. The Saar had been separated from Germany under the Treaty of Versailles in 1919. Almost all the 5,000 Jews of the Saar choose French or Belgian citizenship and leave for France and Belgium.				Joseph Green, film producer, comes to Poland from the U.S. to make *Yidl Mitn Fidl* (*Little Jew with a Fiddle*), a Yiddish film starring Molly Picon as a girl masquerading as a boy violinist who falls in love with a young musician. In 1937, Green will make *A Brivele der Mamen* (*A Little Letter to Mother*) and *Mamele* (*Little Mother*).	**Jan. 1935**
Adolf Hitler* denounces the disarmament clauses of the Versailles treaty and announces the reintroduction of compulsory military service and an increase in the size of the German army.		Jews are excluded from military service as Germany enacts the Conscription Law.		Issachar Ryback, Russian-born painter who settled in Paris in 1926, unexpectedly dies on the eve of the opening of a one-man retrospective organized by the major art dealer Georges Wildenstein. He is considered a master of contemporary Jewish art, adapting a cubistic style to his knowledge of Jewish folklore and life in the shtetl.	**Mar. 1935**
France and the Soviet Union enter into a five-year treaty of mutual assistance, each promising to come to the aid of the other in the event of war. Germany is angered by the agreement. Marshal Józef Pilsudski,* Poland's leader, dies.				Joseph Budko (1888–1940), printer and graphic artist who left Germany in 1933 to settle in Palestine, becomes director of the new Bezalel School of Arts and Crafts in Jerusalem.	**May 1935**
	The Central Conference of American Rabbis (Reform) adopts the resolution that Zionism is "a matter of personal conscience." The conference takes no official stand for or against Zionism.			A documentary film, *The Land of Promise*, is made in Palestine by Jewish film professionals from Germany. It describes the achievements of the Jewish community in Palestine and is shown throughout the world. Franz Weidenreich (1873–1948), German physical anthropologist who attacked the distorted Nazi racial views, leaves the	**June 1935**

	A. General History	B. Jews in North and South America	C. Jews in Europe	D. Jews in the Middle East and Elsewhere	E. Jewish Culture
July 1935		Demonstrators board the German ship SS *Bremen*, then in New York Harbor, and rip down the swastika from its mast. Magistrate Louis Brodsky later dismisses charges against them on the ground that the sight of the "pirate" flag naturally incited them.			University of Heidelberg for a professorship at the Peking Union Medical School. He continues the researches on the Peking man—one of the earliest known hominids. In 1941, he will leave China as a result of the Japanese invasion and continue his researches on the Peking man fossil at the American Museum of Natural History in New York.
Aug. 1935	President Franklin D. Roosevelt* signs the Neutrality Act, which prohibits the sale of arms and other materials to belligerent nations. The act was a victory for U.S. isolationists. The U.S. government organizes the Works Progress Administration.		The 19th Zionist Congress convenes in Lucerne under the leadership of Nahum Sokolow. Revisionists do not participate. The congress approves the "transfer agreement" with Germany. Chaim Weizmann is reelected president, and David Ben-Gurion, chairman of the Jewish Agency Executive, as labor dominates the congress.		
Sept. 1935			Nazi Germany adopts the Nuremberg laws, which officially disenfranchise Jews and classify them as noncitizens. The population is divided into two classes— Reich citizens, of Aryan ancestry, and state subjects, Jews. Jews can no longer have government jobs, serve in the army, vote, marry non-Jews, engage in extramarital sexual relations with Aryans, or hire female non-Jewish domestic workers. The *Times* of London, commenting on the Nuremberg laws, declares: "Nothing like the complete disinheritance and segregation of Jewish citizens, now announced, has been heard since medieval times."		
Oct. 1935	The *New York Times* advocates a boycott of 1936 Olympic Games scheduled to be held		Two English government officials discuss emigration of German Jews to		

A. General History	B. Jews in North and South America	C. Jews in Europe	D. Jews in the Middle East and Elsewhere	E. Jewish Culture	
in Germany as a moral protest against the Hitler* regime. Approximately two-thirds of U.S. newspapers commenting on the 1936 Olympic Games favor a U.S. boycott. Italian forces invade Ethiopia.		Palestine with members of the German Economics Ministry in Berlin. They report to the British Foreign Office their view that the intention of "German policy is clearly to eliminate the Jew from German life, and the Nazis do not mind how this is accomplished. Mortality and emigration provide the means."			**Oct. 1935**
		A wave of anti-Jewish riots occurs in Polish universities. Special seats are assigned to Jewish students.			**Dec. 1935**
The Palace of the League of Nations in Geneva is completed, having been designed by the Swiss architect Julian Flegenheimer (1880–1938).	Richard Courant, German mathematician, settles in the U.S. as professor and head of the department of mathematics at New York University. In 1933, the Nazis forced him to leave his directorship of Goettingen's Mathematics Institute. John Dos Passos,* U.S. novelist, completes his trilogy, *U.S.A.*, which tells the story of the first three decades of the 20th century in the U.S. A Jewish radical, Ben Compton, is a central character.		Moshe Avigdor Amiel (1883–1946), chief rabbi of Antwerp, Belgium, and religious Zionist, is elected chief rabbi of Tel Aviv. In Tel Aviv, he establishes a modern high school yeshiva, combining secular and religious studies.	Under the leadership of Max Weinreich, Yiddish scholar, the Institute for Jewish Research adopts a set of orthographic rules to standardize Yiddish with normative usage, grammar, and spelling. Israel Joshua Singer, Yiddish novelist who emigrated to the U.S. from Poland in 1933, writes *The Brothers Ashkenazi*. It describes, on a grand scale, how the Jewish textile barons of Lodz helped develop this large urban center. Aaron Copland (1900–1990), U.S. composer, uses Mexican folk materials in his orchestral piece *The Mexican Salon*. He will also use folk materials in his ballets *Billy the Kid* (1938), *Rodeo* (1942), and *Appalachian Spring* (1944).	**1936**
The Gestapo (State Secret Police) becomes a "Supreme Reich Agency." Heinrich Himmler,* chief of the SS and the Gestapo, gains absolute control over German internal security.		David Frankfurter, a 25-year-old medical student from Yugoslovia, assassinates Wilhelm Gustloff,* Adolf Hitler's personal representative in Switzerland, as a protest against the persecution of the Jews in Germany. Frankfurter is sentenced to 18 years' imprisonment. In 1945, at the end of the war, he will be released and emigrate to Palestine, where he will die in 1982.		Jack Levine (b. 1915), U.S. painter of protest and social comment, gains recognition as his painting *Feast of Pure Reason* is shown at a Museum of Modern Art exhibition. An unpleasant underworld	**Feb. 1936**

	A. General History	B. Jews in North and South America	C. Jews in Europe	D. Jews in the Middle East and Elsewhere	E. Jewish Culture
Feb. 1936					setting includes millionaire banker John Pierpont Morgan.* Levine also paints biblical themes and subjects drawn from modern Jewish life.
Mar. 1936	Adolf Hitler* sends German troops into the Rhineland province, in defiance of the Versailles treaty, which requires it to be demilitarized.		A pogrom in Przytyk, Poland, results in three Jewish deaths and 60 wounded. A Pole is killed in subsequent clashes with Jewish defense groups. The jailing of the Jewish assailant causes a general strike by a majority of Jewish workers, joined by some Poles, throughout Poland.		Barney Balaban is elected president of Paramount Pictures in the U.S.
Apr. 1936				The Arab Higher Committee is established in Palestine. It demands of British authorities total cessation of Jewish immigration, prohibition of the sale of land to Jews, and the establishment of an Arab "democratic government," i.e., the imposition of the Arab majority will on the Jewish minority. A six-month general strike is declared, and an armed uprising occurs. Within one month, 21 Jews are killed.	Benny Goodman (1909–1986), U.S. jazz clarinetist and band leader, organizes the Benny Goodman Trio with drummer Gene Krupa* and black pianist Teddy Wilson.* It is the first time that a black publicly plays jazz music on a national scale with whites. Otto Loewi (1873–1961), Austrian biochemist, is awarded the Nobel Prize in physiology or medicine for his discoveries relating to chemical transmission of nerve impulses. The Germans will imprison him for two months and deprive him of his possessions when they occupy Austria in 1938. He will settle in the U.S. in 1940.
May 1936	Italy occupies Addis Ababa and Ethiopia surrenders.				
June 1936			Leon Blum is the first Jew and first Socialist to become premier of France. He serves until June 21, 1937.		Meir Balaban (1877–1942) becomes associate professor of Jewish history at the University of Warsaw. Acknowledged as the founder of Polish Jewish historiography, he wrote histories of the Jews of Lemberg (1906), Lublin (1919), Cracow (1931–1936), as well as a history of the Frankist movement (1934–1935). He dies in Warsaw before the liquidation of the ghetto.
July 1936	Civil war erupts in Spain. The Loyalists are anticlerical and antimonarchy leftists, and the nationalists are conservatives led by General Francisco Franco.* Germany and Italy begin military assistance to the nationalists, and Russia, to the Loyalists.			At the request of British authorities, Iraqi Foreign Minister Nuri es-Said* persuades the Arab Higher Committee to negotiate the end of the uprising and strike in Palestine. High Commissioner Arthur Wauchope* suggests that if the strike and uprising are ended, a Royal Commission of Inquiry would come to Palestine to look into the "roots of the problem."	Judah Leib Maimon (1875–1962), Orthodox rabbi and leader of religious Zionism, establishes Mosad haRav Kook, the

A. General History	B. Jews in North and South America	C. Jews in Europe	D. Jews in the Middle East and Elsewhere	E. Jewish Culture	
The Anglo-Egyptian Treaty reserves to Great Britain special rights over the Suez Canal for 20 years. Lev Kamenev, Grigori Zinoviev, and their followers are placed on trial by Joseph Stalin* as Trotskyists and for plotting against the Soviet regime. They openly confess and are executed.		The Polish Ministry of Commerce, in an act of obvious antisemitic intent, requires all shops throughout the country to include as part of the shop sign the name of the owner as it appeared on his birth certificate.		publishing house of the Mizrahi movement. It will publish hundreds of rabbinic works by contemporary authors as well as new editions of old texts. Maimon settled in Palestine in 1913, was the Mizrahi representative to the Zionist Executive, and will serve, after the establishment of the state of Israel, as minister of religion and in the first Knesset.	**Aug. 1936**
Germany and Italy form an alliance (the Rome–Berlin Axis).			The Arab Higher Committee calls off a general strike in Palestine and violence dies out. During this period 197 Arabs, 80 Jews, and 28 British personnel are killed. The cease-fire will last until the summer of 1937, when the Arab rebellion flares up again after the British government's endorsement of the Peel Plan to partition Palestine.	The Palestine Symphony Orchestra is founded by the well-known European violinist, Bronislaw Huberman (1882–1947). Arturo Toscanini* conducts the opening concerts. The orchestra immediately becomes internationally known.	**Oct. 1936**
Franklin D. Roosevelt* is reelected the U.S. President, defeating Republican Governor Alf Landon* of Kansas.	The Jewish vote in the U.S. presidential election is estimated at 85% for Franklin D. Roosevelt* and 15% for Alf Landon.*		The British Royal Commission headed by Lord Peel* (1867–1937) arrives in Palestine to examine the situation. It holds 66 meetings prior to publishing its findings in July 1937. The Arabs boycott the proceedings until the 56th meeting.		**Nov. 1936**
King Edward VIII* of England abdicates the throne to marry an American divorcée, Wallis Warfield Simpson.*					**Dec. 1936**
John Gunther* (1901–1970), U.S. foreign correspondent, writes a best-seller, *Inside Europe*, in which he reports of the depth and breadth of Nazi Germany's antisemitism. Walt Disney* produces *Snow White and the Seven Dwarfs*, the first full-length movie cartoon.	Moses Feinstein (1895–1986), U.S. Orthodox rabbinical leader, emigrates to the U.S. from Russia. He is appointed head of New York's Mesivta Tiferet Jerusalem. He is a leading halakhic authority, and his opinions on contemporary society and modern science in the light of the	The Nazis order all works by Marc Chagall in German museums taken down. The Nazis hold the exhibition Degenerate Art in Munich, which includes works of famous 20th-century Jewish artists. F. L. Destouches,* the French doctor who used the pen	The Haganah establishes the Committee for Illegal Immigration to rescue European Jews and facilitate their illegal entry and absorption into the Palestinian population. The Haganah reaches an agreement with the Polish government for the supply of rifles, machine guns, and	Meyer Levin, U.S. novelist and journalist, writes *The Old Bunch*, a "collective" novel of a "bunch" of second-generation Jews growing to young adulthood in the Chicago of the 1930s. Arthur Kober (1900–1974), U.S. playwright, writes *Having a Wonderful Time*, a comic play	**1937**

	A. General History	B. Jews in North and South America	C. Jews in Europe	D. Jews in the Middle East and Elsewhere	E. Jewish Culture
1937	The NBC Symphony Orchestra is established for Arturo Toscanini.*	*halakhah* guide Orthodox Jewry throughout the world.	name Celine, writes the antisemitic diatribe, *Bagatelle pour un Massacre*, arguing that France is a country occupied by Jews and that a German invasion would be a liberation. Jean-Richard Bloch (1884–1947), French political journalist, and Louis Aragon* found the Communist daily newspaper *Ce Soir*. Polish anti-Jewish boycott activities receive the official approval of Prime Minister Felicjan Slawoj-Skaladowski.* In Poland there are 136 yeshivot with about 12,000 students.	ammunition to be clandestinely transported to Palestine in steamrollers and other types of machinery. Haganah instructors are permitted to train Jews in Poland expecting to settle in Palestine and to utilize Polish arms. The South African Aliens Act closes a loophole in the Quota Act of 1930 and halts the entry of Jews fleeing from Nazi Germany into South Africa. Arthur Biram (1878–1967), principal of Haifa's Reali High School, initiates a paramilitary training program for his students.	describing summer resort life of Bronx Jews of the type he popularized in his *New Yorker* sketches. Jerome Weidman writes *I Can Get It for You Wholesale*, the story of Harry Bogen and how he ruthlessly rose from shipping clerk to wealthy garment manufacturer. This portrayal of an unpleasant Jewish character will be continued in a sequel, *What's in It for Me?* (1938). Leo Rosten's (b. 1908) stories, originally published in *The New Yorker* magazine, are collected into the best-selling *The Education of Hyman Kaplan*. The stories are of Kaplan and other new Americans in Mr. Parkhill's English classroom. Kaplan, the "greenhorn," is immune to the correction or refinement of his speech. Marc Blitzstein (1905–1964), U.S. composer, writes *The Cradle Will Rock*, a play in music with an anticapitalist theme. Originated as a Works Progress Administration theater project, it is banned by the government and is performed privately. Paul Muni (Muni Weisenfreund, 1895–1967) stars in the *Life of Emile Zola*, which receives an Academy Award for best picture. The main theme of the film is the Dreyfus case. Antisemitism, which destroyed Dreyfus' career, is completely ignored. The word *Jew* is absent from the script.
Jan. 1937	Karl Radek (1885–1939?) and other Soviet leaders are arrested by Joseph Stalin* and placed on "show trials" and convicted. Later in the year, Stalin* purge trials continue as Marshal Tukhachevsky* and other Soviet generals are tried and executed. The purge trials will continue in 1938.				
Mar. 1937	Pope Pius XI (1857–1939) issues an encyclical "With Burning Anxiety," which rejects the race-conscious myths of "race" and "blood" as contrary to Christian truth but does not mention nor directly criticize antisemitism.				
Apr. 1937	In April, German aircraft, assisting the nationalists in the Spanish civil war, destroy the city of Guernica. Guernica becomes an anti-Fascist symbol and will be memorialized by				

A. General History	B. Jews in North and South America	C. Jews in Europe	D. Jews in the Middle East and Elsewhere	E. Jewish Culture	
Pablo Picasso's* famous painting.				Joseph Schildkraut (1895–1964), as Dreyfus, wins an Academy Award as best supporting actor.	**April 1937**
Neville Chamberlain* succeeds Stanley Baldwin* as prime minister of Great Britain.	The Central Conference of American Rabbis (Reform), meeting in Columbus, Ohio, adopts a new platform, superseding the Pittsburgh Platform of 1885, that is more traditional in the observance of Judaism and affirms the obligation of Jews to aid in rebuilding a Jewish homeland in Palestine.				**May 1937**
				The Jewish Museum in Berlin holds an exhibition in honor of the 500th anniversary of the birth of Don Isaac Abrabanel (1437-1508), with a catalog by Rachel Wischnitzer (1892–1989). Later in the year, it holds an exhibition on the 100th anniversary of the death of Akiba Eger (1761-1837), the grand rabbi of Posen, with a catalog by Rachel Wischnitzer. It is probably the last Jewish exhibit in Germany before the Holocaust.	**July 1937**
Japan attacks China, triggering a full-scale Sino-Japanese war that lasts until 1945. U.S. President Franklin D. Roosevelt's* plan to increase the number of Supreme Court justices is defeated by Congress. Pastor Martin Niemoller is arrested because of his opposition to the control of the Protestant church by the German government. He is acquitted but will be rearrested in 1938 and sent to a concentration camp. The Nazis open the Buchenwald concentration camp. It first houses professional criminals. Jewish political prisoners will begin arriving in June 1938.	THE PEEL COMMISSION PARTITION PLAN, 1937 		The Peel* Commission recommends the partition of Palestine into a Jewish state and an Arab state and a British enclave around Jerusalem, Bethlehem, Lydda, Ramleh, and Jaffa. The British government issues a White Paper approving the commission's recommendations. The Zionist leadership welcomes the plan and the Arabs reject it.	Jiri Langer (1894–1943), Czech poet and author, writes *Nine Gates to the Chassidic Mysteries*, a volume of Hasidic tales, later translated from Czech into German, Italian, and English. Born to an acculturated upper-class family, Langer left his native Prague in 1913 for the Hasidic community of Belz. He taught Hebrew to his friend Franz Kafka (1883–1924). He will flee to Palestine after the Nazi invasion of Czechoslovakia.	
			An Arab congress convenes in Bludan, Syria. Plans for an armed struggle against the British in Palestine are formulated and the Arab revolt resumes. Arabs assassinate Lewis Andrews,* British district commissioner in Galilee. In retaliation, the British disband the Arab Higher	Yehezkel Kaufmann (1889–1963), biblical scholar who emigrated to Palestine from Europe in 1928, begins publishing his *History of the Israelite Religion*, a history from ancient times to the end of the Second Temple. He writes that Israel's monotheism was a distinctly new idea characterizing the Israelite religion from the time of Moses. This work will be	**Sept 1937**

	A. General History	B. Jews in North and South America	C. Jews in Europe	D. Jews in the Middle East and Elsewhere	E. Jewish Culture
Sept. 1937				Committee, arrest its leaders, and expel them to the Seychelle Islands.	completed in 1957. In 1949 he will be appointed professor of Bible at the Hebrew University, a post he will hold until his death.
Oct. 1937			Anti-Jewish riots inspired by local Nazis break out in the free city of Danzig. Half of the city's Jews leave within one year.		
Dec. 1937	The Japanese capture the Chinese city of Nanking. They destroy a third of the city and kill over 200,000 civilians in what is known as the Rape of Nanking. Japanese aircraft bomb and sink a U.S. naval gunboat, the *Panay*, on China's Yangtze River.		King Carol II* of Romania names Octavian Goga,* an antisemitic Fascist, to head the government. Goga establishes a dictatorship and restricts and harasses Jews.		
1938	The Committee on Un-American Activities of the U.S. House of Representatives is formed to investigate Communist, Fascist, Nazi, and other "un-American" groups. The commercial production of nylon begins.	Msgr. John Oesterreicher arrives in the U.S. from Nazi Europe, where he militantly defended Jews against Nazi antisemitism, and founds the Institute of Judeo-Christian Studies at Seton Hall University. Admiral Claude Bloch (1878–1967) is named commander-in-chief of the U.S. fleet, a post he holds until 1940. Barney Josephson (1902–1988) opens the Cafe Society nightclub in New York. His club breaks rigid racial barriers by being the first to open its doors to racially mixed audiences. He presents black performers such as Billie Holiday* and Hazel Scott.* Three thousand Landsmanschaften organizations in New York are recorded in a Works Progress Administration survey.	Graham Greene,* English novelist, writes *Brighton Express*, a novel in which the notorious Jewish gang leader Colleoni leads Pinkie, the hero, to damnation.	To combat Arab terrorism, the British and Jewish Agency, under the auspices of the Haganah command, establish the Notrim and the Jewish Settlement Police to guard government facilities and Jewish settlements. Orde Wingate* (1903–1944), British officer sympathetic to Zionism, organizes special Jewish "night squads" of Haganah and British troops to use guerilla tactics to clear areas of Galilee of Arab terrorists. This period of British–Jewish cooperation in the mandate is known as "the honeymoon." George Antonius,* a Western-educated Arab, writes *The Arab Awakening*, a serious presentation of the Arab Palestine case to the Western world. He condemns Adolf Hitler's* treatment of the Jews. "To place the brunt of the burden on Arab Palestine is a	Henry "Hank" Greenberg, first baseman of the Detroit Tigers, ties the major and American League baseball record for the most home runs (58) by a right-handed batter. Beatrice Bisno, U.S. novelist, writes *Tomorrow's Bread*, a novel of a Russian Jew in Chicago's garment industry during the 1890s. Irving Berlin's famous patriotic song "God Bless America" is sung for the first time by Kate Smith.* The song is soon considered America's second national anthem. Eugene Ormandy (1899–1985) becomes the music director and principal conductor of the Philadelphia Orchestra, from which he will retire 40 years later in 1980. Benny Goodman performs jazz with his swing band in concert at New York's Carn—

A. General History	B. Jews in North and South America	C. Jews in Europe	D. Jews in the Middle East and Elsewhere	E. Jewish Culture	
		*Founding of Hanita, a "tower and stockade" settlement in western Galilee.*	miserable evasion of the duty that lies upon the whole of the civilized world. It is also morally outrageous. No code of morals can justify the persecution of one people in an attempt to relieve the persecution of another."	egie Hall, featuring solos by Ziggy Elman, Lionel Hampton,* Harry James (1916–1953), and Gene Krupa.* Jerry Siegel and Joe Shuster introduce a new comic strip character, Superman, which will influence American comic strip development.	**1938**
		Romania adopts a law abrogating the minority rights of Jews—established in 1918—resulting in the deprivation of citizenship to many Jews living in Romania since 1918.		Burrill Bernhard Crohn, U.S. gastroenterologist, describes granulomatous colitis, or Crohn's disease of the colon. Mordecai Gebertig (1877–1942), Yiddish folk singer and composer, writes his most famous song, "Undzer Shtetl	**Jan. 1938**
Germany invades and annexes Austria. At the time of the Anschluss (Annexation), there are 181,778 Jews in Austria, of whom 165,946 live in Vienna. Restrictions and discrimination against German Jews are extended to Austrian Jews.		The Nazis impound Sigmund Freud's passport and take his money in order to prevent him and his family from leaving Austria, resulting in a horrified world reaction.	Four hundred Haganah troops found Hanita, a "tower and stockade" settlement in Western Galilee. It is one of 52 such settlements established to guard the Jewish community during the three-year period of the Arab revolt.	Brent" ("Our Town Is Burning"), after the pogrom in Przytyk. It becomes an anthem sung by the ghetto fighters of World War II. Gebertig and his family will be murdered by the Germans. Sergei Eisenstein, Russian film director, wins the Order of Lenin for his film *Alexander Nevsky.*	**Mar. 1938**
	A public opinion poll reveals that about 60% of Americans believe that persecution of European Jews was either entirely or partly their own fault.	German Jews are required to inform authorities of their property worth over 5,000 marks. The Nazi party newspaper, *Volkischer Beobachter*, begins a new antisemitic campaign. "Jews, abandon all hope. Our net is so fine that there is not a hole through which you can slip." Within one month of the Nazi occupation, more than 500 Jews commit suicide in Austria.		Harry Torczyner (Naphtali Herz Tur-Sinai, 1866–1975), Israeli philologist and Bible scholar, writes *The Lachish Letters*, in which he deciphers a collection of Hebrew letters from the biblical period. He left Germany in 1933 for Palestine, where he became professor of Hebrew language at the Hebrew University. He will write commentaries on the Book of Job, espousing the theory that Job is a translation of an Aramaic original, and will complete the	**Apr. 1938**

Jews forced to scrub streets of Vienna, March 1938.

	A. General History	B. Jews in North and South America	C. Jews in Europe	D. Jews in the Middle East and Elsewhere	E. Jewish Culture
May 1938			Hungary adopts the first Jewish law, restricting to 20% the number of Jews in the liberal professions, in commercial and industrial enterprises, and in the government.		17-volume historical dictionary of Hebrew begun by Eliezer Ben-Yehuda (1858–1922).
June 1938			The Nazis require the registration and marking of German Jewish-owned businesses.	The British execute Shelomo Ben-Yosef (Tabachnik, 1913–1938). The first Jew executed by the British in Palestine, he was caught on April 21 in a failed attempt to attack an Arab bus in retaliation for the Arab murder of Jews. He was an illegal immigrant from Poland, arriving in 1937.	
July 1938	A *Fortune* magazine public opinion survey reveals that less than 5% of Americans favor expanding immigration quotas, while 67% favor exclusion of refugees. U.S. President Franklin D. Roosevelt* convenes a conference on the German refugee problem at Evian, France. It is held because of the League of Nations' inability to deal with conditions in Germany and is attended by 32 nations. The results are negligible with only the Dominican Republic offering to accept refugees. The Australian delegate tells the conference, "It will no doubt be appreciated that as we have no racial problem, we are not desirous of importing one."	The Roman Catholic priest James E. Coughlin, whose antisemitic diatribes are aired over the radio and printed in his magazine, *Social Justice*, charges in the magazine that Jews are guilty of deicide and unscrupulous money-lending practices, control international banking, and are responsible for the success of the Russian Revolution. Coughlin, "the radio priest," holds Jews responsible for the nation's ills and is considered the most dangerous antisemite of the decade.	Munich's main synagogue is demolished on Adolf Hitler's* express orders. Licenses of German Jewish physicians and in September licenses of German Jewish lawyers are withdrawn.	British troops are sent to Palestine to assist in suppressing the Arab uprising and controlling terrorism.	
Aug. 1938			Nuremberg's main synagogue and communal center are demolished by the Nazis.		

A. General History	B. Jews in North and South America	C. Jews in Europe	D. Jews in the Middle East and Elsewhere	E. Jewish Culture	
		Finland refuses to permit 53 Austrian Jewish refugees arriving by sea to disembark and orders their return to Germany. The official in the Finnish embassy in Vienna gave entry visas to the Jews without obtaining governmental permission. German Jews are ordered to use only Jewish first names. Those with Aryan first names had to substitute "Israel" or "Sarah" for their names. SS Officer Adolf Eichmann* (1906–1962) establishes a Center for Jewish Emigration in Vienna, Austria, to supervise Jewish emigration.			**Aug. 1938**
Leaders of Germany (Hitler*), Italy (Mussolini*), France (Daladier*), and Great Britain (Chamberlain*) meet at the Munich Conference and agree to the annexation of part of Czechoslovakia, the Sudetenland, to Germany.		The Italian government passes "racial" legislation against the Jews, barring them from studying or teaching in a school of higher learning and revoking the citizenship of all foreign Jews obtained after January 1919 and decreeing their expulsion within six months. In November, further discriminatory legislation will be passed, including the prohibition of marriages between Jews and Aryans and the exclusion of Jews from military and civil administrative positions. Pope Pius XI, in an address to a group of Belgian pilgrims, declares, "It is not possible for Christians to take part in anti-Semitism. Spiritually we are Semites." This statement is omitted			**Sept. 1938**

	A. General History	B. Jews in North and South America	C. Jews in Europe	D. Jews in the Middle East and Elsewhere	E. Jewish Culture
Sept. 1938			from all Italian newspaper accounts of the address.		
Oct. 1938	German troops occupy the Sudetenland, annexing 10,000 square miles of Czech territory with a population of 3.5 million. More than 20,000 Jews live in the Sudetenland. Most flee to the Czechoslovakian provinces of Bohemia and Moravia.		The Nazis require the stamping of the letter *J* on all passports of German Jews. At the end of October, 15,000 Jews living in Germany who are Polish citizens are forcibly returned to the Polish border. At first, Poland does not allow them to reenter the country, and they are trapped in a no-man's-land or held in the border town of Zbaszyn. After international public opinion is aroused, some are reluctantly taken into Poland, others are returned to Germany, and some are sent to concentration camps.	Great Britain sends more troops to Palestine as riots continue. The Arab assault on the Jewish community reaches a new height when 19 Jews are killed in an attack on Tiberias. British reinforcements reconquer the Old City of Jerusalem, which was in control of Arab bands for five days.	
Nov. 1938		The *New York Times* in an editorial, opposes the partition of Palestine and suggests the resettlement of Jews on the African continent. President Franklin D. Roosevelt* recalls American Ambassador Hugh Wilson* from Germany to express U.S. outrage at *Kristallnacht.*	Herschel Grynszpan (1921– ?) assassinates Ernst vom Rath,* counsellor at the German embassy in Paris. He declares he avenged the injustice done by Nazis to his parents, who were expelled to Poland. Under the pretext of retaliation of the Vom Rath* assassination, *Kristallnacht* (Night of the Broken Glass) riots occur in Germany and Austria. The Nazis set fire to 191 synagogues. Ninety-one Jews are killed. More than 30,000, or more than one in 10 of Germany's remaining Jews, are arrested and sent to concentration camps. The Nazis break into and loot thousands of homes and shops. A fine of 1 billion marks is imposed upon all German Jewry. The Nazis require the Aryanization and/or liquidation of German	The high costs of providing security to the Jewish community in Palestine is met by a tax, Kofer ha-Yishuv, voluntarily levied to finance Haganah activities. November 1 is designated as a day for donating jewelry.	

A. General History	B. Jews in North and South America	C. Jews in Europe	D. Jews in the Middle East and Elsewhere	E. Jewish Culture
		Jewish-owned retail businesses.

Hermann Goering* Nazi leader, at a high-level meeting, states: "Should the Reich become involved in an international conflict in the foreseeable future, we in Germany will obviously have to think about settling our accounts with the Jews."

Jewish children are prohibited from attending German public schools. | | **Nov. 1938** |
| | | The remaining 6,000 Jews of the free city of Danzig develop an "orderly" plan with the Nazi government to leave Danzig by May 1939 (later extended until the fall of 1939). Under an agreement with Nazi officials to finance the emigration, they negotiate the sale of Jewish communal property, including the historic Danzig Great Synagogue, which will be torn down in 1939, and the cemetery. The American Joint Distribution Committee "purchases" the ritual collection, which is sent to the Jewish Theological Seminary of America.

Lise Meitner (1878–1968), German physicist, who fled to Sweden earlier in the year, and her nephew, Otto Robert Frisch, German physicist, who fled to Denmark, meet to discuss the research of former colleagues Otto Hahn* and Fritz Strassmann.* They realize that Hahn* and Strassmann* had achieved atomic fission by splitting the uranium atom | The Arab revolt has deteriorated to blood feuds and civil war among Arab clans. The Nashashibi family of Jerusalem organizes the Peace Bands, who initiated campaigns of counterterror against the Mufti and the Arab Higher Committee. During the Arab revolt, more Arabs are killed than Jews or Englishmen. | **Dec. 1938** |

	A. General History	B. Jews in North and South America	C. Jews in Europe	D. Jews in the Middle East and Elsewhere	E. Jewish Culture
Dec. 1938			resulting in a tremendous release of energy. They advise their colleague Niels Bohr, who informs scientists in the U.S. Frisch coins the term *nuclear fission*. The British cabinet decides to allow 10,000 German Jewish children to enter England on the condition that refugee organizations agree to maintain them. It rejects an appeal from the Jewish Agency for an additional 21,000 certificates for admission to Palestine. The Nazis require the Aryanization and/or liquidation of German Jewish-owned industrial enterprises.		
1939	Cardinal Pacelli (1876–1958) is elected Pope Pius XII. The Baseball Hall of Fame at Cooperstown, New York, is dedicated.	The Jewish community of Danzig sends its collection of Jewish art to the Jewish Theological Seminary of America for safekeeping. The collection will be displayed in 1980 at a Jewish Museum of New York exhibition, Danzig 1939: Treasures of a Destroyed Community. It will then tour worldwide. Joseph Breuer, German Orthodox rabbi, emigrates to the U.S. from Frankfurt and becomes the spiritual leader of the German Jewish community of Washington Heights, New York. It is a continuation of the the Orthodox community established in Frankfurt in 1849 and led by Samson Raphael Hirsch (1808–1888), his maternal grandfather. Agudat Israel of America is founded. It is part of a worldwide		Max Brod, Czech author and composer, settles in Palestine and becomes a drama adviser to the Habimah Theater. Brod was the first to recognize the brilliance of novelist Franz Kafka (1883–1924) and arranged in the 1930s for the posthumous publication of Kafka's works. Umberto Cassuto (1883-1951) leaves a professorship of Hebrew at the University of Rome to become professor of Bible at the Hebrew University. Italian racial laws made it impossible for him to remain in Italy. The Nazis will murder his son, Nathan, in 1945.	The publication of *The Universal Jewish Encyclopedia*, edited by Isaac Landman (1880–1946), begins in the U.S. This 10-volume work will be completed in 1943. Milton Steinberg (1903–1950), U.S. Conservative rabbi, writes *As a Driven Leaf*, a novel set in talmudic times dealing with the conflict of religion and philosophy that the life of the heretic Elisha ben Avuyah represents. Edna Ferber writes her first autobiography, *A Peculiar Treasure*. It is dedicated "to Adolf Hitler, who made me a better Jew and a more understanding and tolerant human being, as he has of millions of other Jews, this book is dedicated in loathing and contempt." She has anti-Zionist feelings, which will not be changed by a visit to Israel after its creation.

1939

movement, founded in Europe in 1912, that represents the largest organized force in the European Orthodox world before the advent of Adolf Hitler.*

The American Association of Jewish Education is founded to promote raising instructional and professional service standards in Jewish education.

Louis Buchalter (Lepke, 1897–1944), U.S. gangster, surrenders to FBI Director J. Edgar Hoover* on a narcotics charge. The surrender was arranged by radio commentator Walter Winchell (1897–1972). Lepke will be tried in New York for a murder committed in 1936, found guilty, and executed in 1944.

Lionel Trilling (1905–1975), critic and English professor, is appointed assistant professor of English literature at Columbia University. He had served as an instructor for several years and overcame antisemitic discrimination to become the first Jewish professor in the department.

Thomas Wolfe's* (1900–1938) posthumous autobiographical novel, *The Web and the Rock*, describes his relationship with Aline Bernstein, his mistress of six years and his ambivalent feelings toward Jews.

Anatole Litvak directs the Warner Brothers film *Confessions of a Nazi Spy*, Hollywood's most determined anti-Nazi statement prior to the U.S. entry into World War II. Based on an ex-FBI

Irving Fineman, U.S. novelist, writes *Doctor Addams*, a novel about the adjustment to the U.S. of a cultivated refugee from Nazism.

Danny Kaye (David Kaminski, 1913–1987), U.S. comedian and actor, puts on *The Straw Hat Revue* at Tamiment, a Pennsylvania Jewish summer resort, in collaboration with his wife, Sylvia Fine. The show makes it to Broadway and launches his career in comedy and music.

Harry James, jazz trumpeter and band leader, forms his own band, which emerges as one of the best-known swing ensembles of the big band era, featuring the singer Frank Sinatra* and the drummer Buddy Rich.

Harold Arlen (Hyman Arluck, 1905–1986), the son of a cantor, composes the musical score for the movie *The Wizard of Oz*, including "Over the Rainbow," the song that brings fame to Judy Garland.*

Sholem Asch writes *The Nazarene*, one of a trilogy of novels on Christological themes, which presents Jesus as the last and greatest Jewish prophet. The other two novels are *The Apostle* (1943), about St. Paul, and *Mary* (1949), about the Virgin Mary. Jewish critics accuse Asch of being an apostate, a missionary trying to convince Jews of the acceptability of Jesus. Asch maintains he had written the novels to place the protagonists within the framework of Jewish life to show how innately Jewish they are. Asch

	A. General History	B. Jews in North and South America	C. Jews in Europe	D. Jews in the Middle East and Elsewhere	E. Jewish Culture
1939		agent's articles, the film combines a semifictional story of Nazi activities in the U.S. with newsreel footage. Jewish characters are absent. Edward G. Robinson heads the FBI team and Paul Lukas heads the American Nazi group.			withdraws from New York Jewish literary circles. Nathanael West, U.S. novelist, writes *The Day of the Locust*, a mélange of degenerate characters in a Hollywood setting, symbolizing his belief in the falsity of American values.
Jan. 1939	Barcelona falls to the Spanish nationalists.	A Gallup poll finds 66% opposed to a plan to allow 10,000 refugee children from Germany to be brought to the U.S. and to be cared for in American homes. Felix Frankfurter is appointed to the U.S. Supreme Court by President Franklin D. Roosevelt.* He replaces the deceased Justice Benjamin Nathan Cardozo and will serve until 1965.	German Jews are required to carry identification cards. The German Foreign Office advises its representatives abroad that "the ultimate aim of Germany's Jewish policy [is] the emigration of all Jews living on German territory." Adolf Hitler,* speaking in Berlin, states: "If international-finance Jewry inside and outside Europe should succeed once more in plunging the nations into yet another world war, the consequence will not be the Bolshevization of the earth and thereby the victory of Jewry, but the annihilation of the Jewish race in Europe."		Cecil Roth, English historian, is appointed reader in Jewish studies at Oxford and will serve until his retirement in 1964. Roth will write the standard history of the Jews of England (3rd edition, 1964) and of Italy (1946). An expert in the field of Jewish art, he will edit a *History of Jewish Art* (1971) as well as facsimile editions of several Haggadot. He will serve as editor-in-chief of the *Encyclopedia Judaica*. Sigmund Freud writes his last book, *Moses and Monotheism*, in which he tries to diagnose the origin and special characteristics of the Jewish people. Moses was an Egyptian and not a Jew; he taught monotheism to the Jews; he was killed by rebellious Jews; and this act of patricide gave rise to an unconscious guilt feeling that is the hidden trauma of the Jews. Today's Jews should abandon their ethnic separatism and assimilate and thus return to health. Jews and non-Jews strongly react to the book.
Feb. 1939		Fritz Kuhn,* leader of the German–American Bund, addressing more than 22,000 followers at New York's Madison Square Garden, denounces Jews for their opposition to German Nazism.	Great Britain convenes the St. James Round Table Conference of Palestine Arabs, Arab states, and the Jewish Agency in London. Arabs refuse to sit with Jews. The Arab states are acknowledged as parties to the Arab–Jewish dispute. The British propose an independent Palestinian state in alliance with Great Britain and phased in over a 10-year period. Seventy-five thousand Jews would be permitted to immigrate within the first five years, with subsequent immigration subject to		The publication of *Yediot Ahronot*, a Hebrew-language daily afternoon newspaper, begins in Tel Aviv. Its tabloid layout is an innovation in Hebrew journalism in Palestine.

A. General History	B. Jews in North and South America	C. Jews in Europe	D. Jews in the Middle East and Elsewhere	E. Jewish Culture	
German troops cross the frontier and occupy Czechoslovakia. The Spanish civil war ends as Madrid is formally surrendered to the nationalist leader, General Francisco Franco.*		Arab agreement. All parties reject the proposals. It is estimated that between 20,000 and 50,000 foreigners fought on the Loyalist side during the Spanish civil war. Of these, it is estimated that Jews numbered between 6,000 and 7,000, and 40% of the Americans in the Lincoln Brigade.	Mohandas K. Gandhi* declares that Palestine belongs to the Arabs.	Pinkhes Kahanovich (1884–1950), Russian Yiddish writer, writes the first volume of his novel, *The Family Mashber*, under the pseudonym Der Nister (The Concealed One). This family saga, of which two volumes are known to exist, depicts traditional eastern European Jewish society from the 1870s to the Russian Revolution.	**Mar. 1939**
Italy invades and annexes Albania. The New York World's Fair opens. Palestine participates with its own pavilion.	A *Fortune* magazine survey finds that 85% of non-Jews polled are opposed to relaxing immigration quotas. Of the Jews polled, 22% are against any change.				**Apr. 1939**
		More than 900 German Jewish refugees arrive at Cuba aboard the German passenger ship SS *St. Louis* and are refused entry on the grounds that their entry permits are invalid. The U.S. also refuses entry, and the refugees return to Europe, where they are admitted to England, Belgium, Holland, and France. Hungary adopts the second Jewish law, further reducing the number of Jews in economic activity to 5% and restricting their political rights.	Zionists establish 12 new settlements in Palestine in protest of the British policy, with seven being formed on one day. British Colonial Secretary Malcolm MacDonald* issues a White Paper proposing an independent Palestinian state within 10 years; permitting 75,000 Jews to enter Palestine within five years, with subsequent immigration subject to Arab consent; and immediately prohibiting the sale of land to Jews. In effect, the British government repudiated the Balfour Declaration. The White Paper is never endorsed by the League of Nations nor agreed to by the Zionists, the Palestinian Arabs, or the Arab states. MacDonald* describes the background of the White Paper in an interview that will be shown on Israeli		**May 1939**

A. General History	B. Jews in North and South America	C. Jews in Europe	D. Jews in the Middle East and Elsewhere	E. Jewish Culture

May 1939

World Jewish Population, 1939

Total World Population 2,296,000,000
Total World Jewish Population 16,648,000

Place	Number	% of World Jewry
Europe	9,462,000	56.8
Americas	5,556,000	33.4
Asia	1,008,000	6.1
Africa	594,000	3.6
Australia & New Zealand	28,000	.1

Countries of Largest Jewish Population, 1939

Country	Jewish Population
United States	4,870,000
Poland	3,300,000
U.S.S.R.	3,060,000
Rumania	800,000
Palestine	475,000
Hungary	403,000
Great Britain	390,000
Argentina	350,000
Czechoslovakia	315,000
France	300,000
Germany	215,000

Major Jewish Cities, 1939

City	Jewish Population	Total Population	Jewish Pop. as % of Total Population
New York City (1940)	2,085,000	7,455,000	28.0
Moscow	400,000	3,663,000	10.9
Warsaw	365,000	1,265,700	28.8
Chicago	363,000	3,384,500	10.7
Philadelphia	293,000	1,951,000	15.0
Leningrad	275,000	3,191,000	8.6
London	250,000	8,655,000	2.9
Lodz	220,000	665,000	33.1
Paris	200,000	2,830,000	7.0
Budapest	180,000	1,586,000	11.3
Odessa	180,000	604,000	29.8
Kiev	175,000	846,000	20.7
Kharkov	150,000	833,000	18.0
Tel Aviv	140,000	140,000	10.0
Boston	118,000	781,000	15.1
Lvov	105,000	317,700	33.0

NOTE: Vienna's population was estimated at 91,500, down from 178,000 in 1933 and Berlin's population was 82,788, down from 160,564 in 1933.

June 1939

July 1939

Column D (continued from above):

television in 1981: "We were very sad . . . that we had to take this decision because of . . . the certajnty of war. We would have liked to have considerably more Jewish immigration. . . . Now, there was a little bit of cynicsm . . . in our policy on Palestine. . . . We knew the Jews would be on our side in the war whatever happened. . . . The Arab position was much more uncertain. . . . Therefore we probably made more concessions to the Arabs than we would otherwise have done, because of the crisis which was going to face us."

The League of Nations Permanent Mandates Commission unanimously decides that Britain's Palestine White Paper is a gross violation of international law and is "not in accordance with the interpretation which . . . the Commission had placed on the Palestine Mandate."

Column C (July 1939):

The Nazis create the Reichsvereinigung. This compulsory organization of all Jews in Nazi Germany replaces the existing Jewish communal organization and is supervised by the security police. It enables the Nazis to funnel some of their deadliest orders through one centralized Jewish organization and thereby play off the Jewish leadership against the Jewish population.

Britain's Prime Minister Neville Chamberlain* writes a private letter in which

A. General History	B. Jews in North and South America	C. Jews in Europe	D. Jews in the Middle East and Elsewhere	E. Jewish Culture

he discusses the Nazi persecution of the Jews. "I believe the persecution arose out of two motives: a desire to rob the Jews of their money and a jealousy of their superior cleverness. . . . No doubt Jews aren't a lovable people; I don't care about them myself; but that is not sufficient to explain the Pogrom."

Albert Einstein writes to U.S. President Franklin D. Roosevelt* advising of the military potential of atomic energy. His letter leads to the Manhattan Project and the development of the atomic bomb. He writes at the urging of Leo Szilard (1898–1964), Hungarian nuclear physicist, who is alarmed that Nazi Germany might develop the bomb.

V. M. Molotov* and Joachim von Ribbentrop,* foreign ministers of the Soviet Union and Germany, sign a German–Russian nonaggression pact in Moscow. They secretly carve out spheres of influence in eastern and central Europe, with Russia getting eastern Poland, Bessarabia, Finland, Estonia, Latvia, and Lithuania.

The 21st Zionist Congress convenes in Geneva under the leadership of Chaim Weizmann. In the aftermath of the White Paper, David Ben-Gurion proposes a program of noncooperation with the British, and the Jewish Agency sanctions illegal immigration.

Chaim Weizmann (hand on briefcase), David Ben-Gurion (arms crossed), and Moshe Shertok (far left) at the 21st Zionist Congress. They have just heard the news of the Nazi-Soviet Non-Aggression Pact. (Central Zionist Archives)

Germany invades Poland. Great Britain and France order total mobilization and on September 3 declare war on Germany. It is the beginning of World War II.

Adolf Hitler* personally orders the first Nazi program of murder, a "euthanasia program." Known as T4, over 70,000 mentally ill or

Reinhard Heydrich* (1904–1942) holds a conference in Berlin of his Einsatzgruppen chiefs and directs them, as the first prerequisite of the "ultimate aim," which is to be kept a "total secret," to clear Jews out of western Poland, concentrate them in ghettoes in larger cities, and near railway junctions or along a railway "so

A ship carrying illegal immigrants is intercepted by the British off the coast of Palestine. Shots are fired, and three Jews are killed. The incident happens on the day Adolf Hitler* invades Poland.

After the outbreak of World War II, David Ben-Gurion states the Jews of Palestine "shall fight the war as

	A. General History	B. Jews in North and South America	C. Jews in Europe	D. Jews in the Middle East and Elsewhere	E. Jewish Culture
Sep. 1939	otherwise "hopelessly" ill Germans—none Jewish—are killed between September 1939 and the late summer of 1941 under this operation. The victims are gassed. The Soviet Union invades Poland from the east. Ten days later, Warsaw surrenders to the Nazi invaders. Germany and the Soviet Union sign a friendship and boundary treaty outlining the Polish territory each will occupy.		that future measures may be accomplished more easily." After the commencement of World War II, the Nazis maintain a policy of permitting mass immigration of Jews from the Greater Reich until the end of 1941. During the period, 71,500 Jews manage to flee. In the six-week period between the end of September and the middle of November, more than 250,000 Polish Jews flee eastward to the Soviet zone of Poland and to the Soviet Union. By September, 109,000 Jews have succeeded in emigrating from Nazi-held Austria, leaving 66,000 remaining at the outbreak of World War II.	if there were no White Paper, and the White Paper as if there were no war." Yaakov Dori becomes chief of staff of the Haganah. He will serve in that post until the end of the War of Independence.	
Oct. 1939	Adolf Hitler* issues a secret order appointing Heinrich Himmler* Reich Commissar for the Strengthening of German Nationhood. He is to (1) repatriate German residents abroad who are suitable for permanent return, (2) eliminate those sections of the population of foreign origin that constitute a danger to the Reich, and (3) form new German settlement areas by transfers of population.		Germany begins deporting Austrian and Czech Jews to Poland. Hans Frank* (1900–1946) is named governor-general of the German-occupied Polish territories under the general government. He becomes responsible for the persecution and plundering of the Polish population and the extermination of its Jews. Frank announces that all Jews between the ages of 14 and 60 will be required to work and will be organized in forced labor teams in labor camps. The Nazis establish the first Polish ghetto, in Piotrkow, to confine the Jews. Emanuel Ringelblum (1900–1944), historian of the Warsaw ghetto,	In Palestine, 136,000 Jews register and volunteer for service on behalf of the Allied war effort. Moshe Dayan (1915–1981) and 42 other Haganah men are arrested by the British for carrying arms while training. The British are determined to suppress the Haganah, since the existence of a Jewish military organization would provoke the Arabs, as the Arabs are still being hanged for the possession of arms. They are sentenced to long prison terms and will not be released until February 1941.	

A. General History	B. Jews in North and South America	C. Jews in Europe	D. Jews in the Middle East and Elsewhere	E. Jewish Culture	
		establishes an underground archive and historical institute. Known by the code name Oyneg Shabes (Sabbath Collation), it is a loose association of about 20 researchers who meet in private homes on Saturdays, from which the code name is derived. As October ends, 5,000 Polish Jews are murdered by Germans in the first 55 days of the German conquest of Polish territory.			**Oct. 1939**
The U.S. Congress repeals the Neutrality Law. The "cash and carry" purchase of arms by belligerents is now lawful if the matériel is shipped under the flag of a foreign nation. The repeal is favorable to the French and British. The Soviet Union invades Finland.		The Germans begin the expulsion of 40,000 Jews from western Poland into one of the towns of the general government region of Poland. The Germans execute 53 Warsaw Jews in reprisal for the murder of a Polish policeman by a Jewish ex-convict. This is the first mass arrest and murder of Jews in Warsaw. The Jews in Nazi-occupied Poland are required to wear Star of David identification badges. Hans Frank,* Nazi governor-general of the general government of Poland, orders the formation of Jewish Councils in every Jewish community in the general government of Poland. The Germans intend to issue orders through these councils, which would be responsible for their obedience.			**Nov. 1939**
The Nazi pocket battleship *Graf Spee* is trapped by British warships off the coast of Uruguay, in the mouth of the River Plate. The ship is		On December 19, Hans Frank* writes: "We have now approximately 2,500,000 of them in the General Government and			**Dec. 1939**

	A. General History	B. Jews in North and South America	C. Jews in Europe	D. Jews in the Middle East and Elsewhere	E. Jewish Culture
Dec. 1939	scuttled and its captain commits suicide.		counting half-Jews, perhaps 3,500,000. We cannot shoot 2,500,000 Jews, neither can we poison them. We shall have to take steps, however, designed to extirpate them in some way—and this will be done." The Germans establish a second ghetto in Poland, at Radomsko.		
1940	Color television, developed by Dr. Peter Goldmark,* is demonstrated for the first time.	The Yiddish Scientific Institute (YIVO) moves from Vilna, where it was founded in 1925, to New York and adopts the name YIVO Institute for Jewish Research. Louis Finkelstein (1895–1991), scholar of classical Judaism, becomes president of the Jewish Theological Seminary of America, succeeding Cyrus Adler. Menachem Mendel Schneersohn, the Lubavitcher Rebbe, leader of the Habad Hasidim, arrives in the U.S. as a refugee from Nazism and settles in the Crown Heights section of Brooklyn, New York. Saul Lieberman (1898–1983), trained as a talmudic scholar in Russian yeshivot and who settled in Jerusalem in 1928, joins the faculty of the Jewish Theological Seminary of America as a professor of Talmud. He produced classical critical studies of the Palestinian Talmud while still in Jerusalem. Louis Epstein, U.S. Conservative rabbi and authority on Jewish marriage law, suggests a method for solving the *agunah* problem (a married woman who cannot			The Reform rabbinate of the U.S. issues a revised Union Prayer Book, which is more traditional than the Union Prayer Book of 1894. Sidney Luckman (b. 1916), U.S. professional football player playing with the Chicago Bears, becomes the first great T-formation quarterback. The Bears become league champions. A. M. Klein (1909–1972), Canadian poet, publishes *Hath Not a Jew*, the first of four books of poetry that emphasize his knowledge of talmudic lore and Yiddish folklore, as well as Canadian themes. The others are *The Hitleriad* (1944), *Poems* (1944), and *The Rocking Chair* (1947). Arthur Koestler (1905-1983), Hungarian-born writer who left the Communist party in 1938 at the height of the Stalin* purges, writes *Darkness at Noon*, a novel that is an indictment of Stalinist Russia. Salvador de Madariaga,* Spanish historian, writes *Christopher Columbus*. He claims that Columbus was of Jewish origin, having

A. General History	B. Jews in North and South America	C. Jews in Europe	D. Jews in the Middle East and Elsewhere	E. Jewish Culture	
	remarry after a separation from her husband either because he will not grant her a divorce or because it is unknown whether he is alive). At first, it is accepted by his colleagues but is later rejected because of Orthodox opposition.			been born in Genoa, Italy, of parents who were Jewish or formerly Jewish refugees from Spain.	**1940**

B. Jews in North and South America

Thomas Wolfe's* second autobiographical novel, *You Can't Go Home Again*, includes material from his trip to Germany and his exposure to Nazism, which he believes to be barbaric, manifested by racial nonsense and cruelty.

Ethel Vance's* best-selling novel *Escape* is adapted to the screen and is one of the few films addressing Nazi persecution before the U.S. entry into World War II.

Frank Borzage's* *The Mortal Storm* is Hollywood's first attempt to confront Nazi Germany and Hitler* antisemitism. The story focuses on Professor Viktor Roth, an eminent scientist, from his dismissal to his arrest and his death. It describes the formation of a dictator state. It never uses the word *Jew* and ignores the Jewish problem.

Charles Chaplin* directs *The Great Dictator*, a parody of Adolf Hitler* that also satirizes Benito Mussolini.* The movie openly discusses antisemitic activities and centers around mistaken identities. Chaplin* plays two roles, a Jewish barber and the dictator Hynkel.

The American Agro-Joint (now the Joint Distribution Committee) purchases land in Sosua, the Dominican Republic, and transfers 600 Jews from Germany, France, Poland, and Czechoslovakia. At the July 1938 Evian Conference, Rafael Trujillo,* the country's dictator, offered to absorb 100,000 Jewish refugees.

The various segments of the Jewish community in Chile form a central body, the Representative Committee of the Israelite Community in Chile, to speak for the community in its relations with the general population.

A. General History	B. Jews in North and South America	C. Jews in Europe	D. Jews in the Middle East and Elsewhere	E. Jewish Culture	
		The Germans establish a labor camp for Jews at Belzec. Thousands of Jews from Lublin build fortifications there until it is closed in the autumn of 1940. Emanuel Ringelblum, historian of the Warsaw ghetto, notes that starvation has begun to take its toll, with 50 to 70 deaths daily.			**Jan. 1940**
		The Nazis officially found the Lodz ghetto, an area in the Old City and Baluty quarter, two of the most neglected districts in the city.	Five hundred Palestinian soldiers, Jews and Arabs, leave for France to carry out fortification work on the western front. When war broke out, Jewish volunteers were not accepted in		**Feb. 1940**

Feb. 1940

> *Sixth "Aliyah" to Palestine, 1939–1945*
> *Number:* 62,531
> *Origin:* Refugees from Nazi Europe, including over 12,000 "illegals"; also including over 15,000 Sephardic and Oriental Jews from Yemen (4,7000), Turkey (4,200) and Bulgaria. There were 5 refugee ship disasters resulting in 2,869 deaths: 1939, *Danube*, at Kladovo, 1,160; 1940, *Salvador*, off Turkish coast, 250; 1940, *Patria*, off Haifa, about 280; 1942, *Sturma*, off Istanbul, 769; 1944, *Mefkura*, off Istanbul, 430.

combat units but were sent to the Auxiliary Military Pioneer Corps. The British will later draft Arabs into this corps.

Great Britain begins implementation in Palestine of the land transfer restrictions of the 1939 White Paper.

Mar. 1940

The Russo-Finnish war ends.

Apr. 1940

Germany invades and occupies Denmark. It invades southern Norway and occupies Oslo.

Allied forces, including British, French, and Polish troops, land in northern Norway.

Heinrich Himmler* orders the establishment of the Auschwitz concentration camp in Poland. Known as Auschwitz I, it will never have a large number of Jewish prisoners.

The Nazis begin construction of a wall to enclose the future Warsaw ghetto.

The Nazis close off the Lodz ghetto from the rest of the city. The ghetto contains 164,000 Jews.

Abraham Isaac Alter (1866–1948), the Gerer Rebbe, arrives in Palestine from Poland. He is considered the most prominent figure in European Orthodox Jewry and is a founder of the Agudat Israel movement. This Hasidic dynasty existed in Poland from 1859 to 1939, when the Nazis seized the town of Gur and, in 1941, transferred its Jews to the Warsaw ghetto.

May 1940

A. General History

German forces invade Holland, Belgium, and France (Blitzkrieg).

Neville Chamberlain* resigns and Winston Churchill* becomes prime minister of Great Britain.

Dutch resistance to the Nazis ends. The Netherlands government flees to Great Britain. Nazi Stuka dive bombers raid Rotterdam and destroy 20,000 buildings.

The evacuation of Allied troops from Dunkirk, France, begins. In one week, a hastily assembled fleet of 861 ships and boats evacuates 225,000 British and 113,000 French and Belgian troops to England.

Belgium surrenders to the Nazis.

June 1940

Norway surrenders to the Nazis, who occupy northern Norway as Allied troops are withdrawn.

Italy invades France and declares war on France and Great Britain.

Nazi troops occupy Paris.

France surrenders to Germany. Marshal Philippe Pétain* signs the surrender documents.

The French army commander in Syria accepts the terms of surrender to Germany.

Great Britain recognizes the Free French government headed by General Charles de Gaulle (1890–1970).

Romania capitulates to the Soviet ultimatum and transfers Bessarabia and northern Bukovina to the Soviet Union. It loses 17% of its territory and a population of 3 million. The ceded area becomes the Soviet Moldavian Republic.

A. General History	B. Jews in North and South America	C. Jews in Europe	D. Jews in the Middle East and Elsewhere	E. Jewish Culture	
The French government is moved to Vichy. Great Britain warns it will not allow the Axis to occupy Syria. Marshal Philippe Pétain* is named head of the French (Vichy) government. The Soviet Union occupies Estonia, Lithuania, and Latvia in accordance with a secret agreement with Germany and incorporates them into the Soviet Union.					**July 1940**
German aircraft launch an offensive to cripple the Royal Air Force. The Battle of Britain begins. Leon Trotsky, Soviet Communist leader and rival of Joseph Stalin* who had been exiled in 1929, is assassinated in Mexico City on Stalin's* orders.		The Nazis begin expelling the 80,000 Jews living in Cracow to Warsaw and other Polish towns. By the end of October, 50,000 will be deported. Romania promulgates anti-Jewish laws. Jews are ousted from government employment and forbidden to own agricultural land and trade in villages, and access to universities and high schools is denied. A CBS news correspondent from Berlin reports on the speech by Hans Frank,* Nazi governor-general of occupied Poland, who in announcing plans to make Cracow free of Jews, added: "the Jews must vanish from the face of the earth."			**Aug. 1940**
The U.S. and Great Britain enter into an agreement for the transfer of 50 old U.S. destroyers to Britain in exchange for rights to British air and naval bases in Newfoundland, Bermuda, the Caribbean, and British Guiana. Through the efforts of Colonel William Friedman, leading U.S. cryptanalyst, the		The German occupiers extend the Nuremberg laws to the 4,000 Jews living in Luxembourg and seize all 355 Jewish-owned businesses and hand them over to Aryans. *Jude Suss*, a Nazi propaganda film filled with hatred of the Jews, begins playing throughout Germany and occupied Europe.			**Sep. 1940**

	A. General History	B. Jews in North and South America	C. Jews in Europe	D. Jews in the Middle East and Elsewhere	E. Jewish Culture
Sep. 1940	first complete message transmitted by the Japanese secret diplomatic code Purple is deciphered. Thereafter, the U.S. can read all secret Japanese messages. Germany, Italy, and Japan enter into a 10-year military and economic agreement (Rome–Berlin–Tokyo Axis).		Franz Rademacher,* of the Jewish desk in the German Foreign Office, drafts detailed plans for transferring Jews to the island of Madagascar, in the Indian Ocean. The French ambassador to the Vatican, Leon Berard,* sends a report to Vichy that the Vatican is not interested in French antisemitic laws. The British cabinet agrees to the formation of a Jewish division on the same basis as the Czech and Polish armies in exile. The army would be trained in England, include troops from Palestine, and be shipped back to the Middle East. British bureaucrats and military experts oppose the idea, fearing an Arab rebellion. Between September and November, 3,600 Jewish refugees from Poland, staying in Lithuania, leave for Palestine (1,200) and Japan (2,400). The transfer is arranged through the efforts of the American Joint Distribution Committee.		
Oct. 1940	Romania permits the entry of German troops. Italy invades Greece. While campaigning for reelection to a third term, President Franklin D. Roosevelt states: "I have said this before, but I shall say it again and again and again: your boys are not going to be sent into any foreign wars."		The Nazis establish the Warsaw ghetto, requiring all Jews to move into the ghetto within six weeks. The Nazis deport more than 6,500 German Jews from the Rhineland to internment camps in France, alongside the Pyrenees Mountains bordering Spain. The general government of Poland orders the cessation of granting exit visas to Polish Jews, explaining that Jewish emigration to the U.S.	German and Italian radio stations broadcast an official proclamation in support of Arab independence.	

A. General History	B. Jews in North and South America	C. Jews in Europe	D. Jews in the Middle East and Elsewhere	E. Jewish Culture
		would assist American Jewry in its battle against Germany. The Nazis require registration of Belgian Jews and their property. All Jews were to have the letter *J* stamped on their identity cards. Marshal Philippe Pétain,* chief of state of Vichy France, promulgates anti-Jewish laws for unoccupied France. Foreign Jews could be interned in special camps and Algerian Jews lose their French citizenship.		**Oct. 1940**
Franklin D. Roosevelt* wins a third-term election, defeating Republican Wendell Willkie.* Roosevelt's vice presidential running mate is Secretary of Agriculture Henry A. Wallace.* Soviet Foreign Minister V. M. Molotov* begins a visit to Berlin for talks with Adolf Hitler* and other German leaders. Hungary, Romania, and Slovakia join the Rome–Berlin–Tokyo Axis.	The Jewish vote in the U.S. presidential election is estimated at 90% for Franklin D. Roosevelt* and 10% for Wendell Willkie.*	The Warsaw ghetto is officially declared to be in existence, and the 400,000 Jews of the ghetto are forbidden to move outside its boundaries. A second Nazi antisemitic propaganda film, *The Eternal Jew*, begins playing throughout Germany and occupied Europe. Jews are compared to rats, the carriers of disease, the corrupters of the world.	The Haganah attempts to disable the illegal immigrant ship *Patria* in Haifa Bay in the effort to prevent its sailing to Mauritius with 1,700 deportees aboard. It sinks, and 250 refugees are drowned. The British allow the survivors to remain in Palestine, deducting their number from the quota allocated under the 1939 White Paper. *Poster of* The Eternal Jew *an antisemitic Nazi propaganda film. (Yad Vashem)*	**Nov. 1940**
From December 1940 until April 1941, the British take the offensive in North Africa and push Italians back into Libya.		On December 12, the *Salvador*, a small vessel of 130 tons with 350 Jewish refugees aboard, sinks in the Sea of Marmora, drowning 200 of the refugees. It set sail from Bulgaria destined for Palestine. T. M. Snow,* the head of Britain's Foreign Office Refugee Section, comments: "There could have been no more opportune disaster from the point of view of stopping this traffic." The Nazis murdered fewer than 100,000		**Dec. 1940**

	A. General History	B. Jews in North and South America	C. Jews in Europe	D. Jews in the Middle East and Elsewhere	E. Jewish Culture
Dec. 1940			Jews between the time of their seizure of power and the end of 1940.		
1941	Penicillin is used clinically on humans.	Reinhold Niebuhr,* professor at New York's Union Theological Seminary, founds and edits *Christianity and Crisis*, a journal dedicated to rallying American Christians against Nazism. Rabbi Aaron Kotler, Talmud scholar, Orthodox leader, and rosh yeshiva in Kletzk in Polish Lithuania, arrives in the U.S. from Japan. He is persuaded to remain and build Orthodox institutions in the U.S. instead of moving to Palestine. He establishes the Beth Medrash Govoha in Lakewood, New Jersey. The choice of site is a deliberate attempt to isolate students from American life and ensure total concentration on Talmud study.			Kurt Lewin (1890–1947), U.S. psychologist who left Germany in 1932, writes the essay *Self-Hatred Among Jews*, which applies his theory both to individuals and to groups, for example, the hostility of German Jews toward eastern European Jews. Budd Schulberg, U.S. novelist, writes *What Makes Sammy Run?* describing the rise of a poor Lower East Side boy to Hollywood studio boss through the use of unscrupulous methods. Schulberg attempts to distinguish Sammy from the stereotype. Unlike Sammy, there are "Jews without money, without push, without plots, without any of the characteristics which such experts on genetics as Adolf Hitler . . . try to tell us are racial traits."
Jan. 1941	British forces overrun Italian forces and capture Tobruk, Libya.	The Nazis begin rounding up Polish Jews for transfer to the Warsaw ghetto. By the end of March, more than 70,000 are transferred, swelling the ghetto population to about 500,000. Romanian Iron Guards begin three days of attacks on Jews, killing 120, looting or burning hundreds of shops and houses, and desecrating 25 synagogues.			Delmore Schwartz (1913–1966), U.S. poet and literary critic, writes *Shenandoah*, a short verse dramatization of events surrounding the ritual circumcision (*bris*) of Shenandoah Fish (Schwartz). Schwartz utilizes the act to dramatize his belief that Jews are "chosen for wandering and alienation."
Feb. 1941	General Erwin Rommel* is appointed head of the German forces in North Africa—the Afrika Corps. British forces penetrate 500 miles into Libya. They halt their advance and		Abraham Asscher (1880–1955) and David Cohen (1883–1967), leaders of Dutch Jewry, are directed by the Nazis to organize an Amsterdam Jewish Council. The Council hopes to alleviate Jewish suffering by		Harry G. Friedman (1882–1965), U.S. businessman and philanthropist, makes an initial gift of 850 art objects to the Jewish Museum of New York. By 1965, his gifts will total 6,000 works of

A. General History	B. Jews in North and South America	C. Jews in Europe	D. Jews in the Middle East and Elsewhere	E. Jewish Culture	
send many of these troops to Greece.		cooperating with the Nazis. Asscher is ultimately imprisoned. Upon his return after the war, he will be denounced by some Jewish survivors. He will sever his connections with the Jewish community and will be buried in a non-Jewish cemetery.		ceremonial and fine art. The Tel Aviv Museum exhibits Wooden Synagogues in Poland, with photographs of about 20 synagogues.	**Feb. 1941**

C. Jews in Europe

Feb. 1941

Beginning on February 15, 1,000 Jewish men per week for five weeks are deported from Vienna to the ghettoes of Kielce and Lublin and from there to work in forced labor camps on the Soviet border.

A two-day general strike in Amsterdam, Holland, is the first public protest anywhere against the Nazi anti-Jewish policies. The demonstration is crushed, and the Nazis take measures that worsen the situation of Dutch Jewry.

In reprisal for an accidental anti-Nazi incident in a Jewish-owned tavern, 389 Jews from Amsterdam, mostly young men, are deported to Buchenwald. The owner of the tavern, Ernst Cahn, is executed, the first person killed by the Nazis since its occupation of Holland.

A. General History	B. Jews in North and South America	C. Jews in Europe	D. Jews in the Middle East and Elsewhere	E. Jewish Culture	
Bulgaria enters the war on the side of the Axis. German troops are stationed in Bulgaria. The U.S. Neutrality Act is amended, permitting lend–lease arms trade. President Franklin D. Roosevelt* requests $7 billion in military credits for Great Britain.		Adolf Eichmann* is appointed head of the Gestapo's section (IV B 4) for Jewish affairs and the expulsion of Jewish populations. Adolf Hitler* personally orders the destruction of the grave of Heinrich Heine, 19th-century German Jewish poet, in the Montmartre section of Paris.			**Mar. 1941**

A. General History

Apr. 1941

A pro-Axis faction seizes power in Iraq. They receive assurances from the Vichy French in Syria that German aircraft operating from Syria would support their action against the British.

Germany invades Yugoslavia and Greece.

British forces liberate Addis Ababa, capital of Ethiopia, from the Italians.

Yugoslavia surrenders to the Germans.

British forces are sent to Iraq to quell a pro-Axis rebellion.

Greece surrenders to Germany. The British begin the evacuation of their troops.

The America First Committee holds a mass rally in New York. Charles A. Lindbergh* is the keynote speaker; he accuses Great Britain of attempting to bring the U.S. into "the fiasco of this war."

Axis forces led by General Erwin Rommel* reach the Egyptian border after defeating the British in North Africa.

	A. General History	B. Jews in North and South America	C. Jews in Europe	D. Jews in the Middle East and Elsewhere	E. Jewish Culture
May 1941	British forces occupy Basra and several oil fields in Iraq. The pro-Axis government led by Rashid Ali* demands the withdrawal of all British troops and requests German aid. Rudolf Hess,* third-ranking German leader, flies to Scotland. He believes he can conclude a peace treaty with Great Britain. Adolf Hitler* denounces him as a lunatic. British aircraft attack Syrian airfields used by the Germans for attacking British troops in Iraq. German paratroopers begin the invasion of Crete. They capture the island within 10 days. The Vichy French sign a protocol with Germany over the use of French possessions. Germany can use Syrian and Lebanese air and naval bases; munitions stored in Syria will be transferred to Iraq for German use; a submarine base in Dakar, on the west coast of Africa, will be made available to German use. British troops reach Baghdad and Rashid Ali's* pro-Axis government collapses. Haj Amin al-Husseini* (1893–1974), Palestinian nationalist leader who assisted Rashid Ali's* pro-Axis coup, flees to Germany.	Samuel Lubell writes in the *Saturday Evening Post* magazine that Nazi agents disguised as refugees had infiltrated the U.S. He describes a Gestapo school where spies are taught to "speak Yiddish, to read Hebrew, pray," and are even circumcised to make their disguise complete.	All German consulates are informed that Hermann Goering,* Nazi leader, has banned the emigration of Jews from all occupied territories, including France, in view of the "doubtless imminent final solution." This is the first mention of any "final solution."	Leaders of the Haganah decide to establish a strike force (Palmah) for the execution of special tasks. Recruited by British intelligence, 23 members of the Palmah set out on an amphibious mission to demolish oil refineries in the Lebanese port of Tripoli. They disappear without a trace, and the cause of their death is not known. David Raziel (1910–1941), commander of the Irgun Zeva'i Le'ummi, is killed in a German bombing attack on his car in the outskirts of Baghdad, Iraq. Raziel led a group of Irgun members to sabotage oil installations in Iraq in cooperation with the British during the British operation leading to the overthrow of the pro-Axis Rashid Ali* regime.	
June 1941	British forces from Palestine and Transjordan invade Syria and Lebanon to eliminate German and Vichy French forces. British forces occupy Damascus, Syria.	Representative M. Michael Edelstein, Democrat of New York, collapses and dies of a heart attack in Congress after responding to anti-semitic attacks from Representative John	The Germans occupy Bialystok and immediately begin shooting Jews, killing 2,000. Romanian soldiers slaughter 260 Jews in Jassy and deport over	Angered over British reoccupation of Baghdad, Arabs stage a pogrom in the Jewish quarter, killing over 600 and injuring 850. Palmah troops led by Yigal Allon	

A. General History	B. Jews in North and South America	C. Jews in Europe	D. Jews in the Middle East and Elsewhere	E. Jewish Culture

June 1941

Three million German troops invade the Soviet Union along an 1,800-mile front from the Arctic to the Black Sea.

Vilna and Kaunas (Kovno) in Lithuania fall to the Germans.

The Germans capture Minsk, 200 miles inside Russia.

Romania joins the German invasion of the Soviet Union.

Rankin,* Democrat from Mississippi.

Marc Chagall arrives in New York from France at the invitation of the Museum of Modern Art.

The U.S. State Department issues a ruling barring immigration by all persons with close relatives in Nazi-occupied Europe. The ruling is issued after May hearings by the House Un-American Activities Committee, at which it was claimed that persons pledging to serve the Gestapo were released from concentration camps.

5,000. Of the deportees, over 2,500 die on the way to or at the camps.

German troops occupy Lvov. Mobs of Ukrainian hoodlums begin attacking Jews, murdering several thousand.

(1918–1980) and Moshe Dayan participate in the British invasion of Syria and Lebanon to eliminate German and Vichy French forces. Dayan loses an eye in this action.

Jews being beaten to death, on June 28, in Kovno, Lithuania, by Lithuanian civilians. German soldiers who captured the city on June 24 are onlookers. (Yad Vashem)

July 1941

German troops capture Riga, Latvia.

Great Britain and the Soviet Union sign a formal mutual assistance treaty.

An armistice ends the fighting in Syria and Lebanon. Great Britain and the Free French will control the two Arab countries, and over 20,000 Vichy French troops are permitted to leave.

The Germans capture Smolensk.

All Jews in the Baltic states are ordered to wear the Star of David badge.

The Germans begin executing Jews at the empty fuel pits at Ponary, outside Vilna, beyond the view of witnesses. In 12 days, 5,000 Jews from Vilna are shot. By the end of December, at least 48,000 Jews will be massacred there.

German and Romanian troops begin executing Jews at Kishinev. During 14 days of slaughter, 10,000 Jews are murdered.

C. Jews in Europe

July 1941

Adolf Eichmann* is directed by Gestapo chief Heinrich Muller* to visit Minsk, Bialystok, and Lvov and observe the mass murder of Jews. At his trial, in 1961, he will testify that he asked not to be sent to witness the mass murders. "There are other men who can look upon such actions. I cannot. At night I cannot sleep, I dream. I cannot do it."

Within five weeks of the German invasion of the Soviet Union, the German Einsatzgruppen kill more Jews than the total number killed by the Nazis in the previous eight years of their rule. They work behind an advancing army and are assisted by many local collaborators.

Major Rosler, the regimental commander of the regular German troops in Zhitomir, observes the slaughter of Jews. In January 1942, he will write: "I saw nothing like it either in the First World War or during the Civil War in

July 1941

Russia or during the Western Campaign. . . . Everything that is happening here seems to be absolutely incompatible with our views on education and morality."

Hermann Goering* issues a memorandum to Reinhard Heydrich,* instructing him to "carry out all the necessary preparations with regard to organizational and financial matters for bringing about a complete solution of the Jewish question in the German sphere of influence in Europe."

Reinhard Heydrich* advises Adolf Eichmann* that Adolf Hitler* had ordered the physical extermination of the Jews. Eichmann* will confirm this event during his pretrial interrogation in Israel by Captain Avner Less in 1960.

	A. General History	B. Jews in North and South America	C. Jews in Europe	D. Jews in the Middle East and Elsewhere	E. Jewish Culture
Aug. 1941	The first Arctic convoy brings war matériel to the Soviet Union. It is the beginning of a four-year Allied supply effort. President Franklin D. Roosevelt* and Winston Churchill* meet near Newfoundland, adopt the Atlantic Charter, and pledge the destruction of the Nazi regime.	In a radio address, Senator Gerald R. Nye* of North Dakota accuses Hollywood studios of making films specifically designed to rouse the nation to a state of war hysteria and of being led by men susceptible to national and racial emotions. Some in the industry accuse him of antisemitism, and he states "if anti-Semitism exists in America, the Jews have themselves to blame."	Reinhard Heydrich* writes Heinrich Himmler,* "It may be safely assumed that in the future there will be no more Jews in the annexed Eastern Territories." The 26,000 surviving Jews of Kovno are forced into a ghetto. Drancy, a small town near Paris, used as a Nazi internment center, is reserved solely for Jews. Between August 27 and 29, 11,000 Jewish forced laborers who had been deported from Hungary to Kamenets Podolsk are machine-gunned to death by the Germans.		
Sep. 1941	The Nazis experiment with the use of Zyklon B gas at the Auschwitz main camp, killing 600 Soviet prisoners of war and 300 Jews in the cellar of Block II. A second experiment using Zyklon B is held at Buchenwald. The Germans begin the siege of Leningrad. It will not end until January 1943. The Germans capture Kiev. Following sinkings by German U-boats, the U.S. declares it will "shoot at sight" in the North Atlantic and	Charles A. Lindbergh* speaks on behalf of the America First Committee at Des Moines, Iowa. He charges that the three most important groups pressing the U.S. toward war are the British, the Jews, and the Roosevelt* administration. The Jews are the most dangerous because of "their large ownership and influence in our motion pictures, our press, our radio, and our government."	Vilna's remaining Jews are herded into a ghetto. German posters throughout Kiev order the assembly of Jews for resettlement. The Jews are brought to the Babi Yar ravine, outside the city, and 34,000 are machine-gunned to death by the SS. The SS reports that "the Jews still believed to the very last moment before being executed that indeed all that was happening was that they were being resettled."	Oliver Harvey* (1893–1968), private secretary to Anthony Eden* (1897–1977), Britain's foreign secretary, receives a private note from Eden* commenting on a pro-Zionist memorandum prepared by Harvey.* "If we must have preferences, let me murmur in your ear that I prefer Arabs to Jews."	

Sep. 1941

provides naval cover to convoys of merchant ships carrying arms to Great Britain.

Oct. 1941

German and Romanian troops capture Odessa after a two-month siege.

As German troops advance to within 60 miles of Moscow, a state of siege is proclaimed in the city.

The Germans capture Kharkov, the industrial center of the Russian Ukraine.

The Germans destroy seven Paris synagogues.

Hans Frank* tells the ministers of the general government of Poland, "As far as the Jews are concerned, I want to tell you quite frankly that they must be done away with one way or another."

One of 129 photos of life in the Warsaw Ghetto taken by German soldier Heinz Jost, on his birthday. In the early 1980s he gave them to the publisher of Stern, *the German periodical. They were never published by Jost. In 1987 his photos were given to the Yad Vashem Archives. (Yad Vashem)*

C. Jews in Europe

At a meeting in Prague, Nazi officials discuss the transportation problems that make difficult the implementation of Adolf Hitler's* order to immediately rid the center of Germany of Jews.

In Odessa, 19,000 Jews are burned alive by Romanian and German troops. The next day they massacre another 16,000 Jews from Odessa in the nearby village of Dalnik.

Gestapo chief Heinrich Muller* forwards an order from Heinrich Himmler* announcing a new, revolutionized policy toward the Jews. Apart from a few exceptions judged to be in the German interest, no more Jews are to emigrate from anywhere in Germany or occupied Europe.

A second concentration camp is established at Auschwitz, called Auschwitz II, or Birkenau, which will become the extermination camp. After March 1942, its inmates are mainly Jews.

Around October, Nazi officials begin discussing a new policy concerning the extermination of the Jews—to murder by gas and not by shooting and to do so in secrecy by methods that involve far fewer people and that are away from the towns and cities.

The British indefinitely postpone the formation of a Jewish division to fight in the Middle East.

On October 26, the S.S. hangs Masha Bruskina, a 17-year-old Jew from the Minsk Ghetto who was active in partisan resistance, along with two men. Until 1987, the Russian authorities described her as an unknown partisan. The photo of her execution was published in The New York Times *on Sept. 15, 1987. (Yad Vashem)*

Nov. 1941

The U.S. extends lend–lease credit to the Soviet Union.

The Germans begin construction of the Belzec extermination camp, with Josef Oberhauser* in charge. In December, Christian Wirth* (1885–1944) will be appointed commander of the camp, and Oberhauser* will become his assistant. The camp will be ready for mass killing by the end of February 1942.

Outside the city of Minsk, 12,000 Jews

Nov. 1941

Haj Amin al-Husseini, Grand Mufti of Jerusalem, meeting Hitler in Berlin, in November. (Central Zionist Archives)

C. Jews in Europe

are slaughtered in pits. Three days later, 1,000 German Jews deported from Hamburg arrive in Minsk.

In the pits near the Rumbuli Forest, 10,600 Jews from the Riga ghetto are executed.

Heniek Grabowski, who had been sent by the Jews of Warsaw to Vilna, returns and reports of the slaughter of Vilna's Jews.

Haj Amin al-Husseini,* the mufti of Jerusalem, meets with Adolf Hitler* in Berlin. He pledges Arab cooperation with Germany and offers to recruit an Arab legion.

The first deportees arrive at the Theresienstadt ghetto. It is to receive Jews from Czechoslovakia, together with elderly, famous, and privileged Jews from Germany and western European countries. The Nazis intend to portray Theresienstadt as a "model ghetto" in order to conceal from the world the extermination of the Jews.

Dec. 1941

A. General History

On December 7, Japanese forces attack the U.S. naval base at Pearl Harbor, Hawaii. On December 8, the U.S. declares war on Japan.

The U.S. declares war on Germany and Italy. They declare war on the U.S.

Guam, Wake Island, and Hong Kong are captured by the Japanese, and Malaya is invaded by Japan.

C. Jews in Europe

Henryk Erlich (1882–1941) and Victor Alter (1890–1941), leaders of the Polish Bund and Jewish trade unions, arrested in October 1939 by Russian authorities, are executed. Their executions arouse worldwide protests from labor and liberal circles.

The Germans begin gassing Jews at Chelmno, Poland, by funneling exhaust fumes back into mobile vans.

A. General History	B. Jews in North and South America	C. Jews in Europe	D. Jews in the Middle East and Elsewhere	E. Jewish Culture	
		From December 7 to 9, a further 25,000 Jews, including the noted historian Simon Dubnow, from the Riga ghetto are executed by the Nazis in the Rumbuli Forest. One account says Dubnow's last words before he died were "write and record."			**Dec. 1941**
		Jacob Edelstein (1903–1944), Czech Zionist leader, is appointed Jewish leader of the Theresienstadt concentration camp by the Nazis. In November 1943 he will be sent to Auschwitz, where he will be killed on June 20, 1944.			
		During 1941 the Nazis murdered 1.1 million Jews.			
	Anti-Zionist Reform rabbis found the American Council for Judaism to protest a resolution of the Central Conference of American Rabbis supporting the creation of a Jewish army in Palestine. Laymen soon assume leadership, with Lessing J. Rosenwald as president. The council maintains that Judaism is a religion of universal values and not a nationality, and becomes the most articulate anti-Zionist spokesman among American Jews.

Ernst Lubitsch directs *To Be or Not to Be*, a black comedy satirizing the Nazis and their ideology, which stars Jack Benny and Carole Lombard,* who lead a group of Polish actors who foil the Nazi invaders. Felix Bessart plays Greenberg, a heroic Jew. | Leon Blum, former French premier, is brought to trial by the Vichy government. In 1943 the trial will be suspended and he will be sent to Buchenwald by the Germans. Blum will be liberated in May 1945.

Pierre Bloch, French Socialist politician and resistance leader, escapes to London, where he becomes chief of the French counterespionage. | During the German occupation of Tunisia, the Nazis try to arouse the Arab masses against the Jews. Habib Bourguiba,* leader of the underground Neo-Destour party, orders that the Jews not be disturbed.

The Ihud (Unity) society is founded in Palestine by Judah L. Magnes, Martin Buber, Ernst Simon (1899–1988), and other Jewish intellectuals. As a successor to the Berit Shalom organization, its objective is Arab–Jewish cooperation in Palestine and the creation of a binational state. | Alfred Kazin (b. 1915), U.S. literary critic, establishes his reputation with the publication of *On Native Grounds*, a history of American literature from 1890 to 1940.

Irving Berlin, U.S. songwriter, writes "White Christmas," a popular holiday song, for the movie *Holiday Inn*.

Herbert Lawrence Block (Herblock), U.S. editorial cartoonist, wins his first Pulitzer Prize. In 1954, he will win his second.

The Museum of Modern Art purchases *The Synagogue*, painted by Hyman Bloom. His early work reflected the world he lived in and knew—cantors, rabbis, and synagogues. The horrors of the Holocaust alter Bloom's approach to his art. He becomes preoccupied with | **1942** |

A. General History	B. Jews in North and South America	C. Jews in Europe	D. Jews in the Middle East and Elsewhere	E. Jewish Culture
Jan. 1942		The Polish underground in Warsaw advises the Polish Government in exile of "a blind and cruel anti-Semitism" among the Polish people, itself the victim of Nazi persecution. The Nazis begin the final destruction of the Jewish community of Odessa with the deportation from its Slobodka suburb of over 19,000 Jews to labor camps where, within a year and a half, almost all will die. A conference of Nazi officials is held at Wannsee, a suburb of Berlin. Reinhard Heydrich* tells assembled Nazi "Jewish experts" from across Europe that Hermann Goering* has placed him in charge of preparations for "the final solution of the Jewish Question" and that implementation is to be carried out in coordination with his own "department head," Adolf Eichmann.* He explains that the "final solution" concerns not only Jews already under German rule, but "some eleven million Jews" throughout Europe. A united fighting organization is established by the Jews in the Vilna ghetto, commanded by Yizhak Wittenberg (1907–1943), Joseph Glazman, and Abba Kovner. They decide to fight in the ghetto rather than to escape to join partisans in the forest. In a Berlin speech marking the ninth anniversary of Nazi rule in Germany, Adolf Hitler* speaks of the Jews: "They are our old enemy as it is, they have experienced at our	Chaim Weizmann, writing in *Foreign Affairs* magazine, calls for the establishment of a Jewish commonwealth in Palestine.	death and paints cadavers of extraordinary paint quality and tragic beauty. Frank Loesser (1910–1969), U.S. composer, writes the words and music of his famous song, "Praise the Lord and Pass the Ammunition." David Oistrakh (1908–1974), Soviet violinist, is awarded the Stalin Prize, the Soviet Union's highest honor. Jankel Adler (1895–1949), Polish-born painter, paints *Two Rabbis*, which appears to be in response to the rumors abounding of the fate of European Jewry. In the 1930s, he was a respected teacher at the Düsseldorf Academy of Arts. He left Germany in 1933. His works were removed from German museums and included in the Degenerate Art exhibition. He fought with the Free Polish army and was evacuated to England, where he was demobilized for health reasons.

A. General History	B. Jews in North and South America	C. Jews in Europe	D. Jews in the Middle East and Elsewhere	E. Jewish Culture

hands an upsetting of their ideas, and they rightfully hate us, just as much as we hate them. . . . The war will not end as the Jews imagine it will, namely with the uprooting of the Aryans, but the result of this war will be the complete annihilation of the Jews.''

From January 1941 to January 1942, 48,662 Jews of Warsaw died of starvation.

Singapore and its garrison of 64,000 Commonwealth troops fall to the Japanese.

Japanese and Allied naval forces clash in the Battle of the Java Sea, which the Japanese will win on March 1.

Michael Weizmann, son of Chaim Weizmann, is killed over the North Sea, flying for the British Royal Air Force.

The *Struma*, a refugee ship from Romania with 769 Jews aboard, is torpedoed and sunk by a Soviet submarine in the Black Sea off the coast of Turkey. It had reached Turkey in December, and the Turks refused disembarkation unless the British Palestine authorities would accept the refugees. The British refused. There are two survivors.

Abraham Stern, who founded Lehi, Freedom Fighters for Israel, a group that split from the Irgun, is captured and killed by the British.

The mandatory government permits 858 orphaned children rescued from Poland and sent overland through Russia to Teheran, Iran, entry into Palestine.

Turkish newspaper photo of the Struma *a refugee ship carrying 769 Jewish refugees from Romania. (Central Zionist Archives)*

Henrietta Szold, director of Youth Aliyah, welcoming "Teheran Children" rescued from Nazi-occupied Poland, in Palestine. (Central Zionist Archives)

The U.S. moves all persons of Japanese ancestry, including U.S. citizens, from the Pacific Coast into internment camps in the interior.

Rangoon, the capital of Burma, falls to the Japanese.

All Allied forces in the Dutch East Indies unconditionally surrender to the Japanese.

The Germans begin killing Jews at the Belzec extermination camp in Poland. Deportations are temporarily halted in the middle of June to facilitate the construction of newer and larger gas chambers. Deportations resume in the middle of July.

Mar. 1942

At the beginning of Operation Reinhard* and 10 days after the killings start at Belzec, Paul Josef Goebbels* notes in his diary: "Beginning with Lublin, the Jews in the General Government are now being evacuated eastward. The procedure is a pretty barbaric one. . . . The ghettos that will be emptied in the cities of the General Government will now be refilled with Jews thrown out of the Reich. The process is to be repeated from time to time."

When Operation Reinhard* starts, the papal nuncio in Bratislava, Giuseppe Burzio,* reports to the Vatican that "the deportation of 80,000 persons to Poland at the mercy of the Germans means to condemn a great part of them to certain death."

Construction of an extermination camp at a wooded area near the village of Sobibor begins. Experimental killings of about 250 Jews take place in the middle of April, and in May, Sobibor begins full operation. Franz Stangl* (1908–1971) is the first commander of the camp, and Karl Frenzel,* Kurt Bolender,* and Gustav Wagner* are among the German overseers.

The first deportation train of Jews from France leaves for Auschwitz.

Hungarian Prime Minister Miklos Kallay* prevents implementation of the "final solution" on Hungarian Jewry until the Nazi occupation of Hungary in March 1944. He imposes a nominal anti-Jewish program and gives only verbal support to the Nazis.

Adolf Eichmann* visits the Chelmno extermination camp. On April 19, 1961, at his trial in Jerusalem, Eichmann will testify that he described the scene at Chelmno to Gestapo chief Heinrich Muller* as "horrible, it's an indescribable inferno."

The gassing of Jews begins at the Auschwitz II (Birkenau) extermination camp.

	A. General History	B. Jews in North and South America	C. Jews in Europe	D. Jews in the Middle East and Elsewhere	E. Jewish Culture
Apr. 1942	The Bataan Peninsula on the Philippine island of Luzon falls to the Japanese. About 35,000 U.S. and Filipino troops are captured. Marshal Philippe Pétain* becomes Vichy head of state, a largely ceremonial position, while Pierre Laval* (1883–1945) becomes chief of the government, assuming actual direction of the Vichy administration. Japan is bombed by 16 B-25 bombers launched from the U.S. aircraft carrier *Hornet* under the command of Colonel James H. Doolittle.*		The Jewish Anti-Facist Committee, established by the Soviet government to mobilize world Jewish support for the war effort against Nazi Germany, issues its first appeal for aid. The committee is headed by Solomon Mikhoels (1890–1948), Yiddish actor. An Einsatzkommando unit, killing inside the Soviet Union, reports that the whole of Crimea has been "purged of Jews." The unit had killed 91,678 Jews in four and a half months.	In the spring, the Jews of Benghazi, Libya, are deported to Giado, a camp in the desert south of Tripoli, where over 500 of them die of starvation and typhus. Conditions will be relieved when the British occupy the camp in January 1943.	
May 1942	Between May 4 and 8, U.S. and Japanese naval forces fight the Battle of the Coral Sea. This is the first naval battle in which the participants never see each other, as		A slave labor camp is established at Monowitz, where I.G. Farben has synthetic rubber and oil plants, and is called Auschwitz III.	In May, Menachem Begin (1913–1992) arrives in Palestine as a member of the Polish army of Wladyslaw Anders* organized in the Soviet Union. Anders*	

only planes from the aircraft carrier are involved in the attacks on naval vessels.

The island of Corregidor in Manila Bay and its garrison of about 16,000 U.S. and Filipino troops surrender to the Japanese.

Herbert Baum (1912–1942), a German Communist, and a number of comrades set fire to an anti-Soviet exhibit in Berlin. The group is caught and Baum and 26 others are executed.

SS General Reinhard Heydrich* is fatally wounded in Prague by members of the Czech underground.

British Royal Air Force bombers raid Cologne, in the first 1,000-bomber raid of the war.

The Sobibor extermination camp begins operation. It functions until October 1943. The peak period of extermination is from May to October 1942. In May, 36,000 Jews, mainly from eastern Poland and occupied areas of the Soviet Union, but also from Holland, Austria, Belgium, France, and Czechoslovakia, are gassed there. The total number of victims in 18 months is estimated at 250,000.

The Nazis open a death camp at Maly Trostenets, the site of a collective farm on the outskirts of Minsk. In addition to Jews from Minsk, Jews from Germany, Austria, and Czechoslovakia are brought there for extermination in mobile gas vans. About 20 survivors will be liberated by the Russians in July 1944.

On the site of an existing slave labor camp, construction of the Treblinka extermination camp begins. It utilizes technology developed in the already operational Belzec and Sobibor camps. Franz Stangl* will become the camp commander in September, and Kurt Franz,* his deputy. The killings begin on July 23.

The Polish Socialist Jewish Bund reports to the West a detailed account of deportations and killings of Jews throughout Poland and the gassings at Chelmno and states "the Germans have already killed 700,000 Polish Jews." On June 2, the BBC broadcasts material from the Bund report.

quarreled with Joseph Stalin* and arranged to take his army to serve under British command. They were taken across the Caspian Sea to Iran and then overland to Palestine.

World Zionist leaders meet a New York's Biltmore Hotel and hold an xtraordinary Zionist conference. David Ben-Gurion, chairman of the Jewish Agency Executive, argues that the Jews can no longer depend on Great Britain to facilitate a Jewish national home in Palestine. The conference adopts the Biltmore Program, calling for mass immigration to Palestine and the establishment of a Jewish commonwealth there.

Chaim Weizmann addressing Extraordinary Zionist Conference held at the Biltmore Hotel in New York, May 1942. (Central Zionist Archives)

A. General History	B. Jews in North and South America	C. Jews in Europe	D. Jews in the Middle East and Elsewhere	E. Jewish Culture
June 1942 U.S. naval forces defeat the Japanese in the Battle of Midway, marking a turning point in the war against Japan. The Nazis burn the Czech village of Lidice to the ground and massacre its 199 male residents, in reprisal for the death of Reinhard Heydrich.* Tobruk falls to General Erwin Rommel's* Afrika Corps, and 33,000 Allied troops surrender. Nine days later, the Afrika Corps reaches El Alamein in Egypt.		Polish authorities in London confirm the Jewish Socialist Bund report of the mass murder by the Nazis of over 700,000 Jews in Poland. From the middle of 1942 to 1945, the Nazis confiscate Jewish possessions of artistic and historical value throughout Bohemia and Moravia. They establish the Museum of an Extinct Race in Prague. Jewish art historians, who are later killed, catalog the collection, which is probably the greatest collection of Jewish art ever assembled. Four major exhibitions for Nazi viewing are held. By 1945, some 140,000 objects will fill 8 buildings and 50 warehouses.	During the retreat of Britain's Eighth army, 1,000 Palestinian Jews serve with the Free French brigade defending Bir Hacheim, near Tobruk in Libya. When relieved in July, only 45 of these troops remain alive.	
July 1942 Leaders of the Egyptian liberation movement confer with Field Marshal Erwin Rommel* to prepare for the German entry into Cairo. The Germans totally occupy the Crimea as Russian resistance ends. The Germans capture Rostov.	Twenty thousand attend a rally at New York's Madison Square Garden to protest Nazi atrocities. For the first time, President Franklin D. Roosevelt,* in his message, makes specific mention of atrocities against Jews and declares the American people "will hold the perpetrators of these crimes to strict accountability in a day of reckoning which will surely come."	At a Berlin meeting presided over by Heinrich Himmler,* it is decided to conduct secret medical experiments of "major dimensions" on Jewish women at Auschwitz. The first 2,000 Jews are deported from Holland to Auschwitz. In Paris, 7,000 French Jews are rounded up and taken to Drancy for deportation to Auschwitz.		

July 1942

C. Jews in Europe

Heinrich Himmler,* noting that a "total cleansing is necessary," sends a secret directive to the head of the general government in Poland ordering "the resettlement of the entire Jewish population of the General Government be carried out and completed by December 31."

The Germans begin deportation of the Jews of Warsaw for "resettlement in the East." In two months, nearly 254,000 will be sent by train from the Warsaw ghetto for extermination in the gas chambers at Treblinka. It is the largest destruction of a single community, Jewish or non-Jewish, during World War II.

Adam Czerniakow (1880–1942), head of the Warsaw Jewish Council (Judenrat), commits suicide rather than sign children's deportation orders. Czerniakow kept a secret diary that serves as a reliable account of the destruction of Warsaw Jewry. His last entry noted, "I am powerless, my heart trembles in sorrow and compassion. I can no longer bear all this."

Heinrich Himmler* writes to a senior SS official, "The Occupied Eastern Territories are to become free of Jews. The execution of this very grave order has been placed on my shoulders by the Führer."

Jacob Gens is appointed head of the Vilna ghetto by the Nazis. Gens is accused by some as a Nazi collaborator, whereas others believe he carries out Nazi orders in order to save as many Jews as possible. On September 15, 1943, he will be accused by the Gestapo of aiding the underground and executed.

Deportations to Belzec resume. From mid-July to mid-December, 414,000 Polish Jews and more than 100,000 Jews from Germany, Austria, Czechoslovakia, and other countries are exterminated. When added to the 93,000 killed between March and June, the total number of Jews exterminated at Belzec comes to over 600,000. Murder at Belzec will cease in December.

Between July 23 and August 28, the first five weeks of operations at Treblinka, 312,500 Jews, including 245,000 from Warsaw, are deported to the camp. Chaotic conditions cause a temporary cessation of deportations; Franz Stangl* is reassigned from Sobibor to Treblinka as camp commander; deportations from Warsaw resume on September 3, and by September 21 nearly 254,000 Jews from Warsaw are murdered there.

A. General History	B. Jews in North and South America	C. Jews in Europe	D. Jews in the Middle East and Elsewhere	E. Jewish Culture	
					Aug. 1942
The Germans and Russians engage in the Battle of Stalingrad.	The Jewish Labor Bund's American publication, *The Ghetto Speaks*, reports the gassing of Jews by the Nazis at Chelmno, Poland. In September the report is published on the back page of the Labor Zionist monthly, *The Jewish Frontier*, as the editors are "psychologically unschooled for the new era of mass carnage."	The first part of the Oyneg Shabes archive of the Warsaw ghetto is buried in a bunker on Nowolipki Street.			
U.S. forces invade Guadalcanal in the Solomon Islands, the first time U.S. forces take the initiative in the Pacific war.		The first Jews from Belgium are deported to Auschwitz. By the end of the month, 5,669 Jews are deported, of whom only 321 survive the war.			
Mohandas K. Gandhi* threatens a campaign of civil disobedience in India if Britain does not grant immediate independence. He and other Indian leaders are arrested for resisting the Allied war effort.	The Riegner report of the Nazi plan to kill the Jews of Europe reaches Rabbi Stephen S. Wise. The report is sent to Wise by Samuel S. Silverman, a Member of the British Parliament.	Gerhart Riegner, World Jewish Congress representative in Geneva, advises U.S. Vice-Consul Howard Elting, Jr.,* of the Nazi plan to kill all the Jews of Europe. The source of information is Eduard Schulte,* German industrialist.			
Winston Churchill* and Joseph Stalin* confer in Moscow.					
Field Marshal Erwin Rommel's* forces are halted in fighting near the Alam el Halfa Ridge in Egypt.		During August, more than 400,000 Jews are murdered in German-occupied Europe.			
	Rabbi Stephen S. Wise sends a cable of the Riegner report to Under Secretary of State Sumner Welles.* Wise asks Welles* to transmit the cable to President Franklin D. Roosevelt* and vouches for Gerhart Riegner's reliability. Welles* asks Wise not	Several days after his arrival at Auschwitz, Dr. Johann Kremer,* a German surgeon, notes in his diary: "Was present for the first time at a special action at 3 A.M. By comparison, Dante's inferno seems almost a comedy. Auschwitz is justly called an extermination camp!"			Sep. 1942

Sep. 1942

to release the Riegner report until it is confirmed by the State Department.

Rabbi Stephen S. Wise writes to Supreme Court Justice Felix Frankfurter, suggesting he inform President Franklin D. Roosevelt* of the Riegner report, as he believes Under Secretary of State Sumner Welles* is unwilling to take the report to Roosevelt.*

Jacob Rosenheim (1870–1965) of New York, president of Agudat Israel, receives a telegram from his Swiss representative, Isaac Sternbuch, outlining the mass murders of Jews in Poland. On that day he sends a copy of the message to President Franklin D. Roosevelt.*

Under Secretary of State Sumner Welles* meets with Jewish leaders and agrees to have U.S. intelligence investigate charges of Nazi mass murder in Poland.

Emanuel Celler (1888–1981), New York congressman, appalled at press reports of Nazi deportation of French Jews, introduces legislation to permit immigration to U.S. of French refugees who could prove they were facing Nazi or Vichy roundup, internment, or religious persecution. The bill dies in a House committee on immigration.

Meir Berliner, an Argentine citizen who was trapped with his family in the Warsaw ghetto and then transported to Treblinka, fatally stabs Max Bialas,* an SS overseer. Although Berliner acted on his own initiative, 150 Jews are randomly selected and shot as punishment.

General Kurt von Gienanth,* commander of the military district of the general government in Poland, sends a memo to the army general staff, objecting to Heinrich Himmler's* July 19 directive that ordered deportation of all Jews from the general government by December 31. He reports that 300,000 Jews, including 100,000 skilled workers, are employed in the war effort. "The immediate removal of Jews would cause a considerable reduction in Germany's war potential."

Martin Luther,* of the German Foreign Ministry, advises his colleagues of Joachim von Ribbentrop's* instructions "to hurry as much as possible the evacuation of Jews from the various countries of Europe." At the outset, negotiations should be had with the governments of Bulgaria, Hungary, and Denmark "with the object of starting the evacuation of the Jews of these countries."

An instruction of the Swiss police explains that "refugees on the grounds of race alone are not political refugees," and Swiss frontier police refuse entry to more than 9,000 Jews from France.

On August 22, Hubert Pfoch, German soldier on way to Eastern Front, photographs Jews boarding railway cars in Siedlce, Poland, for transport to Treblinka. Pfoch kept a diary and noted that shortly after he took this photo he saw the Ukrainian S.S. guard kill a Jew with a single blow of his rifle butt. (Yad Vashem)

Two Jews who were killed and whose bodies lay alongside the railway track as the train to Treblinka left the station. (Yad Vashem)

A. General History	B. Jews in North and South America	C. Jews in Europe	D. Jews in the Middle East and Elsewhere	E. Jewish Culture
		A German plan to deport 200,000 Romanian Jews to Belzec does not materialize because of a protest submitted by the U.S. to the Romanian government, various efforts by Romanian Jewish leaders, and disagreements within the Romanian administration.		**Sep. 1942**
U.S. General Mark Clark* arrives in Algiers by submarine for a secret meeting with friendly French officials to facilitate the upcoming Allied North African invasion. Among those whom he meets is José Abulker, one of the leaders of the Algerian resistance. British forces led by General Bernard Montgomery* launch the second Battle of El Alamein against Field Marshal Erwin Rommel's* Axis forces.	*National Jewish Monthly*, the B'nai B'rith magazine, questions reports that Jews were deported east for forced labor and states "it is feared that the Nazis may be resorting to wholesale slaughter, preferring to kill all Jews rather than use their labor."	Heinrich Himmler* replies to the German general staff's request for a delay in ridding the general government of Jews by December 31. He writes that Jewish workers in real war industries will be gradually replaced by Poles and a small number of Jewish concentration camp enterprises will be located in the eastern part of the general government. "But there, too, in accordance with the wish of the Führer, the Jews are some day to disappear." At a London mass meeting to protest Nazi persecution of Jews, William Temple, the archbishop of Canterbury, declares it is "hard to resist the conclusion that there is a settled purpose to exterminate the Jewish people if it can be done." Deportations and killing operations are renewed at Sobibor. About 250,000 Jews from Poland and other countries of Europe are exterminated there. The camp will be closed after the uprising in October 1943. The Italian military commander in Croatia refuses to hand over Jews in his zone to the Nazis.		**Oct. 1942**

	A. General History	B. Jews in North and South America	C. Jews in Europe	D. Jews in the Middle East and Elsewhere	E. Jewish Culture
Oct. 1942			More than 20,000 Jews from Piotrkow are deported to Treblinka. All are gassed.		
Nov. 1942	Allied forces land on the Algerian and Moroccan coasts. German forces invade Tunisia, landing by air. The Allies occupy Casablanca. German troops occupy Vichy France except the area around the Mediterranean coast. A Soviet counteroffensive traps the German Sixth Army in the Stalingrad area. Field Marshal Erwin Rommel's* defeated forces begin a retreat from El Alamein. The British capture 30,000 Axis troops.	Under Secretary of State Sumner Welles* confirms to Stephen S. Wise Nazi extermination plans. Wise holds a press conference in Washington, D.C., reporting that State Department sources confirm that 2 million Jews had been killed in an "extermination campaign." Wise states Nazis are moving Jews from all over Europe to Poland for mass killing. A special issue of the *Jewish Frontier* magazine publishes documented information of Nazi mass murder "whose avowed object is the extermination of a whole people." Congress denies President Franklin D. Roosevelt's* request for a third war powers bill, which would give him power to suspend immigration laws. *Newsweek* magazine reports "the ugly truth is that anti-Semitism was a definite factor in the bitter opposition to the President's request . . ."	The Nazis round up over 100,000 Jews from the Bialystok region for deportation to Treblinka. The Nazis deport 513 Norwegian Jews to Auschwitz. The selection and gas chambers begin operation at Majdanek, near Lublin, which was established in July 1941 as a slave labor camp. Altogether, 130,000 Jews are sent to Majdanek in 1942–1943, of whom about 60% are either shot or gassed upon arrival. An estimated 125,000 Jews will be exterminated at Majdanek before its liberation by the Russians on July 24, 1944.	The Jewish press in Palestine reports a Nazi mass murder program, including construction of gas chambers in eastern Europe and crematoria at Auschwitz. The sources of the reports are Polish Jews arriving in Palestine in exchange for German citizens from British-controlled territories. José Abulker, son of the head of the Algerian Jewish community, having been supplied with American weapons, leads a resistance insurrection in Algiers, which prevents any effective Vichy resistance to the American landings in Algeria.	*Local militia and civilians execute Jewish men and boys in Lithuania. Victims are required to undress and dig a pit which is to become their grave. (Yad Vashem)*
Dec. 1942	Enrico Fermi* and Leo Szilard, Hungarian-born nuclear physicist who left Germany in 1933, split the atom and achieve the first controlled nuclear reaction, which opens the way to the atomic bomb.	A day of mourning and prayer on behalf of European Jewry is observed throughout the U.S. and in 29 foreign countries. In New York, 500,000 Jewish workers stop work for 10 minutes in protest. The following day the Jewish workers make up the 10 minutes of lost time. President Franklin D. Roosevelt,* at Rabbi	Paul Josef Goebbels* notes in his diary that "the Italians are extremely lax in the treatment of the Jews. They protect the Italian Jews both in Tunis and in occupied France. . . . The Jewish question is causing us a lot of trouble. Everywhere, even among our allies, the Jews have friends to help them." He adds: "I believe both the British and	José Abulker and his father are interned at a prison camp in central Algeria by Vichy officials, who the Allies permit to remain in power after the liberation of Algeria. After two months' imprisonment they will be released through American efforts.	

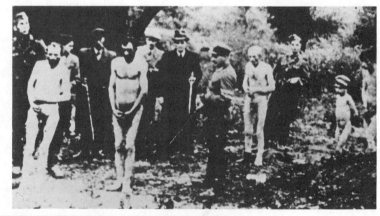

A. General History	B. Jews in North and South America	C. Jews in Europe	D. Jews in the Middle East and Elsewhere	E. Jewish Culture

B. Jews in North and South America

Stephen S. Wise's request, meets with Wise, Henry Monsky (B'nai B'rith), Rabbi Isaac Rosenberg (Union of Orthodox Rabbis), Maurice Wertheim (American Jewish Committee), and Adolph Held (Jewish Labor Committee). They ask the president to warn the Nazis they will be held to strict accountability for their crimes.

Christian Century, a nondenominational Protestant weekly, discusses Rabbi Stephen S. Wise's disclosure of Nazi mass extermination, questioning whether "any good purpose is served by publication of such charges" and arguing that he exaggerates the number of Jews killed.

For the first time, the Allied nations issue a declaration on the German policy of murdering the Jews. It commits the U.S., Britain, and the Soviet Union to postwar prosecution of those responsible.

A *New York Times* editorial notes the official indictment of the Nazi murderers of the Jews and states "the most tragic aspect of the situation is the world's helplessness to stop the horror while the war is going on."

C. Jews in Europe

Americans are happy that we are exterminating the Jewish riff-raff."

Rabbi Michael Dov Weissmandel (d. 1957), Slovakian Orthodox rabbi involved in rescue efforts, appeals to world Jewry for aid: "We cannot understand how you can eat and drink, how you can rest in your beds, how you can stroll in the streets—I am sure you are doing all those things—while this responsibility rests upon you. We have been crying out for months and you have done nothing."

The Germans ambush a Jewish partisan group in White Russia organized earlier in the year by Tobias Belsky and kill 19 of the 150 members of the group.

By the end of the year, the Nazis have destroyed the Jewish community of Yugoslavia, murdering more than 30,000. Four thousand five hundred Jews escape and join the partisans.

During 1942, the Nazis murdered 2.7 million Jews. It is the year of the greatest coordination of the "final solution."

AREA OF MAXIMUM AXIS RULE, 1942

A. General History

J. Robert Oppenheimer (1904–1967), U.S. physicist, becomes director of the laboratories at Los Alamos, New Mexico, and is in charge of the construction of the first atomic bomb.

B. Jews in North and South America

Raphael Lemkin (1901–1959), international lawyer who escaped from Poland to the U.S. in 1941, coins the term *genocide* under the impact of news about the Nazis' extermination of the Jews of Europe.

Bruno Bettelheim (1903–1990), German-

C. Jews in Europe

The Centre of Contemporary Jewish Documentation is established within the underground movement in occupied France, under the presidency of Isaac Schneersohn (1879–1969), to collect and preserve documents of the Nazi persecution.

D. Jews in the Middle East and Elsewhere

Menachem Begin becomes commander of the Irgun Zeva'i Le'ummi in Palestine upon his release from the Polish army located in the Middle East.

The Soviet Union permits the Palestinian Communist party to divide into Jewish and

E. Jewish Culture

Marc Chagall expresses his distress caused by the Nazi destruction of Europe in numerous works painted in the U.S., including *War*, *Obsession*, and *Yellow Crucifixion*.

Maurice Samuel (1895–1972), U.S. author and translator, writes *The World of*

A. General History	B. Jews in North and South America	C. Jews in Europe	D. Jews in the Middle East and Elsewhere	E. Jewish Culture
1943	born psychoanalyst drawing on his experiences at Dachau and Buchenwald in 1938, writes *Individual and Mass Behavior in Extreme Situations*, an essay that describes the Nazi efforts to dehumanize their victims and turn them into "docile masses from which no individual or group act of resistance could arise." Samuel Belkin (1911–1976) becomes president of Yeshiva College in New York. Under his leadership, the institution will grow to include medical and law schools, and achieve university status.		Arab groups. This concession is a reflection of wartime concern over the Arab response to German advances in the Middle East and in recognition of Jewish war efforts.	*Sholom Aleichem*, the first of three books on the development of Yiddish literature. The second will be *Prince of the Ghetto*, on Isaac Leib Peretz (1852–1915), written in 1948, and the third, *The Praise of Yiddish*, will be written in 1971. Israel Joshua Singer, Yiddish novelist who emigrated to the U.S. from Poland in 1933, writes *The Family Carnovsky*. It is the story of German Jewish assimilation, with special emphasis on the youngest family member, the child of a mixed marriage.
Jan. 1943	President Franklin D. Roosevelt* and Winston Churchill* meet at Casablanca to plan future Allied strategy. Roosevelt* suggests a policy of requiring unconditional surrender of the Axis. The Russians lift the German siege of Leningrad. The Royal Air Force conducts the first daylight bombing attack on Berlin.	At the Casablanca Conference, President Franklin D. Roosevelt* proposes that North African resettlement projects restrict the number of Jews allowed to practice such professions as law and medicine. He speaks of "the understandable complaints which the Germans bore towards the Jews in Germany, namely that while they represented a small part of the population, over 50% of the lawyers, doctors, schoolteachers, college professors in Germany were Jews" (the actual figures were 16.3, 10.9, 2.6, and 0.5%, respectively). In January, 29% of respondents to a Gallup poll believe the reports of 2 million Jews killed in Europe since the beginning of the war to be a rumor. Forty-seven percent of respondents believe reports to be true, and 24% have no opinion.	Mordecai Anielewicz (1919–1943) leads the first armed resistance in the Warsaw ghetto, as the Nazis begin a roundup of 5,000 Jews for deportation to Treblinka after nearly four months without a single deportation. Heinrich Himmler* writes to the German minister of transport seeking his help in accomplishing "the removal of Jews": "If I am to wind things up quickly, I must have more trains for transports." The Nazis round up more than 4,000 Jews in Marseilles for deportation under Action Tiger. The Italians refuse to cooperate with the Nazis in rounding up the Jews living in the zone of France under their control. In March, they will prevent the Nazis from deporting Jews living in their zone. Beginning early in the year, as the Russian army begins advancing		Delmore Schwartz, U.S. poet and literary critic, writes in prose and poetry *Genesis*, a description of his "genesis" from his grandfather's life in Russia to his own early American elementary education. Leonard Bernstein (1918–1990), U.S. composer and conductor, is appointed assistant conductor of the New York Philharmonic Orchestra. William Gropper (1897–1977), U.S. cartoonist and painter who is a leading painter of the social realism school, paints *De Profundis* as a memorial to the victims of the Holocaust. In 1935, he painted *The Senate*, an angry satire typical of his work, which had led him to be called the American Daumier. Jacques Lipchitz, Lithuanian-born sculptor who moved to Paris in 1909, where he gained a worldwide reputation,

A. General History	B. Jews in North and South America	C. Jews in Europe	D. Jews in the Middle East and Elsewhere	E. Jewish Culture	
		on the eastern front, the Nazis decide to destroy the evidence of mass murder by digging up the mass graves of murdered Jews and burning the remains. SS Colonel Paul Blobel* commands the personnel, which includes Jews and Russian prisoners of war, assigned to this task. They are known as the Blobel Commando, or Special Commando 1005. In January, Herbert Morrison* (1888–1965), Britain's home secretary, rejects public demands led by the archbishop of Canterbury that Britain lead the world in providing an immediate refuge in the territories of the British Empire for Jews threatened with death. Morrison* fears it will stimulate antisemitism, which was "always beneath the pavement." Morrison* is an outspoken opponent of antisemitism and supporter of Zionism.		and escaped to the U.S. in 1941, sculpts *The Prayer*, an old, disemboweled man performing the Kapparot (expiation) prayer before the Day of Atonement. To Lipchitz it is a prayer for the Jewish victims of the Nazis. Richard Rodgers (1902–1979) writes the music and Oscar Hammerstein II, the lyrics for *Oklahoma!*, the first of several American musical theater smash hits. Others include *Carousel* (1945), *South Pacific* (1949), *The King and I* (1951), and *The Sound of Music* (1959). Selman A. Waksman (1888–1973), U.S. microbiologist, discovers the antibiotic streptomycin. It is the first real cure for tuberculosis. Otto Stern (1888–1969), U.S. physicist, is awarded the Nobel Prize in physics for his work on the magnetic momentum of	**Jan. 1943**
German resistance ends at Stalingrad. The German Sixth Army led by Field Marshal Friedrich Paulus,* who surrenders, is destroyed. The Soviet army recaptures Rostov and Kharkov.	C. L. Sulzberger reports in the *New York Times* that the Romanian government offers to move 70,000 Jews from Transnistra to any place of refuge chosen by the Allies. Romania suggests Palestine and offers to provide Romanian ships for the voyage. The State Department dismisses this rescue possibility. The *New York Times* prints an advertisement headed, "For Sale to Humanity 70,000 Jews," sponsored by the Committee for a Jewish Army of Stateless and Palestinian Jews.	Eight Jews from Finland are deported to Auschwitz. Thereafter, Finland refuses to agree to the Nazi request for the deportation of any of its more than 2,000 Jews. Bulgaria agrees to allow the Nazis to deport 11,000 Jews from the former Yugoslav region of Macedonia and the former Greek region of Thrace, two areas occupied by Bulgaria in 1941. Italian military authorities in Lyons, France, force the French to rescind an order for the deportation of several		molecular beams. A professor of physical chemistry at Hamburg, Stern left Germany for the U.S. in 1933, when the Nazis came to power. George Charles de Hevesy (1885–1966) is awarded the Nobel Prize in chemistry for the development of radioactive tracing. Of Hungarian birth, he taught in Germany until the Nazis came to power and then moved to Denmark. He escaped to Sweden in 1943. Natan Alterman (1910–1970), Palestinian poet, begins writing a weekly satirical	**Feb. 1943**

	A. General History	B. Jews in North and South America	C. Jews in Europe	D. Jews in the Middle East and Elsewhere	E. Jewish Culture
Feb. 1943			hundred French Jews to Auschwitz. Joachim von Ribbentrop* complains to Benito Mussolini* that "Italian military circles . . . lack a proper understanding of the Jewish question." The Hungarian government refuses to comply with the Nazi request for 10,000 Hungarian Jews to be forced laborers in the copper mines at Bor, in Yugoslavia. Several months later, it will yield to the Nazi request. The second part of the Oyneg Shabes archive of the Warsaw ghetto is buried in a bunker on Nowolipki Street.		feature in verse, "The Seventh Column," for the Labour daily *Maariv*, which expresses and shapes public opinion. Many of his poems are censored by the British authorities. For a time he is considered the most influential poet since Hayyim Nahman Bialik. He began his newspaper career in 1934 and in 1968 will win the Israel Prize for Literature.
Mar. 1943	In March, the U.S. Navy defeats the Japanese in the Battle of Bismarck Sea.	On March 1, the American Jewish Congress sponsors a rally at New York's Madison Square Garden to "Stop Hitler Now." Attended by 75,000 people in the Garden and surrounding streets, rally leaders present a rescue plan to President Franklin D. Roosevelt.* The Committee for a Jewish Army (Bergson group) stages a Ben Hecht pageant, *We Will Never Die*, at New York's Madison Square Garden. Over 40,000 attend. President Franklin D. Roosevelt* refuses a message of support, and major Jewish organizations intervene to prevent repeat performances. The U.S. Senate and the House of Representatives pass a resolution condemning Nazi atrocities and urging punishment of those responsible. The resolution is silent on advocating rescue efforts.	In what will become known as a miracle of the Jewish people, Bulgaria releases all of its Jews taken into custody for deportation. At Nazi insistence, the Bulgarian government had ordered the deportation of its 48,000 Jews. A public outcry forces the government to rescind the deportation order. Trude Neumann, the daughter of Theodor Herzl (1860–1904), dies of starvation at the Theresienstadt ghetto. The Nazis begin the deportation of more than 48,000 Jews from Salonika, Greece, for extermination in Poland. The first of four new gas chambers and crematoria begins operation at Auschwitz II. In three months, all four will be operating. One million five hundred thousand Jews are murdered at Auschwitz II.		

B. Jews in North and South America

The Joint Emergency Committee on European Jewish Affairs is organized. The membership includes the American Jewish Committee, the American Jewish Congress, B'nai B'rith, the Jewish Labor Committee, the Synagogue Council of America, Agudat Israel of America, the Union of Orthodox Rabbis, and the American Emergency Committee for Zionist Affairs. Not included is the Committee for a Jewish Army (Bergson group), although it had asked to join.

Rabbi Stephen S. Wise and Joseph Proskauer, president of the American Jewish Committee, meet with British Foreign Secretary Anthony Eden* in Washington, D.C. Eden* rejects their plea for the Allies to ask Germany to receive food for Europe's Jews, to let them leave occupied Europe, and to assist in the removal of 60,000–70,000 Bulgarian Jews to Turkey. According to Harry Hopkins,* Eden* said: "Hitler might well take us up on any such offer and there simply are not enough ships . . . in the world to handle them."

Mar. 1943

NAZI CONCENTRATION CAMPS

A. General History	B. Jews in North and South America	C. Jews in Europe	D. Jews in the Middle East and Elsewhere	E. Jewish Culture
Germany reports the uncovering of a mass grave of thousands of Polish army soldiers killed by the Russians at Katyn, near Smolensk.	On the day of the Warsaw ghetto uprising, the Allies convene an international conference in Bermuda to study the refugee question. No government expresses a willingness to accept Jewish victims of Nazism. Palestine is excluded from consideration. Israel Goldstein of the Synagogue Council of	Adolf Hitler* personally urges the leader of Hungary, Admiral Miklós Horthy,* to permit the "resettlement" of Hungary's Jews. Horthy* refuses and insists that "the Jews cannot be exterminated or beaten to death." The third part of the Oyneg Shabes archive of the Warsaw ghetto	Oliver Harvey,* private secretary to Anthony Eden,* Britain's foreign secretary, records in his diary: "Unfortunately A.E. is immovable on the subject of Palestine. He loves Arabs and hates Jews."	

Apr. 1943

A. General History	B. Jews in North and South America	C. Jews in Europe	D. Jews in the Middle East and Elsewhere	E. Jewish Culture
Apr. 1943	America declares, "Victims are not being rescued because the democracies do not want them."	is buried in a bunker on Swietojerska Street. The next day, the Nazis begin the destruction of the ghetto using SS troops led by General Juergen Stroop.* Twelve hundred Jewish fighters led by Mordecai Anielewicz resist and hold off the Nazis for five weeks. By the end of April, the Germans finish the cremation of more than 600,000 Jews exterminated at Belzec, and all signs of the camp are liquidated. There were only two Jewish survivors from Belzec, Rudolf Reder and Chaim Hirszman. Hirszman will be killed by Polish antisemites in March 1946.		
May 1943	All Axis troops in North Africa surrender to the Allies.	While in Europe, Haj Amin al-Husseini,* the mufti of Jerusalem, complains to the Bulgarian foreign minister about permitting Jewish children to leave for Palestine. He recommends their transport to Poland. Mordecai Anielewicz, leader of the Warsaw ghetto uprising, is killed in the command bunker at 18 Mila Street. Shmuel Zygielbojm (1895–1943), a member of the Polish Bund who was smuggled out of Poland to alert the world to the fate of Poland's Jews, commits suicide in London. In his suicide note he wrote, "By my death I wish to express my vigorous protest against the apathy with which the world regards and resigns itself to the slaughter of the Jewish people." General Juergen Stroop* reports that		

Jewish fighters in the Warsaw Ghetto uprising after their capture in May. This photo appears in the Stroop report, under the caption "These bandits offered armed resistance." (Yad Vashem)

A. General History	B. Jews in North and South America	C. Jews in Europe	D. Jews in the Middle East and Elsewhere	E. Jewish Culture

<table>
<tr><td></td><td></td><td>"there is no more Jewish quarter in Warsaw," the action ending that evening "by blowing up the Warsaw synagogue" (the Great Synagogue onTlomackie Street). According to Stroop's* calculations, 7,000 Jews had been killed in the fighting, 30,000 had been deported to Treblinka, and 631 bunkers had been destroyed. The uprising is the first significant urban revolt against the Nazis.

Josef Mengele,* an SS doctor, arrives at Auschwitz. He begins to conduct medical experiments on Jews.</td><td>

S.S. General Juergen Stroop's report on the quelling of the uprising in the Warsaw Ghetto in April and May, titled "There Is No More Jewish Quarter in Warsaw." Stroop was hanged after a war crimes trial in Warsaw in 1951. (Yad Vashem)</td><td>**May 1943**</td></tr>
<tr><td></td><td></td><td>Heinrich Himmler* orders the liquidation of the ghettoes in Nazi-occupied Poland and Nazi-occupied Soviet Union. The Nazis begin dismantling the remnant of the Lvov ghetto.

Jewish fighters resist the Nazi destruction of the Czestochowa ghetto.</td><td></td><td>**June 1943**</td></tr>
<tr><td>The Germans launch a major offensive at the Kursk region of the Russian central front. It is repulsed by the Soviet army in a major turning point of the war.

The Allies invade Sicily.

Benito Mussolini* is deposed. The new Italian government is led by Marshal Pietro Badoglio (1871–1956).*</td><td>The Bergson group sponsors the Emergency Conference to Rescue the Jewish People of Europe, in New York. The conference calls for the establishment of a U.S. government agency charged specifically with rescuing Jews. Hearst* newspapers are strong supporters of the conference.</td><td>Heinrich Himmler* issues an order not to dismantle Sobibor, but to transform it into a concentration camp, to be used as a depot for ammunition captured from the enemy.

Martin Bormann* (1900–?), head of the Nazi party secretariat, issues a circular on the "final solution," on orders from Adolf Hitler.* Whenever there is public discussion of the Jewish question, "there may be no discussion of a future overall solution. It may however be mentioned that the Jews are taken in groups for appropriate labor purposes."</td><td></td><td>**July 1943**</td></tr>
</table>

459

C. Jews in Europe

July 1943

The Nazis establish a concentration camp at Bergen-Belsen, near Hanover, Germany. It is intended as a prisoner-of-war camp as well as a place for Jews whom they wish to exchange for Germans in Allied custody. Fewer than 400 Jews will be exchanged and 37,000 inmates will die before liberation.

The Spanish government successfully prevents the deportation of 367 Sephardic Spanish subjects living in Salonika to Auschwitz. They are sent, instead, to Bergen-Belsen and six months later to safety in Spain.

The Jewish public in the Vilna ghetto demands that the underground surrender their leader, Yitzhak Wittenberg, to the Nazis, fearing liquidation of the entire ghetto if they did not. Wittenberg turns himself over to the Gestapo and is tortured and executed.

After four months of activity beginning in April, over 700,000 corpses are unearthed and cremated at Treblinka, while the camp continues to receive new transports of Jews for extermination.

	A. General History	B. Jews in North and South America	C. Jews in Europe	D. Jews in the Middle East and Elsewhere	E. Jewish Culture
Aug. 1943	Axis resistance in Sicily ends.	The American Jewish Conference is convened in New York and calls for the establishment of a Jewish commonwealth in Palestine, unlimited immigration to Palestine, and the withdrawal of the White Paper.	During an address at Cracow, Hans Frank,* head of the general government of Poland, states: "We started here with three and a half million Jews, and what remains of them—a few working companies only."		

Aug. 1943

C. Jews in Europe

Seven hundred Jewish prisoners at Treblinka stage a revolt, set fire to several camp buildings, explode the arsenal, and kill about 20 German and Ukrainian guards. More than 150 succeed in escaping, and the rest are killed in the camp. No more than 70 will remain alive at the end of the war.

On August 3, Jews resisting the Nazis during the liquidation of the Bedzin ghetto are all killed.

The Nazis begin the final action to destroy the Bialystok ghetto, rounding up 40,000 Jews for deportation to Treblinka. The Jewish underground resists, but the revolt led by Mordecai Tenenbaum and Daniel Moskowicz is crushed.

Jews from Bialystok are the last of 840,000 Jews to be killed at Treblinka. In September, the gas chambers are destroyed, the barbed wire fencing is removed, the killing site is ploughed up, and the guards are transferred to other camps.

Raymond Raoul Lambert (1894–1943), French Jewish official, is exterminated at Auschwitz. He was arrested after protesting Nazi excesses against Jews to Pierre Laval.* His diary reveals a belief that he was easing the lot of the Jews as he worked with Vichy and the Germans.

	A. General History	B. Jews in North and South America	C. Jews in Europe	D. Jews in the Middle East and Elsewhere	E. Jewish Culture
Sep. 1943	The Allies begin the invasion of Italy when British forces land at Calabria, near the toe of Italy. The capitulation of Italy to the Allies is announced. U.S. forces establish a beachhead at Salerno, Italy. German forces take control of Rome,	Nahum Goldmann of the World Jewish Congress asks Breckinridge Long* of the U.S. State Department for help in providing food and medicine to Jews still alive in Poland, Czechoslovakia, and the Balkans. The State Department refuses. New York Representative	There is armed Jewish resistance to the liquidation of the Tarnow ghetto. No Jews survive. German forces, having occupied the former Italian zone of Nice, France, begin raiding the homes and properties of Jews. The Vilna ghetto is liquidated.		

A. General History	B. Jews in North and South America	C. Jews in Europe	D. Jews in the Middle East and Elsewhere	E. Jewish Culture
occupy most of Italy, and disarm Italian forces in northern Italy. The Germans rescue Benito Mussolini* from Italian imprisonment. The Soviet army recaptures Smolensk.	Samuel Dickstein (1885–1954) introduces a bill in Congress to allow refugees who would not endanger public safety to come to the U.S. temporarily. The Roosevelt* administration opposes the bill, which never reaches the floor of Congress.	At the Babi Yar camp, 325 Jews and Soviet prisoners of war revolt. Only 14 survive. Two of the survivors, David Budnik and Vladimir Davydov, will testify in 1946 at the Nuremberg trials. Beginning at the end of September, and over a three-week period, Danish sea captains and fishermen ferry about 7,000 Danish Jews and about 700 Christians married to Jews to safety in neutral Sweden.		**Sep. 1943**
Italy declares war on Germany.	The Bergson group organizes a visit of 400 Orthodox rabbis to Washington, D.C., to petition for a U.S. rescue agency for European Jews. They meet with Vice President Henry A. Wallace,* as President Franklin D. Roosevelt* refuses to see them.	In an address to SS generals in Poznan, Heinrich Himmler* says: "Among ourselves it should be mentioned quite frankly, and yet we will never speak of it publicly. . . . The extermination of the Jewish race . . . is a page of glory in our history which has never been written and is never to be written." Jewish prisoners at the Sobibor camp revolt. Led by Alexander Pechersky, a Soviet Jewish prisoner of war, they kill several German and Ukrainian guards. About 230–270 Jews are killed inside the camp or in the surroundings; 100 of the 300 who escape are captured and shot; about 130–150 will find their death before the war's end; and only 50–70, including Pechersky, will reach Soviet partisans and freedom. After the revolt, the Sobibor camp is closed. The Germans deport to Auschwitz 1,015 Italian Jews seized in Rome. Pope Pius XII orders assistance to be given to the remaining Jews of Rome, and 4,715 are given		**Oct. 1943**

	A. General History	B. Jews in North and South America	C. Jews in Europe	D. Jews in the Middle East and Elsewhere	E. Jewish Culture
Oct. 1943			sanctuary in the Vatican and in monasteries and convents. A Jewish woman about to be gassed at Auschwitz seizes the revolver of an SS man and kills him and wounds another. The incident sparks other women to attack SS men. The women are killed by camp commandant Rudolf Hoess* and other SS men.		
Nov. 1943	The Soviet army recaptures Kiev. It has been occupied by the Germans since September 1941. U.S. troops invade Tarawa in the Gilbert Islands and end the Japanese resistance after a several-day battle. President Franklin D. Roosevelt* and Winston Churchill* meet with Chiang Kai-shek* at the Cairo Conference. Franklin D. Roosevelt,* Winston Churchill,* and Joseph Stalin* meet at the Teheran Conference. They agree that a U.S. and British invasion of France will receive the highest priority. The Soviet Union will join the war against Japan after the defeat of Germany. Lebanon wins independence from France. The Christian and Muslim communities conclude an unwritten national covenant that guards the country against domination by either other Arab states or commitments to the West. The agreement also provides that the president must be a Christian, while the prime minister and	Senator Guy Gillette* and Congressmen Will Rogers* and Joseph Baldwin* introduce a congressional resolution urging President Franklin D. Roosevelt* to establish a commission to save Europe's remaining Jews. The resolution is withdrawn when Roosevelt* issues an executive order establishing the War Refugee Board.	The Nazis liquidate the remnants of the Riga ghetto. Rabbi Riccardo Pacifici, of Genoa, Italy; 200 members of his congregation; and 100 Jewish refugees from northern Europe who found shelter there are deported and gassed at Auschwitz. Fearing that the uprising at Sobibor might influence prisoners in other camps, the Nazis round up Jews from the labor camps in the Lublin region, transport them to the ditches behind the Majdanek concentration camp gas chambers, and shoot 50,000. The operation is code-named Harvest Festival. Following this massacre, only 612 Jews remain at Majdanek. Romanian dictator Ion Antonescu,* fearing retribution from the Allies, advises his cabinet to resist Nazi plans to deport Jews from the eastern Romanian territory of Transnistra. Many Jews are saved from death, and in March and April 1944, over 1,200 orphans will be permitted to leave Romania for Palestine.		

A. General History	B. Jews in North and South America	C. Jews in Europe	D. Jews in the Middle East and Elsewhere	E. Jewish Culture	
the speaker must be Muslims.		The approximately 30 Jews remaining at the Janowska camp, near Lvov, revolt. It is not known how many Germans are killed or how many Jews escape.			**Nov. 1943**
U.S. General Dwight D. Eisenhower* is appointed supreme commander of the Allied Expeditionary Force.	Congress makes public testimony of the State Department's Breckinridge Long* to the House Foreign Affairs Committee. His claim of admission to the U.S. of 580,000 refugees from Nazism is refuted as false and results in his removal from refugee responsibilities in the State Department.	Felix Nussbaum (1904–1944), German artist, paints *Self-Portrait with Jewish Identity Card* while in hiding from the Germans in Brussels. This work by a relatively unknown artist symbolizes the experiences of an entire generation of artists who were exiled, hunted, imprisoned, and murdered but who were never silenced by the Germans. Nussbaum will be denounced to the Germans in 1944 and deported to Auschwitz, where he will be gassed one month before the Allies liberate Brussels. By the end of the year, Jews number more than 10% of the Soviet partisan movement. By the end of the year, several Jewish resistance groups are active throughout France. Included in these groups are the Jewish Scout Movement and the Organization Juif de Combat. During 1943, the Nazis murdered 500,000 Jews.			**Dec. 1943**
The decision to relocate Japanese-Americans from the Pacific Coast is upheld by the U.S. Supreme Court.	Theodore von Karman (1881–1963), U.S. physicist, is appointed chairman of the U.S. air force scientific advisory board. Of Hungarian origin, he settled in the U.S. in 1930 as head of the Guggenheim Aeronautical Laboratory at the California Institute of Technology. He and his students	Jacob Wiernik, while in the underground at Warsaw, writes *A Year in Treblinka*, the first eyewitness account of the extermination camps. His manuscript will be brought to England by a Polish underground courier at the end of the year and published in the U.S. and Palestine.		Solomon B. Freehof (1892–1990), U.S. Reform rabbi, writes *Reform Jewish Practice and Its Rabbinic Background*, which describes present-day Reform Jewish practices and the traditional rabbinical laws from which they are derived. The Jewish Theological Seminary	**1944**

1944

developed the science of aerodynamics and applied it to aircraft design. He influenced the development of high-speed aircraft.

The National Community Relations Advisory Council, composed of national and local Jewish community relations organizations, is organized to enable its members to exchange views and work together on community relations problems.

Lewis Milestone directs *The Purple Heart*, in which Navigator Lieutenant Wayne Greenbaum (Sam Levene) is a spokesman for the Doolittle raiders of 1942 who were shot down over Tokyo and are tried as spies. Wartime films featuring major Jewish characters are set in the Pacific theater, as filmmakers are wary of featuring a connection between American Jews and their European brethren lest antisemites conclude they are fighting for personal rather than patriotic reasons.

Address Unknown, depicting a relationship of two partners in the art business, is one of the few films addressing Nazi antisemitism. Martin Schultz (Paul Lukas) sends art objects from Germany to Max Einstein (Morris Carnovsky) in San Francisco. Their children are in Germany where Einstein's daughter is tracked down and shot as Schultz's son refuses her sanctuary from the Nazis.

Tomorrow the World, another film dealing

Aaron Rokeah (1880–1957), the Belzer Rebbe, escapes from the Nazis and settles in Palestine.

Ernst Julius Cohen (1869–1944), Dutch physical chemist who served as first president of the Dutch Chemical Society and as president of the International Union of Pure and Applied Chemistry, refuses to flee Holland and is gassed at Auschwitz.

Mendel Grossman (1912–1944), the most famous Jewish camera chronicler of the Holocaust, is deported from the Lodz ghetto to a German work camp, where he dies. Grossman took over 10,000 photographs of daily life in the Lodz ghetto. His hidden negatives will be unearthed after the war and sent to Israel but destroyed during the War of Independence. Some of his prints will survive and, in 1977, 70 will be printed in *With a Camera in the Ghetto*, which is published in the U.S.

of America inaugurates the Eternal Light radio program, which presents dramatizations of Jewish historical subjects. It reaches an audience of several million people.

A Century of Jewish Life (1839–1939), written by Ismar Elbogen (1874–1943), German Jewish scholar who emigrated to the U.S. in 1938, is published posthumously. The work is a sequel to Heinrich Graetz's (1817–1891) *History of the Jews*.

Leonard Bernstein writes the music and Betty Comden (b. 1919) and Adolph Green (b. 1915) write the lyrics for the Broadway musical *On the Town*, which includes the song "New York, New York."

Photograph taken by Mendel Grossman of a child being fed by her older brother in the Lodz Ghetto. (Ghetto Fighters House)

A. General History	B. Jews in North and South America	C. Jews in Europe	D. Jews in the Middle East and Elsewhere	E. Jewish Culture	
	with Nazi antisemitism, involves a 12-year-old German boy, Emil Bruckner, indoctrinated in Nazi ideology, who is brought to U.S., where he attacks his cousin but is accorded a fair trial, thus contrasting American democracy with Nazi despotism.			John von Neumann (1903–1957), U.S. mathematician, and Oskar Morgenstern (1902–1977), U.S. economist, write *Theory of Games and Economic Behavior*, which originates the mathematical theory of games. Von Neumann will be a member of the U.S. Atomic Energy Commission from 1955 until his death. Morgenstern will be the White House consultant on atomic energy matters from 1959 to 1960.	**1944**
The Soviet army drives across prewar Polish borders. Allied forces land at Anzio, 35 miles south of Rome. U.S. forces invade the Japanese-held island of Kwajalein and other islands in the Marshall Islands.	Aides to U.S. Treasury Secretary Henry Morgenthau, Jr. (1891–1967), submit a report to him: "Report to the Secretary on the Acquiesence of This Government in the Murder of the Jews." One of his aides, Josiah DuBois,* threatens to resign and make the story public if President Franklin D. Roosevelt* does not take action. Secretary of Treasury Henry Morgenthau, Jr., and his aides meet with President Franklin D. Roosevelt* to discuss the plight of Jews and suggest an executive order establishing a War Refugee Board. Roosevelt* agrees. He signs the executive order drafted by Oscar Cox,* Milton Handler, and Benjamin V. Cohen. John Pehle* is executive director and the order directs the State, Treasury, and War Departments to assist the board in rescue efforts. In 16 months of action, the board spends $1 million in government funds and $16 million raised by Jewish organizations.		The Irgun declares an armed revolt against the British authorities in Palestine as the British continue to implement immigration restrictions of the White Paper. The Jewish community leadership condemns the decision, which they believe will hamper the Allied war effort against Nazi Germany. Britain's Prime Minister Winston Churchill* asks his cabinet to approve, in principle, the decision to establish a Jewish state in part of Palestine. The discussion remains secret. In the late 1970s, it will be revealed that Sir Harold MacMichael,* the high commissioner in Palestine who was believed to lack sympathy for Zionist aims in fact supported the plan for a Jewish state.	Isaac Stern (b. 1920), violinist, makes his debut as soloist with the New York Philharmonic Orchestra. He has since performed as soloist with that orchestra more than any violinist in its history. Ben Hecht, U.S. novelist and journalist, writes *A Guide for the Bedevilled*, in which he records his regained faith in the Jewish people and his concern for antisemitism in Europe and the U.S. *Jacobowsky and the Colonel*, a play written by S. N. Behrman (1893–1973), U.S. playwright, with Franz Werfel (1890–1945), is produced on Broadway. It is a tragicomedy about the flight of a Jew and a Polish aristocrat before the German advance into France. Joseph Erlanger (1874–1965), U.S. physiologist, is awarded the Nobel Prize in physiology or medicine for his studies of blood mechanics and neurology.	**Jan. 1944**
German troops occupy Hungary, fearing that its ally will defect to the Allies. A pro-German government, led by General Dome	President Franklin D. Roosevelt* authorizes two prominent Zionist leaders, Stephen S. Wise and Abba Hillel Silver, to issue a statement suggesting	Hans Frank,* at a meeting of Nazi party members in Cracow, declares: "the Jews are a race which must be wiped out."	Between March and August, Ira Hirschmann (1901–1989), War Refugee Board representative in Turkey, arranges the	Isidor Isaac Rabi, U.S. physicist, is	**Mar. 1944**

	A. General History	B. Jews in North and South America	C. Jews in Europe	D. Jews in the Middle East and Elsewhere	E. Jewish Culture
Mar. 1944	Sztojay,* is installed and, in May, the "final solution" of Hungarian Jewry is quickly implemented. Soviet troops advance into northern Romania. British General Orde Wingate* is killed in a plane crash in Burma.	future U.S. support for a Jewish national home in Palestine. He then congratulates Speaker Sam Rayburn* for keeping the House in line against passing a resolution favoring a Jewish commonwealth. A few days later he assures six Arab leaders that no decision on Palestine would be made without consultation on both sides.	Emanuel Ringelblum, historian of the Warsaw ghetto, and his family are among a group of 38 in hiding in "Aryan" Warsaw who are betrayed to the Nazis. He is executed several days later. While in hiding he wrote in a history of Polish–Jewish relations during the war: "The blind folly of Poland's anti-Semites . . . has been responsible for the deaths of hundreds of thousands of Jews who could have been saved despite the Germans. . . . Poland has given asylum at the most to one percent of the Jewish victims of Hitler's persecutions." Adolf Eichmann* and his assistants meet at the Mauthausen concentration camp and plan a deportation program for Hungary's 750,000 Jews. The Nazis round up 800 Greek Jews in Athens and, early in April, will send them to Auschwitz.	safeguarding of the remaining Romanian and Bulgarian Jews. He also assists 7,000 Balkan Jews to reach Palestine. The Irgun simultaneously attacks three police stations at Jerusalem, Jaffa, and Haifa, killing six British policemen.	awarded the Nobel Prize in physics for discovering the resonance method for studying atomic nuclei. Herbert Spencer Gasser (1883–1963), U.S. neuro-physiologist, is awarded the Nobel Prize in medicine or physiology for his studies in understanding the complexities of nerve impulse transmission.
Apr. 1944	U.S. and British warplanes begin bombing Budapest and other Hungarian cities, now under German control. The Soviet army recaptures Odessa. It had been under Nazi occupation since October 1941.		The German Propaganda Ministry urges the German press to reiterate "In the case of the Jews there are not merely a few criminals, but all of Jewry rose from criminal roots. The annihilation of Jewry is no loss to humanity." Klaus Barbie,* a middle-ranking Gestapo officer, deports 44 Jewish children and 7 adults to Auschwitz from the village of Izieu, 50 miles east of Lyons. One adult survives. Barbie will become known as "the butcher of Lyons."	The Jewish Agency Executive in Jerusalem decides to isolate the Jewish terrorist groups in Palestine from the Jewish community through a campaign of propaganda. The effort fails.	

A. General History	B. Jews in North and South America	C. Jews in Europe	D. Jews in the Middle East and Elsewhere	E. Jewish Culture
		The first deportation of Jews from Hungary to Auschwitz takes place.		**Apr. 1944**
		After Rudolf Vrba and Alfred Wetzler escape from Auschwitz, Vrba pleads with Hungarian Jewish leaders to resist deportations. His pleas go unheeded.		
Great Britain releases Indian leader Mohandas K. Gandhi* from custody. He had been imprisoned since August 1942.

Christian Wirth,* the SS officer who was inspector of the Operation Reinhard* extermination camps at Belzec, Sobibor, and Treblinka and developed the entire system of extermination, is killed by Josip Broz's* partisans near Trieste. Broz, later known as Marshal Tito, is the leader of the communist resistance movement in Yugoslavia. | A *New York Times* news story reveals that the Hungarian government "is now preparing for the annihilation of Hungarian Jews." | Mass deportations of Hungarian Jews commence and by May 31, 204,312 have been deported to Auschwitz.

The Nazis expand the industrial plants in the Auschwitz region in expectation of the arrival of several hundred thousand Hungarian Jews, some of whom will be chosen for slave labor. Those not selected for labor are gassed and cremated.

Rabbi Michael Dov Weissmandel, Slovakian Orthodox rabbi involved in rescue efforts in Bratislava, sends coded message to the Swiss Orthodox Jewish community. He urges Allied aerial bombardment of the railway lines to Auschwitz to interrupt the deportation of Hungarian Jews.

Joel Brand (1906–1964), a Hungarian Jew, is flown by the Nazis to Istanbul, Turkey, to advise the Jewish Agency of an offer from Adolf Eichmann* to release 1 million Jews in return for 10,000 trucks to be used only on the eastern front. Brand is arrested by the British, and held in Cairo, where it is believed he meets Lord Moyne,* the British minister of state in the Middle | Five years after the promulgation of the MacDonald White Paper, vigorous implementation of its immigration clause by British colonial authorities results in the nonutilization of 20,000 of the 75,000 certificates available for immigration.

The Irgun raids the British radio station at Ramallah, Palestine. | **May 1944** |

	A. General History	B. Jews in North and South America	C. Jews in Europe	D. Jews in the Middle East and Elsewhere	E. Jewish Culture
May 1944			East, who advises him, "What shall I do with those million Jews? Where shall I put them?" The deal never goes through.		
June 1944	The U.S. army liberates Rome. On June 6, the Allies invade Normandy, on the French coast. It is the greatest amphibious operation in history. Within 24 hours, 176,000 troops are landed from 4,000 ships. The SS massacre 624 at the French village of Oradour in reprisal for the killing of an SS man by French partisans. Among those killed are several Jews who found refuge in the village. The Germans launch unmanned V-1 rocket bombs against Great Britain. U.S. forces invade Japanese-held Saipan in the Marianas Islands. U.S. naval forces decisively defeat the Japanese in the Battle of the Philippine Sea. The GI Bill of Rights is signed into law. It provides war veterans educational and other benefits to facilitate their adjustment to civilian life.	The U.S. establishes a "free port" at Oswego, New York, for 1,000 refugees from Nazism. President Franklin D. Roosevelt* obtained congressional approval for the effort and stressed that refugees would be kept "under appropriate security restrictions." He pledges that at the war's end they will be sent back to their homelands. At its convention, the Republican party declares that free Jewish immigration into Palestine was guaranteed by the Balfour Declaration and mandate. It demands the restoration of the right and condemns President Franklin D. Roosevelt's* failure to insist on British adherence. In July, the Democratic party will demand the same immigration policy and adds its hope that a free and democratic Jewish commonwealth will result.	The Nazis take 260 Jews living on the island of Crete to Candia and board them on a ship together with 400 Greek hostages and 300 Italian soldiers. The ship is taken out to sea and scuttled. All are drowned. The day the Allies land in Normandy, the Nazis round up 1,795 Jews on the island of Corfu, in the Adriatic. All are sent directly to Auschwitz, where 1,500 are immediately gassed. Hannah Szenes (Senesh, 1921–1944), a member of a group of Haganah parachutists, is captured by Hungarian police upon entering Hungary to help organize the Jewish resistance. Szenes had parachuted into Yugoslovia in March, where she stayed among Marshal Tito's* partisans until she tried to enter Hungary. By June 17, 340,142 Hungarian Jews have been deported to Auschwitz. Allied officials receive the report of Rudolf Vrba and Alfred Wetzler detailing Auschwitz killing operations. In response to a Jewish request, Adolf Eichmann* permits a train with 1,686 Hungarian Jews to leave for Belsen and then to Switzerland.		
July 1944	The Soviet army recaptures Minsk. It	Forty thousand Americans attend a	As Soviet forces are advancing on Vilna,	In July, 222 Dutch Jews imprisoned in	

A. General History	B. Jews in North and South America	C. Jews in Europe	D. Jews in the Middle East and Elsewhere	E. Jewish Culture	
had been occupied by German forces since July 1941. U.S. forces defeat the Japanese and secure Saipan. The Soviet army recaptures Vilna. It had been occupied by the Germans since June 24, 1941. A group of German army officers fail in an attempt to assassinate Adolf Hitler.* The Soviet army occupies Lublin and liberates the nearby Majdanek concentration and extermination camp.	mass demonstration at New York's Madison Square Park to endorse the implementation of Admiral Horthy's* offer to release Hungarian Jews.	2,000 Jewish laborers remain there. The Nazis kill 1,800 and 200 manage to hide until the Russians arrive. Britain's Prime Minister Winston Churchill* tells Foreign Secretary Anthony Eden* to have Britain's air force bomb Auschwitz. Officials at the Foreign Office subvert Churchill's* request. Between July 7 and November 20, the Allied air forces bomb an oil refining complex 47 miles from the Auschwitz death camps 10 times. On August 20, the U.S. air force bombs the Auschwitz factory area within five miles of the death camps.	Bergen-Belsen and 52 Jews from France arrive in Palestine. German and British officials, the Jewish Agency, and the International Red Cross secretly arranged the exchange for a group of German women and children who had been interned by the British in Palestine as enemy aliens.		**July 1944**

C. Jews in Europe

Admiral Horthy,* Hungarian head of state, stops deportation of Jews to Auschwitz after worldwide protests. He offers to permit emigration of all Jewish children under 10 who possess visas to other countries and all Jews of any age who have Palestine certificates.

Raoul Wallenberg,* a Swedish businessman turned diplomat, begins operating from the Swedish embassy in Budapest, Hungary, and uses bribery, bluff, and deception to save thousands of Jews from Nazi extermination. He is financed by the American Jewish Joint Distribution Committee and supported by his own government.

Britain's Prime Minister Winston Churchill* writes to Foreign Secretary Anthony Eden* describing the "final solution" as "probably the greatest and most horrible crime ever committed in the whole history of the world."

About 437,000 Hungarian Jews have been deported to Auschwitz. More than 170,000 remain in Budapest.

As the Russian army advances, the remaining 8,000 Jews of the Kovno ghetto are taken by train to Stutthof.

The Nazis round up 1,651 Jews of Rhodes and 94 from Kos. They are taken to the mainland by ship and then by train to Auschwitz. Only 151 Jews from Rhodes and 12 from Kos survive the war.

Erich Salomon (1886–1944), pioneer German photojournalist, his wife, and one of his sons are killed at Auschwitz. His informal pictures of important figures and his documentation of political and cultural events influenced the development of photojournalism.

A. General History	B. Jews in North and South America	C. Jews in Europe	D. Jews in the Middle East and Elsewhere	E. Jewish Culture	
The Soviet army liberates Kovno. The Polish underground army in Warsaw begins a revolt against the Germans.	U.S. Assistant Secretary of War John J. McCloy* writes to the World Jewish Congress denying their request to bomb Auschwitz gas chambers and rail lines.	The Nazis separate the remaining 3,000 Jews at the Strassenhof camp, near Riga. All below the age of 18 or over 30 (2,400) are gassed and the remaining 600	The Irgun attacks the Tel Aviv–Jaffa British police headquarters. The Stern group, an extremist wing of the Irgun, makes an unsuccessful attempt to assassinate Sir		**Aug. 1944**

	A. General History	B. Jews in North and South America	C. Jews in Europe	D. Jews in the Middle East and Elsewhere	E. Jewish Culture
Aug. 1944	U.S. and Free French troops land in southern France. The Soviet army crosses the Danube River into Romania. The Allies liberate Paris. It had been occupied by the Germans since June 14, 1940. Romania declares war on Germany. A few days earlier, it surrendered to the Soviet Union and began fighting German forces who attempted to seize control of Bucharest. Germany withdraws its troops from Bulgaria. Guam is recaptured by the U.S. from the Japanese.	The British and American governments issue a public statement, arranged by the War Refugee Board, accepting the responsibility to care for all Jews allowed out of Hungary. However, the Nazis prevent transfer.	are evacuated by sea to Stutthof. The family of Anne Frank is discovered during a search for hidden Jews in Amsterdam. One month later they are deported to Auschwitz. About 67,000 Jews of the Lodz ghetto, where the largest number of Jews still live and who survive by doing forced labor for the Nazis, are deported to Auschwitz shortly before the Soviet army liberates the city. More than 60,000, including Chaim Rumkowski (1877–1944), Elder of the Jews, and his family, are exterminated. Sixteen thousand Slovak soldiers and partisans revolt against Nazi rule. More than 1,500 Jews, from the labor camp at Novaki, fight in the uprising. Of the 2,100 partisans killed, 269 are Jews. Jewish paratroopers sent from Palestine join the uprising.	Harold MacMichael,* the outgoing British high commissioner in Palestine.	
Sep. 1944	The Allies liberate Brussels, Belgium. Bulgaria declares war on Germany. The Germans launch the first unmanned V-2 rocket bombs against Great Britain. The Polish underground army in Warsaw appeals for Allied aid. U.S. forces invade Peleliu Island in the Japanese-held Palau group of islands. The Soviet army occupies Sofia, Bulgaria.	*Life* magazine writes of the Majdanek Nazi extermination camp near Lublin, Poland, overrun by the advancing Russian army. The story features photos of a warehouse filled with 800,000 shoes taken from Nazi victims. Piles of discarded Zyklon B gas canisters were found.	As Russian troops approach the Klooga labor camp in the Baltic area, the Nazis murder 3,000 slave laborers, including 1,500 Jews from the Vilna ghetto, 800 Soviet prisoners of war, and 700 Estonian political prisoners. Paul Eppstein (1901–1944), German Jewish community leader who was appointed Jewish leader of the Theresienstadt concentration camp, is killed by the Gestapo. Darius Paul Dassault, French army officer, is appointed governor of newly liberated Paris with the rank of general of the army.	The Irgun attacks British police buildings in Palestine at Bet Dagon, Qalqilya, Haifa, and Katar. Prime Minister Winston Churchill* announces the formation in the British army of a Jewish brigade of Palestinians. Churchill* overruled the objections of his war minister. It will not serve in the Middle East, and is not allowed to wear its Jewish insignia while in transit through Egypt.	

A. General History	B. Jews in North and South America	C. Jews in Europe	D. Jews in the Middle East and Elsewhere	E. Jewish Culture

A. General History

The Warsaw uprising of the Polish underground army is crushed by the Germans. About 250,000 Poles are killed. The anti-Communist underground army accuses the Soviets of intentionally delaying their advance into Warsaw.

The Soviet army liberates Riga, Latvia. It had been occupied by the Germans since July 1, 1941.

German Field Marshal Erwin Rommel* commits suicide. He was facing a trial for his suspected involvement in an anti-Hitler* plot.

British troops liberate Athens, Greece.

U.S. forces land on Leyte and begin the liberation of the Philippines from the Japanese.

U.S. naval forces defeat the Japanese in the Battle of Leyte Gulf. It is the greatest battle in the history of naval warfare.

B. Jews in North and South America

President Franklin D. Roosevelt* announces in a letter to Senator Robert F. Wagner* his approval of the Palestine plank in the Democratic party platform: "I know how long and ardently the Jewish people have worked and prayed for the establishment of Palestine as a free and democratic Jewish commonwealth. . . . If reelected I shall help to bring about its realization."

C. Jews in Europe

One thousand Jews fight with the Polish underground during the uprising against the Germans in Warsaw. At least 500 are killed.

Jewish inmates at Auschwitz who are forced to assist in the extermination process revolt and blow up one of the four crematoria.

The Arrow Cross Hungarian Fascist organization seizes power and sets up a pro-Nazi government in Hungary. The Germans return to Budapest. Deportations of Jews to death camps are resumed.

The Nazis evacuate the Plaszow camp near Cracow, including Oscar Schindler's* factory, where 1,200 Jews work under his protection. Schindler,* a German Catholic, sets up a new factory in the Sudetenland and arranges for the relocation of all his Jewish laborers, thus saving them from extermination.

Adolf Eichmann* returns to Budapest. He demands that 50,000 able-bodied Jews be marched to Germany. Deportations resume.

At Auschwitz, the Nazis burn documentary evidence of their mass killings. During the last 10 days of human killing, thousands of Jews are marched away from Auschwitz to other camps and factories in central and western Germany.

Hungary exempts from deportation Jews with foreign passports

D. Jews in the Middle East and Elsewhere

The Haganah begins the Saison (hunting season), in which they attempt to paralyze the independent activities of the Stern group and the Irgun. The Stern group ceases activity and the Haganah arrests members of the Irgun.

Corpses of victims killed at Birkenau (Auschwitz) gas chambers being burned in open pits. This photograph was taken by David Szmulewski, a sonderkommando, *and is one of three smuggled out of the camp to alert the world to what was happening there. (Yad Vashem)*

A group of naked Jewish women on the way to a gas chamber at Birkenau (Auschwitz). David Szmulewski took this photograph from the roof of a building in the area. (Yad Vashem)

	A. General History	B. Jews in North and South America	C. Jews in Europe	D. Jews in the Middle East and Elsewhere	E. Jewish Culture
Oct. 1944			or foreign nationality. Swiss Consul Charles Lutz* begins issuing protective documents. Within a few weeks, he has 76 buildings in Budapest under Swiss diplomatic protection in which 25,000 Jews find shelter and are saved. Raoul Wallenberg,* the Swedish representative, also continues to issue protective documents—about 4,500. The gas chambers at Auschwitz stop operating.		
Nov. 1944	U.S. B-29 aircraft from Saipan begin the bombing of Japan. The British army liberates Salonika, Greece. Franklin D. Roosevelt* is elected for a fourth term as U.S. president, defeating Republican Thomas E. Dewey.* Senator Harry S. Truman* of Missouri is elected vice president.	The Jewish vote in the U.S. presidential election is estimated at 90% for Franklin D. Roosevelt* and 10% for Thomas E. Dewey.* U.S. Secretary of State Edward R. Stettinius, Jr.,* notes in his diary that President Franklin D. Roosevelt* stated: "Palestine should be for the Jews and no Arabs should be in it. . . . He has definite ideas on the subject. . . . It should be exclusive Jewish territory." A Gallup poll reports that 76% of Americans believe that the Germans murdered many in concentration camps. Of this number, only 16% believe that 2–6 million people were murdered, and just over 50% believe the number to be 1 million or less. Almost 36% said the deaths amounted to 100,000 or less.	The destruction of crematoria and gas chambers at Auschwitz begins. On November 26, the last 204 members of the Sonderkommando are killed. Heinrich Himmler* ordered the destruction of the gas chambers and crematoria to remove evidence of extermination from advancing Allied forces. By November, more than 1,500 Jewish twins had been experimented on by Josef Mengele* since his arrival at Auschwitz in May 1943. Less than 200 survive. Mengele* was seeking to become an expert on the medical and genetic problems of twins. The Nazis execute several of the Palestinian Jews who were captured after they parachuted behind Nazi lines. They were Hannah Szenes in Budapest; Enzo Sereni in Dachau; Haviva Reik, Rafael Reiss, and Zvi Ben Ya'akov in Kremnica (Slovakia). A total of 34 Palestinian parachutists jumped into Nazi-occupied Europe.	Two members of Lehi (Freedom Fighters for Israel organized by Abraham Stern in 1940) assassinate Lord Moyne,* the British minister of state in the Middle East, in Cairo. The killing arouses sharp reaction from Winston Churchill,* and Zionists disapprove of the act. The Jewish Agency Executive decides to extend the Saison (Hunting Season) operation in the aftermath of the assassination of Lord Moyne.* Haganah intelligence operatives provide the British with information resulting in the detention of 241 Irgun members by the end of February 1945. The Saison causes resentment in the Yishuv.	

A. General History	B. Jews in North and South America	C. Jews in Europe	D. Jews in the Middle East and Elsewhere	E. Jewish Culture	
Germany launches a counteroffensive against the Allied forces in the Ardennes Forest of Luxemburg, the Battle of the Bulge. During the Battle of the Bulge, unarmed U.S. prisoners of war are massacred by an SS unit near the Belgian town of Malmedy. After Malmedy, Americans fully comprehended that the Nazis deliberately killed millions in cold blood and that Americans could be directly affected by such mass murders.	On December 5, Milton Bracker, *New York Times* correspondent, reports of Natzwiller, an abandoned Nazi concentration camp in Alsace, overrun by the Allies: "It is certain that the crematorium, the hooks, the gas orifices, the dissection slab and the urns were not used for mere decoration."	During 1944, the Nazis murdered 600,000 Jews. Hungarian Jewry made up a substantial number of those murdered.			**Dec. 1944**
	Anna M. Rosenberg (1902–1983), U.S. labor relations and manpower expert, receives the Medal of Freedom for service on the president's combined War Labor Board and for apportioning manpower priorities during the war. She is the first woman recipient of the award.		Henry Gluckman, chairman of the South African National Health Services Commission (1942–1944), is appointed minister of health in the government of Prime Minister Jan Christian Smuts.* The only Jew ever to hold a cabinet post in South Africa, he will serve until the Smuts government leaves office in 1948.	The Reconstructionist movement issues a new, revised prayer book. Although it is less radical than the standard Reform prayer book, Reconstructionist leader Mordecai M. Kaplan is excommunicated by the Union of Orthodox Rabbis. The prayer book is also denounced by Alexander Marx, Louis Ginzberg, and Saul Lieberman, who are Kaplan's colleagues at the Jewish Theological Seminary of America. The publication of *Commentary*, a monthly magazine edited by Elliot Cohen (1899–1959), begins under the sponsorship of the American Jewish Committee. Arthur Miller (b. 1915), U.S. playwright and novelist, writes *Focus*, a novel in which non-Jewish Lawrence Newman is mistaken as a Jew and is exposed to antisemitism. He assists his corner newsdealer,	**1945**
U.S. forces land on the island of Luzon in the continuing effort to liberate the Philippines from the Japanese. The Soviet army liberates Warsaw. It had been occupied by the Germans since September 27, 1939. No more than 200 Jews, who were in hiding, survive. The Soviet army liberates Lodz, Poland. The Battle of the Bulge ends in the defeat of the Germans as the Allies regain ground lost in December 1944.		The last transport of Jews, a small group from Berlin, arrives at Auschwitz. Soviet military forces enter Budapest, Hungary, and 120,000 Jews are saved from further attacks. However, Raoul Wallenberg,* summoned to Soviet military headquarters, disappears and is never heard from again. Heinrich Himmler* orders the evacuation of concentration camps in eastern Europe and forces a westward march of all inmates able to move to avoid the advancing Soviet army. This massive transfer of			**Jan. 1945**

	A. General History	B. Jews in North and South America	C. Jews in Europe	D. Jews in the Middle East and Elsewhere	E. Jewish Culture
Jan. 1945			about 700,000 Jews and non-Jews in the dead of winter results in the death of about one-third of them. About half of the victims are Jews. As the Russians approach Auschwitz, the Nazis evacuate about 50,000 remaining slave laborers in the Auschwitz region by train or foot to a hundred different camps in western Germany. The Soviet army liberates Auschwitz, but unlike the worldwide publicity given by the western Allies to the discovery of death camp horrors, the Soviets impose secrecy, and for several weeks the West hears nothing. When a report is released in May, the broadcast version does not mention the word *Jew*.		Finkelstein, in resisting antisemitism. Richard Tucker (Rubin Ticker, 1913–1975), a noted cantor, makes his New York Metropolitan opera debut as Enzo in Ponchielli's *La Gioconda*. His tenor voice is compared to that of the great Italian Enrico Caruso.* Aaron Copland is awarded the Pulitzer Prize in music for his composition *Appalachian Spring*. William Schuman (1910–1992), U.S. composer, becomes head of the Juilliard School of Music in New York. In 1962 he will leave this post to become president of New York's Lincoln Center. In 1943 he won the first Pulitzer Prize awarded in music. He is a noted champion of the cause of modern American classical music. Eugene Rabinowitch (1901–1973), U.S. physical chemist and atomic scientist who left Germany in 1933, founds and edits the *Bulletin of the Atomic Scientists*. From 1944 to 1946 he is senior chemist on the Manhattan Project. Ernst Boris Chain (1906–1979), British biochemist, is awarded the Nobel Prize in physiology or medicine, sharing the prize with Sir Alexander Fleming* and Lord Florey* for their work in developing penicillin. Chain left Germany for England when the Nazis came to power. Avrom Sutskever, Yiddish poet, publishes *The Fortress*,
Feb. 1945	President Franklin D. Roosevelt,* Winston Churchill,* and Joseph Stalin* meet at the Yalta Conference. U.S. and British bombers begin two days of incendiary bombing of Dresden. At least 35,000 are killed in the firestorms. U.S. forces invade the Japanese-held island of Iwo Jima, 775 miles from the Japanese mainland. The Soviet army liberates Poznan, Poland. Egyptian Prime Minister Ahmed Maher Pasha* is assassinated after reading a royal decree declaring war on Germany and Japan.	Associated Press photographer Joe Rosenthal photographs the raising of the American flag over Mt. Suribachi on Iwo Jima. It is probably the best-known picture of the Second World War. On the way home from Yalta, President Franklin D. Roosevelt* meets King ibn Saud* of Saudi Arabia. Roosevelt* offers increased American aid in return for Saudi assistance in gaining Arab support to resolve the Palestine question. Ibn Saud* rejects Roosevelt's* approach and suggests that Jewish refugees be given the choicest homes and lands of the defeated Germans.	Twelve hundred Jews held at Theresienstadt reach Switzerland as a result of ransom negotiations between Isaac Sternbuch, Union of Orthodox Rabbis representative, and Jean-Marie Musy,* pro-Nazi Swiss with contacts to Heinrich Himmler.* When Adolf Hitler* becomes aware of the transfer, he orders no further releases. Soviet General Ivan Danilovich Chernyakhovski (1906–1945) dies of wounds received in battle as his troops capture Koenigsberg in East Prussia. His troops had previously liberated Kiev, Minsk, Vilna, and Grodno.		
Mar. 1945	U.S. forces liberate Manila, the capital of	In an address to Congress, President	The Jewish Brigade under the command	After a trial in an Egyptian court,	

A. General History	B. Jews in North and South America	C. Jews in Europe	D. Jews in the Middle East and Elsewhere	E. Jewish Culture	

the Philippines, from the Japanese.

U.S. forces cross the Rhine River at Remagen and enter Germany.

U.S. B-29 bombers firebomb Tokyo, killing 83,793 Japanese.

The Japanese resistance on Iwo Jima ends.

The Arab League is founded in Cairo by Egypt, Iraq, Lebanon, Transjordan, Saudi Arabia, and Syria. Its principal purpose will become the prevention of the creation of a separate Jewish state in Palestine.

The Soviet Union pressures King Michael* of Romania to accept a Communist-led coalition government.

Franklin D. Roosevelt,* ad libs a phrase: "On the problem of Arabia, I learned more about the whole problem, the Moslem problem, the Jewish problem, by talking to Ibn Saud for five minutes than I could have learned in the exchange of two or three dozen letters." Harry Hopkins,* his trusted assistant, will later write that the only thing Roosevelt learned "which all people well acquainted with the Palestine cause knew, is that the Arabs don't want any more Jews in Palestine."

of General Ernest Benjamin (1900–1969) goes into action in north Italy as part of the British Eighth Army.

Anne Frank and her sister, Margot, die of sickness and starvation at Bergen-Belsen.

Eliahu Hakim and Eliahu Bet Tzuri, two members of Lehi who in November 1944 assassinated Lord Moyne* in Cairo, are executed.

a collection of poems written during the war. He was in the Vilna ghetto during the Nazi occupation and escaped to join the Jewish partisans. His poems are historically significant and also exemplify the defiant imagination capable of creating art during the Holocaust. He will move to Israel in 1947.

Marc Lavry (1903–1967), Israeli composer and conductor, composes the first opera in Palestine featuring contemporay problems, *Dan the Guard*, based on a play by Sim Shalom and adapted as a libretto by Max Brod. Born in Latvia, he was active as a composer and conductor between 1929 and 1934 in Berlin. He emigrated to Palestine in 1935, where he became one of the founders of the national school of Israeli music.

Mar. 1945

Apr. 1945

U.S. forces invade Okinawa, a Japanese island 360 miles south of the mainland.

The Soviet army clears Hungary of all German troops.

U.S. troops liberate a concentration camp outside the German town of Ohrdruf. Hundreds of Jews, as well as Polish and Russian prisoners of war, were shot by the Nazis on the eve of the liberation.

The Buchenwald concentration camp is liberated by Allied forces. Percy Knauth,* *Time* magazine correspondent, witnesses the liberation and writes, "Buchenwald is beyond all comprehension. You just can't understand it, even when you've seen it."

Almost all the Jews at the Buchenwald concentration camp, many of whom had recently arrived from other camps, are marched out to the concentration camp at Flossenberg, leaving the non-Jewish prisoners to await the arrival of U.S. troops.

Adolf Eichmann,* on his last visit to Theresienstadt, is heard to say: "I shall gladly jump into the pit, knowing that in the same pit there are five million enemies of the state."

Count Folke Bernadotte* (1895–1948), a Swedish diplomat, negotiates the release from Theresienstadt of 423 Danish Jews and their return to Denmark.

A train carrying 109 Jews from Vienna

Survivors of Buchenwald concentration camp in their barracks after their liberation in April. Elie Wiesel, winner of the Nobel Peace Prize in 1986, is the farthest right on the second tier from the bottom. (Yad Vashem)

	A. General History	B. Jews in North and South America	C. Jews in Europe	D. Jews in the Middle East and Elsewhere	E. Jewish Culture
Apr. 1945	U.S. President Franklin D. Roosevelt* dies. He is succeeded by Vice President Harry S. Truman.* U.S. army Generals Dwight D. Eisenhower,* Omar Bradley,* and George S. Patton* visit Ohrdruf labor camp and see various torture devices and a shed piled to its ceiling with corpses. Eisenhower* orders nearby army units to tour the camp and states, "We are told that the American soldier does not know what he is fighting for. Now, at least, he will know what he is fighting against."		arrives at Theresienstadt. It is the last deportation arranged by Adolf Eichmann's* department. Heinrich Himmler* agrees to permit 7,000 women, half of them Jewish, to be taken from Ravensbruck to Sweden.	 *On April 24, thirteen days after Buchenwald was liberated by U.S. troops, U.S. Senator Alben W. Barkley of Kentucky visits the concentration camp and views the corpses of victims.*	

Apr. 1945

A. General History

Soviet troops capture Vienna, Austria.

British troops liberate the Bergen-Belsen concentration camp. They find 10,000 unburied bodies. In the ensuing days, photographs, films, and articles about the camp receive wide circulation in Britain.

The Nordhausen labor camp is liberated by the U.S. army. They find 700 barely surviving slave laborers and 3,000 corpses. Al Newman, *Newsweek* magazine correspondent who witnessed the liberation, described it as "a hell factory worked by the living dead."

Attempting to flee Italy, Benito Mussolini* is caught and killed by Italian partisans.

The U.S. army liberates the Dachau concentration camp.

On April 30, Adolf Hitler* commits suicide in the Reich Chancellery in Berlin.

The Soviet army enters the Ravensbruck concentration camp and liberates 23,000 women, Jews and non-Jews. They also overtake "death marchers" from Ravensbruck, saving several thousand other inmates.

President Harry S. Truman* appoints U.S. Supreme Court Justice Robert H. Jackson* the American chief counsel for the prosecution of Nazi war crimes.

	A. General History	B. Jews in North and South America	C. Jews in Europe	D. Jews in the Middle East and Elsewhere	E. Jewish Culture
May 1945	All fighting in Italy ends as 1 million German soldiers surrender. Soviet troops are in control of Berlin. U.S. General James Gavin's* 82nd airborne division liberates Woebblin, a camp in northern Germany established as a transit camp for prisoners evacuated	President Harry S. Truman* receives a State Department memo advising that although President Franklin D. Roosevelt* at times expressed sympathy for certain Zionist aims, he also gave assurances to Arabs, regarded by them as a commitment, that no decision altering the basic situation in Palestine would be	Joseph Pulitzer, of the *St. Louis Post-Dispatch*, leads a tour of concentration camps by American journalists. "I came here in a suspicious frame of mind, feeling that I would find that many of the terrible reports . . . were exaggerations, and largely propaganda. They have been understatements."	Chaim Weizmann writes to British Prime Minister Winston Churchill* emphasizing the desperate position of the Jews of Europe. "This is the time to eliminate the White Paper, to open the doors of Palestine and to proclaim the Jewish state."	

A. General History	B. Jews in North and South America	C. Jews in Europe	D. Jews in the Middle East and Elsewhere	E. Jewish Culture	
from areas in the path of the Allied advance. Outraged by what he sees, Gavin* orders the people of nearby Ludwigslust to visit the camp and rebury the dead. The International Red Cross takes over the Theresienstadt concentration camp. The SS leave the next day. About 1 million German troops surrender in the Netherlands, Denmark, and northwest Germany. The U.S. army liberates the Mathausen concentration camp. There are 110,000 survivors, including 28,000 Jews. The Americans find nearly 10,000 bodies in a huge communal grave.	made without full consultation with both Arabs and Jews.	When the Soviet army captures Berlin, there are 162 Jews in hiding, another 800 half-Jews hiding in the cellars of the Jewish hospital, 4,790 Jews married to non-Jews, 992 people of mixed parentage admitting to be Jews by religion, and 46 Jews who are citizens of countries not at war with Germany. Odilo Globocnik* (1904–1945), SS and police leader of the Lublin district and officer in direct charge of the Operation Reinhard* extermination camps, commits suicide while in British custody.			May 1945

A. General History

May 1945

On May 5, Hans Frank,* Nazi governor-general of occupied Poland, is taken prisoner by U.S. troops.

Japanese kamikaze pilots sink 17 U.S. naval vessels off Okinawa.

On May 8, the war in Europe ends as V-E day is declared.

Soviet troops occupy Prague, Czechoslovakia.

SS General Richard Glueks,* head of the concentration camp directorate, is found dead at the Flensburg naval hospital. It is uncertain whether he committed suicide or was killed by Jews who were tracking down those who had carried out the mass murders.

Dr. Alfred Rosenberg,* chief Nazi ideologist, is arrested by Allied forces.

Heinrich Himmler* is arrested by British forces. Two days later, he commits suicide.

Fighting breaks out in Syria and Lebanon between the French and Arabs.

A. General History	B. Jews in North and South America	C. Jews in Europe	D. Jews in the Middle East and Elsewhere	E. Jewish Culture	
British forces arrest Joachim von Ribbentrop,* German foreign minister, in a Hamburg boardinghouse. The Japanese resistance ends as U.S. forces capture Okinawa. The United Nations Charter is signed at	President Harry S. Truman* adopts a suggestion of his assistant, David Niles (1890–1952), and appoints Earl G. Harrison,* dean of the University of Pennsylvania Law School, to investigate the condition of Jewish refugees in Europe.		British Prime Minister Winston Churchill* rejects Chaim Weizmann's plea for the creation of a Jewish state. "There can, I fear, be no possibility of the question being effectively considered until the victorious Allies are definitely seated at the Peace Table." Zionist		June 1945

	A. **General History**	B. **Jews in North and South America**	C. **Jews in Europe**	D. **Jews in the Middle East and Elsewhere**	E. **Jewish Culture**
June 1945	the San Francisco UN Conference.			leaders believe that Churchill* had ceased his support for their cause in the aftermath of the assassination of Lord Moyne.*	
July 1945	U.S. General Douglas MacArthur* announces the liberation of the Philippines from the Japanese. Joseph Stalin,* President Harry S. Truman,* and Winston Churchill* (later replaced by Clement Attlee*) begin the final conference of the war at Potsdam, Germany. Plans for Japan's surrender are drawn. The U.S. explodes the first atomic bomb at its New Mexico test facility. The British Labour party wins the parliamentary elections. Winston Churchill* is replaced as prime minister by Clement Attlee* (1883–1967).		Representatives of liberated Jews housed in displaced persons camps in the American, British, and French zones of Germany hold a conference at the St. Ottilien camp near Munich. The 94 delegates call for the immediate creation of a Jewish state in Palestine.		
Aug. 1945	A U.S. B-29, the *Enola Gay*, drops an atomic bomb on Hiroshima, Japan. The U.S. drops a second atomic bomb on Nagasaki, Japan. On August 14, Japan surrenders unconditionally. V-J Day is proclaimed on August 15. The Soviet Union occupies Manchuria and several of the Japanese Kurile islands. The Allied occupation of Japan begins with the arrival of U.S. troops. The U.S., Britain, France, and the Soviet Union agree on the basic structure and	Earl G. Harrison,* Truman's* representative investigating the conditions of European Jewish refugees, criticizes conditions in camps housing them, confirms the refugees' desire to emigrate to Palestine, and recommends the immediate admission of 100,000 there. Truman* adopts the suggestion.	Anti-Jewish riots take place in Cracow, Poland. During World War II, over 1,397,000 Jewish soldiers served in the Allied forces, including the U.S., 550,000; the Soviet Union, 500,000; Poland, 140,000; Great Britain, 62,000; France, 46,000; Palestinian units in the British army, 35,000.	At the time of the Japanese surrender, there are 14,874 European Jewish refugees in Shanghai, China.	

A. General History

scope of Nazi war crimes trials. One of the categories, crimes against humanity, includes atrocities against Jews, whatever their nationality.

During World War II, approximately 100 million soldiers fought on both sides, of whom 15 million were killed. It is estimated that there were between 26 and 34 million civilian deaths.

B. Jews in North and South America

U.S. Secretary of State James F. Byrnes* delivers a personal letter from President Harry S. Truman* to Prime Minister Clement Attlee* asking Britain to admit 100,000 Jewish refugees to Palestine. Attlee* rejects the request, instead suggesting an Anglo-American Committee of Inquiry, to which Truman* assents.

Jewish Victims of the Holocaust

It is estimated that 2 million were killed by the Einsatzgruppen,* 3.5 million in the gas chambers,† and about 500,000 died in the ghettos of Eastern Europe of hunger, disease, and exhaustion, and as victims of random terror and reprisals. See Lucy S. Dawidowicz, *The Holocaust and the Historians* (1981), pp. 12–13.

Polish-Soviet area	4,565,000
Germany	125,000
Austria	65,000
Czechoslovakia (in the pre-Munich boundaries)	277,000
Hungary, including northern Transylvania	402,000
France	83,000
Belgium	24,000
Luxembourg	700
Italy	7,500
The Netherlands	106,000
Norway	760
Romania (Regat, southern Transylvania, southern Bukovina)	40,000
Yugoslavia	60,000
Greece	65,000
Total loss	5,820,960

*Einsatzgruppen, special duty troops of the SS's security service and security police, were assigned to each of the German armies invading the Soviet Union. They rounded up the Jews and killed them. The Jews were loaded on trucks or marched to remote areas. They were machine gunned into natural ravines, antitank trenches or the mass graves they were ordered to dig.
†Later, starting in 1942, the Nazis constructed six installations with large scale gassing facilities and with crematoria for the disposal of bodies. They were Auschwitz, Belzec, Chelmno, Majdanek, Sobibor and Treblinka. All were located in Poland. Gilbert notes that 1,500,000 Jews were murdered at Auschwitz; 360,000 at Chelmno; 250,000 at Sobibor; 600,000 at Belzec; and 840,000 at Treblinka. See Martin Gilbert, *The Holocaust* (1985), p. 257, n. 6.

A. General History

The United Nations is created as its charter comes into force.

The International Military Tribunal at Nuremberg begins a 10-month trial of major Nazi figures for war crimes. The 22 defendants are Hermann Goering,* Rudolf Hess,* Joachim von Ribbentrop,* Wilhelm Keitel,* Ernst Kaltenbrunner,* Alfred Rosenberg,* Hans Frank,* Wilhelm Frick,* Julius Streicher,* Walther Funk,* Hjalmar Schacht,* Karl Doenitz,* Erich Raeder,* Baldur von Schirach,* Fritz Sauckel,* Alfred Jodl,* Franz Papen,* Arthur Seyss-Inquart,* Albert Speer,* Konstantin von Neurath,* Hans Fritzsche,* and Martin Bormann* in

C. Jews in Europe

In mid-October, Czech Foreign Minister Jan Masaryk* provides trains to the Berihah (Escape) branch of the Haganah to transport Jews from the Polish border to the Austrian frontier and to the U.S. zone in Germany.

Anti-Jewish riots take place in Sosnowiec, Poland. Polish anti-semites kill eight Jews in Boleslawiec.

Rachel Auerbach visits Treblinka as a member of a Polish delegation investigating Nazi war crimes. She observes "masses of pilferers and robbers with spades and shovels . . . digging and searching and raking and straining the sand. . . . Would they not come upon even one hard coin or at

D. Jews in the Middle East and Elsewhere

Palestine's railway system is paralyzed in a coordinated attack by the Haganah, Irgun, and Stern Group.

The first Haganah ship, the *Berl Katznelson*, bringing refugees to Palestine is intercepted by the British off the coast of Palestine, but most of the passengers reach land and scatter before the vessel is captured. Between November 1945 and the end of April 1948, 54 ships, most of them intercepted by the British, will bring more than 67,000 refugees to Palestine.

Anti-Zionist riots break out in Egypt and Libya. In Cairo, over 100 Jewish businesses are looted. In Alexandria, five Jews are killed. In Tripoli, a pogrom

	A. General History	B. Jews in North and South America	C. Jews in Europe	D. Jews in the Middle East and Elsewhere	E. Jewish Culture
Oct. 1945	absentia. Robert Ley* commits suicide before the trial.		least one gold tooth? They even dragged shells and blind bombs there, those hyenas and jackals in the disguise of man."	lasting over three days results in more than 130 Jewish dead.	
Nov. 1945			Anti-Jewish riots take place in Lublin, Poland.	Thousands of Jews in Tel Aviv riot for two days in response to remarks seen as antisemitic made by British Foreign Secretary Ernest Bevin* (1881–1951). British troops open fire, and six Jews are killed. Many Jews and British troops are injured. Bevin* states that Britain never promised to create a Jewish state, but only to create a Jewish home in Palestine. Jewish refugees seeking to leave Europe should not try to get to the head of the queue. Haganah troops blow up the Sidna Ali coast guard station on the Palestine coast, which is part of the lookout system for illegal immigrant ships.	
Dec. 1945		President Harry S. Truman* meets Chaim Weizmann, and they establish a cordial relationship.	Polish antisemites kill 11 Jews in Kosow-Lacki, a village less than six miles from Treblinka. By the end of the year, and more than seven months after the end of the war, Polish antisemites have murdered 350 Jews in Poland. During 1945, the Nazis murdered more than 100,000 Jews. Although Allied victories disrupted the Nazi extermination machinery, death marches and chaos in the camps accounted for many Jewish deaths.	The Irgun attacks Jerusalem and Jaffa police headquarters, killing 10 soldiers and police.	
1946	The size of the U.S. armed forces is greatly reduced. Lend–lease ends.		Klaus Barbie*, head of the Gestapo in Lyons, France, is arrested in Germany by U.S. forces. He escapes.		The Rabbinical Assembly, the organization of Conservative rabbis, publishes the Sabbath and Festival Prayer

A. General History	B. Jews in North and South America	C. Jews in Europe	D. Jews in the Middle East and Elsewhere	E. Jewish Culture	
Between 1946 and 1949, Greece wages a civil war. The U.S. Atomic Energy Commission is organized, and promotes international control of atomic weapons.		Maxim Litvinov, prominent Jewish Soviet diplomat, who was the Soviet foreign minister from 1930 to 1939 and ambassador to the U.S. from 1941 to 1943, is relieved of his duties without explanation. He will die in obscurity.		Book. Edited by Rabbi Morris Silverman, it follows traditional liturgy, is translated into modern English with supplementary readings, and makes a number of minor changes, such as a reference to sacrifices as a past rather than a future obligation.	**1946**
The first General Assembly of the UN, with 51 nations represented, convenes in Great Britain.		General Sir Frederick Morgan,* senior British relief officer with the UN in Germany, is dismissed. Morgan* had said that thousands of Polish Jews had entered his area with plenty of money, rosy cheeks, and a well-organized, positive plan to get out of Europe. Jewish leaders consider the remarks as brutal antisemitism.	The Anglo-American Committee of Inquiry to examine the Palestine question and the situation of the Jews in Europe commences its investigation. Composed of an equal number of American and English members, they visit displaced persons camps in Europe and Palestine.	Schocken Books, a German book publishing house founded by Salman Schocken, begins publishing books of Jewish interest in the U.S. Isaac Rosenfeld (1918–1956), U.S. literary critic, writes his only novel, *Passage from Home*, whose autobiographical main character explores his ultimate homelessness and alienation.	**Jan. 1946**
Trygve Lie,* a Norwegian, is appointed the first secretary general of the UN.		Polish antisemites murder four Jews on a train from Lodz to Cracow, where they were to attend a Jewish communal convention. The headline to a *Manchester Guardian* article on the condition of the Jews in Poland reads "Jews Still in Flight from Poland—Driven Abroad by Fear—Political Gangs Out to Terrorize Them—Campaign of Murder and Robbery."	Palmah troops raid and damage the radar station on Mt. Carmel. Four days later, they raid police stations at Shafa Amr, Kefar Vitkin, and Sarona. At Sarona, four Palmah men are killed. Irgun troops raid three Royal Air Force airfields and damage or destroy 22 aircraft.	Max Weinreich, Yiddish scholar, writes *Hitler's Professors*, a study of the role German scholarship played in the Nazi crimes against the Jewish people. Franz Landsberger (1883–1964), Hebrew Union College professor of Jewish art history, writes *A History of Jewish Art*, the first survey in English. In the same year, his *Rembrandt, the Jews and the Bible* is	**Feb. 1946**
Winston Churchill* delivers his "iron curtain" speech at Fulton, Missouri. He warns of Soviet expansionism and of irreconcilable differences between East and West. Great Britain grants independence to Transjordan. Abdullah ibn Hussein* becomes king.		Chaim Hirszman, one of two survivors of the Belzec death camp, is murdered the day he testifies in Lublin of what he witnessed at Belzec.	Meir Vilner, spokesman for the Communist party in Palestine, expresses the Soviet line that calls for the withdrawal of the British from Palestine and the creation of an Arab–Jewish state. He opposes a partition.	published. In 1933, the Nazis caused his dismissal as professor at the University of Breslau. In 1935, he was appointed director of the Jewish Museum in Berlin. In 1938, he was sent to a concentration camp by the Nazis. After his release he joined the Hebrew Union College faculty.	**Mar. 1946**
Syria, a former League of			The Stern gang kills seven British soldiers	Ben Hecht writes a drama-pageant, *A Flag Is Born*, a lyrical	**Apr. 1946**

	A. General History	B. Jews in North and South America	C. Jews in Europe	D. Jews in the Middle East and Elsewhere	E. Jewish Culture
Apr. 1946	Nations–mandated territory under French control, is granted independence.			in an attack on a military compound in Tel Aviv. The Anglo-American Committee of Inquiry publishes its report recommending admitting 100,000 refugees to Palestine, revoking the prohibition against the sale of land to Jews, and UN trusteeship leading eventually to a binational state of Arabs and Jews. President Harry S. Truman* hails recommendation. The British do not carry out the report's recommendations.	portrayal, with music by Kurt Weill, of the efforts of survivors from the Treblinka extermination camp to reach a haven in Palestine in the face of British obstruction. Meyer Levin, U.S. novelist and journalist, makes the first feature film of the Yishuv in Palestine, *My Father's House*. Joshua Loth Liebman (1907–1948), U.S. Reform rabbi, writes *Peace of Mind*. It becomes a best-seller, goes through 40 printings, and fosters a closer working relationship between psychology and religion.
May 1946	The Soviet Union withdraws its forces from Iran. Czechoslovak elections result in the emergence of the Communists as the strongest party. Klement Gottwald* heads the coalition government and Eduard Benes*, a non-Communist, is reelected president.		British authorities grant permission for Bergen-Belsen to be organized as a separate Jewish displaced persons camp, including representatives from other Jewish communities in the British zone of occupation. The camp committee is headed by Joseph Rosensaft.	Britain requests Italy to prevent the departure of two ships, the *Eliyahu Golomb* and *Dov Hos*, with about 1,000 displaced persons from La Spezia. The refugees go on a hunger strike. Worldwide publicity focuses on the clandestine immigration to Palestine, which is called illegal. The ships are permitted to sail for Haifa, but passengers are transferred to detention camps on arrival.	YIVO (The Institute for Jewish Research) begins publication in New York of the *YIVO Annual of Jewish Social Science*, in the English language. Sholem Asch writes *East River*, a novel of Jewish life in New York at the turn of the century. Irving Berlin composes the music for the musical comedy *Annie Get Your Gun* and includes the popular songs "There's No Business Like Show Business," "Doin' What Comes Natur'lly," and "Anything You Can Do."
June 1946	Bernard Baruch, U.S. representative to the UN Atomic Energy Commission, proposes the creation of an international atomic development authority, empowered to control all dangerous uses of atomic energy and to inspect all atomic installations. The plan will be vetoed by the Soviet Union in 1948.	Eddie Jacobson (1891–1955), a friend of President Harry S. Truman,* arranges for Truman* to meet Rabbi Arthur J. Lelyveld, a Zionist leader. This is the first of many of Jacobson's efforts on behalf of the Zionist cause.		Haj Amin al-Husseini,* former mufti of Jerusalem, escapes from a French prison, where he was detained as a war criminal. In a few days, he arrives in Egypt. British Foreign Secretary Ernest Bevin* accuses the U.S. of agitating for Jewish immigration into Palestine "because they do not want too many of them in New York." The Haganah blows up 10 of the 11 bridges connecting	George Szell (1897–1970) is engaged as the music director and principal conductor of the Cleveland Orchestra, a position he holds until 1970. Herman Joseph Muller (1890–1967), U.S. geneticist, is awarded the Nobel Prize in physiology or medicine for his work

> *Seventh "Aliyah" to Palestine, 1946–May 15, 1948*
> *Number:* 56,476
> *Origin:* Mostly Holocaust survivors from Europe.

June 1946

Palestine with its neighboring countries. This is the second attack by the Haganah.

On what will become known as Black Sabbath, the British commence a two-week search for Jewish leaders and arms caches in Palestine. Over 2,500 are arrested, including members of the Jewish Agency. David Ben-Gurion is in Europe at the time.

in producing genetic mutations by using X rays.

Arthur Koestler, Hungarian-born writer, writes *Thieves in the Night*, a novel describing the Arab–Jewish conflict before the British withdrawal from Palestine.

Uri Zvi Greenberg (1891–1981), Hebrew and Yiddish poet, publishes a collection of his poems, *Streets of the River*, written on the theme of the Holocaust and on the Jews' will to survive. He emigrated to Palestine in 1923, where he abandoned Yiddish for Hebrew, and became a leader of the revisionist Zionists.

July 1946

King David Hotel in Jerusalem after the Irgun bombing. (Israel Government Press Office)

Poles murder 42 Jews in a pogrom at Kielce. They were aroused by rumors of the Jewish abduction of Christian children for ritual purposes. Following the pogrom, 100,000 Jews, more than half the survivors, flee Poland through Czechoslovakia, assisted by the Berihah movement.

The Czech government, on the recommendation of Premier Klement Gottwald* and Foreign Minister Jan Masaryk,* recognizes the Berihah and agrees to aid its activities. The Polish government, influenced by this decision, opens its borders. A daily exodus of 2,500–3,000 Jews from eastern to western Europe ensues.

The King David Hotel in Jerusalem, which houses the British military headquarters, is blown up by an Irgun operation, headed by Amichai Paglin. Ninety-one Britons, Arabs, and Jews are killed. The Irgun insists, and the British deny, that ample warning to evacuate was given.

General Evelyn Barker,* commander of the British troops in Palestine, issues a directive forbidding British troops from having social or business intercourse with Jews, in the wake of the King David Hotel bombing.

Thousands of British troops place Tel Aviv under a curfew as they search for the King David Hotel attackers. Among those seized is Yitzhak Shamir (Yzernitzky), the Lehi second in command. He is sent to detention in Eritrea. Menachem Begin escapes detection.

The Morrison–Grady Committee, created at Britain's suggestion to evaluate the Anglo-American Committee of Inquiry report, proposes the

	A. General History	B. Jews in North and South America*	C. Jews in Europe	D. Jews in the Middle East and Elsewhere	E. Jewish Culture
July 1946				partition of Palestine into four areas: Arab (40%), Jewish (17%), and two British districts (43%). The central government would be British with Arab and Jewish provinces managing their domestic affairs. The committee also recommends immediate immigration of 100,000 Jews; thereafter the British would regulate immigration. The Plan is rejected by Jews and Arabs.	
Aug. 1946				The British announce that henceforth all illegal Jewish immigrants to Palestine will be sent to camps in Cyprus. The detention camps in Palestine are full, the British wish to deter further Jewish emigration without permits, and they wish to reassure the Arabs of their good intentions. In reponse to the Morrison–Grady plan, the Jewish Agency, meeting in Paris, decides to abandon the Biltmore Program and to settle for a viable state in part of Palestine, i.e., it accepts the principle of the partition.	
Sep. 1946			The Jewish Historical Commission of Poland excavates Warsaw ghetto documents compiled by Emanuel Ringelblum's Oyneg Shabes (Sabbath Collation) group buried on Nowolipki Street. It is a main source of research material of the history of Polish Jewry under Nazi occupation.		
Oct. 1946	The International Military Tribunal at Nuremberg, after a 10-month war crimes trial, renders verdicts: hanging—Goering,*	In a Yom Kippur message to the American Jewish community, President Harry S. Truman* reiterates his support		In October, the Irgun sabotages the Jerusalem railway station. An Arab railway worker and British sapper are	

A. General History	B. Jews in North and South America	C. Jews in Europe	D. Jews in the Middle East and Elsewhere	E. Jewish Culture

A. General History

Ribbentrop, Keitel,* Kaltenbrunner,* Rosenberg,* Frank,* Frick,* Streicher,* Sauckel,* Godl,* Seyss-Inquart,* Bormann*; life—Hess,* Funk,* Raeder*; 20 years—Schirach,* Speer*; 15 years—Neurath*; 10 years—Doenitz*; acquitted—Schact,* Papen,* Fritzsche.*

Those Nazis sentenced to death by the International Military Tribunal at Nuremberg are hanged. Hermann Goering,* however, kills himself the day before his scheduled execution by swallowing cyanide.

B. Jews in North and South America

for the entry of 100,000 Jewish refugees into Palestine and for the creation of a Jewish state in Palestine. The speech creates the impression that Truman* is publicly endorsing the establishment of a Jewish state.

Thomas E. Dewey,* Republican governor of New York, running for reelection, urges immigration to Palestine not of 100,000 Jewish refugees, "but of several hundreds of thousands."

President Harry S. Truman* writes to Senate Finance Committee Chairman Walter George*: "I sincerely wish that every member of Congress could visit the displaced persons camps in Germany and Austria and see just what is happening to 500,000 human beings through no fault of their own."

President Harry S. Truman* replies to King ibn Saud's* reaction to his Yom Kippur statement. He advises ibn Saud* that the American people have supported the concept of a Jewish home in Palestine since the First World War and denies that this policy statement broke a promise since there was consultation with both sides during the year.

D. Jews in the Middle East and Elsewhere

killed. Two attackers, Moshe Barzani and Meir Feinstein, are captured. They are sentenced to death. They will blow themselves up with grenades smuggled into their prison cells.

On the evening following Yom Kippur, 11 settlements are established in the Negev in one night. Settlement of the Negev is forbidden by the mandatory authorities.

The accused in the dock at the Nuremburg War Crimes Trial (Yad Vashem)

A. General History

The Soviet Union consolidates control over eastern Europe.

The first supersonic flight is made by Air Force Captain Charles E. Yeager.*

Jackie Robinson* becomes the first black baseball player to play in the U.S. major leagues.

B. Jews in North and South America

The National Jewish Welfare Board publishes *American Jews in World War II: The Story of 550,000 Fighters for Freedom*, which contains records of heroism and lists of those who were wounded or who lost their lives.

To meet the needs of Conservative Jewish

C. Jews in Europe

Klaus Barbie* begins working as an agent in Germany for the U.S. Army Counterintelligence Corps. In December he is arrested. He is freed six months later and resumes intelligence work.

Catholic, Protestant, and Jewish representatives meet

E. Jewish Culture

Marie Syrkin (1899–1989), U.S. author and educator, writes *Blessed Is the Match*, a study of Jewish resistance to the Nazis during World War II.

Harry A. Wolfson, Harvard professor of Hebrew literature and philosophy, writes *Philo: Foundations of*

	A. General History	B. Jews in North and South America	C. Jews in Europe	D. Jews in the Middle East and Elsewhere	E. Jewish Culture
1947		youth, the Ramah summer camps are founded under the educational guidance of the Teacher's Institute of the Jewish Theological Seminary of America. Nelson Glueck (1900–1971), noted archaeologist, is elected president of the Hebrew Union College. The American Jewish Archives are established at the Hebrew Union College in Cincinnati under the direction of Jacob R. Marcus. The archives contain the largest collection of source material on the history of Jews in the Western Hemisphere. *Crossfire*, directed by Edward Dmytryk,* is the first postwar U.S. film to confront antisemitism. John Horne Burns* (1916–1953), U.S. novelist, writes *The Gallery*, a novel of the American army in Italy during World War II, which includes a "portrait" of sweet, saintlike Lieutenant Moses Shulman, an ex–taxi driver from Brooklyn who is the author's symbol of human dignity. Fred Zinnemann directs *The Search*, a film depicting the continuing problems confronting children who managed to escape the Holocaust in Europe.	at the Swiss town of Seelisberg and issue the Ten Points of Seelisberg. Influenced by the French–Jewish historian Jules Isaac (1877–1963), the proposals deal with the need to emphasize the close bonds between Judaism and Christianity, to present the Passion in a way that will not arouse hostility toward the Jews, and to eliminate from Christian teaching and preaching that Jews are accursed.		*Religious Philosophy in Judaism, Christianity, and Islam*, a two-volume work in which he attempts to demonstrate that Philo Judaeus, the Alexandrian philosopher, was the founder of religious philosophy in Judaism, Christianity, and Islam. Milton Steinberg (1903–1950), U.S. Conservative rabbi, writes *Basic Judaism*, in which he attempts to describe the essentials of the Jewish religion. The book enjoys wide popularity. Solomon Grayzel (1896–1980), U.S. rabbi and historian, writes *A History of the Jews*, a one-volume comprehensive history widely used as a textbook. Saul Bellow, U.S. novelist, writes *The Victim*, in which he studies antisemitism through the story of the relationship of a Jewish writer, Asa Leventhal, and an antisemite. Arthur Miller, U.S. playwright, writes *All My Sons*, about a businessman who manufactures defective airplane parts during World War II and causes the death of his son and other pilots. Roman Vishniac (1897–1990), photographer, publishes *Polish Jews*, a collection of his photographs of Polish Jewish life taken just before the Holocaust. The best-known photographer of eastern European Jewry, he traveled throughout central and eastern Europe between 1933 and
Jan. 1947				President Harry S. Truman* replies to a letter from ibn Saud* of Saudi Arabia and states he is convinced that the Jews in Palestine have no interest in expelling Arabs or in using Palestine as a base for aggression against	

A. General History	B. Jews in North and South America	C. Jews in Europe	D. Jews in the Middle East and Elsewhere	E. Jewish Culture	
Great Britain decides to evacuate India and informs the U.S. that it can no longer carry the military burdens of protecting Greece and Turkey from Communist encroachment.			neighboring Arab states. British Foreign Secretary Ernest Bevin* announces that Britain is referring the Palestine mandate to the UN without specific recommendation. A week later, he accuses President Harry S. Truman,* before the House of Commons, of causing an impasse in solving the Palestine question by playing domestic politics with the issue.	1939. Vishniac's photographs were first exhibited in the U.S. at YIVO (The Institute for Jewish Research) in 1944. Laura Z. Hobson (1900–1986), U.S. author, writes *Gentleman's Agreement*, a novel of antisemitism in the U.S., which becomes a best-seller and is quickly adapted to the screen. The film wins the Academy Award as the best movie of the year.	**Feb. 1947**
U.S. President Harry S. Truman* announces the Truman Doctrine, which serves to protect Greece and Turkey from communism in Europe.			The Irgun attacks the Officer's Club at the Goldschmidt House in Jerusalem. Twelve British officers are killed.	The poetry of Samuel Bernard Greenberg (1893–1917) is posthumously published. He lived in poverty on New York's Lower East Side. Hart Crane* became aware of his manuscripts in 1923	**Mar. 1947**
		Rudolf Hoess,* first commandant of the Auschwitz extermination camp, is sentenced to death after a trial in Warsaw, Poland. He is executed on a site overlooking the camp.	Four Irgun members are hanged by the British at Acre prison.	and was greatly influenced by his poetry. Abraham S. W. Rosenbach (1876–1952), U.S. rare book dealer, purchases the *Bay Psalm Book* for	**Apr. 1947**
			An Irgun-led attack on the British prison at Acre frees 251 prisoners. Soviet UN representative Andrei Gromyko* tells the General Assembly of the Soviet support of the Zionist aspirations for the establishment of a Jewish state in Palestine. His speech is a reversal of three decades of Soviet support of the Arab world. A special meeting of the UN General Assembly establishes the United Nations Special Committee on Palestine (UNSCOP). The investigative body is composed of Australia, Canada, Czechoslovakia,	$151,000, the highest price until then paid for any book on public sale. He is considered the most eminent bibliophile of the first half of the 20th century, and his unique collection of early American Judaica will be donated to the American Jewish Historical Society. He is president of the society for many years. The Jewish Museum moves to the former Warburg mansion on New York's Fifth Avenue. The Warburg mansion was donated to the Jewish Theological Seminary of America by Frieda Schiff Warburg (1876–1958), the	**May 1947**

	A. General History	B. Jews in North and South America	C. Jews in Europe	D. Jews in the Middle East and Elsewhere	E. Jewish Culture
May 1947				Guatemala, India, Iran, the Netherlands, Peru, Sweden, Uruguay, and Yugoslovia. The Haganah ship *Yehuda Halevi* brings about 400 Moroccan "illegal" immigrants to Palestine.	widow of Felix M. Warburg. The museum had been located at the seminary and opened to the public on November 23, 1931. The Cincinnati Art Museum exhibits Jewish Art Objects from the Collection of the Hebrew Union College with the catalogue by Franz Landsberger.
June 1947	The U.S. launches the Marshall Plan to aid European economic recovery.				
July 1947	 *Illegal immigrants aboard the Haganah ship* Exodus *in Haifa Harbor.* (*Central Zionist Archives*)			*Exodus 1947*, an immigrant ship bearing 4,550 Jews from displaced persons camps in Germany, is escorted into Haifa Harbor by the British navy. Foreign Secretary Ernest Bevin* orders the refugees to be returned to their port of origin in southern France rather than be interned in Cyprus. Several UNSCOP members, then in Palestine, witness the transfer of refugees to British ships for return to France. The British hang three members of the Irgun captured during the attack on Acre Prison that freed 251 prisoners. Several hours later, the Irgun hangs two British sergeants who had been abducted on July 12 and held hostage in the effort to thwart the British action.	Arnold Schoenberg (1874–1951), composer, writes *A Survivor from Warsaw* for narrator, men's chorus, and orchestra, which recounts the fate of Polish Jews under Nazism. In 1898 Schoenberg left Judaism to become a Lutheran. In 1925, he was appointed professor of composition at Berlin's Prussian Academy of Arts. Dismissed in 1933 because of his Jewish background he formally returned to Judaism and settled in the U.S. Yehudi Menuhin, violinist, is the first Jewish artist after World War II to perform with the Berlin Philharmonic Orchestra under conductor Wilhelm Furtwangler.* Menuhin is criticized by Jewish groups because Furtwangler* held his position during the Nazi era.
Aug. 1947	Britain's 150-year rule of India ends with the establishment of two independent states, India (Hindu) and Pakistan (Muslim). Ten million persons become refugees in an exchange of populations between the two countries.			Zionist underground activists from Iraq arrive in Palestine on a secret direct flight from Baghdad led by Shlomo Hillel. The UNSCOP report unanimously recommends the prompt ending of the British mandate and, by a 7 to 3 majority with 1 abstention, the partition of Palestine into an Arab state and a Jewish state, with an	In New York, Maurice Schwartz's Jewish Art Theater presents *Shylock and His Daughter*, a Yiddish production of the story of Shakespeare's Shylock from the Jewish point of view. Mikhail Botvinnik, Soviet chess master, wins his first world chess title.

| | | | international zone containing the holy places. Zionists reluctantly support the plan, which is rejected by the Arabs. | Meyer Levin, U.S. novelist and journalist, makes a documentary film, *The Illegals*, describing the emigration of Holocaust survivors to Palestine. | **Aug. 1947** |

James V. Forrestal* becomes the first secretary of defense as all U.S. armed forces are consolidated into the Defense Department.

Jewish refugees on the *Exodus 1947* are forcibly disembarked by the British at Hamburg and returned to displaced persons camps in Germany. When the French government refused to accept the refugees unless they debarked voluntarily in France, the British government ordered their return to Germany despite worldwide protests requesting their admission to Palestine.

A U.S. State Department position paper recommends that the Negev should be included in the prospective Arab state. The UNSCOP majority report assigned most of the Negev to the prospective Jewish state.

Sep. 1947

Seven Dead Sea Scrolls are found by Bedouins in various locations west of the Dead Sea. Eliezer Sukenik (1889–1953), Israeli archaeologist, acquires three of them (the Second Isaiah Scroll, the Thanksgiving Psalms, and the War Scroll) for the Hebrew University. He will be the first person to suggest that the scrolls belonged to the Essenes. The father of Yigael Yadin, he settled in Palestine in 1912 and led excavations of the synagogues at Beth-Alpha (1928) and Hammath-Gader (1932).

The publication of an encyclopedia tracing the laws and institutions of the Talmud through its traditional development begins in Palestine. *Entsiqlopedya Talmudit le-Inyenei Halakhah* will be completed in 1989 with the publication of Volume 20.

Oct. 1947

UN PARTITION PLAN, 1947

MEDITERRANEAN SEA

LEBANON

SYRIA

Acre

Safed

SEA OF GALILEE

Haifa

Jenin

Tel Aviv
Jaffa

Nablus

Jerusalem

Gaza

Bethlehem

Hebron

JORDAN

Rafah

Beersheba

El Arish

THE NEGEV DESERT

EGYPT

0   25   50
MILES

THE ARABAH VALLEY

Eilat   Aqaba

Taba

Proposed Jewish state
Proposed Arab state
Jerusalem and suburbs to be international zone
△ Jewish settlements to be included in Jewish state

The U.S. support for partition is announced by UN Ambassador Herschel V. Johnson.* Johnson* suggests territorial changes be made to the UNSCOP majority report to make the partition plan workable.

Ernest Bevin,* British foreign secretary, writes a private letter to Hector McNeil,* an aide: I am sure [the Russians] are convinced that by immigration they can pour in sufficient indoctrinated Jews to turn it into a Communist state in a very short time. The New York Jews have been doing their work for them.''

Britain advises the UN that it will not

Oct. 1947

accept responsibility, either alone or in concert with other nations, of any Palestine settlement antagonistic to either the Jews or Arabs or both, which would likely necessitate the use of force.

The U.S. delegation to the UN decides to recommend a change in the UNSCOP majority report and to recommend a transfer of the Negev to the prospective Arab state.

Nov. 1947

Voting chart of the U.N. General Assembly approving the Partition of Palestine on November 29.

U.S. Secretary of State George C. Marshall* advises the UN delegation to reaffirm its stand that the Negev be transferred to the prospective Arab state. He reasons that the Negev is historically Arab and has little chance of large-scale development, and the construction of the Red Sea port is questionable.

Chaim Weizmann has a private meeting with President Harry S. Truman* and discusses Jewish enthusiasm for the development of the Negev. The meeting foils the State Department plan to reject the UNSCOP majority report. Truman* calls Major General John H. Hilldring,* of the UN delegation, and orders that the U.S. accept the UNSCOP majority report giving the Negev to the Jews.

U.S. Ambassador Herschel V. Johnson,* withdraws the UN delegation proposal to award the Negev to the Arabs.

Soviet UN representative Andrei Gromyko* defines the Soviet support for the partition. "The solution of the Palestine problem into

			two separate states will be of profound historical significance, because this decision will meet the legitimate demands of the Jewish people."		**Nov. 1947**
			The UN General Assembly votes in favor of the partition of Palestine into independent Jewish and Arab states with Jerusalem internationalized.		
A Communist-led Romanian People's Republic is established. King Michael* abdicates.			Ehud Avriel, head of Rechesh (Haganah arms purchasing mission), concludes the first arms deal with Czechoslovakia for the purchase of 10,000 rifles, 4,500 heavy machine guns, and 3 million rounds of ammunition. The Soviet Union sanctions sales. The weapons were manufactured for the Germans at the Skoda arms factory.		**Dec. 1947**

Dec. 1947

D. Jews in the Middle East and Elsewhere

Several days after the UN partition decision, an Arab mob attacks the Jewish quarter of Aden, Yemen's largest port and a British protectorate. Eighty-two Jews are killed and hundreds of houses and Jewish communal facilities are burned to the ground.

The U.S. announces a total embargo on arms shipments to the Middle East. As the Arab countries have obtained ample arms from Great Britain, the embargo hurts the Jewish cause.

Great Britain announces its intention to terminate its responsibility under the mandate on May 15, 1948. British forces in Palestine would be used only in self-defense and, would not intervene in fighting breaking out between Palestinian Arabs and Jews.

A pogrom is staged in Aleppo, Syria, by the Muslim Brotherhood. Twelve synagogues, 150 houses, 50 shops, and 5 Jewish schools are destroyed. Several thousand Jews flee to Turkey and Lebanon.

Hans Beyth (1901–1947), Youth Aliya leader and Henrietta Szold's assistant, who arranged for the absorption of 20,000 European Jewish youths into Palestinian life, is murdered by Arabs.

A. General History	B. Jews in North and South America	C. Jews in Europe	D. Jews in the Middle East and Elsewhere	E. Jewish Culture	
Dwight D. Eisenhower* writes *Crusade in Europe*, a straightforward account of the Allied invasion of Europe in 1944. It is the best-selling nonfiction book of the year. There is a rapid increase in the	Synagogues are being built on a large scale throughout the U.S. The two Reform rabbinical seminaries in the U.S., the Hebrew Union College, in Cincinnati, and the Jewish Institute of	The Jewish population in the Birobidzhan region of Soviet Siberia numbers about 30,000, the largest ever for the region. The last edition of the Papal *Index librorum prohibitorum* includes Jewish publications,	Yitzhak Ben-Zvi founds the Institute for the Study of Oriental Jewish Communities in the Middle East in Jerusalem. In 1952 it will be renamed the Ben-Zvi Institute. Ernst David Bergman, organic chemist	The first volume of the Yale Judaica Series, translations of ancient and medieval Jewish classics, is published. It is Saadia Gaon's *The Book of Beliefs and Opinions*, a major philosophical work of the 10th century.	**1948**

	A. General History	B. Jews in North and South America	C. Jews in Europe	D. Jews in the Middle East and Elsewhere	E. Jewish Culture
1948	number of motion picture drive-in theaters, where open-air screens are viewed by patrons from inside their automobiles. Public demand for television receivers exceeds the supply, as production reaches 800,000. The most popular receiver is the 10-inch table model. The number of U.S. television stations in operation increases from 18 to 46. The long-playing phonograph record is developed by Dr. Peter Goldmark.* Alfred C. Kinsey* publishes *Sexual Behavior in the Human Male*, a study based on thousands of interviews that shows wide differences between actual sexual practices and conventional beliefs about them.	Religion, in New York, merge. Brandeis University opens in Waltham, Massachusetts, with Dr. Abram L. Sachar as president. Under Jewish auspices, it is a nonsectarian venture in the integration of Jewish and secular studies. Carey McWilliams* writes *A Mask for Privilege*, a history of antisemitism in America. Jorge Garcia-Granados,* member of the special UN Commission on Palestine, writes *The Birth of Israel: The Drama as I Saw It*.	listing those of Edmond Fleg (1874–1963) and Henri Bergson (1859–1941). Carmel College at Wallingford, near Oxford, England, is founded by Rabbi Kopul Rosen. Modeled after the British public school, it combines secular and Jewish studies at a high level. Jean-Paul Sartre* writes *Anti-Semite and Jew*, an incisive analysis of the psychology of the Jew-baiter and an appraisal of the situation of the modern Jew.	trained in his native Germany, becomes scientific director of the science department of the Israel Ministry of Defense. Father Butros Sowmy of the Syrian Orthodox Convent in Jerusalem makes available to the American School of Oriental Research and to the Hebrew University certain scrolls found near the Dead Sea. The scrolls include a complete copy of the Book of Isaiah, dated about 100 BCE, and a fragmentary commentary on Habakkuk.	Mordecai M. Kaplan writes *The Future of the American Jew*, in which he demonstrates that the basic premise of the Reconstructionist movement is that Judaism is not merely a religion, but a religious civilization. Mark Wischnitzer (1882–1955), historian and communal worker who left Germany in 1938, writes *To Dwell in Safety*, a history of Jewish migration from central, eastern, and southeastern Europe since the beginning of the French Revolution. I. F. Stone (1907–1989), U.S. journalist, writes *This Is Israel*, with photographs by Robert Capa (1913–1954), U.S. photographer. Herman Wouk (b. 1915), U.S. novelist, writes *City Boy*, a novel of the experiences of Herbie Bookbinder, an 11-year-old boy from the Bronx. Irwin Shaw (1913–1984), U.S. novelist, writes *The Young Lions*, a novel of the lives of three men in World War II, one a Christian from New York; one a Jewish youth from the Midwest, Noah Ackerman; the third, an Austrian Nazi. In 1958, it will be adapted to the screen. Norman Mailer (b. 1923) writes his best-selling first novel, *The Naked and the Dead*. The plot of this wartime story includes two Jewish soldiers, Roth and Goldstein, who are differentiated by the way each reacts to antisemitism in the platoon.
Jan. 1948	On January 30, Mohandas K. Gandhi,* Indian political and spiritual leader, is assassinated by a Hindu extremist at New Delhi, India.			On January 15, the Arab League announces that the armies of its members —Egypt, Lebanon, Iraq, Saudi Arabia, Syria, Transjordan, and Yemen—will occupy all of Palestine when the British withdraw on May 15, 1948.	

Jan. 1948

D. Jews in the Middle East and Elsewhere

On January 19, the U.S. State Department Policy Planning staff, headed by George Kennan,* recommends no further U.S. initiative in implementing or aiding the UN partition resolution. Since the Arabs will not cooperate, and a Jewish state would not survive without outside help, the issue of Palestine should be returned to the UN General Assembly with a recommendation that it investigate the alternative of a trusteeship.

Jewish Agency representative Golda Meir (Myerson) (1898–1978) visits the U.S. to urge Jews to furnish funds for Palestine.

Arab troops enter Palestine from Lebanon, Transjordan, Iraq, and Syria.

U.S. Secretary of State George C. Marshall* says the U.S. will maintain an embargo of arms to Palestine.

On January 23, U.S. Democratic Senator Warren Magnuson* (Washington) urges the State Department to relax the Palestine arms embargo to permit sales of surplus arms to Jews. He notes $37 million of arms sales to the Arab League states.

A. General History	B. Jews in North and South America	C. Jews in Europe	D. Jews in the Middle East and Elsewhere	E. Jewish Culture	
The Czechoslovakian Communist minority wins complete control of the nation when President Eduard Benes* accedes to Premier Klement Gottwald's* demand that he approve a new cabinet composed of Communists and their supporters. President Benes* later resigns, and in June, a Communist government is formed.	The largest Jewish institution in Santiago, Chile, the Circulo Israelita, is damaged by an explosion, widely believed to be the work of antisemites. A special congressional election in the Bronx, New York, congressional district, which is 55% Jewish, is won by a 2-to-1 margin by Leo Isaacson, an American Labor party member and a backer of Henry A. Wallace.* The vote is a protest against President Harry S. Truman's* wavering Palestine policy.		Arab explosive charges damage the *Palestine Post* building in Jerusalem. The *New York Times* reports the totally unsubstantiated British charge that 1,000 Communist agents are among 15,000 Jewish immigrants attempting to enter Palestine without visas aboard the *Pan Crescent* and the *Pan York*, which had sailed from Bulgaria. The ships were intercepted and debarked at Cyprus on January 1, 1948. Arabs set off explosive charges on Ben Yehuda Street, a main thoroughfare in Jerusalem. The U.S. ambassador to the UN, Warren Austin,* in a speech to the Security Council, states that the partition cannot be enforced and that the Security Council is not empowered to implement the General Assembly decision on the partition.	Delmore Schwartz, U.S. author and critic, publishes *The World Is a Wedding*, consisting of two short novels and five stories outlining a naturalistic treatment of middle-class Jewish families and their friends during the Great Depression. Nathan Ausubel, U.S. scholar, writes *A Treasury of Jewish Folklore*. It will be reprinted more than 20 times. Reuben "Rube" Goldberg (1883–1970), U.S. cartoonist, best known for his comic strips and humor cartoons, wins the Pulitzer Prize for his political cartoon "Peace Today." Rachel Wischnitzer, Jewish art historian, writes *The Messianic Theme in the Paintings of the Dura Synagogue*. The excavations at Dura Europos uncovered many valuable art objects and synagogue mosaics. Wischnitzer demonstrates that these ancient decorations were based on prevalent Jewish ideas concerning the messianic era.	**Feb. 1948**
In *Illinois ex. rel. McCollum* v. *Board of Education*, the U.S. Supreme Court holds that released-time religious education taught in public schools, even if private teachers are used, is a violation of the First Amendment of the Constitution.	The U.S. Conservative rabbinate, the Rabbinical Assembly, holds a conference on Jewish law. It considers but does not resolve the problem of how to amend or revise the law in conformity with modern needs, with special reference to the *agunah*, the widow whose husband's death has not been properly attested to and consequently may not remarry.		Arab explosive charges damage the Jewish Agency building in Jerusalem. President Harry S. Truman* meets with longtime friend Eddie Jacobson, who implores him to see Chaim Weizmann. Five days later, Truman* has a secret meeting with Weizmann, who pleads for the lifting of the American arms embargo and for continued support of the partition. Truman* reassures Weizmann that the U.S. favors the partition, but the arms embargo is maintained. At a UN Security Council meeting, U.S.	The Museum of Modern Art, in New York, exhibits sculpture by Elie Nadelman (1882–1946). His first exhibition, at which he achieved fame, was in 1917. Known as an innovator and one who experimented with new materials and techniques, Nadelman had refused to exhibit after 1930, and was almost forgotten as an artist at the time of his death. Cole Porter's* musical *Kiss Me Kate*,	**Mar. 1948**

Mar. 1948

D. Jews in the Middle East and Elsewhere

Ambassador Warren Austin* calls for the suspension of the partition implementation, a special session of the General Assembly to reconsider the whole problem, and a temporary trusteeship for Palestine to be established under the UN Trusteeship Council.

At a press conference, President Harry S. Truman* states that despite American support for the partition, it cannot be carried out peacefully, and American troops are not to be used as a matter of national policy. A trusteeship is not proposed as a substitute for the partition but will temporarily fill the vacuum at the end of the mandate.

The first shipment of Czech arms, purchased by the Haganah, sails from the Yugoslav port of Sibenik on board the *Nora*. Unmarked crates are concealed beneath a huge delivery of Italian onions. The *Nora* arrives in Palestine on April 3, 1948.

The *Lino*, a vessel chartered by the Syrians to transport 8,000 rifles and 10 million rounds of ammunition purchased from Czechoslovakia in November 1947, sets sail for Beirut from Fiume. The *Lino* is sunk by Jewish frogmen, led by Munya Mardor of Rechesh. The contents are salvaged and reshipped to Beirut aboard the Italian vessel the *Agiro*, under the command of Haganah operatives. The weapons are transferred to Haganah vessels in midocean and taken

E. Jewish Culture

with libretto written by Bella and Samuel Spewack, opens. Built around Shakespeare's *Taming of the Shrew*, it will have 1,070 performances.

Edwin H. Land gives the first public demonstration of the one-step Polaroid Land camera, at the Photographic Society of America annual convention in Cincinnati, Ohio.

Abraham M. Klein's (1909–1972) *The Rocking Chair and Other Poems* wins the Canadian Governor General's Award for Poetry.

Jules Isaac, French Jewish historian, writes *Jesus and Israel*, in which he identifies three themes of Christian "teaching of contempt" that must be eliminated as historically and spiritually inaccurate. (1) Jews were dispersed by God as punishment for the crucifixion of Christ; (2) Judaism was degenerate in the time of Jesus; (3) Jews were guilty of deicide. Isaac's writings influence Catholic theological circles.

The Musée d'Art Juif, in Paris, is founded.

Fanny Blankers-Koen of the Netherlands is the first woman to win three Olympic track events. She finishes first in the 100-meter dash, the 200-meter dash, and the 80-meter hurdles at the 14th Olympiad held in London, England, in July and August.

Maariv, a Hebrew daily afternoon newspaper, founded and edited by Ezriel Carlebach

A. General History	B. Jews in North and South America	C. Jews in Europe	D. Jews in the Middle East and Elsewhere	E. Jewish Culture	

| | | | immediately to Palestine. This is the only purchase of Czech arms by any Arab state in 1948. | (1908–1956), begins publication in Tel Aviv. In 1970, it will have the largest circulation of any newspaper in Israel, with an average weekday circulation of 160,000, and on Friday, 210,000. | **Mar. 1948** |

In column D:

A Dakota DC-3 airplane, chartered by a private U.S. company, arrives in Czechoslovakia and immediately flies weapons to a British-built airfield in southern Palestine, Beit Daras. This is the first shipment of Czech arms to the Jews of Palestine. In the next seven weeks, more than 107 tons of arms are flown to Beit Daras.

In column E:

Jacob Nahum Epstein (1878–1952), talmudic scholar who, in 1925, was appointed professor of Talmudic Philology at the newly founded Hebrew University, publishes *Mavo le-Nusah ha-Mishnah* (*Introduction to the Original Text of the Mishnah*), a two-volume work considered to be the most authoritative study of the original text of the Mishnah.

Apr. 1948

Column A:

President Harry S. Truman* signs the Foreign Assistance Act of 1948, which includes $5.3 billion earmarked for European recovery (the Marshall Plan).

The Organization of American States is established for mutual defense and general cooperation by the U.S. and 20 Latin American countries at Bogotá, Colombia.

Column D:

Between April 3 and 15, Operation Nahshon is undertaken by the Haganah to clear a corridor from the coastal plain to Jerusalem. The objective is to relieve the Arab siege of Jerusalem. It is the first time the Haganah operates on a brigade level and attacks for the purpose of taking territory. The supplies enable the beleaguered city to hold out for another two months.

Column E:

The Habimah Theater troupe, from Palestine, makes a six-week Broadway appearance. It performs four plays in Hebrew.

D. Jews in the Middle East and Elsewhere

Arab attempts to isolate Haifa by attacking Mishmar Haemek, an agricultural settlement overlooking the Jezreel Valley, fail.

A combined Irgun and Lehi force attacks Deir Yassin, an Arab village on the outskirts of Jerusalem, killing 254 villagers. In the Arab world, the attack is given wide publicity as a deliberate massacre. David Ben-Gurion expresses outrage and apologizes to King Abdullah ibn Hussein* of Transjordan.

A convoy of 80 civilians, mostly doctors and nurses, is ambushed by Arabs as it passes through the Jerusalem suburb of Sheikh Jarrach on its way to the Hadassah Hospital on Mt. Scopus. The killing takes place in view of British soldiers, who do not intervene.

Units of the Golani Brigade secure control of Tiberias.

Jews secure control of Haifa.

Rechesh signs a contract with the Czech government for the purchase of 10 Messerschmitt 109 fighter planes. The contract contains a provision for the secret training of Jewish pilots and technicians in Czechoslovakia. American volunteer instructors, under the command of Al Schwimmer, will train 50 to 75 pilots between May and September 1948.

A supply convoy nears Jerusalem as the siege is broken in April. (Central Zionist Archives)

Apr.
1948

President Harry S. Truman* instructs Samuel Rosenman to tell Chaim Weizmann that if a trusteeship is not adopted by the UN General Assembly, the U.S. will recognize the Jewish state when it is established.

Operation Yiftah, led by Yigal Allon, captures Safed, a strategically important town in Galilee.

A. **General History**	B. **Jews in North and South America**	C. **Jews in Europe**	D. **Jews in the Middle East and Elsewhere**	E. **Jewish Culture**
May 1948 In *Shelley* v. *Kramer*, the U.S. Supreme Court holds that a racially restrictive covenant limiting the ownership or occupancy of real estate is unenforceable by state or federal courts. In a subsequent opinion, the attorney general interprets the Supreme Court's ruling as being applicable to religious or ethnic, as well as racial, restrictions.	This Government has been informed that a Jewish state has been proclaimed in Palestine, and recognition has been requested by the provisional Government thereof. The United States recognizes the provisional government as the de facto authority of the new State of Israel. Harry Truman Approved May 14, 1948. 6:11 *Original draft of White House press statement announcing recognition of Israel. President Truman signed statement adding date, time, and "approved." Press Secretary Charles G. Ross inserted handwritten corrections.*		Arabs capture and destroy Etzion villages on the outskirts of Jerusalem, killing or capturing 500 Jewish soldiers. A White House meeting is called by President Harry S. Truman* to advise on the U.S. recognition of Israel. Secretary of State George C. Marshall* argues against and Special Counsel Clark Clifford* argues in favor.	

May
1948

D. Jews in the Middle East and Elsewhere

Jews secure control of Jaffa after several weeks of fighting.

Golda Meir, accompanied by Ezra Danin, meets secretly with King Abdullah ibn Hussein* in Transjordan. She fails to dissuade him from joining the Arab invasion of Palestine to take place upon the departure of the British.

David Ben-Gurion convenes the Provisional Council (later to become the Knesset, or Parliament) in the Municipal Museum of Tel Aviv. He declares the establishment of a Jewish state in Palestine to be known as the State of Israel. Ben-Gurion is elected prime minister and Chaim Weizmann, president.

The U.S. grants full and unconditional de facto recognition to the provisional government of Israel (established on May 15, Israel time). De jure recognition is not granted for the technical reason that the new government is provisional.

As the British withdraw, the armies of Egypt, Transjordan, Syria, Lebanon, and Iraq begin their invasion. Saudi Arabia sends a formation to fight under Egyptian command. Yemen considers itself at war with Israel but sends no contingent.

The Israelis repulse the Syrian invasion of the Jordan Valley.

The Soviet Union recognizes the State of Israel, according it full de jure diplomatic status.

Israel names Ehud Avriel as ambassador to Czechoslovakia, its first official representative abroad.

Ten dismantled Messerschmitt 109 fighters are flown aboard cargo planes from Zatec, Czechoslovakia, to Ekron, Israel.

The UN General Assembly appoints Count Folke Bernadotte,* president of the Swedish Red Cross, as mediator in the Arab–Israeli conflict.

Kibbutz Yad Mordekhai is abandoned by its defenders after resisting and slowing the Egyptian advance toward Tel Aviv.

The Jewish Quarter of the Old City of Jerusalem surrenders to the Arab Legion.

John Phillips,* *Life* photographer who accompanied the Arab Legion in the battle for the Old City of Jerusalem, photographs the surrender of the Jews. He smuggles out his pictures of the looting of the Jewish Quarter, which causes him to be sentenced to death in absentia by the Jordanians.

David Ben-Gurion proclaims the establishment of the State of Israel on May 14, in the Municipal Museum of Tel Aviv. (Central Zionist Archives)

Formalities establishing the Israel Defense Forces (IDF) are completed. Two dissident organizations, Irgun Zeva'i Le'ummi and Lohamei Herut Israel (Lehi), agree to discontinue independent activities, except in Jerusalem, and to be absorbed into the IDF. Their units in Jerusalem are disbanded in September following an ultimatum by the IDF.

The Egyptian advance toward Tel Aviv is halted near Ashdod, only 20 miles from Tel Aviv.

The Israel Defense Forces, in Operation Pitchfork, succeed in consolidating all Jewish areas in the New City (West) of Jerusalem.

The Israel Defense Forces, attempting to link Jerusalem to the coastal plain, fails to capture Latrun. However, an alternative link, called the Burma Road, is made serviceable for vehicles, thus relieving the siege of Jerusalem.

Front page of The New York Times, *May 15, 1948.*

May 1948

A. **General History**	B. **Jews in North and South America**	C. **Jews in Europe**	D. **Jews in the Middle East and Elsewhere**
Mt. Palomar Observatory, with the world's largest reflector, opens in the U.S.	The Democratic party platform includes a plank that reads: "We approve the claims of the State of Israel to the boundaries set forth in U.N. resolution of November 29, 1947, and consider that modification thereof should be made only if fully acceptable to the State of Israel." The Republican platform has a similar plank.		The first truce between Israel and the Arab Legion, arranged by the UN, goes into effect. It is to last 28 days and UN observers are to ensure that neither side gains any military advantage by the acquisition of additional arms or fighting personnel.

June 1948

The U.S. Senate adopts the Vandenberg* Resolution (64–4), which favors the U.S. entering collective security agreements with non–Western Hemisphere nations, as permitted by Article 51 of the UN Charter. This resolution leads to the NATO alliance.

The Republican party nominates Governor Thomas E. Dewey* of New York for president and Governor Earl Warren* of California for vice president.

The Soviet Union begins a blockade of all land traffic between West Berlin and West Germany. The U.S. and Allies begin a large-scale airlift of food and other supplies to thwart the Soviet effort to force western Allies to give up control of the western part of the city.

A new Selective Service Act is signed by President Truman.*

President Harry S. Truman* reluctantly signs the Displaced Persons Act. The bill provides for admission to the U.S. of 205,000

Colonel David "Mickey" Marcus (1902–1948) is accidentally killed outside Jerusalem. Marcus was a retired U.S. Army officer and West Point graduate who had come to Israel to help the Israeli forces.

The Yugoslav government permits Israeli landing rights at the Podgorica airfield, which becomes the standard refueling point for all flights of arms from Czechoslovakia to Israel.

Altalena, *carrying arms for the Irgun, set afire off the coast of Tel Aviv, in a clash with the Haganah. (Photo by Hans Pinn. Israel Government Press Office)*

On June 21, the *Altalena*, a vessel carrying arms for the Irgun, attempts to

	A. General History	B. Jews in North and South America	C. Jews in Europe	D. Jews in the Middle East and Elsewhere	E. Jewish Culture
June 1948	displaced persons (DPs). However, the bill limits the definition of DPs. Truman* says: "The bill discriminates in callous fashion against displaced persons of the Jewish faith." Tito* refuses to allow Yugoslavia to become a vassal Soviet satellite. The result is the excommunication of Yugoslavia from the world Communist movement.			land its cargo near Tel Aviv. When the Irgun refuses to hand over its weapons to the Israel Defense Forces (IDF), the vessel is set afire, with Irgun and IDF casualties. Golda Meir is named the Israeli ambassador to the Soviet Union. Count Folke Bernadotte* proposes to the Jews and the Arabs that the Negev be transferred to the Arabs, and western Galilee, already occupied by Israel during the war, be included in Israel. Muslims riot against Jews in the Libyan cities of Benghazi and Tripoli. Jews defend themselves and limit losses to 14 dead.	
July 1948	The Democrats renominate President Harry S. Truman* and nominate Senator Alben W. Barkley* of Kentucky for vice president. Southern Democrats walk out of the convention in protest against a strong civil rights plank, and later that month, they nominate Governor Strom Thurmond* of South Carolina on a States' Rights (Dixiecrat) ticket. The newly formed Progressive party, made up of Democrats who oppose President Harry S. Truman's* foreign policy, nominates former Vice President Henry A. Wallace* for president. President Harry S. Truman,* by Executive Order 9980, sets up administrative machinery to implement the Ramspeck Act of 1940, which bars racial		Thirteen I. G. Farben officials are sentenced by the Nuremberg Tribunal to prison terms ranging from 18 months to 8 years after having been convicted of looting conquered countries or exploiting slave labor. They are acquitted of participating in aggressive warfare. Alfred Krupp* (1907–1967) is sentenced by the Nuremberg Tribunal to 12 years' imprisonment. He is convicted of the war crimes of having looted conquered countries and exploited slave labor. He will be released in 1951 and his property and companies will be restored to him.	Hostilities resume as the June 11 truce expires. The only agreement Count Folke Bernadotte* was able to arrange during this first truce was the demilitarization of the Mt. Scopus area in Jerusalem. Three B-17 Flying Fortresses, piloted by American volunteers flying from Zatec, Czechoslovakia, bomb Cairo, Gaza, and El-Arish. This is Israel's single long-range bombing mission. The Czechs and Israelis enter into an agreement for the sale of 59 British Spitfire fighter planes, which had been turned over to Czechoslovakia by the Royal Air Force at the end of World War II. By the end of the year, 24 of these planes will be flown to Israel. Thirty-three planes will be shipped by sea from a Yugoslav port and	

A. General History	B. Jews in North and South America	C. Jews in Europe	D. Jews in the Middle East and Elsewhere	E. Jewish Culture	
and religious discriminatory practices in the federal establishment. The order establishes fair employment practices. Idlewild Airport opens in New York.			arrive in Israel on February 18, 1949. A second truce between the Israelis and Arabs goes into effect. Between July 9 and 18, the Israel Defense Forces captured Lydda Airport on the central front and Nazareth on the northern front. They also obtain a direct land connection with the Negev on the southern front. From July through November, the Arab Legion, in breach of the second truce, bombards Jewish Jerusalem almost every night.		**July 1948**
Whittaker Chambers,* former Communist, testifies at a House Un-American Activities Committee hearing that Alger Hiss,* former State Department official, had been a Communist. Hiss* sues for slander and Chambers* produces State Department classified documents allegedly given to him by Hiss.*		Josef Buehler* (1900–1948) is hanged in Cracow, Poland, after his conviction by a Polish court of planning and organizing the extermination of an incalculable number of Jews. He was deputy to Hans Frank,* the Nazi governor-general of the general government of Poland after the Nazi occupation.	The Czech government, submitting in part to American diplomatic pressure, orders the evacuation of Israelis from the Zatec base. The Arab Legion destroys the Latrun water pumping station. Israel then lays a pipeline along the Burma Road to keep Jerusalem supplied. A Soviet diplomatic mission, headed by Pavel Yershov,* arrives in Israel.		**Aug. 1948**
In a Roper Poll, only 10% of respondents are in favor of admitting large numbers of displaced persons to the U.S. Most want other countries to take either all or at least a proportionate share of the refugees.		Israeli Ambassador Golda Meir arrives in Moscow. She receives a tremendous spontaneous welcome from Moscow's 500,000 Jews. A Pravda article by Ilya Ehrenberg, Soviet journalist, warns of official displeasure with the public displays of Soviet Jewry's enthusiasm for Israel.	UN mediator Count Folke Bernadotte* is assassinated by Jewish terrorists in Jerusalem. Ralph J. Bunche* of the U.S. succeeds him as mediator. Count Folke Bernadotte's* final report to the UN on Palestine is published posthumously. It calls for recognition of Israel but advocates the transfer of the Negev area to the Arabs, incorporation of western Galilee into Israel, and placing Jerusalem under UN control.		**Sep. 1948**

	A. General History	B. Jews in North and South America	C. Jews in Europe	D. Jews in the Middle East and Elsewhere	E. Jewish Culture
Sep. 1948	 *New immigrants arrive at a ma'abarah. (Central Zionist Archives)*			U.S. Secretary of State George C. Marshall* announces the U.S. support of Count Folke Bernadotte's* final plan for securing peace in Palestine. Shafiq Adas, an Iraqi Jewish millionaire, is hanged in Basra, having been convicted of selling surplus British army scrap metal to Israel.	
Oct. 1948	All of Manchuria comes under the control of Chinese Communist forces. Governor Thomas E. Dewey,* Republican candidate for president, accuses President Harry S. Truman* of vacillation on Palestine and reaffirms his support of the Republican platform commitment to Israel's boundaries. Dewey states his support for the original UN partition arrangement, which awarded the Negev to Israel.		Joseph Stalin* begins the implementation of an antisemitic and anti-Zionist campaign by initiating a purge of officials friendly to Israel. The Jewish Anti-Fascist Committee is closed down as a center of subversion.	The Israeli army's Operation Yoav clears most of the Negev of Egyptian troops. The Israelis capture Beersheba. President Harry S. Truman* reverses his position and reaffirms the Democratic platform provisions on Israel's boundaries. The original UN partition boundaries should be modified only if acceptable to Israel. He goes beyond the party position by promising prompt financial aid and to extend de jure recognition upon the election of a permanent government. The Israeli army's Operation Hiram clears the entire Galilee of Arab forces.	
Nov. 1948	Harry S. Truman* is reelected President. The Democrats regain control of Congress. Former Premier Hideri Tojo* and six other Japanese leaders are sentenced to death and 18 others are given prison terms by an 11-nation international military tribunal in Tokyo after being found guilty of war crimes. A dry printing process, known as *xerography,* is developed by the	The Jewish vote in the presidential election is estimated at 75% for Harry S. Truman,* 15% for Henry A. Wallace,* and 10% for Thomas E. Dewey.*	Itzik Fefer (1900–1952), Yiddish poet and secretary of the Soviet Union's Jewish Anti-Fascist Committee, "disappears."	The *Christian Science Monitor* runs an exposé of activities at Zatec air base in Czechoslovakia. The story of the Israeli–Czech training and transport of arms through Zatec is true. However, the story falsely reports the presence of Soviet army personnel at the base and Israeli training on Soviet jets. El Al, the Israel airline, is founded. Its primary mission is to transport Jewish immigrants to Israel,	

A. General History	B. Jews in North and South America	C. Jews in Europe	D. Jews in the Middle East and Elsewhere	E. Jewish Culture	
Batelle Memorial Institute of Columbus, Ohio, and the Haloid Co. of Rochester, New York. This process gives promise of being a revolutionary step in the reproduction of printed matter and photographs.			mainly from Middle Eastern countries.		**Nov. 1948**
In Alger Hiss's* hearing, Representative Richard M. Nixon* of the House Un-American Activities Committee charges that the Truman* administration is more interested in concealing embarrassing facts than in finding out who stole classified documents. The UN General Assembly adopts the Universal Declaration of Human Rights. The vote is 48–0, with the Soviet Union and its satellites, Saudi Arabia, and the Union of South Africa abstaining. The principal draftsman is René-Samuel Cassin (1887–1976), French jurist, who served as a member and president of the UN Commission on Human Rights. Alger Hiss* is indicted for perjury by a federal grand jury in New York.			Operation Horev expels Egyptians from the Negev and pursues them into the Sinai. A cease-fire becomes effective on January 7, 1949. A UN General Assembly resolution establishes the Palestine Conciliation Commission to arrange a binding peace settlement between Israel and the Arabs, to facilitate resettlement and repatriation of Arab refugees, and to formulate a plan for a permanent international regime in Jerusalem. The commission members are the U.S., France, and Turkey. The airlift of most Jews from Yemen and Aden, Operation Magic Carpet, begins. When it is completed in September 1950, 45,000 Jews from Yemen and 3,000 from Aden will have been flown to Israel.		**Dec. 1948**
Simone de Beauvoir* writes *The Second Sex*. It becomes a landmark for the modern women's movement and will be translated from French into English in 1953.	Emanuel Celler, U.S. congressman from Brooklyn, New York, becomes chairman of the House Judiciary Committee. He serves in Congress from 1922 to 1972 and is the author of the 1960 Civil Rights Act. Pinkhos Churgin (1894–1957) becomes president of the Mizrahi Organization of America, a religious Zionist organization.	The Soviet Union begins a consistent purge of Jews from party, military, and diplomatic positions as well as scientists, physicians, journalists, and other professionals. Those Jews who are active in public life are charged with *cosmopolitanism*, a derogatory term. "Cosmopolitans" are accused of hating the Soviet people and of supporting Zionism.	The UN Economic Survey Commission, headed by Tennessee Valley Authority chairman Gordon Clapp,* unsuccessfully tries to move the Arab refugee problem from the political to the economic sphere. The commission believes that resettlement of the refugees in various parts of the Middle East could lead to significant economic	A "million dollar trio" of chamber music musicians is formed, including violinist Jascha Heifetz, cellist Gregor Piatigorsky (1903–1976), and pianist Arthur Rubinstein (1887–1982). Arthur Miller, U.S. playwright and novelist, writes *Death of a Salesman*, a Pulitzer Prize–winning play, which portrays	**1949**

A. General History	B. Jews in North and South America	C. Jews in Europe	D. Jews in the Middle East and Elsewhere	E. Jewish Culture
1949	He is the chief architect for the creation of Bar-Ilan University in Israel and in 1955 will leave the U.S. to head the new university.

Ezra Pound* (1885–1972) is awarded the Bollingen Prize for Poetry. The award arouses much controversy as Pound* is an avowed antisemite who embraced Fascism and, while living in Italy during World War II, broadcast treasonous Fascist propaganda. Returned to the U.S., he was adjudged to be of unsound mind and thus escaped trial. Bigotry permeates his poetry.

Benjamin Buttenweiser, U.S. banker, is appointed assistant high commissioner for Germany by High Commissioner John J. McCloy.* An advisor on economic matters and de-Nazification, he will serve until 1951.

Hollywood's first film dealing with the creation of Israel, *Sword in the Desert*, stars Dana Andrews* as an American ship captain who lands illegal immigrants in Palestine in the face of British hostility. Andrews* joins the Jewish underground led by Jeff Chandler. The British are the villains of this film, and the Arabs are not an issue. | The first volumes of the new *Soviet Encyclopedia*, published between 1949 and 1953, fail to mention almost all Jewish artists, writers, and notable personalities included in the first edition (1927). | improvements in the area.

France and Israel begin scientific contacts when the French learn that Dr. Israel Dostrovsky, Israeli scientist, invented a process for producing heavy water.

Joseph Klausner, historian, literary critic, and Zionist, is nominated by the Herut party as their candidate for the presidency of Israel in opposition to Chaim Weizmann. A prolific Hebrew writer who attended the First Zionist Congress, he emigrated from Russia to Palestine in 1917, where he became professor of Hebrew literature, and later of Jewish history at the Hebrew University. Beginning in 1930, he identified with the right-wing nationalists and is considered the ideologist of their movement.

The Mount Scopus College, a Jewish day school, is founded in Melbourne, Australia.

The Weizmann Institute of Science is established in Rehovot. This scientific institution developed from the Daniel Seiff Research Institute, founded in 1934.

Selig Brodetsky (1888–1954), British mathematician and professor at the University of Leeds since 1920, succeeds Judah L. Magnes as president of the Hebrew University in Jerusalem. He will resign in 1952 and return to England. | traveling salesman Willy Loman, who lives in a world of his own and America's false values.

Morris Raphael Cohen's (1882–1947) autobiography, *A Dreamer's Journey*, is published posthumously. Cohen taught philosophy at New York's City College from 1912 to 1938 and wrote of the immigrant generation under the conditions of freedom in the U.S.

Louis Finkelstein, chancellor of the Jewish Theological Seminary of America, edits the two-volume *The Jews: Their History, Culture and Religion*, a comprehensive work by 34 scholars.

Charles Goren, U.S. bridge player, writes *Point Count Bidding in Contract Bridge*, in which he formulates a new system for bidding. Goren wins the National Bridge Championship of America 31 times.

Etta Cone (1870–1949) bequeaths her and her sister Claribel's (1864–1929) world renowned art collection to the Baltimore Museum of Art. Their friendship with Gertrude Stein (1874–1946) brought them into contact with such artists as Henri Matisse* and Pablo Picasso,* whose works are featured.

Jule Styne (b. 1905), U.S. composer, composes the music for *Gentlemen Prefer Blondes*, including the song "Diamonds Are a Girl's Best Friend." His later hit musicals include *Bells Are Ringing* (1956), *Gypsy* (1959), and *Funny Girl* (1964). |
| **Jan. 1949** | | | Britain presents an ultimatum to Israel. Unless Israeli forces | |

A. General History	B. Jews in North and South America	C. Jews in Europe	D. Jews in the Middle East and Elsewhere	E. Jewish Culture	
			withdraw from Sinai, Britain will invoke the Anglo-Egyptian Treaty of 1936 and come to the aid of the Egyptians. A week later, Israeli warplanes shoot down five British warplanes over the Sinai Peninsula. The same day, as Israelis prepare to attack Rafah, in the Sinai, the Egyptians ask for a cease-fire, which is granted.

The U.S. Export-Import Bank announces a decision to grant Israel a loan of $35 million and to earmark an additional $65 million for later use. The loan is used to finance projects to stimulate transportation, communications, industry, and construction.

Israel holds national elections for the First Knesset, with 434,684 votes cast. The Mapai wins 46 seats; Mapam, 19 seats; Herut, 14 seats; and the religious parties, 16 seats. The government is installed on March 10, with David Ben-Gurion as prime minister and minister of defense, and Moshe Sharett as minister of foreign affairs.

Britain grants de facto recognition of Israel. | "The Goldbergs," a hit radio show starring Gertrude Berg as Molly, is adapted to television. It also features Philip Loeb, in the role of Jake, Molly's husband. It will remain a popular television show until 1955.

Karl Schwarz (1885–1962), who was curator of Jewish museums in Berlin and later Tel Aviv, writes *Jewish Artists of the 19th and 20th Centuries*.

Martin Buber's *The Prophetic Faith* appears in English translation from the Hebrew. Buber analyzes Hebrew prophetic writings and their contemporary influence.

Arthur Koestler, Hungarian-born author, writes *Promise and Fulfilment: Palestine, 1917–1949*, a philosophical and psychological history of events from the Balfour Declaration to the establishment of Israel.

Max Brod, who left Czechoslovakia for Palestine in 1939, writes *Unambo*, a novel of Israel's War of Independence.

The Inbal Dance Theater of Israel is founded. Its dancers are drawn primarily from the Yemenite Jewish community, and it specializes in the dances of that community. | **Jan. 1949** |
| | | | Israel concludes a bilateral armistice agreement with Egypt, which terminates the military phase of the War of Independence. The negotiations, chaired by UN mediator Ralph Bunche,* have resulted in an agreement that leaves Egypt in control of the Gaza Strip, but otherwise it withdraws beyond the previous | The first volume of a general, Jewish, and Israeli encyclopedia, *Ha-Entsiqlopedya ha-Ivrit*, is published in Israel, a year late as a result of the War of Independence. The 35th and final volume will appear in 1985. | **Feb. 1949** |

A. General History	B. Jews in North and South America	C. Jews in Europe	D. Jews in the Middle East and Elsewhere	E. Jewish Culture

Feb. 1949

frontier. The Egyptian brigade, which had been surrounded at Faluja, is released and the area turned over to Israel.

Mar. 1949

An American B-50 bomber flies the first nonstop round-the-world flight.

The North Atlantic Treaty Organization (NATO) is formed.

Israeli troops take control of an abandoned police station at Umm Rashrash at the Red Sea. A new city, Eilat, will be built at this southern tip of the Negev.

Israel concludes a bilateral armistice agreement with Lebanon at Rosh ha-Nikrah, which terminates the military phase of the War of Independence. Talks are chaired by Henry Vigier,* UN mediator Ralph J. Bunche's* deputy. Israel withdraws from areas occupied in Lebanon, and the demarcation line follows the previous frontier.

Apr. 1949

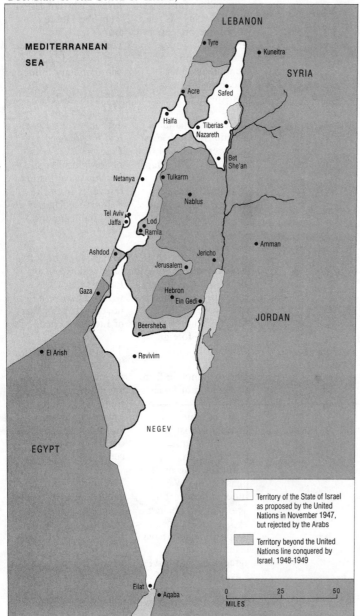

BOUNDARY OF THE STATE OF ISRAEL, 1949–1967

Territory of the State of Israel as proposed by the United Nations in November 1947, but rejected by the Arabs

Territory beyond the United Nations line conquered by Israel, 1948-1949

0 25 50
MILES

Israel concludes a bilateral armistice agreement with Jordan, which terminates the military phase of the War of Independence. Talks are chaired by UN mediator Ralph J. Bunche.* Transjordan remains in control of a large part of the West Bank of the Jordan River, including the Old City of Jerusalem. Transjordan never keeps the agreement to permit free access to the Wailing Wall.

Pope Pius XII issues a Second Encyclical on Palestine, which calls for the full territorial internationalization of Jerusalem.

Kibbutz Lohamei ha-Getta'ot (Ghetto Fighters) is founded on the northern coastal plain of Israel, primarily by Polish and Lithuanian Jews.

A. General History	B. Jews in North and South America	C. Jews in Europe	D. Jews in the Middle East and Elsewhere	E. Jewish Culture	
			They soon establish Ghetto Fighters' House and Holocaust Museum, which includes a document section, a film archive, and a publishing house.		**Apr. 1949**
Great Britain recognizes Ireland's independence. The Soviet Union lifts the Berlin blockade.		Hungarian Foreign Minister Laszlo Rajk is arrested and charged, among other things, with complicity in a Zionist conspiracy. In September, he will be found guilty and summarily executed.	Israel is admitted as a member of the UN. A food rationing system is introduced in Israel; every citizen is allowed about 2,500 calories of food value per day. The Palestine Conciliation Commission meets in Lausanne, Switzerland, with Israel and its Arab neighbors. They fail to reach any agreement. President Harry S. Truman* expresses "deep disappointment" at Israel's failure to show flexibility on the Arab refugee problem. He warns that the U.S. might reconsider its attitude toward Israel.		**May 1949**
			The Hashemite Kingdom of Jordan is established. This change of name is a prelude to the annexation of West Bank Palestine, occupied by the Arab Legion during the War of Independence.		**June 1949**
			Israel concludes a bilateral armistice with Syria at Mahanayim, which terminates the military phase of the War of Independence. Talks are chaired by Henry Vigier,* UN mediator Ralph J. Bunche's* deputy. Syria withdraws to the Syria–Palestine frontier, with a demilitarized zone created out of the line of their farthest advance and the international frontier.		**July 1949**

	A. General History	B. Jews in North and South America	C. Jews in Europe	D. Jews in the Middle East and Elsewhere	E. Jewish Culture
July 1949				At the second Lausanne conference of the Palestine Conciliation Commission, Israel offers to repatriate 100,000 Arab refugees, provided it is linked to peace negotiations.	
Aug. 1949			A Munich newspaper, the *Sueddeutsche Zeitung*, publishes a letter to the editor expressing regret that not all Jews were gassed by the Nazis. Several hundred Jewish displaced persons (DPs) converge on the newspaper's offices at Möhlsträsse to protest. German police intervene and a dozen DPs are injured.	After anti-Jewish press attacks, the synagogue in the Jewish quarter of Damascus, Syria, is bombed.	
Sep. 1949	President Harry S. Truman* announces that the Soviet Union has developed the atomic bomb. The Federal Republic of Germany is established. Konrad Adenauer* (1876–1967), Mayor of Cologne, is elected chancellor. The newly elected Bundestag (Parliament) of 402 members includes more than 50 former Nazis.			The Palestine Conciliation Commission proposes a permanent international regime for Jerusalem. Israel and Jordan would govern separate sectors and a UN commissioner would protect holy places and supervise the stability of the demographic equilibrium. Israel and Jordan refuse to discuss the plan. The Israeli Knesset enacts the Defense Service Law. Modeled after the Swiss army mobilization plan, it establishes a citizen army. All men age 18–29 and all unmarried women age 18–26 are to be drafted for two years' army service. All men up to 49 are to be trained in the reserves and then be called for one month's annual service. The Israeli government establishes the Ulpan, an institution for teaching Hebrew to large numbers of immigrant adults.	

A. General History	B. Jews in North and South America	C. Jews in Europe	D. Jews in the Middle East and Elsewhere	E. Jewish Culture	
The German Democratic Republic is established in the Soviet zone under the leadership of Walter Ulbricht.* The People's Republic of China is declared by the Chinese Communists. The civil war ends in Greece.					**Oct. 1949**
			The Weizmann Institute at Rehovoth is formally opened. Almost exclusively financed by American Jewry, it aims to promote scientific research on the technical level, as distinguished from that of the Hebrew University, which is to promote scientific knowledge and scholarship on a theoretical level.		**Nov. 1949**
The UN General Assembly establishes the office of high commissioner for refugees. The Chinese nationalist government transfers to Taiwan. The Netherlands grants independence to Indonesia. Sukarno* is elected president.		The Communist party of Czechoslovakia, under pressure from the Soviet Union, purges all Jews in the office of the premier and in the ministries of foreign affairs, foreign trade, and information. Included are Milan Rejman, head of the office of the premier, and Evzen Loebl, deputy minister of foreign trade.	The UN General Assembly, led by a coalition of Arab, Muslim, Catholic, and Soviet bloc states, votes for the internationalization of Jerusalem. In reaction, the Israeli government proclaims Jerusalem to be its capital and the Knesset is transferred there. Most countries refuse to move embassies there.		**Dec. 1949**
	The Law Committee of Conservative Judaism's Rabbinical Assembly submits majority and minority reports on the problem of Sabbath observance. The majority permits the use of electric lights and driving on the Sabbath for the purpose of participating in Sabbath worship in the spirit of a living and developing *halakhah* responsive to the changing needs of Jewish people. The minority is concerned	The Prague Jewish Museum is expropriated by the state on the pretext that the Jewish community does not have the means to maintain it. In this museum the Nazis had concentrated Jewish books, manuscripts, and religious and art objects confiscated from many European countries. The Czech government rejects an appeal to transfer some of the objects to Israel.	Israel is among the first group of non-Communist nations to recognize the People's Republic of China. However, diplomatic relations between the two countries are not established.	Three volumes of the American Jewish Committee's Studies in Prejudice are published: *Anti-Semitism and Emotional Disorder* by Nathan W. Ackerman and Marie Jahoda; *The Authoritarian Personality* by Theodor Adorno et al., and *Dynamics of Prejudice* by Bruno Bettelheim and Morris Janowitz. Together with those published in 1949 - *Prophets of Deceit* by Leo Lowenthal and Norbert Guterman and *Rehearsal for*	**1950**

A. General History	B. Jews in North and South America	C. Jews in Europe	D. Jews in the Middle East and Elsewhere	E. Jewish Culture
1950	about the hazards involved in yielding to convenience. The first Conservative day school is organized by Rabbi Robert Gordis at Temple Beth El in Rockaway Park, New York. It is the first in a network of Solomon Schechter Day Schools, which offer Judaic as well as secular studies. Anna M. Rosenberg, U.S. labor relations and manpower expert, is appointed assistant secretary of defense by Secretary of Defense George C. Marshall.* It is the highest post in the military establishment ever held by a woman. She is in charge of coordinating military manpower. John Hersey* (b. 1914), U.S. novelist, writes *The Wall*, a novel of the extinction of the Warsaw ghetto by the Nazis in World War II.	Adolf Eichmann,* Nazi SS officer, arrives in Argentina and begins living in Buenos Aires, with his wife and three sons, under the assumed name of Ricardo Klement.		*Destruction* by Paul W. Massing—they have a decisive impact on contemporary social science. Abraham Joshua Heschel (1907–1972), U.S. rabbinic scholar and theologian, writes *The Earth Is the Lord's*, a personal history of the creative and spiritual forces in Hasidism. Morris U. Schappes, U.S. historian, edits *A Documentary History of the Jews in the United States, 1654–1875*. J. C. Hurewitz, U.S. foreign policy expert, writes *The Struggle for Palestine*, a study of its role in world affairs since 1936. Anzia Yezierska, novelist and writer of short stories, writes *Red Ribbon on a White Horse*, an autobiographical novel describing her poverty-stricken life on New York's Lower East Side, unhappy experiences in Hollywood as a script writer, and return to her early surroundings. Robert Capa, well-known war photographer, and Irwin Shaw, U.S. novelist, collaborate on *Report on Israel*, one of the first journalistic accounts of Israel. Isaac Bashevis Singer (1904–1991), Polish-born author of Yiddish fiction, publishes in English *The Family Moskat*, a realistic novel depicting the degeneration of the lives of various members of a wealthy Warsaw family. The novel spans the years 1912 to World War II.

A. General History	B. Jews in North and South America	C. Jews in Europe	D. Jews in the Middle East and Elsewhere	E. Jewish Culture	
President Harry S. Truman* orders the production of the hydrogen bomb.			The Israeli Government is transferred to Jerusalem. On the same day, Jordan confers citizenship on all Arabs of the West Bank, including Jerusalem.	Saul Lieberman, noted talmudic scholar of the Jewish Theological Seminary of America, writes *Hellenism in Jewish Palestine*, which, together with his *Greek in Jewish Palestine* (1942), traces the influence of Hellenistic culture on Palestine Jewry during the Roman period.	**Jan. 1950**
			The UN General Assembly establishes the UN Refugee Works Administration (UNRWA), with a $54 million budget, to assist in employing refugees on relocation projects in Arab lands. Arab governments refuse to cooperate with any plan designed for economic integration, and the UNRWA remains a relief agency.	An English edition of the Israel Passover Haggadah, arranged and edited by Rabbi Menachem Kasher, is published in the U.S.	**Mar. 1950**
				Arnold "Red" Auerbach (b. 1917) becomes coach of the Boston Celtics of the National Basketball Association. In 1957, his team will win the first of many championships.	
			The Council of the Arab League adopts a resolution forbidding its members to conclude peace with Israel.		**Apr. 1950**
			The Soviet Union reverses its position and no longer supports the 1949 UN resolution calling for the internationalization of Jerusalem. Jacob Malik,* the UN representative of the Soviet Union, advises the secretary-general, "It has become clear that the General Assembly resolution does not satisfy the Arab or Jewish populations of either Jerusalem or Palestine as a whole." Jordan annexes the West Bank of the Palestine territories (including the Old City of Jerusalem) occupied by the Arab Legion during the War of Independence. The Arab League states refuse to recognize the annexation, calling it illegal.	Tadeus Reichstein, Swiss organic chemist, is awarded the Nobel Prize in physiology or medicine, jointly with E. C. Kendall* and P. Hench* for their discovery of cortisone and its medical uses. Mane-Katz (Emanuel Katz, 1894–1962), born in Russia, who arrived in Paris in 1913 and became a representative of the painters of the school of Paris, paints *Homage to Paris*. His early works were primarily of Jewish subject matter. He later painted the sights of Paris and French scenes. He will die in Israel and leave his collection to the city of Haifa. Menachem Begin, Israeli statesman and former commander of the Irgun, writes *The Revolt*, an account of his underground activities as leader of the Irgun Zeva'i Le'ummi during the	

Box:

World Jewish Population, 1950

Total World Population	2,175,090,000
Total World Jewish Population	11,500,000

Place	Number	% of World Jewry
Europe	3,550,000 (1)	30.9
Americas	5,819,930	50.6
Asia	1,374,350	12.0
Africa	702,400	6.1
Australia & New Zealand	44,000	.4

Countries of Largest Jewish Population, 1950

Country	Jewish Population
United States	5,000,000
U.S.S.R.	2,000,000
Israel	1,115,000
Great Britain	450,000
Argentina	360,000
Rumania	335,000
Morocco	260,000
France	235,000
Canada	198,000
Hungary	160,000
Algeria	135,000

Major Jewish Cities, 1950

City	Jewish Population
New York City	2,1000,000
Chicago	325,000
Tel Aviv	310,000
London (greater)	280,000
Los Angeles	250,000
Philadelphia	245,000
Buenos Aires (1948)	165,000
Bucharest (1948–49)	160,000
Haifa	154,000
Boston	140,000
Paris	125,000
Jerusalem	117,000
Budapest (1958–49)	110,000
Casablanca (1948–49)	100,000

	A. General History	B. Jews in North and South America	C. Jews in Europe	D. Jews in the Middle East and Elsewhere	E. Jewish Culture
May 1950				Egypt closes the Suez Canal to Israeli ships and Israeli commerce. The U.S., Britain, and France issue a Tripartite Declaration expressing their opposition to the use of force or threats of force between Israel and its Arab neighbors and guaranteeing the existing armistice lines. The airborne emigration of Jews from Iraq to Israel commences, with Iraq insisting on an 800-mile detour with a landing at Nicosia, Cyprus, both going and coming, on the round trip from Baghdad to Lydda, Israel. In March 1951, Iraq will authorize direct trips to and from Israel. Operation Ali Baba is the largest air emigration ever undertaken. When it ends in December 1951, 120,000 Iraqi Jews will have been flown to Israel.	last years of the British mandate. The publication of a scholarly encyclopedia of the Bible begins in Jerusalem. *Ha-Entsiqlopedya ha-Miqra'it* will be completed in 1988, when the ninth volume, an index, appears. Israeli scholar Yitzhak Heinemann (1876–1957), who fled his post at the Jewish Theological Seminary of Breslau in 1939, publishes a comprehensive study of rabbinic methods of interpretation, *Darkhei ha-Aggadah* (*The Ways of Midrash*). In 1955 Heinemann will receive the Israel Prize for his contributions to the study of Jewish thought.
June 1950	North Korea invades South Korea. The UN Security Council, acting in the absence of the Soviet Union, votes military sanctions and calls on its members to repel the invasion. President Harry S. Truman* authorizes the use of American forces. In July, the UN will establish a unified force, under U.S. command.			Israel joins the 45 nations who vote for UN sanctions against North Korea in response to its invasion of South Korea. A wave of anti-Israel propaganda ensues in the Soviet Union, with the press calling Israel a satellite of Western imperialism.	
July 1950				The Swedish government announces the exchange of notes with Israel over the assassination of Count Folke Bernadotte* in Jerusalem and considers the case as closed. It notes, with satisfaction, "that the government of Israel admits without circumlocution, and regrets the shortcomings of the	

| | | | Israeli police inquiry into the case of [Count Bernadotte*] which have been pointed out by the Swedish authorities." | | **July 1950** |

D. Jews in the Middle East and Elsewhere

July 1950

Israeli Foreign Minister Moshe Sharett, in an address at the Hebrew University, states: "Of the two conflicting conceptions of the social order now locked in ideological struggle—the democratic and the communistic—Israel has definitely chosen the former."

Israel announces the rationing of clothing and footwear. Public resentment results in a consumer revolt and a thriving black market. In October, David Ben-Gurion will offer his resignation, which will be rejected, and the government will be reorganized with a view to alleviating criticism of its economic policy and administration.

Israel enacts the Law of Return, which guarantees the right of every Jew to immigrate to Israel and to become a citizen immediately upon arrival. The law contains a provision permitting an Israeli citizen to retain his or her previous nationality.

A. General History	B. Jews in North and South America	C. Jews in Europe	D. Jews in the Middle East and Elsewhere	E. Jewish Culture	
		Many Romanian Zionist leaders are arrested and held incommunicado for months despite protests from worldwide Jewish organizations. In spite of propaganda and intimidation, Jewish emigration from Romania continues during 1950–1951.	Israeli Prime Minister David Ben-Gurion and Jacob Blaustein, president of the American Jewish Committee, exchange statements clarifying the relationship between Israel and American Jews. Israel explicitly recognizes the full independence of Jewish communities in the Diaspora and of aliyah as the free choice of each American Jew.		**Aug. 1950**

D. Jews in the Middle East and Elsewhere

Sep. 1950

Israel and Great Britain sign an air pact, making Lydda an important link in the air communications of the British Commonwealth and permitting Israel's national air line to operate a Lydda–America service via London.

The UN Palestine Conciliation Commission, consisting of France, Turkey, and the U.S., reports to the General Assembly that (1) Israel wants direct negotiations, while the Arabs want indirect negotiations; (2) Arabs condition negotiations upon Israel receiving back and compensating refugees, while Israel offers to take 100,000 as part of a peace settlement; (3) Arabs insist on the reversion to partition borders, while Israel wants to maintain existing boundaries.

India accords de jure and de facto recognition to Israel.

The UN Palestine Conciliation Commission issues a supplemental report to the secretary-general recommending Arabs and Israelis engage in direct negotiations for peace under the auspices of the UN, and the return of as many Arab refugees to Israel as would be consistent with their own best interests, payment of compensation to those who did not return, and their resettlement in Arab countries with UN technical and financial assistance.

Oct. 1950

A. General History	B. Jews in North and South America	C. Jews in Europe	D. Jews in the Middle East and Elsewhere	E. Jewish Culture
Dec. 1950		The second part of the archives collected by Emanuel Ringelblum during the Nazi occupation is discovered on the site of Novolipki 68 in Warsaw. In the last weeks of the year, antisemitic disturbances occur in numerous Hungarian localities, including Miskolz, Szeged, Tokaj, and Sopron. During the year, the overwhelming majority of the Jewish population has been driven from their jobs by the decision of the Hungarian Communist government. Many are deported to the Soviet Union.		
1951	James G. McDonald* (1886–1964), the first U.S. ambassador to Israel, writes *My Mission to Israel, 1948–1951*.	SS General Juergen Stroop,* who directed the destruction of the Warsaw ghetto, is tried in Warsaw, sentenced to death, and hanged. In 1947, a U.S. military court in Dachau tried and sentenced him to death for the shooting of American airmen but extradited him to Poland. The Parisian colony of Yiddish writers and journalists form an association, Tlomackie 13, named after the association of Yiddish writers that flourished in Warsaw before World War II. Paris has become the most important Yiddish literary center in Europe. Excavations in Rome by the British School of Archaeology find the remains of a small synagogue built into the southwestern chapel of the Severan basilica at Leptis Magna in the 5th century.	Commercial relations with Turkey continue to grow, and Israeli merchant ships begin to arrive in Turkish ports. At Shaar Hagolan, a kibbutz in Israel's Jordan Valley, Dr. Moshe Stekelis of the Hebrew University finds the first known evidence of a Stone Age civilization having existed in Palestine about 65 centuries before the common era. Stekelis unearths utensils and art objects, including a feminine figurine known as the Venus of Shaar Hagolan.	Hannah Arendt (1906–1975), German-American philosopher, writes *The Origins of Totalitarianism*, in which she analyzes the political and psychological factors that lead to antisemitism and points out the basic similarities between Nazism and Soviet Communism. Bertram W. Korn (1918–1979), U.S. Reform rabbi and historian, writes *American Jewry and the Civil War*. Wolf Leslau, U.S. Semitics scholar, edits *The Falasha Anthology*, a scholarly treatment of the life and sacred literature of these little-known Ethiopian Jews. Alfred Kazin, U.S. literary critic, writes *A Walker in the City*, recollections of his experiences as a boy in the Brownsville section of Brooklyn. J. D. Salinger (b. 1919), U.S. novelist, writes *Catcher in the Rye*. Compared by critics to Mark Twain's *Huckleberry Finn*, it sells over a million copies.

A. General History	B. Jews in North and South America	C. Jews in Europe	D. Jews in the Middle East and Elsewhere	E. Jewish Culture	
The French parliament enacts a law granting amnesty to French traitors who had collaborated with the Nazis during World War II.		The U.S. high commissioner in Germany passes a Clemency Act, which results in the release of many war criminals in U.S. custody.		Two books published in the U.S., *Judaism for Modern Man*, by Will Herberg (1901–1977), and *Man Is Not Alone*, by Abraham Joshua Heschel, signal the growth of interest in Jewish thought and theology.	**Jan. 1951**
		Israel presents a claim for $1.5 billion as compensation from Germany to the four occupying powers, U.S., Great Britain, France, and the Soviet Union. Klaus Barbie,* sought by the French for Nazi war crimes, travels with his family from Genoa, Italy (with papers supplied by American officials), to South America and settles in Bolivia.	Iraq passes legislation sequestering the property of Jews who had registered for emigration to Israel and of all Jews who had left Iraq legally after January 1, 1948, unless they return to Iraq within two months after publication of a notice in the press of the capital of the country in which they are residing. The government later freezes the property of those Jews who have not registered for emigration. Israel begins drainage of the Huleh marshes to reclaim 12,500 acres of fertile soil for cultivation.	Charles Angoff (1902–1979), U.S. novelist and editor, writes *Journey to the Dawn*, the first in a series of autobiographical novels tracing the integration of a Russian Jewish immigrant family, the Polonskys, into American society. Herman Wouk, U.S. novelist, writes *The Caine Mutiny*, a novel of cruelties and cowardice aboard a navy minesweeper in the Pacific during World War II. In it, Wouk defends the regular military establishment for its delaying actions while the nation mobilizes for war and includes a court martial trial featuring Lt. Barney Greenwald as defense attorney. The novel will win him the 1952 Pulitzer Prize, be a best-seller for over two years, and be adapted to the stage and screen.	**Mar. 1951**
Julius and Ethel Rosenberg are sentenced to death by U.S. District Judge Irving Kaufman following their conviction for stealing U.S. atomic bomb secrets for the Soviet Union. President Harry S. Truman* recalls General Douglas MacArthur* from his Korean War command, concluding that the general is unable to support his policies. General Matthew B. Ridgway* replaces him as head of the UN forces in Korea. Muhammad Mossadeq* is named prime minister of Iran. Iran promulgates a law calling for the nationalization of Iran's oil resources and cancellation of the Anglo-Iranian Oil Co.'s concession.	From April to December there are about 16 bombings in the Miami area of Florida. Half are against Jewish centers and synagogues, the most serious occurring in December against the Miami Hebrew School and Congregation.		Poland stops all emigration to Israel.	The Jewish Museum in New York exhibits antique ceremonial objects and paintings from the collection of Michael Zagayski (1895–1964). Zagayski built an outstanding collection of Jewish art in the U.S. after having lost all he owned when the Germans occupied Warsaw in 1939. A. M. Klein, Canadian poet and novelist, writes *The Second Scroll*, an	**Apr. 1951**

	A. General History	B. Jews in North and South America	C. Jews in Europe	D. Jews in the Middle East and Elsewhere	E. Jewish Culture
May 1951		Professor Robert MacIver* of Columbia University submits a report on the Jewish Community Relations Agencies, which they commissioned to consider ways to make Jewish community relations work more effectively and efficiently. The State of Israel bond campaign is inaugurated in the U.S., with Rudolf G. Sonneborn as the first president of the organization.	Beginning in May, about 14,000 Hungarian Jews from Budapest and another 8,000 from the provinces are deported to slave labor camps in Siberia. In July, U.S. President Harry S. Truman* will declare that the Hungarian government is "accountable before the world for its infamous conduct." An article in Moscow's *Pravda* asserts that the visit of Israeli ministers to the U.S. was the culmination of the transformation of Israel into an American colony and that Israel's general staff held secret conferences with American intelligence agents.	Israel's El Al airline begins direct flights from Lydda to New York.	allegory on the theme of the "wandering Jew," whose last journey is from the Holocaust to the State of Israel. The Tel Aviv Museum exhibits artistic works by Marc Chagall. It consists of 60 oils, including his latest painting, *King David*, more than 100 gouaches and water colors, and sketches for theater and opera.
July 1951			During the summer, mass deportations of Jews from border areas of the Soviet Union to Siberia are extended to the Jews of Georgia and Daghestan in the Caucasus. After an announcement by the U.S., Great Britain, and France of the termination of the state of war with Germany, the Israel Foreign Office comments that as long as the German people made "no expiation or reparation for the crimes committed by the Nazis . . . Germany's war against the Jewish people cannot be regarded as having come to an end."	King Abdullah ibn Hussein* of Jordan is assassinated as he leaves the Al-Aqsa mosque in Jerusalem. His murder is attributed to his willingness to negotiate with Israel. Israel holds national elections for the Second Knesset. Mapai wins 45 seats; Liberals, 23 seats; Mapam, 15 seats; and the National Religious party, 10 seats. The government is installed with David Ben-Gurion as prime minister and minister of defense and Moshe Sharett as minister of foreign affairs.	
Aug. 1951				The 23rd Zionist Congress is held in Jerusalem and is the first to meet after the creation of the State of Israel. Israeli and American Zionists clash over the definition of Zionism. The Israelis equate	

A. General History	B. Jews in North and South America	C. Jews in Europe	D. Jews in the Middle East and Elsewhere	E. Jewish Culture	
			Zionism with personal immigration to Israel, a concept opposed by the majority of American Zionists. The congress adopts a program defining the task of Zionism as "the consolidation of the State of Israel, the ingathering of the exiles in Israel, and fostering the unity of the Jewish people."		Aug. 1951
The U.S., Britain, and France complete the transformation of the relationship of West Germany and the Allies. The Occupation Statute is to be replaced by freely arrived at contractual relationships, and West Germany is to participate in Western defense and be included in the European community on the basis of equality. The Allies sign a peace treaty with Japan. The Soviet Union refuses to sign.	Nationally syndicated columnist Stewart Alsop* writes a series of articles during and after a visit to the Middle East. He criticizes the U.S. for favoring Israel over the Arab states and for failing to win the cooperation of the Arabs against the Soviet threat of aggression.	West German Chancellor Konrad Adenauer* wins the approval from the Bundestag to make amends for Nazi crimes in the form of material payments to Israel and the Jews at large. Addressing the Bundestag, he acknowledges that "unspeakable crimes were perpetrated in the name of the German people which impose on us the obligation to make moral and material amends."	The UN Security Council adopts a resolution, with the Soviet Union, India, and Nationalist China abstaining, calling on Egypt to lift the blockade of Israeli-bound shipping through the Suez Canal. Egypt indicates it will disregard the resolution.		Sep. 1951
Egypt unilaterally nullifies the Anglo-Egyptian Treaty of 1936, but Great Britain does not evacuate its troops from the Suez Canal area. Egypt also rejects the proposal of the U.S., Great Britain, France, and Turkey to join the Allied command for the defense of the Middle East. Winston Churchill* returns to power, succeeding Clement Attlee* as prime minister of Great Britain.	The Conference on Jewish Material Claims against Germany is established. Presided over by Nahum Goldmann, the conference agrees to support Israel's $1.5 billion claim and to demand satisfaction of all other Jewish claims against Germany.		The U.S. gives Israel a $65 million grant in aid, with $50 million to be used in the absorption of new immigrants and the remainder for economic development. Twenty-seven Iraqi Jews are tried in Baghdad for alleged membership in a Zionist terrorist gang and for terrorist acts. Two are sentenced to death and hanged.		Oct. 1951
		Rudolf Slansky (1901–1952), secretary-general of the Czech Communist party, is arrested and charged with being the leader of a treasonable conspiracy	A second group of 21 Jews goes on trial in Iraq for crimes against the state. Included is an Israeli who "confessed" to having been sent to Iraq to collect economic and		Nov. 1951

	A. **General History**	B. **Jews in North and South America**	C. **Jews in Europe**	D. **Jews in the Middle East and Elsewhere**	E. **Jewish Culture**
Nov. 1951			aimed at overthrowing the government and restoring capitalism. The arrest of Slansky, a Jew, is followed by the arrest of a number of Jews in government positions accused as co-conspirators. Most of the victims are Communists. None is a Zionist or a religious Jew.	financial information. Sixteen are convicted and sentenced to prison terms and six are acquitted. The Soviet Union warns Israel not to join the planned Allied Middle East Command. Israel replies that it has not been invited to join.	
Dec. 1951		The New York State Board of Regents authorizes Yeshiva University to grant degrees in medicine and dentistry.	Mordecai Oren, an Israeli citizen and member of the Knesset, disappears in Czechoslovakia while on a visit to investigate reports of the antisemitic purges and the arrest of his cousin Shimon Ohrenstein. In March 1952, Israel will be informed that Oren was arrested on charges of "crimes against state security." In London, Nahum Goldmann, chairman of the Jewish Agency, secretly meets German Chancellor Konrad Adenauer* to discuss German reparations to Israel and to the Conference on Jewish Material Claims against Germany, a group of 22 Jewish organizations.	Israeli Prime Minister David Ben-Gurion expresses doubts about American Zionists. Mrs. Samuel Halperin, national president of Hadassah, takes issue and states that "the sole criterion of Zionist leadership cannot be personal immigration to Israel."	

Immigration to Israel
May 1948–December 1951
Countries of major immigration:

Iraq	121,512
Rumania	118,940
Poland	103,732
Yemen	45,199
Bulgaria	37,231
Turkey	34,213
Morocco	30,750
Libya	30,482
Iran	24,804
Czechoslovakia	18,217
Egypt	16,508
Hungary	13,631
Tunisia	13,139
Total	684,201

	A. **General History**	B. **Jews in North and South America**	C. **Jews in Europe**	D. **Jews in the Middle East and Elsewhere**	E. **Jewish Culture**
1952	The U.S. Congress adopts the McCarran–Walter Immigration Act of 1952, over the veto of President Harry S. Truman.* It codifies the existing immigration and nationality statutes, and leaves the national origins system unchanged. The U.S. successfully tests the hydrogen bomb. Edward Teller (b. 1908), U.S. physicist, is credited with its invention. Born in Budapest, Hungary, he worked in Göttingen, Germany,	The American Jewish Committee conducts a sociological study of "Riverton," a medium-sized Northeastern Jewish community. The study reveals that 80% of parents and 97% of adolescents conceive religion to be one of the principal attributes of the Jew. Eighty-one percent of grandparents and 16% of parents view themselves as Orthodox; 5% of grandparents and 30% of parents as Reform; and 11% of grandparents and 43% of parents as Conservative.	Jacob Berman, leading Polish Communist, is appointed deputy premier in the government headed by Boleslaw Bierut,* a post he will hold until 1956, when Wladislaw Gomulka* assumes power and accuses him of Stalinism. Throughout the year the Czech Communist party and the press wage an antisemitic campaign of denunciation of Jews as "cosmopolitans," "Zionists," and people who are prone to become traitors in the service of capitalism.	Regarding immigration from those countries where there is opportunity for selection, the government of Israel and the Jewish Agency agree to lessen the proportion of old, sick, and invalid individuals and others requiring social care and to increase the proportion of healthy immigrants of working age, young people, and children. The agreement does not apply to Eastern European countries and where immigration is a matter of rescue.	Michael Blankfort, U.S. novelist, writes *The Juggler*, a novel whose hero, Hans Muller, is a famous juggler who spent 10 years in concentration camps and who has difficulty in adjusting to life in Israel. It will be adapted to the screen in 1953, starring Kirk Douglas (Issur Danilovich, b. 1916), and filmed on location in Israel. S. N. Behrman publishes *Duveen*, a revision and expansion of his *New Yorker* magazine articles on the well-known art dealer Joseph Duveen

A. General History	B. Jews in North and South America	C. Jews in Europe	D. Jews in the Middle East and Elsewhere	E. Jewish Culture	
until the rise of Adolf Hitler.* He moved to the U.S. in 1935 and worked on the Manhattan Project in Los Alamos, New Mexico, during World War II.		Klaus Barbie* is convicted in absentia of Nazi war crimes by a Lyons, France, military tribunal and sentenced to death.	Most Jews of Algeria are completely emancipated. They comprise 22% of the nation's dentists, 21.5% of its doctors, 16.3% of its lawyers, and 18% of its administration.

Helen Suzman (b. 1917) is elected to the South African Parliament from a Johannesburg district with a significant Jewish population. Continuously reelected, she is an opponent of the apartheid system.

Sir Andrew Cohen (1909–1968), British colonial administrator, is appointed governor of Uganda, and will serve until 1957. He introduces political and economic reforms, which prepare this African colony for independence. | (1869–1939), who was the grandson of a Dutch Jewish blacksmith.

Salo Baron (1895–1989) begins publication of a revised version of his *A Social and Religious History of the Jews*, which by 1985 will number 18 volumes and deal with events ending in 1650. Baron portrays Jewish history in the context of world history and rebuts "lachrymose" presentations of Jewish history by emphasizing Jewish social and religious creativity.

Max Kadushin (1895–1980), U.S. rabbi and scholar, writes *The Rabbinic Mind*, a study of rabbinic concepts of God, man, and social values. | **1952** |
| | | | Black Saturday, a mass demonstration against the British in Cairo, develops into a full-scale riot in which nearly all Jewish-owned shops and stores in Cairo's business center are destroyed. In addition, the well-known Jewish school in the 'Abbassia district is totally destroyed.

A third group of 17 defendants are tried in Iraq for espionage for Israel. They include 8 Iraqi Jews, 7 Muslim Arabs, 1 British subject, and the same Israeli convicted at the second trial. The Israeli, the British subject, and 2 Iraqi Jews are convicted, and 13 other defendants are acquitted.

Prime Minister David Ben-Gurion wins approval of the Knesset to submit a | Mark Zborowski and Elizabeth Herzog, U.S. anthropologists, write *Life Is with People*, an anthropological study of the Jewish shtetl in Eastern Europe.

Marc Blitzstein, U.S. composer, adapts Bertolt Brecht's* German lyrics into English for Kurt Weill's (1900–1950) 1928 musical play, *The Threepenny Opera*.

Construction of Lever House, an award-winning New York office building, is completed. It is designed by Gordon Bunshaft, noted U.S. architect.

Anne Frank: The Diary of a Young Girl, appears in English translation from the Dutch. The diary describes the life and thoughts of this Dutch adolescent, born in 1929, during the two years (1942–1944) she | **Jan. 1952** |

517

	A. General History	B. Jews in North and South America	C. Jews in Europe	D. Jews in the Middle East and Elsewhere	E. Jewish Culture
Jan. 1952				collective claim to the West German government for $1 billion in reparations for the expense of absorbing 500,000 refugees. The Claims Conference asked for $500 million for victims living outside Israel. Ben-Gurion overcomes the opposition by proclaiming: "Let not the murderers of our people be also their heirs."	and her family were hiding from the Nazis in Amsterdam. An act of betrayal led to their discovery. Anne died in March 1945 in the Bergen-Belsen concentration camp. The diary was first published in 1947 under the title *Het Achterhuis* (*The Annex*). It is widely translated and acclaimed. Selman Abraham Waksman (1888–1973), U.S. microbiologist, is awarded the Nobel Prize in physiology or medicine for his investigations of antibiotics, especially streptomycin. He coined the term *antibiotic*.
Feb. 1952		President Harry S. Truman* instructs the director of the Bureau of the Budget to increase economic aid to Israel for the fiscal year 1953 from $25 million to $80 million.	Beginning in February, Romania deports about 100,000 families, mostly Jews, from urban centers to detention camps and other areas in the country's interior.		
Apr. 1952	In *Zorach* v. *Clauson*, the U.S. Supreme Court rules that the New York City public school released-time system is constitutional. "The first amendment, however, does not say in every and all respects there shall be a separation of church and state. . . . We are a religious people whose institutions presuppose a Supreme Being."				Felix Bloch (1905–1983), U.S. physicist, is awarded the Nobel Prize for Physics for his work in measuring nuclear magnetic fields. In 1934, Bloch left Germany for the U.S. after the Nazis came to power. The 10-volume *Encyclopedia Judaica Castellana* is completed in Mexico. It places special emphasis on the Jewish communities of Latin America.
May 1952				Israel announces it will move its Foreign Office to Jerusalem. The U.S. and other Western powers oppose the move. Israel defers action.	Darius Milhaud (1892-1974), French composer, writes the biblical opera *David* to celebrate the 3,000th anniversary of Jerusalem as the capital of David's kingdom. Throughout his long career he creates many works of particular Jewish significance. Ilya Ehrenburg, Soviet writer and journalist, is awarded the Stalin Prize in the same year in which fellow Jewish writers and journalists are executed by the Soviets.
June 1952		Several Reform rabbis recommend the establishment of Reform programs and congregations in Israel. The Orthodox Rabbinical Council of America expresses concern about the efforts of the Reform movement "to plant the seed of religious dissension in the Holy Land."			

A. General History	B. Jews in North and South America	C. Jews in Europe	D. Jews in the Middle East and Elsewhere	E. Jewish Culture	
	Look magazine features an article by Rabbi Morris N. Kertzer, "What Is a Jew?" which receives wide acclaim.			Lea Goldberg (1911–1970), Hebrew poet and critic, organizes the department of comparative literature at the Hebrew University, where she teaches until her death. She arrived in Palestine from Europe in 1935, and her first volume of Hebrew verse, *Smoke Rings*, appeared that year. She is also a writer of popular children's books, translator, and novelist.	**June 1952**
King Farouk* of Egypt is dethroned by a bloodless coup led by Gamal Abdel Nasser,* Anwar al-Sadat,* and others. Major General Mohammed Naguib* assumes the titular leadership of the uprising.		Ana Pauker (1890–1960), Romania's minister of foreign affairs and a Jew, is removed from office, and her allies in state and party positions are purged.			**July 1952**
	Brandeis University President Abram L. Sachar announces university policy on Sabbath observance: the university will be closed on the Sabbath and all Jewish holy days, including their second day of observance. Friday night basketball games will not be scheduled, but football games will be played on Saturday.	Leaders of the Jewish Anti-Fascist Committee, including famous Yiddish writers Peretz Markish, Itzik Fefer, and David Bergelson, are executed after a secret trial by the Soviet authorities. They were accused of conspiring to separate the Crimea from the Soviet Union and convert it into a Jewish bourgeois republic that would serve as a base for the Soviet Union's enemies.	Prime Minister David Ben-Gurion, in a Knesset speech, extends the "hand of friendship" to the new Egyptian regime and privately offers economic and political assistance, which Egypt responds to favorably. Private conversations will continue until December 1954.		**Aug. 1952**
	Jacob M. Arvey, Chicago politician, is credited with masterminding the campaign that leads to Adlai E. Stevenson's* nomination as the Democratic candidate for the presidency.	Israel and West Germany sign a reparations agreement, which states that (1) Germany will send Israel, over 14 years, $715 million in goods; (2) Germany agrees to enact legislation to provide individual restitution to victims of Nazi persecution; (3) Germany will pay the Conference on Jewish Material Claims against Germany $107 million, through Israel, for the rehabilitation of Nazi victims living outside Israel. The Dutch commute the death sentence of W. P. F. Lages,* Nazi Gestapo head in Amsterdam from 1940 to 1945, to life			**Sep. 1952**

	A. General History	B. Jews in North and South America	C. Jews in Europe	D. Jews in the Middle East and Elsewhere	E. Jewish Culture
Sep. 1952			imprisonment. Lages* was responsible for the deportation of over 70,000 Jews.		
Nov. 1952	The Republican Eisenhower*–Nixon* ticket defeats the Stevenson*–Sparkman* Democrats. The Republicans win majorities in both houses of Congress.	The Jewish vote in the presidential election is estimated at 64% for Adlai E. Stevenson* and 36% for Dwight D. Eisenhower.*	Rudolf Slansky, former secretary-general of the Czech Communist party, is tried in Prague as a Zionist conspirator. Thirteen Czech Communist leaders, most of whom are Jewish, are tried with Slansky. All confess. Slansky and 10 others are hanged and two are given life imprisonment. Two Israelis, Shimon Ornstein and Mordecai Oren, were arrested in 1951 and used as prosecution witnesses.	After the death of Chaim Weizmann, Israel's first president, Albert Einstein declines an offer from Prime Minister David Ben-Gurion to become a candidate for the presidency of Israel. He writes that he "was deeply touched by the offer but not suited for the position."	
Dec. 1952				Yitzhak Ben-Zvi is elected president of Israel by the Knesset, succeeding Chaim Weizmann. He will be reelected to two five-year terms and die in office.	
1953		The movement of the U.S. Jewish population to the suburbs continues to gain momentum. Conservative and Reform groups continue to establish new synagogue centers in suburban areas. Yeshiva University announces that its medical school will be named the Albert Einstein College of Medicine. The Jewish Theological Seminary of America begins participation in the "Frontiers of Faith" television series devoted to studies of Catholicism, Protestantism, and Judaism. Columbia University and the Jewish Theological Seminary of America agree that students may	A wave of antisemitism and anti-Zionism spreads throughout Hungary. Lajos Stoeckler, Communist-imposed leader of the Jewish community, and important Communist officials of Jewish descent, including Gabor Peter, head of the secret police, are arrested.	France secretly opens many of its nuclear installations to Israeli scientists. Discrimination continues throughout the Arab world. Jordan denies permission to foreigners of the Jewish faith who wish to cross the armistice lines to visit the holy places in Jerusalem and Bethlehem, and the American University in Beirut refuses to admit American students of the Jewish faith. There are 25 daily newspapers in Israel, of which 10 are published in a foreign language. The Israeli Knesset adopts the Law for the Supreme Institute for the Hebrew Language. The law	The Partisan Review magazine publishes Saul Bellow's English translation of a short story "Gimpel the Fool" by Isaac Bashevis Singer, Polish-born author of Yiddish fiction. Singer emigrated to the U.S. in 1935 and began writing Yiddish fiction in the Forward. This translation brings Singer to the attention of the English-speaking world. Sidney B. Hoenig, U.S. scholar, writes The Great Sanhedrin, a study of the origin and development of this supreme council of state during the Second Jewish Commonwealth. The first volume of Rabbi Menachem Kasher's Encyclopedia of Biblical Interpretation, an anthology of biblical

A. General History	B. Jews in North and South America	C. Jews in Europe	D. Jews in the Middle East and Elsewhere	E. Jewish Culture	
	exchange credits between the two institutions. An independent U.S. lobbying committee in support of Israel is formed. Years later, it will be renamed the American Israel Public Affairs Committee. Arthur Burns (1904–1987), U.S. economist, is appointed chairman of the Council of Economic Advisers by President Dwight D. Eisenhower.*		establishes the Academy of the Hebrew Language, which succeeds the Hebrew Language Committee established in 1890. Its function is the development of Hebrew. N. H. Tur-Sinai is chosen as the president of the 23-member academy. Kibbutz Ein Hod is founded on the initiative of Marcel Janco (1895–1984). Janco, a painter born in Romania, was one of the artists who founded the dada movement. He arrived in Palestine in 1941. The kibbutz includes an artist's village and the Janco-Dada Museum.	interpretations from the literature of the Talmud and Midrash, with modern commentaries, appears in English translation. Nahum Glatzer, U.S. scholar who left Germany in 1933, edits *Franz Rosenzweig: His Life and Thought*, an introduction to the philosophy of the 20th-century western European Jewish thinker, with excerpts from his writings. Saul Bellow, U.S. novelist, writes *The Adventures of Augie March*, a picaresque novel depicting the adventures of a Jewish boy from Chicago during the Depression years of the 1930s. It wins Bellow a National Book Award.	**1953**
		The Stalin* regime arrests nine physicians, seven of whom are Jewish, and accuses them, in what is known as the Doctors' Plot, of murdering Soviet leaders and of being Western espionage agents. About one month after Joseph Stalin's* death on March 5, official Soviet organs announce that the charges against them are false, and they are released.		Gerald Reitlinger, English historian, writes *The Final Solution: The Attempt to Exterminate the Jews of Europe, 1939–1945*. David Horowitz, former director of the Jewish Agency's economic department, publishes *A State in the Making*, which describes the negotiations that led to the establishment of the State of Israel.	**Jan. 1953**
			A bomb explodes outside the Soviet legation in Tel Aviv, injuring three Soviets. The Soviet government breaks off diplomatic relations with Israel, which are not restored until July.	Arthur Miller, U.S. playwright and novelist, writes *The Crucible*, a play about the Salem witch trials of 1692. Written and performed during the time of Senator	**Feb. 1953**
Joseph Stalin* dies. His death brings a halt to the major antisemitic campaign he had launched. Georgi M. Malenkov* becomes head of the Soviet government.	The Union of American Hebrew Congregations (Reform) reports the results of a congregational survey. The trend is toward traditional forms of worship and observance: 31% of Reform Jews attend services regularly,	Egypt proposes to Israel adjustments of their border, a land link to Jordan through the southern Negev, and refugee compensation. Israel agrees to negotiate provided the boycott and blockade are ended. Contact is maintained through		Joseph McCarthy's* anti-Communist campaign, it is a play about freedom of conscience and guilt by association. Fritz Reiner (1888–1963) becomes conductor of the Chicago Symphony Orchestra, a post he holds until	**Mar. 1953**

	A. General History	B. Jews in North and South America	C. Jews in Europe	D. Jews in the Middle East and Elsewhere	E. Jewish Culture
Mar. 1953		with Friday evening services being the norm for Sabbath worship; and 12% limit attendance to the High Holy Days. The popularity of home rituals also gained: 74% conduct a Passover seder; 60% observe blessing of Friday night candles, and 80% light the Hanukkah candles. Conservative rabbis and faculty of the Jewish Theological Seminary of America recommend the establishment of a national Jewish religious court, in cooperation with the Orthodox and Reform rabbinate, to deal with domestic relations problems. The Orthodox rabbinate opposes the idea, stating that Conservative and Reform rabbis generally are not capable of dealing with problems of Jewish law (*halakhah*). President Dwight D. Eisenhower,* after receiving Saudi Arabia's foreign minister, "expressed his concern over some evidence [of] a deterioration in relations between the Arab nations and the United States." Eisenhower* added that he would "seek to restore the spirit of confidence and trust."		the efforts of Robert Anderson* of the U.S. and British intermediaries.	ill health forces nis resignation in 1963. The publication of *The Jewish Quarterly*, a journal blending the past, present, and future in Jewish literature, arts, and documentary, begins in England under the editorship of Jacob Sonntag (1905–1984). Fritz Albert Lipmann, U.S. biochemist, is awarded the Nobel Prize in physiology or medicine for his discovery of enzyme A and its importance for intermediary metabolism. He fled Germany for Denmark when the Nazis came to power and emigrated to the U.S. in 1939. Sir Hans Krebs, British biochemist, is awarded the Nobel Prize in physiology or medicine for his research on the conversion of food elements into energy. Krebs fled Germany for Britain when the Nazis came to power. The publication of *Comentario*, a Spanish cultural quarterly magazine, begins in Argentina. The first text of the Hebrew Bible to be printed entirely in Israel is published by the Magnes Press of Hebrew University.
Apr. 1953	Dag Hammarskjold,* Swedish diplomat and economist, is elected secretary-general of the UN after Trygve Lie's* resignation.		The Romanian government continues its persecution of Jews and conducts secret trials during the year and into 1954.	Israel and Jordan exchange gunfire for over two hours across the Jerusalem demarcation line.	The Bezalel National Museum in Jerusalem exhibits ritual objects from all parts of the Diaspora, with a catalogue by its director, Mordecai Narkiss (1898–1957).
May 1953			The Czechs try and convict Richard Slansky, Rudolf's diplomat brother, Eduard Goldstucker, minister to Israel, and Pavel Kavan, also a diplomat. They are sentenced to lengthy	Hussein,* son of King Talal* of Jordan, assumes the throne. Grandson of King Abdullah ibn Hussein,* assassinated in 1951, Hussein* replaces his father, who is mentally unfit.	Kariel "Dosh" Gardosh (b. 1921), Israeli cartoonist, joins the staff of the newspaper *Ma'ariv* as editorial cartoonist. He utilizes a little

A. General History	B. Jews in North and South America	C. Jews in Europe	D. Jews in the Middle East and Elsewhere	E. Jewish Culture	

| | | prison terms. In August, Shimon Ornstein, an Israeli citizen, will receive a life sentence. In October, Mordecai Oren, his cousin and a Mapam party member of the Israeli Knesset, will be sentenced to 15 years in jail. | President Dwight D. Eisenhower* tells B'nai B'rith's Philip Klutznick that he was not sure whether he would have supported the establishment of the State of Israel if he had been president at the time. | sabra, Little Israel, to portray his comic irony.

Menachem Begin, Israeli statesman and former commander of the Irgun, writes *White Nights*, an account of his escape from Poland and imprisonment by the Soviet authorities in Siberia at the beginning of World War II.

The first Israel Prizes are awarded, on Independence Day, to distinguished writers, artists, and scientists who are residents of Israel. | |

| | Congregation Beth El in Springfield, Massachusetts, dedicates a new synagogue featuring works by the noted artists Adolph Gottlieb, Ibram Lassaw, and Robert Motherwell.* Beth El is typical of the nationwide trend of stressing original art forms in synagogue construction. | Robert (b. 1941) and Gerald (b. 1942) Finaly are turned over by the French authorities to Israeli relatives. During the war their parents placed them in a Catholic school to protect them from the Germans. The parents perished in the Holocaust. The Catholic woman responsible for their safekeeping resisted efforts of relatives to obtain the return of the boys after the war. | U.S. Secretary of State John Foster Dulles,* after touring the Middle East, outlines the Eisenhower* administration's Middle East policy. The U.S. would adhere to a principle of exact neutrality so as to win the respect of both the Arabs and Israelis and favor direct negotiations to establish peace; Jerusalem should be internationalized, but there should be "some political status in Jerusalem for Israel and Jordan"; some Arab refugees should be resettled within Israel, but most in Arab countries. | | |

| The UN and North Korea sign a truce agreement, ending the North Korean invasion of South Korea. | The U.S. Senate ratifies, by a vote of 86–1, the Treaty of Friendship, Commerce, and Navigation between the U.S. and Israel, which will be signed on August 23, 1951.

The New York State Board of Regents reports a study of admissions policies of the state's nine medical schools. For the years 1950 and 1952 the median test scores of Jewish applicants was 15% higher than the Catholic and Protestant applicants. In 1950, the acceptance rate of Jewish applicants was about the same as the non-Jewish applicants. In 1952, the Jewish acceptance rate was | Harrison E. Salisbury,* Moscow correspondent of the *New York Times*, is allowed to travel in Siberia. He will write of meeting many Jews in Siberian cities who were sent there from other parts of the Soviet Union. | Diplomatic relations between the Soviet Union and Israel, severed on February 12, 1953, are renewed.

Israel moves its Foreign Office to Jerusalem. The U.S. announces it will not transfer its embassy from Tel Aviv to Jerusalem. | | |

Postwar Jewish Immigration to the United States:
May 1945–June 1953

Date	Total	DPs	Non-DPs	To NYC Area	Elsewhere in U.S.
1945 (May–Dec.)	4,000			2,800	1,200
1946	15,535			10,870	4,665
1947	25,885			18,116	7,769
1948	15,982			11,187	4,795
1949	37,700	31,381	6,319	20,571	17,129
1950	14,139	10,245	3,894	8,861	5,278
1951	16,973	13,580	3,393	8,416	8,557
1952	7,236	3,508	3,728	4,307	2,929
1953 (Jan.–June)	2,383	765	1,618	1,571	812
TOTAL	139,833	59,479	18,952	86,699 (63%)	53,134 (37%)

	A. General History	B. Jews in North and South America	C. Jews in Europe	D. Jews in the Middle East and Elsewhere	E. Jewish Culture
July 1953		about 10% higher. The board concludes there is a substantial decrease in the discriminatory treatment of Jews.			
Aug. 1953	The Soviet Union announces it has developed the hydrogen bomb. President Dwight D. Eisenhower* signs into law the Refugee Relief Act of 1953. It authorizes, over a three-year five-month period and outside the regular quotas, the admission of 214,000 refugees, orphans, and certain close relatives of American citizens and aliens. The Shah of Iran,* supported by the army and the CIA, ousts Premier Muhammad Mossadeq* and his left-wing supporters, and assumes control of the country.			Five Israeli citizens are murdered by Arabs in the Negev. The Israeli Knesset passes the state public education bill, i.e., a state-controlled network of schools with a separate division for religious schools. The Israeli Knesset adopts a law establishing the Heroes' and Martyrs' Authority (Yad Vashem) to perpetuate the memory of the Holocaust and for research and documentation.	
Sep. 1953				Eric Johnston,* President Dwight D. Eisenhower's* personal envoy, begins a mission to urge a plan for the joint Arab and Israeli use of the Jordan River water resources. In 1955, the Israelis will cautiously acquiesce, but the Arab League will reject it.	

Oct. 1953

D. **Jews in the Middle East and Elsewhere**

An Israeli mother and two infants are murdered by Arabs in Moshav Yahud.

Israeli troops raid the Jordan village of Kibya in retaliation for several Arab infiltration attacks in which Israelis were murdered. The Israelis kill 53 Arabs and destroy more than 40 buildings. The U.S., Great Britain, and France condemn the raid and sponsor the UN Security Council resolution strongly censuring Israel, which is adopted.

Israel reports that since May 1950, Arabs have killed or wounded 421 Israeli citizens, and there have been 866 armed attacks and 3,263 cases of theft.

The U.S. suspends aid to Israel at the request of the UN Truce Supervision Organization when Israel refuses to stop work on its hydroelectric project on the upper Jordan River. Israel agrees to temporary suspension and the U.S. resumes aid.

	A. General History	B. Jews in North and South America	C. Jews in Europe	D. Jews in the Middle East and Elsewhere	E. Jewish Culture
Nov. 1953		A United Synagogue of America (Conservative) survey of religious practices			

A. General History	B. Jews in North and South America	C. Jews in Europe	D. Jews in the Middle East and Elsewhere	E. Jewish Culture	
	reports that 60% of Conservative Jews have no religious education beyond bar mitzvah; fewer than 50% of synagogue board members have knowledge of the "aims, tendencies, and practices of the Conservative movement"; 13% recite daily prayers; and 37% observe the dietary laws.				**Nov. 1953**
Lavrenti Beria,* former chief of the Soviet secret police, and his aides are tried and executed in the Soviet Union, bringing to an end his struggle for power with Georgi Malenkov.*			An exhausted Prime Minister David Ben-Gurion resigns and is succeeded by Moshe Sharett as prime minister and Pinhas Lavon (1904–1976) as defense minister. Moshe Dayan succeeds Mordechai Makleff as chief of staff of the Israel Defense Forces.		**Dec. 1953**
	American Jews celebrate the tercentenary of Jewish settlement in the U.S. with a year-long program of cultural and educational activities.

On the occasion of the 300th anniversary of the settlement of Jews in the U.S., the American Jewish Historical Society sponsors a conference of historians on the writing of American Jewish history. The proceedings of the conference, edited by Moshe Davis and Isidore S. Meyer, will be published in 1957.

The History of the Jewish Khazars, a nomadic people who lived in an area north of the Caucasus in the 8th century and who adopted Judaism, is written by the Arabist D. M. Dunlop.*

The Hebrew Union College (Reform) establishes a West | The West German government enacts a restitution law on behalf of individuals oppressed by the Nazis for racial, religious, or political reasons, establishing four categories of indemnification: loss of property, freedom, health, and economic realization. Jews, mostly living in Israel, are the law's principal beneficiaries.

Klaus Barbie* is again convicted in absentia of Nazi war crimes by a Lyons, France, military tribunal and sentenced to death. | | Oscar Handlin (b. 1915), U.S. historian, writes *Adventure in Freedom*, an interpretative study of 300 years of Jewish life in the U.S.

The New York Public Library exhibits The People and the Book, a collection of rare Jewish books and manuscripts from its own collections and those of other libraries in the New York area.

An American Synagogue for Today and Tomorrow, edited by Peter Blake, is published by the Union of American Hebrew Congregations (Reform) to assist its congregations to establish "more honest, sincere, genuinely and intrinsically Jewish houses of worship."

Ben Hecht, U.S. journalist, playwright, and novelist, writes his autobiography, *A Child of the Century*. In | **1954** |

	A. General History	B. Jews in North and South America	C. Jews in Europe	D. Jews in the Middle East and Elsewhere	E. Jewish Culture
1954		Coast branch in Los Angeles, California. Gordon W. Allport,* U.S. sociologist, writes *The Nature of Prejudice*, a study of the roots of hostility, including antisemitism.			the 1940s Hecht was a vigorous supporter of the Irgun's efforts in Palestine. Abraham Joshua Heschel, U.S. rabbi and philosopher, writes *Man's Quest for God*.
Jan. 1954	The first nuclear-powered submarine, the USS *Nautilus*, is commissioned. Hyman Rickover (1900–1986), who came to the U.S. in 1904 from Poland with his parents and graduated from the Naval Academy in 1922, is responsible for the ship's development and is known as the father of the nuclear navy.			The *New York Times* reports that King ibn Saud* of Saudi Arabia urged the sacrifice of 10 million Arabs to "uproot" the "cancer" of Israel.	Irving Berlin receives a special gold medal from President Dwight D. Eisenhower* for his patriotic song "God Bless America," which he composed in 1938. S. N. Behrman, U.S. playwright, writes *The Worcester Account*, in which he describes his boyhood among Jewish immigrants in Massachusetts.
Feb. 1954				Israel abolishes capital punishment for murder. Ultra-Orthodox Jews picket the Israeli consulate in New York, seeking the abolition of women's conscription in Israel's armed forces. Leading Orthodox rabbinical bodies deplore the "shameful riotous conduct."	*Sacred Service*, composed by Darius Milhaud, French composer, is premiered in Israel by the Kol Yisrael Orchestra. Gregory G. Pincus (1903–1967), U.S. biologist who pioneered the development of oral contraceptives, and John Rock* begin clinical testing of birth control pills. Their method proves to be almost totally effective in preventing conception.
Mar. 1954		Yeshiva University announces the establishment of Stern College for Women, after the receipt of a $500,000 gift from Max Stern, U.S. businessman and philanthropist.		Eleven Israelis are killed in an Arab ambush of a civilian bus in the Negev's Scorpion Pass. The UN Mixed Armistice Commission does not censure Jordan for the attack. Israeli forces attack the Jordan village of Nahalin, killing 9 Jordanian military personnel and wounding 19. The UN Mixed Armistice Commission condemns Israel for the raid. The Soviet Union casts its 59th Security Council veto when it blocks a resolution	Leon Poliakov, French historian, writes *Harvest of Hate*, a history of the Nazi program for the destruction of the Jews of Europe. Max Born (1882–1970), German physicist, is awarded the Nobel Prize in physics for his research into quantum mechanics and nuclear physics. He fled Germany for England when the Nazis came to power and returned to Germany in 1953.

A. General History	B. Jews in North and South America	C. Jews in Europe	D. Jews in the Middle East and Elsewhere	E. Jewish Culture	
			calling on Egypt to permit Israeli-bound shipping through the Suez Canal.	Ilya Ehrenburg, Soviet writer and journalist, writes *The Thaw*, a novel that signals the post-Stalin	**Mar. 1954**
The U.S. agrees to grant military aid to Iraq. In February, it had agreed to grant military aid to Pakistan. President Dwight D. Eisenhower* emphasizes an American guarantee that such military aid is not to be used for aggressive purposes.

Pakistan and Turkey enter into a mutual defense treaty. | The U.S. assistant secretary of state for the Near East, Henry Byroade,* admonishes Israel to drop its policy of retaliatory killings and the Arabs to accept the existence of Israel. However, he urges the Israelis "to truly look upon yourselves as a Middle Eastern State and see your own future in that context rather than as . . . peoples of a particular religious faith who must have special rights within and obligations to the Israeli state." | Romania tries Lucretiu Patrascanu, a prominent Jewish Communist lawyer who had been minister of justice in the first postwar cabinet, for being an agent of the Gestapo, the prewar Romanian secret police, and the Americans. He is executed. Many other Jews are defendants in "show" trials throughout the year. | | "thaw." It describes the inhumanity and tyranny of Stalinism. A Jewish physician receives sympathetic treatment as a victim of trumped-up charges of the Doctors' Plot and is saved from execution by Stalin's death.

Joseph Baratz (1890–1968), a founder of Kibbutz Deganyah in Palestine in 1910, writes *A Village by the Jordan: The Story of Deganyah*. It is translated into 13 languages. | **Apr. 1954** |
| In *Brown* v. *Board of Education*, the U.S. Supreme Court rules that compulsory racial segregation in state-supported public schools is unconstitutional and orders lower courts to use "all deliberate speed" to integrate public schools.

French power in Indochina ends with the defeat of their troops at the Battle of Dienbienphu by the Communist Viet Minh forces. The Geneva settlement divides the area into two countries—North Vietnam (Communist) and South Vietnam. | Henry Byroade,* assistant secretary of state, explains and amplifies his April remarks, stating he did not mean to intrude into Israel's internal affairs but believed the matter of immigration into Israel and its continued call for greater immigration to be a matter of grave concern and a cause of the Arab world's fear of Israeli expansionism. | | Israeli immigrants from Romania begin a five-day hunger strike to protest antisemitic trials in Romania against Romanian Jewish leaders. The Knesset passes a vote of formal protest. | | **May 1954** |
| J. Robert Oppenheimer, U.S. physicist, has his security clearance canceled by a government panel that finds him a loyal citizen but not a good security risk. Oppenheimer associated with Communists in the 1930s and was opposed to the development of the hydrogen bomb. | The Rabbinical Assembly (Conservative) amends the form of the marriage contract (*ketubbah*), which requires the bride and groom to turn over their rights to a court of Jewish law (*bet din*) to enforce family law. The amended *ketubbah* was drafted by Saul Lieberman, noted talmudic scholar. | Pierre Mendes-France (1907–1982), French statesman, becomes premier of France, introduces a plan for a Western European defense community, and promises to grant Tunisia independence. He is the third Jew to be premier of France since the Second World War, the others being Leon Blum (1872–1950) in 1946 | Jordanians kill three members of Kibbutz Mevo'ot Betar.

Two Israeli policemen on a vessel in the Sea of Galilee are killed by Syrians, who dispute the right of movement by fishermen and policemen granted by the armistice agreement.

Three days of shooting in Jerusalem | | **June 1954** |

	A. General History	B. Jews in North and South America	C. Jews in Europe	D. Jews in the Middle East and Elsewhere	E. Jewish Culture
June 1954	Senator Joseph McCarthy* concludes two months of hearings in which he accuses the U.S. Army of allowing Communist influence. His chief counsel is Roy M. Cohn, and G. David Schine is a committee investigator.		and René Mayer in 1953. The first large synagogue built in Holland since the end of World War II is dedicated in Rotterdam. During the year, the Great (1671), New (1752), and Uilenburg (1766) synagogues of Amsterdam are sold to the municipality, which is expected to turn them into historical museums.	begins with three Jews and five Arabs killed and many wounded.	
July 1954	Great Britain and Egypt sign an agreement under which the British garrison of 80,000 troops would leave the Suez Canal area within 20 months to be replaced by British civilians who, with Egyptians, would operate the Suez Canal under the terms of a new Anglo-Egyptian Treaty of seven years' duration.	Rabbi Joseph B. Soloveitchik, noted Orthodox talmudic scholar, emphasizes the need for strong resistance to the modernist trend, as observed in mixed pews and the use of microphones on the Sabbath.		Israeli agents in Egypt seek to demonstrate the irresponsibility of the Nasser* regime by exploding bombs in U.S. and British buildings. The objective is to persuade the British to remain in Egypt. Prime Minister Moshe Sharett and Defense Minister Pinhas Lavon may have been unaware of the operation. Egypt uncovers the plot and the agents are placed on trial.	
Sep. 1954				Egypt seizes the Israeli vessel *Bat Galim* in the Suez Canal. On January 1, 1955, Egypt will free the crew.	
Oct. 1954		A survey conducted by Rabbi David Max Eichhorn indicates that about 2,000 non-Jews are being converted annually to Judaism. Most are women, and 1 out of 20 is converted out of conviction rather than for marriage purposes. At least 1,000 of the conversions are by Reform rabbis.			
Nov. 1954	A rebellion against France breaks out in Algeria.			Details of Israel's atomic research and that Israel and France have agreed to cooperate in the development of nuclear energy are made public.	

A. General History	B. Jews in North and South America	C. Jews in Europe	D. Jews in the Middle East and Elsewhere	E. Jewish Culture	
The U.S. Senate censures Senator Joseph McCarthy* for his conduct during hearings on alleged Communist influence in the government and the army. The word *McCarthyism* is coined to describe political accusations using sensational tactics and unsupported evidence.		Antisemitic purges of Jews from Czech governmental and party positions have continued throughout the year. By the end of the year, there are no Jews in party or cabinet positions. François Mauriac,* French Nobel Prize winner, addresses the International League against Racism and Anti-Semitism and states that "the virulence of the anti-Semites has not diminished." A seminary of Jewish studies is opened in Strasbourg, France. West Germany issues a postage stamp with the picture of Jewish social worker and feminist Bertha Pappenheim (1859–1936), who, in 1904, founded the Jewish Women's League of Germany.	The French Socialist government approves a request for the sale of 12 Ouragon jet fighters to Israel. Egyptian Minister Salam Salim* announces that Egypt will never make peace with Israel. At this time, there is considerable ex-Nazi influence on Nasser's* government, and Egypt is a prime organizer of fedayeen attacks on Israel. U.S. diplomats stationed in the Middle East hold a conference in the American embassy in Damascus. They define U.S. policy as (1) complete and strict impartiality between the Arab states and Israel; (2) friendship for all Middle Eastern countries; (3) support of these countries in their efforts to create strong and stable governments; (4) reaffirmation of the Tripartite Declaration of 1950; and (5) support of the UN Truce Supervision Organization. Israel captures several Arab saboteurs and marauders who acknowledge they were acting under the direction of Egyptian military intelligence based in Gaza.		**Dec. 1954**
	The Rabbinical Assembly, the organization of Conservative rabbis, rules that during religious services women may be called to the Torah for *aliyot*. There are 345 Jewish community centers in the U.S., located in approximately 215 cities in addition to metroplitan New York. In 1946, they numbered 295.	During the year, under the pressure of world opinion, the Romanian government releases some prominent Jewish prisoners who had been held for Zionist activities. Hersch Lauterpacht (1897–1960), Whewell professor of international law at Cambridge, is appointed a judge of the International Court of Justice at	One million *dunams* of Israeli land are under irrigation. In 1948, 230,000 *dunams* were under irrigation. Israel's first cotton harvest exceeds expectations. It is predicted that by 1960 imports of cotton will cease. Bar-Ilan University in Ramat Gan, Israel, opens. It is supported by the Mizrachi Orthodox movement	Marshall Sklare (1921–1992), U.S. sociologist, writes *Conservative Judaism*, the first in-depth analysis of the American religious movement. He notes the failure of its religious leaders to develop a distinctive Conservative ideology but acknowledges the movement's contribution to survivalism. Of Orthodoxy he writes: "The history of their	**1955**

	A. General History	B. Jews in North and South America	C. Jews in Europe	D. Jews in the Middle East and Elsewhere	E. Jewish Culture
1955		The Conference of Presidents of Major American Jewish Organizations is organized with Dr. Nahum Goldmann as its first chairman. The Leo Baeck Institute is founded in New York by the Council of Jews from Germany. Named in honor of Rabbi Leo Baeck, it chronicles the history of German and central European Jewry from the emancipation period until the rise of Adolf Hitler. Beginning in 1956, it publishes *The Leo Baeck Yearbook*. John Higham* writes *Strangers in the Land: Patterns of American Nativism, 1860–1925*, in which he outlines the factors that influenced the passage of restrictive immigration laws. Nathan Phillips is elected mayor of Toronto. The first Jew to hold that office, he will serve until 1962. David Arnold Croll, Canadian lawyer, is appointed member of the Canadian Senate, the first Jewish senator in Canadian history. He was mayor of Windsor between 1931 and 1939, a member of the Canadian Parliament, and minister of labor and of public welfare in the provincial government of Ontario.	The Hague. He was born in Galicia and educated at Lvov and Vienna before immigrating to Great Britain.	and is the first American-sponsored liberal arts university in Israel. It is named after Meir Bar-Ilan (Berlin, 1880–1949), leader of religious Zionism and president of the World Mizrachi Center. The archaeological discoveries of the ancient fortress of Massada and the palace of Herod are announced. *Hill 24 Doesn't Answer*, a major film, is produced in Israel. The film's background is the War of Independence.	movement in this country can be written in terms of a case study of institutional decay." Solomon B. Freehof, U.S. Reform rabbi and scholar, writes *The Responsa Literature*, a study of the development of Jewish law as displayed in the literature of rabbinic responsa. Samuel Chotzinoff (1889–1964), U.S. pianist and music critic, writes *A Lost Paradise*, reminiscences of his early years in London and New York's Lower East Side. As a consultant to the NBC radio network, he assembled the NBC Symphony Orchestra in 1937 and induced Arturo Toscanini* to be its conductor. Will Herberg (1901–1977) writes *Protestant–Catholic–Jew: An Essay in American Religious Sociology*, in which he discusses the importance of religion in American life and traces the development of the three groups in the U.S. Herman Wouk, U.S. novelist, writes *Marjorie Morningstar*, depicting middle-class American Jewish life in New York and its summer havens. Arthur Miller, U.S. playwright and novelist, writes *A View from the Bridge*, a play about two Italian longshoremen illegally in the U.S. It wins him his second Pulitzer Prize in drama.
Jan. 1955			Jacob Kaplan is appointed chief rabbi of France.	Israeli agents in Egypt are convicted of espionage after a public trial. Israel's reputation with the Western powers is damaged, and there are widespread repercussions in Israel. Defense Minister Pinhas Lavon denies knowledge of	*Satan in Goray* by Isaac Bashevis Singer, Polish-born author of Yiddish fiction, is translated into

A. General History	B. Jews in North and South America	C. Jews in Europe	D. Jews in the Middle East and Elsewhere	E. Jewish Culture	
			the operation, and the findings of an inquiry commission appointed by Prime Minister Moshe Sharett are inconclusive.	English. Written in 1935, it is the story of Polish Jews of the 17th century turning to a messianic sect with mystic and erotic beliefs after surviving a pogrom.	**Jan. 1955**
Turkey and Iraq enter into the Baghdad Pact defense organization. Iran, Pakistan, and Great Britain later join the pact. The U.S. supports the pact, while Egypt rallies Arab support against the pact. The French government headed by Pierre Mendes-France falls on a vote on his handling of the Tunisian situation. Edgar Faure* succeeds as premier, and the rumor that he, too, is Jewish is probably related to the fact that his wife is Jewish. Soviet Premier Georgi M. Malenkov* resigns and is replaced by Nikolay Bulganin* as premier and Nikita Khrushchev* as party first secretary. Khrushchev* is the leader of the Soviet Union.			Defense Minister Pinhas Lavon resigns following the uncovering of an Israeli intelligence network in Egypt. David Ben-Gurion returns as minister of defense. The Israeli army launches a reprisal attack against Egyptian military headquarters in Gaza. Thirty-eight Egyptian soldiers are killed and 24 wounded. The raid is in response to a series of Egyptian provocations. Gamal Abdel Nasser* uses the raid as a pretext for a Czech arms deal.	*The Collected Stories of Isaac Babel* (1894–1941), Russian writer, appears in English translation with an introduction by the noted critic Lionel Trilling. Some stories describe his experiences as a Jew serving as a political officer in a Cossack regiment during the Russian Revolution, and others concern Jews in his native Odessa. Lillian Hellman, U.S. playwright, is associated with a dramatization of *The Diary of Anne Frank* that obscures the Jewish element of this Nazi tragedy. The script by Albert and Frances Hackett* is preferred to one by Meyer Levin. Rachel Wischnitzer, scholar of Jewish art, writes *Synagogue Architecture in the United States*, a profusely illustrated interpretative history.	**Feb. 1955**
			Egyptians raid the Israeli village of Patish, killing 1 and wounding 18. Several other raids from Gaza will take place in April and May. The UN Security Council adopts a U.S.–British–French resolution condemning Israel for the February Gaza raid.	The Metropolitan Museum of Art in New York exhibits Art of the Hebrew Tradition, a collection of Jewish ceremonial objects for the synagogue and home. It is arranged by the Jewish Museum in commemoration of the American Jewish Tercentenary.	**Mar. 1955**
Anthony Eden* becomes prime minister of Britain, succeeding the retiring Winston Churchill.* The Bandung Conference of 29 Third World countries adopts a charter			The first West German ship not carrying reparations goods docks in Israel. The *Arcturus* loads 45,000 cases of citrus fruit for Germany.	Stephen S. Kayser and Guido Schoenberger edit a catalogue, *Jewish Ceremonial Art*, which is later published as a book. The American Jewish Historical Society and the Theodor Herzl	**Apr. 1955**

	A. General History	B. Jews in North and South America	C. Jews in Europe	D. Jews in the Middle East and Elsewhere	E. Jewish Culture
Apr. 1955	affirming equality between races and nations. Jawaharlal Nehru,* Tito,* Sukarno,* and Gamal Abdel Nasser* are dominant personalities at the conference.				Foundation sponsor a conference on the early history of Zionism in America. In 1958, the proceedings of the conference, edited by Isidore S. Meyer, will be published.
May 1955	West Germany gains full sovereignty as the Allied occupation comes to an end. The Warsaw Pact, militarily unifying the Eastern bloc nations, is created to counter NATO. The pact nations are the Soviet Union, Poland, Czechoslovakia, Hungary, Romania, Bulgaria, Albania, and East Germany. Austria gains its independence. All Allied occupation troops are to be removed by the end of the year.		Gerhard Peters,* German chemical manufacturer who sold Zyklon B to the Auschwitz death camp knowing it would be used to exterminate Jews, is acquitted of war crimes. The *London Jewish Chronicle* publishes an interview with Selig Segal, a Romanian Jew recently released from a Soviet labor camp. Segal reports he had worked in various camps in the Soviet Union, the Urals, and Siberia and "everywhere he had met many Jews who had been deported because of their [suspected] loyalty to Israel." The newspaper publishes similar interviews with other recently released prisoners.		Jonas Salk (b. 1914), U.S. epidemiologist, develops the Salk polio vaccine, the first effective weapon to combat the polio scourge. *Pillar of Salt*, a novel written by Albert Memmi (b. 1920), Tunisian-born French novelist and sociologist, appears in English translation. Largely autobiographical, it depicts the emergence of a young North African Jew from the narrow Jewish society into the French colonial culture and his ultimate disillusionment with Western society. Robert Brunschvig, French orientalist, is appointed director of the Institute of Islamic Studies at the Sorbonne. During World War II, he worked to protect the rights of Algerian Jews persecuted by the Vichy regime.
June 1955				The Jerusalem District Court rules that Israel Kastner (1906–1957) had not been criminally libeled by Malkiel Gruenwald, who accused him, when he was a wartime leader of Hungarian Jewry, of collaborating with the Nazis and being indirectly responsible for or assisting in the murder of Hungarian Jewry. The verdict is appealed to Israel's Supreme Court. The trial becomes a campaign issue as Kastner is a prominent Mapai figure.	Four Dead Sea Scrolls (the first Isaiah scroll, the commentary on Habakkuk, the Manual of Discipline, and the Genesis Apocryphon) are purchased in New York by Professor Yigael Yadin (1917–1984) with the financial help of Samuel Gottesman and are removed to the Hebrew University in Jerusalem. They are purchased from the Syrian Orthodox Metropolitan in Jerusalem.
July 1955			A Bulgarian air force plane shoots down an El Al passenger plane that strayed over Bulgarian air space in error, killing all aboard.	Between July and September, Elmore Jackson,* an American Quaker serving at the UN, shuttles three times between Cairo	

			and Jerusalem in an attempt to mediate a settlement between Egypt and Israel. Egypt demands repatriation of refugees and ceding of the Negev. Israel offers compensation, some union of families, and limited boundary adjustments with a right of passage through Israeli territory. Israel holds national elections for the Third Knesset, with 853,219 votes cast. Mapai wins 40 seats; Herut, 15 seats; Liberals, 13 seats; Ahdut ha-Avodah, 10 seats; Mapam, 9 seats; and the National Religious party, 11 seats. The government is installed on November 3, with David Ben-Gurion as prime minister and minister of defense and Moshe Sharett as minister of foreign affairs.	Tel Aviv holds a traditional Purim parade, the *Adloyada*, for the first time since 1935. More than 500,000 persons take part in the celebration.	**July 1955**
		Israeli newspaper editor Haim Shurer, who spent 40 days in the Soviet Union in 1954, reports that at least half the Soviet Jewish population was interested in Jewish communal life but there was none, "no Jewish theater, school, library, bookshop, or restaurant."	Secretary of State John Foster Dulles,* in a speech approved by President Dwight D. Eisenhower,* proposes a program to end the war between Israel and the Arab states. There should be agreement on borders; an international guarantee of these borders, sponsored by the UN, with U.S. participation through formal treaty obligations; an international loan, with heavy U.S. participation, to enable Israel to pay compensation to Arab refugees; and U.S. assistance to help create more arable land where the refugees will reside. The speech is a broad outline of Project Alpha.		**Aug. 1955**

	A. General History	B. Jews in North and South America	C. Jews in Europe	D. Jews in the Middle East and Elsewhere	E. Jewish Culture
Aug. 1955				Egyptian fedayeen start a series of coordinated attacks against Israeli border settlements and settlements deep in Israeli territory. Israeli forces attack and destroy all military installations at the Khan Yunis fedayeen training camp.	
Sep. 1955	Pakistan joins the Turkish–Iraqi alliance. Iran will join in October, and the U.S. welcomes the event, whereas the Soviet Union protests. The U.S. begins discussions of military aid to Arab countries, including Egypt. In October, representatives of American Jewish organizations will protest to Secretary of State John Foster Dulles* the exclusion of Israel from the U.S. military aid program. President Gamal Abdel Nasser* announces an agreement to exchange Egyptian cotton for massive military aid from Czechoslovakia. The deal is completed under Soviet sponsorship. Nasser* states Western nations refused his requests for arms. The Soviet move is aimed at keeping Egypt from joining the Baghdad Pact.	A September newspaper advertisement listing the Reform synagogues in the metropolitan New York area highlights the movement's suburban growth. Nassau County, with fewer than 150,000 Jews, has 22 Reform congregations; Westchester County, with fewer than 50,000 Jews, has 11 Reform congregations; Brooklyn and the Bronx, with about 870,000 and 475,000 Jews, respectively, have a total of 14 Reform congregations.	Ilya Ehrenburg, Soviet writer and journalist, who has often been an official Soviet spokesman, tells Western Jewish journalists in Geneva that he is an assimilationist and an anti-Zionist and believes Soviet Jews should be Russified. The Van den Nestlei synagogue in Antwerp, rebuilt after being destroyed by the Nazis, is consecrated.	Egyptian troops guarding the Straits of Tiran at the tip of the Sinai Peninsula prevent passage of vessels of all nations to the Israeli port of Eilat. In 1953, they had closed off only Israeli shipping.	
Oct. 1955	Late in the year, Egypt begins to supply money and Soviet bloc weapons to Algerian nationalists fighting the French in Algeria.		During the visit of Israeli Prime Minister Moshe Sharett to Paris, French Prime Minister Edgar Faure* announces the shipment of 12 additional Ouragon jet fighters and of 12 new Mystère 4 jet fighters to Israel. The French react to Gamal Abdel Nasser's* support of Algerian	The Arab League announces the deferral of acceptance of Eric Johnston's* proposal for utilization of Jordan River waters. Johnston,* President Dwight D. Eisenhower's* special envoy, negotiated a plan for the utilization of the waters of the Jordan, the Yarmuk, and their tributaries,	

A. General History	B. Jews in North and South America	C. Jews in Europe	D. Jews in the Middle East and Elsewhere	E. Jewish Culture
		rebels and to the Czech arms pact with Egypt. The U.S. compels France to delay the shipment of the Mystère jets. As of October, Jewish scholarly workers in the Soviet Union number 24,620 or 11% of the national total.	with Israeli, Jordanian, Syrian, and Lebanese experts. Egypt's Gamal Abdel Nasser* concludes a mutual defense treaty with Syria.	Oct. 1955
			Israel attacks the demilitarized zone at El Auja on the Egyptian border, killing 50 and wounding 40 Egyptians, with the loss of 4 Israelis. Sultan Sidi Mohammed ben Youssef* declares that when Morocco achieves independence, "Jews will enjoy full rights with absolute equality and will be associated with every aspect of national life." Israeli Prime Minister David Ben-Gurion, in an address to the Knesset, rejects Project Alpha as an attempt to crush Israel, as it will require Israel to give up the Negev.	Nov. 1955
Pro-Nasser* and anti-Western rioters in Jordan, objecting to British efforts to have Jordan join the Baghdad Pact, cause the resignation of the cabinet. The new government promises not to join the pact. The U.S. and Britain give Egypt assurances of financial aid to help with the construction of the Aswan Dam. Eugene R. Black,* president of the International Bank, begins negotiations with Egypt over a $200 million loan. Egypt accepts the offer and rejects the Soviet one. Dr. Martin Luther King, Jr.,* leads a			In a speech to the Supreme Soviet, Soviet Prime Minister Nikita Khrushchev* condemns Israel as a tool of imperialist states used to threaten its Arab neighbors. After numerous Syrian attacks against Israeli fishermen, Israel attacks Syrian positions in the northeast corner of the Sea of Galilee, killing 56 Syrians, taking 29 prisoners, with 6 Israelis killed.	Dec. 1955

	A. General History	B. Jews in North and South America	C. Jews in Europe	D. Jews in the Middle East and Elsewhere	E. Jewish Culture
Dec. 1955	black boycott of segregated city bus lines in Montgomery, Alabama. Dr. King* achieves national prominence for advocating passive resistance to segregation in public places.				
1956		Eleven heads of Orthodox rabbinic academies of advanced study and the leader of the Hasidic Lubavitch movement issue a ban on Orthodox participation in U.S. rabbinic organizations that include non-Orthodox rabbis. Only four rabbis serve the 300,000 Jews of Buenos Aires, and there are no rabbis in the provinces, as the Jews of Argentina show little interest in religion.	Robert Briscoe (1894–1969) begins service as lord mayor of Dublin, Ireland. He serves until 1957 and again in 1961–1962. In addition to being Dublin's first Jewish lord mayor, he was the first Jewish member of the Irish Dail (Parliament), serving from 1927 to 1965 as a member of Eamon De Valera's* party.	Tel Aviv University is established.	Lawrence H. Fuchs, U.S. political scientist, writes *The Political Behavior of American Jews*, in which he traces the history of Jewish voting from Colonial days to the present. Leo W. Schwarz (1906–1967), U.S. author and editor, edits *Great Ages and Ideas of the Jewish People*, which includes essays by Salo Baron and other noted historians. Maurice Samuel, U.S. author and translator, writes *The Professor and the Fossil*, in which he takes issue with the treatment of the Jews by Arnold J. Toynbee* in his *A Study of History*.
Jan. 1956	French elections return the new Socialist government headed by Guy Mollet.*			The UN Security Council unanimously adopts a U.S., French, and British resolution condemning Israel for its December attack on Syrian positions near the Sea of Galilee. The new Socialist government of France headed by Guy Mollet* establishes strong ties to Israel and informs the U.S. that Mystère jet fighters will be sent to Israel. Former President Harry S. Truman,* Eleanor Roosevelt,* and labor leader Walter Reuther* issue a statement urging the U.S. provision of defensive arms to Israel to help it protect itself from the introduction of Communist arms to Arab countries in the Middle East.	Meyer Levin, U.S. novelist and journalist, writes *Compulsion*, a novel based on the notorious murder of a young boy by Nathan Leopold and Richard Loeb in the 1920s. Allen Ginsberg (b. 1926), U.S. poet, publishes *Howl and Other Poems*. Acknowledged as the leading poet of the "beat generation," Ginsberg, in *Howl*, despairs of what society did to his generation. Gerald Green (b. 1922), U.S. novelist, writes *The Last Angry Man*, a novel of a Brooklyn slum and of Dr. Samuel Abelman, the neighborhood doctor.
Feb. 1956	The U.S. agrees to ship 18 M-41 light tanks to Saudi Arabia.	U.S. Secretary of State John Foster Dulles* acknowledges		U.S. Secretary of State John Foster Dulles* advises a	

A. General History	B. Jews in North and South America	C. Jews in Europe	D. Jews in the Middle East and Elsewhere	E. Jewish Culture	
It is believed the action is related to the renewal of the U.S. lease of Dhahran Air Base that is to expire in June.

Soviet party leader Nikita Khrushchev* denounces Joseph Stalin.* He airs the secrets of 25 years of terror and begins to ease repression. | and accepts Saudi Arabia's insistence on its right to exclude Jewish military personnel from the American air base at Dhahran. | | congressional group that Israel would lose the arms race with the Arabs. Its security should be assured by the UN.

The U.S. makes it known it would not object to the sale of arms to Israel by France or Britain, while continuing to defer action on Israel's request for U.S. arms. | Barbara Miller Solomon, U.S. historian, writes *Ancestors and Immigrants: A Changing New England Tradition*, in which she analyzes the emerging attitude of Boston's leading citizens—the Brahmins—in the post–Civil War era toward the foreigners in their midst. | **Feb. 1956** |
| Jordan's King Hussein,* in response to pressure from Egypt's Gamal Abdel Nasser,* dismisses John Bagot Glubb,* British commander of the Arab Legion, and orders him to leave Jordan.

Tunisia gains independence from France. Habib Bourguiba's* Neo-Destour party is victorious in the elections. Bourguiba* is appointed premier. His cabinet includes a Jew, André Barouch.

Morocco achieves independence from France.

Dr. Martin Luther King, Jr.,* is found guilty of promoting the Montgomery, Alabama, bus boycott. | | | Fedayeen raiders from Gaza wound 11 Israeli settlers near Gevulot.

President Dwight D. Eisenhower* selects former Deputy Secretary of Defense Robert Anderson* to secretly mediate directly with David Ben-Gurion and Gamal Abdel Nasser* in an effort to resolve the Israeli–Egyptian dispute. Eisenhower* concludes from Anderson's* debriefing that while Israel was not ready to make serious concessions, it was Nasser* who had "proved to be a complete stumbling block." | Sensing the threat to their way of life from immigrants, they fashioned pseudoscientific theories of intellectual racism that led to the Immigration Restriction League and the implementation of the restrictionist immigration policy in the 1920s.

Henry "Hank" Greenberg, who spent most of his baseball career with the Detroit Tigers, is elected to the Baseball Hall of Fame. He is the first Jew accorded that recognition. He was selected as the most valuable player of the American League in 1935 and 1940. He led the Tigers to league pennants in 1934, 1935, 1940, and 1945. He hit 58 home | **Mar. 1956** |
| Egypt's Gamal Abdel Nasser* concludes a five-year trilateral military alliance with Saudi Arabia and Yemen. | | The *New York Times* reports the release of all 200 Jews jailed in Romania for Zionist activities. | Fedayeen raiders from Gaza kill one Israeli soldier amd wound three near Nirim. The next day raiders kill three Israeli soldiers near Kisufim.

Israeli troops shell the town of Gaza, killing 56.

U.S. Secretary of State John Foster Dulles,* alarmed at the shift in the Middle East power balance, requests Canada to provide Israel with a squadron of American-licensed jet fighters. | runs in 1938, tying the major league record for right-handed batsmen.

Frederick Loewe (1901–1988) composes the music and Alan Jay Lerner (1918–1986) writes the lyrics for *My Fair Lady*, a Broadway musical based on George Bernard Shaw's* play *Pygmalion*.

Members of the British Parliament present a menorah sculpture by Benno Elkan (1877–1960) to Israel's Knesset in | **Apr. 1956** |

	A. General History	B. Jews in North and South America	C. Jews in Europe	D. Jews in the Middle East and Elsewhere	E. Jewish Culture
Apr. 1956				The U.S. announces that in the event of an Arab–Israeli war it would act through the UN, an approach that would involve the Soviet threat of the use of a Security Council veto. This is a retreat from the Tripartite Declaration of 1950.	Jerusalem. The reliefs depict the history of the Jewish people. Elkan fled his native Germany in 1933 and settled in London. David Daiches, English literary critic, writes an autobiography, *Two Worlds: An Edinburgh Jewish Childhood*. He draws a loving portrait of his father, an Orthodox rabbi, and then outlines the stages of his own estrangement from Orthodox Judaism.
May 1956	Egypt's Gamal Abdel Nasser* enters into an agreement with Jordan to coordinate their armies. Egypt recognizes Communist China.		The Czechs free Mordecai Oren, Israeli citizen and Mapam member of the Knesset, who was arrested in Czechoslovakia in 1952. However, they do not exonerate him. Soviet leader Nikita Khrushchev* expresses his frank opinion of Jews: "At the beginning of the revolution the Jews were more educated than the average Russian. . . . Since then we have created new cadres . . . and now if the Jews were to occupy first place, it would spread discontent among the inhabitants who have roots in the country." The duke of Edinburgh and the prime minister attend a banquet in celebration of the 300th anniversary of the resettlement of the Jews in England under Oliver Cromwell,* following Manasseh ben Israel's petition of 1656. It is the first time that a Jewish gathering is addressed by both a member of the royal family and a prime minister.		The Victoria and Albert Museum in London holds an exhibition of Anglo-Jewish art and history in commemoration of the 300th anniversary of the resettlement of Jews in the British Isles. Richard David Barnett, head of the British Museum's department of western Asiatic antiquities, organizes the exhibition. A Bible illustrated with 105 etchings by Marc Chagall is published in Paris. The Romanian Jewish community begins publication of *The Jewish Religious Review*, edited by Chief Rabbi Moses Rosen (b. 1912). Published biweekly in Romanian, Yiddish, and Hebrew, it is the only Eastern European periodical with a Hebrew section. An ancient Aramaic translation, or *targum*, of the Torah deriving from Galilee is discovered in the Vatican library by a Spanish scholar, A. Diez-Macho.* The *targum*, called Neofiti I, had been mislabeled and untouched for centuries.
June 1956	Britain withdraws from Egypt, ending 74 years of military occupation. Workers riot in Poznan, Poland, to protest working conditions, wages, and taxes.			Golda Meir replaces Moshe Sharett as foreign minister in the Ben-Gurion government. Egypt's Gamal Abdel Nasser* proclaims: "We must be strong in order to regain the	

A. General History	B. Jews in North and South America	C. Jews in Europe	D. Jews in the Middle East and Elsewhere	E. Jewish Culture	
U.S. Secretary of State John Foster Dulles* announces the withdrawal of the U.S. offer to finance Egypt's Aswan Dam after a belated Egyptian agreement on the terms. The U.S. is concerned about the economic viability of the project and the increasingly friendly relations of Egypt with the Soviet Union. A week later, Nasser* announces nationalization of the Suez Canal in retaliation of the U.S. reneging and says the canal's revenues will finance the dam construction. Britain and France consider the action a threat to world peace, raise the issue at the UN, and begin secret planning for military action.		A West German information agency begins distribution of *Night and Fog*, a French documentary film directed by Alain Resnais* that depicts the horrors of the Nazi concentration camps.	rights of the Palestinians by force." King Hussein* of Jordan wires Gamal Abdel Nasser* of Egypt: "We look forward to the future when the Arab flag will fly over our great stolen country." The chief rabbinate of Israel issues a formal prohibition against the establishment of the Reform movement in Israel. In August, the Jerusalem Municipal Council will approve the construction of the Reform-sponsored American School for Archaeology in Jerusalem, which will contain a synagogue in its library.	Nehama Leibowitz (b. 1905) is awarded the Israel Prize for her decades of teaching Bible to teachers and lay adults, applying her method of closely reading the Bible through the eyes of its classic Jewish commentators. Leibowitz's mimeographed lessons on the weekly Torah reading gain worldwide distribution and will be collected in book form beginning in 1966 in Hebrew and 1972 in English. She will be appointed to Tel Aviv University in 1957 and will continue to teach in a variety of settings. Jerry Lieber (b. 1933) and Mike Stoller (b. 1933), U.S. songwriters, write	**July 1956**
U.S. Secretary of State John Foster Dulles* advises Britain's Prime Minister Anthony Eden* that the U.S. opposes armed intervention in the Suez Canal crisis. The British and French assemble a military team to prepare for landings in Egypt to regain the Suez Canal.			The French minister of defense, Maurice Bourges-Maunoury,* asks Israel's Shimon Peres, who is in France on an arms supply mission, "If we make war on Egypt, would Israel be prepared to fight alongside us?" Peres says, "Yes." The U.S. Democratic party national convention adopts its platform, which attacks the Republican Middle East policy and supports arms shipments to Israel "to redress the dangerous imbalance of arms in the area," as well as the conclusion of security guarantees. The Republican party national convention adopts a platform that avoids a commitment of arms shipments to Israel. It declares, "We shall support the independence of Israel against armed aggression."	"Hound Dog," which becomes a national hit as a recording by Elvis Presley.* The song heralds the birth of rock and roll. Lieber and Stoller write many more rock and roll hits.	**Aug. 1956**

	A. General History	B. Jews in North and South America	C. Jews in Europe	D. Jews in the Middle East and Elsewhere	E. Jewish Culture
Sep. 1956	The U.S. again warns Britain's Prime Minister Anthony Eden* against the use of force in the Suez Canal crisis. Eden* replies, comparing Gamal Abdel Nasser* to Adolf Hitler,* and states, "It would be an ignoble end to our long history if we accepted to perish by degrees." Egypt's Gamal Abdel Nasser* rejects the declaration of the London Maritime Conference, which recognizes Egypt's right to compensation for the use of the Suez Canal but insists on international control of the canal. British and French Prime Ministers Anthony Eden* and Guy Mollet* present their case against Egypt to the UN Security Council. The Soviet Union vetoes the resolutions censuring Egypt.		A stage adaptation of *The Diary of Anne Frank* has a simultaneous premiere in about a dozen West German cities. It is the year's outstanding stage event.	The Israeli army attacks a Jordanian army post at Qariya, killing 16 Arab Legionnaires in response to a fedayeen attack that killed 6 Israeli soldiers. The U.S. announces that it has no objection to the sale of 24 jet fighters by Canada to Israel. Israel's Moshe Dayan and Golda Meir fly to Paris to seek additional weapons. The French agree, and begin shipping half-tracks, transport planes, and other arms immediately. Rabbi Amram Blau, leader of the Neturei Karta, and some of his followers are arrested in Jerusalem in a demonstration against Sabbath road traffic. It is reported that he had been arrested 153 times since 1934 for disrupting Sabbath traffic.	
Oct. 1956	A revolt against Soviet influence and for political change breaks out in Hungary. Imre Nagy* becomes prime minister with Soviet consent.		The de-Stalinization program of the Gomulka* regime in Poland is accompanied by a wave of antisemitism.	On October 2, Moshe Dayan advises the senior staff of Israel's impending collaboration with the French to destroy the Egyptian army in the Sinai, eliminate fedayeen bases in Gaza, and open the Straits of Tiran.	

Oct. 1956

D. Jews in the Middle East and Elsewhere

On October 11, Israel uses tanks, artillery, and planes in a retaliatory attack against a Jordanian police fortress at Qalqilia. Jordan invokes the Anglo-Jordanian treaty of 1948, obliging Britain to come to Jordan's aid. The British advise Israel that the Iraqi division would enter Jordan to protect it.

On October 16, Britain's Prime Minister Anthony Eden* and Foreign Secretary Selwyn Lloyd* meet with French counterparts Guy Mollet* and Christian Pineau* and agree on the utilization of Israeli military collaboration against Egypt. Britain calls off plans to protect Jordan.

On October 22, David Ben-Gurion, Moshe Dayan, and Shimon Peres meet at Sèvres, France, with Guy Mollet,* Christian Pineau,* Maurice Bourges-Maunoury,* and Abel Thomas.* Mollet* agrees to utilize French warplanes and warships to protect Israel's population centers while Israel attacks the Egyptians in the Sinai. An Israeli threat to the Suez Canal would justify an Allied intervention. Selwyn Lloyd* and British Foreign Officer for Middle Eastern Affairs Patrick Dean* accept the plan, and on October 24, Ben-Gurion, Pineau,* and Dean* sign the Treaty of Sèvres, a secret accord.

D. Jews in the Middle East and Elsewhere

On October 24, Egypt, Syria, and Jordan sign a tripartite military agreement. They are concerned about the preemptive Israeli attack against Jordan.

Oct. 1956

On October 29, Israel begins Operation Kadesh with a paratroop drop near the Mitla Pass, about 30 miles from the Suez Canal. The same day, Israeli border police kill 48 Arab men, women, and children returning from the fields near Kfar Kassim. The villagers were unaware of a curfew in connection with the Sinai campaign. Israel agrees to pay compensation to the families of the victims and to court-martial the responsible border police.

On October 30, President Dwight D. Eisenhower* sends a message to David Ben-Gurion urging the withdrawal of forces. Ben-Gurion ignores the request. The U.S. seeks a UN Security Council resolution calling for an Israeli withdrawal. Britain and France veto the U.S. resolution and address a joint ultimatum to Egypt and Israel to withdraw from the Suez Canal area.

On October 31, French and British warplanes destroy most of the Egyptian air force in raids on air bases near the Suez Canal. The Soviets inform Gamal Abdel Nasser* they will not go to war over the Suez. Jordan and Syria reject his appeal for military support. He orders a withdrawal from Sinai to concentrate forces to repel the impending British and French invasion.

A. General History	B. Jews in North and South America	C. Jews in Europe	D. Jews in the Middle East and Elsewhere	E. Jewish Culture
Soviet troops invade Hungary. Prime Minister Imre Nagy* declares Hungary's neutrality; withdraws from the Warsaw Pact; appeals to the UN; and urges his people to defend a free, independent, and neutral Hungary. Nagy* appeals to the UN Security Council to counter the Soviet invasion, and the General Assembly approves the resolution, but it remains unenforced. Three days after the invasion, Soviet armed forces take control of Budapest and crush the Hungarian revolt. The Eisenhower*–Nixon* Republican ticket wins the election by a landslide, defeating the Democratic Stevenson*–Kefauver* ticket. However, Congress becomes Democratic in both houses, the first time in 108 years that the party of the incoming president did not control at least one house of Congress. The Soviet Union agrees that Polish	The Jewish vote in U.S. presidential election is estimated at 60% for Adlai E. Stevenson* and 40% for Dwight D. Eisenhower.*		John Foster Dulles* and Abba Eban meet in Washington, D.C. Dulles* expresses pleasure at Gamal Abdel Nasser's* defeat but also fears that the UN might collapse. He advises Eban, Israeli ambassador to the U.S. and chief delegate to the UN, that the U.S. will support the UN Charter. The UN General Assembly, by a vote of 64–5, approves the U.S. resolution calling for an immediate cease-fire and withdrawal of all occupying forces from Egyptian territory. Israel and Egypt accept a cease-fire, but Israel later renounces it under pressure from Britain and France, as a cessation of hostilities would reduce their justification for intervention. The UN General Assembly votes to create the UN Emergency Force, which would separate combatants along the Suez Canal and	

Nov. 1956

	A. General History	B. Jews in North and South America	C. Jews in Europe	D. Jews in the Middle East and Elsewhere	E. Jewish Culture
Nov. 1956	nationals living in the Soviet Union since World War II may return to Poland. It is estimated that 240,000 Poles would return home, including 30,000 Jews. By the end of June 1957, 15,000 Jews will return to Poland, and 4,000 leave for Israel. The U.S. expresses concern to Syria over its receipt of substantial Soviet arms shipments.			elsewhere in the Sinai. British and French paratroops drop near Port Said followed by amphibious landings of additional troops. The Soviet leader Nikolay Bulganin* threatens use of atomic weapons against Britain and France. The U.S. continues to urge the cessation of the operation and threatens to obstruct an impending British $1 billion loan application to the International Monetary Fund. Britain and France agree to a cease-fire. Israel's "hundred hour campaign" ends with the occupation of all of the Sinai Peninsula and Gaza strip, at a cost of 180 men killed. Israel shatters three Egyptian divisions, kills 2,000, and captures about 6,000 prisoners and considerable war matèriel. Soviet leader Nikolay Bulganin* sends a note to Israel saying that its action "places in question the very existence of Israel as a state." David Ben-Gurion makes a "victory" speech as President Dwight D. Eisenhower* writes to him suggesting the termination of friendly cooperation with Israel unless it withdraws from the Sinai. He warns that Israel should not count on U.S. aid in the event of a Soviet-assisted attack.	
Dec. 1956	The last French and British forces leave the Suez Canal area.			Israeli forces withdraw about 30 miles from the Suez Canal area.	
1957				The Moriah synagogue on Mt. Carmel in Haifa and	Nathan Glazer (b. 1923), U.S. sociologist, writes

A. General History	B. Jews in North and South America	C. Jews in Europe	D. Jews in the Middle East and Elsewhere	E. Jewish Culture	
			the Emet ve-Emunah congregation in Jerusalem affiliate with the United Synagogue of America (Conservative).	*American Judaism*, a sociological history that is one of the volumes in the University of Chicago's History of American Civilization series.	**1957**
Anthony Eden* resigns as prime minister of Great Britain and is succeeded by Harold Macmillan.*

President Dwight D. Eisenhower* addresses a joint session of Congress and proposes the Eisenhower Doctrine to secure the Middle East against Soviet aggression by aiding any nation against overt armed aggression from any nation controlled by international communism. In March, Congress will adopt the doctrine.

Saudi Arabia's King ibn Saud* visits Washington, D.C., at the invitation of President Dwight D. Eisenhower,* the first official visit of an Arab head of state. During Eisenhower's* eight years in the presidency, no Israeli leader is so honored. | | A rabbinical seminary is opened in Moscow after decades of a total absence of rabbinical training in the Soviet Union. | Rabbi André Ungar, Reform rabbi of a Port Elizabeth congregation, is ordered to leave South Africa for describing the government as "Nazi." He had already accepted a pulpit in England and rejected appeals from his congregation not to discuss politics.

David Ben-Gurion announces that Israel will leave the Sinai by January 22, with the exception of the Sharm es-Sheikh area. The Gaza strip would also be held. | Bernard Baruch, U.S. financier and statesman, writes his memoirs, *Baruch: My Own Story*, and in 1960 a sequel, *Public Years*.

Bernard Malamud, U.S. novelist, writes *The Assistant*, depicting a struggling Jewish grocer, Morris Bober, and his gentile assistant, Frank Alpine, who eventually takes over the store and inherits his suffering. Bober is eulogized by a rabbi as "a true Jew because he believed in the Jewish experience. He suffered, he endured, but with hope."

West Side Story, with music by Leonard Bernstein, libretto by Arthur Laurents, and lyrics by Stephen Sondheim and conceived by Jerome Robbins (b. 1918), opens on Broadway and has a run of over 980 performances. | **Jan. 1957** |
| The U.S. expresses concern over renewed Soviet arms shipments to Egypt.

The U.S. and Saudi Arabia issue a communiqué: the U.S. will supply Saudi Arabia with military equipment, services, and training for defense and internal security. The U.S. lease of Dhahran Air Base is extended for five years. No mention is made of the Saudi right to exclude American Jewish servicemen from the air base. | | | The UN General Assembly adopts a resolution by a vote of 74–2 (France and Israel oppose) calling for Israeli withdrawal from Gaza and Sharm es-Sheikh.

President Dwight D. Eisenhower* again writes David Ben-Gurion, saying continued disregard of UN resolutions would damage relations between Israel and the U.S., and U.S. Secretary of State John Foster Dulles* declares that the U.S. would give "serious consideration" to applying sanctions against Israel. | Philip Friedman (1901–1960), Polish Jewish historian, writes *Their Brothers' Keepers*, a history of non-Jews who saved Jewish lives during the Nazi occupation of Europe.

Gerald Reitlinger, English historian, writes *The SS: Alibi of a Nation, 1922–1945*, a detailed examination of the SS and the part they played in the Nazi extermination of Europe's Jews.

Jacob Presser (1899–1970), Dutch | **Feb. 1957** |

A. General History	B. Jews in North and South America	C. Jews in Europe	D. Jews in the Middle East and Elsewhere	E. Jewish Culture
Feb. 1957			John Foster Dulles* sends Israel a memo outlining the U.S. position. The U.S. believes the UN Emergency Force (UNEF) should be stationed in Gaza, as the strip "has been a source of armed infiltration and reprisals," the UNEF should be stationed at Sharm es-Sheikh, the U.S. assumes no littoral state (Egypt, Jordan, or Saudi Arabia) would "obstruct the right of free and innocent passage" to the Gulf of Aqaba, and the U.S. would publicly use its influence to implement these measures following an Israeli withdrawal. Senate Majority Leader Lyndon Johnson* writes John Foster Dulles* of the opposition to "coercion" in American relations with Israel. Previously, the Republican Senate leader, William Knowland,* opposed applying sanctions against Israel, as sanctions had not been imposed on the Soviet Union for its military intervention in Hungary. President Dwight D. Eisenhower,* in a nationwide radio and television speech, insists on an unconditional Israeli withdrawal from Gaza and Sharm es-Sheikh. John Foster Dulles* meets with eight U.S. non-Zionist Jewish leaders at his invitation to express U.S. views on a request for Israeli withdrawal. The group is unanimous in supporting Israel's request for "reasonable assurances" prior to withdrawing	writer and historian, writes The Breaking Point, a novel about Jewish life in the concentration camp at Westerbork. He relies on the then still unpublished diaries of Etty Hillesum, to which he had access, as he had never been in the camp. Yitzhak Ben-Zvi, Israel's second president, writes The Exiled and the Redeemed, a history of Jews in Oriental lands, many of whom emigrated to Israel, and of ancient Jewish communities of which there is scant knowledge. A. B. Yehoshua (b. 1936), Israeli novelist, short-story writer, and playwright, writes his first story, "Mot ha-Zaken" ("Death of an Old Man"), which will typify his style of writing allegorical tales with a political and cultural awareness. Yigael Yadin, Israeli archaeologist and soldier, writes The Message of the Scrolls, a description of the Dead Sea Scrolls, whose significance was first recognized by his father, Eliezer Sukenik. Yad Vashem, the Martyrs' and Heroes' Authority of Israel, begins publication of Yad Vashem Studies in English. Paul Ben-Haim (1897–1984), composer who emigrated to Palestine from Germany in 1933, wins the Israel Prize for his symphonic movement Sweet Psalmist of Israel. The Fredric Mann Auditorium in Tel Aviv is opened as the

A. General History	B. Jews in North and South America	C. Jews in Europe	D. Jews in the Middle East and Elsewhere	E. Jewish Culture	
			from Gaza and Sharm es-Sheikh.	new home of the Israel Philharmonic Orchestra.	**Feb. 1957**
			UN Secretary-General Dag Hammarskjold* advises Israel that any proposal to evacuate the UN Emergency Force (UNEF) from Gaza or Sharm es-Sheikh must first be submitted to a special General Assembly committee. U.S. Secretary of State John Foster Dulles* informs President Dwight D. Eisenhower* that Israel had been assured that a purpose of the UNEF would be to restrain the exercise of belligerent rights that would prevent passage through the Straits of Tiran.		
The Suez Canal reopens after clearance by the UN salvage crews of hulks sunk there by the Egyptians during the Suez crisis.			Georges Picot,* France's UN ambassador, addresses the Security Council. France recognizes Israel's right to free passage through the Straits of Tiran. Any interference would fully entitle Israel to use its inherent right of self-defense.		**Mar. 1957**

D. Jews in the Middle East and Elsewhere

Israeli Foreign Minister Golda Meir makes a statement to the UN General Assembly that was jointly drafted by U.S. and Israeli officials and personally approved by John Foster Dulles.* Israel would complete withdrawal from the Sinai on certain "assumptions": The UN Emergency Force would remain in the Sinai and Gaza until a peace accord is reached, fedayeen raids would cease, and the Straits of Tiran would reopen. Repetition of fedayeen raids or interference with free passage through the straits would be regarded as an attack entitling Israel to exercise its inherent right of self defense.

President Dwight D. Eisenhower* writes Prime Minister David Ben-Gurion that "Israel will have no cause to regret" its decision to withdraw, and the U.S. would "seek that [Israel's] hopes prove not to be in vain."

The last Israeli troops leave Sharm es-Sheikh and Gaza.

Israel Kastner, former leader of wartime Hungarian Jewry who settled in Israel and was accused of collaborating with the Nazis, is assassinated in Tel Aviv.

A. General History	B. Jews in North and South America	C. Jews in Europe	D. Jews in the Middle East and Elsewhere	E. Jewish Culture	
Jordan's King Hussein* dismisses a leftist-oriented government influenced by Egypt.			The U.S. tanker *Kern Hills* arrives at the Israeli port of Eilat in the Gulf of Aqaba with a cargo of oil from Iran. The tanker's passage		**Apr. 1957**

	A. General History	B. Jews in North and South America	C. Jews in Europe	D. Jews in the Middle East and Elsewhere	E. Jewish Culture
Apr. 1957	The U.S. sends the Sixth Fleet to the eastern Mediterranean as a gesture of support to Hussein.*			fulfills the U.S. pledge to Israel to establish the right of passage in the Gulf of Aqaba.	
May 1957				Jordanian forces kill four Israeli policemen and a UN truce supervisor, Lieutenant Colonel George A. Flint,* in the Scopus area. Throughout the year, there is tension with Jordan over that Israeli enclave.	
June 1957	By the end of June, 174,277 refugees from Hungary have arrived in Austria since November 1956; 33,542 (including 3,926 assisted by HIAS) were resettled in the U.S.			By the end of June, 20,000 Jewish refugees from Egypt, 40% of Egyptian Jewry, have arrived in Europe since November 1956; by March 21, 1957, Israel had admitted 7,500 of these refugees; by the end of June, 24 gain admission to the U.S.	
July 1957			Nikita Khrushchev* achieves the ouster of V. M. Molotov,* Georgi M. Malenkov,* Dmitri P. Shepilov,* and Lazar Kaganovich (1894–1991) from the Soviet Politburo. Kaganovich is the last Jew among the party leadership.	It is announced that the late James de Rothschild (1878–1957) of London bequeathed 6 million pounds for the construction of a permanent home for the Knesset in Jerusalem and that Joseph Klarwein (1893–1970) has won the architectural competition for the design of the building.	
Aug. 1957	Syria expels four U.S. diplomats on charges they were conspiring to overthrow the government. The U.S. expels the Syrian ambassador to the U.S. and one of his assistants. The U.S. Congress enacts the Civil Rights Act. It is designed to assure voting rights for blacks and other minorities. President Dwight D. Eisenhower* establishes the Civil Rights Commission.		The first Dutch Liberal synagogue is opened in Amsterdam.		

A. General History	B. Jews in North and South America	C. Jews in Europe	D. Jews in the Middle East and Elsewhere	E. Jewish Culture
Governor Orval Faubus* of Arkansas calls out the state National Guard to prevent integration at Little Rock's Central High School. President Dwight D. Eisenhower* sends federal troops to enforce the court-ordered desegregation, and nine black students enter the school.				**Sep. 1957**
The Soviet Union launches *Sputnik*, the first man-made satellite to orbit the earth. The Soviet feat astonishes the Western world.		Soviet leader Nikita Khrushchev,* in a conversation with Eleanor Roosevelt,* admits it is difficult for a Soviet Jew to emigrate or even visit Israel. He adds: "If Israel continues her present policy she will be destroyed." Professor Carl Ludwig's* report to the Swiss Parliament on the country's policy toward refugees maintains that thousands of refugees from Nazism, particularly Jews, had been shut out between 1933 and the war's end because of rigid rules of asylum.	A new Israeli immigrant with grievances against the authorities throws a hand grenade onto the floor of the Knesset from the public gallery, wounding Prime Minister David Ben-Gurion, Foreign Minister Golda Meir, and several other ministers. Israeli President Yitzhak Ben-Zvi begins his second five-year term of office.	**Oct. 1957**
	A bomb is discovered outside Temple Beth-El in Charlotte, North Carolina. At its convention, the United Synagogue of America, the lay arm of the Conservative movement, adopts a set of standards for synagogue practice. *Kashrut* and Sabbath observance are basic tenets of the Conservative movement. Synagogue laity are to recognize the congregation rabbi as the authority on all matters of Jewish law and practice and the interpreter of decisions and principles established by the Rabbinical Assembly.			**Nov. 1957**

	A. General History	B. Jews in North and South America	C. Jews in Europe	D. Jews in the Middle East and Elsewhere	E. Jewish Culture
1958		Congress enacts the Humane Methods of Livestock Slaughter Act. It declares Jewish ritual slaughter (*shehitah*) to be humane. Karl Arnstein, designer of the U.S. dirigibles *Los Angeles* and *Akron*, receives the U.S. Navy Distinguished Public Service Award. Herman Wouk's best-selling novel *Marjorie Morningstar* is adapted to the screen. The film preserves the novel's ethnic integrity by including a bar mitzvah scene in a synagogue and a Passover seder service in a New York City apartment.	Jews' College of London, England, is reorganized under the direction of Rabbi Isidore Epstein as a seminary for the training of rabbis and cantors, with an affiliated teacher's institute. Sir Charles Percy Snow,* English novelist, writes *The Conscience of the Rich*, the seventh in a series of novels chronicling English life. This volume is devoted to the affairs of a wealthy Jewish family.		Bernard Malamud, U.S. writer of short stories and novelist, publishes *The Magic Barrel*, a collection of stories that receives the National Book Award. In 1963, he will publish *Idiots First* and, in 1973, *Rembrandt's Hat*, additional collections of his stories, many of which are on Jewish themes. Marshall Sklare (1921–1992), U.S. sociologist, edits *Jews: Social Patterns of an American Group.* *Hasidism and Modern Man*, an interpretation of Hasidism by Martin Buber, noted philosopher, is edited and translated into English from the German by Maurice Friedman.
Jan. 1958				Israel's Supreme Court overturns a 1955 lower court ruling in the Israel Kastner (1906–1957) case. The court clears Kastner's name and rules he had been criminally libeled by Malkiel Gruenwald.	Harry Golden (1902–1981), U.S. journalist, writes *Only in America*, a best-selling collection of his essays that appeared in his newspaper, *The Carolina Israelite*. He began publishing the *Israelite* in 1941, a 16-page tabloid that appeared six times a year. By 1963 it will have 45,000 paid subscribers. Later essay collections will also be best-sellers. They include *For 2 Cents Plain* (1959), *Enjoy, Enjoy!* (1960), *You're Entitled* (1962), and *So, What Else Is New?* (1964).
Feb. 1958	In an effort to become the dominant force in the Middle East, Egypt and Syria establish the United Arab Republic, with Yemen joining as a partner.	A bomb is discovered at the entrance to Temple Emanu-El of Gastonia, North Carolina.			
Mar. 1958		A bomb explosion causes extensive damage to the school portion of Miami's Temple Beth-El. An anonymous caller threatens similar treatment to other advocates of integration. On the same day, Nashville's Jewish Community Center is extensively damaged by a bomb explosion.			Leon Uris (b. 1924), U.S. novelist, writes *Exodus*, a best-selling novel that becomes a source of popular knowledge about some of the events surrounding the birth of the State of Israel.
Apr. 1958	An insurrection, inspired by the United Arab Republic, threatens the pro-Western	A bomb explodes outside the Jewish Center of Jacksonville, Florida, damaging the	Soviet leader Nikita Khrushchev* tells Paris's *Figaro* that although the government	The new Jerusalem campus of the Hebrew University is opened on Givat Ram.	Karl Shapiro, U.S. poet, publishes his collection, *Poems of a Jew*. In 1945, he won the Pulitzer Prize for

548

A. General History	B. Jews in North and South America	C. Jews in Europe	D. Jews in the Middle East and Elsewhere	E. Jewish Culture	
government in Lebanon. In a month the fighting will spread to the streets of Beirut.	structure. An anonymous caller to a newspaper says, "Jews must be driven out of Florida except in Miami Beach. . . . The bombings will continue until segregation is restored everywhere in the South." The same day, a bomb is discovered at Birmingham, Alabama's, Temple Beth-El.	encouraged Jewish settlement in Birobidjan, it failed because of the historical Jewish predisposition to individual endeavors and their distaste of collective labor and group discipline. After publication, Moscow radio denies that Khrushchev* made the remarks.		*V-Letter and Other Poems.* Leonard Bernstein becomes the first American-born musician to be appointed music director and conductor of the New York Philharmonic Symphony Orchestra. He begins conducting nationally televised New York Philharmonic Young People's Concerts.	**Apr. 1958**
As a result of the Algerian crisis, General Charles de Gaulle* becomes premier of France and is given special powers by the French Parliament.		It is announced that the old Pinkas synagogue in Prague, dating to medieval times, will be restored as a memorial to the Jewish victims of Nazism; the names of 77,257 victims will be inscribed on its walls.	General Charles de Gaulle,* new premier of France, replies to David Ben-Gurion's message of congratulations. "I salute the courageous nation of Israel, with which France maintains solid ties of friendship and shares the same spiritual ideal."	The series, which will last until 1972, introduces great music to millions of new listeners. Itzhak Perlman (b. 1945), violinist and child prodigy, born in Tel Aviv, Israel, gains U.S. fame by appearing on Ed Sullivan's* television show.	**May 1958**
Imre Nagy,* head of the government at the time of the November 1956 Hungarian revolution, and four other leaders are executed after a secret trial. Miklos Gimes and Jozsef Szilagyi, two of those executed, are of Jewish origin.		The Austrian Parliament passes the War and Persecution Damages Law, which limits the indemnification of individuals to claimants with incomes less than $2,769 per year and only for the loss by individuals of household goods, tools, machines, and other possessions indispensable for the exercise of a profession or conduct of a business. The Jewish community expresses its disappointment with the legislation. Liuba Kishinevski, the last Jewish member of the Romanian Communist party leadership, is purged.	Tunisia's President Habib Bourguiba,* in an American television interview, states: "Tunisian Jews are completely assimilated with Tunisian Moslems. They have the same rights and the same duties. . . . They participated in the struggle; some of them were put in concentration camps along with us. Israel? I think that's a different question. We have made the Tunisian Jews citizens. But we have not recognized the State of Israel because we believe it was created by an act of violation and spoliation."	New York University renames its mathematics institute the Courant Institute of Mathematical Sciences in honor of Richard Courant. Courant fled from Germany in 1933 and is credited with the development of mathematical and mechanical theories that facilitated the practical use of electronic computers. The Solomon R. Guggenheim Museum, designed by Frank Lloyd Wright,* and named after the U.S. industrialist and philanthropist (1861–1949), opens in New York. Joshua Lederberg (b. 1925), U.S. geneticist, wins the Nobel Prize in physiology or medicine for his studies on the organization of genetic material in bacteria.	**June 1958**
An army officer's revolt overthrows Iraq's pro-Western regime. King Faisal II* and Premier Nuri es-Said* are murdered.			The Jewish Theological Seminary of America (Conservative) dedicates a student center in Jerusalem.	Joel Brand, a leader of the wartime Hungarian Jewish	**July 1958**

	A. General History	B. Jews in North and South America	C. Jews in Europe	D. Jews in the Middle East and Elsewhere	E. Jewish Culture
July 1958	Lebanon's President Camille Chamoun* appeals to the U.S., Britain, and France for military aid as a revolution in Iraq stirs renewed unrest in Lebanon. The next day, following the invocation of the Eisenhower Doctrine, U.S. troops arrive in Lebanon to protect it from a United Arab Republic or Communist invasion. King Hussein* of Jordan seeks military aid from Britain to withstand United Arab Republic and Communist threats after the revolt in Iraq. British paratroops land in Jordan and will remain there until October 29.				underground, writes *Desperate Mission*, in which he recounts his 1944 mission, made at the direction of Adolf Eichmann,* to present to the Jewish Agency a proposition of exchanging Hungarian Jews for supply trucks and other equipment to be furnished to the Germans. *Notes from the Warsaw Ghetto*, written during the Nazi occupation by Emanuel Ringelblum (1900–1944), historian of the Warsaw ghetto, is edited and translated by Jacob Sloan. The *Jewish Journal of Sociology* begins publication in England under the leadership of Morris Ginsberg and Maurice Freedman.
Aug. 1958	France begins to normalize relations with Egypt and other Middle Eastern countries that had severed ties with her.			Soviet newspapers publish a note from the Soviet Union that warned Israel of dangerous consequences if it permitted U.S. and British aircraft to fly over its territory to Jordan during the Iraqi revolution.	Arnold Wesker (b. 1932), English playwright, writes *Chicken Soup with Barley*, the first of three plays dealing with working-class Jewish life in England. The others of what will be known as the Wesker trilogy are *Roots* (1959) and *I'm Talking About Jerusalem* (1960).
Sep. 1958	The French electorate approves a new constitution for a Fifth French Republic proposed by General Charles de Gaulle,* and he is named president.				The Czech Jewish State Museum publishes A *Catalogue of Paintings of Jewish Children in the Theresienstadt Ghetto*.
Oct. 1958	The Soviet Union announces it will lend Egypt up to $100 million and furnish specialists for the construction of the Aswan Dam. The last of 14,300 U.S. troops leave Lebanon as the area is stabilized.	The school section of the leading Atlanta Reform synagogue, the Temple, is bombed. President Dwight D. Eisenhower* orders the FBI to assist the Atlanta police in its investigation of the incident.	Boris Pasternak (1890–1960), Soviet poet and novelist and apostate Jew, refuses to accept the Nobel Prize in literature. His novel *Dr. Zhivago* revealed his estrangement from Judaism. His refusal is prompted by intense internal political pressure.	The first of two submarines purchased by Israel from Great Britain is delivered. The second will be delivered in February 1959. An Israeli military court convicts eight border patrol policeman for the murder of 48 Israel Arabs at Kfar Kassim on October 29, 1956. They receive sentences ranging from 7 to 17 years.	Habimah, upon celebration of its 40th anniversary, is officially recognized as the Israel National Theater. Walter Eytan (b. 1910), Israeli diplomat who headed the 1949 delegations to the Rhodes armistice negotiations and to the Lausanne Conference with the

A. General History	B. Jews in North and South America	C. Jews in Europe	D. Jews in the Middle East and Elsewhere	E. Jewish Culture	
	The New York State Commission against Discrimination, relying on U.S. State Department advice, dismisses a complaint brought against the Arabian–American Oil Co. (ARAMCO) for failure to employ Jews at its installations in Saudi Arabia.			Arab states, writes *The First Ten Years: Diplomatic History of Israel*. An exhibition of archaeological discoveries made by the Hebrew University expedition in the biblical city of Hazor opens at the British Museum.	**Nov. 1958**
			Syrian forces shell and machine-gun six Israeli settlements along the border and kill a shepherd near Gonen. The firing is repeated on three more days. Israel complains to the UN Security Council.		**Dec. 1958**
George Lincoln Rockwell* founds the American Nazi party, with headquarters in Arlington, Virginia. Alaska and Hawaii are admitted to the Union as the 49th and 50th states. Polaris ballistic missiles are installed on U.S. atomic submarines.	Mr. and Mrs. Samuel Melton, of Columbus, Ohio, donate $180,000 to the Teachers Institute of the Jewish Theological Seminary of America for research in Jewish education. The gift is the largest ever made for such research. The informal group of presidents of 16 Zionist and non-Zionist American Jewish organizations is formally constituted as the Presidents' Conference. Philip M. Klutznick is president and Yehuda Hellman is executive director. Gerald Green's popular novel *The Last Angry Man* is adapted to the screen starring Paul Muni in the role of the doctor, Samuel Abelman. Muni plays a clearly well-rounded Jewish character, a dedicated old-world physician who is unable to adjust to a changing environment. Julio Meinvielle,* an Argentine Jesuit priest, writes *The Jew in the Mystery of History*, an antisemitic book accusing the Jews of advancing the	Venjamin Dymshyts, Soviet economist and engineer, becomes chairman of the State Planning Committee and deputy premier. He is the only Jew in the highest levels of the Soviet regime.		Albert I. Gordon, U.S. rabbi, writes *Jews in Suburbia*, a sociological study based on an analysis of about 100 communities. Herman Wouk, well-known U.S. novelist, writes *This Is My God*, a description of Judaism and its practices from an Orthodox viewpoint. Dr. Nelson Glueck, noted archaeologist and Hebrew Union College president, writes *Rivers in the Desert: A History of the Negev*, in which he reconstructs the successive civilizations that flourished and died there over the centuries. Arthur Hertzberg, U.S. historian and rabbi, edits *The Zionist Idea: A Historical Analysis and Reader*, in which he presents the entire range of Zionist thought from the early 18th century to the present. Philip Roth (b. 1933), U.S. author, writes *Goodbye, Columbus*, a novella, and five short stories depicting contemporary Jewish	**1959**

	A. General History	B. Jews in North and South America	C. Jews in Europe	D. Jews in the Middle East and Elsewhere	E. Jewish Culture
1959		cause of Communism under the cloak of capitalism. It is very popular in Argentina. Meyer Levin's novel and play *Compulsion*, based on the Leopold and Loeb case of 1924, is adapted to the screen. The film ignores the characters' Jewishness and self-hatred.			life in suburban New Jersey and New York. It wins him a National Book Award and a Jewish Book Council Award. However, some in the Jewish community believe his satire to be antisemitic and self-hating. It will be adapted to the screen in 1969. Moss Hart writes his best-selling autobiography, *Act One*. As a playwright, his collaborations with George S. Kaufman include *You Can't Take It with You*. He directed the award-winning musical *My Fair Lady* and wrote the screenplay for the award-winning *Gentleman's Agreement*.
Jan. 1959	The Cuban dictatorship of Fulgencio Batista* ends and Cuba comes under the leadership of the revolutionary Fidel Castro.*		About 8,000 Romanian Jews emigrate to Israel. In late 1958, Romania permitted emigration and about 120,000 out of an estimated 220,000 Jews registered to do so. In March 1959, Romania again will stop emigration, after about 15,000 Jews leave for Israel. Many Jews are prosecuted for "illegal Zionist activities."	There are seven additional Syrian attacks along the Israeli–Syrian border. Israel appeals to the UN Security Council, which takes no action.	Delmore Schwartz, U.S. poet and literary critic, publishes a volume of collected poetry, *Summer Knowledge*, which includes poems on biblical themes. He wins the 1960 Bollingen Prize.
Feb. 1959	Great Britain agrees to surrender its control of the island of Cyprus, which is to become an independent republic. Greece and Greek Cypriots give up their demand for the union of the island with Greece, and Turkey and the Turkish Cypriots give up their demand for the partition of the island between Greece and Turkey.			Egypt resumes its pre-1957 practice of searching foreign ships for cargoes originating in or bound for Israel and confiscating such goods.	Paddy Chayevsky (1923–1981), U.S. playwright and screenwriter, writes *The Tenth Man*. He revives the legend of the Dybbuk, setting his story in the Bronx. Irving Berlin composes "Israel," a song that reflects his emotional attachment to the State of Israel.
Mar. 1959	The U.S. signs separate defense treaties with Iran, Turkey, and Pakistan to assure these Baghdad Pact nations that the U.S. would support them in the face of Communist aggression.		Pope John XXIII declares that the phrase *pro perfidis Judaeis* be deleted from the Good Friday service. This prayer, translated in the American Catholic Missal as "let us pray for the unbelieving Jews," was susceptible of even more derogatory interpretations.		*Six Characters in Search of an Author*, an opera composed by Hugo Weisgall, is produced by the New York City Opera to acclaim. He will become chairman of the faculty of the Cantors Institute of the Jewish Theological Seminary of America and professor of music at Queens College.
May 1959				Egypt detains the Danish freighter *Inge Toft* in the Suez Canal, refusing to permit the passage of	Arthur Kornberg, U.S. biochemist, is

A. General History	B. Jews in North and South America	C. Jews in Europe	D. Jews in the Middle East and Elsewhere	E. Jewish Culture	
			vessels carrying Israeli cargo. B'nai B'rith holds its convention in Jerusalem. It is the first time in its 116-year history that it holds a convention outside the U.S. The International Court at The Hague decides that it has no jurisdiction over Israel's claim for damages resulting from the shooting down of an El Al airliner over Bulgaria in July 1955.	awarded the Nobel Prize in physiology or medicine for his synthesis of DNA in a cell-free preparation. Emilio Segre, U.S. nuclear physicist, is awarded the Nobel Prize in physics for his research in the elementary particle, the antiproton. Segre left Italy for the U.S. in 1938 when racial legislation was enacted. Sir Jacob Epstein (1880–1959), one of the greatest sculptors of the 20th century and who was knighted in 1954, sculpts *Saint Michael Killing the Devil* for England's Coventry Cathedral.	**May 1959**
			UN Secretary-General Dag Hammarskjold* publishes a report emphasizing economic measures necessary for the integration of the refugees in the Middle East. The Arabs agree to the extension of the UN Relief and Works Agency but reject any measure that might be construed as an abandonment of their repatriation demand. A German magazine, *Der Spiegel*, reports that Israel is to manufacture small arms for the West German army. This disclosure causes a cabinet crisis, with some ministers calling for the cancellation of the deal. A majority upholds the sale.	Immanuel Jakobovits (b. 1921), English rabbi, writes *Jewish Medical Ethics: A Comparative and Historical Study of the Jewish Religious Attitude to Medicine and Its Practice.* Cecil Roth, British Jewish historian, writes *The Jews in the Renaissance*, a study of the contributions of the Jews in Italy to the Renaissance. *Hellenistic Civilization and the Jews*, written by Victor Tcherikover (1894–1958), Israeli historian, is published in English translation.	**June 1959**
			Moroccan and other Middle Eastern immigrants to Israel riot in Haifa, Beersheba, and Migdal Ha'emek as a result of housing and employment discrimination. Israel signs an agreement with a group of international investors headed by Baron Edmond de Rothschild to construct a 16-inch oil pipeline from Eilat to Haifa.	Marc Chagall (1887–1985) completes his first stained glass window at the Metz cathedral. The set of windows, based on biblical themes, is completed in 1963. André Schwarz-Bart's novel *The Last of the Just* is awarded France's Goncourt Prize. It traces Jewish martyrdom through 36 generations of the Levy family, ending	**July 1959**

	A. General History	B. Jews in North and South America	C. Jews in Europe	D. Jews in the Middle East and Elsewhere	E. Jewish Culture
Sep. 1959	Nikita Khrushchev* is the first Soviet leader to visit the U.S. He discusses disarmament and the exchange of scientists and cultural figures with President Dwight D. Eisenhower.*				with the death of Ernie at Auschwitz. It is a reflection on Schwarz-Bart's personal tragedy and a poetic meditation on Jewish fate throughout the ages. In 1960, it will appear in English translation.
Oct. 1959	When Iraq withdraws from the Baghdad Pact, the remaining members, Britain, Turkey, Pakistan, and Iran, rename the alliance the Central Treaty Organization.				Primo Levi's (1919–1987) *If This Is a Man*, a first hand account of the horrors of Auschwitz, appears in English translation from the Italian 1947 edition. A writer and chemist, in 1963, Levi will write *The Reawakening*, in which he describes his long journey home to Turin after being liberated from the camp by Soviet soldiers. In 1984, he will write *The Periodic Table*, a third autobiographical volume.
Nov. 1959				Israel holds national elections for the Fourth Knesset, with 969,337 votes cast. Mapai wins 47 seats; Herut, 17 seats; Ahdut ha-Avodah, 7 seats; Mapam, 9 seats; and the National Religious party, 12 seats. The government is installed on December 17, with David Ben-Gurion as prime minister and minister of defense, and Golda Meir as minister of foreign affairs. The National Yiddish Theater of Poland, headed by Ida Kaminska, begins a six-week tour of Israel.	Leon Dujovne (1899–1983), Argentine philosopher, writes *Theory of the Values and Philosophy of History*, which is awarded the first National Prize for philosophy in Argentina. Active in Jewish affairs, he will collaborate in a translation of the Bible into Spanish in 1961 and write *Judaism as Culture* in 1980.
Dec. 1959			On Christmas Eve, two 25-year-old Germans defile the synagogue in Cologne with swastikas and the slogan "Jews get out." Their act sets off a rash of similiar incidents in West Germany and throughout the world.		Slovakian-born Israeli scholar Yehezkel Kutscher (1909–1971), a leading Hebraist and Aramaist, publishes a monumental study in Hebrew of the language of the complete Isaiah scroll from Qumran, showing how its deviations from the Masoretic text reflect the contemporary Hebrew of the Roman period. In 1960 Kutscher will be appointed professor at the Hebrew

A. General History	B. Jews in North and South America	C. Jews in Europe	D. Jews in the Middle East and Elsewhere	E. Jewish Culture	
				University and receive an Israel Prize for his research.	**Dec. 1959**
				Mordecai Richler (b. 1931), Canadian novelist, writes *The Apprenticeship of Duddy Kravitz*, the portrayal of a Jewish boy who creates a financial empire through ruthless manipulation and cunning. Some critics denounce the novel as an example of Richler's Jewish self-hatred, whereas others praise it as an accurate satire of today's society at large. It will be adapted to the screen in 1974, starring Richard Dreyfuss as Duddy.	
Sixteen newly independent African countries join the UN, and the General Assembly adopts the Declaration on the Granting of Independence to Colonial Countries and Peoples.	The Law Committee of the Rabbinical Assembly, the organization of U.S. Conservative rabbis, votes to permit the use of electricity on the Sabbath and to permit travel by car, bus, or train to the synagogue for the purpose of attending Sabbath services. William L. Shirer* (b. 1904), U.S. foreign correspondent, writes *The Rise and Fall of the Third Reich*. Otto Preminger directs *Exodus*, a film (based on Leon Uris' best-selling novel) that is a huge box-office success and lends a sense of grandeur to the experience of the creation of Israel. It stars Paul Newman.	Ilya Ehrenburg, veteran Communist writer, publishes a series of articles in the Moscow magazine *Novye Mir* (*Men, Years, Life*) about his youth and life in Paris before World War I. He gives much space to Jewish themes, which is interpreted as a plea to the Soviet intelligentsia to do something about the plight of Soviet Jews.		Rabbi David de Sola Pool (1885–1970), U.S. Orthodox rabbi, edits and translates into English a new edition of the Ashkenazi Orthodox prayer book, *Siddur: The Traditional Prayer Book for Sabbath and Festivals*. It was authorized by the Rabbinical Council of America. Edgar Rosenberg writes *From Shylock to Svengali: Jewish Stereotypes in English Fiction*. *Felix Frankfurter Reminiscences* is published. These recorded talks with Harlan B. Phillips* discuss aspects of the life of the U.S. Supreme Court justice. Isaac Bashevis Singer, Polish-born author of Yiddish fiction, writes *The Magician of Lublin*, a novel of early Polish Jewish life.	**1960**
Construction of Egypt's Aswan Dam begins. The Soviet Union affirms that it will see this enormous project through to completion.				Bruno Bettelheim, who was an inmate at Dachau and Buchenwald in 1938 before emigrating to	**Jan. 1960**

555

	A. General History	B. Jews in North and South America	C. Jews in Europe	D. Jews in the Middle East and Elsewhere	E. Jewish Culture
Feb. 1960				The Danish ship *Inge Toft*, which had been detained by Egypt in the Suez Canal in May 1959, returns to Haifa, after her Israeli cargo is confiscated. The U.S. Navy announces elimination of the Haifa Clause from its contracts with oil-carrying cargo vessels. This clause, in effect since the spring of 1958, permitted the navy to cancel a contract with an oil-carrying cargo ship if the Arabs refused to accommodate the vessel. Its effect was to prevent U.S. shipowners doing business with Israel from bidding for the navy's cargo shipping.	the U.S., writes *The Informed Heart*, a book of essays and reviews that includes criticism of the Jewish masses for failing to revolt against the "final solution." Frederick Loewe writes the music and Alan Jay Lerner, the lyrics for *Camelot*, a Broadway musical based on the Arthurian legend. Donald A. Glaser, U.S. physicist, is awarded the Nobel Prize in physics, for his design of the bubble chamber, an indispensable research tool in nuclear physics.
Mar. 1960				Israeli Prime Minister David Ben-Gurion visits the U.S., where he has a private visit with President Dwight D. Eisenhower.* The Arab states object to the meeting.	Erik Homberger Erikson, psychoanalyst who emigrated to the U.S. from Germany in 1933, is appointed professor of human development and psychiatry at Harvard University.
Apr. 1960				The Seafarers International Union and the International Longshoremen's Association begin picketing the Egyptian vessel *Cleopatra* when it docks in New York, declaring that the Arab boycott of U.S. ships trading with Israel threatens job opportunities for U.S. seamen. The court challenges to the picketing are unsuccessful. In May, when the U.S. State Department will issue a statement deploring the Arab boycott and affirm freedom of seas, the picket lines will be lifted.	An English version of *Night*, a novel in autobiographical mode by Elie Wiesel (b. 1928), describes his experiences at Auschwitz. Wiesel, the sole survivor of a Hungarian Jewish family, wrote the book in Yiddish in 1956 at the suggestion of François Mauriac,* French Catholic writer, whom he met in France. Two succeeding memoir-novels, *Dawn* (1961) and *The Accident* (1962), complete the trilogy. Harold Pinter (b. 1930), British dramatist, writes *The Caretaker*, a play that establishes his reputation. Its central theme is how to maintain an identity in a world that demands conformity
May 1960	A U.S. U-2 spy plane is shot down over Soviet territory, and Soviet leader Nikita Khrushchev* cancels a planned meeting in			Adolf Eichmann,* Nazi SS officer, is abducted from Buenos Aires, Argentina, by Israeli agents and flown to Israel to	

A. General History	B. Jews in North and South America	C. Jews in Europe	D. Jews in the Middle East and Elsewhere	E. Jewish Culture	
Paris with President Dwight D. Eisenhower.*			stand trial for crimes against the Jewish people. Argentina complains to the UN Security Council, where Israel expresses regret for violation of Argentine law. For the first time since 1948, the U.S. and the USSR both support Israel. A *Washington Post* editorial opposes a trial of Adolf Eichmann* in Israel and charges that everything about the proceeding is "tainted by lawlessness." The abduction violated international law; the crimes were committed not in Israel but in Germany and Austria. Israel could try Eichmann only under ex post facto statutes, and Israel has no authority to speak for Jews elsewhere or in the name of "some imaginary Jewish ethnic entity."	as the price of survival. He will be considered England's foremost postwar playwright. Synagoga, an exhibit of Jewish ritual objects, manuscripts, and works of art, is opened in the Recklinghausen Museum by West German President Heinrich Lübke.* The exhibit was compiled by Israeli and West German scholars, with many objects lent by European Jewish and Israeli museums. Mikhail Tal, Soviet chess master, wins the world championship by defeating fellow countryman, Mikhail Botvinnik. Dov Joseph, who was military governor of Jerusalem during the War of Independence, writes *The Faithful City*, describing the siege of Jerusalem in 1948.	**May 1960**
			A *New York Times* editorial urges that Adolf Eichmann* be tried by an international tribunal "for it was not against Israel but against humanity that his crimes were committed. . . . A clear violation of Argentine sovereignty and of international law . . . that cannot be condoned irrespective of the heinousness of Eichmann's crimes. . . . The rule of law must protect the most depraved of criminals if it is also to stand as a bulwark against the victimization of the innocent."	Yehezkel Kaufmann's *The Religion of Israel: From Its Beginnings to the Babylonian Exile* appears in an English abridged edition. Billy Rose (1899–1966), U.S. show business entrepreneur, announces the gift of his million dollar collection of modern sculpture to the Israel National Museum in Jerusalem. An archaeological expedition led by Yigael Yadin discovers in Judean desert caves 14 letters, one on wood and the rest on	**June 1960**
In July, a UN peace-keeping force is dispatched to the Congo.			The Israeli air force buys its first Fouga Magister jet training plane assembled in Israel under license from a French aircraft	papyrus, by Simon Bar-Kokhba, leader of the Jewish revolt against the Romans in 132 BCE–35 CE. Bar-Kokhba is called	**July 1960**

	A. General History	B. Jews in North and South America	C. Jews in Europe	D. Jews in the Middle East and Elsewhere	E. Jewish Culture
July 1960				manufacturer. All parts of the plane, except the engine and instruments, are of local make.	Shimon ben Kosiba in the letters.

July 1960

D. Jews in the Middle East and Elsewhere

The party platform adopted at the Democratic National Convention includes encouragement of "direct Arab-Israeli peace negotiations, the resettlement of Arab refugees in lands where there is room and opportunity for them, an end to boycotts and blockades, and unrestricted use of the Suez Canal by all nations."

The party platform adopted at the Republican National Convention pledges continued efforts "to eliminate the obstacles to a lasting peace in the area, including the human problem of the Arab refugees; to seek an end to transit and trade restrictions, blockades and boycotts; to secure freedom of navigation in international waterways."

Egypt breaks off diplomatic relations with Iran after the Shah reiterates Iran's de facto recognition of Israel.

Aug. 1960

Democratic presidential candidate John F. Kennedy,* who stated to the national convention of the Zionist Organization of America, "friendship for Israel is not a partisan matter, it is a national commitment," proposes a three-point Middle East program: (1) declaration of friendship for all peoples in the Middle East; (2) reaffirmation of the Tripartite Declaration of 1950, and (3) the use of White House authority to convene a private meeting of Arab and Israeli leaders to consider their common problems.

Republican presidential candidate Richard M. Nixon* declares "the preservation of the state of Israel is what I regard as one of the essential goals of United States foreign policy."

	A. General History	B. Jews in North and South America	C. Jews in Europe	D. Jews in the Middle East and Elsewhere	E. Jewish Culture
Sep. 1960	In a Houston, Texas, speech before Protestant ministers, Democratic presidential candidate John F. Kennedy,* a Catholic, reaffirms his belief in the separation of church and state: "I believe in an America that is officially neither Catholic, Protestant, nor Jewish—where no public official either requests or accepts instructions on public policy from the Pope, the National Council of Churches, or any other ecclesiastical source . . . and where religious liberty is so indivisible that an act against one church is treated as an act against all." U.S. presidential candidates Richard M. Nixon* and John F. Kennedy* meet in the first televised debates. The Organization of Petroleum Exporting			In an address to the UN General Assembly, Egypt's Gamal Abdel Nasser* states: "The only solution to Palestine is that matters should return to the condition prevailing before the error was committed—i.e., the annulment of Israel's existence." Nasser,* along with Nehru* of India and Tito* of Yugoslavia, become leading Third World spokesmen at the UN. A governmental committee created to review new evidence in the Lavon Affair clears Pinhas Lavon of responsibility for the collapse of an Israeli intelligence network in Egypt in 1954. Prime Minister David Ben-Gurion refuses to accept the verdict and demands that his government choose between him and Lavon. In February	

A. General History	B. Jews in North and South America	C. Jews in Europe	D. Jews in the Middle East and Elsewhere	E. Jewish Culture	
Countries is formed by Venezuela, Iran, Iraq, Saudi Arabia, and Kuwait.			1961, Lavon will be dismissed from his post of secretary-general of Histadrut, a post he has held since September 1956. However, in January 1961, Ben-Gurion will tender his resignation, and in March, the Knesset decides to hold general elections on August 15.		**Sep. 1960**
The Democratic Kennedy*–Johnson* ticket wins a close election defeating the Republican Nixon*–Lodge* ticket with 50.1% of the major party vote. Both houses of Congress remain Democratic. Kennedy* is the first Catholic president. French President Charles de Gaulle* speaks of an "Algerian republic [which] will some day exist," thus ruling out Algeria's integration into France.	The Jewish vote in the presidential election is estimated at 82% for John F. Kennedy* and 18% for Richard M. Nixon.*				**Nov. 1960**

D. Jews in the Middle East and Elsewhere

Dec. 1960

The Central Intelligence Agency and the State Department brief the U.S. Senate Joint Committee on Atomic Energy on the Israeli construction in the Negev of a nuclear reactor capable of weapons production.

A mob of Algerian FLN (National Liberation Front) Muslims loots the Great Synagogue of Algiers.

David Ben-Gurion addresses the 25th World Zionist Congress in Jerusalem, stating that immigration is the central problem of the State of Israel and that, according to a talmudic precept, Orthodox Jews remaining in the Diaspora are violating a religious commandment. His speech arouses considerable resentment among American Jews, Zionist and non-Zionist, who believe Jews could be fully observant in the Diaspora.

A. General History	B. Jews in North and South America	C. Jews in Europe	D. Jews in the Middle East and Elsewhere	E. Jewish Culture	
	By the first half of the year, an estimated 5,000 of 11,000 Jews living in Cuba at the time Fidel Castro* came to power emigrate. Thirty-five hundred go to the U.S., and others go to Israel, other Latin American countries, and Canada. Stanley Kramer directs *Judgment at Nuremberg*, a film about the war crimes trials held in	The first trial held in the Soviet Union pursuant to legislation enacted to fight economic crimes involves two Jewish defendants, Rokotov and Faibishevich. During the next two years, about 56 trials are held, and 111 defendants (60% of them Jews) are sentenced to death.	Wolfgang Lutz, a "German businessman," arrives in Egypt and for the next 3½ years transmits to Israel intelligence on the Egyptian rocket program being developed by German scientists. The son of a German mother and Jewish father, he will be caught, sentenced to life imprisonment, and in 1968	Charles Bezalel Sherman (d. 1970), U.S. sociologist, writes *The Jew Within American Society*, a study in ethnic individuality. Ben Halpern, U.S. sociologist, writes *The Idea of the Jewish State*, a study of the background and rise of Zionism and its effect on Jews and Jewish organizations throughout the world.	**1961**

	A. General History	B. Jews in North and South America	C. Jews in Europe	D. Jews in the Middle East and Elsewhere	E. Jewish Culture
1961		postwar Germany, which reflects on the question of German guilt. The movie shows documentary films of the liberation of Buchenwald and its victims.		exchanged for nine Egyptian generals captured in the Six-Day War. The Israel Academy of Sciences and the Humanities is established in Jerusalem through the adoption of a law by the Israeli Knesset. Its function is to advise the government in sciences and humanities and to represent Israel at international conferences.	Joseph Heller (b. 1923), U.S. novelist, writes *Catch-22*, a satire on military illogicality. Edward Lewis Wallant (1926–1962), U.S. novelist, writes *The Pawnbroker*, a novel dealing with the memories and present life of Sol Nazerman, a Harlem pawnbroker who was a respected teacher in Poland and whose wife and children were murdered by the Nazis. In 1965, it will be adapted to the screen, starring Rod Steiger (b. 1925). Ben Hecht, U.S. journalist, novelist, and playwright, writes *Perfidy*, an attack on those he believes made compromises in the struggle to create the State of Israel.
Jan. 1961	The French electorate overwhelmingly endorses by referendum President Charles de Gaulle's* proposal to grant self-determination to Algeria. Patrice Lumumba,* leader of the Congo, is assassinated, becoming a martyr in the eyes of the Third World.				
Feb. 1961				Moroccan King Mohammed V* dies and the country's 160,000 Jews publicly participate in the mourning of this Arab sovereign. He is succeeded by Crown Prince Hassan.* In 1942, Mohammad V* had refused to permit the application of anti-Jewish measures of the Petain Vichy government, although Morocco was then a French protectorate.	Allen Ginsberg, U.S. poet, writes *Kaddish and Other Poems*. The title poem is a moving lament for his recently deceased mother. Leon Uris, U.S. novelist, writes *Mila 18*, a novel about the 1943 uprising of the Jews in the Warsaw ghetto. Raul Hilberg, U.S. historian, writes *The Destruction of the European Jews*, based on the first detailed study of German documents on the Holocaust. His criticism of Jewish passivity, i.e., an almost complete lack of resistance to the implementation of the "final solution," will arouse controversy, but he will maintain this view in his revised edition, published in 1985. The sculptor Jacques Lipchitz donates 300 original castings of his
Mar. 1961	Saudi Arabia announces it will not renew its five-year agreement, due to expire on April 1, 1962, with the U.S. under which the U.S. maintains a military base at Dhahran. The great South African treason trial, which had received wide media attention throughout the second half of the 1950s, ends with the release of the accused. It	The New York Court of Appeals, the state's highest court, sends back to the State Commission on Discrimination the case of Arabian–American Oil Co.'s discrimination against American Jews, advising the state agency to "immediately endeavor to eliminate the unlawful employment practice complained of."		Israel Beer (1912–1966), a high-ranking member of David Ben-Gurion's ministry of defense, is arrested by the Israeli Secret Service and accused of treason for having passed Israeli secrets to Soviet agents. In June, at a closed trial, he will be found guilty of spying for the Soviet Union.	

A. General History	B. Jews in North and South America	C. Jews in Europe	D. Jews in the Middle East and Elsewhere	E. Jewish Culture	
involved 156 people of all races; 23 were white and more than half of them were Jews. The leading defense attorney was Israel Maisels, who is a leader in the Jewish community.				works to the Israel National Museum in Jerusalem, and the widow of Sir Jacob Epstein donates to the museum 200 original molds of his sculptures.	**Mar. 1961**
An attempted coup by French generals in Algeria to seize power and preserve Algeria for France fails.

Cuba crushes the Bay of Pigs invasion of Cuban exiles supported by the U.S. Central Intelligence Agency.

Yuri Gagarin*, a Soviet cosmonaut, is the first man successfully launched into space and to orbit the earth. | *Commentary* magazine publishes a symposium, with 31 participants, entitled "Jewishness and the Younger Intellectuals." Readers note a general attitude of detachment from the Jewish community. Milton Himmelfarb wrote, "Most of the symposiasts have a smattering of Jewish kitchen culture—a peculiar position for intellectuals to be in." | | The UN General Assembly adopts a resolution requesting the Palestine Conciliation Commission, consisting of the U.S., France, and Turkey, to implement a 1948 resolution regarding repatriation or resettlement of the Arab refugees.

The trial of Adolf Eichmann,* Nazi SS officer, for crimes against the Jewish people and humanity opens in the Jerusalem District Court before Presiding Judge Moses Landau of the Supreme Court of Israel and District Court Judges Benjamin Ha-levi and Isaac Raveh. Prosecuted by Gideon Hausner and defended by Robert Servatius,* Eichmann will be convicted and sentenced to death on December 15, 1961. On December 17 the defense will file an appeal. | Melvin Calvin, U.S. biochemist, is awarded the Nobel Prize in chemistry for his studies of photosynthesis.

Robert Hofstadter, U.S. physicist, is awarded the Nobel Prize in physics for his investigation of the structure of atomic nuclei and nucleons.

The first volume of Fritz Baer's two-volume work *History of Jews in Christian Spain* appears in English translation, and it is considered the standard history. Baer teaches at the Hebrew University in Jerusalem.

Jacob Katz, Israeli historian, writes *Tradition and Crisis: Jewish Society at the End of the Middle Ages*, a study of eastern and central European Jewish society and the attitude of the Jews toward the gentile world. | **Apr. 1961** |
| | | | | | |

Adolf Eichmann on trial in Jerusalem for crimes against the Jewish people and humanity. (Israel Government Press Office)

A. General History	B.	C.	D. Jews in the Middle East and Elsewhere	E. Jewish Culture	
The Republic of South Africa is established. Unwilling to accept a British Commonwealth resolution condemning racial discrimination, the new republic withdraws its application for membership.

The first American in space, Alan B. Shepard, Jr.,* reaches an altitude of 116.5 miles in a 15-minute rocket flight. | | | President John F. Kennedy* addresses individual letters to the heads of Arab states giving assurances of U.S. friendship and U.S. support for UN General Assembly resolutions on the Arab refugee problem. The letter is intended to allay Arab suspicion about the impending visit of David Ben-Gurion.

Israeli Prime Minister David Ben-Gurion has a private meeting with President Kennedy.* | Leonard Stein, British Zionist historian, writes *The Balfour Declaration*, a history based on first-hand accounts and including unpublished material.

Netanel Lorch's *The Edge of the Sword* appears in English translation from the Hebrew. It is a history of Israel's War of Independence.

Geza Vermes (b. 1924), English historian, writes *Scripture and Tradition in Judaism*, in which he outlines a | **May 1961** |

	A. General History	B. Jews in North and South America	C. Jews in Europe	D. Jews in the Middle East and Elsewhere	E. Jewish Culture
May 1961				The U.S. State Department later denies Ben-Gurion's statement that he found "a large measure of agreement" with the president on the Arab refugee problem.	tradition-historical approach to the study of *midrash*, which includes delineating how the exegesis of a specific biblical theme or passage developed in early Jewish literature. In 1965, he will succeed Cecil Roth as reader in Jewish studies at the University of Oxford.
June 1961	Kuwait gains its independence and ceases to be a British protectorate. It immediately asks Britain for military assistance in resisting Iraqi territorial claims. British troops will be replaced by Arab League forces in September.			El Al, the Israel airline, inaugurates the first nonstop service between New York and Tel Aviv. It is one of the world's longest scheduled nonstop commercial flights.	Cecil Roth, British Jewish historian, edits *Jewish Art, an Illustrated History*, first published in Hebrew in 1957. A revised English edition will be published in 1971.
July 1961		A new community of Hasidim is incorporated as New Square in Rockland County, New York. They are led by the Skvirer rebbe, Rabbi Joseph Jacob Twersky, originally from the Russian town of Skvir. They move to New Square from the Williamsburg section of Brooklyn.	The publication of a Yiddish periodical, *Sovetish Heymland*, under the editorship of party functionary Aron Vergelis, begins in the Soviet Union. Twenty-five thousand copies of the bimonthly magazine are printed.	Israel fires a rocket, *Shavit II*, which was planned and constructed by Israeli scientists. The rocket is described as a research instrument for the stratosphere and ionosphere. Three Republican U.S. senators (Kenneth Keating* and Jacob Javits of New York and Hugh Scott* of Pennsylvania) criticize President John F. Kennedy's* May letter to the heads of Arab states for his failure to mention resettlement as a solution to the Arab refugee problem. Israeli Prime Minister David Ben-Gurion and Upper Volta President Maurice Yameogo* announce a treaty of friendship between their nations and jointly state that the Africans, who form a majority of South Africa's population, have a fundamental right to respect for their dignity.	The orally administered polio vaccine developed by Albert Sabin, Russian-born microbiologist who came to the U.S. in 1921, begins to be widely used. As a consequence, the disease is almost totally eradicated. In 1970, he will become president of the Weizmann Institute of Science and settle in Israel. Brian Epstein (1934–1967), owner of a Liverpool, England, record shop, discovers the Beatles in the Cavern, a local nightclub. He shepherds them to worldwide prominence.
Aug. 1961	East Germany begins construction of the Berlin Wall.			Israel holds national elections for the Fifth Knesset, with 1,006,964 votes cast. Mapai wins 42 seats;	

A. General History	B. Jews in North and South America	C. Jews in Europe	D. Jews in the Middle East and Elsewhere	E. Jewish Culture
			Herut, 17 seats; Liberals, 17 seats; Ahdut ha-Avodah, 8 seats; Mapam, 9 seats; and the National Religious party, 12 seats. The government is installed on November 2, with David Ben-Gurion as prime minister and minister of defense, and Golda Meir as minister of foreign affairs.	**Aug. 1961**
UN Secretary-General Dag Hammarskjold* dies in an air crash while on a mission to the Congo. Anti-Egyptian opposition in Syria breaks up the United Arab Republic formed in February 1958.		Yevgeny Yevtushenko's* poem "Babi Yar" is published. Babi Yar is a ravine on the outskirts of Kiev where the Nazis had murdered over 30,000 Jews in September 1941. The poem denounces those who reject Jewish martyrdom and is a symbol of the opposition to the official and popular antisemitic climate in the Soviet Union. It arouses severe criticism in official literary circles and from Nikita Khrushchev,* the leader of the Soviet government.	On the second day of the Jewish New Year, in reprisal for the assassination by some Muslims of a Jew in the Jewish quarter of Oran, Jewish youths massacre numerous Muslims. The Algerian Jewish community quickly condemns the act.	**Sep. 1961**
Romania begins asserting its independence of the Soviet Union. Also, Albania, keeping faith with Stalinism, becomes estranged from the Soviet Union. The UN General Assembly censures South African Foreign Minister Eric Louw* for his speech defending apartheid. The Netherlands and Israel join the Afro-Asian states, the Soviet bloc, and some Latin American states in voting for the censure motion.		Three leaders of the Leningrad Jewish community and three leaders of the Moscow Jewish community are arrested, tried, and convicted of supplying information to a capitalist state embassy. All receive prison terms. Soviet press reports deny that Jews are being persecuted and accuse Israeli agents of involving them in espionage activities.	Prime Minister David Ben-Gurion addresses the Knesset, saying the proposal to give Arab refugees freedom of choice is calculated to destroy Israel; the refugees should be resettled among their own people in countries with good land and in need of manpower; Israel will assist in such resettlement, using its own experience. Israel's supreme rabbinical court rules there is no doubt concerning the Jewishness of the 5,000-member Bene Israel community from India.	**Oct. 1961**

	A. General History	B. Jews in North and South America	C. Jews in Europe	D. Jews in the Middle East and Elsewhere	E. Jewish Culture
Oct. 1961				Louis Isaac Rabinowitz, chief rabbi of Johannesburg's Orthodox United Hebrew Congregation for 16 years, leaves South Africa to settle in Israel.	
Dec. 1961			The World Council of Churches, representing over 200 Protestant and Orthodox denominations, condemns antisemitism as a sin against God and man. "In Christian teaching the historic events which led to the crucifixion should not be so presented as to fasten upon the Jewish people of today responsibilities which belong to our corporate humanity and not to one race or community." Anneke Beekman,* a Dutchwoman who as a child was entrusted by her Jewish parents to a Christian family for safekeeping during World War II, appears in public and expresses a desire to remain a Roman Catholic. Relatives of her deceased parents were frustrated in their efforts to trace her. Her foster mother, who hid her and refused to return her to relatives, is an exception to the many Christians who returned Jewish children when claimed by their relatives after the war.	The *New York Times* editorializes that Adolf Eichmann* be imprisoned for life at hard labor "to witness to the end of his days the miracle of Israel's resurrection." The U.S. votes against a draft resolution sponsored by 16 members of the UN General Assembly calling on Israel and its Arab neighbors to undertake direct negotiations to settle all questions in dispute between them, including the question of the Arab refugees. Israel favors and the Arab states oppose the resolution. The South African government forbids the transfer of funds raised by South African Jewry for the Jewish Agency in Israel. This prohibition reflects resentment of Israel's support of black African states against the South African regime. The ban remains in force until the Six-Day War of 1967, when sympathy for Israel's plight results in its being lifted.	
1962	The U.S. establishes the Peace Corps to assist the undeveloped world. War breaks out between India and China along the Himalayan frontier.	Katherine Anne Porter* (1890–1980), U.S. novelist, writes *The Ship of Fools*, about a passenger ship bound from Vera Cruz to Germany in 1931 on the eve of Adolf Hitler's* rise to power, whose generally unpleasant passengers include Loewenthal, a Jew who is anti-Gentile and a caricature of Jewish	Rabbi Louis Jacobs (b. 1920), lecturer at Jews' College and former rabbi of London's New West End synagogue, is not offered the previously assured position of principal of Jews' College because some of his teachings on biblical criticism run counter to traditional Orthodox interpretation. When		The Jewish Publication Society of America publishes The Torah: The Five Books of Moses, the first section of a new "official" English translation of the Bible, the first since 1917. Harry Orlinsky (b. 1908) is editor-in-chief and is assisted by a committee of consultants. The

A. General History	B. Jews in North and South America	C. Jews in Europe	D. Jews in the Middle East and Elsewhere	E. Jewish Culture	
	vulgarity, and antisemitic Germans. It will be adapted to the screen in 1965 under the direction of Stanley Kramer.	he attempts to return to the New West End synagogue, Great Britain's chief rabbi, Dr. Israel Brodie, denies him a certificate authorizing him to officiate. Some supporters resign from New West End and establish the independent St. John's Wood synagogue, with Dr. Jacobs as rabbi. At a meeting of Soviet writers, Soviet leader Nikita Khrushchev* attacks the poet Yevgeny Yevtushenko* for his poem "Babi Yar" and accuses him of lying about antisemitism in the Soviet Union.		committee includes Ephraim A. Speiser (1902–1965), professor of Semitic languages at the University of Pennsylvania, and H. L. Ginsberg (1903–1990), professor of Bible at the Jewish Theological Seminary of America. Isaac Bashevis Singer, Polish-born author of Yiddish fiction, publishes *The Slave* in English. After the massacre of the Jews of a Ukrainian community in the 17th century, a Jew is sold into slavery in Poland. His love for his master's daughter is frowned upon both by Jews and Poles.	1962
John H. Glenn, Jr.,* U.S. astronaut, is the first American to orbit the earth.				Solomon Zeitlin, U.S. scholar, writes the first volume of a multivolume history, *The Rise and Fall of the Judean State*, a political, social, and religious history of the Second Commonwealth.	Feb. 1962
In *Baker* v. *Carr*, the U.S. Supreme Court rules that federal courts have jurisdiction in the voters' suit charging a state apportionment statute deprived them of their constitutional rights. The decision compels state legislatures to give suburban and urban voters a more equal voice.	Bet El, a Conservative synagogue, is founded by 70 families in a suburb of Buenos Aires, Argentina. Led by Rabbi Marshall Meyer, its membership grows to over 350 families by the end of the year.		Israeli troops attack Syrian positions in the demilitarized zone north of the Arab village of Nuqeib after several weeks of rifle and machine-gun firing from Syrian posts at Israeli fishermen in the Sea of Galilee and workers along the border.	Bob Dylan (Robert Allen Zimmerman, b. 1941), U.S. singer and songwriter, releases his first album, *Bob Dylan*. Dylan will spark the merger of American folk, rock, and country music. His songs call attention to social issues.	Mar. 1962
Pope John XXIII issues an encyclical, Peace on Earth, declaring that every human being has the right to honor God according to the dictates of his or her own conscience. At the same time, he appoints Augustin Cardinal Bea president of the Secretariat for the Promotion of Christian Unity to propose to the forthcoming Ecumenical Council measures to improve relations between the Catholic church and other religions.			The UN Security Council adopts a resolution, sponsored by the U.S. and Great Britain, declaring the March 16 Israeli raid on Syrian posts near the Sea of Galilee to be a violation of a 1956 Security Council Resolution condemning armistice breaches by Israel, even in retaliation for attacks. France abstains from the 10–0 Security Council vote. Shortly after his release from French internment, Ahmed ben Bella* of the	Frank Loesser writes the music and Abe Burrows (1910–1985), the libretto for the Pulitzer Prize–winning musical comedy *How to Succeed in Business Without Really Trying*. Max Ferdinand Perutz, British biochemist, is awarded the Nobel Prize in chemistry for research into the structure of globular proteins. He had left Austria for England when the Nazis assumed power.	Apr. 1962

	A. General History	B. Jews in North and South America	C. Jews in Europe	D. Jews in the Middle East and Elsewhere	E. Jewish Culture
Apr. 1962	Cardinal Bea states that the problem of antisemitism and alleged Jewish responsibility for the death of Jesus will be examined by the Ecumenical Council.			Algerian provisional government declares that the Algerian revolution will not be complete until Algeria contributes its armed assistance to the liberation of Palestine. He promises to contribute 100,000 Algerian soldiers.	Giorgio Bassani, Italian Jewish author, writes *The Garden of the Finzi-Continis*, a novel of the author's youth in Ferrara, where an aristocratic Jewish family is unable to face the social upheaval brought about by Fascism and World War II. Its sale of 300,000 copies sets a record for Italian publishing.
May 1962				The Israel Supreme Court dismisses Nazi SS Officer Adolf Eichmann's* appeal of his conviction. Israeli President Yitzhak Ben-Zvi rejects his plea for clemency, and on May 31, he is hanged in Ramleh Prison. His remains are cremated and his ashes scattered over the Mediterranean Sea.	Albert Memmi, of Tunisian Jewish birth and living in France, writes *Portrait of a Jew*, which appears in English translation from the French. He writes of the position of the Jew in the non-Jewish world, the Islamic world of his Jewish youth, and the Christian and secular world of France. All are hostile to Judaism, including the Marxist left.
June 1962	In *Engel* v. *Vitale*, the U.S. Supreme Court holds the school prayer adopted by the New York Board of Regents in 1951 to be unconstitutional. Five parents of school children, two of them Jewish, brought the suit. A September editorial in the Catholic magazine *America* warns that efforts of a few Jews to remove religious practices from public schools might lead to an outbreak of antisemitism.	The most serious of numerous antisemitic attacks in Argentina, which are intensified after Adolf Eichmann's* execution, occurs when a university student, Graciela Narcisa Sirota, is kidnapped, driven to an isolated place, and swastikas are carved on her body. In protest, the Jewish community organizes a 12-hour communal work stoppage, which is joined by many non-Jews. Closed store windows bear the sign: "Closed as a protest against Nazi aggression in Argentina."		President John F. Kennedy* backs Israel's contention that it could unilaterally implement its part of the Johnston* Plan for allocation of the Jordan River waters, in the face of persistent Arab opposition.	Lev Davidovich Landau (1908–1968), Russian physicist, is awarded the Nobel Prize in physics for his pioneering theories of condensed matter, especially liquid helium. He had been imprisoned from 1937 to 1939 during Joseph Stalin's* purge, although he had already won three Stalin Prizes for his work in theoretical physics.
July 1962	Algeria becomes independent.			Israel expels Dr. Robert Soblen, who jumped bail after being sentenced to life imprisonment in the U.S. for espionage on behalf of the Soviet Union and entered Israel under an assumed name. In response to criticism of the expulsion, Prime Minister David Ben-Gurion declares, "We are thinking of a refuge for Jews who do not wish or are	Marc Chagall's stained glass windows *The Twelve Tribes of Israel* are installed in the synagogue of Jerusalem's Hadassah Medical Center. In 1961 and earlier this year, prior to their installation, the windows were exhibited in Paris and New York.

A. General History	B. Jews in North and South America	C. Jews in Europe	D. Jews in the Middle East and Elsewhere	E. Jewish Culture	
			unable to remain where they are, not of an asylum for criminals."		**July 1962**
			Ten-year-old Yossele Schumacher, missing for 2½ years, is returned to his parents after being found in New York by Israeli agents. He had been left in the care of his Orthodox grandfather while his parents, who arrived from Russia in 1957, were settling in Israel. The grandfather was concerned that the boy would not be given an Orthodox education and refused to return him to his parents. Yossele was found in the Brooklyn home of a follower of the Satmar rebbe.		
			After Algeria achieves its independence, a great majority of its Jews leave the country, most emigrating to France.		
	President John F. Kennedy* announces the appointment of U.S. Labor Secretary Arthur J. Goldberg (1908–1990) to the U.S. Supreme Court to replace Justice Felix Frankfurter, who resigns because of poor health.				**Aug. 1962**
The Yemen monarchy is overthrown. A civil war breaks out, with Egypt supporting and Saudi Arabia and Jordan opposing the revolutionary government.	The New York State Commission for Human Rights orders the New York office of the Arabian–American Oil Co. to stop refusing to hire Jews because of ancestry or creed.	A new synagogue is dedicated in Leghorn, Italy, to replace the famous synagogue destroyed in World War II.	In the first U.S. agreement to supply arms to Israel, the Kennedy* administration sells Israel Hawk ground-to-air defensive missiles. The U.S. is attempting to rectify a Middle East arms imbalance caused by the flow of Soviet arms to Egypt. Israel becomes the first non-NATO nation to receive Hawks.		**Sep. 1962**
	In *Tradition*, the magazine of the Orthodox Rabbinical Council of America, Professor Michael Wyschogrod suggests that the Orthodox community should not join those segments of the Jewish community that oppose state aid to private schools. "Orthodox Jewry knows that the				

	A. **General History**	B. **Jews in North and South America**	C. **Jews in Europe**	D. **Jews in the Middle East and Elsewhere**	E. **Jewish Culture**
Sep. 1962		survival of Torah Judaism in this country is inextricably tied to the fate of the day-school movement. Just like the Catholic community . . . we cannot supplement the child's public school education with afternoon instruction and expect to produce someone conversant with his tradition and loyal to it."			
Oct. 1962	The Second Vatican Council convened by Pope John XXIII begins its first session. The U.S. learns that the Soviet Union has brought nuclear missiles to Cuba and is constructing launching stations. The Kennedy* administration issues an ultimatum demanding their immediate withdrawal and advises that it would use military measures to ensure their removal. The U.S. institutes a quarantine around Cuba, and the Soviets remove the missiles.		By the fall, after the establishment of the independent Algerian state, the mass movement of Algerian Jews to France, together with the previous influx of Tunisian and some Moroccan Jews, raises the French Jewish population to an estimated 500,000. The French Jewish community becomes the largest in Western Europe and the world's fourth largest. An estimated 10,000 Jews attend Yom Kippur services at Moscow's Central Synagogue. Large attendances are reported at services in Leningrad, Kiev, and other Russian cities.		

Nov. 1962

D. Jews in the Middle East and Elsewhere

Israel joins 66 other nations in the UN General Assembly and votes for an Afro-Asian resolution that includes a demand for sanctions against South Africa.

The new town of Arad, in the Negev overlooking the Dead Sea, is inaugurated. Its population of 25,000 is to be employed at the Dead Sea potash works and in new industries utilizing the area's natural resources.

Dec. 1962

Joseph Johnson's* mission to resolve the Palestinian refugee problem fails. In 1961, President John F. Kennedy* had arranged for the appointment of Johnson* as a UN official to make proposals for the repatriation of refugees to Israel. His proposals are rejected by Israel and neighboring Arab states.

President John F. Kennedy* meets with Israeli Foreign Minister Golda Meir at Palm Beach, Florida, and describes the U.S. policy of combining close ties with Israel with initiatives toward the Arab world. "I think it is quite clear that in case of any invasion, the U.S. would come to the support of Israel."

	A. **General History**	B. **Jews in North and South America**	C. **Jews in Europe**	D. **Jews in the Middle East and Elsewhere**	E. **Jewish Culture**
1963	In Iran, there are demonstrations against the Shah.*	Membership in the Zionist Organization of America is 87,000. This is a decline from 250,000 in 1948.	The Ukrainian Academy of Sciences in Kiev publishes *Judaism Without Embellishment*, a book	Brother Daniel, born in 1922 as a Polish Jew, Oswald Rufeisen, who converted to	Hannah Arendt, German-American philosopher, writes *Eichmann in Jerusalem: A Report on the*

A. General History	B. Jews in North and South America	C. Jews in Europe	D. Jews in the Middle East and Elsewhere	E. Jewish Culture	
	Father Edward Flannery writes *The Anguish of the Jews*, in which he decries Christian antisemitism.	on the Jewish religion written by Trofim Kichko,* an antisemite. He writes that the Bible and Talmud preach hatred of non-Jews and that Jews are swindlers and exploiters. The book is illustrated with Nazi-like cartoons. After protracted negotiations, Bulgaria agrees to pay Israel $195,000 for the loss of 22 Israelis when an El Al airliner was shot down by Bulgaria in 1955.	Christianity in 1942 and became a Carmelite monk in 1945, is denied his petition to be recognized as a Jew under Israel's Law of Return by Israel's Supreme Court. Speaking for the court, Judge Silberg agreed that Brother Daniel was a Jew according to *halakhah* but said that the Law of Return is based on Jewish national historical consciousness and on the ordinary secular meaning of the term *Jew*. He is offered citizenship by naturalization. Haifa University College is established by the Haifa municipality. It will function under the supervision of the Hebrew University until granted independent status in 1970. Israeli military advisers begin assisting General Joseph Mobutu* of the Congo in a civil war in which pro-Communist forces led by Antoine Gizenga* are aided by Egypt. Congolese troops are trained in Israel and, in 1964, will rout the rebels.	*Banality of Evil*, in which she criticizes the Israeli court judging Adolf Eichmann* for not indicting wartime Jewish leadership, who performed vital tasks for the Nazis that facilitated the "final solution." The book originated as a series of reports on the Eichmann* trial written for the *New Yorker* magazine and both produce much controversy and censure from Jewish scholars and leaders. Max Arzt, leading Conservative rabbi, writes *Justice and Mercy: A Commentary on the New Year and Day of Atonement*. Moshe Davis (b. 1916) writes *The Emergence of Conservative Judaism*, a study of the historical school of Judaism in 19th-century America. Maurice Samuel, U.S. author and translator, writes *Little Did I Know: Recollections and Reflections*, an account of his boyhood in Romania, his adolescence in England, and his mature experiences in Israel and the U.S.	**1963**
		A Dutch court in Arnhem directs that a bronze sculpture by Honoré Daumier,* purchased by a Dutch art collector at a 1941 Nazi art auction, be returned to the estate of Jakob Goldschmidt, a German Jewish banker. It is expected that this decision might affect millions of dollars of confiscated Jewish properties disposed of by the Nazi regime.		Elmer Rice, U.S. playwright, writes his autobiography, *Minority Report*, which includes reminiscences of his New York boyhood and his career in the theater. Nathan Glazer and Daniel Patrick Moynihan* write *Beyond the Melting Pot*, a sociological study of the Negroes, Puerto Ricans, Jews, Italians, and Irish of New York.	**Jan. 1963**
A Baathist-inspired coup overthrows the Iraqi government of				Abraham Joshua Heschel, U.S.	**Feb. 1963**

	A. General History	B. Jews in North and South America	C. Jews in Europe	D. Jews in the Middle East and Elsewhere	E. Jewish Culture
Feb. 1963	Premier Kassim.* A Baathist military coup in Syria a month later will replace the anti-Nasser* regime. Both governments are recognized by the U.S., Great Britain, and the Soviet Union.		*The Deputy*, a play written by Rolf Hochhuth,* a German Protestant, opens in Berlin. It indicts Pope Pius XII for his failure to protest publicly and officially against the mass murder of Jews by the Nazis. The pope is portrayed as a cold and calculating figure, more interested in protecting the financial and institutional interests of the Church than in his moral responsibility as the vicar of Christ. The Soviet press publishes an exchange of letters between Nikita Khrushchev* and Britain's Lord Bertrand Russell.* Russell* expresses dismay at the death sentences meted out to Jews for alleged economic crimes. Khrushchev* denies Soviet anti-Jewish feelings and brands such accusations "a vicious slander on the Soviet people."		theologian, publishes *The Prophets*, emphasizing divine pathos and the prophets' empathy with God. Betty Friedan (b. 1921), U.S. feminist leader, writes *The Feminine Mystique* in which she articulates the premise of female inferiority on which the American notions of family and gender roles are based. Joseph L. Blau and Salo W. Baron (1895–1989) edit a documentary history, *The Jews of the United States, 1790–1840.* In Tel Aviv, Leonard Bernstein conducts his *Kaddish*, an oratorio for narrator, chorus, and orchestra. Barbra Streisand (b. 1942), popular singer, is invited to perform at the White House by President John F. Kennedy.*
Mar. 1963				Israeli Foreign Minister Golda Meir informs the Knesset that "a number of German scientists and hundreds of German technicians are helping to develop offensive missiles in Egypt, and even armaments banned by international law." The Hebrew Union College opens its Biblical and Archaeological School in Jerusalem. The school is the only permanent American academic institution of higher learning in Israel and serves as a postdoctoral research center for U.S. and other universities.	The Jewish Museum in New York exhibits The Hebrew Bible in Christian, Jewish, and Muslim Art and the silver and Judaica collection of Mr. and Mrs. Michael Zagayski. A reproduction of the Sarajevo Haggadah, one of the most famous Hebrew illuminated manuscripts of the medieval period, is published with explanatory text by Cecil Roth. Paul Celan (Anczel, 1920–1970), German Jewish poet, publishes a collection of his poems, *The no-man's-rose*, which contains numerous Jewish themes and illusions.
Apr. 1963		A survey conducted by the Union of Orthodox Rabbis, reported in the *Wall*	The Warsaw Jewish newspaper, *Folks-shtimme*, publishes a report on	President John F. Kennedy* comments at a press conference that the German	Several of his poems commemorate the victims of the

A. General History	B. Jews in North and South America	C. Jews in Europe	D. Jews in the Middle East and Elsewhere	E. Jewish Culture	
	Street Journal, notes the increased demand for kosher products in the U.S. The survey finds approximately 2,000 kosher products are produced by more than 400 companies, compared to 1,000 products produced by 225 companies four years earlier.	military honors awarded to Jews in the Soviet army in World War II. It is estimated that 500,000 Jews served in the Soviet army during World War II, and 160,772 Jews, or 1.74% of all persons so honored, received various military awards and medals.	scientists working on missiles in Egypt "do affect tensions in the Middle East." He notes, also, the displeasure of the West German government. Yitzhak Ben-Zvi, Israel's second president, dies and is succeeded by Zalman Shazar (1889–1974).	Holocaust. He is a survivor of Nazi labor camps, where his parents perished. Ladislav Fuks' first novel, *Mr. Theodor Mundstock*, whose hero is a simple Jew "from the street," wins the prize for the best book issued by the Publishing House of the Association of Czech Writers.	**Apr. 1963**
The Organization for African Unity is formed.	The U.S. State Department reports that it has informed Saudi Arabia that American Jewish servicemen would not be eliminated from personnel assigned to the Dhahran air base.			The State Museum of Cologne, Germany, mounts "Monumenta Judaica," an exhibition of 2,000 years of Jewish history and culture on the Rhine. It is documented in an 800-page catalogue and attracts tens of thousands of visitors from Germany and abroad.	**May 1963**
Pope John XXIII dies between the first and second sessions of the Second Vatican Council. The U.S. Supreme Court holds unconstitutional a Pennsylvania statute requiring the reading of 10 verses of the Bible, without comment, at the opening of each school day and Baltimore, Maryland's, rule requiring the recitation of the Lord's Prayer or the reading of the Bible at the opening of the public school day.			David Ben-Gurion resigns from the Israeli government "because of personal needs," and retires to Sde Boker. On his recommendation, he is succeeded by Minister of Finance Levi Eshkol (1895–1969) as prime minister and minister of defense.	Yaacov Agam (b. 1928), Israeli painter, wins First International Prize at the São Paulo Biennale for his artistic research into the third dimension and movement in painting. Natalia Ginzburg, Italian novelist and playwright, writes *Family Sayings*, a psychological novel based on recollections of her youth, including bourgeois assimilated Italian Jewish life in Turin. She wins Italy's most prestigious literary award, the Strega Prize.	**June 1963**
The Sacred College of Cardinals elevates the archbishop of Milan, Giovanni Battista Cardinal Montini, to the papal throne. He assumes the name Paul VI and immediately announces his decision to carry on the Second Vatican Council. Seventeen leaders of the African National Congress underground are arrested. Five are white, all of them Jews. In August,				Stan Getz (1927–1991), U.S. jazz musician, releases *Jazz Samba*, a record album that includes songs that make Brazilian bossa nova music an international sensation. Getz was already a major figure in jazz as one of the Four Brothers in the Woody Herman band	**July 1963**

	A. General History	B. Jews in North and South America	C. Jews in Europe	D. Jews in the Middle East and Elsewhere	E. Jewish Culture
July 1963	while awaiting trial in a Johannesburg jail, four will escape. Two of the escapees are Jews.				in the late 1940s and as the father of a "cool school" of modern jazz saxophone playing.
Aug. 1963	More than 210,000 persons of all faiths and races march on Washington, D.C., to demonstrate for equal rights and opportunities for all citizens. An estimated 2,000 Jews participate in the march, which is addressed by the Reverend Martin Luther King, Jr.* The U.S. and Soviet Union sign a partial test ban treaty, prohibiting nuclear testing or any other nuclear explosions in the atmosphere, including outer space and under water, if the explosion could spread radioactive debris beyond the territory of the country setting the explosion. The U.N. Security Council votes a voluntary arms embargo against South Africa.			A number of shooting attacks by Syrian forces along the Sea of Galilee culminate in the killing of two settlers from the Israeli border village of Almagor. American Orthodox leaders warn that the Conservative synagogue movement "constituted a serious threat to Israeli Jewry." They complain about Conservative and Reform institutions in Israel and demand that marriages and divorces solemnized by non-Orthodox rabbis be invalidated.	*The Art of Warfare in Biblical Lands*, written by Yigael Yadin, Israeli archaeologist and soldier, is translated into English from Hebrew.
Sep. 1963				The U.S. and Great Britain introduce a UN Security Council resolution condemning "the wanton murder at Almagor in Israel territory of two Israeli citizens on August 19." The Soviet Union vetoes the resolution, which receives eight votes. Rabbi Bernard Moses Casper, former dean of students at the Hebrew University in Jerusalem, assumes the post of chief rabbi of the United Hebrew Congregation of Johannesburg, succeeding Rabbi Louis Isaac Rabinowitz, who retired to settle in Israel.	

A. General History	B. Jews in North and South America	C. Jews in Europe	D. Jews in the Middle East and Elsewhere	E. Jewish Culture	
Konrad Adenauer,* chancellor of West Germany for 14 years, resigns and is succeeded by Ludwig Erhard.* In a farewell interview, Adenauer* says Jews can live in confidence in Germany, German youth is free of antisemitic feelings, Germany is willing to aid Israel after the expiration of the reparation agreements, and diplomatic relations will be established with Israel in the foreseeable future. In October, France hands over the last French Tunisian base, Bizerte, to Tunisia.		During Simhat Torah services, 15,000 Jews, mostly young people, sing and dance in front of the Moscow synagogue, and 10,000 crowd into the Leningrad synagogue and surrounding streets.			**Oct. 1963**

A. General History

Nov. 1963

President John F. Kennedy* is assassinated. He is succeeded by Vice President Lyndon B. Johnson.*

At the second session of the Second Vatican Council, Cardinal Augustin Bea submits a draft of Attitude of Catholics toward Non-Christians, Particularly toward the Jews. It is not discussed by the council but is postponed to the third session, to be held in August 1964.

Jack Ruby, Dallas nightclub owner, kills President John F. Kennedy's* assassin, Lee Harvey Oswald,* The shooting is witnessed by millions of television viewers.

South Vietnamese leader Ngo Dinh Diem* is assassinated.

A. General History	B. Jews in North and South America	C. Jews in Europe	D. Jews in the Middle East and Elsewhere	E. Jewish Culture	
China detonates its first atom bomb.			The government of Israel declares the Bene Israel from India to be Jews in every respect, equal in their rights to all other Jews. The decision follows public demonstrations resulting from rabbinic hesitancy regarding matrimonial matters affecting them. By 1969, over 12,000 Bene Israel will have emigrated to Israel.	Saul Bellow, U.S. novelist, writes *Herzog*, a novel of Moses Herzog, a professor of history, and his involvements with two wives, his children, a friend who betrays him, and his careers in writing and teaching. Bellow's *Herzog* is a humorous attack on higher education in America. It wins him a second National Book Award.	**1964**
			Pope Paul VI visits Christian holy places in Jordan and Israel.	Salo W. Baron, U.S. historian, writes *The Russian Jew under Tsars and Soviets*.	**Jan. 1964**
The UN Security Council dispatches a peace-keeping force to Cyprus.			The *Shalom*, flagship of Israel's Zim line, completes her maiden luxury cruise. The	Ephraim A. Speiser, U.S. orientalist, translates and annotates Genesis, the	**Mar. 1964**

	A. General History	B. Jews in North and South America	C. Jews in Europe	D. Jews in the Middle East and Elsewhere	E. Jewish Culture
Mar. 1964				ship serves an exclusively kosher cuisine in deference to religious objections to dual cuisine, preferred by the ship's operators as an attraction to passengers.	first book in the Anchor Bible series, a publishing effort to make the Bible accessible to the modern reader, utilizing outstanding Protestant, Catholic, and Jewish scholars as editors.
May 1964	Jawaharlal Nehru,* Indian leader, dies.		A memorial at the Treblinka extermination camp in Poland is dedicated in the presence of high Polish officials and many Jewish delegations from abroad. A huge stone holding a menorah surrounded by smaller stones representing cities and villages where the Jewish victims lived, the memorial is situated on the spot where the gas ovens once stood.	The Palestine Liberation Organization (PLO) is founded. Israeli Prime Minister Levi Eshkol visits President Lyndon B. Johnson* in Washington, D.C., the first official visit of an Israeli prime minister to the U.S.	Isaac Bashevis Singer, Polish-born author of Yiddish fiction, publishes *Short Friday, and Other Stories*. Arthur Miller, U.S. playwright, writes *After the Fall*, a play in which a young Jewish lawyer tries to comprehend why he has failed in his relationships with his mother, his wives, and his friends.
June 1964	Three civil rights workers are murdered in Mississippi while working on a summer civil rights project. They included Michael Schwerner and Andrew Goodman of New York. After an extensive search, their bodies are recovered, on August 4.		Spain's General Francisco Franco* establishes a center for Hispanic–Jewish (Sephardic) studies and designates El Transito synagogue of Toledo, erected in the 14th century by Samuel Abulafia (c.1320–1361), as a museum.	Israeli Prime Minister Levi Eshkol visits France and meets with President Charles de Gaulle,* who repeatedly refers to Israel as "our friend and ally."	Rachel Wischnitzer, scholar of Jewish art, writes *The Architecture of the European Synagogue*, an illustrated historical survey. Elie Wiesel's novel *The Town Beyond the Wall* is translated from French into English. A Jew returns to Hungary to confront a man who had been indifferent while the Jews were being sent to concentration camps.
July 1964	President Lyndon B. Johnson* signs into law the Civil Rights Act of 1964, the most comprehensive civil rights legislation in U.S. history. There are race riots in Harlem in New York. Throughout the year there are race riots in other northern urban areas.			The Republican party platform, for the first time since 1944, makes no reference to Israel's aspirations in the Middle East. "Respecting the Middle East, and in addition to our reaffirmed pledges of 1960 concerning this area, we will so direct our economic and military assistance as to help maintain stability in this region and prevent an imbalance of arms."	Franz Meyer writes *Marc Chagall*, a comprehensive study of the Russian-born Jewish artist's work. Meyer is the artist's son-in-law. The Broadway musical *Fiddler on the Roof*, with a score by Sheldon Harnick and Jerry Bock and choreography by Jerome Robbins, opens. It is based on Yiddish stories by Sholom Aleichem (1859–1916). Zero Mostel (1915–1977) plays the role of Tevya.
Aug. 1964		The Seminario Rabínico Latinoamericano is inaugurated in Buenos Aires, Argentina. This first modern rabbinical seminary on the South American continent is founded under the guidance of the U.S.		The Democratic party platform pledges "using our best efforts to prevent a military imbalance, to encourage arms reductions . . . to encourage the resettlement of Arab refugees in lands	

A. General History	B. Jews in North and South America	C. Jews in Europe	D. Jews in the Middle East and Elsewhere	E. Jewish Culture	
	Conservative movement.		where there is room and opportunity. The problems . . . must be peacefully resolved and the territorial integrity of every nation respected."	Paul Simon (b. 1941) and Art Garfunkel (b. 1941), a singing duo known for their gentle folk–rock style, release their first album, *Wednesday Morning, 3 A.M.*	**Aug. 1964**
		Mordecai Oren, an Israeli who had been a prosecution witness in the 1952 trial of Rudolf Slansky, is officially exonerated by the Czech judicial authorities. Oren was released after serving 3 years of his 15-year term. He waged a long battle to clear his name and that of his cousin Shimon Ornstein, who was also used to falsely incriminate Slansky.		Konrad Bloch, U.S. biochemist, is awarded the Nobel Prize in physiology or medicine for his discoveries of the mechanism of cholesterol and fatty acid metabolism. Bloch had left Germany in 1936 for the U.S. after the Nazis came to power. Marc Chagall's ceiling painting in the Paris Opera House is inaugurated.	**Sep. 1964**
Nikita Khrushchev* is ousted from his position as premier of the Soviet Union and is replaced by Leonid Brezhnev.*	Barry Goldwater,* the Republican candidate for the U.S. presidency, responds to a question concerning his Jewish origins. "I am proud of my heritage. My grandparents and my father were Jews. My mother was a Christian. I was baptized a Christian, an Episcopalian. I have a high regard for the American Jewish community."	Between October 12 and August 24, 1965, 10 SS men who served at Treblinka, including Kurt Franz,* deputy commander of the camp, are tried for war crimes by the West German government, at Dusseldorf. Franz and three others who are convicted are sentenced to life imprisonment; five are sentenced to 3½ years of imprisonment; one is acquitted.	The new town of Carmiel, the center of the Galilee development plan initiated by Prime Minister Levi Eshkol, is inaugurated. It is planned for a population of 50,000.	The permanent exhibition Synagogal Textile Treasures from the 16th to the 20th Centuries is opened in the Jewish State Museum in Prague. The museum has approximately 10,000 ceremonial objects, Torah curtains, mantles, draperies, and so on that the Nazis had stored in a central warehouse during World War II—part of a vast collection of	**Oct. 1964**
The Democrat Johnson–Humphrey* ticket wins the popular vote by a landslide. The Shah* of Iran exiles the Ayatollah Khomeini.*	The Jewish vote in the presidential election is estimated at 90% for Lyndon B. Johnson* and 10% for Barry Goldwater.*	At the close of the third session of the Second Vatican Council, the Council Fathers specifically repudiate the notion of the Jewish people as "rejected, cursed or guilty of deicide" and admonish Catholics not to "teach anything that could give rise to hatred or contempt of Jews in the hearts of Christians."		Jewish religious objects and other materials appropriated by the Nazis for the alleged purpose of creating a research center for the study of the Jewish people. The Bezalel National Museum in Jerusalem holds an exhibition of the collection of Jewish art of Heinrich Feuchtwanger.	**Nov. 1964**
Nicolae Ceauşescu* becomes the Communist party leader of Romania. James Michener* (b. 1907), U.S. novelist, writes *The Source*, a		The Roman Catholic church officially repudiates the blood libel of Trent (1475) by canceling the beatification of Simon and the celebrations in his honor.	The second and final season of excavations at Masada is completed under the leadership of Yigael Yadin, Israeli archaeologist, general, and politician. Masada	W. Gunther Plaut, U.S. and Canadian rabbi, writes *The Growth of Reform Judaism*, which chronicles the development of the Reform movement	**1965**

A. General History	B. Jews in North and South America	C. Jews in Europe	D. Jews in the Middle East and Elsewhere	E. Jewish Culture
1965 popular novel about the history of the land of Israel.		Roger Peyrefitte,* a former French diplomat, writes *The Jews*, which professes to be a philosemitic investigation of Jewish life but makes Judaism appear to be odious and ridiculous. Libel suits result in the alteration of objectionable passages in a new edition and the publisher pays a large sum to Jewish charities. The book has three large printings. *The Shop on Main Street*, a Czech film, stars Ida Kaminska as an aged Jewish woman who owns a button shop in a German-occupied Slovakian village and her relationship with her Aryan "controller."	was the site of King Herod's palace and the last stand of the Jewish rebels against the Romans in the years 66–73 CE. The University of the Negev at Beersheba is established and functions under the supervision of the Hebrew University. In 1973, it will be renamed the Ben-Gurion University of the Negev. The al-Fatah terrorist organization, conducting most of its operations from bases in Jordan, plants explosive charges in more than 30 installations and houses in Israeli territory.	until 1948 through a selection of sources and with his commentary. It is a companion volume to his *The Rise of Reform Judaism* (1963). Alfred Kazin, U.S. literary critic, writes *Starting Out in the Thirties*, a description of his exposure to the literary world, which is a continuation of his 1951 memoir, *A Walker in the City*. E. R. Goodenough* (1893–1965), U.S. scholar, completes *Jewish Symbols in the Graeco-Roman Period*, a monumental study begun in 1953. A specialist in Hellenic Judaism, he describes the development of Jewish figural art in the classical period, apparently in defiance of rabbinic proscriptions.
Jan. 1965		Josef Oberhauser,* who was in charge of constructing the Belzec extermination camp, is tried in Munich by the West German government for war crimes. He is convicted and sentenced to 4½ years' imprisonment.	News that the U.S. had secretly given permission to West Germany in the fall of 1964 to sell American M-48 Patton tanks to Israel as part of an $80 million arms deal between West Germany and Israel becomes public. In February, West Germany will cancel the balance of the arms shipments after Egypt threatens to recognize East Germany. The U.S. agrees to supply 200 Patton tanks to Israel and agrees, in principle, to send additional arms if Israel cannot balance Arab arms superiority through purchases from European suppliers. Eli Cohen (1924–1965), an Egyptian-born Israeli intelligence officer who infiltrated high Syrian political circles, is arrested as a spy. He is publicly tried and hanged in Damascus.	*This People Israel: The Meaning of Jewish Existence*, written by Leo Baeck (1873–1956), German rabbi, is published posthumously. It discusses Jewish peoplehood and outlines a political theory of Jewish existence in the uniquely Jewish religious context. Jacob Robinson writes *And the Crooked Shall Be Made Straight: The Eichmann Trial, the Jewish Catastrophe, and Hannah Arendt's Narrative*, in which he refutes the points made by Arendt in her *Eichmann in Jerusalem* (1963). Robinson is a Lithuanian diplomat who fled to the U.S. in 1941. In 1952, he was involved in drafting Israel's reparation agreement with West Germany.

A. General History	B. Jews in North and South America	C. Jews in Europe	D. Jews in the Middle East and Elsewhere	E. Jewish Culture	
Malcolm X,* Black Muslim leader, is murdered at a rally in New York.				Arthur Miller, U.S. playwright and novelist, writes *Incident at Vichy*, a play that concerns the treatment of a group of Frenchmen, including Jews, arrested in 1942 by the Nazis during their occupation.	**Feb. 1965**
Martin Luther King, Jr.,* civil rights leader, leads 25,000 demonstrators on a 50-mile freedom walk from Selma, Alabama, to the state capitol in Montgomery. The first U.S. combat troops are sent to South Vietnam by President Lyndon B. Johnson.* He orders continuous bombing of North Vietnam.	Herbert A. Cukurs,* a Latvian-born Nazi war criminal living in Brazil, is murdered in Montevideo, Uruguay, causing a series of antisemitic outbreaks.		Egypt's Gamal Abdel Nasser* asserts: "We shall not enter Palestine with its soil covered in sand. We shall enter it with its soil saturated in blood."	Sanford "Sandy" Koufax (b. 1935), Los Angeles Dodger pitcher, sets a baseball record when he pitches his fourth no-hit game in four years.	**Mar. 1965**
		Pope Paul VI, in his Passion Sunday sermon, recalls that the day's gospel lesson was a "grave and sad page narrating the clash between Jesus and the Jewish people—the people predestined to await the Messiah but who . . . did not recognize him, fought him and slandered him, and finally killed him." Jewish leaders believe the sermon indicates a retreat from the preliminary declaration on the Jews adopted at the third session of the Second Vatican Council. West Germany extends the statute of limitations for Nazi war crimes for about five years.		New York City's new Metropolitan Opera House is adorned by two murals painted by Marc Chagall, *The Sources of Music* and *The Triumph of Music*. Richard Phillips Feynman (1918–1988) and Julian Seymour Schwinger (b. 1918), U.S. physicists, are awarded the Nobel Prize in physics for their creation of the modern field of quantum electrodynamics. André Lwoff and François Jacob, French biologists, are awarded the Nobel Prize in physiology or medicine for their work on cellular genetic function and the influence of viruses. In World War II, Lwoff served in the French Resistance.	**Apr. 1965**
		Egypt, Jordan, Iraq, Syria, Lebanon, Yemen, Saudi Arabia, Algeria, Kuwait, and Sudan sever diplomatic relations with West Germany in protest over West Germany's recognition of Israel.	Chancellor Ludwig Erhard* and Prime Minister Levi Eshkol formally agree to establish diplomatic relations between West Germany and Israel. The Israel Museum in Jerusalem is opened. The museum consists of four major divisions: the Bezalel National Art Museum; the Samuel Bronfman Biblical and	Jerzy Kosinski (1933–1991), Polish-born author who came to the U.S. in 1957, writes *The Painted Bird*, a novel of a six-year-old's nightmarish childhood in Poland during the Nazi occupation. The Israel Museum in Jerusalem exhibits The Bible in Art and Archaeology, a	**May 1965**

	A. General History	B. Jews in North and South America	C. Jews in Europe	D. Jews in the Middle East and Elsewhere	E. Jewish Culture
May 1965				Archaeological Museum; the Billy Rose Art Garden; and the Shrine of the Book, housing the Dead Sea Scrolls and the Bar Kokhba letters.	comprehensive exhibition including etchings and drawings by Rembrandt van Rijn* and biblical paintings of other old masters.
June 1965	U.S. astronaut Edward White* takes the first American space walk.	President Lyndon B. Johnson* signs the Export Control Act, which contains a requirement making it mandatory for American businessmen to notify the Department of Commerce whenever they receive Arab requests for boycott information.		Wolfgang Pilz* and most of his team of West German scientists leave Egypt. They were engaged in a missile development program.	Dani Karavan, Israeli artist, creates *Memorial Monument for Negev Brigade* near Beersheba, Israel. Ephraim Kishon (b. 1924), Israeli humorist and satirist, writes and directs *Sallah*, a film satirizing the absorption of Sephardic immigrants into Israel in 1948 and starring Haim Topol. It receives an Academy Award nomination as the best foreign film of the year. Kishon emigrated to Israel in 1949 from Hungary. He writes a news column that is one of the most popular in the country.
July 1965	President Lyndon B. Johnson* persuades Associate Justice Arthur J. Goldberg to resign from the Supreme Court to replace Adlai E. Stevenson,* who had died of a heart attack, as U.S. ambassador to the UN. President Johnson* appoints Abe Fortas (1910–1982) to succeed Goldberg on the Supreme Court.	New York Governor Nelson Rockefeller* signs a Fair Sabbath Law, which extends statewide the right of family businesses to remain open on Sunday if they were closed on Saturday in observance of the Sabbath. This right had previously existed only in New York City.		David Ben-Gurion, having rejected the Mapai confirmation of Levi Eshkol as the party's candidate for prime minister, leads six other Mapai members of the Knesset, including Shimon Peres, in the formation of a new political party, Rafi.	Ben Shahn, U.S. painter, illustrates a Passover Haggadah, which is printed by the Trianon Press in Paris.
Aug. 1965	Egypt and Saudi Arabia, who had been supporting opposing sides, agree to end the civil war in Yemen. Egyptian troops will withdraw and the Saudis will cease aid to the Yemeni royalists. Riots in the Watts section of Los Angeles result in 34 dead, over 1,000 wounded, and $40 million in property damage. President Lyndon B. Johnson* signs into law the Voting Rights Act of 1965. Its aim is to secure full voting rights, primarily for blacks, by eliminating literacy tests, poll taxes, and other obstacles.	Many Jewish store owners who had remained in the Watts area of Los Angeles after it changed from a mainly Jewish to a mainly black neighborhood suffer heavy losses in the riots there. The Los Angeles Jewish Federation denies the riots had antisemitic implications. However, *Newsweek* magazine states that "looting and burning revealed a virulent strain of anti-Semitism—not so much blind race hatred as fury against individual Jewish store owners."	West Germany's first ambassador to Israel, Rolf Pauls,* presents his credentials in Jerusalem and Asher Ben-Natan, Israel's first ambassador to West Germany, presents his credentials in Bonn. In Frankfurt, Germany, the trial of overseers of the Auschwitz concentration camp ends with many SS men sentenced to long prison terms. The trial began on December 20, 1963, and continued for 183 sessions.		

A. General History	B. Jews in North and South America	C. Jews in Europe	D. Jews in the Middle East and Elsewhere	E. Jewish Culture	
		Between September 6, 1965, and December 20, 1966, in Hagen, 12 SS men who served at the Sobibor extermination camp, including Kurt Bolender,* the commander of an extermination area, are tried for war crimes by the West German government. During the trial, Bolender* commits suicide. The others are convicted and receive prison terms.	The Tel Aviv Hilton Hotel opens. When construction plans were announced in 1961, the Arab states threatened closure of the Nile Hilton and the termination of any plans for Hilton hotels in the Arab states. Conrad Hilton* rejected the Arab boycott threats. A new Hilton Hotel opens in Tunis in September, and Egypt contracts for three additional Hilton hotels.		**Sep. 1965**
President Lyndon B. Johnson* signs into law the Immigration Act of 1965. The law abolishes the national origins quota system. New immigrants will be admitted on the basis of their skills and their close relationship to those already here.		The Second Vatican Council, at the urging of Augustin Cardinal Bea, promulgates a declaration on the relationship of the Church to non-Christian religions. It declares that the Jews of Jesus' time and of today should not be burdened with the guilt of the crucifixion and that the Church decries antisemitism.	The UN General Assembly's Third Committee debates a Draft Convention on the Elimination of All Forms of Racial Discrimination. The U.S. and Brazil seek an amendment to specifically condemn antisemitism. The Soviet Union, sensitive to criticism of treatment of its Jews, introduces an amendment condemning "anti-Semitism, Zionism, Nazism, neo-Nazism and all other forms . . . of colonialism, national and race hatred, and exclusiveness." The Soviet maneuver results in a compromise convention that makes no reference to any specific form of racial discrimination.		**Oct. 1965**
			Israel holds national elections for the Sixth Knesset, with 1,206,728 votes cast. The alignment (Mapai and Ahdut ha-Avodah) wins 45 seats; Gahal (Herut–Liberal bloc), 26 seats; Rafi, 10 seats; Mapam, 8 seats; and the National Religious party, 11 seats. The government is installed on January 12, 1966, with Levi Eshkol as prime minister and minister of defense and Abba		**Nov. 1965**

	A. General History	B. Jews in North and South America	C. Jews in Europe	D. Jews in the Middle East and Elsewhere	E. Jewish Culture
Nov. 1965				Eban as minister of foreign affairs.	
Dec. 1965	An Austrian court acquits Robert Jan Verbelen,* who had been sentenced to death in absentia in 1947 by a Belgian court on charges of participation in mass killings of Belgian resistance fighters. He was located in Vienna in 1962 by former resistance fighters, but the Austrian government refused extradition on the ground he was an Austrian citizen. Belgian newspapers expected an acquittal since former Nazi judges continued to function in Austria. The acquittal arouses strong indignation in Belgium.				
1966	Throughout the year, the U.S. increases its military strength in Vietnam. It bombs Hanoi and Haiphong and other areas of the north and attacks targets in Cambodia for the first time. The Cultural Revolution, led by Mao Tse-tung,* takes place in Communist China. Communist leaders with Western tendencies are purged. Red Guards attack dissidents. Kwame Nkrumah* is ousted from power in Ghana.	Charles Y. Glock and Rodney Stark, U.S. sociologists, publish their American survey, *Christian Beliefs and Anti-Semitism*, which reports that well into the 20th century, Protestant Sunday School texts repeat the myth that the Jews were responsible for the death of Jesus and Jewish suffering for this act will persist until their collective conversion.	Dr. Immanuel Jakobovits is elected the chief rabbi of the United Hebrew Congregations of the British Commonwealth. Educated in England, he served as chief rabbi of Ireland before coming to the U.S. in 1958, where he served as rabbi of New York's Fifth Avenue synagogue until the time of his election. Sir Isaiah Berlin (b. 1909), English philosopher and political scientist, is appointed president of the newly created Wolfson College at Oxford University.		Bernard Malamud, U.S. writer of short stories and novels, writes *The Fixer*, a novel in which Yakov Bok, a Russian Jewish handyman, is falsely accused of ritual murder, based on the historic Beilis case. Malamud writes: "My story is about imprisonment and the effort of liberation through the growth of a man's spirit." Malamud wins the Pulitzer Prize and a National Book Award. Isaac Bashevis Singer, Polish author of Yiddish fiction, publishes in English translation *In My Father's Court*, a memoir of incidents from his childhood in Warsaw, where his father was a rabbi in a poor quarter of the city. Eli Ginzberg (b. 1911), U.S. economist, writes *Keeper of the Law*, a memoir of his father, Louis Ginzberg (1873–1953), who
Jan. 1966				King Hussein* of Jordan attacks the PLO for its "treasonable" attempts to undermine Jordanian unity. It is announced that a $4.1 million Harry S. Truman Center for the Advancement of Peace will be built in Jerusalem with private	

A. General History	B. Jews in North and South America	C. Jews in Europe	D. Jews in the Middle East and Elsewhere	E. Jewish Culture	
			American contributions.	taught for many years at the Jewish Theological Seminary of America.	**Jan. 1966**
			The U.S. announces it will sell 200 M-48 Patton tanks to Israel to maintain arms stabilization in the Middle East, as the Soviets are shipping arms to Egypt and Syria. In May, the U.S. will announce it is shipping A-4 Skyhawk jet fighters to Israel.	Avram Kampf (b. 1919), U.S. scholar of Jewish art, writes *Contemporary Synagogue Art*, a critical survey of the renaissance of synagogue art in the U.S. since World War II.	**Feb. 1966**
	About 70,000 books in the library of the Jewish Theological Seminary of America in New York are destroyed by fire. Many important collections, including that of Moritz Steinschneider (1816–1907), the Jewish bibliographer, are lost.		King Hussein* arrests scores of PLO officials on charges of illegal activities. The Anti-Defamation League accuses the Coca-Cola Co. of acceding to the Arab boycott by refusing to grant a franchise to an Israeli bottler. Coca-Cola denies the charge and enters into an agreement to establish a bottling plant in Israel. In November, the Arab League will vote to boycott Coca-Cola.	Elie Wiesel, Romanian-born American Jewish novelist and essayist, writes *The Jews of Silence*, an eyewitness report of Jewish persecution in the Soviet Union, which brings the plight of Soviet Jewry to wider attention. Albert Halper, U.S. novelist, writes *The Fourth Horseman of Miami Beach*, about lonely retired and semiretired Jews in Miami Beach, Florida.	**Apr. 1966**
			Soviet Premier Alexei Kosygin* visits Cairo and pledges Soviet support for Egypt's "struggle against imperialism." Egypt extends the use of naval facilities and airfields to the Soviets, who increase their supply of arms and technicians to Egypt. West Germany grants Israel economic aid in the form of long-term loans amounting to 160 million deutsche marks. This program follows the expiration of a 1952 agreement.	Kirk Douglas plays the lead role in *Cast a Giant Shadow*, a film about the role of U.S. Colonel David (Mickey) Marcus in Israel's War of Independence. The Jewish Museum in New York exhibits The Lower East Side: Portal to American Life (1870–1924), curated by Allon Schoener. In 1968, it will be shown at the Smithsonian Institution, in Washington, D.C.	**May 1966**
			King Hussein* of Jordan publicly denounces PLO leaders and their Arab supporters for their "subservience to international communism."	Shmuel Yosef Agnon (1888–1970) and Nelly Sachs (1891–1970) are awarded the Nobel Prize in literature. Agnon left Galicia for Palestine in 1907, and Sachs left Germany in 1940 to live in Sweden. Agnon's prize is the first granted a Hebrew	**June 1966**

	A. General History	B. Jews in North and South America	C. Jews in Europe	D. Jews in the Middle East and Elsewhere	E. Jewish Culture
July 1966			In Britain, 130 members of Parliament sign a petition expressing their concern over "the continuing difficulties confronting Jews in the Soviet Union."	A monument to President John F. Kennedy* is dedicated in the center of the Kennedy Peace Forest, on the outskirts of Jerusalem.	writer. Sachs remarks, "Agnon represents the State of Israel. I represent the tragedy of the Jewish people." The second volume of Yitzhak Baer's *A History of Jews in Christian Spain* is published in English translation from the Hebrew. It spans the history of the Jews in Spain from the 14th century to the expulsion in 1492.
Aug. 1966				An Iraqi pilot flies his Soviet-built MiG-21 jet fighter to Israel and asks for asylum. It is assumed that inspection of the plane is made available to Western powers. The Israeli Knesset building, designed by Joseph Klarwein and paid for in large part by the Rothschild Foundation, is dedicated in Jerusalem.	Gideon Hausner, the prosecutor for the State of Israel at Adolf Eichmann's* trial, writes *Justice in Jerusalem*, a description of Israel's actions and his view of Eichmann's* guilt. Dan Jacobson (b. 1929), British novelist, writes *The Beginners*, a novel set in South Africa, England, and Israel that spans three generations of a Jewish family. He was born in South Africa, and his novels and stories depict the tensions between black and white, as well as Jewish life, under the apartheid system.
Oct. 1966	The UN General Assembly strips South Africa of its mandate to govern South West Africa (Namibia) but is unable to establish a provisional UN authority.		After nearly 500 years, Jews return to the Toledo synagogue for the first Jewish public ceremony since the expulsion. The ceremony is attended by Spanish government officals as well as members of the Catholic clergy. Two members of the Nazi leadership, Baldur von Schirach,* governor of Austria, and Albert Speer,* Adolf Hitler's* minister of war production, are released from the Spandau Prison in West Berlin. The only remaining prisoner in Spandau is Rudolf Hess.*		

Nov. 1966

D. Jews in the Middle East and Elsewhere

After three Israeli soldiers are killed and others wounded near Mt. Hebron, Israeli troops cross the armistice line and evacuate the village of Samoa and blow up 40 houses. They destroy trucks carrying Arab Legionnaires. Eighteen Jordanians and one Israeli officer are killed. The UN Security Council censures Israel for the raid. Israel reiterates its right of self-defense.

Following the Israeli raid at the village of Samoa, King Hussein* responds to antigovernment demonstrations by ordering the arrest of hundreds of PLO followers and the seizure of PLO headquarters in Jerusalem. PLO leader Ahmad Shukairy* calls for a holy war against Hussein.*

The Arab League votes to blacklist the Ford Motor Co. because it licensed an Israeli dealer to assemble British and American Ford trucks and tractors. Henry Ford II* reaffirms Ford's plans for Israel: "We feel we have the . . . right to compete in any market in the world willing to accept us as an industrial citizen."

A. General History	B. Jews in North and South America	C. Jews in Europe	D. Jews in the Middle East and Elsewhere	E. Jewish Culture	
The UN Security Council imposes mandatory sanctions against Rhodesia.		Anti-Jewish bias among the people of France is confirmed by a poll conducted by the French Institute of Public Opinion. However, 17% believe that French Jews are not really French, which compares favorably with 43% who held that view in 1946.			**Dec. 1966**
Throughout the year, the war in Vietnam continues. The strength of U.S. troops in Vietnam is nearly 475,000, more than the number that fought in the Korean War. China explodes its first hydrogen bomb.	Ezra Pound,* poet and critic, admits to Allen Ginsberg that "the worst mistake I made was that stupid, suburban prejudice of antisemitism. All along, that spoiled everything." In *Afroyim* v. *Rusk*, the U.S. Supreme Court rules unconstitutional a section in the Nationality Act of 1940. The court holds that Congress cannot deprive an American of his citizenship unless he either voluntarily renounces it or gives it up. Afroyim, a naturalized U.S. citizen, had moved to Israel, become a citizen under the Law of Return, and voted in the 1951 Israeli election. He had been told by the U.S. State Department he had lost his citizenship. Gary T. Marx, U.S. sociologist, writes *Protest and Prejudice: A Study of Belief in the Black Community*, which is based on his 1964 survey. Marx finds that generally there is less antisemitism in the black community than in the country as a whole. The National Conference of Catholic Bishops in	Sylvain Wijnberg writes *The Jews of Amsterdam*, a sociological study that reports that most Jews in Amsterdam no longer practice their religion or attend synagogue although they continue to identify themselves as Jews. Jewish leaders question whether the study is representative of the Jewish community. Jean-François Steiner's* *Treblinka* is published in an English edition. Steiner,* the son of Isaac Kadmi Cohen, a French Zionist lawyer who perished at Auschwitz, and a Catholic mother, arouses controversy among Holocaust survivors with his work, which is a mixture of fact and fiction. The Jews of Spain regain religious liberty, as Spain enacts a law extending religious freedom to all denominations.		Gerson D. Cohen (1924–1991), U.S. scholar, edits a critical edition of Abraham ibn Daud's *The Book of Tradition*, analyzing the faulty chronology of Daud's biblical, talmudic, and geonic history and stressing its importance as a source of the history of the Spanish Jewish community during the 11th and 12th centuries. Chaim Potok (b. 1929), U.S. author, writes *The Chosen*, the story of the struggle between ultra-Orthodox Hasidim and more flexible Mitnagdim in an American setting as seen through the development of two Brooklyn yeshiva students, Danny Saunders and Reuven Malter. Its immense commercial success startles the literary world. Lucy S. Dawidowicz (1915–1990), U.S. historian, edits *The Golden Tradition: Jewish Life and Thought in Eastern Europe*, which documents the social and intellectual life of the community. Norman Podhoretz (b. 1930), since 1960 editor of *Commentary* magazine and social critic, writes *Making It*, an autobiographical memoir tracing his	**1967**

	A. General History	B. Jews in North and South America	C. Jews in Europe	D. Jews in the Middle East and Elsewhere	E. Jewish Culture
1967		the U.S. issues Guidelines for Catholic–Jewish Relations, which follows the Second Vatican Council declarations affecting the Jews. The prominent German Jewish families of New York are treated in the popular history *Our Crowd* by Stephen Birmingham.*			growth from childhood in Brooklyn's Brownsville section to acceptance in New York's intellectual community. Isaac Bashevis Singer, Polish-born author of Yiddish fiction, publishes in English *The Manor* and, in 1969, its sequel, *The Estate*. They depict the lives of the Jacoby family from the time of the Polish insurrection of 1863 to the end of the 19th century.
Jan. 1967	The U.S. and Soviet Union sign an outer space treaty, prohibiting the sending of nuclear weapons into earth orbit or stationing them in outer space. The treaty also prohibits the establishment of military bases and testing on celestial bodies.		The 677-year-old Amsterdam Maastricht synagogue, the second oldest in Europe, which had been looted and partly destroyed by the Nazis in World War II, is completely restored at the Dutch government's expense.	On January 17, Israeli Prime Minister Levi Eshkol reports 23 Syrian attacks since the beginning of the year, including attacks on farmers inside and outside the demilitarized zones, mine laying on roads, and sabotage of water installations.	Saul Lieberman, professor of Talmud at the Jewish Theological Seminary of America, adds three volumes to his classic critical edition of the Tosafta.
Apr. 1967				After Syrian forces shell Israeli villages for four days, Israeli aircraft attack Syrian artillery positions and Israeli jet fighters down six Syrian MiG-21s. Two weeks after the Israeli–Syrian air battle, Soviet Deputy Prime Minister Jacob Malik* warns the Israelis that they are endangering the "very fate of their State."	Shlomo Dov Goitein (b. 1900), Oriental scholar, writes *A Mediterranean Society: The Jewish Communities of the Arab World as Portrayed in the Documents of the Cairo Genizah*. This first volume of his research discusses the economic life of ordinary people from the 10th to the 13th centuries. Shalom Spiegel's *The Last Trial: On the Legends and Lore of the Command to Abraham to Offer Isaac as a Sacrifice: The Akedah* is

May 1967

D. Jews in the Middle East and Elsewhere

On May 13, the Soviet Union warns Egypt of an impending Israeli attack on Syria. Egyptian military visitors to Syria do not see Israeli troop concentrations and report of a low state of readiness of the Syrian army. Gamal Abdel Nasser* decides to move his forces into the Sinai in an effort to relieve any potential Israeli threat against Syria and satisfy his critics.

On May 15, Egypt's Gamal Abdel Nasser* announces a state of military emergency, accuses Israel of threatening aggression against Syria, and sends two armored divisions into the Sinai.

On May 16, Gamal Abdel Nasser* orders a partial withdrawal of the 3,400-man UN Emergency Force that had been stationed on the Egyptian–Israeli border since 1957. He does not ask for a withdrawal from Gaza or Sharm es-Sheikh. UN Secretary-General U Thant* advises Nasser* that the UN will accept no half measures. It will fulfill its total mission or fully withdraw.

published in English translation from the Hebrew. Spiegel is professor of Hebrew medieval literature at the Jewish Theological Seminary of America.

The 23rd volume of Menachem Kasher's *Torah Shelemah*, an encyclopedic commentary on the Bible, is published. It ends with Chapter 34 of the Book of Exodus.

On May 17, Gamal Abdel Nasser* notifies U Thant* that he is ordering a complete UN Emergency Force withdrawal from Egyptian territory, including Gaza and Sharm es-Sheikh.

On May 18, U Thant* meets with delegates of seven nations whose troops make up the UN Emergency Force. Upon learning that they will remove their troops, U Thant* remains oblivious to U.S. and Israeli demands that UNEF could not be withdrawn without the consent of the UN General Assembly.

On May 19, Egyptian troops begin reinforcing garrisons in the Sinai.

On May 20, Israel orders a general mobilization.

On May 22, in a speech made the same day but before Gamal Abdel Nasser's* speech, Israeli Prime Minister Levi Eshkol disclaims any Israeli intention to attack Egypt or Syria and urges a mutual withdrawal of troop concentrations near the borders.

On May 22, having placed a military garrison at Sharm es-Sheikh, Gamal Abdel Nasser,* in a speech at an air base in the Sinai, announces the closing of the Straits of Tiran to Israeli ships and to all ships transporting "strategic material" to Israel. He adds: "The Jews threaten war; we tell them: Welcome. We are ready for war."

On May 22, the U.S. appeals to Israel not to react to the Egyptian blockade and send no ship through the Straits of Tiran for 48 hours while the U.S. seeks a peaceful solution.

On May 22, French and British Foreign Ministry spokesmen announce that the Tripartite Declaration of 1950 opposing force in the Middle East is no longer valid.

On May 23, a full mobilization of Israel is completed.

On May 23, Israeli Chief of Staff Yitzhak Rabin suffers a nervous breakdown. After what is officially described as a "nicotine poisoning," he returns to his command a few days later.

On May 23, President Lyndon B. Johnson* seeks former President Dwight D. Eisenhower's* advice on how, in 1957, the U.S. viewed Israel's right to free passage through the Straits of Tiran. "General Eisenhower sent me a message stating his view that the Israelis' right of access to the Gulf of Aqaba was definitely part of the 'commitment' we had made to them."

On May 23, President Lyndon B. Johnson* reaffirms the long-held American position that the Gulf of Aqaba is an international waterway and that the blockade of Israeli shipping is, therefore, illegal.

On May 23, U.S. Secretary of State Dean Rusk* briefs the Senate Foreign Relations Committee on the Middle East crisis. He reports to President Lyndon B. Johnson* that Congress would support Israel, but is opposed to unilateral U.S. action.

On May 23, the Soviet Union issues a formal statement on the crisis without any reference to the Egyptian blockade and warns, "Should anyone try to unleash aggression in the Near East, he would be met not only with the united strength of Arab countries but also with strong opposition to aggression from the Soviet Union."

On May 23, the UN Security Council meets in an emergency session at the request of Denmark and Canada. The debate lasts for several days without any resolution due to Soviet opposition to efforts to compel Egypt to lift the blockade.

On May 24, British and American officials meet to discuss the British proposal that an international maritime flotilla be established to run the Egyptian blockade under a naval escort.

On May 24, Israeli Foreign Minister Abba Eban meets with President Charles de Gaulle* of France. De Gaulle* refuses to acknowledge the 1957 French

Neil Simon (b. 1927), U.S. playwright, has four plays running simultaneously on Broadway. *Barefoot in the Park* (1963), *The Odd Couple* (1965), and *Sweet Charity* (1966) are still running when *The Star-Spangled Girl* opens in December 1966. His plays often depict Jewish family life.

Dustin Hoffman, U.S. actor, gains fame as he stars in the film *The Graduate*. The film's soundtrack is by Paul Simon and Art Garfunkel.

The Jewish Museum in New York exhibits Masada and the Finds from the Bar Kochba Caves.

Hans Albrecht Bethe, U.S. nuclear physicist, is awarded the Nobel Prize in physics for describing the nuclear reactions in the energy production of stars. The son of a Jewish mother, he left Germany in 1933 and in 1937 became the director of the theoretical physics division of the Los Alamos Scientific Laboratory.

George Wald, U.S. biologist, is awarded the Nobel Prize in physiology or medicine for discoveries about the eye and the perception of color.

Mordecai Ardon (b. 1896), Israeli painter, paints the triptych *At the Gates of Jerusalem*, which is presented to the Israel Museum. The painting celebrates the reunification of Jerusalem and expresses his longing for a heavenly Jerusalem.

May 1967

May 1967

commitment to Israel's right of free passage through the Straits of Tiran. He also issues a warning to Israel not to shoot first.

On May 25, Gamal Abdel Nasser* addresses the Egyptian National Assembly: "The problem presently before the Arab countries is not whether the port of Eilat should be blockaded or how to blockade it—but how to totally exterminate the State of Israel for all time."

On May 25, Jordan mobilizes its armed forces and invites Iraqi troops to take up positions along the Israeli frontier. Saudi Arabia, Algeria, and Kuwait announce they are putting troops at Gamal Abdel Nasser's* disposal.

On May 25, President Lyndon B. Johnson* has an inconclusive meeting with Israeli Foreign Minister Abba Eban. He cautions Israel not to initiate hostilities; he will continue to try to induce Nasser* to lift the blockade but needs congressional authority to act, as he is mired in the Vietnam War; he would seek UN Security Council action; and would consider a multinational naval force to run the blockade.

On May 27, the Soviets inform President Lyndon B. Johnson* they have information that Israel is planning an attack, and if this is so, they will assist the attacked state. Johnson* informs Levi Eshkol, "I repeat even more strongly than I said yesterday to Mr. Eban. Israel just must not take preemptive miltary action and thereby make itself reponsible for the initiation of hostilities." Israel accedes to the request.

On May 28, following a report of Abba Eban to the Israeli cabinet of his Washington, D.C., trip, Levi Eshkol declares in a speech that the cabinet has decided on "the continuation of political action in the world arena" to find ways to reopen the Straits of Tiran.

On May 29, Gamal Abdel Nasser* declares before the Egyptian National Assembly, "The issue today is not the question of Aqaba or the Strait of Tiran, or UNEF. The issue is the rights of the people of Palestine, the aggression against Palestine that took place in 1948, with the help of Britain and the United States. . . . [People] want to confine it to the Strait of Tiran, UNEF, and the right of passage. We say: We want the rights of the people of Palestine—complete."

On May 30, Jordan's King Hussein* flies to Cairo to sign a mutual defense pact with Egypt that places Jordan's armed forces under Egyptian command in case of war. Hussein* reconciles himself with the PLO, and its leader, Ahmad Shukairy,* returns to Jordan with him. Egypt sends General Abdul Riad* to take command of Arab forces on the Jordanian front.

On May 31, at the request of the U.S., the UN Security Council proposes that Arabs and Israelis use "international diplomacy" to resolve their dispute. Even this proposal is rejected by Egypt, India, and the Soviet Union.

June 1967

On June 1, in response to public demand, Moshe Dayan replaces Levi Eshkol as minister of defense. Eshkol remains prime minister and forms the Government of National Unity. Menachem Begin joins the government as minister without portfolio.

On June 2, Iraq's President Abdel Rahman Aref* addresses his air force officers: "This is the day of the battle to avenge . . . 1948. . . . We shall, God willing, meet in Tel Aviv and Haifa."

On June 3, the Israeli cabinet votes for a preemptive strike against Egypt. Forces facing Syria and Jordan are to remain in a defensive posture even if they are attacked. Moshe Dayan holds a press conference implying a further Israeli delay of the commencement of hostilities.

On June 4, it is announced that U.S. Vice President Hubert Humphrey* will visit Cairo and Egyptian Vice President Zakariya Muhieddine* will visit Washington, D.C., to hold talks on the crisis.

On June 4, it is reported that Algeria, Libya, and Sudan are preparing to send troops to Egypt; Kuwaiti troops have already arrived; Iraqi troops are

Moshe Safdie (b. 1938), Israeli architect, arouses world interest with his revolutionary modular housing project Habitat, exhibited at the Montreal Expo '67 World Exhibition.

continuing to enter Jordan; and Egyptian airlift of troops and equipment to Jordan continues.

On June 5, the Six-Day War begins with early morning Israeli air attacks on Egyptian air fields. Three hundred of three hundred and forty Egyptian planes are destroyed on the ground and another 20 in the air, virtually eliminating the Egyptian air force. Later in the day, the Israelis destroy the air forces of Jordan and Syria and in retaliation for an Iraqi air strike against Israel inflict considerable damage on the Iraqi air force.

On June 5, Israeli forces, led by Generals Israel Tal, Avraham Yoffe, and Ariel Sharon, attack the Egyptians in the Sinai. By the end of June 6, the second day, Gaza, Rafah, El Arish, and Abu Ageila are captured; the Egyptians are routed all over the Sinai, and the Egyptian commander, Field Marshal Abdel Hakim Amer,* orders all Egyptian units to withdraw behind the Suez Canal.

On June 5, Jordan's King Hussein,* misinformed by Egypt of the war's progress, permits Egyptian General Riad,* commanding his forces, to attack Israeli Jerusalem. Hussein* disregards Levi Eshkol's appeal, transmitted through the UN, to refrain from entering the war. The Israelis, led by General Uzi Narkiss and Colonel Mordecai Gur, attack Jordanian positions and by June 7, the third day, capture Jerusalem's Old City. Bethlehem, Hebron, Ramallah, Jenin, and Nablus also fall to the Israelis.

On June 5, Soviet Premier Alexei Kosygin* uses the "hot line" for the first time to communicate with President Lyndon B. Johnson.* They agree that the superpowers should stay out of the war and encourage a cease-fire.

On June 6, Gamal Abdel Nasser* accuses the U.S. and Britain of aiding Israel in its attacks on Egypt. The U.S. denies the accusation. Israel monitored the radio conversation between Nasser* and Hussein* when they agreed to accuse the U.S. of aiding Israel. Accusations stop after Israel releases the tape of the conversation. Most Arab states break diplomatic relations with the U.S.

On June 7, at the end of the third day, Jordanian forces withdraw across the Jordan River.

On June 7, Israeli forces seize Sharm es-Sheikh and open the Straits of Tiran.

On June 7, a Gallup Poll finds that 56% of Americans express sympathy toward Israel, whereas only 4% sympathize with the Arabs.

On June 7, Naomi Shemer, Israeli musical artist, composes a new version of her ballad, "Jerusalem the Golden," which becomes the anthem of the Six-Day War.

On June 8, Jordan's Hussein* and Egypt's Nasser* agree to a cease-fire with Israel.

On June 8, Israeli aircraft mistakenly attack a U.S. electronic surveillance vessel, USS *Liberty*, off Egypt's coast. The vessel is severely damaged and 10 U.S. sailors are killed. The U.S. accepts Israel's apology.

On June 9, Gamal Abdel Nasser* announces his resignation. He returns to office the next day after popular demonstrations in his favor take place throughout Egypt.

On June 10, Israeli forces, led by General David Elazar, capture the Golan Heights on the sixth day after routing the Syrian forces. A cease-fire is observed by both sides at 6:30 P.M., and the Six-Day War ends.

On June 10, at 9 A.M. Washington, D.C., time, Soviet Premier Alexei Kosygin,* fearing that Israel would threaten Damascus, uses the "hot line" to warn of Soviet military action if Israel does not stop the advance into Syria. President Lyndon B. Johnson* assures Kosygin* that the Israelis will stop and directs the U.S. Sixth Fleet to head toward the Syrian coast, as a signal that Soviet military action would be countered by U.S. military action.

On June 10, the Soviet Union severs diplomatic relations with Israel. Other Soviet bloc states, with the exception of Romania, quickly follow.

Isreali paratroopers at the Western Wall after capture of the Old City of Jerusalem. (Photograph by David Rubinger. Israel Government Press Office)

Front page, The New York Times, *June 8, 1967.*

June 1967

On June 13, a Soviet-proposed UN Security Council resolution condemning Israel and ordering an unconditional withdrawal to the 1949 armistice lines fails passage.

On June 19, in a speech, President Lyndon B. Johnson* unveils a U.S.–Middle East policy. The U.S. would not press Israel to withdraw in the absence of peace. Five principles essential to peace are enunciated: the recognized right to national life; justice for the refugees; innocent maritime passage; limits on the arms race; and political independence and territorial integrity for all.

In June, the Six-Day War produces an unexpected and widespread reaction of American Jewry. Hundreds of millions of dollars are raised for Israel's support.

On June 23, U.S. President Lyndon B. Johnson* and Soviet Premier Alexei Kosygin* begin a summit conference in Glassboro, New Jersey. The conference ends on June 25 without any concrete agreements on the Middle East.

On June 27, the Israeli Knesset formally adds Arab East Jerusalem and the surrounding area to the area of Israeli sovereignty. An additional statute protects the holy places from desecration and assures freedom of access to them.

In South Africa, 1,800 Jews volunteer for noncombatant service in Israel. Seven hundred and eighty-two arrive in Israel before the Jewish Agency advises that they cannot use any more volunteers. The South Africans comprise proportionately the largest group of Diaspora volunteers and the second largest in actual number.

A. **General History**	B. **Jews in North and South America**	C. **Jews in Europe**	D. **Jews in the Middle East and Elsewhere**	E. **Jewish Culture**

BOUNDARY OF ISRAEL AFTER SIX-DAY WAR

July 1967

On July 4, the UN General Assembly resolution on the Arab–Israeli conflict, drafted by Latin American nations, fails to receive the required vote. The U.S. is prepared to support the resolution's call on Israel to "withdraw all its forces from all territories occupied by it as a result of the recent conflict."

The UN General Assembly, by a vote of 99 to 0, adopts a resolution declaring the changed status of Jerusalem to be invalid.

Leonard Bernstein, U.S. composer and conductor, leads the Israel Philharmonic Orchestra in a performance on Jerusalem's Mt. Scopus one month after the liberation of Jerusalem during the Six-Day War.

A. General History	B. Jews in North and South America	C. Jews in Europe	D. Jews in the Middle East and Elsewhere	E. Jewish Culture	
The Association of South East Asian Nations is founded. George Lincoln Rockwell,* the head of the American Nazi party, is assassinated by a disgruntled party member.		Charles H. Jordan, executive vice chairman of the Joint Distribution Committee, disappears while on a visit to Prague, Czechoslovakia. His body is found four days later. Czech officials intimate that he committed suicide by drowning, but U.S. and Israeli officials suspect foul play. The cause of his death has never been established.	The Khartoum Conference of Arab nations, held from August 19 to September 1, issues a proclamation of no peace with Israel, no recognition of Israel, and no negotiation with Israel concerning any Palestinian territory.		**Aug. 1967**
Che Guevara,* chief aide to Cuba's Fidel Castro,* dies in Bolivia.			An Egyptian missile sinks the Israeli destroyer *Eilat* off the Egyptian coast. Three days later, Israeli troops shell the major oil installations in the Egyptian port city of Suez in retaliation. The Israeli UN delegate calls for a concerted action against South Africa in a UN debate on apartheid.		**Oct. 1967**
			The UN Security Council passes Resolution 242. It calls for Israeli withdrawal "from territories occupied in the recent conflict." The Council rejected use of the words *all* and *the*, which the Arabs and Soviets wanted inserted before the word *territories*. The resolution calls for the end of the state of belligerency and the right of every state in the area to be acknowledged as sovereign and "to live in peace within secure and recognized boundaries."		**Nov. 1967**
The first human heart transplant is performed in South Africa by Dr. Christiaan N. Barnard.*					**Dec. 1967**
Wilbur J. Cohen is appointed secretary of	A group of young Jews educated within	*Judaism and Zionism*, an antisemitic book by	Israel Abrahams, leading South African	David M. Feldman, U.S. Conservative	**1968**

	A. General History	B. Jews in North and South America	C. Jews in Europe	D. Jews in the Middle East and Elsewhere	E. Jewish Culture
1968	health, education and welfare by President Lyndon B. Johnson.* Cohen was the Democratic party's chief strategist and expert in the field of social welfare legislation for over 30 years. His tenure in the Johnson* administration will see the enactment of the Medicare and Medicaid health programs.	the Conservative movement establish the first *havurah* group in Somerville, Massachusetts. The *havurah* movement initially was an attempt to develop a religious experience outside a formal synagogue affiliation. By the 1980s, the *havurah* movement will develop to offer synagogue members a more intimate fellowship within the congregation. The Reconstructionist movement establishes the Reconstructionist Rabbinical College, in Philadelphia.	Trofim Kichko,* is published in the Soviet Union. Kichko* directly links the practices and beliefs of Judaism to a hostile political ideology, i.e., Zionism. Throughout the year there is an intense official antisemitic campaign in Poland, exacerbated by political-party infighting between factions led by party leader Wladislaw Gomulka,* former secret police chief Mieczyslaw Moczar,* and Politburo member Edward Gierek.*	Orthodox rabbi for over 30 years, retires and settles in Israel.	rabbi and scholar, writes *Birth Control in Jewish Law*, a comprehensive review of marital relations, contraception, abortion, and related issues. It is based on primary sources collected from the Talmud, posttalmudic codes, and responsa through modern times. *The English–Yiddish Yiddish–English Dictionary*, edited by Uriel Weinreich (1926–1967), Yiddish scholar and linguist, is published posthumously. It will become the most widely used Yiddish dictionary.
Jan. 1968	Alexander Dubcek* replaces Antonin Novotny* as first secretary of the Czech Communist party. A period of liberalization, the Prague Spring, is inaugurated. The Soviet Union expresses deep misgivings.			Haim Bar-Lev (b. 1924) becomes chief of staff of the Israel Defense Forces.	Anthony Hecht, U.S. poet, wins the Pulitzer Prize for his collection of poems, *The Hard Hours*. Arthur Miller, U.S. playwright and novelist, writes *The Price*, a play about the conflict between two brothers who meet after a long separation to dispose of their parents' possessions. A central character is an old Jew who acts as a wise commentator. Arthur Hertzberg (b. 1921), U.S. Conservative rabbi and scholar, writes *The French Enlightenment and the Jews*, describing the internal life and diversity of the Portuguese, Sephardic, and Alsatian French Jewish communities in the preemancipation period. He suggests that French circles of the 18th century were responsible for the political emancipation of the Jews as well as for modern antisemitism and Jewish assimilation. Mel Brooks (Melvin Kaminsky, b. 1926),
Feb. 1968			*Fiddler on the Roof*, the hit U.S. musical, opens in Hamburg as *Anatevka*. It has an attendance over 300,000 at its 274 performances before it tours other West German cities.		
Mar. 1968	The Kerner Commission issues its report on the 1967 U.S. civil disorders that the president appointed it to investigate. It concludes, "Our nation is moving toward two societies, one black, one white—separate and unequal. Reaction to last summer's disorders has quickened the movement and deepened the division."		Student demonstrations in Poland become a pretext for the Gomulka* government's antisemitic campaign. Many Jews are fired from their jobs. Approximately 25,000 Jews emigrate.	A series of terrorist raids from Jordan is climaxed when a bus carrying high school students strikes a mine near Eilat, killing 2 and injuring 28. Israeli troops raid Karameh, Jordan, killing 150 terrorists and taking many prisoners. Arab Legion troops intervene, and heavy fighting results in 100 Jordanians killed and 90 wounded. Israeli losses are 27 dead and 70 wounded. The UN	

A. General History	B. Jews in North and South America	C. Jews in Europe	D. Jews in the Middle East and Elsewhere	E. Jewish Culture	
President Lyndon B. Johnson* announces that he will not run in the presidential election.			Security Council condemns Israel for the Karameh raid.	writes and directs *The Producers*, a film comedy satirizing Nazism. Zero Mostel plays Max Bialystock, a theatrical producer of the play *Springtime for Hitler*. Brooks wins an Oscar for the best original screenplay.	**Mar. 1968**
Civil rights leader Dr. Martin Luther King, Jr.,* is assassinated in Memphis, Tennessee. A three-day riot in Washington, D.C., is the most violent of the civil disorders that follow. President Lyndon B. Johnson* signs into law the Civil Rights Act of 1968, which is intended to end racial discrimination in the sale and rental of 80% of the nation's homes and apartments.				Arnold Newman (b. 1918), U.S. photographer who is world renowned for his environmental portraits where the setting and surrounding objects symbolize or describe the sitter's accomplishments, photographs David Ben-Gurion on Israel's 20th anniversary in the Tel Aviv Museum, where he had announced Israel's independence.	**Apr. 1968**
Peace talks between the U.S. and Communist Vietnam are begun in Paris.		Israel accuses the Soviet Union of antisemitic discrimination against its Jews during a UN Security Council debate.		Marshall W. Nirenberg, U.S. biochemist, is awarded the Nobel Prize in physiology or medicine for his work in deciphering the genetic code by which sequences of the units of DNA "spell out" instructions for the synthesis of proteins.	**May 1968**
U.S. Senator Robert F. Kennedy* of New York, a presidential contender, is assassinated in Los Angeles by Sirhan Sirhan,* a 24-year-old Jordanian who was born in Jerusalem. President Lyndon B. Johnson* selects U.S. Supreme Court Justice Abe Fortas to replace Chief Justice Earl Warren,* who announced his intention to retire. In October, Johnson* will withdraw Fortas's nomination in the face of opposition by Republican and southern Democrat senators.		Israel and Romania enter into a trade agreement after Romania's acting foreign minister visits Israel.	The 27th Zionist Congress, meeting in Jerusalem, revises the 1951 Jerusalem Program, making it more outspokenly Zionist. It calls for the centrality of Israel in Jewish life and the ingathering of the Jewish people in Israel through aliyah from all countries.	*The Non-Jewish Jew and Other Essays*, written by Isaac Deutscher (1907–1967), Marxist historian and journalist, is published posthumously. Well known for his political biographies of Stalin* and Trotsky, he categorizes Spinoza, Marx, Freud, and Trotsky in this book of essays as "non-Jewish" Jews.	**June 1968**
The U.S. and the Soviet Union sign a nonproliferation treaty, prohibiting the transfer of nuclear weapons to other countries and prohibiting assistance to nonnuclear countries to	John F. Hatchett* is appointed director of New York University's Afro-American Center. While a teacher in the public school system, Hatchett* wrote that Jews practice "misery, degradation, racism		George Ball,* U.S. ambassador to the UN, visits Jordan and is authorized by the Israelis to convey the Israeli offer to King Hussein* to return the West Bank, with minor modifications,	French novelist Romain Gary's (1914–1980) novel *The Dance of Genghis Cohn* is published in English. Adapting the Dybbuk legend, the novel depicts the haunting of an ex-Nazi by the spirit of Cohn, a Jewish	**July 1968**

	A. General History	B. Jews in North and South America	C. Jews in Europe	D. Jews in the Middle East and Elsewhere	E. Jewish Culture
July 1968	manufacture or acquire nuclear weapons.	and cultural genocide . . . against my people." He will be removed in October, when he calls Vice President Hubert Humphrey* and Richard M. Nixon* "racist bastards." The Jewish Defense League in New York, a militant group that assumes responsibility for the physical protection of Jews, is organized by Rabbi Meir Kahane. Kahane's motivation is an upsurge of antisemitism.		to Jordan in return for peace. Iraq decides to keep 12,000 troops in Jordan despite King Hussein's* wish to have them withdrawn. On July 23, an Israeli El Al airliner flying from Rome to Lod is hijacked and forced to land in Algeria. Algeria first releases 23 passengers carrying non-Israeli passports and later releases 10 Israeli women and children. The Israeli men will not be released until August 31. Israel agrees to free 16 Arab prisoners as a "humanitarian gesture."	entertainer whom he had murdered during World War II. André Chouraqui, Israeli lawyer and government official who emigrated from North Africa to Israel, writes *Between East and West: A History of the Jews of North Africa*. René-Samuel Cassin, French expert on international law and editor of the first draft of the Universal Declaration of the Rights of Man in 1948, is awarded the Nobel Peace Prize. Cassin is president of the Alliance Israelite Universelle.
Aug. 1968	The Democratic National Convention, held in Chicago, is disrupted by anti–Vietnam War protesters. The Soviet Union and its allies, Poland, East Germany, Hungary, and Bulgaria, invade and occupy Czechoslovakia and reverse a democratization trend begun earlier in the year by a new government headed by Alexander Dubcek.*		The Soviet defense ministry publication *Red Star* asserts that Jews in Communist countries were recruited as spies for Israel's intelligence agency and the U.S. Central Intelligence Agency. At least one-third of Czechoslovakia's Jewish population of 15,000 leaves the country after the Soviet invasion.		Israel Through the Ages, organized by André Malraux,* French minister of state for cultural affairs, opens at the Petit Palais Museum in Paris. Artur London, one of the three survivors of the Slansky trial of the 1950s, writes *The Confession*, which describes his experiences as a Czech Communist party official forced to confess to crimes he did not commit.
Sep. 1968		Black–Jewish relations in New York are exacerbated by a school strike of the United Federation of Teachers (largely Jewish in membership) against the governing board (largely black) of the Ocean Hill–Brownsville public school district. Whitney Young,* head of the National Urban League, writes, "Jews who are caught in such conflict aren't singled out because they are Jews but because they are whites whose presence in some	The Soviet newspaper *Pravda* writes that Jiri Hayek,* the non-Jewish Czech foreign minister before the occupation, was a Nazi collaborator and had changed his name from Karpeles, an obvious Jewish name.	An artillery duel along 80 miles of the Suez Canal, during which Egypt fires over 10,000 shells, kills 10 Israeli soldiers and wounds 18. At a B'nai B'rith convention, Richard M. Nixon* urges the U.S. to give Israel "sufficient military power to deter an attack." This is the first time it is proposed that the U.S. give Israel a decided military advantage. At the convention, both presidential candidates, Richard	Abba Eban, Israeli diplomat and author, writes *My People: The Story of the Jews*, a highly personalized general Jewish history with special emphasis on the rise of the State of Israel. David Flusser, Israeli scholar and specialist on the history of early Christianity, writes *Jesus*. He writes of Jesus as a Jewish figure, and his observations arouse controversy among Jewish and Christian scholars.

A. General History	B. Jews in North and South America	C. Jews in Europe	D. Jews in the Middle East and Elsewhere	E. Jewish Culture	
		ghetto institutions is resented."	M. Nixon* and Hubert Humphrey,* issue statements supporting the sale of Phantom jets to Israel.	Ya'akov Kirschen (b. 1938), cartoonist, emigrates to Israel from the U.S. and shortly thereafter creates "Dry Bones," a daily political cartoon strip that appears in the Israeli press and achieves worldwide popularity.	**Sep. 1968**
			On the third day of the Sukkot holiday, 47 are injured in Hebron when a hand grenade explodes on the steps of the Tomb of the Patriarchs. A sudden Egyptian artillery barrage along the Suez Canal kills 15 Israeli soldiers and wounds 34. In reply, Israel bombards Egyptian oil refineries at Suez, starting many fires. Israeli troops attack deep into Egypt, blowing up the Qena and Naj Hammadi bridges and the Naj Hammadi transformer station on the Nile River.		**Oct. 1968**
The Republican Nixon*–Agnew* ticket wins one of closest elections in U.S. history. The popular vote is 31,375,000 to 31,125,000 for the Democratic Humphrey*–Muskie* ticket, with American Independents Wallace*–LeMay* receiving 9,775,000 votes. The Democrats retain control of both houses of Congress.	The Jewish vote in the U.S. presidential election is estimated at 81% for Hubert Humphrey,* 17% for Richard M. Nixon,* and 2% for George C. Wallace.*		King Hussein* of Jordan enters into an agreement with the PLO and al-Fatah, who agree not to interfere with Jordan in return for freedom to pursue their terrorist activities against Israeli territory. Twelve are killed and 52 are injured in Jerusalem's Mahane Yehuda market when a car bomb explodes.		**Nov. 1968**
U.S. astronauts orbit the moon.		At the opening ceremonies in Madrid of the first public synagogue built in Spain since the expulsion, the Spanish government explicitly recognizes that the 1492 order of King Ferdinand* and Queen Isabella* expelling Jews from the kingdom is void.	Two Arab terrorists attempt to blow up an Israeli El Al airliner at the Athens airport, killing an Israeli engineer and injuring several passengers. Israeli Transport Minister Moshe Carmel holds the Lebanese government reponsible because "we know that the men came from Beirut."		**Dec. 1968**

Dec. 1968

The Johnson* administration announces that the U.S. will sell Israel 50 Phantom F-4 jet fighter bombers.

Israeli troops land at the Beirut airport and, after evacuating nearby people, destroy 14 Arab commercial aircraft without any loss of life. The UN Security Council unanimously condemns Israel for the raid. It does not consider Israel's complaint of the Athens incident.

By the end of the year, there were 1,280 incidents since the Six-Day War. A total of 281 Israelis and 600 Arabs were killed.

By the end of the year, the Soviet Union has supplied the Arab states with $2.5 billion worth of arms since the 1967 Six-Day War. There are about 2,000 to 3,000 Soviet military advisers in Egypt.

	A. General History	B. Jews in North and South America	C. Jews in Europe	D. Jews in the Middle East and Elsewhere	E. Jewish Culture
1969		There are 10 member congregations of the Reconstructionist movement. The Law Committee of the Rabbinical Assembly, the organization of U.S. Conservative rabbis, votes to permit congregations to abandon the second day of all festivals except New Year's (Rosh Hashanah) to conform to Israeli practice. The decision evokes conflict within the Conservative movement. Gertrude J. Selznick and Stephen Steinberg write *The Tenacity of Prejudice: Anti-Semitism in Contemporary America*, an Anti-Defamation League–sponsored survey. They find over one-third of the sample rated "high" on antisemitic beliefs and report that while "conventional antisemitism [has] undoubtedly declined since the 1930's and 1940's, [it has] not declined radically and [is] still far from vanishing." The board of directors of the University of Chile establishes a Center for Jewish Studies, directed by Bernardo Berdichevsky.	The Diamond Club in Antwerp, Belgium, celebrates its 75th anniversary. Among those given high Belgian awards are several prominent Jewish diamond dealers. Raymond Aron (1905–1983), French philosopher and World War II editor of the Free French press, writes *De Gaulle, Israel and the Jews*. He concludes that Charles de Gaulle's* post–Six-Day War attitude toward Israel encouraged anti-Jewish sentiments in French society.		Harry Orlinsky, U.S. biblical scholar, edits *Notes on the New Translation of the Torah*, describing the modern archaeological, historical, and linguistic research underlying the recent Jewish Publication Society of America's English translation. Orlinsky was editor in chief of the translation project. Theodor H. Gaster (b. 1906), biblical scholar, writes *Myth, Legend, and Custom in the Old Testament*, in which he attempts to gather "all that can be derived from comparative folklore and mythology for the interpretation of the Old Testament." Philip Roth, U.S. author, writes *Portnoy's Complaint*, the autobiography of Alexander Portnoy as told to a psychiatrist, including his relations with Sophie, his possessive "Jewish mother," and his obsession with sex. It will be adapted to the screen in 1972. Salvador Luria (1912–1991), U.S. biologist, is awarded the Nobel Prize in physiology or medicine. His research extends the principles of genetics to viruses and bacteria

A. General History	B. Jews in North and South America	C. Jews in Europe	D. Jews in the Middle East and Elsewhere	E. Jewish Culture	
The Soviet spaceship *Soyuz-5* performs the first linkup in space with a transfer of cosmonauts from one spaceship to another. The commander of *Soyuz-5* is Lieutenant Colonel Boris Volynov, reported to be Jewish.	"Harlem on My Mind," an exhibition at New York's Metropolitan Museum of Art, opens. The exhibition catalog contains a preface by 18-year-old Candice Van Ellison,* who writes "Behind every hurdle that the Afro-American has yet to jump stands the Jew who has already cleared it. . . . Our contempt for the Jews makes us feel more completely American in sharing a national prejudice." Museum director Thomas Hoving* refuses demands for deletion of the preface. On January 31, the museum withdraws the catalog after continued pressure from political leaders and Jewish organizations. The Anti-Defamation League issues a study, "Anti-Semitism in the New York City School Controversy," charging that black separatists deliberately created a pattern of antisemitism in order to gain greater control within the public school system.		A jet engine factory is founded at Beit Shemesh, near Jerusalem, by French industrialist Joseph Shidlovsky, owner of the Turbomeka Co. Nine Jews are publicly hanged in Iraq after being arrested in October 1967 with 17 others and accused of espionage for Israel. Later, two more will be hanged.	and leads to the new science of molecular biology. Murray Gellmann (b. 1929), U.S. physicist, is awarded the Nobel Prize in physics for his research in the behavior of subatomic particles. Martin Gilbert, British historian, edits a *Jewish History Atlas*, a collection of maps on the course of Jewish life from its earliest beginnings to the present. Leni Yahil writes *The Rescue of Danish Jewry: Test of a Democracy*, which describes the courageous and successful Danish effort to save its Jews from the Nazis during World War II. Ben Zion Dinur's *Israel and the Diaspora* appears in English translation from the Hebrew. Dinur, a founder of the Israeli school of Jewish historiography, maintains that the unique feature of Israel in the Diaspora "is not to be found in the expulsion of Jews from their homeland	**Jan. 1969**
		Four Arab terrorists attack an El Al plane at the Zurich airport, killing one and wounding several others. An Israeli security guard kills one terrorist. The guard is tried in December with the three surviving terrorists and is acquitted of firing at a disarmed man, while the three terrorists are convicted and sentenced to 12 years in prison. The first volume, *Overture*, of a 10-volume study, *The Netherlands in the Second World War*, is published. The author	A terrorist bomb explosion at a Jerusalem supermarket kills two and injures nine. Israeli Prime Minister Levi Eshkol dies and will be succeeded on March 17 by Golda Meir, who re-forms the National Unity Government without any change in its membership. Yasir Arafat* (b. 1929), leader of al-Fatah, becomes head of the PLO.	to foreign countries, but in the continuation of collective Jewish life in the Dispersion and in spite of the Dispersion." Yad Vashem, the Martyrs' and Heroes' Authority of Israel, publishes a study of the Jewish community of Romania, the first in a series on the destruction of the Jewish communities of Europe during the Holocaust. Bezalel Narkiss, Israeli scholar of Jewish art, writes *Hebrew Illuminated Manuscripts*. The 60	**Feb. 1969**

	A. General History	B. Jews in North and South America	C. Jews in Europe	D. Jews in the Middle East and Elsewhere	E. Jewish Culture
Feb. 1969			includes a detailed account of the government's return of Jewish refugees to Germany in 1938–1939 when they were ruled "undesirable persons" by Justice Minister Carel Goseling.*		reproductions prove that the Second Commandment did not inhibit Jewish artistic expression in Spain, France, Germany, or Italy during the Middle Ages.
Mar. 1969	Soviet and Chinese armies clash along their Asian border and relations between the two Communist countries worsen throughout the year.			Egyptian Chief of Staff General Abdul Riad* is killed in an artillery exchange along the Suez Canal front. U.S. Secretary of State William Rogers* declares before the Senate Foreign Relations Committee that the U.S. will play a more active role in Middle East. The 1967 Arab–Israeli borders "should not reflect the weight of conquest" and UN Resolution 242 affirms "the need for a just settlement of the refugee problem."	Marc Chagall's tapestries *Exodus, Entry into Jerusalem,* and *Isaiah's Prophecy* are installed in Israel's Knesset. An exhibition of the work of Anna Ticho (1894–1980), Israeli landscape artist, is held at the Jewish Museum in New York.
Apr. 1969	Charles de Gaulle* resigns as the head of France after a defeat in a national referendum. Georges Pompidou* is elected to succeed him.			Gamal Abdel Nasser* denounces the cease-fire resolution between Israel and Egypt and proclaims a "war of attrition," and his forces begin a daily shelling of Israeli positions along the Suez Canal.	
May 1969	Justice Abe Fortas resigns from the U.S. Supreme Court after *Life* magazine reveals that in 1966, soon after joining the Court, Fortas accepted a $20,000 fee from a charitable foundation established by financier Louis Wolfson, who was then under investigation by the Securities and Exchange Commission.		Two Arabs bomb the El Al airline office in Brussels, injuring two employees. Jewish communal and Israeli offices are placed under constant police protection. Boris Kotschubiesky, a Soviet Jewish engineer, is tried for "anti-Soviet slander" and sentenced to three years in a labor camp. He objected to Soviet policy toward Israel and to limitations put on Jewish life and openly demanded the right to emigrate to Israel. A rumor begins to spread in the French		

A. General History	B. Jews in North and South America	C. Jews in Europe	D. Jews in the Middle East and Elsewhere	E. Jewish Culture
		city of Orléans that several women have disappeared and that six Jewish merchants had drugged and smuggled them out of the country to a life of prostitution abroad. This antisemitic falsehood is spread by word of mouth and ultimately fades away during the summer. The episode will become the subject of a book written by the sociologist Edgar Morin.*		**May 1969**
U.S. astronauts Neil Armstrong* and Edwin E. Aldrin, Jr.* land on the moon; Michael Collins* remains in lunar orbit in the Command Module.			The U.S. joins in a unanimous UN Security Council resolution that calls all Israeli actions regarding Jerusalem invalid and urges Israel to rescind all actions taken by it to change Jerusalem's status. Israel restates its view that Jerusalem is Israel's eternal capital and rejects the U.S. view that East Jerusalem is occupied territory.	**July 1969**
		Israel and Romania announce the upgrading of their diplomatic missions from legations to embassies. Romania's independent foreign policy increases its differences with its Communist allies.	Israeli jet fighter bombers raid terrorist bases in Lebanon in reprisal for attacks on Israeli settlements. The U.S. joins in unanimous UN Security Council condemnation of Israel. A deranged Australian tourist, Michael Rohan,* sets fire to Jerusalem's al-Aqsa mosque, causing limited damage to the Muslim shrine. Worldwide Muslim outrage ensues. A U.S. TWA airliner is hijacked by two Arab terrorists while on flight from Rome to Athens and diverted to Damascus, Syria. The Syrians release all but two Israeli men, who will be held hostage until December 5, when they are released as part of a prisoner-exchange deal.	**Aug. 1969**

	A. General History	B. Jews in North and South America	C. Jews in Europe	D. Jews in the Middle East and Elsewhere	E. Jewish Culture
Sep. 1969	King Idris'* conservative pro-American Libyan monarchy is overthrown in an army coup. The new regime, led by Colonel Muammar Qaddafi,* is anti-American, pan-Arab, and radical in tone and gradually develops a foreign policy following the Soviet line.			Israeli Prime Minister Golda Meir is warmly received by President Richard M. Nixon* at the White House during an official state visit. There is no official U.S. response to her request for additional military supplies for Israel, but she declares that she is going home "with a lighter heart than when I came."	
Oct. 1969	Willy Brandt* is elected chancellor of West Germany.			Israel holds national elections for the Seventh Knesset, with 1,367,743 votes cast. Mapai wins 56 seats; Liberals, 26 seats; and the National Religious party, 12 seats. The government is installed on December 15 with Golda Meir as prime minister, Moshe Dayan as minister of defense, and Abba Eban as minister of foreign affairs.	
Nov. 1969	Anti-Vietnam moratorium day rallies held throughout the U.S. are believed to be the largest nationally coordinated antiwar demonstration in U.S. history.				
Dec. 1969	Vice President Spiro T. Agnew* attacks the mass media for bias, referring to a "little group of men who wield a free hand in selecting, presenting and interpreting the great issues." He complains that television commentators "live and work in the geographical and intellectual confines of Washington, D.C., or New York City."		Five missile boats built by France for Israel but impounded under the French embargo of Israeli weapons after the Six-Day War leave Cherbourg without French permission. Manned by Israeli personnel who were in France awaiting the lifting of the embargo, the boats will arrive in Israel on January 1, 1970. France demands Israel recall the head of its arms purchasing mission. By the end of the year, all Jewish supporters of the Dubcek* regime have been expelled from the Czech Communist party as a result of a	U.S. Secretary of State William Rogers* proposes a Middle East settlement known as the Rogers Plan. Israel would withdraw from occupied territory and the Arabs would agree to some contractual arrangement guaranteeing a permanent peace with Israel. Alterations in the 1967 borders should be "insubstantial" and only for "mutual security." A "binding agreement" is not the formal peace treaty sought by Israel, and Israel rejects the plan. President Richard M. Nixon* instructs his assistant, Leonard	

598

A. General History	B. Jews in North and South America	C. Jews in Europe	D. Jews in the Middle East and Elsewhere	E. Jewish Culture	
		campaign that included antisemitism under the guise of anti-Zionism by Soviet and Slovak party leadership to rally popular support for the new regime.	Garment, to convey private assurances to Israeli Prime Minister Golda Meir that he would not press the Rogers Plan. U.S. Ambassador Charles Yost* presents a proposal for an Israeli–Jordanian settlement at the Big Four (i.e., the U.S., Britain, France, and the Soviet Union) talks. The proposal calls for Israel to return to the pre-1967 borders in exchange for guarantees, improved access to Jerusalem's holy places, and an agreement prohibiting violence across the Jordanian border. Israel would have to accept some Palestinian refugees. By the end of December, 47 Egyptian aircraft have been shot down during the year along the Suez Canal front. Israeli mastery of the air prevented any large-scale Egyptian effort to cross the canal, despite almost continuous hostilities.		**Dec. 1969**
Libya's Colonel Muammar Qaddafi,* leader of the revolutionary council that ousted King Idris,* orders the expulsion of 25,000 Italian settlers and the expropriation of their property.	Bora Laskin becomes the first Jewish appointee to the Supreme Court of Canada. The Argentine economy is disrupted by the collapse of credit cooperatives as a result of mismanagement and embezzlements by managers. Of the 242 cooperatives, 124 are Jewish owned. The Jewish community is harmed as Jewish businessmen are deprived of credit, the cooperatives cease support of Jewish communal, social, and educational institutions, and a negative impression is	Franz Stangl,* commander of the Sobibor and Treblinka extermination camps who escaped to Brazil after World War II and was caught in 1967 and extradited to West Germany, is tried for war crimes by the West German government at Dusseldorf. He is convicted and sentenced to life imprisonment. Bruno Kreisky (1911–1990), Austrian statesman, is elected prime minister (chancellor) of Austria. He is the first Jew to hold such office. He fled Austria for Sweden in 1938 after the Nazi	David Ben-Gurion resigns from the Knesset and retires from public life. Ceylon, which has maintained diplomatic relations with Israel since 1957, suspends them and closes Israel's legation in Colombo.	Jacob R. Marcus, U.S. historian, writes *The Colonial American Jews, 1492–1776*, a three-volume survey. Arthur Goren, U.S. historian, writes *New York Jews and the Quest for Community: The Kehillah Experiment, 1908–1922*. Goren, who wins the Bancroft Prize for his work, describes the social and political background of the most notable effort to centralize Jewish community organization in the U.S. Henry Feingold, U.S. historian, writes *The Politics of Rescue: The Roosevelt*	**1970**

A. General History	B. Jews in North and South America	C. Jews in Europe	D. Jews in the Middle East and Elsewhere	E. Jewish Culture
1970	left on the non-Jewish world. Karl A. Schleunes,* U.S. historian, writes *The Twisted Road to Auschwitz: Nazi Policy Toward German Jews, 1933–1939*. He maintains that although Adolf Hitler* encouraged and even forced emigration in an effort to rid Germany of its Jews, he had no preconceived plan to exterminate the Jews of Europe. He suggests that Hitler* turned Jewish matters over to the SS in 1939. John Updike* (b. 1932), U.S. novelist, writes *Bech: A Book*, assembled as a novel from a series of short stories around a Jewish writer, Henry Bech, written for the *New Yorker* magazine. It is a satirical treatment of a Jewish writer seeking recognition.	occupation and returned after the end of World War II. He was foreign minister from 1959 to 1966. Hermann Bondi, mathematician, is appointed chief scientist of Britain's ministry of defence. Born in Vienna, he moved to England in 1937, but his studies at Cambridge were interrupted when he was interned and sent to Canada as an alien at the outbreak of World War II.		*Administration and the Holocaust, 1938–1945*. Feingold describes the failure of the Roosevelt* administration to move the U.S. in any useful way to alleviate the desperate plight of Europe's Jews. Leonard Slater, U.S. author, writes *The Pledge*, describing the American Jewish contribution to the creation of the State of Israel. Jacob Neusner, U.S. historian, completes his five-volume *A History of the Jews in Babylonia*. Leon Uris, U.S. novelist, writes *QB VII*, a novel based on the trial of an American novelist charged with libeling a Polish surgeon by contending that he performed experimental sterilization of Jews in a Nazi concentration camp.
Jan. 1970			Gamal Abdel Nasser* travels secretly to Moscow. The Soviets agree to supply Egypt with advanced Soviet anti-aircraft missiles and missile crews to stop Israeli air raids. Israeli Defense Minister Moshe Dayan states that Israel will continue to disrupt Egyptian war preparations in reply to the "war of attrition" by continuing air attacks and commando raids on Egyptian military targets. A message from President Richard M. Nixon* to American Jewish leaders does not disavow the Rogers Plan, but assures that the U.S. will not impose a peace settlement.	Mark Harris, U.S. novelist, writes *The Goy*, a novel portraying a gentile professor's relations with Jewish colleagues. Saul Bellow, U.S. novelist, wins his third National Book Award for *Mr. Sammler's Planet*, which depicts the odyssey of Arthur Sammler, a survivor of a Nazi concentration camp who, with all his experience of man at his worst, has not lost his faith in human values. Isaac Bashevis Singer, Polish-born author of Yiddish fiction, publishes in English translation *Enemies, a Love Story*, his first novel in an American setting. It chronicles

A. General History	B. Jews in North and South America	C. Jews in Europe	D. Jews in the Middle East and Elsewhere	E. Jewish Culture	
			Israel's Supreme Court grants the petition of Major Benjamin Shalit, who is married to a non-Jew, to enter the nationality of his two children as Jews in the ministry of the interior's population register. The decision reopens the controversy, Who Is a Jew? On March 10 the Knesset will adopt a law providing that only persons born of a Jewish mother or converted to Judaism would be registered as Jewish by nationality. The law does not specify that conversion must be according to *halakhah*, and it is presumed that Reform or Conservative conversions performed abroad would be recognized.	the life of a Polish Jew who marries the girl who helped him escape from the Nazis after he believes his wife is dead. In 1989, it will be adapted to the screen under the direction of Paul Mazursky. Yehuda Bauer, Israeli historian, writes *From Diplomacy to Resistance: A History of Jewish Palestine, 1939–1945*, describing how the Jews prepared for the postwar struggle that was to lead to statehood. He also writes *Flight and Rescue: Brichah*, a history of the illegal immigration of almost 300,000 Holocaust survivors from Europe to Palestine. Paul Anthony Samuelson, U.S. economist, is awarded the Nobel Prize in economics for his efforts to raise the level of scientific analysis in economic theory.	**Jan. 1970**
The conspiracy trial of the Chicago Seven ends. It was presided over by Judge Julius Hoffman. The defendants included Jerry Rubin, Abbie Hoffman, and David Dellinger, who were charged with inciting to riot and convicted of intent to incite riot at the Chicago Democratic National Convention in 1968.		El Al passengers on board a bus in the Munich airport are attacked by Arab terrorists, with 1 Israeli killed and 11 others injured, including actress Hanna Meron. After the attack, West Germany's Jewish community centers and synagogues are placed under police protection. The Munich Jewish community's home for the aged is set afire, and seven occupants lose their lives. The West German government contributes 1 million deutsche marks toward rebuilding the home. A Swissair airliner bound for Tel Aviv explodes within 15 minutes after taking off from Zurich. The 47 passengers and crew are killed. The Palestinian Front for the Liberation of Palestine claims responsibility.	Egypt charges that an Israeli air attack killed 70 and injured 49 at a factory near Cairo. Israel acknowledges that the pilots mistook the factory for an army camp.	Sir Bernard Katz, British physiologist, and Julius Axelrod, U.S. scientist, are awarded the Nobel Prize in physiology or medicine for research in the nature of both the nerve impulse and nerve–muscle connections. The Canadian Writers Series publishes studies of three Jewish authors: A. M. Klein, Leonard Cohen (b. 1934), and Mordecai Richler (b. 1931). A group of works by Mark Rothko (1903–1970), U.S. abstract painter, is permanently installed in the Rothko Room of the Tate Gallery, in London.	**Feb. 1970**

	A. General History	B. Jews in North and South America	C. Jews in Europe	D. Jews in the Middle East and Elsewhere	E. Jewish Culture
Mar. 1970	In Cambodia, Prince Sihanouk* is overthrown in a coup. Lon Nol takes power.		The Soviet government organizes a press conference attended by Aron Vergelis, Benjamin Dymshyts, General David Dragunsky, and other Jews affiliated with the government, who state that Soviet Jewry is content and that the discontent among some is caused by "Zionist traitors." The Soviet Union commences an intensive campaign of anti-Israel and anti-Zionist vilification in reponse to Western and Israeli protests of the treatment of Soviet Jews. The Soviets maintain that Russian Jews have no desire to emigrate to Israel.	The Jewish War Veterans demonstrate in Chicago against visiting President Georges Pompidou* of France to protest the sale of French jet warplanes to Libya. Irritated by this action, President Richard M. Nixon* delays a decision responding to an Israeli request for additional Phantom jet warplanes.	Otto Klemperer (1885–1973), conductor, becomes an Israeli citizen. He gained fame as a European conductor, especially in Germany. In 1919, he converted to Roman Catholicism. He fled Germany in 1933 to escape the Nazis who attacked him for his Jewish origins. He reverted to Judaism in 1967. The Israel Institute for Talmudic Publications under the direction of Rabbi Adin Steinsaltz begins publication of a multivolume Hebrew edition of the Babylonian Talmud in which the Hebrew and Aramaic source is printed with vowels and is accompanied by a plain explanation of the text in modern Hebrew, seeking to facilitate the study of Talmud for everyone. The English edition will begin publication in 1989.
Apr. 1970				Egypt charges that an Israeli air attack killed 30 schoolchildren and wounded 36 near Kantara. Israel denies the charge, stating they were attacking a military target, and Egypt refuses access to the site to journalists for over a week. Israeli planes on a mission over Egypt encounter Soviet-piloted aircraft.	
May 1970				Israeli forces cross into Lebanon and destroy Fatah camps in a 39-hour operation. During the first five months of 1970, 140 attacks on Israel were carried out from Lebanese territory. The UN Security Council condemns the Israeli operation, with the U.S. abstaining. A school bus from the Upper Galilee village of Avivim is hit by bazooka shells fired from Lebanese territory, killing 8 children and 4 adults and injuring 20.	

A. General History	B. Jews in North and South America	C. Jews in Europe	D. Jews in the Middle East and Elsewhere	E. Jewish Culture	
Parliamentary elections in Great Britain return the Conservative party to power in an upset victory over the Labour party. Edward Heath* replaces Harold Wilson* as prime minister.			U.S. Secretary of State William Rogers* advises Congress that the Soviet Union is involved in Egypt's air defense, and Soviet military personnel are stationed in a country outside the Warsaw Pact. Rogers* starts a new peace initiative aimed at achieving a new Israeli–Egyptian cease-fire along the Suez Canal and to begin indirect peace talks with UN Special Envoy Gunnar Jarring.*		**June 1970**
			Seventy-nine U.S. senators endorse a bipartisan letter to Secretary of State William Rogers* warning that recent Soviet actions in the Middle East are a threat to world peace and a challenge to U.S. strategic interests and urging that the U.S. supply aircraft to Israel.		
			Israeli and Syrian forces commence a battle along the entire cease-fire line in the Golan Heights. This battle lasts several days and is a culmination of several months of sporadic fighting.		
Construction of the Aswan Dam in Egypt is completed. The Soviet Union aided the project.			In a television interview, President Richard M. Nixon* threatens U.S. action if the Soviet Union upsets the balance of power in the Middle East. He charges that Israel's aggressive neighbors, Syria and Egypt, want to "drive Israel into the sea" and suggests that Israel is entitled to "defensible borders."		**July 1970**
			Sophisticated Soviet missiles along the Suez Canal down four Israeli jets, and five pilots are captured; Israel downs nine MiGs, including four reliably reported to have been flown by Soviet pilots.		

	A. General History	B. Jews in North and South America	C. Jews in Europe	D. Jews in the Middle East and Elsewhere	E. Jewish Culture
Aug. 1970				As a result of U.S. efforts, and apparent Soviet acquiescence, Egypt and Israel accept a Suez Canal cease-fire and begin diplomatic talks. However, in violation of the military standstill agreement, Egypt immediately deploys a large number of Soviet ground-to-air missiles near the Suez Canal. Israel denounces the violation and refuses to return to the talks.	
Sep. 1970	Egyptian President Gamal Abdel Nasser* dies. He is succeeded by Vice President Anwar al-Sadat.*				

Sep. 1970

D. Jews in the Middle East and Elsewhere

Four airliners are attacked by George Habash's* Popular Front for the Liberation of Palestine (PFLP). (1) An attempt to hijack an El Al airliner over England is foiled, and Leila Khaled,* one of the terrorists, is captured. (2) A Pan Am 747 is hijacked to Cairo, where it is blown up after evacuation of passengers and crew. (3, 4) A Swissair airliner and a TWA airliner are flown to Dawson Field in Jordan and are joined by a BOAC airliner, and they are blown up. More than 300 passengers are exchanged for 7 Arab terrorists. The PFLP attacks arouse universal condemnation and highlight Jordan's King Hussein's* inability to control Palestinian terrorists.

King Hussein* orders Jordan's army to move against Palestinians threatening his regime. Syria moves 300 tanks into Jordan. President Richard M. Nixon* denounces the Syrian intervention. Israel, encouraged by the U.S., mobilizes and threatens Syria.

Syria withdraws from Jordan and the crisis ends with thousands of Palestinian casualties. The PLO charges that there were more casualties inflicted on them by the Jordanians in three days than by the Israelis in two decades of hostilities.

Israeli Prime Minister Golda Meir has a private meeting with President Richard M. Nixon* in Washington, D.C. She advises that Israel will not rejoin peace discussions until the Suez Canal military situation is restored to the pre–cease-fire status. She requests large-scale economic and military assistance not to be contingent on agreement with the details of U.S. peace proposals.

	A. General History	B. Jews in North and South America	C. Jews in Europe	D. Jews in the Middle East and Elsewhere	E. Jewish Culture
Oct. 1970		The Jewish Defense League (JDL) holds a sit-in at the Federation of Jewish Philanthropies of New York and demands the expenditure of $6 million for Jewish education. Major Jewish organizations react critically to the JDL action.	On the Simhat Torah holiday, more than 15,000 Moscow Jews, the largest group ever, congregate in front of the Moscow synagogue, dancing and singing Hebrew and Israeli songs. Similar groups assemble in Leningrad and other cities.		
Nov. 1970	General Charles de Gaulle* dies.				

A. General History	B. Jews in North and South America	C. Jews in Europe	D. Jews in the Middle East and Elsewhere	E. Jewish Culture	
Poland's Communist leader, Wladislaw Gomulka,* is forced out of office following rioting in Gdansk in protest against rising prices and is succeeded by Edward Gierek.* Both Gomulka* and Gierek* were involved in Poland's postwar antisemitic campaigns.		Twelve Soviet Jews are tried in Leningrad and convicted of attempting to hijack an airliner at Smolny Airport in June and fly it to Sweden. Two, Mark Dymshits and Edward Kuznetsov, are sentenced to death. Under pressure from the West, the death sentences are commuted to 15 years' imprisonment. West Germany granted Israel 150 million deutsche marks in economic aid during the year.	Israel announces it will return to Gunnar Jarring's* peace talks, which were suspended after the Egyptian violation of the cease-fire agreement. Jordan's King Hussein* and Israeli Defense Minister Moshe Dayan, on separate visits to Washington, D.C., receive assurances of additional military aid. Hussein* is reported to have urged the U.S. not to speak of a Palestinian entity, and when asked by the press of his promise to grant Palestinian self-determination, he replied he was confident they would always vote to remain in "the Jordanian family." The London-based Institute for Strategic Studies reports that during the year, the Soviet Union sent a total of $2.5 billion in arms aid and 20,000 military personnel to Egypt.		**Dec. 1970**
Indira Gandhi* is elected leader of India. India signs the Treaty of Peace, Friendship and Co-operation with the Soviet Union.	In New York, the decision of Mayor John V. Lindsay* and other city officials to build three 24-story low-income apartment houses in white, heavily Jewish middle-class Forest Hills, Queens, contributes to the growing tension between the city's black and Jewish communities. Reinhold Niebuhr's* widow requests the removal of his name from the masthead of *Christianity and Crisis* because of an article criticizing Israel. Niebuhr* founded the magazine in 1941 to rally American Christians against Nazism.	The Spanish government completes the restoration of Toledo's famed El Transito synagogue to what it had looked like in the 14th century. Marcel Ophul's film *The Sorrow and the Pity*, a documentary on the attitude of the French population under the Nazi occupation, is shown throughout France. The film includes the depiction of the general indifference of the French to the Jewish plight under the Pétain* regime.	Hebrew University professor Benjamin Mazar announces discovery of a large parapet stone at Jerusalem's Temple Mount, the first to bear a Hebrew inscription, and reading "belonging to the trumpet-blowing place." The stone and inscription confirm a statement by Josephus in his *The Jewish War* that a trumpet was sounded by a priest atop the Temple Wall every Sabbath to signal the approach and close of the holy day.	Cynthia Ozick (b. 1928), U.S. novelist, short story writer, and essayist, publishes *The Pagan Rabbi and Other Stories*, which includes her widely acclaimed story "Envy: or, Yiddish in America," believed to be a description of the relations of most Yiddish writers to Isaac Bashevis Singer. E. L. Doctorow (b. 1931), U.S. novelist, writes *The Book of Daniel*, a biographical novel of a boy recalling his parents who resemble Julius and Ethel Rosenberg and are executed for providing secret information to an enemy nation.	**1971**
General Idi Amin* seizes power in Uganda.				Herman Wouk, U.S. novelist, writes *The Winds of War*, a	**Jan. 1971**

	A. General History	B. Jews in North and South America	C. Jews in Europe	D. Jews in the Middle East and Elsewhere	E. Jewish Culture
Feb. 1971	The U.S. and the Soviet Union sign a seabed treaty, prohibiting the placement or storage of nuclear weapons or launchers on the seabed or ocean floor beyond a country's 12-mile limit.		A World Conference on Soviet Jewry, attended by 800 delegates from 38 countries, meets in Brussels, Belgium. It proclaims the Brussels Declaration, which is a commitment to escalate the protest movement in support of Soviet Jewry. Jewish activists from the Soviet Union express their solidarity.	UN mediator Gunnar Jarring* presents Egypt and Israel with a memorandum calling for Israel's withdrawal from the Sinai contingent on security arrangements in the Sinai and provisions for Israeli maritime rights in the Suez Canal and Straits of Tiran. Israeli and Egyptian conditions for the acceptance of the proposal end in a suspension of the Jarring* talks.	best-selling saga of World War II.

Yosef Hayim Yerushalmi, U.S. historian, writes *From Spanish Court to Italian Ghetto: Isaac Cardosa.* His study of this 17th-century Marrano physician shows the transition from his life among the privileged minority of royal Madrid to his precarious existence as a secret Judaizer and finally as a professing Jew in the ghettoes of Venice and Verona. |
| **Mar. 1971** | | *Newsweek* magazine's March 1st cover story is "The American Jew Today." | An International Consultation on Soviet Jewry is held in London as a follow-up to the Brussels Conference. It notes the "more realistic" emerging Soviet emigration policy and cautions that those being allowed to leave "represent only a fraction of the number who have applied to emigrate." | | Abraham E. Millgram, U.S. author, writes *Jewish Worship*, a comprehensive and readable study of Jewish liturgy.

Raphael Mahler's *A History of Modern Jewry, 1780–1815* appears in English translation. Mahler, professor of history at Tel Aviv University since 1961, discusses the development of the economic life of the Jews in western and eastern Europe during this transitional period. |
| **May 1971** | Egyptian President Anwar al-Sadat* foils an attempted coup and arrests Vice President Ali Sabry* and other officials on the charge of treason. Sabry* is regarded as sympathetic to the Soviet Union. In December, they will be tried by a revolutionary tribunal, and Sabry* will be sentenced to death. Sadat* will commute his sentence to life imprisonment.

Egypt and the Soviet Union sign a 15-year Treaty of Friendship and Cooperation after the Soviets decide to abandon Ali Sabry* and his supporters. | | | U.S. Secretary of State William Rogers* visits Egypt and Israel to explore an interim settlement proposal. His effort fails. | *The Encyclopaedia Judaica* is published in Israel. Begun in pre-Hitler* Germany, it was continued in the U.S. and completed in Israel.

Shlomo Dov Goitein writes a second volume to his *A Mediterranean Society: The Jewish Communities of the Arab World as Portrayed in the Documents of the Cairo Genizah.* This volume discusses the composition and organization of the Cairo Jewish community. The five-volume study will be completed in 1985. |
| **June 1971** | The U.S. Supreme Court upholds the right of the *New York Times* and the *Washington Post* to print the Pentagon Papers, classified documents about the | | | A reconstituted Jewish Agency meets in Jerusalem. Half of its governing bodies represent the World Zionist Organization (WZO) and half represent major | Ellis Rivkin, U.S. historian, writes *The* |

A. General History	B. Jews in North and South America	C. Jews in Europe	D. Jews in the Middle East and Elsewhere	E. Jewish Culture	
U.S. involvement in Vietnam. They were leaked to the newspapers by Daniel Ellsberg, who is indicted for unauthorized possession of secret documents.			Jewish fund-raising and other organizations. The agency controls immigration, land settlement and social services in Israel, and the WZO concentrates on ideological and youth activities and Jewish education in the Diaspora. Max Fisher of the U.S. is elected chairman of the board of governors and Louis Pincus of Israel, chairman of the executive.	*Shaping of Jewish History*. This brief historical interpretation espouses the "unity concept" of Jewish history. Jewish adherence to one form or another of the unity concept explains their ability to adapt repeatedly to foreign influences without the loss of Jewish identity.	**June 1971**
			Syria severs diplomatic relations with Jordan, ostensibly to demonstrate solidarity with the Palestinian struggle, but some observers suspect the motive is to prevent Palestinians fleeing from Jordan from entering Syria.	Sanford "Sandy" Koufax, left-handed pitcher of the Los Angeles Dodgers, is elected to the Baseball Hall of Fame. In 1959, he struck out 18 batters in a nine-inning game to equal a major league record. He was the first pitcher to average more than one strikeout an inning during his career. He led the Dodgers to two World Series championships, winning two games each in the 1963 and 1965 Series. He never played on Rosh Hashanah and Yom Kippur.	**Aug. 1971**
The U.S. and the Soviet Union sign a nuclear accidents agreement, providing for immediate notification in case of an accidental or unauthorized detonation of a nuclear weapon. The agreement also requires advance warning if one nation is planning to launch a missile outside its national territory in the direction of the other country. The John F. Kennedy Center for Performing Arts, in Washington, D.C., is opened with the première of *Mass*, composed by Leonard Bernstein in honor of the late president.			There is a brief engagement in the air over the Suez Canal, which is the only outbreak of the year, as Egypt and Israel observe the cease-fire. The UN Security Council adopts a resolution deploring Israel's failure to adhere to previous UN resolutions regarding the status of Jerusalem. The U.S. votes for the resolution, but UN Ambassador George Bush* reaffirms the U.S. position that the ultimate status of Jerusalem be determined by negotiations between Israel and Jordan in the context of a peace settlement and that the U.S. does not advocate the return to an artificially divided city and favors a unified city with free access to all.	The New York Historical Society exhibits City of Promise, featuring aspects of Jewish life in New York from 1654 to 1970. It is sponsored by the Central Synagogue on the occasion of its 100th anniversary. Simon Kuznets, U.S. economist, is awarded the Nobel Prize in economics. Dennis Gabor, British physicist, is awarded the Nobel Prize in physics for his development of holography. Of Hungarian birth, he did his research in Germany until 1933 when he left for England after the Nazis came to power.	**Sep. 1971**
The UN General Assembly recognizes				Mozes Heiman Gans writes *Memorabilia:*	**Oct. 1971**

607

	A. General History	B. Jews in North and South America	C. Jews in Europe	D. Jews in the Middle East and Elsewhere	E. Jewish Culture
Oct. 1971	and seats the People's Republic of China and expels Nationalist China.			Egyptian President Anwar al-Sadat* visits Moscow and receives promises of increased Soviet military assistance. However, they advise him they do not believe his forces are capable of defeating the Israelis. Sadat* concludes that the Soviets want to avoid the risk of a confrontation with the U.S. on the eve of a summit meeting.	*Picture Atlas of Jewish Life in Holland from the Middle Ages to 1940*, which goes through several printings and arouses much interest throughout the Netherlands. Amos Elon (b. 1926), Israeli journalist and author, writes *The Israelis: Founders and Sons*, an account of generational change in Israel.
Nov. 1971	Jordan's prime minister and minister of defense, Wasfi Tal,* is assassinated in Cairo by four Palestinians seeking revenge for the Jordanian crackdown on terrorist groups during September 1970.				Raphael Patai, U.S. scholar and editor, edits a two-volume *Encyclopedia of Zionism and Israel*, a comprehensive reference work. The Museum of Ethnography and Folklore in Tel Aviv exhibits Polish Synagogues and Cemeteries and Their Destruction, featuring photographs by Zalman Gostynski and Adam Buyak.
Dec. 1971	Kurt Waldheim,* Austrian diplomat, is elected UN secretary-general.		During the year, a dramatic change occurs in the Soviet policy toward Jewish emigration. There is a steady flow of departures and 12,897 Jews leave, with 12,839 emigrating to Israel.	Israeli Prime Minister Golda Meir visits Washington, D.C. The U.S. agrees to its first long-term arms assistance program. Aircraft will be supplied to Israel over a three-year period. During the year, Jordan's King Hussein* and Israel normalized relations de facto. There were few border incidents, and the bridges across the Jordan River carried a steady flow of goods and Arab visitors in both directions. A disagreement on territorial demands prevented progress toward a peace treaty.	
1972		Moises Cohen is appointed minister of finance in the Uruguayan government of President Juan Bordaberry.* He is the first Jew in Uruguay's history to become a minister. A study of Reform rabbis and laymen commissioned by the	Dr. Augusto Segre, head of the culture department of the Union of Italian Jewish Communities, conducts a lecture course at the Pontifical Lateran University on postbiblical Judaism as a continuation and evolution of classical Judaism. Segre is the first Jew invited to	During the year, the first 250 dwellings of the new Jewish quarter of Kiryat Arba are completed. Israeli Defense Minister Moshe Dayan and the Arab mayor of Hebron entered into an agreement that designated specific hours of prayer by Jews and Arabs at the Tomb of the	The Rabbinical Assembly, the organization of Conservative rabbis, publishes a *Mahzor for Rosh Hashanah and Yom Kippur*. Edited by Rabbi Jules Harlow, the *Mahzor* follows tradition but also includes modern readings and poems relevant to the

A. General History	B. Jews in North and South America	C. Jews in Europe	D. Jews in the Middle East and Elsewhere	E. Jewish Culture	
	Central Conference of American Rabbis reports: "More than one in three congregants, aged 20 to 24, is now married to a spouse who was born non-Jewish. One in four of this age group is married to a spouse who has not converted. . . . On every issue of Jewish identity on which they were queried, Reform youth seem to be more detached from Judaism and Jewishness than their parents."	occupy a chair at the university. Newspapers report that Klaus Barbie,* Nazi war criminal, is living in Peru. He returns to Bolivia under pressure from Peruvian authorities.	Patriarchs (Cave of Machpelah), which has served as a mosque.	contemporary historical experience. Marshall Sklare, U.S. sociologist, writes an augmented edition of his *Conservative Judaism*, written in 1955, an in-depth analysis of the American religious movement. Revising his views on American Orthodoxy, he writes that a "renaissance of American Orthodoxy" is taking place and that it has "transformed itself into a growing force in American Jewish life."	**1972**
		Israel cancels the sale by the Assumptionist Fathers of the Notre Dame de France convent in Jerusalem to Hadassah after protests from the Vatican.	U.S. officials reveal the signing of a U.S.–Israel arms agreement in November 1971, authorizing Israel to manufacture various kinds of American weapons and equipment.	Mark Spitz, U.S. champion swimmer from California, competing at the Munich Olympic Games, becomes the first person to win seven Olympic gold medals.	**Jan. 1972**
U.S. President Richard M. Nixon* visits Communist China. An agreement to increase contacts between the two countries is reached.			France agrees to reimburse Israel for 50 Mirage jets purchased but embargoed since the June 1967 Six-Day War. Israeli forces attack terrorist bases in southern Lebanon's Fatahland after three persons were killed and seven injured in terrorist strikes. The UN Security Council adopts a resolution calling on Israel to stop military action on Lebanon. The U.S. abstains after its effort to insert into the resolution a sentence deploring "all actions which have resulted in the loss of innocent lives" is defeated.	Bobby Fischer (b. 1943) of the U.S. defeats Boris Spassky (b. 1937) of the USSR at Reykjavik, thus becoming the first U.S. world chess champion. Kenneth Joseph Arrow, U.S. economist, is awarded the Nobel Prize in economics. William Howard Stein, U.S. biochemist, is awarded the Nobel Prize in chemistry for research in proteins, peptides, and amino acids. Gerald Maurice Edelman, U.S. immunologist, is awarded the Nobel	**Feb. 1972**
		The Dutch Parliament votes not to release three Nazi war criminals, Ferdinand Funten,* Franz Fischer,* and Joseph Kotalla,* serving life sentences since their conviction in 1948 of deporting thousands		Prize in physiology or medicine. He established the chemical structure of gamma globulin, which defends the body against foreign bodies and disease.	**Mar. 1972**

	A. General History	B. Jews in North and South America	C. Jews in Europe	D. Jews in the Middle East and Elsewhere	E. Jewish Culture
Mar. 1972			of Jews to the death camps. Parliament overruled the recommendation of Dutch Minister of Justice Andries van Agt* after a mass protest by Jewish and non-Jewish groups.		The fifth and concluding volume of European historian Simon Dubnow's (1860–1941) *History of the Jews* is published in English translation. Dubnow's history concludes with the rise of Adolf Hitler.*
Apr. 1972		*Time* magazine's April 10 cover story is "What It Means to Be Jewish." National Solidarity Day for Soviet Jews is observed in more than 100 American cities. Over 1 million sign petitions urging President Richard M. Nixon* to make emigration of Soviet Jews a priority agenda item in his forthcoming summit meetings with Soviet leaders.	Iraq and the Soviet Union sign a 15-year treaty that includes a pledge to "continue their determined struggle against imperialism and Zionism."	Uganda leader Idi Amin* breaks off diplomatic relations with Israel. Israel maintains that Uganda sacrificed good relations with Israel to obtain financial assistance from Arab countries.	Isaiah Trunk, research associate of the YIVO Institute for Jewish Research in New York, writes *Judenrat*, a study of Jewish Councils set up by the Nazis in occupied eastern Europe. He emphasizes that the Nazis forced Jews to establish the councils, forced individuals to serve on them, and forced the councils to provide services for the Germans to facilitate the "final solution." The book wins a National Book Award.
May 1972	U.S. President Richard M. Nixon* and Soviet leaders hold summit meetings in Moscow and enter into a treaty limiting each country's defensive strategic weapons to 200 antimissile missiles.			Israel's Prime Minister Golda Meir pays an official visit to Romania, the first by an Israeli prime minister to a Communist country. Israeli paratroopers recover a Belgian airliner that was forced to land at Lod airport by Black September terrorists. On behalf of the Popular Front for the Liberation of Palestine, three Japanese terrorists massacre 23 passengers at Lod airport, among them Christian pilgrims from Puerto Rico and world-renowned scientist Aharon Katzir of the Weizmann Institute of Science. The UN Security Council fails to adopt a resolution condemning this act.	Art Spiegelman (b. 1948), U.S. cartoonist, creates "Maus" a cartoon strip, which is a moving and horrifying tale of the Holocaust around the metaphor of the Nazis cast as cats and the Jews as mice. He is the son of an Auschwitz survivor. The first volume of Israel Zinberg's (1873–1939) *A History of Jewish Literature*, in 12 volumes, appears in English translation from the Yiddish by Bernard Martin. Zinberg was a Russian historian of Hebrew and Yiddish literature. His work is a study of Jewish literary activity from the Spanish period to the Russian Haskalah. The original Yiddish volumes were published between 1929 and 1937 when he was arrested and deported to Vladivostok, where he died.
June 1972		Sally J. Priesand graduates from the Hebrew Union College (Reform) and is ordained as the first		Yitzhak Rabin, Israel's ambassador to the U.S., publicly notes that President Richard M. Nixon* has been	

A. General History	B. Jews in North and South America	C. Jews in Europe	D. Jews in the Middle East and Elsewhere	E. Jewish Culture	
	woman rabbi in the U.S.		more supportive of Israel than any previous U.S. president. Rabin is accused of interfering in U.S. domestic politics during the presidential campaign.	*My Michael*, a novel by the Israeli novelist and social critic Amos Oz (b. 1939), is his first fiction to appear in English translation. An examination of the chasm developing between a content husband and his despairing wife who gradually loses touch with the reality of modern Israeli life, the book is perceived as the personification of the schizophrenic city of Jerusalem.	**June 1972**
Yemen and the U.S. agree to resume diplomatic relations. Yemen is the first of the six Arab states that had severed diplomatic relations with the U.S. after the 1967 Six-Day War to restore formal relations. Several weeks later, the Sudan and the U.S. resume diplomatic relations. Egyptian President Anwar al-Sadat* announces the expulsion of all Soviet military advisors and experts and directs that all Soviet bases and equipment be placed under Egyptian control.			At a press conference held in Kuwait, U.S. Secretary of State William P. Rogers* recommends direct negotiations between Israel and the Arab states. The Democrats adopt a party platform that pledges a long-term commitment to supply military assistance to Israel, have all parties enter into direct negotiations toward a permanent settlement, "recognize and support the established status of Jerusalem as the capital of Israel," move the U.S. embassy from Tel Aviv to Jerusalem, and calls on the world community to recognize its responsibility "for a just solution of the problems of the Jewish and Arab refugees."		**July 1972**
		The Soviet government issues a "diploma tax" decree, requiring would-be emigrants who had acquired a higher education to pay a large fee, which in effect would make it prohibitive for educated Jews to emigrate. American Jews launch a campaign of protest.	The Republicans adopt a party platform that pledges "to prevent the development of a military imbalance . . . by providing Israel with support essential for her security"; economic assistance, including special aid to help Israel resettle Russian immigrants; and "to help in any way possible to bring Israel and the Arab states to the conference table, where they may negotiate a lasting peace." No mention is made of Jerusalem.		**Aug. 1972**
The Philippine government of	U.S. Senator Henry Jackson* outlines a legislative proposal	Cyril K. Harris, Britain's national Hillel director, writes	On September 5, eight Black September Palestinian		**Sep. 1972**

A. General History	B. Jews in North and South America	C. Jews in Europe	D. Jews in the Middle East and Elsewhere	E. Jewish Culture
Sep. 1972	Ferdinand Marcos* declares martial law.	tying trade benefits to the Soviet Union to their removal of curbs on emigration. The Soviet Union would be barred from the most-favored-nation trade status if it denies its citizens the right and opportunity to emigrate or imposes more than a nominal tax on emigration until such time as the president determines it is no longer in violation. Several days after the Munich massacre, the Israel Philharmonic Orchestra, conducted by Zubin Mehta,* performs before an audience of 4,000 in Buenos Aires, Argentina. The audience stands in silence to the memory of the victims.	in the *Jewish Chronicle* that one in three of Britain's Jewish student population is likely to marry out of the religion; seven of eight have no active connection with Jewish life; and nine of ten know next to nothing about Judaism. The PLO representative in Paris, France, Mahmoud Hamchari,* is wounded and later dies from an explosion set off when he lifts his telephone receiver. Police experts attribute his assassination to Israeli agents.	terrorists kill two and seize and hold hostage nine Israeli Olympic athletes at the Olympic Village in Munich, West Germany. On September 6, a shoot-out at Munich airport with West German police, who are attempting to free the hostages, results in the death of all the Israelis, five terrorists, and one policeman. The remaining three terrorists are taken prisoner. The games are postponed for 24 hours. The UN Security Council takes no action. Israeli war planes attack Arab terrorist bases in Syria and Lebanon in retaliation for the Munich Olympic massacre. Three Syrian jets are shot down over the Golan Heights. The UN Security Council adopts a resolution calling for an end of military operations by "the parties concerned." A U.S. resolution deploring the Munich massacre is not considered. Israeli forces cross into Lebanon, search 16 villages, destroy about 150 fortifications and buildings used by Arab terrorists, kill about 60 terrorists, and take prisoners. The Lebanese army intervenes and suffers 60 casualties. Israel's Supreme Court rejects the appeal of Meyer Lansky (1902–1983), U.S. underworld figure, to override the refusal of the Interior Ministry to grant him an immigration visa. The court said he was "a person with a criminal past likely to endanger public welfare." Lansky returns to the U.S.	

A. General History	B. Jews in North and South America	C. Jews in Europe	D. Jews in the Middle East and Elsewhere	E. Jewish Culture	
The U.S. and the Soviet Union enter into a comprehensive trade agreement. The Soviet Union is to repay a portion of the World War II lend–lease debt and the Nixon* administration will seek congressional authorization to extend to the Soviet Union most-favored-nation treatment.			West Germany releases three Arab terrorists held for the massacre of Israelis at the Munich Olympic Games as ransom for a German airliner hijacked over Cyprus by two Black September terrorists on a flight from Beirut, Lebanon.		**Oct. 1972**
The Republican Nixon*–Agnew* ticket is reelected to a second term, defeating the Democratic McGovern*–Shriver* ticket and sweeping 49 states. The Democrats retain control of Congress.	The Jewish vote in the presidential election is estimated at 65% for George McGovern* and 35% for Richard M. Nixon.*	Cambridge University announces that University College will be renamed for Sir Isaac Wolfson (1897–1991) in recognition of a 2 million pound grant from his foundation.	Syrian and Israeli forces engage in air, artillery, and tank battles on the Golan Heights. Six Syrian MiGs are downed, with no Israeli losses.		**Nov. 1972**
	Robert Strauss (b. 1918), U.S. attorney from Texas, is elected chairman of the Democratic National Committee.	During the year, the Soviet Union permitted 34,733 Jews to emigrate.	The UN General Assembly, by a vote of 86 to 7, with 31 abstentions and 8 absent, adopts a resolution calling "upon all States not to recognize any such changes and measures carried out by Israel in the occupied Arab territories" and invites them to avoid actions, including aid, that would constitute recognition of the occupation. The U.S. abstains. During the year, the Suez Canal and Jordan River cease-fire lines were almost completely quiet. There was no interim arrangement for the opening of the Suez Canal, but the open bridges policy on the Jordan River continued, with regular traffic of people and goods between the West Bank and East Bank, which many regard as an interim de facto settlement with Jordan.		**Dec. 1972**
The United Nations and the Organization for African Unity	The Rabbinical Assembly, the organization of	The Bolivian Supreme Court denies a French request to extradite		Sharon and Michael Strassfeld and Richard Siegel, U.S. authors,	**1973**

	A. General History	B. Jews in North and South America	C. Jews in Europe	D. Jews in the Middle East and Elsewhere	E. Jewish Culture
1973	recognize the South West Africa People's Organization as the sole representative of the Namibian people.	Conservative rabbis, rules that during religious services women may be counted toward the making of a minyan. The Central Conference of American Rabbis (Reform) adopts a resolution declaring opposition to officiation at mixed marriages but also recognizes that its members "have held and continue to hold divergent interpretations of Jewish tradition." Thus the right of each Reform rabbi to decide whether to officiate at a mixed marriage is preserved. "Bridget Loves Bernie," the Saturday-night television situation comedy dealing with Jewish–Catholic intermarriage, is dropped by the Columbia Broadcasting System from its fall season. CBS claims the decision is unrelated to criticism from Jewish and Catholic religious organizations. The U.S. government issues a commemorative stamp in honor of George Gershwin (1898–1937). It is the first in the American Artists series. This is the fourth American postage stamp honoring a Jew. The first, in 1948, honored Rabbi Alexander D. Goode, who with three other chaplains in World War II gave their life belts to other soldiers as their troopship sank; the second, in 1950, honored labor leader Samuel Gompers (1850–1924); the third, in 1966, honored Albert Einstein (1879–1955).	the Nazi war criminal Klaus Barbie*.		compile and edit *The Jewish Catalog*. The *Catalog* provides information to enable Jews to live a more involved and creative Jewish life. It is an outgrowth of the *havurah* movement. *The Second Jewish Catalog* will be published in 1976 and *The Third Jewish Catalog*, in 1980. The catalogs enjoy great commercial success, selling over 500,000 copies. Max Weinreich's *History of the Yiddish Language: Concepts, Facts, Methods* is posthumously published in Yiddish in four volumes. In 1925, Weinreich (1894–1969) was a co-founder of the YIVO Institute of Jewish Research in Vilna. He was the first professor of Yiddish in an American university. He taught at City College of New York. Philip Roth, U.S. author, writes *Reading Myself and Others*, a collection of articles, interviews, and essays, among which he responds to criticism of his attitude toward Jews and Jewishness. Arthur A. Cohen, U.S. author, writes *In the Days of Simon Stern*, a novel that employs fantasy to assist in projecting Judaism's messianic beliefs. Bernard D. Weinryb, U.S. historian, writes *The Jews of Poland: A Social and Economic History of the Jewish Community in Poland from 1100 to 1800.* Alexander Altmann (1906–1987), professor of Jewish philosophy at Brandeis University, writes

A. General History	B. Jews in North and South America	C. Jews in Europe	D. Jews in the Middle East and Elsewhere	E. Jewish Culture	
A cease-fire takes place in Vietnam.			Israeli Prime Minister Golda Meir and Pope Paul VI hold a meeting at the Vatican. Meir is the first Israeli prime minister to visit the Vatican.	*Moses Mendelssohn: A Biographical Study*, an examination of his life and work, and of Jewish thought and history against the background of intellectual life of 18th-century Europe.	Jan. 1973
	At an American–Soviet trade conference, U.S. Senator Edmund G. Muskie* advises that the Soviet emigration policy is a major roadblock to expanded East–West trade. "Soviet leaders would be profoundly mistaken if they underestimated American feelings . . . Americans properly perceive the exorbitant tax on Jewish emigrants . . . as being in violation of fundamental human rights and freedoms."		A Libyan airliner strays over the Israeli-held Sinai. It ignores signals of Israeli interceptors to land and makes maneuvers that alarm the Israelis, who had received warnings of an Arab terrorist plan to fly an explosives-laden plane into an Israeli city. The Israelis down the airliner, with the loss of 106 lives. Israel is condemned by the international civil aviation organization. Israel, while not acknowledging legal liability, makes payments to the families of the victims.	Gershom Scholem's biography of the pseudo-Messiah, *Sabbati Sevi: The Mystical Messiah, 1626–1676*, is published in an English translation of the Hebrew original. Scholem's account of this important messianic movement, from its emergence in Turkey and of the events leading to Sevi's apostasy, depicts its repercussions in Europe. Scholem is professor of Jewish mysticism at the Hebrew University.

Leonard Baskin (b. 1922), U.S. artist, illustrates the new official Reform Passover Haggadah. | Feb. 1973 |
| The last American troops leave Vietnam. | Senator Henry Jackson* introduces an amendment to a proposed trade bill linking trade benefits to the Soviet Union with the right of Soviet citizens to emigrate. Jackson* refers to the Universal Declaration of Human Rights, which holds that "everyone has the right to leave any country, including his own, and to return to his country."

Victor Louis, Soviet journalist with close government connections, publishes an article in an Israeli newspaper stating that the Soviets would no longer enforce the "diploma tax" on emigration and acknowledges that the decision is a result of U.S. congressional pressure. | | Egypt's Anwar al-Sadat* sends emissaries to Syria to propose a joint military action against Israel. Syria's Hafiz al-Assad* declares readiness to go to war against Israel. | The Jewish Museum of New York acquires 600 artifacts from ancient Israel obtained by museum director Joy Ungerleider-Mayerson, from the New York University classics department. It greatly enhances the museum's archaeological collection.

Brian David Josephson, British physicist, is awarded the Nobel Prize in physics for his work on conductors and semiconductors.

The National Museum of the Biblical Message of Marc Chagall is inaugurated in Nice, France. Suggested by André Malraux,* minister of cultural affairs to President Charles de Gaulle* in | Mar. 1973 |

615

	A. General History	B. Jews in North and South America	C. Jews in Europe	D. Jews in the Middle East and Elsewhere	E. Jewish Culture
Apr. 1973	President Richard M. Nixon* sends to Congress a comprehensive Trade Reform Act, which includes a provision authorizing most-favored-nation status to the Soviet Union. The bill contains no provisions responding to congressional concern over the emigration problem. Nixon* states he did not believe "a policy of denying most-favored-nation treatment to Soviet export is a proper or even effective way of dealing with the problem."	Over 100 Soviet Jewish activists write an open letter to Congress pleading for the passage of the Jackson* amendment and asserting that "everyone's fate is determined by unknown people acting . . . in a totally arbitrary way." President Richard M. Nixon* has an extraordinary meeting with U.S. Jewish leaders. Nixon* advises he made a commitment to the Soviet Union which he considers integral to the policy of détente. He asks Jewish leaders to reconsider their support for the Jackson* amendment. After receiving pleas from Soviet Jewish activists, U.S. Jewish leaders reaffirm their support.		An attempt by Arab terrorists to hijack an Israeli El Al passenger plane at Nicosia, Cyprus, is thwarted by Israeli security forces. The residence of the Israeli ambassador is also attacked. Israeli commandos raid Beirut, Lebanon, and kill three Palestinian terrorist leaders. Ephraim Katzir, professor at the Weizmann Institute of Science, is elected the fourth president of Israel, succeeding Zalman Shazar, who is ineligible by law to serve a third term.	1969, it is the only national museum in France devoted to the work of a living artist. Claude Lanzmann, French film director, produces *Why Israel?* a documentary on Israel that receives acclaim for its artistic film technique and approach. The State Museum in Goettingen, West Germany, holds an exhibition on the 700-year history of the Jews in South Lower Saxony. The Israel Museum in Jerusalem holds an exhibition dealing with all aspects of Jewish life in Morocco.
May 1973	Criminal charges brought against Daniel Ellsberg for leaking the Pentagon Papers to the press are dismissed.			In May, and again in June, Egypt's Anwar al-Sadat* visits Syria to confirm arrangements for war against Israel.	
June 1973	The U.S. and the Soviet Union sign an agreement on the prevention of nuclear war, providing that they will refrain from the threat or use of force against each other or their allies and will act in a manner consistent with avoiding nuclear war.		Marc Chagall visits Moscow and Leningrad after a 50-year absence. He is reunited with two of his sisters. He refuses to go to Vitebsk. "I would have been afraid not to recognize my town, and in any event I have carried it forever in my heart."	Willy Brandt,* chancellor of West Germany, is the first West German head of state to visit Israel.	
July 1973		O. N. Miller,* chairman of Standard Oil Co. of California, sends a letter to 262,000 shareholders and 41,000 employees asking them to urge the U.S. to show a greater understanding of the Arabs and to give greater support to the Arab efforts toward peace. Members of Congress and Jewish		Yosef Allon, assistant air attaché assigned to Israel's Washington, D.C., embassy, is murdered outside his Washington home. The U.S. vetoes a UN Security Council resolution, sponsored by Egypt, calling for the Israeli withdrawal from occupied territories and for a Palestinian homeland.	

A. General History	B. Jews in North and South America	C. Jews in Europe	D. Jews in the Middle East and Elsewhere	E. Jewish Culture	
	community leaders protest.		The U.S. states the resolution would have fundamentally changed Resolution 242 of 1967. Israeli agents in Lillehammer, Norway, kill the wrong man in their hunt for an Arab terrorist.		**July 1973**
The U.S. ceases bombing in Cambodia, ending more than nine years of U.S. air warfare in Indochina. President Richard M. Nixon* announces that he will nominate National Security Adviser Henry Kissinger as secretary of state to replace William Rogers.* Kissinger is the first non–American-born and non-Christian to become secretary of state.			Israeli warplanes intercept a Lebanese commercial airliner and force it to land in Israel, mistakenly believing that George Habash* and other terrorist leaders are aboard. The UN Security Council unanimously condemns Israel. Egypt's Anwar al-Sadat* visits Saudi Arabia and obtains the assurance of a Saudi oil embargo in the event the renewed fighting against the Israelis goes badly. The Soviets accelerate the shipment of arms to Syria and begin anew to supply Egypt with the latest ground and anti-aircraft missiles.		**Aug. 1973**
	Andrei Sakharov,* Soviet human rights leader, writes an open letter to Congress appealing for support of the Jackson* amendment, asserting its passage is essential to assuring détente.	In Austria, three armed Arab terrorists seize Soviet Jewish émigrés on a Soviet train en route to Vienna for transshipment to Israel. The Austrian chancellor, Bruno Kreisky, announces that he will close the transit center. Israeli Prime Minister Golda Meir tries unsuccessfully to persuade Kreisky to change his decision.	Syria's Hafiz al-Assad* and Jordan's King Hussein* meet Anwar al-Sadat* in Cairo and reach a tactical agreement on an impending attack on Israel. Israeli jet fighters down 13 Syrian MiGs in an air battle over the Mediterranean Sea. One Israeli Mirage jet is lost, but the pilot is rescued.		**Sep. 1973**
U.S. Vice President Spiro T. Agnew* resigns and pleads no contest to one count of income tax evasion. President Richard Nixon* nominates Gerald R. Ford,* Republican leader of			The Egyptian war minister, General Ahmad Ismail Ali,* flies to Damascus to inform Hafiz al-Assad* that the "zero hour" for the attack on Israel would be 2 P.M. on October 6, which is		**Oct. 1973**

A. General History	B. Jews in North and South America	C. Jews in Europe	D. Jews in the Middle East and Elsewhere	E. Jewish Culture
Oct. 1973	the House of Representatives, to succeed Agnew.*		Yom Kippur, the most solemn day in the Jewish year.	

Oct. 1973

D. Jews in the Middle East and Elsewhere

In the first week of October, the Soviets evacuate families of advisers to Egypt and Syria, launch satellites into orbit to photograph Israeli defenses, and dispatch an electronics surveillance ship toward Egypt.

On October 5, in the face of overwhelming evidence of large-scale Arab military preparations, the Israeli general staff alerts its standing army but does not order full mobilization.

On the morning of October 6, Israel orders the mobilization of the armored corps reserves, rejects Chief of Staff David Elazar's plea for a total mobilization, and asks the U.S. to restrain the Arabs. U.S. Secretary of State Henry Kissinger advises Israel not to launch a preemptive strike.

On October 6, at 2 P.M., Egypt and Syria launch massive coordinated attacks on Israeli positions in the Sinai and Golan Heights. They achieve complete tactical surprise. The Egyptians cross the Suez Canal and bypass the Bar-Lev Line, and the Syrians capture the Israeli post on Mt. Hermon and penetrate Israeli defenses on the Golan. Soviet-supplied anti-aircraft missiles cause serious damage to Israeli air support on both fronts.

On October 8, Egypt claims control of the entire eastern bank of the Suez Canal. Israeli counterattacks in the Sinai are repulsed with heavy losses. The Israelis dig in, and the Egyptians consolidate their bridgeheads. Syria claims control of a large part of the Golan Heights.

On October 9, after the Syrians launch FROG (Free Rocket Over Ground) missiles against Israeli civilian areas, the Israeli air force launches attacks against Syrian industrial targets, seaports, fuel storage depots, power stations, and the defense ministry in Damascus. The attacks seriously affect the Syrian economy and last until October 21.

On October 9, the Israeli general staff decides to move reserves to the Golan Heights and to concentrate their effort against the Syrians. By October 11, Israeli forces break through the Syrian defenses and push past the 1967 cease-fire line toward Damascus.

On October 9, during a visit of Algerian President Houari Boumedienne* to Moscow, Soviet Defense Minister Andrei Grechko* publicly urges all Arab nations to supply troops to Egypt and Syria and suggests that the Arabs advance beyond the pre-1967 borders. *Pravda* exhorts the Arabs to use an oil embargo.

On October 9, Israeli Ambassador Simcha Dinitz advises the U.S. of staggering Israeli losses in the Sinai and that Egypt has the best of the fight so far. President Richard M. Nixon* orders Henry Kissinger to advise the Israelis that the U.S. will replace all its losses. Several days elapse before a resupply airlift begins. Nixon* decides to resupply Israel because of a massive Soviet airlift to Egypt and Syria.

On October 13, John J. McCloy,* lawyer for the Arabian–American Oil Co., delivers a letter signed by the chairmen of Exxon, Mobil, Texaco, and Chevron to the White House, urging the U.S. not to support Israel.

On October 14, Egypt stages an all-out offensive in the Sinai, following a three-day lull in which they moved large amounts of men and matériel across the Suez Canal and into the Sinai. The Israelis crush the Egyptians, inflicting massive losses, particularly in tanks.

On October 14, the first U.S. air transports arrive in Israel. In 4½ weeks, 566 flights will transport 22,000 tons of military equipment from the U.S. to Israel.

On October 15, Israeli troops establish a bridgehead on the west bank of the Suez Canal and begin attacking Egyptian missile sites and other targets.

Beginning on October 15, Israeli troops in the Golan repulse Iraqi and Jordanian counterattacks, inflicting severe casualties. By October 19, Israeli control of the Damascus Plain is uncontested.

Beginning on October 16, Egyptian troops in the Sinai unsuccessfully attempt to close the Israeli corridor leading to the west bank of the Suez Canal. This "battle of the Chinese farm" will be concluded by October 18, and the Israelis will expand the bridgehead into Egypt.

On October 17, Arab oil producers, meeting in Kuwait, announce they will cut oil production 5% a month and raise prices 17% in order to force the U.S. to change its Middle East policy.

On October 19, U.S. President Richard M. Nixon* asks Congress for $2.2 billion to cover the cost of military aid to Israel "to maintain a balance of forces and thus achieve stability in the Middle East."

On October 19, Soviet leader Leonid Brezhnev* invites U.S. Secretary of State Henry Kissinger to Moscow for "urgent consultations." Kissinger arrives in Moscow on the evening of October 20.

On October 20, Israeli troops push out in three directions from their bridgehead on the west bank of the Suez Canal and continue to inflict much damage on Egyptian forces.

On October 21, Kuwait, Bahrain, Qatar, and Dubai join Saudi Arabia and Libya and announce an embargo of oil shipments to the U.S.

On October 21, Henry Kissinger and Leonid Brezhnev* agree on terms for a cease-fire. President Richard M. Nixon* urges Israel to accept it, noting that the agreement calls for a cease-fire in place and that the Soviets endorse the principle of direct negotiations, as does Anwar al-Sadat.* Israel accepts the proposal.

On October 22, just before the cease-fire becomes effective, Israeli forces retake their Mt. Hermon position.

On October 22, the UN Security Council adopts Resolution 338, which calls for a cease-fire, immediate negotiations between the parties with the aim of establishing a just and durable peace, and the implementation of UN Resolution 242 of 1967 in all its parts.

On October 23, despite the cease-fire, fighting continues on the Suez front, and Israel captures the territory covering the remaining escape routes of Egypt's Third Army, trapped in the Sinai.

On October 23, the UN Security Council adopts Resolution 339, demanding Egypt and Israel end hostilities and return to positions occupied on the October 22 deadline. A second cease-fire begins on October 24.

On October 24, when Israel turns back a Red Cross convoy bringing supplies to the trapped Egyptian Third Army, Soviet leader Leonid Brezhnev* cables the White House threatening unilateral Soviet military action. The U.S. orders a worldwide military and nuclear alert to counter the Soviet threat.

On October 27, Israeli General Aharon Yariv and Egyptian General Abd al-Ghani al-Gamazi* begin disengagement talks at Kilometer 101 on the Suez Canal's west bank. Israel agrees to allow the resupply of Egypt's Third Army.

On October 27, a UN Security Council resolution establishes a 7,000-man peace-keeping force to enforce the cease-fire in the Golan and the Sinai. No U.S. or Soviet troops would participate in the force.

Israeli casualties in the Yom Kippur War are 2,552 dead and over 3,000 wounded.

OCTOBER 24, 1973, YOM KIPPUR WAR
CEASE-FIRE LINES. ABOVE, SYRIA; BELOW, EGYPT

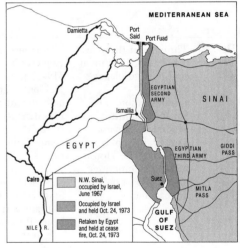

	A. General History	B. Jews in North and South America	C. Jews in Europe	D. Jews in the Middle East and Elsewhere	E. Jewish Culture
Nov. 1973	Following a meeting between Secretary of State Henry Kissinger and President Anwar al-Sadat,* the U.S. and Egypt announce their intention to resume diplomatic relations, which were ended six years before.	Abraham D. Beame is elected the first Jewish mayor of New York. Dr. Gerson D. Cohen is installed as the fifth chancellor of the Jewish Theological Seminary of America, succeeding Dr. Louis Finkelstein.		European Economic Council foreign ministers release a statement aimed at placating the Arabs. It calls for Israel to return the territories occupied since 1967 and to take into account the rights of the Palestinians. Egyptian and Israeli military representatives at Kilometer 101 agree on a prisoner-of-war exchange, involving 241 Israelis and 8,031 Egyptians. The Israeli government appoints a commission to investigate events connected with the Yom Kippur War, headed by Shimon Agranat, president of Israel's Supreme Court.	
Dec. 1973	Throughout the year, the Watergate scandal continues to plague the Nixon* administration. The Senate committee headed by Senator Sam Ervin* holds hearings. The House Judiciary Committee investigates a possible impeachment.	The House of Representatives votes 319–80 in favor of the Jackson*–Vanik* amendment to President Richard M. Nixon's* comprehensive trade bill. U.S. Secretary of State Henry Kissinger is awarded the Nobel Peace Prize for his role in the negotiations leading to the end of U.S. involvement in Vietnam. Bora Laskin, justice of the Supreme Court of Canada, is appointed chief justice of Canada.	In London, an Arab terrorist assassination attempt on Joseph Edward Sieff, president of Marks and Spencer Ltd. and Zionist leader, fails.	David Ben-Gurion, Israel's first prime minister, dies. The Geneva Peace Conference is convened under UN auspices. Israel, Egypt, Jordan, the U.S., and the Soviet Union attend. Syria boycotts it. No real progress is made, and Henry Kissinger's shuttle diplomacy replaces the Geneva talks. Israel holds national elections for the Eighth Knesset, with 1,601,098 votes cast. The Alignment (Labor–Mapam) wins 51 seats; Likud (Herut–Liberals), 39 seats; and the National Religious party, 10 seats. The government is installed on March 10, 1974, with Golda Meir as prime minister, Moshe Dayan as minister of defense, and Abba Eban as minister of foreign affairs.	

A. General History	B. Jews in North and South America	C. Jews in Europe	D. Jews in the Middle East and Elsewhere	E. Jewish Culture	
Rosemary Radford Reuther,* revisionist Catholic thinker, edits *Religion and Sexism*, a ground-breaking anthology that brings together essays by Christian and Jewish women to show the critical role of "the Judeo-Christian tradition in shaping the traditional cultural images that have degraded and suppressed women."	Mitzvah buses, boldly marked vans sponsored by the Lubavitch movement, begin visiting university campuses with the objective of convincing non-Orthodox Jews to intensify their religious observance. Rosemary Radford Reuther* writes *Faith and Fratricide: The Theological Roots of Anti-Semitism*, in which she concludes that the early Christians, and the author of the Gospel of John in particular, falsified the events surrounding the crucifixion of Jesus when they shifted the blame for this act from the Roman political authorities to the Jewish religious authorities. Mel Brooks produces *Blazing Saddles*, a parody of American western films. It is described by Brooks as a "Jewish western with a black hero." Joan Micklin Silver directs *Hester Street*, a film adaptation of Abraham Cahan's 1896 novel *Yekl, a Tale of the Ghetto*. It depicts the clash of old and new values confronting the Jewish immigrant.		The Gush Emunim (Bloc of the Faithful) movement is founded. It is a religious organization whose purpose is to establish permanent Jewish control over the territories occupied by Israel in the 1967 Six-Day War. Its spiritual guide is Rabbi Zvi Judah Kook (1891–1982), son of the late chief rabbi of Palestine, Abraham Isaac Kook (1865–1935). It will evolve into a politically active movement.	Benno Jacob's commentary *The First Book of the Torah: Genesis*, is translated into English in an abridged edition. Jacob (1862–1945), a German rabbi and biblical scholar, first wrote his commentary in 1934 in German. It was considered a learned treatise, using modern methods of scholarship, faithful to the Jewish tradition. Reuben Ainsztein writes *Jewish Resistance in Nazi-Occupied Eastern Europe*, which describes the fight of the partisans, resistance in the ghettoes, and revolts in the death camps to prove that all Jews did not go to their death as "sheep to slaughter." The Hebrew Union College Skirball Museum in Los Angeles inaugurates its first long-term exhibit, A Walk Through the Past, a display of ceremonial art and archaeological artifacts. The museum was established in 1913 in Cincinnati and was reorganized in 1972 in Los Angeles. The publication of *The Journal of Jewish Art*, edited by Bezalel Narkiss, Israeli scholar of Jewish art, begins under the auspices of Spertus College, Chicago, Illinois.	**1974**
			Israel and Egypt sign the first Sinai disengagement agreement after the shuttle diplomacy by Secretary of State Henry Kissinger. Israel withdraws from the Suez Canal's west bank to a line 15 to 20 kilometers east of the canal; Egypt reoccupies the east bank in a zone 8 to 10 kilometers wide; a UN buffer zone is established between them. Egypt secretly	Aharon Appelfeld (b. 1932), Israeli novelist, writes *Badenheim 1939*, which depicts the false tranquility of European Jewry before World War II. His works concentrate on the effect of the Holocaust on its victims.	**Jan. 1974**

	A. General History	B. Jews in North and South America	C. Jews in Europe	D. Jews in the Middle East and Elsewhere	E. Jewish Culture
Jan. 1974				agrees to clear and reopen the Suez Canal and allow passage of nonmilitary cargoes bound for Israel and to rebuild adjacent cities. Syria is not a party to the agreement.	
Feb. 1974	U.S. Secretary of State Henry Kissinger warns Arab countries that their Yom Kippur War oil embargo on the U.S. "must be construed as a form of blackmail." The U.S. and Egypt announce resumption of full diplomatic relations.			Israeli troops complete their withdrawal from the west bank of the Suez Canal. U.S. Secretary of State Henry Kissinger delivers a list to the Israelis of their prisoners of war held by Syria. Israel later declares that the receipt of this list fulfilled a condition for holding disengagement talks with Syria.	
Mar. 1974	Arab oil producers end their Yom Kippur War oil embargo on the U.S. and Western nations, except the Netherlands. The Arab oil embargo resulted in quadrupling world oil prices and was the largest and most sudden transfer of wealth in the world's history.			Prime Minister Golda Meir and her new coalition cabinet, including Moshe Dayan as defense minister, are sworn in as the government of Israel.	
Apr. 1974	Egypt's Anwar al-Sadat* ends 18 years of reliance on Soviet military matériel. The Soviet Union failed for 6 months to honor resupply requests. Sadat* announces that Egypt will seek other sources of arms. A military junta seizes power in Portugal.	The Supreme Court rules the Marco Defunis case to be moot as DeFunis was to graduate from another law school. DeFunis, a white applicant and Phi Beta Kappa graduate from the University of Washington, was denied admission to the university law school. He sued, alleging discrimination, as the school admitted minority candidates with lower test scores. The suit causes friction between the black and Jewish communities.		The Agranat Commission interim report on the Yom Kippur War is released. It recommends the dismissal of Chief of Staff David Elazar, intelligence chief Eliahu Zeira and his three deputies, and the suspension of southern front commander Shmuel Gonen. It absolves Defense Minister Moshe Dayan and Prime Minister Golda Meir of direct personal blame. Elazar resigns. The public and press criticize the commission for absolving Dayan. A government crisis ensues and Golda Meir resigns as prime minister, bringing	

A. General History	B. Jews in North and South America	C. Jews in Europe	D. Jews in the Middle East and Elsewhere	E. Jewish Culture
			down the month-old coalition government.	Apr. 1974
			Palestinian terrorists infiltrate from Lebanon and kill 16 civilians, mostly women and children, at Kiryat Shemonah. Israel retaliates by raiding villages in Lebanon.	
			Israel's Labour party elects former Chief of Staff and Ambassador to the U.S. Yitzhak Rabin to form a new government.	
Helmut Schmidt* succeeds Willy Brandt* as chancellor of West Germany following Brandt's* resignation in the wake of a spy scandal.			Three Palestinian terrorists infiltrate from Lebanon into Ma'alot, where they take about 120 schoolchildren hostage. Their demand for the release of imprisoned Palestinian terrorists is rejected. When Israeli troops storm the school, 20 children, 1 Israeli soldier, and the 3 terrorists are killed. Israel retaliates with jet raids on villages in Lebanon.	May 1974
			Yitzhak Rabin forms a new Labour government. Notably absent are Moshe Dayan, Abba Eban, and Pinhas Sapir.	
			Israel and Syria sign a Golan Heights disengagement agreement after one month of shuttle diplomacy. Israel returns all territory captured in the Yom Kippur War plus the town of Kuneitra, taken in 1967. The Syrians will renege on their agreement to repopulate Kuneitra with civilians. Israel gains an exchange of prisoners of war. Buffer zones are established, separated by a neutral zone occupied by UN forces.	

	A. General History	B. Jews in North and South America	C. Jews in Europe	D. Jews in the Middle East and Elsewhere	E. Jewish Culture
June 1974		President Richard M. Nixon* returns from a one-week tour of Egypt, Saudi Arabia, Syria, Israel, and Jordan. He signs an agreement of friendship and cooperation with Egypt, announces the resumption of diplomatic relations with Syria, and promises Israel military and economic aid.		Several Palestinian terrorists infiltrate from Lebanon and attack Kibbutz Shamir, in Upper Galilee, killing three women. Five days later, infiltrating by sea, three Palestinian terrorists attack a family in a Nahariya apartment house. A mother and two children are killed, as well as an Israeli soldier. Israel retaliates with air attacks on Lebanon. Israeli troops complete their withdrawal from the Golan Heights. An exchange of 56 Israeli prisoners of war for 382 Arabs, including 10 Iraqis and 5 Moroccans, takes place.	
July 1974	Democracy is restored in Greece as the military dictatorship turns over power to a civilian government.				
Aug. 1974	U.S. President Richard M. Nixon* resigns after admitting complicity in the Watergate cover-up. Vice President Gerald R. Ford* is sworn in as the 38th president of the U.S. and later selects Nelson Rockefeller* to be vice president. In September, President Ford* will pardon Nixon.* Turkey invades Cyprus. The island is divided into Turkish and Greek enclaves.		Sylva Zalmanson, Soviet dissident jailed in 1970 for her part in the plot to hijack an airliner from Leningrad to reach Israel, is freed and leaves for Israel.	Archbishop Hilarion Capucci, Greek Catholic patriarchal vicar in East Jerusalem, is arrested for smuggling arms into Israel for use by terrorists.	
Sep. 1974	Ethiopian emperor Haile Selassie* is ousted in a military coup after 58 years of rule.			A TWA airliner en route from Israel to New York crashes into the Ionian Sea, killing all 88 aboard. In January 1975, the U.S. will confirm the crash was caused by a bomb explosion.	
Oct. 1974	The Hirshhorn Museum opens in Washington, D.C. It is the gift of art	In a lecture at Duke University, General George Brown,* chairman of the joint	Oscar Schindler,* a German Catholic who saved more than 1,500 Jews during the	The Arab Summit at Rabat, including King Hussein* of Jordan, recognizes the PLO as	

A. General History	B. Jews in North and South America	C. Jews in Europe	D. Jews in the Middle East and Elsewhere	E. Jewish Culture	
collector Joseph Hirshhorn.	chiefs of staff, complains of the Jewish lobby in favor of Israel. "They own, you know, the banks in this country, the newspapers." Brown* will issue a retraction one day after newspaper accounts of his lecture.	Holocaust by employing them in his factory, dies. More than 400 Jews whom he saved attend his funeral at the Latin Cemetery in Jerusalem.	the "sole legitimate representative of the Palestinian people" and issues a declaration calling for the creation of an independent Palestinian state.		**Oct. 1974**
The UN General Assembly bars the participation of South Africa.	Richard Stone, Democrat of Florida, is the first Jewish U.S. senator elected by popular vote in the Deep South. Elliot Levitas, Democrat of Atlanta, 1 of 21 Jews to win a seat in the U.S. House of Representatives, is the first Jew to be elected to Congress from Georgia.		Three Palestinian terrorists shoot their way into a Beit Sh'an apartment house, killing 4 and wounding 23 civilians. Yasir Arafat* addresses the UN General Assembly. The General Assembly recognizes the PLO as the sole spokesman for the Palestine Arabs, grants the PLO observer status at the UN, and affirms the Palestinian right to national independence and sovereignty. Over 100,000 Israel supporters rally in New York to protest Arafat's* appearance at the UN.		**Nov. 1974**

D. Jews in the Middle East and Elsewhere

Nov. 1974

The UN Educational, Scientific, and Cultural Organization's (UNESCO) Commission for Social Sciences, Humanities and Culture votes to invite the UNESCO director general to withhold assistance to Israel for Israel's persistent alteration of the historical features of Jerusalem. Later, UNESCO votes to exclude Israel from the European regional group, making Israel the only member not part of a regional group. A storm of protest ensues, with the U.S. Congress threatening to withhold contributions to UNESCO until the body rescinds its anti-Israel measures.

Russian ballet dancers Valery and Galina Panov make their debut in Israel. They were granted permission to emigrate to Israel, as the Soviet Union responds to world opinion.

A. General History	B. Jews in North and South America	C. Jews in Europe	D. Jews in the Middle East and Elsewhere	E. Jewish Culture	
	The Senate passes the Trade Reform Act, including the Jackson* amendment, and both houses of Congress adopt the Senate version of the act, which later becomes law. Several days later, the Soviet government publicly rejects the Jackson* amendment provisions.		Archbishop Hilarion Capucci, Greek Catholic patriarchal vicar in East Jerusalem, is sentenced to 12 years' imprisonment by an Israeli court for smuggling arms into Israel for use by terrorists.		**Dec. 1974**
	The states of New York and Illinois pass		Golda Meir's autobiography, *My*	The Central Conference of	**1975**

	A. General History	B. Jews in North and South America	C. Jews in Europe	D. Jews in the Middle East and Elsewhere	E. Jewish Culture
1975		laws making it illegal for corporations to comply with the Arab boycott of Israel. Well-known Argentine antisemite Horacio Calderon* is appointed as head of the Buenos Aires University press department and his antisemitic book *Jewish Argentina*, which blames the Jews for the country's ills, is published. Antisemitism is widespread in Argentina.		*Life*, is published in the U.S. About the Arab surprise attack in the Yom Kippur War of 1973, she wrote, "I should have listened to the warnings of my heart and ordered a call-up. . . . I shall live with this terrible knowledge for the rest of my life."	American Rabbis (Reform) publishes *Gates of Prayer*, the first of a series of new prayer books that contain more prayers in Hebrew than the older prayer books, as well as a range of commentaries from classical and contemporary sources. *Gates of Prayer* is followed by *Gates of Repentance* (1977), *Gates of the House* (1977), *Gates of Mitzvah* (1979), *Gates of the Seasons* (1983), *Gates of Forgiveness— Selichot* (1987), and *Gates of Understanding* (1987).
Jan. 1975		Secretary of State Henry Kissinger announces that the Soviet Union has canceled the trade agreement of October 1972, ostensibly on the grounds of its objection to the Jackson*–Vanik* amendment linking it with freer emigration from the Soviet Union. The Soviets also objected to limitations on Eximbank credits.	The Vatican publishes Guidelines and Suggestions for Relations with Judaism, designed to implement the Vatican II Declaration on the Jews. The guidelines surpass the declaration and clearly reject widespread teaching that Judaism is a rigid religion calling for neither love of God nor love of men. The guidelines state the history of Judaism did not end with the destruction of Jerusalem but continued to develop, creating new religious values. The document calls on Catholics to fight antisemitism.		Yosef Hayim Yerushalmi, U.S. historian, writes *Haggadah and History*, a survey of the evolution of the printed Passover Haggadah from the beginnings of Hebrew printing in the 15th century. Saul Bellow, U.S. novelist, wins a Pulitzer Prize for his novel *Humboldt's Gift*, in which he examines the nature of boredom through the lives of Charlie Citrine and his friend and mentor, the poet Von Humboldt Fleisher, modeled after Bellow's friend Delmore Schwartz.
Feb. 1975		Edward H. Levi (b. 1911) is appointed attorney general of the U.S. by President Gerald Ford.* He is the first Jew to hold the post.			E. L. Doctorow, U.S. novelist, wins a National Book Award for *Ragtime*, a novel of early 20th-century America that meshes tales of fictional characters with real people such as J. P. Morgan,* Scott Joplin,* and Emma Goldman.
Mar. 1975	King Faisal* of Saudi Arabia is assassinated in Riyadh by his nephew. No major change in Saudi policies results. Iran and Iraq end a long-standing border conflict. Iran wins Iraqi agreement to modify the frontier line in Iran's favor. In return, Iran agrees to end military support for Kurdish rebels in Iraq.	President Gerald R. Ford* criticizes the Arab boycott of U.S. firms doing business with Israel, saying discrimination against "institutions or individuals on religious or ethnic grounds" is repugnant to American principles.		Eight Fatah terrorists come ashore at Tel Aviv and occupy the small seafront Savoy Hotel. When Israeli troops attack, they detonate explosives. Eight civilians, three Israeli soldiers, and seven terrorists are killed. U.S. Secretary of State Henry Kissinger's efforts for a second Israeli–Egyptian	Lucy S. Dawidowicz, U.S. historian, writes *The War Against the Jews, 1933–1945*, a systematic and scholarly treatment of the "final solution."

A. General History	B. Jews in North and South America	C. Jews in Europe	D. Jews in the Middle East and Elsewhere	E. Jewish Culture	
			agreement fail. The U.S. blames Israel for the negotiation failure, and President Gerald R. Ford* orders the reassessment of the U.S. policy.	Antisemitism was at the core of Adolf Hitler's* beliefs and the central motivation of his policies. She notes the willingness of people to accept Hitler's* policies. The Jewish experience simply did not prepare them for the situation they faced and to say Jews cooperated or collaborated with the Nazis is a historical misrepresentation.	**Mar. 1975**
A civil war between Christian and Muslim forces breaks out in Lebanon. PLO activities based in Lebanon heighten tensions between Christians and Muslims. Saigon falls to the Communist Vietnamese.				Simon Dubnow's (1860–1941) *History of the Jews in Russia and Poland* is reprinted with a supplement by Leon Shapiro, updating the history of Russian Jewry between 1912 and 1974.	**Apr. 1975**
Egypt's Anwar al-Sadat* accuses Libya's Muammar Qaddafi* of offering the Soviet Union naval bases in Libya as part of a $12 billion arms deal concluded with Soviet Premier Alexei Kosygin.*			Seventy-six of the U.S. Senate's then 99 members write to President Gerald R. Ford* implicitly rejecting the administration's attempts to blame Israel for the breakdown in negotiations with Egypt and explicitly opposing the withholding of American aid to Israel.	*The Sunshine Boys*, a play by Neil Simon written in 1972, is adapted to film, starring George Burns and Walter Matthau. Simon deals with the serious problems of old age in a humorous way, and his characters are patterned after the well-known vaudevillians Smith and Dale (Joe Sulzer and Charlie Marks).	**May 1975**
Eight years after its closure in the 1967 Arab–Israeli war, the Suez Canal is reopened to shipping.			U.S. President Gerald R. Ford* and Egypt's Anwar al-Sadat* meet in Salzburg, Austria, to discuss the resumption of negotiations for a Sinai accord with Israel. Sadat* proposes that the Umm Khisheiba surveillance station be operated by U.S. civilians rather than Israelis. In Washington, D.C., Israeli Prime Minister Yitzhak Rabin has talks with President Gerald R. Ford* and Secretary of State Henry Kissinger about renewing negotiations for an Israeli–Egyptian accord.	*A Chorus Line*, a musical with music by Marvin Hamlisch and lyrics by Edward Kleban, opens on Broadway. "The Pious Ones," a photographic essay of the Hassidic community in the Williamsburg neighborhood of Brooklyn, New York, appears in the August issue of the *National Geographic* magazine. David Baltimore (b. 1938), U.S. microbiologist, and Howard Martin Temin (b. 1925), U.S. geneticist, are awarded the Nobel Prize in physiology	**June 1975**
			A bomb explosion in Jerusalem's Zion Square kills 14 and injures 72.		**July 1975**

A. General History	B. Jews in North and South America	C. Jews in Europe	D. Jews in the Middle East and Elsewhere	E. Jewish Culture

Aug. 1975

Thirty-five nations sign the Helsinki accord. President Gerald R. Ford* and Soviet leader Leonid Brezhnev* are present to symbolize this consummation of détente. The accord recognizes human rights principles, including the provision for the reunion of families.

or medicine for discovering how certain cancer-causing viruses affect genes.

Benjamin R. Mottelson, U.S.-born physicist who lives in Denmark, and Aage Bohr,* Danish physicist, are awarded the Nobel Prize in physics for their researches on the inner structure of the atom. Bohr,* son of Niels Bohr, is of partly Jewish descent.

Sep. 1975

As a result of Henry Kissinger's mediation, Egypt and Israel reach a second disengagement agreement. The Israelis agree to withdraw from the Mitla and Gidi passes and return the Abu Rudeis oil fields; Egypt agrees to allow Israel to ship nonmilitary goods through the Suez Canal. U.S. civilians are to operate an early warning system in the passes. Both sides are to limit troops in the Sinai to 8,000. Both sides agree not to use force to resolve conflict and to reach a final peace settlement by means of negotiations called for by UN Resolution 338. On the same day, the U.S. and Israel sign an unpublished agreement as a companion to the Israeli–Egyptian disengagement agreement. The U.S. is to help Israel meet its requirements for arms, economic assistance, and energy and support Israel's right to free passage through the Strait of Bad el Mandeb and the Strait of Gibraltar; pledges not to recognize or negotiate with the PLO as long as it does not accept Israel's right to exist or UN Resolutions 242 and 338; and reiterates its long-standing

Leonid Kantorovich, Soviet economist, is awarded the Nobel Prize in economics. He is considered the leading representative of the mathematics school in Soviet economic planning.

The Jewish Museum of New York exhibits "Jewish Experience in the Art of the Twentieth Century," curated by Avram Kampf.

The Spertus Museum of Judaica in Chicago exhibits "Magic and Superstition in the Jewish Tradition."

Ephraim E. Urbach's *The Sages: Their Concepts and Beliefs* is translated from Hebrew into English. It is a comprehensive and scholarly analysis of the religious and social thought of the Mishnaic and talmudic sages. Urbach emigrated to Palestine from Germany in 1938.

David Vital, Israeli historian, writes *The Origins of Zionism*, the first in a three-volume work.

The Jewish National and University Library in Jerusalem exhibits The Portuguese Jews of Amsterdam in the

---

Resolution 3379

Adopted by the U.N General Assembly on November 10, 1975, which "determines that Zionism is a form of racism and racial discrimination."

IN FAVOR – 72

Afghanistan	Guinea-Bissau	Pakistan
Albania	Guyana	Poland
Algeria	Hungary	Portugal
Bahrain	India	Qatar
Bangladesh	Indonesia	Rwanda
Brazil	Iran	Sao Tome and
Bulgaria	Iraq	Principe
Burundi	Jordan	Saudia Arabia
Byelorussian SSR	Kuwait	Senegal
Cambodia	Laos	Somalia
Cape Verde	Lebanon	Sri Lanka
Chad	Libyan Arab Republic	Sudan
China	Madagascar	Syrian Arab Republic
Congo	Malaysia	Tunisia
Cuba	Maldives	Turkey
Cyprus	Mali	Uganda
Czechoslovakia	Malta	Ukranian SSR
Dahomey	Mauritania	USSR
Democratic Yemen	Mexico	United Arab Emirates
Egypt	Mongolia	United Republic of
Equatorial Guinea	Morocco	Cameroon
Gambia	Moambique	United Republic of
German Democratic	Niger	Tanzania
Republic	Nigeria	Yemen
Grenada	Oman	Yugoslavia
Guinea		

AGAINST – 35

Australia	Finland	Liberia
Austria	Swaziland	Luxembourg
Bahamas	France	Malawi
Barbados	Germany, Federal	Netherlands
Belgium	Republic	New Zealand
Canada	Haiti	Nicaragua
Central African	Honduras	Norway
Republic	Iceland	Panama
Costa Rica	Ireland	Sweden
Denmark	Israel	United Kingdom
Dominican Republic	Italy	United States
El Salvador	Ivory Coast	Uruguay
Fiji		

ABSTENTIONS – 32

Argentina	Greece	Philippines
Bhutan	Guatemala	Sierra Leone
Bolivia	Jamaica	Singapore
Botswana	Japan	Thailand
Burma	Kenya	Togo
Chile	Lesotho	Trinidad and Tobago
Colombia	Mauritius	Upper Volta
Ecuador	Nepal	Venezuela
Ethiopia	Papua New Guinea	Zaire
Gabon	Paraguay	Zambia
Ghana	Peru	

A. General History	B. Jews in North and South America	C. Jews in Europe	D. Jews in the Middle East and Elsewhere	E. Jewish Culture	
			commitment to Israel's right to survival. Israel's Moshe Dayan and Egyptian Deputy Premier Hassan el-Tuhami* hold a secret meeting in Morocco to discuss a possible peace treaty between Israel and Egypt.	17th Century to mark the 300th anniversary of the opening of the Portuguese synagogue in Amsterdam. Yeshayahu Liebowitz (b. 1903), Israeli scientist and philosopher, publishes *Judaism, the Jewish People, and the State of Israel*, a collection of articles and lectures	**Sep. 1975**
			The Greek freighter *Olympus* passes through the Suez Canal. It is the first time in more than 15 years that Israeli-bound cargo is allowed through the canal. The UN General Assembly, by a vote of 72 to 35 with 32 abstentions, adopts Resolution 3379, which declares that Zionism is a "form of racism and racial discrimination." Both houses of the U.S. Congress unanimously adopt a resolution calling on the UN General Assembly to rescind Resolution 3379. U.S. Secretary of State Henry Kissinger declares that the "United States will ignore this vote." A terrorist bomb explosion on Jerusalem's Jaffa Road kills 7 and injures 42.	describing his "unorthodox orthodoxy." He criticizes traditional authorities responsible for the religious law and the Israeli government and its foreign policy. Emigrating to Palestine from Europe in 1935, he has seven doctoral degrees and is considered an intellectual giant as well as one of Israel's most controversial personalities.	**Nov. 1975**
During a U.S. visit, President Anwar al-Sadat* of Egypt addresses a joint session of Congress. Sadat* is the first Egyptian president to officially visit the U.S. Juan Carlos I* becomes the first king of Spain in over 44 years.					
Elena Bonner, wife of Andrei Sakharov,* Soviet dissident leader, accepts his Nobel Peace Prize. He was refused an exit visa to Oslo. She reads his remarks, which include the condemnation of UN Resolution 3379.	Leaders of the Jewish community of Brazil meet with President Ernesto Geisel* after Brazil's UN General Assembly vote in favor of Resolution 3379. Geisel* reassures them that the government intends no restrictions on Zionist activities. Editorials in leading Brazilian newspapers criticize the vote as contrary to Brazilian tradition.	Eleven OPEC oil ministers are taken hostage at Vienna. The terrorists broadcast a communiqué denouncing any compromise involving the Arab acceptance of Israel's existence. The hostages are flown to Algiers and Tripoli, where they are released.			**Dec. 1975**

	A. General History	B. Jews in North and South America	C. Jews in Europe	D. Jews in the Middle East and Elsewhere	E. Jewish Culture
1976	Supporters of black majority rule wage guerrilla war throughout Rhodesia against the white government. Chou En-lai,* Chinese premier, and Mao Tse-tung,* Chinese Communist party chairman, die. The "Gang of Four," including Jiang Qing, Mao's* wife, fails in a bid to seize power. The U.S. and the Soviet Union sign a peaceful nuclear explosions treaty, prohibiting underground tests for peaceful purposes of devices yielding more than 150 kilotons and for the exchange of testing information and limited access to test sites.		John Toland,* U.S. author, writes the best-selling biography *Adolf Hitler*, in which he speculates that Hitler's* hatred of the Jews may have been in reaction to a Jewish physician who had treated his mother when she was dying from cancer.	Yahel, the first kibbutz sponsored by U.S. Reform Judaism, is established in Israel.	Irving Howe (b. 1920), U.S. social and literary critic, writes *World of Our Fathers*, a social and cultural history of eastern European Jewish immigrants on New York's Lower East Side. It wins him a National Book Award and becomes a best-seller. Saul Bellow, U.S. novelist, is awarded the Nobel Prize in literature for his "exuberant ideas, flashing irony, hilarious comedy and burning compassion." He has won the National Book Award three times, and, in 1976, the Pulitzer Prize. Saul Bellow, U.S. novelist, writes *To Jerusalem and Back: A Personal Account*, which reports his observations on contemporary Israeli society. "What you do know is that there is one fact of Jewish life unchanged by the creation of a Jewish state: you cannot take your right to live for granted."
Jan. 1976	Syria's Hafiz al-Assad* shifts support in Lebanon's civil war from Lebanese and Palestinian Muslims and uses Syrian troops to restore the military balance that had been turning against the Christians.			Faruq Khaddoumi,* PLO spokesman, addresses the UN Security Council and declares that the PLO regards Israel's creation as a violation of the UN Charter. The U.S. vetoes the UN Security Council resolution that calls for an Israeli withdrawal from all Arab territories occupied since 1967 and the establishment of a Palestinian Arab state. Israeli Prime Minister Yitzhak Rabin addresses a joint session of Congress, the first Israeli prime minister to do so.	*Lilith* magazine is founded in the U.S. It becomes a vehicle for the discussion of Jewish feminist issues. Howard M. Sachar (b. 1928), U.S. historian, writes *A History of Israel: From the Rise of Zionism to Our Time*. James Levine (b. 1943), the grandson of a cantor and composer of liturgical music, is appointed music director of New York's Metropolitan Opera.
Feb. 1976		Harvard University announces plans for a $15 million Center for Jewish Studies.	The Second World Conference of Jewish Communities on Soviet Jewry is held in Brussels, Belgium, with 1,200 delegates from 32 countries in attendance.		Milton Friedman (b. 1912), U.S. economist, wins the Nobel Prize in economics. His philosophy is
Mar. 1976	Egypt's Anwar al-Sadat* abrogates the 15-year				

A. General History	B. Jews in North and South America	C. Jews in Europe	D. Jews in the Middle East and Elsewhere	E. Jewish Culture	
Soviet–Egyptian Treaty of Friendship and Cooperation concluded in 1971 and orders the Soviets to close their naval bases in Alexandria. The Soviets refused to resupply Egypt with military spare parts and did not agree to Egypt's request to restructure their outstanding debt to the Soviet Union.				generally associated with a laissez-faire, or hands-off, policy in regard to business and trade. Baruch S. Blumberg, U.S. researcher, wins the Nobel Prize in physiology or medicine for his research on blood leading to discoveries of the origins and spread of infectious diseases.	**Mar. 1976**
Syria sends troops into Lebanon to support Christians in response to gains made by the alliance of Palestinians and Christian leftists. In June, the Arab League will support the move. Portugal holds its first free elections in over half a century.			In a major speech on Middle East policy, Democratic presidential candidate Jimmy Carter* expresses his view that "the Jewish people are entitled to one place on this earth where they can have their own state, one given to them from time immemorial." He emphasizes that sympathy for the Palestinians should "not lead us to recognize the existence of brutal terrorists who masquerade as their representatives in the world forum."	Burton Richter, U.S. physicist, wins the Nobel Prize in physics for the discovery of the subatomic psi particle. The Jewish Museum in New York holds a retrospective exhibition of the art of Ludwig Yehuda Wolpert (1900–1981), a major designer. He is the first metalworker to apply the Bauhaus aesthetic principles—form and function are mutually dependent, fine design should be aimed at mass production, and ornament should be banned—to the fabrication of Jewish ceremonial art.	**Apr. 1976**
The first Helsinki watch committee is organized in Moscow. Its purpose is to inform the signatory states of any violations of the 1975 Helsinki accord. Among its members are Yuri Orlov,* who serves as chairman; Elena Bonner, the wife of Andrei Sakharov;* Vladimir Slepak; Aleksandr Ginzburg; and Anatoly Sharansky (b. 1948).			At its national meeting in Johannesburg, the South African Jewish Board of Deputies unanimously condemns the policy of apartheid.	Two autobiographical accounts of Israeli military–political leaders, Moshe Dayan's *Story of My Life* and Yigael Allon's *My Father's House*, are published in the U.S. Rina Mor-Messinger of Israel wins the Miss Universe title. The Israel Museum in Jerusalem exhibits "Archaeological Discoveries in the Jewish Quarter of Jerusalem" from the Second Temple period.	**May 1976**
The U.S. ambassador to Lebanon, Francis E. Meloy, Jr.,* and his economic counselor are murdered in Beirut. Blacks in Soweto, a suburb of Johannesburg, and Capetown riot against			An Air France plane en route from Israel to Paris with 247 passengers is hijacked by pro-Palestinian terrorists shortly after takeoff from Athens. The plane is flown to Entebbe, Uganda, where President Idi Amin* tells the	Jacques Derrida (b. 1930), French philosopher born in Algeria, publishes in	**June 1976**

	A. General History	B. Jews in North and South America	C. Jews in Europe	D. Jews in the Middle East and Elsewhere	E. Jewish Culture
June 1976	South Africa's apartheid policy.			hostages he supports the Palestinian cause and the hijackers' demand for the release of imprisoned terrorists.	English one of his major works, *Of Grammatology*. In contrast to virtually all other philosophers, Derrida understands writing to be the most apt metaphor for reality because it represents the trace of what is no longer there. Derrida's analytical method of "deconstruction," which shows that meaning is unstable, makes a significant impact on literary criticism.
July 1976			The Soviet Union's only Jewish cosmonaut, Colonel Boris Volynov, commands the two-man *Soyez-21* spacecraft.	On July 2, all non-Israeli passengers are released from the Air France plane hijacked to Entebbe, Uganda, as a result of French government efforts. On July 3, Israeli commandos under the command of General Dan Shomron fly to Entebbe and rescue the Israeli hostages. Seven terrorists, twenty Ugandan soldiers, three hostages, and two Israeli soldiers, including the leader of the rescue force, Lieutenant Colonel Jonathan Netanyahu, are killed. Dora Bloch, a 74-year-old hostage who had been taken to a local hospital, is later killed by the Ugandans.	Israeli archaeologist Ze'ev Meshel announces the discovery of several Hebrew inscriptions at what he believes was an 8th-century BCE way station and shrine on the border between the Negev and the Sinai Peninsula at modern Kuntillet Ajrud. One of the large jars features a painting of a god and goddess and an inscription invoking the blessing of "YHWH [the Lord] and his consort[?] /Asherah[?]/shrine[?]." Many scholars see in this evidence of a nonbiblical Israelite worship of male and female deities.

Passengers deplaning at Ben-Gurion Airport after the Entebbe rescue. (Israel Government Press Office)

	A. General History	B.	C.	D. Jews in the Middle East and Elsewhere	E. Jewish Culture
				The Democratic party platform pledges to continue "our consistent support" for Israel. It recognizes "the established status of Jerusalem as the capital of Israel" and declares the U.S. embassy will be moved from Tel Aviv to Jerusalem.	*The Eighty-First Blow*, a film documentary, describes the Holocaust in chronological detail. It is one of a trilogy of documentary films produced for the Ghetto Fighters' House in Israel. The other films are *The Last Sea* (1984), describing survivors when they reach Palestine, and *Flame in the Ashes* (1987), which examines Jewish resistance in the Holocaust.
Aug. 1976				The Republican party platform reiterates the "fundamental and enduring commitment" to Israel. The platform is silent on the Jerusalem issue. Israel opens the "good fence," an official border crossing point with customs and money exchange, at the Lebanese border.	
Sep. 1976				Democratic presidential candidate	

A. General History	B. Jews in North and South America	C. Jews in Europe	D. Jews in the Middle East and Elsewhere	E. Jewish Culture	
			Jimmy Carter* endorses congressional efforts to block the sale of Maverick air-to-surface missiles to Saudi Arabia. "We should not simply sell weapons to get oil." The weapons sale is approved.		**Sep. 1976**
There are nearly 30,000 Syrian troops in Lebanon. Leaders of Saudi Arabia, Egypt, Syria, Lebanon, and the PLO hold a summit at Riyadh. The Syrian army in Lebanon is legitimized as a peace-keeping force and Yasir Arafat* is urged to suspend PLO military activities.	In a campaign speech in New York, President Gerald R. Ford* acknowledges that "we must do better in terms of Soviet Jewish emigration," promises that he will not "tolerate" another Arab oil embargo, and declares that "the PLO will not be a participant in any future conference on peace in the Middle East."				**Oct. 1976**
Democrats Jimmy Carter* and Walter Mondale* defeat Republicans President Gerald R. Ford* and Robert Dole* for the presidency.	The Jewish vote in the presidential election is 68% for Jimmy Carter* and 32% for Gerald R. Ford.*		A new Israeli political party, the Democratic Movement, is formed by Professor Yigael Yadin. He calls for electoral reform, a quest for peace with the Arabs even at the expense of territorial compromise, and an effort to improve social and economic conditions.		**Nov. 1976**
Kurt Waldheim* of Austria wins approval of the UN Security Council for a second five-year term as secretary-general.			Prime Minister Yitzhak Rabin and his government resign. In January 1977, the Knesset will decide on its own dissolution and will set the date for national elections. Rabin's government remains in power as a caretaker government.		**Dec. 1976**
Prime Minister Ian Smith* of Rhodesia begins to develop a settlement for black majority rule.	Rabbi Norman Lamm (b. 1927), U.S. Orthodox rabbi, is elected president of Yeshiva University in New York, succeeding Dr. Samuel Belkin (1911–1976). The chancellor of the Jewish Theological Seminary of America, Gerson D. Cohen, establishes the Commission for the	David Irving,* British author, writes *Hitler's War*, in which he suggests that Adolf Hitler* had nothing to do with the "final solution." He bases his assertion on the inability of scholars to discover written orders from Hitler to kill all the Jews of Europe.	Rabbi Emanuel Rackman (b. 1910), U.S. Orthodox rabbi, becomes president of Bar Ilan University in Israel.	Neil Simon, U.S. playwright, writes *Chapter Two*, a play dealing with the death of his first wife and his remarriage. Lucjan Dobroszycki and Barbara Kirshenblatt-Gimblett, under the auspices of the YIVO Institute for Jewish Research, write *Image Before My Eyes: A Photographic*	**1977**

	A. General History	B. Jews in North and South America	C. Jews in Europe	D. Jews in the Middle East and Elsewhere	E. Jewish Culture
1977		Study of the Ordination of Women as Rabbis, drawn from the faculty, rabbis, and laity of the Conservative movement. *Annie Hall*, a film by Woody Allen (Allen Stewart Konigsberg, b. 1935), wins an Oscar as the best picture of the year. Allen wins the award as best director. The film touches on such issues as Jewish self-hatred, Jewish feelings about White Anglo-Saxon Protestants (WASPs), and WASP antisemitism. The Union of American Hebrew Congregations (Reform) resolves to admit homosexual congregations. In 1973, Solomon Freehof, leading Reform Jewish halakhic authority, wrote a responsum ruling that "homosexuality is deemed in Jewish law to be a sin. [But] . . . it would be in direct contravention to Jewish law to keep sinners out of the congregation."			*History of Jewish Life in Poland, 1864–1939*. The exhibition of the photographs is later shown in the Jewish Museum in New York and other museums in the U.S. and Tel Aviv, Israel. Rosalyn Sussman Yalow wins the Nobel Prize in physiology or medicine for her role in developing the radioimmunoassay, a technique now widely used for measuring the concentration of biologically active substances in the body undetectable by any other method. She is affiliated with New York's Mt. Sinai hospital. Her partner in this research, Solomon Berson, died in 1972. Andrew Schally, of Tulane University, who was born in Vilna, Poland, is awarded the Nobel Prize in physiology or medicine for his research in pituitary hormone deficiencies. The Jewish Museum in New York exhibits Fabric of Jewish Life: Textiles from the Jewish Museum Collection. This collection of ceremonial textiles for the synagogue and home was taken primarily from the museum's Harry G. Friedman, Benjamin Mintz, and Ephraim Benguiat collections. The Yeshiva University Museum in New York exhibits Families & Feasts: Paintings by Moritz Daniel Oppenheim (1799–1882) and Isidor Kaufmann (1853–1921), with the catalog by Alfred Werner. Dannie Abse (b. 1923), Welsh-born
Jan. 1977			Abu Daoud,* a leader of the Fatah terrorist organization who organized the murder of the Israeli athletes at the 1972 Munich Olympics, is released and flown to Algiers after his arrest by French counterespionage agents. Israel protests the French action.		
Feb. 1977	Mengistu Haile Mariam* assumes power in Ethiopia, which becomes Marxist. Ethiopia and Somalia begin to wage war over the Ogaden region.			The Carter* administration vetoes the impending sale of Israeli-made Kfir jet fighters to Ecuador. U.S. approval was required because the planes had American-made engines. The Israelis	

A. General History	B. Jews in North and South America	C. Jews in Europe	D. Jews in the Middle East and Elsewhere	E. Jewish Culture	
			regard the veto of the $200 million sale as a serious blow to their aircraft industry. The U.S. says the veto is part of the U.S. policy to restrain the Latin American arms race. Yitzhak Rabin is chosen as the Labour nominee for the premiership, narrowly defeating Shimon Peres (1455 to 1404).	playwright, poet, and physician, publishes his *Collected Poems, 1948–1976*. Abse has sophisticated knowledge of midrashic, Hasidic, and Kabbalistic legends, which he adapts and utilizes in his poems. R. B. Kitaj (b. 1932), U.S. artist who lives in England, paints *The Jew Etc.*, a portrait of	**Feb. 1977**
	Seven members of the Hanafi Muslim sect occupy several floors of the national headquarters of B'nai B'rith in Washington, D.C. They threaten to kill their Jewish hostages and accuse the Jews of control of the courts and the media. They surrender two days later and are convicted and sentenced to prison for armed kidnapping and other crimes.	Soviet Jewish dissident leader Anatoly Sharansky is arrested on charges of treason. He is accused of being a CIA agent.	At a town meeting in Clinton, Massachusetts, President Jimmy Carter* declares that the creation of Israel was "one of the finest acts of the world nations that has ever occurred." He notes that the Palestinians have never given up on their desire to destroy Israel, but declares "there has to be a homeland for the Palestinian refugees who have suffered for many, many years." President Jimmy Carter* addresses the UN General Assembly and shakes hands with the PLO's UN observer at a reception following the address. This deliberate and symbolic act, made while the Palestine National Council was meeting in Cairo, fails to bring about any modification of the PLO policy of refusing to accept Israel's right to exist.	a man traveling on a train into presumed exile. The Holocaust and the condition of the modern Jew are major subjects of his work. Israeli archaeologist Yigael Yadin, whose father Eliezer Sukenik (1889–1953) had helped Israel acquire some of the first Dead Sea Scrolls and who himself had won the Israel Prize in 1956 for his study of the Scroll of the Sons of Light against the Sons of Darkness, publishes a three-volume edition of and commentary on the large Dead Sea Temple Scroll, which Yadin had helped Israel acquire after the Six-Day War. The Temple Scroll presents an interpretation of the Torah's ritual laws in which God speaks in the first person.	**Mar. 1977**
In the two years since its eruption in April 1975, the civil war in Lebanon has taken about 60,000 lives and about three times as many have been wounded.	Argentine military authorities arrest Jacobo Timerman (b. 1923), editor of the liberal daily *La Opinión*. Jewish efforts from around the world fail to obtain Timerman's release. The American Civil Liberties Union (ACLU) agrees to go to court to defend the constitutional rights of Frank Collin,* who		PLO leader Yasir Arafat* is officially received by Soviet leader Leonid Brezhnev* in Moscow. They issue a joint statement, calling for a comprehensive Middle East settlement that includes the right of Palestinians to create an independent state and for the participation of the		**Apr. 1977**

	A. General History	B. Jews in North and South America	C. Jews in Europe	D. Jews in the Middle East and Elsewhere	E. Jewish Culture
Apr. 1977		was seeking to organize a Nazi march through Skokie, a predominantly Jewish suburb of Chicago, Illinois. Skokie's population of 69,000 contains approximately 40,000 Jews, of whom an estimated 7,000 are Holocaust survivors. The town enacted legislation aimed at banning the march. ACLU officials will later report that 40,000 of its 250,000 members resigned in 1977.		PLO at the Geneva Conference. Yitzhak Rabin withdraws as Labour's candidate for the premiership in the upcoming Israeli elections as a result of the revelation that his wife, violating Israeli law, opened a bank account in the U.S. while he was Israeli ambassador. Defense Minister Shimon Peres is unanimously elected to succeed him and will serve until the May elections.	
May 1977				Fifty-four Israeli paratroopers and airmen are killed in a helicopter crash during a training exercise. Israel holds national elections for the Ninth Knesset, with 1,771,726 votes cast. Likud wins 43 seats; the Alignment (Labour–Mapam), 32 seats; the Democratic Movement for Change, 15 seats; and the National Religious party 12 seats. Two days after his election to be Israel's prime minister, Menachem Begin visits the Gush Emunim settlement of Elon Moreh on the West Bank and declares that "there will be many Elon Morehs."	
June 1977		President Jimmy Carter* signs a new antiboycott law directed primarily at the Arab boycott of Israel.	President Jimmy Carter* declares that Soviet dissident Anatoly Sharansky was not a CIA agent. His arrest is perceived by the U.S. as a direct challenge to the Helsinki accord and seriously detrimental to détente.	Israeli Prime Minister Menachem Begin's government is installed. The cabinet includes Moshe Dayan as foreign minister, Yigael Yadin as deputy prime minister, Ezer Weizmann as defense minister, and Ariel Sharon as agriculture minister. The nine-nation European Economic	

A. General History	B. Jews in North and South America	C. Jews in Europe	D. Jews in the Middle East and Elsewhere	E. Jewish Culture	
			Community (EEC) issues a statement calling on Israel to "recognize the legitimate rights of the Palestinian people" but does not grant formal recognition to the PLO.		**June 1977**
Anwar al-Sadat's* Egypt and Muammar Qaddafi's* Libya engage in a short and bloody border war.			Israeli Prime Minister Menachem Begin meets with U.S. President Jimmy Carter* at the White House. Carter* indicates his pleasure with Begin's statements that all issues are negotiable and that he looks forward to the Geneva Conference in October. At a press conference after Begin's departure, Carter* says he advised Begin of the U.S.'s concern over the creation of West Bank Israeli settlements. Israeli settlements in the occupied territories had "always been characterized by our government . . . as an illegal action."		**July 1977**
			Israeli Prime Minister Menachem Begin visits Romania and holds talks with President Nicolae Ceauşescu.* It is later reported in the press that this visit lays the groundwork for Anwar al-Sadat's* historic visit to Jerusalem.		**Aug. 1977**
The U.S. and Panama sign a treaty that will end U.S. control of the Panama Canal in 1999.			Israeli Foreign Minister Moshe Dayan holds a secret meeting with Egyptian Deputy Prime Minister Hassan Tuhami* in Morocco. Dayan is said to have offered to return the whole of the Sinai to Egyptian rule in return for a peace treaty.		**Sep. 1977**
Delegates from the 35 nations who participated in the 1975 Helsinki accord assemble at Belgrade,			The U.S. and the Soviet Union issue a joint statement on the Middle East designed to facilitate the		**Oct. 1977**

A. General History	B. Jews in North and South America	C. Jews in Europe	D. Jews in the Middle East and Elsewhere	E. Jewish Culture
Oct. 1977	Yugoslavia, for a follow-up conference.			resumption of the Geneva Conference no later than December 1977. President Jimmy Carter* addresses the UN General Assembly and tries to soften congressional and Israeli criticism of the joint U.S.–Soviet statement. He says that the U.S. does not intend to impose a Middle East settlement, and that the basis for peace is provided in Resolutions 242 and 338, which was not mentioned in the U.S.–Soviet statement. He reaffirms as "unquestionable" the U.S. commitment to Israel's security, but again states that "the legitimate rights of the Palestinians must be recognized."	
Nov. 1977	The UN Security Council imposes a mandatory arms embargo against South Africa.	Edward I. Koch is elected mayor of the city of New York.	Helmut Schmidt* is the first West German chancellor to visit Auschwitz. "The crimes of Nazi fascism, the guilt of the German Reich under Hitler's leadership, lie at the bottom of our responsibility. We Germans of today are not guilty as individuals, but we must take upon us the political heritage of those who were guilty. In this lies our responsibility."	In response to a plea by Pope Paul VI for clemency, Israeli authorities free Archbishop Hilarion Capucci.	

D. Jews in the Middle East and Elsewhere

On November 9, Egypt's Anwar al-Sadat,* in an address to the People's Assembly in Cairo, broadcast nationwide, declares: "I am ready to go to the ends of the earth if this will prevent a soldier or an officer of my sons from being wounded—not being killed, but wounded. Israel will be astonished when it hears me saying now before you that I am ready to go to their house, to the Knesset itself and to talk to them."

On November 10, Israel's Menachem Begin states that if Anwar al-Sadat* would come to Jerusalem, he would be received with all honor. An official Israeli invitation is extended to Sadat* through the offices of the U.S. ambassador.

On November 16, U.S. President Jimmy Carter* praises Anwar al-Sadat's* decision to go to Jerusalem as a step in the right direction. Taken by surprise, the Carter* administration still envisions a U.S. and Soviet–sponsored Geneva peace conference. It is believed that Sadat* acted as a result of his dismay at the U.S. involvement with the Soviets after he had eliminated them from Egypt.

Nov. 1977

On November 19, Anwar al-Sadat* arrives in Israel and receives a cordial welcome.

On November 20, Anwar al-Sadat* addresses the Israeli Knesset. He admits that the Arabs had previously rejected Israel but goes on to say, "Yet today I tell you, and I declare it to the whole world, that we accept living with you in permanent peace based on justice." However, he insists on a complete Israeli withdrawal from the occupied territories, including Arab Jerusalem, and the right of the Palestinian people to establish their own state. He warns that he did not come to Israel to conclude a separate peace between Egypt and Israel.

On December 5, Libya, Syria, Iraq, Algeria, South Yemen, and the PLO meet in Tripoli, Libya. They condemn Anwar al-Sadat's* peace initiative as "high treason" and form an anti-Egyptian front. Sadat* breaks off relations with these countries.

Dec. 1977

On December 16, Israel's Menachem Begin visits President Jimmy Carter* in Washington, D.C., to present his peace plan before conveying it to Anwar al-Sadat* at Ismailia. Carter* calls the Israeli proposals "constructive" and a "fair basis for negotiation."

On December 25 and 26, Menachem Begin and Anwar al-Sadat* discuss peace proposals at Ismailia. They announce continuation of negotiations through 2 committees: one on political affairs, headed by Israeli Foreign Minister Moshe Dayan, and the other on military affairs, headed by Egyptian Defense Minister Abdul Ghani Gamasy.*

On December 28, U.S. President Jimmy Carter* discusses what he means by a Palestinian homeland. "We do favor a homeland or an entity wherein the Palestinians can live in peace. . . . My own preference is that they not be an independent nation but be tied in some way with the surrounding countries, making a choice, for instance, between Israel and Jordan."

Great Britain officially welcomes Israeli Prime Minister Menachem Begin, ending Britain's ostracism of the former leader of the Irgun Zeva'i Le'ummi.

A. **General History**	B. **Jews in North and South America**	C. **Jews in Europe**	D. **Jews in the Middle East and Elsewhere**	E. **Jewish Culture**	
	Reform, Conservative, and Traditional (modern Orthodox) rabbis in Denver, Colorado, establish a joint *bet din* to oversee conversions in order to assure that rabbis in Denver would recognize converts. Orthodox rabbis refuse to join. The *bet din* will be dissolved in 1983, when the Central Conference of American Rabbis (Reform) adopts its resolution recognizing patrilineal descent. During its existence, the *bet din* will supervise over 750 conversions.	In France, Robert Faurisson,* a professor of literature at the University of Lyon, writes a history of Nazi concentration camps in which he concludes that the gas chambers never existed. *Madame Rosa*, a French film directed by Moshe Mizrahi, stars Simone Signoret as an ex-whore in the Belleville section of Paris who makes a living raising children abandoned by prostitutes. She is a Jewess who survived Auschwitz. A major	Sir Zelman Cowen is appointed governor-general of Australia. A leading legal scholar, he is the second Australian-born Jew to be named governor-general. Sir Isaac Isaac held the post in the 1930s.	Herman Wouk, U.S. novelist, writes *War and Remembrance*, a continuation of his saga of World War II begun in 1971 with *The Winds of War*. Both books will be adapted to television. Alfred Kazin, U.S. literary critic, writes *New York Jew*, a continuation of his memoir of American literary life into the 1970s. Theodore H. White (1915–1986), U.S. journalist, writes *In Search of History*, a memoir. Well known	**1978**

	A. General History	B. Jews in North and South America	C. Jews in Europe	D. Jews in the Middle East and Elsewhere	E. Jewish Culture
1978			theme is her raising the child of an Arab to be a faithful Arab. It will win the Academy Award for Best Foreign Film.		for his reports from China during World War II and for his books on presidential election campaigns. White's memoir includes a description of his youth in Boston's Jewish community.
Jan. 1978				Meeting at Aswan, Egypt, President Jimmy Carter* and Anwar al-Sadat* issue a joint statement, the Aswan principles: peace must be based on normal relations, not just an end to belligerency; Israel must withdraw from territories occupied in 1967; there must be agreement on secure and recognized borders in accordance with UN Resolutions 242 and 338; the Palestinian problem in all its aspects must be resolved, including the recognition of the legitimate rights of the Palestinian people.	Isaac Bashevis Singer, Polish-born author of Yiddish fiction, publishes in English *Shosha*, a novel of ghetto life in Poland before World War II. Howard Nemerov (1920–1991), U.S. poet, wins the Pulitzer Prize and National Book Award for his *Collected Poems*. The English translation of Israel Zinberg's monumental *A History of Jewish Literature* is completed with the publication of the 12th volume.
Feb., 1978				Anwar al-Sadat* arrives in Washington, D.C., for talks with President Jimmy Carter* and urges the U.S. to act as "the arbiter" in talks with Israel. Carter* stresses the U.S. intention to be "mediator," not arbiter.	Isaac Bashevis Singer, Polish-born author of Yiddish fiction, who emigrated to the U.S. in 1935, is awarded the Nobel Prize in literature for his contributions to Yiddish literature. In accepting the award he says: "I never forget that I am only a storyteller."
Mar. 1978	Left-wing terrorists kidnap former Italian Premier Aldo Moro.* His bullet-riddled body is found 3½ weeks later.			President Jimmy Carter* states that the abandonment or rejection by the Israeli government of the applicability of UN Resolution 242 to the West Bank would be a complete reversal of Israeli policy and a serious blow to peace prospects. Later, former UN Ambassador Arthur J. Goldberg, the principal architect of Resolution 242, writes that 242 envisaged withdrawal on all three fronts. PLO terrorists operating out of Lebanon land on the beach south of Haifa	Arno A. Penzias, U.S. physicist, is awarded the Nobel Prize in physics for the discovery of a faint electromagnetic radiation that appears to permeate the entire universe. Penzias left his native Germany with his parents in 1940. Herbert A. Simon, U.S. economist, is awarded the Nobel Prize in economics for his publications on the structure and decision-making

A. General History	B. Jews in North and South America	C. Jews in Europe	D. Jews in the Middle East and Elsewhere	E. Jewish Culture	
			and kill 35 Israelis and wound 76 on buses and in cars on the Tel Aviv coastal road. They also kill an American, Gail Rubin, a nature photographer, near Kibbutz Maagan Michael. Nine terrorists are killed and two captured. The Israel Defense Forces begin an incursion into southern Lebanon to root out PLO terrorist positions. Five days later, the IDF is in control of the entire area between the border and the Litani River. The UN Security Council adopts the U.S. resolution calling upon Israel to withdraw its troops from Lebanon and the establishment of a UN interim force (UNIFIL) to ensure the peaceful character of southern Lebanon and to take measures to restore Lebanese control. The Israelis accuse the U.S. of yielding to Saudi pressure and deleting a resolution phrase that would have authorized UNIFIL to prevent entry of unauthorized armed persons into the zone. Menachem Begin begins a visit to Washington, D.C., for talks with Jimmy Carter.* When the difficult talks end, Carter* advises the Senate Foreign Relations Committee that the "diplomatic process has come to a halt."	within economic organizations. Daniel Nathans, U.S. researcher, is awarded the Nobel Prize in physiology or medicine for the discovery of enzymes that break the giant molecules of DNA into manageable pieces. Vladimir Horowitz (1904–1989), renowned pianist, gives a recital at the White House. Born in Berdichev, Russia, Horowitz left Russia in 1925 and later settled in the U.S. in 1939. President Jimmy Carter* introduces him as a "national treasure." Saul Steinberg (b. 1914), U.S. painter and graphic artist, has a one-man show at New York's Whitney Museum. Born in Romania, he studied architecture and was a cartoonist in Italy between 1933 and 1940, when he fled Nazi Europe by way of Portugal and the Dominican Republic, arriving in the U.S. in 1942. A *New Yorker* magazine cartoonist, he is a rare artist whose work was known by mass audiences before being recognized by the critics as an important painter. Some of his work utilizes unintelligible rubber stamps and forged passports, an autobiographical reminder of his road to the U.S.	**Mar. 1978**
Noor Mohammed Taraki* overthrows Afghan President Mohammed Daud,* which greatly increases Soviet influence in Afghanistan and brings 3,000 military advisers to the country.	NBC televises "Holocaust," a 9½-hour, four-part fictionalized drama dealing with the fate of European Jewry under the Nazis during World War II. The series is seen by 120 million viewers and spurs a number of		Lieutenant General Rafael Eitan is appointed chief of staff of the Israeli Defense Forces, succeeding Lieutenant General Mordecai Gur. In Tel Aviv, 25,000 Israelis hold a rally	The Jewish Museum of New York mounts a retrospective exhibition of the paintings, drawings, and graphics of Jack Levine, social realist painter.	**Apr. 1978**

	A. General History	B. Jews in North and South America	C. Jews in Europe	D. Jews in the Middle East and Elsewhere	E. Jewish Culture
Apr. 1978		efforts to teach children about the Holocaust.		calling on Menachem Begin to give preference to ending the Arab–Israeli conflict over retaining lands in the West Bank. They favor territorial compromise: "Better a land of peace than a piece of land." The movement becomes known as Peace Now. The Israeli Knesset passes a law providing for free but not compulsory secondary education.	An exhibition on Judaism in the Middle Ages is held in Eisenstadt, Austria. In 1902, Sandor Wolf founded a private museum to illustrate the life of the Jews in the city. After World War II, his collection was incorporated into the collections of the local museums. Peter Kapitza (1894–1984), Soviet physicist, is awarded the Nobel Prize in physics for his research on the liquefaction of helium. He went to England in 1921, where he taught and did research. In 1929, he was the first foreigner in over 200 years to be elected a Fellow of the Royal Society. He returned to the Soviet Union in 1934, where he headed the new Institute of Physical Problems in Moscow. He played a key role in Soviet atomic and nuclear bomb research.
May 1978	Widespread antigovernment riots in Iran spread to Teheran, its capital.		Three Palestinian terrorists attempt to attack El Al passengers gathered in a waiting room at Paris' Orly Airport. Their attack fails, and the three are killed along with a French security officer.	At a White House ceremony attended by more than a 1,000 Jewish leaders marking the 30th anniversary of the State of Israel, U.S. President Jimmy Carter* declares: "For 30 years we have stood at the side of the proud and independent nation of Israel. I can say without reservation. . . . the United States will never support any agreement or any action that places Israel's security in jeopardy." The U.S. Senate approves an arms deal that ties the sale of previously promised 15 F-15 and 75 F-16 aircraft to Israel to congressional approval of the sale of 50 F-5Es to Egypt and 60 F-15s to Saudi Arabia. A senior Carter* official is reported to have boasted in private about having "broken the back of the Jewish lobby." Yitzhak Navon (b. 1921) becomes Israel's fifth president, succeeding Ephraim Katzir. He is the first Sephardi and first Sabra to hold the post. The Museum of the Diaspora (Beth Hatefutsoth), costing $10 million, opens on the campus of Tel Aviv	The Israel Museum in Jerusalem exhibits Architecture in the Hanukkah Lamp, showing architecture as a unifying motif in the design of the back wall of the Hanukkah lamp. It also exhibits Script, Scroll and the Book, including the Aleppo Codex and the Temple Scroll, on the occasion of the nation's 30th anniversary.

A. General History	B. Jews in North and South America	C. Jews in Europe	D. Jews in the Middle East and Elsewhere	E. Jewish Culture	
			University. During the year, it exhibits Beyond the Golden Door, on the history of the Jewish community in New York, and The Last Jews of Radauti, a photographic record of a dying Jewish community in Romania.		**May 1978**
The U.S. Supreme Court votes 5–4 to uphold the decision of the California Supreme Court requiring the University of California to admit Allan Bakke to its medical school. Bakke, a white, claimed he was denied admission solely on the basis of race. The Court holds unlawful the use of racial or ethnic quotas where there had been no finding of past discrimination but holds that affirmative action is permissible. The decision strains relations between Jews, who are pleased, and blacks, who are dismayed by it.	American Nazis seeking to hold a march in Skokie, Illinois, gain a legal victory when U.S. Supreme Court Justice Warren Burger* denies Skokie's request for a stay of the march. Having gained a victory, the Nazis cancel their plans to march in Skokie in favor of a rally in Marquette Park in Chicago.		Israel ends its phased withdrawal from Lebanon and turns over the last occupied area to Major Saad Haddad's* Lebanese Christian troops rather than to the UN interim force, thus honoring Israel's commitment to Lebanese Christians who cooperated with it. Israel's ambassador to South Africa, Yitzhak Unna, refuses an invitation to be guest of honor at the opening of the play *Golda*, because it is to be performed in a Pretoria theater closed to blacks.		**June 1978**
A French newspaper quotes Andrew Young,* U.S. ambassador to the UN: "there are hundreds, perhaps thousands, of people whom I would call political prisoners" in U.S. prisons. He is publicly rebuked by President Jimmy Carter.* Syrian troops in Lebanon attack Christians in the heaviest fighting in two years. At least 200 are killed.	President Jimmy Carter* again states that the Soviet charge that Anatoly Sharansky had committed espionage on behalf of the U.S. is "patently false."	Soviet Jewish dissident leader Anatoly Sharansky is convicted of espionage and receives a 13-year sentence, 3 in prison and 10 in a forced labor camp. Avital Sharansky, Anatoly's wife, meets with Vice President Walter Mondale* and congressional leaders. She tells them, "In your hands is the fate of the Jewish movement in the Soviet Union."	Vice President Walter Mondale,* accompanied by 28 American Jewish leaders, makes an official three-day goodwill visit to Israel. When it is announced that he will not make an official visit to East Jerusalem, Jerusalem Mayor Teddy Kollek threatens to boycott the visit. As a compromise, Mondale* and his family, accompanied by Kollek, make a personal visit to the Western Wall.		**July 1978**
An explosion destroys a nine-story building in Beirut, Lebanon, killing at least 150 persons belonging to several Palestinian terrorist organizations.			After meeting with Menachem Begin in Jerusalem and Anwar al-Sadat* in Cairo, U.S. Secretary of State Cyrus Vance* announces that the two leaders have agreed to a tripartite summit conference at Camp David.		**Aug. 1978**

	A. General History	B. Jews in North and South America	C. Jews in Europe	D. Jews in the Middle East and Elsewhere	E. Jewish Culture
Sep. 1978	Thousands of demonstrators defy the Iranian government imposition of martial law. They demand the removal of the Shah and the establishment of an Islamic state headed by the Ayatollah Khomeini,* a religious leader living in exile.			From September 5 to 16, secret discussions are held at Camp David. Agreement is announced and two documents are signed, with President Jimmy Carter* signing as a witness: One, A Framework for Peace in the Middle East, and the other, A Framework for the Conclusion of a Peace Treaty Between Israel and Egypt. Anwar al-Sadat* writes two side letters to Carter*: (1) All Israeli settlers must leave the Sinai; (2) Arab Jerusalem is an integral part of the West Bank. Menachem Begin writes a letter: Jerusalem is one city indivisible, the capital of Israel. Carter's* letter to Sadat* reaffirms the U.S. position, which is close to Egypt's. The signing ceremony is televised live around the world.	
Oct. 1978	Karol Cardinal Wojtyla, archbishop of Cracow, is elected pope and takes the name John Paul II. He is the first non-Italian to be elevated to the papacy in over four centuries. France grants asylum to the Ayatollah Khomeini, Muslim spiritual leader expelled from Iran by the Shah.				
Nov. 1978	An Arab League summit meeting is held at Baghdad. The Camp David accords are denounced, and it is agreed that if Egypt signs a treaty with Israel, it will be suspended from the Arab League, the Arab League headquarters will be moved from Cairo, and sanctions on Egypt will be imposed. An 88-day New York newspaper strike	John Updike,* U.S. novelist, interviewed by an Israeli newspaper about the American literary scene, observes: "Jewish writers do have a facility with the rhythms of urban American life that gentile writers seem to lack." However, he also observes that "Jews have penetrated all aspects of publishing from sales and promotion to editing and reviewing. I do think that Jewish	West Germany marks the 40th anniversary of *Kristallnacht*. President Walter Scheel* states: "After November 9, 1938, few Germans had the courage to face the consequences of the pogrom. But we today, being able to see the larger contexts, must not evade the truth, even where it is distressing and shameful. . . . We must not forget the November days of 1938. This we owe	Israeli and Egyptian negotiating teams agree on the text of a treaty. However, a further delay ensues. Egyptian President Anwar al-Sadat* and Israeli Prime Minister Menachem Begin are jointly awarded the Nobel Peace Prize for their efforts in bringing peace to Egypt and Israel.	

A. General History	B. Jews in North and South America	C. Jews in Europe	D. Jews in the Middle East and Elsewhere	E. Jewish Culture	
ends, and the *New York Times* resumes publication.	critics . . . do tend to respond more warmly to Jewish writers."	the Jewish people; we owe it to the world and we owe it to ourselves." Six years after he applied for an exit visa, Jewish refusnik Valentin Levich, a prominent scientist, is granted one and leaves for Israel.			**Nov. 1978**
			President Jimmy Carter* bluntly states that it is up to Israel to accept or reject the treaty with Egypt. American Jewish leaders write to Carter,* objecting to his blaming Israel for the impasse and stating that Israel's objections to Egyptian revisions were reasonable. Israel is visited by 132,000 West German tourists, a record number. The Israeli consumer price index has risen by 50% during the course of the year.		**Dec. 1978**
	The Conservative movement's Commission for the Study of the Ordination of Women as Rabbis issues a report arguing there are no halakhic barriers to women's ordination. However, the legal responsibility for the ordination of women rests with the seminary's faculty. William Styron* (b. 1925), U.S. novelist, writes *Sophie's Choice*, a novel about the relationship between Nathan Landau and his beloved Sophie, an émigré Polish Catholic beauty, in postwar New York. Central to the novel are Sophie's experiences in a Nazi concentration camp. It will be adapted to the screen in 1982.		The problem of Jews who leave the Soviet Union with permits to go to Israel but, after arriving in Vienna, emigrate to the U.S. or some other country continues to be a matter of great concern to Israel, which wants immigrants.	Joseph Heller, U.S. novelist, writes *Good as Gold*, a comic novel with a farcical treatment of Jewish family life and the Washington political scene. The Jewish Theological Seminary of America publishes *A Guide to Jewish Religious Practice* written by Rabbi Isaac Klein (1905–1979), a leading traditional scholar in the Conservative movement. The Yeshiva University Museum in New York exhibits Purim: The Face and the Mask, featuring the holiday in art, drama, parody, music, food, costume, and ritual in different cultural environments. Sheldon Glashow and Steven Weinberg,	**1979**

	A. General History	B. Jews in North and South America	C. Jews in Europe	D. Jews in the Middle East and Elsewhere	E. Jewish Culture
1979		Ron Liebman, who plays Reuben Warshofsky, a union organizer from the North, stars with Sally Field* in *Norma Rae*, a film portraying the efforts of textile workers in an Alabama town to rid themselves of exploitation by plant owners.			U.S. physicists, are awarded the Nobel Prize in physics for discovering the link between electromagnetic interaction and the so-called weak interaction of elementary particles. Both are New York natives and they were classmates at Bronx High School of Science.
Jan. 1979	The U.S. and Communist China establish diplomatic relations. The Shah* flees Iran and the Ayatollah Khomeini* returns in triumph on February 1.		About 20 million West Germans view the TV miniseries "Holocaust." It results in a nationwide demand for dissemination of information about the Third Reich. In 1979, the memorial at Dachau has 764,000 visitors, more than ever before.	In an interview with the German news magazine *Der Spiegel*, the Ayatollah Khomeini* declares that his Islamic republic would "break off relations with Israel because we do not believe there is any legal justification for its existence."	*The Warsaw Diary of Adam Czerniakow: Prelude to Doom* is published in English. Czerniakow (1880–1942) was the head of the Warsaw Judenrat (Council) who struggled to maintain Jewish communal existence. He committed suicide in the summer of 1942 when faced with Nazi demands for deportees from the ghetto.
Feb. 1979	The U.S. ambassador to Afghanistan, Adolph Dubs,* is murdered by Islamic insurgents.			A second Camp David conference is attended by Israel's Moshe Dayan and Egypt's Mustapha Khalil.*	The Museum of the Diaspora (Beth Hatefutsoth) in Tel Aviv exhibits Ghettos in Italy: Venice—Rome and Moses Mendelssohn and His Time.
Mar. 1979	In a meeting at Baghdad, the Arab League calls for the complete severance of diplomatic and economic relations with Egypt. Anwar al-Sadat* notes that his Arab critics have become rich from oil revenues while the Egyptians sacrificed their lives and wealth in four wars with Israel. *Front page*, The New York Times, *March 27, 1979.*		Thirty are wounded by an explosion in the area of a Paris kosher restaurant frequented by Jewish university students. 	Menachem Begin and Jimmy Carter* meet in Washington, D.C., to discuss peace proposals. President Jimmy Carter's* visit to Jerusalem and Cairo results in a treaty between Egypt and Israel. Carter* announces the resolution of the final points of difference, and on March 26, the treaty of peace between Israel and Egypt is signed by Carter,* Menachem Begin, and Anwar al-Sadat* at the White House in Washington, D.C.	The Israel Museum in Jerusalem exhibits Turner and the Bible. Bernard Wasserstein, British historian, writes *Britain and the Jews of Europe, 1939–1945*, in which he describes Britain's almost complete ban on Jewish immigration, its restrictive immigration policy on Palestine, and its failure to aid the Jewish resistance in occupied Europe during the Second World War.
Apr. 1979	The Presidential Commission on the Holocaust, created in 1978 and headed by Elie Wiesel, holds its first meeting at the White House.		Five Soviet dissidents are exchanged for two Soviet spies sentenced to long prison terms in the U.S. Two Jewish dissidents, Mark Dymshyts and Edward Kuznetsov, had been sentenced to death in 1970 for the attempted hijack of a	Israeli Prime Minister Menachem Begin is cordially received on his official visit to Cairo, Egypt. The U.S. and Israel sign an agreement for the construction of two air bases in the Negev to replace	

A. General History	B. Jews in North and South America	C. Jews in Europe	D. Jews in the Middle East and Elsewhere	E. Jewish Culture	
		Soviet airliner from Leningrad to Israel. Their sentences were later reduced to long prison terms.	bases in the Sinai that Israel is scheduled to evacuate by April 1982. PLO terrorists, who arrived by sea from Lebanon, seize a house in the coastal town of Nahariya and kill four, including two infant girls. The first ship flying the Israeli flag passes through the Suez Canal.		**Apr. 1979**
Margaret Thatcher,* Conservative party leader, becomes Great Britain's first woman prime minister.			The Sinai town of El-Arish is returned by the Israelis to the Egyptians eight months ahead of schedule. President Jimmy Carter* appoints Robert Strauss to be his special Middle East envoy. In November, Strauss will resign to head Carter's* reelection campaign and be replaced by Sol Linowitz (b. 1913).		**May 1979**
The U.S. and the Soviet Union sign a second strategic arms limitation treaty. The U.S. Senate does not ratify the treaty, but both sides informally observe the limits.			Israeli and Syrian jets clash in an air battle over Lebanon. Six Syrian MiGs are shot down.		**June 1979**
Sandinista rebels in Nicaragua oust President Anastasio Somoza.* Saddam Hussein* becomes Iraq's head of state.		The West German Bundestag votes to abolish the statute of limitations for murder, allowing for the further prosecution of Nazi war crimes. Austrian Chancellor Bruno Kreisky receives PLO chairman Yasir Arafat* with honors usually accorded a head of state. Israel protests.	The Carter* administration announces plans to sell arms valued at $594 million to Egypt and $580 million to Israel. This is in addition to an $800 million grant and $2.2 billion loan to Israel to relocate the Sinai bases to the Negev.		**July 1979**
Iraq's head of state, Saddam Hussein,* accuses Syrian President Hafiz al-Assad* of a recent coup attempt in Iraq.	Andrew Young,* U.S. ambassador to the UN, resigns after violating U.S. policy by meeting with PLO UN observer Zehdi Labib Terzi.* Secretary of State Cyrus Vance* threatened to resign if		President Jimmy Carter* instructs his special Middle East envoy, Robert Strauss, to discuss with Menachem Begin and Anwar al-Sadat* a proposed amendment to UN Resolution 242 that had referred to		**Aug. 1979**

	A. General History	B. Jews in North and South America	C. Jews in Europe	D. Jews in the Middle East and Elsewhere	E. Jewish Culture
Aug. 1979		Young* remained on. Young explicitly blames Israel for leaking an account of the meeting. Black–Jewish relations become strained, and American Jews resent the president's failure to clarify the affair.		Palestinians only as "refugees." The proposed amendment would call for "Palestinian rights." Its objective is to obtain PLO support for 242 so they can enter the peace talks. Begin and Sadat* reject Carter's* suggestion.	
Sep. 1979				At the swearing-in ceremony of Andrew Young's successor as UN ambassador, Donald McHenry,* President Jimmy Carter* declares that no "American Jewish leaders or anyone else" urged him to seek Young's* resignation.	
Oct. 1979	Iran's deposed Shah* arrives secretly in the U.S. for medical treatment.			Israeli Foreign Minister Moshe Dayan resigns from the Begin government. He disagrees over the manner in which the autonomy discussions are being conducted and proposes that if they fail, Israel should unilaterally replace its governance of the territories with a civilian Palestinian administration and return only if the PLO overran the areas. Israel's Supreme Court declares the West Bank settlement of Elon Moreh, near Nablus, to be illegal and orders it dismantled.	

Nov. 1979

A. General History: Militants seize the U.S. embassy in Teheran, Iran, and take about 90 hostages in protest over the Shah's* admission to the U.S. for medical treatment. They release some blacks and women, retaining about 50 hostages.

Arabs seize and occupy the Grand Mosque in Mecca, Saudi Arabia. The

U.S. Military and Economic Aid to Israel, 1977–1989 ($ million)									
	Economic Aid			Military Aid			Total Economic & Military Aid		
Year	Loans	Grants	Total	Loans	Grants	Total	Loans	Grants	Grand Total
1977	245	490	735	500	500	1,000	745	990	1,735
1978	260	525	785	500	500	1,000	760	1,025	1,785
1979	260	525	785	2,700	600	3,300	2,960	1,125	4,085
1980		525	525	500	500	1,000	760	1,025	1,785
1981		764	764	900	500	1,400	900	1,264	2,164
1982		806	806	850	550	1,400	850	1,356	2,206
1983		785	785	950	750	1,700	950	1,535	2,485
1984		910	910	850	850	1,750	850	1,760	2,610
1985		1,950	1,950		1,400	1,400		3,350	3,350
1986		1,898	1,898		1,723	1,723		3,621	3,621
1987		1,200	1,200		1,800	1,800		3,000	3,000
1988		1,200	1,200		1,800	1,800		3,000	3,000
1989		1,200	1,200		1,800	1,800		3,000	3,000
Total	765	12,778	13,543	7,750	13,273	21,023	8,775	26,051	34,826

A. General History	B. Jews in North and South America	C. Jews in Europe	D. Jews in the Middle East and Elsewhere	E. Jewish Culture	
occupation lasts two weeks, and 244 people are killed before Saudi security forces restore order.					**Nov. 1979**
A Libyan mob sets fire to the U.S. embassy in Tripoli. They are supporting the Iranians who took over the U.S. embassy in Teheran. Soviet troops invade Afghanistan. Western sources believe the Soviet Union is unwilling to permit the pro-Soviet Marxist regime on its southern border to be overthrown by a Muslim tribal rebellion.			Israel's economy is hampered by rapidly increasing inflation. The consumer price index in December was 114% higher than at the end of 1978. By the end of the year, an estimated 30,000 of Iran's 80,000 Jews have left, with about half going to Israel and half to the U.S.		**Dec. 1979**
	President Jimmy Carter* presents the Medal of Freedom to Admiral Hyman Rickover (1900–1986). The president states: "With the exception of my father, no other person has had such a profound impact on my life." Rickover will retire in 1982 after serving for 63 years, longer than any other naval officer in American history.			Walter Laqueur (b. 1921) writes *The Terrible Secret*, in which he details the many ways in which information of the "final solution" became known to the West. Herbert Brown, U.S. chemist, is awarded the Nobel Prize in chemistry for his study of boron-containing compounds.	**1980**
President Jimmy Carter* embargoes grain sales and high-technology exports to the Soviet Union in retaliation for its invasion of Afghanistan. Andrei Sakharov,* 1975 winner of the Nobel Peace Prize, and his wife, Elena Bonner, are exiled to the city of Gorky. He had demanded withdrawal of Soviet troops from Afghanistan.				Paul Berg, U.S. biochemist, is awarded the Nobel Prize in chemistry for his fundamental studies of the biochemistry of nucleic acids, with particular regard to recombinant deoxyribonucleic acid (DNA). Baruj Benacerraf, of Venezuelan birth and a professor of pathology at the Harvard Medical School, is awarded the Nobel Prize in physiology or medicine for the discovery of the role of antigens in organ transplants.	**Jan. 1980**
		Kurt Lischka,* former deputy Gestapo chief in Paris, and two others are convicted in Cologne of the responsibility for deportation of about	Egypt and Israel formally exchange ambassadors. Israeli war hero and a Labour party leader Yigael Allon dies	Walter Gilbert, Harvard professor of molecular biology, is awarded the Nobel Prize in chemistry for developing ways of	**Feb. 1980**

	A. General History	B. Jews in North and South America	C. Jews in Europe	D. Jews in the Middle East and Elsewhere	E. Jewish Culture
Feb. 1980			70,000 Jews from France to the Nazi death camps. Serge Klarsfeld, a Jewish lawyer, and his wife, Beate,* gathered the evidence of their guilt. Lischka* receives a 10-year sentence.	suddenly while campaigning to become the leader of the Labour party.	finding the order in which the individual links are present in the chainlike molecules of nucleic acids. Lawrence R. Klein, U.S. economist, is awarded the Nobel Prize in economics for developing computer models of the world's economy.
Mar. 1980	Oscar Arnulfo Romero, archbishop of San Salvador, is assassinated. El Salvador's polarization intensifies and civil war escalates.	Massachusetts Senator Edward Kennedy* defeats President Jimmy Carter* in the New York presidential primary. He receives the majority of Jewish votes.		The U.S. joins all other members of the UN Security Council and votes in favor of Resolution 465, calling on Israel to dismantle existing West Bank settlements and to cease establishing new ones in Arab territories occupied since 1967. It also contains numerous references to Jerusalem as occupied Arab territory. President Jimmy Carter* disavows the U.S. vote for UN Security Council resolution 465. His instructions were that all references to Jerusalem should be deleted before the U.S. voted in favor. American Jewish leaders express dismay over the handling of the issue.	The Jewish Museum in New York exhibits Danzig 1939: Treasures of a Destroyed Community. It describes the Jewish community of Danzig from the 17th century to the Nazi era. It also exhibits Andy Warhol: Ten Portraits of Jews of the 20th Century and Remembrances of the Near East: Photographs by Bonfils, 1867–1907. Felix Bonfils* (d. 1885), a French photographer, made his home in Beirut, where he established a photographic group. The images recorded by Bonfils and his associates reached a worldwide audience.
Apr. 1980	The U.S. breaks diplomatic relations with Iran after Islamic militants continue to hold American embassy employees taken hostage in November 1979. The U.S. military effort to rescue the hostages held by Iran fails. U.S. Secretary of State Cyrus Vance* resigns. He opposed the use of military force to secure the release of U.S. hostages held by Iran. He is replaced by Senator Edmund G. Muskie.*			Five Arab terrorists from Lebanon penetrate the Misgav Am kibbutz, near the Lebanese border, and seize the nursery. Holding the children and some adults hostage, they demand the release of terrorists held by the Israelis. The terrorists are killed and the hostages rescued by a crack Israeli assault unit. Two kibbutz members and one soldier are killed. El Al security personnel find a bomb on a flight from Zurich to Tel Aviv and foil the attempt to blow up the plane.	The Museum of the Diaspora (Beth Hatefutsoth) in Tel Aviv exhibits Libya: An Extinct Jewish Community; Kafka—Prague; Judaism in Medieval Art; and The Closed Curtain: The Moscow Yiddish State Theater, depicting the history of the theater from its creation to 1949. The Tel Aviv Museum exhibits El Lissitzky: Eleven Original Gouaches for the Had Gadya, Kiev, 1919.

A. General History	B. Jews in North and South America	C. Jews in Europe	D. Jews in the Middle East and Elsewhere	E. Jewish Culture	

After 90 years of British rule, Rhodesia becomes the independent nation of Zimbabwe, led by Robert Mugabe.*

Apr. 1980

The Rabbinical Assembly, the organization of U.S. Conservative rabbis, approves the ordination of women rabbis.

Arab terrorists kill 6 Jews and injure 17 at Hebron. Israeli military authorities order the deportation of the mayors of Hebron and the nearby village of Halhoul for incitement to violence. The mayors appeal to Israeli courts, which affirm the order. In December, they will be deported to southern Lebanon.

Israeli Defense Minister Ezer Weizmann resigns from the Begin government. He disagrees with the government over the autonomy talks and settlement policy.

May 1980

The Arab mayors of Nablus and Ramallah are seriously injured by explosives planted in their cars. A third device, planted in the car of the mayor of El Bireh, explodes as it is being dismantled by an Israeli bomb disposal expert, blinding him. Menachem Begin condemns these attacks, which are believed to be perpetrated by Israeli extremists.

The European Economic Community adopts the Venice Declaration which acknowledges the right of existence of Israel and all states in the region, and the right of the Palestinian people to exercise fully its right to self-determination. It does not call for an independent Palestinian state nor recognize the PLO as

June 1980

Soviet Jewish Emmigration, 1968–1991		
Year	_Jews Leaving USSR_	_Jews Arriving in Israel_
1968	231	231
1969	3,033	3,033
1970	999	999
1971	12,897	12,839
1972	31,903	31,652
1973	34,733	33,277
1974	20,767	16,888
1975	13,363	8,435
1976	14,254	7,250
1977	16,833	8,350
1978	28,756	12,090
1979	51,331	17,278
1980	21,648	7,570
1981	9,448	1,762
1982	2,692	731
1983	1,314	861
1984	896	340
1985	1,140	348
1986	904	201
1987	8,060	2,015
1988	18,965	2,329
1989	71,217	12,924
1990	186,815	183,770
1991	179,720	147,495
Total	732,119	512,668

	A. General History	B. Jews in North and South America	C. Jews in Europe	D. Jews in the Middle East and Elsewhere	E. Jewish Culture
June 1980				the sole representative of the Palestinian people. It calls for the end of Israel's territorial occupation, the creation of Israeli settlements and an agreed-upon status for Jerusalem.	
July 1980	President Jimmy Carter's* brother, Billy*, registers as a foreign agent of the Libyan government with the U.S. Justice Department. He acknowledges that he had accepted $220,000 from the radical Arab regime.

Sixty-eight U.S. senators write to President Jimmy Carter* opposing the sale of extra fuel tanks, bomb racks, and missiles to Saudi Arabia for their F-15 jet fighters. They remind the president of his 1978 assurance that the U.S. did not intend to sell the Saudis systems of armaments enhancing their range or ground attack capability. The Saudi request is postponed until after the elections.

The U.S. boycotts the Olympic Games held in Moscow because of the 1979 Soviet invasion of Afghanistan.

The deposed Shah* of Iran dies in exile in Egypt. | | Terrorists attack a group of Jewish children in Antwerp, Belgium, killing 1 and injuring 17 other persons. | Israel receives 4 American F-16 jet fighters. They will receive about 4 per month, a total of 75.

The Israeli Knesset Defense and Foreign Affairs Committee receives an intelligence estimate that the amount of uranium supplied by France to Iraq and other help from France for Iraq's French-made nuclear reactor would enable Iraq to produce atomic bombs by the mid-1980s.

The Israeli Knesset adopts a new basic law, Jerusalem, the Capital of Israel. Few political leaders are prepared to oppose this private bill, even though it will undoubtedly arouse international disapproval. Venezuela and Uruguay immediately announce their intention to move their embassies from Jerusalem to Tel Aviv. | |
| **Aug. 1980** | After two weeks of crippling strikes led by Lech Walesa,* the Polish government agrees to give workers the right to strike and organize independent unions (Solidarity). It is the first time the right to strike is permitted in the Soviet bloc. | | | Israel conducts the largest operation since Operation Litani in 1978: 18 terrorist targets are hit in an area extending about 20 miles into Lebanon from the Israeli border.

The UN Security Council passes a resolution calling on all nations to remove their embassies from Jerusalem. The vote | |

American Immigrants to Israel, 1950–1991

1950–59	3,610
1960–63	2,213
1964	1,006
1965	924
1966	749
1967	665
1968	932
1969	5,738
1970	6,882
1971	7,364
1972	5,515
1973	4,393
1974	3,089
1975	2,803
1976	2,746
1977	2,571
1978	2,291
1979	2,950
1980	2,312
1981	2,384
1982	3,037
1983	3,909
1984	2,866
1985	2,199
1986	2,251
1987	2,141
1988	1,822
1989	1,590
1990	1,715
1991	1,763
Total	84,422

A. General History	B. Jews in North and South America	C. Jews in Europe	D. Jews in the Middle East and Elsewhere	E. Jewish Culture
			is 14–0, with the U.S. abstaining.	**Aug. 1980**
The Iran–Iraq conflict escalates into major warfare. In fierce fighting in the following months, they cripple each other's oil installations and severely damage civilian population centers. The U.S. deploys four AWACS (radar command early-warning surveillance airplanes) with supporting personnel to Saudi Arabia in the wake of the Iran–Iraq war.			Republican presidential candidate Ronald Reagan* emphasizes that "Israel is a major strategic asset to America." He attacks the Carter* administration on its arms sales to Saudi Arabia, voting record at the UN, and position on Jerusalem, and says, "President Carter refuses to brand the PLO as a terrorist organization. I have no hesitation in doing so." President Jimmy Carter* declares that "the United States government and I personally oppose an independent Palestinian state—and unless and until they recognize Israel's right to exist and accept Resolution 242 as a basis for peace, we will neither recognize nor negotiate with the PLO."	**Sep. 1980**
		On Simhat Torah, a bomb explodes in front of the rue Copernic synagogue in Paris. Four passersby are killed and nine worshipers are wounded. More than 200,000 Parisians hold a protest march.	Israeli Energy Minister Yitzhak Moda'i and U.S. Secretary of State Edmund G. Muskie* sign an agreement ensuring that Israel will have sufficient oil supplies until 1994. Israeli President Yitzhak Navon makes a successful visit to Egypt. Navon is the first Israeli head of state to visit an Arab country. His welcome by Anwar al-Sadat* is carried live on Egyptian radio and television.	**Oct. 1980**
Republicans Ronald Reagan* and George Bush* defeat Democrats President Jimmy Carter* and Vice President Walter Mondale* in the U.S. presidential election. The Republicans gain	The Jewish vote in the presidential election is estimated at 45% for Jimmy Carter,* 37% for Ronald Reagan,* and 17% for John Anderson.* For the first time since 1928,			**Nov. 1980**

	A. General History	B. Jews in North and South America	C. Jews in Europe	D. Jews in the Middle East and Elsewhere	E. Jewish Culture
Nov. 1980	control of U.S. Senate for first time since 1956. The ailing Republican U.S. senator from New York, Jacob Javits, is defeated in the Republican primary. *Voyager 1* sends spectacular pictures back to Earth revealing that the planet Saturn has scores of rings, not six.	most Jews do not vote for the Democratic candidate.			
Dec. 1980	Right-wing death squads in El Salvador are blamed for the murder of three Roman Catholic nuns and an American lay worker. The U.S. halts aid and requests the restructuring of the government. José Napoleon Duarte* becomes the new leader.		Soon after the establishment of Solidarity, a group of Polish intellectuals publishes an open letter calling for the reexamination of Polish–Jewish relations of 1968, when Wladislaw Gomulka's* regime carried on an antisemitic campaign.	The Israeli Knesset passes an amendment to the anatomy and pathology law restricting medical discretion to perform autopsies and organ transplants. The bill implements a coalition agreement with Agudat Israel (an Orthodox party) and is passed over the protests of the Israel Medical Association that it would hamper progress of medical science. In 1980, Israel's annual inflation rate is 132.9%.	
Jan. 1981	On his last day in office, President Jimmy Carter* announces an agreement for the release of the hostages held by Iran. After the inauguration of President Ronald Reagan,* 44 hostages are released.				Robert Alter (b. 1935), U.S. literary critic and Hebrew scholar, writes *The Art of Biblical Narrative*, in which he analyzes the literary form and content of the Bible. He will continue these studies in 1985 with the publication of *The Art of Biblical Poetry*.
Feb. 1981			Pope John Paul II appoints the bishop of Orleans, Jean-Marie Lustiger, archbishop of Paris. Lustiger was born in Paris to a family of Polish Jewish immigrants and converted to Christianity during World War II at the age of 14. He identifies himself as a Jew in accordance with the Christian tradition that Christianity is the fulfillment of Judaism.	At a press interview, President Ronald Reagan* responds to a question on the Israeli West Bank settlement activity. "I disagreed when the previous administration referred to them as illegal; they're not illegal." Deputy Prime Minister Yigael Yadin announces his retirement from political life and the dissolution of his political party, the	Blu Greenberg writes *On Women and Judaism*, which becomes a primer for modern American Orthodox women struggling to combine Orthodoxy and feminism. Janet Blatter and Sybil Milton write *Art of the Holocaust*, which describes artists who immortalized themselves by their

A. General History	B. Jews in North and South America	C. Jews in Europe	D. Jews in the Middle East and Elsewhere	E. Jewish Culture	
			Democratic Movement, when the term of the Knesset ends.	paintings and drawings of life in the camps. More than 350 of these works are reproduced.	**Feb. 1981**
President Ronald Reagan* is shot in the chest by John W. Hinckley, Jr.*				Anne Roiphe, U.S. author, writes *Generation Without Memory: A Jewish Journey in Christian America*, in which she reevaluates her own relationship with Judaism.	**Mar. 1981**
The U.S. launches the world's first space shuttle, *Columbia*, from Cape Canaveral, Florida. It completes 36 orbits of the earth during its 54½-hour flight. President Ronald Reagan* lifts the grain embargo imposed on the Soviet Union by President Jimmy Carter* after their invasion of Afghanistan.			Following a Syrian bombardment of Christian strongholds on the Damascus–Beirut road, Israeli Foreign Minister Yitzhak Shamir declares: "Israel cannot sit idly by and watch Syrian troops massacre Lebanese Christians." A week later, Israeli troops attack Syrian-supported terrorist targets in Lebanon. Israel publicly acknowledges it is supplying Lebanese Christians "with means and equipment to protect themselves." Israeli warplanes shoot down two Syrian helicopters involved in a Syrian offensive against the Lebanese Christians. The Syrians deploy Soviet surface-to-air missiles in Lebanon's Bekaa Valley, posing a threat to Israeli aircraft. U.S. special envoy Philip Habib* spends the ensuing months attempting to resolve the crisis. The Reagan* administration decides to sell five airborne warning and control system planes (AWACs) and other military equipment to Saudi Arabia. Israel opposes the sale as a grave threat to its security.	*Spiritual Resistance: Art from Concentration Camps, 1940–1945*, a selection of drawings and paintings from the collection of Kibbutz Lohamei ha-Getta'ot, Israel, is published. The book includes essays by Miriam Novitch, Lucy S. Dawidowicz, and Tom L. Freudenheim. The publication of *Prooftexts: A Journal of Jewish Literary History*, a scholary journal, begins in the U.S. under the editorship of Alan Mintz and David G. Roskies. It will examine literary approaches to classical Jewish sources, the study of modern Hebrew and Yiddish literature, American and European literature, and Jewish writing in other languages. The publication of *Modern Judaism*, a scholarly journal, begins in the U.S., edited by Steven T. Katz. It will be a forum for the discussion of all aspects of Jewish life since the Haskalah, the Jewish enlightenment, in the 18th century.	**Apr. 1981**
Pope John Paul II, riding in an open car in St. Peter's Square, in Vatican City, is shot and seriously			Prime Minister Menachem Begin demands that Syria remove its surface-to-air missiles	Roald Hoffmann, born in Poland and who emigrated to the U.S. in 1949, is awarded the Nobel Prize in chemistry for the application of laws of	**May. 1981**

	A. General History	B. Jews in North and South America	C. Jews in Europe	D. Jews in the Middle East and Elsewhere	E. Jewish Culture
May 1981	wounded by a Turkish terrorist, Mehmet Ali Agca.* The U.S. closes the Libyan embassy in Washington, D.C.			from Syrian territory bordering Lebanon, as well as from Lebanon's Bekaa Valley. He acknowledges that planned Israeli attacks on the missiles had been postponed at the urging of the U.S.	quantum mechanics to chemical reactions. The Jewish Museum in New York exhibits Artists of Israel: 1920–1980; Mordecai and Esther in Persia, including paintings and manuscripts from its collection and the Library of the Jewish Theological Seminary of America; and Paintings by Moritz Oppenheim: Jewish Life in 19th Century Germany. It also enhances its collection of antiquities, particularly in the period of the Second Temple, with the donation of the Betty and Max Ratner collection.
June 1981	The U.S. Center for Disease Control announces an "unusual" occurrence in five homosexual men in Los Angeles of a deadly form of pneumonia. This will later be acknowledged to be the first official notice of acquired immunodeficiency syndrome (AIDS).			Menachem Begin and Anwar al-Sadat* hold a summit meeting at Sharm es-Sheikh. Labour accuses Begin of electioneering. Israeli warplanes completely destroy Iraq's Osirak nuclear reactor near Baghdad. Prime Minister Menachem Begin justifies the preemptive attack because Israel believes that the Iraqis intend to produce atomic weapons and use them against Israel. Neither the U.S. nor Egypt had advance information of the attack, which comes three days after the Begin–Sadat* meeting and several weeks before Israeli elections. The U.S. joins other UN Security Council members in condemning the Israeli raid on the Iraqi nuclear reactor. An Israeli statement asserts it "will continue with all means available to it to protect its people and prevent its enemies from developing weapons of mass destruction." Israel holds national elections for the 10th Knesset, with 1,937,366 votes cast. Likud wins 48 seats; the Alignment, 47 seats; and the National Religious party, 4 seats. The government is installed on August 5, with Menachem Begin as prime minister,	The Judaic Museum of the Jewish Community Center of Greater Washington exhibits The Jews in the Age of Rembrandt. Supported by the Netherlands–American Bicentennial Commission, in 1982, the exhibition will tour the Jewish Museum in New York, the Hebrew Union College Skirball Museum in Los Angeles, and the Maurice Spertus Museum of Judaica in Chicago. Jacobo Timerman, Argentine journalist who founded the newspaper La Opinión in Buenos Aires in 1971, writes Prisoner Without a Name, Cell Without a Number. It describes how, although no charges were ever brought against him, he was imprisoned by the military government in Argentina, was tortured, and eventually was expelled from the country. Elias Canetti (b. 1905), Bulgarian-born novelist, essayist, and dramatist who writes

A. General History	B. Jews in North and South America	C. Jews in Europe	D. Jews in the Middle East and Elsewhere	E. Jewish Culture	
			Ariel Sharon as minister of defense, and Yitzhak Shamir as minister of foreign affairs. The Hebrew University dedicates its restored Mt. Scopus campus, the school's original 1925 site, in Jordanian hands from 1948 until the 1967 Six-Day War.	in German, is awarded the Nobel Prize in literature. A Museum for Jewish Art from Italy opens in Jerusalem. Mainly from the collection of U. S. Nahon, the museum houses almost 1,000 objects, including the original synagogue of Conegliano Veneto, which was built in 1701 and brought to Israel in 1952.	**June 1981**
The U.S. Congress approves President Ronald Reagan's* request for the largest tax and budget cuts in U.S. history.			Between July 10 and 24, violence flares in northern Israel and Lebanon, with Israeli attacks on terrorist targets in Lebanon and the PLO shelling of population centers in northern Israel. Israeli warplanes bomb PLO headquarters in Beirut. Several hundred persons are killed. In reaction, the U.S. postpones delivery of six F-16s to Israel. On July 24, a cease-fire arranged by U.S. special envoy Philip Habib* takes effect. Israel, Egypt, and the U.S. sign an agreement on the nature of the multinational force that is to monitor security arrangements after Israel evacuates the Sinai in April 1982. A dispute erupts over the archaeological activities at a site in Jerusalem's City of David. Orthodox authorities wish to halt the excavation because they believe the site to be an ancient Jewish cemetery. The Israeli Supreme Court will rule that excavation at the site is legal.	Ziva Amishai-Maisels, Israeli scholar of Jewish art, writes *Jacob Steinhardt: Etchings and Lithographs*, which contains a classified catalogue of 246 etchings and lithographs. Steinhardt (1887–1968), painter and printmaker and an early disciple of German expressionism, left Germany for Israel in 1933. T. Carmi (b. 1925), Hebrew poet and historian, edits *The Penguin Book of Hebrew Verse*, in which he traces the development of Hebrew poetry from biblical times to the contemporary period. The Israel Museum in Jerusalem exhibits Hebrew Micrography: One Thousand Years of Art in Script and The Jews of Kurdistan: Daily Life, Customs, Arts and Crafts. The Museum of the Diaspora (Beth Hatefutsoth) in Tel Aviv exhibits La Nación—The Spanish and Portuguese Jews in the Caribbean; Jews from the Konkan: The Bene Israel Communities in India; The Wonderful Island of Djerba: An Ancient Jewish Community on the	**July 1981**
U.S. warplanes shoot down two Libyan warplanes over the Gulf of Sidra, off the coast of Libya.					**Aug. 1981**

	A. General History	B. Jews in North and South America	C. Jews in Europe	D. Jews in the Middle East and Elsewhere	E. Jewish Culture
Aug. 1981	President Ronald Reagan* dismisses striking air traffic controllers, crippling their union and inflicting a major blow on the labor movement.		Arab terrorists attack a Vienna, Austria, synagogue, killing 2 and wounding 19.	Saudi Crown Prince Fahd* announces an eight-point peace plan for the Middle East to replace the Camp David accords. It is rejected by Israel and the PLO. Menachem Begin and Anwar al-Sadat* hold a summit meeting at Alexandria and discuss the resumption of autonomy talks.	Tunisian Coast; and The Jews in France under the Revolution and the Empire.
Sep. 1981	Sandra Day O'Connor* is sworn in as the first woman associate justice of the U.S. Supreme Court. She was nominated by President Ronald Reagan to replace retiring Associate Justice Potter Stewart.* The U.S. Congress raises the debt limit to $1.08 trillion, the first time the ceiling is raised over the $1 trillion mark.			Prime Minister Menachem Begin meets with President Ronald Reagan* in Washington, D.C. An agreement is reached on wide-ranging cooperation on military matters. The U.S. will purchase $200 million of Israeli-produced military equipment. In an apparent misunderstanding, Begin continues to denounce the proposed U.S. sale of arms, including AWACs, to Saudi Arabia.	
Oct. 1981	Egypt's President Anwar al-Sadat* is assassinated during a military parade marking the eighth anniversary of the Yom Kippur War. The assassins are Muslim fundamentalists opposed to Sadat's peace with Israel and his liberal interpretation of Islamic law. He is replaced by Vice President Hosni Mubarak.*			Menachem Begin attends Anwar al-Sadat's* funeral in Cairo and later meets with Egyptian President Hosni Mubarak.* They pledge "to each other peace forever." At a press conference, President Ronald Reagan* declares that he will not permit Saudi Arabia to be another Iran and implies American intervention to forestall any takeover. He also states, "It is not the business of other nations to make American foreign policy" in an apparent reference to Israel's opposition to the proposed Saudi arms sale. Administration lobbyists portray the issue as Menachem Begin versus Reagan.*	

A. General History	B. Jews in North and South America	C. Jews in Europe	D. Jews in the Middle East and Elsewhere	E. Jewish Culture	
			The U.S. Senate approves the Reagan* administration's proposal to sell $8.5 billion worth of military aid to Saudi Arabia. The House had rejected the sale.		**Oct. 1981**
			Israel and the U.S. sign a memorandum of understanding on strategic cooperation to deter Soviet threats in the Middle East. In response to Arab criticism, the U.S. notes that the memorandum is not addressed to any country other than the Soviet Union.		**Nov. 1981**
Javier Pérez de Cuéllar,* Peruvian diplomat, is elected UN secretary-general, succeeding Kurt Waldheim.* After a year of unrest, Poland's leader, General Wojciech Jaruzelski,* declares martial law and outlaws the Solidarity movement.			Israel adopts a law extending "Israeli law, jurisdiction, and administration" to the Golan Heights, which had been captured from Syria in the 1967 Six-Day War. Although reported as an annexation, it is not; the Golan Heights were not declared to be Israeli territory. The U.S. suspends a memorandum of strategic cooperation it signed with Israel on November 30 after Israel adopts the Golan Heights law. In 1981, Israel's annual inflation rate is 101.5%.		**Dec. 1981**
	The National Gallery of Art in Washington, D.C., exhibits Lessing J. Rosenwald: Tribute to a Collector. It is described as the finest collection of prints and drawings ever formed by a single individual in the U.S. Letty Cottin Pogrebin, U.S. feminist leader, writes "Anti-Semitism in the Women's Movement," in *Ms.* magazine. It calls to the attention of feminists the parallels between	The Jewish Museum in Venice, established in 1956, is restored and reopened.		Yosef Hayim Yerushalmi, U.S. historian, writes *Zakhor: Jewish History and Jewish Memory*. He focuses on the relationship between Jewish history and collective memory and the place of the historian within that relationship. The Jewish Museum in New York installs a permanent exhibition, Israel in Antiquity: From David to Herod. It is an archaeological exhibition of Israel's religion, home life,	**1982**

	A. General History	B. Jews in North and South America	C. Jews in Europe	D. Jews in the Middle East and Elsewhere	E. Jewish Culture
1982		antifeminism and antisemitism.			and political environment from 1000 BCE to 70 CE. It
Jan. 1982			A bomb blast at an Israeli-owned West Berlin restaurant injures 25 persons. Arab terrorists claim responsibility.		also exhibits A Tale of Two Cities: Jewish Life in Franfurt and Istanbul, 1750–1870, a comparison between a typical Ashkenazic community and a center of Sephardic Jewry, and Fragments of Greatness Rediscovered: A Loan Exhibition from Poland, reflecting nine centuries of Jewish life in Poland.
Feb., 1982	The northern Syrian city of Hama is sealed off for three weeks while Hafiz al-Assad's* government troops crush the opposition Muslim Brotherhood that had been assassinating Syrian officials and Soviet advisers. When reporters visit the city three months later, they report an estimated 10,000 to 20,000 civilian deaths and widespread destruction. The U.S. surgeon general, C. Everett Koop,* calls smoking the nation's most important health issue and warns of the dangers of "passive smoking"—breathing someone else's tobacco fumes.				Irving Abella and Harold Troper write None Is Too Many: Canada and the Jews of Europe, 1933–1948. They describe Canadian governmental bigotry and indifference toward the Jewish victims of Nazism. They assert that Prime Minister W. Mackenzie King* feared the influx of Jews during the Depression might arouse antisemitism. Aaron Klug, born in Lithuania, raised in South Africa, and affiliated with Great Britain's Cambridge Medical Research Council, is awarded the Nobel Prize in chemistry for developments in electron microscopy and study of acid-protein complexes.
Mar. 1982	Iran launches a spring offensive to retake territory lost to Iraq. Heavy fighting continues throughout the year. The U.S. bans imports of Libyan crude oil, the first of a series of economic sanctions.	The New York Times reports Alonzo Mann* as stating Leo M. Frank did not kill Mary Phagan* in 1913. "She was murdered instead by Jim Conley."* Mann* was a 14-year-old office boy working for Frank at the time he witnessed Conley carrying the limp body of Phagan* to the basement. A witness at the trial, Mann* volunteered no information out of fear of Conley.		Drew Middleton,* veteran military analyst, reports in the New York Times of the PLO military buildup in Lebanon. The PLO is "now able to attack most of the cities and towns in northern Israel at long range." He notes that well-trained volunteers from Iraq, Libya, and South Yemen are reinforcing the Soviet-supplied PLO forces.	Thérèse and Mendel Metzger, French scholars of Jewish art, write Jewish Life in the Middle Ages. Utilizing miniatures in illuminated Hebrew manuscripts, they reconstruct a detailed account of Jewish life in Europe in the Middle Ages. The volume contains about 400 illustrations, including 200 in full color.
Apr. 1982	Argentine troops seize the British-administered Falkland Islands, claiming sovereignty over the islands 240 miles off its coast.			Yaacov Bar-Simantov, second secretary of Israel's embassy in France, is killed by Arab terrorists in Paris. Allan Harry Goodman, a recent American	

A. General History	B. Jews in North and South America	C. Jews in Europe	D. Jews in the Middle East and Elsewhere	E. Jewish Culture	
			immigrant to Israel, kills 2 Arabs and wounds 12 on the Temple Mount. The act is denounced by the Israeli government. He will be sentenced to life plus two 20-year terms for murder and attempted murder. The UN Security Council circulates a resolution, which is vetoed by the U.S., implicitly condemning Israel for the incident. The Israeli air force attacks terrorist bases in southern Lebanon for the first time since July 1981 after an Israeli soldier is killed by a land mine in southern Lebanon. After forcibly evacuating Israeli residents, Israel razes the Sinai settlement of Yamit prior to turning it over to Egypt. Three years after the signing of the Israeli–Egyptian peace treaty, the Sinai is completely turned over to Egypt. One issue remains unresolved—the status of the Taba area, just south of Eilat.	Bezalel Narkiss, Israeli scholar of Jewish art, writes *Hebrew Illuminated Manuscripts in the British Isles: A Catalogue Raisonné*. The Israel Museum in Jerusalem exhibits Jewish Treasures from Paris: From the Collections of the Cluny Museum and the Consistoire and Towers of Spice: The Tower Shape Tradition in Havdalah Spice Boxes. The tower was the most popular shape for spice boxes among the Jewish communities of Europe. Joshua Sobol (b. 1930), Israeli playwright, writes *Soul of a Jew*, based on the life, ideas, and identity crisis of Otto Weininger, a Jewish philosopher who left the faith and was known for his antisemitic ideas. Weininger committed suicide in 1903, when he was 23 years of age.	Apr. 1982
British troops land on the Falkland Islands and engage Argentine troops in battle to regain control.			Israeli warplanes down two Syrian MiGs while on reconnaissance patrol near Beirut.	The Museum of the Diaspora (Beth Hatefutsoth) in Tel Aviv mounts 6 exhibits: Synagogues in 19th Century Germany; A Worthwhile Philanthropic Empire: The Life Work of Baron Maurice de Hirsch; The Jews in	May 1982
King Khalid* of Saudi Arabia dies. He had ruled since 1975 and is succeeded by Crown Prince Fahd.* Argentine troops surrender to the British, and Britain regains control of the Falkland Islands. Britain imposes a news blackout during the Falkland operation. At the same time there is worldwide news			Shlomo Argov, Israel's ambassador to Great Britain, is seriously wounded by Arab terrorists in London. Israeli armed forces bomb and shell Arab terrorist positions from southern Lebanon all the way to Beirut. The PLO retaliates with rocket and artillery shelling of 23 Israeli settlements in western and northern Galilee and of Major	Romania in Modern Times; The Jewish Community of Basel; The Jews of San'a; and The Golden Age of Amsterdam Jewry. Yaffa Eliach, U.S. historian and survivor of the Holocaust, writes *Hasidic Tales of the Holocaust*, a collection of 89 stories based on oral histories and interviews.	June 1982

	A. General History	B. Jews in North and South America	C. Jews in Europe	D. Jews in the Middle East and Elsewhere	E. Jewish Culture
June 1982	coverage of the Israeli incursion into Lebanon. U.S. Secretary of State Alexander Haig* resigns. He is succeeded by George Shultz.*			Saad Haddad's* enclave in Lebanon. Israel launches Operation Peace for Galilee, citing Israel's right of self-defense under Article 51 of the UN Charter. The Israeli armed forces are instructed to push the terrorists back 40 kilometers to place Israeli settlements out of range and not to attack the Syrian army unless it attacks. Prime Minister Menachem Begin declares, "We do not covet even one inch of Lebanese soil." The U.S. vetoes a UN Security Council resolution condemning Israel for its actions in Lebanon. On June 9, the Israeli air force downs 22 Syrian MiG fighters and destroys 19 surface-to-air missile (SAM) batteries in Lebanon without the loss of a single aircraft. On June 10, the Israel air force shoots down 25 more Syrian MiGs and 2 more SAM batteries. By June 12, Israeli forces virtually encircle Beirut, linking up with Christian Phalangist troops, and cut off PLO escape routes by closing off the Beirut–Damascus highway. Over 130 Israeli soldiers are killed and about 600 are wounded. Vast PLO arsenals are overrun and confiscated. Over 9,000 PLO members or supporters are detained. While attending the funeral of King Khalid,* U.S. Vice President George Bush* and Defense Secretary Caspar Weinberger* advise the Saudis that the	

A. General History	B. Jews in North and South America	C. Jews in Europe	D. Jews in the Middle East and Elsewhere	E. Jewish Culture	
			U.S. will not allow the Israelis to enter West Beirut.		**June 1982**
			Prime Minister Menachem Begin holds talks with President Ronald Reagan* in Washington, D.C. President Reagan* tells the press: "It's clear that we and Israel both seek an end to the violence in Lebanon under a strong central government. . . . Israel must not be subjected to violence from the north."		
			Fierce fighting resumes around Beirut. Israeli forces drive Syrian forces from the city. A new cease-fire takes hold on June 26. The siege of Beirut continues, as do negotiations led by U.S. special envoy Philip Habib* for the removal of the PLO from Beirut.		
		Seven persons are injured by a bomb blast at the El Al ticket counter at the Munich airport.	One hundred thousand antiwar demonstrators attend a rally sponsored by Peace Now in Tel Aviv.		**July 1982**
			As sporadic fighting continues in Lebanon, Israeli forces destroy over 70 Syrian tanks in eastern Lebanon.		
Bashir Gemayel,* a Maronite Christian, is elected president of Lebanon by its Parliament.		The Abu Nidal* Palestinian terrorist group opens fire and throws grenades at patrons of Goldenberg's Restaurant in Paris, killing 6 and wounding 22. French President François Mitterand* attends the memorial service for the victims.	President Ronald Reagan* advises that Israel–U.S. relations would be affected if Israel invades West Beirut.		**Aug. 1982**
			Prime Minister Menachem Begin advises Secretary of State George Shultz* that Israel would agree to a multinational force occupying West Beirut after most of the PLO forces depart.		
			Israeli planes bombard West Beirut. President Ronald Reagan* phones		

	A. General History	B. Jews in North and South America	C. Jews in Europe	D. Jews in the Middle East and Elsewhere	E. Jewish Culture
Aug., 1982				Prime Minister Menachem Begin to express his outrage. A cease-fire is implemented and the PLO accepts the evacuation terms. PLO and Syrian forces, under the protection of U.S., French, and Italian troops, begin their departure from Beirut by land and sea. By September 1, about 15,000 PLO terrorists and Syrian forces will have left. Israel lost 345 soldiers, with another 2,130 wounded. Between 450 to 500 Syrian tanks were destroyed; 86 planes were lost; and at least 19 surface-to-air missile batteries were destroyed. The PLO had over 1,000 killed with another 6,000 held prisoner.	
Sep. 1982	Bashir Gemayel,* president-elect of Lebanon, is assassinated in a bomb blast at Christian Phalangist headquarters in East Beirut.		A terrorist submachine gun attack in front of Brussels' main synagogue wounds four persons.	President Ronald Reagan* unveils his Middle East peace plan. He urges self-government by the Palestinians in association with Jordan, calls upon Israel to freeze all settlement activity, and states that Israel cannot be expected to return to the narrow and indefensible pre-1967 borders; Jerusalem must remain undivided, its final status to be negotiated. The plan is rejected by the Begin cabinet and the Arabs. Following the assassination of Bashir Gemayel,* Israeli forces enter West Beirut and surround the three remaining PLO and Muslim strongholds, including the large refugee camps of Sabra and Shatilla. Hundreds of unarmed civilians are massacred by Christian	

A. General History	B. Jews in North and South America	C. Jews in Europe	D. Jews in the Middle East and Elsewhere	E. Jewish Culture
			Phalangist forces in the Sabra and Shatilla refugee camps. Worldwide anger is directed at Israel for permitting the Phalangists to enter. Nine days later, 400,000 Israelis hold the largest public rally ever in Tel Aviv to denounce the government and demand a formal judicial investigation of Sabra and Shatilla. The Israeli government establishes a commission of inquiry headed by the president of the Israeli Supreme Court, Yitzhak Kahan, who appoints Supreme Court Justice Aharon Barak and retired General Yona Efrat as the other members. Israeli forces leave Beirut and are replaced by a multinational force of U.S., French, and Italian troops. Egypt recalls its ambassador from Israel.	**Sep. 1982**
		Terrorists open fire and throw grenades at worshipers leaving the main synagogue in Rome after Simhat Torah services. A two-year-old girl is killed, and 35 are injured.		**Oct. 1982**
Soviet leader Leonid Brezhnev* dies. He is succeeded by Yuri V. Andropov,* the former head of the KGB.			Israeli military head-quarters in Tyre, Leb-anon, is destroyed by an explosion, killing 76 Israeli soldiers and 14 Arabs and wound-ing another 27 Israelis and 28 Arabs. An in-quiry finds the explo-sion was caused by poor construction and a gas leakage.	**Nov. 1982**
Dr. Barney B. Clark* becomes the first recipient of a permanent artificial heart. He will live almost four months after the surgery.			The U.S. Congress approves $2.485 billion in aid for Israel for fiscal year 1983. The total is $300 million more than the year before, and	**Dec. 1982**

	A. General History	B. Jews in North and South America	C. Jews in Europe	D. Jews in the Middle East and Elsewhere	E. Jewish Culture
Dec. 1982	The first Boland amendment, barring the use of federal money for the support of the contras in Nicaragua, becomes effective.			Congress stipulates that $1.535 billion be in the form of a grant.	
1983		At a convention, the Central Conference of American Rabbis (Reform) votes to recognize as Jews—even without conversion—persons with one Jewish parent, father or mother, as long as they publicly identify with the Jewish community. Opponents of the resolution on patrilineal descent argue that it would turn the Reform movement into a sect, with offspring who would not be acceptable as marriage partners for other Jews. President Ronald Reagan* signs into law a congressional bill granting honorary U.S. citizenship to Raoul Wallenberg,* the disappeared Swedish World War II diplomat credited with saving thousands of Hungarian Jews from the Nazi death camps. Previously only Winston Churchill* and the Marquis de Lafayette* had been so honored. Peter Grose* writes *Israel in the Mind of America*. Regarding President Franklin D. Roosevelt's* efforts to save Jewish lives during the World War II Holocaust, he claims "The options open to the United States government were pitifully few. But even the possibilites scarcely came up for discussion. . . . Roosevelt's guilt, the guilt of American Jewish leadership and	Nozyk synagogue in Warsaw, blown up by the Nazis in 1943 and now restored, is reopened. World Jewish and Lutheran leaders meet in Stockholm at a conference celebrating the 500th anniversary of the birth of Martin Luther,* leader of the Protestant Reformation. The Lutherans proclaim: "We cannot accept or condone the violent verbal attacks that the Reformer made against the Jews. Lutherans and Jews interpret the Hebrew Bible differently. But we believe that a Christological reading of the Scriptures does not lead to anti-Judaism, let alone anti-Semitism."	The U.S. Congress earmarks $350 million of its military aid project to Israel for the development of the Lavi jet fighter plane.	The new English translation of the entire Bible, undertaken by the Jewish Publication Society of America, is completed with the publication of *Writings*. A *Writings* committee was formed in 1966, which included Nahum Sarna, Moshe Greenberg, and Jonas C. Greenfield. All are American-trained scholars. Cynthia Ozick, U.S. novelist, short story writer, and essayist, writes *The Cannibal Galaxy*, the story of school principal Joseph Brill, who establishes a primary school with a dual curriculum in which traditional Jewish and modern European cultures are brought together. Brill believes he can decide which students will succeed and which will not. Ozick's main theme is idolatry, and she is deeply concerned by anyone who dares to rival God. David Mamet (b. 1947), U.S. playwright, writes *Glengarry Glen Ross*, a play depicting with bitterness yet compassion the sleazy world of a Chicago real estate office. It wins him a Pulitzer Prize. Neil Simon, U.S. playwright, writes *Brighton Beach Memoirs*, the first of three autobiographical plays. It will be followed by *Biloxi Blues* in 1985 and *Broadway Bound* in

A. General History	B. Jews in North and South America	C. Jews in Europe	D. Jews in the Middle East and Elsewhere	E. Jewish Culture	
	of the dozens and hundreds of others in positions of responsibility, was that most of the time they failed to try."			1987. They are concerned with the maturation of Eugene Morris Jerome (Simon). In *Biloxi Blues*, Jerome confronts antisemitism. The first two will be adapted to the screen, and *Broadway Bound* will be adapted for television.	**1983**
			Israeli Defense Minister Ariel Sharon visits Zaire, the first African nation to resume formal ties with Israel after the Yom Kippur War. He concludes military agreements that would involve Israel in reorganizing the Zaire army.	Roman Vishniac, photographer of eastern and central European Jewry during the 1930s, publishes *A Vanished World*, a collection of his work. Of the 16,000 photographs he took, he rescued only 2,000. Some negatives were sewn into his clothing when he came to the U.S. in 1940, and most were hidden with his father in a village in France during the war. A selection was first published in 1947.	**Jan. 1983**
		Klaus Barbie,* wartime chief of the Gestapo in the Lyon area of France, is extradited from Bolivia to France at the initiative of Nazi hunter Serge Klarsfeld and is charged with crimes against humanity. He is accused of organizing the roundup and deportation of several hundred Jews, including 44 children of Izieu, to Auschwitz, as well as the torture and deportation to death camps of non-Jewish French Resistance members.	The Kahan Commission investigating the Sabra and Shatilla massacres absolves Israeli political and military authorities of any direct responsibility. However, it finds indirect responsibility, through negligence and lack of forethought, to rest with Defense Minister Ariel Sharon, Chief of Staff Raphael Eitan, Chief of Military Intelligence Yehoshua Saguy, and divisional commander Amos Yaron. The cabinet accepts the findings, and Sharon resigns as minister of defense. He is replaced by Moshe Arens. A grenade is hurled at a group of Peace Now activists demonstrating in front of the prime minister's office in Jerusalem, killing Emil Grunzweig, a Peace Now activist and reserve paratroop officer. He is the first Jew to be killed at a political demonstration in Israel's history.	Barbra Streisand, popular singer and actress, directs, produces, and stars in *Yentl*. The movie is based on a short story by Isaac Bashevis Singer. Yentl is a young woman in a Polish shtetl who masquerades as a man so she can study to be a rabbi. The Jewish Museum of New York exhibits The Immigrant Generations: Jewish Artists in Britain, 1900–1945. Artists represented are Jacob Epstein (1899–1959), Alfred Wolmark (1872–1961), David Bomberg (1890–1957), Mark Gertler (1891–1939), Jacob Kramer (1892–1962), Bernard Meninsky (1891–1950), Jankel Adler (1895–1949), Josef Herman (b. 1911), and Jacob Bornfriend (1904–1976). It also	**Feb. 1983**

	A. General History	B. Jews in North and South America	C. Jews in Europe	D. Jews in the Middle East and Elsewhere	E. Jewish Culture
Mar. 1983	President Ronald Reagan* proposes Star Wars, a space-based missile defense system. The digital compact disc player is mass-marketed in U.S. retail stores.			The Knesset elects Chaim Herzog (b. 1918) to be the sixth president of Israel. The son of Rabbi Isaac Herzog, a chief rabbi of Palestine, he served as an Israeli Defense Forces general, as director of military intelligence, as ambassador to the UN, and as a member of the Knesset.	exhibits Kings and Citizens: The History of the Jews in Denmark, 1622–1983. The Jewish Museum of New York permanently installs in its collection the sculpture *The Holocaust* by George Segal (b. 1924), U.S. sculptor. Commissioned by the city of San Francisco as a memorial to the six million victims of the Holocaust, a bronze cast of the sculpture is installed in a park overlooking San Francisco's Golden Gate Bridge. The Israel Museum in Jerusalem exhibits The Illustrated Haggadot of the Eighteenth Century and Bezalel, 1906–1929, depicting the history of the Bezalel Museum, its painters and artists, and its objects.
Apr. 1983	The U.S. embassy in Beirut is destroyed by a car bomb, which kills 63, including 17 Americans.	At a gathering of 10,000 Holocaust survivors in Maryland, President Ronald Reagan* announces the transfer of two large buildings in Washington, D.C., for use as a Holocaust museum.	Jews from around the world participate in ceremonies commemorating the 40th anniversary of the Warsaw ghetto uprising. Marek Edelman, the only surviving leader of the Jewish Fighting Organization in the Warsaw ghetto and a Polish Solidarity leader, does not participate and calls for a boycott of the ceremonies.	Issam Sartawi,* a PLO aide to Yasir Arafat* and a moderate, is assassinated while representing the PLO at a conference of the Socialist International in Portugal. The Syrian-backed PLO faction headed by Abu Nidal* claims responsibility. After months of consultation with Yasir Arafat,* Jordan announces it will not participate in negotiations on the basis of President Ronald Reagan's* September 1982 peace plan. King Hussein* is reported to be annoyed with the PLO's lack of realism. President Ronald Reagan* announces that Secretary of State George Shultz* will visit the Middle East to try to achieve secure borders for Israel and withdrawal of all foreign forces from Lebanon.	
May 1983	The U.S. Supreme Court decides that the Reagan* administration policy of granting tax exemptions to private schools that practice racial discrimination is unconstitutional.			Israel approves the U.S.-sponsored plan for the simultaneous withdrawal of Israeli and Syrian troops from Lebanon. Syria rejects the agreement when Secretary of State George Shultz* meets with President Hafiz al-Assad.* Lebanon and Israel sign an agreement for the Israeli withdrawal from Lebanon. The	

A. General History	B. Jews in North and South America	C. Jews in Europe	D. Jews in the Middle East and Elsewhere	E. Jewish Culture
			agreement is, in effect, a treaty between Israel and Lebanon in which Israel is recognized by Lebanon and that ends the state of war between them. Lebanon, under Syrian pressure, fails to ratify the agreement. Syrian forces begin actively aiding anti-Arafat* forces led by Abu Musa* in the Lebanese battle to control the PLO.	**May 1983**
The Conservatives, led by Margaret Thatcher,* win Great Britain's election.		Twenty-eight Jews are elected to Great Britain's Parliament, including a record 17 from the Conservative party. The Thatcher* government includes Leon Brittan as home secretary, Sir Keith Joseph as secretary of state for education and science, and Nigel Lawson as the first Jew to be appointed chancellor of the exchequer.	The Syrians declare Yasir Arafat* persona non grata and order him out of the country. An antiwar rally sponsored by Peace Now is attended by 150,000 in Tel Aviv. Ariel Sharon files a libel suit in New York against *Time* magazine, which reported that he had met with members of the Gemayel* family after the assassination of Bashir Gemayel* to discuss revenge.	**June 1983**
			Aharon Gross, a yeshiva student, is stabbed to death in the Hebron market. Three weeks later, several gunmen kill 3 Arab students and wound 30 in an attack at Hebron's Islamic College. Prime Minister Menachem Begin deplores this "loathsome crime." The Israeli cabinet approves a plan to withdraw troops from the suburbs of Beirut and the Shouf Mountains and to redeploy them south along the Awali River. Redeployment will begin in early September and allow Israel to reduce its troops in Lebanon. Following the	**July 1983**

	A. General History	B. Jews in North and South America	C. Jews in Europe	D. Jews in the Middle East and Elsewhere	E. Jewish Culture
July 1983				redeployment, rival Lebanese factions resume fighting.	
Aug. 1983	The U.S. Navy launches the USS *Hyman G. Rickover*, a nuclear-powered attack submarine. It is the second time a navy ship is named for a living person.	The U.S. Justice Department releases a report admitting misconduct by American officials in shielding Klaus Barbie,* former Nazi Gestapo leader in Lyon, France, from French prosecutors and facilitating his escape to Bolivia in 1951. Seventeen hundred educators attend the annual meeting of the Conference of Alternatives in Jewish Education, held at Brandeis University, Waltham, Massachusetts.		Liberian President Samuel Doe* visits Israel, the first black African leader to visit Israel in 10 years. Liberia becomes the second African country to resume diplomatic relations with Israel following the Yom Kippur War. Israeli Prime Minister Menachem Begin announces his decision to resign. It is widely believed the resignation is a consequence of the findings of the Kahan Commission. In October, a new caretaker government headed by Likud's Yitzhak Shamir takes office. The U.S. vetoes a UN Security Council draft resolution calling on Israel to dismantle its West Bank settlements. Several days later, Secretary of State George Shultz* says "one could foresee them staying right where they are, but the residents of those settlements would live under the legal jurisdiction of whatever jurisdiction resulted from the negotiations" but reiterates the U.S. position that new settlements are not constructive to peace. At the end of August, President Ronald Reagan* calls the new settlements an "obstacle to peace." El Salvador announces the return of its embassy to Jerusalem. Costa Rica had done so earlier in the year. All foreign embassies had moved from Jerusalem following the passage of the Jerusalem Law in 1980.	

A. General History	B. Jews in North and South America	C. Jews in Europe	D. Jews in the Middle East and Elsewhere	E. Jewish Culture	
A suicide car bomb attack kills 241 U.S. troops and injures 70 at Marine Corps headquarters in Beirut. Another car bomb kills 58 French paratroopers as it crashes into the Beirut building housing them. James G. Watt,* U.S. secretary of the interior, quits amid controversy after his description of a commission becomes public: "I have a black, I have a woman, two Jews and a cripple."	The faculty of the Jewish Theological Seminary of America votes 34 to 8 to admit women into the Conservative movement's rabbinical program of study.	Soviet refusenik Josif Begun is sentenced to seven years' imprisonment and another five years of internal exile for anti-Soviet propaganda. He had been teaching Hebrew.	On October 9, trading on the Tel Aviv stock exchange is suspended. On October 11, the shekel is devalued by 23% and the government announces a 50% increase in the price of subsidized goods. Trading resumes on October 24, and in November the Knesset will pass a series of tax increases. New York Senator Daniel Patrick Moynihan* introduces a bill in the Senate to move the U.S. embassy in Israel to Jerusalem. He stresses that Israel is the only nation whose own choice of its capital the U.S. fails to accept.		Oct. 1983
At a news conference, U.S. Defense Secretary Caspar Weinberger* states that the U.S. has reliable evidence that the car bombing of the Marine Corps headquarters in Beirut was undertaken with "the sponsorship, knowledge and authority of the Syrian government."	Black candidate Harold Washington* is elected mayor of Chicago. Although his opponent is Jewish, Washington receives 43% of the Jewish vote. Jewish voters for Washington outnumbered his other white voters by a substantial margin.		A car bomb explodes at Israel Defense Forces headquarters at Tyre, killing 61, including 29 Israelis, with 40 injured, including 28 Israelis. Israeli warplanes retaliate with bombing raids of terrorist headquarters and objectives, the first such raids in Lebanon since October 1982.		Nov. 1983

D. Jews in the Middle East and Elsewhere

Nov. 1983

Israel and PLO forces under Yasir Arafat's* control exchange 4,500 Arab prisoners for 6 Israelis held by the PLO for more than one year. Israel is compelled to make "painful concessions" for fear of safety of Israeli captives held in Tripoli, where rival PLO factions are engaged in fierce fighting.

The U.S. and Israel announce an agreement on expanded American–Israeli cooperation, including joint military exercises and prepositioning U.S. military equipment in Israel.

Israeli Defense Minister Moshe Arens reports that Syria, with the financial aid of Saudi Arabia, has received during the year Soviet arms enabling it to establish an army of over 400,000.

A. General History	B. Jews in North and South America	C. Jews in Europe	D. Jews in the Middle East and Elsewhere	E. Jewish Culture	
Two U.S. Navy jets are shot down by Syrian missiles during a raid on Syrian anti-aircraft positions in Lebanon. One pilot			A bomb explodes in a crowded Jerusalem bus, killing 5 and wounding 46. The PLO claims responsibility.		Dec. 1983

	A. General History	B. Jews in North and South America	C. Jews in Europe	D. Jews in the Middle East and Elsewhere	E. Jewish Culture
Dec. 1983	is killed and another captured, but he will be freed by the Syrians in a month. The U.S. Navy battleship *New Jersey* and other American ships bombard Syrian positions in the hills east of Beirut after Syrian missiles are fired at American reconnaissance jets. For the second time in 16 months, Yasir Arafat* and his PLO fighters are driven from Lebanon. They are evacuated from Tripoli aboard Greek ships flying the UN flag with French naval protection. His enemy is a rival PLO faction supported by Syria. Israel is dismayed by Arafat's* reception by Egypt's President Hosni Mubarak.* Raúl Alfonsín* assumes the presidency of Argentina. The country returns to democracy after the election of this civilian who replaces the military dictatorship disgraced by the Falklands War. The U.S. decides that General Motors and Japan's carmaker Toyota can jointly build Japanese-designed cars at a California plant.			At the end of 1983, Israel had lost 563 soldiers and 3,200 wounded since the start of Operation Peace for Galilee in June 1982 and still occupied 2,800 square miles of Lebanese territory where more than 500,000 Lebanese live. The 1983 inflation rate in Israel is 190.4%. At the end of the year, the U.S. Congress approves $2.6 billion in military and economic assistance for Israel for fiscal year 1984. It inserts a provision in the State Department authorization act requiring the U.S. to withhold payment or suspend participation in the UN if it expels Israel or denies its right to participate in the General Assembly or any other UN agency.	
1984	The U.S. Supreme Court, by a 5–4 vote, rules that Pawtucket, Rhode Island, may publicly finance a Nativity scene as part of a traditional Christmas display. The crèche, like Santa Claus, Christmas trees, and Christmas carols, has become so accepted as part of traditional Christmas displays that government funding poses no serious threat to the First Amendment.	David S. Wyman,* U.S. historian, writes *The Abandonment of the Jews: America and the Holocaust, 1941–1945*, in which he calls the indifference of President Franklin D. Roosevelt to the plight of Europe's Jews "the worst failure of his Presidency."	Soviet attacks against Israel and Zionism continue. Typical is the publication of a 330,000-copy edition of Boris Kravtsov's *Flight from the Ghetto*, a supposed report of a Soviet Jew who emigrated first to Israel and then to the U.S. before returning to the Soviet Union. The French Ministry of Cultural Affairs declares synagogues in Nancy, Mulhouse,	"Heritage: Civilization of the Jews," a nine-part portrayal of Jewish history, is televised over the U.S. Public Broadcasting System. Narrated by Abba Eban, it is seen by millions. The series describes the writing down of the Bible as a human process, which results in criticism from Orthodox Jewish circles.

A. General History	B. Jews in North and South America	C. Jews in Europe	D. Jews in the Middle East and Elsewhere	E. Jewish Culture	
		Soultz, Colmar, and Guebwiller to be monuments of national historical importance. The designation means they cannot be altered and are eligible for government assistance toward restoration. In *Hitler and the Final Solution*, British historian Gerald Fleming* demonstrates that Adolf Hitler* was determined to exterminate the Jews as early as the 1920s and that there were statements from Heinrich Himmler* and other Nazi officials that Hitler* initiated the "final solution." Fleming is rebutting David Irving's* theory that Hitler* was not involved.		Mesorah Publications, in New York, publishes *The Complete Art Scroll Siddur*. Mesorah is identified with right-wing Orthodoxy. The Rabbinical Council of America, representing modern Orthodoxy, later adopts this *siddur* as its official prayer book, replacing the one edited by Rabbi David de Sola Pool. The council added an introduction and inserted the Prayer for the State of Israel, which was omitted by the non-Zionist editors. Mesorah publications and Bible commentaries have a wide readership. Barry W. Holtz, U.S. scholar, edits *Back to the Sources*, an introduction to the classical Jewish texts written by the younger generation of American Jewish scholars.	**1984**
After a meeting with and personal appeal from the Reverend Jesse Jackson,* a black minister and candidate for the Democratic presidential nomination, Syria's President Hafiz al-Assad* releases U.S. Navy pilot Lieutenant Robert O. Goodman,* who was captured after being shot down over Syria. An Arab League donation of $100,000 to PUSH for Excellence, Inc., a Chicago organization headed by the Reverend Jesse Jackson,* candidate for the Democratic presidential nomination, is disclosed.			Major Saad Haddad,* commander of the Israeli-supported Christian militia in southern Lebanon, dies of cancer. In April, Major General Antoine Lahad* will take over Haddad's command. Israeli police arrest Yona Avrushmi and accuse him of having thrown the grenade that killed Emil Grunzweig at the 1983 Peace Now rally in Jerusalem. West German Chancellor Helmut Kohl* criticizes the Arab refusal to recognize Israel and Israel's West Bank settlements. His country supports Palestinian self-determination and the security of all Middle East nations.	Avram Kampf, U.S. scholar of Jewish art, writes *Jewish Experience in the Art of the Twentieth Century*. Isaac Bashevis Singer, Polish-born author of Yiddish fiction, publishes in English *Love and Exile: A Memoir*. Consisting of three previously published books, *A Little Boy in Search of God*, *A Young Man in Search of Love*, and *Lost in America*, and a new autobiographical introduction, *The Beginning*, it is a memoir of his youth in Poland, his emigration to America, and his many loves in both places.	**Jan. 1984**
Yuri V. Andropov,* Soviet head of state, dies. He is succeeded by 72-year-old Konstantin U. Chernenko.*	The Reverend Jesse Jackson* acknowledges that he referred to Jews as "Hymies" and to New York as		The Reagan* administration provides funds for continued research and development of the Lavi project,	The Jewish Museum of New York exhibits The Jewish Heritage in American Folk Art and a painting by Larry Rivers (b. 1923), U.S. painter,	**Feb. 1984**

	A. General History	B. Jews in North and South America	C. Jews in Europe	D. Jews in the Middle East and Elsewhere	E. Jewish Culture
Feb. 1984	Muslims and leftist militias seize control of West Beirut, driving out Christian forces. Chaos ensues and hundreds are killed as rival militias battle each other.	Hymietown" in a private conversation. "It was not done in a spirit of meanness [but] it was wrong."		which contemplates the Israeli manufacture of an advanced jet fighter aircraft.	*Larry Rivers' History of Matzah: The Story of the Jewish People*. It is a triptych covering 4,000 years of Jewish history, with over 60 scenes and pieces of text, set against the tan background of the matzah.
Mar. 1984	Iran accuses Iraq of using chemical warfare in the Iran–Iraq conflict. Iraq denies the charge, which is later conclusively confirmed.	Arthur Rudolph,* one of a group of over 100 German scientists brought to the U.S. after World War II and director of the *Saturn V* program, leaves the U.S. and returns to West Germany. Although a U.S. citizen, he leaves after the publication of charges that he was involved with brutality toward slave laborers in a Nazi rocket factory.		Lebanon formally abrogates its May 17, 1983, accord with Israel to which the U.S. was a signatory. The U.S. suggests to Israel that the Lebanese government of Amir Gemayel* could not survive unless it succumbed to Syrian pressure to renege on the agreement.	*The Precious Legacy*, an exhibition of Judaic treasures from the Czechoslovak State Collections, tours the U.S. The State Collections are a unique repository of historic and artistic artifacts obtained by the Czech government after World War II from Jewish possessions confiscated by the Nazis.
Apr. 1984	Lebanon's President Amir Gemayel* appoints Rashid Karami,* a Sunni Moslem leader, as premier. Karami* is known as a close supporter of Syria.			Three Arab gunmen open fire on passersby near Jerusalem's main intersection, wounding 48, 1 of whom later dies. Arab terrorists hijack an Israeli passenger bus going from Tel Aviv to Ashkelon. It is overtaken and stormed by Israeli troops and the terrorists are killed. Israeli press reports accuse the troops of killing some of the terrorists after retaking the bus. An investigatory commission confirms that two of the terrorists were killed during the retaking and two afterward by blows to the head, presumably by Israeli security forces. Israeli security forces arrest a number of Jews and accuse them of planting bombs beneath six Arab-owned buses in the Jerusalem area. Twenty-seven Jews are indicted and accused of forming an organization to perpetrate violent acts against Arabs.	Cesar Milstein, a citizen of both Argentina and Great Britain and affiliated with the Cambridge Medical Research Council, is awarded the Nobel Prize in physiology or medicine for discovering a method for producing antibodies of unprecedented purity. The Tel Aviv Museum holds a retrospective exhibition of the works of Nahum Gutman (b. 1898), who is a leading Israeli painter and illustrator. The third volume of Eliyahu Ashtor's (1914–1984) *The Jews in Moslem Spain* is published in English translation. Joshua Sobol, Israeli playwright, writes *Ghetto*, which depicts life in the Vilna ghetto under Nazi occupation through the development of a theater group there. The Museum of the Diaspora (Beth

Population of Israel, 1948–1989

Year	Jews	Non-Jews	Total
1948 (5/15)	650,000	156,000	806,000
1951	1,404,000	173,000	1,577,000
1960	1,911,300	239,100	2,150,400
1970	2,582,000	440,100	3,022,100
1973	2,834,200	497,600	3,331,800
1974	2,890,300	518,700	3,409,000
1976	3,020,400	555,000	3,575,400
1977	3,077,300	575,900	3,653,200
1980	3,282,700	639,000	3,921,700
1984	3,471,700	728,300	4,200,000
1986	3,562,500	770,600	4,333,100
1989	3,717,100	843,900	4,561,000

A. General History	B. Jews in North and South America	C. Jews in Europe	D. Jews in the Middle East and Elsewhere	E. Jewish Culture	
The Soviet Union announces it will not participate in the summer Olympic Games to be held in Los Angeles.	Former SS Colonel Walter Rauff,* who had been living in Chile since 1958, dies. His extradition had been sought by West Germany, France, and Israel for the murder of 97,000 Jews during World War II. He was protected from extradition by the Chilean statute of limitations.		President Ronald Reagan* declares his opposition to Senator Daniel Patrick Moynihan's* bill calling for moving the U.S. embassy in Israel to Jerusalem. "Jerusalem has to be part of the negotiations if we're going to have peace talks." Israel announces the resumption of diplomatic relations with Sri Lanka, which were suspended for 14 years.	Hatefutsoth) in Tel Aviv exhibits The Story of the Jews in Hungary and The Jews of Germany from Roman Times to the Weimar Republic.	**May 1984**
	Louis Farrakhan,* head of a Muslim group and a supporter of the Reverend Jesse Jackson,* describes Judaism as a "gutter religion" and Israel and its supporters as "engaged in a criminal conspiracy." Jackson* calls Farrakhan's* remarks "reprehensible and morally indefensible" but refuses to directly repudiate him.		Yitzhak Rabin, Labour candidate for defense minister in the upcoming national elections, criticizing Likud's Lebanese policy, alleges that Lebanon is under virtual Syrian control and there are about 20,000 terrorists in Lebanon, including Shiite Khomeinists. He calls for a staged Israeli withdrawal, with the UN interim force and Antoine Lahad's* southern Lebanon army taking its place. The Democratic party platform emphasizes the need for Israel to have secure and defensible borders; that the basis for peace is the unequivocal recognition of Israel's right to exist; that there should be a resolution of the Palestinian issue; and that negotiations with the PLO must be preceded by their recognition of Israel, abandonment of terrorism, and adherence to UN Resolutions 242 and 338. Supporters of Reverend Jesse Jackson* prevent the adoption of a resolution condemning antisemitism.		**June 1984**

	A. General History	B. Jews in North and South America	C. Jews in Europe	D. Jews in the Middle East and Elsewhere	E. Jewish Culture
July 1984			While attending a scientific meeting in Leningrad, Ephraim Katzir, former president of Israel and a distinguished scientist, is detained, interrogated, and expelled from the country by the KGB for attempting to meet refusniks.	Israel holds national elections for the 11th Knesset. The Alignment wins 44 seats; Likud, 41 seats; Tehiya–Tzomet, 5 seats; and the National Religious party, 4 seats. A national unity government is installed on September 14, with Shimon Peres as prime minister, Yitzhak Shamir as minister of foreign affairs, and Yitzhak Rabin as minister of defense. It is agreed that at the end of the first half of the 50-month term, Shamir will replace Peres as prime minister. Rabin will be defense minister for the entire period.	
Aug. 1984				The Republican party platform links relations with Israel to countering the Soviet expansion in the Middle East. "Israel's strength, coupled with U.S. assistance, is the main obstacle to Soviet domination of the region. The sovereignty, security, and integrity of the state of Israel is a moral imperative."	
Sep. 1984	Twenty-three are killed as a car bomb blows up in front of the U.S. embassy annex in East Beirut. The Islamic Jihad claims credit in retaliation for the U.S. veto of the September 6 UN Security Council resolution. West German Chancellor Helmut Kohl* asks President Ronald Reagan* to accompany him to a concentration camp and to a German military cemetery during his planned visit to Germany in the spring of 1985. Kohl* is upset at the Allies' refusal to invite			On September 6, the U.S. vetoes a UN Security council resolution calling on Israel to remove restrictions and obstacles imposed on civilians traveling through Israeli-occupied southern Lebanon. The U.S. calls the resolution unbalanced. Jordan resumes diplomatic relations with Egypt. Syria warns that King Hussein* risks assassination for this move and for contemplating peace negotiations with Israel.	

A. General History	B. Jews in North and South America	C. Jews in Europe	D. Jews in the Middle East and Elsewhere	E. Jewish Culture
him to the 40th anniversary celebration of D day in France. Kohl believes that the 1985 V-E Day anniversary ceremonies would demonstrate U.S.–German reconciliation.			In an effort to curb inflation, the new Israeli unity government trims its budget, devalues the shekel, increases the prices of subsidized basic commodities, and imposes a freeze on all goods and services. President Ronald Reagan* asserts his administration strengthened ties with Israel in three ways: (1) upgraded and formalized strategic cooperation, (2) increased economic assistance from 1981 to 1984, including a changeover from loans to grants, and (3) began negotiations for a free trade area between Israel and the U.S. From late 1984 until January 6, 1985, over 7,000 Ethiopian Jews are airlifted to Israel from the Sudan. The Israeli airlift ends suddenly, leaving over 1,000 stranded in refugee camps after a premature press disclosure by Israeli officials.	**Sep. 1984**
U.S. Secretary of State George Shultz* delivers a speech on terrorism and the modern world at a New York synagogue. He praises Israel for raising international awareness of the global scope of the terrorist threat and calls for a U.S. policy of prevention, preemption, and retaliation. Indian Prime Minister Indira Gandhi* is assassinated by two of her Sikh bodyguards. Her son, Rajiv,* succeeds her.				**Oct. 1984**
Republican President Ronald Reagan* wins reelection, trouncing	The Jewish vote in the presidential election is estimated at 65–69% for Walter		At the invitation of King Hussein,* Yasir Arafat's* Palestine National Council	**Nov. 1984**

	A. General History	B. Jews in North and South America	C. Jews in Europe	D. Jews in the Middle East and Elsewhere	E. Jewish Culture
Nov. 1984	Democrat Walter Mondale.* The U.S. and Iraq resume diplomatic relations, which Iraq had broken for alleged American support for Israel during the Six-Day War. The Iraqi foreign minister states that Iraq would no longer oppose the efforts of Israel's Arab neighbors to make peace with her.	Mondale* and 31–35% for Ronald Reagan.* A survey of 2,900 Jewish voters concluded that a fear of growing ties between government and religion and concern for social justice resulted in the heavy Jewish vote for Mondale.* Denominational patterns characterized the vote: Secular Jews voted 83% for Mondale; Reform Jews, 72%; Conservative Jews, 71%; and Orthodox Jews, 49%. Charles Percy,* Republican U.S. senator from Illinois, is defeated for reelection by Paul Simon,* who receives support from groups that consider several of Percy's actions as chairman of the Senate Foreign Relations Committee unfriendly to Israel.		meets in Amman, Jordan. The meeting marks a reconciliation of Hussein* with Arafat.* Hussein* addresses the meeting and calls upon the PLO to abandon an armed struggle against Israel and to join him in seeking a negotiated settlement on the basis of UN Security Council Resolution 242.	
Dec. 1984	Bell Laboratories announces it has perfected a one-megabit chip, which can store an unprecedented amount of information on a tiny piece of silicon. More than 3,000 people in Bhopal, India, are killed by toxic fumes emitted from a Union Carbide insecticide plant. Great Britain and China sign an agreement to transfer the crown colony of Hong Kong to Chinese sovereignty in 1997.			Israeli efforts to curb inflation and restore economic viability begin to bear fruit as December's rise in the consumer price index is only 3.7%. For the year, the inflation rate is 444.9%; the standard of living declines by 7.5%; and unemployment is about 7% at the end of the year.	
1985	In an out-of-court settlement, the Lockheed Corp. agrees to pay a $10,000 fine and forgo exports to Saudi Arabia for one year as a consequence of charges that it violated	The Union of American Hebrew Congregations (Reform) decides to support the establishment of Reform Jewish day schools. This is viewed as a significant	Protests halt the presentation in Frankfurt of Rainer Werner Fassbinder's* play *Garbage, the City and Death.* The play focuses on the character of a real estate speculator	The Israel National Parks Authority opens an archaeological park at Jericho, which is thought to be the oldest continuously inhabited city in the world.	The Rabbinical Assembly, the organization of Conservative rabbis, publishes *Siddur Sim Shalom*, a prayer book for Sabbath, festivals and weekdays. It appears about four

A. General History	B. Jews in North and South America	C. Jews in Europe	D. Jews in the Middle East and Elsewhere	E. Jewish Culture	
antidiscrimination provisions of the Export Administration Act. From 1979 to 1984, penalties imposed on U.S. companies for violating the antiboycott law amounted to $4,088,500.	change by a movement that supports public education and emphasizes universal rather than particular Jewish concerns.	referred to as "the rich Jew" and deals with the destruction of a Frankfurt residential area for a commercial development. The play's antisemitism is denounced, yet its censorship evokes charges of catering to Jewish power. Claude Lanzmann (b. 1925), French filmmaker, produces and directs *Shoah*, a 9½-hour documentary recording the memory of the survivors, the perpetrators, and the bystanders of the Holocaust. *Shoah* contains no photographs or film of the Holocaust. It receives worldwide acclaim.		decades after publication of the Conservative movement's first prayer book. Philip Roth, U.S. author, publishes the trilogy of novels (*The Ghost Writer*, 1979; *Zuckerman Unbound*, 1981; *The Anatomy Lesson*, 1983) depicting the life of Nathan Zuckerman in one volume under the title *Zuckerman Bound*, with an added epilogue, "The Prague Orgy." Charles E. Silberman, U.S. journalist, writes *A Certain People: American Jews and Their Lives Today*, a portrait of the present state of American Jewry, in which he argues that antisemitism is no longer the major factor in American Jewish life that it had been in an earlier generation.	**1985**
	The jury in a trial of a suit brought by Ariel Sharon against *Time* magazine in a New York federal court finds that *Time* did not libel Sharon as it accepted the article in good faith. However, the jury finds the *Time* correspondent acted negligently and carelessly as he provided no substantial evidence supporting his assertions of Sharon's complicity in the massacre of Arabs in the Sabra and Shatilla refugee camps in West Beirut.		Yona Avrushmi, who was convicted of murdering Emil Grunzweig and wounding nine others at a Peace Now demonstration in Jerusalem in February 1983, is sentenced to life imprisonment. Israel begins a three stage phased withdrawal from Lebanon. It decides not to link the withdrawal to a comparable Syrian withdrawal or to a political agreement with the Lebanese government. The first phase will be completed in February when the port city of Sidon reverts to Lebanese authority. The Knesset defeats an effort to have the Law of Return amended, such that conversions to Judaism take place "according to halakhah." Religious parties sought passage of the amendment, which was opposed by spokesmen of the U.S. Conservative and Reform movements.	E.L. Doctorow, U.S. novelist, writes *World's Fair*, describing a Jewish boy's New York childhood in the 1930s. Lis Harris writes *Holy Days: The World of a Hasidic Family*. Harris, a staff writer for *The New Yorker* magazine, was invited into the Lubavitch community of Crown Heights to research this Orthodox group. The book first appeared as a series of articles in the magazine. *Sunday in the Park with George*, a musical drama by Stephen Sondheim, wins the Pulitzer Prize for drama. The Jewish Museum of New York exhibits The Circle of Montparnasse: Jewish Artists in Paris, 1905–1945. It	**Jan. 1985**

	A. General History	B. Jews in North and South America	C. Jews in Europe	D. Jews in the Middle East and Elsewhere	E. Jewish Culture
Feb. 1985	Libyan leader Muammar Qaddafi* addresses a conference of Louis Farrakhan's* Nation of Islam by satellite and urges black soldiers to "leave the American army" and join with other blacks to fight "your racist oppressors" and establish a separate nation. U.S. White House aide Lieutenant Colonel Oliver North* and two associates begin secret purchases of arms for Nicaraguan contras in violation of the Boland amendment of 1982. The money comes from a secret $24 million contribution by King Fahd* of Saudi Arabia.	After an eight-week trial, Ernst Zundel* is convicted in Canada of willfully publishing statements that he knew to be false and that caused injury or mischief to a public interest. Zundel* runs a Toronto publishing house that disseminated material denying the historicity of the Holocaust. Rudolph Vrba, an Auschwitz survivor, and historian Raul Hilberg were prominent prosecution witnesses.		Speaking in New York, Israeli Defense Minister Yitzhak Rabin states that "Syria came out of the war in Lebanon with the upper hand vis-à-vis Israel in terms of deciding the political future of Lebanon. [Syria] won in that respect."	describes the first generation of Jews to become professional visual artists in the West—including Marc Chagall, Moise Kisling, Jacques Lipchitz, Mane-Katz, Amedeo Modigliani, Jules Pascin, Chaim Soutine, and Max Weber. It also exhibits Art and Exile: Felix Nussbaum, 1904–1944, a retrospective of the German painter who died at Auschwitz. The people of his hometown, Osnabruck, located his paintings after World War II and installed them in the city's historical museum.
Mar. 1985	Mikhail Gorbachev* succeeds Konstantin U. Chernenko,* who died, as Soviet Communist party leader. He strikes a theme of glasnost, more openness and frankness, in Soviet society. In a 4–4 vote, the U.S. Supreme Court affirms a lower court ruling that required the Village of Scarsdale, New York, to permit the display of a privately sponsored Nativity scene on public land as a free-speech right.			Twelve Israeli soldiers are killed and 14 wounded by a suicide car-bomber who detonates his vehicle as it passes an open military truck just north of Metullah, in Lebanon. Over 800 Ethiopian Jews are secretly flown to Israel from the Sudan aboard U.S. aircraft. Details of plan were worked out by Vice President George Bush* during a Sudan visit.	Herman Wouk, U.S. author, writes Inside, Outside, a novel whose hero is I. David Goodkind, a Jewish presidential speechwriter and adviser. Goodkind, an Orthodox Jew, is an insider religiously and an outsider in his relations with the workaday world. The B'nai B'rith Klutznick Museum in Washington, D.C., exhibits Hooray for Yiddish Theater in America, which includes over 250 posters, photographs, costumes, and other memorabilia.
Apr. 1985	The White House announces President Ronald Reagan* will visit a West German military cemetery at Bitburg. The subsequent discovery that among the 2,000 soldiers buried there are 47 members of the Waffen SS results in a storm of protest.	At the White House ceremony at which Elie Wiesel is awarded a Congressional Gold Medal of Achievement, Wiesel requests President Ronald Reagan* to cancel his Bitburg cemetery visit. Wiesel tells the president before a live television audience, "That place, Mr. President, is not your place. Your place is with the		Israel completes the second stage of its Lebanon withdrawal, pulling out of a 300-square-kilometer area in and around Nabatiyeh. Israel remains in control of 2,000 square kilometers of Lebanon. The U.S. and Israel sign a free trade agreement, later implemented by congressional	David Bercuson writes Canada and the Birth of Israel, which describes the reluctance of Prime Minister W. Mackenzie King* to support proposals for the establishment of Israel. Lester Pearson,* Canadian diplomat, was the leading supporter of the drive to obtain Canada's vote in favor of the partition.

A. General History	B. Jews in North and South America	C. Jews in Europe	D. Jews in the Middle East and Elsewhere	E. Jewish Culture	
	victims of the S.S." After the ceremony, it is announced that the Bergen-Belsen concentration camp is added to the president's itinerary.		approval, which would gradually eliminate tariffs on exports of the two countries to each other. In a visit to Israel, U.S. Secretary of the Navy John Lehman* announces that the U.S. and Israel would jointly build three submarines for the Israeli navy, that coproduction of a missile would be undertaken, and that the U.S. would lease a second squadron of Kfir fighters from Israel.	Irving Layton, Canadian poet, writes a memoir, *Waiting for the Messiah*, in which he recalls childhood experiences of antisemitism and reacts with anguish to the Holocaust. Considered the most prolific Canadian poet, and a literary figure, he is a professor of English at York University, Toronto. Yeshayahu Nir, Israeli scholar, writes *The Bible and the Image: The History of Photography in the Holy Land, 1839–1899*.	**Apr. 1985**
President Ronald Reagan* visits the Bergen-Belsen concentration camp for over one hour and the Bitburg military cemetery for 10 minutes. At Bergen-Belsen, addressing survivors of the Holocaust, Reagan* says, "Many of you are worried that reconciliation means forgetting. But I promise you, we will never forget." West German President Richard von Weizsacker* addresses Parliament several days after President Ronald Reagan's* visit and while acknowledging that "execution of the [Nazi] crimes lay in the hands of a few and was hidden from the eyes of the public" states that "everyone who opened his ears and wanted to be informed could not fail to observe that the deportation trains were on their way." Children and the unborn are not responsible, but "their forefathers have left a heavy heritage. . . . We are all concerned by its consequences	Amy Eilberg is the first woman to receive ordination from the Jewish Theological Seminary of America. A month later she is admitted to the Conservative movement's rabbinical organization, the Rabbinical Assembly.	The French government bans a television documentary of the story of 21 non-French World War II resistance fighters—mostly eastern European Jews—executed by the Gestapo after betrayal by the Communist party, which objected to "foreigners" receiving credit for exploits against the Nazis. Reports indicate the ban is a result of Communist party pressure. Pope John Paul II visits the Netherlands. He does not meet with Jewish leaders because he refuses to meet their demands that he publicly recognize the State of Israel and admit the role of the Church and the Vatican in the persecution of the Jews, specifically the failure of Pope Pius XII to condemn Nazi persecutions.	Israel releases 1,150 convicted Arab terrorists held in prison in exchange for three Israeli soldiers held in Damascus by the Popular Front for the Liberation of Palestine. This desire to close the final chapter of the stay in Lebanon is severely criticized, as the exchange includes the release of 167 convicted murderers. The Israel National Parks Authority opens the City of David in Jerusalem. This archaeological park contains the remains of a room burned when the First Temple was destroyed by the Babylonians in 586 BCE.	The Israel Museum in Jerusalem opens three new galleries: one containing the permanent display Israel Communities: Tradition and Heritage; a gallery of Asian art; and a gallery of 15th–19th-century old masters. Later in the year, a two-story gallery housing Israeli art is opened. The museum is three times as large as it was when it opened 20 years ago. The Israel Museum in Jerusalem exhibits From Secular to Sacred: Everyday Objects in Jewish Ritual Use. It examines the social and economic conditions that caused the conversion of everyday objects into ritual use. The Tel Aviv Museum holds retrospective exhibitions on the Israeli painter Mordecai Ardon and Jankel Adler (1895–1949), Polish-born painter who lived in Great Britain after World War II.	**May 1985**

	A. General History	B. Jews in North and South America	C. Jews in Europe	D. Jews in the Middle East and Elsewhere	E. Jewish Culture
May 1985	and are held responsible for them." Louis Farrakhan,* leader of the Nation of Islam movement, announces the receipt of a $5 million interest-free loan from Muammar Qaddafi,* Libyan leader, that is to be used by blacks to build economic enterprises in the U.S.				The Jewish National and University Library in Jerusalem exhibits Selected Manuscripts and Prints from the Treasures of the Jewish National and University Library. Jehuda Reinharz, U.S. historian, writes *Chaim Weizmann: The Making of a Zionist Leader*. This volume of a projected complete biography ends when Weizmann, at the age of 40 as World War I begins, enters the center stage of world politics as the major negotiator for the Balfour Declaration.
June 1985	TWA Flight 847 is hijacked by Shi'ite Muslims from Athens to Beirut, with 39 Americans aboard. U.S. serviceman Robert Stethem* is murdered by the hijackers, who demand the release of 766 Lebanese Shi'ites held by Israel as result of attacks on Israeli army units in southern Lebanon. The hostages are released on June 30, and the Israelis later release the detainees.		During a visit to London, Israeli Foreign Minister Yitzhak Shamir reiterates Israeli objections to the continued British embargo on oil and arms shipments to Israel, while weapons are sold to Jordan and Saudi Arabia. The remains of a man who had drowned in 1979, believed to be former SS doctor Josef Mengele,* are exhumed in Embu, Brazil. West German, American, and Brazilian scientists examine the remains and confirm Mengele's* identity.	The judicial commission on inquiry into the 1933 murder of Chaim Arlosoroff, appointed in March 1982 by Prime Minister Menachem Begin, concludes that neither Avraham Stavsky nor Zvi Rosenblatt, both members of the revisionist movement, had any connection with the crime. Israel completes the third stage of its Lebanon withdrawal. What remains is a security zone, 8–15 kilometers wide. Following the deaths in a road accident of 17 schoolchildren and 4 adults from Petah Tikvah, Interior Minister Rabbi Yitzhak Peretz asserts that the deaths were the result of divine retribution for Sabbath violations. The city's laws had been amended to permit film screenings on Friday evening. His comment provokes widespread outrage.	
July 1985	By a 5–4 vote, the U.S. Supreme Court holds unconstitutional the spending of millions of dollars to send public schoolteachers in New York and Michigan into religious schools to teach remedial courses.	The Institute for Historical Review is ordered by the Superior Court of Los Angeles to pay Mel Mermelstein, a Holocaust survivor, the $50,000 reward it offered for "proof" that Jews were gassed by the Nazis in concentration camps. In 1980, Mermelstein		Twenty five members of a Jewish terrorist organization from the West Bank and Golan Heights are convicted of various crimes, including a 1983 attack on Hebron's Islamic college and a conspiracy to blow up the Dome of the Rock shrine on Jerusalem's Temple Mount.	

A. General History	B. Jews in North and South America	C. Jews in Europe	D. Jews in the Middle East and Elsewhere	E. Jewish Culture	
Israeli government officials tell Robert McFarlane* of the U.S. National Security Council that Iran wishes to open a "political discourse" with the U.S. Contacts lead to a shipment of American arms to Iran and the release of an American hostage.	submitted to the institute declarations by Auschwitz survivors who had witnessed friends and relatives taken away and gassed.		An economic recovery plan is introduced in Israel. The inflation rate is reduced to 14% in the final five months of the year from 150% in the first seven months of the year.		**July 1985**
An earthquake in Mexico City, measuring 7.8 on the Richter scale, causes widespread devastation and more than 5,000 deaths.			Three PLO terrorists attack an Israeli yacht anchored in a marina at Larnaca, Cyprus, and murder its three civilian passengers. Before surrendering to Cypriot police, they demand the release of 20 PLO terrorists held in Israeli prisons.		**Sep. 1985**
	Louis Farrakhan,* leader of the Nation of Islam, addresses a crowd of 25,000 at New York's Madison Square Garden and calls Jews "blood suckers whom Jesus condemned in the plainest of language." And charges that the "Jewish lobby has a stranglehold on government."	At a press conference, Soviet leader Mikhail Gorbachev* states, "If there is any country in which Jews enjoy the political and other rights that they do in our country, I would like to hear about it. . . . The Jewish population, which makes up 0.69 percent of the country's total population, is represented in its political and cultural life on the order of at least 10 to 20 percent."	The Israeli air force bombs PLO facilities in Tunisia in retaliation for the Lanarca and other terrorist attacks. Yasir Arafat's* headquarters are destroyed, and 60 are killed. The UN Security Council adopts a resolution, with the U.S. abstaining, denouncing the attack as a violation of international law and an infringement on Tunisian sovereignty. Seven Israelis, including four children, vacationing at Ras Burka, in the Sinai, are shot by an Egyptian security man, and five bleed to death as Egyptian personnel prevent medical assistance from reaching them. The culprit will be sentenced to life imprisonment. PLO terrorists of the Abu Abbas* faction hijack the *Achille Lauro,* an Italian cruise ship bound for Israel from Alexandria, Egypt. They kill Leon Klinghoffer, a 69-year-old disabled American Jewish		**Oct. 1985**

	A. General History	B. Jews in North and South America	C. Jews in Europe	D. Jews in the Middle East and Elsewhere	E. Jewish Culture
Oct. 1985				tourist, and throw his body and wheelchair overboard. Syria refuses to assist the hijackers, who return the ship to Egypt. Egypt allows the four terrorists and Abu Abbas* to leave aboard an Egyptian airliner, which is intercepted over the Mediterranean Sea by U.S. Navy jets and forced to land in Sicily. Italy detains the terrorists but allows Abu Abbas* to flee to Yugoslavia.	
Nov. 1985	Palestinian terrorists of the Abu Nidal* faction hijack an Egyptian airliner bound from Athens to Cairo and divert it to Malta where they begin shooting passengers. The Egyptian rescue effort results in 60 deaths, including two of the three hijackers. Two Israeli women are aboard, and one survives. A summit meeting between Soviet leader Mikhail Gorbachev* and U.S. President Ronald Reagan* takes place in Geneva. They issue a statement supporting a 50% reduction in strategic nuclear arms and outline an agreement on intermediate-range nuclear forces. Two weeks later, an agreement on academic cooperation is signed, which includes projects of cataloging and publishing the collections of Judaic manuscripts in libraries in Moscow and Leningrad. A volcano erupts in Colombia, killing 25,000 people.	Jonathan Jay Pollard, American Jewish U.S. Navy intelligence analyst, is arrested on charges of spying for Israel. His wife, Anne Henderson Pollard, is charged as an accomplice. Pollard supplied secret U.S. data to Israeli officials on Arab armies and on Soviet weapons supplied to Arab states. Israel apologizes, calls the operation "rogue," disbands the unit responsible, and allows U.S. officials to come to Israel to investigate.	After viewing excerpts of Claude Lanzmann's documentary *Shoah*, Jerzy Turowicz,* the editor of a Catholic newspaper published in Cracow, criticizes Lanzmann as having "anti-Polish, anti-Catholic and anti-peasant prejudices" and states that "Polish anti-Semitism, which we do not mean to diminish or justify, had nothing to do with the extermination of the Jews." A Vatican document on Christian–Jewish relations, The Common Bond: Christians and Jews; Notes for Preaching and Teaching, is issued. "Jews and Judaism should not occupy an occasional and marginal place in catechesis; their purpose there is essential and should be organically integrated." For the first time, the Holocaust and the State of Israel are mentioned in an official Vatican document. Catholics are to recognize and teach the spiritual significance to Jews of these events.		
Dec. 1985	Major Muslim and Christian militia leaders sign a		Palestinian terrorists of the Abu Nidal* faction coordinate		

A. General History	B. Jews in North and South America	C. Jews in Europe	D. Jews in the Middle East and Elsewhere	E. Jewish Culture	
Syrian-arranged peace treaty. President Amin Gemayel* of Lebanon undermines the treaty as it involves major political concessions by the Christians. The fighting renews.		attacks near the El Al counters in the Rome and Vienna airports, killing 20, including 5 Americans. Security police kill three of the four terrorists in Rome and one of the three in Vienna.			**Dec. 1985**
	The Rabbinical Assembly, the organization of Conservative rabbis, adopts a resolution opposing patrilineal descent and providing for sanctions against any member rabbi who accepts as Jewish someone neither born of a Jewish mother nor converted according to Jewish law. McGill University establishes the first endowed chair in Jewish studies in Canada. Professor Ruth R. Wisse is appointed to the chair.	Stanley Waterman and Barry Kosmin compile *British Jewry in the Eighties: A Statistical and Geographical Guide*, which reports British Jewry to be a declining population, with more people over the age of 55 and fewer under 45 than the national average. There is a steadily rising Jewish divorce rate, although it is not as high as in the general population. The Netherlands State Institute for Documentation on the Second World War publishes a scientific edition of the *Diaries of Anne Frank*, which refutes neo-Nazi claims that the work was a forgery and contains all the passages omitted in the edition edited by her father, Otto Frank, because he believed them to be too personal. The remains of a synagogue dating from the 4th century CE are uncovered by archaeologists in Bova Marina in southern Italy.	Anton Shammas,* an Israeli Arab, writes *Arabesques*, an autobiographical novel depicting 150 years of history in the author's home village of Fassuta in Upper Galilee. It is the first significant work of Hebrew literature written by a non-Jew.	Elie Wiesel, literary interpreter of the Holocaust, is awarded the Nobel Peace Prize. Deborah Lipstadt, U.S. historian, writes *Beyond Belief: The American Press and the Coming of the Holocaust: 1933–1945*. She demonstrates that the significance and scope of the news events were persistently ignored, as the editors were skeptical of the accuracy of the reports of the "final solution." Walter Laqueur and Gerald Breitman, U.S. historians, write *Breaking the Silence*, in which they reveal the story of Eduard Schulte,* a leading German industrialist who in July 1942 was the first to alert the Allied governments of the Nazi plan to exterminate the Jews. Schulte* passed word of the "final solution" to the American legation in Berne, Switzerland.	**1986**
The space shuttle *Challenger* explodes on lift-off, killing all seven aboard. The U.S. space program is halted.			Israel agrees to submit to arbitration the ownership of Taba. A tiny coastal strip south of Eilat containing a hotel, Taba has been the subject of an Egyptian–Israeli dispute since the signing of the 1979 peace treaty.	Philip Roth, U.S. author, writes *The Counterlife*, an experimental novel in which he attempts to convince the reader not to equate Nathan Zuckerman with Roth. It includes a consideration of Israeli nationalism in the disputed territories. Geoffrey Wigoder writes *The Story of the Synagogue*. He surveys the history of the	**Jan. 1986**
Ten members of the Order, a neo-Nazi group, are convicted	John Demjanjuk,* a retired Cleveland autoworker, is the first	Anatoly Sharansky, leading Soviet refusnik, is released	Israel intercepts a Libyan civilian jet flying from Tripoli to	synagogue from the	**Feb. 1986**

| **Feb. 1986** | by a U.S. court in Seattle of a series of violent acts, including the 1984 machine-gun slaying in Denver of Alan Berg, Jewish radio personality.

Italy and the Vatican sign a concordat abolishing Roman Catholicism as the state religion in Italy. Control of the ancient Jewish catacombs in Rome is relinquished by the Vatican to the government, and Catholic religious instruction in public schools is changed from a compulsory to an elective subject.

At the Communist party congress, Soviet leader Mikhail Gorbachev* calls for radical reform of the Soviet economy.

Jean-Claude Duvalier* flees Haiti into exile, ending his family's 28-year dictatorship.

President Ferdinand Marcos* of the Philippines is forced into exile after losing an election to Corazon C. Aquino.* | alleged Nazi war criminal extradited by the U.S. to Israel. In 1981, he was stripped of his U.S. citizenship for misrepresenting his past when he arrived in the U.S. in 1952. U.S. courts in Cleveland heard testimony that he had been a guard at the Treblinka concentration camp, was known as "Ivan the Terrible," and brutalized camp inmates as they were led to the gas chambers. | from prison and exchanged in Berlin for persons held by the West. He receives a tumultuous welcome on his arrival in Israel. | Damascus, mistakenly believing Palestinian terrorist leaders are aboard. Syria sponsors a UN Security Council resolution condemning Israel, which the U.S. vetoes. The U.S. deplores the Israeli action but says the resolution does not recognize the right of states to intercept aircraft under "exceptional circumstances."

Israel and Spain establish diplomatic relations.

Jordan's King Hussein* announces the termination of year-long discussions with Yasir Arafat* about possible Middle East peace initiatives.

Dov Zakheim, U.S. Defense Department official, estimates that Lavi jet fighter production costs would far exceed Israel's estimates. Israel continues the development of the fighter.

Israel's Knesset defeats an amendment to the Law of Return that specifies that a person is Jewish for the purpose of the Law of Return only if the conversion was performed according to *halakhah*. The change would have rendered invalid conversions done by non-Orthodox rabbis. | classical period to the present and includes photographs and descriptions of the 18 models of the synagogue in the Museum of the Diaspora (Beth Hatefutsoth) in Tel Aviv.

The Book of Abraham, an epic novel by Marek Halter (b. 1932), French novelist and activist, appears in English translation. It is a fictional account of Jewish survival, spanning the history of the Diaspora as experienced by one family. An escapee of the Warsaw ghetto, Halter is active in French Jewish communal affairs and was appointed the first director of the Center of Judaism in Paris by President François Mitterrand.*

The Metropolitan Museum of Art in New York exhibits Treasures from the Holy Land: Ancient Art from the Israel Museum.

The Jewish Museum in New York exhibits Treasures of the Jewish Museum, 90 pieces from its permanent collection, and Moshe Zabari: A Twenty-Five-Year Retrospective.

The announcement is made of the proposed Museum of Jewish Heritage—A Living Memorial to the Holocaust to be built in New York. |
| **Mar. 1986** | Libya fires missiles at U.S. aircraft in the Gulf of Sidra; the U.S. retaliates by firing missiles at Libyan patrol boats and land-based missile sites on the Libyan coast.

The World Jewish Congress releases information linking Kurt Waldheim,* former UN secretary-general and | The U.S. Supreme Court rules that the air force did not have to alter its dress code to allow Captain Simcha Goldman to wear his yarmulke while on duty.

The National Jewish Center for Learning and Leadership, whose president is Rabbi Irving Greenberg, holds a conference on the | | Four Israelis are attacked in Cairo. One, the wife of an Israeli diplomat, is killed.

Nablus Mayor Zafr al-Masri* is assassinated by Palestinian terrorists, who warn against any Arab West Bank cooperation with Israel or Jordan. | A 2,000-year-old boat is uncovered beneath the waters of the Sea of Galilee, the first ancient vessel ever to be retrieved in Israel.

Israel's Antiquities Department announces that the remains of a vessel |

A. General History	B. Jews in North and South America	C. Jews in Europe	D. Jews in the Middle East and Elsewhere	E. Jewish Culture	

current candidate for the presidency of Austria, to Nazi actions against civilians during World War II. Austrian news magazine *Profil* and the *New York Times* report the discovery of documents linking him to Nazi activity in the Balkans in 1942–1943, although his autobiography states he ended his military service in 1941. The accusations are criticized by veteran Nazi hunter Simon Wiesenthal for lack of any real evidence of "crimes" by Waldheim.*

issue Will There Be One Jewish People by the Year 2000?

The Georgia Board of Pardons and Paroles grants a posthumous pardon to Leo M. Frank, who was convicted in 1913 of the murder of Mary Phagan.* The pardon is granted "in recognition of the state's failure to protect the person of Leo Frank and thereby preserve his opportunity for continued legal appeal of his conviction, and in recognition of the state's failure to bring his killer to justice, and as an effort to heal old wounds."

discovered off the Mediterranean coast in 1985 near Kibbutz Ma'agan Michael is probably the first Phoenician ship found anywhere. According to pottery found on the ship, it was dated to the late 5th or early 6th century BCE.

The Israel Museum exhibits two tiny silver amulets on which were etched the oldest biblical text ever found. Dating to the 6th century BCE, the inscriptions contain versions of the threefold priestly benediction found in Numbers 6. It predates the Dead Sea Scrolls by 400 years. The amulets were excavated in Jerusalem's Hinnom Valley in 1979.

A terrorist bomb explodes at a West Berlin discothèque used by American servicemen. Two die and 200 are injured. The U.S. accuses Libya of the attack, and President Ronald Reagan* describes Muammar Qaddafi* as "this mad dog of the Middle East."

U.S. aircraft bomb targets in Tripoli and Benghazi, Libya. A number of civilians are killed. President Ronald Reagan* states the attack was ordered in retaliation for the West Berlin discothèque bombing and to deter future Libyan terrorism.

A nuclear reactor in a Chernobyl plant in the Soviet Ukraine explodes. Radioactive debris spreads throughout parts of the Soviet Union and Scandinavia, causing high levels of radiation. Mikhail Gorbachev* publicly announces the accident and invites visitors to the area. It is the first

Israeli security personnel at London's Heathrow Airport discover a bomb concealed in a bag carried by a pregnant woman boarding an E1 A1 flight to Tel Aviv. British police arrest Nezar Hindawi,* whom they accuse of tricking the woman, his friend, into carrying the bomb.

Pope John Paul II visits the Central Synagogue in Rome. No pope has ever before entered a Jewish house of worship. The ceremony is broadcast live around the world.

Vladimir Horowitz, world-famous pianist, returns to perform in the Soviet Union for the first time since 1925. His concerts are part of a cultural exchange agreement concluded by Ronald Reagan* and Mikhail Gorbachev.* In 1980 Horowitz had said: "I don't like the Russian approach to music, to art, to anything. I lost all my family there. I never want to go back and I never will."

A judicial commission of inquiry into the regulation of bank shares headed by Supreme Court Justice Moshe Beisky calls for the resignation of leaders of Israel's major banks and the governor of the Bank of Israel. In June, a Hebrew University professor of economics, Michael Bruno, will be named governor of the Bank of Israel.

The Israel Museum exhibits 600 items from Moshe Dayan's antiquities collection, which it purchased from his wife for $1 million. The purchase is criticized, as it is alleged that Dayan acquired many of the objects through questionable methods.

The Museum of the Diaspora (Beth Hatefutsoth) in Tel Aviv exhibits From Carthage to Jerusalem: The Jewish Community in Tunis; Kovno Ghetto—Images from a Hidden Camera; Passage Through China: The Jewish Communities of Harbin, Tientsin, and Shanghai; and In the Footsteps of Columbus: Jews in America, 1654–1880.

The Israel Defense Forces produces *Ricochets*, a feature-length film describing an infantry unit in combat in Lebanon, which

	A. General History	B. Jews in North and South America	C. Jews in Europe	D. Jews in the Middle East and Elsewhere	E. Jewish Culture
Apr. 1986	acknowledgment of an error by the Soviet Union in almost 70 years.				becomes a box office success.
May 1986	Robert McFarlane,* U.S. national security adviser; Lieutenant Colonel Oliver North*; and others fly to Iran, carrying spare parts for Iran's Hawk anti-aircraft missiles. They spend four days meeting with Iranian officials, unsuccessfully trying to win the release of all U.S. hostages.		British Prime Minister Margaret Thatcher* visits Israel. Hers is the first visit to Israel of an incumbent British prime minister.		
June 1986	Kurt Waldheim,* former secretary-general of the UN, is elected president of Austria.	Jonathan Jay Pollard pleads guilty in a U.S. district court in Washington, D.C., to participating in an Israeli-directed espionage conspiracy against the U.S. After the Reform representative to the Jewish Welfare Board Commission on Jewish Chaplaincy certifies a female rabbi, the Orthodox objection to this action results in each movement's rabbinic organization certifying its own candidates.	Ernst Nolte,* leading German historian of the revisionist school, suggests that Auschwitz resulted from the Nazi fear of the Soviets and accuses critics of Nazism of ignoring the fact that the Nazis had done what others had previously done "with the sole exception of the gassing procedures."		
July 1986			A doctoral degree awarded by the University of Nantes to Henri Roques* is rescinded. His dissertation, which analyzed the writings of Kurt Gerstein,* former Nazi SS officer, concluded that Gerstein's* main evidence of the operation of gas chambers in the concentration camps was worthless. In the summer, Italy brings to trial the hijackers of the *Achille Lauro*. The confessed murderer of Leon Klinghoffer is sentenced to 30 years in prison, instead of life, as requested by the prosecution. The judge and jury	Israel unveils a prototype of the Lavi jet fighter. U.S. officials urge Israel to abandon the project as it is too costly and, instead, purchase an updated F-16 fighter, which will use technology developed for the Lavi. Israeli Prime Minister Shimon Peres visits Morocco and confers with King Hassan.* The meeting has symbolic value, with Morocco being the second major Arab country to confer with Israel. Radical Arab states condemn the meeting, and Syria severs diplomatic relations with Morocco.	

A. General History	B. Jews in North and South America	C. Jews in Europe	D. Jews in the Middle East and Elsewhere	E. Jewish Culture	
		accepted his claim of "extenuating circumstances" as he "had grown up in tragic conditions." The Italian Supreme Court repeals the 1930 law that requires Jews to affiliate with the organized Jewish community and pay a tax for support of communal institutions.			July 1986

D. Jews in the Middle East and Elsewhere

The U.S. and Israel sign an agreement for the construction of a $250 million Voice of America relay station in the Negev that would make it more difficult for the Soviets to jam broadcasts. The station will take five years to build.

Israeli and Soviet officials hold a brief meeting at Helsinki, their first official contact since the Soviet Union severed relations in 1967.

Israel's cabinet approves the construction of a Mormon center for Near Eastern studies in Jerusalem in the face of Orthodox opposition. One hundred fifty-four members of the U.S. Congress urged support for the construction of the center.

A. General History	B. Jews in North and South America	C. Jews in Europe	D. Jews in the Middle East and Elsewhere	E. Jewish Culture	
The U.S. Senate confirms President Ronald Reagan's* nominations of William Rehnquist* to be chief justice and Antonin Scalia* to be associate justice of the Supreme Court. The U.S. Congress enacts legislation overhauling the income tax system, changing brackets and eliminating deductions.		Jagellonian University in Cracow, Poland, holds a conference on Polish Jewish history, with the participation of Israeli scholars. The university announces the formation of an institute for the study of the history and culture of Polish Jews.	Palestinian terrorists massacre 22 worshipers in an attack on the Neve Shalom synagogue in Istanbul. A survey of Arab public opinion in Israel records that over 90% believe the PLO is the sole and legitimate representative of the Palestinian people and that 78% prefer the establishment of a democratic Palestinian state. An Israeli report records 60,000 Jews living on the West Bank. Over 66% reside in suburbs of Tel Aviv and Jerusalem, including 12,000 in Ma'ale Adumim, a Jerusalem suburb, on the road to Jericho. John Demjanjuk* is indicted in a		Sep. 1986

A. General History	B. Jews in North and South America	C. Jews in Europe	D. Jews in the Middle East and Elsewhere	E. Jewish Culture
Sep. 1986			Jerusalem district court of crimes under the Nazi and Nazi Collaborators Punishment Law of 1950. He says: "I was never in a place you call Treblinka and I never served the Nazis. I myself was a prisoner of war." His trial is scheduled for 1987.	
Oct. 1986	President Ronald Reagan* and Soviet leader Mikhail Gorbachev* hold a summit meeting in Reykjavik, Iceland. Reagan* advises before the meeting that human rights issues would receive equal priority with arms control matters. They shock the world by agreeing to eliminate almost all ballistic missiles from their inventories.	Nezar Hindawi* is convicted of having plotted to place a bomb on an El Al aircraft at London's Heathrow Airport in April. Britain severs diplomatic relations with Syria, stating that it has "conclusive evidence" that Syria trained Hindawi,* supplied the bomb, and directed the plot. The U.S. and Canada recall their ambassadors to Syria.	The London *Sunday Times* publishes a story, "Inside Dimona, Israel's Nuclear Bomb Factory," which asserts that the Dimona facility produced an arsenal of 100–200 nuclear weapons. The newspaper lists Mordecai Vanunu as the source. He is a former technician at Dimona who was dismissed in 1985.

Terrorists attack new Israel Defense Forces recruits and their families with grenades outside the Dung Gate in Jerusalem's Old City. One person is killed and 70 are wounded.

Israel's Supreme Court orders the creation of the Ethiopian Heritage Institute in the religious affairs ministry as part of an arrangement by which Ethiopians would not have to undergo a ritual immersion before being permitted to marry.

Yitzhak Shamir replaces Shimon Peres as Israel's prime minister. | |
| **Nov. 1986** | Iranian sources are quoted in a Lebanese magazine, claiming that Robert McFarlane,* former U.S. national security adviser, offered to send arms to Iran in exchange for the | After the November elections, the U.S. Senate includes eight Jews: Republicans Rudy Boschwitz (Minn.), Chic Hecht (Nev.), Warren Rudman (N.H.), Edward Zorinsky | | Israel announces that Mordecai Vanunu, dismissed Dimona nuclear facility technician, is under detention.

Israel signs an agreement with the | |

				Nov. 1986
release of hostages held in Lebanon. U.S. news reports confirm the story and that the U.S. had encouraged third parties, including Israel, to make similar shipments. President Ronald Reagan* announces that between $10 million and $30 million in profits from the sale of U.S. arms to Iran had been secretly diverted to assist contra rebels fighting the Nicaraguan government. He accepts the resignation of national security adviser John Poindexter* and his assistant, Lieutenant Colonel Oliver North.* Ivan Boesky, stock trader, pleads guilty in New York to illegally using corporate "insider" information to make huge profits. Boesky, a well-known Jewish community leader and philanthropist, agrees to pay $100 million in penalties and is banned from stock trading.	(Neb.), and Arlen Specter (Penn.), and Democrats Carl Levin (Mich.), Howard Metzenbaum (Ohio), and Frank Lautenberg (N.J.), Israel confirms that it helped transfer arms from the U.S. to Iran upon the request of the U.S. but denies that it had served as a channel for the transfer of funds to the contras.		U.S. to participate in the Strategic Defense Initiative, joining Great Britain and West Germany in the Star Wars program. Israel will undertake research in tactical ballistic missile systems. A yeshiva student is stabbed to death by terrorists in Jerusalem's Old City. Retaliation by local Israelis forces Arab families living near the yeshiva to flee their homes.	

				Dec. 1986
President Ronald Reagan* asks for the appointment of an independent counsel to investigate the Iran–contra arms deal. Lawrence Walsh* is selected by a three-judge panel as the independent counsel. Soviet leader Mikhail Gorbachev* advises leading dissident physicist Andrei Sakharov* and his wife, Yelena Bonner, that they are free to leave internal exile at Gorky.			The Israel Supreme Court rules against Interior Minister Rabbi Yitzhak Peretz in the matter of Shoshana Miller, a Reform convert to Judaism whose request for citizenship under the Law of Return was granted. Miller had objected to Peretz's requirement that the word *convert* be printed on her identity card. The court rules that traditional Jewish law forbade shaming a convert. A prototype of the Lavi jet fighter makes its maiden flight.	

	A. General History	B. Jews in North and South America	C. Jews in Europe	D. Jews in the Middle East and Elsewhere	E. Jewish Culture
1987		The Rabbinical Assembly, the organization of Conservative rabbis, reaffirms its commitment to matrilineal descent as the sole determinant (aside from conversion) of halakhic Jewish identity. Conservative Judaism continues to differ with the position of Reform Judaism on this issue. The Jewish Theological Seminary of America (Conservative) announces that it will grant cantorial diplomas to women. The North American Jewish Data Bank, directed by Barry Kosmin, estimates American Jews to be divided as follows: 2% Reconstructionist, 9% Orthodox, 29% Reform, 34% Conservative, and 26% "other" or "just Jewish."	French film director Louis Malle*—a Catholic—produces *Au Revoir les Enfants*, a movie about his memory of a rural priest who, during World War II, is deported by the Germans to a concentration camp for hiding Jewish boys in his school. The movie wins the French equivalent of an Oscar. *Commissar*, a film made in the Soviet Union in 1967 under the direction of Alexander Askoldov,* is shown in the West. The film, set in 1922, implies a link between Soviet antisemitism and Nazism and was suppressed for 20 years. It will be shown in the Soviet Union in 1988. Paul Johnson,* British journalist and historian, writes *A History of the Jews*, in which he describes the Jewish development of ethical monotheism and the role the Jews played in the creation of the modern world, the origin of secular ideas, the evolution of capitalism, and the development of 19th- and 20th-century culture.	The Israel Museum opens its renovated and expanded Judaica wing. It exhibits Joseph Stieglitz's important collection of Jewish ritual objects.	Joseph Brodsky (b. 1940), Russian poet living in exile in the U.S. since 1972, is awarded the Nobel Prize in literature. He does not generally write of Jewish subjects, but his long poem "Isaac and Abraham" deals with the Akedah, and "The Jewish Cemetery near Leningrad" is considered an outstanding example of Soviet Jewish poetry. Cynthia Ozick, U.S. novelist, short story writer, and essayist, writes *The Messiah of Stockholm*, a novel dedicated to Philip Roth, who introduced her to the writings of Bruno Schulz, a Polish Jew who was killed by the Nazis in 1942. Lars Andemening is a Stockholm book reviewer who obsessively believes he is the son of Bruno Schulz. The Jewish Museum in New York exhibits The Dreyfus Affair: Art, Truth & Justice, a compilation of paintings, sculpture, and graphic art relating to the Dreyfus Affair, curated by Norman Kleeblatt.
Jan. 1987				U.S. Defense Department official Dov Zakheim visits Israel to advise that the Lavi fighter plane project is too costly for Israel's defense economy and not a military necessity.	Michael Marrus, University of Toronto history professor, writes *The Holocaust in History*, a study of the historiography of the Holocaust. He includes a discussion of the argument between *intentionalists*, who assert that from the early 1920s Adolf Hitler* was intent on exterminating the Jews, and *functionalists*, who maintain there was no preestablished plan of extermination, but the "final solution"
Feb. 1987	The Tower Commission, established by President Ronald Reagan* to investigate the Iran–contra affair, issues its report, declaring that the U.S. government is		Great Britain's United Synagogue sells its oldest synagogue, the New Synagogue in Stamford (North London), to the Bobover Hassidim, who will use the premises for	Israel is officially designated by the U.S. as a major non-NATO ally. This is an acknowledgment of Israel's strategic value to the U.S.	

A. General History	B. Jews in North and South America	C. Jews in Europe	D. Jews in the Middle East and Elsewhere	E. Jewish Culture	
responsible for its own decisions and must bear responsibility for the consequences, even if the government of Israel actively worked to begin the initiative. Syrian troops deploy in West Beirut, ending three years of anarchy during which dozens of foreigners were kidnapped, mainly by pro-Iranian Shiites.		educational purposes. The membership of the synagogue fell below 270 from a peak of 2,000 in the 1950s. The Union of Italian Jewish Communities and the Italian government sign an agreement that the community will no longer be a public body that is controlled by the state. However, contributions to the community can be deducted from taxes, up to a maximum of 10% of personal income, and Jews can observe the Sabbath and holidays wherever employed and obtain kosher food in public institutions. European Jewish leaders and Catholic officials from Poland, France, and Belgium sign an agreement requiring that the Carmelite convent near the Auschwitz–Birkenau extermination camps be closed and that the nuns living in the convent be relocated to an interreligious center about a mile from the camps.		emerged out of a series of increasingly harsh steps against the Jews, ending in a policy of mass murder. The Pushkin Fine Arts Museum in Moscow exhibits 90 paintings and 200 graphic works by Marc Chagall to celebrate the centenary of the birth of the Russian-born artist. The Israel Museum in Jerusalem exhibits Tradition and Revolution: The Jewish Renaissance in Russian Avant-Garde Art, 1912–1928. The exhibition features El Lissitzky (1890–1941), Nathan Altman (1889–1970), Issachar Ryback (1897–1935), Joseph Tchaikov (1888–1986), Boris Aronson (1898–1980), and Marc Chagall (1897–1985) and their efforts to create a new, modern Jewish art by fusing the folk sources of the Jews with the modern artistic motifs of the day. The exhibition will be shown at the Jewish Museum in New York in 1988.	**Feb. 1987**
The Mormons' Jerusalem Center, on Mt. Scopus, opens.	Jonathan Jay Pollard is sentenced to life imprisonment and his wife, Anne Henderson Pollard, to two concurrent five-year terms by U.S. District Judge Aubrey Robinson* for spying against the U.S. on behalf of Israel.		Colonel Aviem Sella, the Israeli air force officer who was the first "handler" of convicted spy Jonathan Jay Pollard, is assigned to command Israel's largest air base. The U.S. protests, and Sella resigns. Natan (Anatoly) Sharansky, leading Soviet refusnik who arrived in Israel in 1986, speaks out against the bungling absorption bureaucracy and the failure to make new immigrants feel at home in Israel.	The Museum of the Diaspora (Beth Hatefutsoth) in Tel Aviv exhibits Jews on the Banks of the Amazon. Benny Morris, Israeli historian, writes *The Birth of the Palestinian Refugee Problem, 1947–1949*, in which he concludes that the refugee problem was a by-product of Arab and Jewish fears resulting from the bitter fighting of the War of Independence. Shabtai Teveth, Israeli historian, writes *Ben-Gurion: The Burning Ground, 1886–1948*, a	**Mar. 1987**

	A. General History	B. Jews in North and South America	C. Jews in Europe	D. Jews in the Middle East and Elsewhere	E. Jewish Culture
Apr. 1987	U.S. government places Kurt Waldheim,* newly elected president of Austria, on the "watch list" of persons barred from entering the U.S. The decision is based on a finding that he "assisted or otherwise participated in the persecution of persons because of race, religion, national origin or political opinion." He is the first head of state to be barred.	Karl Linnas,* commandant of a concentration camp in Tartu, Estonia, during World War II, is deported by the U.S. to the Soviet Union. In 1962, he was sentenced to death in absentia by the Soviet Union. In 1981, he was stripped of his U.S. citizenship. He is the first ex-Nazi forcibly deported to the Soviet Union by the U.S. In July, he will die of natural causes in Leningrad.		President Chaim Herzog becomes the first Israeli head of state to visit West Germany. Shimon Peres becomes the first Israeli foreign minister to visit Spain. While Syrian President Hafiz al-Asad* visits Moscow, Soviet leader Mikhail Gorbachev* publicly states that the Soviets "unambiguously recognize . . . Israel's right to peace and a secure existence. At the same time, the Soviet Union continues to categorically oppose Tel Aviv's policy of force and annexation."	biography ending in the year David Ben-Gurion became Israel's first prime minister.
May 1987		A U.S. district judge decides that the Satmar Hasidic community of Kiryas Joel, in New York's Rockland County, could not insist that publicly provided school buses for their schools be driven only by men. The U.S. Supreme Court rules that the Civil Rights Act of 1966, outlawing racial discrimination, also permits private lawsuits against discrimination based on ancestry or ethnic identity. A synagogue in Silver Spring, Maryland, had sued to recover damages from eight men accused of defacing the edifice with antisemitic slogans and swastikas in 1982.	Sister Teresia Benedicta is beatified by Pope John Paul II. Born Edith Stein, she converted in 1922 and became a Carmelite nun. She was murdered by the Nazis in 1942. This first case of a Jewish-born Catholic being beatified results in criticism from some Jews who assert she was murdered because she was Jewish and, therefore, was not a martyr for the Catholic faith. The new Jewish Historical Museum in Amsterdam opens. The museum operates under government auspices and is housed in a converted complex of four former Ashkenazic synagogues erected in 1671, 1686, 1700, and 1752 that were badly damaged in World War II. They were sold to the city of Amsterdam, which donated 80% of the $11 million cost of renovation.		

A. General History	B. Jews in North and South America	C. Jews in Europe	D. Jews in the Middle East and Elsewhere	E. Jewish Culture	
Pope John Paul II receives Austrian President Kurt Waldheim* on an official state visit despite worldwide protests. He praises Waldheim* for his activities to promote peace and does not mention the controversy surrounding his activities during the Second World War. The Supreme Soviet enacts a law proposed by Mikhail Gorbachev* embodying his policy of *perestroika* (economic restructuring), which requires competition among state-owned enterprises, less central control over planning and pricing, and more responsibility for local organizations.	The U.S. Presbyterian church promulgates A Theological Understanding of the Relationship Between Christians and Jews. It confirms the authenticity of Judaism and calls for an end to the teaching of contempt for Jews, but says "the State of Israel is a geopolitical entity and is not to be validated theologically."	England's Conservative Margaret Thatcher* wins an unprecedented third term as prime minister. The number of Jews elected to Parliament falls to 23 (16 Conservative and 7 Labour) from 28 (17 Conservative and 11 Labour). An analysis of Jewish voting patterns reveals a gradual movement to the political right. Labour had become more hostile to Israel.	The U.S. and Israel sign a more detailed agreement than the August 1986 accord for the construction of a Voice of America radio transmitter in the Negev. The agreement provides that the U.S. would lease the land from Israel for 25 years. The Jewish Agency Assembly meeting in Jerusalem adopts reforms demanded by American Jews, including removal of partisan considerations from the agency, equal partnership between the Zionist movement and Diaspora philanthropists, accountability of board officers, reiteration of a 1986 decision forbidding agency funding for non-Zionist (i.e., ultra-Orthodox) religious schools, and the cutting off of allocations to any Israeli body that refuses to accept Ethiopian immigrants as Jews.		June 1987
Millions of Americans watch the testimony of Lieutenant Colonel Oliver North* during the congressional hearings on the Iran–contra affair.	The United Church of Christ adopts a resolution declaring that "Judaism has not been superseded by Christianity," that "God has not rejected the Jewish people," and asking for forgiveness for the Christian church's violence to Jews resulting from the denial of "God's continuing covenantal relationship with the Jewish people."	Klaus Barbie,* "the butcher of Lyons," is found guilty by a French court in Lyons of the 17 crimes against humanity he was accused of and sentenced to life imprisonment. Barbie* was defended by Jacques Verges,* who argued that crimes against humanity were not limited only to Nazi Germany, accusing France of such crimes in Algeria, and Israel against Arabs.			July 1987
			The Israeli cabinet votes to end the Lavi fighter plane project.		Aug. 1987
		Pope John Paul II meets with American Jewish leaders in Miami. Earlier he met in Rome with another delegation and	Israel releases an abridged version of the indictment of Mordecai Vanunu, former technician at the Dimona Nuclear		Sep. 1987

	A. General History	B. Jews in North and South America	C. Jews in Europe	D. Jews in the Middle East and Elsewhere	E. Jewish Culture
Sep. 1987			discussed the Waldheim* visit, the Holocaust, antisemitism, and the Vatican's relations with Israel. Jean-Marie Le Pen,* leader of France's right-wing National Front party, declares that the issue of Nazi gas chambers was one "discussed by historians" and "a question of detail in the history of World War II." The French National Assembly, in protest, will open its fall session with a minute of silence in memory of victims of Nazism.	Research Center. He has been on trial in secret for passing top secret information about the facility to the London *Sunday Times*.	
Oct. 1987	The U.S. Senate rejects President Ronald Reagan's* nomination of Robert H. Bork* to a seat on the U.S. Supreme Court. The second nominee, Douglas Ginsburg, withdraws after acknowledging that he had smoked marijuana. The third nominee, Anthony M. Kennedy,* is confirmed. The New York stock market crashes, plunging the Dow Jones industrial averages 22.6%, the largest one-day decline since 1914.			Ida Nudel, leading Soviet refusnik, arrives in Israel. She had been refused an exit visa for 17 years, including 4 in exile in Siberia.	
Nov. 1987	The congressional committee investigating the Iran–contra affair issues a majority report finding that Lieutenant Colonel Oliver North,* not the Israelis, conceived of the scheme to divert arms money obtained from selling weapons to Iran to the Nicaraguan contras. On the 70th anniversary of the Russian Revolution, Soviet leader Mikhail Gorbachev* criticizes Soviet dictator Joseph			A lone Palestinian gunman flies a hang glider from Syrian-occupied Lebanon into Israel, near Kiryat Shemonah where he kills six soldiers and wounds seven before he is killed.	

A. General History	B. Jews in North and South America	C. Jews in Europe	D. Jews in the Middle East and Elsewhere	E. Jewish Culture	
Stalin,* asserting that "the guilt of Stalin is enormous and unforgivable." Censorship of books, films, and speech is loosened.					**Nov. 1987**
U.S. President Ronald Reagan* and Soviet Secretary Mikhail Gorbachev* sign a treaty in which they agree to dismantle all Soviet and U.S. medium- and shorter-range missiles and to establish an extensive weapons investigation system, including placing technicians in each other's countries. It is the first treaty requiring the reduction of nuclear arsenals.	Two hundred thousand demonstrators from throughout the U.S. assemble in Washington, D.C., on the day before the summit meeting of Soviet leader Mikhail Gorbachev* and President Ronald Reagan* to call attention to the Soviet Union's human rights and emigration policies.		An accident between an Israeli truck and Palestinian cars kills four Palestinians in the Gaza strip. Rioting ensues, and the Palestinian uprising called the *intifada* begins. The World Zionist Congress, meeting in Jerusalem, elects Simcha Dinitz chairman of the Jewish Agency Executive. Two Zionist movements that stress religious pluralism, Arza (Reform) and Mercaz (Conservative) win a total of 53 seats. The Religious Zionist movement, which supports the religious status quo in Israel, is accorded 14.		**Dec. 1987**
	Rabbi Norman Lamm, president of Yeshiva University, discusses centrist orthodoxy in an address that highlights three areas in which centrists differ from right-wing orthodoxy: (1) openness to secular culture, (2) support of Zionism, and (3) respect and tolerance for divergent opinions. His assertion that non-Orthodox forms of Judaism are "valid groupings" if "sincere in their commitments" is criticized by the Orthodox right wing. The Rabbinical Assembly issues Emet VeEmunah, the first official statement of principles of Conservative Judaism. It advocates increased attention to ritual practice in the home and halakhic flexibility to permit Judaism to adapt to social change.	A new Jewish Museum in Frankfurt is officially opened by West German Chancellor Helmut Kohl.*	The remains of a 5,000-year-old temple near the town of Beit Shemesh, southwest of Jerusalem, are discovered by a team of Israeli and French archaeologists in an excavation funded by the National Geographic Society.	Under the auspices of the YIVO Institute for Jewish Research, Zvi Gitelman writes *A Century of Ambivalence: The Jews of Russia and the Soviet Union 1881 to the Present*, containing over 380 photographs and accompanying text. The photographs are exhibited at the Jewish Museum in New York. Arno Mayer, U.S. historian, writes *Why Did the Heavens Not Darken?: The Final Solution in History*. He maintains that the decision to exterminate the Jews resulted from military frustration, first perceived in December 1941, over the failure of the campaign against the Soviet Union. The German generals played as important a role as Adolf Hitler,* Heinrich Himmler,*	**1988**

	A. General History	B. Jews in North and South America	C. Jews in Europe	D. Jews in the Middle East and Elsewhere	E. Jewish Culture
Jan. 1988	A parliamentary All-Party War Crimes Group reports that 3,000 Nazis entered Great Britain after World War II. In February the House of Commons will establish an independent War Crimes Inquiry to investigate accusations against former Nazis living in Britain.			The *intifada* uprising continues. Israel deports 9 Palestinians, the first of 32 deported during the year. Many Palestinians are jailed. The Israeli army begins a series of curfews. Rather than shooting stone throwers on sight, the army sets a policy of beating demonstrators to discourage further disorder.	and the SS in the "final solution." The New York Public Library exhibits A Sign and a Witness: 2000 Years of Hebrew Books and Illuminated Manuscripts. The three-month exhibition is attended by 150,000, the largest attendance for any exhibition ever held at the library.
Feb. 1988	The U.S. Congress enacts the Proxmire Act, a bill to implement the UN Convention Against Genocide. Its passage ends a 20-year effort to make genocide a crime in the U.S. An international panel of historians assembled by the Austrian government to investigate the World War II activities of Austrian President Kurt Waldheim* reports that no proof was found that he committed war crimes. They criticize him, however, for failing to protest or intervene in atrocities he knew were happening. Soviet leader Mikhail Gorbachev* announces that he will withdraw all Soviet troops from Afghanistan by early 1989.	Jacob Tannenbaum, a concentration camp survivor, loses his U.S. citizenship after confessing that he was a *kapo* who brutalized Jewish prisoners at the Goerlitz concentration camp. Tannenbaum, 76 years old, whose family was killed during the Holocaust, is not deported.	The Soviet newspapers *Pravda* and *Izvestia* condemn Pamyat, a Russian nationalist organization, for its antisemitism.	Israeli President Chaim Herzog is reelected by the Knesset to a second five-year term.	Rabbi Irving Greenberg, U.S. scholar and leader of the Center for Jewish Learning and Leadership, writes *The Jewish Way*. His description of the cycle of Jewish holidays includes an analysis of the effect of the Holocaust on the Jewish religious experience. Ida Huberman, Israeli art historian, writes *Living Symbols: Symbols in Jewish Art and Tradition*. The Jewish Museum in New York exhibits Golem: Danger, Deliverance and Art, a comprehensive gathering of visual material relating to the golem tale. Franz Kafka's (1883–1924) handwritten manuscript of his novel *The Trial* is sold at auction for $1.98 million to a West German book dealer, the highest price ever paid for a modern manuscript. The purchaser described the novel as "perhaps the most important work in 20th century German literature, and Germany had to have it." Philip Roth later wrote to the *New York Times* of the sale's Kafkaesque irony: If Kafka had lived, he probably would have been
Mar. 1988	The Reverend Jesse Jackson* wins the Michigan Democratic caucuses. His is the first victory by an African-American presidential candidate in a large state, and it establishes him as a serious contender for the Democratic presidential nomination. White House officials Oliver North* and			Mordecai Vanunu, a former employee at the Dimona Nuclear Research Center who was indicted for passing secret information about the center to the *London Sunday Times*, is convicted after a trial held in camera and sentenced to 18 years' imprisonment. Leaders of the *intifada* call for a reprisal	

A. General History	B. Jews in North and South America	C. Jews in Europe	D. Jews in the Middle East and Elsewhere	E. Jewish Culture	
John Poindexter* and others involved in the Iran–contra affair are indicted on charges of conspiring to defraud the government.			against Palestinian collaborators with Israel.	gassed at Auschwitz with his three sisters, and the manuscript would have been destroyed by the Nazis if not taken to Palestine by Max	**Mar. 1988**
		Several months after the death of Werner Nachmann, chairman of the Central Council of Jews in Germany since 1969, it is revealed that he had embezzled $15 million from accounts intended for victims of the Holocaust.

Three thousand Jews, including government representatives from Israel, commemorate the 45th anniversary of the Warsaw ghetto revolt at ceremonies in Warsaw. Marek Edelman, the only survivor of the ghetto revolt still living in Poland, organizes an alternative ceremony, to protest the current repressive government. | Khalil al-Wazir* (Abu Jihad) is assassinated in Tunis by unknown assailants. He was Yasir Arafat's deputy in charge of the PLO's military arm and chairman of its Committee on the Occupied Territories. Thirteen Palestinians are killed in widespread rioting throughout the occupied territories in Israel following news of his death.

An Israeli court finds John Demjanjuk* guilty of killing thousands of Jews during World War II at the Treblinka death camp. The 68-year-old retired autoworker from Cleveland, Ohio, denied he was the Ukrainian-born "Ivan the Terrible." In June, he will appeal the verdict to the Israeli Supreme Court.

At a meeting in Moscow with PLO leader Yasir Arafat,* Soviet leader Mikhail Gorbachev* supports the Palestinians' right to "self-determination," but urges Arafat* to recognize the State of Israel and consider its security interests as a necessary element for the establishment of peace.

The U.S. and Israel sign a five-year memorandum of understanding formalizing cooperation in military, economic, political, and intelligence matters. | Brod while escaping from the Nazis.

The East German government and the Jewish community of East Berlin mounts a comprehensive exhibit on Jews in Berlin, And Teach Them Not to Forget.

A small ivory pomegranate, 1.68 inches high, believed to be the first relic attributed to the First Temple era nearly 3,000 years ago, is anonymously donated to the Israel Museum. It bears an inscription in ancient Hebrew, "Belonging to the Temple of the Lord, holy to the priests."

The Museum of the Diaspora (Beth Hatefutsoth) in Tel Aviv exhibits Remnants: The Last Jews of Poland, 1980–1985.

Natan Sharansky, prominent Russian dissident, writes Fear No Evil, in which he describes his trial and imprisonment that resulted from his efforts to emigrate to Israel from the Soviet Union.

Ruth R. Wisse, Canadian scholar, writes A Little Love in Big Manhattan: Two Yiddish Poets, a dual biography of Mani Leib and Moshe Leib Halpern (1886–1932), who were part of the group of young American Jewish writers and poets known as Di Yunge. | **Apr. 1988** |
| A new U.S. immigration law becomes effective. More than 1.4 million illegal aliens seek | | During his first trip to the Soviet Union, U.S. President Ronald Reagan* meets with | The Supreme Court of Israel rules that Leah Shakdiel, an Orthodox woman who was elected to the | Michael A. Meyer, U.S. scholar, writes Response to Modernity: | **May 1988** |

	A. General History	B. Jews in North and South America	C. Jews in Europe	D. Jews in the Middle East and Elsewhere	E. Jewish Culture
May 1988	amnesty under the law. Their action can lead to legal status and eventual citizenship.		dissidents and refusniks.	Religious Council in the Negev town of Yeroḥam, could not be denied service solely because of her sex. Orthodox circles had objected to her service. She becomes the first woman to participate in a Religious Council as a full member.	*A History of the Reform Movement in Judaism.* Hugh Nissenson, U.S. novelist and essayist, publishes *The Elephant and My Jewish Problem: Selected Stories and Journals, 1957–1987,* which includes his journals on the trial of Adolf Eichmann* in 1961 and the trial of Klaus Barbie* in 1987.
June 1988	Soviet leader Mikhail Gorbachev* calls for sweeping governmental changes, including a limit of two five-year terms for a new and enhanced Soviet presidency, multicandidate elections, and diminished party authority over economic matters.		Pope John Paul II meets Austrian president Kurt Waldheim* in Vienna. Jewish leaders protest.	The U.S. and Israel sign an agreement for the joint development of the Arrow antiballistic missile. The U.S. will contribute 80% toward the $130 million expected cost. The Knesset defeats an amendment to the Law of Return proposed by Orthodox factions that would consider as Jews only those converts who entered into Judaism according to Orthodox practice. American Jewish communal leaders strongly urged the amendment's defeat.	
July 1988	An Iranian airliner is destroyed in the Persian Gulf by a missile fired from a U.S. Navy cruiser. Navy officials say they mistook the airliner for an Iranian jet fighter. More than 290 people are killed. Iran and Iraq agree to a cease-fire in their eight-year-old war.			King Hussein* renounces Jordan's legal and administrative ties to the West Bank, thereby surrendering his claims to the Israeli-occupied territory to the PLO.	
Sep. 1988	The six-year term of Lebanon President Amin Gemayel* ends. Parliament is unable to agree on a successor. Gemayel* appoints army commander General Michel Aoun* interim prime minister. Muslims reject the appointment. The U.S. announces its belief that Libya is able to produce chemical weapons and			Israel announces it launched an experimental satellite, *Ofek-1,* which orbits the earth once every 90 minutes. An international arbitration panel awards the disputed Sinai territory of Taba to Egypt. This is the last item to be resolved in the implementation of the 1979 peace treaty with Egypt.	

A. General History	B. Jews in North and South America	C. Jews in Europe	D. Jews in the Middle East and Elsewhere	E. Jewish Culture
is on the verge of full-scale manufacturing.				**Sep. 1988**
Republican Vice President George Bush* defeats Democratic Massachusetts Governor Michael Dukakis* in the U.S. presidental election. Benazir Bhutto* becomes president of Pakistan, succeeding her adversary, Mohammad Zia.* Zia* and the U.S. ambassador were killed three months earlier in a suspicious plane crash. Bhutto* is the first Muslim woman to become a head of state.	The Jewish vote in the presidential election is estimated at about 65–72% for Dukakis and 28–35% for Bush. An all-time high of 31 Jews are elected to the U.S. House of Representatives. The Senate continues to have eight Jewish senators.		Israel holds national elections for the 12th Knesset. Likud wins 40 seats; the Alignment, 39 seats; Sephardi Torah Guardians (Shas), 6 seats; and Agudat Israel, 5 seats. Altogether, religious lists win 18 seats. The national unity government is installed on December 22, with Yitzhak Shamir as prime minister, Shimon Peres as vice premier and finance minister, Moshe Arens as minister of foreign affairs, and Yitzhak Rabin as defense minister. At a meeting in Algiers, the Palestine National Council proclaims the independent "State of Palestine." It does not define its boundaries.	**Nov. 1988**
An earthquake, measuring 6.9 on the Richter scale, devastates Soviet Armenia, killing over 25,000 people. Pan Am Flight 103 explodes over Lockerbie, Scotland, killing over 270 people. Investigators suspect terrorists from the Middle East placed a bomb on the plane. Soviet leader Mikhail Gorbachev* announces his intent to cut Soviet troops by 500,000.	As a result of the liberalization of the Soviet policy toward the emigration of Jews, U.S. immigration officials announce they will no longer automatically grant Soviet Jews refugee status. The requirement of "well founded fear of persecution" to be considered a refugee would have to be proven. Israel welcomes the move as it assures more immigration to Israel and lessens the "dropout" problem when Soviet Jews reach Austria.		On December 7, in Stockholm, Sweden, PLO Chairman Yasir Arafat* meets with five U.S. Jews from the International Center for Peace in the Middle East. After the meeting, Swedish Foreign Minister Sten Andersson* reads a document, ratified by Arafat,* declaring that the PLO has accepted Israel's right to exist, will participate in an international peace conference on the basis of UN Resolutions 242 and 338, and rejects terrorism "in all its forms."	**Dec. 1988**

D. Jews in the Middle East and Elsewhere

On December 14, at a press conference, PLO Chairman Yasir Arafat* recognizes Israel's right to exist and states that "we totally and absolutely renounce all forms of terrorism, including individual, group and state terrorism." U.S. President Ronald Reagan* authorizes the State Department to enter into a substantive dialogue with the PLO.

Dec. 1988

Dec. 1988

U.S. President Ronald Reagan* sends a message to Israeli Prime Minister Yitzhak Shamir explaining the U.S. decision to open a dialogue with the PLO. "Nothing in this decision should be construed as weakening the United States' commitment to Israel's security."

According to Israeli sources, 293 Palestinians were killed by Israeli forces in the first year of the *intifada*. Sixteen Israeli Jews died as a result of *intifada* violence. About 20 Palestinians were killed by Palestinians for "collaborating" with Israel.

At years' end, the Jewish population in the West Bank and Gaza strip is estimated at 71,000. The Arab population is about 1,500,000.

	A. **General History**	B. **Jews in North and South America**	C. **Jews in Europe**	D. **Jews in the Middle East and Elsewhere**	E. **Jewish Culture**
Jan. 1989	The U.S. accuses West German companies of assisting Libya in constructing a chemical weapons plant at Rabta. Libya claims the plant manufactures pharmaceuticals. West Germany at first denies but later acknowledges involvement of West German companies. U.S. naval aircraft shoot down two Libyan fighters over the Mediterranean Sea. The U.S. says the fighters approached U.S. forces in a "hostile manner." In Paris, 145 nations attend a conference on chemical weapons. The conference issues a statement reaffirming the 1925 pact banning the use of chemical weapons and endorses the role of the UN secretary-general in investigating their use. The conference convenes at a U.S. initiative to express concern over the use of chemical weapons by Iraq in the war with Iran. Saudi Arabia, Algeria, Bahrain, Iraq, United Arab Emirates, Jordan, Qatar, and China have upgraded their PLO missions to embassy status in recognition of the PLO's November	Former U.S. officials including Undersecretary of State George Ball,* file a complaint with the Federal Election Commission, charging the American–Israel Public Affairs Committee and 53 political action committees of violating federal election laws. The complaint charges the groups with illegal collusion in working to elect or defeat political candidates based on their positions toward Israel. The Union of American Hebrew Congregations (Reform) issues a guide for couples contemplating divorce, "When There Is No Alternative."	The Dutch Parliament pardons two Nazi war criminals who were responsible for the deportation of over 100,000 Dutch Jews and who have been imprisoned since 1949. Ferdinand aus der Funten,* 79, was SS commander of security police, based in Amsterdam, and Franz Fischer,* 87, held a similar post in the Hague.	Israel adopts an austerity program to revive a troubled economy. The plan includes budget reductions of $550 million and government subsidy cuts on food and gasoline of $220 million. The shekel is devalued by 8%. The plan is proposed by Finance Minister Shimon Peres. Israel deports 13 Palestinians accused of aiding in the organization of the *intifada*. In a radio broadcast, PLO Chairman Yasir Arafat* warns that "whoever thinks of stopping the *intifada* before it achieves its goals, I will give him 10 bullets in the chest." The threat is reportedly aimed at Mayor Elias Freij* of Bethlehem. PLO Chairman Yasir Arafat* holds his first official talks with the European Community. The committee of the foreign ministers of Spain, France, and Greece does not recommend recognition of the state proclaimed by the PLO. Israel releases Faisal al-Husseini,* most prominent West Bank PLO leader. He has spent 18 of the last 21	Nahum Sarna, U.S. biblical scholar, writes the commentary to Genesis, the first volume in the Jewish Publication Society of America Torah Commentary Series. In 1990 Jacob Milgrom will write the commentary to Numbers, Baruch A. Levine, to Leviticus; and in 1991, Nahum Sarna, to Exodus. The series will be completed by Jeffrey H. Tigay's commentary on Deuteronomy. Two of U.S. novelist Cynthia Ozick's short stories that were published in the *New Yorker* magazine, "The Shawl" (1980) and "Rosa" (1983), appear in a book entitled *The Shawl*. It centers on the prewar, Holocaust, and postwar experiences of Rosa Lublin, the death of her baby daughter Magda in a concentration camp, and her niece Stella who survives and comes to America with Rosa. Stephen Sondheim, U.S. composer and lyricist, has three hits on Broadway: first, a revival of *Sweeney Todd*, produced in 1979; second, a revival of *Gypsy*, a 1959 musical with lyrics by Sondheim and music by Jule Styne; third, Jerome

A. General History	B. Jews in North and South America	C. Jews in Europe	D. Jews in the Middle East and Elsewhere	E. Jewish Culture	
declaration of an independent state.

An article in the Soviet weekly *Literaturnya Gazeta* confirms that Joseph Stalin* personally ordered the 1940 assassination of Leon Trotsky in Mexico City.

The U.S. Supreme Court strikes down a 1983 Richmond, Virginia, plan requiring that the city award minority contractors 30% of the amount of every construction contract. It rules that racial quotas must always be avoided in awarding such contracts and affirmative action used only in specific, well-documented cases of discrimination. | | | months in administrative detention on charges of fomenting unrest.

While testifying before the Senate, U.S. Secretary of State designate James A. Baker* refers to the U.S. dialogue with the PLO and states: "the existence of the dialogue should not lead anyone to misunderstand our overall policy or to question our enduring support for the State of Israel. Nor have we altered our belief that an independent Palestinian state will not be a source of stability or contribute to a just and enduring peace." | Robbins's *Broadway*, which contains scenes from two shows in which Sondheim was the lyricist, *West Side Story* and *Gypsy*, and one, *A Funny Thing Happened on the Way to the Forum* (1962), for which Sondheim did both music and lyrics.

American Jewish theater is booming with five plays on the New York stage in March. They are *Cafe Crown*, a recollection of Second Avenue's Cafe Royale; *Songs of Paradise*, a Yiddish revue that interprets events in the Book of Genesis; *Chuchem*, a tale drawn from the history of the Jews in Kaifeng; *Cantorial*, a comedy about a couple moving into a chic apartment that was a Lower East | **Jan. 1989** |
| General Alfredo Stroessner,* dictator of Paraguay since 1954, is ousted and sent into exile.

The last Soviet troops leave Afghanistan.

Iran's Ayatollah Khomeini* denounces the novel *Satanic Verses* as blasphemy and demands the execution of its author, Salman Rushdie.*

Algerian voters overwhelmingly approve a new constitution. It paves the way for a multiparty system for the first time since Algeria achieved independence from France in 1962.

Algerian voters overwhelmingly approve a new constitution. It paves the way for a multi-party system for the first time since Algeria achieved independence from France in 1962. | Jewish students and faculty at the University of Michigan picket the offices of the student newspaper, *The Michigan Daily*, to protest editorials that suggested that Israeli security officials might be behind the destruction of Pan Am Flight 103 and that the rescue of Ethiopian Jews was designed to displace Palestinians. The editorial page editor describes herself as Jewish and states that none of the editorials are antisemitic.

President George Bush* appoints Morris Abram, former chairman of the Conference of Presidents of Major Jewish Organizations, as the U.S. ambassador to the European headquarters of the UN in Geneva. | The first officially sanctioned Jewish cultural center is opened in Moscow. It is named after Solomon Mikhoels, Yiddish actor, cultural leader, and chairman of the Jewish Anti-Facist Committee who was killed in 1948 during a Stalinist purge.

The Vatican issues a document entitled The Church and Racism, which contains the Vatican's first statement on anti-Zionism. It calls antisemitism "the most tragic form that racist ideology has assumed in our century." After distinguishing anti-Zionism, which "questions the State of Israel and its policies," from antisemitism, it comments that anti-Zionism "serves at times as a screen for anti-Semitism, feeding on it and leading to it." | A U.S. State Department 1988 report on human rights conditions in 169 countries accuses Israel of a "substantial increase in human rights violations" in the West Bank and Gaza. It states that Israel's army was "untrained and inexperienced in riot control." The report notes the ability to assemble information about conditions in Israel because it is an open society with a free press.

Israeli forces kill five PLO terrorists in southern Lebanon and thwart an attempt to infiltrate Israel. The PLO admits responsibility. Israel requests the U.S. to break off dialogue with the PLO. Secretary of State James A. Baker decides to continue.

Israeli Foreign Minister Moshe Arens meets Soviet Foreign Minister Eduard | Side synagogue; and *The Education of Hyman Kaplan*, a musical based on Leo Rosten's hilarious stories.

Dr. Harold Varmus, U.S. virologist, wins the Nobel Prize in medicine, shared with his colleague Dr. J. Michael Bishop,* for their cancer research.

Hotel Terminus: The Life and Times of Klaus Barbie, a documentary film produced and directed by French filmmaker Marcel Ophuls wins an Academy Award.

The Jewish Museum in New York exhibits Gardens and Ghettos: The Art of Jewish Life in Italy. It traces the evolution of Jewish life in Italy from Roman times to the modern era.

Amos Oz, Israeli novelist, writes *To Know a Woman*, a story about Yoel Ravid, a retired Israeli | **Feb. 1989** |

	A. General History	B. Jews in North and South America	C. Jews in Europe	D. Jews in the Middle East and Elsewhere	E. Jewish Culture
Feb. 1989			A yeshiva for the training of rabbis, scholars, and teachers opens in Moscow. This first yeshiva in the Soviet Union is a joint project of the New York-based Aleph Society and the Soviet Academy of Sciences. There will be 80 students. Three rabbis from Israel and two from the U.S. will comprise the initial faculty.	Shevardnadze* in Cairo. Arens advises that Israel will not negotiate with the PLO. Shevardnadze* later states that the Soviet Union may resume ties with Israel if Israel takes part in an international peace conference that includes the PLO. Israel and Egypt sign agreements returning the Taba strip to Egypt, settling a seven-year-old border dispute. The Soviet freighter *Vita Novitsky* docks at Ashdod to load 80 tons of food and clothing donated by Israeli citizens for victims of the November earthquake in Soviet Armenia. It is the first Soviet vessel in 22 years to call at an Israeli port. Likud candidates for mayor in municipal elections win seven cities that Labour had controlled. They include Tiberias, Beersheba, Petah Tikva, Ashdod, Ramat Gan, and Holon. Jerusalem's Mayor Teddy Kollek wins reelection but loses his majority on the city council.	spy, and his efforts to escape his past. A literary metaphor for Israel's permanent state of siege, the novel sells 45,000 copies within two weeks of its publication, a record for book sales in Israel. *The Summer of Aviya*, an Israeli film, wins the Silver Bear Award, the second highest, at the Berlin International Film Festival. It is the first Israeli film to take an award at the festival. It is the story of a 10-year-old, Aviya, and her mother, Henya, a Holocaust survivor. Israeli archaeologists who searched caves near the Dead Sea announce the discovery of a 2,000-year-old jug containing three cubic inches of once-fragrant oil, believed to be of the kind used to anoint the kings of Judah. The jug was found in the summer of 1988, but the announcement was delayed until early 1989, until tests verified that the oil was truly ancient.
Mar. 1989	The *New York Times* reports that U.S. and Swiss officials believe Egypt has acquired the main elements of a plant designed to produce poison gas from a Swiss company. Egypt denies the charge. A federal jury in Washington, D.C., convicts Fawaz Yunis* of the 1985 hijacking of a Royal Jordanian airliner in Beirut. The verdict is the first application of a 1984 U.S. law asserting U.S. jurisdiction over the taking of	The Rabbinical Assembly (Conservative) announces a program to train circumcision and divorce specialists and to build ritual baths for conversions. The move is designed to lessen reliance on Orthodox colleagues. There has been a growing refusal of Orthodox rabbis to perform such rites and to share facilities with the non-Orthodox.		The U.S. permits three PLO members to attend a private conference on the Middle East in New York. The State Department obtains a waiver of the 1974 law prohibiting entry into the U.S. of members of groups advocating violence. The action is believed to be part of a U.S. effort to encourage Israeli–PLO contacts as several left-wing members of the Knesset attend the conference. Israeli Foreign Minister Moshe Arens	Lucy S. Dawidowicz, U.S. historian, writes *From That Time and Place: A Memoir, 1938–1947*, in which she describes her year in Vilna in 1938 as an American student at the YIVO Institute. Wolf Blitzer, U.S. journalist, writes *Territory of Lies: The Exclusive Story of Jonathan Jay Pollard, the American Who Spied on His Country for Israel—and How He Was Betrayed*. Arthur Hertzberg, U.S. rabbi and historian, writes *The*

A. General History	B. Jews in North and South America	C. Jews in Europe	D. Jews in the Middle East and Elsewhere	E. Jewish Culture	
American hostages regardless of where it takes place. Iraq agrees to pay the U.S. $27.3 million in compensation to the families of 37 U.S. sailors killed in the May 1987 missile attack on the frigate USS *Stark* in the Persian Gulf. For the first time in 70 years, Soviet people elect a new Congress from slates of competing candidates. Factional fighting in Lebanon resumes as Christian soldiers and militia led by General Michel Aoun* begin an effort to expel 40,000 Syrian troops from Lebanon. Soviet leader Mikhail Gorbachev* acknowledges the total failure of Stalinist collectivization and centralized control of agriculture. He proposes to return the land to families.			meets U.S. Secretary of State James A. Baker.* After the meeting, Baker* tells reporters, "We can and must find a way to move ahead which . . . addresses Israel's legitimate security needs and addresses the legitimate political rights of the Palestinian people." Ultra-Orthodox Israelis attack Jewish women holding a prayer service at the Western Wall in Jerusalem. The women intended to read from the Torah scoll and are wearing prayer shawls. An intelligence agency report to the Israeli cabinet concludes that Israel has no choice but to talk to the PLO in an effort to end the *intifada*. There are no serious leaders other than the PLO, and the PLO has moved toward moderation. In March, U.S. Secretary of State James A. Baker* tells a congressional committee that the U.S. opposes a Palestinian state but does not retreat from the statement of a possibility of an eventual Israel–PLO dialogue. "It would be wrong for us to . . . rule out . . . any dialogue that might lead us to peace. . . . We are committed totally and completely to the security of Israel. And that commitment . . . will never change." In its first contact with the Bush* administration, PLO officials in Tunis reject a request to reduce violence in the West Bank and Gaza. PLO leader Yasir Arafat* is elected	*Jews in America: Four Centuries of an Uneasy Encounter.* Ernst Pawel, U.S. novelist and biographer, writes *The Labyrinth of Exile: A Life of Theodor Herzl.*	**Mar. 1989**

	A. General History	B. Jews in North and South America	C. Jews in Europe	D. Jews in the Middle East and Elsewhere	E. Jewish Culture
Mar. 1989				president of the self-proclaimed Palestinian state by the PLO Central Committee in Tunis. The PLO claims 114 nations have recognized the state.	
Apr. 1989	After one month of factional fighting in Lebanon, 234 have been killed, including Spain's ambassador, and about 874 wounded. Christian soldiers and militiamen totaling 30,000 are engaged with 20,000 Muslim soldiers and militia backed by 40,000 Syrian troops. Syria controls about 65% of Lebanon. Riots erupt throughout Jordan over government-imposed price increases on such items as gasoline and irrigation water. At least eight are killed and a number of dissidents are arrested. Price increases resulted from economic reforms worked out in conjunction with the International Monetary Fund. The Polish government sets elections and legalizes the Solidarity movement. The *New York Times* reports the Soviet Union has sold about 15 SU-24 bombers to Libya and is training Libyan pilots to fly these supersonic aircraft. It has also agreed to refit a Libyan transport plane with air refueling capability. Soviet leader Mikhail Gorbachev* secures the ouster of more than one-third of Central Committee party leaders. Almost all opposed his reforms.			Egyptian President Hosni Mubarak* confers with President George Bush* in Washington, D.C. President Bush* says, "Egypt and the U.S. share the goal of security for Israel, the end of the occupation [of the West Bank and Gaza strip], and the achievement of Palestinian political rights." Israeli Prime Minister Yitzhak Shamir confers with U.S. President George Bush* in Washington, D.C. Shamir proposes "free, democratic elections" to select representatives to negotiate with Israel to establish a "self-governing administration" in the West Bank and Gaza. Following an interim period, "a vital test of coexistence and cooperation," negotiations would begin. Bush* expresses support for the plan. PLO leader Yasir Arafat* rejects Yitzhak Shamir's proposal for elections among the Palestinians in the West Bank and Gaza. Rabbi Moshe Levinger, leader of the Gush Emunim West Bank settlers organization, is indicted for manslaughter by an Israeli court in the killing of a Palestinian. PLO leader Yasir Arafat* rejects Yitzhak Shamir's peace plan. He insists on UN supervised elections after the Israelis have	

A. General History	B. Jews in North and South America	C. Jews in Europe	D. Jews in the Middle East and Elsewhere	E. Jewish Culture	
			withdrawn from the West Bank and Gaza, leading to the selection of representatives for negotiations of an independent Palestinian state.		**Apr. 1989**
Lebanese factions agree to a cease-fire to end the fighting in Beirut. According to a UN report, 290 people have been killed, 3,000 buildings have been damaged, and 100,000 have fled the country since the fighting began in March. Several days later, the cease-fire collapses. Amnesty International report accuses Egypt of torturing political detainees (Islamic fundamentalists). The report charges "that there is a pattern of torture in Egypt and that there are insufficient safeguards to protect detainees." The spiritual leader of Lebanon's Sunni Moslems, Sheik Khaled,* is killed in a car bomb explosion in West Beirut. A moderate, he supported talks between Christians and Moslems to end the 14-year-old civil war. Mohammed Ali Hamadei,* a pro-Iranian Lebanese terrorist, is convicted by a court in Frankfurt, West Germany, of the 1985 hijacking of a TWA airliner and the murder of a U.S. serviceman. He is sentenced to life imprisonment. Egypt returns to the Arab League. It had been suspended from the 22-member organization after its 1979 peace treaty with Israel.	Oprah Winfrey's* daytime national television show broadcasts accusations by a guest, identified as mentally disturbed and under psychiatric care, that she had witnessed the ritual murder of a Jewish child and that such practices took place in other Jewish families. After hundreds of protests, the show expresses regrets for this appearance.	French police capture Paul Touvier,* France's most wanted war criminal. A colleague of Klaus Barbie,* the Lyons Gestapo chief, he was in hiding in a Catholic priory in Nice operated by Archbishop Marcel Lefebvre, who in 1988 was excommunicated by the Vatican.	U.S. Secretary of State James A. Baker* threatens to withhold U.S. contributions to the World Health Organization (WHO) if it votes to admit the PLO as a member state. The WHO defers the PLO application until 1990. While on an official visit to France, PLO leader Yasir Arafat* responds to a question about the PLO charter provision that calls for the destruction of Israel. "I was elected on a political program founded on the basis of two states. As for the Charter, I believe there's an expression in French, *c'est caduc*—or null and void." In a speech at an American–Israel Public Affairs Committee conference, Secretary of State James A. Baker* calls on Israel "to lay aside once and for all the unrealistic vision of a greater Israel" and calls on Palestinians to "reach out to Israelis and convince them of your peaceful intentions." Amnesty International reports that 1,000 Palestinians are being held by Israel in administrative detention. Israel argues that administrative detention is not illegal and is sanctioned under international law under special emergency conditions.		**May 1989**

	A. General History	B. Jews in North and South America	C. Jews in Europe	D. Jews in the Middle East and Elsewhere	E. Jewish Culture
May 1989	The Arab League summit conference ends after failing to pressure Syria to withdraw its 40,000 troops from Lebanon.				
June 1989	Abdel Kader Helmy,* U.S. rocket expert, pleads guilty in a federal district court in Sacramento, California, of attempting to smuggle sophisticated weapons technology to Egypt. He was recruited for the smuggling ring by Egypt's defense minister, Abdel Halim Abu Ghazala.* Egyptian President Hosni Mubarak* denies that the ring existed. Demonstrators in Tiananmen Square in Peking, urging reform, are crushed by the Chinese military. Hundreds are killed. Iran's leader, the Ayatollah Khomeini,* dies. The Solidarity movement wins the first free elections held in Poland since the Communists took over after the end of World War II. In August Tadeusz Mazowiecki,* an associate of Lech Walesa,* will become prime minister.	At its annual convention, the Central Conference of American Rabbis (Reform) debates whether to admit homosexual rabbis into its organization. It decides to study the issue at the rabbinic and congregational level for at least one year before bringing it to a vote at a future convention.		In a meeting in Tunis, the U.S. formally asks the PLO to allow Palestinians in the West Bank and Gaza to take part in Israeli-sponsored elections. The U.S. vetoes a UN Security Council resolution deploring Israeli policies in the West Bank and Gaza. Ninety-two U.S. senators write to Secretary of State James A. Baker* in support of Israeli Prime Minister Yitzhak Shamir's peace plan. Israel deports eight Palestinians from the West Bank and Gaza to Lebanon, bringing to 55 the number of Palestinians forced into exile since the *intifada* began. The U.S. criticizes the action.	
July 1989	The U.S. Supreme Court rules that states can place new restraints on a woman's right to have an abortion. However, it does not overrule *Roe* v. *Wade*. The U.S. Supreme Court rules that the display of a Christmas nativity scene in a Pittsburgh court house violates the First Amendment. At the same time, it rules that posting a menorah and a Christmas tree outside	By a 97–1 vote, the U.S. Senate adopts legislation forbidding U.S. talks with any PLO representative known to have committed terrorist acts against U.S. citizens. The action is in response to talks with Yasir Arafat's* principal deputy, Salem Khalef,* also known as Abu Iyad,* who was implicated in the 1973 killing of the U.S. ambassador to the Sudan, Cleo A. Noel, Jr.* Khalef* is the founder and		Israeli Prime Minister Yitzhak Shamir amends his peace plan in response to pressure from his own Likud party. He adds four conditions: (1) There will be no participation in the elections by East Jerusalem residents; (2) there will be no elections until the *intifada* ends; (3) Israel will not give up any territory and no Palestinian state will be created; (4) Jewish settlements will continue to be	

A. General History	B. Jews in North and South America	C. Jews in Europe	D. Jews in the Middle East and Elsewhere	E. Jewish Culture

A. General History

Pittsburgh's city hall is constitutionally permissible, because they are part of a seasonal display that "has attained a secular status in our society."

A pro-Iranian Shiite Moslem terrorist group claims it hanged U.S. Colonel William Higgins,* held hostage since February 1988, in retaliation for the Israeli abduction of Sheik Abdul Karem Obeid* from southern Lebanon. They produce a videotape of the hanged hostage.

B. Jews in North and South America

leader of the Black September group responsible for the massacre of Israeli athletes at the 1972 Olympic Games held in Munich.

D. Jews in the Middle East and Elsewhere

established in the West Bank and Gaza. The move risks the government coalition with Labour.

Sixteen Israelis are killed when an Israeli bus from Tel Aviv plunges into a ravine on the outskirts of Jerusalem as an Arab passenger wrenches the steering wheel from the driver.

Israeli Labour party leaders vote to leave the governing coalition. Later, the Israeli cabinet reaffirms Yitzhak Shamir's peace plan for Palestinian elections on the West Bank and Gaza as originally proposed. The cabinet action defuses a crisis that threatens the coalition government.

The Israeli Supreme Court rules the government must recognize conversions performed abroad by Reform and Conservative rabbis. In a separate ruling, the Court decides that Reform rabbis cannot perform marriages in Israel.

It is reported that the PLO would accept Yitzhak Shamir's peace plan if the U.S. and Egypt send observers to oversee the elections, the residents of East Jerusalem vote, and Israel agrees to exchange land for peace.

Israeli commandos abduct Sheik Abdul Karem Obeid,* leader of the Party of God, a pro-Iran group, from his home in southern Lebanon. He is accused of supporting terrorist attacks into Israel. The kidnapping is criticized by the U.S. and UN.

WORLD JEWISH POPULATION 1989

Total World Population	5,318,000,000
Total World Jewish Population	13,276,300

Place	Number	% of World Jewry
Europe	2,558,400	19.3
Americas	6,727,700	50.7
Asia	3,750,700	28.3
Africa	149,900	1.1
Australia & New Zealand	89,600	0.7

Countries of Largest Population 1989

Country	Jewish Population	% of World Jewry
United States	5,981,000	45.1
Israel	3,717,100	28.0
U.S.S.R.	1,370,000	10.3
France	530,000	4.0
Great Britain	320,000	2.4
Canada	310,000	2.3
Argentina	218,000	1.6
South Africa	114,000	0.9
Brazil	100,000	0.8
Australia	85,000	0.6

	A. General History	B. Jews in North and South America	C. Jews in Europe	D. Jews in the Middle East and Elsewhere	E. Jewish Culture
Aug. 1989	The fighting renews in Beirut between Christians and Muslims aligned with Syria. In a four-day period, more than 70 are killed and 300 wounded. Since fighting began in March, about 650 have been killed and 2,700 wounded. On August 15, Pope John Paul II calls Syrian shelling of Beirut "genocide" and says that Syria is seeking Lebanon's destruction. It is reported that 310,000 ethnic Turks living in Bulgaria have fled to Turkey since June when Turkey permitted entry. They say they faced a Bulgarian campaign of religious and cultural assimilation.		Cardinal Jozef Glemp, Poland's Roman Catholic primate, criticizes Jews who object to a convent at the site of the Auschwitz death camp and advises them not to talk "from the position of a people raised above all others. . . . Do you, esteemed Jews, not see that your pronouncements against the nuns offend the feelings of all Poles, and our sovereignty, which has been achieved with such difficulty? Your power lies in the mass media that are easily at your disposal in many countries." His remarks are criticized in a front-page editorial of Solidarity's daily newspaper. YIVO enters into an agreement with the Lithuanian government, allowing it to photocopy 40,000 pages of documents, newspapers, and books left by YIVO in Vilna during World War II.	The U.S. urges the PLO to accept Yitzhak Shamir's peace plan for Arab elections in the West Bank and Gaza. The PLO insists on a direct role in the negotiations and that a Palestinian state would be a result.	
Sep. 1989	The U.S. evacuates its embassy in Beirut in response to Christian threats. The Christians claim the U.S. supports Syria in Lebanon's civil war. New York's Mayor Edward I. Koch is defeated in the Democratic mayoral primary by Manhattan Borough President David Dinkins,* thus thwarting his effort for an unprecedented fourth term. In November, Dinkins* will be elected New York's first African-American mayor. Hurricane Hugo devastates the Carolinas area of the U.S. and parts of the Caribbean, and an		The Vatican urges the removal of the Carmelite convent from its site at Auschwitz. In its first public declaration on the controversy, it backs the 1987 accord signed by Catholic bishops and Jewish leaders and rejects the opposition of Poland's Cardinal Jozef Glemp. Yehuda Bauer, director of Holocaust Studies at the Hebrew University, writes that frequently cited figures of 2.5 million Jewish and 1.5 million other victims at Auschwitz are "patently false." He asserts that about 1.6 million people, of whom 1.35 million were Jews, were gassed or otherwise	Israeli Defense Minister Yitzhak Rabin meets with Egyptian President Hosni Mubarak* to discuss an Egyptian 10-point peace plan. It includes a free election held under international supervision in West Bank, Gaza, and East Jerusalem; setting a date for the beginning of negotiations for the final status of occupied lands; Israel is to agree to negotiate land for peace, while also protecting Israel's security; the halt of construction and expansion of settlements. Israel would not be required to talk to the PLO or accept the idea of a Palestinian state.	

earthquake measuring 7.1 on the Richter scale hits San Francisco and the Bay area, killing 67 people. Saudi Arabia beheads 16 pro-Iranian Kuwaitis involved in bombings and other terrorism during the annual Muslim pilgrimage to Mecca in July.		killed at Auschwitz. He contends that Polish nationalists and Communists promoted the larger figure, casting both Jewish and Polish losses in such large numbers that the distinction between the fates of the two groups was blurred.	Hungary reestablishes full diplomatic relations with Israel, ending a breach dating from the 1967 Six-Day War.		**Sep. 1989**
Huge protests erupt in East Germany. Thousands of refugees flee to the West. Party leader Erich Honecker* is ousted. The Hungarian Communist party changes its name. Parliament decides to allow a multiparty system, with elections in 1990. Lebanese legislators meeting in Saudi Arabia endorse an Arab League peace plan that reduces Christian power and gives greater say in the government to Muslims. Christian forces led by General Michel Aoun* reject the plan because it fails to provide a timetable for the Syrian withdrawal.		Joseph Wybran, a physician and head of the Coordinating Committee on Jewish Organizations in Belgium, is shot to death in a hospital parking lot in Brussels.	The Soviet Union abstains from a UN General Assembly vote to reject Israel's credentials. It is the first time in seven years that the Soviet Union has not joined efforts, led by Muslim nations, to expel Israel from the UN. Israel is seated by a vote of 95–37, with 15 abstentions. The U.S. accuses Israeli Prime Minister Yitzhak Shamir of hampering peace efforts with "unhelpful" statements. Secretary of State James A. Baker* says, "Our goal all along has been to assist in the implementation of the Shamir initiative."		**Oct. 1989**
Lebanon's Parliament elects René Moawad,* a Maronite Christian, president. He attempts to form a government of national reconciliation, despite threats by General Michel Aoun.* On November 22, President Moawad* is assassinated. He will be succeeded by Elias Hrawi.* East Germany opens the Berlin Wall. In Czechoslovakia, demonstrations force the Communist party to cede absolute power. In Bulgaria, Stalinist leader Todor	U.S. Roman Catholic bishops adopt a statement declaring that Palestinians have the right to an independent homeland. Israel should have the right to secure its borders. Israel must modify its definition of adequate security, and the Palestinians should disavow claims to other territory in Israel and accept the limitations on the sovereignty of their homeland to ensure Israel's security.	West German Chancellor Helmut Kohl* ends a trip to Poland with a visit to Auschwitz. He writes in the visitors' book: "The warnings emanating from this place must never be forgotten. Unspeakable hurt was inflicted on various peoples here, but above all on European Jews, in the name of Germany." More than 11,000 Jews leave the Soviet Union, the first time the figure exceeds 10,000 a month. Over 71,000 Jews leave during 1989.	Israel agrees to accept the U.S. plan to choose negotiators for limited self-rule in the West Bank and Gaza but seeks assurance that the PLO will not be involved in the negotiations. Israeli Prime Minister Yitzhak Shamir meets with U.S. President George Bush* in Washington, D.C. They fail to clear the way for peace talks. Israel blames the PLO for the delay. Bush* expresses concern about Israeli methods used to suppress the *intifada* and about Israel's military		**Nov. 1989**

	A. General History	B. Jews in North and South America	C. Jews in Europe	D. Jews in the Middle East and Elsewhere	E. Jewish Culture
Nov. 1989	Zhivkov* is forced out. These actions are a result of a shift in Soviet policy. Mikhail Gorbachev* had announced that the Soviet Union would not utilize military force to maintain existing regimes and would not resist an end to the Communist monopoly on political power. Jordanians vote in the first nationwide elections in 22 years. Militant Muslims win at least 26 seats in the 80-member Parliament. Women vote for the first time. The vote formalizes Jordan's separation from the West Bank. King Hussein* retains power to dissolve Parliament and to rule under martial law provisions in force since the 1967 Six-Day War.			cooperation with South Africa. The U.S. threatens to suspend all financial support for the UN if the General Assembly recognizes the PLO as "the Provisional Government of Palestine." The U.S. also condemns as "objectionable" a proposal to channel UN food aid in the West Bank and Gaza through the PLO. In December, Arab governments will withdraw these proposals.	
Dec. 1989	Egypt and Syria agree to restore diplomatic relations after a 12-year rift. Syria severed ties after Egyptian President Anwar al-Sadat* traveled to Jerusalem in 1977 to open peace talks with Israel. The Augusto Pinochet* era ends as Chileans elect a new leader, Patricio Aylwin,* in free elections. The U.S. invades Panama, asserting the right to protect its citizens, democracy, and the Panama Canal. General Manuel Antonio Noriega* is ousted. Prodemocracy forces oust Romanian leader Nicolae Ceauşescu.* Thousands are killed in the fighting.		More than 700 Soviet Jews, representing 175 Soviet Jewish organizations from 75 cities, and observers from around the world meet in Moscow in the first national conference of Soviet Jews in more than 70 years.	U.S. Vice President Dan Quayle* formally commits the Bush* administration to repealing UN General Assembly Resolution 3379, which defines Zionism as "a form of racism and racial discrimination." It is the first time any U.S. administration has formally committed itself to securing a repeal. Later in the month, the Soviet Union announces it would oppose repeal of the resolution. B'tselem, an Israeli human rights organization, reports that about 607 Arabs have been killed by Israeli security forces since the *intifada* began in December 1987. Another 28 apparently have been killed by Israeli civilians, and 166 alleged collaborators with Israel have been killed by Arabs.	

712

The Emergence of non-European Centers of Jewry

Approximate Number of Jews in the Year	United States	Canada	Argentina	Palestine/ Israel (since 1948)	South Africa	Brazil	Uruguay	Chile	Mexico	Egypt	Australia and New Zealand
1800	2,000	. . .	. . .	10,000	. . .	. . .	. . .	. . .	. . .	. . .	. . .
1850	50,000	500	. . .	12,000	1,000	. . .	. . .	. . .	. . .	. . .	. . .
1880	230,000	2,400	. . .	25,000	. . .	. . .	. . .	. . .	. . .	. . .	. . .
1890	500,000	6,400	1,000	35,000	. . .	. . .	. . .	. . .	. . .	. . .	. . .
1900	1,000,000	16,400	30,000	55,000	30,000	3,000	. . .	. . .	1,000	27,000	16,000
1910	2,200,000	70,000	90,000	80,000	50,000	5,000	. . .	1,000	2,000	40,000	18,000
1920	3,200,000	120,000	130,000	75,000	60,000	7,000	1,000	2,000	. . .	60,000	24,000
1930	4,400,000	150,000	220,000	170,000	. . .	40,000	10,000	5,000	12,000	65,000	. . .
1933	4,500,000	170,000	240,000	220,000	80,000	45,000	12,000	7,000	12,000	70,000	27,000
1939	4,870,000	170,000	350,000	475,000	95,000	80,000	25,000	15,000	20,000	70,000	28,000
1950	5,000,000	198,000	360,000	1,115,000	103,400	115,000	40,000	40,000	25,000	65,000	44,000
1960	5,531,500	250,000	400,000	1,880,000	110,000	125,000	45,000	30,000	26,000	13,500	68,500
1970	5,870,000	280,000	500,000	2,560,000	119,900	150,000	50,000	35,000	35,000	1,000	77,000
1980	5,690,000	308,000	242,000	3,282,700	108,000	110,000	40,000	25,000	35,000	250	74,000
1989	5,515,000	310,000	218,000	3,717,000	114,000	100,000	24,400	15,000	35,000	200	89,500

1990

Spike Lee,* noted African-American filmmaker, produces *Mo' Better Blues*, the story of a troubled black jazz musician. The film includes two minor characters, Josh and Moe Flatbush, club owners who exploit the African-American musicians in the film. Lee* portrays them with despicable traits typically used to disparage Jews. The ADL (Anti-Defamation League of B'nai B'rith) accuses Lee* of dredging up age-old and highly dangerous antisemitic stereotypes.

Life magazine's list of the 100 most important Americans of the 20th century includes 16 Jews: Irving Berlin, Leonard Bernstein, Bob Dylan, Albert Einstein, Abraham Flexner, Betty Friedan, Milton Friedman, Edwin Land, William Levitt, Louis B. Mayer, J. Robert Oppenheimer, William Paley, Richard Rodgers, Jonas Salk, Alfred Stieglitz, and Walter Winchell.

Nasty Girl, a German film written and directed by Michael Verhoeven,* is a fictional depiction inspired by the factual experience of Anja Rosmus, who set out to learn what happened in her hometown, Passau, during the Nazi era, and the ostracism and harassment she encountered. The film wins an award at the Berlin Film Festival.

Dr. John Strugnell,* Harvard Divinity School professor, who has been chief editor of the Dead Sea Scrolls, is dismissed because of antisemitic remarks made in a newspaper interview. The scrolls are kept at the Rockefeller Museum in Jerusalem.

Philip Roth, U.S. author, writes *Patrimony: A True Story*, a nonfiction portrait of his father, Herman, and of his father's struggle with a fatal illness.

Judith Plaskow writes *Standing Again at Sinai*, a comprehensive exploration of Judaism from a feminist perspective.

Judith Miller, U.S. journalist, writes *One, by One, by One: Facing the Holocaust*, in which she investigates how six different countries, the U.S., Germany, the Soviet Union, Austria, the Netherlands, and France, engage in remembering the Holocaust. She describes the forgetting, distorting, and political manipulation of the Holocaust.

Harry A. Markowitz, professor of finance at Baruch College of the City University of New York, and Merton H. Miller, of the University of Chicago's Graduate School of Business Administration, are two of three American

	A. General History	B. Jews in North and South America	C. Jews in Europe	D. Jews in the Middle East and Elsewhere	E. Jewish Culture
Jan. 1990			Israeli officials acknowledge they paid Nicolae Ceauşescu's* Romanian government $2,000 to $3,000 for each Jew allowed to emigrate over the past two decades. Chief Rabbi Moses Rosen would not confirm the human trade but stated, "I suppose it is true."	The U.S. reduces its annual payment to the UN Food and Agricultural Organization (FAO) from $61.4 million to $18 million because of its support of the PLO and intimates it might withdraw from the FAO altogether.	winners of the Nobel Prize in economics. Jerome I. Friedman, U.S. physicist, is one of three to win the Nobel Prize in physics. David Kazhdan, a Harvard University mathematician who emigrated to the U.S. from the Soviet Union in 1975, wins a
Feb. 1990	Nelson Mandela,* 71-year-old African National Congress leader, is freed by the South American government after 27 years in prison. The Spanish government signs an accord officially granting the Protestant and Jewish faiths privileges comparable to those of Roman Catholics. In effect, the accord ratifies the Constitution of 1978 that guarantees "freedom of ideology, religion and worship" and overturns the 1492 expulsion decree of King Ferdinand* and Queen Isabella.* It is estimated that there are 15,000 Jews and 60,000 Protestants in Spain.		Austria concludes an agreement with the Committee for Jewish Claims of Austria, which will pay nearly $200 million in social insurance benefits to about 5,000 Jews who were 8 to 14 years old when the Nazis annexed the country. The average pension will be about $3,500 per year and will be paid for an average of 10 years. In 1987, legislation was enacted making Jews who were over 14 at the annexation eligible for such pensions. Czechoslovakia appoints Rita Klimova ambassador to the U.S. and Rudolf Slansky ambassador to the Soviet Union. Both are Jews, and Slansky is the son of Rudolf Slansky, former general secretary of the Czech Communist party, who was hanged in 1952 after a Stalinist show trial.	Terrorists attack a tour bus carrying about 30 Israeli tourists near Cairo, killing 11 Israelis and wounding 17. The U.S. State Department annual report on human rights says 432 Palestinians were killed in 1989 compared to 366 in 1988 by Israeli security forces or settlers, 128 were killed by other Palestinians compared to 13 in 1988, and 13 Israelis were killed by Palestinians in the territories, compared to 11 previously killed since the *intifada* began. The report concludes that Israeli soldiers continued to violate rights of Palestinians, causing "avoidable deaths and injuries." Poland and Czechoslovakia resume diplomatic relations with Israel after a 23-year break. Nelson Mandela,* South African anti-apartheid leader, meets PLO chairman Yasir Arafat* in Zambia. Mandela* says Arafat* "is fighting against a unique form of colonialism, and we wish him success in his struggle."	coveted MacArthur Foundation fellowship with its $275,000 stipend. A golden calf 4½ inches long and 4½ inches tall that was an object of worship dating from the 2nd millennium BCE is unearthed by Harvard University archaeologists excavating Canaanite ruins near the ancient port city of Ashkelon. Martin Gilbert, British historian, edits *Surviving the Holocaust: The Kovno Ghetto Diary* of Avraham Tory which describes life in the ghetto of Kovno, Lithuania, from June 1941 to January 1944. The four-volume *Encyclopedia of the Holocaust* published by Yad Vashem in Jerusalem is edited by Israel Gutman. The editor of the English edition is Geoffrey Wigoder.
Mar. 1990	Walter H. Annenberg, former U.S. ambassador to Great			Israel and Bulgaria announce they will resume diplomatic	

714

A. General History	B. Jews in North and South America	C. Jews in Europe	D. Jews in the Middle East and Elsewhere	E. Jewish Culture	
Britain, donates $50 million to the United Negro College Fund. It is the largest single donation to the fund, which was established in 1944, and is a consortium of 41 black colleges in the U.S. The Arab League agrees to move its headquarters back to Cairo. It was transferred to Tunis in 1979 because of Egypt's peace treaty with Israel. Lithuania declares itself a sovereign and independent state and secedes from the Soviet Union. The Soviet Union does not recognize this action. Lithuania was forcibly annexed in 1940. The U.S. and Great Britain halt an attempt to ship nuclear devices to Iraq. Five people are arrested in London.			relations after a break of 23 years. At a news conference, U.S. President George Bush* states: "The United States [does] not believe there should be new settlements in the West Bank and East Jerusalem." After protests by U.S. Jewish leaders, the administration issues a statement that reiterates the long-standing U.S. policy on Jerusalem—that it must be a united city and its final status should be determined through negotiations. It does not disavow Bush's statement. Israel's 15-month-old coalition government collapses in a dispute over Arab peace talks. It is the first Israeli government to fall as a result of a no-confidence vote. Labour party leader and Foreign Minister Shimon Peres and Likud leaders could not agree on a peace plan. The Israeli Knesset dissolves the government. Prime Minister Yitzhak Shamir will head the caretaker regime.		Mar. 1990

D. Jews in the Middle East and Elsewhere

Mar. 1990

Former U.S. president Jimmy Carter* visits Syria and then Israel. He says Syrian President Hafiz al-Assad* authorized him to advise Israeli leaders that Syria was willing to open peace talks and negotiate the future of the Golan Heights. Carter* accuses Israel of violating Palestinian rights in the territories. Israeli officials say he privately told them not to settle Soviet Jews in Jerusalem.

In a letter dated March 16, U.S. Secretary of State James A. Baker* writes to California Congressman Mel Levine: "I am also very aware of the great significance which Jerusalem has for the Jewish people as well as for people of all religions. Clearly, Jews and others can live where they want, East or West, and the city must remain undivided."

A. General History	B. Jews in North and South America	C. Jews in Europe	D. Jews in the Middle East and Elsewhere	E. Jewish Culture	
	Over 20,000 Jews celebrate Siyum HaShas, or completion of the Talmud, at New York's Madison	East Germany's first freely elected democratic government apologizes for the Holocaust,	President Saddam Hussein* of Iraq says Iraq has advanced nerve gas weapons and threatens to		Apr. 1990

	A. General History	B. Jews in North and South America	C. Jews in Europe	D. Jews in the Middle East and Elsewhere	E. Jewish Culture
Apr. 1990		Square Garden. Sponsored by Agudat Israel, it celebrates the completion of 7½ years of a page-a-day study of Talmud by Jews throughout the world.	ending 40 years of official denial. It accepts joint responsibility for Nazi crimes, expresses willingness to pay reparations to victims, and seeks diplomatic ties with Israel. A survey of 506 adults in the Moscow area reveals that antisemitism in the Soviet Union is on the rise. Sponsored by the American Jewish Committee, it is the first survey to be conducted since the 1920s.	destroy "half of Israel" if it attacks his country. He denies Iraq has nuclear weapons. Israel launches its second experimental satellite, *Ofek II*. It can last about two months before it falls back to earth. One hundred fifty thousand Israelis rally to demand a change in the electoral system.	

Apr. 1990

D. Jews in the Middle East and Elsewhere

One hundred fifty Jewish settlers rent the St. John's Hospice, unoccupied buildings owned by the Greek Orthodox church in the Christian Quarter of Jerusalem's Old City. Palestinian and Christian clerics close holy sites in protest. After a denial, the Israeli government acknowledges that it secretly cofinanced the rental. The Israeli Supreme Court will order the settlers to leave the buildings.

Acting Prime Minister and Likud party leader Yitzhak Shamir is asked by President Chaim Herzog to form a government after Labour party leader Shimon Peres fails to do so.

Israel's President Chaim Herzog calls for changes in the nation's electoral system. "How can citizens . . . watch calmly the present political phenomena revealing a total contempt for the principles of democracy?"

	A. General History	B. Jews in North and South America	C. Jews in Europe	D. Jews in the Middle East and Elsewhere	E. Jewish Culture
May 1990		An English-language weekly edition of the *Forward* begins publication in New York.	French President François Mitterrand* joins about 200,000 silent marchers in Paris who protest antisemitism and the desecration of 34 graves at a Jewish cemetery in Carpentras, in southern France. The Jewish Theological Seminary of America and YIVO establish a Jewish studies program at the Moscow State Institute of History and Archives. Its purpose is to train Soviet students, Jewish and non-Jewish, in skills necessary to understand and catalog the vast quantities of Jewish	Ami Popper, an Israeli gunman who was dishonorably discharged from the army, kills 7 Arab laborers and wounds 11 in Rishon Lezion, a town 10 miles southeast of Tel Aviv. He is apprehended, and Israeli leaders condemn the attack. Riots erupt in the territories, and more Arabs are killed. At an Arab summit meeting held in Baghdad, President Saddam Hussein* of Iraq threatens to use "weapons of total destruction" in response to an Israeli attack against Arabs. The main item on the summit agenda is immigration of Soviet	

A. General History	B. Jews in North and South America	C. Jews in Europe	D. Jews in the Middle East and Elsewhere	E. Jewish Culture	
		manuscripts now being found in the Soviet Union.	Jews to Israel, which is denounced as a grave threat to Arab security. Syria and four other Arab nations do not attend the meeting. Greece establishes full diplomatic relations with Israel.		**May 1990**
The Islamic Salvation Front, which advocates turning Algeria into an Islamic republic, wins the country's first free local elections since gaining independence from France in 1962. Most of the front's leaders are in prison.	At its 101st annual meeting, the Central Conference of American Rabbis (Reform) votes to admit acknowledged, sexually active homosexuals into its rabbinate.	The Prince of Asturias Foundation, a private foundation linked to the Spanish royal family, grants its annual Concord Prize to the 700,000 Sephardic Jews around the world. It is an effort at reconciliation 500 years after the expulsion of Jews from Spain.	At a Bush*–Gorbachev* press conference, Soviet leader Mikhail Gorbachev* threatens to halt the immigration of Soviet Jews to Israel unless he is assured they will not be settled in the occupied territories. Israel responds by saying it has no plans to settle Soviet Jews in the territories. However, acting Prime Minister Yitzhak Shamir says a democracy cannot restrict where people live.		**June 1990**

D. Jews in the Middle East and Elsewhere

Yitzhak Shamir succeeds in forming a new Israeli government. With 62 votes in the 120-member Knesset, he forms the first right-wing government since 1984. David Levy is foreign minister, Moshe Arens is defense minister, and Ariel Sharon is minister of construction and housing.

U.S. Secretary of State James A. Baker* criticizes conditions for peace talks advanced by Israel's new government. Testifying before Congress, he says, "everybody over there should know that the telephone number [of the White House] is 1-202-456-1414. When you're serious about peace, call us."

U.S. President George Bush* suspends the 18-month dialogue with the PLO. He declares the U.S. to be ready to resume talks "any time" the PLO more clearly condemns the May 30 attempted attack on the Tel Aviv beaches and disciplines those responsible.

June 1990

A. General History	B. Jews in North and South America	C. Jews in Europe	D. Jews in the Middle East and Elsewhere	E. Jewish Culture	
About 1,400 Moslems die in a stampede of pilgrims in an air-conditioned tunnel while observing the annual Hadj, or pilgrimage, to Mecca, Saudi Arabia. Iraq's president Saddam Hussein* openly threatens to use force against Arab oil-producing nations unless they curb their production. His			It is reported that about 15,000 Ethiopian Jews are stranded in Addis Ababa. About 500 Jews per month had been allowed to leave for Israel. In the last several months exit visas have been held up as a way to encourage Israel to supply more military assistance in the war against insurgents. Israeli officials say the		**July 1990**

	A. General History	B. Jews in North and South America	C. Jews in Europe	D. Jews in the Middle East and Elsewhere	E. Jewish Culture
July 1990	warning is aimed at Kuwait and the United Arab Emirates. The U.S. conducts naval exercises in the Persian Gulf amid rising tensions over the oil dispute between Iraq and Kuwait. Kuwait says Iraq is massing 30,000 troops and 200 tanks along its border. It is reported that Iraqi troops will start pulling back from the Kuwaiti border as a result of mediation efforts by Egypt's President Hosni Mubarak* and Saudi King Fahd.* The Lebanese government imposes an economic and diplomatic blockade on Christian General Michel Aoun's* forces in a move to oust him from his enclave near Beirut.			suspension is a joint decision as Israel is concerned that non-Jews are among those seeking to emigrate. About 3,000 Ethiopian Jews have left for Israel in 1990. At month's end, emigration returns to normal.	
Aug. 1990	On August 2, Iraq invades and seizes Kuwait. The UN Security Council adopts a resolution demanding an Iraqi withdrawal. The U.S. freezes Iraqi assets. On August 5, U.S. President George Bush* says the Iraqi assault on Kuwait "will not stand." Their withdrawal is the only acceptable outcome. On August 6, the UN Security Council votes, 13–0, to embargo trade with Iraq and occupied Kuwait. On August 7, the U.S. orders combat troops and planes to Saudi Arabia at a Saudi invitation. Turkey orders a shutdown of Iraqi oil pipelines. On August 8, Iraq annexes Kuwait. On August 9, the UN Security Council declares Iraq's annexation void. On August 10, 12 Arab nations agree to send a pan-		West Germany indicts Josef Schwammberger* in the deaths of 3,000 people, mostly Jews, in Poland during World War II while a commandant of concentration camps. A fugitive for nearly 40 years, he was extradited in May from Argentina.	Saddam Hussein* says Iraq will withdraw from Kuwait if Israel agrees to withdraw from the West Bank and Syria from Lebanon. The U.S. and Israel reject the "linkage." Three hundred Egyptian soldiers arrive in Saudi Arabia.	

A. General History	B. Jews in North and South America	C. Jews in Europe	D. Jews in the Middle East and Elsewhere	E. Jewish Culture

Arab force to protect Saudi Arabia. Egypt, Syria, Morocco, Lebanon, Bahrain, Oman, Djibouti, Qatar, United Arab Emirates, Somalia, Saudia Arabia, and Kuwait vote for the force. Iraq, Libya, and the PLO reject the resolution, Algeria and Yemen abstain, and Tunisia is absent. On August 16, Iraq seeks peace with Iran and offers to accede to all of Iran's demands for settling their eight-year war. The same day, Iraq orders 6,500 U.S. and British citizens trapped in Kuwait to assemble in two hotels, and if they refuse, they will be rounded up. On August 20, U.S. President George Bush* demands the release of over 3,000 Americans held in Iraq and Kuwait, calling them "hostages." On August 25, the UN Security Council adopts a resolution, 13–0, giving the U.S. and other nations the right to enforce the economic embargo against Iraq by halting shipping to and from Iraq. On August 26, Saddam Hussein* says captive foreign women and children can leave Iraq.

Estimated Jewish Population in the U.S., 1790–1990

Year	U.S. Population	U.S. Jews	% of Population
1790	3,929,000	1,400	0.04
1800	5,308,000	2,000	0.04
1820	9,638,000	2,700	0.03
1830	12,866,000	4,000	0.03
1840	17,069,000	15,000	0.09
1860	31,443,000	150,000	0.48
1880	50,156,000	230,000	0.46
1900	75,995,000	1,058,000	1.39
1920	105,711,000	3,389,000	3.20
1930	122,775,000	4,228,000	3.44
1940	131,669,000	4,870,000	3.69
1950	150,697,000	5,000,000	3.31
1960	179,323,000	5,531,000	3.08
1970	203,302,000	5,800,000	2.85
1980	226,546,000	5,921,000	2.61
1990	248,710,000	5,981,000	2.40

The Bush administration asks Congress to forgive Egypt's $7 billion military debt to the U.S.

On September 9, U.S. President George Bush* and Soviet leader Mikhail Gorbachev* meet in Helsinki. They issue a joint statement warning Iraq to leave Kuwait.

Soviet President Mikhail Gorbachev* announces a sweeping plan to create a Soviet

An appellate court in New York State denies a request of the Israeli government to halt publication and sale of *By Way of Deception: A Devastating Insider's Portrait of the Mossad*, a book written by Victor Ostrovsky, a former Mossad agent. Israel alleges that book would disseminate information that "could endanger the lives of various people in the employ of the State of Israel." The

Dr. George Habash,* leader of the Popular Front for the Liberation of Palestine, cuts his ties with Syria and moves his base to Iraq as a result of Syria's anti-Iraqi stance in the Persian Gulf crisis.

U.S. officials advise Israel that any attack on Israel by Iraq would result in a vigorous American response in support of Israel.

Israel and the Soviet Union agree to

	A. General History	B. Jews in North and South America	C. Jews in Europe	D. Jews in the Middle East and Elsewhere	E. Jewish Culture
Sep. 1990	market economy within 18 months. Palestinian fighters loyal to PLO chairman Yasir Arafat* rout those loyal to a breakaway PLO faction allied with Abu Nidal* after three days of fighting near Sidon, Lebanon. About 78 are killed in the battles.	court action spurs book sales. Madison, Wisconsin, police guard synagogues during the New Year holiday as a result of more than 20 acts of antisemitic vandalism during the past two months.		establish formal consular ties.	

Sep. 1990

A. General History

The U.S., Great Britain, France, and the Soviet Union, the four World War II allies, sign a treaty relinquishing all their occupation rights in Germany, leaving West and East Germany free to unite on October 3.

On September 23, Saddam Hussein* threatens to attack oil installations in Saudi Arabia and other Arab states in the region and Israel if the West tries to "strangle" Iraq's people. On September 25, the UN Security Council adopts a resolution authorizing an air embargo of Iraq.

The Soviet Parliament gives initial approval to a law on the freedom of conscience, formally ending decades of religious oppression.

Lebanon's President Elias Hrawi* orders his predominantly Muslim army to blockade Christian General Michel Aoun's* enclave in Beirut.

	A. General History	B. Jews in North and South America	C. Jews in Europe	D. Jews in the Middle East and Elsewhere	E. Jewish Culture
Oct. 1990	On October 1, U.S. President George Bush* addresses the UN and hopes for a peaceful end to the Persian Gulf crisis. After the Iraqi withdrawal, steps could be taken "for all the states and the peoples of the region to settle the conflicts that divide the Arabs from Israel." Seeming to make a step toward conciliation, he later states that "this was not designed to convey flexibility or a shift in position." East and West Germany unite after 45 years of division. The Lebanese government officially asks for Syrian military intervention to oust Christian General Michel Aoun* and his 15,000 troops from the areas they control in Beirut.	Brandeis University researchers publish *Intermarriage and American Jews Today: New Findings and Policy Implications.* Surveying data from population studies in eight communities between 1985 and 1989, they find that 29% of Jewish marriages today involve a spouse who was not born Jewish. They find great differences between "conversionary" marriages, in which one spouse converts to Judaism, which are more prone to give their children a Jewish education and have a higher level of ritual observance, and "mixed marriages," where one spouse remains non-Jewish.	A Moscow city court sentences a leader of Pamyat, a Russian nationalist group, to two years in jail for disrupting a writers' forum and shouting, "Kikes, go home to Israel." He was found guilty of fanning interethnic enmity in violation of a new law. His sentence will be appealed. An international commission of experts established to determine the fate of Raoul Wallenberg,* Swedish diplomat missing since 1945, believes he may still be somewhere in the Soviet Union's vast penal system. They are certain he did not die in July 1947 of a heart attack in Lubyanka Prison, as was claimed in February 1957 by the then Soviet Foreign Minister Andrei Gromyko.*	Israel announces plans to distribute gas masks and other chemical warfare gear to the Israeli public. General Mikhail A. Moiseyev,* Chief of the Soviet General Staff, in an interview at the *New York Times* to discuss the Persian Gulf crisis says that Israel's bombing of the Iraqi nuclear reactor at Osiraq in 1981 was understandable. "There was . . . reason for taking the action that Israel undertook." Twenty-one Arabs are killed and over 100 wounded as Israeli police open fire on rioting Palestinians after they hurled stones from the Temple Mount in Jerusalem onto thousands of Jews gathered below at the Western Wall to celebrate the festival of Sukkot.	

A. General History	B. Jews in North and South America	C. Jews in Europe	D. Jews in the Middle East and Elsewhere	E. Jewish Culture
Syrian troops begin deployment.

Rifaat al-Mahgoub,* Egypt's second-ranking official and Speaker of the Parliament, is assassinated in Cairo.

Christian General Michel Aoun* surrenders after a Syrian air and ground assault that kills 750 and wounds thousands. He flees to France's embassy in Beirut, where he is granted asylum.

The Bush* administration decides to send as many as 100,000 more troops to augment the 240,000 deployed in Saudi Arabia. | | | The U.S. gives its support to a proposed UN resolution condemning Israel for the killings of Arabs on the Temple Mount and calling for a UN investigation of the event. The U.S. rebukes Israel for not acting "with more restraint."

Saddam Hussein* threatens to attack Israel, implying that the attack would be carried out with long-range missiles.

The U.S. joins the rest of the UN Security Council in deploring Israel's refusal to cooperate with an investigation by the secretary-general of the Temple Mount killings.

The Israeli government-appointed panel investigating the Temple Mount killings blames Muslim clerics for inciting the riot and justifies the use of live ammunition by the police. However, it criticizes the police for not averting the violence. | **Oct. 1990** |
| U.S. President George Bush* orders more than 150,000 U.S. troops to the Persian Gulf, citing the need for an "adequate offensive military option."

The National Council of Churches, representing 32 member denominations and about 42 million American Christians, passes a resolution calling for the immediate withdrawal of U.S. troops from the Persian Gulf and criticizes the Bush* administration for "reckless rhetoric" and "imprudent behavior" and a | Two new Jewish members are elected to the House of Representatives, bringing the number of Jews in the House to 33, a record high. The number of Jews in the Senate remains at eight. However, the defeat of Minnesota Republican Senator Rudy Boschwitz by Paul Wellstone, a Democrat, is attributed in part to an appeal to Jewish voters that criticized Wellstone for raising his children as "non-Jews" and for having "no connection" with the Jewish community. Raising the religious | | The UN secretary general, reacting to the Temple Mount killings, suggests a meeting of the 164 nations that signed the Fourth Geneva Convention to discuss means of protecting Palestinians in the West Bank and Gaza.

Israel rejects a UN report suggesting that 164 signatories to the Fourth Geneva Convention meet to discuss protection of Palestinians in the territories, saying, "For the 40 years since the Geneva Convention was signed there have been dozens of wars with millions killed | **Nov. 1990** |

	A. **General History**	B. **Jews in North and South America**	C. **Jews in Europe**	D. **Jews in the Middle East and Elsewhere**	E. **Jewish Culture**
Nov. 1990	precipitous military buildup. It also links the Persian Gulf crisis with the Israeli–Palestinian issue. Accusing the U.S. of practicing a double standard, it calls for an international conference to resolve it. Margaret Thatcher* resigns as Britain's prime minister after 11½ years service. She is succeeded by John Major.* U.S. President George Bush* meets with Syrian President Hafiz al-Assad* in Geneva. Bush* says Syria supports the use of force against Iraq. On November 29, the UN Security Council approves a resolution authorizing the use of force to eject Iraq from Kuwait if it does not withdraw by January 15.	issue offended many voters. The Council of Jewish Federations supports the Bush* administration's Persian Gulf policy by adopting a resolution in favor of a firm posture of opposition to Saddam Hussein's* belligerence. A study of Canadian Jewry, *The Persistence of Invisible Poverty Among Jews in Canada*, reveals that one out of every six Canadian Jews lives in poverty. Tom Watson,* noted U.S. professional golfer, resigns from the Kansas City Country Club after the application of Henry Bloch is withdrawn because his sponsors feared he would not be accepted. Watson's* wife and children are Jewish. "I see acts of anti-Semitism on the rise around the world . . . It hurts. It's a family matter and it's something I can't accept." Several weeks later, Bloch is admitted into membership.		and wounded. The international community has not found reason to convene the signatories even once." Meir Kahane, 58-year-old founder of the Jewish Defense League and of the Kach party in Israel, is assassinated while speaking in New York. The assassin is alleged to be Egyptian-born El Sayyid A. Nosair.* Israel invites Jean-Claude Aimee,* a senior UN official, to visit Israel and investigate the Temple Mount killings. An infiltrator slips across the Egyptian border into Israel and ambushes a bus and three military vehicles, killing 4 and wounding 27 Israelis. Two days later, five Israeli soldiers are killed fighting in southern Lebanon.	
Dec. 1990	Saddam Hussein* announces that Iraq will release all foreign hostages. Eduard Shevardnadze* resigns as foreign minister of the Soviet Union and warns of a new dictatorship taking place.	The Federal Election Commission announces that it had cleared American–Israel Public Affairs Committee (AIPAC) and 27 pro-Israel political action committees (PAC) on charges brought against them by seven former government officials in January 1989.	Poland's Roman Catholic bishops issue a document condemning antisemitism and acknowledging that some Poles assisted Nazis in killing Jews during World War II. The document is to be read at all masses said on January 20, 1991.	Israeli Prime Minister Yitzhak Shamir meets with U.S. President George Bush* in Washington, D.C., to discuss the Persian Gulf crisis. At the conclusion of the two-hour meeting, Shamir states Bush* told him, "There will not be any deal at the expense of Israel."	

Dec. 1990

D. Jews in the Middle East and Elsewhere

Three Israelis are stabbed and killed by Arabs at an aluminum factory in Jaffa.

U.S. President George Bush* states he is convinced the U.S.-led coalition of Western and Arab nations would not fall apart if Iraq attacked Israel. He also praises Israel for its "low profile position" in the crisis. "It's not easy. They have their security they feel could well be at stake from some radical act of Saddam Hussein."

The U.S. supports a unanimous UN Security Council resolution criticizing Israel for the deportation of Palestinians. The text includes Jerusalem in the "Palestinian territories occupied by Israel since 1967." It is the third resolution hostile to Israel adopted by the UN Security Council since the outbreak of the Persian Gulf crisis.

Israeli sources report that after three years of *intifada*, Palestinian casualties total 13,017 wounded, 628 killed by Israelis, and 368 killed by Palestinians. Israeli casualties are 2,880 soldiers wounded, 10 soldiers killed, 1,189 civilians wounded, and 12 civilians killed. Palestinians held in administrative detention without charges number 1,076. Palestinians in prison for *intifada* crimes number 9,840.

A. General History	B. Jews in North and South America	C. Jews in Europe	D. Jews in the Middle East and Elsewhere	E. Jewish Culture	
		Europa, Europa, a French–German film by Angieszka Holland,* tells the astonishing true story of how Solomon Perel, German Jewish teenager, survives the Holocaust. It includes his experience as a member of the Hitler Youth. Polish filmmaker Andrzej Wajda* produces *Korczak*, the story of Janusz Korczak (Henryk Goldsmit, 1878–1942). An assimilated Jewish doctor, he refuses to flee the Warsaw ghetto and stays to care for 200 Jewish orphan children. He goes with them to death at Treblinka. The film is criticized by Claude Lanzmann, who questions why it omits any mention of Polish complicity with the Nazis during the Holocaust.		Neil Simon, U.S. playwright, writes *Lost in Yonkers*, set in an apartment over a candy store, where the ruthless will-to-live philosophy of Grandma Kurnitz is juxtaposed against the need for love and understanding of her children and grandchildren. The play opens 30 years after his first Broadway show, *Come Blow Your Horn*. In between, there have been 24 other openings, including two revivals. Joseph Brodsky, Russian poet exiled from the Soviet Union in 1972, is named the fifth poet laureate of the U.S. He is the first foreign-born poet to be named laureate. He won the Nobel Prize in literature in 1987.	1991
PLO leader Yasir Arafat* addresses a rally in Baghdad and asserts that if the U.S. and its allies want to fight, "then, I say welcome, welcome, welcome to war. . . . Iraq and Palestine would be 'together, side by side.' On January 8, President George Bush* asks the U.S. Congress to authorize		Israel opens a consulate in Moscow nearly 24 years after the Soviet Union severed ties in the aftermath of the Six-Day War.	After a futile meeting with U.S. Secretary of State James A. Baker,* Iraqi Foreign Minister Tariq Aziz* asserts that Iraq will attack Israel if a war starts in the Persian Gulf. President George Bush* sends a mission headed by Deputy Secretary of State Lawrence Eagleburger* to Israel	The Jewish Museum in New York exhibits *Painting a Place in America: Jewish Artists in New York, 1900–1945*. It traces the experience of immigrant and first-generation American Jewish artists and surveys their impact on American art. Included in the exhibit are works by Louise Nevelson, Mark Rothko, Ben	Jan. 1991

A. General History	B. Jews in North and South America	C. Jews in Europe	D. Jews in the Middle East and Elsewhere	E. Jewish Culture
Jan. 1991	the "use of all necessary means" to get Iraqi forces out of Kuwait. On January 12, the U.S. Congress votes to give President George Bush* authority to send U.S. troops into combat to drive Iraqi forces from Kuwait. On January 16, after the expiration of the January 15 UN deadline for Iraqi withdrawal, the U.S. and Allied forces go to war against Iraq. Air attacks are launched on targets in Iraq and Kuwait. President George Bush* states, "The liberation of Kuwait has begun. . . . We are determined to knock out Saddam Hussein's nuclear bomb potential. We will destroy his chemical weapons facilities." From Iraq's invasion of Kuwait until the Allied attack of January 16 more than 1.5 million people left Iraq, Kuwait, and the other Persian Gulf countries, including 250,000 Jordanians and Palestinians, 30,000 of whom fled to Israeli occupied territories. South Africa's President F. W. de Klerk* announces that he will introduce legislation repealing the "remnants of racially discriminatory legislation which have become known as the cornerstones of apartheid."		to urge it to stay out of the conflict and to inform Israel that the U.S. will attempt to protect it from Iraqi attack if war breaks out. Earlier, Bush* asked Israel not to undertake a preemptive action against Iraq and Israel agreed. Two PLO officials, including Abu Iyad,* considered the second highest PLO official after Yasir Arafat,* are assassinated in Tunis. The PLO blames Israel, but other reports indicate the shootings were on orders of Iraq and carried out by the Abu Nidal* Palestinian group. On January 18, Iraq launches a SCUD missile attack against Israel. Eight missiles are fired. Casualties and damage are light. The next day, Iraq launches a second SCUD attack against Israel. President George Bush* telephones Israeli Prime Minister Yitzhak Shamir. Bush urges Israeli restraint and hopes Israel will let the U.S. retaliate on its behalf. The U.S. rushes Patriot antimissile batteries to Israel, which are manned by U.S. soldiers. Germany begins delivering $670 million in military aid to Israel, which includes gas masks, gas-proof vehicles, and poison gas antidotes. An Israeli defense spokesman comments, "I think everyone can understand why the Germans are offering us this aid. . . . We are hearing every day about the aid given by German elements . . . to the Iraqi ability to	Shahn, Raphael Soyer, and Max Weber. The Tel Aviv Museum of Art exhibits In the Flower of Youth: Maurycy Gottlieb, 1856–1879. Despite his death at age 23, Gottlieb became a celebrated painter in Poland and among Jewish circles in eastern Europe during his lifetime. Many of his works were destroyed by the Nazis. The exhibit is shown also at the Warsaw National Museum. The Israel Museum exhibits The Jewish Art of Solomon Yudovin (1892–1954): From Folk Art to Socialist Realism. He traveled as a recorder with the famous Anski Jewish ethnographic expedition through the Pale of Settlement between 1911 and 1914 and kept painting Jewish themes throughout his career. The 100 or so items on view are from the collection of Tsilya Menjeritsky, a recent Russian refusnik immigrant. Seven murals painted by Marc Chagall in Moscow in 1920 and 1921, for the Moscow Jewish Art Theatre, depicting the Jewish life of his youth in Vitebsk, are exhibited in a museum in Martigny, Switzerland. They were banned by Joseph Stalin* as formalist non-Socialist art. They will go on exhibition in Moscow and Leningrad. David Mamet, U.S. playwright and filmmaker, writes and directs Homocide, the story of Bobby Gold, an assimilated Jewish cop and his search for

A. General History	B. Jews in North and South America	C. Jews in Europe	D. Jews in the Middle East and Elsewhere	E. Jewish Culture	
			fire missiles at Israel and to Iraq's chemical warfare capability."	his Jewish identity as he becomes involved in solving the murder of an old Jewish woman who ran a pawn shop in an urban ghetto.	**Jan. 1991**
Jordan's King Hussein* abandons neutrality and aligns himself with Iraq in the Gulf War. "This war is a war against all Arabs and all Muslims and not against Iraq alone." On February 23, thousands of Allied troops led by U.S. General H. Norman Schwarzkopf* drive into Kuwait to oust Iraqi forces. They meet little resistance and capture thousands of Iraqi soldiers. Iraq sets fire to about one-half of Kuwait's 1,000 oil wells. On February 27, U.S. President George Bush* declares victory and orders a halt to the offensive in the Gulf War. He declares, "Iraq's army is defeated, our military objectives are met." It is later estimated that 100,000 Iraqis have been killed and 300,000 wounded. On March 3, Iraq will accept terms set by the U.S.-led coalition and the UN to end the war.			The U.S. releases $400 million of loan guarantees to Israel for the construction of housing for Soviet immigrants. The U.S. had held up the guarantees for more than a year to obtain assurances the money would not be spent on settlements in the West Bank and Gaza strip. On February 25, Iraq launches its 39th and last SCUD missile attack on Israel. In these attacks, one person was killed by a missile, 12 died indirectly, and nearly 200 were injured; 4,095 buildings were damaged, and 1,644 families were evacuated from Tel Aviv and Ramat Gan.	Nadine Gordimer (b. 1923), South African novelist, is awarded the Nobel Prize in literature. South Africa's President F. W. de Klerk* calls the award "an honor to South Africa." Her novels and short stories portray the trauma of racial segregation. Several were banned by the South African government.	**Feb. 1991**
Walter H. Annenberg, U.S. publisher, announces he will bequeath $1 billion of paintings, including works by Manet,* Monet,* Renoir,* Degas,* Cézanne,* Van Gogh,* and Picasso,* to the Metropolitan Museum of Art upon his death. In the aftermath of the Gulf War, Iraq suppresses rebellions of Shiites in the south and Kurds in the north, as the U.S. adopts a hands-off policy. In late March and early April, UN sources report that 1.5		Lech Walesa,* president of Poland, in a meeting with Jewish leaders in New York, concedes there has been a resurgence of antisemitism in Poland. "Though this is just a marginal part of life, I am ashamed of it. As long as I have anything to say in Poland, I will oppose antisemitism."	The U.S. grants Israel $600 million in cash aid to help cover its increased military and civil defense costs incurred as a result of the Gulf War. In an address to Congress, U.S. President George Bush* says the Gulf War illustrates that "geography cannot guarantee security" and "a comprehensive peace must be grounded in U.N. Security Council Resolutions 242 and 338 and the principle of territory for peace. . . . The time		**Mar. 1991**

	A. General History	B. Jews in North and South America	C. Jews in Europe	D. Jews in the Middle East and Elsewhere	E. Jewish Culture
Mar. 1991	million Kurds flee Iraq to Turkey and Iran. Lebanon's government orders Palestinian and Lebanese militias to disarm by the end of April. The government warns that the Lebanese army, supported by 40,000 Syrian troops stationed in Lebanon, will enforce the order.			has come to put an end to Arab-Israeli conflict." During the week of March 10, U.S. Secretary of State James A. Baker* meets with the foreign ministers of Egypt, Syria, Saudi Arabia, Kuwait, Qatar, Bahrain, Oman, and the United Arab Emirates, in Saudi Arabia, with Israeli Prime Minister Yitzhak Shamir and with Palestinian leaders in an effort to encourage peace negotiations. Israeli Air Force Brigadier General Rami Dotan pleads guilty to taking $10 million in kickbacks on the purchase of U.S. military equipment. He is sentenced to 13 years in prison.	
May 1991	The *New York Times* reports that Kuwait has decided not to allow 170,000 Palestinians who lived in Kuwait and fled the Iraqi invasion to return. Before the Iraqi invasion there were about 320,000 Palestinians living in Kuwait. Many Kuwaitis believe the Palestinians betrayed the country that harbored them. Ninety percent of Croats vote for independence from the Yugoslav federation. The Soviet Parliament passes a law to take effect in 1993 that would allow citizens unhindered travel and emigration. Ethiopia's Marxist leader, Mengistu Haile Mariam,* quits and flees into exile. Eight days later rebels		Addressing Israel's Knesset, Poland's President Lech Walesa* apologizes for antisemitism in Poland's history. "Here in Israel, the land of your culture and revival, I ask for your forgiveness." Israeli Prime Minister Yitzhak Shamir says he hopes the first visit to Israel by a Polish president would ease Polish–Israeli relations.	U.S. Secretary of State James A. Baker* drives from Amman, Jordan to Jerusalem. The trip takes about 90 minutes. Baker* says, "You realize when you drive like that . . . just how short the distances are and how important, therefore, it is to promote peaceful co-existence." Testifying before Congress, U.S. Secretary of State James A. Baker says, "Nothing has made my job of trying to find Arab and Palestinian partners for Israel more difficult than being greeted by a new [West Bank] settlement every time I arrive" in the Middle East. Israeli aircraft begin airlifting 14,000 Ethiopian Jews from Addis Ababa to Israel. The airlift is	

A. General History	B. Jews in North and South America	C. Jews in Europe	D. Jews in the Middle East and Elsewhere	E. Jewish Culture	
will seize Addis Ababa, the capital.

Syria and Lebanon sign a treaty providing for close cooperation in matters of security, commerce, foreign policy, and education that some experts say amounts to Syrian annexation of Lebanon.

The U.S. and its allies agree to forgive one-half of the $20.2 billion that Egypt owes them.

U.S. President George Bush* proposes a plan to control weapons in the Middle East. The plan would ban chemical and biological weapons, end sales and production of surface-to-surface missiles, and block the introduction of new nuclear weapons. | | | completed in 36 hours. Afterward, Israel confirms that it paid the Marxist government $35 million for the release of the Ethiopian Jews.

The *Wall Street Journal* reports, "Though [President Bush's] plan doesn't single out Israel, it would have the effect of requiring Jerusalem to end its production of nuclear weapons." | | **May 1991** |
| Boris Yeltsin,* Russian political and economic reformer, is elected president of the Russian republic, defeating a Communist party opponent.

An Iraqi defector supplies information to the UN that Iraq has hidden a substantial amount of nuclear materials. The UN orders new inspections.

South Africa's Parliament repeals the Population Registration Act, the legal foundation of apartheid. | The Council of Jewish Federations reports the results of the National Jewish Population Survey of 1990, the broadest national survey of American Jews ever undertaken. It reports 5.5 million core Jews (i.e., those who consider themselves Jews by religion or secular Jews). There is increasing acceptance of intermarriage. Since 1985, Jews married other Jews—including converts to Judaism—48% of the time. This compares to 91% before 1965. | | | | **June 1991** |
| The Warsaw Pact disbands. For 36 years this military alliance bound the Communist regimes of the Soviet Union and eastern Europe.

Iraq admits it had an extensive, secret program for making | | U.S. Assistant Secretary of State Richard Schifter and Elie Wiesel, in Romania to dedicate a memorial to the 400,000 Romanian Jews who were killed in World War II, visit Jassy, the scene of a pogrom in June 1941 | Israeli Judge Ezra Kama concludes an inquiry on last October's Temple Mount riot and finds that the violence was not planned by either side; the rioting started after a tear gas grenade was accidentally dropped | | **July 1991** |

	A. General History	B. Jews in North and South America	C. Jews in Europe	D. Jews in the Middle East and Elsewhere	E. Jewish Culture
July 1991	nuclear weapons, in violation of the nuclear nonproliferation treaty to which it is a signatory. A curfew imposed by the army in Algeria throughout the country since early June is lifted. In June, Islamic fundamentalist opposition provoked a series of strikes and demonstrations resulting in about 60 deaths. Algeria is burdened with a 30% unemployment rate, a 20% inflation rate, and $26 billion in debts. UN weapons specialists report that Iraq possesses four times the chemical weapons it admitted to earlier.		that took the lives of 8,000 Jews. They express U.S. and American Jewish concerns about the Romanian Parliament's rehabilitation of Ion Antonescu,* who initiated mass killings. There are estimated to be 20,000 Jews in Romania.	by a policeman and rolled toward the demonstrators, who then threw stones at police and Jewish worshippers at the Western Wall. He finds that the police fired at random without reasonable care. His findings contradict an earlier Israeli government report. U.S. President George Bush* and Soviet President Mikhail Gorbachev* issue a joint statement in Moscow reaffirming "their strong mutual commitment to promote peace and genuine reconciliation among the Arab states, Israel and the Palestinians." They add that peace can only result from direct negotiations between the parties.	
Aug. 1991	On August 19, Soviet President Gorbachev* is ousted from power as the result of a coup dominated by the KGB, the military, and hard-line Communist leaders. Two days later, the coup fails as Russian President Boris Yeltsin* leads the popular resistance. Mikhail Gorbachev* returns to Moscow to resume power. Communism as an ideological and political force is defeated, and on August 23, Gorbachev* resigns as head of the Communist party. On August 25, Estonia Latvia, Lithuania, the Ukraine, and Byelorussia declare independence. On August 29, the Supreme Soviet bans communists from all political activity in the Soviet Union. General Michel Aoun,* Christian army	In New York, African-Americans riot in Brooklyn's Crown Heights neighborhood after a car driven by a Lubavitch Hasid accidentally kills a seven-year-old child, Gavin Cato. Yankel Rosenbaum, an Australian Hasid, is accosted and stabbed by a gang of African-American youths. He later dies. The unrest continues for several days.		Albania and Israel agree to establish diplomatic relations. In April, most of Albania's Jewish population secretly emigrated to Israel.	

Population of Jerusalem, 1844–1990

Year	Total	Jews	Non-Jews	% Jews
1844	15,510	7,120	8,390	45.9
1876	25,030	12,000	13,030	47.9
1896	45,420	28,122	17,298	61.9
1905	60,000	40,000	20,000	66.6
1913	75,200	48,400	26,800	64.3
1922	62,578	33,971	28,607	54.3
1931	90,053	51,222	38,831	56.6
1948	165,000	100,000	65,000	60.6
1967	263,309	195,000	68,309	74.3
1977	376,000	272,300	103,700	72.4
1985	457,700	328,000	129,700	71.7
1990	493,500	353,900	139,600	71.7

A. General History	B. Jews in North and South America	C. Jews in Europe	D. Jews in the Middle East and Elsewhere	E. Jewish Culture
leader of the fight to drive Syrian forces out of Lebanon, is granted asylum in France under a special pardon by the Lebanese government.				**Aug. 1991**
Lebanon and Syria sign an accord ensuring daily coordination of military and security matters. The U.S. officially recognizes the independence of Lithuania, Latvia, and Estonia. The Soviet legislature dissolves itself and sets up a transitional government dominated by the republics. It passes a human rights declaration that promises equality, privacy, freedom of speech and religion, and free choice of work. Saudi Arabia's UN representative, Samir Shihabi,* is elected president of the General Assembly. Born in Jerusalem in 1925, he joined the Saudi foreign service in 1949, after studying law at Yale and Cambridge University. The Huntington Library in California, which photographed the complete Dead Sea Scrolls in 1980, decides to make them immediately available without restriction to all researchers. The scrolls had been under the exclusive control of a small number of researchers for decades. The UN Security Council imposes an arms embargo against Yugoslavia, calling for an end to the civil war raging throughout the country.			At a press conference, U.S. President George Bush* demands that Congress delay for four months the debate regarding Israel's request for $10 billion in housing loan guarantees to resettle newly arrived Soviet Jews until after a Middle East peace conference scheduled for October. "I'm up against some powerful political forces, . . . something like a thousand lobbyists on the Hill . . . We've got one lonely little guy down here doing it." Congress agrees to the delay. U.S. President George Bush* writes to the president of the Conference of Major Jewish Organizations. "I am concerned that some of my comments at the Thursday press conference caused apprehension within the Jewish community. My reference to lobbyists and powerful political forces were never meant to be pejorative in any sense." It is reported that Bush* was alarmed by the antisemitic tone of some of the supportive letters and phone messages he received. In a speech at the UN General Assembly, U.S. President George Bush* urges the repeal of its 1975 resolution equating Zionism with racism. "This body cannot claim to seek peace and at the same time challenge Israel's right to exist." The Soviet Union supports	**Sep. 1991**

	A. General History	B. Jews in North and South America	C. Jews in Europe	D. Jews in the Middle East and Elsewhere	E. Jewish Culture
Sep. 1991				Bush's* call for a repeal.	
Oct. 1991	A UN team of nuclear arms inspectors reports, "Contrary to Iraq's claims . . . the team found documents showing that Iraq had been working on a nuclear weapons design and a surface-to-surface missile project intended, presumably, as a delivery system for the weapon." UN inspectors locate 16 previously undeclared SCUD missile sites in western Iraq. U.S. intelligence officials acknowledge that Allied forces failed to destroy two important Iraqi nuclear weapons installations during the Gulf War.		Soviet President Mikhail Gorbachev* condemns antisemitism in a statement issued at Babi Yar, commemorating the killings of thousands of Jews by the Nazis 50 years ago. He acknowledges that hatred of Jews still exists in the nation's "everyday life," and he regrets the hundreds of thousands of "gifted and enterprising citizens" now emigrating because of it. Lithuania suspends the rehabilitation of thousands of people who were sentenced by Soviet courts after World War II on war crimes charges. A Lithuanian Supreme Court judge discovered that several exonerations of people convicted of killing Jews were unjustified.	The U.S. and the Soviet Union invite Israel, Egypt, Jordan, Syria, Lebanon, and Faisal al-Husseini,* a Palestinian leader in the occupied territories, to a peace conference to begin on October 30 at Madrid, Spain. Israel and the Soviet Union restore full diplomatic relations. Israel, Jordan, Syria, Lebanon, Egypt, and representatives of the Palestinians meet for peace talks in Madrid, Spain. U.S. President George Bush* addresses the conference and tells the Israelis "territorial compromise is essential for peace" and tells Arabs "it is not simply to end the state of war in the Middle East and replace it with a state of nonbelligerency. . . . We seek peace, real peace. And by real peace I mean treaties. Security. Diplomatic relations. Economic relations. Trade. Investment. Cultural exchange. Even tourism."	
Dec. 1991	The Soviet Union dissolves. Mikhail Gorbachev* resigns as president. Eleven former republics constitute themselves as the Commonwealth of Independent States. Estonia, Latvia, Lithuania, and Georgia do not participate. The first free parliamentary elections are held in Algeria. The Islamic Salvation Front, a militant Muslim fundamentalist movement, wins by a wide plurality. Its objective is to turn	A New York Supreme Court jury acquits El Sayid A. Nosair* of murdering Meir Kahane. Nosair* is convicted of assault and weapons possession.		Arab–Israeli peace talks begin in Washington, D.C., with the Israelis meeting with separate Lebanese, Syrian, and joint Palestinian–Jordanian groups. They adjourn eight days later after a failure to advance the discussions beyond procedures and agendas. The talks are scheduled to resume in January 1992. The UN General Assembly revokes Resolution 3379, the 1975 "Zionism is racism" resolution, by a vote of 111 to 25	

Algeria into an Islamic republic in the Iranian mold.

Roll-Call at U.N. on Zionism Issue

Special to The New York Times

UNITED NATIONS, Dec. 16 —Following is the 111-to-25 roll-call vote today by which the General Assembly adopted a resolution revoking the 1975 resolution equating Zionism with racism:

IN FAVOR—111

Albania	Kenya
Antigua & Barbuda	Latvia
	Lesotho
Argentina	Liberia
Australia	Liechtenstein
Austria	Lithuania
Bahamas	Luxembourg
Barbados	Madagascar
Belgium	Malawi
Belize	Maita
Benin	Marshall Islands
Bhutan	Mexico
Bolivia	Micronesia
Botswana	Mongolia
Brazil	Mozambique
Britain	Namibia
Bulgaria	Nepal
Burundi	Netherlands
Byelorussia	New Guinea
Cambodia	New Zealand
Cameroon	Nicaragua
Canada	Nigeria
Cape Verde	Norway
Central African Republic	Panama
	Papua
Chile	Paraguay
Colombia	Peru
Congo	Phillippines
Costa Rica	Poland
Cyprus	Portugal
Czechoslovakia	Romania
Denmark	Rwanda
Dominica	St. Kitts & Nevis
Dominican Republic	St. Lucia
Ecuador	St. Vincent
El Salvador	& the Grenadines
Estonia	Samoa
Fiji	Sao Tome
Finland	& Principe
France	Seychelles
Gabon	Sierra Leone
Gambia	Singapore
Germany	Solomon Islands
Greece	Soviet Union
Grenada	Spain
Guatemala	South Korea
Guyana	Suriname
Haiti	Swaziland
Honduras	Sweden
Hungary	Thailand
Iceland	Togo
India	Ukraine
Ireland	United States
Israel	Uruguay
Italy	Venezuela
Ivory Coast	Yugoslavia
Jamaica	Zaire
Japan	Zambia

AGAINST—25

Afghanistan	Mauritania
Algeria	North Korea
Bangladesh	Pakistan
Brunei	Qatar
Cuba	Saudi Arabia
Indonesia	Somalia
Iran	Sri Lanka
Iraq	Sudan
Jordan	Syria
Lebanon	United Arab
Libya	Emirates
Malaysia	Vietnam
Mali	Yemen

ABSTENTIONS—13

Angola	Myanmar
Burkina Faso	Tanzania
Ethiopia	Trinidad-Tobago
Ghana	Turkey
Laos	Uganda
Maldives	Zimbabwe
Mauritius	

ABSENT OR NOT VOTING—17

Bahrain	Kuwait
Chad	Morocco
China	Niger
Comoros	Oman
Djibouti	Senegal
Egypt	South Africa
Equatorial Guinea	Tunisia
Guinea	Vanuatu
Guinea-Bissau	

---

with 13 abstentions. The repeal resolution is sprearheaded by the U.S. and cosponsored by 85 countries, including the Soviet Union. It is only the second time that the General Assembly has overturned one of its own resolutions.

GLOSSARY

Adonai: The traditional Jewish pronunciation of the personal name of God, the tetragrammaton, YHWH (*see below*). During the Second Temple period, Jews treated the sacred name YHWH as unsayable and stipulated that it be read "Adonai," meaning "my Lord."

Aggadah: Nonlegal rabbinic interpretation, or *midrash*, of the Bible including homilies, stories elaborating Scripture, stories about rabbis, and other genres.

Agudat Israel: The Orthodox Jewish political movement organized in 1912 in Europe, seeking to sustain the values of traditional eastern European Jewry. The Agudah, as it is known, became the major religious political bloc within the Israeli government in 1948.

Agunah: A woman who does not receive a Jewish bill of divorce (*get*) from her husband either because he is missing or because he refuses to grant it to her when their marriage otherwise dissolves. According to *halakhah*, she may not remarry.

Ahdut ha-Avodah: The Zionist Labor movement seeking to unite workers founded in Palestine in 1919. In 1965 it joined the Labor party coalition in the Israeli government.

Aktion: A Nazi euphemism for the operation of rounding up, transporting, and murdering European Jews during the Shoah.

Aleinu: An early rabbinic prayer affirming acceptance of the Jewish covenant with God and looking toward the perfection of the world through universal recognition of God's kingship. Originally part of the New Year service, *Aleinu* came to be used at the end of nearly every prayer service.

Aliyah: (1) Immigration to Israel, derived from the term for "going up" to Jerusalem. It refers to each wave of immigration, beginning in 1882. (2) "Going up" to the Torah when it is publicly read, an honor given to individuals during a synagogue service.

Amidah: The central prayer of every Jewish service, named for the "standing" position in which it is said. The daily *Amidah* includes 19 (originally 18) blessings; the holiday versions contain fewer because they exclude personal petitions.

Amora: The Aramaic term for a rabbinic scholar of the post-Mishnah generations, from the 3rd through the end of the 5th centuries, quoted in the Palestinian or Babylonian Talmud. It means "expounder."

Anusim: Jews "forced" into Christianity throughout the Middle Ages, especially in Spain and Portugal, where many continued practicing Judaism in secret as Marranos.

Apocrypha: The corpus of Jewish books from the period between the Hebrew Bible and the Christian Scriptures. Excluded from the Jewish canon, the Apocrypha, or some of it, is included in some Christian Bibles.

Arenda: "Leasing" to individuals of various fixed assets or prerogatives, such as land, industries, and tax collection, by the authorities in Poland and Lithuania. In the 16th century the Polish government, pressured by Gentiles competing for such leases, prohibited Jews from receiving them.

Aron ha-Kodesh: The holy ark in which Torah scrolls are held in the synagogue, based on the sacred box in which the two stone tables of the covenant were placed by Moses in biblical tradition.

Ashkenaz: The Jewish name first applied in the 9th century to the area of Franco-Germany and later Poland, too. It is derived from the Bible. It will be contrasted with Sepharad, the Jewish name for Spain, the other major community of European Jews.

Astral cult: The worship of the sun, moon, and/or stars, characteristic of ancient Israel's pagan neighbors, explicitly forbidden in Deuteronomy.

Atonement, Day of: The solemn day for expurgating the sins of the Jewish people, observed on the 10th day of the New Year, known in Hebrew as Yom ha-Kippurim.

Auto-da-fé: The Portuguese term for "act of faith," referring to the exposure of Christian heretics, many of them converted Jews, during the Church's Inquisition.

Badhan: The Hebrew term for "jester," an entertainer at Jewish weddings and other festivities, from the talmudic period on.

Bar: Aramaic for "son" (ben in Hebrew), used in the names of many Jews in Greco-Roman times.

Bar mitzvah: Coming of age for a Jewish boy at age 13, at which time he becomes fully responsible for performing the commandments (*mitzvot*). Traditionally the event is marked by calling the bar mitzvah to the Torah in the synagogue.

Bat: Hebrew for "daughter," used in forming traditional Jewish names (e.g., Esther bat Avihayil).

Bat mitzvah: Coming of age for a Jewish girl, traditionally at age 12 but among liberal Jews at 13, at which time she becomes fully responsible for performing the commandments (*mitzvot*). The event is marked in various ways in most synagogues, beginning in the mid-20th century.

Ben: Hebrew for "son," used in forming traditional Jewish names (e.g., David ben Yishai).

Beraitot (sg., beraita): Rabbinic statements from the period of the Mishnah that are not quoted in Rabbi Judah ha-Nasi's Mishnah. The Aramaic term means "the ones outside."

Berakhah: The formula acknowledging God as the source of one's blessing, ordinarily rendered "blessing, benediction."

Berit Shalom: An organization founded in 1925 to promote a binational Arab–Jewish state in Palestine. Called "Covenant of Peace," the group dissolved during the tense 1930s.

Betar: A right-wing Zionist youth organization formed in 1923 named for the Jewish fortress holding out against the Romans. It is associated with the Herut (freedom) movement in Israel, now centered in the Likud party.

Bet Din: The Hebrew term for a "house of judgment," a rabbinic court.

Bet ha-midrash: A traditional "house of study," harking back to Roman times.

Bilu: A movement of eastern European Jews in the first aliyah (immigration wave) to Israel in 1882 named for the initials of a Biblical phrase meaning "House of Jacob, come, let us go."

Bimah: A platform in the center or front of a synagogue on which the Torah is read. (*See also* Aliyah, definition 2.)

Black Hundreds: Gangs of czarist Russians organized to attack Jews and revolutionaries, responsible for the pogroms of 1905.

Black September: A terrorist group connected to the Palestine Liberation Organization responsible for the massacre of Israeli athletes at the 1972 Olympic Games in Munich and other acts.

Blood libel: Spurious accusation that Jews murder a Gentile child to obtain ritual blood, especially for Passover matzah.

Bund: A political organization of Jews formed in Vilna in 1897 to promote labor causes, Jewish nationalism, and Yiddish in eastern Europe and opposed to Zionism.

Caliph: The Anglicized form of the Arabic term for a ruler, literally "deputy" of God.

Cherubim: A biblical term for compound creatures including the body of a bull or lion, wings of an eagle, and head of a man. Such winged sphinxes serve as guards or pedestals for deities and kings in the ancient Near East in general, as well as for Israel's God in the biblical tabernacle and temple.

Circumcision: The removal of the foreskin of the male organ, practiced in Judaism on all males, on the eighth day of birth or at the time of conversion, symbolizing the covenant between God and the Jewish people and accordingly called *berit milah* (covenant of circumcision).

Cohen (or kohen): A priest descended from the tribe of Levi. In traditional Judaism, *kohanim* (pl.) serve certain ritual functions.

Conservative Judaism: An American religious movement begun in the early 20th century to promote the conservation of tradition at the same time as change to adapt tradition to modernity. An Israeli offshoot called Masorti Judaism seeks to provide a "traditional" religious alternative to Orthodoxy.

Consistory: The term given by Napoleon in 1808 to the umbrella organization of Jewish religious institutions in France.

Conversos: Jews "converted" to Christianity in Spain and Portugal during the Middle Ages. Some continued to practice Judaism in secret.

Cossacks: A Ukrainian group of paramilitary horsemen who attacked Jews in Russia and Poland in the 17th century.

Council of the Four Lands: The Jewish self-governing body in Russia–Poland originating in the 16th century. Named for the four regions of Major Poland, Minor Poland, Red Russia, and Lithuania, it was called in Hebrew Va'ad Arba Aratzot.

Court Jew: Beginning in the 16th century, European rulers would often name a Jew to the court to assist the government in matters of taxation and finance.

Crypto-Jew: A Jew formally converted to another religion but secretly practicing Judaism; the best-known instance is the Marranos of late medieval Spain.

Cuneiform: The writing developed in Mesopotamia by pressing a cut reed stylus into wet clay. Signs are made through conventional patterns of wedge-shaped impressions that originally imitated line-drawn pictures.

Dayyan: "Judge" in a rabbinic court. (*See Bet Din.*)

Dead Sea Scrolls: Scrolls and fragments of parchment found in caves above the northwest shore of the Dead Sea. They contain texts of the Hebrew Bible as well as original works preserved and copied by a community of Jews who lived there in Roman times.

Derash: The rabbinic interpretive method of "searching" Scripture for esoteric and/or traditional meaning. (*See also Midrash.*)

Desecration of the Host: A libel

leveled by medieval Christians against Jews alleging that Jews had desecrated the bread that Christians believed had become in the Eucharist the body of Jesus. As in cases of blood libel (*see above*), Christians would often attack Jews on the basis of the charge.

Dhimma: Arabic term for "protection" that non-Muslims must pay to live securely under Muslim rule. *Dhimmi* are the protected people.

Diaspora: An overall term designating the aggregate of Jewish communities living outside the land of Israel. Because such communities often originated through an expulsion from Israel, the term is Greek for "dispersion."

Disputation: An argument over doctrine, grounded in the interpretation of Scripture, between Christian groups or between Christians and Jews, especially in the medieval period.

Dybbuk: In medieval Jewish mysticism, a dead, sinful soul "clinging" to and often tormenting the body of a living person.

Einsatzgruppen: Nazi "mobile" killer "units" in areas occupied during World War II.

Emancipation: The extension of fundamental civil rights to Jews in Europe beginning in the early 19th century.

Eretz Israel: The "Land of Israel," the biblical name for what is later sometimes called Palestine.

Eruv: The technical means of overcoming a certain restriction in rabbinic law, especially erecting a fence around a community allowing Jews to carry within this artificially constructed private domain on the Sabbath.

Etrog: A citron. Fruit taken in hand with the palm branch (*lulav*) in celebrating the festival of Sukkot (Booths).

Essenes: Groups of Jews living in exclusive communities in Israel under Rome and preparing for the Messiah. The community that preserved the Dead Sea Scrolls may have been Essene.

Exegesis: The process of drawing meaning out of a text, used primarily regarding Scripture.

Exilarch: The title of the appointed head of the Babylonian Jewish community in the first millennium CE, *resh galuta* (head of the exile) in Aramaic. Tradition had it that the exilarch was descended from King David.

Fatah: The Arabic acronym for Palestine Liberation movement, formed by Palestinians in Kuwait in the 1950s. After the Six-Day War in 1967, al-Fatah, led by Yasir Arafat,* became the major component of the Palestine Liberation Organization (*see below*).

Fedayeen: The Arabic term for the "self-sacrificing" Arab terrorists infiltrating Israel in the 1950s.

Final solution: The Nazi euphemism for the extermination of the Jewish people.

Frankists: The followers of the Sabbatean (*see below*) false messiah of the 18th century, Jacob Frank.

An antinomian European Jewish sect some of whom sought acceptance within the Christian church.

Gabbai: The "collector" of taxes and charity within the Jewish communities of the talmudic era and later the title of a synagogue official, particularly one who dispenses aliyot to the Torah.

Gahal: The Hebrew acronym for the Bloc of Herut–Likud, the major right-wing Israeli political party organized in 1965.

Galut: The Hebrew term for "exile," used abstractly for alienation of the Jewish people and God from one another and concretely for the removal of the Jews from the land of Israel from biblical through modern times.

Gaon, geonic: The *gaon*, or eminent one, was the head or dean of a rabbinical academy in Babylonia from the 6th through the 11th centuries. After the Talmud was edited, the various *geonim* decided questions of Jewish law based on its traditions.

Gemara: The edited commentary on and discussion of the Mishnah incorporated into the Palestinian and Babylonian Talmuds. The term is Aramaic for "learning."

Gematria: An ancient method of interpretation by which the letters of a Hebrew word are decoded according to an assigned numerical value and then equated with another word of the same numerical value. The term is probably derived from the Greek "gamma = tria" (the third letter of the alphabet = three).

Genizah: The "store room" of a synagogue used since the early Middle Ages for discarding unused Hebrew books and documents. *The Genizah* is the rich mine of medieval source material discovered in the late 19th century in the synagogue of Old Cairo.

Get: Aramaic for "document," specifically a Jewish bill of divorce.

Ghetto: Originally a walled quarter of a city in which all Jews were compelled to live; the first such ghetto was that in Venice in 1516. Recently, it refers to any urban area with a particular ethnic concentration.

Golem: Legendary "lump" brought to life as an artificial man by mystical magic, especially a formula containing names of God. The classic story of the Maharal of Prague's golem was to have taken place at the turn of the 17th century.

Gush Emunim: "Bloc of the Faithful," an ultranationalist religious organization formed in Israel in 1974 for the purpose of establishing permanent Jewish control over the territory occupied by Israel in 1967.

Ha'avara: A business company set up in 1933 to "transfer" German Jews' capital from Nazi Germany to Palestine in the form of trade goods and thereby facilitate Jewish emigration.

Habad Hasidism: Hasidism fol-

lowing the teaching of Rabbi Shneur Zalman of Ladi, who emphasized the intellectual as well as the emotional. Habad, a Hebrew acronym for "wisdom, understanding, and knowledge," is embodied in the Lubavitch Hasidim, a large worldwide group best known for its efforts to get nonobservant Jews to adopt traditional observances.

Habimah: "The Stage," Jewish theater group originating in Moscow in 1917 and evolving into the national Israeli theater company, based in Tel Aviv.

Hadas: The Hebrew term for the "myrtle" branches taken in hand as one of the four species with which one celebrates the festival of Sukkot (Booths).

Hadassah: The Women's Zionist Organization of America, founded in 1912 by Henrietta (Hadassah) Szold and named for her in 1914. Active in providing medical and educational services to Israel, it is the largest Zionist organization.

Haftarah: The prophetic selection chanted at the "conclusion" of the reading of the Torah on the Sabbath and festivals.

Haganah: The clandestine Jewish defense organization set up in Palestine in 1920 under the British mandate. With the establishment of the State of Israel, it was developed into the Israeli Defense Forces, the state's army.

Haggadah: The "narration" of the Exodus at the Passover meal, the seder (*see below*). The book incorporating the entire liturgy of the seder comes to be called the Haggadah.

Hakham: Originally a functionary of the medieval rabbinic court, the "sage" became the title of the rabbinic leader of a Sephardic (*see below*) Jewish community.

Halakhah: Traditional Jewish law based on rabbinic interpretation (*midrash*) of the Bible and later decided on the basis of rabbinic codes and precedents.

Halitzah: The ceremony of "removing" the shoe of a man who refuses to obey Jewish law and marry the widow of his brother when that union produced no offspring.

Hallel: The service recited preceding the Torah reading on festivals comprised of the series of Psalms 113 through 118.

Halukkah: The "distribution" of funds collected from Diaspora Jews for the support of Jewish settlers in the land of Israel in the centuries preceding the modern Zionist movement.

Halutzim: The "pioneers" who settled and especially farmed the land of Israel from 1882 through the 1930s.

Hametz: "Leavened" foods, mainly baked goods, that are traditionally forbidden during the festival of Pesah (Passover).

Hannukah: The Jewish holiday at the onset of winter commemorating the "rededication" of the Jerusalem Temple by the Maccabees in 165 BCE. It is observed by kindling lights for eight nights in thanksgiving to God for delivering

the few and weak from the hand of the numerous and powerful.

Hashemite: A family that claims direct descent from the Muslim prophet Mohammed and the title given by the British in the 1920s to the kingdoms of Iraq and the Transjordan. The Hashemite dynasty of Iraq was overthrown in 1958: that of Jordan's King Hussein* continues to rule as of this writing.

Ha-Shiloah: The Hebrew periodical established in Russia by the cultural Zionist Ahad ha-Am in 1896 and published until the First World War. The name, referring to the biblical Jerusalem water source Siloam, puns on Hebrew for "dispatch."

Ha-Shomer: "The Watchman," a defense organization of Jewish pioneers in Palestine from 1909 to 1920 forming the core of the Jewish army under the British mandate, the Haganah (*see above*).

Hasidism: The Jewish religious revivalist movement originating in eastern Europe in the late 18th century. It maintains many characteristics of early modern Polish life, including its dress. Diverse sects of Hasidim hail from different towns and follow different leaders, or rebbes (*see below*).

Haskalah: European Jewish "enlightenment," which introduced Jews to modern ways of expression and thought from about 1750 to about 1880.

Haskama: The rabbinic "imprimatur" inserted in a Jewish book, mainly from the 15th century on. At first such approval was advised to avert censorship; later, it was intended to bolster a book's authority.

Hasmonean: The family of the 2nd-century BCE nationalist Jewish priest from Modin, Mattathias, father of Judas (Judah) the Maccabee.

"Hatikvah": The song of the Zionist movement and the national anthem of the State of Israel; Hebrew for "the hope."

Havdalah: The ritual marking the "separation" between the sacred time of the Sabbath or a festival and the work week.

Havurah (pl., havurot): An exclusive Jewish religious community or fellowship in the Roman period. It was revived by traditional progressive American Jews in the 1960s.

Hazzan: The designated cantor in a synagogue; in talmudic times, an administrative synagogue official.

Heder: A traditional "one-room" European Jewish schoolhouse.

Herem: A "ban" of excommunication from the Jewish community imposed occasionally in the Middle Ages.

Herut: The right-wing Israeli political party inspired by Zev Jabotinsky and formed in 1948. (*See also* Gahal.)

Heter Iskah: The Jewish legal arrangement to bypass the biblical prohibition against taking interest from Jews: A creditor and debtor go into limited partnership, enabling the creditor in effect to lend to the debtor at a profit.

Hevrah: A communal committee, popular in Europe, for taking care of Jewish social needs; for example, the *hevrah kadishah* attends to a family's needs concerning burial and mourning.

Hieroglyphic: A writing system representing word concepts and consonants by conventional pictures, first evidenced in Egypt around 3000 BCE.

High Holy Days: The English term for the Days of Awe, Rosh Hashanah (New Year) and Yom Kippur (Day of Atonement), a period of penitence falling around September.

Histadrut: General Federation of Labor organization, founded in 1920, the main labor union in the State of Israel.

Holocaust: The Western term meaning "fully burned" sacrifice, designating the destruction of European Jewry during World War II. The parallel Hebrew term, Sho'ah, means "annihilation."

Hoshana Rabbah: The seventh day of the fall festival of Sukkot (Booths), on which worshippers encircle the synagogue seven times carrying the four species—myrtle, willow, palm, and *etrog*—and reciting hosannas.

Hovevei Zion: "Lovers of Zion," the 19th-century Russian Jewish Zionist movement.

Huppah: A Jewish wedding canopy, and by extension the wedding ceremony itself.

Ice Age: The most recent cycle of ice covering a large part of the globe ended its severe phase around 9000 BCE but is not over yet.

Iggeret: Postbiblical Hebrew for "epistle." It is used for manifesto-like letters written by medieval authorities.

Ihud: "Unity," an unsuccessful group of Jews and Arabs seeking a binational state in Palestine. Founded in 1942 by Judah L. Magnes and other Jewish intellectuals.

Inquisition: The investigation by Christian church officials into whether Jewish converts to Christianity were true to their new faith or were secretly practicing their former religion.

Israel: The name of the ancient Hebrew people, after their ancestor Jacob whose name was changed to "Israel"; later, a name of the Jewish people; since biblical times the name of the land of Israel, selected in 1948 as the name of the newly established Jewish state.

IZL: Pronounced "Eitzel," a Hebrew acronym for the right-wing Jewish underground organization in the British mandate of Palestine— "Irgun Zva'i Le'ummi," the National Military Organization.

JAC: Jewish Anti-Fascist Committee. A group of Soviet Jews organized in 1942 to oppose Nazism.

JDC: Joint Distribution Committee. An American Jewish organization founded in 1914 to provide relief to European Jews during the First World War, later reorganized

and expanded to service Jewish communities worldwide.

Jewish Agency: The executive arm of the World Zionist Organization, created as part of the League of Nations' mandate plan (*see below*) in 1922 and established in 1929 to develop the Jewish settlement of Palestine. It continues in the State of Israel to facilitate the absorption of immigrants (*olim*).

Jewish National Fund: A financial institution established in 1901 by the Zionist Organization for the purchase of land for Jewish settlement in Palestine. It continues to rehabilitate the land through the planting of forests.

Kabbalah: The esoteric "tradition" passed on among Jewish mystics beginning in Roman times and continuing in diverse forms through the Middle Ages and into the modern era. The term is used this way from the 12th century on.

Kahal: Hebrew for "congregation," used to denote the organized Jewish community in eastern Europe in the preemancipation era. (*See* Kehillah.)

Karaites: Sectarian Jews who, beginning in Mesopotamia in the 8th century, reject rabbinic interpretation of the Bible and seek to base Jewish law on a more direct reading of Scripture. The name *Karaite*, first used in the 9th century, means "Scripturalist."

Kehillah: The local communal organization of eastern European Jewry. (*See* Kahal.)

Ketubbah: The traditional Jewish "document" delineating the amount a husband must pay his wife in the event of divorce. It is signed and witnessed prior to the marriage proper.

Kosher: The Hebrew term meaning "fit," referring to food that is permitted according to Jewish religious law. The term has entered modern English in the sense of "legitimate."

Ladino: The Judeo-Spanish language developed among Jews of Spanish extraction beginning in the 16th century.

Landsmannschaften: The Yiddish name for associations of eastern European Jewish immigrants from the same town formed for the purpose of economic assistance; in time they take on more social functions.

Likud: The "bloc" of right-wing Israeli parties formed in 1973 around Gahal (*see above*).

Lulav: The "palm branch" taken in hand with three other species of plants to celebrate the festival of Sukkot (Booths).

Ma'abarah: The initial "transit" camp for new immigrants to the State of Israel in the early 1950s.

Maftir: The last person called to read the Torah on the Sabbath and festivals and who chants the Haftarah (*see above*).

Magen David: The "Shield of David," often called the "Star of David," a six-pointed star used as a symbol of Jewishness since the 17th century.

Maggid: Eastern European, itin-

erant Hasidic "preacher" (lit., storyteller).

Magic Carpet: The operation in 1949–1950 to airlift about 30,000 Jews from Yemen to the newly independent State of Israel.

Mahzor: A prayer book containing services for the "cycle" of festivals.

Mandate for Palestine: The administration of Palestine by the British from 1922, when the League of Nations charged England with this responsibility, until 1948, when the State of Israel was established.

Mapai: Zionist-Socialist labor party in Israel founded in 1930, joining the Labor party coalition in 1965, whose full Hebrew name is Mifleget Po'alei Eretz Yisrael (Israel Labor party).

Mapam: Left-wing Israeli political party, sometimes joined to the Labor coalition, whose full Hebrew name is Mifleget ha-Po'alim ha-Me'uhedet (United Workers party).

Marrano: The Christian name for Jews in Spain and Portugal who converted to Christianity but continued to practice Judaism in secret and their descendants; Spanish for "pig."

Maskil: A Jew participating in the Enlightenment (*see* Haskalah), open to viewing Jewish life and culture outside of a strictly religious framework.

Masorah, Masoretic: The "tradition" of preserving the text of Scripture and its vocalization by standardizing the Hebrew consonants; by insertion of diacritic marks to indicate vowels, accentuation, and punctuation; and by marginal notes on unusual forms. The Masoretic text was established in Babylonia and the land of Israel from about the 7th through the 9th centuries.

Matzah: Unleavened crackerlike bread eaten on the festival of Passover. According to the Torah, matzah commemorates the Israelites' exodus from Egypt when they were too hurried to let their bread rise.

Me'assefim: The Hebrew term for contributors to the Haskalah periodical in Germany, Ha-Me'assef.

Megillah: Hebrew for "scroll," one of the five biblical books that are read on special days; the Book of Esther is read on the festival of Purim from a parchment scroll and is accordingly known as *the* Megillah.

Melammed: The Hebrew term for a "teacher" of children in premodern times.

Mellah: The North African Arabic term for the Jewish quarter of a town.

Menorah: "Candelabrum," the seven-branched solid-gold lamp that, according to the Torah, stood in the inner sanctum of the Tabernacle in the wilderness after the Israelites left Egypt and in the First and Second Temples. It was the main symbol of Judaism in antiquity and remains an important one. An eight-branched menorah is used on the holiday of Hanukkah.

Meshummad: An "apostate" Jew, mostly in the form of conversion to Christianity by force or by choice.

Mezuzah: Literally "doorpost," it is a small case containing a parchment on which the Shema is inscribed, traditionally affixed beside the door of one's home and rooms in which one dwells.

Messiah: The "anointed" king from the House of David, understood from the Hellenistic period on as a savior who would rule the community Israel in the end of days.

Midrash: The "searching" of Scripture to discover divinely encoded meaning. The term comes to refer to all classical rabbinic interpretation of the Bible and is used to designate collections of such interpretation.

Mikveh: A "reservoir" of water used for ritual bathing.

Minhag: "Custom," often used for rituals developed out of popular practice rather than law. Ashkenazic and Sephardic Jews differ in many of their *minhagim*.

Minyan: A "quorum" for public prayer, traditionally comprising 10 men (bar mitzvah age or above); more recently in egalitarian communities, it includes women, too.

Mishnah: The edition of rabbinic legal traditions and teachings by Rabbi Judah ha-Nasi in Israel around 215. The Mishnah forms the basis of the Palestinian and Babylonian Talmudim, which take it as their starting point. The Hebrew term means "teaching."

Mitnagdim: "Opponents" of the emerging Hasidic movement, formed after Rabbi Elijah the Gaon of Vilna placed the Hasidim under ban (*see Herem*) in 1772. The division into Hasidic and Mitnagdic camps persists among ultra-Orthodox Jews.

Mitzvah: A "commandment" of the Torah, traditionally incumbent upon all Jews; more popularly, a good deed.

Mizrah: "East," often indicated in synagogues and ritually observant homes with a sign on the east wall, toward which Jews pray. The sign, which is commonly fashioned as an object of art, is also termed a *mizrah*.

Mizrahi: The Orthodox Zionist movement founded in Vilna in 1902. The name, meaning "eastern" (i.e., Zion oriented), is abridged from Merkaz Ruhani (Spiritual Center).

Mohel: "Circumciser," the person, usually a trained officiant, who performs the ritual circumcision. (*See* Circumcision.)

Moshav (pl., moshavim): Cooperative agricultural "settlements," established in the land of Israel since 1921, in which land and large machinery are owned commonly.

Mossad: "Institution [for Intelligence and Special Missions]," the State of Israel's secret service.

Mufti: A Muslim "jurist," the title of a local Muslim leader.

Musaf: An "addition" to the service on Sabbaths and festivals derived from the additional offering on holy days in the ancient temple.

Musar: "Ethics," emphasized in the 19th-century eastern European movement by that name founded by Rabbi Israel Salanter.

Nagid: The biblical term for a political-military "commander," applied to leaders of the Jewish community in medieval Arab societies

Nahal: The branch of the Israeli military in which male and female soldiers establish agricultural settlements to protect border areas. The name is an acronym for Noar Halutzi Lohem (Fighting Pioneer Youth).

Nasi: Usually rendered "prince," the term refers in the Bible to the head of a tribe and in Roman times designates the chief of the rabbinic court or Sanhedrin.

Nazarene: A Jewish follower of Jesus, named after Jesus' home in Nazareth.

Neilah: The final service on the Day of Atonement (Yom Kippur), named for the liturgical image of the imminent "closing" of the gates of repentance.

Neolithic: Late Stone Age.

Neolog: The Reform movement in Hungary, which began more conservatively than its German counterpart in 1868.

New Christians: The Christian name for Jewish converts and their descendants in Spain and Portugal in the late Middle Ages. (*Compare Conversos.*)

NILI: Jewish underground fighting organization in Palestine during World War I who assisted the British in the hope of establishing a Jewish state. The name is an acronym of the biblical phrase *"Netzah Yisrael Lo Yeshaqqer"* (the Eternal One of Israel will not break faith).

Ninth of Av: See Tisha B'Av.

Olim: Immigrants to Israel, literally, "those going up." (*See also* Aliyah, definition 1.)

Omer, Counting of: The period of counting days from the second day of Passover until the festival of Shavuot (Weeks) seven weeks later derived from the biblical commandment of setting aside, beginning at Passover, a "measure" (*omer*) of barley from the harvest to present to the priests on Shavuot. The period of counting (*sefirah*) traditionally entails certain ascetic practices.

Oral Torah: The corpus of all rabbinic legal and aggadic interpretation of the written Torah (Pentateuch), understood traditionally as having been revealed together with the written Torah to Moses and transmitted from generation to generation. In Hebrew, *Torah she-be'al peh.*

ORT: Organization for Rehabilitation and Training. This Jewish organization was founded in St. Petersburg in 1880 to develop skilled job training. Beginning in 1921, ORT spread to western Europe, and later to Israel and other lands, setting up vocational schools and programs. Its name was originally a Russian acronym.

Orthodox Judaism: The traditionalist movement in Judaism. Founded in central Europe around the turn of the 19th century as a reaction to Reform, it maintains the centrality of *halakhah* (*see above*) as strictly interpreted.

Ossuaries: Boxlike containers into which the bones of decayed corpses were deposited for memorialization, used in the Greek and Roman periods.

Ostraca: Potsherds used for written communications; common in Iron Age Israel (the biblical period).

Pale of Settlement: The area to which Jews were restricted to reside in czarist Russia.

Palestine Liberation Organization (PLO): The umbrella group of Arab organizations determined to return the territory of Palestine (Israel) to Arab control. Originally formed in 1964 as the Eyptian counterpart of the Syrian-backed Fatah (*see above*), the PLO, as it became known, was reorganized in 1968 with al-Fatah as its main component. Since 1974, the PLO, the agent of numerous terrorist acts in Israel and worldwide, has claimed to be the "sole legitimate representative of the Palestinian people" and subsequently declared itself a government of the Palestinian state in exile.

Palestine National Covenant: The declaration of aims of the Palestinian liberation movement. Formulated in 1964 and revised in 1968 (*see* Palestine Liberation Organization), it seeks to take over the territory of the British mandate (*see above*) of Palestine, including the State of Israel and Kingdom of Jordan, by "armed struggle" and to eliminate "Zionism in Palestine."

Palmah: The "shock troops," more literally "assault companies" (Peluggot ha-Mahatz) of the Haganah (*see above*), formed in 1941 and incorporated within the Israeli army (Israel Defense Forces) in 1949.

Papyrus: Writing material produced in Egypt from papyrus plants growing in the Nile marshes, and the predecessor of paper.

Parashah: The "section" of the Torah (Pentateuch) that is read on the Sabbath in the synagogue. It is also called the sidrah (*see below*).

Parnas: The lay leader (lit., "provider") of a synagogue in medieval and early modern times.

Parokhet: The "curtain" that covers the ark containing the Torah scrolls in the synagogue, named for the curtain that divided the holy of holies from the outer chamber of the tabernacle (*Mishkan*) and temple in ancient times.

Partition plans: Various proposals for dividing the British mandate of Palestine into Jewish and Arab lands, resulting in the UN partition of 1947, leading to the establishment of the State of Israel and the administration of the remaining land by Egypt (Gaza) and the Hashemite Kingdom of Jordon (West Bank).

Passover: *See* Pesah.

Patriarchs: Hebrew forefathers of the Israelite people about whom we read primarily in the Book of Genesis: Abraham, Isaac, Jacob, and the 12 sons of Jacob, most prominent among whom are Judah and Joseph. The wives of the patriarchs are the matriarchs, principally Sarah, Rebecca, Leah, and Rachel.

Pentateuch: The Bible's Five Books of Moses, known in Judaism as the Torah.

Pe'ot: The "corners" of the head, above the ears, at which ultra-Orthodox Jewish men and boys let the hair grow uncut, also known as *sidecurls.*

Pesah (Passover): The biblical and later Jewish spring festival celebrating the land's renewed fertility and the exodus of the Hebrews from Egyptian bondage.

Peshat: The meaning of the Bible as determined within the parameters of its historical, linguistic, and literary contexts. *Peshat*, a Hebrew term meaning "plain" sense, becomes a major mode of Jewish Bible interpretation beginning in the 10th century.

Phalanges: Military arms of the Maronite Christians in Lebanon.

Pharaoh: Hebraized Egyptian title for the king.

Pharisees: A party of Jews that apparently originated in the 2nd century BCE, affirming such doctrines as resurrection of the dead and a high degree of ritual purity. The rabbis of the late 1st and subsequent centuries CE are Pharisees, a term (Hebrew, *perushim*) probably referring to "separation" from the impure.

Pilpul: The dialectical mode of talmudic argument developed into a method of making ever sharper distinctions. *Pilpul* ("peppering") becomes prominent in talmudic education in 16th-century Poland; its detractors regard it as hairsplitting casuistry.

Pinkas: A "notebook" registering data about the membership of a Jewish community, especially in eastern Europe.

Piyyut: Jewish religious "poetry" composed for use at various points in the liturgy, especially from the 6th century on.

PLO: (*see* Palestine Liberation Organization.

Po'alei Zion: "Workers of Zion," a Marxist Jewish party founded in 1906 adopting the ideology of Dov Ber Borochov, with branches in Russia, Austria, and the U.S., in tension with other Zionist groups on one side and the Communists on the other.

Pogrom: A Russian term used to designate a violent, unprovoked attack on a Jewish community. Though the term took on this usage only in the 19th century, it has come to be applied to anti-Jewish attacks in earlier times, too.

Protocols of the Elders of Zion: Spurious tract composed by an antisemite in Russia at the turn of the 20th century describing an international conspiracy for Jewish domination of the world. Confirming common anti-Jewish stereotypes, the work has fueled antisemitism and has remained in circulation among Arabs and even in the West until today.

Pseudepigraph: A composition attributed to a well-known figure of the past. In the Hellenistic and Roman periods, many Jewish pseudepigraphs were written.

Purim: The late winter/early spring holiday celebrating the success of ancient Persian Jewry in overcoming an attempt to annihilate them by antisemites. The Scroll of Esther, narrating the biblical story, is read aloud, and merrymaking as well as charity are ordained.

Pyramid: A monumental tomb constructed for Egyptian royalty, mainly in the mid-3rd millennium BCE, a millennium before the Hebrews are said to have been in Egypt.

Rabbi: "Master," that is, teacher, the title taken by Pharisaic sages after the destruction of Jerusalem in 70 CE. The rabbi becomes the religious teacher and authority in a Jewish community.

Rakah: The small Arab–Israeli political party formed in the 1960s, the "New Communist List" (Reshimah Komunistit Hadashah).

Rebbe: Yiddish for "rabbi," used by Hasidim. The leading rebbe of a Hasidic sect (also known as the zaddik) is often held to possess wondrous mediatory powers with the divine.

Rebbetzin: Yiddish term for a rabbi's wife.

Reconstructionism: The conception of Judaism as an "evolving religious civilization," developed in the U.S. in the early 20th century by Rabbi Mordecai M. Kaplan. Viewing Jewish tradition as folkways rather than as binding *halakhah* (*see above*), Reconstructionism promotes living in two civilizations, the Jewish and the surrounding one.

Reform Judaism: A movement to accommodate Jewish life and worship to the contemporary surrounding culture, originating in Germany in the early 19th century and spreading mainly to western Europe and the U.S. Stressing the universal ethical teachings of Judaism, Reform turned from consistently opposing Jewish distinctiveness to supporting the State of Israel.

Responsa: The Latin term for Hebrew *teshuvot* (replies; sg., *teshuva*), referring to legal opinions given by a rabbinic authority who is asked to clarify an unprecedented point of *halakhah* (*see above*).

Revisionists: Followers of the radically nationalist Zionist movement led by Zev Jabotinsky. (*See also* Betar, Herut.)

Rishonim: The "first" commentators on the Talmud and other works of Jewish law, from the early *geonim* (9th century) through the composition of the *Shulhan Arukh* (16th century) (*see below*).

Rosh Hashanah: The Jewish New Year, literally "Head of the Year," beginning the 10 Days of

Repentance culminating in the Day of Atonement (Yom Kippur). The two days of Rosh Hashanah entail a longer synagogue service that features the theme that all God's creatures stand in judgment.

Rosh Hodesh: "New Moon," the first day of a month, celebrated as a minor holiday in the traditional liturgy and the occasion for women's prayer groups to meet in recent years.

Rosh yeshiva: The "head of a yeshiva," the religious authority, sometimes also the principal, of a traditionalist school or rabbinic academy.

Sabbatean: A follower of the 17th-century messianic pretender Shabbetai Tzvi. Sabbateanism persisted in small circles even after Shabbetai Tzvi was discredited in the eyes of other Jews.

Sabbath (Hebrew, Shabbat): The seventh day of each week, ordained by the Torah as a sacred day on which to "desist" from work, since God rested on the seventh day of creation.

Saboraim: Rabbinic scholars engaged in compiling the traditions and materials of earlier sages (*amoraim; see above*) for inclusion in the Babylonian Talmud (5th–6th centuries).

Sadducees: Named for the Zadokite group of Jerusalem priests, the Sadducees were apparently upper-class Jews, emerging in the 2nd century BCE, opposed to key Pharisaic doctrines such as resurrection. Their opponents, the Pharisees, supersede them after the Roman destruction of the Temple in 70 CE.

Saison: The code word indicating the collaboration of the Haganah (*see above*) with the British in Palestine in 1944–1945 to suppress the radical Jewish Irgun (*see* IZL).

Sanhedrin: The Hebraized Greek word for "council," applied to the chief judicial and legislative body of the Jews in the land of Israel in late Greek and Roman times. In 1807 it is the name given to the Jewish assembly convoked by Napoleon in Paris.

Sanjak: The administrative province of the Ottoman Empire.

Seder: The traditional ceremonial meal observed on the first and second nights of Passover (only the first night in Israel and among Reform Jews). The seder (order) involves an elaborate recitation of the exodus story (*see* Haggadah) and a number of symbols that recall the ancient temple practices and reflect the themes of the festival.

Selektion: The Nazi term used to designate Jews for deportation and for separation upon arrival at a concentration camp of those marked for immediate death from those assigned to labor.

Selihot: Prayers asking forgiveness (*selihah*), recited on fast days as well as preceding Rosh Hashanah (*see above*) and during the 10 Days of Repentance.

Semikhah: The "laying on" of the hands of a master rabbi to a disciple, indicating ordination as a

rabbi. The ancient talmudic practice was revived by rabbinical seminaries and private rabbis in premodern times, and the term came to refer to ordination itself.

Sephardic: Pertaining to the Jews whose ancestors lived in Spain and Portugal, most of whom were expelled in the 1490s, and their culture, which is distinguished from that of Ashkenaz (Franco-Germany; *see above*).

Septuagint: The Greek translation of the Torah (Pentateuch) made by Jews in Alexandria, Egypt, in the mid-3rd century BCE. Its name, the "Seventy," derives from the legend by which the rendering was performed by 72 Jerusalem sages, each working alone and producing the exact same text. The term becomes extended to refer to the ancient Greek translations of the remaining books of the Hebrew Bible, too.

Shadkhan: The Hebrew–Yiddish term for a "matchmaker," who arranges a *shiddukh* (match) between a prospective husband and wife.

Shammash: (1) The "service-provider" in a synagogue, the beadle. (2) The candle used to light the others on a Hannukah menorah (*see above*).

Shavuot: The Festival of "Weeks," occurring seven weeks after Passover. Originally a celebration of the grain harvest, it becomes the festival of the giving of the Torah to Israel on Mt. Sinai.

Shehitah: The traditional ritual "slaughter" of animals for food performed according to regulations designed to minimize the animal's pain and drain its blood.

Sheitl: A wig worn by highly traditionalist married women to hide their hair from men other than their husbands.

Skekhinah: The divine presence (lit., indwelling), used in rabbinic literature and especially mystical circles to refer to the immanent female manifestations of God in contrast to the generally male images of divine transcendence, such as "Master of the World."

Shema: Three paragraphs from the Torah developing the theme of covenant obligations between God and Israel, a centerpiece of the daily morning and evening liturgy. The recitation begins with Deuteronomy 6:4: "Hear, O Israel, the Lord our God, the Lord is One."

Shemini Atzeret: The last two days (in Israel the last day) of the festival of Sukkot (Booths), a particularly joyous occasion [lit., the eighth (day), an assembly]. Since about the 16th century, the second day is also a celebration for renewing the annual cycle of reading the Torah, Simhat Torah (*see below*).

Shemoneh Esreh: The "18" blessings of the central daily prayer, the *Amidah* (*see above*).

Shiksa: A pejorative Yiddish term for a non-Jewish woman; the male counterpart is *sheigitz.*

Shivah: The initial period of mourning the loss of an immediate relative, ordinarily "seven" days, beginning at the time of burial.

Shnorrer: The Yiddish term for a perpetual "beggar."

Shofar: The "horn" of an animal, usually a ram, made into a trumpet to announce the approaching New Year and to symbolize the call to repentance during services on Rosh Hashanah (*see above*). In ancient times, the shofar announced the onset and end of various holy days and other occasions.

Shohet: A person qualified to perform ritual slaughter. (*See Shehitah.*)

Shtadlan: A lobbyist for Jewish interests at the courts of heads of state in Europe in late medieval and early modern times, derived from the Hebrew–Aramaic verb, "to press, persuade."

Shtetl: "Little town" in Yiddish, the eastern European village in which many Jews lived in the early modern period.

Shtibl: "Little house" in Yiddish, the small eastern European synagogue in early modern times, transported by Hasidim to their new communities in Israel and the West.

Shulhan Arukh: The code of Jewish law compiled by Rabbi Joseph Caro in Israel about 1542 and amended for use by European Jews by Rabbi Moses Isserles. It remains the standard source for traditional observance.

Shund: The Yiddish term for "trash," used to refer to a form of theater and other arts.

Siddur: The "arrangement" of the Jewish liturgy, hence, the daily prayer book. The first *siddurim* are attested in the geonic period (from the 10th century CE).

Sidrah: One of the 54 sections of the Torah (Pentateuch) that is "arranged" to be read out in synagogue on the Sabbath (*see also* Parashah).

Simhat Torah: "Celebration of the Torah," when the new annual reading of the Torah commences, coinciding with the second day of Shemini Atzeret (*see above*). The festive rituals for this day, originating in the late Middle Ages, include encircling the synagogue with Torah scrolls and dancing around the Torah.

Sinai Campaign: The invasion of the Sinai Peninsula by Israeli forces in the fall of 1956 to end an Egyptian blockade of Israel and a series of terror attacks.

Six-Day War: Israeli strike against Egypt in June 1967 to open its blockade of Israel. When Syria and Jordan joined the fight, Israel defeated them, too, capturing the Sinai Peninsula, the Gaza strip, the Golan Heights, and the West Bank including East Jerusalem.

Solel Boneh: "Paves and Builds," the name of the Israeli construction company created by the Histadrut (*see above*). Providing needed roads for Jewish settlements in the 1930s and for the British army during World War II, the company continued to build in Israel and by contract abroad.

SS: Schutzstaffel (Protection Detachment), the elite armed Nazi corps responsible for directing the

roundup and annihilation of Jews and others during World War II.

Stele: A standing monument often used in ancient times for recording official declarations and as a cultic prop.

Sukkah: A "booth." (*See* Sukkot.)

Sukkot: The Festival of "Booths" (or Tabernacles), commemorating the ancient Israelites' temporary dwellings in the Sinai wilderness following the exodus from Egypt and celebrating the fall harvest. It occurs in September–October and serves as the prototype for the American holiday Thanksgiving.

Synagogue: This Greek term for a house of "assembly," corresponding to the Hebrew *beit knesset* (house of assembly), designates the building in which Jews would gather to study, worship, or otherwise meet. Synagogue remains date back to the Roman period, but the institution of a Jewish prayer house may have originated as early as the 6th century BCE.

Synod: A council or assembly convoked by the Christian church.

Tallit: Prayer "shawl" with fringes (*tzitziyot*) on the four corners, as ordained by the Torah.

Tallit katan: A "small prayer shawl" traditionally worn under one's shirt or coat all day in contrast to the large outer "tallit" (*see above*) that is worn during morning worship. It is also called *arba kanfot* (four corners) or *tzitzit* (fringe).

Talmud: The "teaching" of Jewish law and lore presented as the discussion of the Mishnah by rabbinic sages in the academies of Israel and Babylonia. The Palestinian Talmud was completed by the end of the 4th century CE, the far more extensive Babylonian Talmud by the 7th century.

Tanna (pl., tannaim): Rabbinic sage (lit., "teacher" in Aramaic) of the Roman period, the era of the Mishnah.

Tashlikh: The custom observed on the New Year (Rosh Hashanah) of casting crumbs, symbolic of one's sins, into a river or stream. The name of the ritual, meaning "you shall cast," is taken from a biblical verse recited during the ceremony.

Targum: The term for an ancient Aramaic "translation" of part of the Hebrew Bible.

Tefillah: This Hebrew term for "prayer" in general is used in classical rabbinic literature to designate the central, standing prayer (*Amidah*).

Tefillin: Phylacteries, two black leather boxes containing passages from the Torah on parchment, fastened to the arm and head with black leather straps, symbolizing one's duties to act and think according to God's teachings. Traditionally worn at weekday morning services, tefillin as such hark back at least to Roman times.

Tehina (pl., tehinnot): "Supplications" of God, private prayers, composed by or for Jewish women in premodern Europe.

Tell: A "mound" formed of the debris of successive towns, built one on top of the other, a common phenomenon in the ancient Near East.

Temple: The Latin-derived term for the ancient "house" of God (Hebrew, *beit ha-miqdash*, "house of the holy") in Jerusalem serving as the central holy place of the ancient Israelites and the Jewish people. The Temple built by King Solomon in the late 10th century BCE was destroyed by Babylonia in 587/586 BCE; the Second Temple, rebuilt in 515 BCE and refurbished by King Herod around the turn of the era, was destroyed by Rome in 70 CE. In the 19th-century, Reform Jews began calling their synagogues temples. Jewish tradition looks forward to rebuilding the Jerusalem Temple in the messianic era.

Temple Mount: The site where the Jerusalem Temple (*see above*) stood, also where according to Muslim tradition the prophet Muhammad ascended to heaven. As the third holiest place in Islam, the Temple Mount (Haram al-Sharif in Arabic) became the site for the Al-Aqsa and Dome of the Rock mosques, which still stand there.

Ten Commandments: More properly, the "ten statements" comprise the set of positive and negative injunctions delivered by God to Israel at Mt. Sinai and recorded in Exodus 20 and Deuteronomy 5.

Terefah: Meat that is not kosher (*see above*), from the biblical term for an animal killed other than by the proper ritual; in common parlance, *treif*, the opposite of kosher.

Tetrarch: The title of a Roman territorial governor.

Tevah: A platform in a Sephardic (*see above*) synagogue supporting the table on which the Torah is read. The term, meaning "box," is taken from the Mishnah (*see above*). (*See also Bimah.*)

Tisha B'Av: The "ninth of (the Hebrew month of) Av," the traditional date on which the First and Second Temples were destroyed and on which these national and religious catastrophes as well as others are commemorated by a daylong fast.

Torah: Literally, divine "instruction," Torah broadly embraces all religious sources and teaching; more narrowly, it refers to the written Torah revealed by God, traditionally to Moses, and embodied in the Pentateuch, as well as the oral Torah, believed traditionally to be the concurrent unwritten yet revealed interpretation of the written Torah.

Tosafot: "Additions" to the extant Talmud commentaries made by the first generations of Rashi's students in Franco-Germany, the Tosafists. These additions often raise critical questions and seek to harmonize seemingly conflicting positions in the Talmud.

Tosefta: A "supplement" to the Mishnah, compiled perhaps 50 years later, overlapping in content and structure but presenting significantly different material, too.

Uganda Scheme: The British proposal in 1903 to found a Jewish homeland in Uganda, central Africa, considered and rejected by Zionist leaders.

UNIFIL: Acronym for the United Nations Interim Force in Lebanon, assigned to monitor the Lebanon–Israel border.

United Hias Service: An international Jewish immigrant and refugee service. HIAS was formed in New York City through the merger of the Hebrew Sheltering House Association (1884) and the Hebrew Immigrant Aid Society (1902). In 1954, a single international agency designed to help refugees to find new homes in the United States, Western Europe and South America was formed through the merger of HIAS, with the United Service for New Americans and the Joint Distribution Committee's Migration department into the United HIAS Service.

Va'ad Le'ummi: The "National Committee" representing the Jewish settlement (*see Yishuv*) under the British mandate for Palestine (*see above*), responsible for security, education, and various welfare functions.

Vilayet: The largest administrative unit within the Ottoman Empire.

Vizier: The title of a high minister of a Muslim state.

Vulgate: The Latin translation of the Hebrew and Christian scriptures made by Jerome around 400 CE, for many centuries the official Latin version of the Bible.

Wannsee Conference: A convocation of leading Nazi thinkers held in Wannsee, a suburb of Berlin on January 20, 1942, to plan the destruction of every last Jew in Europe.

War of Independence: The war between Jews and surrounding Arabs in Israel, from 1947 to 1949, following the partition of Palestine (*see above*); in Hebrew, Milhemet Ha-Shihrur.

White Papers: A series of six reports issued by the British government in Palestine from 1922 to 1939, delineating its policy concerning Jews and Arabs there, severely limiting Jewish immigration (aliyah) in order to mollify the Arabs.

Wissenschaft des Judentums: The "science of Judaism," the application of general scholarly tools to the study of Jewish texts, history, and religion, beginning in Germany in the early 19th century and continuing in modern seminaries and universities.

World Zionist Organization (WZO): The world-wide organization of Zionists founded in 1897 under the leadership of Theodor Herzl. Originally called the Zionist Organization, it came to be known in 1960 as the WZO.

Yad Va-Shem: Hebrew for "memorial-monument," the name of the Israeli institution authorized to research and educate concerning the Sho'ah (Holocaust), memorialize the 6 million Jewish victims, and honor the Jewish resistance fighters and the "righteous Gentiles" who rescued Jews. Officially called the Israel Martyrs' and Heroes' Remembrance, Yad Va-Shem is a many-faceted museum and memorial in Jerusalem.

Yarmulke: "Skullcap" in Yiddish, worn traditionally by men to signify humility before God. It is known in Hebrew as *kippah*.

Yeshiva: A school for training younger students in traditional Jewish sources and an academy for training older students in Talmud and codes to prepare them as rabbis.

Yevsektsiya: The sections of the Russian Communist party charged with educating Jews in Communist doctrines, functioning from 1918 to 1930.

YHWH: The four-letter personal name of the biblical God, the tetragrammaton, probably related in some way to the verb *to be*. The original pronunciation of the name went into disuse in Greco-Roman times, and in its place the epithet Adonai (my Lord) was introduced. Traditional Jews replace even this epithet, except in prayer, with the term *ha-Shem* (the Name).

Yiddish: A Jewish language that developed beginning in the Middle Ages as Jews who were pushed eastward from Germany wove many Hebrew and some Slavic terms into the Germanic base of the language that they preserved as their ethnic tongue. Yiddish was spoken among Jews in eastern Europe and in places to which they migrated.

Yishuv: The Jewish "settlement" of the land of Israel, particularly the Zionist settler population from the first aliyah in 1882 until the establishment of the state in 1948.

Yivo: A Yiddish academic institute founded in 1925 in Vilna, on the initiative of Max Weinreich (1894–1969) and Nahum Shtif (1879–1933). YIVO is an acronym from its Yiddish name: Yidisher Visnshaftlekher Institut. It was known in English as the Yiddish Scientific Institute until its relocation to New York City, in 1939, when its English name was changed to the YIVO Institute for Jewish Research.

Yom Kippur: The "Day of Atonement." (*See* Atonement, Day of.)

Yom Kippur War: The war between Israel and Egypt and Syria, when the latter two attacked Israel by surprise in October 1973 in order to regain the territories Israel won in the Six-Day War of 1967. It took Israel weeks to reverse the Arabs.

Yordim: Israeli citizens who leave their homeland to live elsewhere, "those who descend" in contrast to *olim* (*see above*).

Zaddik (or tzaddik): A "righteous man," leader of a Hasidic sect. (*See also* Rebbe.) More generally, a person who displays exceptional generosity and other personal qualities. Legend holds that the world exists by virtue of 36 zaddikim.

Zealots: Radical Judean nationalists of the 1st century CE.

Ziggurat: A Mesopotamian temple tower resembling a pyramid with a rectangular shrine at the top, probably the model of the Bible's Tower of Babel.

Zionism: The political movement, initiated in the mid-19th century in Europe, to reestablish a Jewish state in the land of Israel, or "Zion" in one of its biblical names; more generally, support of the State of Israel.

Zionist Congress: The parliament of the Zionist movement. Initially it met every year, then every second year. Following World War II it meets at irregular intervals.

Zizit (or tzitzit): The fringe ordained by the Torah to be worn on the four corners of one's garment; (*See* Tallit.)

Zohar: The major work of the Jewish mystical tradition, a commentary on the Torah incorporating traditional and innovative ideas of Kabbalah (*see above*). Meaning "shining, splendor," the book is traditionally attributed to the 2nd-century sage Simeon bar Yohai, but it is ascribed by historians to Moses de Leon in 13th-century Spain.

INDEX

NOTE: Jewish communities are listed nationally and geographically without indication of the relation between the one and the other; for example: Polish Jews; Warsaw Jews.

References are to years, months (numbers following colons), and columns (letters A through E).